Triumph

The Life and Art of Captain Adrian Jones

M.V.O., M.R.C.V.S., F.R.B.S.

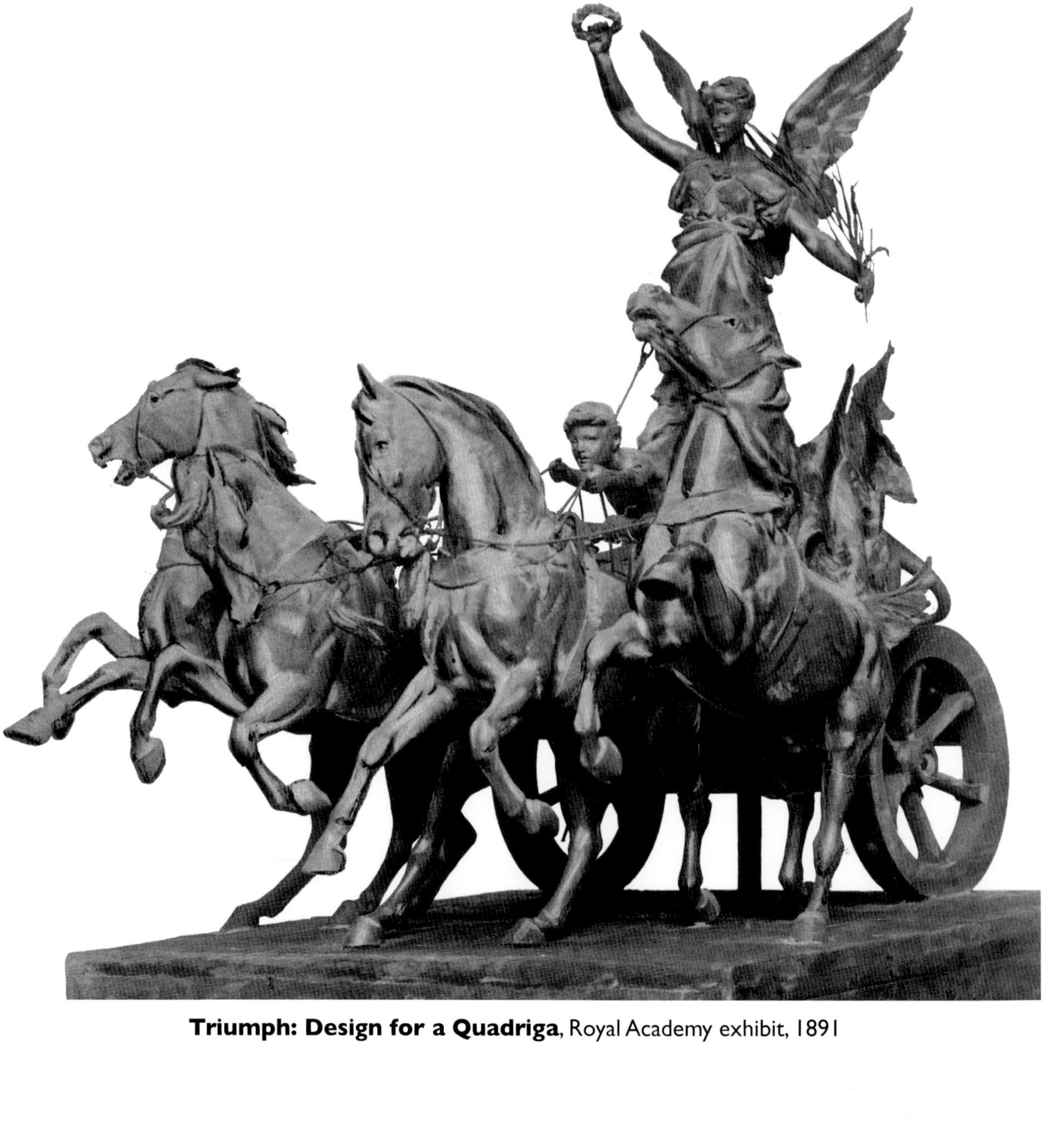

Triumph: Design for a Quadriga, Royal Academy exhibit, 1891

To Ken,

With best wishes and with happy memories of over half a century of friendship,

Triumph

The Life and Art of Captain Adrian Jones

M.V.O., M.R.C.V.S., F.R.B.S.

by

Robert S. Burns

Bobbie

The Quadriga was at first called 'Triumph' and at last that is what indeed it is.

James Manson
(First Secretary of the Camden Town Group of Painters), 1912

Nothing is more valuable than understanding comment ... The appreciation of those who understand is the thing that all artists strive to obtain.

Adrian Jones
Memoirs of a Soldier Artist, 1933

Logaston Press

LOGASTON PRESS
Little Logaston Woonton Almeley
Herefordshire HR3 6QH
www.logastonpress.co.uk

First published by Logaston Press 2010

ISBN 978 1 906663 44 5

Typeset in Garamond by Logaston Press
and printed and bound in Poland
www.polskabook.pl

Front cover photograph of the Peace Quadriga by John Lush
Frontispiece from the Jones family collections

Contents

Author's Foreword

The firm of Stanley Paul published Adrian Jones's autobiography, *Memoirs of a Soldier Artist*, in the late autumn of 1933. A news item headlined 'Contrasts in Best Sellers' in the *Times* reported that the most successful books of that year's pre-Christmas season were written either by the young or by 'distinguished veterans'. Adrian Jones's *Memoirs* was one of the latter. As he approached his ninetieth year he had set down his mainly happy recollections of a life filled with action and art, accurately summarised by one book review heading as 'A Story of Stupendous Tasks'. In the foreword to the autobiography, Lord Baden-Powell implicitly evaluated the soldier artist's impact on the London scene as comparable to that of Sir Christopher Wren and St Paul's Cathedral by quoting the Latin tag *Si monumentum requiris circumspice* ('If you seek his monument, look around'). He went on to claim that the history of so versatile a personality could not fail to be of interest to many, while his human characteristics would appeal to all. However, despite his fame during the reigns of Victoria, Edward VII and George V, despite the continuing major presence of his public art sculptures in London, and despite his unique interest as an amalgam of soldier, veterinary surgeon, painter and sculptor, Adrian Jones has never received a full biography. He deserves one, because of the timeless quality of his figurative art; and he needs one because his *Memoirs* are far from comprehensive. Also, having been written well after events about which he had not kept a diary, they are at times inaccurate.

This biography adds to the story told in *Memoirs*, and aims to do so in a style which Adrian Jones would approve and which will draw the twenty-first century reader into the world of an imperial Britain long vanished. Those two aims led to a set of decisions, listed below. The first four decisions echo Adrian Jones's practice in his autobiography:

1) The biography is chronological, but also partly thematic. 2) As a raconteur, Adrian Jones liked beguiling diversions. They are indulged here also. 3) Footnotes are eschewed and scholarly apparatus kept limited. 4) Measurements, given only when significant, are imperial; places are given their Victorian names, e.g. Peking, not Beijing; Indian and Middle Eastern place names about which there is no unanimity when Anglicised are given in the spelling used in *Memoirs*; but the sometimes misspelt surnames are corrected where necessary.

The story of Adrian Jones's military life is fully covered, whereas in the autobiography there is, for example, no account of the author's army service in England, and no illustration of him in uniform. However, this is not a military history, so no space is given to campaign maps. The interested reader will find them readily available in war books.

Invaluable full access to the Jones family archives has made it possible to give some account of the family. In *Memoirs*, because of Victorian reticence over private matters, Adrian wrote very little about his family. The archives held also photographs, taken in the artist's studio, of the first models of various statues. These, most never previously published, give insights into how Adrian Jones later modified his initial ideas.

The opening words of each chapter title are usually a quotation from *Memoirs*.

Finally, in a most un-Victorian or Edwardian manner, because the tribe of Joneses is large, the anachronism has been used of mainly referring to 'Adrian', not to 'Jones'.

Acknowledgements

It is no hyperbole to say that without the great help received from many individuals over the past two years it would have been impossible to write this biography. Adrian Jones's collateral descendants, Mark Cunningham and Kate Measham, sought out all the photographs, press cuttings and documents in their family archives and generously loaned them. Ruth Capper, a friend of the family, provided further archive material via Betty Lee of Ludlow. Edward Horswell, who curated the Sladmore Gallery's 1984 Retrospective Exhibition of Adrian Jones's art, made available all his copyright material, and he and his assistant Sonia Harman were always helpful and encouraging to the project. John Lush, educated at the same school as Adrian Jones, tramped through much of London, motored through much of England, and was able to visit Adelaide in Australia, to photograph the public art statues, and the statuettes and paintings in private collections and institutions. In addition, when necessary he (ably assisted by his son Howard) and the Ludlow photographer Gareth Thomas worked on aged prints from the nineteenth and early twentieth century to make them fit for modern publishing. Staff Sergeant David Turner, Royal Artillery, took a series of photographs of the Royal Horse Artillery bronze 'Action Front'. Judith Channon and Shirley Leviseur typed – and often uncomplainingly retyped – the text and its revisions. Mark Cunningham, the Shropshire figurative sculptor Jemma Pearson, Frances Houston of the Archives and Historical Collection of the Royal Veterinary College, Rollo Clifford of the Royal Gloucestershire Hussars Association, the late Ludlow historian David Lloyd, and my son Arthur and daughter Catriona all read particular chapters to check on the correctness of the information or to comment as necessary on style and interest.

No one could write a book such as this one without gaining feelings of highest regard for the curators and staff of Britain's regimental museums. Their cordial willingness to help makes each contact a delight. Particular thanks are owed to Clive Morris at the Queen's Dragoon Guards Museum, home of the historical records of the Queen's Bays; to Captain Holtby at the Queen's Royal Lancers' Museum, Grantham; to Colonel Quarrelle and Major Begbie at the Royal Artillery Institution, Larkhill; to Amy Wegerhoss at the Queen's Own Hussars' Museum, Warwick; and to the staffs of the Soldiers of Gloucestershire Museum at Bristol, the Firepower Royal Artillery Museum at Woolwich, and most of all to the Army Medical Services Museum, Aldershot, which preserves the history of the army veterinary service. Outside the orbit of regimental museums, the staffs of the Imperial War Museum, especially Pauline Allwright in the Art Department, and of the Templer Study Centre in the National Army Museum were equally helpful. John Lush and I are grateful also for the welcome and help we received from David Cowdery at the Cavalry and Guards Club, Brigadier Lennox and Major Atkins at the Victory Services Club, Dr Eyal and Jen Walker at the Royal United Services Institute, David Tudor of the Shropshire Society in London, and to all staffs who rearranged lighting and provided stepladders as necessary to facilitate good photographic results.

For information on and access to paintings and indoor sculptures by Adrian Jones I am indebted to many institutions and individuals. Space could not be found in the book for illustrations of and comments on everything, but all contributed to an overall picture and were therefore valuable. My thanks to Dr Minne at the Royal British Society of Sculptors (as, reflecting the changed ethnicity of Britain, the Royal Society of British Sculptors has been renamed); to Alison Marks, the Art and Exhibitions Officer at Northampton

Museums and Art Gallery, and William Lowther and Caroline Houghton at Holdenby House; to Nathan Pendlebury and the staff at the Walker Art Gallery and Croxteth Hall; to staff at the National Portrait Gallery, the National Horse Racing Museum, English Heritage, Ipswich Town Hall and Ludlow College; and to John and Mary Hyde, Gordon and Jeannie Lees, William Fergusson, Rollo Clifford, Gordon Place and John Williams.

Graham Verow used his expertise in computer-based genealogical research to find exact information on Adrian Jones's family. I was glad to receive help from Paul Grier and Mike the barman at the Savage Club; and for information on Chelsea Arts Club and Adrian Jones's role in it I am greatly indebted to the Club's historian, Tom Cross, who generously referred me to his book *Artists and Bohemians*. Caro Skyrme, past chairman of the Equestrian Artists Association, took an encouraging interest in the idea of this biography. Jen Davies, President of the Old Ludlovians, loaned her collection of information on Adrian Jones. Anyone interested in his art must be grateful for the various writings of Selwyn Hodson Pressinger which have helped to keep the name of Adrian Jones known to the public. My wife Barbara has read much and travelled much to help my writing and research. Andy and Karen Johnson at Logaston Press have been wonderfully patient and supportive. To each and all, thank you.

Illustrations Credits

Numbers refer to the page on which the illustrations appears; a = above, b = below, l = left, r = right. An asterisk indicates that the work is shown by kind permission of its private owner.

Chapter One	pages 4, 5: Jones family collections 7: by kind permission of Ludlow College
Chapter Two	13: Jones family collection
Chapter Three	23, 33, 34, 36: Jones family collections 34, Photo: John Lush
Chapter Four	42a, 50, 51, 52: Jones family collections 42b*: Photo: John Lush 43, 44: Colindale Newspaper Library
Chapter Five	48: by kind permission of the Cavalry and Guards Club. Photo: John Lush 49: by kind permission of the Royal Dublin Society 50, 51, 52: Jones family collections
Chapter Six	65: Photo: John Lush 67: Jones family collections
Chapter Seven	73a*, 73b*, 85*: Photo: John Lush 74, 75, 76, 78, 79, 81, 83, 87: Jones family collections. 76, 87: Photo: John Lush 80: Photo: John Lush 86: by kind permission of the King's Royal Hussars

Chapter Eight	90, 93, 94, 102, 104, 109, 110: Jones family collections 91, 95: Photos: John Lush 96: by kind permission of Ludlow College 107: by kind permission of Northampton Museums and Art Gallery. Photo: John Lush
Chapter Nine	113, 114, 124l, 124r: Jones family collections. 119, 124: Photo: John Lush 114, 115: by kind permission of National Museums, Liverpool 116*, 117*, 120*, 121*, 122*, 123a*, 123b*, 126*. 116, 117: Photo: John Lush 118: by kind permission of the Sladmore Gallery
Chapter Ten	128, 130: by kind permission of Winchester Cathedral. Photo: John Lush 133: by kind permission of the Queen's Royal Lancers Regiment 135a, 135b: Jones family collections 136, 137a, 137b, 138, 139, 140, 141, 142: Photos: John Lush
Chapter Eleven	144, 145, 150, 151, 153, 154al: Jones family collections. 145: photo John Lush 148, 149, 154, 155, 158: Photo: John Lush 157*: private postcard collection
Chapter Twelve	161, 163, 164, 166r, 169: Jones family collections 166al, 166bl, 171, 172, 173: Photo: John Lush
Chapter Thirteen	176, 178, 180, 181, 184: Jones family collections 182l, 182r: by kind permission of the Shropshire Society in London. Photos: John Lush
Chapter Fourteen	186, 189, 191, 192, 194, 195, 198: Jones family collections. 186: Photo: John Lush 199, 200, 201, 202: Photos: John Lush
Chapter Fifteen	206 copyright RUSI: by kind permission of the Royal United Services Institution Council. Photo: John Lush 207 by kind permission of Ipswich Town Hall. Photo: Barbara Burns 210, 214, 215, 218: Jones family collections 211, 219, 220, 221, 222: Photos: John Lush 212: by kind permission of the Victory Services Club. Photo: John Lush
Chapter Sixteen	224, 225, 227: by kind permission of the Royal Artillery Institution and the King's Troop, RHA 226l, 226r, 229: Photos: John Lush 230, 232, 234, 236, 240a, 240b, 241, 242: Jones family collections
Chapter Seventeen	244, 246, 247, 253, 256: Jones family collections 248, 249a, 249bb, 250, 251: Photos: John Lush
Chapter Eighteen	261, 263a, 263b, 265, 268, 272, 273a, 273b: Jones family collections 264*, 265*: Photos: John Lush 270, 271: Photos: John Lush

Introduction

An enormous pleasure in the course of researching and writing this book has been visiting the homes of people who enjoy living with Adrian Jones's artworks. Without exception, the owners had collected more than one piece. The art of Adrian Jones is addictive, so much so that one collector's wife refers to her living room with its examples of the artist's equestrian works as 'the loose box'. Some owners have a family history of descent from the original commissioner of a work, or a link to the army, the hunt or the turf which partly accounts for their interest, but others' enthusiasm has been ignited by the chance sighting of a work by an artist previously unknown to them. One private collector told me that his admiration for Adrian Jones stemmed from a Saturday morning visit to a local art gallery where he noticed two portraits of horses. He was immediately impressed by the excellence of the brushwork and the precise, skilful way in which the subjects had been portrayed. The precision had included such details as a saddle sore on the back of one horse and spittle on the flank of the other, each telling of recent hard riding and hard exercising, and making the horses vibrantly real.

This observer had noticed that in Adrian Jones's art even a small commissioned painting of a single standing horse is more than just an attractive pose. Whilst ensuring that looking at the finished painting would give his patron much the same pleasurable feeling as when he gave the subject a pat in real life, Adrian Jones nevertheless painted horses with total truthfulness (though in his large sculptures he aimed to produce 'an artistic monument ... the resemblance ... yet not a transcript of nature'). Some of his artistic lifetime was contemporaneous with the Aesthetic Movement, but he did not practise 'art for art's sake'. He painted and sculpted with purpose. Part of that purpose was to record; and the record was there partly with the motive of creating a work which would have emotional significance – not for its own sake, but to affect the viewer's attitude towards, for example, the animal kingdom, or bravery and death in battle, or comradeship between nations and races. This is done with superb craftsmanship and without overt moralising. Those who do more than glance at Adrian Jones's work typically become enthusiasts for his art. The casual Saturday morning visitor to a local gallery went on to purchase; then went to a major art gallery to view the Jones works on display and to request sight of those in the basement; and when he learned of the Duke of Edinburgh's Appeal for the conservation and casting in bronze of Adrian's 'Duncan's Horses' statue, he subscribed, and afterwards attended the unveiling ceremony at the Royal Veterinary College in June 1985.

Another present at that ceremony was the largest contributor to the Appeal, the late Paul Mellon KBE. An American art connoisseur, formerly President of the National Gallery of Art in Washington, he had promoted the cause of high quality animal painting and sporting art in Britain, and as his generosity to the Appeal reflects, he too was a great admirer of Adrian Jones's talent, especially as a sculptor. In 1980 his friend and associate John Baskett, the first curator of the Paul Mellon Art Collection, had brought out a magnificent illustrated history of *The Horse in Art.* In 2006 Yale University Press published a second edition, with an added chapter on 'The Twentieth Century and the Modern World'. In that chapter appears Pablo Picasso's 'The Horse', dated 1901, and his 'Jester on Horseback', dated 1905. On the next page is Franz Marc's painting, 'Little Yellow Horses', of 1912. On the page after that is Adrian Jones's sculpture of the same year, the four-horsed chariot of the Peace Quadriga, to which the book applies the term 'masterpiece'. To appear next to works by Picasso and Marc is an unaccustomed experience for a work by Adrian Jones. In any general account of the twentieth century, art historians will certainly – and rightly – refer fully to Picasso. They might dutifully inform readers that 'The Horse' is an early example of Picasso's 'Blue Period', whereas by the time he painted 'Jester on Horseback' Picasso had moved on to his more cheerful 'Rose Period'. Marc might well be included as a painter who had been influenced by Impressionism and then been part of the significant Blaue Reiter school. Jones, by contrast, did not move on to help to invent Cubism (unlike Picasso), nor did he develop towards abstract painting (unlike Marc). He exists in a space beyond the planets of the abstract expressionists, the minimalists, the Vorticists, the Fauvists, the Cubists, the Futurists and the Surrealists, so the art historian may pass by without observing his star.

There may be an element of caricature in that metaphorical account. Nevertheless it remains broadly true that in the middle years of the twentieth century Victorian artists from Lord Leighton downwards were treated dismissively. The adjective 'modern' in front of 'art' was transmuted from its straightforward sense of 'recent' to mean 'experimental', thereby excluding a traditional artist such as Adrian Jones, who was still active in the 1930s. In contrast, Adrian's Victorian and Edwardian contemporary William Frith, the painter of such popular pictures of the Victorian scene as 'Life at the Seaside', 'Derby Day' and 'The Railway Station', at the end of his autobiography, published in 1887, complained that 'the bizarre, French 'impressionist' style of painting recently imported into this country will do incalculable damage to the *modern* (my italics) school of English art'. Frith, painter of 'modern' scenes, was soon forgotten and literally undervalued. Adrian, reflecting in his autobiography of 1933 on such somersaults in art fashions, wrote, 'Sincerity has very little quality of immortality in it, and it is disconcerting to recall the number of artists who did their very best throughout a long life, achieved honour and recognition, and today are forgotten and neglected. Whether there is another lease of life before them when a later generation comes along is a question I find easy to ask but difficult to answer.'

Could Adrian visit the twenty-first century to seek the answer he would feel at least partly encouraged. His great equestrian artist predecessor, George Stubbs, is now highly regarded. Stubbs, like Adrian, had been expert in using his detailed understanding of horse anatomy when he painted, and had forcefully felt that the Royal Academy had treated him unfairly. For many decades after his death he was largely ignored. But now the Royal Veterinary College has on permanent display his painting of 'Eclipse', taking pride of place with Adrian's own 'Duncan's Horses', and the National Gallery considers 'Whistlejacket' one of its outstanding and most popular exhibits. Adrian would notice also that interest has revived in mainstream Victorian art; that new public art – often figurative statues – decorate the major cities of Britain, and not least that his own major works have been conserved and his memorials, such as that to the Royal Marines, rededicated.

Adrian had a strong sense of 'life's ever-rolling stream', for he outlived many of his friends: 'They enjoyed their hour before they went their ways, and I enjoyed it with them.' It is my wish that readers will equally enjoy sharing Adrian Jones's 'hour', that of a man who loyally served his Monarchs and his Muse. Though he was an outsider in establishment eyes, alienation is not amongst the themes of his art, and unlike such artists as the orientalist Alma Tadema he did not retreat from his own world in either his art or his life. Both were markedly influenced by what was then an important aspect of the national identity, Britain as the mother-country of an empire. He is a British artist who brings us part of the British past at the height of its imperial, military and financial power, and then in the cataclysm of 1914-18. He does so not as a historian, either for or against such concepts as 'Victorianism' or 'Imperialism', but through the eyes of an artist who was actively involved. He watched the fifty thousand troops in Queen Victoria's Diamond Jubilee procession, but he had also *served* with her gunners, her dragoon guards, her hussars, her household cavalry, her Indian soldiers and her veterinary service. And afterwards he painted and sculpted the royal horse named Diamond Jubilee.

Chronology

(Sculptures are indicated by bold type)

1845 9 February, born in Ludlow, Shropshire; 12 February, christened Alfred Adrian Jones, fifth son and sixth child of James Brookholding Jones, Veterinary Surgeon, and Jane Jones. (Second daughter born 1847; sixth son 1848.)

1849 25 August, death of his mother, Jane Jones. Family employs housekeeper and servant.

1850s Schooling at Ludlow Grammar School. Weekly drawing lessons. Outside school, informal tuition in watercolour painting from Henry Ziegler, and riding with Ludlow Foxhounds.

1863 3 October, enters London Veterinary College (which will become Royal Veterinary College in 1875)

1865 25 April, graduates Member of the Royal College of Veterinary Surgeons (MRCVS)

1867 11 January, joins Army Veterinary Service. Gazetted veterinary surgeon officer to Royal Horse Artillery battery at Ahmed-nuggur, India. 7 October, ordered to Bombay to embark for Abyssinia.

1868 Veterinary surgeon with General Napier's advance strike force in Abyssinian War. 10 April, at the battle of Aroghee, and 13 April at storming of fortress of Magdala. Campaign medal. 23 June, rejoins Royal Horse Artillery, now at Kirkee, India.

1869 30 June, gazetted to 3rd Hussars at Ahmed-nuggur. Rides winners at Poona racecourse, but health undermined from Abyssinia. Ordered six months sick leave.

1870 31 January, begins sick leave in Britain. 13 July, on medical advice resigns army commission. 23 July, marries Emma Beckingham at Ross-on-Wye, Herefordshire. Becomes landlord of Swan Hotel there.

1871 10 June, health restored, rejoins army. Gazetted to Royal Artillery at Weedon, Northants. 27 September, gazetted to 2nd Dragoon Guards (Queen's Bays) at Aldershot, Hants.

1872 The Queen's Bays move to Brighton. Also ceremonial duties in London.

1874 Bays return to Aldershot. March past for Army Commander-in-Chief, Duke of Cambridge.

1875 Bays posted to Leeds. Mid-May, provide escort for Duke of Edinburgh opening Exhibition of Arts and Manufactures. 14 July, ordered to march to Liverpool to embark for Dublin. 28 July, Bays HQ with Adrian reach Newbridge, Co. Kildare.

1876-80 In Ireland, summers at The Curragh, winters in various locations. 1876-77 season is elected huntsman of Queen's Bays pack. Paints self-portrait, brother officers' horses, and racehorses. 10 October 1878, son Adrian born in Dublin.

1881 27 February, embarks at Dublin with 7th Hussars for the Transvaal (First Boer) War. Delays on voyage. 22 April, arrives Cape Town. Truce already declared. May onwards, attached to Inniskilling Dragoons. Is one of Sir Evelyn Wood's cavalry escort to Zululand, for conference with Zulu chiefs. Draws the conference scene.

1882 19 January, returns to Britain. Posted to St. John's Wood Barracks, London. Is befriended by the sculptor Charles Birch, ARA. Begins sculpting.

1883 1 April, appointed Veterinary Surgeon 1st Class and promoted Captain. 16 August, death of first wife Emma at their home in Adelaide Road, London.

1884 **A Hunter: One of the Right Sort** statuette accepted for RA Exhibition. Enters **Gone Away** for Goldsmiths Company competition. Posted to Nile Expeditionary Force for the Relief of General Gordon campaign. 11 November, arrives Egypt.

1885 Marches camel convoy from Luxor and Aswan to Korti, Sudan, arriving 31 January. Hears **Gone Away** has won Goldsmiths First Prize. Inspects camels' conditions. Submits adverse report. Egypt medal and Khedive of Egypt's Star. 3 July, return to St. John's Wood. Devotes free time and leaves to painting and sculpting.

1886 **Camel Corps Scout** statuette exhibited at RA. Bronze and silver versions sold to brother officers. 10 April, elected to Savage Club membership.

1887 **Gone Away**, bronze, exhibited RA.

1888 16 May, gazetted to 2nd Life Guards at Windsor. Presented to Prince of Wales at Levee. **The Last Arrow**, wax, exhibited RA. **Fred Archer on Ormonde** cast in silver.

1889 July, **The Last Arrow**, bronze, exhibited Grosvenor Gallery. Sir Coutts Lindsay commissions Quadriga driven by an Assyrian for next year's exhibition. **Waterloo: The Charge Well Fought** statuette exhibited RA.

1890 **Waterloo** statuette, featuring Duke of Wellington and Life Guards officer, exhibited RA. Sculpts Derby winner **Sainfoin**, silver statuette. Chelsea Arts Club founded.

1890s A decade of numerous commissioned portraits, both paintings and sculptures, of Derby and Grand National winners. Main patrons Prince of Wales and Lord Wavertree.

1891 10 June, on twentieth anniversary of rejoining army, placed on retired half pay. 23 June: marries Emma Wedlake. They move to 147 Church Street, Chelsea. Large studio built in garden. **Triumph, Design for a Quadriga**, exhibited at RA. 4 Nov, **Icicle**, silver statuette, presented to Captain Oakeley of Atherstone Hunt.

1892 **Duncan's Horses**, plaster statue, exhibited RA. Goes to France to paint outstanding French racehorses on commission. July edition of *Magazine of Art* prints anonymous paragraph alleging a sculptor used a 'ghost' to create an RA exhibit. Adrian seemingly target of the accuser. Slander never substantiated, and withdrawn.

1893 **Maternal Care**, plaster statue, exhibited RA. 2nd Life Guards commission **Royal Standard Bearer**, silver statuette, as wedding present for Duke of York. Sculpts Grand National Winner **Cloister**, statuette, and life-size foxhound statue **Forager**. 20 October, attends funeral of Charles Birch.

1894 **Rape of the Sabines**, plaster statue, exhibited RA; afterwards at Alexandra Palace. **Mare and Foal**, bronze version of Maternal Care statue but with dog removed, exhibited Earls Court Industrial Exhibition. Sculpts Grand National Winner **Why Not**, bronze statuette, and **Polo Player**, bronze statuette.

1895 With Emma, visits New York, Philadelphia and Boston, USA. 20 November, **Derby Cup Trophy** presented to winner of main race at Derby racecourse.

1896 His portrait by Jamyn Brooks exhibited at RA. Princess of Wales commissions **Persimmon**, bronze statuette. Lord Wavertree commissions Grand National Winner **The Soarer**, silver and bronze statuettes, and silver on ebony base inkstand.

1898 May, one-man show, Graves Gallery, Pall Mall. Sculptures include **Breaking a Two Year Old Horse**. Models bas relief **Memorial for Berkeley Pigott**, Winchester Cathedral.

1899 March, on Show Sunday exhibits 'ten footer' painting, 'Charge of 21st Lancers at Omdurman'.

1900 Five royal commissions from Prince of Wales, including pair of 20"x20" statuettes of Grand National winner **Ambush II** and Derby winner **Diamond Jubilee**. Also paints those horses, and exhibits war and agricultural scenes at London Sketch Club.

1902 Sculpts **Meditation**, nude bronze statuette.

1903 12 April, **Royal Marines Memorial**, the Mall, unveiled by Prince of Wales (later King George V). **Colonel Afsur Dowla**, silver equestrian statuette, and **For the Faith**, bronze equestrian statuette, exhibited at RA.

1904 6 June, **South Australia Boer War Memorial**, Adelaide, unveiled. 9 November: bronze statuettes of equine brothers **Florizel II**, **Persimmon** and **Diamond Jubilee** given to King Edward VII by Prince of Wales as birthday present.

1905 10 June, opens Church St. Studio to exhibit plaster cast of **Persimmon** statue, commissioned by Jockey Club. 8 September, plaster cast of Adelaide horse unveiled in Ludlow Town Hall by Lord Windsor.

1906 15 May, larger than life size **Persimmon** bronze statue placed in Royal Stud, Sandringham. 23 June, Lord Roberts unveils **Carabiniers Boer War Memorial**, Chelsea Embankment. Sculpts marble bust of **General Buller**. 6 September, Lord Lieutenant of Devon unveils **General Buller**, bronze equestrian statue, Exeter.

1906-07 Chairman of Chelsea Arts Club.

1907 15 June, life size bronze equestrian statue of **Duke of Cambridge** unveiled by Edward VII. Summoned to Buckingham Palace, awarded M.V.O. (Member of Victorian Order). October, begins work on the **Peace Quadriga**.

1908 July, Chairman of Hanging Committee for large Allied Artists Association exhibition of sculptures and paintings in Albert Hall. Exhibits plaster casts of **General Buller** statue and **Joy of Living** statue. 23 July, one of eleven former pupils of Ludlow Grammar School who meet to found Old Boys Club. 27 July, distributes art awards at Crystal Palace School of Art, Music, Science and Literature.

1909 His portrait, with **Triumph** in the background, painted by Alfred Priest.

1910 Sculpts Grand Military Gold Cup winner **Vinegar Hill** with owner rider Dermot McCalmont up, bronze statuette. 4 April, **Mullagh**, favourite hunter of Lord Lonsdale, bronze statuette, presented to him by Cottesmore Hunt farmers.

1911 3 October, view day for the press of the **Peace Quadriga** at Burton's Foundry, Thames Ditton. Designs **Cottesmore Hunt Medal**, gift to retiring MFH, Lord Lonsdale.

1912 2 April, George V and Queen Mary inspect **Peace Quadriga**. 1 August, Guest of Honour at Ludlow Grammar School Speech Day.

1913 For first time exhibits paintings at R.A: 'Lord Roberts with Kitchener in South Africa' and 'Enid and Geraint'. Sculpts best racing son of Persimmon, **Prince Palatine**, bronze statuette.

1914 Second life-size painting of Lord Roberts, on Volney in India, exhibited RA. Sculpts the late **Sir George White VC**, marble bust, exhibited RA. Becomes President of Shropshire Society in London. Designs **Webb Medal**. Aged sixty nine, attempts to rejoin army.

1915 Queen Alexandra buys 'A Thoroughbred', shown in RA. War Relief Exhibition. Paints 'Royal Artillery on the Dunes, Flanders'.

1916 Sculpts **Steward**, foxhound of the Heythrop pack, silver statuette. 21 December, statue of **Captain Sturt** unveiled, Adelaide. Paints Lord Kitchener portrait; and 'Uhlan Débâcle in Pripet Marshes' painting exhibited RA.

1917 **To Commemorate A Nation Regaining Its Independence**, plaster memorial statuette, exhibited RA.

1919/20 Paints portraits of Earl Haig ('Dawn') and of 'General Allenby before Jerusalem'.

1921 **Action Front**, plaster statuette, exhibited RA. Sculpts **The Tetrarch**, bronze statuette, for Dermot McCalmont.

1922 9 March, **Bridgnorth Great War Memorial** unveiled by Private Eli Jones, K.S.L.I. 29 April, **Royal Gloucestershire Hussars Memorial** unveiled by General Chetwode. Sculpts equestrian bronze statuette, **Lord Lonsdale on Patsy** with pair of Cottesmore Hunt foxhounds, exhibited RA.

1923 **General Masceo of Cuba**, equestrian bronze statuette, exhibited RA.

1924 21 May, **Cavalry of the Empire Great War Memorial** unveiled by Prince of Wales (afterwards Edward VIII). **Bas relief side panel** exhibited RA. 9 November, **Uxbridge Great War Memorial** unveiled. Joie de Vivre, under title **The Joy of Life** included in Empire Exhibition, Wembley, in Palace of Arts grounds.

1925 **Action Front**, now a bronze group, exhibited RA. **The Empty Saddle**, bronze statuette, also exhibited RA.

1926 Two statuettes, **John Hassall, Esq., RI**, bronze, and **A Thoroughbred** exhibited RA. June, holds exhibition of his works in Chelsea studio. October, shows **Action Front** at Army Officers Art Society exhibition.

1927 Another two statuettes, **The Tetrarch**, bronze, and **Sir Ross Smith**, exhibited RA. 17 July, **Queen's Bays (Portable) War Memorial** unveiled by General Fanshawe.

1929 10 May, **The Empty Saddle**, Inniskilling Dragoons (Portable) War Memorial, unveiled at York by Field Marshal Allenby.

1931 **Over**, equestrian bronze statuette, exhibited RA.

1932 **Maternal Care** as bronze statuette, exhibited RA.

1933 Publication of 'best seller' autobiography, *Memoirs of a Soldier Artist.* **St George**, equestrian statuette, exhibited RA.

1935 February, Chelsea Arts Club celebrates his 90th birthday with a party for him. 9 April, at Annual Dinner of Royal Society of British Sculptors receives its highest honour, the Society's Gold Medal. **General Botha**, equestrian statuette, exhibited RA.

1938 24 January, dies. 28 January, funeral at Chelsea Old Church, followed by cremation at Golders Green. Ashes later buried at St Laurence's, Ludlow, beside commemorative plaque. Emma moves out of 147 Church Street, the marital home for forty seven years.

Note: Most of Adrian Jones's sculptures, including some not discussed nor illustrated in the book, are listed in this chronology of events. The mention of his very numerous paintings is limited to major canvases.

Chapter One: 'Early Days'
1845-1867: From Ludlow to Camden Town

The 9th of February 1845 was not an obviously propitious moment to be born in the historic Shropshire market town of Ludlow, even when that birth took place in a family 'in easy circumstances'. As was frequent practice in those precarious times, his parents had Alfred Adrian Jones, their fifth son, baptised just three days after his birth. That year the town was to be pockmarked by a scourge of smallpox and many funerals. Should the child survive, a look ahead to the kind of schooling for which a middle-class family might hope revealed only an ancient local grammar school tumbling in both reputation and pupil numbers. Yet when, ninety years later, Adrian Jones wrote his autobiography, *Memoirs of a Soldier Artist*, the story of his 'youth, middle age, old age, anecdotage', even though he suspected that distance lent enchantment, he was convinced that it was his first years that were 'best worth living and remembering'.

This was far from a mindless repetition of the Englishman's mantra that your schooldays are the best days of your life. Indeed, his zestful reminiscence is very largely about life out of school, and afterwards about life outside the routine regimental duties of an army officer. But a considered view of what is best worth remembering about Adrian Jones's life must be different from his own assessment. What finally was best in his life was his art. His reflections on his boyhood and early manhood are often implicitly or explicitly more evaluative than his treatment of his later life. (Thus he assesses the performance of his drawing master, but not the actions of politicians in the troubled Ireland in which he served, nor the controversial leadership in the Boer and Great War of the British generals whom he later sculpted or painted.) But on fuller reflection, he would surely have accepted that his best 'vigour and striving' went into his art. Revealingly, towards the end of his Introduction to his *Memoirs* it is his home in Chelsea, not that in Ludlow, which he categorises as the 'birthplace of my best endeavour'.

Thus, although he may have had fond memories of his boyhood days as 'the best worth living', we know all the same that it was his artist's studio that produced his 'best endeavour'. The most emphatic writing in *Memoirs* is on the call of Art which cannot be denied. Adrian Jones was keen on horses and hounds but he does not begin his autobiography with a quotation from the fox-hunting stories of R.S. Surtees which were so popular in the 1850s, nor with any nostalgic reference to the 'blue remembered hills' of A.E. Housman (next to whose ashes and memorial plaque on the north aisle wall of St. Laurence's parish church, Ludlow, his own were to be laid). Rather he opens with a quotation from W.E. Henley's poem 'Invicta':

> I am the Master of my Fate,
> I am the Captain of my Soul.

His experience as a small country boy had made him doubt the truth of those lines, for so strong was his sense that he must become an artist that he felt predestined. It was a feeling that was to persist despite all discouragements.

His father was scornfully dismissive of such a career ambition: 'Art means bread and cheese in a garret.' Wisely, his son did not for the present pursue his case. Nor in his *Memoirs* does he criticise his parents. However, his opinion of the town of his birth and boyhood is perhaps coloured by his sense that he might have received greater encouragement in a different environment.

Yet he was deeply fond of Ludlow, 'most delightful and picturesque of towns'. His perception of it went far deeper than simply appreciation of its physical beauty. Looking back from the 1930s, he wrote:

> Even today there is that in its atmosphere which keeps progress in place but makes for the content which, for all we know to the contrary, may be better for us ... Although in this era of motor cars and picture-palaces it cannot retain its old-world aloofness, it still contrives to impose upon visitors in some subtle fashion all its own a sense of satisfaction with a somnolent and decorous town. Ludlow has never lost her self respect; indeed she impresses it upon her residents at all hours of the day and night through the medium of the chimes in the belfry of her church.

But he also calls the town a 'sleepy hollow' and 'hardly a centre of progressive thought'; and his last word on his birthplace is that at the end of his boyhood 'I left peaceful, happy, unprogressive Ludlow and came to London'. Are those adjectives unconnected, or is there a causal link, with 'unprogressive' the cause and 'peaceful' and 'happy' the effect? What he says about Ludlow captures something important about the place, but it cannot be the whole truth; his memory of the somnolence of the town must be in contrast to the bustling London in which he spent most of his later life. It is not entirely accurate even to describe Ludlow as being in a hollow. Approached from three points of the compass, most spectacularly via the steep decline from Clee Hill, the town does indeed seem to nestle below the hills, but the town centre is built on a ridge and, approached from the north, stands dominant above the Teme and Corve rivers. But it is the epithet 'sleepy' which, like 'unprogressive', is open to debate. Those art historians who have neglected Adrian Jones on the ground that he was not significant in the development of 'modern' art might well see his describing anything as 'unprogressive' as an instance of pot accusing kettle. In his old age, however, Adrian had much sympathy with new developments in sculpture, and referred to Epstein as 'a man of genius, of great, great genius'. So, just as a description of Adrian himself as 'unprogressive' would not be wholly fair, the Ludlow of his youth was not unbrokenly 'sleepy'. The town's population was expanding rapidly; it had a lively intellectual life; it saw new industry and employment in transport replacing a past of glove-making and malting; and it was certainly not always a calm idyll of political harmony.

Early Victorian Ludlow had inherited from the town's Georgian and Regency heyday some impressive architecture and offered a cultivated and enjoyable lifestyle for those who could afford it. For gentle and genteel exercise, promenade walks had been laid out around the castle, while for the more energetic, the area offered good hunting, steeple-chasing and flat races, and the Ludlow pack of foxhounds. The upper room of the market hall had been made fit for assemblies and balls, and cultural life embraced a theatre, a circulating library and bookstalls. Nor was Victorian Ludlow content merely to inherit. The 1840s and 1850s were years of initiatives which brought both material and cultural progress. In 1840 spacious new Assembly Rooms were opened, allowing larger and more glittering balls to be held; and in the 1850s Ludlow's first professional photographer set up a studio, a local paper, *The Ludlow Advertiser,* was founded, the interior of the parish church of St Laurence was modernised, the organ being moved from the rood screen into the north transept so that the whole length of the church could be viewed, and, most importantly, the railway arrived, the line coming from Shrewsbury and then being extended to Hereford. The 1852 arrival of the railway must certainly have impinged upon Adrian Jones's consciousness. It was greeted with huge celebrations. The Mayor declared a general holiday, a cannon fired in salute, the church bells rang, crowds gathered at the station to meet the first train, and sports were held in the castle's outer bailey. This last event included a race for women which the Methodist minister castigated as 'degrading and demoralising'. Clearly one person at least thought that Ludlow was becoming *too* progressive. Schoolboys would also have been aware of the large engineering works, including a lengthy tunnel, needed to extend the line to Hereford in 1853. The extension was later to bring a particular bonus to Adrian Jones, as on it was to travel once a week an art master from Hereford. Later also he would use the photographer Thomas Jones to take *carte de visite* photographs of him in his cavalry uniforms of the Royal Horse Artillery and subsequently the 3rd Hussars.

The advent of the train symbolised the future, but the horse remained important, so the prosperity of Adrian's father, James Brookholding-Jones, as the town's only veterinary surgeon, was not affected, and he remained one of the comfortably-off professional men. The town had over a dozen solicitors and about ten doctors. In addition, the 1841 census had shown that one in twenty of the population was of independent means. The quarter of the townsfolk involved in manufacturing produced enough wealth to support an expanding population, albeit the distribution of that wealth from manufacturing was uneven, and leisure was provided for the upper middle and middle classes by the usual Victorian army of domestic servants. So although Ludlow was a rural market town, it was not dominated by agriculture; indeed, only marginally more people were fully employed in agriculture than were of independent means, although of course some other labourers undertook casual agricultural work.

It was nevertheless the rural rather than the urban aspects of Ludlow life that most shaped Adrian's growing up. He took part in the popular sport of ratting, the one blood sport he did not really enjoy, because the rats, caught alive, were destined to be thrown into a rat pit where bets were placed on which terriers in the pit could kill the largest number of rats in the shortest time. Adrian called this 'an ugly sight'. He kept ferrets and nets for rabbiting, but muzzled the ferrets to keep them from driving the rabbits into an end hole 'and then eating them alive as their horrid habit is'. His family was on the periphery of the equally popular sport of cock-fighting; his father kept game fowls, though he did not breed them specifically for the cock-fighting ring, and circumspectly he did not match them in the ring on his own account. In his *Memoirs* Adrian did not defend cock-fighting, nor any bloodsport, but he considered that cocks had a better chance than deer, fox, pheasant or partridge. Cocks, like rutting stags, are keen to prove their superiority in a fight, whereas the other animals are far from keen to be chased or shot. However, very much his greatest enthusiasm was horsemanship and following the Ludlow Foxhounds.

James Brookholding-Jones provided good mounts for his sons as they reached their early teens. Adrian took to riding instantly, enthusiastically and ably, as precociously as another boy with different gifts might take to a musical instrument, and his deep interest and excitement was much more than delight in the physical exercise and the thrill of a chase. From the time he started riding he sought to understand something of the movements of horses. The fundamental appeal was to his latent artist's observant eye: 'I found myself watching the pull of their muscles, their aspect as they trotted, cantered, galloped or jumped.' In his nineties, reviewing his youthful experience, he remained certain that the child had been the father of the man, and that his boyish passion for close observation had been 'of the greatest use' to him in his later life as an equine artist. The first piece of art that strongly appealed to the schoolboy was a portrait of the Master of the Ludlow Foxhounds: 'I could not keep away from it, the likeness was so striking.' As might be expected of someone keen on art but as yet inexpert at it, his first reaction was to be impressed by the striking resemblance between the painted portrait and the real man. But then he went on to appreciate the equine and equestrian elements. The horse was clearly a hunter, not a carriage horse; and the master's seat was that of a man clearly capable of

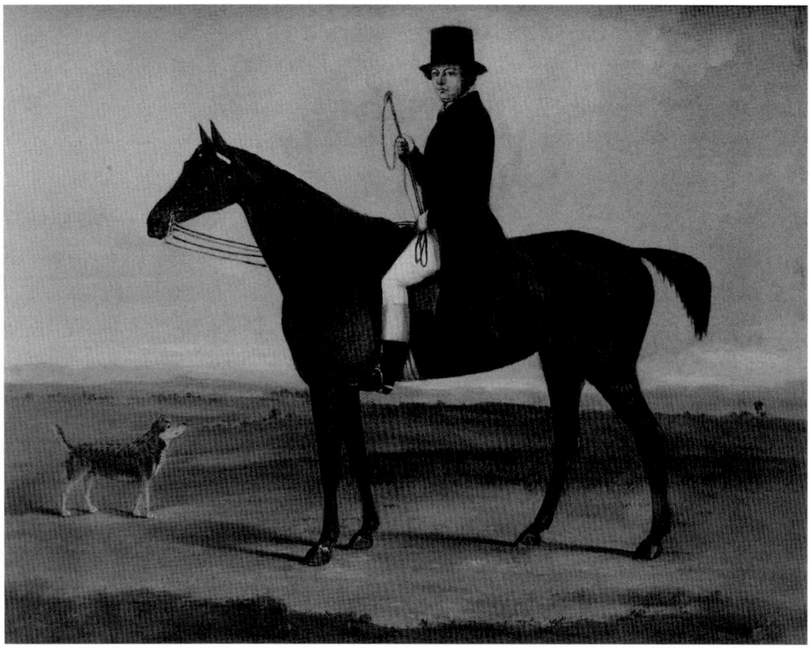
Portrait of James Brookholding Jones, Adrian Jones's father

staying in it. Adrian's father was also painted on horseback. The pose is static. A dog, tail erect, stands gazing devotedly up at his master on the stationary horse. The setting is open country, but there is no sense that the horse is about to gallop across it. The rider sits straight-backed in the saddle rather than crouched, with the reins held lightly in his left hand, while his right poses the whip idly across his chest, and his gaze is not towards the country ahead but turned towards the painter. In his own mature work Adrian Jones was usually to portray horses in movement or ready for movement, but this painting of his father's horse seems to have provided the template for the first statuette he successfully submitted to the Royal Academy, 'One of the Right Sort'.

When James came to consider the education of his sons, he must have had misgivings. Certainly he had choice. The town offered over a dozen private schools, of variable quality but the better of them giving tuition in the modern subjects needed for the new age as well as the classics. Two of these better ones were sited in Mill Street, in close competition with the grammar school that stood in the same street. The family's Anglican instincts favoured the grammar school, which had been in the town since medieval times and on its present site since 1527, and had produced a remarkable number of distinguished men, including William Owen, who over a span of thirty-two years from 1792 had had more than two hundred of his paintings hung at the Royal Academy, who had painted many of the eminent men of his era, not least the Prime Minister William Pitt, and who had been appointed Principal Portrait Painter to the Prince Regent.

Not that any of that would have carried much weight with James – and it was he who made the decisions. In his son's words, 'he was emphatically the man who mattered'. On 27 October 1836, at the age of twenty-four, James had married Jane Marshall at Tetbury in Gloucestershire. There may have been an element of shotgun marriage, for their eldest son, Frederick James, was born just under seven months later. During the first four years of the marriage, Jane gave birth to a son or a daughter annually, and in the following almost eight years she completed a family of six boys and two girls. Adrian was her sixth child and fifth son. Eleven months after the birth of her last son, Thomas, she died in August 1849, aged thirty-five. Adrian was just four. In his autobiography he mentions neither his mother nor his stepmother Lucy, a local girl from nearby Brimfield whom his father married in the 1860s. Lucy lived on into the 20th century and took pride in her stepson's achievements as a sculptor, making a point of informing the local press when an Australian from Adelaide wrote to her, after his visit to what he termed 'your quaint old town', praising 'the exceptional ability' Adrian had put into sculpting 'the beautiful bronze statue' in Adelaide commemorating the Australian Troopers who fought in the Boer War, and assuring her that 'this masterpiece takes the highest place amongst the statues in our city'.

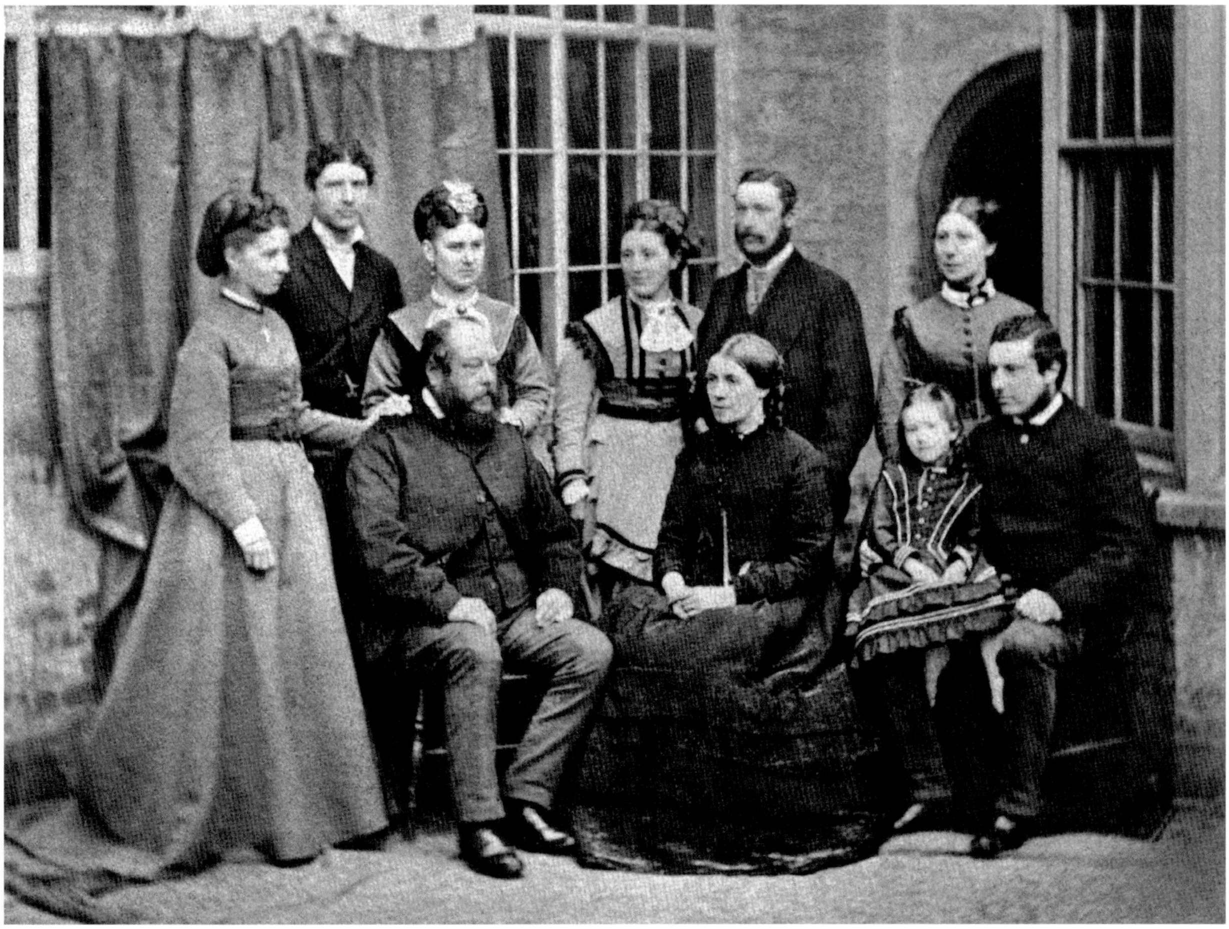

The family of James B. Jones. He sits on the left; on his left is Adrian's stepmother Lucy, and beyond her the eldest son Frederick with his daughter on his knee and his wife standing behind. The recently wed Adrian and his first wife Emma (née Beckingham) stand behind James. On Adrian's right is his elder sister Emily, and centre back are his younger sister Fanny and elder brother Edward.

Adrian's omission of his mother, his stepmother and of his sisters from his memoirs does not reflect an antagonistic relationship with home. He remembered a vigorously happy home life, his leisure time being spent mainly with his brothers, and after leaving Ludlow he often went back to visit his family. On this, as on other matters, writing in the 1930s he still observed a Victorian reticence about his private life, reinforced by the army officer tradition of not discussing ladies in the Mess.

Regrettably, through its headmaster the grammar school had become caught up in bad-tempered politics as national reforming legislation thrust change upon Ludlow in the wake of the 1832 Reform Bill. The Municipal Corporation Act had demanded that charity and municipal property be separated. In the first proposed division in 1837 of the income from property, the charities received only an unfairly niggardly amount. A revised settlement in 1841 raised the charities' income to £859 per annum and the town clerk went off to London to promote the requisite Parliamentary Bill, whereupon two petitioners, considering the amount still too little, objected. One of these petitioners was the Reverend Arthur Willis, since 1838 headmaster of the grammar school. It took five years of furious litigation which caused much ill-feeling before the charities' final settlement was agreed at £1,525, and the borough council was left with legal costs of £37,000. The town's anger at this impoverishment fell upon Willis. Town parents withdrew their sons, leaving him with just a handful of boarders and a few day boys. His salary was not paid from 1846, and then a quarrel over school times was used as a reason to give him notice of dismissal in 1850. In the same year C. Brice's booklet *Ludlow Grammar School as It Is and Was*, published locally, narrated scandalous but true stories about disputes between Willis and his assistant master John Williams, who taught the lower school boys at the lower end of the medieval schoolroom. Among other incidents the older boys hung a labelled effigy of Williams above his desk and greeted his entry with 'uproarious jibes and jeers'.

So there was much to give James pause when thinking about the education of his sons. Yet one of Willis's pupils, John Harley, valued his education enough to make him the school's largest benefactor in later years, and reminiscing at a Speech Day he described not only how Latin grammar had been 'thoroughly impressed, compressed and driven into us by iteration' and caning, but also described the school of 1843 as a confident institution 'having all the advantages that age and experience could give it'. In the end that heritage of history decided the father. Also he had three years in which to estimate the calibre of the new headmaster, James Banks, before Adrian was sent to the school in 1855. In a typical year the school was now averaging about forty boys, of whom up to a dozen were headmaster's boarders, so still comparatively few town boys were in attendance. Opinions differed as to whether this was because of too much emphasis on Latin and Greek, or too severe a regime run by the headmaster. As one of his former pupils expressed it, 'it was only by much tribulation that we could enter the temple of knowledge'. Six strokes of the cane on the hand were commonplace. The regime was also arduous. The school bell rang at 7 a.m. to start the day in summer and at 7.30 a.m. in winter. There were breaks for breakfast and lunch, and unless a boy was in detention his day ended around 4 p.m. Wednesdays and Saturdays were half holidays, but (except for nonconformists) there was morning school on Sundays at 8 a.m. for religious teaching, followed by attendance afterwards in the school seats in the parish church for both matins and evensong.

One of Banks's first actions was to found a school library in 1853, but books for the classroom were an expense and therefore not always in sufficient supply – even Latin dictionaries sometimes had to be shared. The penalty for translating a word incorrectly was writing out the column in the dictionary in which the word appeared, which made the dictionary with the shortest columns very popular for impositions. To tax the boys further, the rules in Wordsworth's *Greek Grammar* were in Latin. Homework could take four or five hours, and harsh retribution fell upon the boy who was found to have used a crib. Parents complained to the Trustees about the severity of both Banks and his successor, Sampson Kingswood. These headmasters could however display a more genial side at such occasions as the Christmas treat, and they were both academically brilliant. Kingswood had gained First Class Honours at Cambridge in 1848, and Banks was a distinguished classical scholar who edited and translated several classical texts. Both these classicists were progressive enough to campaign for the better teaching of mathematics in the school. Banks was a believer in the developing Victorian ethos of the public schools and therefore sought to promote manly character. Following the example of many another Victorian classical scholar, in the third year of his headship he produced his 'slim volume' of verse, *Nugae: The Solace of Rare Leisure*. In one poem he wishes manliness for his sons:

> My sons, oh they should stand erect,
> Above all lying arts,
> Whose open brows should well reflect,
> Their honest manly hearts.

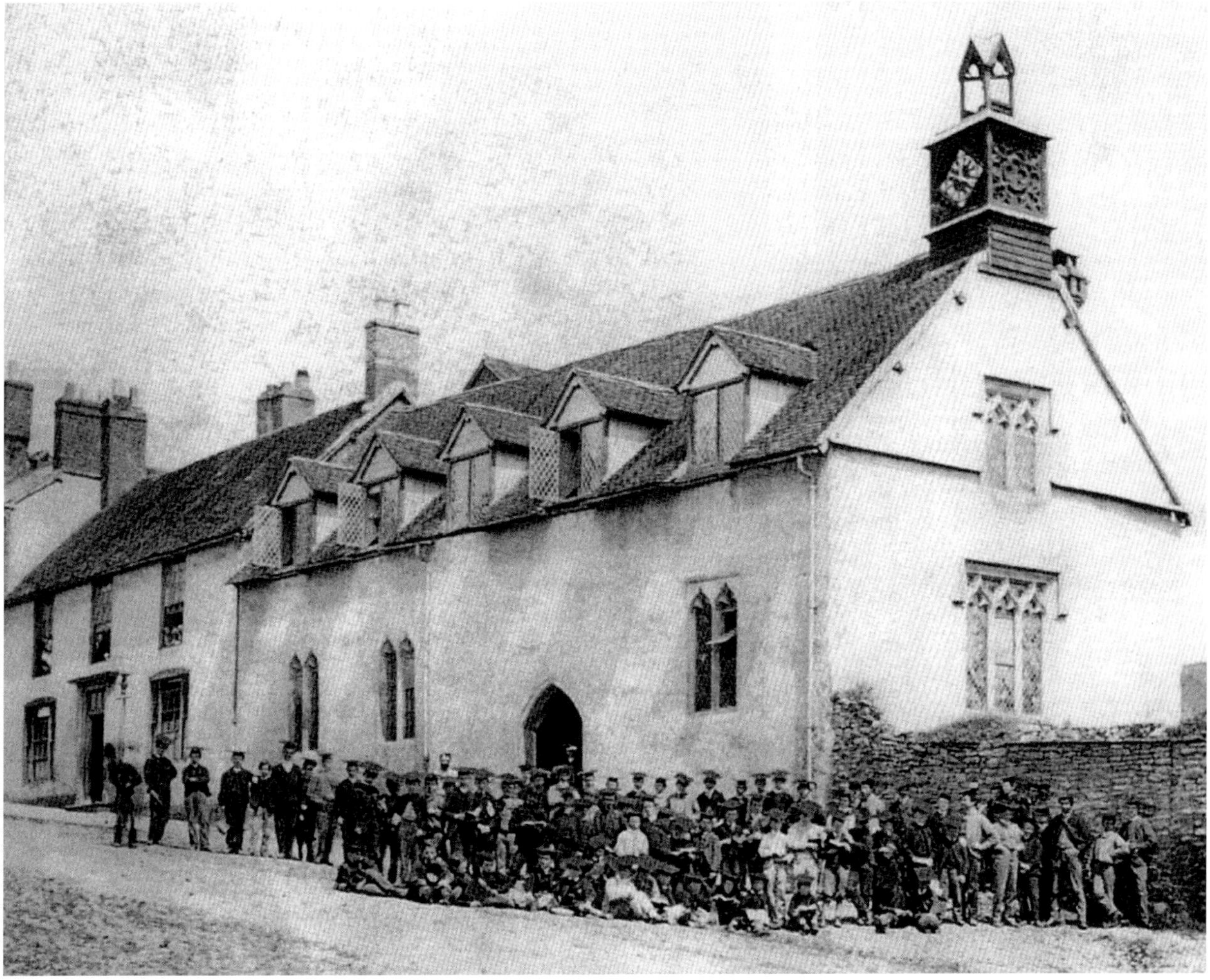

Wearing their mortarboards, the pupils of Ludlow Grammar School in the nineteenth century.
Since 1527 all its pupils had been educated in the Schoolroom behind.

This was something which Adrian Jones took from his education, physically as well as ethically. Even when he was in his nineties, people were to remark upon his ramrod-straight back, and his great amiability of character was accompanied by moral rectitude. He also took from his arduous schooling what another former pupil termed appreciation of 'having to do uncongenial tasks cheerfully as a matter of duty'. He left having received straightforward instruction in writing from the school's newly appointed English master and, significantly, weekly practice in drawing. He recorded in his *Memoirs* that 'not one of the lessons appealed to me quite so much as that which came in the drawing class on a Monday afternoon. I used to look forward to that with the keenest anticipation'. He went on to complain that he did not receive any personal attention in these lessons, because the drawing master took no individual interest in any pupil in the class. The master's failure to pay attention to individual characteristics, however, had the useful benefit for his pupil that Adrian not only did his own drawings but also helped those classmates who did not enjoy the subject. He thereby gained extra practice – and won school Art prizes.

The art master's failure to foster Adrian's bent and gifts did not deter him from the idea that he wanted to be an artist. Out of school he spent much of his leisure making drawings and watercolour paintings. In

Memoirs he terms these efforts 'immature'. The choice of word is probably evaluative as well as descriptive. While it is not clear whether this is the schoolboy's perception or the judgement with hindsight of the 1930s author, the likelihood is that the young Adrian was already discerning. Importantly, he had the good fortune to meet the artist Henry Ziegler, a meeting which appears to have been as significant for the development of his painting as his later meeting with C.E. Birch was to be for the development of his sculpture. Unlike the drawing master, 'he took a personal interest in me and gave me my first serious lessons in construction and painting in watercolour from nature'. This was now the great decade of the Pre-Raphaelites, their Brotherhood having been founded in 1848 and their declared aims including 'to study Nature attentively'. Ziegler had been travelling in Europe with the Duke of Rutland and other patrons, and was therefore able to show Adrian 'a large portfolio of sketches from Norway, Sweden, the Tyrol and many coastal towns', i.e. not scenes from the classical 'Grand Tour'. Ruskin would have approved – and presumably Ziegler would have read Ruskin's first two volumes of *Modern Painters*, published in 1843 and 1846, which covered his attitude to nature and learning to draw what was really there, and played down the importance of 'composition'. But much of Ziegler's painting predated Ruskin's writings, and he was not going to abandon 'construction' in his advice to Adrian. Ziegler was neither a native Salopian nor a permanent Ludlow resident, but he was a frequent visitor from the time when Thomas Knight employed him to sketch the scenery around Downton Castle. He liked working in the borderland Marches, and during visits to Downton in 1826 had painted six views of Ludlow. These were engraved in 1846, and so were widely available when Adrian knew him. During the time of their acquaintance, Ziegler was painting watercolour portraits, so could give Adrian advice on that art as well as on landscape painting. Probably he also learned the importance of having patrons, including royal patrons. Over many years Ziegler had received commissions from Queen Adelaide (the consort of King William IV) and from lesser royalty, and in the years in which he was taking an interest in Adrian's development he was also teaching many members of the royal family to paint and draw.

Appreciating the role of commissions was an important lesson for Adrian, and he would make use of it in later years. Nevertheless, despite the example of Ziegler's social and professional success, Adrian's father remained convinced that 'art means bread and cheese in a garret'. But unlike the participants in the Great Lawsuit, father and son finally reached an amicable compromise. Adrian already had a precocious understanding and appreciation of horses, their movements, their qualities and their nature, and he accepted the idea of taking up a profession that would bring him into contact with horses. He was sent to the Veterinary College in Camden Town. As he left Ludlow, a town which then boasted not a single piece of public statuary, he could not know that he would one day remedy that deficiency with the plaster cast of one of his monumental memorials, which would be installed in the town's most prestigious site.

'Under orders but fairly content': veterinary studies

In Adrian Jones's autobiography of some 50,000 words, *Memoirs of a Soldier Artist*, ten pages are given to his youth and education in Ludlow, but just half a sentence to his undergraduate career. At the start of the sentence he leaves Ludlow, and then continues 'and [I] came to London and graduated at the Veterinary College in Camden Town and took my finals at the Royal College of Veterinary Surgeons and found myself at the ripe age of twenty one with my degree and qualifications'. Having dismissed his veterinary studies in less than a breath, he adds decisively, 'but I had no intention of practising'.

This might suggest that to the would-be artist veterinary science was not important. Nothing could be further from the truth. It was with complete justification that the historian of the Royal Veterinary College, Professor Cotchin, lamented that the memorial tablet to Adrian Jones on the outside of St Laurence's church in Ludlow 'does not state his veterinary qualification'; and Adrian's fellow Ludlovian E.T. Evans made the confident if impossible to verify claim that 'probably no sculptor of the present, or any past, age had a superior knowledge of equine anatomy'. While Evans might be accused of letting local patriotism inflate his judgement, he is not alone in his view that Adrian Jones became to English horse sculpture what George Stubbs was to English horse painting. At its Hawkshead site the Royal Veterinary College exhibits two main works of art: 'Eclipse', painted by Stubbs and 'Duncan's Horses', sculpted by Jones.

As witnessed by the copperplate signature of his name – 'Alfred A. Jones' – in the entrance register, Adrian entered College on 3 October 1863, aged eighteen. The institution was then the London Veterinary College in Great College Street in Camden Town. ('London' in its title would not be replaced by 'Royal' until 1875, when the College was incorporated by Royal Charter.) Adrian followed the London College course of two nine-month sessions. He was examined *viva voce* in chemistry, pharmacy and the science of substances used in medicine; the anatomy and physiology of the horse and the recognition and treatment of equine diseases and ailments; and the anatomy and physiology of the ox and other domesticated animals. Success there qualified the London students for entry to the Diploma examinations of the Royal College of Veterinary Surgeons, which had received its Royal Charter in 1844. The examinations were held in the Freemasons tavern, so opportunity for drowning sorrow or celebrating joyous outcome was close at hand. Adrian graduated successfully, and on 25 April 1865 received the qualification of Member of the Royal College. This entitled him to term himself 'Veterinary Surgeon', which distinguished him from the humbler trades of 'farrier' and 'cow leech'. Though the arrangers of his memorial plaque omitted the letters, he placed MRCVS after his name on the title page of his *Memoirs*, giving it equal importance to the distinctions of MVO (Member of the Victorian Order) and FRBS (Fellow of the Royal British Sculptors Society) that he earned as an artist.

In the 1860s, despite the advance of the railways, horse welfare was still vital to both civilian and military society. The value of the College was acknowledged in the additional funding it received from businesses such as breweries and from carriers who depended on horse-drawn transport. Its range of students broadened Adrian's acquaintance. While some like him came from a veterinary or farming family, others came from backgrounds in medicine or chemistry, and a sprinkling came from Ireland or abroad, including several nations in the Empire, the United States and France. Student behaviour during the courses was variable, but the authorities sought to impose discipline where necessary. Cotchin records that during or around Adrian Jones's time there, one student was suspended for thieving from fellow students, one for disturbing lectures, and, more unusually, one for using College notepaper when offering betting information for five pounds. After graduating, a proportion of students enterprisingly made their careers abroad or, like Adrian, joined the army, with which the College had a close connection (the two immediately previous Principals had been much involved with the Army Veterinary Service).

Adrian Jones arrived during the tenth year of the Principalship of Professor Charles Spooner. He could indubitably not have applied the term 'unprogressive' to the College of 1863. Most students thought Spooner an exceptionally fine and forward-looking teacher. He protested against vivisection in unnecessary demonstrations, he campaigned for the chloroforming of animals before they were subjected to experimentation, and he served on the council of the Society for the Prevention of Cruelty to Animals. In his early years he had been handicapped by inadequate lecturing and practical rooms, and by the low educational level of some entrants, because then there was no matriculation examination. Such an examination was only introduced the year after Adrian's entry, but he would have had no difficulty with it, for it was essentially a straightforward test in English and arithmetic (though a 21st-century applicant might be defeated by its requirement to parse simple sentences). Notably, by 1863, although a larger lecture theatre still lay four years in the future, new buildings were in position: a dissecting room, a separate covered enclosure for the slaughter and dissection of animals and for post mortem examinations, and a chemistry laboratory. Equally importantly, recent appointments included three of the four best teachers of Spooner's regime. In the chair of chemistry since 1860 was Professor Tuson. A researcher of repute, he was co-editor of the journal of the profession, the *Veterinarian*, and of the standard work *Veterinary Pharmacopoeia*. He boosted the morale of his vets in training by telling them they were a better group than medical students. Appointed at the same time as Tuson was a new demonstrator in anatomy, William Pritchard, described by the College historian as 'an unsurpassed clinical observer and a skilled operator'. He was a stern controller of order and good conduct in the dissecting room, and the students benefited. But probably the most beneficial teacher of all was George Varnell, who was appointed Professor of Anatomy in the year before Adrian began his training. Apart from being a thorough master of Adrian's favourite subject, horse anatomy, and lecturing on it clearly, he demonstrated two further skills – clever draughtsmanship, and the habit of putting observations on record. Adrian admired the former skill and was to use the latter to good effect in his first military campaign. Meanwhile he followed the routine of student life. Each working day began with the anatomy lecture at 9.15 a.m. At 11 a.m. chemistry and cattle pathology lectures alternated, and at 1 p.m., except on the half day, came lectures on the physiology and pathology of the horse.

The College bicentennial history is unequivocal: 'two great men qualified from the College in Spooner's reign – the sculptor, Adrian Jones, and the scientist Griffith Evans'. Their two distinguished lives had a number of parallels. Evans, from a Welsh farming family, graduated before Jones. Like him, he joined the army as a commissioned officer, serving initially with the Artillery. Both saw warfare, in Evans's case the American Civil War, and both in their old age in the 1930s wrote of their experience of it, Jones in his *Memoirs* and Evans at length in a 1935 issue of the *Veterinary Record*. But whereas Jones combined his army duties with art, Evans combined his with studying medicine. Posted to Montreal, he followed the medical course at McGill University, and when posted back to Ipswich and then Woolwich in England he continued medical studies at three hospitals and at King's College. Twice he was ordered to India to investigate diseases which were killing army animals. His second posting was to the Punjab to study the disease 'surra'. He quickly demonstrated that the numerous fatalities to horses and camels were the effect of a disease-causing unicellular organism which was parasitic in the animals' blood. This was the first discovery of a pathogen of this type. Like Jones, Evans has his memorial: he is remembered in the organism now called *Trypanosoma Evansi*. He received other honours also and lived to be 100, an anniversary which was commemorated by the College.

To Adrian Jones, the College's bicentennial history devotes a page of text and full page illustrations of two of his major sculptures. It might seem odd that a history of undergraduate veterinary studies should include illustrations of sculptures, but that use of space is justified. Veterinary studies were as important to Jones's art as to Evans's science, perhaps even more so. As the magazine *Punch* put it, 'It is not too much to say that, aided to a large extent by his knowledge of comparative anatomy, Adrian Jones stands absolutely alone as an exponent of animal life.' Without tuition in veterinary science, Adrian Jones's art would not have been of that first rank which in his lifetime received so much public acclaim – albeit, as we shall see, not from those members of the Royal Academy who were reluctant to recognise a talent which had been trained in vet school rather than art school.

Meanwhile Adrian's first task was to persuade his father that he was 'a fully qualified veterinary surgeon who felt that it was impossible to settle down to the humdrum life of a young practitioner'. He was prepared to put the call of art on hold for the moment but was determined that his immediate destiny should be 'something more moving and adventurous' than a country veterinary practice. Finally, with parental goodwill, in January 1867, at the age of nearly twenty-two, he joined the Army Veterinary Service. Apart from a brief break, it was to be his career for the next twenty-four years.

Chapter Two: 'The Spirit of Adventure'
1867-1871: Army Service in India and Abyssinia

The army had been appointing trained veterinary surgeons to cavalry regiments since 1796. Originally the appointments had carried warrant officer rank only, but gradually commissions had been introduced, which had helped to raise the status of the profession generally. As yet army vet officers did not have their own regiment. The Army Veterinary Corps was not to be formed until 1903 and the prefix 'Royal' was added only in 1918 in recognition of its invaluable performance in the Great War, when it expanded from about 500 all ranks at the start of hostilities to nearly 42,000 by the time of the Armistice. In 1867 the new officer was gazetted not to a corps but to a regiment and wore that regiment's uniform. However, the Indian Mutiny had enhanced the reputation of vet officers, partly because they suffered just as others did. Two were murdered at Meerut on the first day of the mutiny in 1857, and others thereafter. So on 1 July 1859, the Wilkinson Warrant (so named after the Principal Veterinary Surgeon at the time) laid down a graded establishment for veterinary surgeons. The army was to have forty veterinary surgeons ranking as lieutenants, twenty-five veterinary surgeons first class, ranking as captains, and three staff veterinary surgeons ranking as majors. In the regimental list, however, the vets were to be considered the junior officer of their rank, except mercifully when it came to the allocation and choice of living quarters. After five years a surgeon became eligible for promotion to surgeon first class, which suggests that a career pattern had been organised, but in practice the pattern was easily disrupted because a vacancy had to arise at the rank above before a promotion could be made. Adrian's father may have feared that to be an artist was to starve in a garret, but a vet officer's life was hardly the way to quick riches. Daily pay was ten shillings on appointment, rising to fourteen shillings daily after twenty-five years' service. First class pay could rise to £1. There was feeling among vet officers that the Wilkinson Contract could have been more generous, but it was not easy for them to give voice and impact to their dissatisfaction. Each officer was serving in a different regiment and therefore isolated from his fellow vets. Nevertheless, in the year before Adrian joined the service, vet officers managed to combine to submit a memorandum asking for improvements. In response the powers that be simply quoted the stern law of supply and demand: there being no shortage of candidates, there was no need for better conditions of service.

Recruit officer Adrian Jones's marching orders were that he was to report in February 1867 to a Royal Horse Artillery battery stationed at Ahmednuggur (modern spelling Ahmadnagar) in India. He was to travel with the Peninsular and Oriental shipping line and he was to pay his own boat fare. (Happily the army afterwards refunded his expenses.) He filled his voyage out 'with day-dreams of adventures to be experienced' amidst the excitement of life in India where the Northwest Frontier was still in wild disorder and the awful scenes of the Mutiny were just ten unforgotten years in the past. For an inexperienced young officer in a strange exotic country, to have to make a journey to the interior to find his unit might almost have been set as a test of initiative. Bombay, the pioneer Indian city for railways, had been building lines out since 1851, but as yet steam would take him only so far. Adrian was fortunate. He met a civil engineer who was also travelling to Ahmednuggur and who invited Adrian to join him. From Poona they travelled onwards in the engineer's light two-wheeled tonga. One of their overnight stops was spent in a Dak (mail house) bungalow. They ordered chicken for supper and while waiting for their meal heard such a wild commotion in the compound outside that Adrian went to see what was happening. The cook was having a chicken hunt, chasing the birds around the compound until he eventually got near enough to a victim to grab it. The unfortunate bird was instantly killed, skinned, slit lengthways, opened out, and grilled over the fire, thus literally becoming a dispatch cock. The spatchcock meal enjoyed, their tonga ride continued until they reached their destination. Adrian allowed himself the leisurely luxury of a couple of days' holiday with his new friend before reporting for duty and starting to master the not very onerous military duties to which he was assigned.

For someone whose voyage out to India had been 'filled with day-dreams of adventures', a posting to the Royal Horse Artillery at Ahmednuggur was not ideal for finding fulfilment. When a few years earlier subaltern Bob Roberts (afterwards to rise to Field Marshal Earl Roberts, and to be painted by Adrian Jones as such) had also joined the Horse Artillery, it had been at Peshawar. He had been able to write in his memoirs:

> Life on the frontier in those days had a great charm for most young men; ... military expeditions were constantly taking place, ... and one lived in hope of being amongst those chosen for active service.

The redoubtable hill-fortress of Ahmednuggur, on the north-western edge of the Nizam of Hyderabad's extensive territory, had been the setting for a great storming capture by Wellesley and his soldiers in the Mahratta wars at the start of the 19th century, ('all done before breakfast', went the story), but it was a very long way from India's North West Frontier, and there had been no rising in a military cantonment during the Mutiny within 150 miles of it. Gunners could tell stirring stories of how they had used India's Ludlow Castle (nothing to do with the Shropshire town, but a British residence just outside Delhi named thus after a Dr Ludlow) as the site for their four batteries of guns which had pounded a breach in the walls of Delhi and enabled the forces of the Crown to enter and drive out the mutineers; but ten years later serving with the artillery in Ahmednuggur was peacetime soldiering.

> I reported myself to Major Blount, who commanded the battery of the Royal Horse Artillery. No youngster can have been more fortunate in his superior officer. I hired a bungalow, joined the Mess, and started to master my military duties ... soon I had the leisure to buy horses.

Though in his *Memoirs* Adrian describes the decade of the 1870s, spent serving with the Queen's Bays, as 'the pleasantest of my life', the months he spent in 1867 with the RHA were equally pleasant – 'having such a good time as only comes to a carefree young man in the best health'.

The RHA had been brought into being in the last years of the 18th century to meet the battlefield demand for guns which could be manoeuvred as swiftly as cavalry. In 1867, British artillery was still organised in batteries rather than larger regiments and was divided into three separate branches. Garrison artillery provided heavy, sometimes static, firepower; mounted field artillery supported the infantry; and horse artillery worked with the cavalry. Their watchwords were speed and dash. Their fast horses, driven by soldiers ideally not much heavier than jockeys, pulled light field guns and were trained to go into action at the full gallop. They

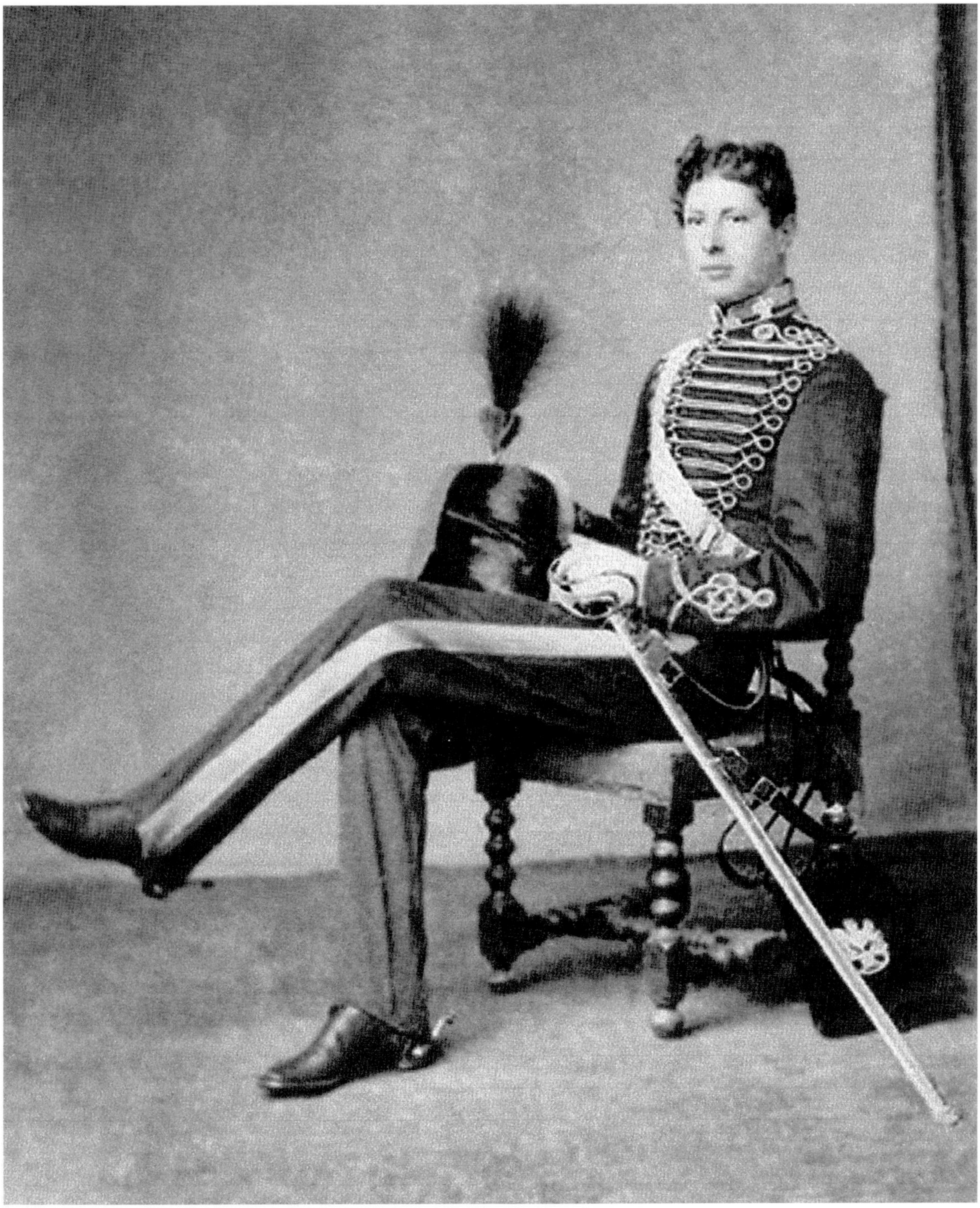

Lieutenant Adrian Jones, Veterinary Surgeon,
Royal Horse Artillery, 1867

could be spectacular at any time, and in peacetime glamorous. The horses, men and guns of an RHA battery charging past was the top attraction at many a 19th-century military review and tournament (and survives into the 21st century in the ceremonial duties of the King's Troop). Since the Mutiny the policy in India had been not to entrust Indian native regiments with cannon so that the artillery was almost entirely manned by British soldiers.

In preparation for the social side of army life, Adrian had gone to Ludlow's professional photographer Thomas Jones to have his picture taken for his *carte de visite*. A trim figure, for as a competitive horseman he had to keep his weight down, he sits leaning back in a padded chair, left hand resting on rather than gripping his sword hilt and his legs casually crossed, almost as if he were modelling for a society portrait of a cavalry officer and gentleman by his contemporary, the painter James Tissot. The neatly fitting jacket expensively features on his chest parallel groups of gold cord fastened to ball buttons and ending in a curl just below his collar, and on the sleeve is a large gold cord Austrian knot, whilst down his leg to his spurred boot runs the regiment's single stripe, nearly two inches wide. His sabretache, though now obsolescent for battlefield use, hangs decoratively from his sword belt. On his thigh perches his black busby, its scarlet bag pulled across the top and down the right hand side nearly out of sight of the camera. There is therefore nothing to distract attention from the prominence of the plume that marks him out from his brother officers: whereas they sport a white ostrich feather, his red plume distinguishes him as the regiment's veterinary surgeon. His chest, half-turned towards the lens, gives similar prominence to the second distinguishing feature, the veterinary officer's white leather shoulder pouch belt. Not surprisingly, his unlined face looks across with quiet confidence to meet the eyes of those who will receive his visiting card.

Adrian hired a bungalow, joined the Mess, and doubtless, as etiquette demanded, presented his card to the commanding officer's wife, Mrs Blount. Artillery officers, like veterinary officers, did not buy promotion. Opportunities came not through purchase but through the retirement or death (all too likely in that climate) of a more senior officer. That could mean frustration for the ambitious, but also meant stable officer staffing, so there developed a strong unit and family spirit. Soon Mrs Blount was helping Adrian with his first racing jacket. She chose his racing colours and had the jacket made for him in her own bungalow. Labour cost little. Mrs Blount could afford house servants, and officers could afford grooms. Though Adrian did not win his first race, other officers soon recognised his skill with horses and entrusted some of theirs to him for training, so one of his morning commitments became riding a string of them over the gallops. By sticking to a jockey's diet and with the aid of a pad of quilted cotton wool intended to prevent the saddle from bruising the horse's withers, he was, in his own words, 'fairly successful in the races'.

Game was plentiful. Near the start of his posting, Adrian went out early one morning for a ride to have a look at the country round the military cantonment. Spotting some black buck, he rode quietly until he knew they would no longer be alarmed and then galloped to his bungalow for a rifle and back again to see if the buck were still there. They were, within range and in the open. 'I jumped off and shot, dropping my quarry cleanly. I hoisted him up on the horse under me and the Mess had venison chops for breakfast.' His impromptu effort caused some hilarity amongst his brother officers, being so different from the usual highly organised big-game hunting expedition. He observed ruefully: 'I found that there was a lot to learn'. But he was learning about the country. In a self-disciplined way, he trained himself to ignore the pangs of thirst, making a practice of having nothing to drink from the time he left camp in the morning until he returned. His self-discipline over eating and drinking was to stand him in good stead. Life in India was going well; but suddenly it ended. On 7 October 1867 Adrian came under orders to proceed to Bombay and then onwards to Abyssinia. His military adventures were about to begin.

The Abyssinia Expedition 1868

At the start of the 21st century, the military historian Ian Hernon published his account of colonial campaigns of the 19th century under the title *Britain's Forgotten Wars*. The book included an account of the campaign to Magdala in Abyssinia in 1868. The soldiers who served in the campaign would have been saddened to think that the action they took part in would in the future be 'forgotten'. Pleased at the successful conclusion of the campaign, their Commander-in-Chief General Sir Robert Napier in his last General Order had assured his troops 'your gallant exploits will live in history'. The war correspondent G.A. Henty, later to become famous as the most prolific writer of patriotic tales of Empire for boys, put together his despatches from Abyssinia in his 1868 book *The March to Magdala*. In purple prose he wrote of it as:

> One of the most interesting and notable campaigns ever undertaken. Since the expedition of Pizarro and Cortes in the Middle Ages, no such novel and hazardous expedition is on record. The country itself was like that of the far-famed Prester John – everything about it smacked of the marvellous. It was more mountainous, more inaccessible, more war-loving, more wild than any other country in the world.

In his understated *Memoirs* Adrian Jones did not wax thus lyrical, and the poor bloody infantry would certainly have cursed Abyssinia rather than viewing it as romantically as newspaper man Henty. So with the passage of time the campaign slipped out of public consciousness, but in February 1936 memory was revived when Mussolini invaded Abyssinia. The *Evening Standard* rushed to interview 'the only British survivor of the Abyssinian War of 1868'. That survivor was Adrian Jones, who was interviewed in the week in which he celebrated his 91st birthday. After reference to Adrian's 'great reputation as a sculptor', the reporter continued:

> He was sitting before the fire in his Chelsea drawing-room, a man with shoulders set in a military line with a head of thick white hair. He wore a high white collar and a black cravat fastened with a neat pin, and his only concession to his years was a red shawl draped over his back. He lit a cigarette as he let his mind wander back ...

His first relevant memory would have been of embarkation at Bombay. A huge fleet of steam and sailing ships carrying soldiers, labourers, stores and animals headed out from Calcutta, Bombay, England and Mediterranean ports to Annesley Bay on the Red Sea coast (now called the Bay of Zula, in present-day Eritrea). Adrian sailed in a convoy of twenty ships, ten steamships towing ten sailing ships. He was in one of the latter. Once arrived at its natural shallow water harbour destination, its cargo of horses and mules was put into flat-bottomed boats and brought as near as possible to the land. The boats were overturned, and the horses and mules were baptised into war by being forced to swim for the shore. Adrian comments laconically that 'it was no easy job to capture, arrange and bring them into camp'. Life was uncomfortable for the humans also. The Commissariat had not yet unpacked its stores, so those who failed in the scramble for a seat in a ship's boat to be taken back to the fleet for food went hungry. Hammocks were rigged in the open and Adrian and his fellows sought what sleep they could find against the noise made by the jackals and hyenas which had scented them.

The purpose of all this activity was to rescue some sixty Europeans, including four English officials, who had been imprisoned, often in shackles and sometimes tortured, by King Theodore of Abyssinia. Various measures of conciliation, including sending with the new British Consul a gift of a matched pair of engraved revolvers from Queen Victoria, had failed. For his pains, the Consul also had been incarcerated. A major problem was that King Theodore was increasingly mentally deranged. He was rumoured to have killed more than 3,000 people in a month. His men had pillaged and burned churches, and cast many priests and young girls alive into the flames. In September 1867 the Foreign Minister, Lord Stanley, had demanded release of the prisoners within three months, warning that in default there would be war. No positive response forthcoming, in November Parliament voted the necessary money and supplies, and Queen Victoria regally ordered Lord Napier, who was to command the British action: 'Break thou the Chains' (which Napier afterwards adopted, translated into Latin, as his motto *Tu Vincula Frange*). In the same month the Commander in Chief of the British Army, the Duke of Cambridge, wrote to Napier from his office on Horse Guards:

> I don't think you will have much real fighting, but you will have great difficulty in bringing him [i.e. Theodore] to stand, and it is to be feared he may do some serious mischief to the unfortunate captives ... your main difficulty, I believe, will be the want of roads.

Historians tend to have a poor opinion of the Duke as C-in-C, for he opposed army reform and stayed in office for too long, but in this forecast at least he was accurate.

Napier had at his disposal a Pioneer Force plus two cavalry divisions of fighting soldiers. The Second Division was to garrison the line of march and communication as a temporary army of occupation. The First Division was to be the strike force. It was to this Division that Adrian found himself attached as Veterinary Surgeon. The Army List shows him still gazetted to the artillery, but *A History of the RAVC* records him as being with the Third Dragoon Guards, and in actuality he served both their two squadrons and the two batteries of artillery which were part of the division's First Brigade. One battery transported on elephants the heavy artillery, four modern Armstrong rifled breech loading guns. Adrian would be more involved with the Dragoons, the only British cavalry on the campaign, and the battery of steel mountain guns commanded by Lieutenant Colonel Penn, which used horses and mules. Major General Staveley commanded the division; and the highly demanding task of surveying the way ahead and the country in its vicinity so that the pioneers could be instructed where best to convert mere tracks from the base at Zula up to the highlands into a road fit for guns, wheeled vehicles and heavy baggage animals, fell upon Colonel Phayre, leading to sarcastic puns about 'Phayre roads'.

To the annoyance of Napier, the Land Transport Corps was not part of the army and therefore not subject to military discipline. The muleteers, who had been recruited from Persia, Egypt and the Mediterranean, proved to be as stubborn as mules are reputed to be. They refused to look after the expected number of five animals each, and when that number was reduced to three they insisted on having one of them to ride on. They demanded double the agreed rate of pay, and went on strike in support of their claim. Roberts, now the senior staff officer at the base, Zula, recorded with dismay that because of the lack of discipline many mules were lost or stolen, starved of food or left short of water. When they were needed to proceed to Senafe, the first station in the hills and the advance depot for supplies, sixty-seven miles distant from the base, a very small proportion managed the march, leaving behind them hundreds of mule carcasses decomposing in the hot sun. Adrian, though not directly concerned with those, nevertheless carried a heavy load of responsibility for the strike force's animals. The combination of direct sun during the day and the heat given off by the rocks after sunset proved fatal to many. As horse sickness raged, Adrian was responsible for giving instructions relating to diagnosis, treatments, and prevention of illness, as well as arranging camps and animal sick depots.

Before they had gone far on the 380-mile route to Magdala, Napier summoned Adrian in person and asked for his recommendations. With some conviction he argued that if the route up a dry pass were abandoned and a way found for the troops to move forward on the higher ground, the crisis would abate. This would not be easy advice to follow. Any such change of plans would involve an even harder slog for the pioneers and the troops. Nevertheless, the General took his subordinate's advice, and it proved to be the right decision. Applying the lessons of his tutor at Veterinary College, Adrian took voluminous notes on the animals' health. After they had spent a few days on the higher plateau, no fresh cases appeared, leaving him to deal only with those animals in which the sickness had already been incubating.

The problem of feeding the army in the field was equally challenging. There was no large trading class amongst the population with whom the commissariat could deal, there was no standard measure, and the only coin accepted was the Austrian Maria Theresa dollar. Furthermore, the part of Abyssinia across which the British had to advance produced few vegetables; butter, eggs and poultry were scarce and dear, and forage for the animals was very scarce. The troops were originally allocated rations which included one pound of vegetables daily, but by the third week in January that had been reduced for the strike force to just two ounces. Fortunately the wild country contained plenty of game which Adrian could shoot, and he hitched a goat to his pack mule so that he had a supply of milk to vary his diet. However, the scarcity of forage combined with hard going caused renewed great mortality amongst the transport animals. All officers and men in the advanced strike force had to reduce kit. The soldiers found themselves crammed twelve to a tent ('like herrings' reported G.A Henty to readers of his newspaper column). For the final forced march to Magdala no personal baggage was permitted, not even a change of clothes. The mules carried only food. So the army advanced, its troops on iron rations and its animals on half or even quarter rations, across a difficult terrain in humid and stormy weather, with sudden strong winds, drenching rain, thunder and lightning. As Napier was to say in his final Order to his troops:

> You have crossed ranges of mountains (many steep and precipitous) more than ten thousand feet in altitude, where your supplies would not keep pace with you. In four days you passed the formidable chasm of the Beshilo [River] ... though with scanty food, and some of you even for many hours without either food or water.

So the First Brigade, now reinforced by a naval rocket battery and another battery of artillery from the Second Brigade, reached the Plain of Aroghee before Magdala. There Adrian had his first experience of fighting. 'I was with Colonel Penn and his mule battery when a great number of men came over the hill and the Colonel asked me whether I thought they were friends or enemies.' Earlier Adrian had almost been involved in an incident of 'friendly fire', for it was sometimes difficult to distinguish friend from foe at a distance. Though Theodore's army generally wore a civilian costume of white shirt, trousers and cotton cloak around their shoulders, the senior officers often wore a scarlet cape, while Napier's own force wore a mixture of traditional redcoats and the new khaki. Field glasses were not as powerful then as they became later. However, the formation Colonel Penn had spotted kept advancing, albeit hesitantly, until it became clear that they were indeed enemy. Possibly they initially thought that Colonel Penn's group was a small baggage train, for it included over fifty laden animals. Each of his six steel guns required one mule to carry it. The gun carriage travelled on a second mule, while a third mule carried the wheels, and about half a dozen others carried its ammunition, tools and stores.

Adrian records in his *Memoirs* that after the identity of the opponents was established, 'the guns were dismounted and placed in position', making it sound as effortless as emptying a shopping basket onto the kitchen table. It was of course a much more elaborate and heavy business than that, but the troopers were trained to be quick. The chief of the enemy party was easily distinguished. He rode a white pony, as did Theodore himself, and carried the standard black hide shield decorated with silver metal plates. He was not close enough for Adrian to see if the shield was further decorated with tufts of lion hair, a mark that the warrior had personally slain a lion, but he certainly came within the range of Colonel Penn's modern weaponry. Those accurate and versatile guns could fire a seven-pound elongated shot, or a shell, or shrapnel. The range was established. 'Then', Adrian told the reporter from the *Evening Standard*, 'The Colonel ... landed a shell very neatly right on the man on his pony.' When the smoke cleared the gunners saw that he and many of his party were casualties. The remainder retreated.

The main battle produced a slaughter. Theodore sought to attack a baggage train which he thought was undefended, but three hundred British Infantry quickly moved into position on the plateau, and the artillery and naval brigade with its rocket guns set up overlooking the battlefield. Theodore's own artillery was in a still more commanding position on cliffs standing three hundred feet high above the plateau, but his gunners were not skilful enough to find the range while allowing for the three hundred-foot difference in height, so their bombardment fell harmlessly beyond the British troops. These were equipped with the new Enfield Snider rifle. It was the first time these breech loaders had been used in battle. They raised the previous rate of fire of about three rounds per minute to ten rounds per minute, and this rapid fire broke up the brave last charges of the Abyssinians. Most of the infantry fired nearly all of their ninety rounds in the first quarter of an hour. ('A great deal too rapid', thought Henty; 'slaughter where natives thickly clustered', but against small groups 'not one shot in a hundred told'.) About seven hundred of Theodore's army of 6,000 were killed and a further 1,200 men were wounded, whereas British losses were a mere twenty wounded, of whom just two died of their wounds. So on Good Friday Adrian saw the devastating effect of European fire power on a fanatically brave enemy. He saw also the British soldiers' hatred of this wholesale slaughter and their admiration for their opponents.

He saw that admiration turn to disgust, however, when during the subsequent advance from Aroghee to storm Magdala they came across a scene of massacre. At the foot of a cliff they found more than 300 mutilated, naked dead Abyssinians chained hand and foot with their throats cut, lying in a putrefying mass. In a fit of temper Theodore had ordered these prisoners to be massacred and then pitched over the cliff. Adrian witnessed also Napier's chivalric compassion, allowing the women, children and animals to leave the citadel of Magdala before his troops stormed it. And 'I saw King Theodore come out of one of the gates of the city on his white pony, as though he were anxious to challenge one of his enemies to single combat but, being greeted with a shot, he retreated hastily and the gate was blocked'. The next time Adrian saw Theodore, he was dead. As he described it to the *Evening Standard* reporter:

> Once we were in the town the enemy fled and the only real danger was their matchlocks which they had thrown down all over the place. It was uncomfortable to walk amongst the guns, for they were all charged and the fuses lit, and they were popping off right and left on the ground. I was one of the first to go into the hut in which King Theodore had shot himself when he realised he was defeated. He lay there, stripped of everything which might betray his identity, and it was some time before we could be quite sure that the body really was that of the King. Two doctors examined it for a long time, too, before they could discover where he had shot himself. Then they found a tiny bullet hole at the back of his head and so discovered that he had fired into his mouth. He had used the revolver which had been given to him years before by Queen Victoria.

The quiet style of narration, never over-dramatising the situation (the euphemism 'uncomfortable' is typical) suggests that the reporter quoted Adrian accurately. Even in the more considered written account of the same scene in his *Memoirs*, the description is low key – though therein the 'stripped of everything which might betray his identity' becomes the more colourful 'without any of the trappings of royalty', and the 'tiny bullet hole at the back of his head' becomes 'a great hole in the top of his head'.

'With the capture of Magdala we returned to our base – the campaign was over.' Yet the return journey had its dangers, though he survived them, unlike his goat, which was eaten one night by a hyena. Going for a walk along a dry river bed, Adrian came face to face with a lion, which to his very great relief, for he was completely unarmed, turned round and went away; on another occasion he became lost in a dense wood; on a third occasion the dry watercourse down which their column was marching was suddenly flooded by an eight-foot wall of water before which packs, wagons and men went down like matchsticks, though with no lives lost. Describing to the reporter how rain could come down 'like water poured from a bucket', he predicted that the modern Italian army would have a hard time of it in the rainy season. He too had endured a hard time, but he had his recognition when the Commander-in-Chief, General Napier, sent for him and gave him his personal thanks for all those times when he had been the only veterinary officer with the attack brigade. In his future life as an artist, when he was sculpting war memorials, or painting or sculpting equestrian likenesses of famous soldiers, he was able to feel satisfaction that the work came from the hands of one who had himself suffered hardships and dangers on campaign.

The Magdala campaign is of interest to Empire historians because it was a war carried out with no imperialist ambitions, but simply the humanitarian intention to free prisoners, most of them not even British, from cruel incarceration. It had other consequences, though: the comprehensive victory and swift exit enhanced national prestige, and the bonds of trust were re-forged between Indian and British soldiers who in the words of Napier had 'forgotten the prejudices of Race and Creed' to march and fight alongside one another. The campaign interests military historians also because it was the first in which the British army was equipped with breech loading rifles that quadrupled the possible rate of rifle fire and obviated the danger of the rifleman having perhaps to rise dangerously to an exposed position when reloading through the muzzle. The campaign was also almost the last occasion in which a British regiment carried its colours into battle: the Duke of Wellington's 33rd Foot Regiment carried its colours during the storming of the Magdala fortress. (Thirty years later Adrian would sculpt a bas relief scene from the very last such occasion, the battle of Laing's Nek in the Transvaal War: beneath the scene he sculpted crossed Queen's and Regimental Colours.)

The campaign is even of particular interest to medal collectors, because uniquely on the Abyssinia medal the name and unit of recipients such as Adrian Jones was embossed on the centre of the reverse side, not engraved on the rim, and the medal was suspended from a Queen Victoria crown – an attractive method, but so weak that it was never used again. Also, of course, the Magdala campaign like all Victorian campaigns produced art, although already the method of recording war was changing: the Duke of Cambridge wrote to thank Napier for 'all the *photographs*' he had sent. But serving officers still sent drawings, later made into engravings, to such journals as the *Illustrated London News*. For instance, among the four drawings sent by Captain James of the Bombay Grenadiers to that journal was the arresting image 'Shipping Elephants at Bombay', which showed elephants being hoisted aboard a sailing ship – a scene also witnessed by Adrian. A couple of years later Captain James was presented by the Viceroy of India with a Certificate of Merit for 'the best original painting' at an art exhibition held at Mian Mir near Lahore on the occasion of the visit to India of HRH the Duke of Edinburgh. The painting was 'The Scene of the Massacre' (of the murdered prisoners). This again was witnessed by Adrian, but he did not paint it. Indeed, given his length of military experience, battlefield scenes are surprisingly rare in his artistic output.

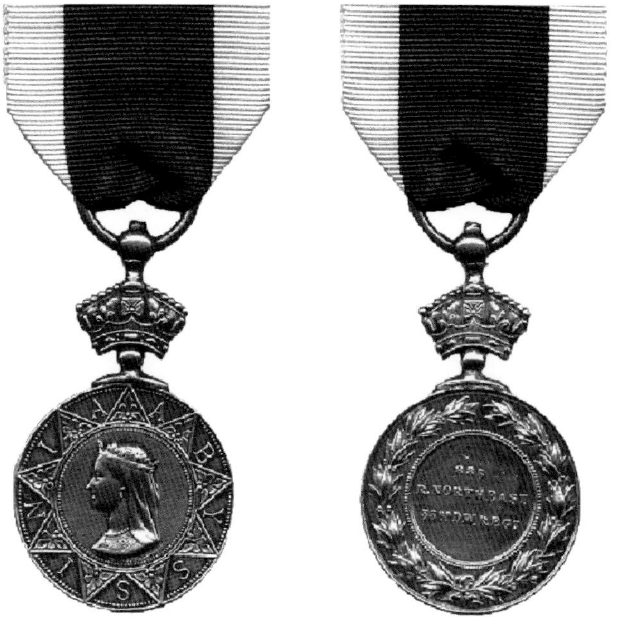

The Abyssinia campaign medal

Napier was back at the Zula base by the beginning of June and entrusted to Major Bob Roberts the task of carrying his final despatches to London. Reaching London just before the end of the month, he checked in at his club and received there a note directing him to take the despatches without delay to the Secretary of State for India. It was evening. Stafford and Lady Northcote were at dinner, but Sir Stafford interrupted his meal to look through the despatches. When he had finished reading them, he asked Roberts to take them, again without delay, to the Commander-in-Chief, the Duke of Cambridge. The Duke however was at a dinner party himself that evening, and a servant told Roberts it was quite impossible to disturb His Royal Highness. Roberts set down the despatches, placed his card on top of them, told the servant to deliver them at once and went back to his club. There after just a short interval, the Duke's Aide-de-Camp appeared and told Roberts he had been ordered to find him and fetch him back with him. Thus finally two months after the storming of Magdala, the Army's Commander-in-Chief was able to question Roberts about the campaign and to read the despatches with their complimentary remarks about the good service of the Army Veterinary Corps.

It had been a 'just war', but nonetheless horrific. What had been its impact upon Adrian Jones, apart from impressing upon him the lesson that a Victorian small war usually demanded many days of hard marching to produce one day of successful battle? It was not in his nature to indulge in retrospective analysis of his emotions. He simply says that he returned to the horse artillery in India feeling 'a seasoned veteran'. But in his future works of art he did little to glorify war spirit; often the emphasis was to be on the wounded or upon 'peace, which is ... the aim and end of every great struggle'.

Another effect of the campaign which would have far-reaching consequences was the undermining of Adrian's robust health by bad food and bad water. In the meantime, though, he found efficient and prompt embarkation at Zula and, having been spared the port's fearful heat and inadequate water supply, he was shipped back to India.

India 1868-1871

Adrian's return to India was a return to peacetime soldiering. He rejoined the Horse Artillery in late June 1868, now stationed at Kirkee and therefore much nearer to Poona and its important racecourse. He had already been successful there, riding a big Australian horse to victory with such firm control that the Aga Khan had taken a coin from his watch chain and presented it to Adrian to commemorate what he apparently said was the best ridden race he had ever seen. Now Adrian bought a smaller Arab horse, Toll-Loll, and was so encouraged by its style and speed that he decided to run it at Poona in a maiden race, even though there would be competition from the Aga Khan's large stud. He won the race and the lottery and 'they did me a great deal of good, morally and financially'.

Then in June 1869 he was gazetted to the 3rd Hussars as replacement for their Veterinary Surgeon, who had died. This meant a return to his first station in India, Ahmednuggur, but now as a member of a famous cavalry regiment. In the 18th century they had charged at Dettingen, where they had captured two silver kettle-drums which were now the regimental kettle-drums. Three further battle honours had been gained under Wellington in the Peninsular War. But the newest name on their list of honours was 'Cabool' [Kabul], added during their previous tour of duty in India. That tour had lasted sixteen years, from 1837. For the initial four years they had not fought a battle, yet had lost eight officers and over twenty times that number of men to 'heat apoplexy' and other diseases of the sub-continent. Then in 1842 the 3rds had gone into action as part of General Pollock's force which had avenged the worst defeat in British military history, the wipe-out (bar one survivor) of a British and Indian army retreating from Kabul. They had marched with Pollock through the Khyber Pass to relieve Jellalabad, then in August and September 1842 advanced with him to Kabul, distinguishing themselves en route at the battle of Tezeen with a traditional hard-riding charge that overwhelmed the Afghan cavalry. More distressingly, their route had been along the line of retreat of the slaughtered army, so they frequently came across what an officer called 'the frightful reality', ghastly strewn heaps of rotting corpses. Later in the 1840s they had been involved, at heavy cost in casualties, under 'fighting general' Sir Hugh Gough in the First and Second Silkh Wars. Among other exploits, at Ferozeshah (First War) they famously charged an entrenched Sikh artillery position, swords waving, and at Chilianwala (Second War) they had been part of Gough's standard attack method, direct frontal assault, on a Sikh army of over 30,000 men and sixty guns. Their tour of duty ended as it had begun with four years of peacetime soldiering – and the attrition of around twenty deaths from disease annually. Of the four hundred and twenty NCOs and men who sailed out as the young Queen Victoria began her reign, only forty-seven returned to Britain in 1853.

In their sixteen years of soldiering in India the 3rds had seen many horrors and displayed much military heroism. They might therefore have viewed the prospect of another spell there without enthusiasm, and no doubt some old soldiers' tales caused apprehension as well as whetting appetite for glory among the new recruits. But this was now late 1868. The interim had been fifteen years of peaceful duty in England, Ireland and Scotland. Spared the Indian Mutiny's cruelties and hardships, their most warlike exploit had been the humane putting down of a bread riot in Exeter. There had been a turnover in personnel. And they could think like a 'new' regiment, because in 1861 they had been re-designated from 3rd Light Dragoon Guards to 3rd Hussars, though they kept their blue uniform tunics with distinctive scarlet collars, the story being that their enemy in the Punjab had called them 'the red-throated cavalry', an allusion to the blood which had flowed so copiously at Chilianwala. A few long service men could wear the campaign medals for the two Sikh Wars. The medal for the First showed on its reverse side the winged figure of Victory holding a laurel wreath with her right arm, which is extended over the pile of emblems of war at her feet. It was a motif which Adrian would use later, with variations, in some important sculptures. His artist's eye would have been even more interested by the Jellalabad medal of 1842. Its splendid ribbon of watered red, white, yellow and blue had been designed by the Governor-General of India, Lord Ellenborough, to symbolise an oriental sunrise, and the medal's reverse side depicted winged Victory flying over Jellalabad fort,. Her foot touches the fort wall, so she can be interpreted as alighting to end the siege, just as decades later Adrian sculpted winged Peace alighting on the chariot of war to arrest its progress. That medal was awarded only to those troops who defended Jellalabad, not to those who marched to its relief, so it was rarely seen in the 3rd Hussars' messroom.

In that officers' mess Adrian found ready acceptance. He was battle-experienced, expert at his work, and, most importantly, an excellent horseman. Among the officers Adrian met when he joined them was Major

Edward Gore, who later transferred to the Inniskilling Dragoons. He was to be Adrian's commanding officer in the Transvaal War in 1881, and would later commission Adrian to paint his horses. But for the moment Adrian's most important new acquaintance was Major Dent, who was the owner of a fine Australian horse. Adrian judged it would make a racer, so took it into training with his own horse. Although he was now stationed further from Poona, he took the horse down to the big meeting there. As it was a big horse and thus expected to carry a greater weight than the smaller Arab horses, Adrian had no difficulty meeting the jockey weight requirements. As he was cantering to the starting post, Lord Beresford came over and offered to back his Australian horse against Major Dent's. Adrian took the bet, they agreed to treble it, and Adrian won. He rode two further winners at Poona, bringing him more financial good fortune, and became confident in his ability to judge the quality of a racehorse.

And thus life might have continued. But now the effect of the bad food and suspect water of the Abyssinian campaign began to take its toll. His health broke down, and he was ordered home. No doubt it seemed a great misfortune at the time, but it was to lead to an entirely new turn of events.

Chapter Three: 'The Pleasantest of My Life'
1871-1880: Army Service in England and Ireland

'Food had been bad and the water was under suspicion; my digestion had been undermined and I was ordered home where I married.' Not many autobiographers would introduce their marriage as a three word tailpiece to a sentence which already contained much information about other life-changing circumstances. This would seem to be carrying Victorian reticence about private life to extremes. The next sentence in his *Memoirs* misprints his new bride's name: 'My wife was Miss E.C. Beckingham.' As the marriage certificate of 23 July 1870 records, she was 'E.E.', Emma Elizabeth Beckingham, the third child and second daughter of a Monmouthshire family, originally from Newport. By the time of Emma's birth, the family had settled near Monmouth in the village of Dixton, where her father, Thomas Beckingham, worked as a coal merchant's clerk. It was evidently secure employment; the family grew, and all five daughters received an education. By the 1860s the household was prosperous enough to employ a live-in female servant to help look after the four younger daughters. Emma's mother had been just sixteen when her only son was born, and she was twenty-seven at the time of Emma's birth. She lived just a further eighteen years, dying in 1866. Her husband died two years later, so neither of them saw the curate of Ross-on-Wye parish church marry Emma and Adrian on 23 July 1870. The family's witness to the ceremony was Emma's closest sister, Bessie, who had her late father's occupation entered on the wedding certificate as 'Accountant'.

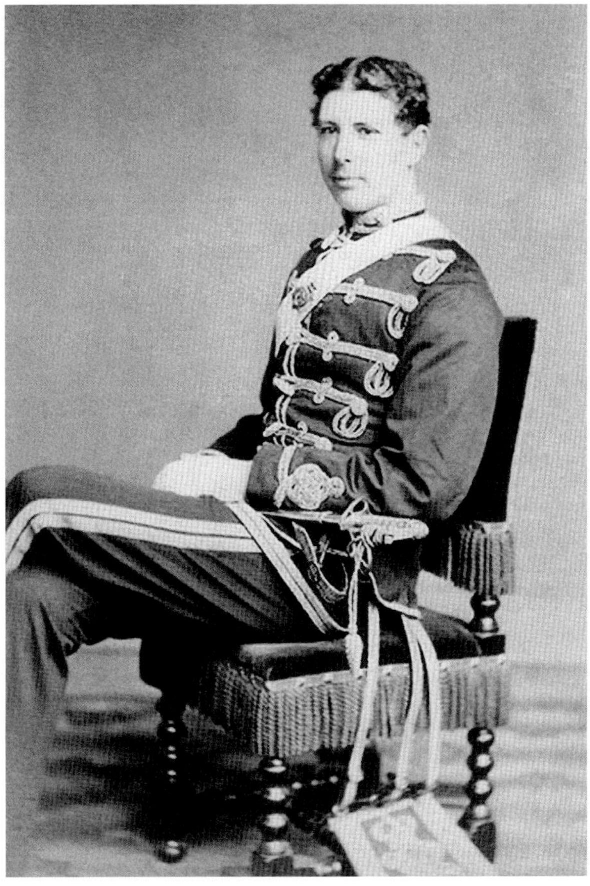

Lieutenant Adrian Jones, VS,
3rd Hussars, 1870

The convention of keeping one's private life private makes Adrian's account of his marriage appear cursory, but there is no reason to think it was not a happy marriage. The *Memoirs* continue more warmly: 'and our marriage was enriched eight years later by a son who carries my name, Adrian. He, in his turn, has a son Adrian, so that there are three generations of us today'. Emma saw her husband through his convalescence, helped him to make a living until he was fit again for army service, travelled with him throughout his future army home station postings, and, as he gratefully acknowledges, gave him an heir.

His six months' sick leave was due to expire in July 1870. The order arrived for him to report back to his regiment in India, but his doctor warned him that if he returned to the East he would very soon be buried there. The medical verdict came as 'a terrible shock'. During his leave Adrian had gone back to the photographer Thomas Jones in his 3rd Hussars uniform, confident that he would soon be wearing it again. Again he took a relaxed pose on the studio upholstered chair, legs casually crossed, his Hussars sabretache hanging by its three slings on his left and his cavalry sword held across his thighs. He now of course wore the Hussars tunic, and down his trouser leg ran the Hussars double stripe, but paradoxically he looked less of a Hussars officer than in his RHA uniform, for whereas in that uniform he had been able proudly to perch a Hussars-type busby on his lap, the Veterinary Surgeon of the 3rd Hussars wore not a busby but a cocked hat. And now the unavoidable decision had to be taken not to wear uniform at all. Three days after his wedding, the *London Gazette* of 26 July 1870 intimated his resignation from the army with effect from 13th July. 'I was ill, young, inexperienced, and I could find nothing better to do than resign.'

Interlude in Ross-on-Wye

Writing in his *Memoirs* about the 1870s, Adrian asserted: 'I think, on looking back over the whole of my career, that this decade was the pleasantest of my life.' It did not, however, begin entirely happily. Having been forced to return to civilian life because of concerns about his health, and having acquired responsibility for his new wife and her orphaned younger sisters, he had to find a way of earning a living. His veterinary qualifications were one obvious source of income. Another less obvious possibility presented itself in the form of Ross-on-Wye's burgeoning tourism. In 1867 a new hotel, the Swan, had been built on the corner of High Street and Edde Cross Street. It replaced the smaller, fading Swan and Falcon Hotel, whose chief fame was that, before boarding a pleasure boat to go down the Wye to Monmouth, Lord Nelson and his party had breakfasted there in 1802. This dated boast was overtaken in 1867 by the visit of the novelist Charles Dickens to Ross's Royal Hotel, which had the further advantage of overlooking the scenic horseshoe bend of the River Wye. So the Swan advertised itself as a 'Family, Commercial and Posting House', and while aiming at a more middle class market than the Royal, sought to be second only to that hotel amongst Ross's twenty taverns. The business outlook held promise. The railway which had reached Ludlow in 1852 and then been extended to Hereford, from there now went via a branch line to Ross, the line having been completed in 1855. The usual joyous civic celebrations – flags and banners, a free tea for children, and evening balls for adults, including one at the Swan and Falcon – greeted the railway's arrival. Beneficially, the Great Western Railway absorbed the local railway company in 1862, and seven years later, in a formidable display of Victorian engineering efficiency, its well-organised gangs of navvies converted its 21½ miles of track from Brunel's broad gauge to standard gauge in just five days. That at once eliminated the delays and damages of unloading and reloading goods because of gauge changes. Finally Ross achieved connections to the national rail network in every direction with the opening of the line to Monmouth in 1870. At that moment of opportunity Adrian Jones took up residence in the Swan as 'Veterinary Surgeon and Hotel Keeper'.

The two married ladies who originally ran the Swan stressed that it was a family hotel. For Adrian its appeal was that it was a Post House, with unusually extensive stabling and a large yard, from which a horse omnibus service ran to and from the station. The 1871 census shows a family concern at work. Adrian was 'mine host', assisted by Emma and his sister-in-law Bessie. His younger sister-in-law, Ellen, aged eighteen, was the barmaid. In addition they employed a second barmaid, a cook, a waitress, and a chambermaid, all of them resident spinsters in their twenties. For Adrian, used to the masculine environment of his own family, veterinary college and the officers' mess, it must have been quite a change to be surrounded by women; but many of the hotel guests and bar patrons were male, and a young lad was employed to double as boots boy and billiard marker. Adrian was highly expert at the billiard table, and continued to be so throughout his life, though when he was in his nineties he complained that he was not as good at the long pots as he used to be.

For the moment his long-term future was uncertain, but soon he felt that he had made a wise decision in resigning his commission and not returning to India. His underlying constitution being fit and robust, recovery soon set in. As an ardent enthusiast for horse-racing, especially steeplechases, he renewed his 'keenest interest' in the fortunes of a horse called The Colonel. Along with his horse-loving brothers, Adrian had long taken that interest in this outstanding stallion because he was a Shropshire hero: 'We felt that he carried the honour of the county in his keeping.' The Colonel had been bred at Little Brampton and trained at Rock Farm, Richards Castle, both places close to Ludlow. For two seasons the horse was hunted, and like his other admirers, Adrian considered him an outstandingly safe and steady jumper. Then he had met The Colonel in a small steeplechase and been 'delighted to note how he cantered easily along, taking all his jumps without effort, while we, on our ordinary horses, were at top speed all the time'. He won races on the flat, over hurdles, and steeplechasing, but his two greatest triumphs, which proved to Adrian that his 'faith in The Colonel was justified', came whilst Adrian was still in the army overseas. In 1869, ridden by George Stevens, the most successful National jockey of all time, The Colonel won the Grand National, and then in 1870, once more with George Stevens up and now the 7 to 2 favourite, he won again. By the time Adrian came to set down his *Memoirs* in 1933, this feat of successive Grand National victories had still been achieved by no other horse. Adrian wrote: 'Only those who know the Aintree course can really understand what this means.' His comment is even truer of the course as it was in 1869/70 than of the twenty-first-century course. Though then as now the track was a marathon highly challenging left-hander round which the horses made two circuits, then it was not fully turfed, so the horses had to cross some plough, the fences had not been modified to be more horse-friendly, and the top weight was seven pounds heavier at twelve and a half stone.

After his second victory in the National, The Colonel was lost to Shropshire. Baron von Oppenheim bought him for 2,000 guineas at Tattersall's and ran him on the Continent, where he triumphed in the Great Vienna Steeplechase, and he was brought back to Aintree for the 1871 National. History does not record if Adrian loyally gambled on him despite his having been given the top weight. If he did not, he saved his money, for George Stevens could only bring The Colonel home just outside the places. What is certain is that Adrian would have loved to paint this good-looking, nearly black horse 'of first-class quality', but the days when his artistic reputation would bring him commissions to paint Grand National runners and winners lay two decades in the future. The Colonel went back to Germany, was put to stud and, it is said, served as a ceremonial charger for Emperor Wilhelm I; and Adrian, now fully recovered in health, just before the first anniversary of his marriage, went back to the army.

The Queen's Bays

Adrian became a commissioned army officer for the second time on 6 June 1871. Again he had to report to the Artillery, but sensibly the army gave him a home posting at Weedon in Northamptonshire, where now the cavalry barracks are remembered only in a couple of street names. It was good hunting country, and near to Earl Spencer's stately home Althorp, where he would later sculpt an outstanding foxhound of the Pytchley pack. However, the posting to Weedon and the Artillery lasted just three months. In September Lieutenant Gudgeon, the veterinary officer of the 2nd Dragoon Guards (Queen's Bays), left the regiment on promotion to Veterinary Surgeon 1st class, and Adrian replaced him. The choice was appropriate. Both he and the Bays had returned from service in India the previous year, and the shared background helped him to fit into the new Mess quickly. The relationship between the regiment and its sporting artist veterinary surgeon was to prove one of mutual affectionate regard which lasted for more than forty years after the end of his posting to it.

Unfortunately, Adrian's account in his *Memoirs* of his service moves with the Bays is misleading. He writes: 'In 1871, to be precise, I was gazetted to the Queen's Bays and quartered at Brighton.' His recording of his gazetting to the regiment is indeed precise, but the regiment's move to Brighton came twelve months later. (Adrian did not keep a diary.) He continues: 'Thence I went to Ireland'. That also is accurate, although it omits the (unimportant) detail that he embarked for Dublin at Liverpool rather than Brighton. But after 'Ireland' he adds, 'where I remained for ten years'. Here his love affair with Ireland has led him astray. It is true that he remained with the regiment for ten years, but the Bays – and their vet – did not sail for Ireland until 1875. Doubtless he made the error because he remembered his time in Ireland with particular enthusiasm ('the pleasantest of my life; chiefly on account of the sport – the hunting and steeplechasing') and he goes on to describe it to the exclusion of his service in England – understandably, for the interests of the Irish he met echoed his own. His first comment on them is: 'To an Irishman of the right sort a horse is a necessity'. Nonetheless, it is a pity that he did not say more about his time with the Bays in England. It would have been interesting to read his account of soldiering in England in the years 1871 to 1875, years of army reforms, where peacetime flogging was abolished for other ranks, the purchase of commissions and promotions was abolished for officers, and the age profile of the army was changed by the introduction of short service enlistments. No doubt he would not have revealed his views on the radicalism of Gladstone's Secretary of State for War Edward Cardwell, as opposed to the conservatism of Queen Victoria's cousin, the Commander-in-Chief the Duke of Cambridge, for he never makes 'political' points, but he might have mentioned some of the strongly favourable inspection reports on the Bays' horses for which he cared. Perhaps in contrast to the perils of campaigning in Abyssinia it seemed too unremarkable to be worth writing about, but it was a life of variety and colour.

At the end of their twelve years' tour of duty in India, the 2nd Queen's Dragoon Guards had sailed from Bombay homeward-bound on the last day of 1869. They disembarked at Portsmouth, and after a few weeks in Chichester moved to an eighteen-month introduction to their new depot, the barracks at Colchester. Before them lay the task of absorbing the army reforms being introduced by Edward Cardwell; behind them lay a history that stretched back to the troubled days of James II and the Battle of the Boyne. 'Queen's' had first entered their title on the accession of George II (1727), when they had become known as the Queen's Regiment of Horse; and twenty years later they had become the 2nd Regiment of Dragoon Guards. They had picked up the name Queen's Bays later in the 18th century when serving in England with the majority of the regiment mounted on bay horses (unlike the rest of the heavy dragoon regiments which, with the obvious exception of the Scots Greys, rode black horses). Now at Colchester, in keeping with tradition, the whole unit was remounted on bays, and the regiment's official designation altered to the 2nd Dragoon Guards (Queen's Bays). They liked to be known simply as 'the Bays', though it was to be 1921 before their title was officially reversed to The Queen's Bays (2nd Dragoon Guards). Later in the 1920s when 'for love of my old regiment' Adrian Jones, without charging a fee, sculpted their transportable 1914-18 regimental war memorial, the Order of Ceremony sheet for the dedication parade he attended at Colchester carried only the legend 'The Queen's Bays'.

In August 1871 the Bays moved to take part in the Aldershot autumn manoeuvres. A month later the renamed, remounted regiment was joined at Aldershot East Cavalry Barracks by its new veterinary surgeon officer, Lieutenant Adrian Jones. His previous experiences with cavalry regiments, in both peace and war, had been abroad. Now he was to experience life in a cavalry regiment in peacetime homeland conditions. Aldershot Garrison then was modern. It had been set up as a huge barracks town and centre of army training as recently as the 1850s, one reaction to failings exposed by the Crimean War. The grey stone East Cavalry Barracks had all the usual features: stables for the horses, with barrack rooms above for the troopers; large riding school;

gymnasium; messes, and some houses for senior married officers; gate and guardhouse; and, defined by its 'if-it-doesn't-move-paint-it' equidistant edging stones, the neatly maintained parade ground, in which took place everything from the pageantry of full dress parades to sword exercises to pack drill for defaulters. From beside it Wellington Avenue led to the garrison church, the chalice of which had been looted and brought home from Magdala, though it would not be until 1883 that the mound behind the church would be surmounted by Wyatt's huge bronze equestrian statue of the Duke of Wellington, removed from the Wellington Arch at Hyde Park Corner, where Adrian's Peace Quadriga would one day replace it. Down the Avenue on Sundays marched the regiment, band playing, on church parade in full dress: gilt metal helmet with black horsehair plume fountaining up from its socket and then falling to the helmet bottom, scarlet tunic, and blue cavalry trousers with a leg stripe. At this time each gazetting to a different regiment meant new uniform expense for the veterinary officer, but Adrian was going to be fortunate in having a posting that was to last for ten years, by the end of which time the Army Veterinary Corps was being created and given its own uniform.

The Bays' day, like that of all cavalry regiments, was punctuated by trumpet calls, but within most weeks officers could find enough time for their own interests, be they hunting or art or wine. The veterinary surgeon's role was unusual in that he had no men to look after directly, for the Veterinary Department was as yet officers only. (Other ranks would be introduced as another of the 1881 changes in organisation.) He shared the fervent almost narcissistic cavalry belief that smart personal turn-out, correct in every particular from the close fit of the stable jacket to the application of pipe clay to the sword slings, enhanced regimental reputation and esprit de corps, and the studio photographs he had taken of himself in full dress show he took pleasurable pride in his own military appearance; but he did not have chain-of-command responsibility for the spit and polish of Bays troopers. Nor did his veterinary – and of course junior – officer status give him any formal input on cavalry battle tactics, though he might have harboured doubts about the professionalism of those who did organise training. On the tough campaign in Abyssinia the cavalry had been critically dependent on working with the infantry, engineers and artillery, but in 1870s Aldershot cavalry training was largely insulated from that of other arms. However, the veterinary surgeon was not a peripheral figure in the regiment. He was part of Head Quarters. Every officer and NCO had to care about the promotion of good horse and stable management, but the vet's specialist skills and knowledge remained the final key to horse health and appearance, and therefore preparedness for war or support of the civil power - or for an approaching Annual Inspection.

Adrian had briefly and not very seriously thought of himself as a 'veteran' after the Abyssinian War, but now he served under men who truly were veterans. The Commanding Officer, Lt Colonel William Henry Seymour CB, had fought in the Light Infantry in the Crimean War 1854-56, and wore on his medal ribbon all four battle clasps which a soldier could earn in that war - Alma, Balaklava, Inkerman and Sebastopol. He had then commanded the Bays during the Mutiny in the Oudh campaign. He had been wounded, had frequently been mentioned in despatches, and had his charger wounded during the Relief of Lucknow, the Oudh capital. In the officers' mess (and years later in the regimental museum in Shrewsbury) hung a dramatic painting of the red-coated, sword-wielding Bays leading the British cavalry charge on Lucknow which had earned them the battle honour 'Lucknow'. So Colonel Seymour had experience of what could be achieved by brave dash and the cavalry spirit. However, as Adrian was to learn when he left the Bays on being posted to the First Boer War, it was a method of warfare that was becoming obsolete. After Adrian had been with the Bays for nine months, Colonel Seymour, having commanded the regiment for almost fourteen years, retired temporarily on half pay. Before leaving he made a gift of £200 to the regiment, the annual interest to be used to provide warm clothing for the children of private soldiers, evidence of the caring paternalism that made the Bays a family as well as a regiment.

The new commanding officer, promoted to Lt Colonel on the same day in June 1872 as Colonel Seymour retired, was Henry Holden Steward. He had been a soldier since 1850, when Adrian was just five, and had purchased promotion to major in March 1870, a year before Cardwell abolished the system of officer commission purchase. The promotion to command was of course on merit. He had a space of six weeks to be ready for the Bays' inspection by the Inspecting General of Cavalry in Great Britain. To quote the regimental record: 'The Inspecting General expressed his satisfaction with the appearance, riding and drill of the regiment and with all that came under his notice.' The headquarters staff, particularly the new commanding officer, his staff major, the adjutant and regimental sergeant major, the riding master and the veterinary surgeon, had successfully negotiated the first test of their military virtues as then demanded. Colonel Steward continued in command until 1877. Those were five years of contented happiness in the life of Adrian Jones, and – while recognising that it was not tested in war – of exemplary performance in the life of the Bays.

The regiment moved out from Aldershot in mid-August 1872 to join in a month of autumn manoeuvres on Salisbury Plain, at the conclusion of which a five day route march took Head Quarters and five troops to Brighton. The attractions of the fashionable seaside resort, with plenty of accommodation possible for wives, made it a popular posting, and the band could easily slip into a second role of playing for residents and holidaymakers. For the regiment as a whole it was a matter of fitting into the routine: winter and spring at home in Brighton, with some generous leave; a summer of drills and, if required, ceremonial escort duties; and an autumn of manoeuvres and the Annual Inspection. Thus in the summer of 1873 six troops were ordered to Kensington Barracks for duties connected to the visit of the Shah of Persia to London. They acted as escort to the Shah and to British royalty, and in the absence of the Household Cavalry stood guard in Whitehall. Regimental Head Quarters remained in Brighton, but with two thirds of the regiment on detachment in Kensington, HQ staff also had to go there at times. It was Adrian's introduction to military life in London, a world which later became very familiar to him. His was a support role: his job was to ensure that the six troops' 240 horses were fit for their escort and guard duties, though as a highly capable rider himself he would certainly embellish rather than lower the standard when on parade. Autumn 1873's month-long manoeuvres, held in Staffordshire, ended in the third week of September, leaving just eight days for Head Quarters to prepare for the visit of the Inspecting General of Cavalry to Brighton. However, he expressed 'entire satisfaction'.

In 1874 ceremonial duties called three troops to London for the public entry of the Duke and Duchess of Edinburgh, when the Bays formed part of the escort of the Royal Procession from Paddington Station to Buckingham Palace. Then in mid-May the whole regiment moved back to Aldershot, this time under canvas at North Camp, initially to take its place in the large review designed to impress the Czar of Russia. So it was farewell to the charms of Brighton, and the regiment left with the final encomium of a letter from the Town Council saying: 'the excellent performance of the regimental band had been a source of great pleasure to the inhabitants' and adding complimentary remarks on the 'exemplary behaviour' of the men. Next, after the review for the Czar, the usual round of drills and manoeuvres culminated in the march past of the Cavalry Division before the Commander-in-Chief of the Army. Thus, probably for the first time, Adrian came under the eye of HRH Field Marshal the Duke of Cambridge. The Duke is unlikely to have noticed Lieutenant Jones, one man among the many hundreds marching past, but although Adrian would not for a moment have foreseen that in the years ahead he would be commissioned to execute a national memorial to the Duke, he took note of him: 'I saw him often when he was reviewing the troops on Laffan's Plain and other historic parts of Aldershot ... a prominent figure riding at the head of his staff, the biggest man and the biggest horse of the lot.'

While the Duke did not notice Adrian the individual, he certainly closely observed the regiment of which he was a part. Its *Digest* records:

> The Field Marshal Commanding in Chief highly commended the excellent turn out of the Bays, the good condition of the horses, and ... said it reflected very great credit on the regiment. His Royal Highness also expressed himself exceedingly pleased with the very excellent manner in which the Queen's Bays marched past on the occasion, and sent a staff officer specially to Colonel Steward to notify the highly flattering notice that had been taken, and desired that the officers, non-commissioned officers and men might be informed.

This lavish praise might seem no more than royal flattery of loyal subjects, and the emphasis on smartness might be gathered as evidence of the Duke's fossilised attitude towards what constitutes military effectiveness, but the Bays had no such reservations. The commendations were received with pride and recorded in the annals: a deal of expertise and equestrian skills as well as polishing had gone into earning them. Adrian could take particular pleasure that 'the good condition of the horses' had been noted. He had shown he could meet the demands of peacetime as well as those of wartime. When in the future he received praise from the Duke for his work as an artist, he could value it the more because by then he knew that this cousin of the Queen could also when he chose deliver a right good rollicking, well larded with swear words.

From Aldershot the Bays marched by parties to their next posting, at Leeds. At Annual Inspection, the Inspecting General of Cavalry seconded all that the Duke of Cambridge had said, and added praise not only for 'every department that came under his notice' but also for the dismounted drill. (When later in Victorian times there was some debate on whether church parade should remain compulsory, one argument advanced was that such parades usefully reminded the soldier that he was a civilised Christian being, and another was that in cavalry regiments, where foot parades are rare, church parades kept men up to the mark at marching.) However, in 1875 Leeds it was mounted ceremonial that was required. The city's civic pride led it to compete with the other northern conurbations such as Manchester, both as a symbol of industrial progress and to show that where there was 'brass' from industrial ugliness there could also be beauty and interest in art. Manchester had already held its Arts Treasures Exhibition, and was currently planning to build a magnificent town hall for which Ford Madox Brown, who in the next decade would be one of Adrian's artistic Savage Club friends, was designing frescoes hymning Manchester's history; then the hall would be opened by a civic procession many thousands strong, with mounted cavalry in attendance. Leeds already had its splendid Renaissance-style towered town hall, and now in May 1875 was staging a prestigious Exhibition of Arts and Manufactures to be opened by Queen Victoria's second son, the Duke of Edinburgh. The Head Quarters troop of the Bays, led by Colonel Steward, furnished the mounted guards of honour and escorts to the Duke. Afterwards Head Quarters received royal compliments on their smartness and their efficiency in their escort duties, though that probably mattered less to Adrian than the opportunity to see an exhibition of such special interest to him. He had continued to paint during his service in England, but his output was not yet in the public domain. It went to brother officers rather than the sale room.

Then, at the end of June the regiment received notice to be ready to move to Ireland. Its marching orders and routes towards embarkation at Liverpool arrived on 14th July. Headquarters and two other troops were last to leave, marching out from Leeds on the 21st and disembarking at Dublin North Wall on the 27th. Next day they marched to their new Irish station, Newbridge in County Kildare. High summer, and for Adrian the 'pleasantest' of times lay ahead.

Ireland

Reviewing Adrian's *Memoirs* in January 1934, the *Irish Independent*'s critic, while on the whole praising 'this interesting volume', wrote: 'While in the Army, Captain Jones spent ten years in Ireland. Although he declares that these years were the pleasantest of his life, he has singularly little of interest to recall concerning them.' It is an understandable observation, and would probably have been no different even had the critic known that the 'ten years' were in reality only six. Adrian's account, written with the serene selective memory of age, is entirely of his personal enjoyment of those features of Irish life which strongly appealed to him: Irish hunting, Irish steeplechasing, Irish humour; nothing else. Yet in the year he arrived in Kildare, the Irish nationalist leader Charles Stewart Parnell was elected Member of Parliament for the neighbouring county of Meath and set about wrecking normal parliamentary business with his filibustering. In the middle of Adrian's time in Ireland, the autumn and winter of 1878 were particularly harsh, with heavy rains, crop failures and consequent rural poverty and threat of food shortages. And by the time he was leaving Ireland early in the next decade, the Bays had been required to aid the civil power several times, and the government of Prime Minister Gladstone was introducing Coercion Acts in response to civil disorders in areas of Ireland, at the cost of suspending habeas corpus and, for some specific offences, trial by jury. Adrian was not writing political memoirs, and there is little point in lamenting the absence of what was never intended to be there, but the result is the thinness of which the *Irish Independent* complained.

When Adrian arrived with the Head Quarters troop of the Bays at Newbridge on 28 July 1875, he became part of a huge British army presence in Ireland. About 26,000 troops, a seventh of the total army strength, was situated there, spread around more than seventy barracks. He instantly had a sense of that size, for the very next day the regiment was pitched into the summer drill season at the Curragh and remained there until its end. The Curragh was Ireland's Aldershot, and equally modern. It had been established as a military base as recently as 1854-55, built on over 5,000 acres of unenclosed common land where farmers still had the right to graze sheep. It was an impressive camp. At its centre was a tall clock tower, on the right of which was the Catholic chapel and on the left, the Protestant church. It had schools, a post office, a telegraph station, a fire engine depot, extensive stabling and no fewer than ten barrack squares, each of which could house a whole regiment, plus further accommodation under canvas. But what made the Curragh particularly attractive to Adrian was that it was a great home of field sports. Some other ranks stationed there managed to keep beagles; a splendid pack of hounds, the flying Kildares, with a military Master of Fox Hounds, provided sport for the wealthier soldiers; and the very name 'Curragh' meant 'racecourse'. The Curragh Races drew large crowds. As a popular rhyme put it:

> On the Curragh of Kildare
> All Ireland will be there.

But first there was the matter of gaining a satisfactory report on the regiment's performance in the summer training. It did not prove too difficult. The Officer Commanding Curragh Military District was Brigadier Seymour CB – the very same William Henry Seymour who had commanded the Bays for nearly fourteen years until 1872. He took the earliest opportunity after the Bays' arrival to visit them, and 'expressed himself quite satisfied with the appearance of both men and horses'. No doubt 'quite' was used in the sense of 'wholly', not in the sense of 'fairly'. The occasion was as much reunion as inspection. Inspecting officers' visits are not normally viewed with keen anticipation, but in their *History of the Queen's Bays 1685-1929* Frederic Whyte and Hilliard Atteridge report that the regiment's former commanding colonel was 'received with a rare burst of enthusiasm'. In his more formal three-day inspection at the end of the drill season, he again expressed full satisfaction. By the following year, 1876, Brigadier Seymour was the Inspecting General of Cavalry in Ireland. After his full inspection of the Bays in June he was 'perfectly satisfied with everything he had seen' and passed on a favourable report to the Duke of Cambridge. In 1877, now promoted to Major General, at the annual inspection 'he was particularly pleased with the excellent turn out of the Bays ... and with the great pains evidently taken everywhere'. He made a very favourable report.

Because of Seymour's long previous connection with the Bays, a cynic might interpret 'very favourable' as favouritism. That would be mistaken and unfair. Whilst his initial early visit was doubtless motivated by a desire to renew auld acquaintance from lang syne, the subsequent annual inspections, each lasting two or three days, constituted a rigorous wide-ranging assessment by the Inspecting General and his staff, whose report went up to the Commander-in-Chief at Horse Guards, where it was read and drew responsive comment. To a more technological age, the Victorian cavalry's stress on exemplary appearance may seem over-emphatic, but pride in smartness in peacetime bred self-confidence and esprit de corps which could translate into endurance and bravery in wartime, and for Adrian and the regiment's horses a healthy appearance and efficiency as a means of waging battle were incontrovertibly linked. Adrian had confidence in his veterinary diagnoses and treatments, and the reiterated positive assessments made at inspections were good for his self-esteem, but although in his *Memoirs* he gives himself some credit for what he achieved with horses, mules and camels under wartime conditions in Abyssinia and the Sudan and quotes the praise he received from very senior officers in the field, nowhere does he boast of the standards he achieved in the routines of peace. Of course in barrack life it was not a solo effort. His brother officers, the regimental shoeing smiths and farriers, the saddle tree maker, the saddler sergeant and the privates all played their parts.

However, at the War Office there must have been a thought that to have the annual assessment of a cavalry regiment carried out exclusively by a senior cavalry officer was riskily incestuous. In 1878 a General Order announced that henceforward the regiments would in addition be inspected every summer by the General Commanding the District. The Inspector General of Cavalry's inspection would be limited to specifically cavalry aspects – such matters as equipment, equitation and horse drill. Discipline and internal administration would come under the review of the General Commanding the District. That year, therefore, before Major General Seymour's autumn inspection, now reduced to one day, (verdict – 'exceedingly pleased; result admirable') the Bays faced a June inspection by Major General Hamilton. He reported that he too was well satisfied. And so it continued until the end of the Bays' tour of duty in Ireland in 1881, with District Generals commending both their very high state of efficiency and their good character, the latter judgement corroborated afterwards by the fact that in the course of a year the Bays had the lowest number of court martials of any cavalry unit stationed in Ireland. Adrian was indeed serving with a regiment of the highest reputation.

Adrian spent the summers of 1875, 1876 and 1878 at the Curragh. Also present at those Drill field-days was Lieutenant French, with the 19th Hussars (then, unlike the Bays, an unhappy regiment with an unpopular commanding officer whose troubles culminated in 1877 with the mutinous refusal of seventy men to appear at an extra parade, which led the ringleaders to years of penal servitude). Almost half a century later, the future 'little field marshal' would unveil Adrian's Cavalry of the Empire memorial. In the future too he would share one thing in common with Adrian's father: he disapproved of his eldest son's practising art, even though his son's fine military paintings included one of the field marshal mounted, wearing full uniform, with in the background a squadron of the 19th Hussars drawn up on parade. For the present, though he was very different from Adrian in physique, temperament and morality, he shared some of his interests. Both were serious students of the welfare of army horses in campaigns; both were keen on hunting; both were brave and successful steeplechase riders. Their next service together would be in the Sudan.

For winter quarters, the Bays left the Curragh. They spent their first winter in nearby Newbridge barracks, but more typical was their experience in subsequent years. Head Quarters with some supporting troops went to a district central location, while most of the regiment's troops were posted to a range of outquarters in other towns. In 1876 after the Curragh drills, Head Quarters and two troops route marched to Cahir, east of Tipperary on the Waterford-Limerick railway line; one and a half troops marched to Waterford, forty miles east of Cahir; two troops went to Fethard, north east, and one to Clogheen to the south; and just half a troop went to each of Clonmel and Carrick-on-Suir (both on the rail line to Waterford) and to New Ross (on the rail spur north of Waterford). As a half troop comprised only a junior officer, a handful of NCOs and twenty-five privates, these arrangements were more in the style of a policing operation than a military one. The next winter, 1877-78, Head Quarters was in Ballincollig in Cork, and outquarters ranged from Bandon, still further south, and Cork itself to Limerick seventy miles to the north, though again there was a railway connection.

These were places where Adrian could easily be happy: rural and horsy, with most of the country towns no bigger than Ludlow and, like it, pleasantly situated on a river. Indeed, as Adrian's duties took him from HQ to the outstations he saw much that was reminiscent of Ludlow. Cahir had a fine castle, New Ross had remains of ancient city gates, and Tipperary's county town Clonmel had Georgian areas, and was partly walled, and its populace loved both fox hunting and hare coursing. Of course the situation was not truly idyllic. In nationalistic Cork and Limerick, many people were pauper poor, unemployed or unskilled underemployed, illiterate or semi-literate, with little hope of betterment except through emigration. Waterford in those late 1870s years of agricultural depression and poor harvests had soup kitchens feeding the poor as well as assembly rooms more glittering than anything Ludlow could show. But for someone serving in the British army the atmosphere was not as grim as it had been during the Great Famine, now thirty years in the past, or as it was to become in the full scale land wars between tenants and landed proprietors in the 1880s. Nor was the relationship between army and populace antagonistic everywhere. The soldiers brought money and trade to the small garrison towns, and in 1878 a fifth of the men were Irish themselves. The Gaelic Athletic Association had not yet been founded so the mingling of garrison and town sides in such 'British' sports as soccer was not forbidden. In his *Memoirs*, Adrian claims bluntly: 'The regiment was popular'. At Cahir it ran a pack of harriers, for which Adrian was elected huntsman in the latter part of the season. Following the hare and the chasing hounds rode a mix of soldiers, townsfolk and the local Catholic priests. These last arbitrated any dispute over who deserved the half crown reward for first spotting a hare in her form at a site near the meet. Adrian's pack also received invitations to hunt other stretches of country. Responding to an invitation from a Mr Moore to hunt on his land at Clonmel, they arrived to find they were popular indeed: 'all the neighbourhood had gathered to the Meet'. Mixing with the officer class was never a social problem for the landowners in Irish society, whose habits were much as they would have been in England and who indeed themselves supplied some of the army's finest officers. Among those whom Adrian had already met or would meet in the years ahead were the future field marshals French, Kitchener and Roberts (who was from Waterford). 'The whole neighbourhood', however, was broader than officers and landowners. A local hard rider was asked to lead the way. He promptly leaped one of the fearsome Tipperary banks and then several others which were equally dramatic. Adrian had his best hunter out that day and as a fearless rider could cope, but it was hard for the hounds and never a hare came into view. Adrian pulled up in protest and complained, 'This is not hunting!' Of course he received assurance that the next field would produce a hare and so, dubiously, he went on. But indeed there was a hare which gave them a splendid run, albeit over demanding country that caused many other riders to fall.

Inevitably Adrian himself fell on other occasions, but he was badly hurt only once. Though discretion is said to be the better part of valour, army ethos may forbid its exercise. Winter was the season for longer leaves as well as for steeplechasing. Returning from a leave spent hunting in Cheltenham, he found that a chestnut mare of his which he had lent to a brother officer to train and ride to hounds had been entered in a steeplechase. When he had last ridden her she had been rough and wild, and he knew that a remarkable improvement would have been necessary if she were to be ready for racing. He envisaged a highly uncomfortable, dangerous ride. 'But I could not refuse to ride on that account: you should not, of course, shrink from personal risk at any time, and in the army you must not.' His apprehension was justified. The mare went wildly at the easy preliminary fence as if it were ten feet high. He managed enough control of her to negotiate two thirds of the course, but then at an easy bank she slipped, turned turtle, and landed on top of him. The well-intentioned man who picked him up grasped far too tightly for the comfort of a man with several broken ribs, and his morale was not improved by hearing one man say: 'Sure, he's as dead as mutton.' But he was not. In the *Memoirs* he dismisses the event with: 'I should have been killed, but my luck was in ... of course, as soon as I was well enough I was on horseback again.'

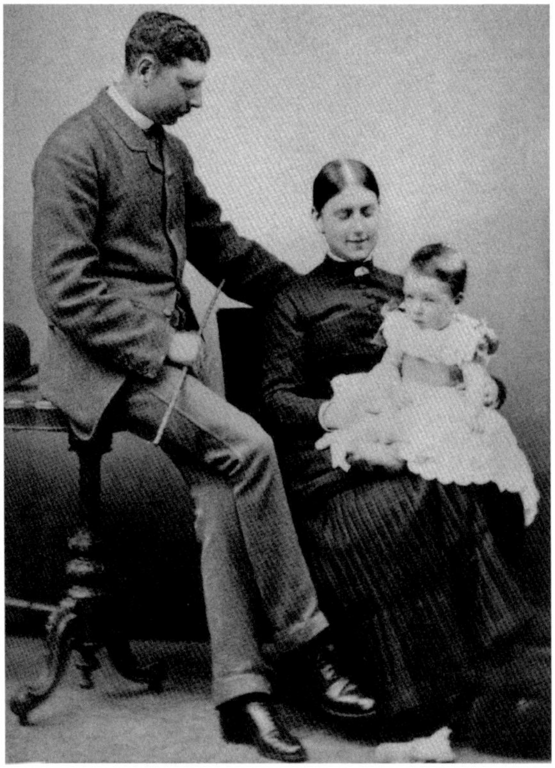

Adrian, his first wife Emma, and their new son, also Adrian, 1879

He rode in steeplechases at Newbridge. At the September 1876 meeting on the six-year-old Phoenix, carrying 12 stone 7lbs he finished unplaced in the Military Steeplechase Plate. At the meeting he describes in the *Memoirs* he did gain a place, but the emphasis in the account is not on the racing but on the conviviality and sheer fun of another occasion enjoyed by Irish and soldiers alike: 'Every horsy man for miles around ... farmers bring their wives and families ... the crowd is extremely happy and excited.' At the end of the meeting he had the thrill of taking the reins of a coach and four for a devil-take-the-hindmost gallop back to the barracks. The infantry guards officers who were on top of the coach as guests yelled in alarm, fearful of being scalped as the coach thundered towards the ominously low barracks gateway arch. They accused Adrian of being a wild Irishman, which delighted his high spirits even more. And they all enjoyed the evening in the mess.

For the winter season 1878-79 the Bays were stationed in Dublin. It was a good time to have the resources of a capital city available, for there in October 1878 Adrian's wife Emma gave birth to a son, christened Adrian. The boy thrived.

Artistic life

In tandem with the satisfactory development of his military career, Adrian's artistic life was burgeoning. While HQ was at Ballincollig in 1877, Lt Colonel Steward completed five years in command, and retired on half pay. His replacement, promoted to Lt Colonel, was Thomas William Sneyd, an efficient soldier, a keen horseman, and a man happy to encourage Adrian's art and raise its profile, and thereby that of the regiment. Adrian, confident in his knowledge of animal anatomy and his powers of observation of animal movement, launched into a debate in the correspondence columns of the *Irish Times* concerning the limb

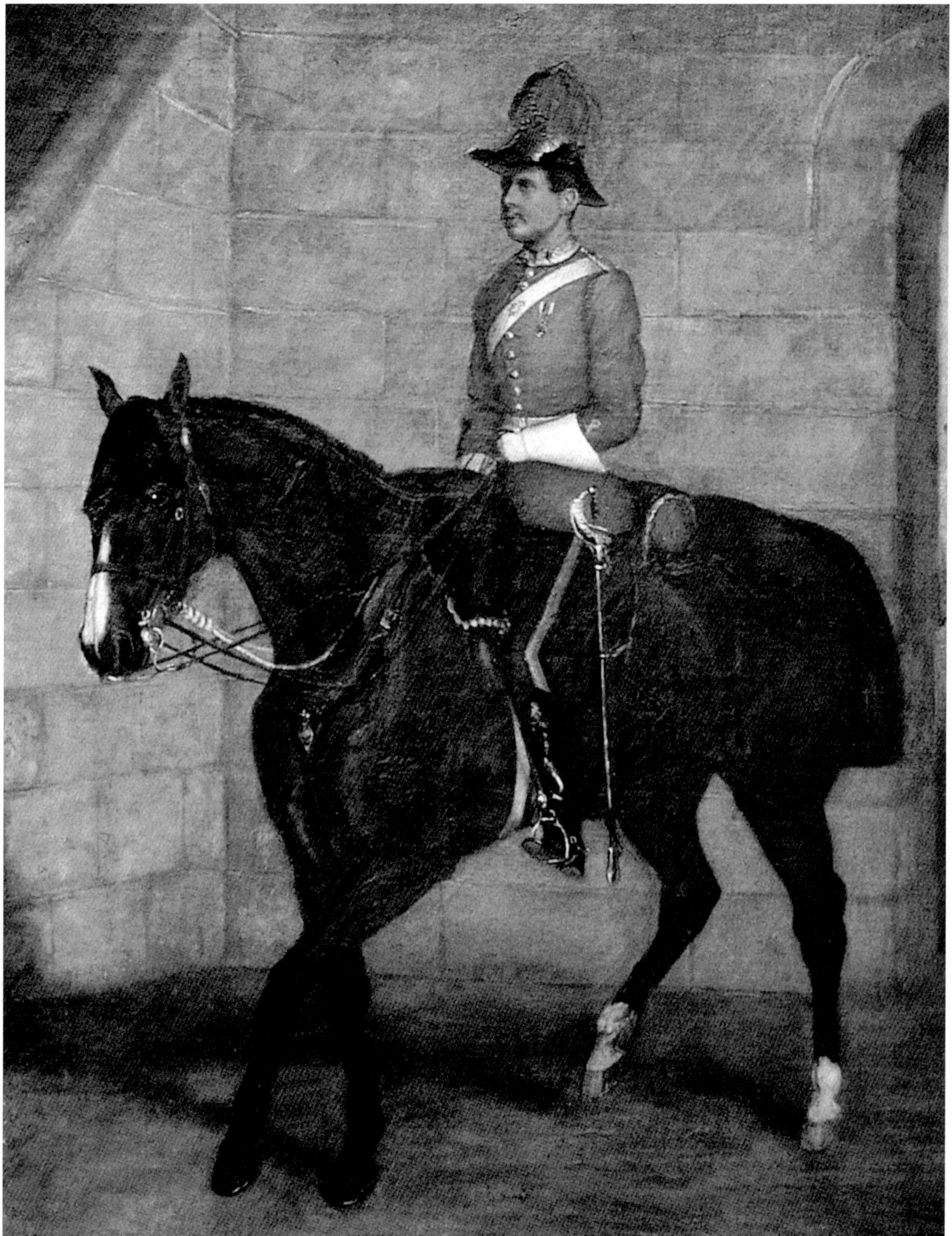

Equestrian Self-Portrait (detail), undated but certainly 1870s. Adrian portrays himself in the uniform of the veterinary surgeon officer of the Queen's Bays, which he wore throughout the 1870s.
(See back cover for colour illustration.)

and body positions of thoroughbreds and greyhounds running at full speed. Non-racegoers might well feel this is hardly a subject to stir the emotions, but Adrian writes with vehement feeling. In a second letter objecting to what he saw as inaccurate, unjustified remarks by a Mr Hayes about his previous letter, he defends and attacks. In defence: 'Remarks I offered in my former letter are true to nature' and 'Regarding my optical illusion, I must tell Mr Hayes that the greyhound's legs must have been in the position I stated, or it could not have been impressed on my retina.' In attack, in addition to emotive phrases like 'the absurdity of the comparison' and 'too ludicrous to need comment': 'As regards the length of forearm in a greyhound interfering with the fact of the animal's body being nearer the ground, at the same time sustaining the weight, has Mr Hayes forgotten the fact of the splendid mechanical arrangement of the shoulders, that they are attached to the trunk by means of muscles and not by a fixed bony joint?' This hectoring criticism is very different from the positive calm that characterises most of his autobiography, but the same passion against the distortion of animals was to fire his approach to sculpting. He signed his letter, from Ballincollig, 27 October 1877, 'Adrian Jones, VS, Queen's Bays, Amateur Animal Painter'.

For portraits in his Royal Horse Artillery and 3rd Hussars officer uniforms, Adrian had sat in the studio of the professional photographer Thomas Jones, who worked next door to the Ludlow house where Adrian was born. Now, however, as one confident enough to sign himself 'amateur painter' when sending a letter to the press, he chose to record his Dragoon Guards service in paint. An *equestrian* self-portrait is an improbable concept. Any anthology of self-portraits is unlikely to contain an example, and it would be ridiculous to imagine the artist taking brush, palette and canvas into the saddle. The horse and uniform may have been taken from life, but the artist worked dismounted. In this small oil painting (26½ by 22½ inches) Adrian paints himself quietly riding his bay charger through an arched barrack entrance. The background inside and outside the arch is left visually uninteresting; the concentration is on foreground man and beast. The rider sits, militarily erect yet relaxed, in dress uniform. Details show that the painting was done before November 1880, when the order was issued for dragoon officers' badges of rank to be worn on the shoulder strap instead of on the collar, but obviously after the Abyssinian War. Adrian's Abyssinia campaign medal, glinting, hangs by its unique Queen's crown suspension from its red-striped, white-edged ribbon. It looks a little dwarfed, not because of any error by the artist but because – most unusually – its diameter is less than the width of its ribbon. The same accuracy is everywhere evident, from the pip on the lace-topped collar of a junior officer (full gold lace collars only for majors and above) and the scarlet-lined plaited gold shoulder cord on the Dragoon Guards' tunic, down past the evenly spaced buttons to the rectangular gilt waist plate and the white leather gauntlets with the single Austrian knot of his lieutenancy protruding above (for this is before his promotion in the next decade to a captain's double knot); and then on down beside the open work handguard of the straight cavalry sword at rest in its scabbard, past the striped blue pantaloons to the regulation cavalry black boot sloping from four inches below the knee at the front to mid calf at the back. He wears also the distinguishing marks of a veterinary surgeon officer, a white shoulder belt and, in place of the other officers' black-plumed metal helmets, a cocked hat with red swan feathers drooping outwards. The saddlery and horse furniture are equally exactly depicted. Behind the saddle the bed roll end bears the Queen's Bays' regimental lettering, a (rather squiggly) 2 above the letters DG, indicating 2nd Dragoon Guards. The 2 reappears on the bit boss.

So this painting is essentially portraiture as documentation. The apprentice artist records himself at a routine moment in his army life. The completed work, presented without complexity or emotional intensity, is chiefly of biographical interest. It makes no claim to be major art, though it has some simple virtues. Museums tend not to display small horse paintings, but if this were on public show a curator's note need carry nothing more than background information: there is no call for 'interpretation'. Nor does Adrian himself 'say' anything, either satirical or laudatory, by way of social commentary. This is art for the family wall, and it still hangs there. In its equestrian military subject, in its painstaking approach, and in its dominant mood of a man confident in his easy oneness with his horse, it prefigures many of Adrian's major public works of art.

Within the next two years his 'amateur' paintings were receiving press coverage. Being stationed now in Dublin, he could often visit Punchestown Racecourse, purpose-built for steeplechasing, in nearby Naas. In July 1879 the Dublin paper *Freeman's Journal and Daily Advertiser*, quoting the London columnist Atlas, reported an unusual painting, a grouped picture by two artists of horses which had won at Punchestown on various dates in 1879:

> A group of Punchestown winners of this year with their riders, painted by Mr Adrian Jones of the Queen's Bays and Mr Reynolds, is in its genre about the most truthful and realistic picture I ever saw. The horses are painted as they showed in the paddock, and not in summer or showyard condition, and are one and all striking likenesses. The riders, among whom the bearded Lord Cloncurry towers, are also admirably presented with their characteristic seats and attitudes. Among the horses are Lottery, Yellow Gown, Dick, Wild Norah the Second, The Parson.

The report concludes by listing some of the jockeys depicted, and informing its readers that 'the proprietor of this phenomenally true representation of chasing cracks' was a Mr Cranfield, of Grafton Street, presumably a dealer. It is tempting to speculate that also 'among the horses' was Sidbury, which belonged to Adrian's commanding officer, Lt Colonel Sneyd, and had won the Punchestown Cup. But even if it was included, that was not sufficient memento for the Commanding Officer. He commissioned a study of Sidbury from Adrian, who depicted the horse in oil on card, 19 by 22 inches. Dated 1879 and signed, it remains in the possession of Colonel, later General, Sneyd's descendants, as does a study of another of his racehorses, of the same size and date. Both paintings featured in the 1984 Sladmore Gallery retrospective exhibition of Adrian's work. The present whereabouts of his Punchestown group painting, as with all too many of his paintings, is sadly not known, at least to this writer.

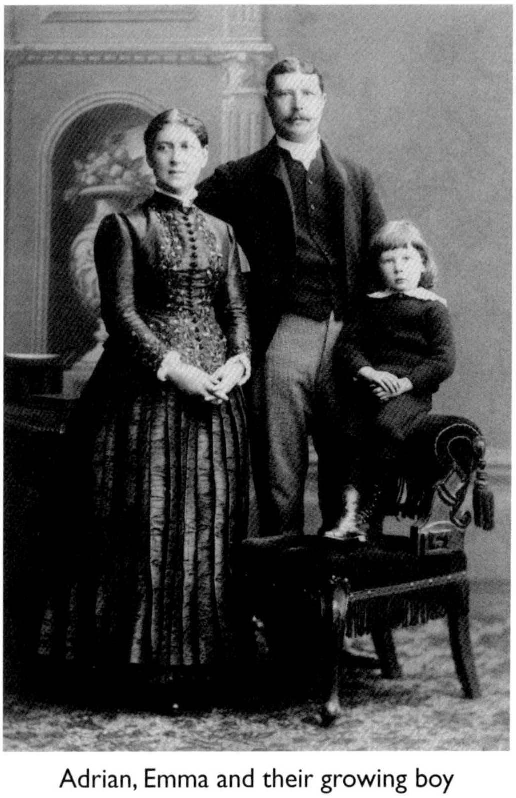

Adrian, Emma and their growing boy

By now Adrian was enough of a public figure for his sailing with his wife and son from Kingstown (now Dun Laoghaire) aboard the royal mail packet for leave in England to be reported in the social column of the *Daily News* on 20 January 1880. But his days in Ireland were numbered. In late April the major general commanding the Dublin District held his marching-out inspection of the Bays, expressing his sorrow at losing the regiment from his command as 'it had borne an exemplary character'. Over the next few days Head Quarters and the other troops route-marched north to Dundalk and outstations in Belfast and Longford. From July to October they had to control civil disturbances several times as troubles worsened in the north of Ireland. The following May they moved to the middle of Ireland, before embarking for England at the end of their Ireland tour of duty. But before then Adrian had been suddenly summoned from them. He was one of eleven veterinary surgeons selected to go out to the First Boer War.

Chapter Four: 'The Easy Tenor Disturbed' 1881-1882: The Transvaal (First Boer) War

The forceful victory of the Germans in the Franco-Prussian War of 1870-71 had rung an alarm bell. The perceived threat led to reforms in army organisation, but Curragh drills and exercises could not encompass anything as large scale as an encirclement-of-Paris mock scenario, and the priority continued to be practising closer-to-home skills such as supporting the civil powers. Meanwhile the real wars the British were fighting were 'small wars' against 'natives'. Amongst other expeditions, in 1873-4 Britain's youngest and brightest general, Garnet Wolseley, helped by his ring of able staff, which included Henry Brackenbury, Redvers Buller and Evelyn Wood, and with Hugh McCalmont from the 7th Hussars as an aide-de-camp, dealt successfully with an Ashanti incursion on the Gold Coast. In his later army career and in his future life as an artist Adrian would come to know all five men well, but for the present his 'easy tenor' of life on a home station continued. Then in 1879 the defeat at Isandlhwana of a British column, equipped with modern weaponry, by a Zulu army mainly wielding cowhide shields and assegais, caused amazed reaction. Perhaps the Zulu nation would prove an underestimated danger to British colonists? Adrian probably felt for the British commanding general, Baron Chelmsford, who had served competently enough as Napier's deputy adjutant-general in the Abyssinian War, but London decided the Zulu War demanded the genius of Wolseley, and sent him to take over command and finish off the brave foe. Wolseley arrived only to find that Chelmsford had by now learned how to counter the Zulus' 'chest and horns' battle formation and had successfully completed the defeat of the Zulus by his victory at Ulundi. So the Zulu threat had been tamed. Wolseley, as High Commissioner for South Africa, could confidently be expected to tidy away any remaining problems. He did not anticipate that the Boers who lived across the Vaal River would pose a big problem. Even though he knew they were dissatisfied and calling for independence, he had been assured the Boer farmers were neither individually brave nor communally capable of concerted action.

The local military commander was Major General Sir George Colley, an Irishman appointed on the recommendation of Wolseley because he had served well at lieutenant colonel level on the Gold Coast and had a brilliant mind (he was the author, no less, of the lengthy *Encyclopaedia Britannica* entry on 'Army'). In late 1880, Colley also did not fear trouble from the voortrekkers. After all, their thinly spread total population was only about a third of the size of the British army. But had he compared his situation with that in his increasingly unsettled native land he might have been less confident. In Ireland, if violent nationalists could band together they would be a potential surprise danger to the handfuls of soldiers in small outstations; and in County Mayo earlier in 1880 the Captain Boycott affair had shown how dissatisfied civilians (encouraged by news of British army defeats in the Zulu War) could inflame a situation through planned and sometimes violent action. Meanwhile the significant statistic in Transvaal was not the size of the Boer population compared with that of the British army but its size compared with the British garrison in their country – fewer than two thousand soldiers dispersed in seven isolated veldt stations. Worse, the stations were unpopular: a monotonous diet and a climate the British found trying adding to the boredom.

Still worse, whereas there had been a full cavalry regiment, the King's Dragoon Guards, in the force, in October 1880 all except two squadrons were posted to India. Numbers were further reduced by more than 200 desertions from this rump of cavalry and the infantry. In his *History of the British Cavalry* the Marquess of Anglesey tells the story of a bright Boer madam who used her brothel to smuggle out deserters, even lending them clothes and money. Had she started earlier, she claimed, 'there would not have been a private left in the King's Dragoon Guards'.

Aware of the military position on the ground, even more encouraged than Irish nationalists by British disasters against the Zulus, and determined not to accept the condition laid down by Gladstone's new British government that they must be part of a South African Confederation, in December 1880 the Transvaalers proclaimed the re-constitution of their own independent republic, and set about attacking the scattered British garrisons. So it was not by Prussians in Europe, nor by Zulus, but by the Dutch in Africa that Adrian found that 'the easy tenor of my way was disturbed'. It was the first occasion since the Crimean War a quarter of a century earlier that the British army had faced Europeans.

Thus for a second time Adrian was unexpectedly summoned to war. Telegrams from South Africa could now reach London within one to four days. The army staff looked to organise reinforcements from home stations. The 6th Inniskilling Dragoons, to whom Adrian would later be attached, embarked at Woolwich, England, to arrive at Durban, South Africa, in mid-February. Adrian, being stationed in Ireland, was ordered to travel to war with a cavalry regiment also stationed there, the 7th Hussars. They were not complete strangers to him, for their recent experience had largely mirrored his. Like him, they had enjoyed peaceful times in India in the latter 1860s, though before that they had been engaged in hectic soldiering in the Mutiny and then on the savage North West Frontier; like him and the Bays they had arrived at Aldershot in 1871 and similarly appreciated its modern infrastructure of gas lighting, running water, and up-to-date soldiers' homes, and then they had been posted to Ireland and served at many of the same stations as the Bays. Their equipment was modern too. In May 1878 they had been issued with the powerful Martini-Henry breech loading rifle, though it was carried in a deep leather bucket secured to the offside of the saddle behind the hussar's leg rather than slung on the hussar's back, an arrangement which had the handicap of probably separating hussar and rifle if his horse was shot. Unfortunately Treasury parsimony severely limited musketry training. Even when the Boer War broke out in December 1880 the allocation per man per annum was only raised to fifty rounds. However, the 7th were successfully carrying out the tasks laid upon them in Ireland. Because of increasing unrest, leave was currently suspended for the officers and NCOs, and the regiment was often deployed in aid of the civil authorities. Their Limerick detachment of two and a half troops was commanded by Hugh McCalmont, already at least a name to Adrian as a fellow cavalry jockey who had ridden in Irish races and as the owner of a Grand National runner, and for whom he would later execute commissioned equine paintings. Because of rather than despite the tense atmosphere, the detachment threw a brilliant ball where champagne flowed like water. Even as the Hussars were recovering from these social exertions, news reached Ireland of the early major British defeats in the Transvaal War. The regiment, though it was not its turn on the cavalry rota for overseas station service, volunteered for South Africa. Its control of behaviour in disaffected Ireland had avoided stoking disturbance and shown an ability to cool threatening situations. That was an ability, in addition to its fighting capabilities, with potential for the Transvaal. Ordered to concentrate in Dublin for embarkation, the 7th routemarched there from their various outstation locations.

On 26 February 1881 HQ and five troops with their horses went aboard the *SS Calabria*, which at sea joined the *SS France*, out from London with another party of the 7th who had gone there to collect extra horses. A day later the other squadrons of the 7th Hussars and their newly attached veterinary surgeon

Adrian Jones sailed from Kingstown (now Dun Laoghaire) on the *SS Nemesis*. It was the one ship's name Adrian could always recall, because the voyage caused him so much trouble. As he wrote in the 1930s in his *Memoirs*, 'Fifty years ago boats had not reached the stage so near perfection they have arrived at today.' The *Nemesis*, despite its classical name (albeit that naming a ship after the goddess of retribution hardly seems a happy choice) was not of the 'A1 at Lloyds' calibre of the Blue Funnel Line's ships bearing names from classical literature. Thus, 'mischance was never far off'.

The British army's performance was to prove so embarrassingly poor in the First Boer War that no campaign medals were issued. Adrian might have felt he almost deserved a medal just for getting to South Africa. Certainly in later years, when he met Colonel Richard Moody of the Buffs, the first Vice-President of the Ludlow Grammar School Old Boys' Club, they could exchange horror stories of their army troopship voyages to South Africa. Moody had first gone out with the Buffs in 1876 on the *St Laurence*. It shared a name with Ludlow's parish church, but had none of that building's charm. In his account in the regimental journal, Moody called it 'a nasty dirty little ship full of rats and only capable of steaming about nine knots'. Ninety miles north of Table Bay it ran at night onto Paternoster Reef – run aground deliberately, Moody speculated, to gain the insurance money. The Buffs paraded on deck as the commanding officer issued orders from the bridge, told off one company commander because his company was not paraded in order of height, and arrested the ship's assistant purser for saying in panic that the ship would only hold together for an hour. Meanwhile the Colonel's lady calmed the women and children until they were loaded into the few lifeboats available and set off in the darkness to find land, leaving the soldiers standing 'at ease' and wondering when they would become food for sharks. Fortunately the sea was calm and at daylight the lifeboats returned and in several trips rescued the troops. They now found themselves, bereft of equipment and supplies, on a deserted stretch of coast with, in those days before universal communication, no means of quickly informing authority that they were safe if not exactly well. An officer discovered a remote farm, commandeered a horse, and rode the ninety miles to Cape Town in eighteen hours.

When Adrian narrated the story of his troopship voyage, it was less dramatic in its denouement, but more filled with suspense. The *Calabria* and *France* arrived in Port Natal on April 4th. The *Nemesis*, which had set out a day later, had not even reached Cape Town by April 5th. Alarm grew as a week passed with no sign of her, and deepened as a second week passed. Other ships searched for her on the route, unavailingly. General opinion, as the second week stretched into a third week overdue, hardened into suspicion that she had gone down.

In military terms it did not matter. Reinforcements were no longer needed, for fighting was finished. This time Britain had lost not only the first battle, which was not uncommon in Victoria's small wars, but also the whole campaign. The first defeat had come within days of the declaration of independence: a Transvaaler commando (i.e. armed force) destroyed a column of the Connaught Rangers regiment. That first engagement had some old-fashioned features reminiscent of peacetime ceremonial. Before battle commenced, the Connaughts' band played the National Anthem, and after the defeat and surrender, those Connaught prisoners of war who were unwounded marched off into captivity to the inappropriate accompaniment of their band's survivors playing 'Rule Britannia', while their fatally wounded commanding officer and the Boer Commander drank champagne together. However, on the Boer side the tactics of the battle itself had been savagely ruthless, intelligent and modern. They offered no target themselves, but mowed down the surrounded Connaughts with modern rifles fired from concealed positions. Their marksmen made a particular point of hitting all nine of the Connaughts' officers.

Next the Transvaalers crossed into Natal and stationed 2,000 men at the best pass through the Drakensberg mountains, Laing's Nek, to stop the British army under Major General Colley entering their homeland to relieve the besieged Transvaal garrisons. Colley's frontal assault on them at the end of January failed. He retired to his camp, but then in early February, as he sought to secure his line of communication with Natal, he was surprised by a mounted Boer commando and lost half his men. Next, having received some reinforcement, he decided on a dash for military glory, to be made before 'Bobs' Roberts arrived to supersede him as commander of the British forces. He would occupy Majuba Hill, a sugarloaf mountain from which he hoped to dominate the Boers entrenched at Laing's Nek. On 26th February his force climbed it by night. The Boers were surprised to see them there, but once they realised the British had no artillery with which to shell them, not unduly perturbed. Moving between sheltering boulders and concealing shrubs, and given covering fire to make the British keep their heads down, one hundred and eighty Boer volunteer good shots climbed to the perimeter crest. That reached, they let loose a hail of short-range enveloping fire. Colley himself and more than ninety of his men fell dead, and more than three hundred fell wounded there or in downhill flight. Historians are divided on whether two Boers were killed or only one. Despite individual feats of heroism, the Majuba disaster meant that the British had fought four battles, and lost four, in a little over two months. Six of the seven besieged British garrisons in Pretoria and smaller Transvaal towns held out still, but in early March the Prime Minister, Gladstone, arranged a truce and then, on 21st March, concluded terms of peace.

Meanwhile Adrian was still on or below the waves. Under the reforms introduced by the Principal Veterinary Officer, he remained an officer of the Army Veterinary Department, one of eleven posted not to a regiment but to a place, South Africa. But in the circumscribed world of a troopship at sea, the new system felt, for all practical purposes, just like the former system of being gazetted to a regiment; and by inclination he always liked to identify with those with whom he messed. In their usual habitat the 7th (Queen's Own) Hussars officers were high spirited. In the mid 1870s Queen Victoria had arranged for her son Arthur, Duke of Connaught, to be appointed to the Hussars, but his royalty had not spared him suffering practical japes perpetrated by brother officers, especially Hugh McCalmont, who set off a detonating firework under the table at which the Prince was playing whist. Its force broke window panes and the mirror over the mantelpiece. Rather shaken, brother officers decided that the irrepressible had verged upon the irresponsible. They trashed McCalmont's room and decorated nearby trees with his belongings. The Prince apparently neither stood on his royal dignity nor bore any grudge. Shipboard, however, was not normal habitat. Hugh McCalmont and Adrian tell in their memoirs that the Hussars on both *Calabria* and *Nemesis* were bad sailors. Once when a heavy swell was running, their commanding officer, unable to hold back seasickness any longer, abruptly dismissed the accused man who was appearing before him for some military offence with the verdict 'Remanded – until the weather is calmer', before rushing out himself. 'Then too,' wrote Adrian, 'many of the soldiers, young and inexperienced as they were, suffered greatly from seasickness and this added nothing to the pleasure of the cruise'. In writing of seasickness he could allow himself archetypal English humorous understatement. But there was no humorous relief in what he labelled the voyage's 'first crisis'. As *Nemesis* reached the tropics, her engines developed faults. One consequence of the loss of power and speed was that little draught of air came through the windsails, the wide canvas tunnels designed to channel air below deck. Without their cooling effect, the badly ventilated 'tween decks, where the horses were stalled near the ailing engines, became unbearably hot. Horses started to succumb to heat exhaustion. By the time the ship was leaving tropical waters, thirty-nine had died. On campaign in Abyssinia and the Sudan, Adrian witnessed larger losses of army animals, especially mules and camels. But for a man who loved horses and who had a particular duty of care for those on board, this was the darkest experience of his veterinary career.

The ship's handicapped progress and the extra watering of horses in attempts to save them now brought on a second crisis. The ship, still crammed with men and many remaining horses, ran low on fresh water.

The Captain called a conference of all the officers to seek their opinion on whether he should divert to St Helena. To consider not hastening with all possible speed to a war to which they had been ordered could not be an easy decision for part of a regiment whose comrades, for all they knew, might already be taking casualties and needing replacement men and horses. Without means of communication to higher military authority, it was impossible to pass the buck upwards. In his *Memoirs* Adrian contrasted the situation with the 1930s world in which the Lords of the Admiralty had 'every unit of the Fleet under direct and immediate control'. The meeting of officers decided to abandon the direct route to Cape Town: on their slow boat, the risk of water shortage was too great. So *Nemesis* put into St Helena, took on water, and so 'set trouble out of reach'. After a happily uneventful final leg, she arrived at Cape Town on 22 April 1881, a belated eighteen days after *Calabria* and *France*.

Now the Hussars heard how the regular route to Cape Town had been searched for any sign of them, and how most people had given up hope of seeing them again. They heard too that peace had been declared a month earlier, though the endorsing Peace Conference still lay in the future. The news of peace caused some angry and glum faces. McCalmont wrote, 'I am thoroughly humiliated and degraded ... Why have Colley and all his men been sacrificed if there was a foregone conclusion there was nothing worth fighting for?' Also, gallant action in a small war could enhance an officer's promotion prospects, but despite the many Victorian small wars a cavalry regiment or infantry battalion could spend decades without earning a campaign medal or battle honour. McCalmont *had* seen action when he had previously gone out to South Africa with Sir Garnet Wolseley at the time of the Zulu War. Ironically, his fighting then had been to help make Transvaal safer for the Boers, who were being menaced by the native King Sekukwni.

'Bobs' Roberts had not arrived in South Africa to take command until after the fighting was over. In disgust he left again after just forty-eight hours. Adrian could not make such a decision. He had the immediate task of transferring the horses to the *Calabria*, then sailing with them and the Hussars up the Indian Ocean to Durban. In those days Durban had no port. Because of an underwater bank, large vessels had to ride at anchor offshore in open sea. If the sea was rough, embarking from or disembarking to a lighter could be an awkward performance. The soldier, probably in full marching order, had to time his jump when the deck of the lighter and the open port of the ship as they rose and fell were roughly level, then pray that strong nautical arms would catch and steady him. The horses had to be unloaded. *Calabria* arrived in a heavy swell, so unloading was difficult as well as laborious: 'Every horse had to be hoisted up and placed in a surf-boat and then had to be battened down to get through the rolling water and past the Bar.'

Transportation troubles overcome, the regiment marched through inland Natal to Pinetown, an unexciting station on the railway line to Pietermaritzburg. They camped there for thirteen tedious months before being recalled to Britain in July 1882. Adrian soon continued upcountry to Newcastle. There, he writes in his *Memoirs*, 'we heard that Peace was declared. I was attached just then to the Inniskilling Dragoons.' As when giving his account of his tour of duty in Ireland, writing fifty years after the events and without benefit of a diary kept at the time, his recall is only partly accurate. The Inniskillings arrived at Newcastle on March 16th, so they were indeed there to hear peace declared on the 21st; but Adrian did not get there before the end of April. His attachment to the Inniskillings was a switch under the new flexible organisation of Army Veterinary Department officers. This was a more 'normal' existence than he had experienced with the Hussars: garrison, as opposed to shipboard, life. The commanding officer was a familiar face. Colonel Edward Gore, formerly of the 3rd Hussars, whom Adrian had known in India, for the past four years had commanded the Inniskilling Dragoons.

There was still soldiering to be done, chiefly escort duties, and there were still some moments of high excitement calling for resolute response, as on the night in the rainy season when a violent

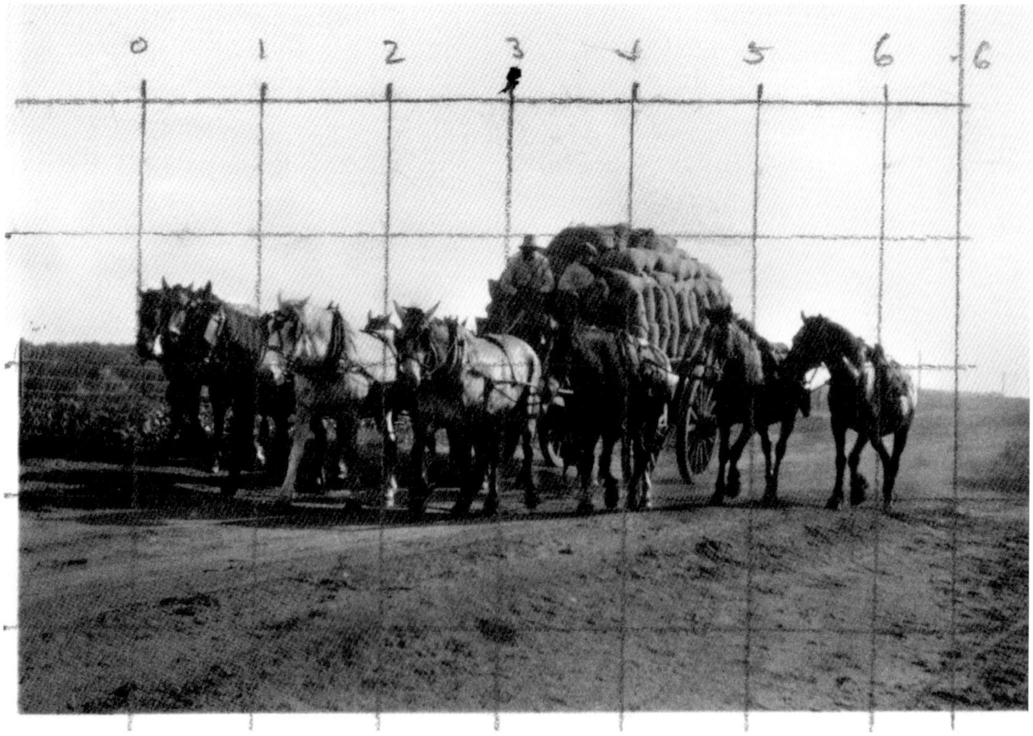

Grid overlay on photograph of horses and cart. Adrian used this as one method of composing a picture. This photograph was sent to him from the American West, but he also brought home from South Africa photographs of Boer horses and carts and combined elements from different photographs in his painting.

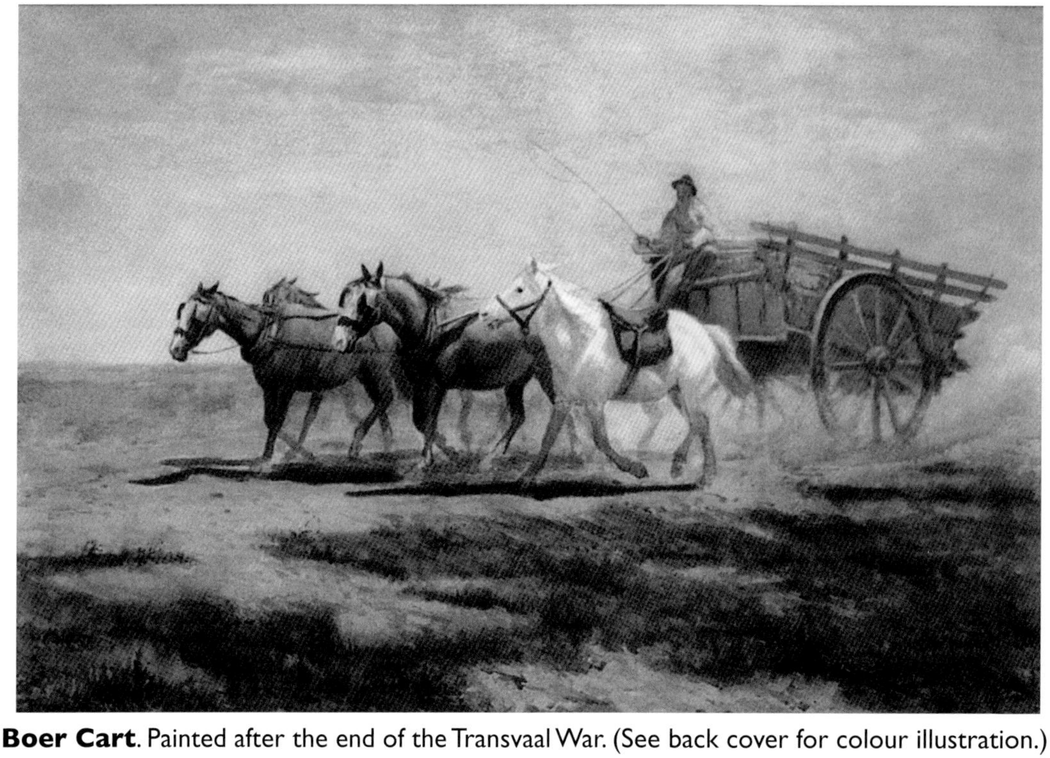

Boer Cart. Painted after the end of the Transvaal War. (See back cover for colour illustration.)

thunderstorm and close-by sheet lightning panicked the horses. They stampeded, breaking their line ropes, scattering tents and galloping off for miles, with Adrian and others after them and determined to retrieve them. It was almost like a cavalry charge of old, but without shot or shell. He never forgot what he downplayed as 'that scamper across the lightning-lit countryside', and used the memory for the painting of an equivalent daytime scene of a herd of horses galloping on the veldt. But there was no longer the pressure of war. He was happy. As with the Queen's Bays, he felt particular affection for a regiment of Irish origins and connections whose commanding officer was also Irish, with a family seat at Derrymore in County Clare. Again, as with the Bays, regiment and veterinary surgeon did not forget each other. In the 1890s Gore, now a general and Honorary Colonel of the Inniskillings, commissioned Adrian to execute paintings of himself and his horses. Even after the Inniskillings in the post-1914-18 War cavalry amalgamations were absorbed into a more senior regiment, the 5th Dragoon Guards, it was to Adrian they turned for their regimental memorial to those of all ranks who fell as Inniskillings in the Great War.

All that lay in the middle or distant future. But there was time for art even now, not yet sculpting, but drawing and painting. At Newcastle he made sketches, later worked up into a large picture, of Gore leading the Inniskillings over Bennet's Drift (ford). Using photographs taken of horses pulling large-wheeled Boer wagons, he composed equivalents of British agricultural or coaching scenes. He also drew scenes in which horses were mere details. At the end of August, for instance, he went with the four squadrons of cavalry which Sir Evelyn Wood took to Zululand. The British Resident, Mr Osborne, had been finding it difficult to maintain peace and harmony among the Zulus, so the Natal Government was worried, and sent Sir Evelyn to confer with the principal chiefs. Adrian felt disappointed that many of the chiefs came without

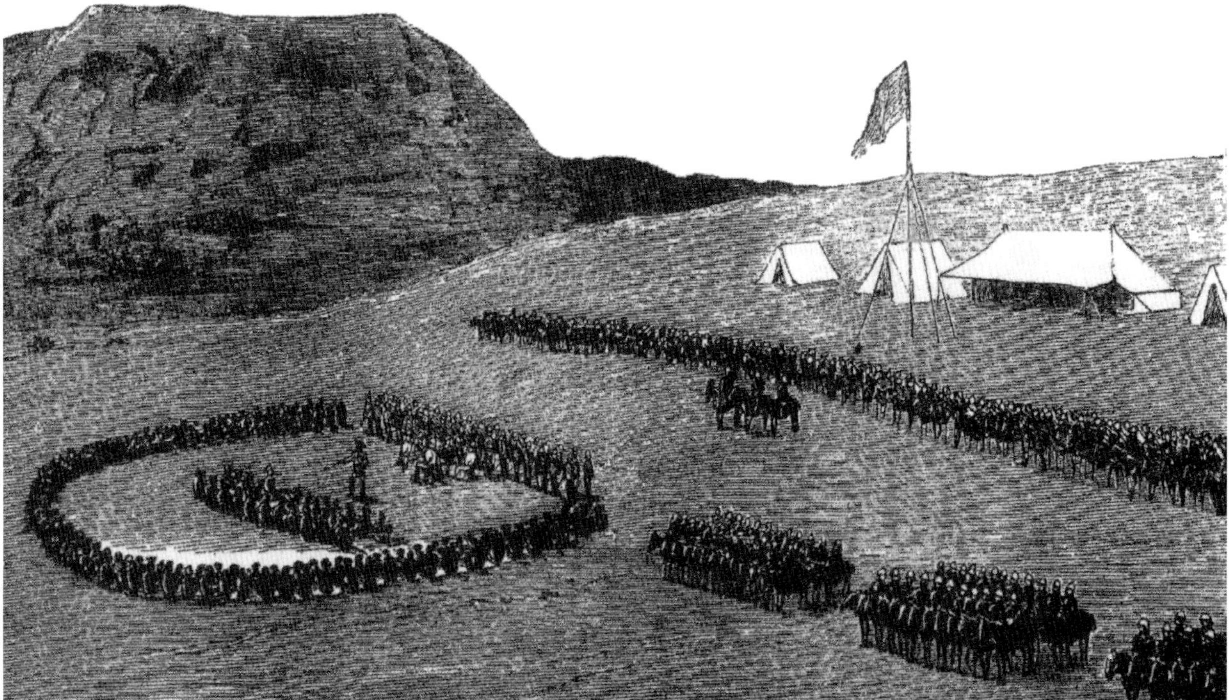

Sketch for the 'Graphic' of General Sir Evelyn Woods's **Conference with the Zulus**, 1882: general view

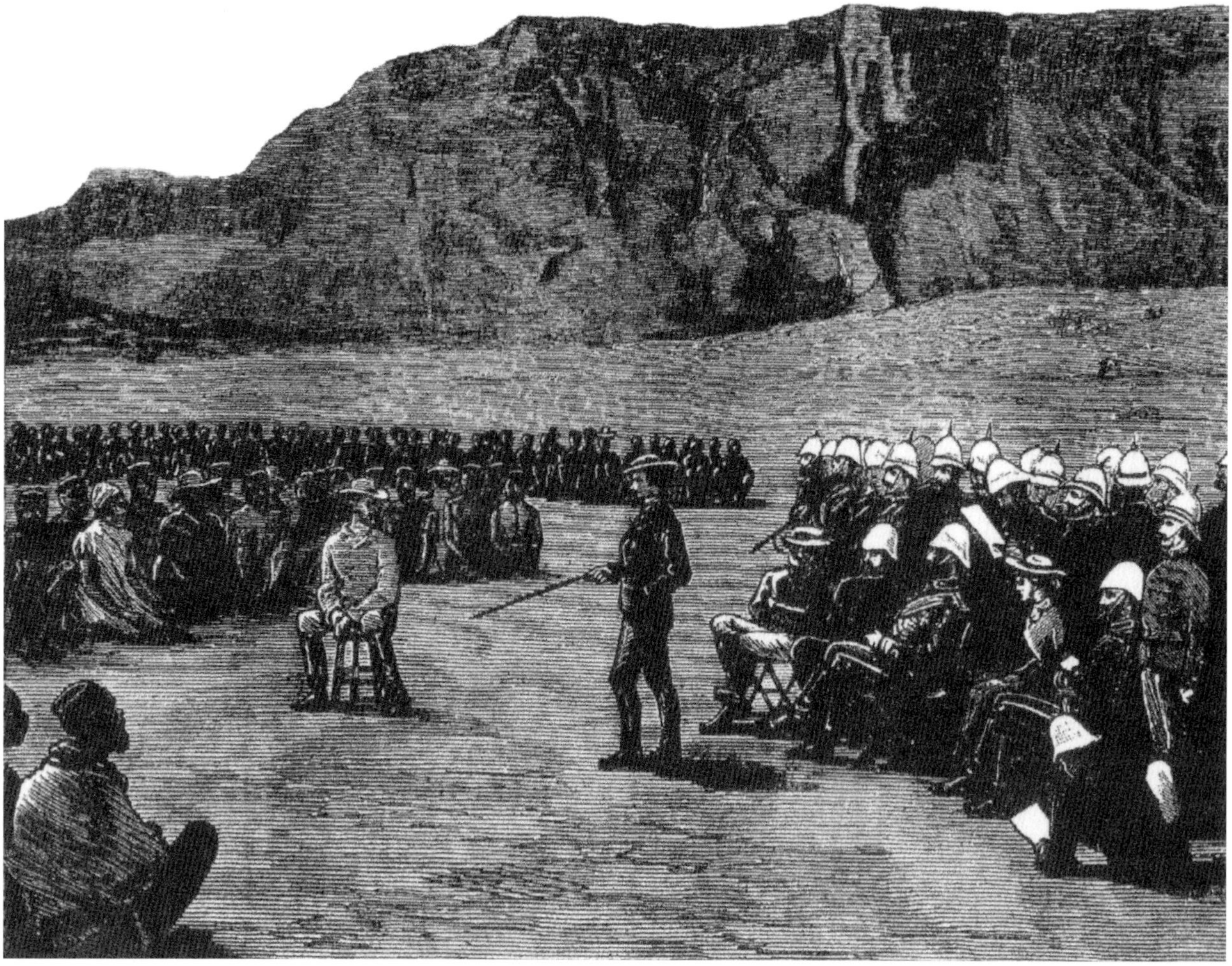

Detail: **Conference with the Zulus**, the interpreter speaking

war paint and wearing European dress, so were less picturesque than he would have wished for a historic scene. Nevertheless, he painted a general view, and a closer view of the main actors. In the broader view, with Imlayatsa Hill looming behind, the ranks of cavalry sit quietly on their mounts, while before them is the conference, ringed by Zulus. In the close-up, the interpreter waves his stick to emphasise a point as he speaks to one of the Zulu chiefs who has been involved in the internecine fighting. In the centre of the facing front row of Europeans Sir Evelyn listens calmly, leaving the staff officer within whispering distance behind him to make notes and provide any prompts needed. On his right is the British Resident, and on his left one of those remarkable intrepid Victorian lady globe-trotters – in this instance, Lady Florence Dixie. On her left is General Redvers Buller, VC, hero of the Zulu War, who just like 'Bobs' Roberts, the Inniskillings, the 7th Hussars and Adrian, had arrived too late to restore British military fortunes in the First Boer War. And perhaps the anonymous figure seen back view in the right foreground as he records the scene is Adrian's quiet insertion of himself in the picture. This is just bread and butter work, but shows he could do crowd scenes if he chose. He sent the results to the *Graphic* magazine in London, and they published them in their November 1881 issue. The audience for his art work was broadening.

Chapter Five: 'My Real Destiny'
1882-1884: Soldier Artist in London

In January 1882, on his return from the Transvaal, Adrian was posted as the veterinary officer for St John's Wood Barracks. There he found three long timbered stable lines, erected as recently as 1876. Gate stables had room for eight further horses, chargers for the sentries. Stationed in the barracks was a Battery of Royal Horse Artillery. It was a familiar scene. Fifteen years ago he had begun his army career with a gazetting to the RHA; life looked as if it might be circling into an unremarkable eddy. As it turned out, however, for an officer who 'had been taking up pencil and brush whenever occasion offered' and who 'had never failed to take the chance to paint the chargers or racehorses of my brother officers', his posting to St John's Wood was to prove life-changing and life-enhancing.

The catalyst was his meeting and growing friendship with sculptor Charles Birch, an enthusiastic part-time soldier in the Artists' Rifles, which although an infantry regiment used horses for such mundane tasks as hauling baggage wagons. Birch befriended him, in a friendship destined to flourish in studio, clubland and dining club until Birch's death in 1893. Soon, in times free from army duties, Adrian was frequenting Birch's studio:

> ... watching the work he was doing with keenest interest, particularly on the anatomical side. Other sculptors, friends of my friend, were in and out of his studio and they soon realised that my feeling for anatomy was based upon close observation, so that they not only listened to what I had to say, but even asked my opinion, saying that a fresh eye, especially when it belonged to a man who was sure of his ground, was a real help to them ... Birch would not only welcome me to his own studio, but he would take me to those of his friends.

So, as he acknowledges in *Soldier Artist*, Adrian owed much to this 'true friend'. On top of the general debt, he was particularly grateful for a chance remark. Composing his memoirs decades after the events described, he was sometimes mistaken or inexact in his memories. But in recording the chance remark he seeks to quote verbatim, and around the remark his writing flames into figurative incandescence:

> Then one day, in his studio, came the chance remark that I think settled the course of my future. He said to me, 'What a pity it is, Jones, that with your genuine love of art, your knowledge of animals and your eye for form, you don't take up sculpture; I'm sure you would make a success of it.' I think that pregnant sentence acted like fire in a powder-magazine. It blew up all my doubts, hesitations and uncertainty and behind them I saw what I took to be my real destiny, not perhaps to be pursued at once but to be regarded as the aim and end of life.

Very happily for Adrian, the 'chance remark' came from the lips of a man similar to him in personality and aptitude, who had himself partly learned his skills in the studio of another sculptor. Twelve years older than Adrian, his age equipped him for filling readily the twin role of friend and mentor. He was then at the height of popular fame, and his generous nature made him ready in every way to assist someone earnestly asking for his aid. Like Adrian, he had shown natural artistic ability in his youth, and he enrolled as a student at the Somerset House School of Design when just twelve. After a year he had gone with his German-translator father to Berlin. There he studied Greek and Roman classical art and attended classes in anatomy, perspective, life and animal life. His combination of industry and talent brought him not only prize medals but also at the age of nineteen, before he returned to London, a royal commission, a marble bust of the British ambassador, the Earl of Westmoreland, commissioned by the King of Prussia. Once back in London he continued his training at the Royal Academy Schools, again winning medals and honorary awards. Thus far his education in art had been the antithesis of Adrian's lack of any orthodox apprenticeship. But next he had entered a working relationship which, though more formal than that he was now proposing to Adrian, had some parallels. He had become an assistant to the prolific sculptor John Foley, RA, working in Foley's studio. Talent ensured that he and another promising sculptor, Thomas Brock, became the chief assistants, and Birch continued to assist Foley for ten years.

When in 1883 Adrian started practising sculpture in Birch's studio, there was much debate in the art world about how far an artist could legitimately use assistants to work on sculptures which on completion would bear the signature only of the master. The debate then involved Brock, and in the next decade would reignite, with Brock and Birch both getting involved, and cause Adrian more obsessive pain than anything else in his life. Forty years after it had been – falsely – insinuated that he used 'ghost' assistants to improve the artistic merit of his work, he devoted a disproportionately lengthy appendix in his *Memoirs* to the accusation and its denial. For the present in 1883, however, the debate did not concern him. The libel case of Belt v. Lawes, in which Belt claimed he had been libelled by Lawes's assertion that much of Belt's statuary of the previous five years had been executed by Brock or another of Belt's assistants, had been intermittently winding through the courts since June 1882, occasionally entertaining the public with tales of assistants being hidden or smuggled out through a trapdoor when visitors came to the studio. But tuition in sculpture in the Royal Academy schools was not as adequate as that in painting, and busy sculptors needed assistants to carry out the more mechanical tasks, so whatever the potential for slander, the system of using assistants continued. It provided experience and needed income to those starting out.

The untrained Adrian could not of course assist Birch. The appreciated help all flowed the other way. Adrian knew he was in good teaching hands which themselves had been well taught. Though Foley's studio had been in London, he was an Irishman whom Dublin generally regarded as its most illustrious sculptor. When Adrian was soldiering near or in that city, Foley's statues were almost ubiquitous. His pair of the statesman and orator Edmund Burke and the novelist, playwright and poet Oliver Goldsmith flanked the main entrance to Trinity College on College Green; his bronze of the greatest Irish parliamentarian, Henry Grattan, posed nearby; his Sir Jonathan Guinness sat in reflective mood beside St Patrick's Cathedral; and outside Leinster House, then the premises of the Royal Dublin Society, rose his large Prince Albert Memorial, with the Prince himself on top, and around the base in tribute four individual statues, emblematic of Science, Art, Industry and Agriculture. Adrian had gone from Dublin to the Transvaal War just before Foley's O'Connell Memorial (completed by Brock after Foley's death) had been erected; but now, stationed back in London, he could contemplate another Foley statue of Albert, that on the elaborate London Memorial to him.

From Foley's works, with Birch's guidance, Adrian absorbed much: the value of naturalism and realism and the use of telling detail; not to be scared of the large and ambitious, and the possibilities for personifying a concept or a virtue. But first he had to master the necessary mechanical skills. Birch showed him how to construct an armature, the support on which a sculpture was built. Next he advised him 'on how to put the clay upon it, adding pieces of clay where required, while avoiding the student's error of piling it on too much and then scraping it down with a tool'. To this advice he added comment on 'the value of big flat planes meeting each other in such a way that no deep cuts are left'.

'And that,' Birch stressed, 'was all'. When later controversy raged over whether Adrian's work was original (see page 97-101), the *Morning* newspaper sent its reporter to interview Birch. He asked if Adrian had done all the work on his first statuette himself. 'All,' Birch replied unequivocally. He was equally robust in response when the reporter referred to those sculptors who had claimed that it was not possible for a man to learn the technique of sculpting in so short a space of time as it had apparently taken Adrian: 'That is all nonsense,' Birch declared, adding that Adrian had had previous studies and experience that gave him a special advantage in regard to the learning of the new art.

Birch was thinking of Adrian's scientific knowledge of and personal experience with horses, for the statuette in question was Adrian's first work of sculpture, a study of one of his own hunters. Having helped Adrian fix up the armature, Birch left him to do the modelling on his own. Sculptor friends of Birch who came and went in his studio were naturally interested in this untutored beginner who could model a horse so competently, but whose career was not that of sculptor but of army officer. As is often the lot of somebody unusual, he had to accept some chaffing; indeed the general joke was that the horse he was shaping was fed on 'chaff'. It proved good feed, the kindly meant bantering comments boosting Adrian's confidence that his statuette, now christened 'One of the Right Sort', was not going to turn out looking miserably 'half-rationed'.

When Adrian finished his modelling, so impressed was Birch with his pupil's work that he suggested that Adrian should send it to the Royal Academy for possible selection for the Academy's 1884 Summer Exhibition. Adrian did not record his emotions on hearing this bold proposal, but he submitted the statuette. No doubt he hoped that it would indeed prove to be one of the right sort.

The hands-on help Birch gave Adrian over armature construction was essential for the apprentice sculptor, but even more propitious for Adrian's artistic evolution were the other benefits Birch's friendship offered. The frequent visits to the studio of fellow artists and potential patrons were part business, part social, and broadened Adrian's range of valuable and companionable contacts. Equally broadening was seeing the range of Birch's work. He learnt that an artist who wished to avoid his father's predicted fate of bread and cheese in a garret must offer more than busts and figures. Adrian already knew and practised two of Birch's alternatives: he painted, and sold his paintings; and he drew for illustrated periodicals. But the industrious and versatile Birch also designed numerous trophy items – medallions, hunt cups, shields – and his example led Adrian to diversify his own output in due course. One instance would be his design for the Derby Cup. This was not for the Epsom Derby but for the most prestigious race at the Derby Racecourse three day November 1895 meeting, patronised by the Prince of Wales, who came with the Duke and Duchess of Devonshire's house party from Chatsworth. The party included the Prince's frequent companion at the races, his mistress Daisy, Countess of Warwick, and also present were others known to Adrian, such as Hugh McCalmont, by then an MP, and members of the Rothschild and Sassoon families, whose horses he would paint. In its account the *Derby Mercury* gave equal prominence to the society spectators, to the 'splendid class' international field of horses that, backed by 'extremely brisk' betting, raced for the Cup, and to Adrian's magnificent prize:

> The Derby Cup trophy takes the form of a tankard of Elizabethan design, bold in execution and very massive. Its salient features are its lip, formed of a satyr's head, its handle of enriched strap work, surmounted by a finely-modelled Pegasus, and its top, or knob, a knight in armour at the salute. Its highly decorated shield is a masterpiece of fine repoussé work, as are the frieze around the

top and the decoration of the base. The cup was specially designed by Captain Adrian Jones.

His hammering of metal from behind, required for repoussé work, shows one more skill mastered.

The most valuable lessons of all Adrian learned from Birch, however, were those imparted by his recent popular successes. In 1879 he had exhibited at the Royal Academy an equestrian work called 'The Last Call'. In the words of the *Queen* magazine, the work 'electrified the public by its power, dramatic force, and intensity'. It showed a cavalry trumpeter and his horse being fatally wounded simultaneously. The rider's head and trumpet arm are thrown up and back; the horse plunges head down and forwards. The next year he had exhibited what was to prove his most famous sculpture, a portrait statue of Lieutenant Walter Hamilton VC, aimed pistol in his left hand, drawn sword in his right, his legs bestriding a prone knife-wielding enemy Afghan. It was a sculptural equivalent of Victorian narrative painting, dramatic in impact and in its use of suspense – is the Afghan or the Lieutenant going to be the one to survive the combat? Most Victorian visitors to the Summer Exhibition knew the answer. Hamilton had fallen at Kabul only the previous year, when he and his men charged out to silence an enemy cannon, and it was said he had first despatched five of the enemy, three with the pistol and two with the sword. Like the general public, Adrian admired the pride in valour that inspired the work, and the vigorous realisation. (In 1891 he acted as the Treasurer to whom the public were invited to send subscriptions in response to an Appeal to purchase the statue for the Royal Dublin Society's museum. In 1985, with southern Ireland long independent of Britain, on the suggestion of Major General Goff Hamilton, a great grandnephew of Lieutenant Hamilton, the RDS presented the statue to the National Army Museum, Chelsea.) Not having been taught in art school, Adrian more than most sculptors had to gain some ideas from works in exhibitions or public spaces. Though, having seen actual battlefield death, he never produced any big sculpture as bloodthirsty as Birch's composition, he frequently used the detail of an empty scabbard or pistol holder, all indicative of actual or imminently expected close mortal combat. The drawn pistol or sword is in the hand; the drawn bayonet is fixed on the rifle.

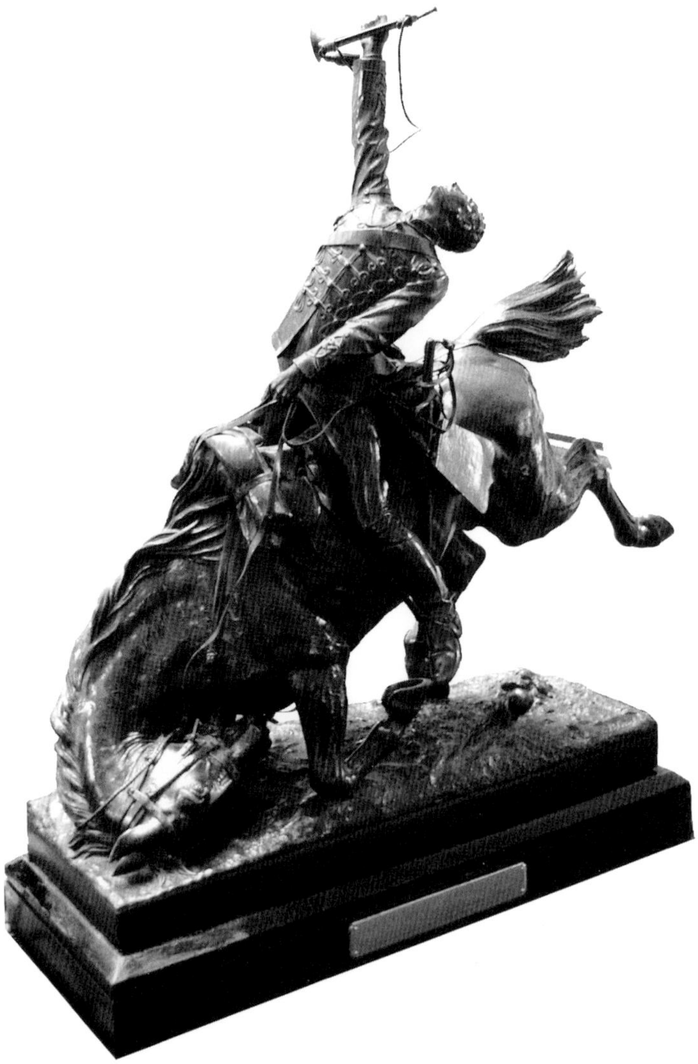

The Last Call,
bronze statuette by Charles Birch, ARA

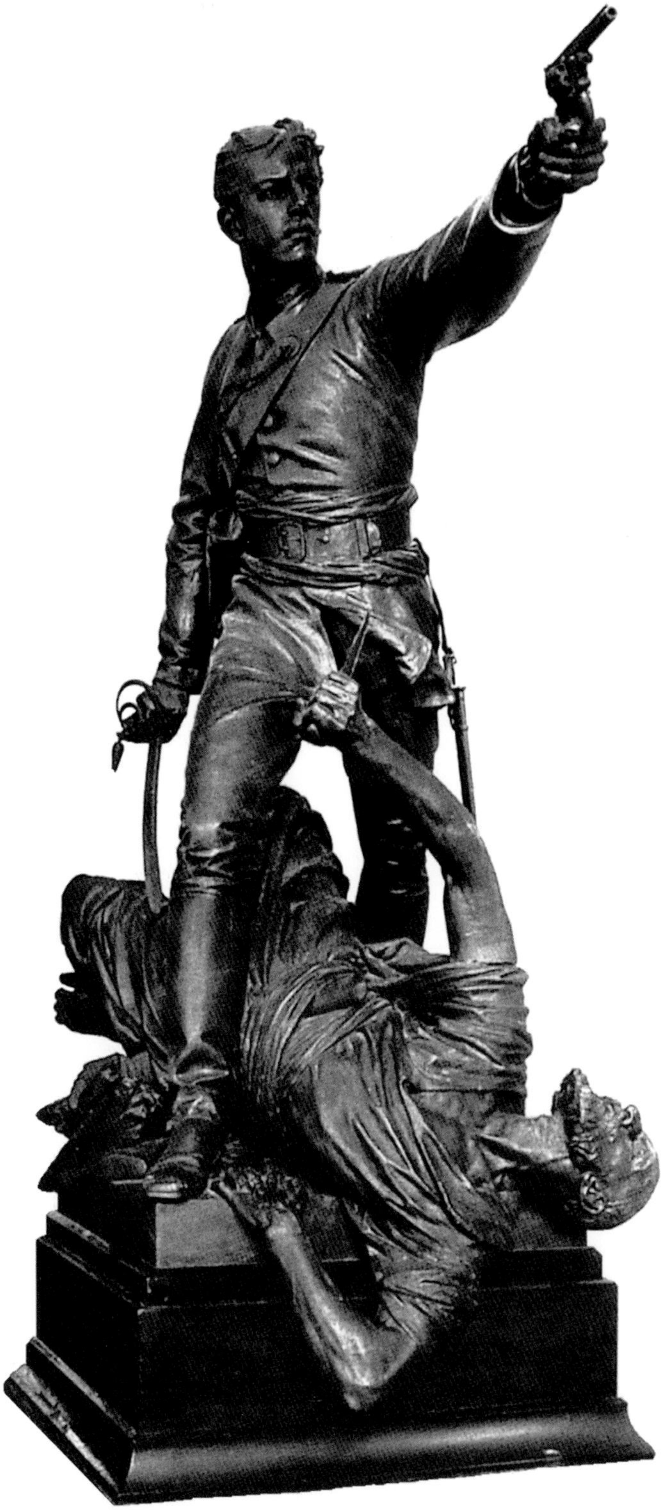

Lieutenant Walter Hamilton, VC,
bronze painted plaster statue by Charles Birch, ARA

Of course, learning from Birch's works brought Adrian larger benefits than simply ideas for significant detail. He learned that placing figures on a sculpted base, such as the fought-over broken cannon pieces in the 'Hamilton' statue, rather than on a plain flat slab, intensified the narrative impact. He also learned the commercial advantage of finishing work while its subject still held public attention. The sculpture of Hamilton's death had been exhibited within a year of the event. Adrian too became a rapid worker, and his speed of execution would help gain him commissions for his paintings and sculptures: 'Happily, I was never afraid of a special effort ... The pace of my work was something that my academic critics could not understand; indeed, they resented it.' A third lesson Adrian absorbed was the merit of keeping in mind the potential market and site for a work. The popular success of the 'Hamilton VC' portrait sculpture brought Birch new commissions: while Adrian was with him in 1883 he was working on statues of Disraeli and Major General Earle for sites beside St George's Hall in Liverpool. But 'Hamilton' itself found no buyer who wanted it cast in bronze. Where would it fit? When afterwards a public subscription appeal brought the bronze-painted plaster to the Royal Dublin Society, it looked incongruous on the black and white tiled floor of a room furnished with such items as a writing table, chairs and a grandfather clock. Adrian sought to ensure that, in addition to fulfilling their intention, his statues suited their site.

Sadly, the main reason why from 1883 onwards Adrian could spend his off-duty hours in Birch's study was bereavement. For years his wife Emma had been suffering from the kidney problems which Victorian doctors labelled Bright's Disease. As always

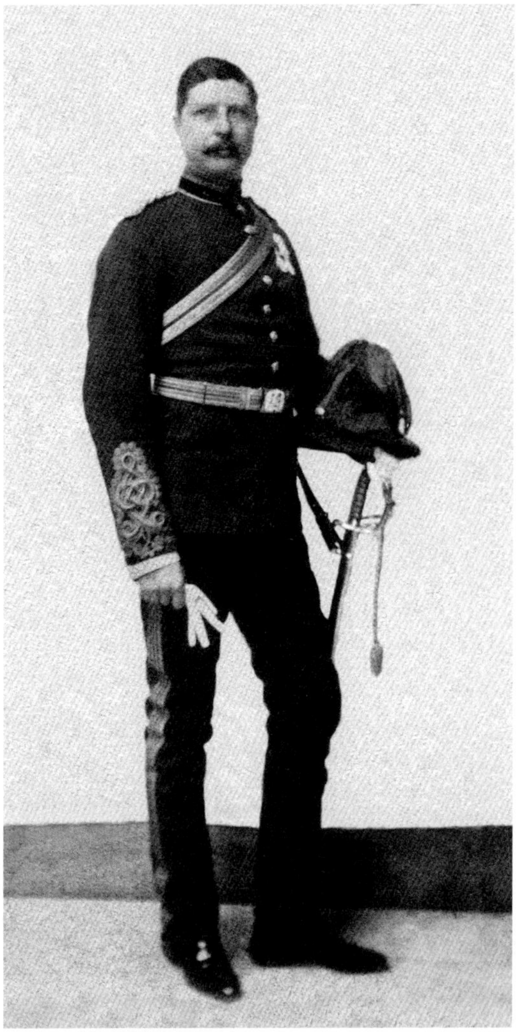

Adrian Jones, promoted to Captain and Veterinary Surgeon 1st class, Army Veterinary Service, 1883

in his *Memoirs,* Adrian is extremely reticent about what is a family matter. He does not mention Emma's death in his third chapter, which includes coverage of his time in London after the Transvaal War. The only mention is a reference in chapter two to the future: 'Unfortunately, I was destined to lose my wife comparatively early in life.' In today's more emotionally forthcoming Britain, or by comparison with the lachrymose mourning of the Widow of Windsor for Prince Albert, the single word 'unfortunately' seems inadequate as an expression of love and sorrow. He wrote the word fifty years after the event, so allowance must be made for the operation of Time, the great healer, and for Adrian's possible feeling of delicacy over giving a fulsome account of emotion felt for his first wife in a book to be published while he was living most happily with his second. But essentially his restraint, in an age when death often came early rather than late, is an expression of Victorian male stoic response in public, the upper lip stiff however intense the private feeling. Emma died in their home on Adelaide Road in Hampstead on 16 August 1883, aged just 35. As when running the Swan Hotel, the Beckingham girls helped one another, and the youngest sister, Minnie, ten years Emma's junior, watched at the death bed. The doctor certified that the cause of death of Emma Elizabeth Jones, wife of Alfred Adrian Jones, Army Veterinary Surgeon, was 'Bright's Disease, 6 years'.

After Emma's death, Adrian immersed himself in the life of art and of the army. He still had to attend to his prospering military career. In the Army Veterinary Department section of the Army List he now ranked as the most senior veterinary surgeon with war experience. On 1 April 1883 he had become a Veterinary Surgeon First Class and received promotion in rank to Captain. The rich suburb of St John's Wood provided a pleasant working environment, as did the barracks themselves, for the new stable lines of 1876 had been built as an interim home for the regimental headquarters of the Household Cavalry, and so to a good standard. As the only veterinary officer for the Royal Horse Artillery now stationed there, Adrian's duties were substantial and of major responsibility but fairly routine. At 6.30 am the barrack gate opened and out rode the gunners for an hour and a half of walking and trotting their horses, the exercise taking place along whatever route took the fancy of the officer in charge. They returned at 8 to feed and water the horses and themselves, then carried out the day's training activities until 'Stables' was sounded at 11. The gunners attended to the smartness of the horses and harnesses and the cleanliness of the stables; Adrian did his round of the lines; and afterwards the horses watered at the troughs. In the afternoon, unless specially required for military exercises or parades, the horses remained in the lines in the care of the duty stablemen. At 6.15 p.m. the picquet guard was mounted to ensure that all would be well during the night, and the not too busy twelve-hour day was over.

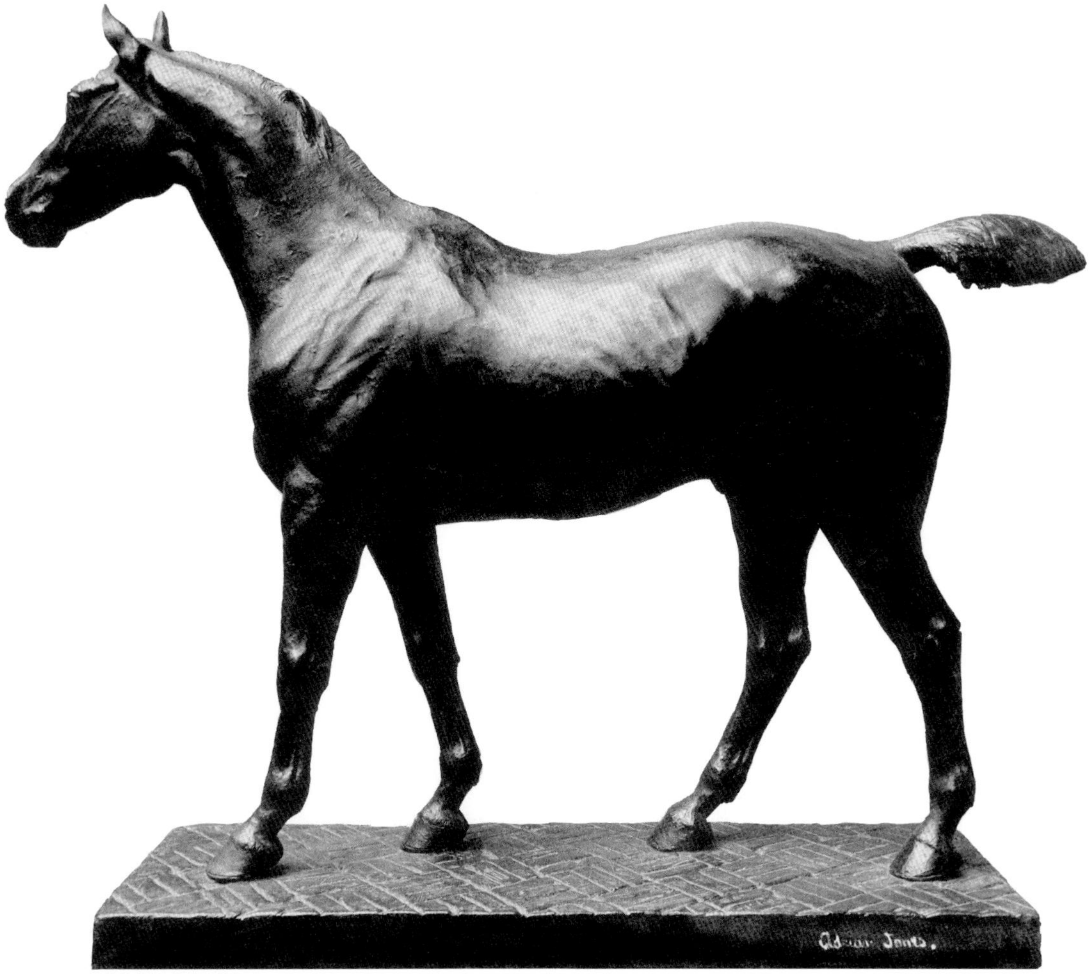

A Hunter: One of the Right Sort: Royal Academy Exhibit, 1884

Outside the barracks, St John's Wood had some artistic life. Until November 1882, a short walking distance away in Grove End Road lived James Tissot, the brilliant and popular painter of Victorian social life particularly famed for his portrait of the cavalry officer Frederick Burnaby. Tissot's young model and mistress Kathleen Newton was the daughter of an Irish army officer who had served with the Indian army, and she herself had gone out to India at the age of seventeen, but though those circumstances gave her something in common with Adrian there was almost no chance of any social relationship developing. The Victorian moral code restricted the social circle of this 'fallen woman', she was dying of consumption, and Adrian's art was in a different field from the elegant ladies who featured in Tissot's. A year after Tissot moved away to Paris because of Kathleen Newton's death, Alma Tadema took over the Grove End house and garden, but his orientalism also had no connection to Adrian's art, though subsequently Adrian sometimes showed paintings in the same exhibitions as Alma Tadema's wife and daughter.

Adrian's second way of life, that of artist, continued in the studio of Charles Birch. The Royal Academy selected 'One of the Right Sort' for its 1884 Summer Exhibition. This marks an astonishing achievement that is probably unique in the history of British art. Has anyone else, before or since, had their very first sculpture accepted for a Royal Academy Summer Exhibition? It was a success possible only for someone who had not attended art school: those who had received formal art training would have worked on their first attempt during their studies and displayed it, if at all, in an exhibition of students' work.

The rarity and magnitude of Adrian's accomplishment compels admiration. Speaking about the working methods of the RA Council, Sir Frederick Leighton stated:

> To judge the pictures and sculptures, and elect those that have sufficient artistic merit to exhibition in the Academy, we absolutely do not know who the author may chance to be. We are perfectly open-minded in our selection and do not enquire who has done the work we select. The veriest novice has an equal chance with the oldest artist. Authorship is nothing to us; our duty is to look after Art and pass nothing that is not worthy of place in the Academy.

Despite this assertion of Leighton's, however, other Royal Academicians such as Thomas Brock continued to maintain that 'fine technique' was impossible without 'long course of study and practice'. It was not easy

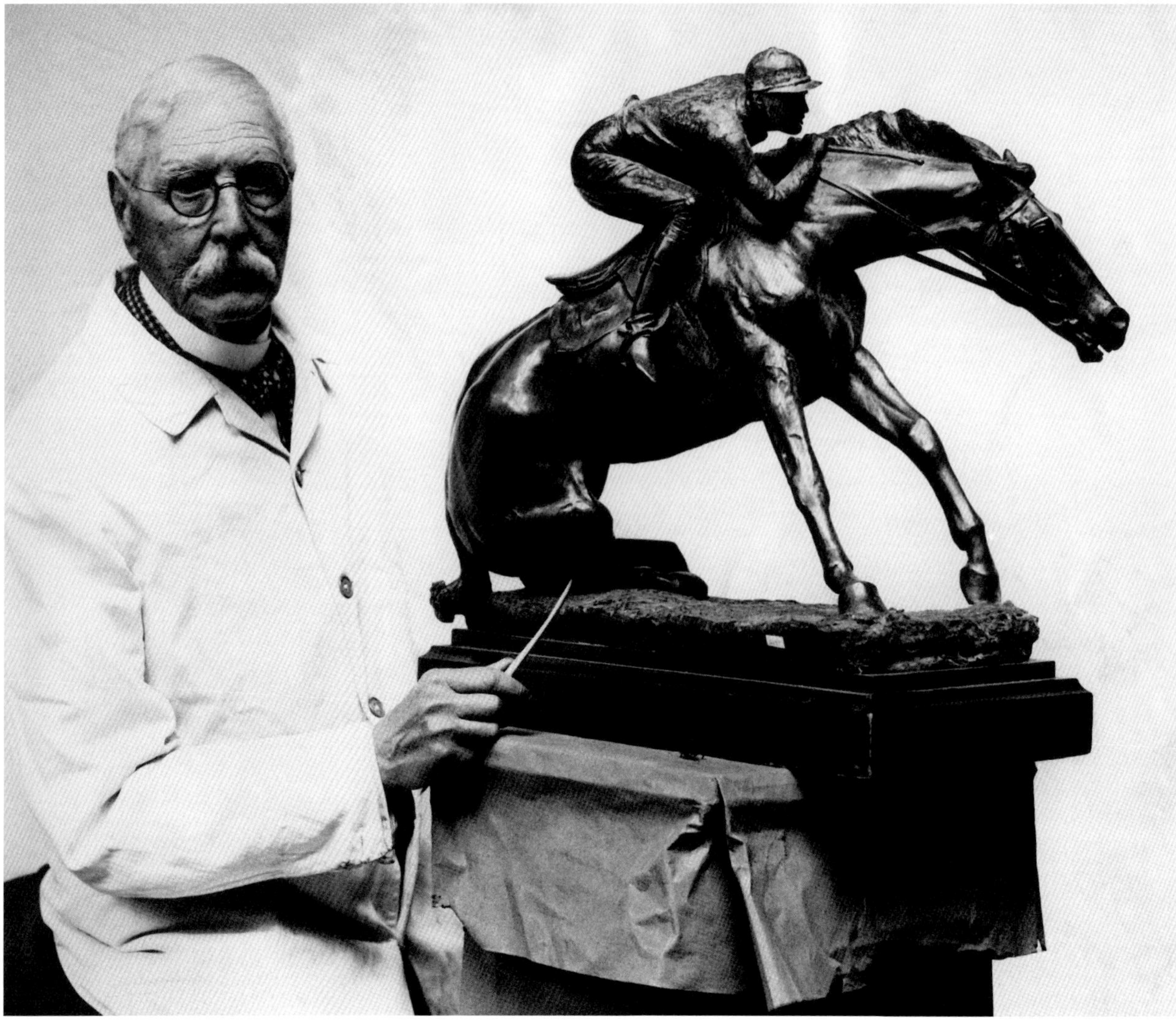

Adrian poses in his studio beside his **Becher's Brook** statuette.

for RAs in a competitive market to avoid jealousy towards someone whose outstanding natural talent had been nourished not in art school but in veterinary school and stable, and on hunting field and racecourse.

The first page of illustrations in the text of Adrian's *Memoirs* shows in the upper half the old painting, owned by his family, of his father on one of his horses. The horse stands facing left. Below is another half-page photograph. In this one stands Adrian's sculpture, 'One of the Right Sort', on a base scored to indicate stable-yard paving blocks. Again the horse faces left. The base's side carries Adrian's obvious, legible signature, and the wording below the title proclaims 'The first piece of sculpture executed by the Author. Exhibited RA 1884'. Clearly his hunter sculpture owes something to the family's portrait of his father's hunter, with the similarities emphasised by the decision as to which way to position the statuette for the photographer.

The pose photographed is the one favoured by many equine artists from the eighteenth century onwards. The horse is seen squarely from the side, standing on level ground, all four legs showing, with the farther apart nearer legs framing the further pair; it looks ahead, ears pricked and tail up. Later, particularly when not working on a commission to model some prize winning racehorse, Adrian often preferred to sculpt dramatic activity. In his later statuette 'Becher's Brook' the horse struggles on crumpled hind legs in an arched upward diagonal, the flanks heaving up but the neck bending down and the front legs stretched as it seeks to recover from the ditch on the landing side. (In Adrian's time the ditch really could be a 'brook' with running water, and the drop over the hedge was notoriously tougher than it is now after being partly filled in.) The jockey is out of his saddle, head well beyond the withers, clinging on and coaxing. The viewer is left uncertain whether man and horse or Becher's will win the test of courage and power. But already in the simply posed 'One of the Right Sort' Adrian showed how well he could portray physique: the hunter's compact muscularity is imbued with vigour. The moulding of the powerful shoulders and hindquarters, complemented by the precise detailing of smaller features such as pasterns, points of hock and fetlock joints, give a sense of what Adrian aimed to create throughout his equine sculpting career – 'a magnificent presence, as it should be'. Magnificent, but different: this horse is 'the right sort', but not the same sort as the slimmer and finer-boned thoroughbred on which his father sits.

The statuette appeared in the RA's show of 1884, exhibit 1760, with its title expanded to 'A Hunter, One of the Right Sort'. Exhibit 1667 was Rodin's 'L'Age d'Airain' (Age of bronze). The *Daily News* recorded: 'A popular little work is Mr Adrian Jones's weight-carrying hunter', and, more equivocally, 'Nothing is better modelled than the nude and not very interesting or intelligible figure which M. Rodin calls 'L'Age d'Airain'. He might as well represent the Stone Age, so far as we can see'.

Naturally pleased and emboldened by this success, Adrian entered a Goldsmiths' Company competition to sculpt a statuette that had to feature a mounted huntsman with two hounds. The subject suited his expert knowledge and appealed to him too. He labelled his work 'Gone Away' and sent it off to the Goldsmiths' Company. As is the way with competitions requiring entries by a certain date, silence then reigned, and before Adrian received news of success or failure, the words 'Gone Away' also applied to him.

General Gordon had been besieged by a Mahdist cordon in Khartoum since mid-March 1884, and British public opinion sought to persuade the Liberal Government that he must not be abandoned. Queen Victoria wrote to her Prime Minister, Gladstone: 'You are bound to try to save him.' Lord Wolseley submitted memoranda arguing the need for a British relief expedition. Gladstone, who had no desire to spend British blood in the inhospitable heat and deserts of the Sudan, prevaricated until his Secretary of State for War threatened to resign. Reluctantly, on 5th August the Government finally voted £300,000 for the operation, and later in the month Wolseley was appointed to command it. In September a corps of specially selected officers and men set sail for Egypt to learn to ride camels. Meanwhile the Principal Veterinary Surgeon to the Forces, George Fleming, was fretting that he could obtain definite information neither on the Nile Expedition's requirements for veterinary surgeons and supplies, nor on the number of camels which would need veterinary supervision. He suspected that this was because the army staff believed that army vets might do well enough caring for horses, but would know little, if anything, of the diseases or management of camels – a belief which, in his submission of reports to the War Office, he labelled 'a fallacy'.

In late August on his own initiative he despatched a supply of medicines, and he followed that on 10th September by sending out three army veterinary surgeons, though he could give them no instructions other than to report to the military authorities in Suez. Suez passed them on to Cairo, with orders to report to the Chief of Staff of the British Army in Egypt. The senior officer of the three, Veterinary Surgeon 1st Class Burt, attempted to do so, but was told he should instead report to the Chief of Staff of the Nile Expeditionary Force itself. General Buller, however, was too busy organising supplies and stores to be sent up the Nile to give Burt a meeting, so Burt suffered what he called 'five days' unaccountable delay' before learning that he would be appointed Senior Veterinary Officer for the Expeditionary Force. Two days later he established that he could have six officers, including himself, though he would have to double as administrative officer and working vet.

Four army vets were already routinely serving in Egypt; two had accompanied him out. So he could provide for the Nile and still leave one vet at base in Cairo, but he would have no one left over for animal welfare in the ports of Alexandria or Suakin. He requested two more from England. Then as now economy being a watchword, he was told he could apply for only one. He decided to ignore the ports, and sent all his available vets to man the major camel depots being formed at Assouan (Aswan), Wadi Halfa and Korti. He stayed behind to make arrangements for the needed veterinary medicine supplies, and then finally reached Assouan himself on 12 October 1884. Assouan was to be the main distribution point of camels to the various transport corps units and camel regiments. There he found one comparatively inexperienced vet officer (the planned second one was delayed with other troops on the river journey) facing the impossibly arduous task of looking after large camel numbers on both banks of the Nile. Clearly more than the envisaged 3,500 camels were going to have to be cared for, and many of those already there were suffering from saddlery galls. Burt, this time successfully, applied for another two officers from England. George Fleming, in response to both applications from Burt, instantly chose and despatched the required vets. Veterinary Surgeon First Class Adrian Jones found himself, in late October 1884, for a third time, suddenly 'gone away' to war. This time, because of the huge total of camels and the huge mileage of military operations involved, it was to be what the Army Veterinary Department termed 'quite an exceptional campaign'.

Chapter Six: 'Across Unknown Country' 1884-1885: The Relief of Gordon Expedition

Summer 1884 had promised well for Adrian. From May to July the first evidence of 'my real destiny', his hunter statuette 'One of the Right Sort', had been on show alongside the works of famous artists in the Royal Academy Summer Exhibition, and had attracted favourable comment. He felt he had also done good work in 'Gone Away', on which he awaited the verdict of the Goldsmiths' judges. It must have been with mixed feelings that in the late autumn he received the belated order to join the Nile Expeditionary Force. The troopships had already steamed away, so, as at the outset of his army career, he was commanded to make his own way – this time to Cairo via Vienna and Trieste. He wrote in his *Memoirs*: 'The route consoled me.' He never paraded the emotions of family life, and for the unaware reader the sense of 'consoled' might just mean that Adrian had enjoyed the new sights, but knowing the circumstances, we can gather that in the journey he found consolation after the distress of Emma's illness and death. The route took him to a part of Europe he had always wished to see, 'a panorama never to be forgotten', the rivers and mountain gorges of the Steining Pass. Sadly, after Austria the journey continued on an ill-found boat down the Adriatic and across the Mediterranean to Alexandria, and ended with 'memories unpleasant and indelible'. He reported to Cairo. His previous call to war had taken him to Natal and the Transvaal, to be part of 16,000 reinforcements who had reached there too late to save Major General Colley's 2,000 men from losing every battle in the Transvaal War. Now he was joining a force that would be victorious in every battle. Yet he would discover that though Wolseley again had his 'Ashanti ring' of talented officers with him, the campaign would struggle to merit the phrase which was popular at the time, 'All Sir Garnet' (that is, well-ordered and working smoothly).

Whereas when Adrian had arrived in South Africa the fighting was over, now, as he reached Cairo in November 1884, Gordon was besieged in Khartoum, and the Nile Expeditionary Force's battles in the Sudan still lay in the future. First, Adrian had to go south to Assouan, five hundred and seventy miles by slow train and Nile steamer. There Inspecting Veterinary Surgeon Burt awaited him, and he learned that Wolseley's requisition for camels had been increased from 3,500 to 4,400. It had now been estimated that the Camel Corps staff and soldiers would need more than 2,000 camels, leaving the rest for transport companies and units such as the Field Hospital. With any fewer, it was feared that the campaign would be logistically doomed. Burt decided that for the present he would send the two other recently arrived vets up the Nile to seek to maintain the health of the camels already purchased, but keep the experienced Adrian with him to execute the task to which he himself had been ordered, the local purchase of more. Stories were circulating of combatant officers having previously been detailed for purchasing duties despite being unable to distinguish a camel's sex or age, or to judge its physical fitness for heavy work. Burt needed to utilise Adrian's good powers of judgement. During the campaign he came to use Adrian as virtually a chief of staff who would work alongside him to mitigate the consequences of unsatisfactory practices stemming from negligence or misguided orders.

Burt and Adrian spent November and the first part of December selecting and buying camels in the area between Assouan and Luxor. In his *Memoirs*, Adrian describes an expedition on which he had orders to contact a designated Arab chief. He travelled by the banks of the Nile, with some of his camel train loaded with packs of Spanish dollars for paying for purchases. One camel's pack struck an overhanging rock, tipping the camel into the river. Fortunately for Adrian, the water was not deep, so he was able to rescue both the animal and its load of dollars. He reached the chief, without further setbacks, by sunset. With veterinary judgement he chose his camels and paid for them. Leaving them with his native camel drivers for the return march, he caught a steamer back to Assouan for his next assignment. No sleeping berth was available, but a crew member made up a bed on a dining table and he was given blankets. These, though he did not realise it, were lice-infested.

The camels having been bought, some were distributed to units of the Expeditionary Force, and Burt set off for Wady Halfa by steamer, entrusting to Adrian the task of leading a large convoy of remount camels along the west side of the Nile to the same destination. The route was 'undulating, with large sandhills and valleys between them, all looking precisely alike, so that it was not easy to carry the country in one's eye, and while the sand was hard in some places, in others it was very soft, and our paces were necessarily slow'. To cover the 212 miles took eleven marches from sunrise to near sunset. Next came the task of watering and feeding the camels and settling them for the night, a process 'long and arduous'. But though it was arduous, Adrian insisted that it was done properly. He knew from what he had seen at Assouan that numbers of camels had been injured early in their march up the Nile (it was reported that in one journey of sixteen days their saddles had been taken off only once), and the veterinary surgeon at Wady Halfa had recorded in November that many more cases of pack-gall had occurred during camel marches starting from Assouan. In his subsequent comments on the campaign George Fleming complained about 'such preventable injuries' and lamented 'the horrible state of the poor animals – saddles buried in the flesh of their backs, or embedded in the granulations of the immense sloughing wounds; bones of the spine laid bare, fractured or carious; and festering sores, a moving mass of maggots, with a stench that was sickening'.

After seeing to the beasts, Adrian had to see to the men. The camel drivers regarded him as doctor as well as vet. They waited for him after his round of duties, and using medicines he had obtained from the Army Medical Department he treated them with pills and the pail of eyewash he had prepared, for the drifting sand and insects of the desert caused many eye inflammations. For himself he avoided bathing in the Nile – 'too many crocodiles about' – so customarily took one of the men down to the river with a bucket to fill and pour over him. He started suffering an unpleasant chest irritation, so he asked the day's water pourer if he knew what was the matter. The man grinned rudely and replied 'Kalmough'. Wondering if he was victim to an obscure Middle Eastern disease, Adrian turned up the unfamiliar word in his dictionary. The translation was 'louse'. He complained to his batman, who defended himself from blame: 'Didn't you know all about it, sir? I have been catching them for the last three days.' Their source must have been the steamer blankets. Adrian generously lathered on sulphur ointment, and as the sun warmed the ointment, went about smelling like a kennel after the hounds have been dressed. Happily the sulphur worked, leaving him to contend just with other insects and the day's physical demands of marching, dealing with the camels and finally hunting to augment his rations. Reminiscing half a century later, he applied to his march with the camel convoy such adjectives as 'busy', 'anxious', 'responsible' and 'fatiguing'. He arrived at Wady Halfa in late December, with no man and no camel lost to illness.

Burt had arrived by steamer a few days earlier, and busied himself inspecting the Sick Camel Depot which had been set up at Sarass, 35 miles farther on. On New Year's Eve he reported to General Buller that all camels were being moved out of Wady Halfa: these included 153 sick animals sent to Sarass. He considered that a quarter of them would not be fit for service again and should be sold forthwith. As 1885 dawned, Burt ordered Adrian to march on to Sarass with the convoy of 101 camels which he had brought from Luxor and Assouan and to bring with them a large supply of veterinary medicines for the Sick Depot. There on 5th January Burt attended a Board of Inspection. It examined 230 sick animals, victims of overwork and inexpert care. By contrast, the '101 remount riding camels from Luxor ... with one exception, a saddlery gall, were all in condition and fit for work'. Other circumstances, demanding heavy loading or greater speed or commitment to combat, could be more challenging than those Adrian had yet faced; but the ninety-nine percent of good camel health on Adrian's convoy was very seldom, if ever, matched elsewhere during the campaign.

The veterinary task at Sarass was unpleasant. Incurable camels had to be shot at once; the seventy cases so bad that they were unlikely to recover in time to serve the military thrust to Khartoum had to be sold off; and the remainder of the sick needed treatment for sore backs and general debilitation. But two days after the Inspection Board Burt was off again on his Inspecting Veterinary Surgeon duties, over the next fortnight establishing the numbers of sick and well camels, donkeys and mules at six depots, and heading always in the direction of Wolseley's headquarters at Korti, three hundred and forty miles from Sarass. He took Adrian with him. Their camels could average over twenty miles daily, and on the longest march had to cover forty. By 23rd January they had reached Dongola, which Adrian thought 'a jolly camp with pleasant surroundings, which I should have been pleased to visit had I not been so eager to reach the front'. Burt was equally eager. The tone of his post-war Veterinary Report to the Duke of Cambridge at the War Office shows that it rankled with him that because of the inadequate and incompetent buying of camels (many of them too young to work hard) by non-vet officers north of Assouan, he had been ordered to stay there to buy more instead of being able to press on to see how camels were faring in the front lines. He and Adrian set off, covered the remaining one hundred and thirty-six miles in six marches, and reached Korti on the last day of January. Their hurrying journey from Sarass had taken twenty-four days, which was eleven fewer than the quickest journey by troops by boat from Sarass, that of the Royal Irish Regiment, who had been rewarded with a £100 prize from Wolseley, and less than half the time taken by the slowest unit, the Duke of Cornwall's Light Infantry. Nevertheless, Burt and Adrian had arrived frustratingly late. The Desert Column of the Camel Corps had set off across the Bayuda Desert to rescue Gordon from Khartoum a month earlier. But still at Korti was Wolseley himself and a third of the 19th Hussars. These cavalry were waiting to be Wolseley's escort when he went forward to take glorious personal command of the Desert Column strike force. Sadly for him, however, Lord Hartington, the Secretary of State for War, had forbidden him to go with the advance. Frustration at delay was the lot of more than just the veterinary surgeons.

The idea of forming a Camel Corps of four composite regiments to relieve Khartoum had been Wolseley's. Nowadays they would be called 'special forces'. Naturally this innovative plan was opposed by the conservative Duke of Cambridge, who feared that a corps selected from forty different units would lack cohesion and regimental spirit. But Wolseley insisted on choosing the best men from a range of regiments. He had formed four regiments. The Heavy Camel Regiment was recruited from household cavalry, dragoon and lancer regiments; the Guards Camel Regiment took men from seven Guards battalions plus Royal Marines redeployed from Suakin on the Red Sea coast; the Mounted Infantry Camel Regiment was formed from thirteen regiments already stationed in Egypt; and a Light Camel Regiment was drawn from nine hussar regiments. The colonel commanding that regiment of hussars was not a Wolseley choice. Instead he owed his appointment to having been an equerry to the Prince of Wales. Wolseley considered him 'useless', and assigned his regiment to Line of Communication duties.

Despite the heterogeneous make-up of the force, esprit de corps did not suffer too much. What the Duke should have worried about was the dependence on camels even though, unlike the cavalry horses of the 19th

Hussars, they were not required for fighting. In his Instructions on the use of Camel Regiments, Wolseley wrote:

> The soldiers of the camel regiments will fight only on foot. They are mounted on camels only to enable them to make longer marches. The camel is a good traveller but he is a slow mover.

The main flaw in his bold campaign strategy was that in a situation which demanded speed of action he had opted for 'a slow mover'. Worse, as Wolseley also warned in his Instructions on camels, 'He cannot be managed as easily as a horse'. That was true of the riding of them, though the difficulty did not concern Lord Cochrane, with whom Adrian would serve in the 2nd Life Guards in the future and who for the present commanded that regiment's contingent in the Camel Corps. Within days of collecting the unit's camels at Assouan he had organised a camel race – indicative, perhaps, of the cavalier attitude of many in the Expeditionary Force towards their new chargers, with which they were still unfamiliar. For the care of the camels was even more difficult to manage than the riding of them. As Adrian put it firmly in the opening words of his *Short Report on the Camels of the Nile Expeditionary Force 1884-85*:

> There was a prevailing idea that the camel, or rather dromedary, was a very hardy animal, and could with impunity work hard on a small quantity of food and water, given at very long intervals. My opinion is, that of all the animals used on a campaign ... this is the most delicate, and therefore requires more care.

Adrian of course had the advantage of having seen the mishandling of camels in the transport trains in the Abyssinian War of 1867, where many of those bought had been young and weak, and then been underfed, so that they were unfit to carry the expected weight of load. That experience was a major reason for his selection for the Nile by George Fleming. The planning staff, however, did not inform themselves adequately about camel management, so the beasts were watered infrequently, some even deliberately kept without water for three day spells to 'train' them for the desert crossing, which meant they started out already debilitated. The camels were given ill-fitting saddles and too heavy loads for too long spells, leaving seventy percent of them with saddle galls; made to walk nose tied to the tail of the camel in front rather than freely; tied down in picket lines and fed with inadequate dry forage rather than allowed to graze. It was a lengthy catalogue of mistreatment, but at times the exigencies of war made a slower pace, freer grazing or better forage supplies impossible. Often at the end of a long hot march the soldiers themselves were too deadbeat to devote enough attention to the animals. The losses of camels were such that even the second estimate of numbers required had been far surpassed. Over 8,200 were bought. Yet still the Desert Column had perforce to set out across the difficult, unwelcoming Bayuda desert with too few in its baggage camels train.

Also too few were the veterinary officers. They were overworked, usually isolated from each other, sometimes without being allocated a batman from the unit they were servicing, except occasionally as a 'favour', and without trained dressers to assist them. None except Burt being in a higher rank than captain, their opinions were overruled by their seniors. It may well be that, even had the camels been properly cared for, the Force would still not have rescued Gordon. But after the expedition was over, George Fleming still held that poor administration could result in 'causing not only loss and delay, but even jeopardising the success of expeditions'.

None of that should detract from the remarkable fortitude, steadfastness and bravery of the troops in the battles that followed against an organised, formidable and fanatical foe. Adrian's autobiography recounts: 'As things happened, I was not among the troops that marched across the desert and so I missed the battle of Abu Klea.' The opening three words of that sentence could refer to almost anything, but the key happening was that the troops had left Korti before he arrived there. (The next sentence, as precise as the previous one was imprecise, states, 'At Korti on 18 December 1884, I received a letter that filled me with delight.' But as the official Veterinary Report on the Nile Expeditionary Force reveals, Adrian did not arrive in Korti until 31 January 1885. The dates he gives in *Memoirs* for major public events, such as the unveilings of his war memorials, are accurate, because he used Durrant's Press Cuttings agency and posted their dated cuttings into a very large album to which he could refer. For events in his private life he relied on his memory of what had happened. In this instance memory had to reach back across forty-nine years, and proved fallible. The letter which had so delighted him came from Goldsmiths' Company. It contained the excellent news that he had been awarded first prize in the Company's competition for a statuette. Amongst all the mail delivered to the troops, the announcement of a prize for sculpture must have been unique: it was a letter he would treasure. Probably 18th December was the date of writing rather than of arrival.)

Adrian was not among the thousand troops who set off in an impressive column forty camels wide, but they included several officers and men whom he knew from his past service, including the war artist Melton Prior, and others whom he would get to know later. Ahead of the troops lay the arid waste of the Bayuda Desert. It was not like the popular image of a desert, sandhills rolling away to the horizon: the surface was part rock, part gravel, part sand and part clay. In front Major John French led thirty-nine hussars on Syrian horses, of wonderful constitution and well suited to the climate, in efficient reconnoitring. Still further ahead scouted the Intelligence Officer, Major Herbert Kitchener, and his frontier force. Years later Adrian would paint a large portrait of him against a background of Sphinx and pyramids in tribute to all he achieved in Egypt and the Sudan. Amid the column, escorted by some of the Light Camel Regiment, came the insufficient thousand baggage camels of the Transport Companies. Because too few camel drivers had been recruited, the camels had been tied in short strings that occasionally broke apart or became tangled, causing stoppages which dismayed the Desert Column commander, Brigadier Herbert Stewart. When they reached water at Jakdul Wells, these camels had little chance to rest. Their supplies were unloaded, and as more were needed, at nightfall Stewart set off with the baggage train back to Korti. More delay. A couple of days later, now under the command of Lieutenant Colonel Stanley Clarke, they were off over the same ground again, heading back from Korti to Jakdul Wells. Accompanying them, driven to despair, went veterinary surgeon Bennett, who shot dead the camels that collapsed from incurable exhaustion, and abandoned others unfit to proceed, in the hope that they might be recovered by a future convoy. The demand for as much pace as possible forbade time for grazing; the demand for as many supplies as possible for the soldiers limited the forage for the camels to one third of normal rations; and at no pause anywhere on the journey were the camels relieved of the hurting saddles. By the end of the campaigning in March 1885 the Bayuda would consume 2,300 camels. Only the Naval Brigade detachment, which brought the Force's Gardner machine-gun, did not lose a camel. Whilst not matching Adrian's record for preventing saddle gall, they successfully caulked the sores with oakum, the tarred rope fibre material used for caulking ships' planking.

The return to Korti for more supplies had cost Stewart ten days' delay. He pressed on to the next source of adequate water in Abu Klea valley, towards an enemy who knew he was coming. Major French, patrolling ahead, warned him that the dervishes were blocking the pass to the Abu Klea Wells. Stewart camped for the night inside a stone and thorn zariba. Melton Prior sketched the men and officers toiling to build it. Then the next day the troops advanced in a traditional British square. Amongst those advancing to the battle of Abu Klea was the junior surgeon who had accompanied the second baggage train from Korti then continued on with the Desert Column as its only vet. Lieutenant Bennett survived the battle (unlike the seventy or so camels killed). He also survived the sniper fire of the next battle two days later at Abu Kru, but when they reached the Nile and entrenched, the strain told: he went down with a mix of sunstroke and typhus and had to be invalided home.

Captain Charles Pigott and his small terrier Smoke, both known to Adrian from Natal days, was in the left front of the square upon which the dervishes, emerging suddenly from a ravine, came sweeping down. Smoke met their advances with angry barking before retreating at the last moment into the comparative safety of the square. The British infantry, now dismounted to fight, their camels tethered behind them inside the square, met the dervish advance with a heavy volley of death-dealing fire from their Martini-Henry rifles. Except for Pigott. He, according to the story related in the Marquess of Anglesey's *History of British Cavalry*, was busy earning the nickname 'bloody-minded Pigott'. He had transferred out of the Rifles into the 21st Hussars, and as the only cavalry officer commanding a company of the Mounted Infantry Regiment he was living up to the cavalry tradition of idiosyncratic military spirit, and in particular to the example of Colonel Burnaby of the Blues (the Burnaby whom Tissot had famously and popularly painted in full dress uniform and languid pose in 1870). At the battle of El Teb, a year before Abu Klea, Burnaby had picked off tribesmen 'like driven hares' with a double-barrelled 12-bore loaded with pig shot. Some who saw his action thought that was not quite playing the game.

Burnaby had freelanced his way on to Wolseley's staff, and now, over the heads of the commanding officer and company commanders of the Heavy Camel Regiment, ordered two companies to open up to let the Naval Brigade's Gardner gun pass out of the square. This dangerous manoeuvre took place just as the dervishes, forced to swing right by the fire of the infantry, now swung left to launch themselves at the gun and the gap in the square. Lord Charles Beresford, in command of the Naval Brigade, sighted the Gardner and at first caused many casualties in the advancing charge. Then the gun jammed. In a moment Baggara warriors swarmed over the gun team, hacking or spearing to death all the sailors manning it except Beresford. Burnaby too, on a borrowed pony because his own had previously been wounded beneath him, had gone outside the square and rode around shouting orders to men to fall back to the square. At this battle he observed the conventions, and sought to defend himself, unavailingly, with his cavalry sword; but Captain Pigott, according to Anglesey's informant, did his utmost to save Burnaby. He used buckshot to riddle the Baggara, and made one tribesman's head look 'like the rose of a watering can'. However, beside the Gardner stood another Pigott, a naval lieutenant, and in his memoirs published thirty years later Lord Charles Beresford tells very much the same story, but therein the wielder of the peppering fowling piece is the navy's Pigott. Pigott RN, like the other sailors around the gun, did not survive to confirm or disown this story. Pigott of the 21st Hussars did survive. Afterwards, in 1888, he earned the DSO for services in Burma operations, and there is no record that he rejected the sobriquet 'bloody-minded Pigott', even though it was a rather back-handed compliment. Whoever was the hero, he failed in his object. Pigott RN lay already dead as three spear thrusts toppled Burnaby from his horse, and he collapsed to the ground, whilst army Captain Pigott and others were swept back deeper into the partly opened square. Ironically, it was the long-suffering camels which saved the men who had misused them. They and their baggage proved an impassable obstacle which prevented the enemy advancing upon the backs of the far side of the square. The Guards Camel Regiment rear ranks about turned, aimed and shot all the invader dervishes (and, unavoidably, a few of their own, including Brigadier Stewart's bugler, despite good marksmanship). In less than fifteen minutes of immensely entangled close combat, the most savage battle of Victoria's wars in Egypt was over. It passed into military legend alongside Rorke's Drift (albeit less filmed) as a supreme example of British soldiers' grit under threat of annihilation.

Henry Newbolt had the battle of Abu Klea in mind when he composed the middle verse of his poem 'Vitai Lampada':

The sand of the desert is sodden red –
Red with the wreck of a square that broke;
The Gatling's jammed and the Colonel dead,
And the regiment blind with dust and smoke.
The river of death has brimmed his banks,
And England's far, and Honour a name,
But the voice of a schoolboy rallies the ranks:
'Play up! Play up! and play the game!'

It was of course not the Gatling but the Gardner (which would have scanned equally well) that jammed. The Colonel died. Burnaby was still alive, just, when after the battle a private of the Queen's Bays found him, cradled him, and offered water. Burnaby uttered his last words, 'Look after yourself', and soon afterwards died. Not surprisingly, the poem makes no reference to the actions of Pigott. The rallying call of the public schoolboy is a fantasy. It was Burnaby who had 'played the game', dangerously so. The square had not really been 'broken'; it had been opened up, probably because of Burnaby's maverick manoeuvre to support Beresford's desire to get his Gardner gun out into action. The river of dead had brimmed: eight officers and seventy-nine men. Adrian's future brother officer Lord Cochrane of the Life Guards, as he wandered around looking at the dead, did not feel that the battle had been a triumph for the public school spirit, even though he had been educated at Eton. Instead, as he wrote in his autobiography *My Army Life*, the dead men left him with the sad and bitter reflection that Britain had built her Empire on low pay.

Two days later the Desert Column was again victorious but bloodied at Abu Kru as it fought its way to the Nile. Brigadier Stewart fell mortally wounded. His successor, Colonel Wilson, proceeded cautiously yet capably, though he received criticism for delaying once he had reached the river. The Mahdi, learning of the pause, decided to storm Khartoum with his 50,000 dervishes. When Wilson's gunboats finally reached there two days later, on 28 January 1885, it was clear to everyone on board that Khartoum had certainly fallen and therefore Gordon was probably dead. As indeed he was. He had dressed in his white tropical uniform to die with heroic dignity. The aftermath was less dignified. His killers cut off his head and carried it impaled on a spear to their camp. Next day it was fixed in the fork of a tree and became a target for stone-throwing.

As Wilson's gunboats ran the gauntlet of retreat from Khartoum downriver, Major Burt and Adrian were urgently active in and around Korti, seeking to improve camel health. On February 1st, his first day at Korti, Burt inspected the camels of the Depot and Transport Companies and found over a hundred 'in very low condition and with severe saddlery galls'. He instantly made it clear to the General Officer Commanding Lines of Communication that he disagreed with that officer's policy of sending out sick animals, under contract for two months, with natives. He considered that grain feeding, browsing and grazing, with rest under veterinary officers' supervision, would be better. 'Nevertheless', as he complained in his Report, three days later, the General sent the camels out, to add to the two hundred and twelve he had despatched in mid-January, under contract, up to twenty miles distant. The only impact Burt's protest had was to authorise him to send a vet to encamp in the vicinity of these animals to see that the terms of the contract were carried out. Burt detailed Adrian.

The General must have felt he could do without this gadfly of a Principal Veterinary Surgeon at Korti. When on 9th February Burt reported that he had inspected another five hundred and thirty-two transport camels, found 'a large proportion ... suffering from saddlery galls of the worst description ... large and deep ... in many instances exposing the bone beneath', and again recommended his means of treatment, the

General acted. Through his Director of Transport he ordered Burt to move to Dal and make that outstation his headquarters until further notice. Enraged, the next day Burt wrote to Buller, told him of the order, and continued:

> I desire to refer the question for your consideration. As Head of the Veterinary Service, Nile Expeditionary Force, should I not receive instructions from your office as to my movements? ... I have been put to great inconvenience in the performance of my duties at this station. I am of opinion that I should be allowed to remain here, considering the enormous proportion of camels ... requiring the constant supervision of myself and Officers of the department under me. By returning to Dal I am ... unable to see how I can carry out my duties.

The letter availed nothing. General Buller, ineffective as Chief of Staff, was now away at Abu Klea in a field command role, decisively and unilaterally deciding to evacuate the Desert Column to its Korti base. So Burt went into exile at distant Dal and Adrian set off to inspect the suitability of the tract of country around Korti for resting and grazing the contracted out camels.

For anyone who knows Adrian's writing only through his *Memoirs*, in which he hardly ever comments adversely on anyone or anything, however controversial the person or incident, it is startling to read his summary report for the War Office: *On the Camels of the Nile Expeditionary Force, 1884-1885*. He writes tersely and bluntly for a private readership in the War Office. Thus in the paragraph titled 'Grazing Sick Animals' he begins:

> In opposition to the opinion of Inspecting Veterinary Surgeon Burt, Veterinary Surgeon Phillips and myself, a large number of sick camels were handed over to natives to feed and be attended to ... I found many tied down, with no sign of food near them, and others turned into the desert to browse upon the scrub, but with no additional food or care.

Not content with such comment on the policy of a General, he adds a damning statistic. 'The result was, I believe, that out of about 300, some three or four were fit for work after two months.' None of this appears in the *Memoirs* account of his inspection, and nowhere in the book does he even hint at criticism of any senior officers in any war, though by then he was long retired from the army and their actions were hardening into history. Contrastingly, the Report is unsparing. On 'Watering': 'Under the impression ... that the camel was such a hardy animal ... and also 'to prepare him for future droughts', an Order was issued to water it only every third day ... I was quite at a loss to understand this order ... especially as the camels were fed almost entirely on dry food, which, on scientific grounds, necessitated ... more water.' On Feeding: 'Dry grain was almost invariably the staple food ... The most noticeable effect was ... impactment and inflammation of the stomach and sudden death.' And so on, home truths spelt out on Working (poor animals loaded up for hours before starting on the march), Diseases (debility caused by starvation and overwork) and Purchasing (camels far too young – many had not even a full set of temporary teeth). All this, written in 1885, was not just benefit of hindsight. During the campaign itself the Veterinary Department had not been used in sufficient numbers, and those vets who had been with the Force had felt that their professional opinions had been too often ignored or overruled. 'The common sense view', Adrian reported, 'would have been to feed, water and otherwise treat the camels so that they should be as healthy and strong as possible to undergo any privation that the exigencies of war required of them, and not have to start on a desert march in a debilitated condition.'

As Burt was in Dal, when Adrian returned to Korti from his daily marches and nightly bivouacs, he reported directly to Wolseley. Perhaps he tempered his criticism, but certainly enough was said to get a change in policy. The next batch of camels sent out was given three times the length of rest and recuperation given to the early batches. All he relates in *Memoirs* is that Wolseley 'complimented me on my work and remarked that I seemed to be able to find my way quite well across unknown country'. He could have informed Wolseley that he had been accompanied by a guide, an interpreter, native camel drivers and three soldiers of the Berkshire Regiment (whom he sent on a long camel ride the day after they said they had 'accidentally' broken his gin flask and the contents had been 'lost'). But as someone who liked quiet jokes in his art and his life, he gave as his explanation: 'I had learned to take my bearings when I was a boy hunting with the Ludlow Foxhounds.'

Meanwhile Wolseley's River Column, led by General Earle, had been making slow progress along the Nile. On February 10th their disciplined firepower overcame Dervish bravery in a battle at the village of Kirkeban. The Dervishes killed only thirteen men of the Column, but one was General Earle, to add to the toll of Generals Stewart and Gordon. Colonel Henry Brackenbury succeeded him and was keen to press on, but despite calls from Queen and Country to avenge Gordon, Gladstone had no stomach for further perilous adventure. Buller marched the Desert Column back, en route destroying or abandoning the veterinary stores at Jakdul Wells; and Brackenbury renegotiated a hundred miles of Nile cataracts and rapids to return the River Column. With the two strike forces wholly back at base by mid-March, Adrian and his fellow vet officer Phillips, having managed to limit the disastrous policy of sending out camels on contract to a fifth of the herd, found themselves supervising the welfare of 2,077 camels. Burt, still sidelined to Dal, in his Report of 23rd March recorded that at Dal he was supervising twenty-six camels, two horses and twelve mules. To imply that this was hardly an adequate role for the Inspecting Veterinary Surgeon, he pointed out in the 'Remarks' column that the Expeditionary Force still had over 3,000 camels on its strength, despite over 4,000 having died or been sold, lost or destroyed.

A fortnight later, in preparation for the Force's withdrawal from Korti, he reorganised the stationing of his officers. The officer who had been with the River Column was sent north to Luxor to purchase yet more camels, and Adrian replaced him on what was now termed General Brackenbury's Column. The last month of his stay at Korti enabled him, as the units of the Columns returned and had their camels inspected, to renew old acquaintances – Buller, McCalmont, French, Pigott, Melton Prior and others – and make new ones. Though he was not yet somebody who might today be called a celebrity, he was at least distinctive: not just a soldier-painter, but a soldier-sculptor who had exhibited at the Royal Academy and won a Goldsmiths' Prize for a tableau on a subject dear to the interests of many a cavalry officer, a hunting scene. He had made a drawing of a Camel Corps Scout, and intended to translate that into a statuette when posted back to Britain. With Brackenbury's Column he marched north 'across the sand under the blazing sun but with the dry heat which is not so trying'. Brackenbury 'chose desert sun', avoiding shade and palm groves as he thought those fostered sickness, 'and although the temperature was 130 degrees in the sun, the men remained healthy'. Finally they took transport, to Cairo, Alexandria and home, Adrian reaching England in July 1885. Buller, not an admirer of Gordon's delaying in Khartoum, said, 'The man was not worth the camels.'

In mid-August 1885 Inspecting Veterinary Surgeon Burt despatched from Army Headquarters, Cairo, his Departmental Report on the part played by his officers in connection with the military operations of the Nile Expeditionary Force, 1884-5. It included Burt's own experience, statistical returns and the reports he had commissioned back in April 1885, on the orders of George Fleming (Principal Veterinary Surgeon to the Forces), from four of his officers. Three had written on their respective experiences with the Desert Column, the River Column and the 19th Hussars, and Adrian had written his summarising indictment of camel maltreatment. When Burt's despatch from Cairo HQ had been read by George Fleming in the War Office in Pall Mall, he submitted it to HRH the Duke of Cambridge in the same building, but not before he had taken time to write a three-page introduction of forceful complaint, verging on recrimination, and of calls for reform. Pertinently Fleming pointed out that the returns 'cannot be regarded as accurate or at all satisfactory' because of the way Burt had been sidelined in Dal and was therefore unable to superintend his officers or obtain requisite information. While recognising that the extremely heavy inefficiency and mortality among the camels were 'mainly due to the nature and urgency of the duty on which these animals were employed', his litany of criticisms was comprehensive. Most particularly he directed the attention of the Duke as Commander-in-Chief to Burt's observations on the position and functions of veterinary surgeons in the field in wartime. The frustrations and indignities which had enraged Burt lie everywhere just underneath the temperate prose in which he catalogues the general staff's failure to plan adequate veterinary services. There had been 'paucity of officers', often in 'isolated position', with 'not a farrier or shoeing smith available for duty', no trained dressers for Sick Line duties, and batmen granted only belatedly 'and this very much in the manner of a favour'. As for the senior Administrative Veterinary Officer, which had been Burt's own role in Sudan, that officer should in future be stationed at front line headquarters rather than as in his own case being deputed as an assistant camel purchaser in the rear area and then exiled to 'a remote station or the Lines of Communication'.

The Veterinary Report amounted to an appeal for new ways. Its criticisms were so comprehensive that four months later Colonel George Furse, who had been the Director of Transport for the Expeditionary Force, was asked to give his side of the story. In his good-tempered 'Observations' he wrote, 'All they (i.e. the vets) say in a veterinary point of view is unquestionable; but they must admit ... many of the faults they bring to notice had their origin in the very unusual peculiarities of the undertaking.' Furse too had had his frustrations. With insufficient camels, 'the food for the troops being the principal requirement, we had to forego carrying the forage for the animals, and though the troops were well fed throughout the animals were nearly starved'. When on Burt's recommendation he had twice telegraphed Buller asking for camel blankets, Buller had written back: 'It is impossible to blanket them; we have no blankets for our men.' Furse's concluding remarks were as damning as the vets' opinions: 'We never have a pack transport ready to take the field and have to create one the best way we can at the very last moment... it becomes impossible to do justice to our transport animals ... and under similar circumstances I have no hesitation whatever in saying that we could never work a transport satisfactorily.'

In his Report Burt had written he was convinced that what he euphemistically termed 'the inconveniences' of the campaign 'must prove very disheartening to young and inexperienced Officers of the Department'. In actuality, he, an experienced senior officer, complained more than his juniors. Adrian, another experienced officer, as ever in his public *Memoirs*, is uncomplaining. He mentions personal misfortunes such as the lice-infested bed made up for him, but nowhere does he hint that the army system was ever at fault. Nor does he claim any credit, however small, for future improvements in army performance that stemmed from lessons learned in 1884-5. But things did improve. For one thing, the Veterinary Department became more valued. Within five years a new statute declared its officers now eligible for awards in the Military Division of the Order of the Bath; later, vets changed from being a Department to members of a Corps, like the medical officers, with other ranks to provide the trained hands whose absence in Wolseley's force had been so lamented. Colonel Furse afterwards wrote an excellent manual on 'Provisioning Armies in the Field'. Most importantly of all, General Kitchener, on the basis of the Report as well as his personal experience, resolved that when he set out to reconquer the Sudan his strategy would be based on transport by rail, not camel. But for Adrian – as for Wolseley – there would be no more active campaigning in the field.

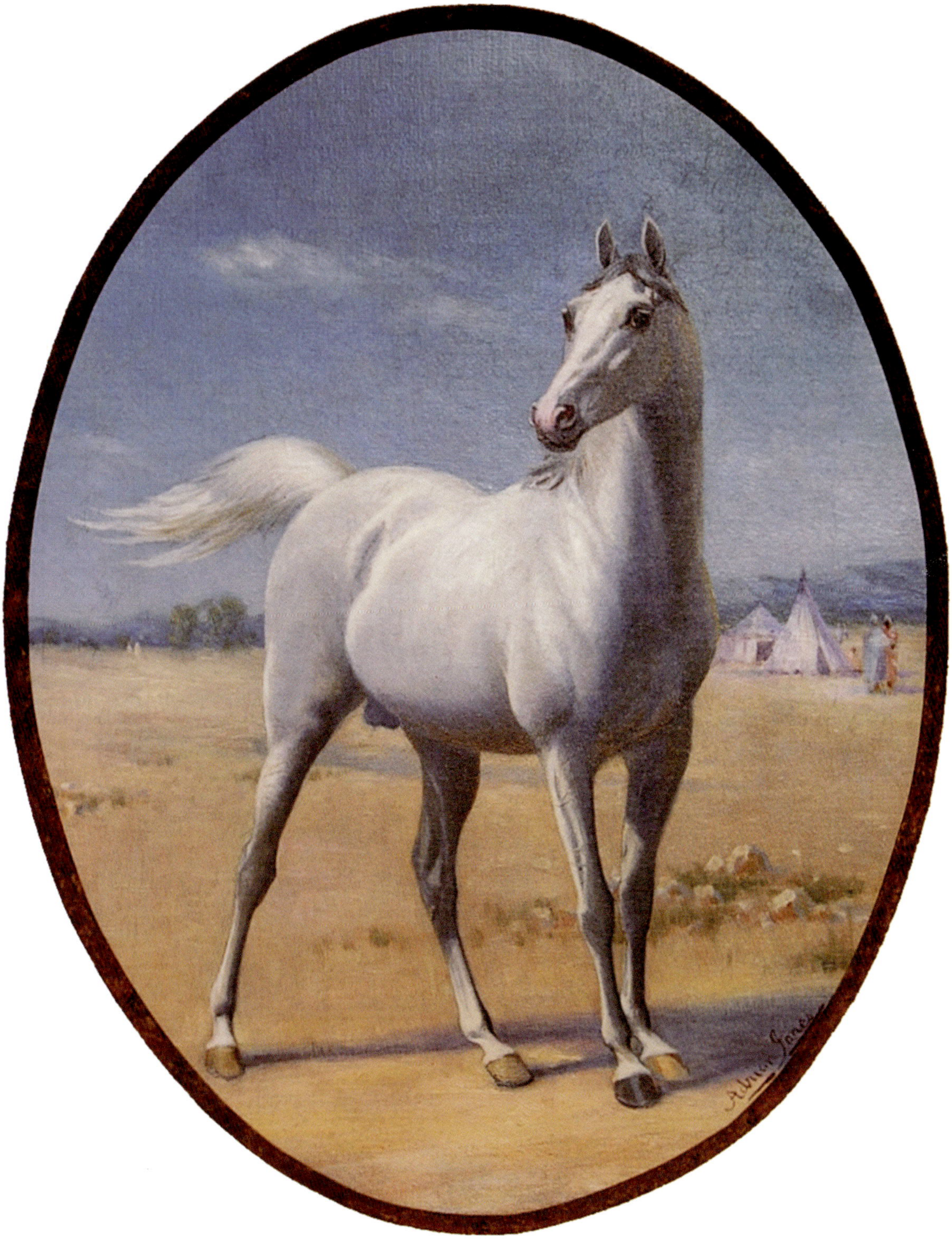

Arab Stallion. Adrian's signature, lower right, must have been placed there when it was decided to frame the painting as an oval. The background desert scene actually fills the whole of its rectangular canvas.

Camel Corps Scout (1885-86)

With confidence in his developing sculpting skill and in the marketing potential, Adrian made a drawing of a Camel Corps trooper while in Sudan and modelled it after his return to England. Towards the end of his Korti posting, when the Desert Column had returned there, he had opportunities to meet officers from seven Guards battalions, ten senior cavalry regiments, ten hussar regiments and fourteen infantry regiments, plus a sprinkling of officers from the artillery and the support services. Many of these were wealthy. A number, including six hereditary members of the House of Lords, were titled. They saw themselves as a selected elite force, and knew that their experience of going to war on camels in an exotic foreign service location was likely to be unique in their military careers. The campaign medal they were to receive disappointed them: it was an undated Egypt medal, originally awarded in 1882 for the British suppression of a revolt against the Khedive of Egypt, which depicted the Egyptian Sphinx beneath the single word 'Egypt'. It seemed inappropriate for a war fought wholly in Sudan, and the clasps on the medal ribbon bearing the words 'The Nile 1884-85' and, for those involved in the battle, 'Abu Klea', offered only slight enhancement. The accompanying Khedive's Star medal similarly made no mention of Sudan and carried an irrelevant Egyptian scene of the Sphinx before a background of pyramids. What was lacking was an accurate memento, representational of the daily life of soldiers with camels in the Sudan, telling not of parade ground ceremonial but of active campaigning in the field, yet free from any immediate reference to war's horrors. So Adrian set about giving sculptural expression to a central experience of Camel Corps service – being up in the saddle. Remembering the example of his acquaintance G.A. Henty rushing his book *The March to Magdala* into print so promptly after the 1868 Abyssinia campaign, he made this his leisure time priority.

The statuette camel is pacing over stony ground. Any officer patron could explain to that great majority of his brother officers who had not been chosen for the regiment's Camel Corps contingent that this was the Bayuda of the Sudan, not the desert sands of Egypt. The 'scout' scans the field of view from beneath the high-crowned, broad-brimmed Wolseley helmet, which has wrapped round it a cloth puggaree that could be used for shading from the burning sun. (Adrian must have considered 'scout', suggesting military activity and potential for bravery, to be a more appealing title than plain 'trooper', and of course much of his time at Korti had been spent scouting the unmapped land around, but he knew that scouting for the enemy – outpost and patrol duties, and forming an advanced cavalry screen – had been very largely the work of the 150 Syrian horses of the 19th Hussars). A heavy bandolier of bullets clings over the scout's left shoulder, and his sword bayonet, long to compensate for the shortness of his carbine, hangs at his left hip. His right hand carries the Martini-Henry carbine, a single shot breech loader which demanded from the sculptor the moulding of not just the usual trigger and trigger guard but in addition under the butt a curved lever which ejected the spent round and opened the breech chamber to receive the next single round. Adrian could have shown the carbine stowed away in its rifle bucket on the camel's right flank, for in reality the Camel Corps had orders to fire dismounted wherever possible, but he wanted the ensemble to suggest a whiff of danger and a scout on the 'qui vive'. (The closed left hand probably held the camel's head rope, but if so that vulnerable detail is not to be seen on the example photographed for *Memoirs.*) The scout's legs are in the Camel Corps uniform of corduroy breeches and cloth puttees, and his ankle boots are in stirrups, used by the British, who liked to treat the camel like a horse if possible, but scorned by the native camel men. To emphasise motion, a haversack swings to the sway of the camel's inimitable walk.

The detailing is meticulous, and the different textures of the scout's jumper, his corduroy breeches and the camel's wrinkly skin are further evidence of Adrian's skilled craftsmanship. When later, after the Great War of 1914-18, Adrian was sending in work to the War Memorial Exhibition, a *Daily Sketch* correspondent, under the heading 'A Great Craftsman', wrote 'he is like Benvenuto Cellini'. Such praise was not wholly welcome,

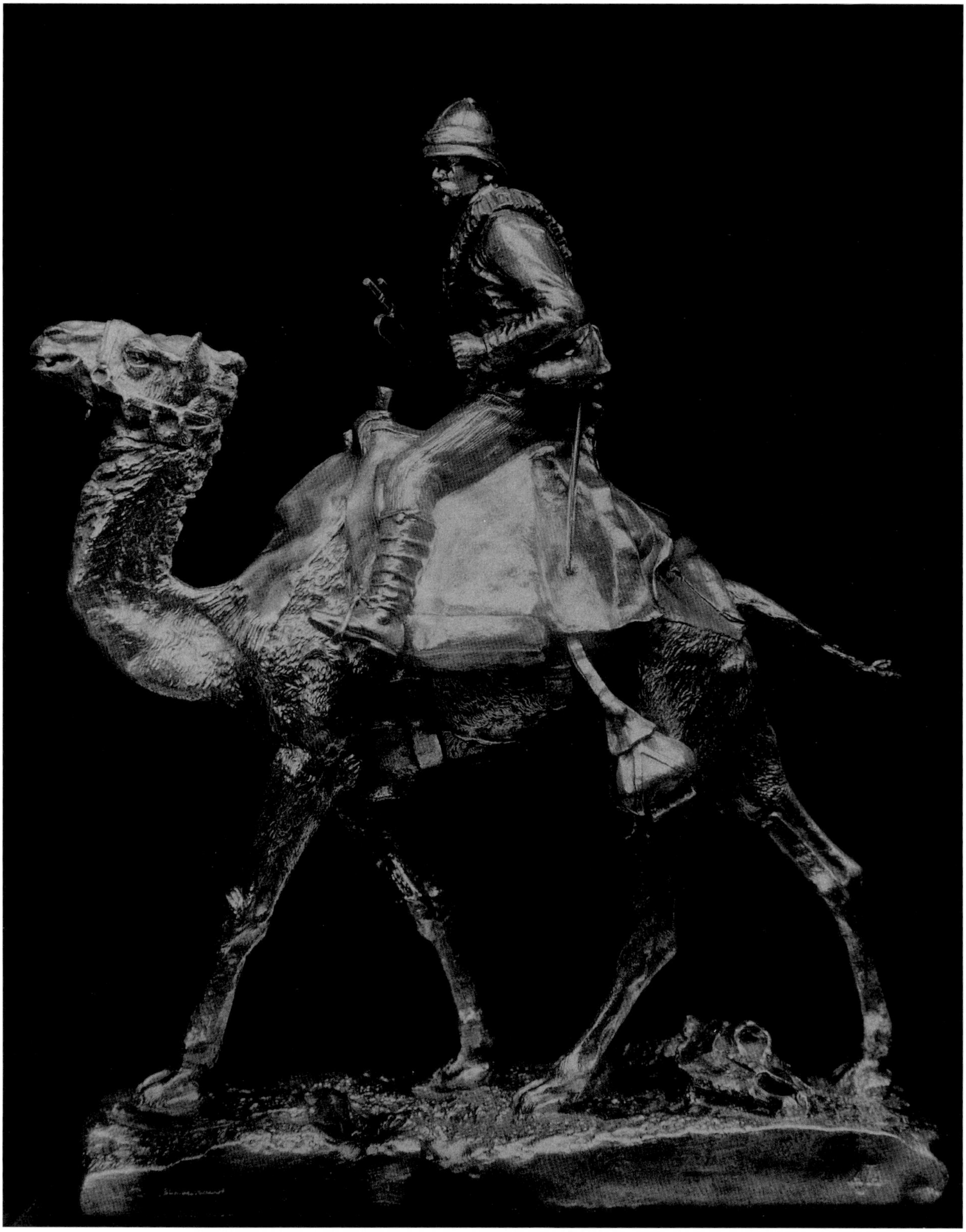

Camel Scout, bronze or silver statuette, 1885/86; RA exhibit, 1886

in that it suggested he was a craftsman rather than an artist. As a stand-up comic would point out, it is nice to be referred to as a good painter, but the effect alters when 'and decorator' is added. 'Artist and craftsman' is not exactly parallel, but in his own writing on his art Adrian liked to argue that he was more than a copier of nature because in his statues he subtly altered planes and masses, modifying proportions for artistic effect. But the Camel Corps statuette is simply a marvellous example of conventional representational modelling. It might be termed 'souvenir art'. Such labelling is potentially derogatory. Indeed, many art critics, conditioned by reading the famous poets and observing the graphic artists of later wars, might be better pleased if the statuette 'spoke' of the brutality or suffering of war. In his capacity as a professional veterinary surgeon Adrian firmly criticised the avoidable sufferings caused to the Nile expedition's camels, but the place for that was the official report for the War Office. In the statuette there is no hint of his concerns. His subject matter is not camel saddlery galls, nor camel emaciation, nor even, for humorous effect, obstreperous camel behaviour. The statuette camel is a companion in arms with a dignified bearing, performing its army role as Wolseley and the British public would wish.

From the decision to pay heed to the demand for a valued campaign souvenir flowed further decisions suited to his personal inclinations as well as his market. In his later civic and regimental war memorials he almost invariably placed the emphasis on other ranks, often to the exclusion of officers. So too in the Camel Corps statuette. A further reason here was that as the purchasers would be officers, an officer rider would inevitably lead to speculation and possible jealousy over whom Adrian had in mind when modelling. Better an anonymous trooper, portrayed without any attempt at individual characterisation. Second, the necessity of providing an accurate memento excused him from an experimental approach and enabled him to stay true to his lifelong attitude towards God's animal kingdom: model nothing in any way grotesque.

The final result is a happy combination of observant recognition and skill by a confident, self-directed artist. The *Memoirs* record that 'the statuette was reproduced in both silver and bronze and copies were purchased by many officers'. Camel scouts may still be seen riding timelessly across the mantelpiece in those homes whose families have traditions of army service. Just a year after Adrian's return from the Sudan it appeared in the 1886 RA Summer Exhibition (exhibit 1850).

Chapter Seven: 'Full of Kindness and Camaraderie' 1885-1891: Club and Army Life in London

Stationed once again at St John's Wood, Adrian now spent nearly three years engaged in routine army life over which his autobiography passes in silence. His main interests were the studio he took in Kensington, the life of art and the life of clubland. Now more than ever, 'I gave every free afternoon and evening and part of my leave' to painting and sculpting. He was determined to master the depiction of animal action completely. Often, but not exclusively, his subjects were horses, singly or in groups. Initially his works were small-scale. But his happiness was already large-scale. On 10 April 1886, with his sculptor friend Charles Birch as one of his sponsors, he was elected a member of the Savage Club. Another member was G.A. Henty; so now, if he wished, he could tease Henty with having slowed down since his time in Abyssinia, for his book *The Dash for Khartoum: A Tale of the Nile Expedition* did not appear until well after Adrian had made his sales of 'Camel Scout'.

Adrian said of the Savage Club:

> It was housed in the Savoy, and I do not think any of its happy members could boast happier hours than I have enjoyed there ... All through the years that I was making my successful debut as an artist ... the Savage was a second home. I was constantly meeting men who had achieved success in art or letters and ... there is freedom of intercourse and a genuine friendliness ... I met some of the most interesting men in London at the Savage; the one who made the most distinct impression upon me at first was James McNeil Whistler.

Whistler had been elected to membership two months earlier. He had been born eleven years before Adrian, and had achieved fame and embraced controversy as a painter whilst Adrian was still training as a veterinary surgeon. In 1877 his legal action against Ruskin, after the latter had accused him of 'Cockney impudence ... two hundred guineas for flinging a pot of paint in the public's face', had bankrupted him, but now his fortunes were partly restored and he had just been elected President of the Society of British Artists. The picture which had so roused Ruskin's disdain when shown in the Grosvenor Gallery's opening exhibition, 'Nocturne in Black and Gold: The Falling Rocket', was different from anything Adrian had painted or would paint in the future, and the two men differed also in personality, but soon Whistler was 'Jimmy' to Adrian, and Adrian's great nephew records that he became 'a great friend'. Both of Whistler's grandfathers had served in the British army, his father and brother had served in the American army, and Jimmy himself had spent three years at West Point military academy. He had also seen war, having gone to Chile with a military equipment sales group and thus been at Valparaiso in 1866 when the enemy Spanish fleet had largely destroyed that town with a naval bombardment. He valued his military background, which had trained his powers of observation (he had come top in drawing at West Point) and his systematic recall of what he had observed. It had also developed a combative edge which made him always fight his corner.

In Adrian he met, possibly uniquely, both now and later in the Chelsea Arts Club, an artist who shared a military background, emphasised in Adrian's case by his habit of wearing a military cape in the club. (On the day Adrian died, a newspaper columnist reminisced about talking to the 90-year-old artist in the Savage Club: 'He was wrapped in an ancient cloak which was said to be seventy years old'.)

Adrian wrote *Memoirs* in 1933, a time when 'Whistler's pictures can hardly be said to command a big market', though he did not rule out 'another lease of life before them when another generation comes along'. Yet although Whistler was then unfashionable, Adrian refers to him in the book (excluding the Appendices) as often as he refers to his mentor Charles Birch, and more often than anyone else except his patron the Prince of Wales, later Edward VII. Nevertheless his friendship with 'Jimmy', unlike that with Charles Birch, is of little significance in the history of art. Lord Baden Powell's Foreword to the autobiography commends 'many-sided' Adrian to the reader 'as a horseman, a horse surgeon, a soldier, an artist, and ... as a humorist'. It was mainly in that last role that he often enjoyed the company of Whistler. 'He was a pretty wit but, unfortunately, when it took him in charge he did not mind whom he stung ... when he was friendly there was no more delightful companion but ... he would sacrifice a friend for a bon mot.' If the victim was a member of the Royal Academy, Adrian would have been less than human if he did not enjoy the joke against that establishment which was never to elect him to membership. (Leighton, President of the RA, to Whistler: 'Tell me, why do you never finish any of your paintings?' Whistler to Leighton: 'Why do you ever start any of yours?')

Adrian relished anecdotes. Amongst the highest praises he could pay to another was that he was a 'witty raconteur' or that he 'always appeared to have a fresh funny story to beguile the moments of leisure'. Those tributes were to friends with whom he went riding in Hyde Park's Rotten Row. Even more he enjoyed yarning in clubland, where he and Whistler were distinctive figures – tall Adrian striking in his military cloak, small Jimmy immaculate in full length frock coat with supporting props of tall silk hat, cane and monocle. Adrian could have sought election to clubs catering chiefly for armed forces officers, but he had that company already in the Mess. He favoured instead clubs with a bias to artists, the Savage, the Chelsea Arts, and the Arts Club, in all of which Whistler too had membership. Jimmy of course was a celebrated and self-celebrated wit, one who talked brilliantly himself and was a celebrity subject for stories told by others.

There is no record of Whistler's seeking to influence Adrian's art. Often in the Victorian art world artists formed groups of those who shared a similar outlook or technique and sought to establish a relationship with a gallery favourable to the group's distinctive creed. But it was the older man's vivid personality to which Adrian responded, not his artistic manifesto as preached in his 'Ten O' Clock Lecture' in 1885, the year before Adrian came to know him well. In the lecture he developed his idea that art is an 'arrangement', to quote the first word of some of his titles, of colour and artistic vision which seeks neither to tell a story nor paint a moral. Art, as the over-simplified expression puts it, is for art's sake. The artist is a 'a monument of isolation', divorced from the world around him and not sending it any messages. In his essay on 'Mr Whistler's Ten O' Clock' Oscar Wilde argued that Whistler's assertion was unachievable in reality because any artist is 'the resultant of a certain milieu and a certain entourage'. He went on to say that Whistler 'is indeed one of the very greatest masters of painting in my opinion'. (Being Wilde, he could not refrain from closing the essay with one more sentence: 'And I may add that in this opinion Mr Whistler himself entirely concurs.') Adrian shared Wilde's high opinion of Whistler's painting, as part of a broad artistic appreciation which embraced most painters. He placed Whistler sincerely amongst the 'big men' of his age and admired his draughtsmanship just as much as he admired the 'extraordinarily good' but different draughtsmanship of Millais and Leighton. He appreciated Leighton's painting despite Leighton's treatment of him as a sculptor; he appreciated Whistler's despite the eccentric waspishness which made some others enemies of Whistler and derogatory about his work. However, in his own approach to art Adrian remained a polar opposite to 'a monument of isolation'.

Half a century later, when he received the gold medal of the Royal Society of British Sculptors, Adrian took the opportunity to look back to the 1880s, 'when I first joined the sculptors' brigade'. His thoughts appeared in the *Times* (10 April 1935) under the heading 'A Testament of Beauty'. He narrates that he 'took a good look round the different memorials in London. Some were good, some were bad ... very saddening to look at. I therefore determined that if I got any to do I would make them more pleasant to look at ... doing their bit as an ornament'. It sounds as if part of him dwelt in Whistler's camp. The 'art' or 'arrangement' was the key: aesthetic appeal was important. In his advice to the 'young men' of 1935 his views still may owe something to Whistler's call for 'perfection of harmony': 'I cannot bring myself to believe that ugliness and incongruity without any beauty can ever be called art.' By 1935 he had had his opportunities to 'ornament' the streets and parks of London and other cities. In 1885-86 they still lay years ahead, but already it was in sculpture, not painting, that he envisaged his future. Influenced by Birch rather than Whistler, his major works would often depend in part on historic narrative or sporting interest, and call forth emotions other than aesthetic appreciation – admiration for courage, pity for suffering in war, desire for lasting peace, patriotic pride in Britain and her Empire.

During the later 1880s, however, the public's attention was on Whistler, and what he said and wrote doubled the influence of his painting on British art. After only two years' membership, in 1886 he was elected President of the Society of British Artists and a year later he gained a Royal Charter for it, so that it became the RSBA. Largely in response to Whistler's impact and that of the French Impressionists on English artists, 1886 also saw the founding of the New English Art Club. Fifty artists who did not wish to practise the academic style of painting favoured by the RA exhibited with the new group. The leading lights were John Singer Sargent, another American, this time with a military surname rather than background, and Wilson Steer, from Ross-on-Wye, where Adrian had once been landlord of the Swan Hotel. Adrian would get to know both men well in art circles and in the as yet unfounded Chelsea Arts Club.

Perhaps initially because of the Ross-on-Wye link, Steer became a friend for life. Like Adrian, he had not been through the Royal Academy Schools. In 1882 he had sought entry and been rejected. He had, however, received training in art. After leaving Hereford Cathedral School he had spent two years at Gloucester School of Art, then a year studying in South Kensington and finally, after his RA rejection, he went to France for two years' further tuition. When he returned to England and took a studio in Chelsea, Adrian was in Sudan, and even when Adrian was back in home service their acquaintance was at first intermittent. Adrian's military duties kept him mainly in London; Steer spent long summers away, usually painting at the seaside in Suffolk or northern France. Greater opportunities for contact rose when Steer became a founder member of the New English Art Club and regularly showed his pictures in its twice yearly exhibitions, and then also at RSBA exhibitions. Nevertheless, it was not until the 1890s, when Adrian had retired from the army and he and Steer became members of Chelsea Arts Club, that the friendship became close. Influenced by Monet as well as by Whistler, Steer experimented with modern styles. Unlike Adrian, he often received harsh criticism, his bright palette colours labelled jarring and the final result even termed ugly. The unconventional pictures did not appeal to conventional tastes: in his studio unsold seaside pictures piled up. He claimed defensively that as an Impressionist painter his vocation was not to be a journalist who sought to record facts; it was to be a poet with selective poetic vision. Adrian, by contrast, at this time was usually a 'journalist' artist. Working often on commission, his brief was to record, for the owner or the illustrated press, fast racehorses and hunters, sometimes the horse alone, sometimes with rider up. The pictures had a sure sale. It went without saying that the subject matter of a commissioned work must be recognisable. Adrian's consequent attention to accurate detailing within his compositions, so different from Steer's atmospheric impressions of young women at the seaside, more often than not with their anonymous backs to the painter, might suggest that artists with such extremely opposed techniques would not find enough in common for friendship. What united them, apart from their rural English-Welsh border upbringing and shared feeling of being outsiders in the RA's eyes, was their joyful response to their surroundings. They liked what nature and life set before them, and painted it with unaffected pleasure.

Most histories of modern painting are largely accounts of artists like Wilson Steer. As art historians trace developments, and sometimes arguments, from this 'group' to that 'school' or '-ism', a painter such as Adrian is overlooked. He may have been fervently admired by contemporary reviewers, but he is not 'significant'. For the same pardonable reason of 'significance', historians write more about Steer's acquaintance with Whistler or Walter Sickert; but it was Adrian's funeral that Steer attended as a mourner. Circumstances brought them closer in the 1890s. Adrian moved to live in Church Street in Chelsea, while Steer did his studio work just across King's Road in Manresa Street. In 1895 Steer's favourite model rejected his offer of marriage, which made him more dependent on the Chelsea Arts Club for company. Then in 1898 he moved to live in Cheyne Walk, at the foot of Church Street. Perhaps most importantly, Steer left behind the influences of Whistler and Monet and changed to landscape painting in a style which owed a debt to Turner. Adrian returned to his roots on occasion to paint Ludlow-sited scenes such as his 'Plough Horses in Harness Near Ludlow', which has Ludlow Castle in the background. He recommended Ludlow to Steer as a suitable summer destination for a painter wanting to continue to develop as a landscape artist. Motivated by that, by his boyhood connection with the nearby area, and by the fact that Turner had painted there, Steer took his friend's advice. In 1898 he painted at least six oils there, including 'Ludlow Walks', a romantic arcadian view of the walks which had been laid out by the banks of the River Teme, and stretching beyond to the distant prospect of Clee Hill. In 1899 he returned to paint at least eight oils and the watercolours 'Landscape Near Ludlow' and 'The River Teme at Ludlow'. In 1900, still not having exhausted the rural inspiration of Ludlow, he was back to paint 'The Teme at Ludlow, Sunset'. Many of these were first exhibited at the New English Art Club. Adrian and Steer were both very 'English' artists, though they were very different in personality. Camaraderie came naturally to Adrian. He could bond with Whistler, who in the ripostes of raillery gave better than he got, and also with Steer, a very different character who, despite twenty-seven years as Professor of Painting at the Slade School, was socially reticent. Mr Tom Cross, the Chelsea Arts Club's historian, writes of the friendship of Adrian with Steer in his atmospheric account of the Club's life. On one occasion, according to Cross, when Adrian showed Steer South African scenes which he had painted in the previous decade, Steer looked at them for a long time without making any comment. Driven to impatience, Adrian asked for his opinion. 'Typically,' says Cross, 'all that Steer came up with was "I've never been in South Africa".'

A more incongruous artist companion for Adrian was the caricaturist Phil May, renowned for his *Punch* cartoons of East London humour. In *Memoirs* Adrian observes that May, 'among the cleverest men of his time, was his own worst enemy', and describes a caricature of him 'shown sitting in a long Ulster [i.e. long loose overcoat] with a cigar and a glass by his side; if that glass had not been there, there is no height on which he could not have stayed'. Adrian and May were both Savages and early Chelsea Arts members:

> One evening, just as I was leaving the Savage Club on my way to Chelsea, Phil May offered me a lift in his cab. I accepted his invitation, but he did not go home directly. He called at the homes of several friends and took refreshment at each place in turn so that when he arrived home his condition was not altogether satisfactory for Mrs May. He told me afterwards that as

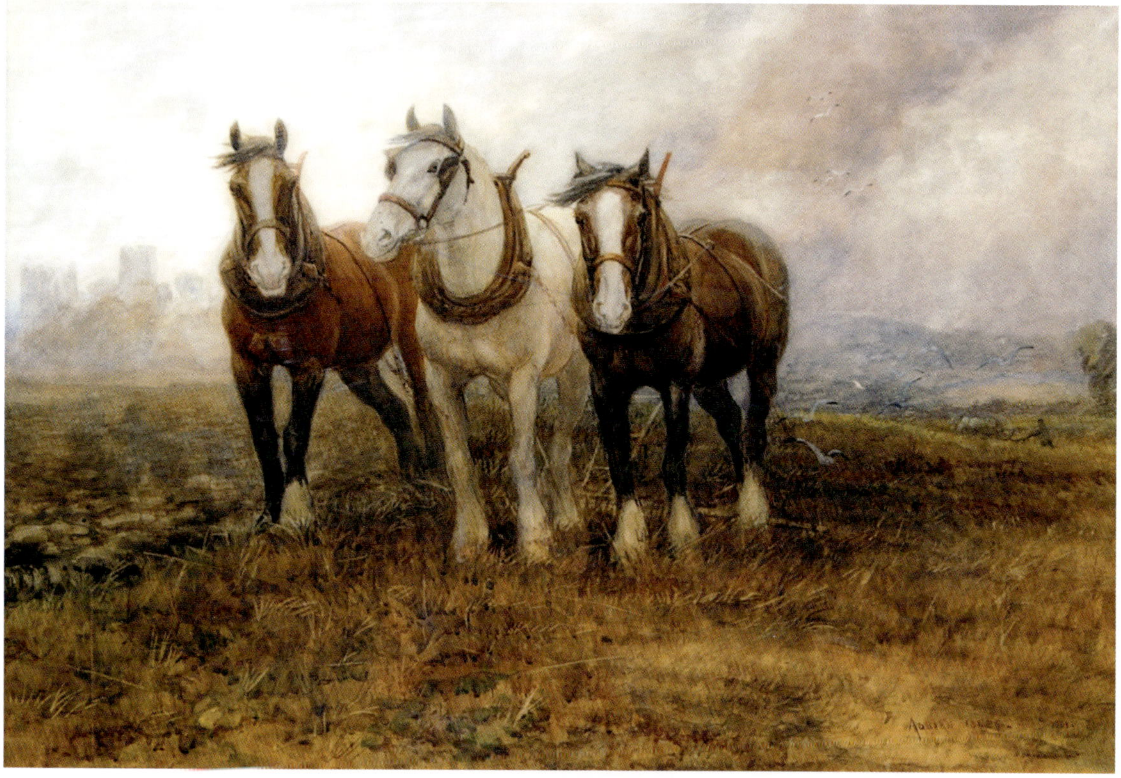

Plough Horses in Harness near Ludlow, watercolour, 1901

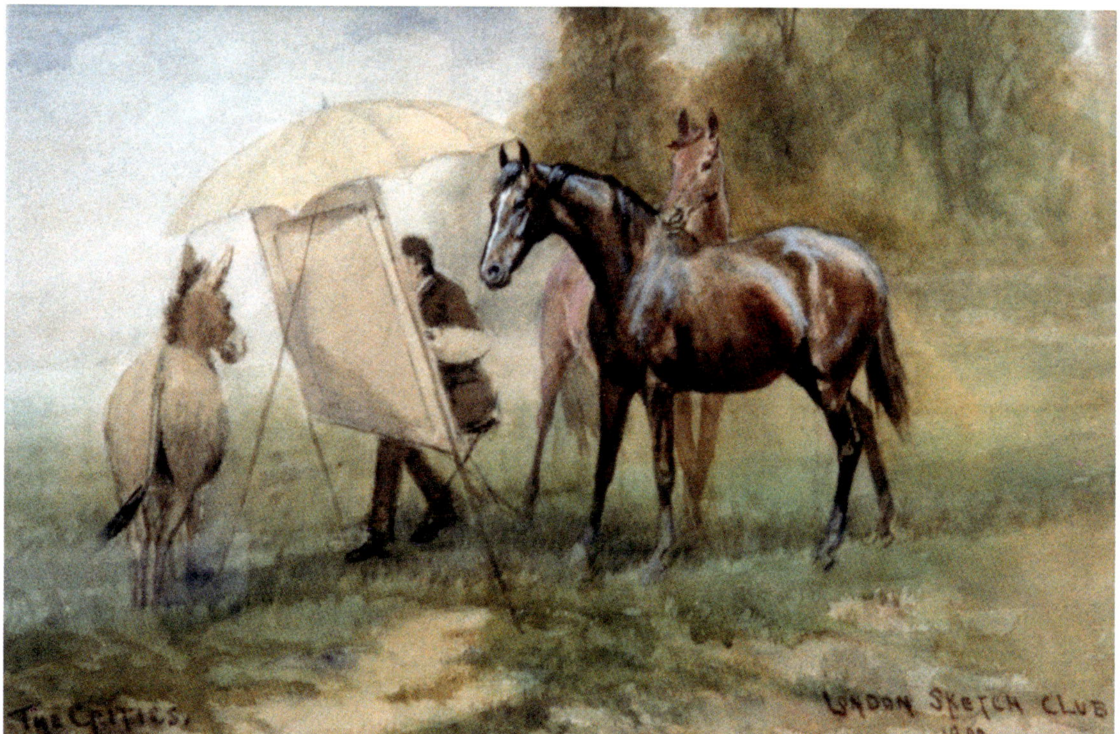

The Critics, watercolour sketch, 1890. Adrian relished funny anecdotes, and on occasion put jokes in his art.

he felt he wanted to indulge a little he had said that he was going to spend the evening with me, as my reputation for sobriety would be useful on that occasion.

Mrs May promoted the friendship, but her husband was, in the words of Tom Cross, 'one of the true Bohemians' as well as a brilliant draughtsman. Thirteen years after Adrian first met him, he died of cirrhosis of the liver, aged just thirty-nine.

Adrian and May both exhibited at the Sketch Club, but Adrian was also busy sculpting. Early in 1886, the year after his return from the Sudan, he exhibited 'Gone Away' at 'Mr Conolly's establishment', 16 Parkside, where it could readily be seen by people passing from Hyde Park Corner to Knightsbridge. The writer of the 'Town and Country Gossip' page in the 16th March issue of *Horse and Hound* enthused about this 'marvellous group' and strongly recommended his readers to go to view 'the wonderful cast of the horse by Mr Jones, who, being a V.S., has in his work most carefully depicted the anatomy of a high-class hunter, and such a design cast in bronze or silver would surpass in merit anything of the kind that has ever come under my notice'.

Encouraged by such heartening comment, Adrian did cast it in bronze and submitted it to the 1887 RA Summer Exhibition. The laudatory words of *Horse and Hound* proved propitious. This second work of his life as a sculptor, like his first, was accepted (exhibit no. 1807). It established his reputation as a 'sporting artist', a term which in some art circles can be belittling as well as descriptive, but which brought him many commissions. During 1887 the bronze of 'Gone Away' in the RA Exhibition (exhibit 1807) continued to prove popular with the public. *The Graphic* of 7th May, having first expressed pleasure that rural life was better represented in the Academy than any other subject except portraiture, commented on 'Gone Away': 'A group in bronze by Mr Adrian Jones should not be overlooked. It is excellent in modelling; seldom have we seen a horse better sculptured. These are the best presentations of "the noble animal" in the show.' It may be that the columnist had some bias in favour of 'Gone Away' because his report appeared in the paper's Rural News feature. This may also explain the report's brevity, as it had to compete for commentary space

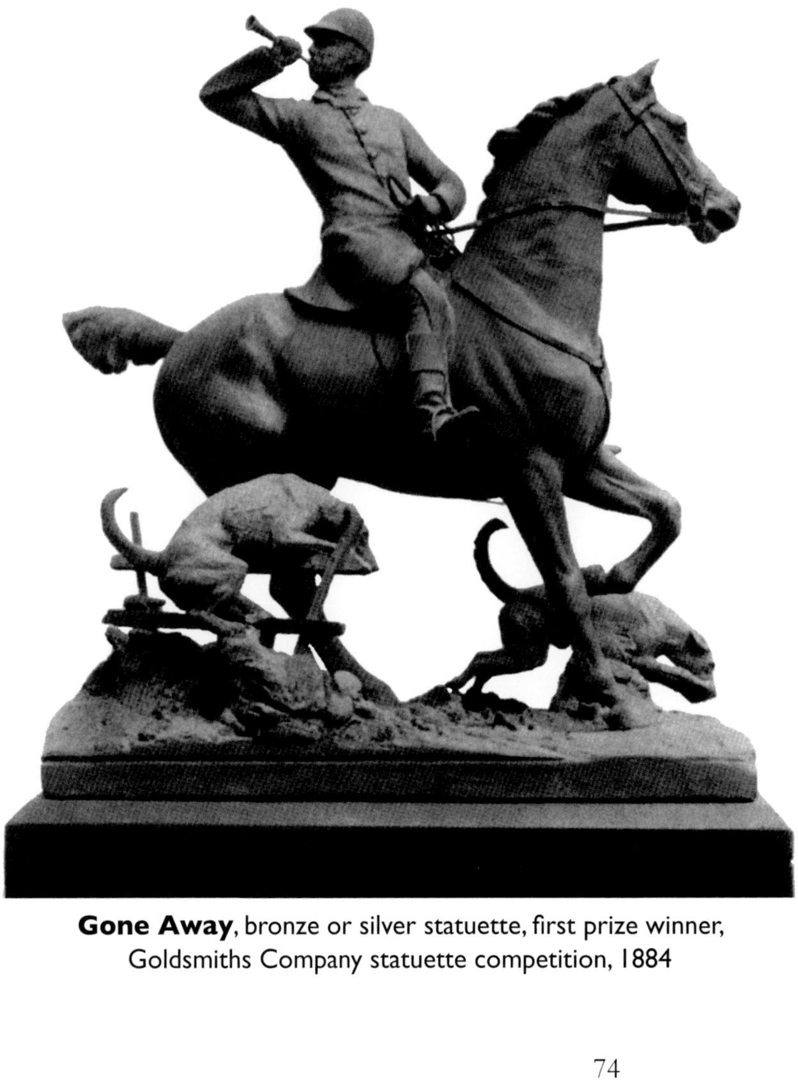

Gone Away, bronze or silver statuette, first prize winner, Goldsmiths Company statuette competition, 1884

with the Exhibition's paintings of cattle and birds and with other events such as the London Orchid Show in King's Road, Chelsea, thronged with 'many botanical and fashionable visitors'. Nevertheless it is typical of the view of animal experts that Adrian was a master of animal sculptures.

When three years later the committee of the Atherstone Hunt came up from Warwickshire to London to choose a silver statuette for a presentation to their Master, they approached the firm Elkingtons rather than an individual artist and asked to see a sample of suitable statuettes. Amongst the sample was 'Gone Away'. The committee members liked it best, were informed that the sculptor was Adrian, and so came to his studio and commissioned him to model another group of mounted huntsman and hounds which Elkingtons would then produce in silver. This time Adrian had not just to model a set subject but also to achieve a likeness. He portrayed the Master, William Oakeley, on his favourite hunter Icicle, waving his hat to encourage three favourite named hounds. Adrian was invited to the presentation at Oakeley's country seat, which took place immediately before a Meet. The courtesy of the hosts extended to asking Adrian to ride with the Hunt, but not to giving him an easy horse. It was fortunate that he was expert in controlling horses, for whereas the Hunt members had their mounts led up to and held at the front door, 'Jones' was directed to the stables to find there a horse which reared up when he tried to get into the saddle and which thereafter 'gave me a lot of trouble'. Patrons still tended to treat artists as tradesmen.

Adrian knew that his knowledge of animal anatomy and physiology enabled him to excel at horse and hound compositions, and over the next thirty years they remained a frequent subject, 'for commissions might almost be said to have come tumbling over one another'. 'Gone Away', the first effort in that field, set the pattern for those of greatest general appeal. Fullest appreciation of the quality of the statuette of a stationary horse requires in the viewer, as in the artist, a knowledge of animal physique. But where the composition is active, as in 'Gone Away', Adrian's eye for capturing animal movement, in harmony with his accurate knowledge of the underlying physical structure, enlivens the work's overall rhythm. The statuette, as befits the work of a beginner, is modest in ambition. It is not votive, nor memorial, nor a comment on the ethics of fox-hunting (already in the nineteenth century sometimes a topic for

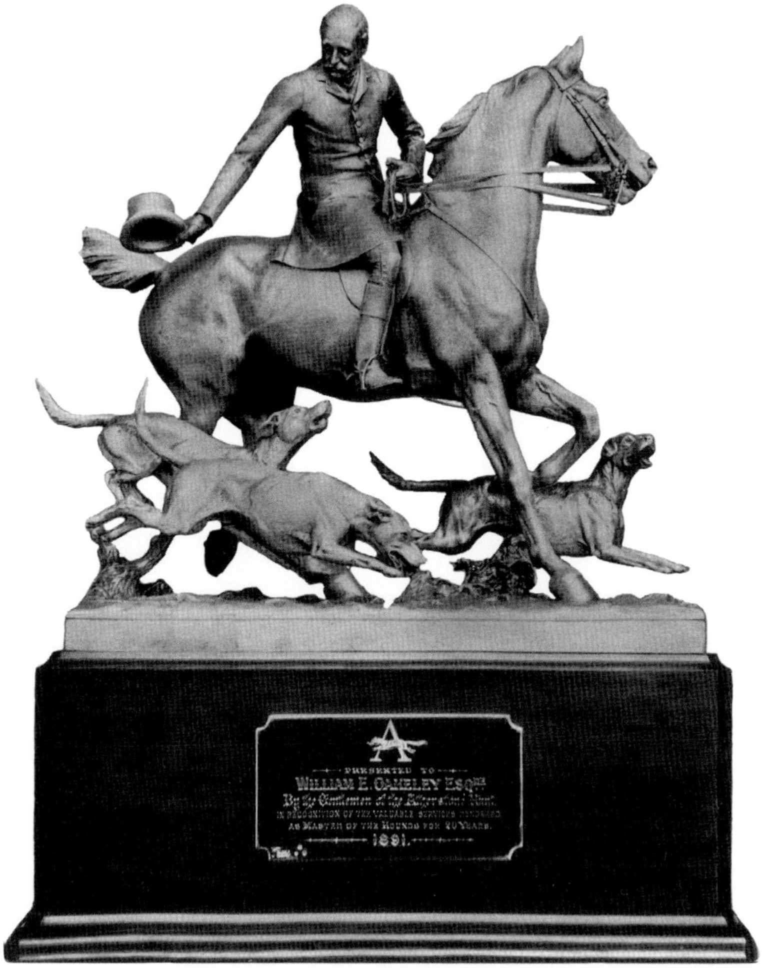

Capping On: William Oakeley, Master of the Atherstone Hunt, on Icicle

dispute, especially when a hunt harmed farmers' crops or fences and the payment of compensation was tardy). The focus of his inspiration could, luckily, be something he knew well, the hunting field, and he concentrates on the look of the real thing. The huntsman on his powerful hunter turns half-round in the conventional 'tally ho' position: nothing strikingly original there. Very probably the judges bestowed first prize on this submission not so much because of the mastery of curve and plane in the whole work but because of the contribution of the hounds to the overall vitality. The two hounds are not just chasing. Both are surmounting obstacles, which energises the composition, and the one scrabbling over the two-bar stile is tribute to Adrian's careful observation of an animal in a particular circumstance. As well as giving a strong sense of activity itself, the group activates the space around it, the horse ready for the chase, the leading hound nose down on the scent ahead, the second scrambling to catch up, and the huntsman summoning the field behind. However, 'Gone Away' is not really a work that calls for extended analytical or explanatory comment. Unstylised, it simply 'does its bit as ornament' (to quote Adrian's remark in 'A Testament of Beauty'), and does it with fine, thoughtful craftsmanship.

One place in which a cast of 'Gone Away' sat as silver ornament for many years was the dining room of Chattis Hill at Stockbridge. There the leading trainer 'Atty' Persse had his racing stable establishment. His nephew, Mr G.A.G. Brooke, described in a magazine article how the statuette was positioned so that it glittered in the morning sunshine, and was gazed at by at least fifty miniature portraits of the heads of horses which 'Atty' had trained to success. The family referred to it as 'The Silver Huntsman' rather than as

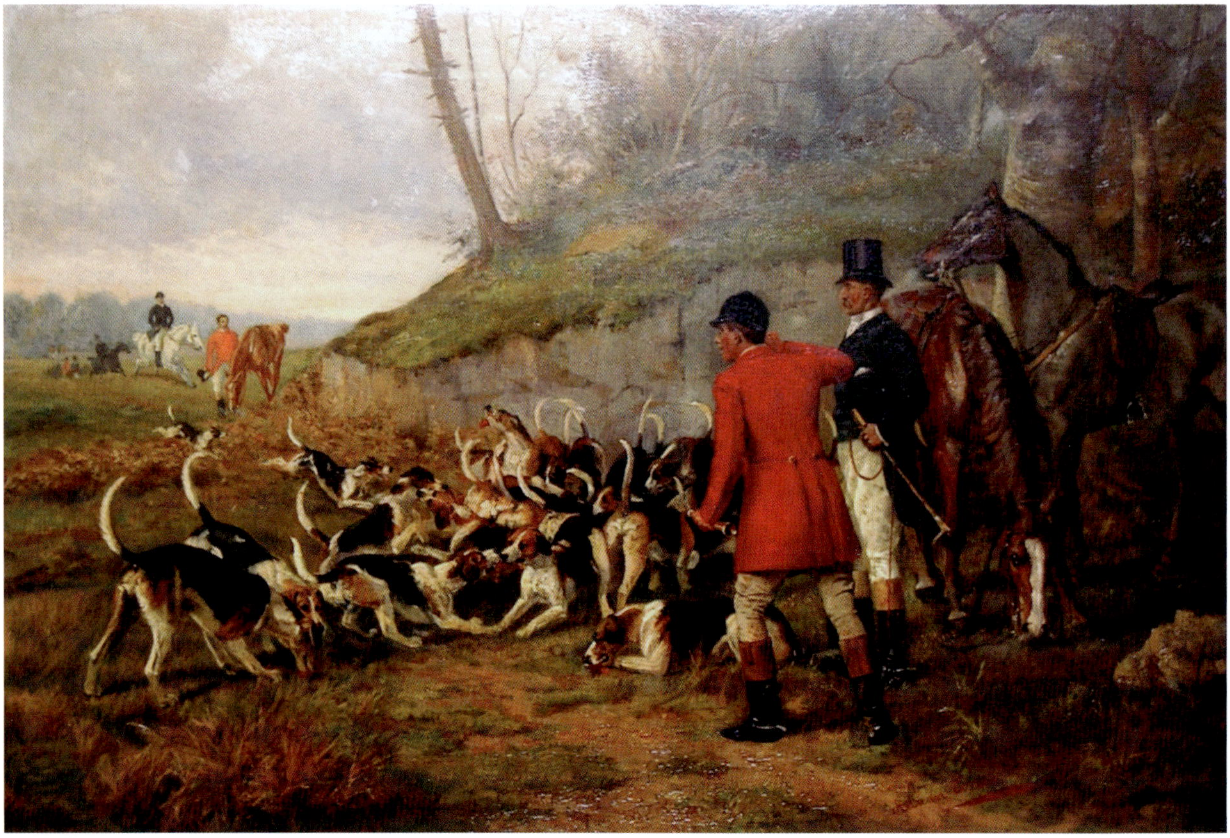

The Kill. The subject will not appeal universally, but the animated depiction of the excited hounds makes this (undated) 32 by 44 inches painting one of Adrian's finest. The scene is particularly well composed, the triangle of horses, Hunt officials and dogs being echoed in the hillside triangle, the apex of which leads the eye on to the approaching Hunt members.

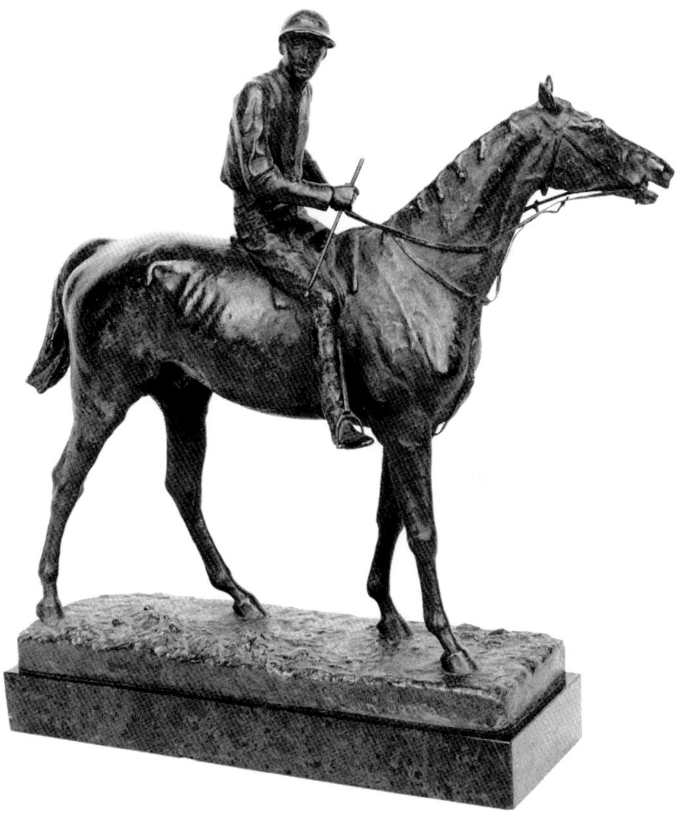

Fred Archer on Ormonde, statuette, 1888

'Gone Away', and an inscription on the plinth read 'The Tally Ho Cup, Cork Park Races 1899. Won by H.G. Persse's B.G. Gillie. Ridden by owner. 23 ran'. Brooke wrote, 'I never saw such statuary ever. By Adrian Jones, it had caught my imagination as a child of six, and I always loved it.' He also thought it 'must have been hell to clean'. Persse's son John was killed serving as an infantry officer in the Second World War. His father presented 'The Silver Huntsman' to his regiment, the Rifle Brigade.

In 1888 Adrian received for the first time a commission to sculpt an outstanding racehorse. The race crowds had seen the Duke of Westminster's horse Ormonde take the Triple Crown of 2,000 Guineas, Derby and St Leger. Adrian cast a bronze statuette, 14 inches by 12, of Ormonde with the jockey Fred Archer in the saddle. It is brilliantly executed. Ormonde looks every inch a thoroughbred, alert, muscled, lean and fit. Archer sits relaxed, his legs low in the long stirrup leathers which look strange to modern racegoers' eyes but which Adrian favoured, and his glance turned to the right as if acknowledging the congratulations of the backers or the owner while he walks the horse quietly. The quality of the artistry ensured that Adrian would attract frequent patronage from successful moneyed owners and become nationally renowned as a first choice sculptor of the Turf's greatest horses.

In the same year, 1888, he was presented to the Prince of Wales at a levee, the beginning of what would be a very long and happy relationship with the future King. Now becoming established as a well-known artist, he stewarded at the Artists' Benevolent Fund Dinner, and he again successfully submitted to the Royal Academy, this time a wax of 'The Last Arrow' (exhibit 1982). As model for the mounted North American Indian, who is galloping to shoot a last arrow into the chased bison, Adrian used an Indian who was then performing in the 'Wild West Show' which 'Buffalo Bill' Cody had put on at Earl's Court Exhibition Hall. Colonel Cody forewarned Adrian that his Indian spoke no English and gave firm instructions that he must not be given money or alcohol, though he could be given as many cigarettes as he wished. For each sitting he came by cab and the session passed in a comfortable haze of tobacco, for both artist and model were inveterate smokers. The Indian meticulously put out each cigarette when he had smoked it far enough down, thereby combining avoidance of any fire risk (a careful habit which Adrian speculated he must have learned on the dry prairies) with the potential economy of saved butt ends. Adrian thought him a 'gentlemanly fellow' and was pleased to find a further way of rewarding him without disregarding Buffalo Bill's instructions, by gifts of coloured handkerchiefs. His collaborative model had proved invaluable: 'He may claim to have helped me make 'The Last Arrow' a definite success.'

The group is a piece of vigorous realism. Clearly creative excitement went into portraying the Indian, riding bareback, hunting down and slaying the wild shaggy humped bison. Its popularity caused Sir Coutts Lindsay to invite Adrian to place a work in the 1889 exhibition to be held in his famed Grosvenor Gallery in New Bond Street, where works appeared not by anonymous competitive submission but by personal invitation. Adrian accepted the invitation. This might surprise those whose idea of the kind of artist who exhibited there is coloured by the story of Ruskin accusing Whistler's exhibited pictures of 'flinging a pot of paint in the public's face' or by the patter song which W.S. Gilbert had written for the operetta 'Patience':

> A pallid and thin young man,
> A haggard and lank young man,
> A greenery-yallery, Grosvenor Gallery
> Foot-in-the-grave young man.

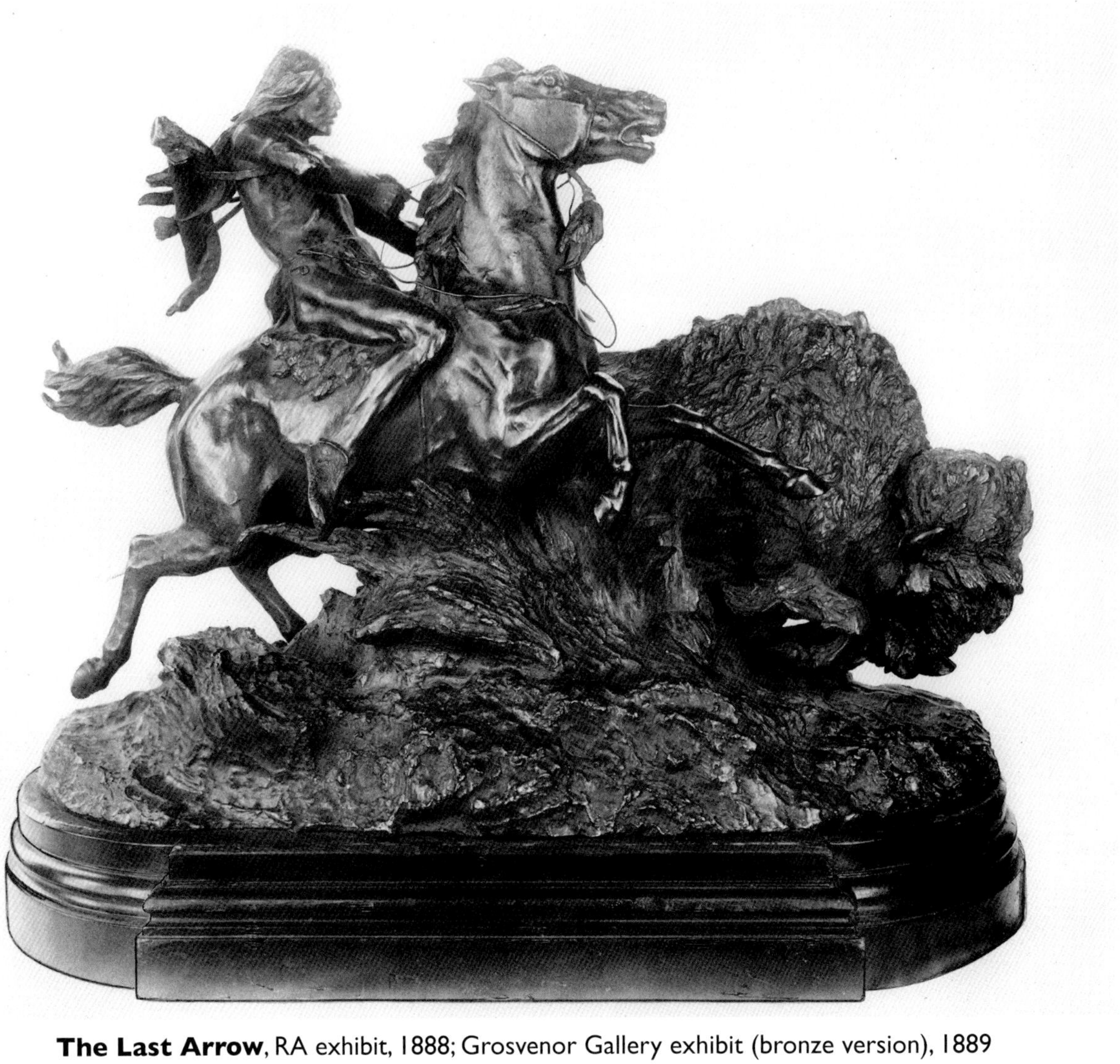

The Last Arrow, RA exhibit, 1888; Grosvenor Gallery exhibit (bronze version), 1889

No artist could less resemble Adrian Jones, whom Gilbert knew as a fellow member of the Savage Club, than the young art-for-art's-sake aesthete satirised in those lines. Obviously Gilbert did not have Life Guards officers in mind when he wrote them. No more did George Grossmith, another of Adrian's Savage Club friends and also D'Oyly Carte Opera's leading comic singer in the 1880s, think for a second that it was the like of Adrian who was being parodied on the Savoy Theatre stage. In reality, though implicit in the founding of the Gallery in 1877 had been some disgruntlement with the Royal Academy's dominance of the British art scene, and some attempt to dispute that, and though leading luminaries of its annual exhibitions – the avant-garde Whistler and the dreamlike Pre-Raphaelite Burne-Jones – were not Royal Academicians, RAs up to and including the President Frederick Leighton also showed there.

So Adrian cast the wax 'Last Arrow' RA exhibit in durable bronze, and it went on display amid the pictures by Millais et al. The *Daily News* review of 10 July 1889 remarked 'The sculpture deserves more attention than usual ... Mr Adrian Jones has put plenty of power and dramatic action into his bronze group.' Adrian's self-assessment was that the group deserved a full-page illustration in *Memoirs*, and he records that it was 'well received' at the Grosvenor. The public liked the work too, and so did Coutts Lindsay, who therefore asked Adrian to model a large group of an Assyrian driving a four-horsed chariot, and promised

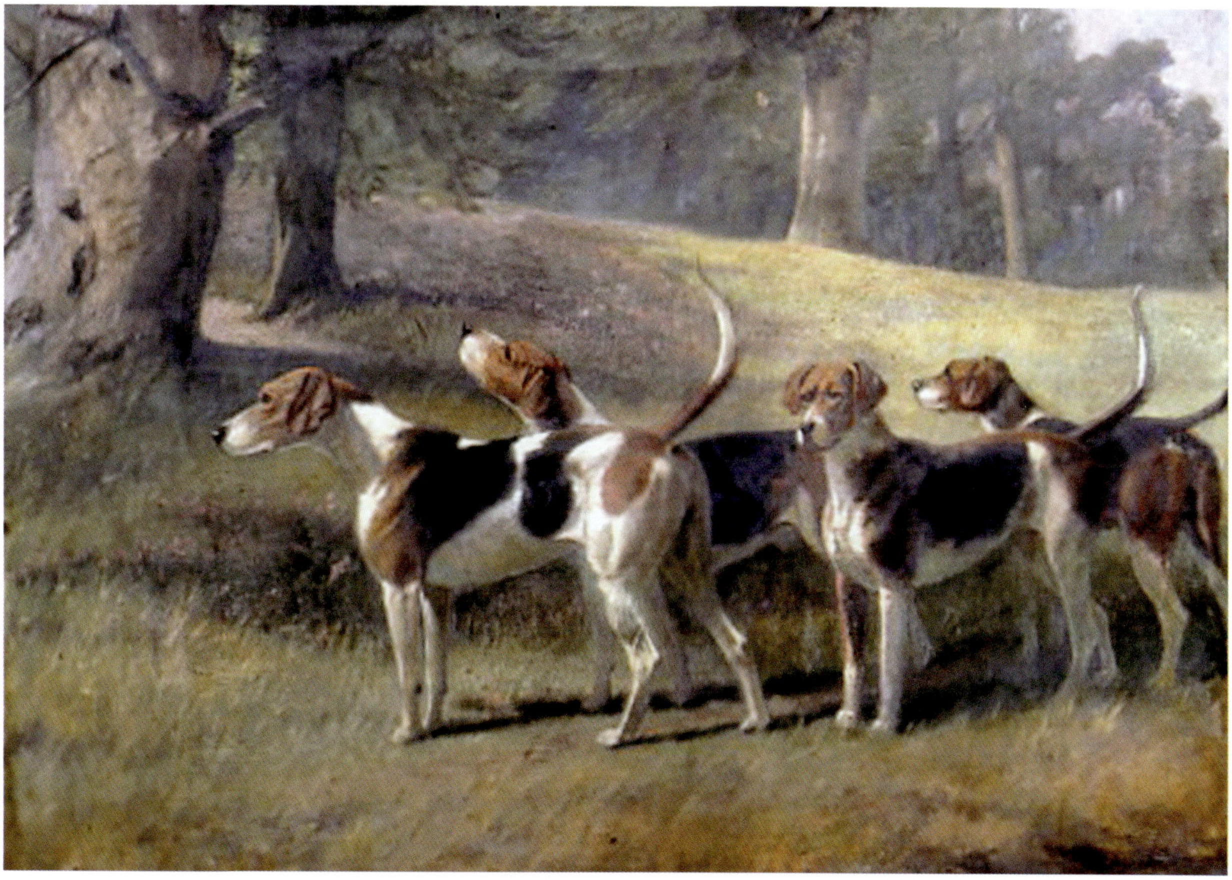

The Earl of Cavan's Foxhounds. Four of Lord Cavan's favourite hounds, painted in 1921 for the farmers of the Hertfordshire Hunt. Adrian also received a commission from the Hunt members for a portrait in oils of Lord Cavan mounted on his favourite hunter. As the Earl was C.I.G.S. [Chief of the Imperial General Staff] as well as Master of the Hertfordshire, the sittings in hunting kit were frequently interrupted by his need to change into uniform and dash off to undertake his military duties.

it pride of place in the Grosvenor. Unfortunately, the Gallery's finances failed, and it had to close before Adrian had finished the group. But more was to come of this model, for it was this that in time would be the prototype for Adrian's greatest triumph, the Quadriga. In the meantime, though, his inspiration for his next submissions to the Royal Academy came from a change not in his artistic but in his military career.

The 2nd Life Guards

Adrian continued successfully to submit statuettes to the Royal Academy, but his scenes were now from military history. In successive years, 1889 and 1890, he showed 'Waterloo: the charge well fought' (exhibit 2133) and 'Waterloo: Picton's Brigade about to advance' (exhibit 2029). The emphasis on Waterloo was inspired by a change in Adrian's military career. On 16 May 1888 he was gazetted to the 2nd Life Guards, who had fought in the battle. It was the bloodiest in their history. The 2nd Life Guards, on the left of the cavalry line in the Household Cavalry Brigade, had awkwardly picked their way forward through the lines of artillery and infantry in front of them. Then, after an inadequate pause to reorganise, the duty trumpeter sounded the charge and they swept down past La Haie-Sainte Farm. They were on their own, split from the centre and right of the line, who had gone past the Farm on the far side. Their charge burst upon the Cuirassiers, the elite of the French cavalry, big men better armoured than the Life Guards and wielding longer swords. Nevertheless, in desperately vicious hand-to-hand combat the Life Guards had broken through, but then, carried away by the exhilaration of victory, they had rampaged on towards the 84 guns of the French Grand Battery, and the easier target of the wagon lines. When French lancers made the inevitable countercharge, the 2nd Life Guards and their tired horses suffered heavily. 87 of the regiment were killed, 63 were wounded, and more than 150 horses were lost.

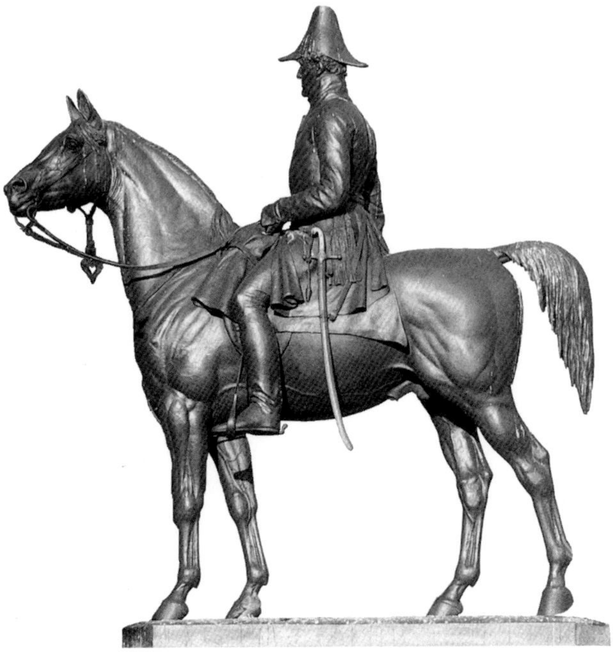

The Duke of Wellington on Copenhagen,
by Sir Joseph Edgar Boehm, 1888.
Sited in front of Apsley House at Hyde Park Corner, it faces away from the Wellington Arch and the Quadriga. (See page 188 for Wellington's Ghost's comments on the horse's build.)

Adrian saw portrayals of the battle on the walls of the Household Cavalry messes. If in tribute to his new regiment's history he was going to make Waterloo a subject for his art, sculpture seemed the more distinctive option. He does not refer to either of his RA exhibits in the text of *Memoirs*, but he chooses as one illustration of his work 'Picton's Brigade about to advance'. The title is surprising. Lieutenant General Sir Thomas Picton had commanded not a brigade but Wellington's Fifth Division; and the calm commanding officer at the front of the group is clearly not Picton, who was renowned for the idiosyncrasy that he always fought dressed in top hat and civilian coat. In fact the calm commander is of course the Duke of Wellington on his charger Copenhagen. Adrian had been a young boy when the Duke died, but he knew well various Wellington images, most importantly equestrian sculptures,

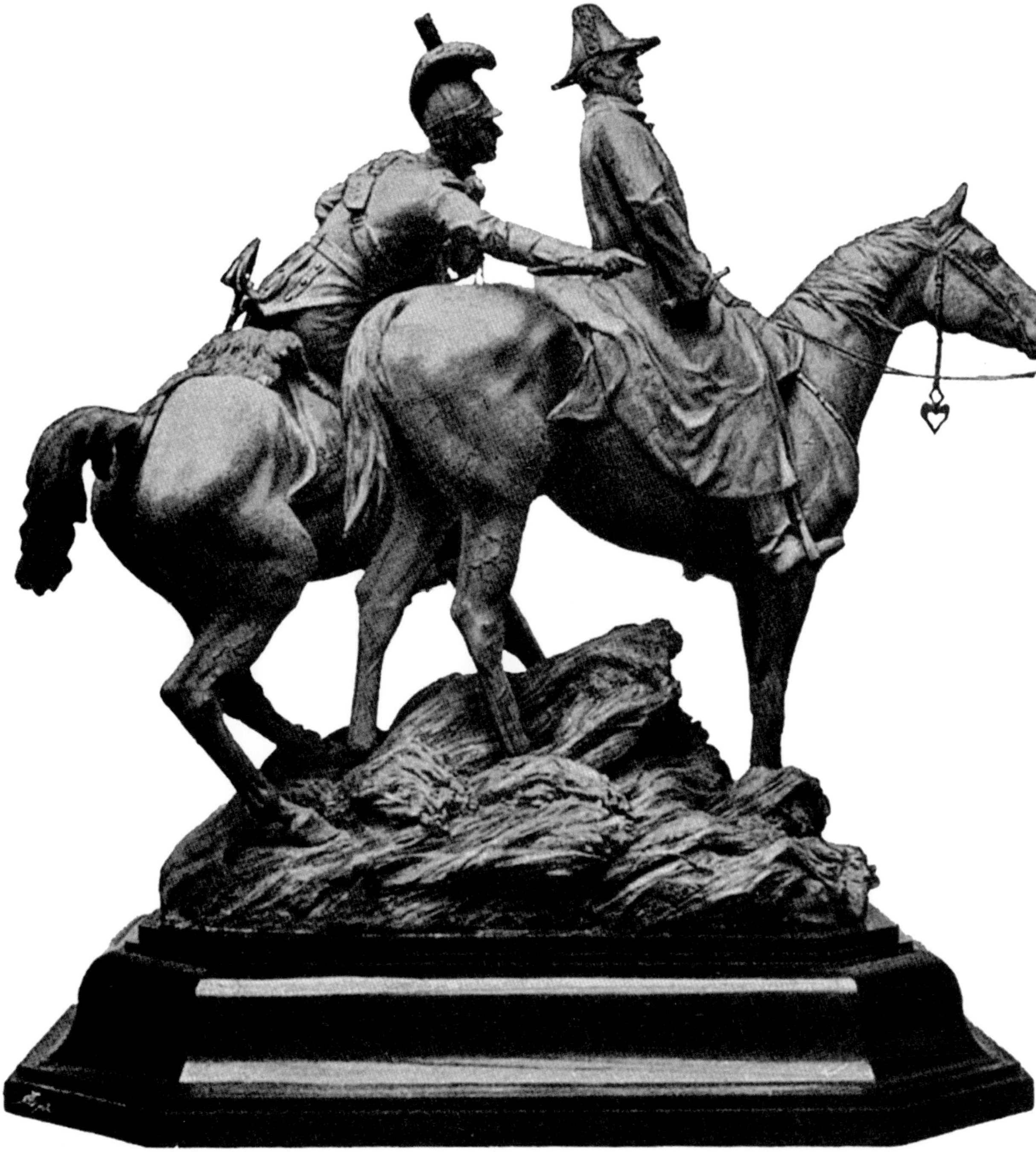

Waterloo, Picton's Brigade about to advance, bronze statuette, R.A. exhibit, 1890.
This title, used on popular postcards of the statuette, is mistaken, because at Waterloo it was Lord Somerset who commanded the Household Cavalry Brigade that included the 2nd Life Guards.
The RA listed the statuette as simply 'Waterloo'.

from his daily life in London. The forty tons of Wyatt's huge – and hugely derided – statue had stood across Decimus Burton's Arch (hence the name 'Wellington Arch') until it was taken down in 1883 for removal to Aldershot; Life Guards duties regularly took Adrian near Apsley House and Boehm's replacement statue there, which had been unveiled in 1888; and though he would not see it so frequently, Adrian must have been aware also of Chantrey's statue at the Royal Exchange and perhaps thought it odd that Chantrey sculpted the Duke hatless and riding without stirrups. Wyatt's and Boehm's statues, however, may have suggested some details. Boehm's more portly Wellington is dressed for post-war ceremonial, but his Copenhagen is more convincing than Wyatt's. Adrian, like Wyatt, shows Wellington dressed for Waterloo's bad weather.

Any resemblances between the works are less important than a crucial difference. The large statues are essentially portraits. The statuette is a scene. Something is happening; the Duke is using his eyes and ears. The statuette is a small example of narrative art, though unlike many Victorian narrative paintings it is not an invitation to moralise. Indeed, the viewer has to use his own imagination to supply a narrative. Presumably the Life Guards officer who has scrambled his horse up the rocky outcrop that is the Duke's observation point is indicating something important in the field of view ahead. The viewer who knows nothing of the details of the battle may imagine his saying something as simple as: 'My lord, the cavalry are ready.' The more knowledgeable viewer can give his imagination free rein; perhaps the officer is checking with the Duke the best line for the cavalry brigades to take in the planned sweep down past La Haie-Sainte Farm in a decisive shock charge against the Cuirassiers. The upward sloping line of the officer's horse, continued by the officer's back, and the leaning turn of his torso and arm to the right across the back of Copenhagen which unifies the group, is artistically pleasing. But the really striking feature in 'Waterloo' is Wellington's pose. In Boehm's and Chantrey's statues, Wellington simply sits inactive; in Wyatt's, disproportionately tall, he sits stiffly upright and for some indeterminate reason holds out a stiff right arm. In Adrian's statuette, Wellington is unmoving yet, paradoxically, active. He is almost standing in the stirrups, and stretches up his slim body to give himself the best possible view over the (imagined) ridged ground ahead where his infantry on the reverse slope were largely concealed from the French. At the same time he leans back the better to hear the words of his staff officer. Contemporary art critics frequently commented on how Adrian's sculpted animals were instinct with action. The same compliment can often equally be paid to his human subjects, particularly in works such as 'Waterloo' which are not portrait commissions. Nor does the figure lack artistry, the curving sweep of the rain cape skirt complementing the curves of Copenhagen's neck, mane and croup. In little space, much is achieved.

As a prestigious regiment, the 2nd Life Guards would certainly expect to have a voice in the appointment of their veterinary officer. Since 1881 only the Household Cavalry regiments had managed to retain the system of having their own vet gazetted to them. Captain Jones would wear the same uniform as the Life Guards captains, apart from three distinguishing features: no cuirass; cocked hat with red swan feathers in place of helmet; and shoulder belt of white patent leather with a Veterinary Department pattern instrument case, though even that professionally useful belt was abandoned when in Review Order, replaced by dress belt and pouch of Life Guards pattern.

The choice of Adrian for the Life Guards in May 1888 was no doubt influenced by his war service. Egypt was the regiment's only recent experience of battle; 'Egypt 1882' and 'Tel-el-Kebir' were its first battle honours since Waterloo. The Commanding Officer, Colonel Townshend, had commanded the 2nd Life Guards squadron of the composite Household Cavalry Regiment in the 1882 Egypt War and so wore the same Egypt Medal and Khedive's Star as Adrian had received after his active service in Sudan 1884-85. One of the regiment's majors, Lord Dundonald, was known to Adrian from that Nile campaign, as he had commanded the 2nd Life Guards contingent of the Camel Corps. Five others on the officer strength of twenty-four had been in Egypt; none of the officers had seen war elsewhere. And though the Colonel of the Regiment, Viscount Templeton, had been an infantryman and commanded footguards units in the battles of the Crimean War, at least he had shared the common cavalry experience of having his horse shot. On top of all that, the regiment's Colonel-in-Chief was the Prince of Wales, who was already getting to know of Adrian as an artist.

So Adrian joined the 2nd Life Guards at Windsor. Again he had his photograph taken for the family album. No longer the slight figure of his steeplechasing days, he stands in the photographer's studio, staring away from the camera, Victorian-style. He wears the regiment's scarlet tunic, bemedalled and gold-corded; he is booted, spurred and gauntleted, and holds the half-basket hilt of his cavalry sword – the epitome of an officer and a gentleman. But that role did not stop him from continuing as an artist also. Like the other two Household Cavalry regiments, the 1st Life Guards and the Royal Horse Guards (the Blues), the 2nd Life Guards rotated barracks annually between Windsor, Regent's Park and Knightsbridge. With two years in three thus being spent in London, home of the Savage Club and the chief art galleries, it was obvious that Adrian's base for his leisure and leave times artistic work should be there also. He took a studio in Cheniston Gardens, just west along Kensington Road from Knightsbridge Barracks.

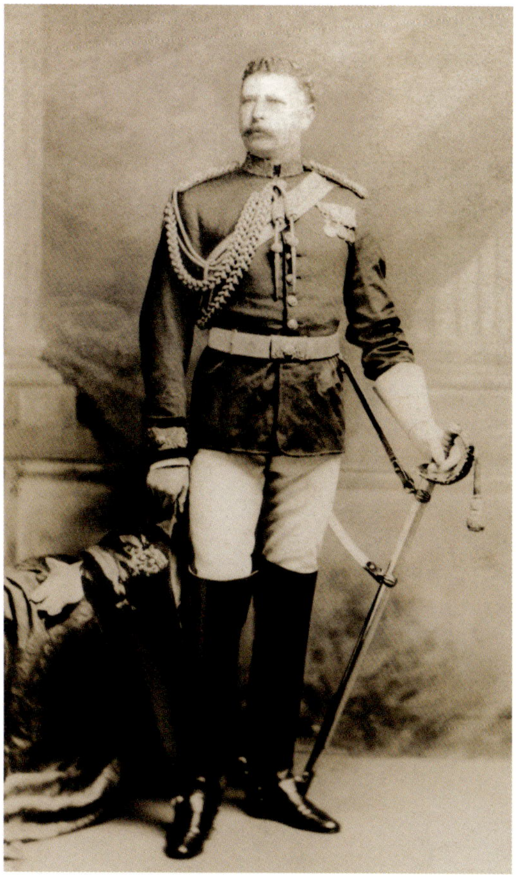

Captain Adrian Jones,
Veterinary Surgeon 1st class, 2nd Life Guards

Life was good. The Household Cavalry had its critics, who thought that regiments whose main London duty was ceremonially to mount Queen Victoria's Lifeguard were not serious professional soldiers. Certainly some officers appeared to join only briefly, to gain social cachet from serving alongside peers of the realm, rather than to make an army career. The abolition of purchase of commissions had not yet much changed the regiments' social composition. Being an officer in them was still an expensive business. Dundonald, seven years younger than Adrian but in terms of army seniority a close contemporary, recounts in his autobiography *My Army Life* that although in 1869 purchasing his commission had cost £1,260, that was less of a burden than the continuing expenses of having to buy and maintain two chargers and their equipment, keep a batman and a civilian groom, pay his mess bills and subscribe towards the cost of the regiment's thirty-four bandsmen. It was not a lifestyle that could be afforded on the daily pay of eight shillings; a private income was essential. Adrian's pay as a captain was higher and his cost of living was lower than that of those with Life Guards commissions, and his art gave him a second source of income, so though he would not become rich as a soldier of the Queen he does not appear to have suffered financial hardship. Also, his personality was such that he was normally very happy with his lot in society. Radicals might on occasion rail against cavalry extravagance, but Adrian, as in his earlier postings, happily identified with his regiment. After all, it was unlikely that a veterinary surgeon would be unhappy in a regiment whose working philosophy was 'horses first'. Twenty years after he had retired from the army he would still enjoy attending a Life Guards officers' reunion dinner.

The life suited him. He was totally familiar with the daily routines of watering and exercising. He was medically as competent as anyone else at the stage veterinary science had then reached. He was a confident judge of a horse's worth as reflected in his frequent attendance at the nearby Albert Gate horse sales. (The regiment's authorised black horses were now supplied by the Remount Establishment. It was said that one economy that the household cavalry did practise was to sell on ageing horses to firms of undertakers.) So his routine work was not stressful; nor, because of his excellent horsemanship, was any occasional demand for ceremonial. Mounting the Queen's Guard at Horse Guards – in Victoria's reign always a full guard, whether or not she was in residence in London – could be time-consuming for other officers, but it was not one of Adrian's roles. In the Mess he met ready companionship. He shared the experience of the handful of senior officers who had served in Egypt, with the further bond that in 1882 as in 1884-85 the commander of the force had been Wolseley, who had personally expressed his debt of gratitude to Adrian for his work with camels, and who felt particularly warmly towards the 2nd Life Guards because their medical officers had restored him to good health when he had become ill on the outward-bound troopship.

Adrian also shared the interest of most officers in horse racing and field sports. Though he himself was not now competing in races, he could certainly hold his own in conversations about them. When Dundonald rode his horse Benita in the 1889 Household Brigade meeting at Windsor and in the Royal Horse Guards regimental meet at Hawthorn Hill, no doubt Adrian complimented or commented as appropriate. He

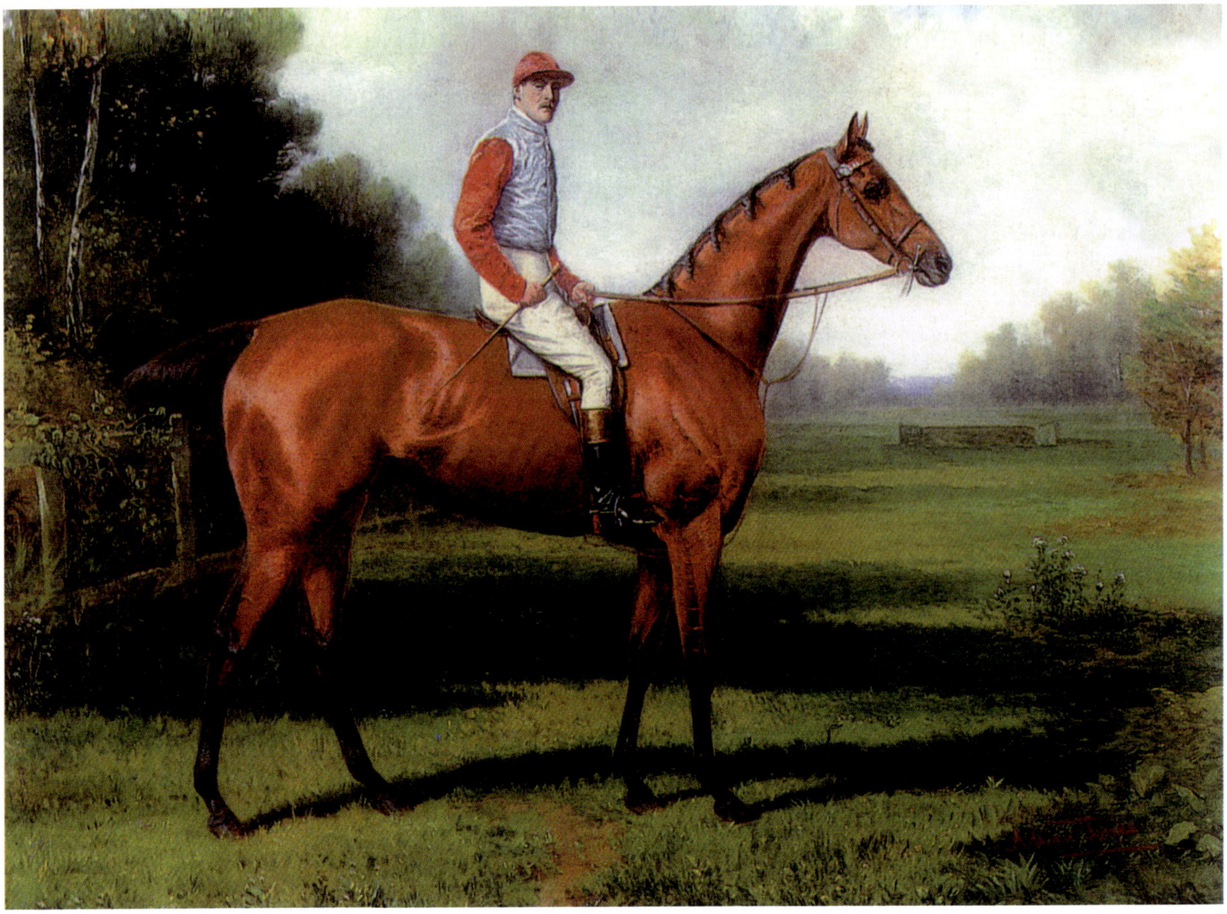

Roman Oak, oil painting, 1890.
At 39 by 47 inches the painting is more generously sized than many of Adrian's studies of a single horse.

attended such meetings, painting the scene or winning horses, and sometimes received commissions, as when Lord Annaly requested a portrait of his brother, Captain the Hon. Henry White, on his mare Lady Sarah, winner of the Grand Military and Household Brigade Cup. As Adrian's reputation spread, he ventured to paint more famous horses, of interest not only in Household Cavalry circles but also among the army and racegoers generally. In 1890 he painted in oils Captain Willie Leetham of the 5th Dragoon Guards on Roman Oak, which that year won the Irish Grand Military Cup and started favourite for the Grand National but fell at the Canal Turn. Thirty-four years later the painting was to reappear as an illustration in Ralph Pomeroy's history of Leetham's regiment. Like many of Adrian's earlier horse portraits it is an attractive side view of a single, quietly standing horse, still awaiting the tap of the whip and the dig of the spurs. When two years later Adrian's portrait of General Byrne's horse Amphion received the army's accolade of being exhibited in the Horse Guards Regent's Park barracks, a press correspondent who had been 'recently favoured' with a view of the oil of this 'clean cut, handsome' racer concluded 'the portraiture of the animal is excellent, the green meadows forming a background in a nice harmony of colour with the rich chestnut of the horse's glossy coat'. The Amphion picture replaces the jockey with a stable boy holding the horse, but the words on its 'nice harmony' could have been equally well applied to Roman Oak's portrait. In commissioned paintings

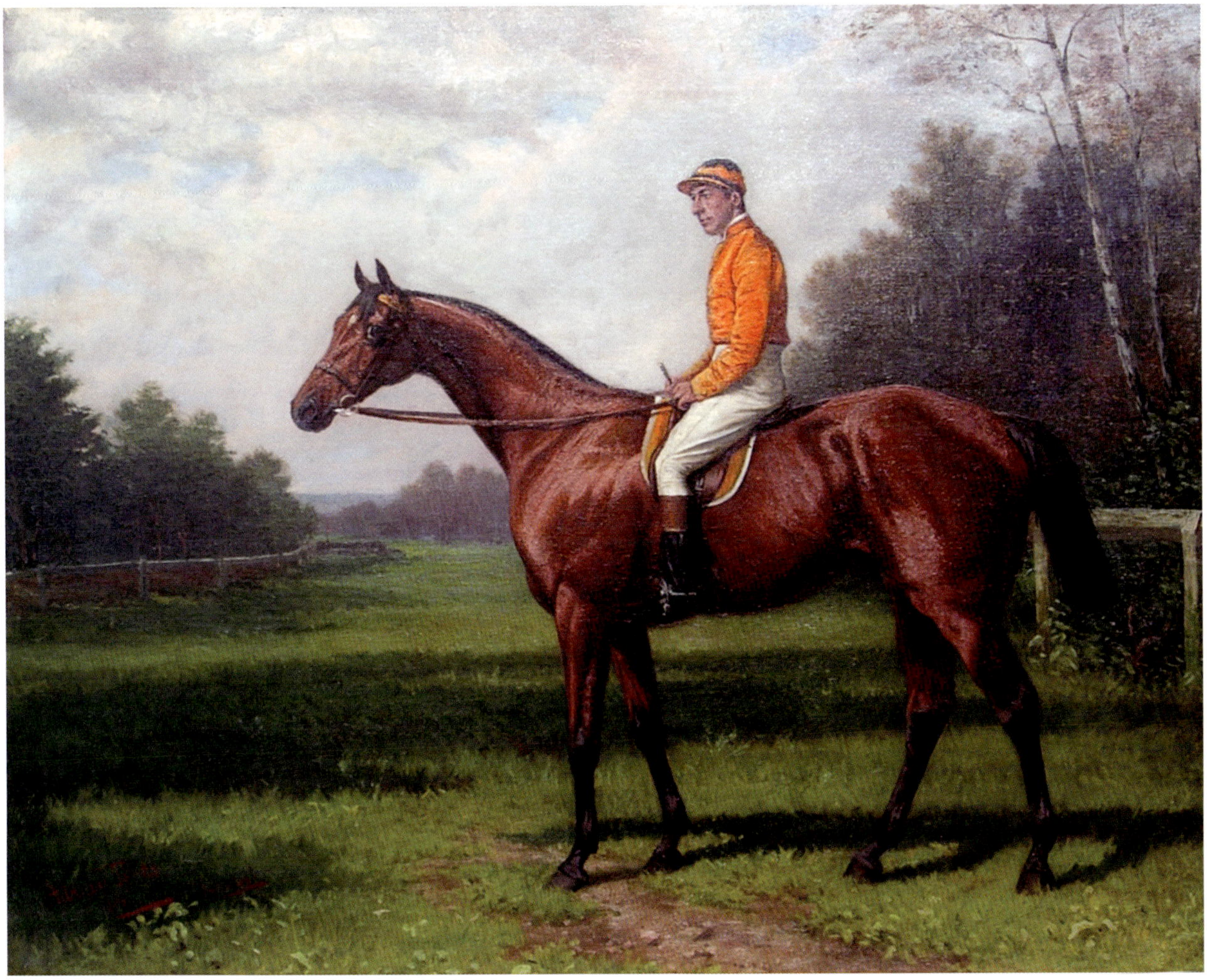

The Swindler with jockey, oil painting, 1890. The horse's pose and the background suggest a companion piece to **Roman Oak**, but the less famed Swindler is on a smaller 23 by 30 inches canvas.

of thoroughbreds, some element of repetitiveness was unavoidable. In 1890 Adrian also painted the Derby winner Sainfoin, again a single animal. Later he would give greater variety of interest by introducing a supporting cast of other famed horses in different poses in the near background.

In addition to affording new subjects and new patrons, service in the 2nd Life Guards 1888-91 was of military and veterinary interest. For his services in the Sudan Dundonald had been promoted to Brevet Colonel and then in June 1889 was further promoted to full Colonel. Within the 2nd Life Guards

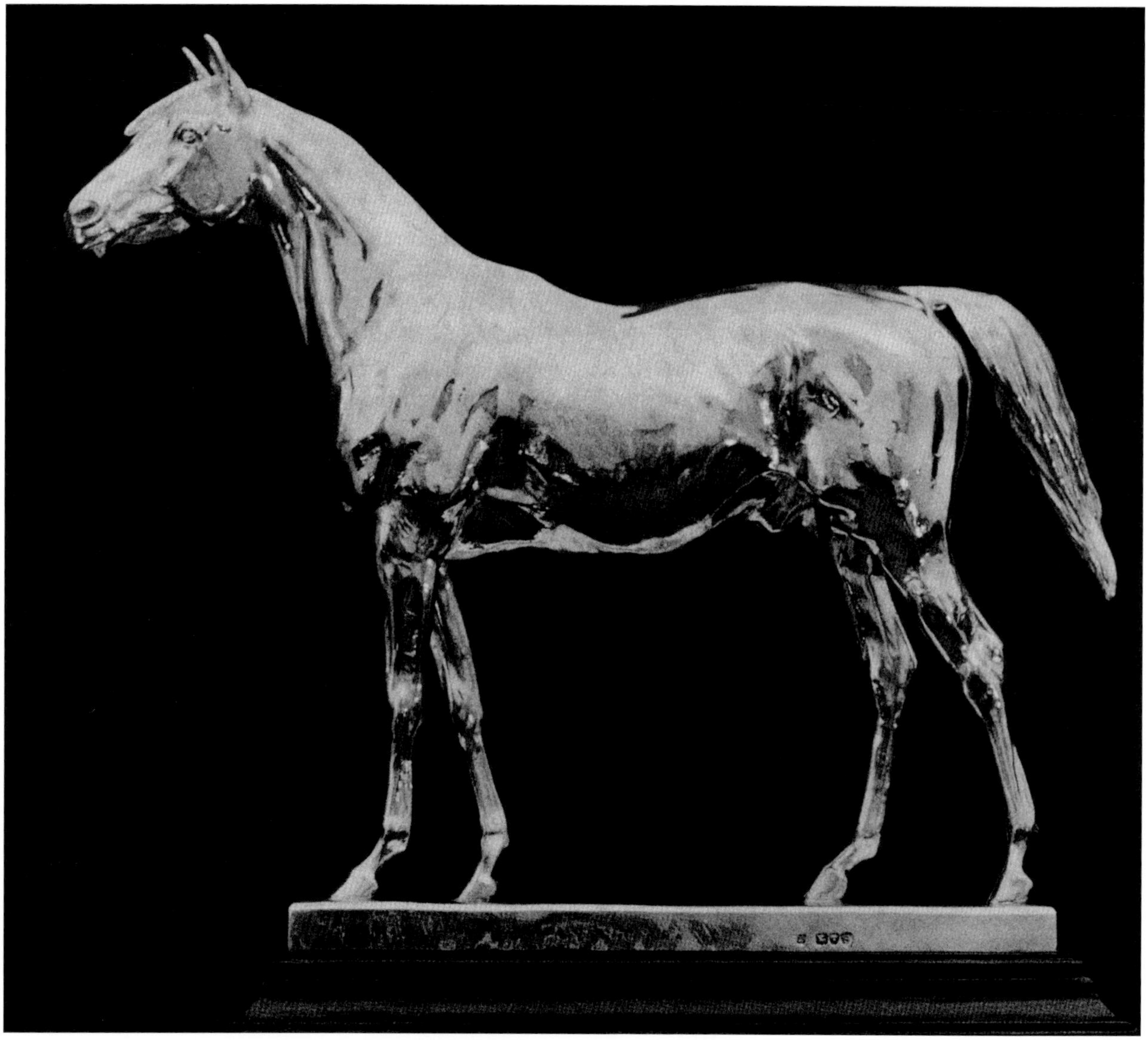

Sainfoin, silver statuette, 1890.

It was sculpted as an officers' mess table centrepiece to celebrate Sainfoin winning the 1890 Derby. The owner was a Hussar, Sir James Miller, and this remains the only time that the Derby's winning owner was a serving officer. The statuette is now part of the mess silver of the King's Royal Hussars. Ten years later, in the Boer War, Captain Miller was ambushed and wounded in the back, and his horse Bustard was shot dead. Bustard was another good horse – winner of the Irish Military Steeplechase and twice winner of the 14th Hussars regimental steeplechase. In a gentlemanly action, the Boers handed over their wounded captive to a band sergeant of the South Staffordshire Regiment. Captain Miller recovered from his wound.

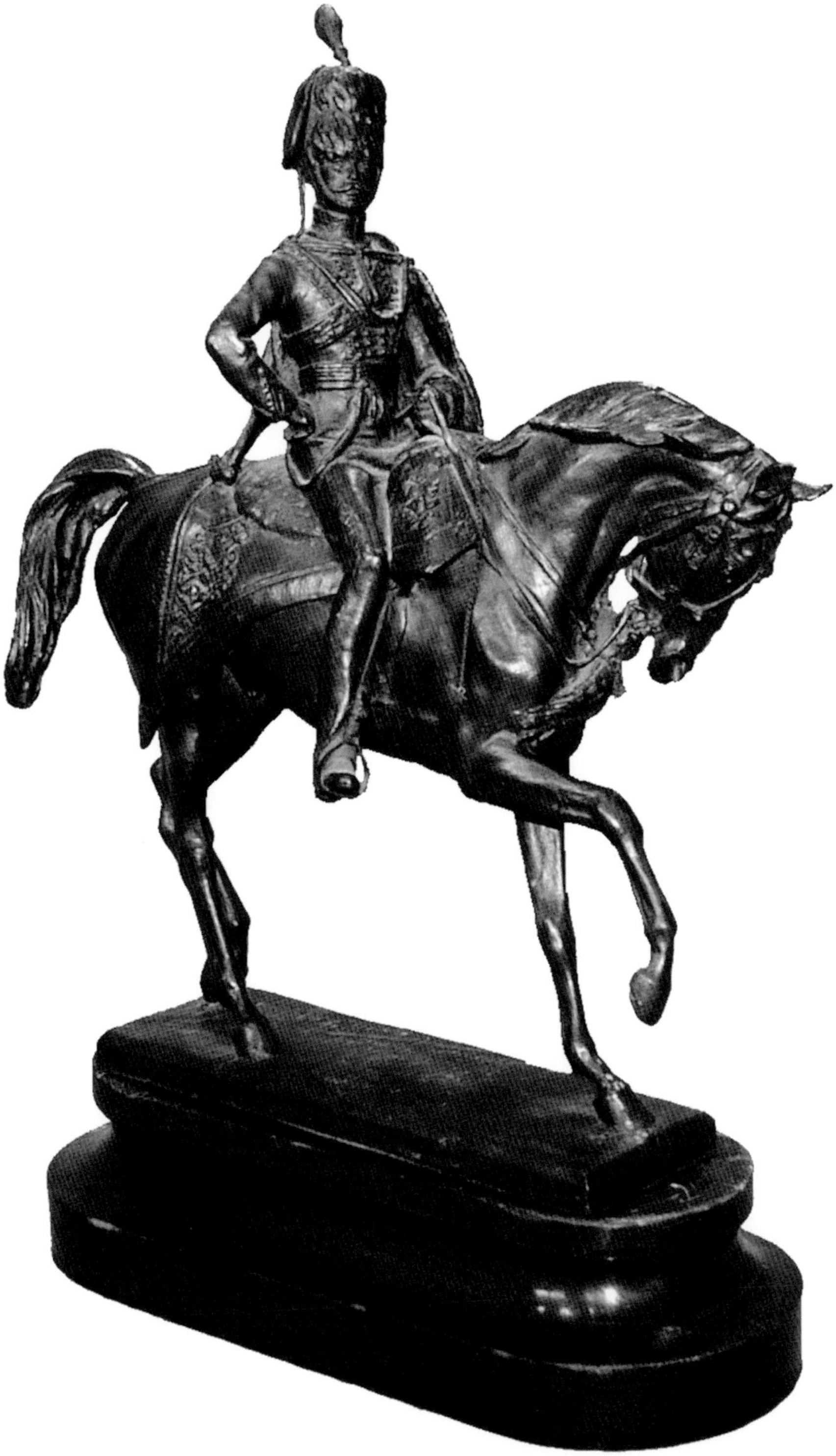

Mounted Officer of the 8th (The King's Royal Irish) Hussars, bronze statuette, 1898.
A limited edition of nine bronzes of the 22 by 17 inches statuette was cast under the direction of Sladmore Editeurs for the Sladmore Gallery's retrospective Exhibition of May, 1984.
Adrian later used a similar pose of man and horse in his Colonel Dowla statuette.

Dundonald continued to hold the lower regimental rank of Major, but on larger formation manoeuvres he sometimes found himself empowered to give orders to his regiment's commanding officer! He could handle that situation coolly, just as a year later when Captain of the Queen's Guard on duty at Horse Guards he handled the unaccustomed job of rescuing the Prince of Wales from Drury Lane Theatre, near which had gathered a potentially threatening mob whilst the Bow Street police were on strike. What made him militarily interesting to serve with, however, was that he constituted the opposite of the public caricature perception of a cavalry officer as an incompetent fop. His opinions, after his Nile Expedition experiences, were determined: the cavalry should act as mounted infantry who then dismounted to shoot, a tactic much more likely to be effective than galloping with sword or lance. He deplored the Duke of Cambridge's custom of insisting at every annual inspection that the three household cavalry regiments should charge in line. That showed that the Duke still believed in shock cavalry tactics. Dundonald asserted in his autobiography that 'we hardly did anything essential for modern conditions of warfare'. He added that the Duke was liked by everyone – as a 'typical old-time gentleman'. It was a double-edged compliment. Dundonald's own insistence when he later became commanding officer was on improving marksmanship and mounting and dismounting skills. For the present he was second in command of the regiment and Adrian had to cope with the fact that he and the current commanding officer had different ideas on horse conditioning. The Commanding Officer, Colonel Hanning Lee, liked to see the chargers sleek and fat, to be the more impressive on ceremonial parade. When Hanning Lee was away on leave, Dundonald would change the regime and work the horses harder to make them fitter. Presumably Adrian ministered to both outcomes with equal care.

His service life was coming to an end. He would continue to live in London. Around him would be frequent reminders of his former profession: the military bands playing the music he enjoyed; the mounted sentries outside Horse Guards, their appearance unchanged until Edward VII ordered their carbines be replaced by the more ornamental cavalry sabres; the sittings for their portraits by the nation's generals and field marshals. But he would no longer be on the active list of officers. On 10 June, 1891, twenty years to the day after he re-entered the army at Weedon, and just under a quarter of a century since he first joined the Army Veterinary Service, he was placed on retired half-pay.

Thirteen days later he married for the second time.

Chapter Eight: 'Happiest Companionship' and 'Ugly Scandal' 1891-1894: Marriage, Chelsea and Controversy over Ghosts

'Miss Emma Wedlake, whom I took to the altar', wrote Adrian in *Memoirs*, referring for the first time to his second wife. His brief clause is not literally accurate. He set out from his Cheniston Gardens studio and she from her home in Chelsea Gardens, and they went not to church but to Kensington Register Office. It was 23 June 1891. Adrian, until the 10th of June an army veterinary surgeon, could now declare his profession to the registrar as solely 'Artist: Sculptor and Painter'. He was forty-six and a widower; his spinster bride was his junior by eleven years, and therefore the age his first wife Emma had been at the time of her death. Knowledge of Adrian's robust, straightforward personality discourages pseudo-psychological speculation along the lines that he wooed her because of her similarities to his first wife, but the resemblances, though probably coincidental, are remarkable. Like Emma Beckingham, Emma Wedlake was from a rural background (the Somerset coastal village of Watchet) and a large family of girls (she was the sixth of seven daughters). Exactly as at Adrian's first wedding, the witness from the bride's family at Kensington was the next daughter, again two years younger, and again named Elizabeth. Their father, Robert Wedlake, was a master mariner who was often away from home. After she finished school Emma worked as a dressmaker in Watchet but while still young had moved to London and by the time of the 1881 census was the head of her household in Clerkenwell with room enough for a visitor from Somerset and an elderly baker/servant. She gave her occupation as 'shopwoman'.

Almost needless to relate, Adrian divulges none of this private family information in *Memoirs*, but he does pay his wife warm tribute, and accepts that his reticence makes his words inadequate: 'Miss Emma Wedlake ... has given me very nearly forty years of the happiest companionship (and) has done much to take away the burden of the business affairs that weigh so heavily upon an artist; indeed, this is but a poor acknowledgement of all she has been to me.' Possibly Adrian drafted Chapter IV of his *Memoirs* early; certainly by the time the book appeared in late 1933 the nearly forty years had stretched to forty-two, and the marriage was to endure for a further four years until Adrian's death. Thereafter Emma continued to care for his works. As a widow, and in her will, she donated statuettes and paintings to bodies which she considered would value them, such as the Royal United Services Institute and Ludlow Grammar School.

Adrian had not led a sheltered life. As a soldier he must have been aware of prostitutes at the barrack gates and the application of the Contagious Diseases Act in garrison towns like Aldershot. As someone who moved in race-going social circles he would know of the Prince of Wales's string of mistresses. As an artist he knew both of models of easy virtue and of the loose life styles of fellow artists such as Rossetti, Whistler, Augustus John, Munnings and Rodin. But to his own married life he brought the same attitude that he brought to his regiment, faithful loyalty. He did not make a parade of this; it was simply part of being a Victorian gentleman. Nowhere in his writing or speeches does he hymn the Victorian middle-class ideal of modest womanhood,

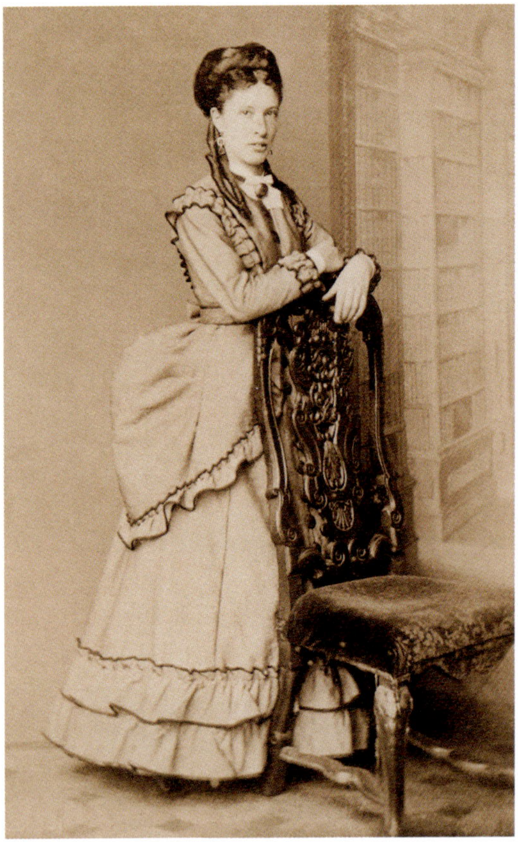

Emma Jones (née Wedlake), c.1891. The studio photograph was taken in London for her carte de visite. As befits a former dressmaker, she wears a highly fashionable dress which features an overskirt at the back.

and nowhere in his art does he indulge in moralising domestic genre canvases. In his sculptures the comparatively few studies of women are mainly of personified virtues such as Peace. As a soldier and a denizen of male clubland he accepted the prevailing view of separate spheres for men and women. But the divide was not absolute. Both his wives helped him in business, and he did not discourage women artists in their artistic hopes, having for them the fellow feeling of one who had sometimes been discouraged himself and who felt that he and they were inadequately recognised by the leading art schools. When Emmeline Lawrence's weekly suffragette journal *Votes for Women* splashed his Quadriga across its front page, he treasured his copy.

After their marriage Adrian and Emma moved to their new home at 147 Church Street (now Old Church Street) in Chelsea. In the garden they had a new studio built, big enough to enable Adrian to house his horse models and execute large-scale statues. The street they had chosen was not then fashionable or expensive. Onslow Gardens to the north and Cheyne Walk on Chelsea Embankment to the south were smarter. Church Street, far from being gentrified, was still a mix of the stables of the London General Omnibus Company and shops and workshops, with an emphasis on serving the neighbourhood's hundreds of horses. Some of the 18th-century houses were dilapidated, and in a survey carried out just six years previously five houses numbered between 125 and 151 and therefore close to 147 were found to be of ill-repute, with links between them arranged so that users of the premises could exit anonymously by a different way. However, the Chelsea scenes Whistler had painted had vanished. Muddy reaches of the Thames had been bulwarked behind the newly built Chelsea Embankment, and Cremorne House grounds, classed as a public nuisance, had closed. But Chelsea had more than maintained its reputation, established earlier by Turner, Holman Hunt, Rossetti, Whistler himself and others, as the place for artists. The area around the intersection of Church Street with King's Road, nicknamed the Latin Quarter, housed countless inexpensive studios and lodgings. These were home both to established artists and to beginners who after their studies, often in the artists' colonies in Antwerp or Paris, had come to Chelsea's colony of artists to start their careers. Church Street continued north to Fulham Road, where the big-name sculptors Edgar Boehm, Alfred Gilbert and Edward Poynter worked in studios which had begun life unglamorously as tradesmen's workshops, though from them had come the handsome end-product of the Onslow Gardens Estate. Other studios had had equally unglamorous origins as workshops built to prepare the 1851 Great Exhibition, but now the area breathed the glamour of bohemianism. It was an atmosphere with which Adrian and his bride were familiar, he through his circle of artist friends, she through having lived in Chelsea Gardens, just two streets west of Church Street. They took on the lease of no. 147 happily, and were to stay there together until Adrian died at home in 1938.

Chelsea had numerous pubs, but lacked the café society of Paris's Left Bank. Among artists, sculptors, who had the larger studios, hosted convivial 'at homes', but something more organised was required. The artist Tom Cross has chronicled the birth and life of the Chelsea Arts Club in *Artists and Bohemians*. In September 1890 the sculptor Stirling Lee called a formal meeting in his studio with the aim of establishing an exhibiting society to be called the Chelsea Art Club, but a month later a follow-up meeting at which Whistler was present decided Chelsea needed a social club more than an exhibiting society and that the club should be 'Bohemian' in character. Stirling Lee became the first chairman, the committee included William Frith and Jimmy Whistler, and six months later the Club was inaugurated at 181 Kings Road. That would be its home, and a second home to the member artists living nearby, for the next decade, until it moved in next door to Adrian at 143-5 Church Street. The main feature of its mess room was a long second-hand dining table seating at least twenty, deliberately chosen to encourage comradeship and discourage cliques. A second room upstairs provided further opportunities for sociability, newspaper reading and playing cards or chess. Whistler, witty clubman and bon viveur, Bohemian in behaviour if not in dress, might have seemed the obvious choice for chairman, but there was some feeling that his Presidency of the Royal Society of British Artists had been high-handed and that his style was therefore potentially inappropriate for a social club, but he did chair the subcommittee which dealt with rules and elections. When the Musée de Luxembourg bought the portrait of his mother at a good price, the members celebrated with a reception at the club in his honour in December 1891. All the Club members signed a parchment of greetings as 'a record of their high appreciation of the distinguished honour that had come to him by the placing of his mother's portrait in the national collection of France'. As Adrian observed, 'We all took the greatest interest in the life and work of our contemporaries who had arrived.' Whistler's speech of thanks concluded with an unexpected witticism: 'It is right at such a time of peace, after the struggle, to bury the hatchet – in the side of the enemy – and leave it there.' To quote Adrian again: 'Undoubtedly, Jimmy combined dignity with impudence.'

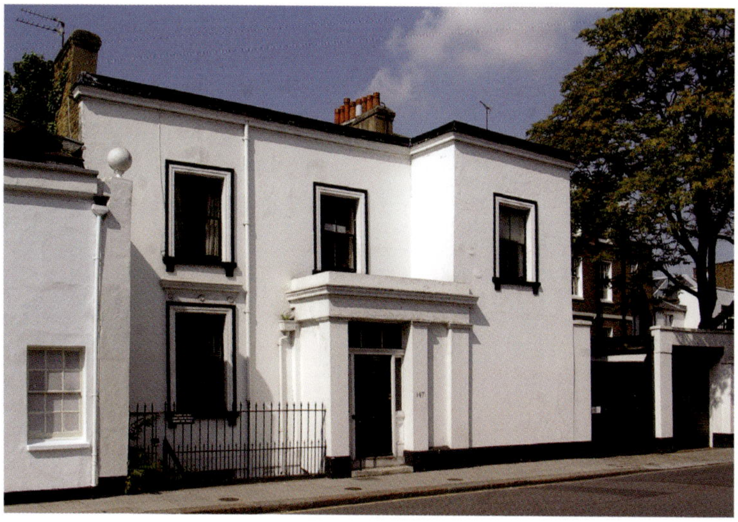

147 Church Street (now Old Church Street), Chelsea, the home of Adrian and Emma from 1891 to 1938. Since then the house has been given the name Adrian House, and the Chelsea Arts Club is still next door, left of picture.

Freed from the army though still in touch with it, he was enjoying his life of marriage, clubland and art. To his membership of the Savage Club he now added membership of the Wigwam, a dining group founded in 1879 by Savage Club members wearied of that club's insufficiently varied menu of traditional fare, familiarly referred to as 'roast or boiled missionary'. The Wigwam members met monthly in the evening at some hospitable hostelry, no guests allowed, and apart from a brief formality of the reading of minutes devoted themselves to dining, perhaps an anecdotal speech, and 'story-telling by some of the best raconteurs in London'. It was the kind of within-bounds conviviality which Adrian enjoyed, in the company of both old acquaintances such as G.A. Henty and Melton Prior, and a widening group of new friends. He remained a member all his life.

Any evening indulgence was worked off the next morning. Early each day Emma and he rode in Hyde Park's Rotten Row. 'To be sure, the regulated paces of that fashionable course were a bit slow for a hunting man', but he found the exercise adequate for keeping him fit, and though he missed galloping over open country he had the compensations of 'happy and pleasant social companionship' and time to appraise the turn-out and seat of the riders. (Lord Ribblesdale 'did as much justice to his horse as he did to his tailor'; and 'the most polished and accomplished horsewoman to be seen in the Row was Miss Haines; none of her sex looked quite so well on horseback'. As the latter judgement was based on side-saddle riding skills rather than any other attribute, presumably it did not grieve Emma.)

As one would expect, *Memoirs* does not mention Lily Langtry's daily canters in Hyde Park. Adrian is more concerned to pay tribute to the mounted policemen who knew precisely when to intervene and when to make allowances for capable riders who could bend the regulations without causing risk to others. In good weather the pleasures of riding might seduce the Joneses into spending longer on the Row than planned, but nevertheless the riding was always the prelude to a morning of vigorous work in the studio. Adrian felt the early work-outs gave him the energy he needed to cope with his heavy workload. That workload was threefold: paintings of their favourite horses for cavalry officers; paintings of winners of the major horseracing classics for their wealthy owners; and the preparation of a major sculpture for exhibition in a gallery or the Royal Academy. Yet despite his seven successful submissions by 1891 to its Summer Exhibitions, the Academy still did not embrace him. In its report on Private View day for the RA's 1890 Old Masters Exhibition the *Daily News* recorded the names from 'society' and from the worlds of politics, letters, the arts and the sciences to whom Sir Frederick Leighton played host, then added, almost at the end of its full account, 'and of the not generally favoured outsiders, those who obtained admission on Saturday included ... Mr Adrian Jones'. Yet Adrian was still unaware that some Royal Academicians felt resentful envy of his successes, which owed nothing to the RA schools: 'I was not conscious of any handicap.' But now the tendency to view him as an 'outsider' transmuted into an attempt at full ostracism.

Duncan's Horses

Still unconscious of all the feeling against him at the Academy, at the 1891 RA exhibition Adrian exhibited a modified version of the Assyrian driving a four-horsed chariot he had made at Sir Coutts Lindsay's request some time earlier. He gave this new version the title 'Triumph, design for a quadriga' (exhibit 1962). To continue the story in his own words:

> This work of mine was so fortunate as to attract the attention of the Prince of Wales who saw it at an Academy banquet and afterwards sent for me. In the course of my visit he made a proposal that filled me with astonishment and pleasure. This was that the Arch on the top of Constitution Hill ... would make an ideal site for a quadriga to be founded on the one he had admired at Burlington House [the home of the Royal Academy] ... With this great encouragement I made an elaborate sketch-drawing and in order to see the ensemble, a photograph of my group was placed on this drawing. When the work was clearly outlined in my mind, I decided to call upon Sir Frederick Leighton and ask him whether, as President of the Royal Academy and of the Art Department of the State, he would say a good word for me, if the idea matured, the sketch-model being then on exhibition at the Royal Academy. Sir Frederick replied quite frankly that 'he had his own friends to look after', and that, moreover, I had not yet gained any experience in modelling a colossal group. This was correct enough but I assured him I could do the large work far better than the sketch-design. He replied dryly:

> 'We all think that we can, until we try,' and he declined to give me any encouragement, but before I left I said: 'Sir Frederick, I will send to the next exhibition at the Royal Academy a life-size group.' I was hardly outside the door before reason began to remonstrate at the top of her voice and to suggest that I had been undertaking too much because I had not in my mind at that moment even an idea for the group.

Rebuffed, without an idea in his mind, but absolutely determined to prove himself, he went for a walk along Chelsea Embankment, near his new home in Church Street. As he walked, his mind was not on the scenery but on visualising in his imagination possible large statuary groups. Perhaps not surprisingly, his own mental calm having been disturbed by Leighton, there came to mind one of those moments in Shakespeare when disorder in the world of man is reflected in disorder in the universe at large. He recalled the discord in Macbeth's Scotland after the murder of King Duncan. Day turned to night and the natural order of things was upset. And the key memory, as anyone who knew his interests might have forecast, was of the moment of disorder in the animal kingdom when Duncan's horses 'turned wild in nature'. He had his idea.

He made sketches, first with two horses and then with three. For modelling the most difficult of the three horse poses, he went to a knacker for a dead horse and fixed the corpse in a field in the exact position required so that he could model accurately. Having worked with furious energy, he sent the completed plaster cast, ten feet high and eight feet wide at the base, to the Royal Academy in 1892 as 'Duncan's Horses'. On varnishing day, Royal Academicians admired it. The *Times* reported: 'Mr Adrian Jones has courage, can model horses and group them', while another critic designated it the finest thing in the Academy's Central Hall, and the *Sporting Life* suggested that 'Duncan's Horses' should be acquired for the nation and erected in a public place.

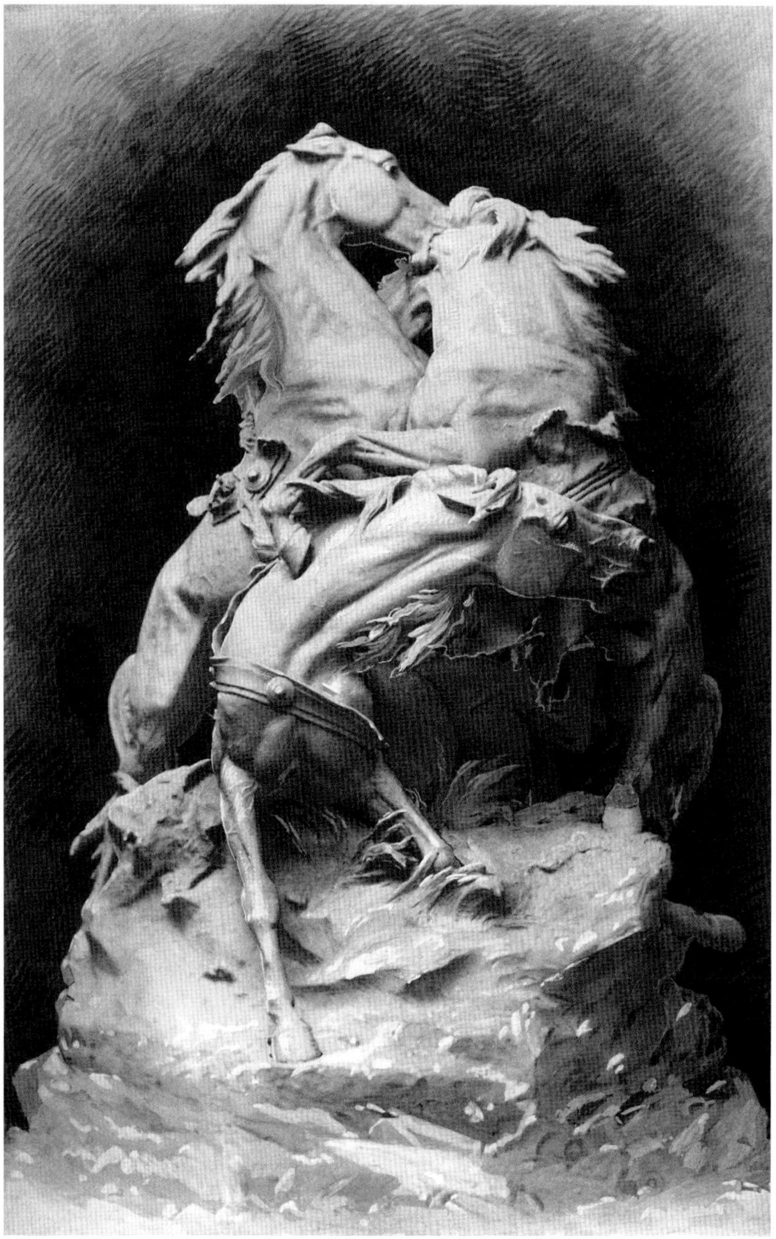

Duncan's Horses, plaster cast statue, RA exhibit, 1892

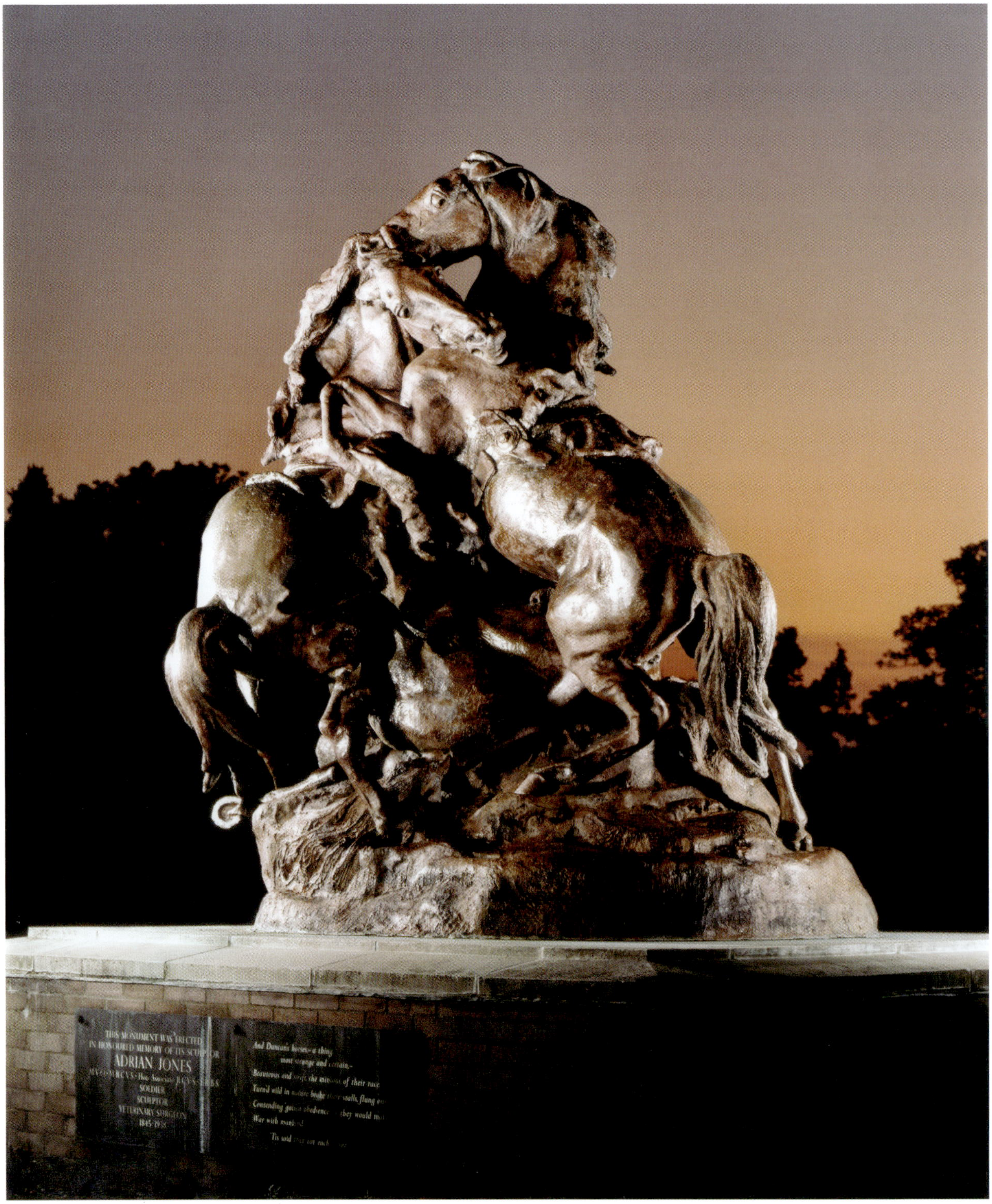

Duncan's Horses, plaster cast, on its plinth at the Royal Veterinary College before conservation and casting in bronze

'The heavens, as troubled with man's act,
Threatens his bloody stage'

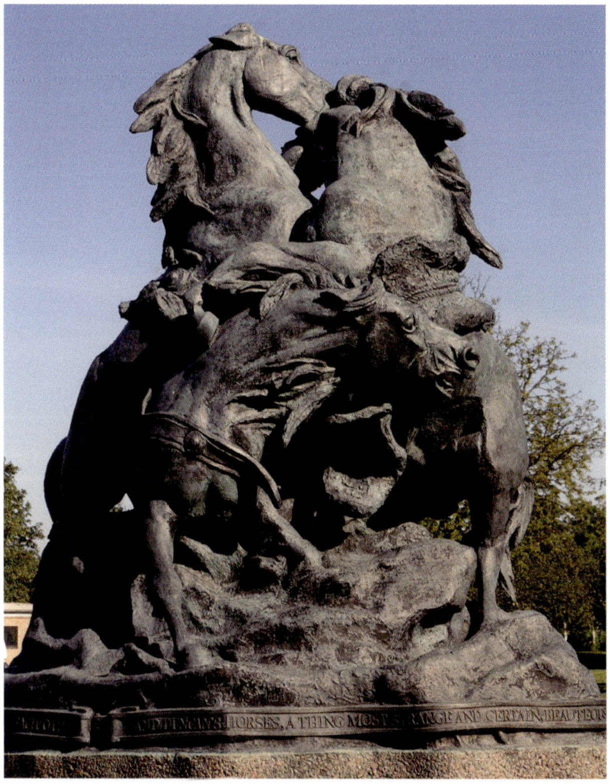

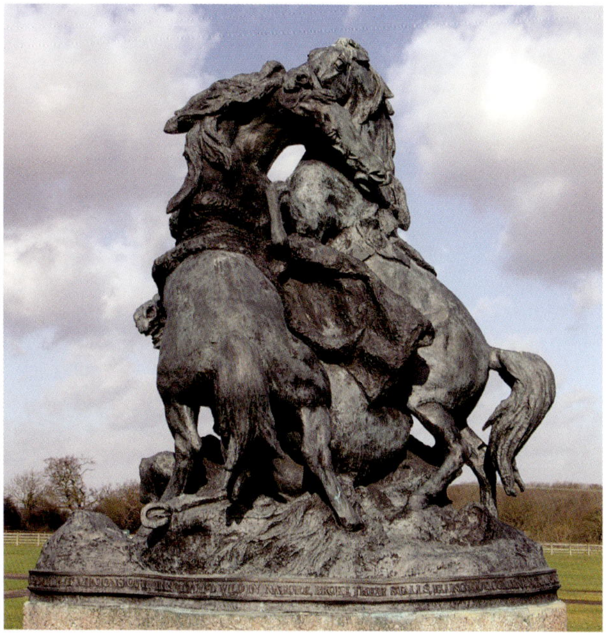

Duncan's Horses:
Right: Close-up as seen from College entrance side
Left: Close-up, far side
Below: Detail: 'Tis said they eat each other'

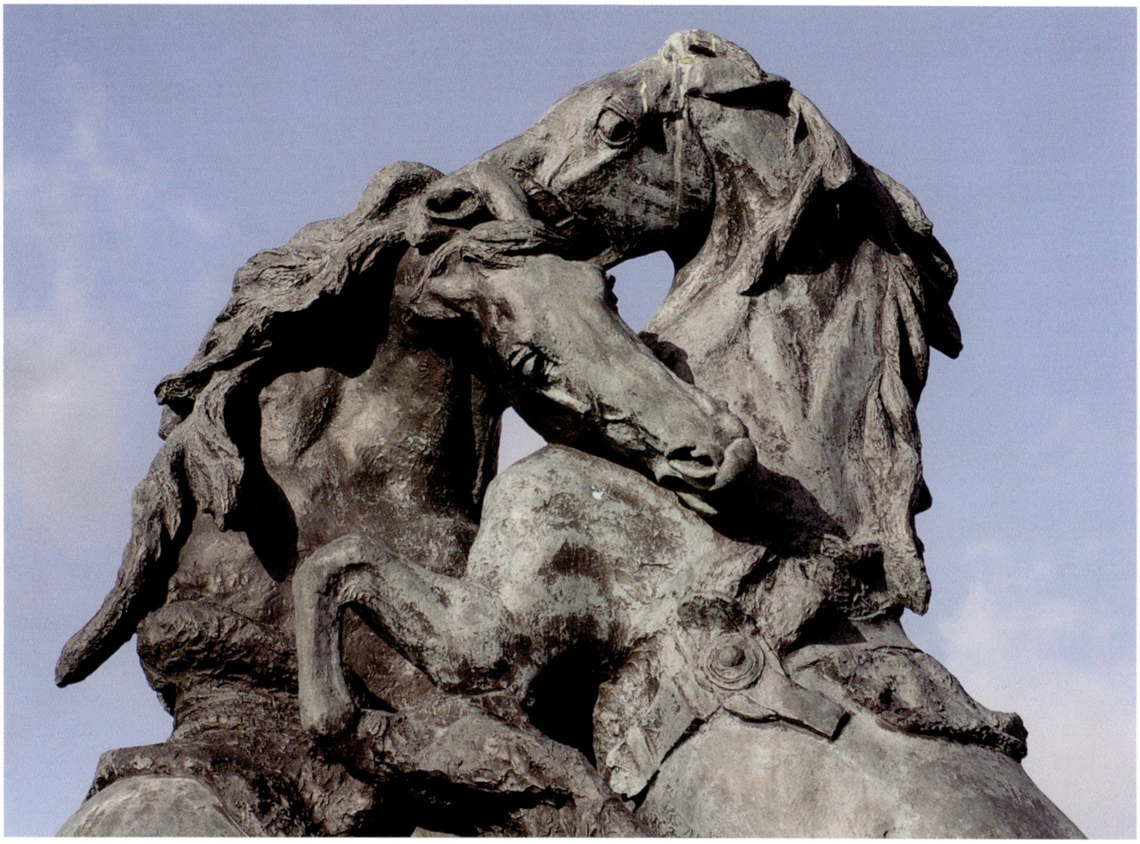

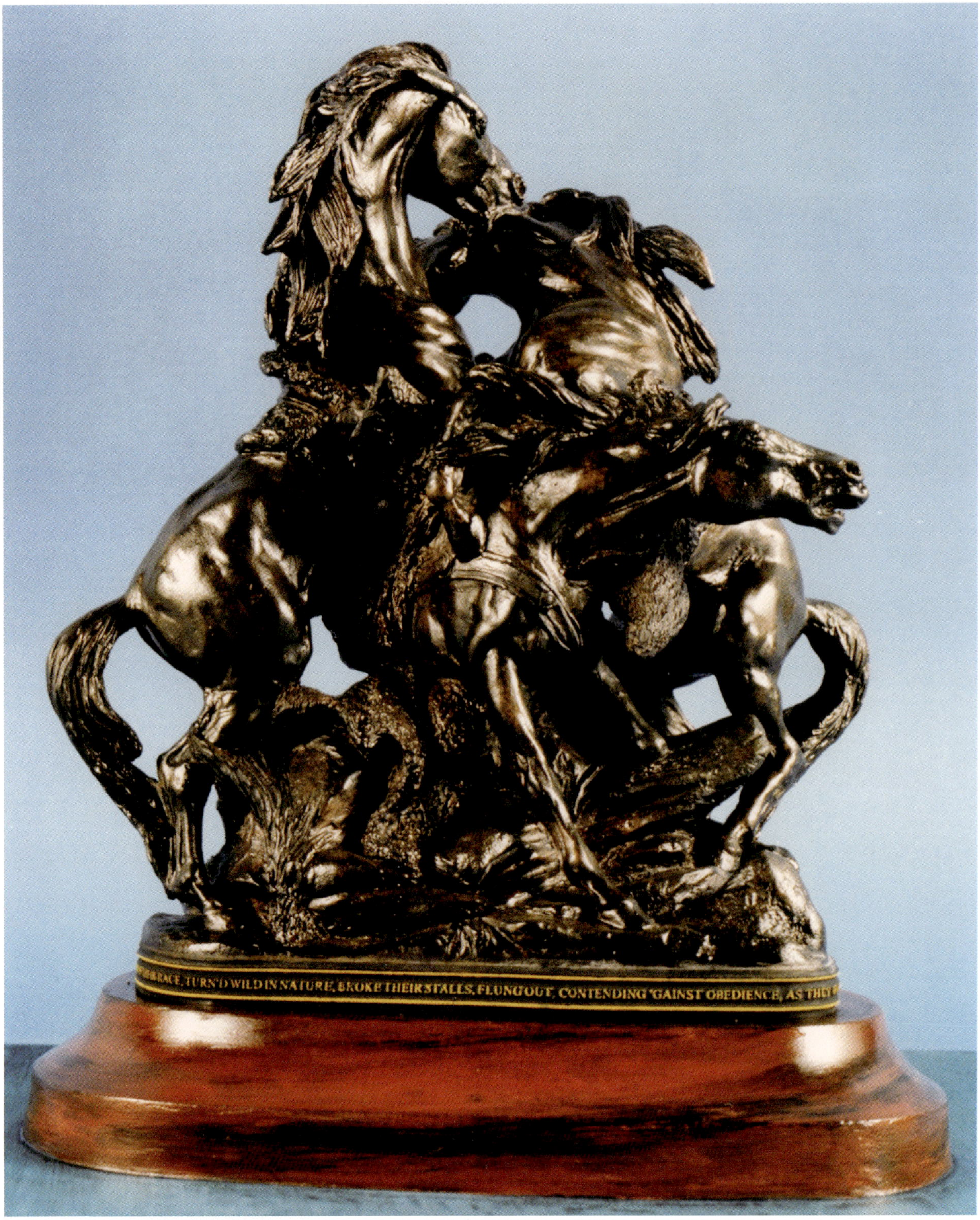

Duncan's Horses, bronze statuette. A limited series of this maquette was sold in aid of HRH The Duke of Edinburgh's Appeal for the casting of the statue in bronze, 1985.

When Adrian encountered the Royal Academicians gathered at the large statue on varnishing day, someone asked, 'Which is the front?' He replied, 'Any part you like. Good sculpture can be regarded from any point of view.' Perhaps the RAs felt that this fellow Jones, who only a year previously had still been a spare-time artist, had overreached himself in thus advising them, products of the Royal Academy schools, on how to view sculpture. He relates that, in a bunch and rather huffily, they deserted him and his statue. Yet his answer, if a touch tactless, was sound enough. 'Duncan's Horses' is a statue which absolutely demands the viewer to walk round it – and not just to read all of the quotation from Shakespeare around its base.

Confident that his reputation had been enhanced, Adrian set off for Paris to fulfil a commission to paint France's finest horses. The *Morning* newspaper saw these commissions as 'one up' to the English. Its correspondent enjoyed reporting 'the interesting fact that a member of the English school [i.e. Adrian] has been for some time on the other side of 'the silver streak' [i.e. the English Channel!] painting the first and second horses in the Grand Prix, together with several French fathers of the stud, and racehorses in training. These commissions may be regarded by Mr Adrian Jones as a distinguished compliment, not only to himself, but through him, to the English school.' The writer, revelling in the greater number of words which could be fitted into a Victorian column because of the packed typesetting favoured in even the most popular press, clearly believed that an 'interesting fact' is enhanced by the occasional decorative circumlocution (and surely 'fathers of the stud' is rather splendid for 'sires'), but he still leaves himself space for interesting observations. He points out that 'an impressionist portrait painter of horses has yet to rise into favour in the land that engendered the Impressionists' – Dufy's horseracing scenes were still far in the future – and is confident that because Adrian is 'of the conservative school' and his works manifest 'anatomical knowledge' there is no reason why he should not eventually prove a successor to such as Stubbs and Landseer 'as a painter of high-mettled cattle' (i.e. horses!)

'Ghost Story'

The *Morning* article, containing no hint of forthcoming troubles for Adrian, appeared in the third week of July, 1892. But when Adrian had been leaving for the Paris painting trip, he had been advised to read the current issue of the *Magazine of Art*. Accordingly, he had read the article 'Ghost Story', though 'without any immediate thought that it could possibly be aimed at me'. The article had named no names; nevertheless, the author clearly sought to impose pack drill followed by dismissal in disgrace. A friend in Paris awoke Adrian to the reality that the unsigned article's insinuations were directed at him. He abandoned his painting trip and returned to London to face the 'Ghost' scandal.

Because the heated controversy hurt him deeply, he gives it great space in his *Memoirs*. Seen from a century later, the length seems disproportionate. The week of the scandal debate, recounted in a brief chapter and a long appendix, occupies a quarter of the book. The other three quarters cover a life which at the date of his autobiography's publication had filled eighty-eight years with interest and incident. It is true that the scars of the week of interviews and correspondence in *The Morning* and other journals persisted much longer, and indeed probably never quite healed, yet Adrian recognised that, as he had succeeded in clearing his name, the wounding allegations would not finally affect history's judgement on him. In the Epilogue which immediately precedes the lengthy Appendix, he looks forward 'to future generations, when all the working of cliques and petty jealousies is dead and forgotten'. In a biography they cannot be 'forgotten', for Adrian's attitude in 1892 and afterwards matters, but they may be considered here more briefly.

The July 1892 issue of the *Magazine of Art* contained an unsigned, unattributed paragraph which informed readers that 'the sculptor's 'ghost' has resumed his work in the exhibition rooms of the Royal Academy ... with extraordinary effrontery'. It went on to give a highly sympathetic portrait of this metaphorical ghost.

Apparently in reality the ghost was 'an artist of talent' whose works because of 'public ignorance and neglect' had not found buyers, and so he has been driven by 'his patient life of unrequited toil, of neglected talent, and unmerited poverty' to take up a position of paid assistant to another sculptor. It is upon this other 'so-called sculptor' that the anonymous writer heaps his 'emphatic condemnation': rogues of that ilk, 'lacking alike artistic intelligence and honesty', exploit the assistant and take the credit and emoluments for the 'artistic merit' supplied by the brains, genius and powers of execution of the assistant. Righteously, Anon proclaims it has been necessary 'to point the matter out in view of the success of at least one prominent work at the Royal Academy'. Happily for Anon, however, in his view the exploiting sculptor's behaviour in fooling the 'purblind and ignorant public' is 'too contemptible to need further exposition'. Therefore he avoids naming him – and equally avoids risk of being sued for defamation.

Nevertheless, at the end of July the *Morning* thought the matter would end up in the law courts, for though the general public were mystified, few in the art world had any doubt as to the person pointed at. Again, no names appeared in print, but the paper's opinion was on the side of the accused. 'He is a man of great ability', it told its readers:

> It remains for the accuser to sustain his charge ... The accuser says that the sculptor, being without artistic training, is incapable of producing the Academy work in question, and the suggestion is that the production in question is really the work of ... an assistant who possesses the artistic education required ... The reply is that certainly the artist has employed an assistant, as do all sculptors engaged in heavy work, but that the sculptor in question was the actual designer.

Warming to Adrian's defence, the paper said of the accusers:

> A curious process of reasoning has been employed, which seems to be academical in the worst sense of the word. A certain sculptor, says Authority, has not had the advantage of proper training, yet he has produced masterly works, therefore, he must get somebody, who has had the orthodox schooling, to do the work for him ... But it is very unsafe to argue about genius as you may argue about academic talent ... English art authorities would do well to remember that genius has continued to find adequate expression, even before the institution of the Royal Academy, or of its half-empty strangely eclectic schools.

With the debate raging so vehemently, and with accusers labelling Adrian a trickster and defenders proclaiming his genius, unsurprisingly, on the Monday after Saturday's *Morning* published its stirring case for the defence, letters to the editor joined in. 'Sculptor' (still more anonymity) referred to the example of the President of the Royal Academy himself, Lord Leighton, who had used Thomas Brock, RA, as an assistant, yet no one had thought to doubt Leighton's ability to do his work without such assistance. 'Sculptor' had taken the trouble to ask brother sculptors whether 'the man aimed at' had done other equally important works without assistance. The answer had been 'undoubtedly'. 'Sculptor' concluded his letter with a general observation: 'The editor of the *Magazine of Art* himself deplores the difficulties an artist has to encounter in his struggle for praise and fortune, and he must know that one of the hardest to overcome is the hostility of brother artists who have made a position and who put everything possible in the way of one who might become a competitor with them for commissions.'

The suspicion that the scandalous accusations were motivated not by a selfless concern for the sanctity of art but by a wish to eliminate unwelcome competition often enters the debate. Adrian mentioned it the day after the letter of 'Sculptor' appeared, when he gave an interview to *The Morning*. He began by using the paper to issue a statement:

> I herewith challenge the President and Council of the Royal Academy, or any other person, to formulate some definite charge against me and publicly to name me as the individual referred to in the *Magazine of Art* ... I undertake to proceed at once by legal action against my accuser or accusers.

That gauntlet thrown down, Adrian told how he had returned to London to search 'for a clue to the circulator of the lie, but without avail'. However, since then, 'one of the best-known men in London has taken my case up and I think we now have sufficient evidence'. Presumably this means he hired or received help from a detective or investigative lawyer. He continues by giving a remarkably detailed, but regrettably not finally revelatory, description of his suspect.

> The man I believe to be my accuser holds one of the highest positions the world of art can bestow – mind you, I do not say it is the highest ... You ask me what object had this gentleman in view when he started the slander? Jealousy and dislike were his chief objects. You must know the man I suspect is eaten up with conceit and self-admiration. He has a great objection – in fact a strong dislike – to any man rising from the ranks; and I have risen from them and am justly proud of it. Some years ago he said to me, 'You have only sent us in small sculpture, why not try something big?' I promised him I would and the next year I exhibited a large piece at the Academy and the work was praised high and low. My success seems to have annoyed him, however, and probably my obtaining some commission, which he had expected to come to his studio, did not increase his love for me.

Even when quoted only in extract, that is an extraordinary interview. Anyone reading it, whether in 1892 or today, must be tempted to play amateur detective with the clues provided. Elsewhere in *Memoirs* Adrian had quoted Leighton's own words that he was 'a prig about drawing' and would never give house-room to any picture not 'wellnigh perfect' in that skill. So is he perhaps the suspect 'eaten up with conceit'? Adrian also comments that Leighton is 'extraordinarily good' as a draughtsman. That might cause 'self-admiration', albeit pardonably, and might perhaps again suggest Leighton? And the story of the unnamed instigator of the scandal provoking Adrian into the promise to produce a large sculpture, and Adrian fulfilling the challenge and exhibiting a major work to broad acclaim at the next year's Academy Summer Exhibition, strongly suggests a retelling of the story of Leighton's role in the genesis of 'Triumph' and 'Duncan's Horses'. But then what interpretation is the reader meant to give to Adrian adding to 'one of the highest positions the world of art can bestow' the qualification 'mind you, I do not say it is the highest'? In 1892 Leighton had been President of the Royal Academy for eighteen years. The Victorian establishment viewed the Royal Academy's President as the art world's equivalent to the Prime Minister in politics. Is Adrian therefore eliminating Leighton from the list of suspects? Is the implication that the scandalmonger was some other member of the RA Council, or perhaps the influential editor of the *Magazine of Art*, Mr Spielmann, who had used the gravitas of the editorial 'we' in publicising the 'ghost' gossip? Or might the qualification be no more than a demeaning aside questioning the status of a top man who did not truly deserve the title? The answer remains unknown.

A second extraordinary feature of the interview is Adrian's outburst of vituperation. Normally he is generous in his references to others. Indeed, those of his 1930s readers who shared the increasing opinion that the British generals of the 1914-18 War had been 'donkeys' might have felt he was generous to a fault. So it is to an extent surprising that he does not make it clear whether he is exculpating or implicating the President of the Royal Academy. After all, there was potential for some sympathy for and some appreciation of Leighton. Because of his part-German background, though he became very much an establishment figure, Leighton had initially been thought of as an outsider. The RA hanging committee had rejected some of his best pictures often enough for him to suspect that they were biased against him. When he had become President of the RA he had encouraged sculptors and given them better display space. The detailed naturalistic musculature of Leighton's own sculpture, 'Achilles Wrestling With A Python', exhibited at the RA in 1877, must have impressed Adrian when he saw it, and was generally credited with giving inaugural impetus to the 'New Sculpture' movement. However, that was one of probably no more than three life-size sculptures Leighton made, and the task had taken him three years. So his volatile temperament may well have been enviously irritated when, having been dismissive of Adrian as not one of 'his own friends' and as someone too inexperienced to be capable of modelling a large group, he was countered by Adrian's promise to produce something life-size within a year. He may also have been piqued that the Prince of Wales, who had helped him to the Presidency of the RA, was now apparently favouring the possibility of a commission for the highly prestigious site of the Wellington Arch being given to this comparatively inexperienced and unquestionably untrained sculptor who had only just ceased being a career army officer. Whatever the trigger or triggers for dislike, it is clear that Adrian, who rubbed along happily with a wide variety of other men, did not get on with Leighton. Their personalities were far apart. The one rejoiced in social companionship; the other, when he designed his palatial house in Holland Park, did not include a single guest bedroom.

Adrian told his interviewer, 'I have called at his house' [that of the suspected accuser] 'with the object of having the matter out face to face with him but, unfortunately for me, he was not at home'. But, just as everywhere else in the press debate on the scandal, no name is given. The identity of the man responsible remains concealed. One wishes that when, forty years after the 'Ghost' scandal, Adrian set down the story of his life, he had left in their dark drawer all the issues of the *Morning* and the other papers which his sense of outrage in 1892 had led him to store as potential ammunition in a legal battle. Their too numerous pages could have been replaced by a brief passage mentioning as matter of historical fact whom he had suspected at the time. The tone, as far as possible, could have reflected 'all passion spent', and there would have been no need to make live accusations. However, if the suspect had been a revered public name, Adrian perhaps felt it better not to revive any debate. Leighton, for instance, although his pictures were not fetching good prices in the 1930s, had been ennobled as a lord just before his death, and his death itself, as his body lay in state in the Royal Academy before burial in St Paul's, had been a national event. Those, art historians and others, wishing for certainty must remain disappointed.

After the reported interview with Adrian, Appendix One to his autobiography continues for a further thirty-seven pages: articles, letters and five more interviews. The subject matter becomes repetitive. On one hand, there are the views of those who argued that the unnamed sculptor had not put in the years of steady practice necessary to achieve the techniques of sculpture and the standard of manual dexterity shown in the unspecified sculpture. On the other hand, there is the evidence of friends, sometimes writing under a nom de plume, that they had personally seen the unnamed sculptor sketching out the original designs for the unspecified sculpture and that as a masterly sculptor he had no superior in his special line of work. The absence of names finally makes the debate, so real to its participants, almost surreal for the reader. The most vivid contributions come from the interviews given by Adrian's mentor Charles Birch and by Sir Frederick Leighton. Birch roundly dismissed as 'all nonsense' the idea that the sculptor had not had time enough to learn the technique of sculpture. Leighton, when asked if 'the group in question' bore the mark of the sculptor's 'particular talent', could not bring himself to say more than 'I am really unable to say', but had no hesitation in declaring 'You want to know who the accuser is? I do not know, and if I did, I should not tell you.'

It was left to a now forgotten journal, the *Hawk,* to place a spirited conclusion on the week of debate:

> This is a terrible business. This man's days are made unendurable and his nights hideous by the consciousness that everywhere the finger of suspicion is pointed against him and that he can do absolutely nothing to clear himself of the charge which is aimed against his fame and his daily bread. Now, is this fair, or what is usually called the English spirit?

Let us allow the debate to rest there.

But there was to be an epilogue. Adrian was by now a committee member of the Savage Club. A decade earlier, a member, C.B. Lawes, had won a court case concerning another sculptor using a 'ghost' and now had given an interview to the *Morning* in which he said he had no personal knowledge of the current debate but made the standard case for the prosecution that only long practice could give a sculptor the power to execute his conceptions. When the Savages reassembled for the autumn Lawes wrote to the Committee. For the first time Adrian's name appeared. 'A man of honour [would] not permit his name to appear upon the Committee of his Club until such time as he was enabled to re-establish his good name before the public. Mr Jones has not taken this course.' He called for Adrian to be taken off the Committee. The Committee's instant response was to invite Lawes to substantiate his slur or withdraw. Of course he could not substantiate it, so without prevarication he withdrew his charge of dishonourable conduct – 'and, at the same time, I desire to express my sorrow and regret at having made any charge against him'.

The allegations against Adrian died. He felt pleased to have his honourable reputation vindicated, and to have retained the confidence of his patrons, as commissions continued to come in. But 1893 ended in sadness, with the death in mid-October of Charles Birch, Adrian's consistently helpful friend, who had first inspired him to take up sculpture. Adrian had stayed close to him and his family; indeed, the second witness at his wedding to Emma Wedlake had been Birch's nephew, Georg von Pirch. In its obituary the *Queen* described Birch as 'singularly amiable in disposition ... incapable of aught that could wound the feelings of others'. The group of friends and relations, including Adrian, who followed his coffin to the graveside was large. The coffin was completely covered in wreaths, noticeable among them those from the Savage and Wigwam Clubs. But only two Royal Academicians, one of them Thomas Brock who with Birch had been a leading assistant to John Foley, attended this funeral of their RA Associate. The *Mid Counties Express* commented:

> It is assumed that Adrian Jones will be the next Associate. That he is Birch's natural successor goes without saying, but the ways of the Royal Academy are so mysterious that we must be prepared for any surprises. By the way, it was generally remarked at the funeral that Burlington House had omitted to send a wreath. If it was an oversight it was unpardonable, and still more so if it arose from any other cause.

The suspicion lingered that even in death Birch remained unforgiven for his tutoring and encouragement of the outsider Adrian Jones.

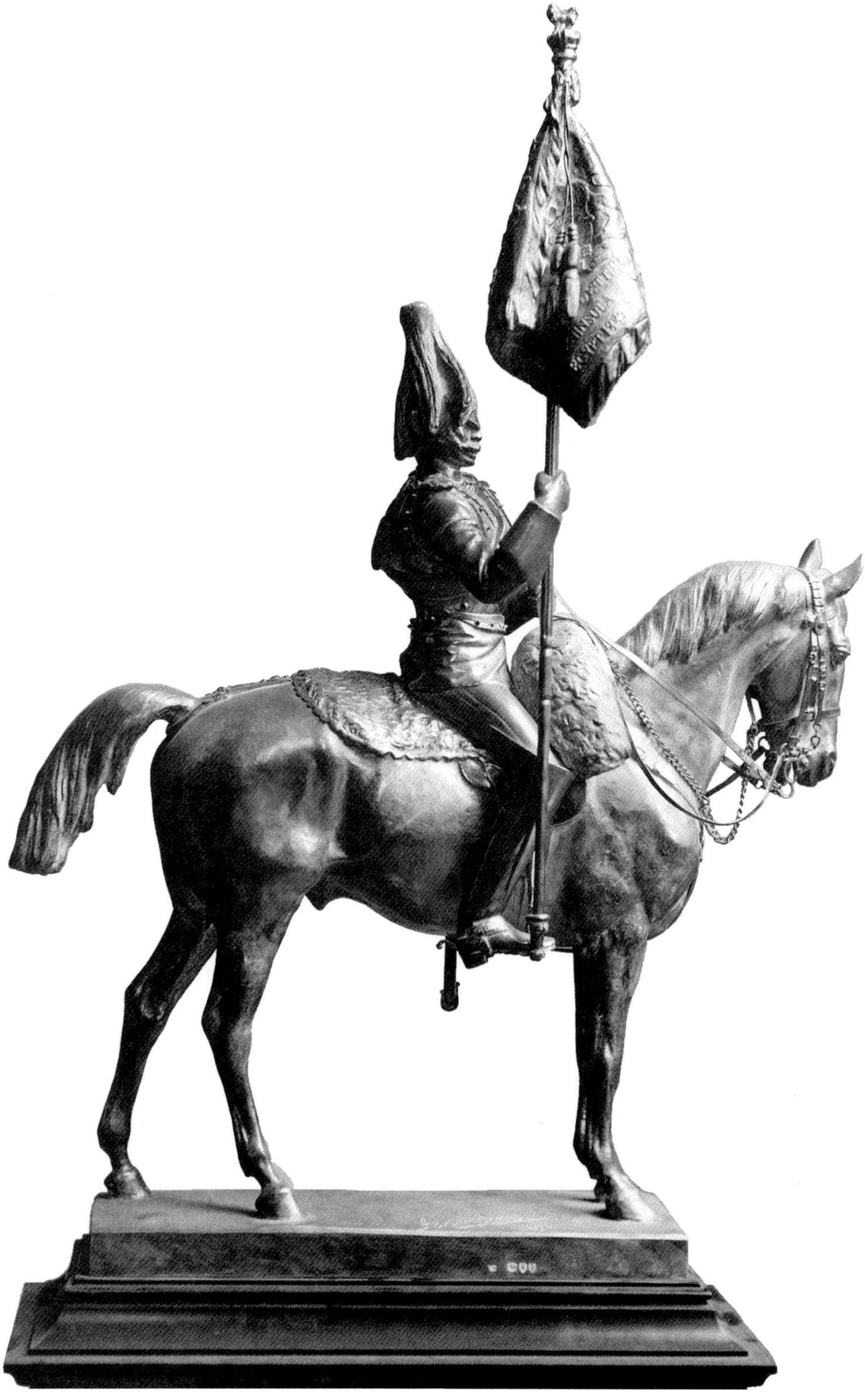

Royal Standard Bearer, silver statuette, 1893

The Royal Standard Bearer

After his account of the 'Ghost' slander in chapter 6 of *Memoirs*, Adrian opened the next chapter in his book and his life with:

> No man who desires to express the best that is in him can afford to brood over his troubles; he must set them aside and get along with the job. This is what I did when the last echoes of the 'Ghost' scandal had died down, and I was left to work in peace. I was fortunate in my friends and a trouble of the kind I had experienced puts friendship to the acid test ... My brother officers did not doubt my *bona fides,* and in 1893 the officers of the 2nd Life Guards commissioned me to model a statuette of a mounted Royal Standard Bearer and to have it cast in silver for presentation to their Royal Highnesses the Duke and Duchess of York, on the occasion of their marriage.

This commission was a vote of trust and confidence indeed, for since the death of his elder brother Eddy the previous year, George, Duke of York, had become after his father the heir to the throne. Doubtless behind the scenes the senior officers of the 2nd Life Guards had checked with Prince Edward, who was Colonel-in-Chief of the Household Cavalry, that the choice of artist to create his son's wedding present was acceptable. Edward had no hesitation. As Adrian put it, 'I was honoured by the confidence of the first gentleman in the land'. The expression 'first gentleman' is foremost an objective description of the Prince of Wales's royal position, but Adrian would not have chosen it had he not wished implicitly to endorse its favourable evaluation. His broad humanity liked Edward's broad humanity. At this time too he probably had some fellow feeling for Edward's own treatment by the press, in which innuendoes often referred to the current royal favourite Lady Daisy Brooke, sometimes without naming names, on occasion using the transparent disguise 'Lady River'.

The Prince's support was not in the public view. The welcome open support was that of the 2nd Life Guards officers alongside whom Adrian had served. Adrian's supporters ranged from Colonel Hanning-Lee, his last commanding officer and still in command in 1893, and Lord Dundonald, the second-in-command, down to the Earl of Longford, who had been the regiment's most junior subaltern when Adrian finished his service. (Six years later Adrian made the gift of an oil painting on the occasion of the Earl's own wedding to Lady Villiers.) When the silver statuette was completed, the regiment arranged a private viewing in Knightsbridge Barracks. Invitations went to Adrian's friends and army acquaintances. Amongst these, the Duke of Cambridge, still the army's Commander-in-Chief, praised the work with the knowledge and discernment of a cavalry officer accustomed to looking at horses. Adrian particularly appreciated that praise, for the general opinion on the Duke after his lifetime of reviews and inspections was that 'there was no better judge of a mounted soldier'.

The wedding of George to Princess May of Teck took place on 3 July 1893 in the Chapel Royal of St James's Palace. The newly wed couple departed on honeymoon to Sandringham. The wedding presents were displayed in the Imperial Institute in South Kensington, opened two months previously by the Prince of Wales and Queen Victoria to the accompaniments of an orchestra conducted by Sir Arthur Sullivan and a gun salute, and the public queued for hours to view the *Royal Standard Bearer* and the other gifts. Once the statuette was restored to the future George V, it sat on his dining table, and on several occasions he told Adrian how pleased he was to see it there. In 1895 another admirer of it, Lord Dundonald, presented a virtually identical silver to the officers of the 2nd Life Guards as a regimental challenge trophy.

The twenty-six-inch-high statuette depicts a corporal major of the Life Guards holding upright the royal standard. He is mounted, on parade on his disciplined horse, ready for state duty. As befits its role, the horse is fit – witness the lean flank – yet sturdy, able to carry the well-built rider and the extra weight of his pieces of dress armour, sword and standard. Adrian has not recorded which horse he used as a model. Had the commission come a few years later, he would certainly have chosen the 2nd Life Guards' most famous horse, Freddy of Paardeburg, which had returned from hard campaigning in the Boer War, and after time for recuperation had uniquely been declared fit again for state duty. A photograph taken in 1902 shows Freddy in exactly the same position as Adrian's statuette, left hind leg slightly back and the royal standard bearer on

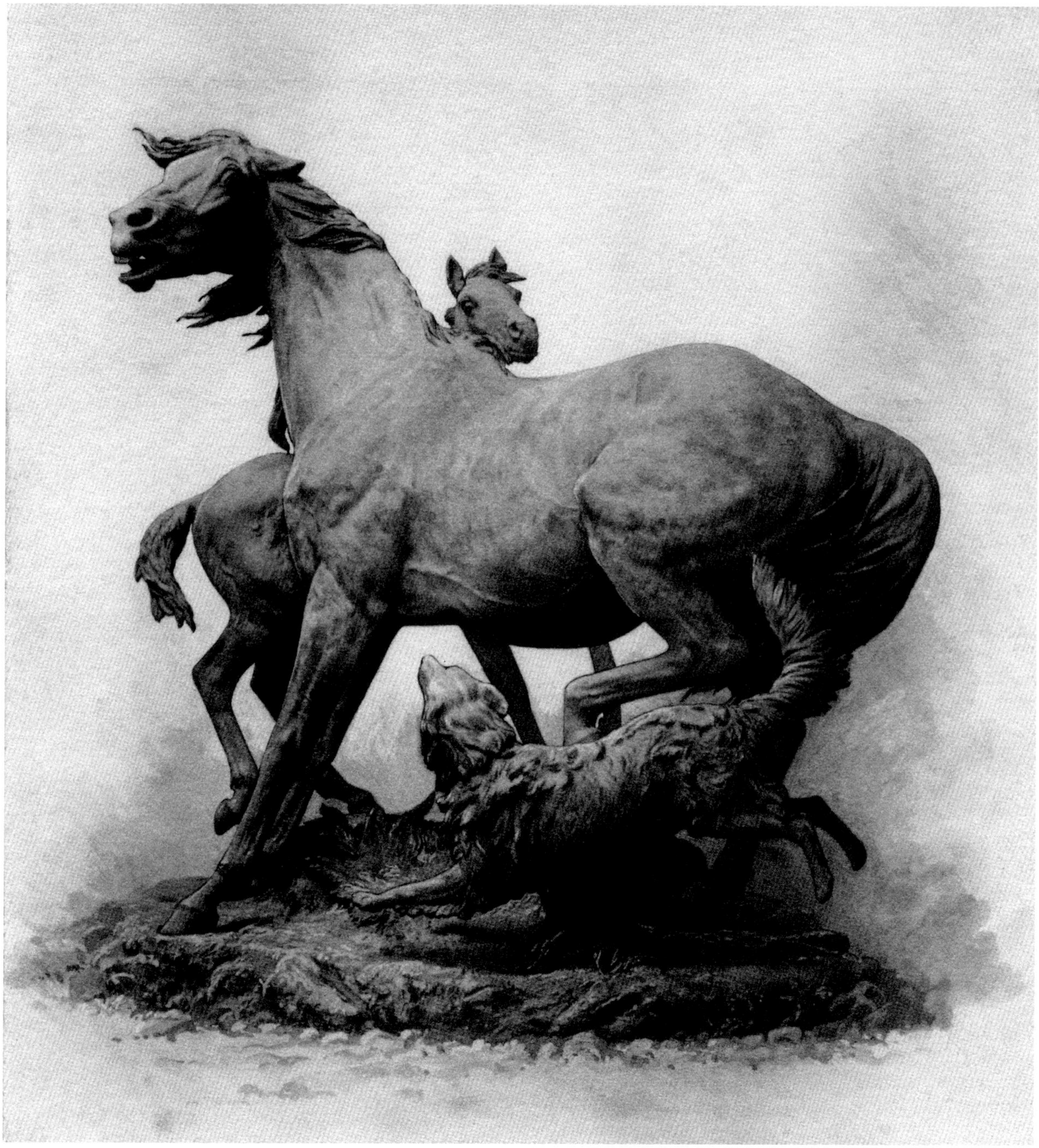

Maternal Care, plaster cast statue, RA exhibit, 1893

his back. One senses that Adrian would have enjoyed working the extra detail of the Queen's South Africa medal with five clasps which Freddy had been officially awarded and which he wore on his harness below the breastplate. While a commission to sculpt a horse and rider was for Adrian 'bread and butter' work, the great importance of the intended recipients and his post-scandal desire to display, if only in miniature, the supreme technical competence of which the scandalmonger whispered him incapable, made him ensure the craftsmanship was excellent. The various surface textures of tassels, standard (on which it is possible even to read the embroidered battle honours), metal helmet and horsehair plume, saddle lambskin, horse mane and horse skin etc. are differentiated. In the horse's harness, every boss, buckle and ring, the two cheek straps for bridle and bridoon, every link in the curb chain, everything is exactly detailed. Everyone can recognise the miracle of the sculptor's hand. Beyond that, those of conservative outlook will get a satisfying sense of history and tradition displayed. Those who prefer sculpture to be liberated from figurative subject matter must look elsewhere. The Royal Standard Bearer is art as sensuous percept, not as intellectual concept.

Gratifying and reassuring as the support of his patrons was, Adrian found time to pursue his own creative instincts as well. Later in his career he would turn gladly to painting as relief from the hard labour of creating the Quadriga, but in the 1890s it was to large sculptures in which subject and artistic vision could be wholly his own choice that he turned 'in my spare time' as a change from executing the wishes of patrons. Immediately after the 'Ghost' scandal he sculpted 'Maternal Care'. The life-size group showed a mare shielding her foal from a gambolling dog. It had been problematic in the making, for three times the clay fell away from the mare's belly. Superstitious friends interpreted this as a sign of bad luck, but the Royal Academy accepted it for the 1893 Summer Exhibition. The *Leeds Mercury* thought it 'well composed' but 'very tame'. The *Standard*, however, felt it should be bought for the nation. 'In this particular class of animal life', wrote their art critic, 'Adrian Jones stands alone', and he went on to complain that the Academy's Council did not pay sufficient attention to the just demands of sculptors. Adrian suspected that seeing his work thus used as a peg on which to hang criticism of the Academy probably made him still less popular with those Academicians who had hoped in the previous year that the veiled accusation of using 'ghost' assistants would have finished his career. He reflected: 'My popularity never strayed within the portals of Burlington House.' The door to membership remained closed against him. The statue did not sell quickly (though in due course it found a home in an estate near Salisbury, since sold off), so when he made a statuette of the composition he removed the dog, which made the work easier to afford.

At around the same time, though, Adrian had the opportunity to depict another dog. The Master of the Pytchley Hunt, Lord Spencer, commissioned a life-size statue of his foxhound Forager. In the sporting art which developed in the 18th century, prints of hunting scenes had become popular. The painter Henry Alken had found a market for a complete hunt scenario, seven paintings in all, rumbustiously tracing the events of a day's hunting right through to its evening close, the hunt members at supper raising their glasses to toast 'the fox'. As sporting art flourished in the 19th century, aristocratic owners commissioned pictures of favourite dogs, although hound sculptures remained comparatively rare.

Rich Masters of Foxhounds such as the Duke of Beaufort at the Beaufort and Lord Spencer at the Pytchley kennels supplemented their love of field sports with an interest in the science of breeding. They sought to produce in a hound the ideal combination of appearance and ability. In 1878 the Peterborough Hound Show was inaugurated to encourage and celebrate this stud book interest. Forager, after winning several minor show prizes, won best dog first prize at Peterborough. That prompted Lord Spencer to invite Adrian to Althorp to model what a later issue of the *Ladies' Field* gushingly termed 'that splendid animal, bred at the Pytchley Kennels, and credited with being one of the best which have come from that centre of high standards'. Adrian, who delighted in hounds as much as in horses, and was interested in the evolution

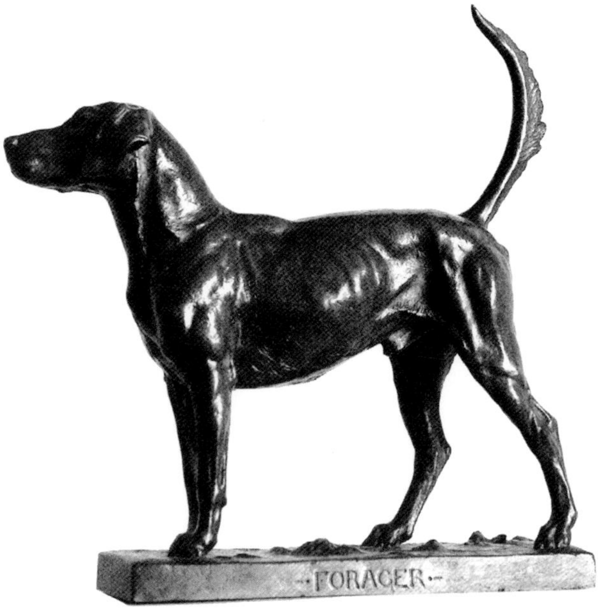

Forager, 1893. Adrian executed a life-size statue for the M.F.H. of the Pytchley Hunt at Althorp House. This photograph, however, is of the smaller bronze statuette, cast to a high standard, which could be purchased by other Pytchley Hunt members.

of their anatomy, set about the task with enthusiasm, his pleasure in it enhanced by the fact of working at Althorp. Distinguished hunting men dropped by to admire the life-size work in progress and he could discuss with them the changes to foxhound configuration which breeding for particular characteristics was producing. Prize judges were now looking for straight forelegs with turned-in toes, but Adrian's visitors could not explain the rationale for this. Adrian thought it through:

> ... and came to the conclusion that this type is desired because it enables the hound to travel many miles on a hard road without injury. If his weight came on the pad of the foot he would soon become footsore, but being supported by his toes and nails he does not tire to the same extent. The evolutionary process of the forelegs causes considerable modification of the tendons and ligaments around the knee-joint and makes the outside of the legs appear straight, hence the term 'straight leg'.

Although the British are a nation of dog lovers, unless they were also keen followers of hounds they would probably soon tire of an art exhibition of repeated representations of single standing hounds. Yet what provokes boredom in many can appeal greatly to those who have a particular interest in the subject. Lord Spencer was succeeded as Master of the Pytchley by Lord Annaly, who wrote Adrian a letter of appreciation. That he wrote it in the midst of the hunting season is unremarkable. But it is surely remarkable that he wrote on Christmas Day, as if Forager was the finest possible Christmas present:

> My Dear Jones,
>
> I must write you a line to tell you how delighted I am with the model you have made of 'Forager'. It is really splendid and does you the greatest possible credit. You have the dog to the life and the work is beautifully artistic. I think it quite the best thing of its sort I have ever seen and, if it is shown, ought to bring you heaps of orders. I don't believe there is another man in England who can do it as well ... Everybody here is delighted with your work ...
>
> Yours, Annaly

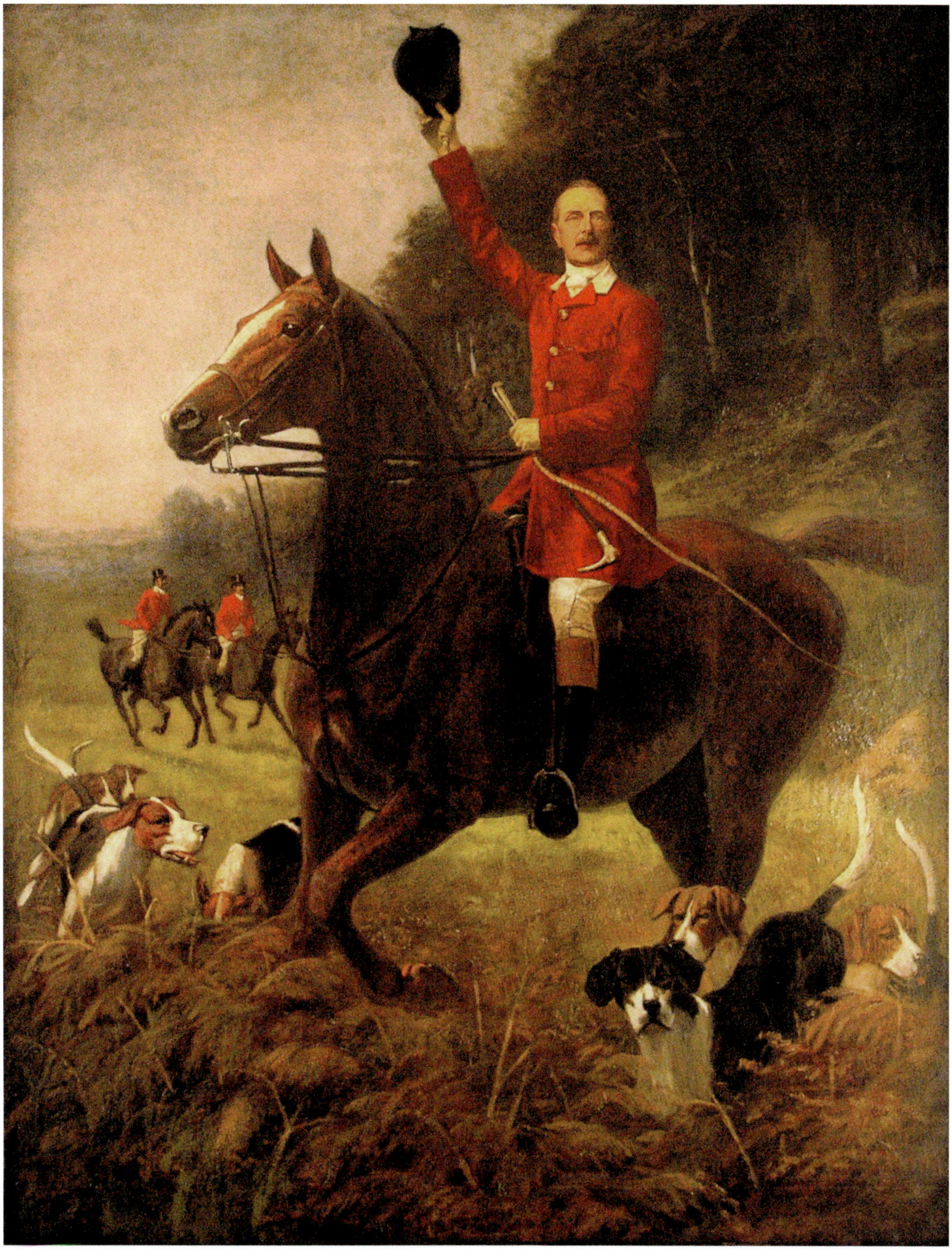

Lord Annaly: A Day with the Pytchley, oil on canvas, *c.*1894. This painting, full of the russet colours of the hunting season, is something very different from the small prints of hunting scenes still found in unmodernised hotels and pubs. Whilst not a 'ten footer', it is yet a large work, 6½ feet by 5¼ feet.

Annaly had a knowledgeable eye. What in the statue made him consider it 'quite the best thing of its sort'? Some desirable features in a foxhound, such as good temper, cannot really be captured in a sculpture, although some viewers may claim they can sense them. Whereas the major preoccupation of an artist portraying a person is usually to capture character, perhaps by emphasising a detail of expression, Adrian could not do much other than give Forager a trustful stare at an unseen huntsman and a joyfully raised stern. This is not to imply that he worked without feeling. His admiration for the subject of this piece of commissioned tribute art is deep; he celebrates the hound's quality by modelling an exact physical resemblance to the hound's well-bred constitution. Hence the lean conical head, the close-lying ears, the long neck and throat line, the flat straight back and wide muscled thighs, and smooth coat. Hence also, and most particularly, the ruler straight forelegs, straight in side view, straight in front view, that end in slightly turned-in toes. One might say that the statue is not so much 'beautifully artistic' as 'beautifully executed'. The scope for artistry here, or in Adrian's similarly posed hound 'Steward' of the Heythorp pack, modelled in 1916, is more limited than when he could use his eye for ensemble in the design of his 1891 Atherstone Hunt silver, in which the Master encourages three running hounds. For Adrian, however, the works, in meeting different demands, were as good as each other. In *Memoirs* he used the Atherstone Presentation group and the Pytchley hound as side-by-side illustrations of his work for the hunting fraternity.

And he had one good story to tell about 'Forager'. The statue was in his studio when another foxhound was brought there for modelling. As soon as the hound saw the statue, he rushed up and licked it nearly all over. (No other breed of dog ever took notice of the statue.) Adrian called the incident 'odd' and 'very curious' – but he appreciated the hound's approval.

In the following year, 1894, Adrian again devoted 'my spare time' to working on a large group statue that he could submit for inclusion in the Royal Academy summer exhibition. He could hardly have chosen a subject more different from his normal run of commissioned works. He did not paint equestriennes. He did not paint and very seldom sculpted the female nude. Yet for his Academy subject he decided on 'The Rape of the Sabines', and his sculpture showed a Roman rider carrying off a Sabine woman. Partly his motivation was a desire to show he could turn his hand to anything, further to disprove the allegation made during the 'Ghost' controversy two years previously that his lack of training made it impossible for him to be the creator of a genuinely original equine group. In choosing a classical subject, he was also challenging the Royal Academy's neo-classic tradition on its own ground. But in reality the sculpture was not a complete change from his usual work. Though the Sabine victim represented a departure, his deeper interest was the horse of the victimiser:

> The Roman rides without stirrups and on a piece of sacking for a saddle. It was an arduous and ambitious effort, but I loved the labour of expressing the excitement of the great, plunging horse of which the rider seems near to losing control. I think I enjoyed the modelling of this animal all the more because I knew from the closest observation how the movements I depicted would express themselves in terms of line, and I had a quiet consciousness that there was not among my critics and traducers any man who had enjoyed so close a study of horses as I ... There was hardly a day I had not been on the saddle or with horses, if only for an hour or two with my eyes, so to speak, always at attention. Moreover, I felt that this group should be a challenge to my critics and so it was.

As that makes clear, Adrian remained unreconciled to his 'traducers'. Moreover, sculptors had to struggle harder than painters to make an adequate living. The work took longer, and the market was more limited.

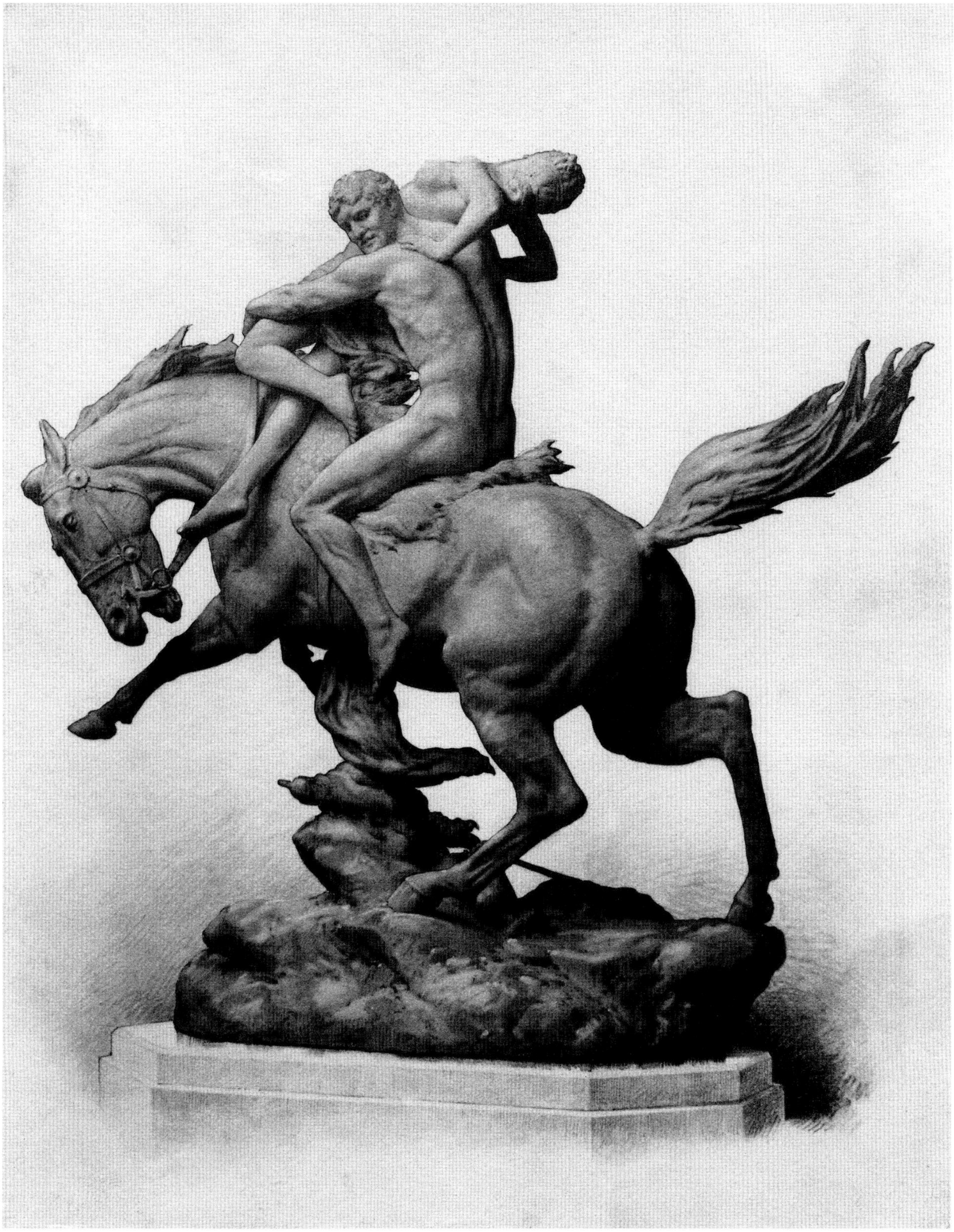

Rape of the Sabines, plaster cast statue, RA exhibit, 1894

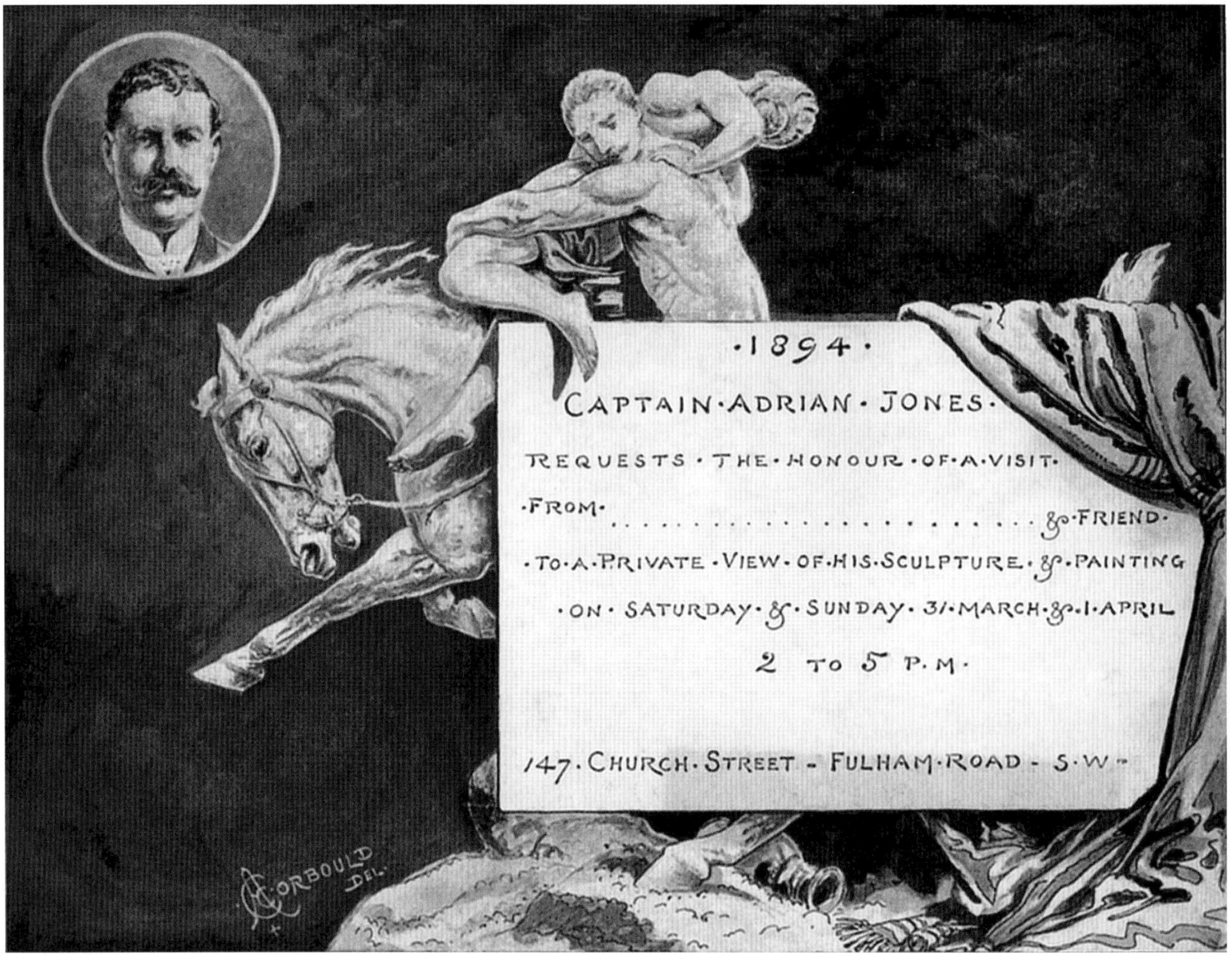

Invitation to Adrian's private view, 1894

Since retiring from the army, Adrian had been able to compete full-time for commissions, and his completed works often led to similar commissions from their admirers. Professional jealousy could stoke animosity. Adrian very rarely uses sarcasm in *Memoirs*, but after describing his motivation for 'Rape of the Sabines' he continues: 'Indeed the old gentlemen of the Royal Academy Hanging Committee expressed their friendly feeling towards me and their entire freedom from bias by relegating it to a very bad position.' The press, aware of the underlying ill-will, commented on the positioning. The *Times* said: 'The best group of its class, "The Rape of the Sabines", by Adrian Jones, is relegated to a place where it cannot properly be seen, and a major portion of the design is lost', and the *Daily Chronicle* made the same criticism, pointing out that Adrian's group 'by singular lack of judgement on the part of those having charge of the business, has been placed ... where it can only be partially seen'. If the poor positioning really was the outcome of malice aforethought, it was both petty and misguided; under Leighton, who was within two years of his death, the Academy had improved the conditions in which sculptors' work was displayed. Adrian had enjoyed modelling the statue, but it would have been unrealistic to expect the subject to attract a private buyer possessed of an appropriate site and the necessary funds for casting the statue in bronze. The plaster cast went on permanent display at Alexandra Palace, and a cartoon of it was drawn by the equestrian and *Punch* artist Alfred Corbould (1852-1920), who added the schoolboy joke of a Victorian moustache to the Roman's upper lip. Adrian used the cartoon on the invitation card to his 1894 private viewing party for his friends.

Chapter Nine: 'Among The Racers'
1895-1899: Racehorses, Patrons and the Prince of Wales

'King Edward was, to my mind, an ideal man and gentleman, and was, moreover, the best friend I ever had.' That sentence constitutes one of the shortest paragraphs in Adrian's *Memoirs of a Soldier Artist*. The previous paragraph gives an account of the King's last visit to view the modelling of the Quadriga, and the next one tells of the compliments Adrian received on the completed statue. On a swift or careless perusal of the book, the reader might move on, having barely noticed the intervening micro-paragraph. Yet it is surely an arresting, doubly startling remark. The first surprise to anyone who knows more revelatory biographies of Edward VII's at times self-indulgent life is Adrian's unqualified tribute, 'ideal man'. That, however, is the lesser surprise, for Adrian, always reticent about private life, loyal and discreet, would never write with the candour of a journalist. The more unforeseen is the claim that Edward was his 'best friend' – not a common claim for a subject to make about a sovereign, especially in a hierarchical society such as the Victorian and Edwardian. Our instinct may be to see it as presumptuous.

But Adrian, though self-confident as a man, veterinary surgeon and artist, was not presumptuous. Not for a moment would he have presumed the complementary sentiment that he was Edward's best friend. He recognised absolutely that Edward was more significant in his life than vice versa. Edward's offer in 1891 of the Wellington Arch as the site for a large Quadriga statue by Adrian must have been the equivalent of a promising sculptor in the twenty-first century being offered *permanent* display in the Turbine Hall at Tate Modern or on the unoccupied plinth in Trafalgar Square. Edward also gave him royal commissions for paintings and sculptures. But the relationship between the two was not just one of patron and grateful recipient. Sir Edward Grey's general remark that there was 'real sympathy of feeling between himself [the King] and his people' is applicable to Edward's individual relationship with Adrian. Though self-indulgent, Edward was not self-centred. He had a range of friends and acquaintances that extended far beyond 'the Marlborough House set', and he liked to see them happy in their lives. Adrian was loyal to him; he stayed loyal to Adrian, something that Adrian particularly appreciated in the aftermath of the 'Ghost' allegations of 1892:

> Few men who entered upon the active and professional practice of their art so late in life could have been more fortunate than I. The Prince of Wales was pleased with my work, and his estimate of my character was decidedly more flattering than that of my detractors, so that while my reputation was, so to speak, on trial, I had the great satisfaction of knowing that I retained his confidence, and whenever there was an opportunity of placing work in my way, he not only took it, but declared himself well satisfied with his choice. I count this, perhaps, as the greatest good fortune of my professional career.

The two men liked each other. Both were companionable, and incorrigible smokers; Edward liked to be amused, and Adrian liked telling entertaining stories; both were members of the Savage Club where 'the great ones of the world relaxed under the Club roof and laid formality aside', though the Prince did not attend as regularly as Adrian; and they had plenty of acquaintances, interests and experiences in common to talk about.

Edward, like his mother before him, knew Ludlow. While still a thirteen-year-old Princess, Victoria had visited the town with her mother in 1832. They had attended church service in St Laurence's, been seated in the front row of the gallery, and heard a sermon preached by the Grammar School Headmaster, the Reverend John Hinde. (His son, in 1832 an impressionable sixteen-year-old, went on to serve as one of Victoria's soldiers for thirty years, commanding the 8th Foot (King's Liverpool Regiment) through most of the Indian Mutiny.)

Travelling by rail from Crewe, Edward had come to Ludlow in October 1861, when Adrian was still at school. After inspecting the castle, the Prince visited the nearby house and estate of Moor Park, which was the main reason for his journey to Ludlow. He had met his future wife Alexandra for the first time the month before, and thereby confirmed the encouraging report sent previously by his elder sister Vicky that Alexandra had 'a lovely figure', 'a complexion as beautiful as possible' and perfect walk, carriage and manner. His thoughts and those of his parents were therefore turning to marriage and the need for a home. The Salwey family solicitor showed Edward over the property. The day was hazy, but the prospect sufficiently open to enable the Prince to judge the great extent and beauty of the scenery. He returned to Ludlow, lunched in The Angel Hotel just across the street from the house in which Adrian had been born, and left by train for Shrewsbury. Whatever his opinion of Moor Park, it was to prove irrelevant, for Prince Albert settled on the then less attractive Sandringham, and as he and the Queen, not Edward, had the necessary finances, Ludlow lost what the local historian Henry Weyman termed 'the incalculable benefit of having a Royal residence in its immediate region'.

In other ways too Edward's life was full of experiences and interests which gave him common ground with Adrian. In his spells at both Oxford and Cambridge he took up hunting and joined the universities' Volunteer Corps. In the summer of 1861 his father sent him to the Curragh Camp in Ireland for military training with the Grenadier Guards. Though that did not prove happy soldiering, as he lacked experience adequate to some of the command tasks imposed upon him, he continued to want to join the army: in 1882 and again in 1884 he volunteered his services for campaigning with General Wolseley in Egypt and Sudan, but whereas Adrian was called to the attempted relief of General Gordon in Khartoum, Edward to his frustration was politely rejected. In 1875 he made a royal progress round India, including landing and spending time in Bombay. He met Adrian's commanding general in the Abyssinian War, Lord Napier, at a pig-sticking hunt where Adrian's services would again have been useful to Napier, whose horse was felled by the enraged boar. But more significant than any of the above for promoting friendly relations between Adrian and the Prince was Edward's fascination with the social ambience and the excitement of horse racing. Its attraction increased as that of yacht racing declined. From 1893 onwards Kaiser Willy started treating Cowes Regatta as an opportunity for display of German imperial might by coming escorted by his latest warship and using a new yacht which regularly beat Edward's *Britannia*, and the regatta lost its appeal for the Prince.

Adrian's informal friendship with Edward, to whom he never referred as 'Bertie', was just one of many similar congenial relationships that characterised Edward's outgoing nature and helped to bring him closer to his people; but the bond of horse racing, horse character and breeding, equine painting and equine sculpture, was a particularly strong one. Edward had been attending race meetings, both the annual society round of Newmarket, Epsom, Royal Ascot and Doncaster, and also lesser courses, since the 1860s. In the 1870s he had started holding a dinner on the evening of Derby Day for members of the Jockey Club, and in the middle of the decade he registered racing colours. However, eleven years were to pass before he became a winning owner, and happily for Adrian the start of Edward's decade of remarkable success, the 1890s, coincided with Adrian's retirement from the army and his exhibiting of 'Triumph' at the Royal Academy. In the years that followed he received numerous royal commissions.

Edward's turf successes stemmed from the purchase in 1885 of the mare Perdita II for the new royal stud at Sandringham. She was mated with the nineteenth century's greatest sire, St Simon, hence her second son's name, Persimmon. Persimmon won around £35,000 in prize money and afterwards earned over £100,000 as a stallion in stud fees, which made him the leading sire in four seasons between 1902 and 1912. He also inspired some of Adrian's finest art, culminating in the Peace Quadriga of 1912. In 1895, Persimmon, then a two year old colt, lost just one race, to St Frusquin, owned by another of Adrian's patrons, Leopold de Rothschild, for whom he painted Lactantius two years later. Adrian did not paint St Frusquin, but he went to Sandringham to sketch Persimmon. The following year both horses, as three year olds, were eligible for the classics. Because of injury Persimmon could not compete in the first of the season, the 2,000 Guineas. St Frusquin won it, and was duly installed as favourite for the Derby. Punters backing Persimmon could

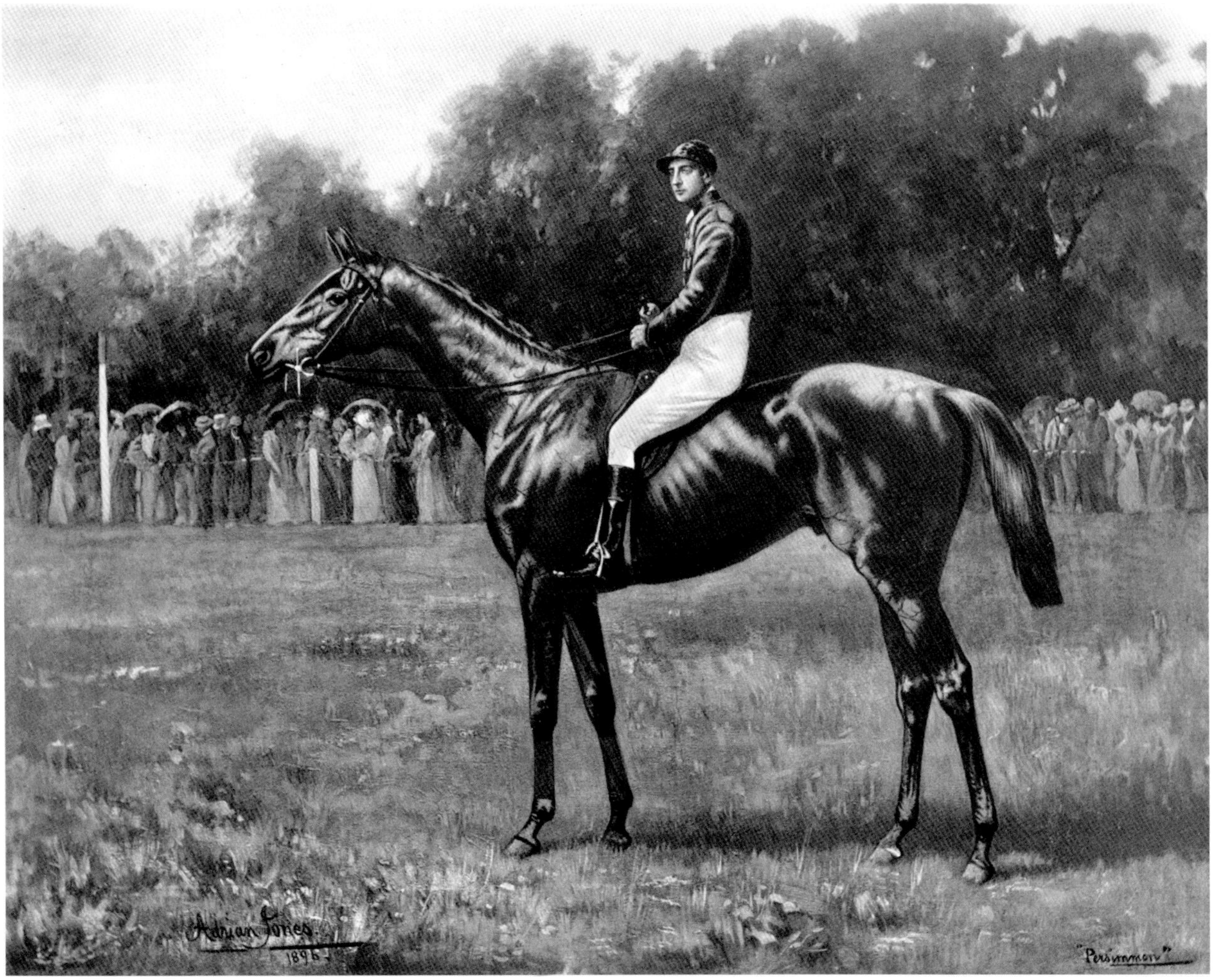

Persimmon with Watts Up, 1896. Before executing this royal commission Adrian made numerous sketches of horse and jockey at Newmarket and Epsom, the last ones done rapidly at the starting post (seen here in the background).

get decent odds of 5 to 1, for he had wintered unpromisingly, and on the morning of the Derby he sweated so profusely as he worked out on the Epsom Downs that his trainer felt deeply pessimistic. However, the 1896 race produced one of the great Derby finishes. With two furlongs to go, Persimmon and his jockey Watts were still behind St Frusquin on the rails, but Watts managed to quicken him until over the last half furlong Persimmon and St Frusquin raced stride for stride, neck-and-neck abreast. The *Times* reported: 'The issue hung in the balance to the end', but Persimmon won by a neck, and his time broke the race record. A celebratory shower of top hats was thrown into the air, and the Prince led his horse into the winner's enclosure. The *Times* continued: 'The enthusiasm of the vast multitude, which found vent in a hurricane of cheering prolonged for something like quarter of an hour, could not but touch and move the Prince and his family, for it was so manifestly spontaneous. Old and young, high and low, rich and poor, winners and losers vied with one another in exuberance of delight.' The combination of excitement at the close finish and delight at the popular Prince's victory certainly produced a memorable occasion. Fortunately, for the first time film makers recorded the scene, and the National Horse Racing Museum in Newmarket screens the film constantly so that visitors can relive it.

Wanting his own memento, Edward approached Adrian personally to commission a painting of Persimmon with Jack Watts in the saddle. Adrian liked painting exceptionally talented horses, and this was a commission he could accept with confidence as well as pleasure; he had previously painted Sir James Miller's 1890 Derby winner Sainfoin with Watts up. The new commission in 1896 from royalty was prestigious, welcome and comparatively undemanding – but also artistically limiting. Essentially he had to record the horse's appearance, sideview, stationary, in the painting's foreground, to show a great, beautiful thoroughbred, the product of the finest pedigree breeding. In his book *Great Racehorses in Art* John Fairley confirms that contemporary observers considered him almost perfectly made for a racehorse. Adrian captures the slim, lightish head and neck, the great depth from the withers, and the powerful hindquarters. The sunshine in the picture is coming from the left, the direction which Persimmon is facing, and so runs along the body, illuminating the rippling fitness of a perfectly trained colt. Adrian liked to have humans also in his paintings. The background ladies in their day coats indicate a racecourse setting, and the jockey complements the horse. Watts uses long stirrup leathers rather than the 'crouch' style which the American jockey Tod Sloan had introduced in 1879 and of which Adrian disapproved on the grounds that high stirrups meant the jockey could not sense with his legs if his horse was distressed, and could be more easily catapulted off.

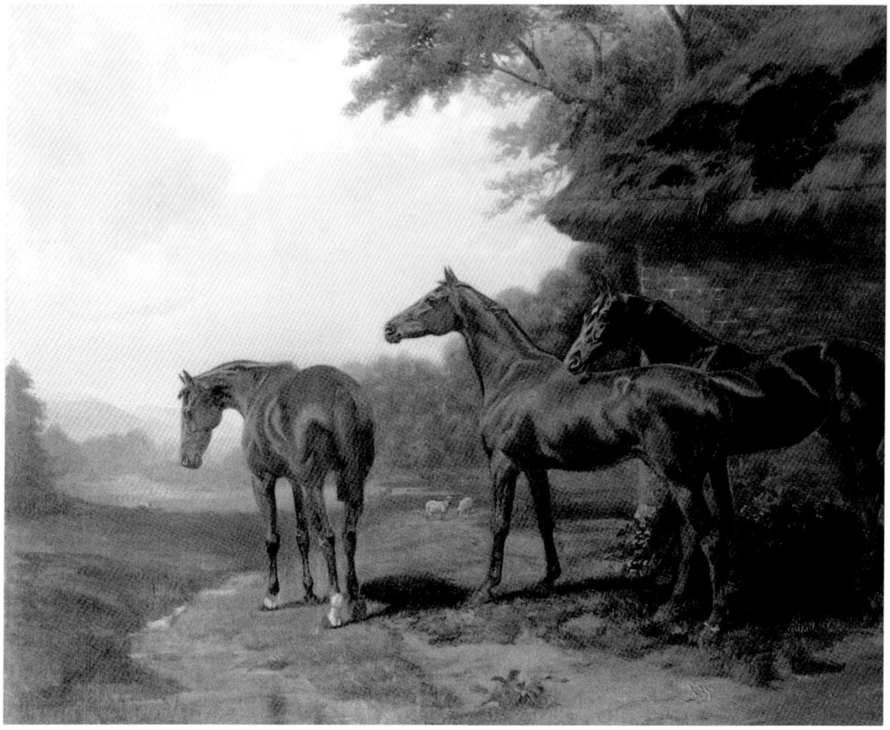

Horses at grass: Coronet, Merryman and Dewdrop, 1895

When possible, Adrian liked to escape from the conventional horse portrait broadside pose. In 1895 Colonel William Hall Walker (later Lord Wavertree) had asked him to paint two pictures of three horses at grass. Horses like company, and Adrian liked grouping them in a painting as it immediately increased interest for the viewer. However, Colonel Walker stipulated that all the horses should be painted broadside on. 'I assured him that if he would allow me to make a group, I could give him two really interesting pictures, and he remarked rather dryly, "Probably if you did I should not recognise them, but let it be as you wish." He was called away for a few days and I was left undisturbed to do my best.' So Adrian was free to place the horses, as he wished, in a chosen setting. He shows Coronet, Merryman and Dewdrop beside a thatched estate building. The thatch and a tall shading tree extend to the top right of the painting, but on the left the sky is open, and as is customary in Adrian's technique the horses face towards the main light source. Thus they face left, Merryman and Dewdrop in slightly angled broadside poses, Dewdrop with his head companionably over Merryman's back, whilst Coronet is shown rear view, but with head and neck turned left as if contemplating a drink from the small stream curling past his hooves. In the middle distance two sheep add a touch of farming interest to the space between Coronet and the other two horses, and beyond Coronet the winding course of the stream draws the eye along the vale to low hills.

Adrian's second group of three horses is a companion piece. Though the horses' shadows show that the sunlight is again coming from the front left, this time the brightness within the composition is on the right and the horses look in that direction. Again two horses, Hornet and Touchstone, are angled side on, and the third, Mystery, end-on, but here facing towards the viewer. Adrian took pleasure in the shining quality of the six handsome animals, at rest away from competition, and the counterbalancing of the compositions strongly suggests that he envisaged them hung side by side as a complete group. When Lord Wavertree returned, he readily picked out all six horses by name in turn. Adrian commented: 'I do not know who was the better pleased, he or I.' In 1933 Lord Wavertree bequeathed his Adrian Jones paintings to the Walker Art Gallery in Liverpool. The six horses are on display in the principal corridor of Croxteth Hall, which like the Walker itself hangs pictures from the National Museums and Galleries on Merseyside group. They hang opposite each other on facing walls, not side by side, but they make an interesting contrast with two paintings of three horses by Lynwood Palmer in the same corridor. Palmer's paintings date from two decades after Adrian's, and each shows three horses standing in line broadside on. Lord Wavertree was seemingly unrepentant about preferring equine paintings to be 'record' rather than 'art'.

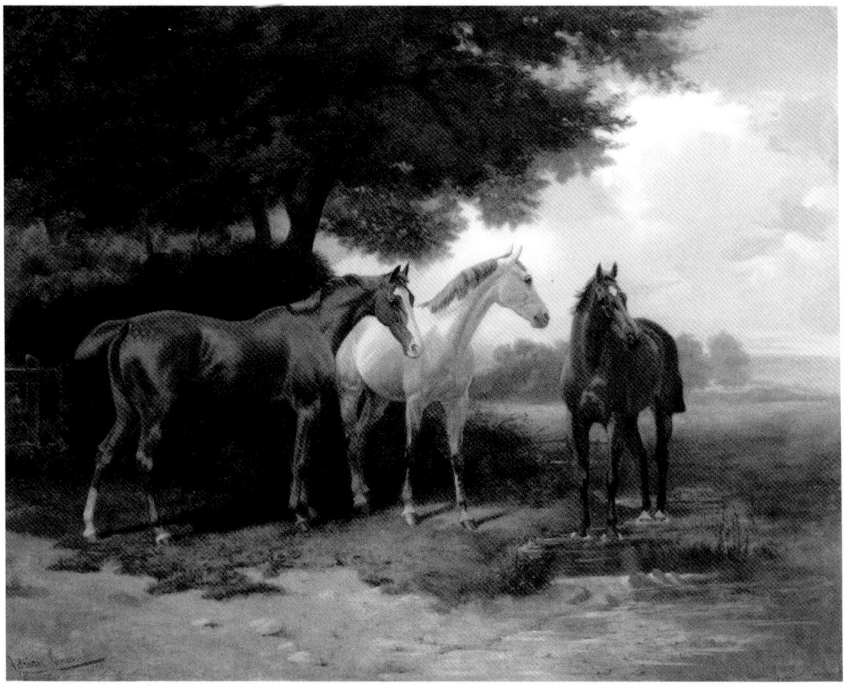

Horses at grass: Hornet, Touchstone and Mystery, 1895.
Like its companion painting opposite, this was bequeathed to Liverpool's Walker Art Gallery, named after its great benefactor, Colonel Walker.

When Adrian had painted oils of 'Roman Oak' and 'The Swindler' in 1890 he had been content to use closely similar backgrounds, even to the extent of the main tree shadow behind each horse appearing to be the same one. By the middle 1890s he tended to make the background more specific. Some commissions required him to record a horse dear to its owner but little known to fame and fortune. Cutty Sark, for instance, painted in 1895, subsequently raced under National Hunt rules for two seasons at Hunt race meetings and minor racecourses. She delighted her owner by gaining five first places in her ten outings in steeplechases, and though an objection was lodged to her victory in the Ladies' Purse Steeplechase of the Tarporley Hunt on the ground that she had not been regularly hunted as required by the conditions, it was withdrawn, so all five wins stood. Even so, her fame fell well short of replicating that of the original Cutty Sark character in Burns's poem *Tam O'Shanter*. (Her name had been drawn from Scots literature because her dam was named after Sir Walter Scott's novel *Waverley*.) Adrian's brief had the familiar limiting factor of requiring a broadside view of a solo horse, but he brought as much affectionate care to delineating the modest bay mare as he would to capturing a Derby winner. A casual look at this painting, or at that of Brave, an attractive polo pony painted a year later (1896), might lead to an impression that the canvases are damaged. In reality the white flecks on the horses' coats are Adrian's faithful, compassionate recording of saddle sores and spittle. The background too is detailed. The initials JMW on the bucket in Cutty Sark's

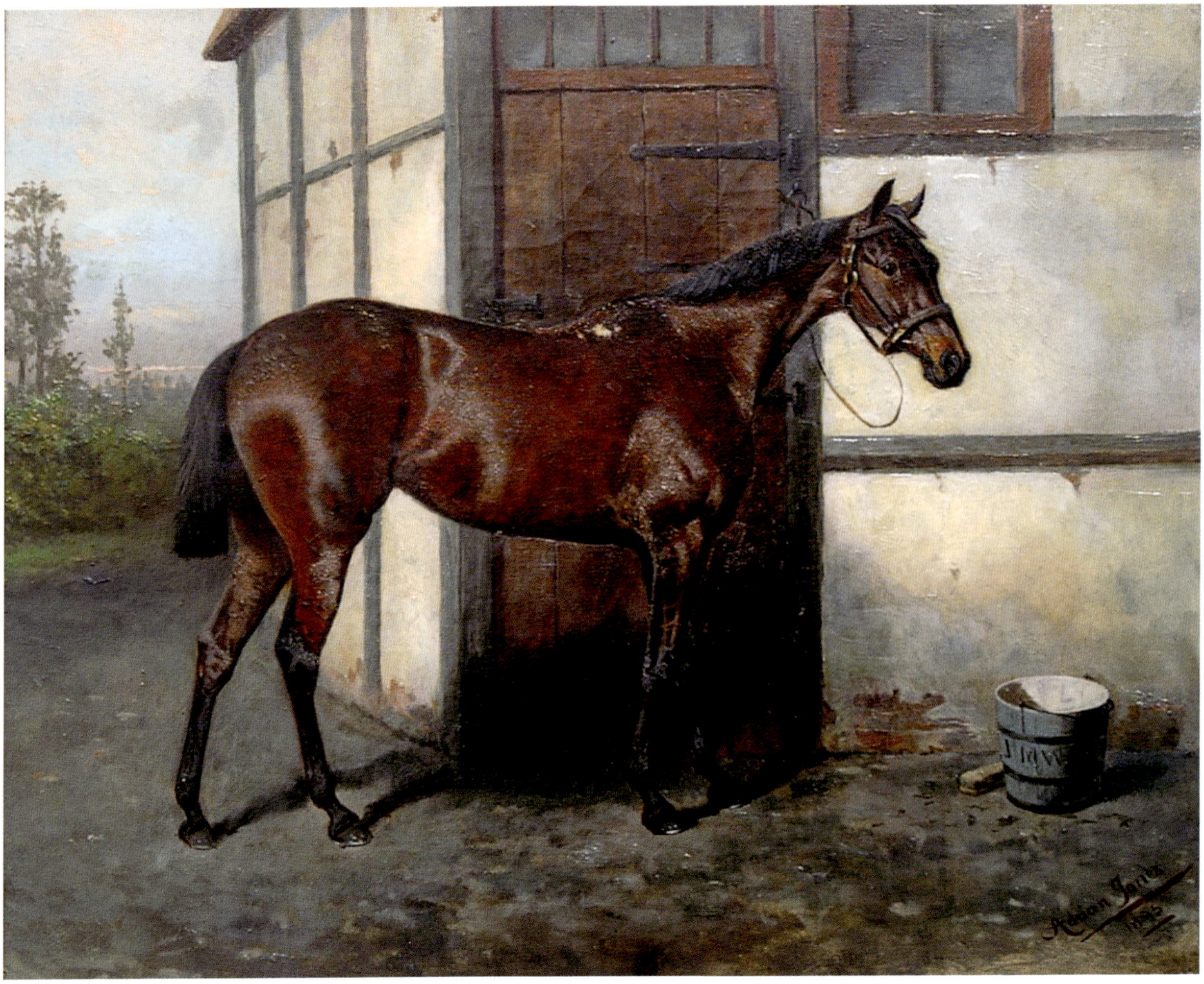

Cutty Sark, 1895. This and **Brave** (opposite) are small paintings, both 16 by 20 inches.

stableyard are those of her owner, James Monro Walker, a brother of William Hall Walker, Lord Wavertree. Obviously such realistic scenes of animal life do not constitute Victorian High Art. Their owners delight in Adrian's imitative skills rather than seek the moral improvement conveyed in the large canvases depicting great stories from mythology, literature, history or religion which were purchased by museums or stately homes. Sometimes of course, as in Lord Wavertree's bequest or because of a gallery's special interest, pictures do end up in public ownership, but even then a similar painting may remain in a private collection because Adrian had been asked to record a horse for, say, both the owner and his racing manager.

In the last years of the nineteenth century Lord Wavertree commissioned several works. Adrian must have particularly enjoyed producing in 1896 the larger 42 by 60 inches painting required for the four horses in 'Changing Polo Ponies at Hurlingham'. Here was an opportunity to display versatility, for the scene embraces in loose formation Nimble, Cicely, Dynamite and Lady Jane, plus Lord Wavertree in the saddle, two standing grooms each holding a polo pony at its head, and a background of distant mounted players, spectators, club grandstand with flag, trees and sky. Though in 1896 polo was a young sport in Britain, brought in by cavalry regiments at the end of the 1860s, and the Hurlingham Club itself was formed only in 1875, already the scene looks thoroughly English – the nobility at play, able to afford four ponies to get successfully through the chukkas. Adrian makes the action clear. Lord Wavertree has dismounted from the

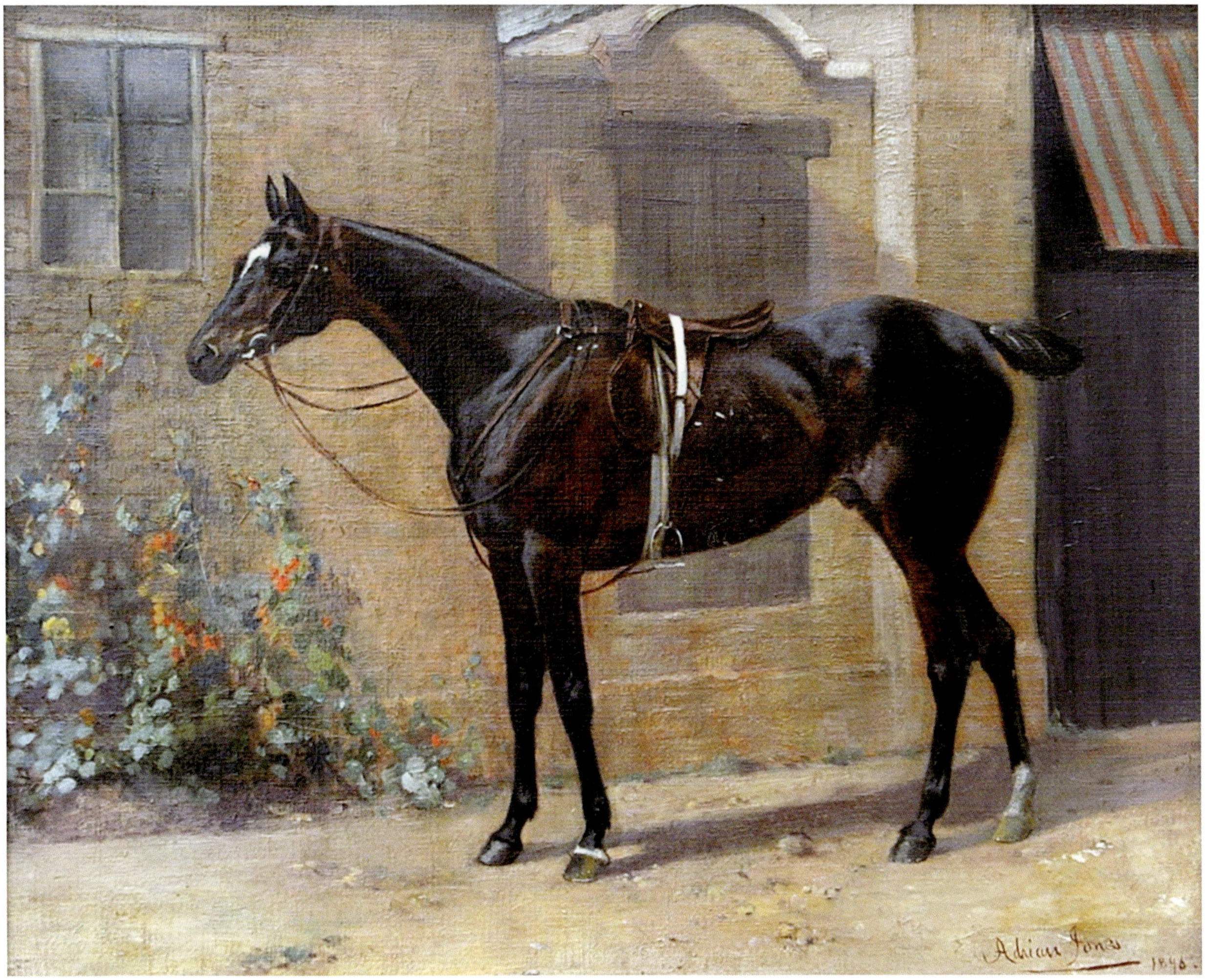

Brave, 1896. The white flecks of spittle on the flanks show the polo pony has just been at exercise.

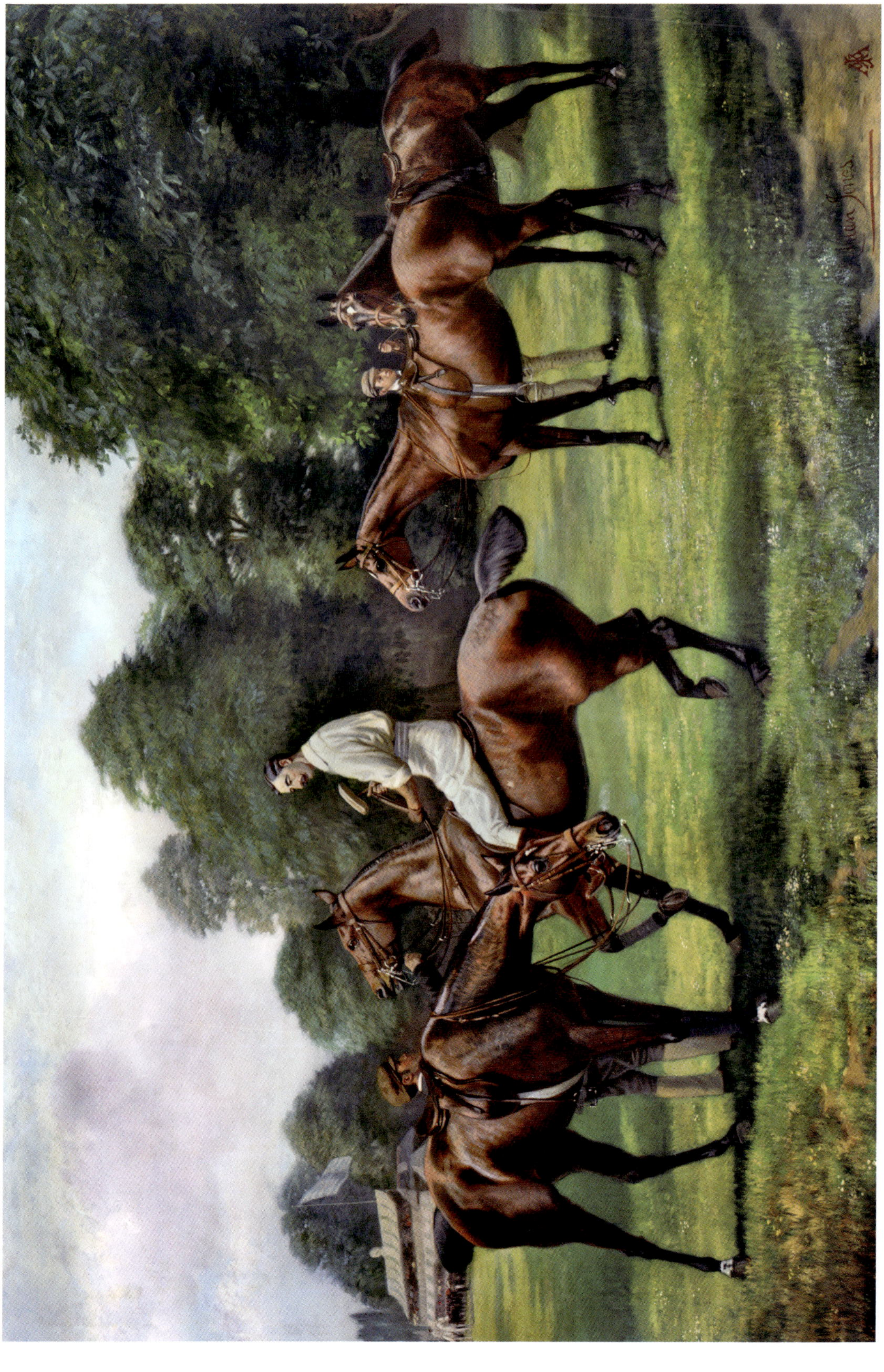

Changing Polo Ponies at Hurlingham, 1896

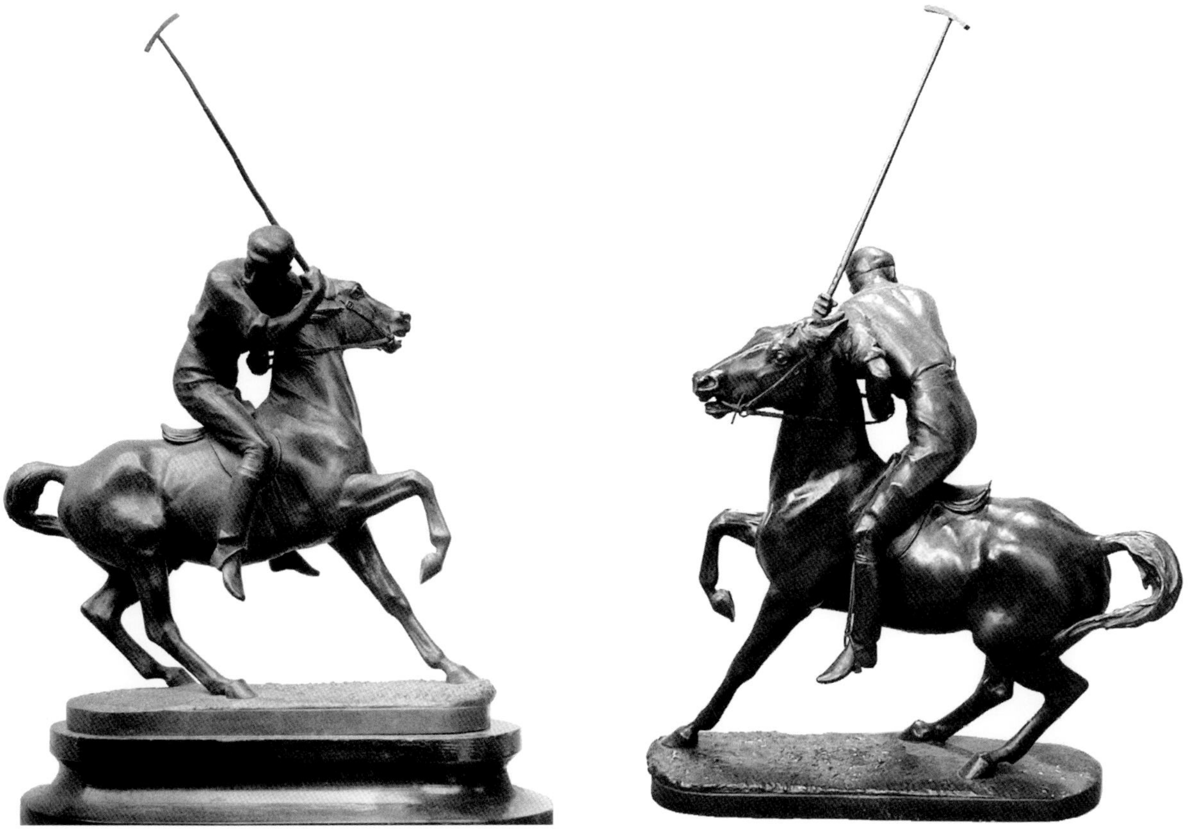

Polo Player, bronze statuette, 22 by 16 inches, 1894, chosen by Adrian as an exhibit for his one-man show in the Graves Gallery, Pall Mall, in May and June 1898. It is shown here from both sides; Adrian always considered the back view of a sculpture as important as the front.

exhausted Nimble on the left. The pony stands with head and neck lowered, and breath steaming. Lord Wavertree now sits on fresh, mettlesome Cicely, who is raising two legs, keen to be off, but for the moment restrained by the groom at her head. His polo mallet is in his right hand, and his waist belt sports the club colours echoed in the stripes waving on the grandstand flag. The picture is a harmony of greens and browns, but with one contrasting highlight: the whites of Lord Wavertree's polo clothes call attention to him as the central figure in the composition. Though only one of the scene's four animals in the foreground is moving, the picture contains a narrative and 'action'. It may seem remarkable that Adrian did not choose to portray a more dramatic moment on the polo field, for a competitive incident in a chukka would have suited his special skill at painting horses and riders twisting and turning. But the commission was essentially to portray his patron's horses, and a match play scene would have meant sharing the canvas with the mounts of his opponents. Also, in 1894 Adrian had sculpted a bronze statuette of a polo player in a match, swinging a backhand stroke of his mallet. In the painting he was happy to undertake something different. (For the retrospective exhibition of his work at the Sladmore Gallery in 1984, his grandchildren Adrian and Monica authorised a limited edition of nine 'Polo Player' statuettes. They sold readily.)

Lord Wavertree's other commissions of 1896 were for three paintings of the Grand National winner of that year, The Soarer, with his amateur jockey Captain Campbell up, silver and bronze statuettes of the horse, and an equine inkstand. This multiple commission reflects the fact that by 1896 Adrian was everywhere recognised as the nation's best artist of Grand National horses. In 1893 the winning owner Mr

Charles Duff had asked him to make a bronze of Cloister, a bold jumping stayer that was the first horse to win carrying the maximum weight of 12 stone 7lb. The admiration that statuette received had led the 1894 winning owner, Captain Fenwick, to ask for a statuette of his horse, Why Not. Then in 1895 the *Graphic* asked him to record whichever horse won the National. His picture of Wild Man of Borneo, with its owner jockey Mr John Widger in the saddle, appeared swiftly in its pages that April. Perhaps not surprisingly, Wild Man is shown still breathing heavily.

But perhaps it was his depiction of 'The Soarer' that made the breakthrough. Lord Wavertree was not a lucky Grand National owner – his final tally was one win from twenty-seven entries. But in 1896 he judged that in buying The Soarer from his friend Captain David Campbell he had found a winner. Campbell was an officer in the 9th Queen's Royal Lancers and a gifted rider and polo player. Later he was to command the regiment in the Great War and lead it in one of the Western Front's rare cavalry charges; later still he was to complete his career as General Sir David Campbell, KCB, Governor of Malta. For the moment, however, what mattered most was his potential as an amateur steeplechase jockey. In their last outing before the 1896 National he and The Soarer fell. They were brought down by another horse, and Campbell was confident that but for that mishap The Soarer would have won. He did not communicate his confidence in the horse to the bookies, so The Soarer started the National at generous odds of 40 to 1. Campbell rode him to victory.

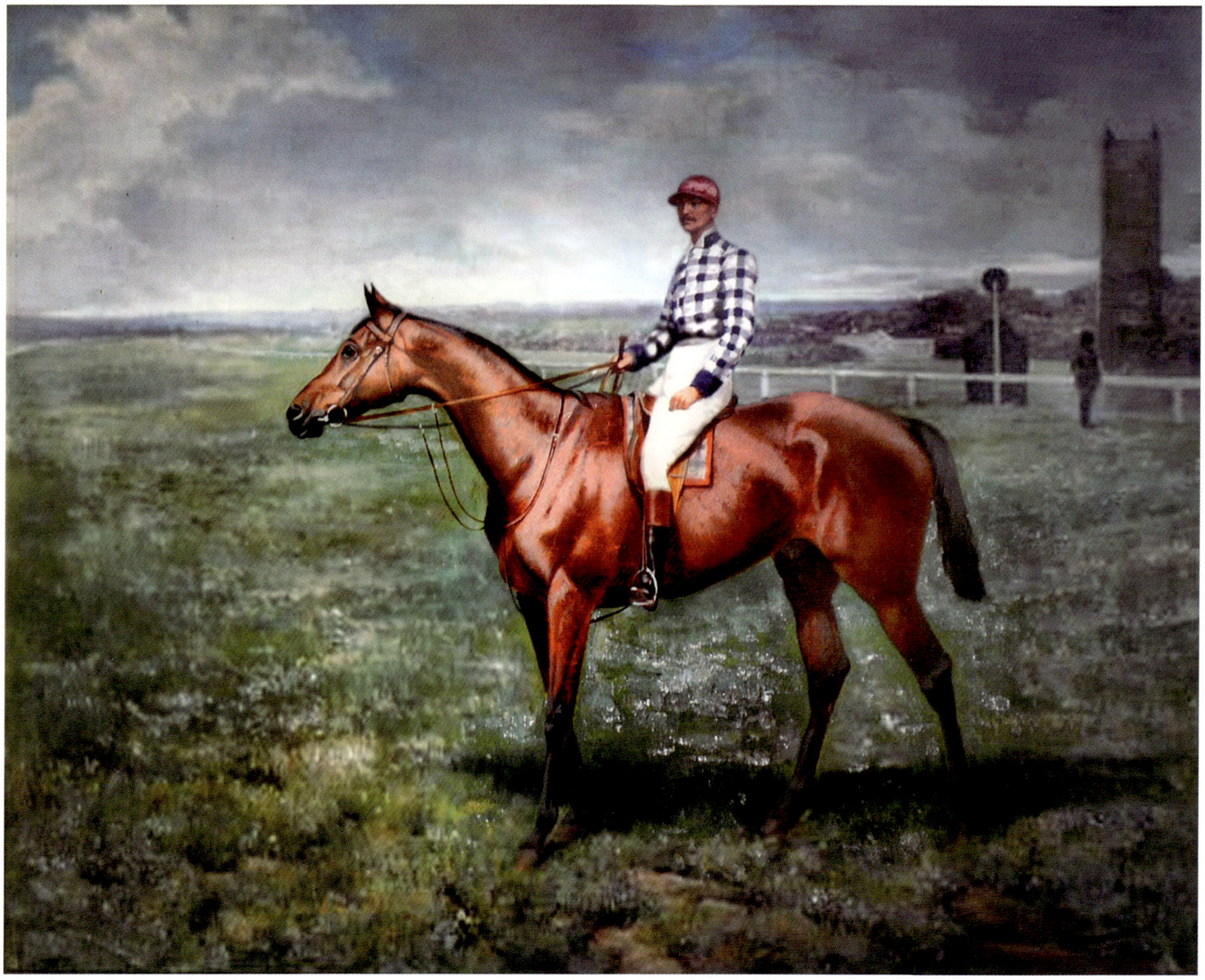

The Soarer with Captain Campbell up, 1896, seen at Aintree

Suddenly the officers of the 9th Lancers found themselves richer and Adrian found his art much in demand. The three paintings – one for the new owner, Lord Wavertree, one for his racing management, and one for the regiment – vary only in minor background detail. Whereas in the painting bequeathed to the Walker Art Gallery a policeman stands inside the course rails and a couple of stable lads lean on the rails to his right, in the version illustrated here a policeman stands alone and in a slightly different position near the list of runners board. Beyond the racecourse is the low outline of the Mersey estuary. But essentially the painting is about the winning horse and David Campbell in the distinctive Wavertree check racing silks. The Soarer is almost scrawny. Lord Wavertree himself termed him 'a scarecrow of a horse'.

It would have been interesting to see what changes Adrian would have captured had he painted him again a year later after the 1897 National, for by then his appearance had improved so much that Lord Wavertree spoke of him as 'a beautiful animal, full of quality' and wanted to be his jockey in the National. The Soarer had been going outstandingly well beneath him when going over fences at the gallops, and as someone who had ridden a great many winners he felt 'quite able to do him justice'. However, when selling The Soarer Campbell had made it a condition that he should have first choice of rides, and now he telegraphed from India, where he was stationed, to claim his right. On homecoming he found The Soarer indeed better than before, so decided not to risk injury by entering any warm-up races. In his Foreword to a later history of the Grand National, Lord Wavertree wrote 'The consequence was that when he started for the National in 1897 he was mad fresh, and I could see him with my glasses, jumping over fences, in front of the others, with considerably more vigour than was necessary'. The Soarer continued jumping fences in front of the field 'until he reached the water jump when ... he increased his speed and put his head up in the air, took off a good length in front ... and landed a good length over it – the most enormous jump I have ever witnessed ... He galloped straight on to the paddock and apparently did not see the white rails, which he snapped like a carrot. Then he charged into the wooden palings which separated the paddock from the course and crashed through them.' His injuries included a fractured skull. Obviously in 1897 there was no call for a celebratory painting, and though The Soarer started again in the 1898 National he ran fearfully and thereafter Lord Wavertree decided not to run him again. But each time he dipped his pen, Lord Wavertree had a reminder of The Soarer's day of glory in 1896. The silver inkstand Adrian made that year must be his most unusual racing memento. The horse's laurel-wreathed head looks toward the letter writer, rather as if he is looking over a field gate, hoping for an apple. Below are inscribed his name and the year of his National triumph. Behind is a pair of flat Pegasuses bounding like steeplechasers, the one taking off and the other stretching out to land. There is not a straight line anywhere in the composition. The play of light from any writing table lamp on the varied planes enhances the piece further, even giving such effects as a blaze on Soarer's face. As a final appropriate touch the ebony base is supported by the pasterns and hooves of four horse legs. The whole work is a joy: spirited, entertaining, and beautiful.

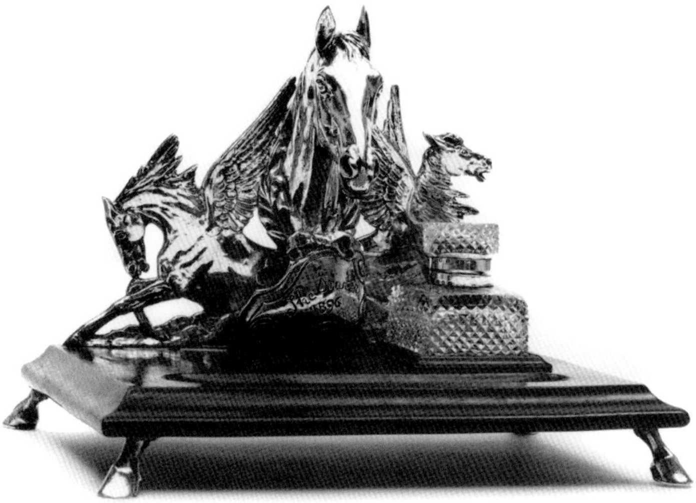

The Soarer, silver and ebony inkstand, 1896.
The stand originally held two stoppered ink bottles.

Colonel Walker continued his patronage. In 1899 Adrian painted him jumping on Raleigh, which like Cutty Sark won the Ladies' Purse at the Tarporley Hunt meeting. In the same year he painted the Colonel's racing manager Jock Fergusson on Glen Royal, winner of the National Hunt Steeplechase; and the following year he painted Merry Gal with, as was increasingly his custom, other horses circling in the background. Then in 1905 he had the chance to paint an outstanding filly, Cherry Lass, winner of the Thousand Guineas and the Oaks. The painting is an unusual arrangement with the focus of interest at the filly's head, below which, carrying whip and saddle, stands the legendary jockey Herbert Jones in discussion with her trainer Jack Robinson. Set in the paddock at Epsom, it is a bright attractive picture of the smart Edwardian racing season of 1905, in which Hall Walker was the leading owner. Immediately after mentioning his paintings of Merry Gal and Cherry Lass, Adrian, writing amid the Depression of the 1930s, continued his autobiography: 'I suppose people must have been very happy in those days to give their horses such cheerful names, and

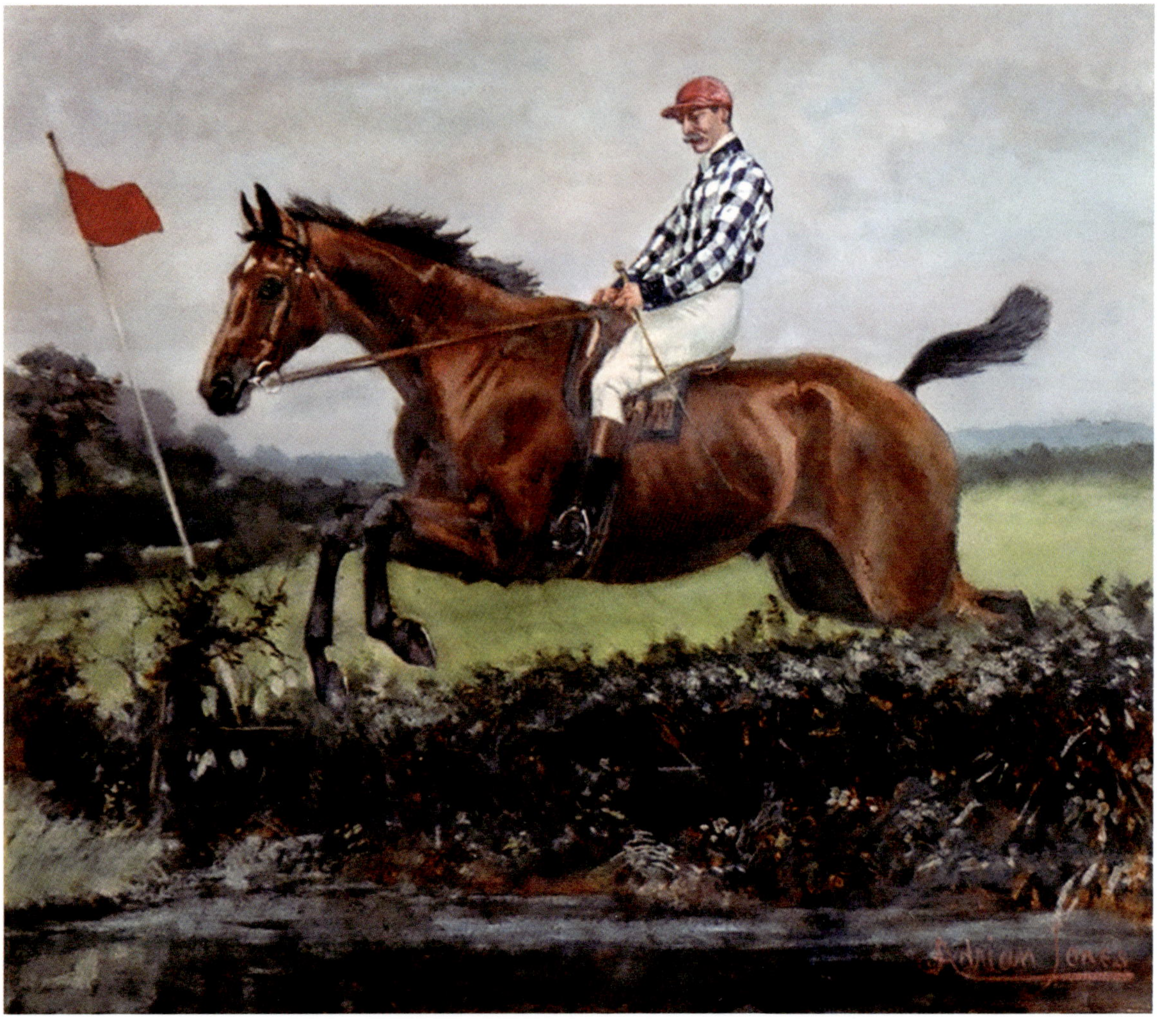

Above: **Raleigh with Colonel Walker up**, 1899
Opposite, top: **Glen Royal, with Jock Fergusson up,** 1899. In this racecourse scene, the spectators are merely background colour to the 1898 National Hunt Steeplechase victor. Emphasising the horse was necessarily Adrian's customary practice. However, in a painting of the Household Brigade Cup race meeting he devoted two thirds of the canvas to the well-dressed crowd, with what appears to be himself in the central foreground.
Opposite, bottom: **Cherry Lass**, 1905

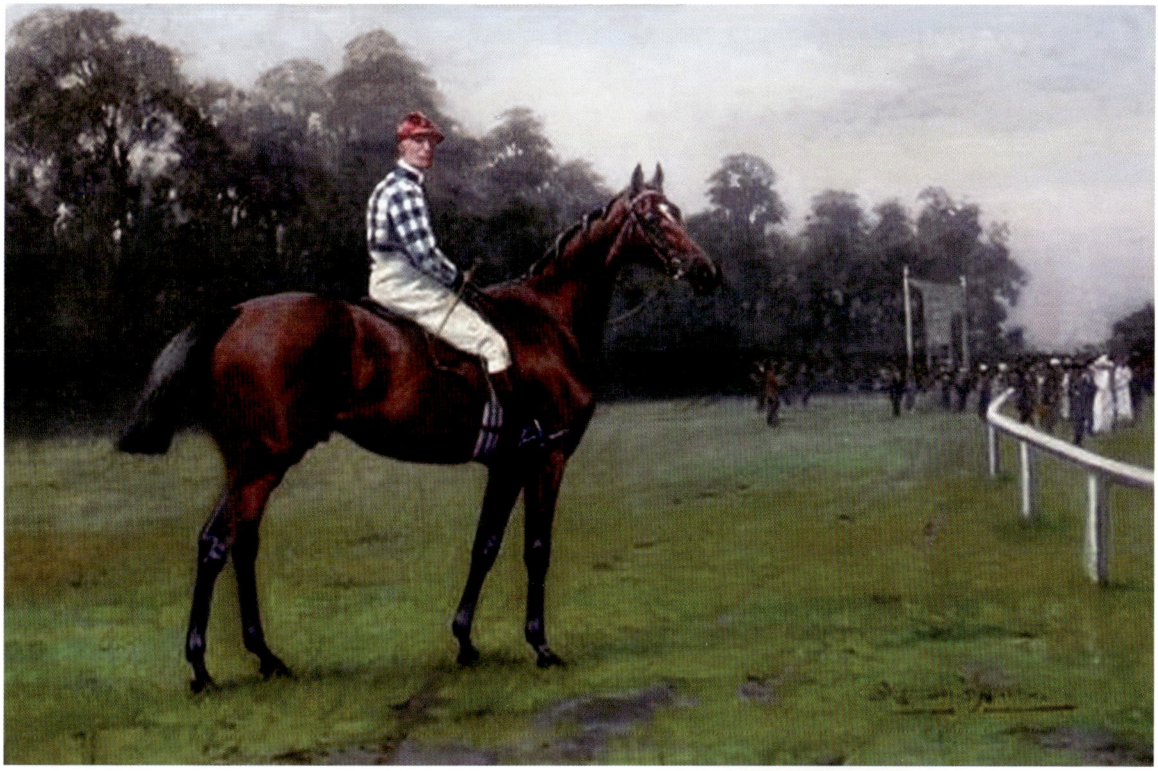

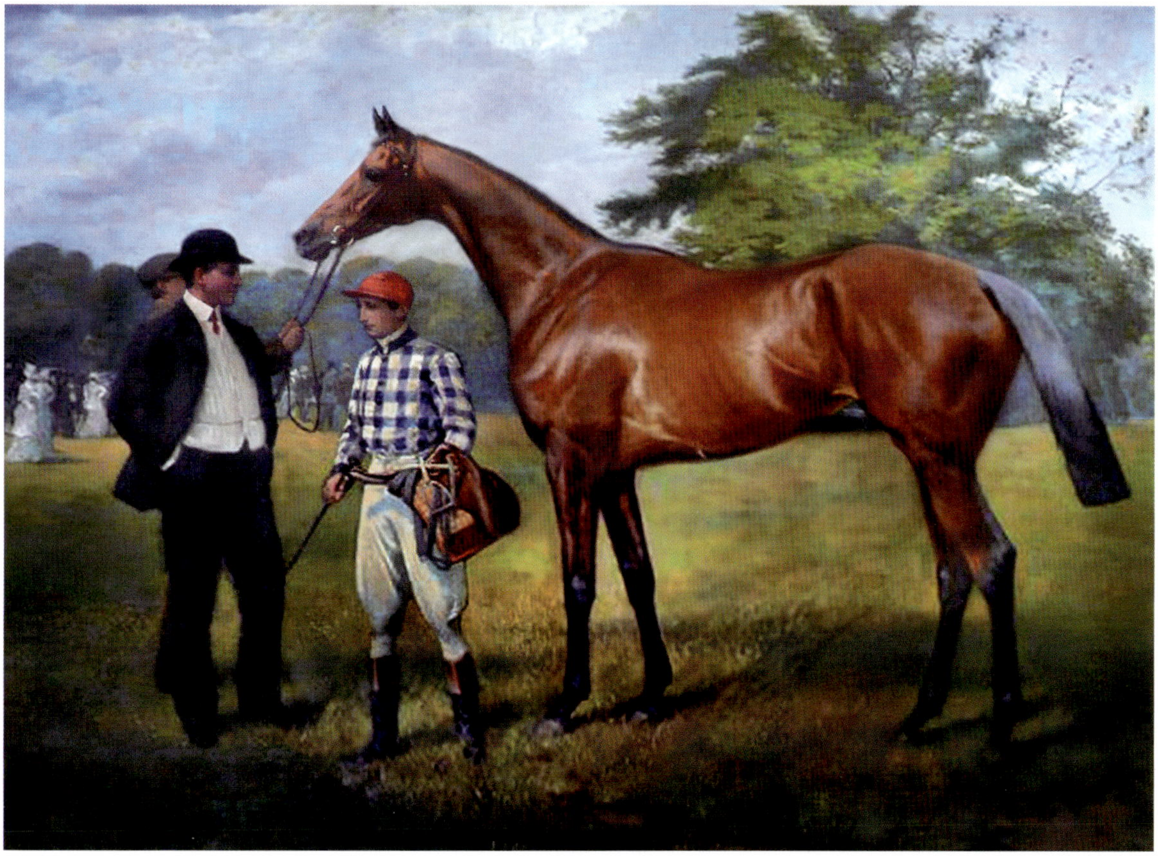

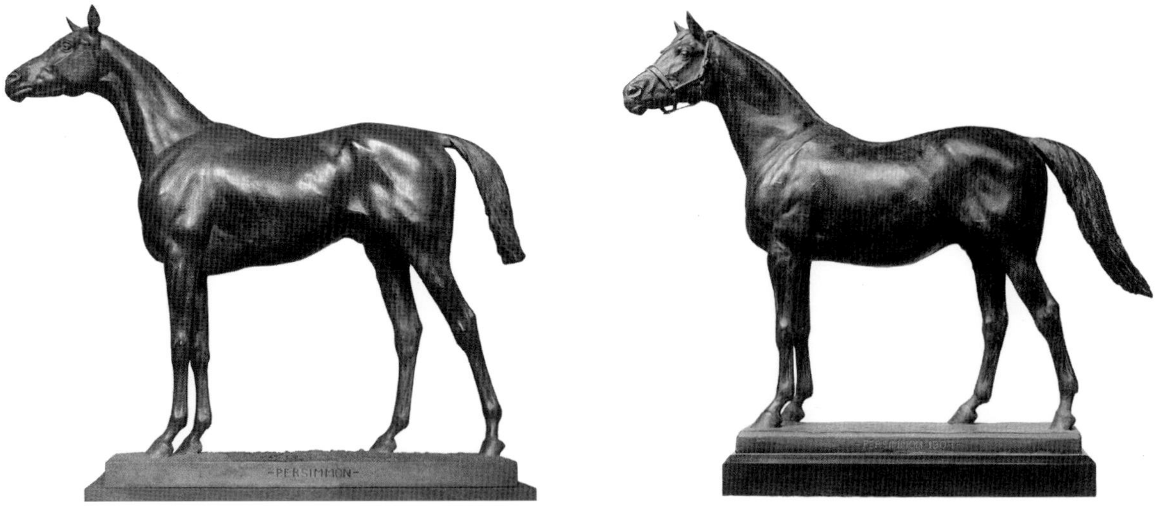

Left: **Persimmon as racehorse**, bronze statuette, 1895
Right: **Persimmon as studhorse**, bronze statuette, 1898. Now that he has been retired from racing, Persimmon's figure has clearly filled out.

certainly the world as I can remember it then was a very jolly place, if only for a minority. Income tax was trifling, business was good, society was festive, money flowed easily and good-fellowship abounded.'

Business was good for Adrian, and paintings and statuettes went from his studio to a variety of patrons. A typical example, exhibited in the National Horse Racing Museum at Newmarket is the equine statuette 'Eager', which was owned by a Mr Cox, and cast to commemorate his three first places in the 1898 and 1899 racing seasons. Adrian's 'business' works, which were not aimed at exhibition in the Royal Academy, were produced at a rate which was the envy of many other artists and which on occasion produced stories in the press. The *Sportsman* of 22 April 1899, under the heading 'City and Suburban Winner', reported :

> There was on exhibition from noon yesterday at 31 New Bond Street an extraordinary picture, the portrait of Newhaven II, Mornington Cannon up, painted on canvas in oils, within less than forty eight hours of the race for the City and Suburban. It was a commission from the Fine Art Military and Sporting Gallery to Mr Adrian Jones ... It is lifelike and complete, and has been done in the amazingly short space of time mentioned. The oils were still wet when we inspected it.

Adrian was able to paint at such speed partly because of his disciplined approach but also because his unerring eye enabled him to get his drawing lines right first time. Quality did not appear to suffer. More surprising, because his public image was as a supreme painter of racehorses, is the variety of his nature paintings. His one man exhibition in the Graves Gallery, Pall Mall, in May and June 1898, had the wordy title 'Sporting, Polo, Hunting and Military Pictures by Captain Adrian Jones', which even at such length did not encompass the range on show. *Lloyd's Weekly Newspaper* told its readers, 'The artist, possessing wide experience of martial and sporting life, gives added interest by a keenly observant eye and a deft, obedient hand in transcribing some very fresh and breezy scenes of nature'. There were the expected hunting scenes – an energetic design of riders and steeds going through a spinney by a brook in 'The First Day of the Season', and huntsmen coming back at sunset in 'After a Good Day'. There were farming scenes: 'The Golden Harvest', replete with ruddy autumn colours, and 'Turning on the Headland', a study of field

working horses. In contrast to those realistic scenes, there was the poetic 'Marmion and the Elfin Knight'. The newspaper also admired 'the true artist-like accomplishment' of the statuettes on display, and rightly described 'The Polo Player' as 'abounding in life and go'. The magazine *Land and Water* complained that the 1898 Royal Academy exhibition was 'very short of sporting subjects; in fact, it does not cultivate or encourage them'. However, it assured its readers, that as compensation 'there was plenty to interest in the Pall Mall exhibition'.

Princess Alexandra loaned the exhibition Adrian's painting of her horse Viva, with her favourite dog Plumpie also in the picture. The Prince of Wales loaned his painting of Persimmon. Unsurprisingly, both visited the exhibition (on separate occasions), for the Prince of Wales was now Adrian's best patron. He had followed his 1895 commissioning of Persimmon as a racehorse by commissioning in 1898 a statuette of the fuller-figured, sturdier Persimmon as stud horse. In 1900 Edward had special cause for celebration. gaining the unique distinction of being the only owner to win in the same year both the Grand National and the flat season classics triple crown of Two Thousand Guineas, Derby and St Leger. A month after the victory of Ambush II in the National, the *Sporting Times* columnist who wrote under the byline 'British Yeoman' spent two hours in Adrian's studio to watch him at work on the Prince's commissioned painting of the horse. He enthused:

> I don't know when I have seen a racing picture that has made such an impression on me. The scene is near the starting post at Aintree, and Barsac and Manifesto are introduced into the picture. Barsac is pricking his ears, and you can almost swear that you see him turn his neck as he always does preparatory to a bit of play at the post. Manifesto looks a bit dignified ... That jaunty air which is so particularly taking in Ambush II is hit off to the life. Anthony's is a speaking likeness, and his seat is admirably portrayed.

Manifesto was Britain's greatest steeplechaser at the end of the 19th century. He had won the National in 1897 and 1899, and was placed another three times. Adrian could not resist painting him, both because of the horse's fame and because when it came to selling prints or engravings a larger number of faces in the picture tended to increase sales. Barsac, another distinguished steeplechaser, shares the painting's middle ground with Manifesto. Ambush II remains the dominant central foreground subject. Adrian also painted for the Prince a version with Ambush II as a solo horse, again with Anthony up, and sculpted for him a bronze statuette which is still at Sandringham.

Prince Edward followed a productive breeding policy of repeatedly sending his mare Perdita to the stallion St Simon to be served. This had added to his racing stable the Ascot and Goodwood Cup winner Florizel II, the outstanding Persimmon, and then his more temperamental younger brother Diamond Jubilee. In the glory year of 1900, Diamond Jubilee, so named because of his birth during Victoria's jubilee in 1897, earned so much prize money by his victories as a three year old colt in the classics' triple crown and the Eclipse Stakes that he eclipsed even Persimmon's performance and made Edward the season's leading owner. Money was therefore plentiful, and Adrian benefited from commissions to paint and model. However, the task of recording Diamond Jubilee proved awkward, particularly in comparison to Adrian's pleasant dealings with Persimmon. It had taken twenty minutes of struggle to saddle Diamond Jubilee for the St Leger, and he approached the starting gate almost entirely on his hind legs – an approach caught in a striking photograph now on display in the National Horseracing Museum. Yet Diamond Jubilee won easily. However, whilst Adrian wanted to capture the 'character' of the horse, to show him misbehaving would have been impolitic. He opted instead to show him waiting placidly for the start of the Derby. The jockey presented no difficulty. Herbert Jones had been Diamond Jubilee's stable lad, and was promoted to jockey because the horse behaved

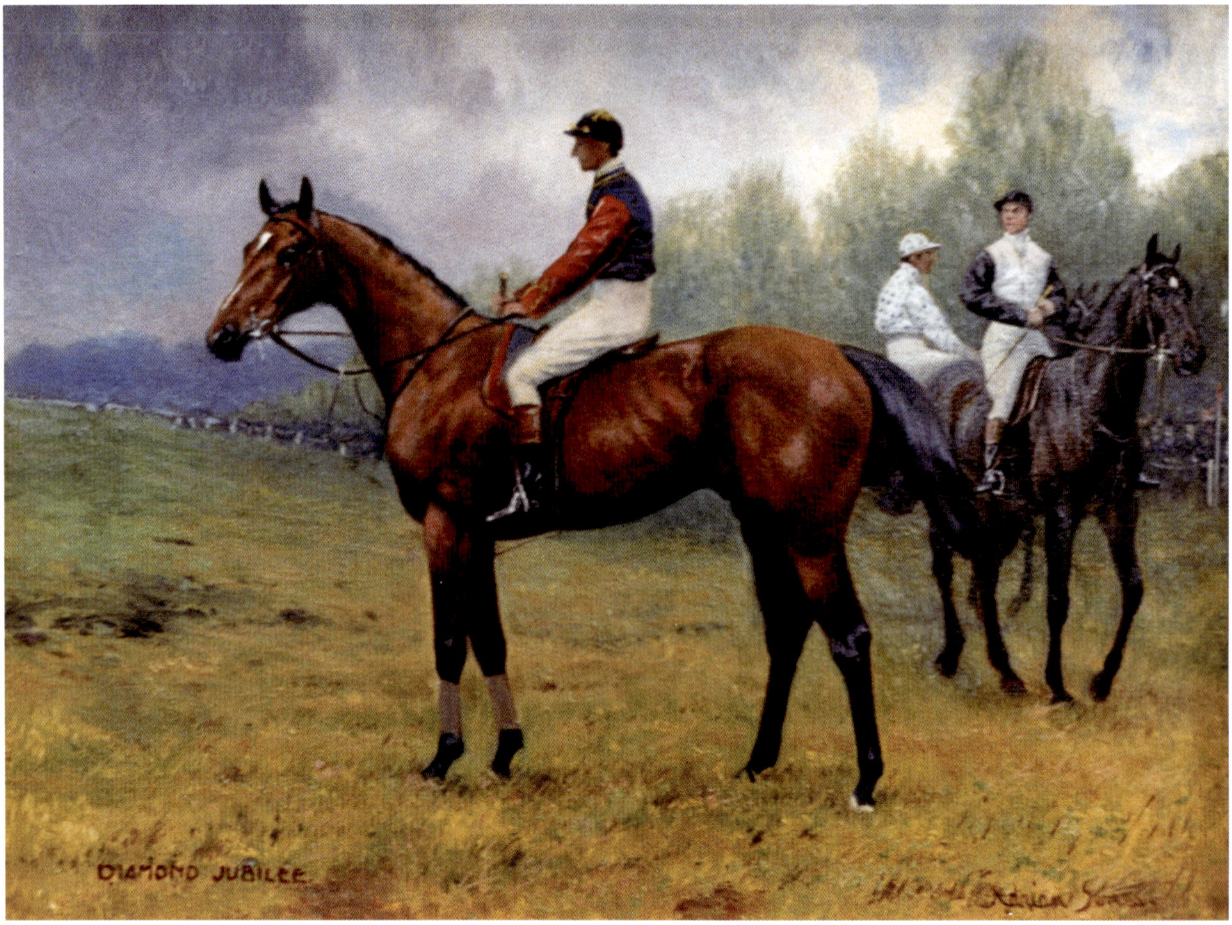

Diamond Jubilee, with Herbert Jones up, 1900

for him, whereas Jack Watts and Mornington Cannon had both on occasion been played up. Adrian records him in the Prince's distinctive racing silks of red sleeves and purple body with gold trimmings. Remembering painting the horse, he exclaimed in his *Memoirs*: 'What a difficult job that was. The horse might be content to put up with jockeys, but he certainly had no use for an artist.' When he attempted to sketch in Diamond Jubilee's box, the colt turned with lightning rapidity and kicked over the easel with his hind legs: 'You could not see the sketch for hoof marks.' When it came to making the statuette he found it impossible to take measurements and had to rely entirely on his eye. He was, however, understanding and forgiving: 'When one considers the life of a racehorse, it is not hard to account for the nerves.' Again he painted variants of the picture of the horse. The dullest area of a conventional side-on horse portrait tends to be the background behind the tail, hence the custom in a typical rectangular composition to leave greater space in front of the head. But in the painting of Diamond Jubilee illustrated here, Adrian has placed two subsidiary horses behind Jubilee, leaving the concentration of interest at the front solely on Jubilee's strong, assertive head. This seems to be part of his effort to express 'what I might call the character of the horse'. Presumably his term 'character' embraces both physique and personality. In his book *Great Racehorses in Art* John Fairley writes that Diamond Jubilee was also characterised by a powerful front and full quarters. Adrian certainly does justice to those; and though Herbert Jones is sitting with the reins relaxed, can we imagine that there is a wicked glint in the horse's eye as it turns towards the painter?

Chapter Ten: 'The realities of the world we live in' 1898-1906: Reminders of Imperial Dangers

Adrian left the army in 1891, but his military experience continued to shape the career as an artist that lay ahead of him. All his connections with high-ranking Army men, together with his knowledge of army life, experience of warfare and expert skill at the portrayal of equine anatomy, made sure that many commissions for portraits, statues and memorial monuments would come his way. But also, his career happened to coincide with an extraordinary transition, from the 'small wars' of Victoria's reign to the great and terrible war which was to come, and which he lived to depict, in an era when public art assumed an importance it had not had before, and perhaps never will again. Then, public commemorations and memorials were a conduit for private emotion, and the artist's values and sensibility was transmitted into bronze, stone and paint in a way that powerfully expressed the sentiments both of the past and the present age. For Adrian, a culminating point was the creation of the Peace Quadriga and its inauguration in 1912; and then came the dreadful realisation that the Quadriga was the herald not of peace, but of a horrific Great War. Before he had to grapple with finding appropriate ways to express the truths and sorrows of that cataclysm, in the 1890s and 1900s he produced a range of works that dealt with the military realities of the age, and allowed him to express wisdom and compassion born of his own experience as an officer and a gentleman.

Memorial to Colonel Charles Pigott (1897-98)

One work he was commissioned to make allowed him to reflect events in which he himself had been involved, though to which he had not been witness, having arrived only when the action was over. This was a memorial to Colonel Charles Berkeley Pigott, who was involved in the disastrous attack at Laing's Nek in the Transvaal in 1881. In his *Memoirs*, Adrian dates the work to 1896, but the strong balance of probability must be against that, as Pigott did not die until 1897, the year inscribed on the memorial. The evidence of his book is that Adrian is fallible on dates, as on the spelling of names, and he is surely a year or two out.

Adrian would first have met Pigott in South Africa, for the 60th Rifles remained there in the aftermath of the war, and would have visited Laing's Nek, just a little over twenty miles north of Newcastle. He met him again in the Sudan in 1884-85, by which time Pigott had changed from the Rifles to the cavalry. He was a captain in the 21st Hussars, and had been appointed commander of D Company of the Mounted Infantry Camel Regiment, a component of the force aiming to rescue General Gordon at Khartoum. His appointment was possibly because of his previous infantry experience: all the other twenty officers in the four companies were from infantry regiments. In 1882 Adrian was a painter artist, but by 1885 he was becoming known to fellow officers as a sculptor. Pigott may have been one of the many officers who bought a cast of Adrian's 'Camel Corps Scout' statuette as a memento of the campaign.

Not many military artists had preceded Adrian in attempting to commemorate the First Boer (or Transvaal) War in art. Unlike the Relief of General Gordon expedition to which Adrian was called two years later, the Transvaal campaign had neither aroused much patriotic feeling nor offered military victories.

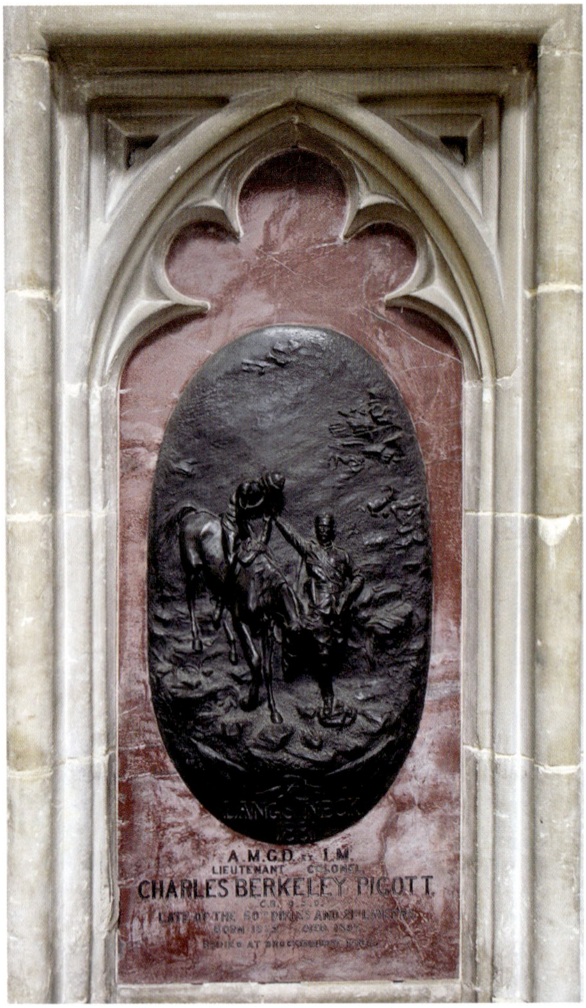

Lieutenant Colonel Pigott Memorial, bas relief, Winchester Cathedral. Adrian particularly admired the selflessness involved in one soldier risking his own life to save another's.

The unpopular war was succeeded by an unpopular peace, seen by its critics as a craven surrender, so the whole affair generated little market for paintings. An exception was a work submitted to the 1882 Royal Academy Exhibition by Lady Elizabeth Butler. Her oil, 'Floreat Etona', depicted a moment in the disaster at Laing's Nek. One Old Etonian officer's mount has just been shot and is collapsing beneath him even as he struggles to maintain his seat. Alongside him gallops another Old Etonian officer, seeking to bolster his comrade's morale by waving his sword aloft and shouting 'Floreat Etona'. The story goes that the words of his school motto were the last he uttered. As they passed from his lips, a Boer shot killed him. The painting, however, freezes the action a moment before that. For civilian visitors to the RA Exhibition, the picture must have seemed essentially an evocation of military spirit and dash. For any forward-thinking military visitor, however, the subtext spoke of futile tactics. Out in front of soldiers on foot, these were infantry officers using impractical cavalry methods as they waved their useless cold steel at the out-of-reach enemy who were firing at them from concealed prone positions. Lady Butler gives some hint of how wasted was their bravery, morally admirable but tactically mistaken: in the background she paints the colonel in command of the British attack on his distinctive white horse. His head is thrown back. He too has been picked off by the Boer marksmen. The visitor could view the painting as tribute to or criticism of the public school ethos, a plus for bravery but a minus for professional inadequacy. Either way, the emphasis on one school narrowed the picture's appeal, and it went into a private collection. While at Newcastle Adrian had, as described earlier, prepared the sketches for his large painting of 'General Gore Leading the Inniskillings over Bennet's Drift'. It and 'Floreat Etona' are the only two paintings of the Transvaal War mentioned by Peter Harrington in his monumental *British Artists and War* of 1993. He knew of it only from Adrian's mentioning it in his *Memoirs*, and its present whereabouts – if any – are not known.

So for the present the only place to see a publicly displayed Adrian Jones work associated with the Transvaal War is Winchester Cathedral. Sited on the north wall of the nave, in an area of Rifle Brigade memorials, is his memorial to Lieutenant Colonel C.B. Pigott. Adrian writes:

> It represents Captain Berkeley Piggot (*sic*) on Laing's Nek, bringing the wounded men out of action under a hail of bullets. I carried out this design in white metal. Every now and again some work associated with the Army would bring back to me the realities of the world we live

in. It would offer stern reminders of the days when I too was facing danger or death, but was finding time, even in hours of crisis, to study the movements of animals in action.

His memorial is a bas relief set on marble in a framed blind arch window, a commission Adrian was happy to undertake. It gave him the opportunity to pay tribute to a soldier he knew, to record the main redeeming feature of the Laing's Nek defeat, and to include a reference to a significant moment in British military history. Also, in 1898 anything that included a reference to the 21st Lancers (as the 21st Hussars had been re-designated) was likely to arouse interest; at the time the 21st were the darlings of public patriotism because of their famed charge at Omdurman, and Adrian was working on a painting of that. The wording below the relief announces that it is to the Greater Glory of God and In Memoriam of Lieutenant Colonel Charles Berkeley Pigott, CB, DSO, Late of the 60th Rifles and 21st Lancers; Born 1859, Died 1897. Immediately above is the year and the anglicised name of the battle site, Langs Neck, and crossed Colours. Crossed regimental Colours and royal Colours flags are not uncommon on military memorials, and Adrian used the motif again seven years later on his Second Boer War Memorial for the Carabiniers. The emphasis there is on the regiment, so his treatment of the flags is detailed. The regiment's emblazoned badges and battle honours show up clearly. But his purpose on the Pigott memorial is different. The usual format for relief sculpture, as conventionally taught in art schools, was a framed rectangle, more often horizontal than vertical, with of course a flat rear plane. Adrian would feature bas relief rectangles to excellent informative and artistic effect on many of his greatest outdoor sculptures – the memorials to the Carabiniers, the Marines, the Gloucestershire Hussars and the Cavalry of the Empire, and the equestrian statue of the Duke of Cambridge. For the indoor, smaller memorial in Winchester Cathedral, however, although the whole is framed by a vertical rectangle, the eye barely notices that. Attention is seized by the unusual oval bas relief. The cleverly positioned flags seem to be giving structural support to the scene.

In the background of her painting, Lady Butler had shown the black silk colours of the 58th Regiment of Foot flying above the battle. She included this significant detail because she knew that by the 1880s colours really had no place on the battlefield. They might well symbolise the spirit of the regiment and make a brave sight, but the colour party was too vulnerable to small arms fire. Painting as soon as possible after the event, she recorded the waving colours as something noteworthy because of its extreme rarity. The practice of carrying them had been just about obsolete even fifteen years earlier, when Adrian had witnessed them carried during the storming of Magdala. By the time he came to sculpt Laing's Nek, another fifteen years on from the event, he knew it had turned out to be the last time in British military history that a regiment would carry its colours into battle (and, despite the defeat, saved them). So he gave them a place on the memorial plaque. Charles Pigott, however, was an officer of the 60th Rifles, so it would have been inappropriate to sculpt the flags of the 58th Foot. The colours are therefore left anonymous, a retrospective support and tribute to the battlefield acts of heroism which they inspired.

There were doubtless a number of instances of Pigott's bravery which Adrian could have chosen to depict, because the 60th Rifles had been in the thick of things. He chose a moment later in the battle than the doomed advance painted by Lady Butler. Pigott, revolver in hand to fight off anyone who tries to stop him, is leading a casualty to safety. Bravery motivated by compassion, at the risk of one's own life to defend another's, had a strong emotional appeal for Adrian. He was to use the theme again on his first large outdoor war memorial sculpture, the Marines monument on the Mall. For Pigott, he had a further reason for choosing this particular act of compassion. Two Victoria Crosses were awarded after Laing's Nek. One went to a Lieutenant of the 58th for making three journeys under heavy fire over open ground to bring in wounded men. The second went to a batman trooper of the King's Dragoons who, though himself shot through both arms, gave up his horse

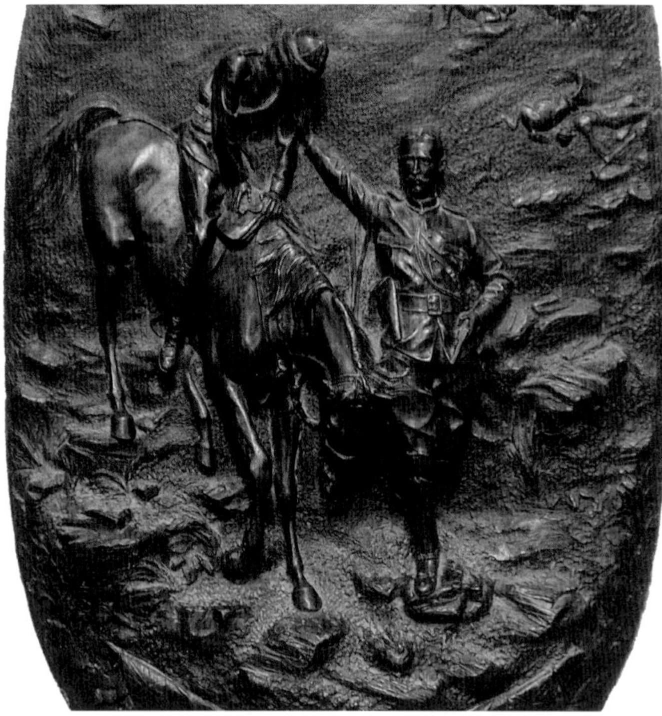

Pigott Memorial, bas relief detail

to the commanding officer of the cavalry who had fallen injured when his horse was shot from beneath him. The trooper, taking the reins beneath his wounded arm, led horse and officer through gunfire to the ambulance. Rescuing the wounded was the definitive image for noble acts at Laing's Nek.

Adrian wrote of representing Pigott 'bringing the wounded men out of action under a hail of bullets', but to have shown such a multiple scene would have involved reduced emphasis on the subject of the memorial, and sculpting 'a hail of bullets' in bas relief is virtually impossible. The hail could only have been shown indirectly through the postures of the men, but to have portrayed Pigott cowering or dodging would have been unacceptably unheroic to Victorian eyes. Sensibly (for this is not art for art's sake but for the family's sake), and of course probably truthfully, Adrian shows Pigott upright, arm extended to support the wounded private whom he has lifted on to his own officer's horse, because Pigott's priority is to save the man rather than to take cover himself; but in the background Adrian sketches the unheroic grim reality of war, as depicted by the casualties of men and horses.

As an experienced scenic painter, Adrian had no problems with perspective. The three-dimensional effect, achieved without straying into high relief, is remarkable, and such details as the reins looped over Pigott's right shoulder are superbly crafted. Adrian has used the opportunity of bas relief to sculpt the horse on a steep downward incline. He avoided that pose in his equestrian and equine statues: those had to look good from all sides. A raised hindquarter cutting across the sightline from below to the rider might not be artistically successful. On a bas relief, however, obviously nobody could view it from the back.

Perhaps Britain's best known work of art depicting suffering in war is 'Gassed', painted by Adrian's friend John Singer Sargent in 1918 and now in the Imperial War Museum. Adrian considered Sargent the greatest portrait painter of his time, and his iconic masterpiece of the line of men blinded by mustard gas (usually only temporarily, though most viewers do not realise that) still evokes a horrified emotional response. It too was a commission, intended for remembrance: the War Office wanted a painting commemorating the men of the Great War. There was little appetite in 1918 for heroic battle scenes, and Sargent recorded a post-battle moment. Any heroism is in the past; now there is just Wilfred Owen's 'the pity of war', and the pity war evokes. 'Gassed' is a major work, while in the overall corpus of Adrian Jones's art, the oval plaque for Charles Pigott is a minor work. But in executing it he had to meet two demands: to pay due tribute to heroic action in an outpost of Empire, and to record in the figure of the slumped, exhausted, wounded private the human cost of imperial action. With the passing of time and the Empire, any sense of a 'hail of bullets' has been lost. Now, like Sargent's, it seems a post-battle scene of suffering and compassion, with the officer's pistol barrel not aimed but lowered. Adrian would surely be pleased that his 'stern reminder of danger and death' is now more likely to be seen as tribute to the nobility of human comradeship and human compassion.

Omdurman (1899)

The Pigott memorial had involved thoughts and feelings generated by a defeat. Different sentiments, those of victory, are associated with another work completed by Adrian at around the same time. Major General Sir Herbert Kitchener's army won the battle of Omdurman, the decisive moment in the reconquest of the Sudan, on 2 September 1898. The commander of Kitchener's 3rd Egyptian Brigade was Brigadier 'Taffy' Lewis, like Adrian a former pupil of Ludlow Grammar School. He kept a diary, now in the National Army Museum, of his eye-witness experience, which included facing the Mahdist army's advance on his brigade:

> Soon began as fine a spectacle as it comes to the lot of most soldiers to see ... Gradually our whole front from the river south to the Kerreri Hills was enveloped by a deep mass of men moving regularly and rapidly, hundreds of flags waving over them, and their deep war chant was carried down to us like the noise of the sea. The order and pace with which they moved struck us so particularly. This was no horde of savages but a well-ordered army.

Numerically that army was twice the strength of Kitchener's. Yet the Anglo-Egyptian firepower annihilated them. As the poet Hilaire Belloc encapsulated it: 'We have got / The Maxim gun and they have not'. From a British perspective, the battle unromantically demonstrated the fighting superiority of modern weaponry. But one minor incident harked back to earlier times: a thundering cavalry charge by the 21st Lancers. Within five months of those few minutes of hand-to-hand bravery, Adrian had completed a ten-foot-wide painting of the scene.

The painting first came to public notice in March 1899 in newspaper accounts of that year's first 'Studio Sunday'. On such Sundays those artists who could not place RA or ARA after their name, and therefore had to send their works to the Burlington House jury for consideration, would open their studio doors to fellow artists, friends and acquaintances to give them an advance viewing of what was being submitted to the Royal Academy. Essentially the occasions were social, but some press correspondents would attend. The *Newcastle Leader* columnist, having put himself through the tiring business of visiting a 'considerable number of studios', picked out only one work for particular comment: 'Captain Adrian Jones has just completed what is perhaps the most important picture he has painted for some time.'

Adrian was far from alone in entering the market with an Omdurman painting. Thirteen years earlier the death of Gordon had called forth a wave of imperial sentiment on which artists had surfed. In retrospect, however, there was no disguising that Wolseley's Nile Expeditionary Force had been unsuccessful in its mission. The view of war correspondent G.W. Steevens expressed in *With Kitchener to Khartoum* was typical. He compared 'the machine-like precision of Kitchener's campaign' to 'the extempore, amateur scrambles of Wolseley' and invited his readers to 'read over the tale again now – the faltering and the folly and the failure ... we blundered when we suffered Gordon to go out, we fiddled and failed when we tried to bring him back'. By contrast, in 1898 'we have gained precious national self-respect'. In his role of correspondent for the *Morning Post* Winston Churchill suggested that 'now the British People may ... tell some stone mason to ... cut on the pedestal of Gordon's statue in Trafalgar Square ... the not unsatisfactory word "Avenged".' Clearly the great and comprehensive victory at Omdurman, an apogee of Empire, called for commemoration, not least in art. But the destruction of the 'fine spectacle' witnessed by Taffy Lewis was too uncomfortably one-sided and bloody for British taste. Independently yet almost as one, painters opted instead for the charge of the 21st Lancers.

Militarily, the charge was folly. Without reconnoitring, the cavalry charged across unknown ground towards an unknown number of enemy marshalled in a defensive formation. But as a Lancers' officer who charged in 'A' squadron with Winston Churchill wrote afterwards: 'Wise or unwise, it was a brave deed nobly done.' The cavalry had shown the admired Victorian virtue of pluck. The British people glorified them, the War Office did not make public its adverse opinion, and the painters could make better pictures of this heroic charge than they could of the well-conducted main battle.

In *With Kitchener to Khartoum* Steevens uses as his illustration (in black and white) a painting by Stanley Berkeley. Like the better known George Rowlandson picture, it shows an early moment in the action when the scene is still chiefly a cavalry charge. Rowlandson's horses, roughly in line, sweep across the canvas from right to left. It is a dashing composition which has lent itself to use on book covers and dust jackets, as the Lancers gallop across the book front, round the spine and then continue across the back cover, led by the upraised arm of their commanding officer, Colonel Martin. The *Illustrated London News* used a contemporary picture sub-titled 'An Exciting Moment'. That moment is the one late in the battle when two officers earned the Victoria Cross trying to rescue an unhorsed fellow officer by lifting him onto one of their own horses.

This theme, however, was too similar to the one Adrian had chosen for his bas relief memorial to Captain Pigott; he wanted a different focus for his Omdurman scene. Like Caton Woodville in the vigorous painting which hangs in the National Army Museum, he depicts the moment the Mahdist Emir commander on his black charger rushed boldly at the Lancers. The ways the two painters composed the scene show many similarities of detail and accurate recording. On the right of each is the crowded mass of Mahdist infantry and their flags; centre right, Colonel Martin, who had disdained to draw either sword or revolver, on his white horse, pointing the way forward; centre, the helmeted, sword-wielding Emir; left, a British officer, sword arm raised, encouraging his men. Neither painter shows British 'victory' (moments later, a lance thrust killed the Emir). However, Caton Woodville's painting is more of a set piece: the Lancers, still in what is recognisably a line-abreast cavalry charge, against the dominant central Emir and his crouching foot soldiers. Adrian's painting, by contrast, could justly be retitled 'Mêlée at Omdurman'.

When his painting was on exhibition, the *Manchester Courier* complained that this 'ambitious battle scene ... lacks concentration'. But that is the point. The battle, though brief, almost instantly became pell-mell confusion. This was old-fashioned every-man-look-out-for-himself-and-his-mates hand-to-hand combat in which superior European battlefield technology such as traversing machine guns played no part. As Churchill commented, concentration was individual – for him, 'eye, bridle-hand and trigger finger'; for most others, eye, bridle-hand and lance or sword arm. Adrian knew his chosen scene, in which the Lancers' Syrian cavalry horses and the Emir's charger could be shown in varied postures rather than all racing forward, suited his veterinary understanding of equine movement, but he took care also artistically to frame the confused scene between the officer's sword held aloft on the left and the Mahdist black flag on the right.

The painting shows the centre of the Lancers' charge. They have galloped forward with their lances lowered in the 'attack infantry' position still held by two attackers in the central middleground, but the wedged crowd of rear ranks have been forced to raise their lances uselessly upright, and the trooper on the black horse still has his carbine redundant in its holster bucket. Adrian was professionally familiar with the British cavalry uniforms; but he also accurately depicts Mahdist dress and weaponry, both standard features like white turbans, jibbahs (tunics) with sewn-on coloured 'poverty patches', leaf-bladed spear and straight-bladed, double-edged sword, and distinctive details like the officer's Turkish style helmet and the flag-bearer's close-fitting decorated cap. Adrian knew that the horses issued to the 21st Lancers had not been of uniform

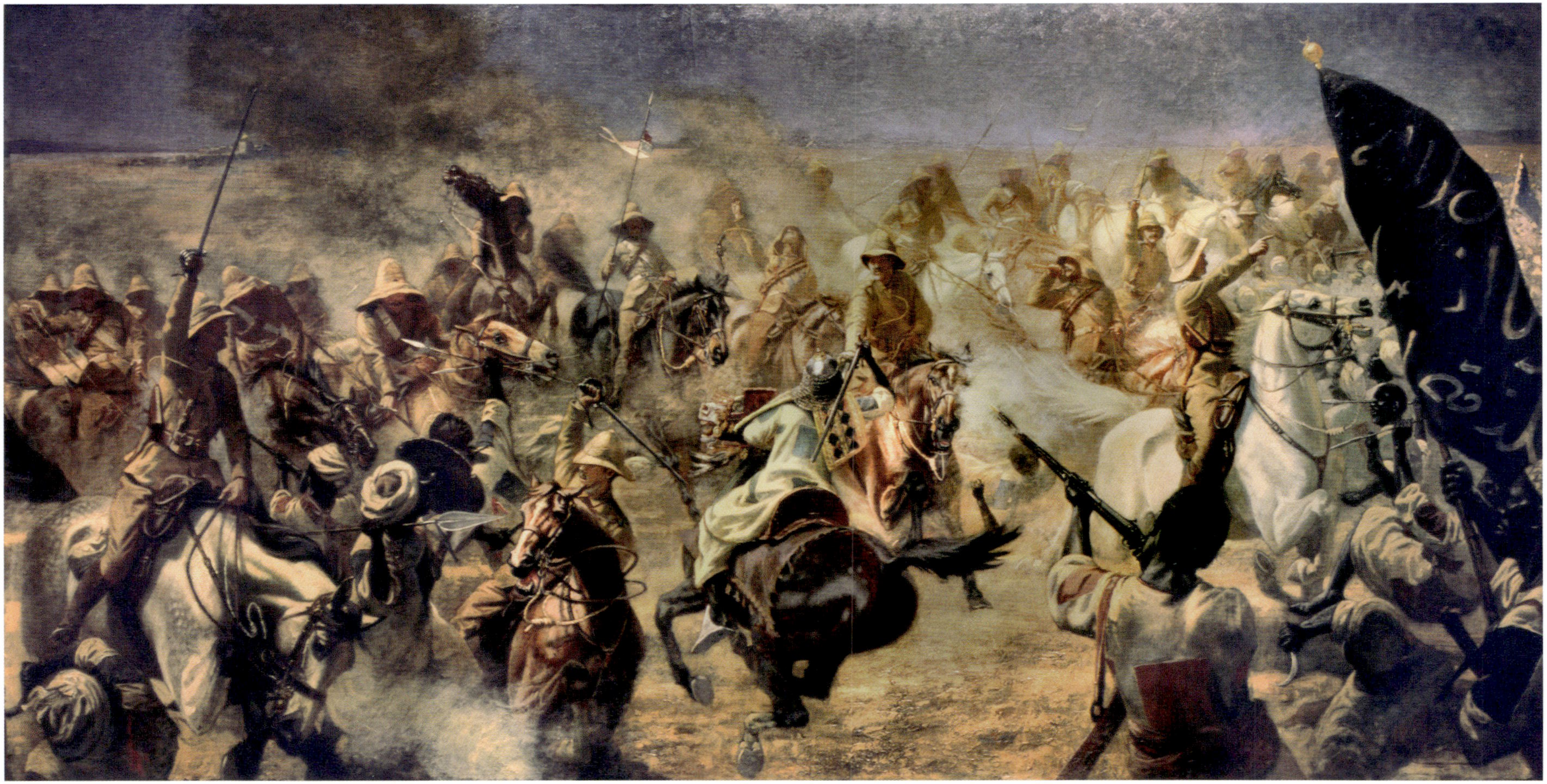

Charge of the 21st (Empress of India's) Lancers at the battle of Omdurman, 1898/99.
The spirited charge earned the regiment three Victoria Crosses, made it famous in a day, and attracted many Victorian artists.

colour and he knew the exact shade of horse ridden by the leading officers of both sides, just as he knew that at this late stage in the reconquest of Sudan campaign many Hadendowa tribesmen had shed their fuzzy-wuzzy hairstyle for the close crop of the right foreground rifleman.

He could not hope to be so exactly true to the participants' actions. No war photographer had been there to freeze the moment. But, as the Manchester newspaper noted, he makes an 'ambitious' attempt. Before the flagbearer a warrior lies prone, hoping to be at least beyond the range of any mounted soldier's sword sweep if not of a lance thrust, whilst he seeks with his curved dagger to land a disabling slash on horse or rider or stirrup leathers. The Emir readies himself to swing over his heavy Mahdist sword which could carve woundingly through the lighter cavalry sabre. Though unlike a film or multi-media art installation the painting cannot reproduce the bedlam of confused battle, a trumpeter is sounding a call to no apparent effect. All the exhorting, yelling, cursing, aiming or thrusting or hacking men are below the picture's dust-shrouded skyline, for they are fighting down in one of the khors (dried water channels) that ran across the Omdurman plain.

The *Newcastle Leader* writer could hardly contain his enthusiasm:

> An episode which gives abundant scope for the display of that knowledge of soldiers and of horses in which Mr Jones is not excelled by any living artist ... This whole scene reeking with heat and dust. It is a stirring picture, but interest will centre less on the men than upon the horses. These are painted with superb skill. In every variety of attitude – galloping, turning, halting ... they always remain living, moving animals. One may almost see the quiver of the flesh and the dilation of the nostrils as the breath comes and goes in quick pants.

The painting was bought from Adrian by two brothers named Brinton who had ridden in the 21st Lancers' charge, and was later bequeathed to the regiment. Its amalgamation with the 17th Lancers brought together the 21st's Omdurman painting and the 17th's statuette by Adrian of the Duke of Cambridge. When in its turn the 17th/21st became part of the Queen's Royal Lancers, the new regiment purchased Adrian's works. The painting is thus the property of the regiment and goes with it on its travels. George Rowlandson's dashing canvas, however, belongs to the regimental museum, so its horses must stay there.

The Royal Marines Memorial (1902-03)

The Boxer Rising of 1899 and the Second Boer War which began in the same year marked the end of a century of British imperial expansion and conflict, and gave rise to a commission which, Adrian later reported in his *Memoirs*, made him feel 'particularly pleased'; he stated, with excusable pride, that 'I thought that my star was really in the ascendant'.

In 1902 the officers of the Royal Marines had formed a committee whose brief was to bring about the erection of a statue to honour the Marines killed in the Boxer Rising and Boer wars. Adrian was invited to submit a model design, and the committee met in his studio to view it, and decided there and then to give him the commission. In career terms, this was a breakthrough. Though the Marines Memorial would not be his first large statue (that was 'Duncan's Horses', ten years previously), it was his first commission, with all the financial certainty which that brought, for a large statue to be sited in a public open space. The site had already been chosen. Although the Marines had a long connection with London, as the first corps of marines had been raised there under the title 'The Admirals' Men' in 1664, until now the city had had no Marines Memorial. Because of the Marines' unique role as seagoing soldiers, the memorial now proposed would stand just off the Mall in St James's Park, near both the Admiralty Arch and the old Army headquarters,

Horse Guards. (During 1939-45 the memorial was slightly damaged in the German blitz on London, so was moved to a storage yard in Nine Elms and then to the grounds of the Royal Hospital at Chelsea, before being returned in 1948, close still to Admiralty Arch, but now on the north side of the Mall. In October 2000 the Marines rededicated it.)

The *Daily Telegraph*, in the 1900s boasting the world's largest circulation of any morning paper, reported to its readership that 'there was a very large attendance' at the original unveiling ceremony in April 1903, and devoted some 1,400 words to describing the event for those readers who had not been present. It was in every way a big occasion. The Prince of Wales (afterwards George V), who unveiled the memorial, was accompanied by Princess May in a pale mauve costume with a fur collar (then acceptable) and a suitably large hat. Their guard of honour was drawn from three separate Marines barracks. Beside them, facing the memorial, paraded the Marines band and the Corps colours. The Prince inspected the parade. In his wake followed Earl Roberts, the Commander-in-Chief of the Army, and the Earl of Selborne, the First Lord of the Admiralty. The watchers included members of the Cabinet, MPs and a host of naval and military officers in full uniform, not least the Marines major who had won the Victoria Cross for his gallantry in the defence of the British Legation at Peking in 1900.

The Prince pulled away the enveloping Union Jacks. As they fell, the guard of honour presented arms, the band played 'When our heads are bowed with woe', officers saluted, and the men in the crowd stood bareheaded until the last notes of 'Last Post' in a specially composed setting died away. The Edwardians did this kind of ceremony well, its symbolic significance emphasised by the presence of so many important officers of state. As the Prince stated in his speech following the unveiling, deep regret for the loss of lives melded with pride and satisfaction that the dead were now honoured at a 'prominent position in the capital of the Empire'. He continued, 'I should like to congratulate the sculptor, Mr Adrian Jones, on the choice of his subject and the able manner in which he has carried out the work of this beautiful statue.' Such public praise, which was followed by private personal congratulations from the Prince after he had inspected the statue more closely, was remarkable recognition for a tyro sculptor of

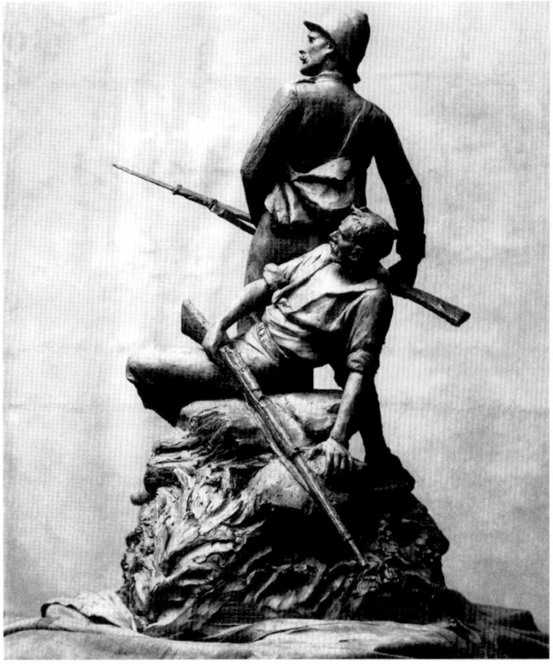

Royal Marines Memorial: initial design, studio plaster statue

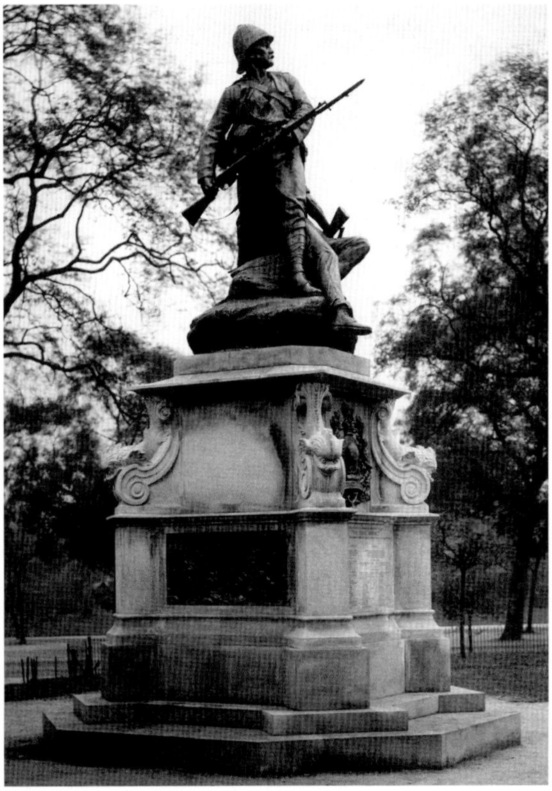

Royal Marines Memorial: 1903, then sited on south side of the Mall

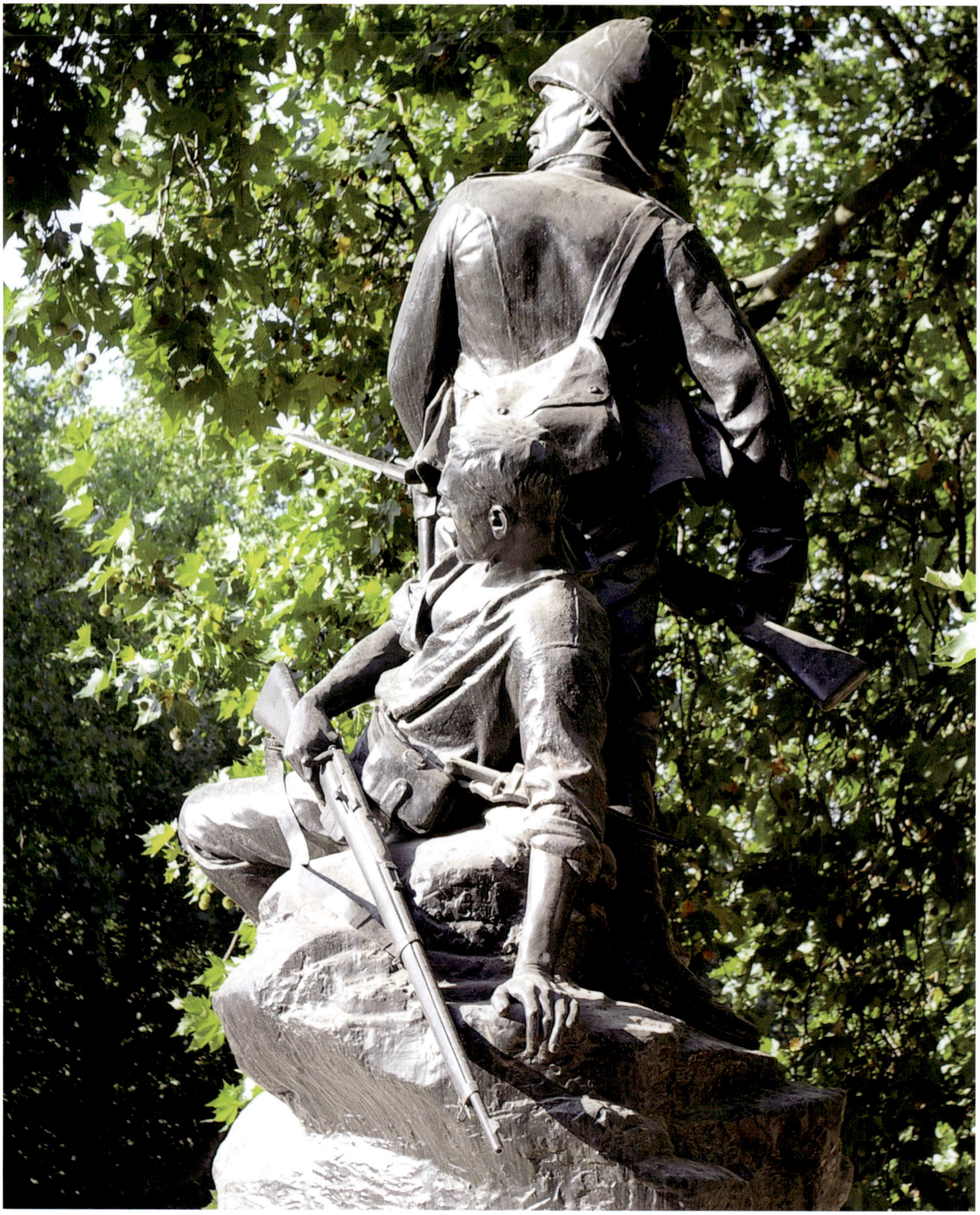

Royal Marines Memorial: the statue, back view. Comparison with the studio model reveals how Adrian has lowered the unimportant rock feature and cleaned up its line, repositioned the wounded Marine closer to the broad back of his defender, and restored his equipment, including a bayonet, so there can be no sense of his having abandoned it.

large public works, and the statue retained public esteem in the years that followed. When a later, greater war broke out in August 1914, *The British Architect* journal in September 1914 looked again at the Marines Memorial: 'There is no need to explain to anyone the tale of courage and resolution which it typifies ... It is to be hoped that when the time comes to memorialise the doings of those who are now protecting our lives and honour, we shall erect nothing less worthy than this adequate and beautiful memorial by Captain Jones.' ('Adequate' of course carries the Edwardian force of 'fully befitting' rather than the 21st-century sense of 'barely satisfactory'.)

The *British Architect* also thought the Marines statue 'one of the few London statues with a really well-designed pedestal'. Often the pedestals of Adrian's large statues are architect-designed, but for the Marines the design was his own, though it owes the stone dolphins that replaced the bronze ones of the original design to the suggestion of Sir Thomas Jackson, who, unlike some Royal Academicians, was constructively supportive of Adrian's work. The four dolphins, outward facing at the four corners of the pedestal's upper tier, refer to the regiment's seaborne history of conflicts around the world: the two on the corners facing the Mall flank the Marines' globe and laurel badge. On the lower tier Adrian positioned two bas reliefs dated 1902, which reveals that this large project had taken a full year to complete. One plaque depicts a sortie: the Marines are scrambling over a wall from the grounds of the British Legation in Peking to force the Chinese attackers to retreat. They are led by a United States Marine Corps captain (the figure on the extreme right, whom Adrian distinguishes by his American hat), because all the senior British officers had been killed or wounded. The scene is savage. In the right foreground a Chinese attacker is being bayoneted; centre foreground another lies dead; to the left, some Chinese, including the plaque's most prominent figure, who is sculpted in higher relief, are turning to flee. The second bas relief is a Boer War scene, the battle at Graspan Heights in which nearly half of the Marines engaged became casualties. Both pictures are carefully composed. In the Peking scene the opposing forces close at the apex of a triangle. The eye is led along the files of advancing British, pauses at the horrific violence of the meeting point where the advance is momentarily checked

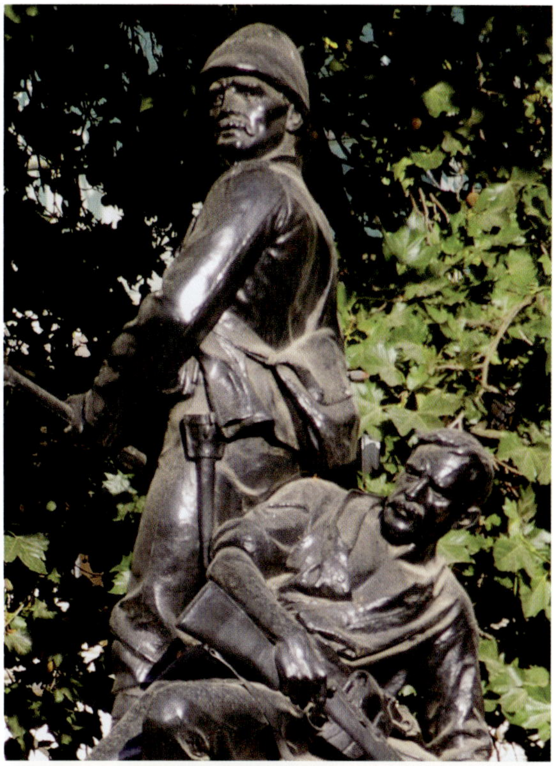

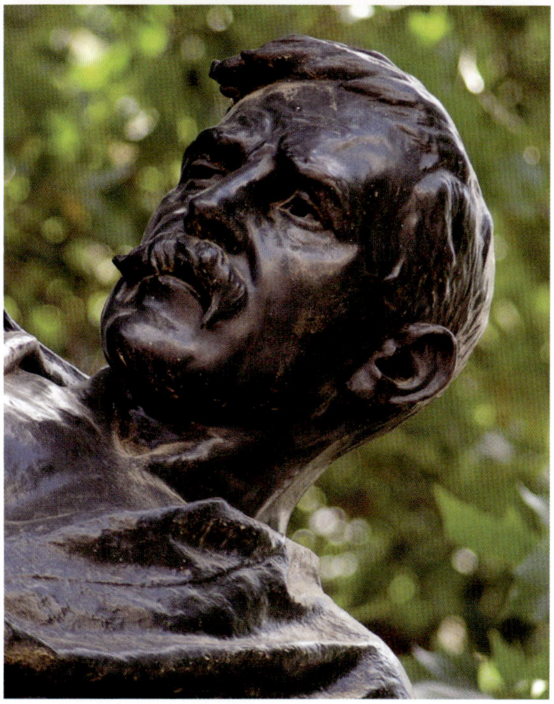

Above: **Royal Marines Memorial**, detail, side view. Greater love hath no man than this ...'
Below: Detail, head of the wounded, exhausted Marine

by a few resolute Chinese riflemen, and then is moved left by the prominent fleeing Chinese man towards the general scene of hurried retreat. (It is a scene that captures the attention of passers by in the Mall: sometimes Chinese tourists pause to be photographed alongside this London reference to an incident in the history of their own capital city.) On the South African plaque, the alignment of the left foreground rocks, the directed binoculars, and the barrel of the field gun all lead the eye diagonally right to the Marines' arduous and hazardous uphill assault.

The bronze statue on the pedestal is of two marines exposed on slightly sloping rock slabs. In his subsequent regimental memorials Adrian usually depicted military action but avoided explicit foreground scenes of war's beastliness. He continued, however, with the choice, already prefigured in his Camel Scout memento, of other ranks rather than officers for his statues. His large painted portraits and his commissioned statues of famous military leaders were necessarily concerned with high-ranking officers, but for war memorial statues he invariably sculpted other ranks in recognition of what they had endured. Here a defiant marine stands guard to defend the life of his exhausted, presumably wounded, comrade; he embodies St John's words: 'Greater love hath no man than this, that a man lay down his life for his friends.' The rear-sight on his rifle is lowered, for the enemy are too close to be picked off by long distance shooting. Instead, his bayonet is fixed for last ditch close combat. The exhausted man supports himself by one arm braced on the rock slab, and though his other hand still clutches his rifle, the sense is that he is too weak to raise it. His bayonet lies uselessly undrawn in its scabbard; he has no strength left for jabbing.

In this composition of heroic action and suffering, Adrian's detailing is, as usual, impressive. He had to model a weapon new to him. The 'long' Lee-Enfield rifle, with which the Marines had been equipped in the Boer War, had been introduced to the army five years after Adrian's retirement. But there is more to the detailing than just accurately reproduced weaponry. Similar exactness distinguishes everything from the folds of the sleeves to the winding of the puttees. Such precise execution is comparable to the particularised realism of the Pre-Raphaelite paintings Adrian had seen during his artistic development, though in 1903 Pre-Raphaelite style was out of fashion. To compare chalk with cheese, it is revealing to walk from the Mall through Admiralty Arch and turn right down Whitehall to pause at Oscar Neman's affectionate statue of

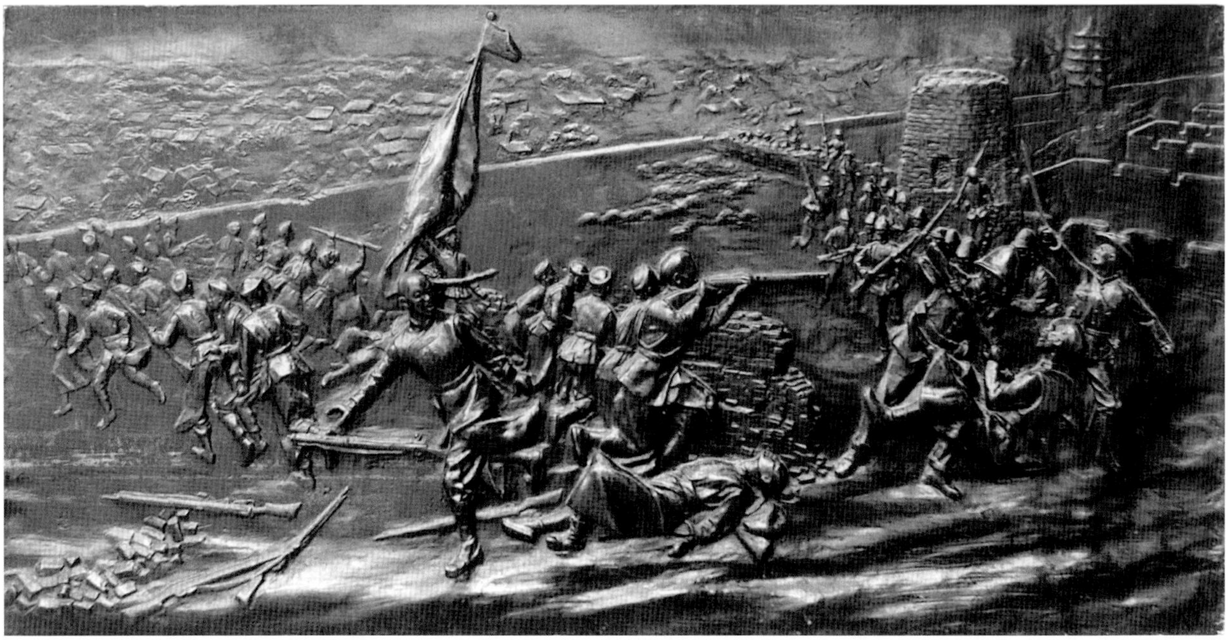

Royal Marines Memorial, bas relief: Marines defending the British Legation, Peking, during the Boxer Rising

Field Marshal Montgomery standing at ease. The sculptor's use of rough bobbling technique on battledress blouse and trousers continues down onto the shoes and the ground, so Monty seems almost to merge with the base. He is totally recognisable, but his 'character' is not clear. He appears unassuming, which he was not, and undifferentiated from his setting, whereas he usually sought to stand out from the competition. The attitude captures his popular style of addressing the Desert Rats, yet leaves much unsaid. The Marines statue, as the *British Architect* noticed, 'tells a tale ... such as all may understand'.

As an artist Adrian is most renowned for his horses, but the admirable Royal Marines memorial owes nothing to his reverence for equine nature or his skill with equine subjects. When it is said of him that he is better at horses than humans, that is a comparative judgement. While he is excellent at horses, the Marines statue is evidence that his depiction of humans could be excellent too, as exemplified by the strained, anxious expression of the wounded soldier.

The Carabiniers (6th Dragoon Guards) Boer War memorial (1905-06)

Adrian was also commissioned to provide a bas relief memorial after the Second Boer War (1899-1902) for the seventy-seven officers and men of the Carabiniers who were killed in action or died of disease while on active service in that war. The commissioners were a regimental committee headed by the colonel of the regiment, Lieutenant General Sir John Frier, and understandably they wanted a grand, large monument and a conspicuous site to honour the fallen. Adrian worked it during 1905-6, and on a Saturday in June 1906, as the monument waited behind crimson curtains and flanking Union Jacks, an appropriately grand parade and large crowd assembled on Chelsea Embankment opposite Chelsea Bridge to view the unveiling by Field Marshal 'Bobs' Roberts, VC. The Paymaster-General represented the Government; present from the army was another field marshal holder of the Victoria Cross, Sir George White, then the Governor of the Royal Chelsea Hospital and for years lauded in popular acclaim as 'the hero of Ladysmith', accompanied by a line-up of Chelsea Pensioners in their red coats; three generals and ten other officers of field rank plus junior officers; the trumpeters of the Royal Horse Guards with their trumpet-major; and to conduct the religious part of the forthcoming ceremony, the Chaplain-General to the Forces. The Carabiniers regiment itself was

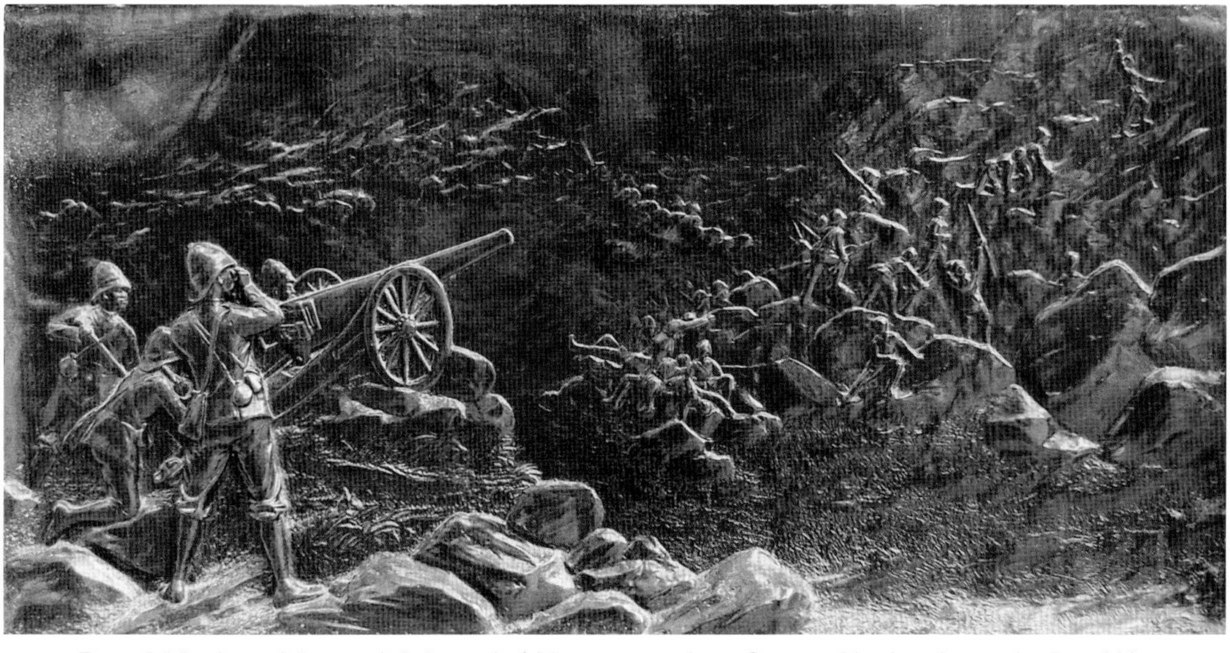

Royal Marines Memorial, bas relief: Marines assaulting Graspan Heights during the Boer War

out in India, but the unveiling was nevertheless a family occasion. A few serving Carabiniers had managed to get home from India, but much the largest section of the informal guard of honour were old comrades in civilian dress who had travelled from all parts of the world. Moving among them, Roberts met one still hale and hearty grizzled veteran who had joined in 1846, a few who had fought in the Crimean War, a few more who had served alongside him at the siege of Delhi during the Indian Mutiny, and large numbers who had been in his force during the Afghanistan campaign of 1879-80 and in the Boer War itself. The regiment had also invited three boys from the Duke of York's School whose father or other close relative had been Carabinier casualties in that war. There too were the ladies of the regiment: the colonel's lady, Lady Frier; widows, wives and orphaned daughters. Adrian was accompanied by his wife Emma.

The trumpeters sounded the Last Post. Speaking with the emotion of a man who had been the commanding officer in Afghanistan and who for almost half a century had been part of a regiment which – as he reminded his listeners – had since 1685 served ten British sovereigns, General Frier honoured his late gallant comrades. He expressed his best thanks 'to the talented sculptor, Captain Jones, not only for the production of this highly artistic memorial, but also for the kindly zeal he has displayed towards his old branch of the cavalry service in carrying it out'. Members of the crowd shouted 'hear, hear'. Lord Roberts expressed his sense of privilege at being invited to honour the dead of the Carabiniers. He valued it especially because he had been

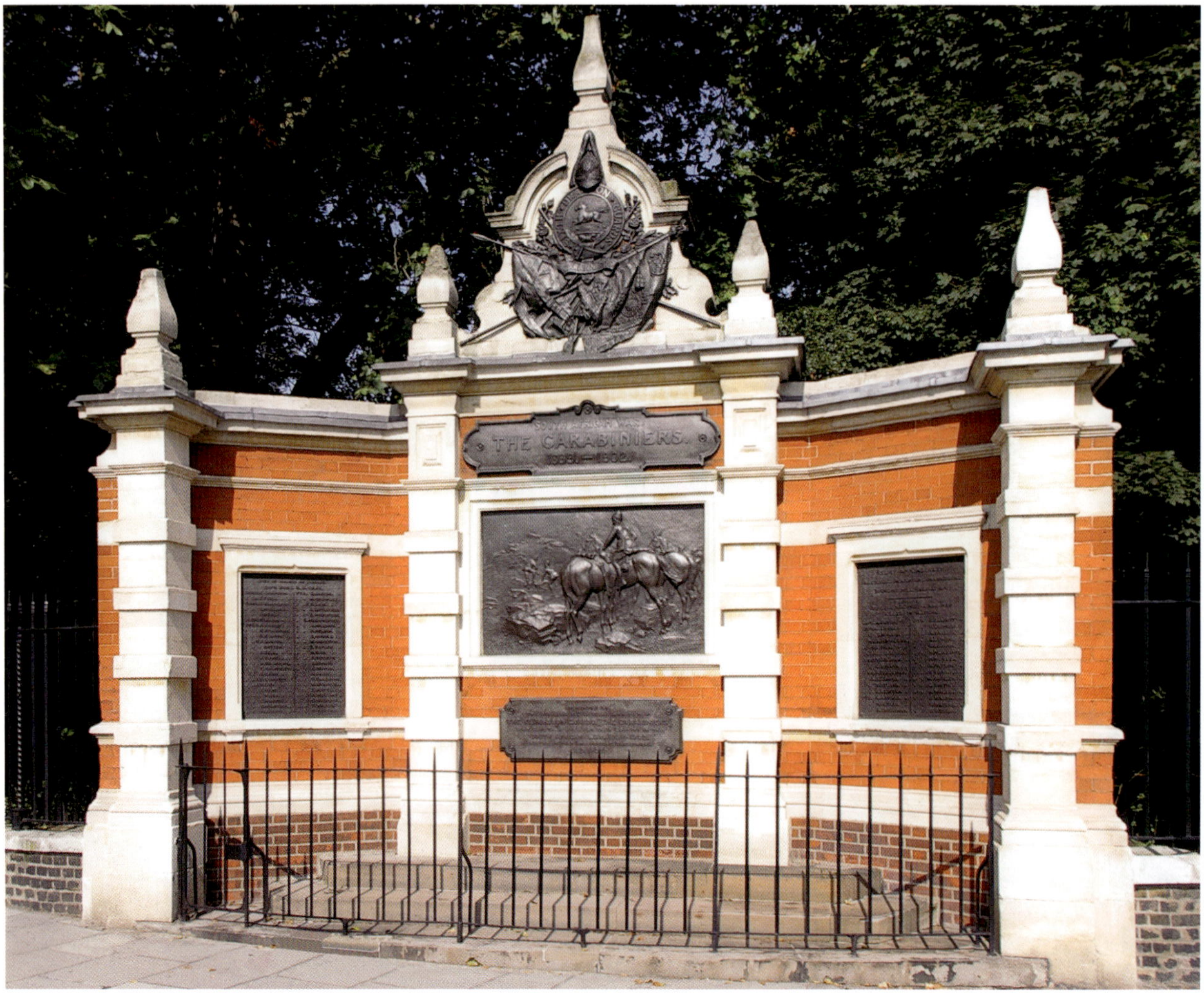

Carabiniers Boer War Memorial, 1906, on Chelsea Embankment, facing Chelsea Bridge

connected with the regiment on several battlefronts, and praised it particularly for being 'the first regiment to reach Kimberley during the memorable ride under Sir John French' (when his cavalry division on half rations and in broiling heat had galloped through the Boers to end the four months' siege of Kimberley, though at the expense of rendering most of the horses unfit for further duty). Roberts unveiled the memorial. The Chaplain-General, with unapologetic confidence in the rightness of the cause, dedicated it: 'May all who look upon it realise the joy of faithful service; the peace of a triumphant death; and the power of an endless life.' The trumpeters sounded reveille.

The memorial's central feature is Adrian's horizontal bronze low relief of four Carabiniers scouting on a kopje in South Africa. Plaques above and below on the dressed stone and red brick surround name the regiment and the war and give a dedicatory inscription and the 1905 date of construction; and on either side on the surround, vertical panels list the six major actions, topped by the Relief of Kimberley, in which the regiment fought, those of all ranks who were killed in action, and those who died from disease. Surmounting the monument is an emblematical trophy, also by Adrian. Crossed colours flags, a cavalry trumpet and, less obvious but to be expected on a Carabiniers monument, crossed carbines, support the regiment's badge of a horse galloping, mane and tail flying, and a plumed regimental cavalry helmet. Everything is exactly detailed.

The emblematic nature of the trophy fronting the top arch is clear. The panel, though not strictly emblematic, is not just any scene haphazardly chosen. It encapsulates the procedures laid down for scouting by cavalry and mounted infantry in an army which had learned the hard way how elusive and surprising Boer movements could be in those days before aerial reconnaissance was available. There are four men in the scout patrol. One, still mounted, holds the reins of all four horses, and remains sheltered in dead ground, ready to facilitate

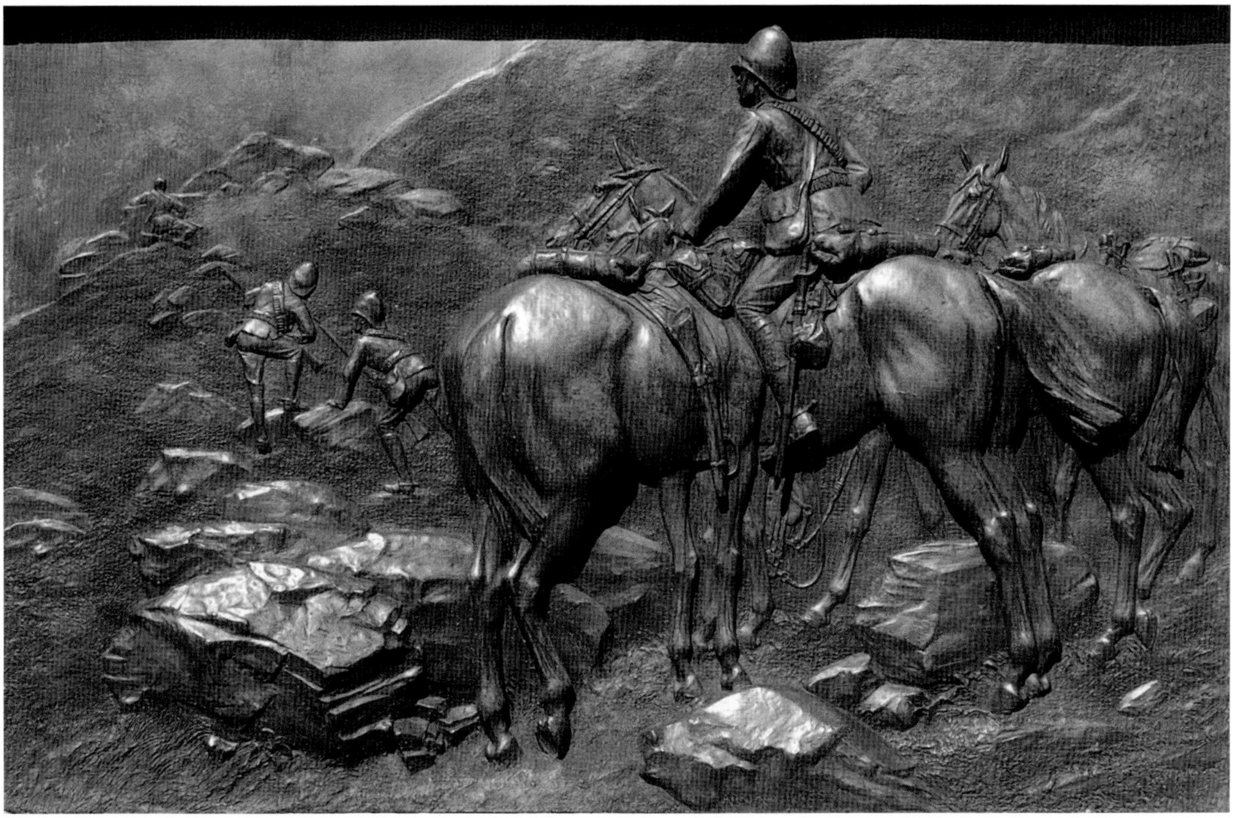

Detail: bas relief of four man mounted scouting patrol on **Carabiniers Boer War Memorial**

a speedy escape, if necessary. Two scale the kopje, their carbines at the carry, prepared to give covering fire to protect the scout ahead who peers over the crest spying for information about the enemy. The whole is artistically composed, the stare of the mounted trooper and the alignment of the two climbers both leading the eye to the small distant figure of the spying scout, who otherwise might not be noticed. Adrian nearly always preferred scenes of soldiering to scenes of slaughter. Here, as in the bas reliefs on his later memorials to the Gloucester Hussars and Cavalry of the Empire, the soldiers are dressed and equipped for campaigning, not for parade ground ceremonial, but there is no immediate evocation of war's horrors. Again too his painterly control of perspective serves him well; the sense of depth achieved in low relief is remarkable.

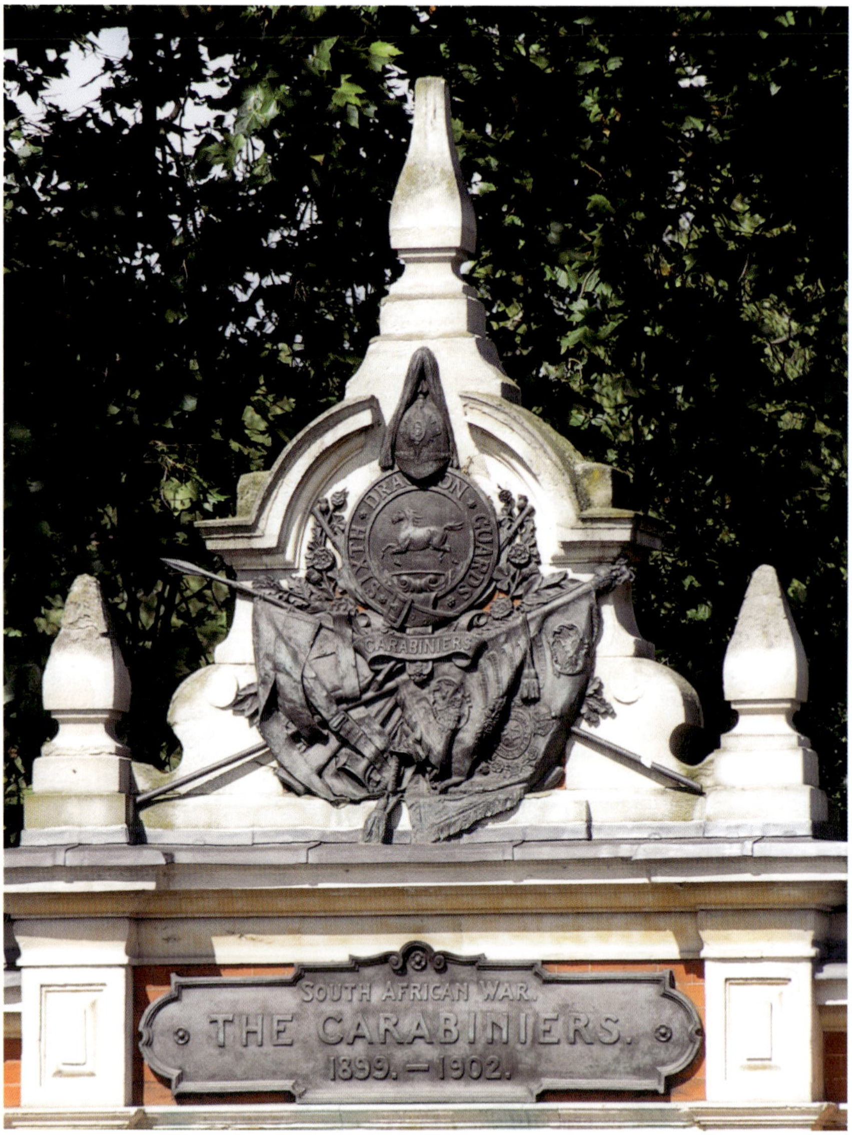

Detail: the emblematic trophy on the **Carabiniers (Sixth Dragoon Guards) Boer War memorial**

Among the extensive national press coverage of the ceremony, the *Morning Post* called the monument 'a handsome and striking work of art', but the *Dundee Courier* from the distant Scottish east coast referred to 'a modest but artistic mural tablet'. Both are right. It does not confront the passer-by as would a three-dimensional statue, and nowadays the 'striking' site has to compete with all the paraphernalia of road traffic engineering. But those who pause to survey Adrian's artistry are well rewarded. The architect of the surround was much put out by the *Times* report that 'the architectural features of the memorial ... have been executed by Mr John Liddell from the designs of the sculptor'. He indignantly wrote to the paper that this misrepresented him 'in a way likely to subject me to ridicule': as someone who had been in the architectural profession for sixty-one years he was no mere contractor. His sense of injured pride was justified, for he had suggested the architectural design to Adrian, who was wholly responsible only for the bronze modelling. The modello of the Carabiniers memorial, a bronze patinated plaster relief, is in the National Army Museum.

Chapter Eleven: 'The dignity and honour of native princes' 1902-1905: Homage to the Sons of Empire

Adrian himself had seen service overseas as part of his life as a soldier of the Queen. Now in his career as an artist he had the opportunity to commemorate not just the British soldiers who took part in the military campaigns of the Empire, but also the soldiers of other countries in the Empire who fought alongside them.

Indian Army Officer statuette: Colonel Afsur Dowla (1902-03)

In the list of exhibits at the 1903 Royal Academy Summer Exhibition, Adrian Jones's equestrian statuette of an Indian army officer appears as no. 1815 'Colonel Afsur Dowla, ADC to HH the Nizam of Hyderabad; statuette, silver'. That is accurate, though in Adrian's autobiography it is termed 'a work in bronze' (and 'Afsur' is misprinted as 'Afsun'). Adrian kept a bronze version which remained in his family until his widow gave it to his old school in March 1939. Its exhibition title is a combination of the sitter's shortened name and his rank of Dowla to which the Nizam had raised him in 1897, in which year also Queen Victoria had made him a Companion of the Most Eminent Order of the Indian Empire (CIE).

Afsur-ul-Mulk was five years younger than Adrian, but they started their army careers in the same year, 1867. In a post-Mutiny proclamation of 1858 Queen Victoria had promised she would 'respect the rights, dignity and honour of native princes as our own'. The Muslim dynasty of Hyderabad was the richest of all India's princely states, and the officers of its army were among India's militarily most efficient and ceremonially most splendid soldiers. Afsur himself, well placed in the state's social hierarchy, within ten years of joining the service was in command of the Nizam's escort at important occasions as far away as Delhi; by 1880 he had been appointed to the Nizam's staff, and a year later he went as a squadron commander with his regiment to troubled Afghanistan. In 1884 he was promoted to command the Nizam's cavalry brigade and so, now a senior officer, he was invited by the Commander in Chief, India, General Sir 'Bobs' Roberts, to the 1886 Camp of Exercise at Delhi. There Roberts organised the Army of India's largest ever manoeuvres, designed to test to the limit the readiness for war of the fighting men, the transport and the commissariat. The British and Indian troops involved were divided into two army corps, with their headquarters and concentration areas initially 150 miles apart. After a fortnight of brigade and divisional exercises, the opposing corps met for a climactic battle on the historic battlefield of Panipat, where the Mogul dynasty had established its supremacy with its victories in 1526 and 1536. Lord Dufferin, the Viceroy, came up from the seat of government in Calcutta to observe the climax, as did a dozen invited officers from America and the principal armies of Europe, including the German army. In his *Forty One Years in India* Roberts comments that these foreign observers were 'somewhat surprised at the fine physique and efficiency of our Native soldiers', and found still more remarkable 'the paucity of British officers in the Indian regiments'. (They might have been yet more surprised to know that later Queen Victoria awarded Afsur the rank of major in the *British* army.) The Camp of Exercise ended with a march past of 35,000 men through a thunderstorm deluge.

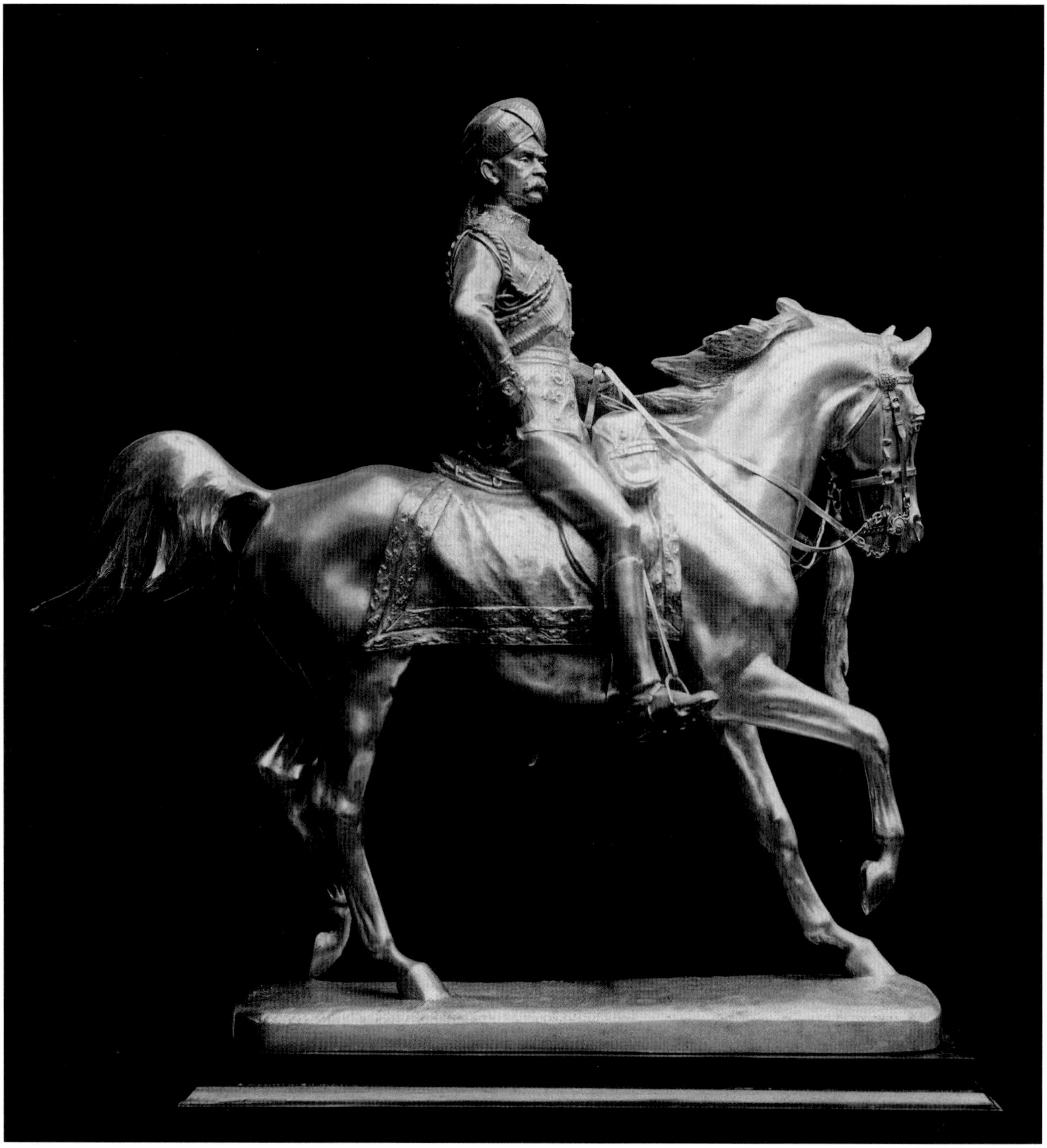

Colonel Afsur Dowla, silver statuette, Royal Academy exhibit, 1903

Two years later British royalty visited Hyderabad. The Nizam placed Afsur in charge of making the arrangements. First he had to host Queen Victoria's son Arthur, Duke of Connaught, and his wife the Duchess, and next the Prince of Wales's eldest son, Prince 'Eddy' Albert Victor. For his trip to India the latter had been promoted to lieutenant-colonel in his regiment, the 10th Hussars, but he was far from being a serious professional soldier. What the disciplined Afsur privately thought of the vacuous Eddy, and whether he had heard the speculation that part of the motivation for the prince's being sent to India was to keep him away from potential involvement in homosexual scandal in London, is not known; but in public he was hospitably genial and satisfactorily organised all the elaborate protocols of precedence in society. In 1900-01 he experienced real warfare again: he went to China as a staff officer in the British-Indian army part of the international force that put down the Boxer Rebellion which had begun with the murder by the Boxers of 'foreign devil' British missionaries and ended with the relief of the foreign legations in Peking, entry to the Forbidden City, and the Boxers' defeat.

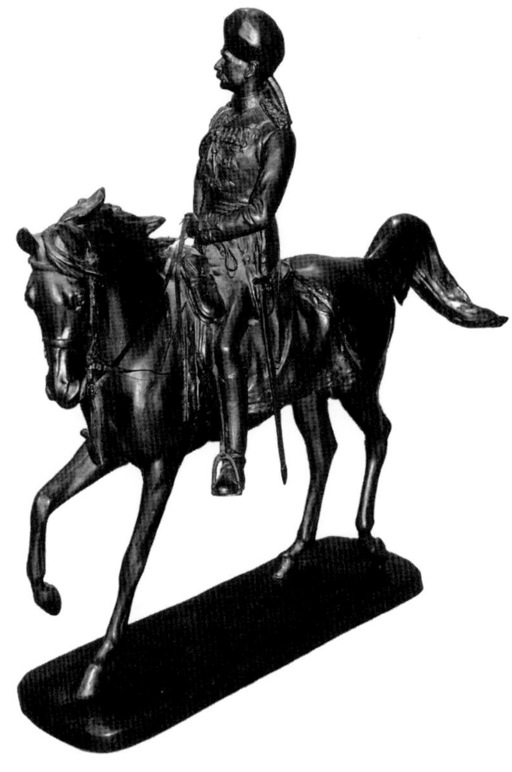

Colonel Afsur Dowla, statuette in bronze

Then in 1902, promoted to full colonel for his role in the China Expedition, he came to London with the Indian Contingent for the coronation of the new King-Emperor, Edward VII, and to receive his China campaign medal to add to his Afghan one. The coronation had to be postponed from its planned date in late June because Edward needed a sudden operation for acute appendicitis. Whilst the crowned heads of Europe could return home until the rearranged date in early August, the contingents from distant parts of the Empire had to stay on in Britain, so Colonel Afsur found his life on hold for six weeks. Adrian was working hard that summer, for he was sculpting his first large public memorial, commissioned by the Royal Marines to commemorate their recent services in the Boxer Rebellion and the Boer War. Meanwhile the troops from almost all parts of the Empire spending the summer in Britain made the British public particularly aware of and enthusiastic about the Empire, and prepared to cheer the coronation as a celebration of empire as much as of monarchy. Adrian could see commercial and artistic potential for coronation memorabilia. For his part, Colonel Afsur wanted a remembrance of his participation in the coronation procession; and in Captain Jones he met a military artist who was carving a bas relief panel, of a battle scene at the Peking legations quarter during the Boxer Rebellion, destined for the pedestal of the Marines Memorial. Thus circumstances made the two men a match. Even apart from the coincidence of their engagement with China, they had much in common. Both had cavalry service; both were good at equine sport; both were acquainted with the royal family; and both were possessors of campaign medals from Victoria's 'small wars'. And of course Adrian had years of experience of undertaking equestrian portraits of soldiers.

After the coronation Colonel Afsur returned to Hyderabad, again as the Nizam's invaluable senior officer, and later he was knighted (KCIE) and appointed ADC to the Viceroy, Lord Hardinge. At his accession in 1911 the last Nizam held a congratulatory parade at which he personally presented Colonel Sir Afsur with a jewelled ornament to be worn over his headdress, a ring, a necklace, and a sword of honour. In the fulsome praise of *The Imperial Coronation Durbar Illustrated*, published in Lahore, Afsur had been 'a pillar and an ornament of the Court of India's greatest Ruler'. And before that he had received one other distinction in common with the sculptor of the equestrian statuette of him. In 1906 the Prince of Wales, later King George V, conferred on him Membership of the Victorian Order for organising the royal visit of that year to Hyderabad, and the next year Adrian was made MVO for his sculpture of another member of the royal family, the Duke of Cambridge.

The equestrian statuette of Colonel Afsur must have made a pleasant change from his large scale Marines Memorial for Adrian as he worked on them both in the summer of 1902. It was a small work. Had it been a life-size statue for a prominent site in Hyderabad it would have been expected to make a statement about the greatness of the ruling dynasty; as a statuette, it could be essentially an authentic memento of a major experience, and the sculptor could approach his task as if he were recording a winning racehorse with the winning jockey up. The arrangements for the sittings are not known. Many of the Empire troops present for the coronation were photographed for illustrated magazines. Adrian may have used photographs as an aid, but chiefly he would have used his customary techniques – quick sketches, more worked-up drawings or paintings, horse measurements, all these taken in the open or in stables, plus sittings in his Chelsea studio.

He used expression and pose to convey the personality of his subject, but though the statuette was linked to the particular event of a coronation procession, he chose not to use setting. The upper surface of the signed and dated (1902) base is very slightly roughened, but there is no attempt to fashion a distinctive London street surface. However, the horse is shown moving at a slow trot. At trot a cavalry officer would normally rise in his stirrups to make life more comfortable for himself, but on ceremonial parade the discipline was to bump along in the saddle. The magnificent steed moves naturally, an image of contained power, looking ahead down the line of march, but Colonel Afsur sits stiffly erect, chin in and chest out in parade-ground style, and gazes slightly to his right as if viewing the police, troops and crowd lining the processional route. His body language (to use an expression which neither he nor Adrian would have used) shows awareness that he himself is not only on parade but also on display. One arm is moved away from the reins and rested on his hip, partly to suggest he is in cool command (the troopers would have both hands on the reins), and partly the better to show his full dress uniform. He is wearing the kurta, richly decorated with facings, rather than the short jacket of British cavalry, and in addition to a shoulder belt wears a cummerbund. From the latter hang slings which hold his sword, a smart arrangement on horseback, though it would have been less impressive if he were marching on foot, as the sword would trail on the ground. The horse too is in full dress, including a splendid waving throat tassel. As ever in Adrian's equine studies, the musculature is magnificently rendered. But though he could work on this sculpture in much the same spirit as he would handle a racehorse study, the approach could not be identical. In an exhibition catalogue a racehorse sculpture would carry the name of the horse alone or placed before the jockey's. This statuette, however, was to be exhibited as 'Colonel Afsur Dowla, ADC' It is a portrait, a good likeness accurate in detail, of a military man at an important ceremonial occasion. It cannot simultaneously be a character study revelatory of the private man, who was renowned for his geniality. Adrian shows Afsur's on-parade face: a serious, unanimated mien, stern-looking, aloof even, with the bold eyebrows and carefully groomed cavalry moustache indicative of the military virtues of bravery and boldness that lie within.

Afsur's lifestyle was not dissimilar to that of a senior officer in, say, the British Household Cavalry, with which Adrian had served. Empire historians now sometimes refer to members of the Indian elite like Afsur as 'Westernised'. It can be used as a dismissive term. But in Adrian Jones's minutely observed and handsome portrayal there is tribute, not disparagement.

South Australia memorial (1902-04)

At the outbreak of the Boer War in 1899 the states of Australia were still separate self-governing colonies. Joseph Chamberlain, in his role as Secretary for the Colonies, approached them for help, and among the responses was that of the South Australia government in Adelaide, who sent contingents totalling more than 1,500 men and horses. (The last contingent, raised after the Federation of 1901, went as Australian Commonwealth Horse.) Though the war dragged on until the signing of peace at the end of May 1902, the first South Australian state contingent landed back in Sydney from Cape Town a year earlier, and on 13 July 1901, they and other early returned South Australia contingents paraded to receive their Queen's South Africa campaign medals.

The silver medal showed the crowned head of the aged Queen Victoria, and on the reverse Britannia holding out to troops in the background – rather prematurely, for much bitter guerrilla warfare still lay ahead – a laurel victory wreath. Amongst the recipients on parade stood Quartermaster Sergeant George Goodall, a descendant of pioneers who had arrived in Australia in 1839. A blacksmith and farrier by trade, before the war he had been a member of the 20th Mounted Rifles and had the reputation of being able to break in and ride any horse. In 1902, now Regimental Quartermaster Sergeant, he sailed for London with the Australian Corps contingent who would take part in the coronation of Edward VII.

The Queen's Medals presentation parade, as well as stimulating patriotic pride, had reminded South Australians of the sorrow they had suffered because not all their boys had returned. Fund raising began for a war memorial. Now the committee, with £3,000 behind it, had authority to commission a large sculpture. It asked Mr Kyffin Thomas, a citizen of Adelaide who with his daughter was planning to be in London for a lengthy visit during 1902, to cooperate with South Australia's Agent General in London in seeking out a sculptor capable of producing a large equestrian statue. Thomas contacted Adrian. In response, Adrian offered to make a sketch model for £50 and an eleven-foot-high bronze for just £1,600, that price to include delivery of the statue to London Docks, and suggested that they meet at the Savage Club on the following Saturday. The date did not suit Thomas, so Adrian wrote again on 12th May, urging Thomas to get authority from Australia to set up a committee empowered to select his quickly prepared design which, he stressed, was 'a *rough* sketch design ... just an idea which could work out into something spirited, warlike and good'. He emphasised also the competitiveness of his £1,600 quotation which 'will only pay for material and mechanics wages', but which nevertheless would satisfy him because he would be able to keep the studio and staff going while he waited in hope of a large commission to celebrate the new independent nation of South Africa. Further to plead his cause, he reminded Thomas that his army service in India and Africa had given him, uniquely among British sculptors, an owner's knowledge of Australian and Arab horses. The urgent tone of the letters makes clear how much it mattered to Adrian to satisfy Adelaide and thereby maintain a continuous flow of studio work. Three days later he wrote again, enclosing magazine articles on his previous works, promising a statue 'second to none', urging again that the matter be expedited, and inviting Thomas to come to meet him at the Savage or his Chelsea studio. Thomas replied reassuringly the same day; he had already written to Adelaide and advocated an early decision. On 20th June the Agent General and Adrian received telegrams authorising the Agent and Thomas to appoint a London committee, approve the sketch design, and order a clay model. Provisionally, Adrian had won his keenly sought commission.

Kyffin Thomas and some of his new committee, very aware of Adrian's wish for a quick final decision but perhaps not appreciating how much work was involved for the preliminary judgement, asked for a model to be ready *in a week.* That was, in Adrian's words, 'a very large order even for a rapid worker'. He promised Thomas he would 'rough up' at once a model 'similar to the sketch I made for you,' added 'I take it that life and action is wanted,' and assured Thomas that if he would come to lunch with Emma and himself on Saturday

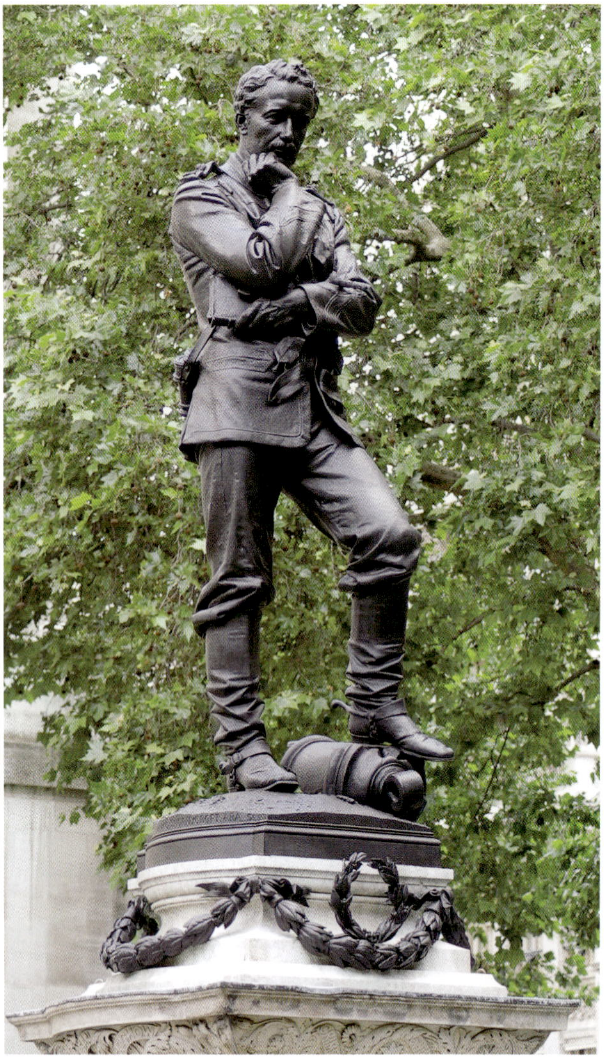

General Gordon, by Sir Hamo Thorneycroft RA, initially sited in Trafalgar Square, 1888. Gordon is shown wearing patrol jacket, not full dress uniform. Now sited in the Victoria Embankment Gardens.

or Sunday to chat things over, the model would be ready for inspection by next Wednesday. Thereupon Adrian, never afraid of a special effort, set to work by night as well as by day. When the committee returned the appointed week later, a model, albeit imperfect, was ready for viewing.

This time the Committee brought with them a knowledgeable judge, the distinguished sculptor Sir Hamo Thorneycroft. Adrian knew his work well; indeed, Adrian's own life-size or larger memorials were probably influenced by a Thorneycroft statue of particular interest to him, the military figure of General Gordon. That bronze now stands on the Thames Embankment, but it was originally erected, in the year Adrian was posted to the 2nd Life Guards, in London's best known central site, Trafalgar Square. When Adrian and others who had served in the Nile Expeditionary Force went there they would have seen Gordon dressed as a soldier in active service uniform though not at this moment involved in actual combat. The statue has realistic 'narrative' details: Gordon's chin rests on his clenched hand in the classic 'thinker' pose, his other hand holds a bible, and at his feet is a broken mortar barrel. Here in detailed bronze are embodied virtues valued by conventional Victorian society – military bravery, Christianity, adventurous Imperial service. On the plinth below bas relief panels allegorically depict associated virtues: Charity, Justice, Fortitude and Faith. Adrian learned from scrutinising such statues. Now the situation was reversed; it was Hamo Thorneycroft's turn to view Adrian's statue (or proposed statue). He circled it to see its impact from every point of view, sat on the floor to judge as far as possible how the statue would look when raised on a plinth, and suggested some alteration to details of the model's kopje rocks groundwork. A Committee member remarked to Thorneycroft that it was unrealistic to expect every detail to have been worked over to best effect because it was only a week ago that Adrian had been commissioned to make the sketch model. Relating the incident in his *Memoirs*, Adrian records: 'Thorneycroft was frankly surprised.' That might be an understatement, for those who had been through normal academic training in art could never quite accept Adrian's speed of work, and indeed resented it, but Sir Hamo's grandfather, father and mother had all been sculptors, so he had intimate personal knowledge of varied rates of work. Assured that nothing of the statue had existed just seven days earlier, he unhesitatingly complimented Adrian: 'Well, I congratulate you. I regard that as a really wonderful achievement.' His endorsement gained Adrian a commission priced at £1,600 to work up the model into a bronze.

The Committee departed 'fully satisfied', but Adrian knew that work remained to be done to put right the imperfections observed by Hamo Thorneycroft and himself. As with his Colonel Dowla statuette, he seized the extra opportunity offered by the postponement due to appendicitis of Edward VII's Coronation. On June 26th, the day the delay until 4th August was announced, he wrote immediately to Major Charles Burt, an army officer involved with the colonials' coronation role:

> Have you any officer or trooper belonging to Adelaide? If so, will you ask him to kindly come to my studio and see a sketch model I am doing for a committee from Adelaide to commemorate the memory of those who fought and died in South Africa. Besides being of much interest to anyone from South Australia, I should like to get a few details, so that the statue then sent to A. shall be correct in every respect ...

Adrian gave the letter to his nephew to deliver, it was passed on to the Commanding Officer of the Australian Coronation Corps, Colonel Cameron, and his response was to despatch RQMS George Goodall to Adrian's studio. Goodall gave Adrian the 'few details' he was hoping for, particularly concerning the equipment worn by the South Australians during the war, and what would be a convincing posture for a scout who had just sighted hostile Boers. Even more rewardingly, Adrian persuaded Goodall to sit as model for him for half a day, during which he made a clay of his head, concentrating on a strong facial likeness. Ever afterwards Goodall would modestly insist that it was only his head which appeared in the final statue, and that he was not selected for the role because of any outstanding merit on his part as a soldier during the Boer War. But when the statue was later erected in Adelaide, it was deliberately positioned so that the sun would fall upon his face and give that aspect of the composition special prominence.

Meanwhile Adrian continued to work in his studio. Following Hamo Thorneycroft's advice, he altered the alignment of the rocky kopje so that it ran uphill from the horse's rear legs to forelegs. Thus the scene became the rider reaching the crest rather than implausibly bestriding it and making himself an easy target. He loaded the horse with the pieces of kit and tack described by Goodall and removed the incorrect saddle roll. Now that he had an individualised face he twisted the torso slightly and the head markedly to the right, enabling a side viewer to see the full face. He tilted the front rim of the slouch hat further up

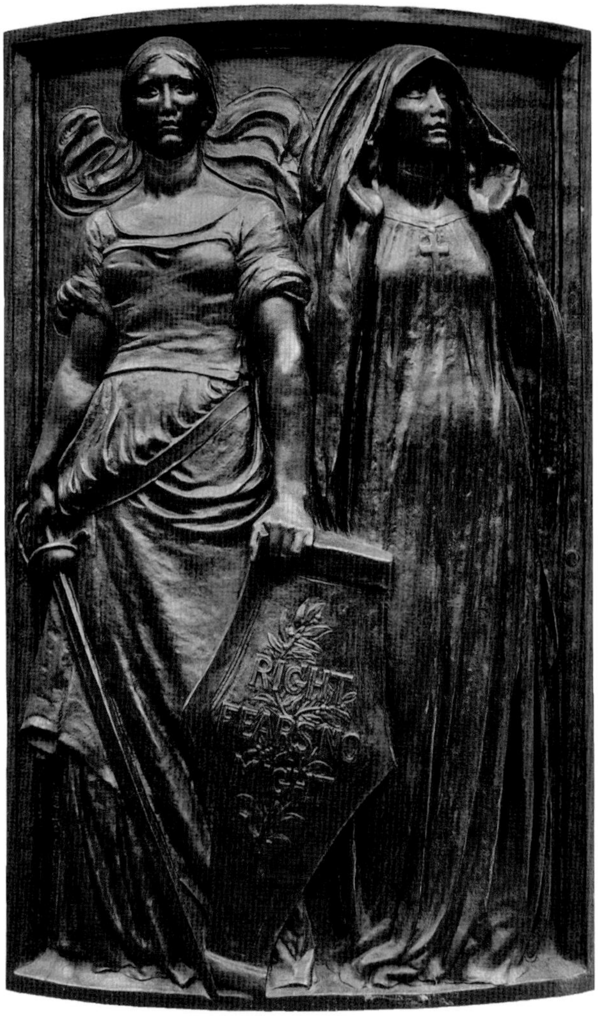

Fortitude and Faith, allegorical reliefs in bronze on pedestal of General Gordon statue. Adrian, like the New Sculptors, frequently used reliefs, but generally portrayed soldiers rather than allegorical virtues.

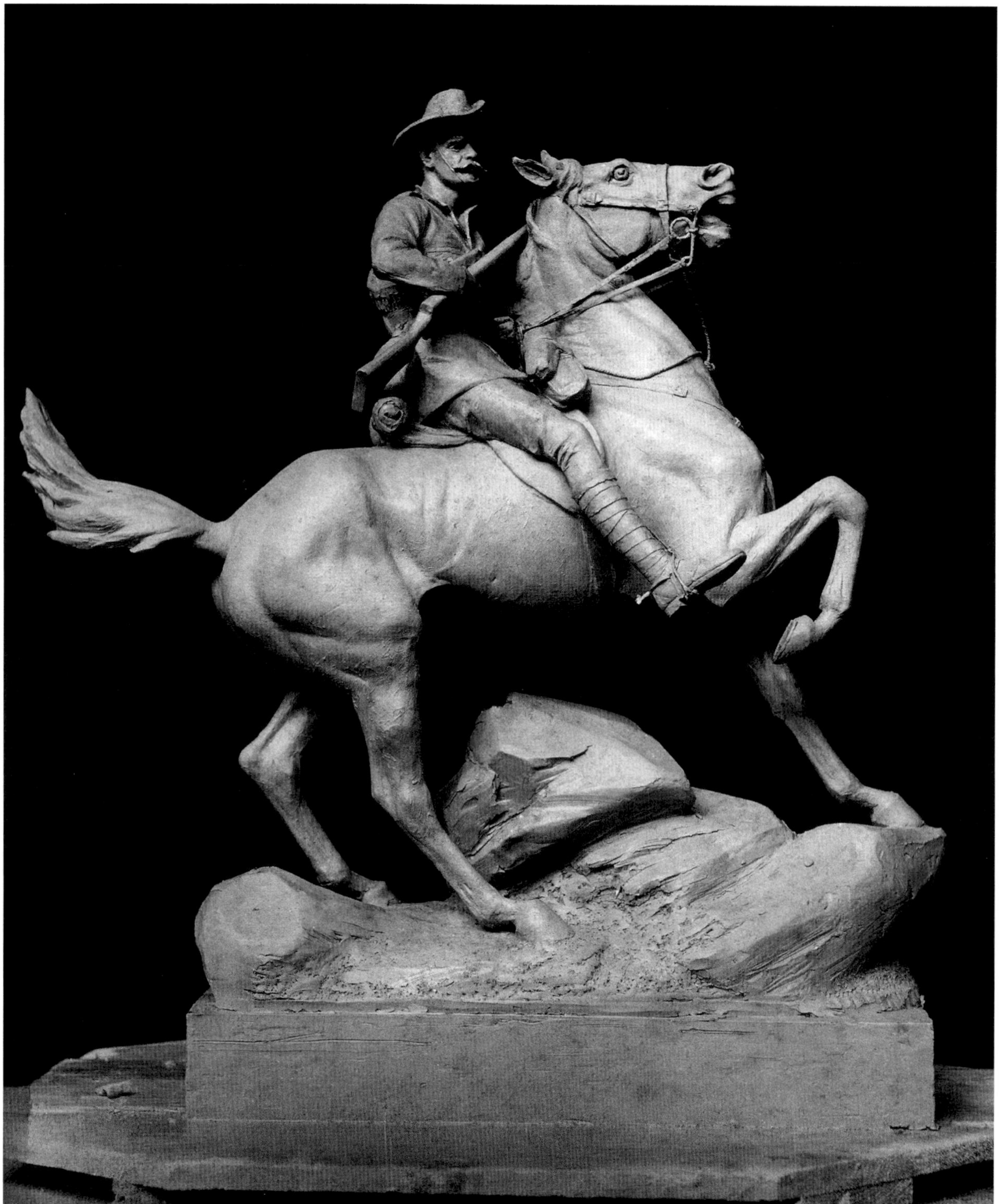

South Australia Boer War Memorial: the initial studio plaster statue to remove shadow from the forehead, and pulled the right arm up and out, so that instead of just casually holding the rifle across his body he appears to be swinging it round ready to use it against foes who have just been spotted to his right. Overall the Scout's pose has been transformed from semi-relaxed to startled and tense. The horse itself was made more powerful 'along the vigorous lines that appeal so strongly to the sturdy Australian people'. He also made changes to improve the artistry of the composition. He pulled in and lowered the angle of the near foreleg to bring it within the 'frame' of the group, and for the same reason drooped the upward frisky tail to a low swish which continued the line of the horse's back and echoed that of the kopje. He achieved this better artistic effect without sacrificing lively realism. As he wrote in *Memoirs*:

> Where equestrian groups are concerned, the sculptor cannot pose his horse or his horses and then merely copy them ... he must be a close observer, able to commit action to memory so that he can reproduce the animal in any position that is necessary to the execution of his idea ... Where a cessation of motion is represented, there must at least be a feeling that the limbs can move, or that they have moved.

Adrian detested any concept of the horse as 'still life'.

Adrian and Kyffin Thomas became friends. After one of Thomas's visits in October 1902 to see the work progressing, Adrian was able to tell him that at Buckingham Palace he had shown King Edward a photograph of the model design and that Edward had 'seemed very pleased with the idea of the memorial' and thought the design 'very spirited'. However, when later in the month Thomas invited him to lunch, Adrian wrote in reply, 'You have been so awfully nice and kind that I do not like to say no to your kind invitation to lunch on Wednesday. I make it a rule not to lunch out as it spoils my whole day. But if this is a special occasion and you very much wish me to come, I must. I know you will excuse me putting it so. I am just warming to my work on your statue and I feel sure it will be a success.' In December Thomas and his daughter set off for mainland Europe, then home (en route sending Adrian from Rome a picture of a 'very good old master'). Adrian wished them 'bon voyage' and gave a final assurance that 'the statue will be A1'.

In late March 1903 Adrian underwent an operation for 'internal complaints', and though afterwards he progressed very favourably, work had to be suspended for most of April. Emma took over the correspondence, acknowledging the receipt of photos of the pedestal design for the statue and forwarding Adrian's comments. Convalescence completed, Adrian resumed work. As usual, he met the deadlines. Burton's Thames Ditton foundry cast the statue in bronze, and by February 1904 it was crated and ready to be shipped on the *S.S. Wahool* . Once in South Australia, the statue received the generous respect due to a national monument. The Customs levied no duty. The railway transported and stored it at no cost. Portland Cement donated the bags of cement for the foundations.

After an open competition with a dozen entries, Adelaide had chosen an oblong red granite pedestal of

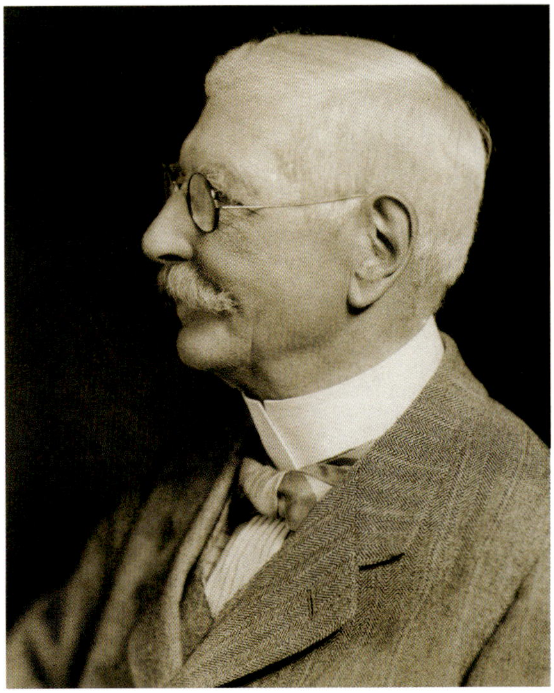

Adrian Jones: early twentieth century photograph

simple design, 12 feet high, to be the base for the equally tall statue, and it was erected in the city's most prominent site, in front of Government House. Over it was set up the necessary scaffolding and Goliath travelling crane. The 4½ ton statue, still crated (the crate weighed another ton) was carted to a position alongside the plinth. Passers by watched with interest as it was uncrated, lifted up and across, then lowered and secured on its pedestal. The sculpted head of George Goodall looked down briefly on the platform for VIP dignitaries built below, and then he was covered in flags and sheeting. All was ready for His Excellency the Governor of South Australia to unveil the memorial on 6 June 1904.

On the day itself, numerous flags flew from Government House and nearby buildings, and spectators lined the rooftops and crammed the streets to watch the parade and unveiling. The Chairman of the Fund, Mr Brookman, addressed the crowds. They were met this day, he said, to do homage to the memory of the brave men who gave their lives in South Africa, and to do honour to those valiant soldiers who rendered such distinguished service to the Empire. The statue was symbolic of the loyalty that united Australia to the motherland. They rejoiced today that their nation was at peace, but no citizen or stranger would be able to look on the emblem of the statue without realising that any foe that struck at England must in future reckon with Australia. All sections of the community had contributed towards this statue, which might therefore be regarded as a national memorial. The Committee felt that in every respect it was worthy of the people of South Australia, and a triumph for the artist, Captain Adrian Jones. It was now his pleasing duty to ask His Worship the Mayor to accept the statue for the citizens of Adelaide.

After the crowd's cheers, the Mayor, Mr Cohen MP, replied that the presentation which had today been made to the city might very well be said to mark another epoch in the history of South Australia. They had indeed assembled there today to do honour to the brave and noble sons of South Australia who had responded to the call of patriotism and laid down their lives in the interests and for the defence of the Empire. It was manifest that in accepting this magnificent monument on behalf of the citizens of Adelaide, they did not accept it merely and simply because it would adorn the city. They accepted it because of the reverence felt for the noble sons of South Australia – whose names they desired should ever remain green – for their patriotism, their loyalty, and their duty to the Empire. The Mayor then formally accepted it on behalf of the city. Yeomanry troopers, on the cue from the State Governor, pulled away the veilings.

The proud words, evocative of an age confident in the Empire and the ties with the motherland, were genuinely sincere. When Germany, which had encouraged the Boer revolt, struck against Britain in 1914, it indeed had to reckon again with Australia. Twenty years after receiving his commission for the Adelaide memorial, Adrian was to be the sculptor of a war memorial for an English yeomanry regiment, the Royal Gloucestershire Hussars, who fought beside the Australians at Gallipoli.

Adrian had not been present in Adelaide, but in his News Cuttings Book he pasted an Australian newspaper review sent to him by Kyffin Thomas:

> Tens of thousands of people from all parts of South Australia were in Adelaide to witness the unveiling by the Governor, Sir George Le Hunte, of the handsome memorial which has been erected in front of Government House ... The bronze emblem is of imposing dimensions, and is typical of a well-mounted Australian soldier with full accoutrements. The regard for the utmost accuracy is manifested in the indication of boot protectors on the soles of the trooper's boots. The monument tells at a glance the story of the arduous work that faced our soldiers in the tedious campaign in South Africa. The trooper ... has reined his horse up to reconnoitre the enemy's position, and one can imagine, as one looks upon the stern and eager visage of the soldier, that he is ready at a moment to give the signal that shall bring the main

> body into action, and save the position. The horse, too, is wonderfully depicted, and is a fine study of an animal. The whole treatment of the broad masses is very fine, and the anatomy is exactly typical of the sturdy stamp of fine chargers supplied by South Australia for the use of the contingents. The creature is instinct with life, and its whole being is strung with nervous excitement ... Four tablets have been placed on the pedestal, two of which bear the names of those who fell. Above each list are a scroll and wreath with the words: 'Who dies for his country dies nobly.'

The article was illustrated by a photograph of the crowds in their best clothes and hats for the occasion, and subscribed 'Unveiling the National Memorial'. Because the state contingents had usually been formed into inter-state operational units, there was the idea that Adrian's statue was to an extent a national as well as a state memorial. Back in London, the *Morning Post* reported: 'The sculptor's work is much appreciated in the colony', and quoted a telegram sent from Adelaide to Adrian's Chelsea address: 'Unveiled statue yesterday, everyone delighted, splendid work, accept thanks, congratulations, South Australia – Le Hunte, Governor'. In *Memoirs* Adrian wrote: 'Many Australians told me that they thought it the best statue they have in the country, but this may have been said to please me.' He too quoted the telegram but modesty or memory lapse led him to omit the garlanding praises 'everyone delighted' and 'splendid work'.

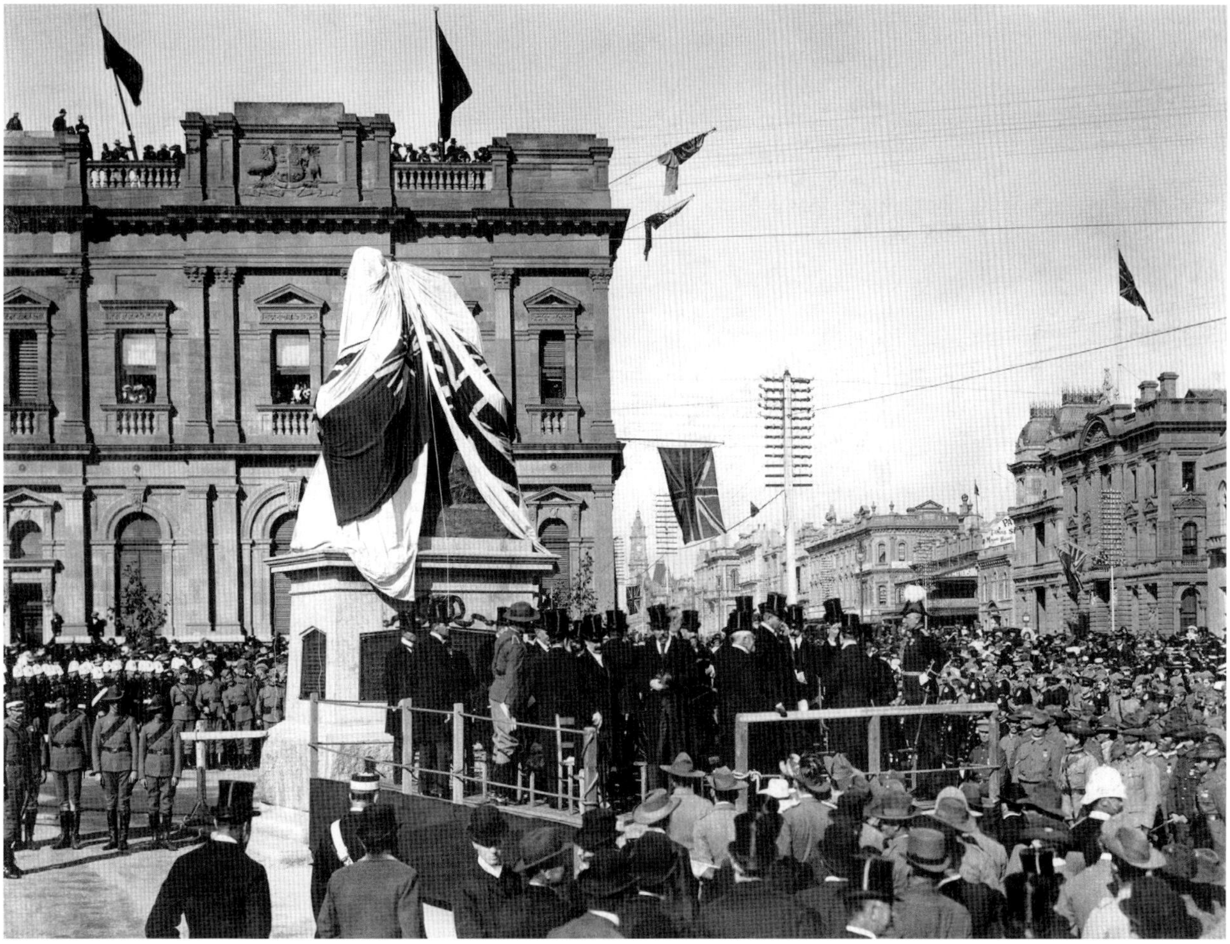

Unveiling the **South Australia Boer War Memorial**, Adelaide

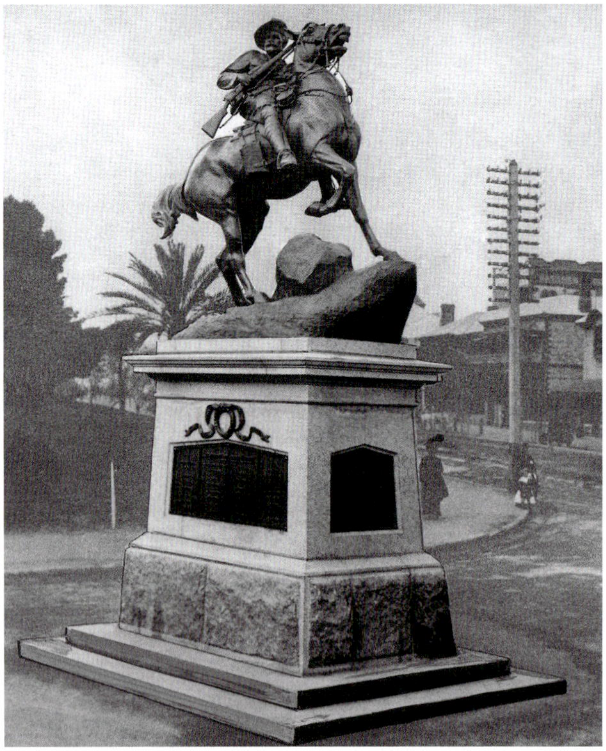

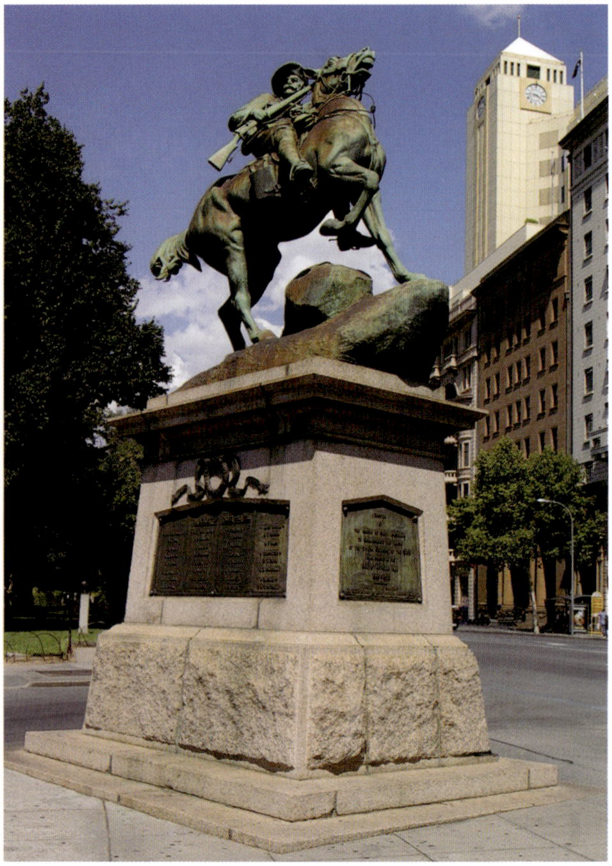

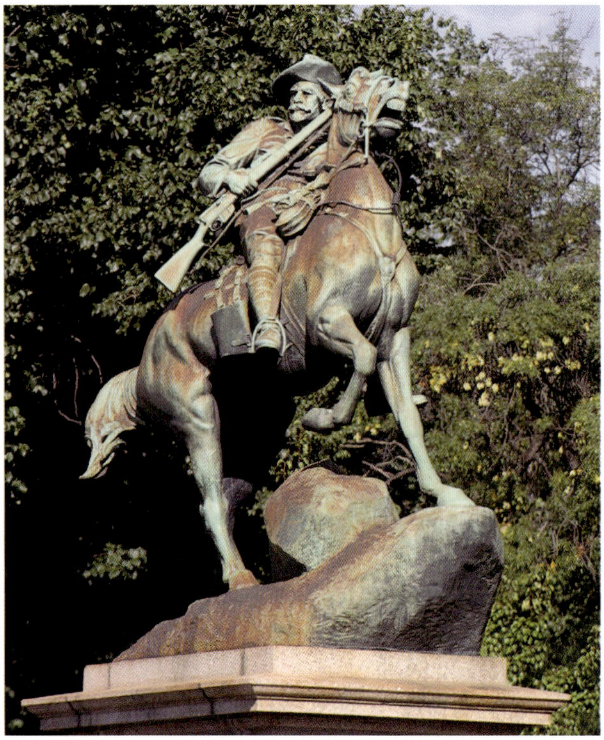

Clockwise from top left:
South Australian War Memorial c.1904;
South Australian War Memorial 2007, bronze statue on red granite plinth;
the statue of the scout, positioned so that the sun would fall full on his face

Opposite:
South Australian War Memorial (Detail)

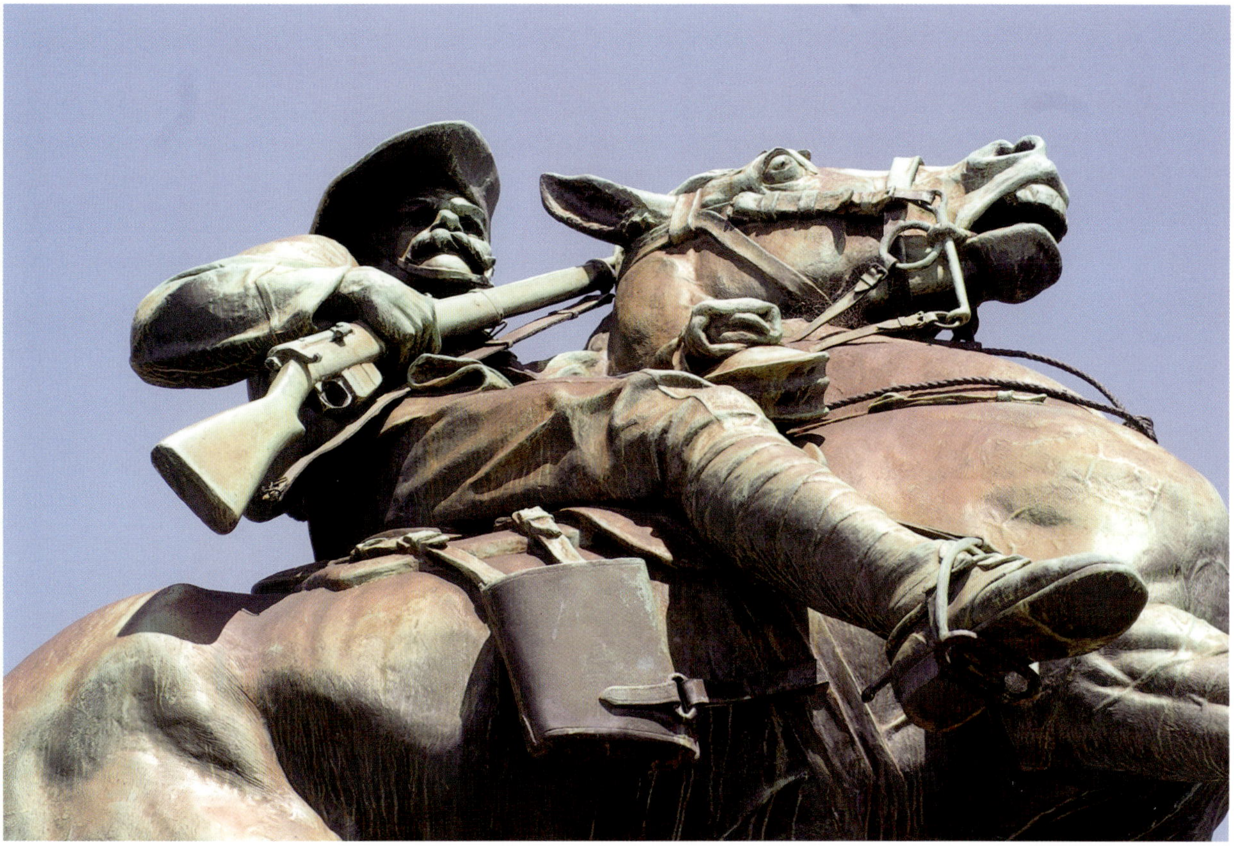

The Australian Scout goes to Ludlow (1905)
In late August 1904, Adrian wrote to the Town Clerk of Ludlow, John Williams, offering to present to his native town the original of the statue which had been so well received as a memorial in Adelaide. From Ludlow, as from South Australia, men had volunteered for Boer War service. The Shropshire Yeomanry had been asked to raise a company for the newly formed Imperial Yeomanry. 130 volunteers who had been passed as being medically sound and physically fit, and able to shoot and ride well enough to fulfil their role as mounted infantry, disembarked from their troopship in February 1900 at Capetown. From there, as the 13th (Shropshire) Company of the Imperial Yeomanry 5th Battalion, they had trekked nearly 3,000 miles with Lord Methuen's column and been involved in about eighty skirmishes or more major engagements. By the time they returned to Shropshire in June 1901 they had lost twelve men and had eleven wounded. A second and a third contingent followed the first. So when the Town Clerk told him that he would lay his offer before Ludlow Town Council at their next meeting in the Town Hall, Adrian must have thought that Ludlow had cause enough for setting up a Boer War memorial, and expected that the matter would be rather easier to expedite than sending a bronze half way round the world to Australia.

However, the matter was not as straightforward as he hoped. In 1887 the Council, after some nervous debate, had decided to emulate the fashion of many larger towns and mark Victoria's Golden Jubilee by funding a prestigious civic building. It would combine utility, as both Market and Town Hall, with Victorian aesthetic, an eclectic polychrome mix of brick and stone and pointed arches, pinnacles, finials, pepper-pot cupola and spires expressive of aspiration. Seventeen years later the loan taken out to meet the costs of the building and its London architect was still far from paid off. Finances were tight. At the January 1905 Council

Meeting, the Finance Committee reported the need to take up a Public Works Loans Commissioners' grant which the Council would have to repay at 3¾% over the next thirty years. The Sanitary Committee reported they would have to budget for potential compensation to persons prejudicially affected by the installation of a new sewerage system. The Borough Surveyor reported that to light new areas of the town the Gas Company was demanding that the Corporation should put up a sum of money in advance and be responsible for excavating certain lengths of road. That would cost about £100. Finally it was the turn of the General Purposes Committee. Its spokesman reported that having considered the estimate for placing the equestrian statue offered by Captain Adrian Jones to the town in the suggested position in the Town Hall, it recommended the Corporation not to incur the expense. The cost of this too would be about £100, and they could not ask the ratepayers to pay that sum. The Council decided to thank Captain Jones for his offer, but to decline it.

It was a rebuff, but though unimaginative, an understandable response from men who considered that their first duty was to the ratepayers. However, the Mayor, Alderman Lloyd, thought that Ludlow should respond more generously. Town Clerk John Williams was equally set on a response befitting the town for which he had been the Clerk for quarter of a century in succession to his father's thirty-seven years as Clerk. Adelaide had funded its memorial through public subscription; Ludlow would do the same. Their Appeal was quickly successful, so that by April 4th the plaster original had been delivered from Burton's Thames Ditton Foundry and fixed high in the Hall lobby. The white plaster was painted bronze to make it closely resemble the Adelaide statue, the archway behind was painted white to throw it into relief, and an unveiling by Lord Windsor was arranged for September 8th.

On that occasion, reported the *Birmingham Daily Post*, 'the ancient borough of Ludlow was much astir', 'the town was gay with flags and banners', and the Hall itself 'prettily decorated'. The ceremony being indoors, the thousands who had watched in Adelaide obviously could not be replicated in Ludlow, but the Town Clerk issued tickets gratis to as many applicants as could be fitted in. Those who gained entry included Adrian's stepmother, happy to tell anyone how proud she was of her stepson's achievements. Lord Windsor was currently Lord Lieutenant of Glamorganshire, and he was therefore entitled to a guard of honour. For this major public ceremony he received one consisting of men from the Ludlow area who had served in the 13th Shropshire Company of the 5th Imperial Yeomanry Battalion or in the Service Volunteers during the Boer War. They escorted Lord Windsor to the Hall, and there paraded on the left of the statue, while the Ludlow Company of the 1st Volunteer Battalion of the King's Shropshire Light Infantry paraded on the right.

Alderman Lloyd said how pleased he was as Mayor to accept the gift of the statue on behalf of the Borough. Shropshire people were said to be very proud, and Ludlow people might well feel proud to claim one of England's greatest sculptors as a Ludlow man. Lord Windsor unveiled the horse and rider and, as one would expect, said to applause that he too was pleased to be in Ludlow to do honour to one of the greatest sculptors of the day. But also, perhaps because he was aware that in his audience were assembled the councillors who had initially declined the gift, he forcefully expressed some far from anodyne sentiments. It was a bad thing when an artist was not honoured in his own country, and it was bad for him to feel that his work was neglected by those with whom he had been brought up; but it was much worse for the people, when, from ignorance or dullness, they failed to detect merit when they saw it, and if they failed to feel any pride in one who had won the appreciation of distinguished artists.

At Ludlow, unlike Adelaide, Adrian was himself present, and so could return thanks for the complimentary references to his art. In his speech, instead of responding to Lord Windsor's other remarks, he explained the motive for his gift. His idea had been that having the bronze statue at Adelaide and the original design at

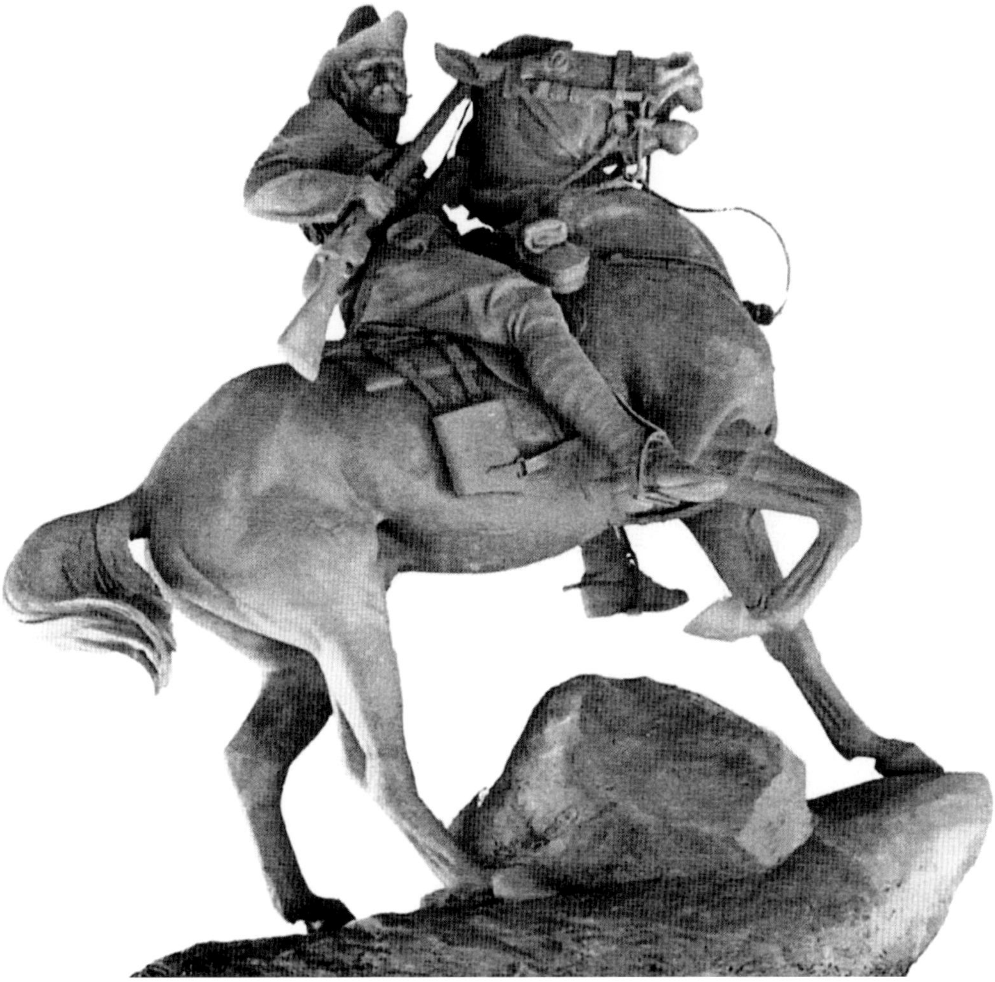

The Ludlow Horse: plaster statue painted bronze shade

the ancient and historic town of Ludlow would bring together the mother country and the young country. Then as the final act Lord Windsor unveiled the three tablets fixed below the statue. One bore the names of the men who served; a second bore the roll of honour of those who did not return; and the third bore the name of the sculptor and donor, Adrian Jones.

In the same year, the survivors in England formed a 13th Company Comrades Association and held their first annual reunion in Ludlow Town Hall, dining beneath two captured Boer flags. Annual dinners continued until the outbreak of the Great War of 1914-18. Not until 1950 did the Association disband, having long exemplified the comradeship expressed in the last words of the last speech at its last Dinner, held in 1913:

> We have seen a ride together,
> We have ridden side by side,
> And it binds us all together
> Like a lover to his bride.

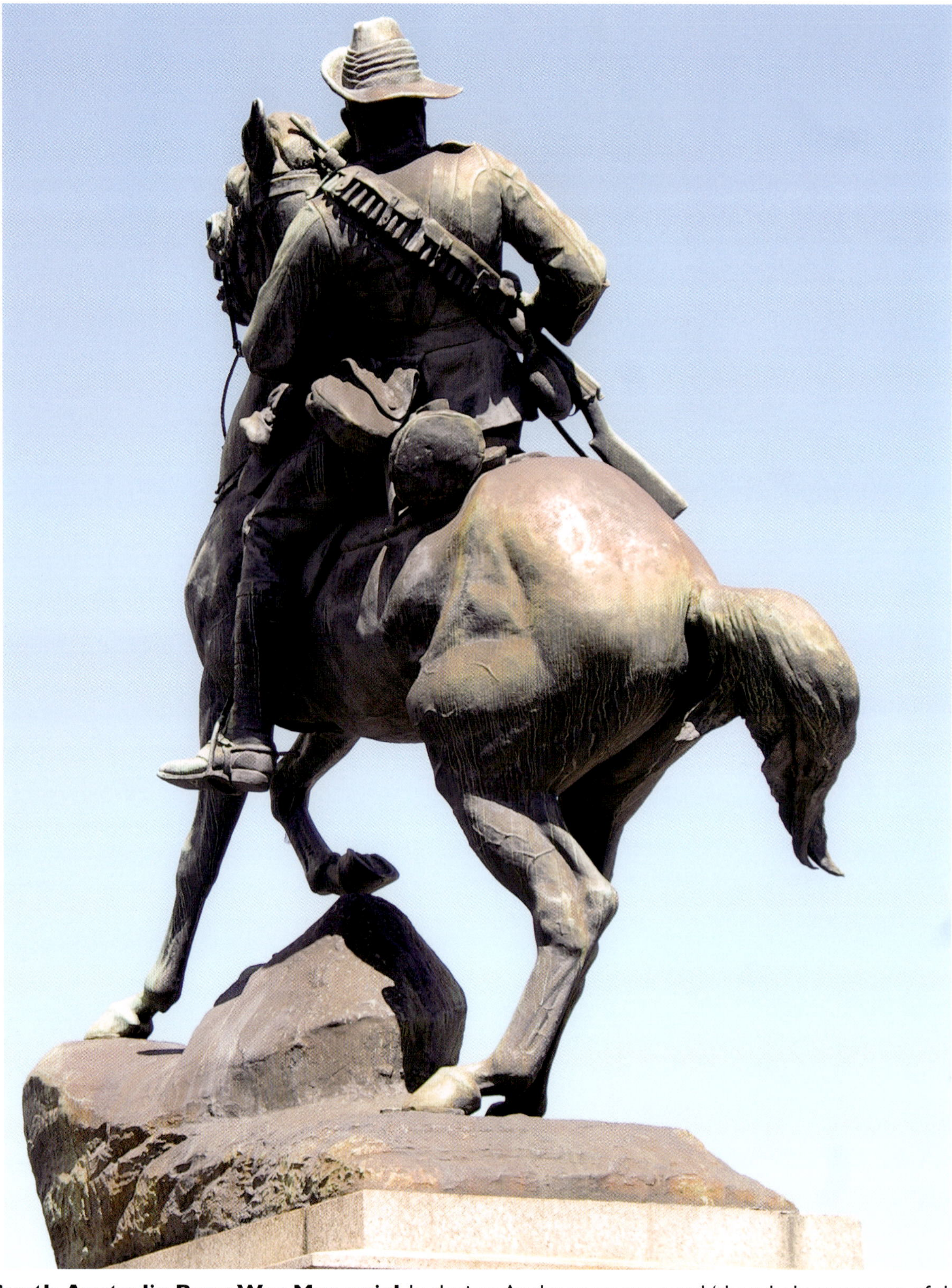

South Australia Boer War Memorial, back view. As the press reported, 'the whole treatment of the broad masses is very fine, and the anatomy is exactly typical of the sturdy stamp of fine chargers supplied by South Australia for the use of the contingents'.

Chapter Twelve: 'An instinctive sympathy' 1904-1907: Statues of Military Commanders

General Sir Redvers Buller (1904-05)

The inscription on the statue commemorating the South Australians who fought in the Second Boer War reads: 'Who dies for his country dies nobly'. That widely felt sentiment would naturally lead a regiment or a nation to wish to commemorate those who fall in conflict, whatever the prevailing views of the justice of the cause or the effectiveness of the campaign. These opinions may carry force, however, when it comes to monuments to commemorate the generals responsible for conducting that campaign. By the end of the Second Boer War in 1902, questions were being asked about the handling of the war, and General Sir Redvers Buller was in the critical firing line. Since the first volume of the publication of the extremely lengthy *Times History of the War in South Africa* had come out in 1902, its principal author, Leo Amery, had been censoriously critical of Buller's generalship, and in 1905 had summarised his opinion by labelling Buller 'the embodiment of the qualities and defects which the British military system tended to produce'. The emphasis was on 'defects'. In his narrative of the war, Amery, freer with his adjectives than Adrian, peppered Buller with, among others, 'bewildered', 'disheartened' and 'unnerved'. One searches in vain for any hints of such an indecisive, pessimistic character in the large equestrian state of General Buller designed and executed by Adrian, and unveiled on 6 September 1905. Amery's verdict on 'Black Week' in the Boer War, when the British lost the battles at Stormberg, Magersfontein and Colenso, was that Buller had failed, whereas the pedestal of Adrian's statue encapsulates Buller's contribution to the War in the three word tribute 'He Saved Natal'.

It does not follow that one view invalidates the other. Amery was passing judgement on events in December 1899; the pedestal's three words commemorated the finally successful relief of Ladysmith in late February 1900 and the subsequent capturing of all Natal, which took until September. Adrian's commission, unusual in that it involved making a statue of someone who was still alive, was to meet popular demand to celebrate a victor. To that task, as an ex-army officer now entering his sixties, he brought a perspective understandably different from that of Leo Amery, an aspiring political journalist in his late twenties. In any case, it was not in Adrian's nature to criticise British commanders, many of whom he had known in the course of his military career. Describing the unveiling of the statue in his *Memoirs*, however, some qualification of 'great' was unavoidable, and he characterises Buller as 'that great *and rather unfortunate* soldier'.

Adrian considered Buller 'unfortunate' because opinion-formers like Amery had judged him on 'Black Week' rather than on his ability and performance across forty-one years of army service. Some of Adrian's own military career had involved him in the same campaigns as Buller, and other parts of it had afforded a parallel experience. He first got to know Buller personally at Sir Evelyn Woods's conference with the Zulu chiefs after the end of the Transvaal War, and had further contact with him in the Sudan when Buller brought Wolseley's Desert Column back to Korti after Wilson's failure to rescue Gordon. On his return to Britain in late 1885, Buller had taken up a London posting at the War Office. Apart from twelve months in 1886-87 spent in Ireland in a civilian role which had the policing purpose of restoring law and order in the Kerry area, he stayed at the War Office until 1897, rising in rank to Adjutant General. Adrian's service in Ireland had been a decade earlier, though the poverty and disaffection Buller encountered were familiar enough to him, and he would have warmly approved of the news of Buller's successes and his attitude that Ireland required the prevention of oppression by landlords just as much as it required restoration of law and order over murderous agitators.

Adrian's final spell of army service in St. John's Wood Barracks and then the Life Guards had coincided with Buller's time in London, and even after Adrian left the army in 1891, the two men still met socially. Buller had a clubbable personality, and like Adrian, he was a member of the Savage Club. Also, though himself an infantryman and someone who considered the cavalry sabre a distinctly out-of-date weapon, he was a keen horseman; and as an amateur sketch artist he was keen on art and moved in art circles. Their common interests and an overlapping circle of acquaintances made for an easy relationship when Buller later came to sit for Adrian, but of course some of the joint acquaintances were not also joint friends. One of Buller's personal friends was the President of the Royal Academy, Frederick Leighton. He had died before Adrian started work on his statue of Buller, but Edward was by then King, and neither he nor the 'Marlborough House set' liked Buller and indeed were suspected of spreading slanders about him when his reputation was in eclipse after the Boer War. On the topic of the King, Adrian would have to be circumspect. Buller viewed Edward not as an 'ideal gentleman' but as someone who had failed to support him when General Roberts demanded his sacking from the army with relegation to half-pay.

When Buller sailed for South Africa in 1899 to take command in the Boer War he stood high in both military and popular opinion. The admiring men and women of Devon saw him as a heroic man of action fit to rank alongside Drake. After the defeats he suffered in the early months of the war, and despite his later advances, when the adverse press reports reduced his reputation to a controversial one, he still did not lose the affectionate goodwill of his troops. They cheered him heartily as he made his farewell visits at the relinquishing of his command in October 1900. He was similarly greeted by cheering crowds in November, when he reached Southampton, whose Corporation awarded him the freedom of the Borough. Next the garrison town of Aldershot celebrated him with a verve apparently unequalled in its previous history. The train that carried him there was beflagged, as was the station when he arrived. Special trains from elsewhere brought more people into Aldershot to augment the crowds. Through the packed streets the men of the Aldershot fire brigade hauled the carriage in which sat Buller, his wife Lady Audrey and his daughter Georgiana, past the flags and congratulatory banners, and past cheers from the specially built grandstands.

When Adrian started work on his equestrian statue in 1904, enthusiasm for Buller still endured in Devon (the General came from Downes, near Crediton, and generations of Bullers had been Members of Parliament for Exeter) and among his old soldiers. Buller might have harsh critics amongst senior officers and journalists in London, but Adrian had no hesitation in accepting the commission, which came from the city of Exeter. He must have appreciated Buller's first decisive reform as Quarter Master General at the War Office. Buller had taken up the QMG post in October 1887. Still fresh in his memory was his experience as Chief of Staff on the Nile Expedition that failed to reach Khartoum in time. He had not obtained sufficient camels to meet the needs of the Desert Column, and many of those obtained were not fit for the job required. Still on the desk lay the Veterinary Department's report of 1885 which included Adrian's summary of the transport problems caused by ignorance, and the Director of Transport's response of 1886 with its bleak conclusion that under existing arrangements 'I have no hesitation whatever in saying that we could never work a transport satisfactorily'. By the following year Buller had established the Army Service Corps. There had briefly been such a corps from 1869 to 1881, but in a reverse image of the Veterinary Department, which was officers only, it had been other ranks only. Buller now set it up as a proper regiment of all ranks, responsible for army transport and supply. Thanks to Buller, the reports on the Nile Expedition had not met the too frequent fate of merely dust-gathering. Thirty years later it remained 'a pleasant thought' for Adrian that because of the commission to sculpt Buller his 'association with that great soldier ... ripened into a friendship that endured to the end of his life'.

After his dismissal from army command in October 1901 Buller spent most of his time on his estate at Crediton. There he was extremely popular, because he was the very best kind of landlord, full of practical concern for the quality of workers' lives, and friendly to all. It is said that in many cottages his portrait hung alongside that of the late Queen. Evidently that popularity was not confined to Crediton or Devon; often when he visited other parts of the country, to his embarrassment people spontaneously cheered him, probably from a mix of admiration and a sense that he had been unfairly treated. It was however the civic leaders of Exeter who determined that he should be publicly commemorated. Artists had depicted in paint the revolver-wielding Buller, astride his agile pony and wearing the practical open-necked fighting uniform of the Frontier Light Horse, rescuing a dismounted officer from Zulu warriors. That fearless act in 1879 during the Zulu War had earned Buller the Victoria Cross. The Exeter committee was now proposing a much grander work of art. It would not be an action piece, but would show General Buller in ceremonial uniform, and astride a statelier horse than the one on which he had won his VC, which stood just fourteen hands high The purpose of the equestrian statue was to be a salute, delivered with recognition of and gratitude for great military leadership. As such, in that Edwardian world, which would not have found acceptable an equivalent of, say, Graham Sutherland's 'tribute' painting of Winston Churchill, it placed certain constraints on the selected sculptor's creativity. A modern equivalent in public statuary would be the great footballer whose statue is commissioned to stand at the ground where the fans adored him. The Exeter committee wanted a sculptor who had the skills to create an authentic general on an authentic horse.

The committee consulted Buller himself. Could he suggest a sculptor to whom his equestrian statue could be entrusted? Telling the story, after the statue had been completed to the admiration of Devonians and its plaster cast had impressed Londoners in the particularly strong sculpture section of the Allied Artists Exhibition, the journal *Ideas* related that Buller 'replied emphatically, "Yes, Adrian Jones, for he is the only sculptor I know of who understands a horse, and is likely to model one properly"'. (The story seconded the journal's own opinion that Adrian was 'probably the only living sculptor who understands the horse from tail-tip to nostrils'.) Buller was not very interested in horse racing, so was probably not so much influenced by Adrian's portrayals of racehorses as by the string of equestrian sculptures which Adrian had successfully submitted for exhibition at the Royal Academy during Buller's years at the War Office. Also, as an active Prime Warden of the Goldsmiths Company he would be aware that Adrian had won a Company first prize with 'Gone Away'. The Committee fell in with Buller's strongly expressed wish.

The commission for the Exeter statue, Adrian's first for a statue of a famous soldier rather than a regiment, was a breakthrough that broadened his field of possibilities. Nor was that his only reason for feeling pleased. It struck a blow against 'the disgruntled, but diminishing, band of Academicians that had stood to hamper my progress', and against 'a fairly general opinion that important works should be entrusted to full-blown Royal Academicians'. In *Memoirs* he adds the comment that it was already clear to him that 'failing a change of heart, I should never receive the honour of a call to the inner circle. They were at least sufficiently powerful to see to that, even though they could not divert commissions from my studio'. He probably felt an instinctive sympathy for Buller, ousted by Roberts's 'India ring' of officers, just as he himself was excluded from the 'inner circle' of the Royal Academy; and certainly he must have been gratified that though in his years at the War Office Buller had been a friend of the Academy's late President, Frederick Leighton, he had nevertheless recommended Adrian to the commissioning committee.

Adrian made arrangements to set about his task. Local tradition asserts that for modelling the horse he used Buller's favourite mount, Biffen, which Buller had brought back from South Africa. But he began with the man. Knowing that the 50,000 admirers from Britain and overseas who had subscribed to the fundraising wanted 'a faithful likeness', he asked Buller if he would be prepared to come to the Church Street studio to sit for a bust. Buller assented, and took his seat with the words of a general to a captain: 'We have now to reverse the order of things; I am entirely at your command.' Lady Audrey accompanied her husband to the sittings. Buller could look dour, could not claim to be handsome, and at times in his career had lost control of his temper, but Adrian relates that Lady Audrey's entertaining conversation during the several sittings 'not only kept the General in the best of humours, but gave him the pleasant expression that was a great help to me in my work'. Just as when King Edward watched him sculpting, Adrian generally sought to respond positively to any useful comments or suggestions made in the studio. He did not see this as undermining artistic integrity, but thought it sensible to give consideration to any remark which might make the work more suited to its intended purpose. When the marble bust was completed, the family admired and cherished it.

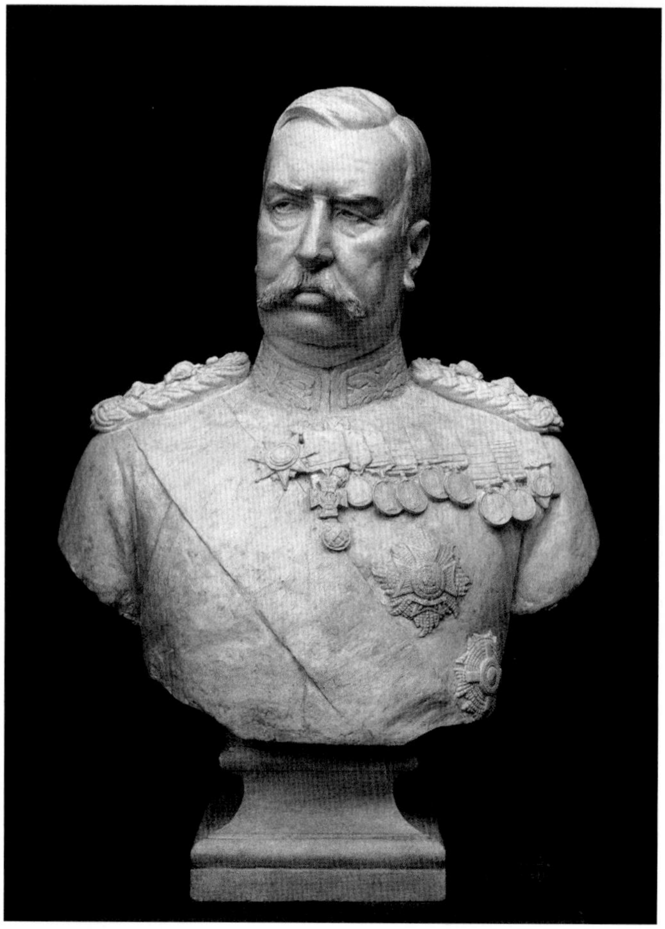

General Sir Redvers Buller, VC, 1905, marble bust. Adrian very seldom worked in marble – like the New Sculptors school he preferred bronze – but this characterful bust shows how readily he could turn his hand to marble portraiture.

(In due course Buller left it to his only child, Georgiana. She too was to suffer the hazards of war. Her fiancé was killed in the Great War, and in the Second World War bomb blast damaged her house in Exeter. When she died in 1953, Dame Georgiana left sums of money to the local charities for which she had worked in her lifetime, but the first item in her list of bequests was the bust of her father by Adrian Jones, which she left to the Dean and Chapter of St. Paul's Cathedral. She must have hoped it might find a modest place among the cathedral's myriad of memorials to military commanders, naval heroes and artists, including men with whom her father's life had entwined – Lord Kitchener, General Gordon and Frederick Leighton among them. But post-1945 the custom of housing statues and busts was dwindling: public taste shifted to simpler commemorations, and space was increasingly at a premium. The field marshals of the Second World War are typical in being remembered in St. Paul's only on finely lettered tablets of British stone; and Adrian's marble bust of Buller is not on the cathedral's inventory.)

To work on the statue, Adrian made visits to the Bullers' country seat at Downes, and Lady Audrey invited him to stay there again prior to the

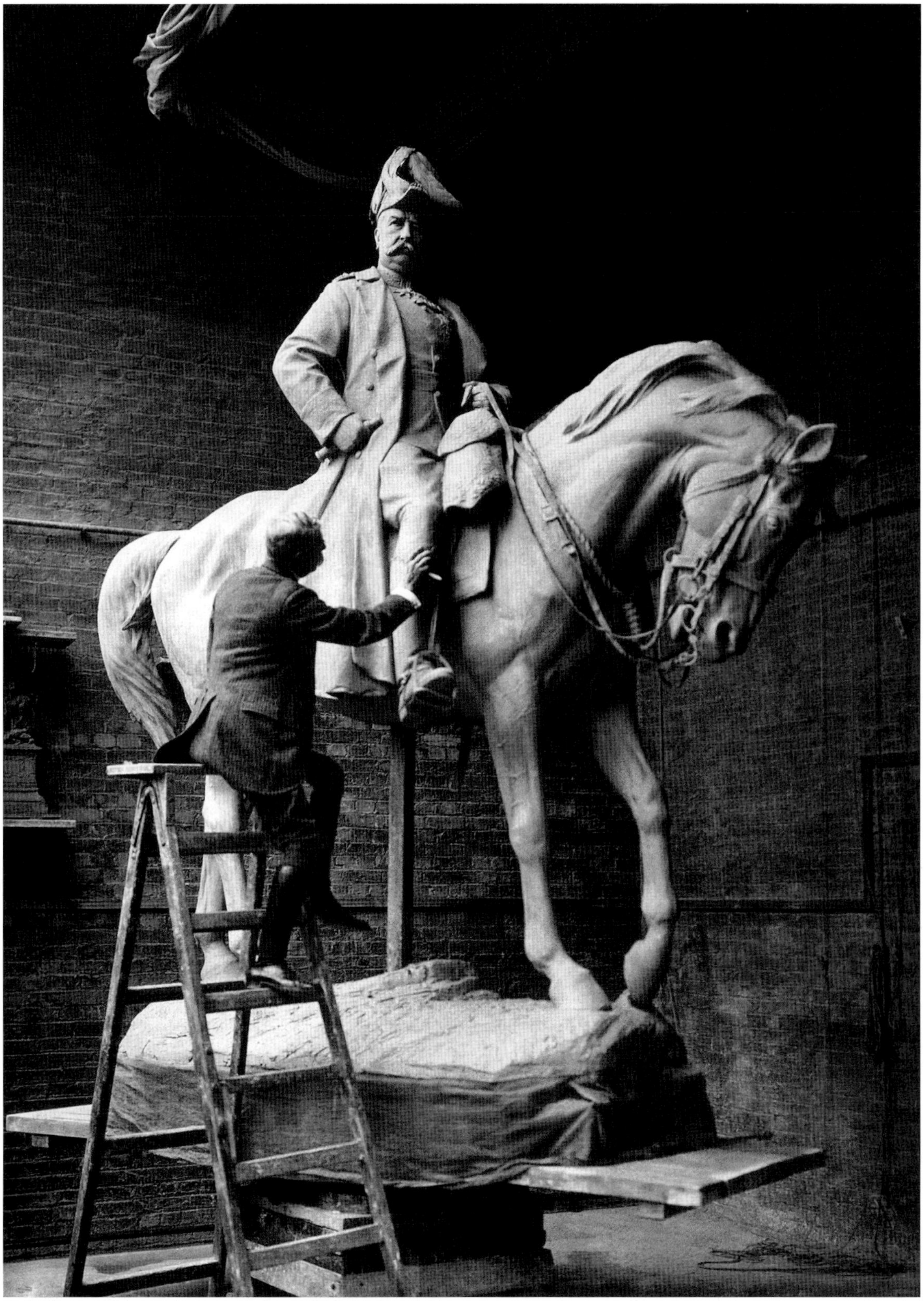

General Buller, studio model for equestrian statue

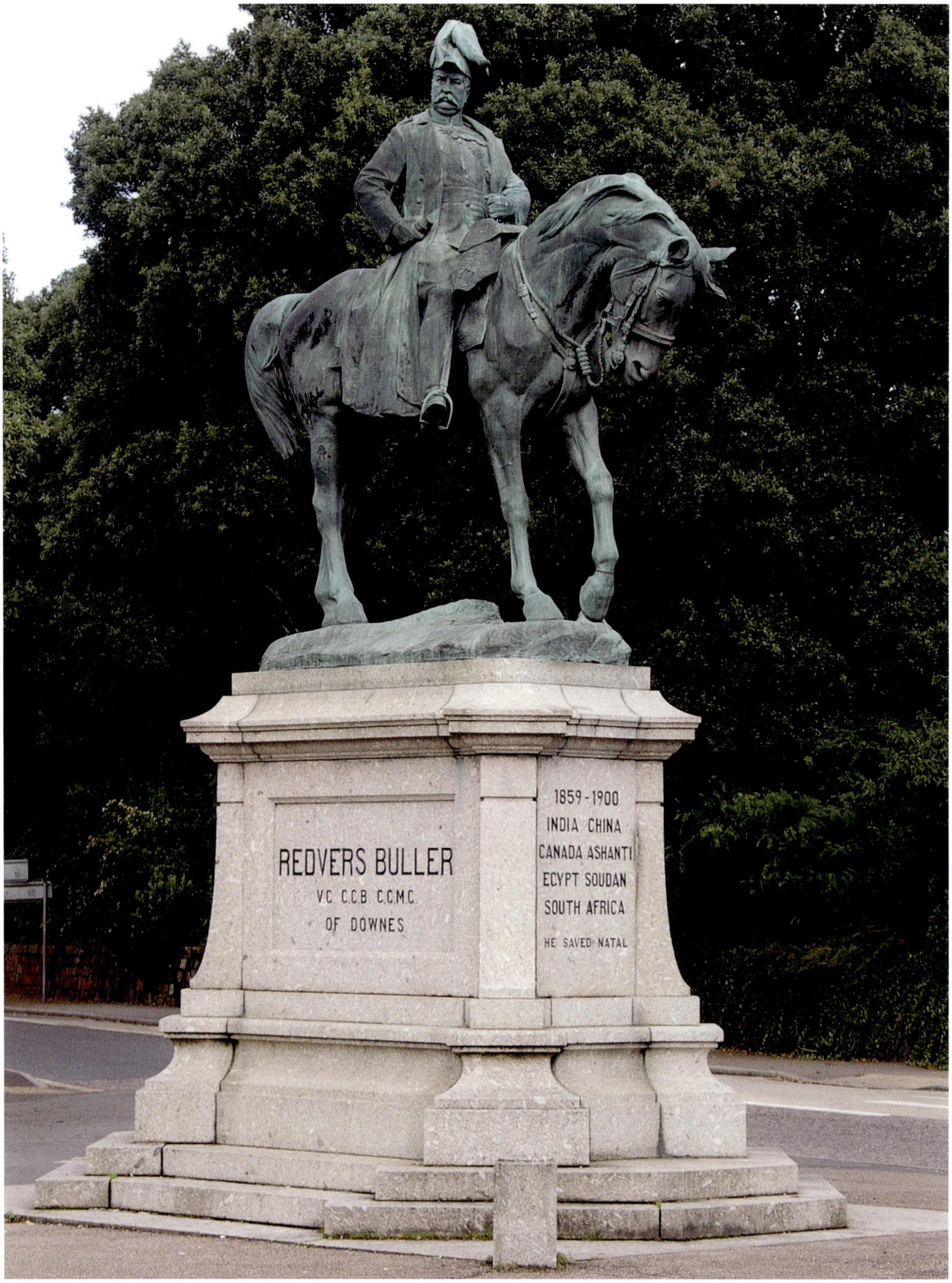

General Buller, bronze statue on plinth, 1905, Exeter

unveiling. The casting of the statue, like that of his other large works, was entrusted to Burton's Foundry at Thames Ditton, and the bronze was then carried by the Great Western Railway to a siding not far from the intended site at the junction of Hele Road and New North Road in Exeter. The Exeter committee had been particularly helpful over arrangements. Adrian's experience was that he had 'no occasion to wear a worried look from start to finish'. Even so, much remained to be done. In the dark small hours of 6th September 1905, Adrian rose early and, with lamps lit, drove horse and carriage from Crediton to Exeter, to reach the siding before daylight had broken. As the statue weighed four tons, it needed respectful handling. Fearing an accident, Adrian asked the railway officials to move nothing until it was light enough to see properly. As dawn broke the statue was transferred to a trolley, transported to the site, and hoisted into position on its ten foot high pedestal of Cornish granite. The railed platform for the unveiling party was in its place next to the pedestal front, and the area was ringed with flagpoles twice as tall as the street gas lamps. It remained only to string the bunting of many nations between the poles and check that the flags on the statue could be moved easily. All this was done before most of Exeter's citizens – and indeed Adrian – had breakfasted.

As the day advanced, special excursion trains ran from Paddington, Waterloo, Bath and Bristol to help bring the thousands expected to join the local Devonians for the ceremony. The huge numbers were of course more due to Buller's fame than to Adrian's reputation as an artist. 'The Organisation for the Reinstatement of General Sir Redvers Buller', which included some prominent citizens amongst its leaders, had been encouraging support, and many old soldier subscribers to the statue fund no doubt wished to view the end product.

Buller had been one of the bright and brave officers whom Wolseley had fostered in their careers, and though on the campaign to rescue Gordon each had at times been critical of the other's performance, when Buller was under attack for his perceived shortcomings in the Boer War, Wolseley had written letters of support to both him and Lady Audrey. So it was Lord Wolseley who was asked to do the unveiling. Adrian writes in *Memoirs* that Wolseley would have done so 'but for an official engagement which it was impossible to cancel'. That was a polite fiction. It may have been the reason given to Adrian to lessen disappointment at not having his statue unveiled by his former commander in the Sudan, but in reality his attendance was forbidden on medical grounds. Wolseley had accepted the invitation without consulting his doctor, and when the doctor learned of Wolseley's intention to attend, he wrote to Lady Audrey to say he must forbid it. Wolseley's health and memory had seriously deteriorated since his retirement in 1900, and the fear was that any emotional strain would cause mental breakdown.

Viscount Ebrington, the Lord Lieutenant of Devon, took Wolseley's place. Buller, his wife and his daughter watched and listened. So too did the top-hatted dignitaries for whom a space was kept near the platform party, the police, the fire brigade, the uniformed soldiers representing Buller's old regiment the 60th Rifles, and the general populace. The customary ceremonial mix of speeches and band music led to the climactic pulling away of the flags to reveal the statue. The general instant opinion on the 13-foot-high statue was 'superb', though it is said that locals from the area around Downes were disappointed that their hero was shown riding away from Crediton rather than towards it.

Adrian shows Buller full of years, but his firm John Bull stare still makes him appear formidable. His bulk is also impressive, and emphasised by the long flowing greatcoat worn open over the full dress uniform which carries on its breast the decorations, orders and campaign medals that tell of a meritorious lifetime of military service. As always in Adrian's statues, the sartorial detail is pinpoint accurate. The sculptured medals, for instance, just as on the marble bust, line up from the Victoria Cross in its position of honour on the right of the medal line, through the campaign medals, each with the correct number of battle clasps on the ribbon, to the Khedive's Egyptian Star, relegated to the left of the line because it is a foreign award.

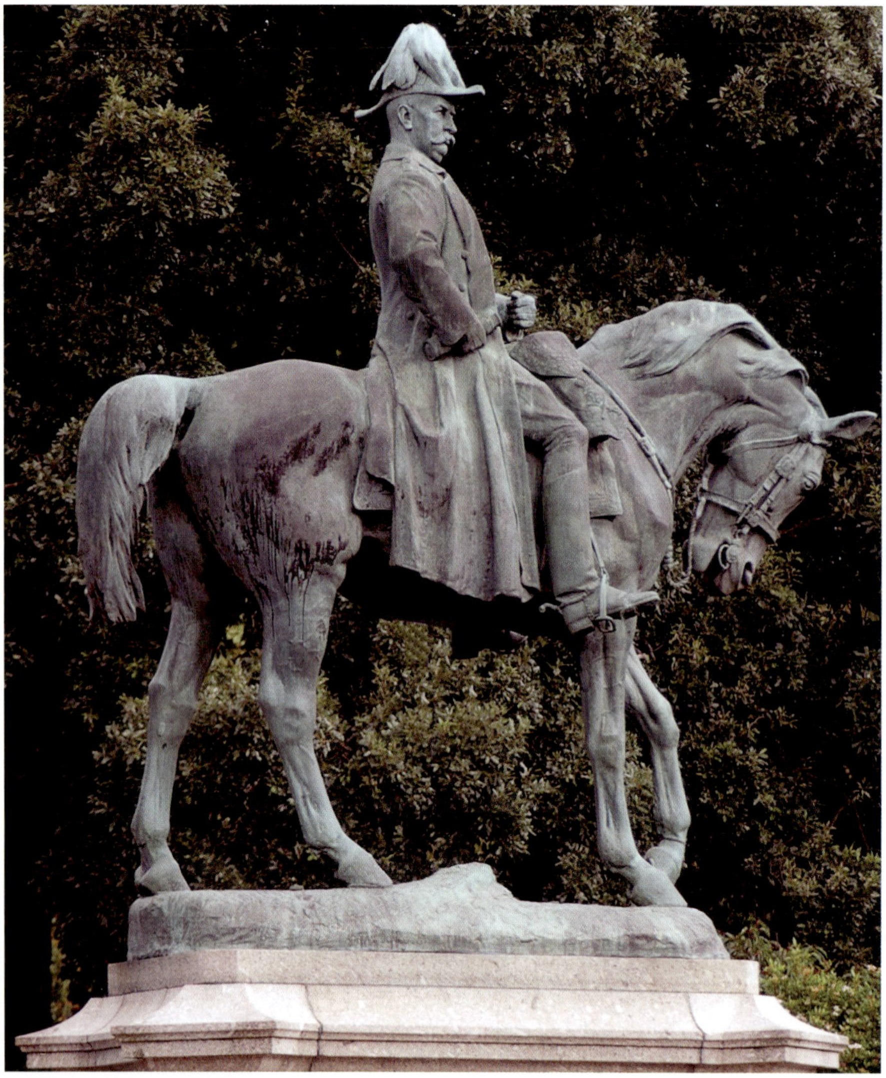

Above: **General Buller**, bronze equestrian statue. The reins are missing.
Below right: Detail, **General Buller**, the head
Below left: Detail, **General Buller**, part of postcard from 1905, showing the reins in position. Imagination leads one to think he looks more relaxed, being in control of his steed, than he does when the reins are missing.

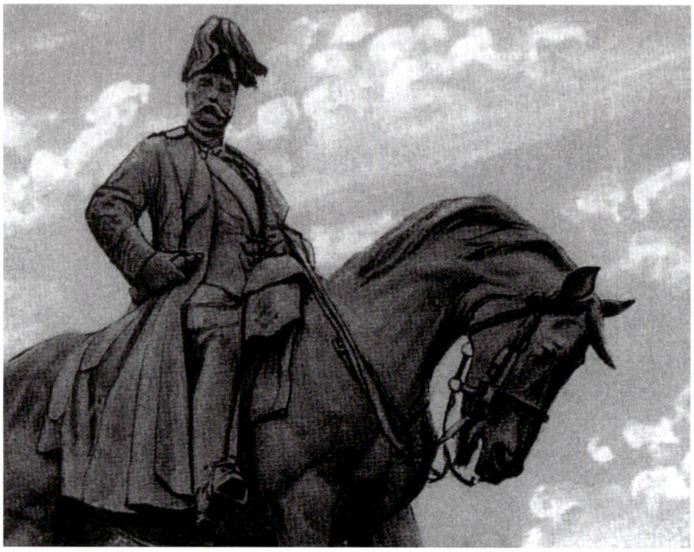

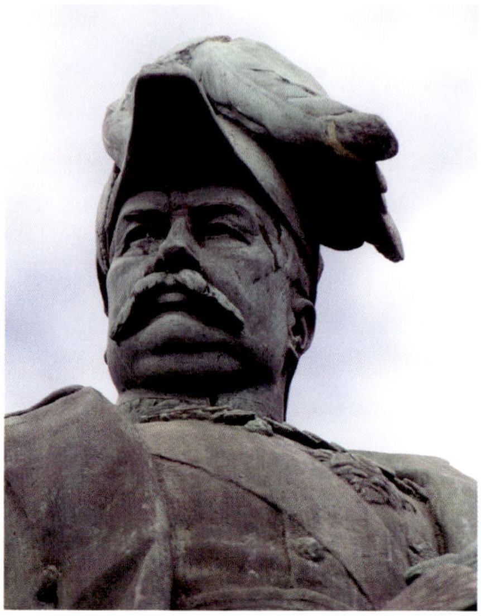

Achieving historical accuracy is painstaking, but for Adrian it was comparatively straightforward. Depicting personality, however, in the expected conventional 'tribute statue' format of an officer sitting on a quiet horse is extraordinarily difficult. Portrait artists seeking a more informal image often have to urge their subject to adopt a less self-conscious pose. But for a military leader, being self-conscious is a professional necessity. He must be aware that the eyes of his men will be upon him, and in facial expression and bodily attitude he must consciously seek to ensure that he does nothing that could lower their performance or morale. The statue's open greatcoat and the telescope in the right hand show that Buller is inspecting an exercise rather than a parade. His concentrated gaze is on how the men are doing in the field. How in such an undramatic composition does the artist animate personality? It would have been easier had Adrian's task been to portray the young, athletic Buller winning his VC. As his earlier Marines memorial had shown, Adrian could certainly sculpt expressive facial emotions in a scene of action. So too, if he had shown Buller lifting a threatened comrade onto his own horse to carry him to safety, it would not have been difficult to characterise him as dashingly fearless. (That subject would have had an incidental benefit. The broad brimmed felt hat with puggaree wound tightly round the crown, the uniform headgear of the Frontier Light Horse, would have been easier to model than the feather plume of a British general's cocked hat. A zoom lens photograph of the latter on the Exeter statue shows that it resembles a dead bird rather more than a plume. Adrian's triumph is that seen as it normally is, with unaided eyesight from twenty feet below, the plume appears exactly right.) In the undramatic, static Exeter composition wherein Buller is performing a routine military duty, it would seem unrealistic to expect much revelation of character.

Nevertheless, Adrian manages to put the viewer in touch with personality as well as with history. History indeed shaped that personality, and the viewer should regard the wording in bold black capitals on the pedestal as part of the statue's narrative. They tell that the elderly soldier above served the nation for forty-one years, fought in seven campaigns around the world in punishing climates and terrain, won the VC and 'saved Natal'. Still he adopts the military pose – head up, chin in, chest out; still his back is resolutely straight; but now his ageing limbs welcome a greatcoat against any nip in the air of his home neighbourhood. He was once a legend of physical strength, the only man of any rank on the Red River Expedition in Canada who could carry a hundred-pound barrel of pork on his back when portage around rapids was required – but those days are over. Perhaps his staring eyes are seeing the past as well as the present. The imaginative observer can empathise with the isolated figure whose role now is to watch the exertions of others. Yet for the sake of the unimaginative observer one must feel a twinge of disappointment that Exeter did not give Adrian a different commission. His own preference was to show men rather than officers, and Buller, though fonder than the next man of the good things in life, was supremely good at mucking in. A scene of him sharing the same hardships as the men on a campaign would surely have made easier the revelation of the personality which made him so popular among those who served under him. However, the public's enthusiastic reception of the Buller statue led to Adrian's receiving a similar commission for a memorial to the Duke of Cambridge, a royal figure for whom such a statue was fully appropriate.

Meanwhile, all viewers of Buller must feel some sadness that in the twenty-first century he has lost control of his horse. Should he wish to turn round and look again towards Crediton and Downes, he would find it difficult, for his left hand, which should be holding the reins, is empty. The reins which Adrian sculpted, clearly visible in the colour postcards of the statue sold in 1905, are gone. 'He saved Natal' is a quotation from a speech made in South Africa at Buller's farewell banquet. In fact, the speaker went further than that, declaiming: 'He saved Natal, South Africa and the British Empire.' The more sober Exeter committee did not have the full assertion engraved on the statue's plinth, but one hopes that today's local government will nevertheless feel that Buller is historically and artistically important enough for his reins to be restored.

The Duke of Cambridge (1906-07)

The Duke of Cambridge (1819-1904) is another figure about whose performance, understandably, military historians have reservations. He served as Commander-in-Chief of the British Army, without any time limit on his holding the office, from 1856 until he was pressed to resign in 1895. A first cousin of Queen Victoria, he had been made a major-general at the inexperienced age of 26, and had not seen active service until the Crimean War of 1854-55, when he became the general of the infantry division (comprising the Brigade of Guards and the Highland Brigade). He proved personally brave enough, and his division, albeit belatedly after one of those battlefield confusions so frequent in that war, showed both heroism and steadiness worthy of a drill review as it made the successful second assault on the Great Redoubt at the battle of the River Alma, and held it against a counter-attack by the Russian infantry. On the whole the infantry division generals were more competent than the Crimean cavalry generals, and the Duke was notably competent at executing parade-ground-style infantry manoeuvres, though a story is told of him once having been dismayed by an order to march his troops south east as marching by a compass point was not part of his repertoire. Obviously his battle honours do not bear comparison with those of his successors as C-in-C, Viscount Wolseley (1895-1900) and Earl Roberts (1900-1904), nor with those of 20th-century military leaders such as Field Marshals Montgomery and Slim, whose statues also stand in Whitehall. Instead, the Duke has to be assessed as an administrator.

In one way the timing of his appointment was unlucky. The Crimean War had highlighted so many failings in British Army practice that in 1856 there was momentum for change. But then in the Indian Mutiny of 1857-59 British forces were successful, and the Duke acted decisively by creating 25 new infantry battalions to serve as the second battalions of existing regiments. Impetus for change thereafter weakened, and when Sidney Herbert left the War Office in 1861 it stopped. In day to day leadership, the Duke was a great improvement on the commander in the Crimean War, Lord Raglan, whom the war correspondent of the *Times*, William Russell, had criticised for not going among the troops, so that 'his person is in consequence unknown to them'. The Duke busily visited regiments and attended field days, so he became a familiar figure, popular with the men, who referred to him by his Christian name 'George', and several Aldershot pubs were named after him. But he was conservative by nature, his critics would say complacent. He did not initiate needed modernisation in the years before Gladstone appointed Edward Cardwell to the War Office, and thereafter he opposed such Cardwell reforms as the abolition of purchase commissions, on the grounds that making the officers 'mercenaries' rather than 'gentlemen' smacked of dangerous republicanism. As the reputation of Wolseley and his ring of bright staff officers rose, the Duke found himself disagreeing with many of Wolseley's modernising ideas, though he liked the strength of Wolseley's passion for the army, and was fair in his comments to Queen Victoria about him. Hence the overall judgement of historians that the Duke was a drag on military progress. Yet, as he reluctantly left office, he could point to the remarkable success rate of the army in Victoria's small wars, its transformed powers of logistical preparation (what a contrast to Crimean days!), and of the army's adaptation to hostile challenges and harsh terrains and climates around the empire on which the sun never set. Another strong point of his career, of course, was his special pleasure in the excellence of his army's turn-out at field days and parades.

Most importantly from Adrian's point of view, 'when the long and strenuous life of the Duke of Cambridge came to an end, there was a general opinion that a memorial should be set up somewhere in the neighbourhood of the War Office where, for so many years, he had served his country with a very wholehearted devotion'. Elsewhere in his *Memoirs* Adrian refers to him as 'that fine old soldier ... a man greatly respected and esteemed by all those who were brought into contact with him, and undoubtedly a very sound judge of military matters'. Then, recognising that there had been critics of the Duke, he argues: 'Had he not belonged to the Royal Family, it is at least quite likely that his high position would have passed unchallenged.' No doubts or reservations about the Duke there, and when in 1906 a committee chaired by Queen Victoria's son the Duke of Connaught invited sculptors to submit designs for an equestrian statue to be sited in Whitehall between Horse Guards and the War Office, Adrian was among those who submitted their designs. The committee duly called at the studio in his garden in Church Street, but as Adrian rotated his design piece on its pedestal so it might be assessed from every direction, it overbalanced and crashed into a thousand pieces. Fortunately, the committee members had seen enough to respond favourably when Adrian apologetically asked them if they would be prepared to return for a second viewing after he had rebuilt the sketch model. On their second visit they gave him the commission on the spot. Afterwards, General Redvers Buller, whom he knew extremely well, having recently made a sculpture of him, privately reassured Adrian that he had won the contest to sculpt the Duke of Cambridge, not through any favouritism on his [Buller's] part but through the unanimous agreement of the committee members that his design was the most attractive.

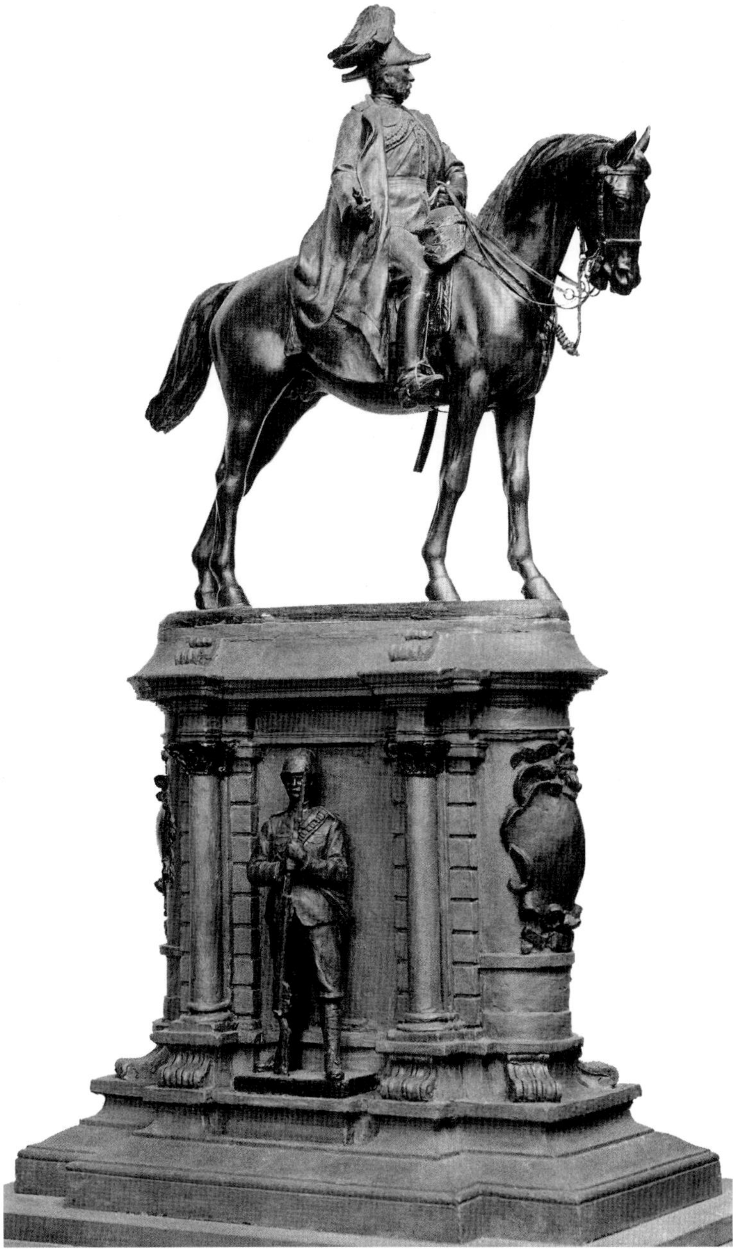

The Duke of Cambridge: initial idea for the plinth

Adrian had seen the Duke frequently: in Aldershot and London during his army service, later riding in the Row in Hyde Park and for the last time close up in Knightsbridge Barracks when he had come with friends to look at Adrian's silver statuette 'Royal Standard Bearer' before it was presented to the Duke of York (afterwards George V) as a wedding present from the 2nd Life Guards. But that meeting had been more than ten years previously. Now the Duke had died, which did not suit the artist's preference for working from a living model. In a post-Great War article for the *Daily Express* entitled 'Why the Statues of London Are So Dull' he was to write:

> It is manifestly unfair to expect a sculptor to make his statue 'live' if he never has an opportunity of seeing the living man and studying and absorbing his personality. Yet that is what often

> happens. The celebrity's clothes are worn by a model, and the face is copied from a photograph ... A work of art must show personality – the personality of the sitter and the personality of the artist – and one must work from the living model to detect and reproduce that vital spark.

On the other hand, another feature of the Cambridge commission suited him:

> The first thing that a sculptor should know is where it is intended that his statue should stand, so that the design not only of the figure but of the plinth that supports it can conform with the architecture of the surrounding buildings and give an effect of harmony instead of discord. It has unfortunately become the fashion to mount statues on a perfectly plain block of stone, under the mistaken impression that it indicates strength. As a matter of fact, it indicates nothing but a lack of imagination, and detracts from the value of the figure by breaking the continuity of design which is essential to an artistic conception.

However, for the model of the Duke of Cambridge, doubtless realising that the committee's choice would depend on the merit of the portrayal of the rider and his steed, Adrian first concentrated on getting those right. He succeeded so well that his initial models were virtually identical to the final bronze. As the Duke was to be posed as if carrying out his familiar role of reviewing troops, there was no call for scenery beneath the horse; a slab as flat as a parade ground would serve. But he did not intend to place the plain slab on top of a despised 'perfectly plain block of stone'. From the beginning he obviously had it in mind to make the pedestal high enough to raise the statue above the Whitehall traffic but at eye level for upper deck passengers on the open top buses, and solid enough to withstand any traffic accident. (When a friend asked him 'What is going to happen if a bus drives into it?' Adrian assured him he would be sorry for the bus.) Also, from the outset he followed his policy of conforming with the architecture of the surrounding buildings: the round columns, flanked by square stones, rising from the lower to the upper base are a direct reference to the building behind. Otherwise at this stage he did not give a lot of thought to the final aesthetic effect. Early drawings show needless scrolls on the bases obtruding on the otherwise smooth lines, unoriginal conventionally elaborate shields on both ends, and a rounded plinth standing on a four-tiered basically rectangular base with which it does not harmonise. In this initial design, he added to the equestrian statue on top statues of standing soldiers in campaign dress at the sides. As so often, his first thoughts were ambitious and would therefore be costly to execute.

The final pedestal design, carefully considered by Adrian in collaboration with his architect, John Belcher, ARA, is quite different from the earlier plan. The street base is slimmed and now echoes the upper base; the rounded pillars are replaced by elegant concave grooves which complement rather than simply reproduce the columns on nearby Whitehall buildings; and to give cleaner lines the obtrusive carved scrolls, squares and shields are eliminated. Most importantly, Adrian dismisses the foot soldier statues. They are replaced on the plinth ends by bas reliefs of a Grenadier Guardsman and a 17th Lancer, standing smartly rigid as if waiting to be inspected by their commander-in-chief, who had himself served in both their regiments. Though attractive, they are not so prominent as to distract attention from the equestrian figure above. Adrian and Belcher could feel they had integrated the granite pedestal with its setting and completed the artistic concept of the statue. Adrian signed his work for all to see beside the lancer's boot.

The making of the full-size statue attracted numerous royal visitors whose close acquaintance with the Duke was a useful compensation for the absence of the man himself. Adrian sculpted the Duke gazing to the left, so that once in position he would look at the new War Office rather than Horse Guards. Perhaps because

Cardwell had evicted the Duke from Horse Guards and moved him to be based under his supervision in Pall Mall, it seemed inappropriate to have him looking back towards Horse Guards. Or was it a little private joke on Adrian's part to show the Duke confronting the War Office which had often disagreed with him?

King Edward himself performed the unveiling. Queen Alexandra, the Prince and Princess of Wales, the Duke of Connaught and other members of the Royal Family, eight officer representatives of the German Emperor, Britain's top generals, the Governor of the Bank of England, the Prime Minister, the Secretary and Under Secretary of State for War, four former Secretaries of State for War, and the Masters of several city

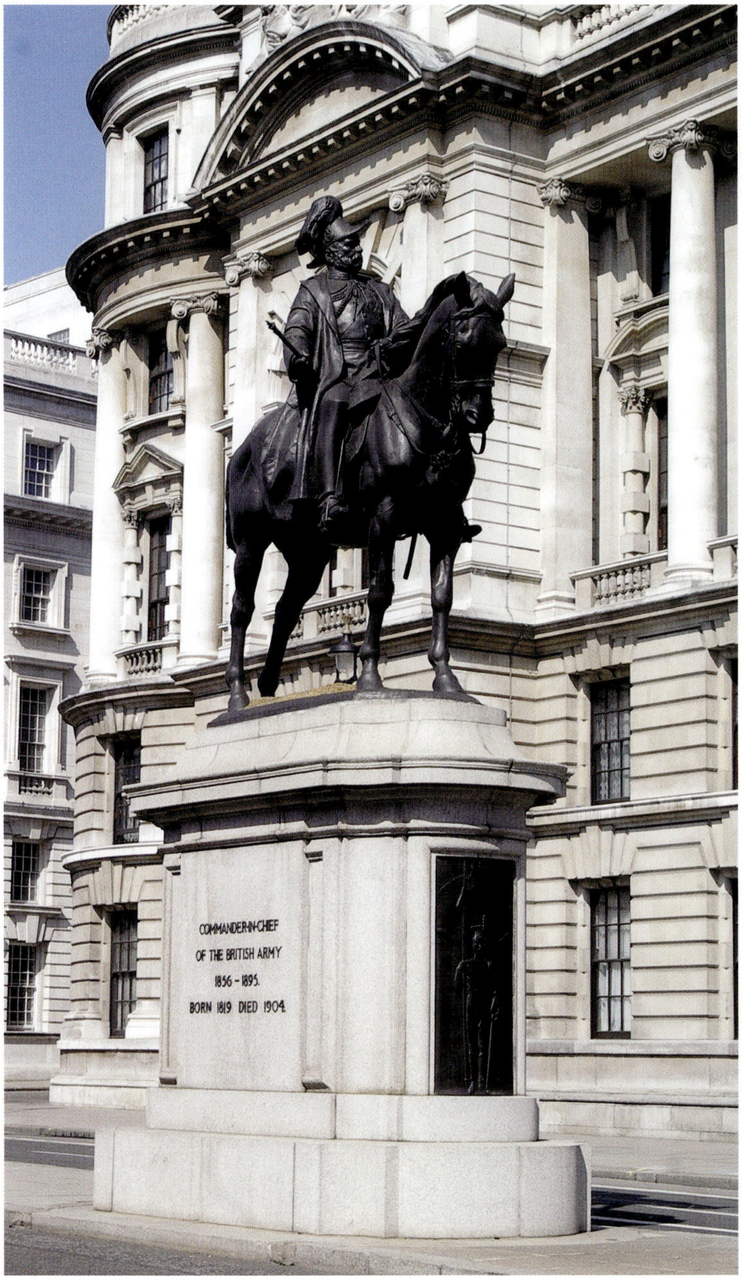

The Duke of Cambridge, bronze equestrian statue, 1907, with cleaner plinth design and bas reliefs replacing standing statues

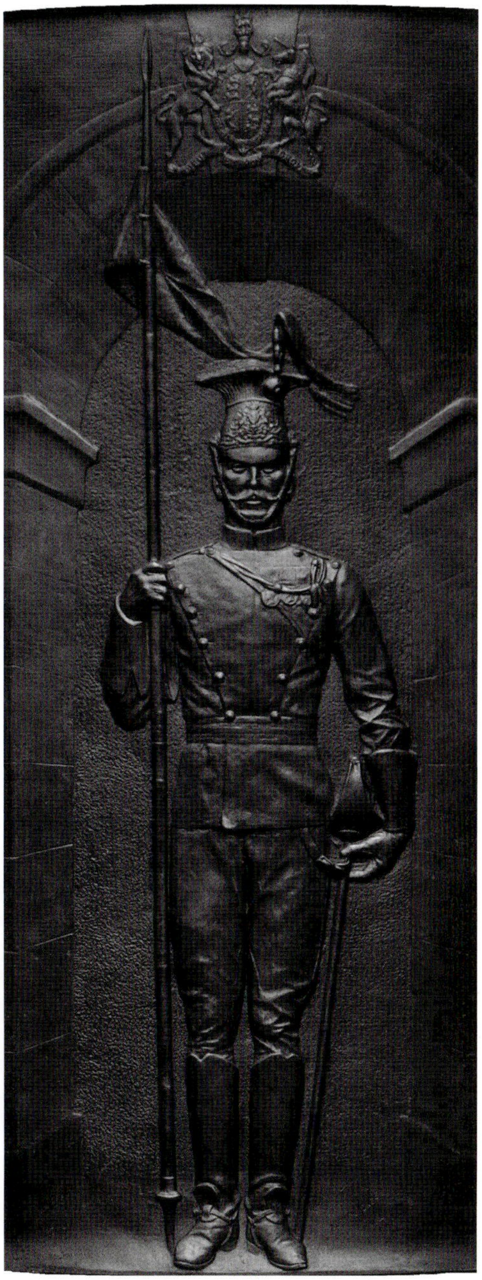

17th Lancer bas relief on plinth of the **Duke of Cambridge** statue, Whitehall

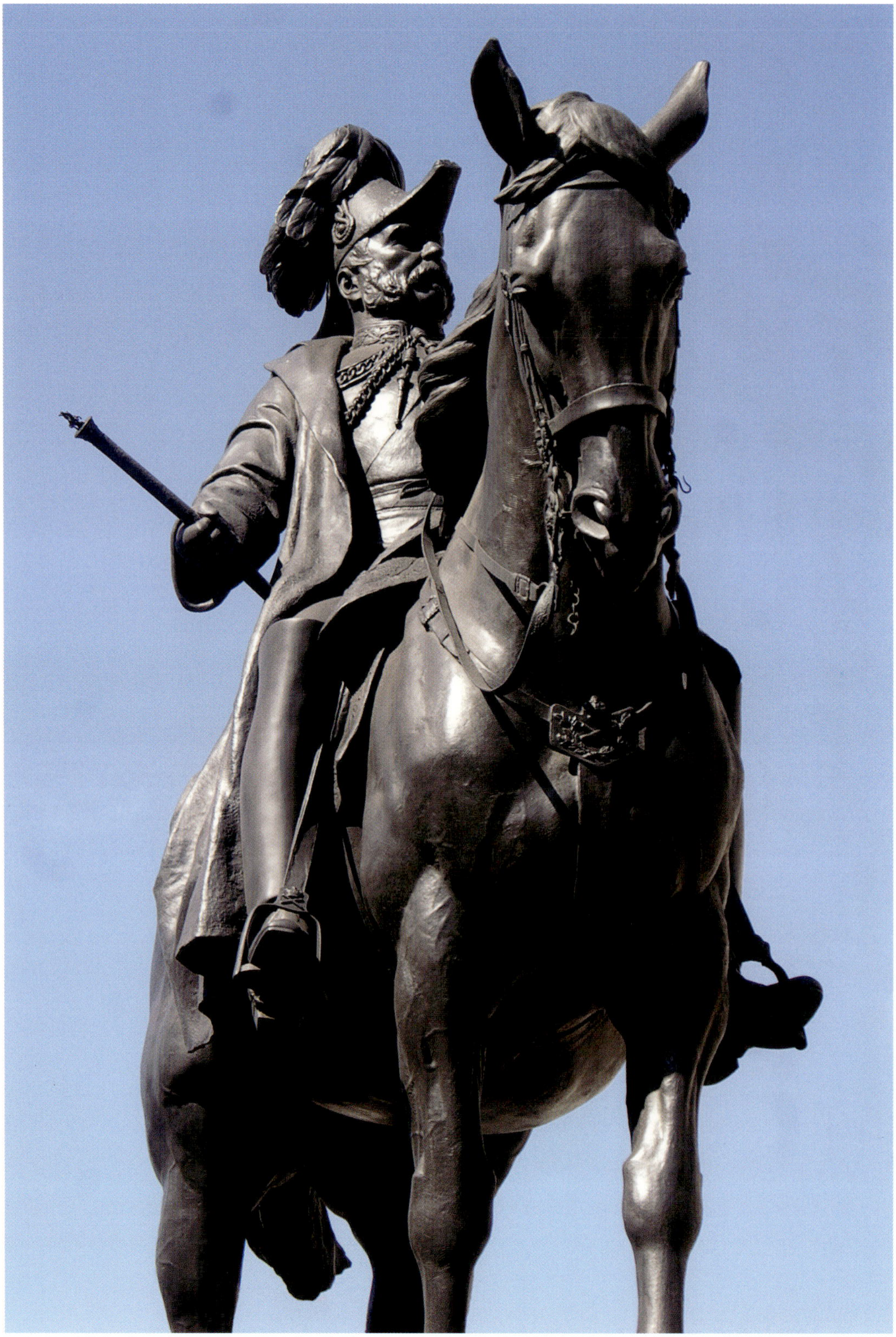

The Duke of Cambridge. The craftsmanship in the meticulous detailing shows Adrian's mastery of precision and historical accuracy.

companies were present, and the Lord Mayor arrived in his state coach. Considerable crowds huddling under umbrellas watched in a heavy downpour. They saw in front of the still-covered statue a red-carpeted dais and beside it, facing up Whitehall, the King's Guard of Honour provided by the Grenadier Guards, carrying the King's Colour and accompanied by their band. Opposite them, beyond the statue and facing south down Whitehall, paraded a tribute guard of Adrian's old regiment, the 2nd Life Guards. To the side paraded parties of twenty-one men from each of the ten regiments, including the 17th Lancers, with which the Duke had been particularly connected. The soldiers were in church parade order, dismounted and not carrying rifles, though the Lancers held their lances, and the scene was not as colourful as it might have been because many detachments had been ordered into greatcoats as some protection against wind and rain. But the dais party of a glittering retinue of royalty and escorting British, Indian and German officers, their many helmet plumes drenched but still fluttering in the wind, was impressive enough. The Guards band played the National Anthem, and the Duke of Connaught invited the King to unveil the statue. The King responded with appropriately gracious words, then pulled the cord to release the covering Union Jacks. Sodden from the gale-driven rain, they stuck stubbornly to the statue. 'Fetch them down at any cost!' ordered Edward. With careful forethought, Adrian had arranged for four warrant officers, one from each of the Guards regiments, to be in position to deal with any hitches such as this. They pulled the flags clear to reveal the imposing five-ton equestrian bronze, already familiar to the King from his visits to Adrian's Chelsea studio and now a new feature of the central London route for major state ceremonies. A few days later the grateful King summoned Adrian to Buckingham Palace and made him a Member of the Victorian Order.

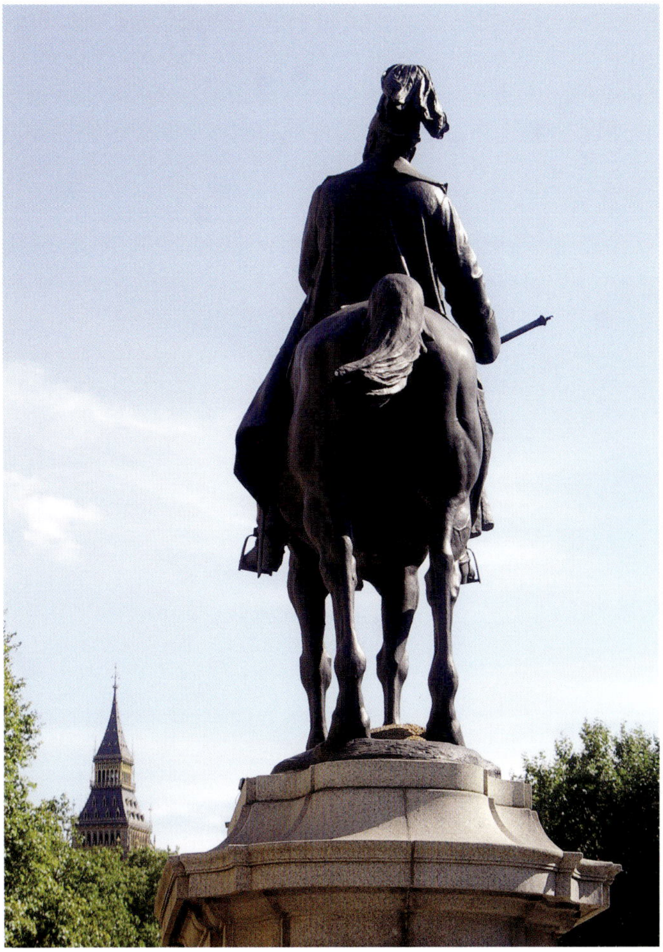

The Duke of Cambridge. The artist in Adrian was pleased when a General told him, 'I like the front very much, but I should have known it was the Duke from the back'.

Very often Adrian liked to create a sense of movement in the horses he portrays, but for the statue of the Duke of Cambridge he chose to rein that in. The disciplined horse dips its head and swishes its tail but otherwise is still. The pose is one associated in the public mind with the Duke. He sits on his stationary horse watching an imaginary march past of the soldiers of the Queen Empress. (It is a pose which can be got wrong. Critics of the Whitehall equestrian statue of Earl Haig, a commission which Adrian did not receive despite some public demand that he should, complain that Haig's horse looks braced for urinating.) In his 'Dull Statues' article Adrian also stated that 'a transcript of nature is not art. Art is something more than this', and on consideration of this statue many onlookers may well feel that the horse has some aspect of personality such as nobility or power or beauty. But the first reaction is probably more simply admiration for the craftsmanship that has been put into every detail of the 'transcript', from the lie of the mane and the exact accuracy of the harness to the rearmost fetlock and hoof. In the Savage Club two members wagered on whether or not the horse had a girth (saddle belly-band). The money was collected by the member who claimed it had. With typical concern for detail and anatomy, Adrian had moulded it sunk unobtrusively into the horse's flesh.

Nevertheless, for this commission the horse had to be no more than the complement to its commemorated rider. Rightly he is shown full of years towards the end rather than the start of his command, but still with a firm seat, upright in the saddle, head erect and gaze fixed. He wears full uniform and in the hand that does not hold the reins he carries his field marshal's baton. In the 'Dull Statues' article another lament of Adrian's is that 'too much attention is paid to the clothes and too little to the man inside them ... A great soldier, or any other man accustomed to command, could be dressed in the humblest of rags and still look a leader of men.' There he arguably exaggerates into the realms of the fanciful, and in sculpting the Duke he has the advantage of field marshal's uniform decorated with his Orders and medals rather than the handicap of drab or humbling clothing, but his artistic aim was to capture what he termed 'inward fire' in his human subjects. Being metaphorical, the expression cannot be pinned down literally, and it would be bizarre to interpret it narrowly and conclude Adrian thought all his soldier figures should be 'fiery'. The general sense is clear enough: a 'great' statue should breathe some animating noble trait. This is more easily achieved if the figure is sculpted physically active, as in the statue of Lt Pollock Hamilton V.C. by Adrian's mentor Charles Birch, or his own defiant Marine sheltering a wounded comrade on his Marines memorial in the Mall. These have an 'inward fire' of courage. But the Duke, like his steed, is still. That does not mean lack of personality. He exudes dignity and authority. At the unveiling, doubtless some who had known him felt moved. But does the pose stir feeling in today's passing pedestrians? Perhaps a sense of pride in British history? The response is again more likely to be one of admiration for the detailed verisimilitude. Certainly that is the response of Major General Sir Frederick Smith in his *History of the Royal Army Veterinary Corps*. He likens Adrian's work to that of the 19th-century French painter Ernest Meissonier, famed for careful attention to detail in his military and historical paintings: 'The equestrian statue of the Duke of Cambridge in Whitehall is Meissonier-like in its accuracy of detail and faithful likeness; he has captured the precise gesture and attitude of the Duke.'

Adrian's Quadriga and Cavalry Memorial masterpieces still lay ahead, but in a newspaper interview he gave to the *Evening News* later in 1907 he said he considered 'Duncan's Horses' his finest imaginative work and the Duke his best statue, and revealed that King Edward had promised to unveil it after inspecting the original design in the studio. The reporter commented that 'no artist could desire higher testimony to his ability'. No such statement will ever receive universal agreement, but certainly the contemporary acclaim that greeted the Duke of Cambridge was near universal.

Chapter Thirteen: 'Sufficient good fellowship' 1906-1914: The Chelsea Arts Club, the Shropshire Society and other diversions

Despite all the work Adrian took on during his career as a London artist, it must not be thought that this was at the expense of his social life. The convivial friendships of club life offered relaxation from working for patrons, and gave welcome and needed support in difficult times such as the period of the 'Ghost' controversy. Adrian said in his *Memoirs*:

> In the intervals of striving I was very faithful to the Savage Club. It had stood by me loyally through my trouble and I always regard with pleasure the jolly Saturday night dinners, when everybody relaxed and there was sufficient good fellowship on the first floor in the house in Adelphi Terrace to have made all Fleet Street and the Strand quite happy.

Very much closer to home was the Chelsea Arts Club, which moved to 143-145 Church Street, next door to Adrian and Emma, thereby offering the companionship of fellow artists and a large billiard room. As the Edwardian age and the twentieth century began, Adrian was approaching his sixties, and becoming, in the words of the Club's historian Tom Cross, 'a truly Victorian figure, and one of the most respected members of the Club'. In 1906-7 he became the Club's Chairman. Under his chairmanship it decided to stage a Ball in London which for glamour would rival anything staged in Paris or Rome. A year of planning led to the Royal Opera House in Covent Garden becoming the setting for the first Chelsea Arts Ball. All the half guinea tickets, to include supper, sold; all the boxes at five to eight guineas were taken; and the student artists and guests who danced the night away produced a healthy profit of £450 and inaugurated the tradition of the annual Chelsea Arts Ball, which became the world's most famous (and eventually notorious) costume ball. 1909 saw the profits doubled, so the Ball moved on to the Albert Hall. A great floor mounted over the arena provided the largest dance floor in the world, and on its more than 16,000 square feet more than 4,000 costumed dancers whirled to the tunes of costumed large bands. (In the Albert Hall, in those pre-amplification days, a band needed to be big: there might be more than a hundred players, and the vocalists sometimes used a megaphone.) Tom Cross relates how because of the vast space, the Club set up signs to serve as meeting places to find one's partner. The *Punch* artist George Belcher contributed a sign which depicted a drunken waiter vainly trying to draw a cork from a soda water syphon. Titled 'Athlete Struggling With a Syphon', it wittily bore remarkable resemblance to Lord Leighton's most famous sculpture, 'Athlete Struggling With a Python'.

The detailed arrangements were the responsibility of the Chairman of the Arts Club House Committee, but other members could offer proposals. For the 1912 Ball, Adrian suggested that a military band play, but was overruled. He had the consolation that at the New Year's Eve Ball 'Auld Lang Syne' was played by army pipers. (The early Arts balls were lively but decorous affairs. After the Second World War they became scandalous, inebriated assaults being launched on the imaginative floats and on other dancers. The tabloid press reported: 'One girl wearing a strapless evening gown was soon wearing a gownless evening strap.' Ironically, the event did not survive into 'the swinging sixties': the 1958 Ball coincided with a night of thickest pea soup fog, and the financial loss killed off the event.)

The Arts Club membership included what some art historians might consider a surprising number who were unimpressed by the techniques and distortions of the modernists. That attitude might be expected among those working artists whose output was for journals. The *Punch* cartoonist H.M. Bateman, who joined the Club in 1910, was one who was angered by the new styles. But so too were others who sought to earn their living in the general art market, exhibited in such outlets as the Sketch Club and the New English Art Club, and now felt in danger of being sidelined by such as Matisse, Braque and Picasso. When in 1912 the second Post-Impressionist Exhibition featured the experimental continental trio and British artists like Stanley Spencer and Wyndham Lewis, the Arts Club in joking retaliation mounted a spoof exhibition about a fictional modernist group named the Racinistes. These imagined artists rejoiced in such names as Rotten and Gaga, and programme notes recounted how the various geniuses had shot themselves, gone mad, or destroyed themselves with drugs in the manner expected amongst extreme artistic types. Doubtless Adrian enjoyed the joke.

Many Chelsea Arts Club members were also involved with the New English Art Club. The Newlyn school of painters from Cornwall and the Glasgow Boys exhibited at the New English Art Club and when

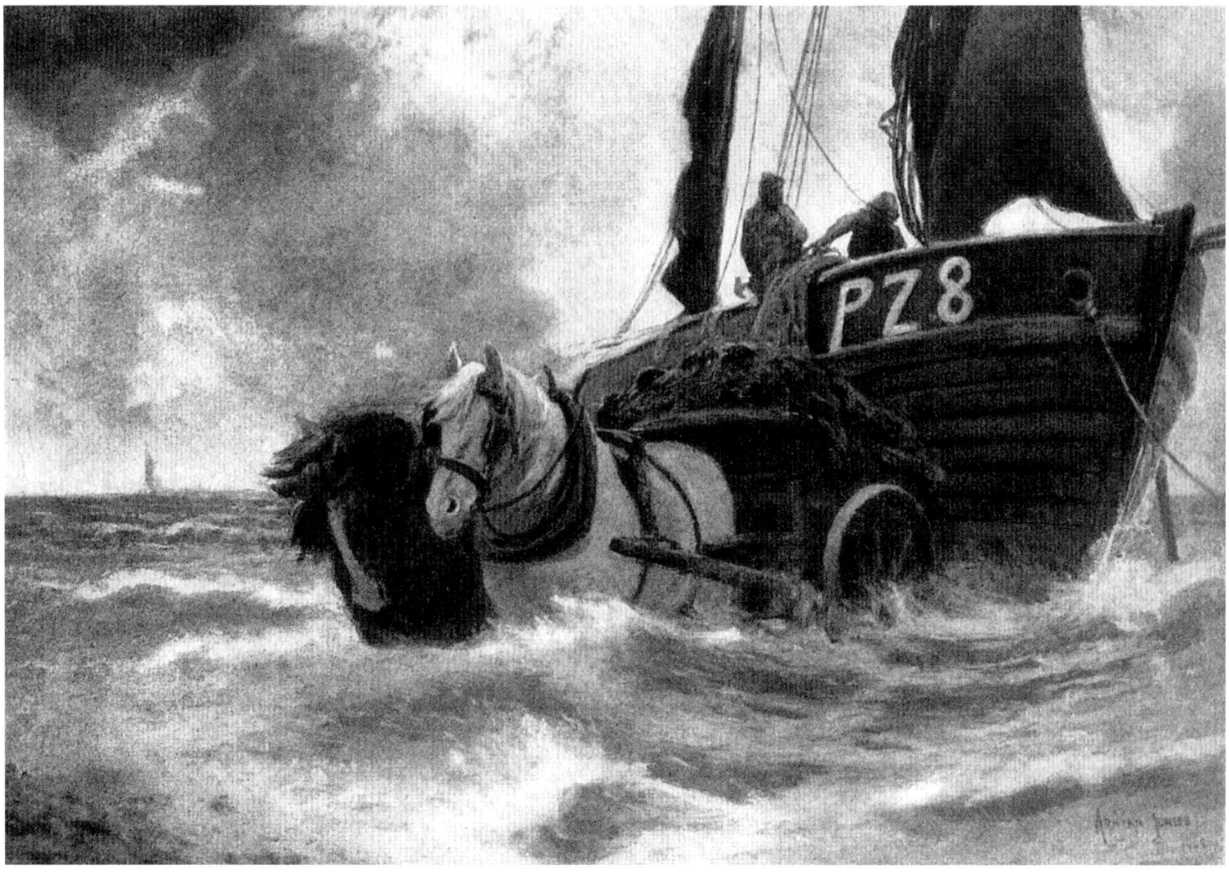

Taking the Nets on Board, 1902. Here Adrian adopts the style of many of the Newlyn School of painters who, initially influenced by Jean-François Millet, liked realistic open air scenes.
The public first saw this picture in a January 1903 issue of 'Illustrated Sporting and Dramatic'.

in London used the Chelsea Arts Club as a social base. Their membership further widened Adrian's range of contacts, and later led him to Cornwall, where in a departure from his customary farming or racing settings for his horse paintings he showed a pair of horses between the shafts of the cart they had pulled out through wind-whipped surf to a Penzance-registered fishing boat so that its load of nets could be manhauled on board. Unlike Whistler, Adrian exhibited very little in Scotland, and though the Scottish press on occasion reviewed his work he remained much less known there than in England. However, he became thoroughly familiar with the paintings of the Scottish colourist J.D. Fergusson, who exhibited annually at the Royal British Society of Artists, and he helped to introduce another colourist, S.J. Peploe, to a London audience when as chairman of the hanging committee at the inaugural exhibition of the Allied Artists Association in the Albert Hall he included several Peploe works.

Adrian was instrumental in helping to establish the Allied Artists Association, which, as a riposte to exhibitions largely limited to a group of like-thinking artists, was open to anyone. Mindful probably of the huge success of the Chelsea Arts Club Balls, the committee made the bold decision to hire the Albert Hall and in their first exhibition in July 1908 displayed some 4,000 works of art. The Association's members had elected the hanging committee by vote and Adrian as that committee's chairman – evidence of his status and popularity amongst fellow artists. The Committee was not a selection jury. Its task was to provide exhibition space for any of the eight hundred members who wished to exercise their right to exhibit up to five works. The stalls were removed from the centre of the arena to provide space for sculptures, while the rest of the building was used to hang oils, watercolours, and black and white sketches. 'There is a confusion of styles greater than the confusion of tongues at Babel', reported the *Morning Post*. 'Yet on the whole,' said the *Yorkshire Post*, 'one cannot but be amazed that with such principles of selection – or lack of principle – the exhibition reaches the standard it does.' The exhibition ranged from unknowns to such as Walter Sickert, Lucien Pissarro, Wilson Steer, Samuel Peploe and Adrian himself (represented by the plaster cast of his General Buller equestrian statue and by his prancing shire horse study 'Joie de Vivre'). Modernists and traditionalists appeared beside each other. The *Morning Post* commented that 'the brilliant revolt of Walter Sickert will cause debate in which scorn and praise will be extreme'. The exhibition was a triumph of inclusiveness.

In 1913, the year after the spoof exhibition on the Racinistes, the Chelsea Arts Club elected another member who hated 'modern' distortion in painting. Like Adrian, Alf Munnings specialised in conventional horse paintings. Adrian had the good fortune to work as an artist during one of horse racing's golden eras, from around 1880 to 1914. Munnings, born in 1878, was of a later generation, gaining his first acceptance for Royal Academy exhibition in 1899. He was a contrast to Adrian in his personality and in his artistic career. He had no veterinary training, but by purchasing a copy of Stubbs's *Anatomy of the Horse* and studying it he gained a sound enough knowledge, enhanced by looking after horses during the Great War and gaining experience as a war artist whilst attached to the Canadian Cavalry Brigade. His rumbustious personality was the right one for leading the wild night of celebrations with which the Arts Club greeted the Armistice, but later his unconventional drunken behaviour led to his expulsion (until re-election in the 1930s). To Adrian as senior member fell the unpleasant task of delivering to Munnings at his studio the notice of expulsion. In her biography of Munnings Jean Goodman records that Adrian, who thought it a terrible thing to be suspended from a club, was much more upset than Munnings, who simply transferred his conviviality to the society of the Café Royal, and was accepted as a member of the more expensive Arts Club off Piccadilly, where Adrian too was a member. Meanwhile, Munnings's career as a painter flourished. His forty-five paintings in the 'Canada at War' exhibition in 1919 established his reputation, he was soon elected an Associate of the Royal Academy, and in 1944 he defeated Augustus John in the election to be its

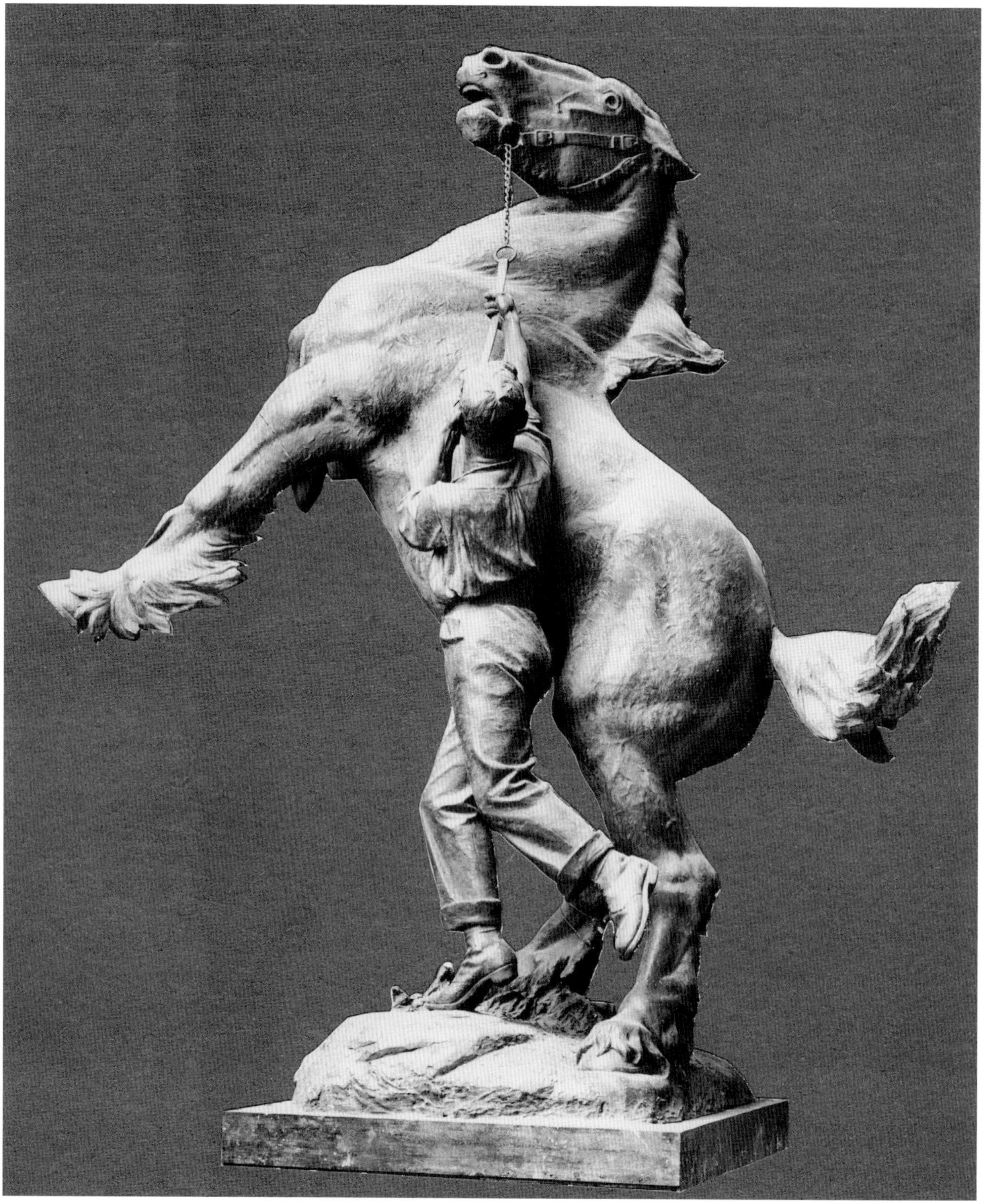

Joie de Vivre, plaster cast statue, Allied Artists exhibit, 1908. Under the anglicised title 'Joy of Life' it was chosen later for exhibition in the Palace of Art grounds at the British Empire Exhibition, 1924.

President. As his output increased and Adrian's declined, he went on to surpass Adrian in popular appeal. In the privacy of Chelsea Arts Club he had vented numerous diatribes against Picasso and other modernists, but his broadcast castigation of Cézanne, Matisse, Picasso and Henry Moore at the 1949 Academy Banquet caused a public uproar that resulted in his resignation from the Academy. Like Adrian, he enjoyed breaking free from commissions and static poses. At his Memorial Service in 1959 Augustus John rated him 'greater than Stubbs. He made it move, had greater narrative quality, and his groupings are better'. Certainly his atmospheric groupings, evocative of the colour and personalities of Epsom and smaller race meetings, were lively and well executed; but a league table of artists' reputations cannot have the validity of tables of games clubs. It may be that the only safe assessment is that in quantity and quality of output the foremost portrayers of horses in the history of British art are George Stubbs, Adrian Jones and Alfred Munnings. (In comparison to Adrian, Munnings did few sculptures, but in the National Horseracing Museum stands one of the five castings of his fine Black Jack equine statuette.)

Adrian continued to be a member of the Chelsea Arts Club until the end of his life, a well-known figure in his scarlet-lined military campaign cloak when talking and smoking, and a regular able performer at the snooker table. By 1914 the Club was financially sound enough to agree a new lease of its premises, to run for sixty years. Adrian was one of the six named leaseholders. In his lengthy, happy membership he had only one falling out with the Club. This was when the ground landlord said he was willing to offer the Club the lease of 147 Church Street – Adrian's house and studio! At an explosive meeting, Adrian, who had not been consulted about this possibility, made it very clear that he was not prepared to sell. Happily, the Club decided it would not be in its financial interest to expand its premises, and the idea lapsed. Later the Club celebrated Adrian's ninetieth birthday with 'a marvellous party': an illustration in *Artists and Bohemians* shows Adrian cutting his birthday cake. The Club history also salutes his art: an illustration of the Quadriga terms it 'one of the great decorative sculptures of London'. Had they still been alive to read it, that artists' verdict would have pleased King Edward VII and Adrian alike.

The Shropshire Society in London

Adrian Jones's career as a soldier and then as an artist working in London took him away from Shropshire, but he had no wish to forsake his roots. He kept in touch with his native county, his birthplace, his family and his school through occasional visits and, because he was a highly clubbable man, through his membership of the Shropshire Society in London. There had been such a Society which met monthly in London as early as the eighteenth century. A press advertisement for its meeting in March 1750 at the Pope Head Tavern in Cornhill in the City of London announced: 'Some regulations are then intended to be made towards carrying on the amiable and laudable society to the universal satisfaction of the members thereof.' The satisfaction cannot have proved universal, because later that society died. Its heir was conceived at the end of the nineteenth century by letters written to Shropshire newspapers advocating a Shropshire Society along the lines of other county societies then active in London. The outcome was a meeting on 9 February 1899 (Adrian's fifty-fourth birthday, as it happens) at the Hotel Cecil in the Strand, attended by about ninety Shropshire men living in or around London. Adrian was among them. The author of the letter, a Mr Rickards, was elected the first honorary secretary, the Right Honourable Earl of Powys was elected President (the first of very many titled persons or honourables or knights who were to hold that office) and a committee of management representing the leading towns of Shropshire, including Ludlow, was formed.

The Society's stated aims chimed happily with Adrian Jones's personality. They included 'to foster patriotism, to spread sociability and cheerfulness, to renew old associations and to preserve records of interesting and historical events, to enable its members to make new friends with the Salopian spirit, feelings and memories, and to provide a timely and enjoyable rendezvous for young people from the County who feel lonely in London. Also to give any Salopian who hit a bad time a helping hand from the Benevolent Fund, all prompted by love for the dear old County of Shropshire'. All these aspirations were subsequently pursued, but significantly the Society's first event was a social one, an inaugural annual dinner held three months later in May, again at the Hotel Cecil. The holding mortar of the Society was always the bonding with fellow Salopians. Essentially the atmosphere was that of clubland – originally all male, with a membership of those who had successfully made a middle or upper class mark in life. The Society was part of a wider web of similar societies. This loose grouping was formalised in 1912 with the formation of the English County Societies Conference. In addition to encouraging County patriotism, the Conference declared a second objective: 'to further the recognition of St George's Day'. This was another aim with which Adrian was in full sympathy. (In the 1920s, when he sculpted St George as the symbol of the cavalry of the empire, there were over twenty London County Societies affiliated to the conference and to the Royal Society of St George. Thereafter there was some decline, but the Shropshire Society has continued to flourish into the twenty-first century.)

From being a founder member, Adrian Jones went on to be active in the Society's service. In 1907 the Society funded a mural tablet to be placed in St Michael's Church, Madeley, to the memory of a past member of the Society, the late Sir Wyke Bayliss, who had been President of the Royal Society of British Artists. Adrian took charge of the work. Maintaining contact with the RSBA, the Society in 1909 and again in 1911 arranged concerts by Shropshire artistes in the RSBA's Suffolk Street galleries. By then Adrian was a leading member of the Society. In 1908, along with the best-selling historical novelist Stanley Weyman

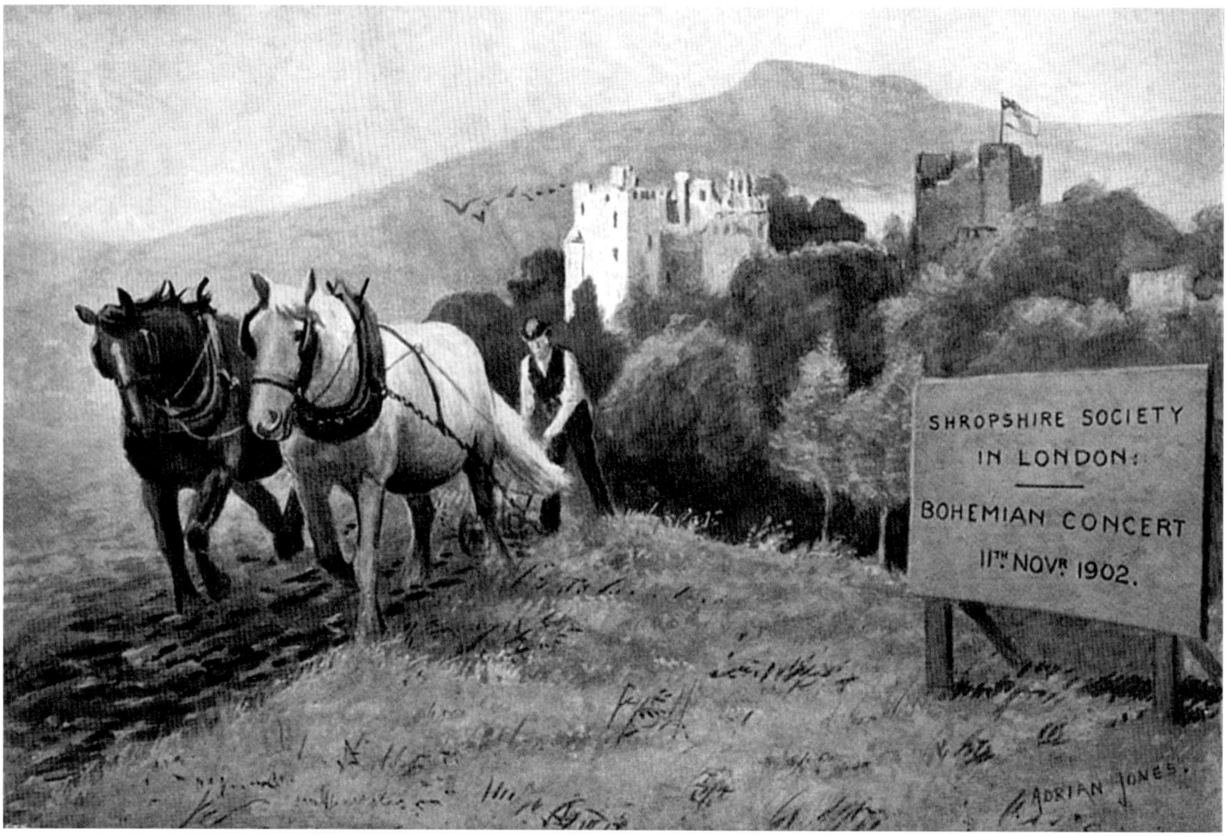

Publicity work by Adrian for the Shropshire Society in London.
The background in the sketch is of Ludlow Castle and Clee Hill.

(also from Ludlow) and the composer Edward German (from Market Drayton), he was elected a Vice-President. Usefully, he was familiar with the RSBA and with major artists who had exhibited there. Under its earlier name, the British Society of Artists, it had liked to see itself as a sort of younger brother to the Royal Academy and a possible route into that top establishment. When Whistler felt that an 'outsider' such as himself might benefit from having the support of an establishment institution, Walter Sickert, an exhibitor there but not a member, had encouraged him to join. In 1884 he was elected. In 1886 he became President and confidently refurbished to his designs the Galleries in which later the Salopian artists would entertain. In the latter 1880s Adrian was stationed in London, beginning to find recognition as an artist and frequently meeting important names of the London art world. His comment on 'Jimmy' Whistler was that at times 'there was no more delightful companion but he was not naturally good tempered'. Whistler quarrelled with the BSA members over the kinds of exhibitions which should be mounted, and two years after his election as President they voted him out. Thereupon his followers resigned, which altered the BSA's complexion: as Whistler put it, playing upon the Society's title (and incidentally providing evidence for Adrian's comment that he 'could not refrain from retort'), 'the artists left and the British remained'.

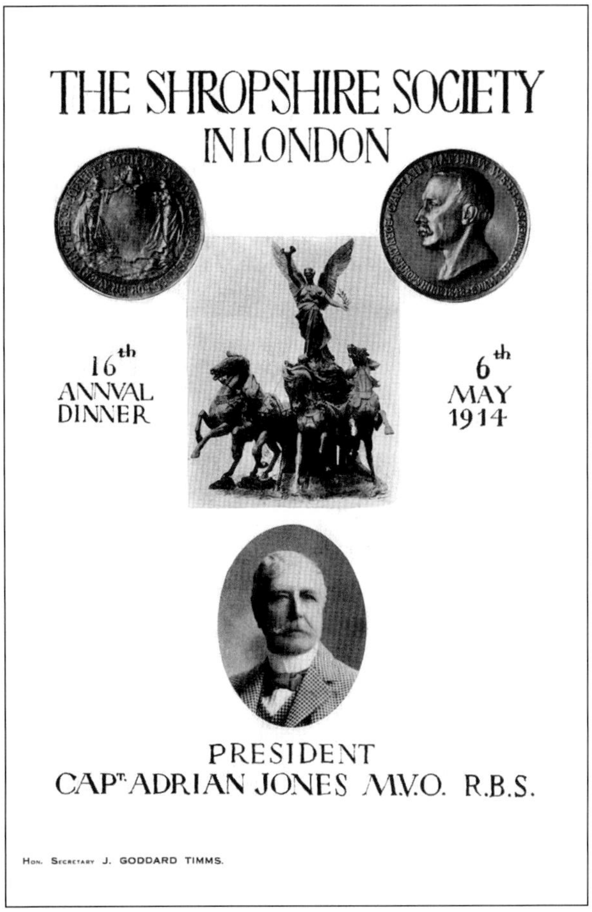

Front cover of Shropshire Society in London 1914 Annual Dinner menu card

In 1913, at a time when a desire to salute civilian heroes was in vogue, the Society arranged to commemorate the late merchant navy Captain Matthew Webb of Dawley in Shropshire, who in 1875 had become the first person to swim the English Channel, achieving the feat using the breaststroke at twenty strokes per minute. In 1883 he had lost his life in the whirlpool below the Niagara Falls when attempting to swim from the USA to Canada. The Society decided that the memorial should be a silver medal, to be awarded for saving life from drowning under difficult circumstances within Shropshire. Understandably, the design and execution of the medal were entrusted to Adrian.

The Webb Medal 1914

The Webb Medal inaugurated by the Shropshire Society in London in 1914 is of silver and hangs from a ribbon originally of blue and gold halves, but now of blue. The front carries a portrait head of Captain Webb. It is conventionally noble. There is no sense of Webb's later, sadder years as a swimming showman undertaking dangerous swims in an effort to make ends meet, because the inscription on the medal refers to his celebrated Channel swim, not to his later tragic death. On the reverse is a shield flanked by Britannia and La France (Marianne). At the bottom in the foreground the swimmer is forcing his passage through the waves away from Britannia and towards Marianne. The wording in the centre records the 'heroic conduct' which earned the medal. By remarkable coincidence the first recipient of the medal in July 1916 was a Ludlow G.S pupil, W.H. Carpenter. He had saved another boy from drowning in Downton Gorge on the River Teme, diving in to rescue the other boy, who was well out in the stream, and after a struggle and being under the water for a considerable part of the rescue time, getting him safely to the bank. Adrian travelled up to Shropshire to present the medal personally on Speech Day. Addressing Carpenter, he told him to look upon his brave act as the first step on the ladder of life.

Altogether nine medals were awarded in the years up to 1930, when a reunion of the recipients still alive and traceable, including Carpenter, was held. They were made life members of the Society. Few medals were presented in later years, until in 1948 'it was agreed that the Webb Memorial Medal would only be presented in future if application was made'. Perhaps not surprisingly, rescuers being modest or ignorant of the award, the medal lay dormant until 2003/4. Through Ludlow Sixth Form College, the successor to the Grammar School, the Shropshire Society contacted Carpenter's descendants and his medal was handed over into the Society's possession. Shortly afterwards the Society organised a special gathering at Shrewsbury School, when in the presence of Carpenter's son, grandson and family, the President and Treasurer of the Old Ludlovians' Association spoke about Carpenter's act of 'bravery in water', and the Webb Medal was officially revived. The criterion for making the award has been altered to cover acts of bravery of any kind.

In 1914 Adrian became the Society's sixteenth President. In twelve of the previous fifteen years the President had been titled; with one exception, all had held office for just a year. Adrian took office before the outbreak of the First World War, and was then re-elected five times so that he presided for the six years 1914-1919 and in his last year chaired the Society's Victory Reunion Banquet. It made sense to the members to keep him in office for such an unusually long spell, because during the war years the Society was much involved in charitable work for Shropshire soldiers, so it was appropriate for it to be led by a military man. There had been another soldier amongst the past Presidents, General Sir William Gatacre, KCB, who had commanded troops in the Relief of Chitral expedition, in the Sudan, and in the Boer War. Gatacre had been President in 1904, the year when Adrian was sculpting General Buller. Adrian would have had to be

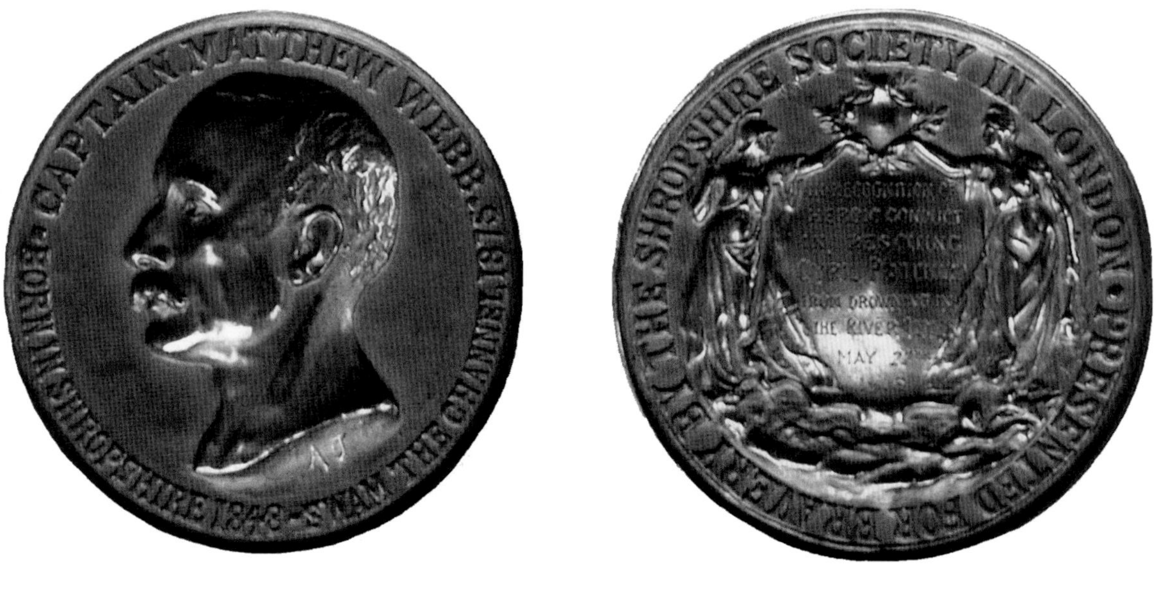

Obverse and reverse faces of the first **Webb Medal** to be awarded for an act of bravery in water by a Salopian

diplomatic in response to any remarks made about Gatacre by Buller, who did not feel that Gatacre had served him well in the Boer War.

Adrian most probably later heard more about Gatacre from Colonel Richard Moody of the Buffs (East Kent) Regiment. Moody and he were two of the former pupils of Ludlow Grammar School who met in 1908 to suggest the formation of an Old Boys' Club. Moody had served in Gatacre's brigade on the North West Frontier of India in the Relief of Chitral expedition of 1895, and had been put in charge of building a road through one of the difficult mountain passes. Gatacre had ordered that it should be built five feet wide along its full length. When Moody was able to report that this arduous task had been completed, Gatacre came to inspect. 'Excellent,' he said. 'Very good indeed. Now widen it everywhere to eight feet.' Such slave-driving had earned him the nickname 'General Backacher'.

Adrian's first big occasion as President of the Shropshire Society was the 1914 annual dinner on 6th May. He had the non-executive support of seventeen Vice-Presidents, who included several members of the House of Lords, seven Members of Parliament and the distinguished composer Edward German. His hard-working executive committee included another Old Ludlovian, the brilliant London journalist Ellis Powell, editor of the *Financial News*. Adrian himself chaired the banquet committee. As such he had overall direction, but one trusts that in modesty he allowed the other six members of the committee to plan the details, for when the menu appeared its front cover held not only an oval photograph of himself, but also photographs of his Peace Quadriga and the face and reverse side of the Webb Medal. Whilst the band played a programme of ten pieces of music, including a selection from Edward German's 'Merrie England', the diners ate their way through a splendidly long menu which appropriately included wild Severn salmon, saddle of Shropshire lamb and Shrewsbury cakes. Adrian proposed the loyal toast to King George and after a singing of the National Anthem, a further royal toast to Queen Mary, Queen Alexandra, the Prince of Wales, and the other members of the Royal Family. There followed five toasts and responses: to the Society itself, to the armed forces of the Empire, to Parliament (proposed by Ellis Powell), to the visitors and finally by the Mayor of Shrewsbury to 'all friends around the Wrekin.' The formalities concluded with a programme of songs performed by Shropshire singers and a second rendering of God Save the King. Such a programme was typical of the peacetime dinners. The 1914 Dinner included one extra item: a presentation to Adrian of the first Webb Medal struck from the die he had designed. A second medal was presented to Captain Webb's brother.

Ludlow Grammar School Revisited

Another link with Shropshire was Adrian's old school. Among other visits, Adrian attended the Speech Day of 1912. He came as the Guest of Honour and distributed the prizes. 'A very large audience came to the speeches this year,' reported the school magazine, 'anxious no doubt to do honour to our distinguished alumnus Captain Adrian Jones.'

The headmaster had carefully ensured that the prizes awarded for the virtue of punctuality reflected Adrian's foreign service in the army. The books came from the *Peep at Many Lands* series: one pupil received the book on India, a second that on Egypt and a third that on South Africa. The school magazine recorded that Adrian 'gave an interesting address mainly to the boys, urging the importance of thoroughness in all that they undertake and pointing out that even the highest positions are open to those who have sufficient energy and perseverance'. He lightened these exhortations with 'a few anecdotes of a life … of exceptional interest and variety' and a few self-deprecatory jokes.

He spoke in an assembly hall which displayed on its walls spears and Arabic-lettered flags captured by Colonel Taffy Lewis in the battle of Omdurman. Adrian himself had placed a Mahdist flag held aloft in the right foreground of his large 1899 painting of that battle, and in this Speech Day setting he and his audience could not avoid being conscious of imperialism. He told the boys that 'they should be proud of their country and of being Britishers'. He supposed that they knew what the Union Jack was, and that it was a symbol of a mighty Empire, and wanted to impress upon them the fact that 'whenever and wherever they saw a Union Jack they should raise their hats and as British citizens they should respect the flag which typified the whole Empire'. He also advocated smart personal appearance. These are not sentiments that would be uttered from a twenty-first-century Speech Day platform. They tell of a Britain long vanished. But the qualities he advocated to the boys were those he himself exemplified – thoroughness, energy, perseverance. Other parts of his advice could still be uttered today: for example, he stressed the value of travel away from one's own environment, and the importance of thinking 'large and broadly.'

Schoolboys are notoriously bad at absorbing the sentiments preached at Speech Days, but one would like to think that those present paid due attention, for as well as being a veteran of imperial campaigns, in that year, 1912, he was at the height of his powers as an artist and famous throughout the land as a celebrity. For that was the year of the inauguration of his Peace Quadriga.

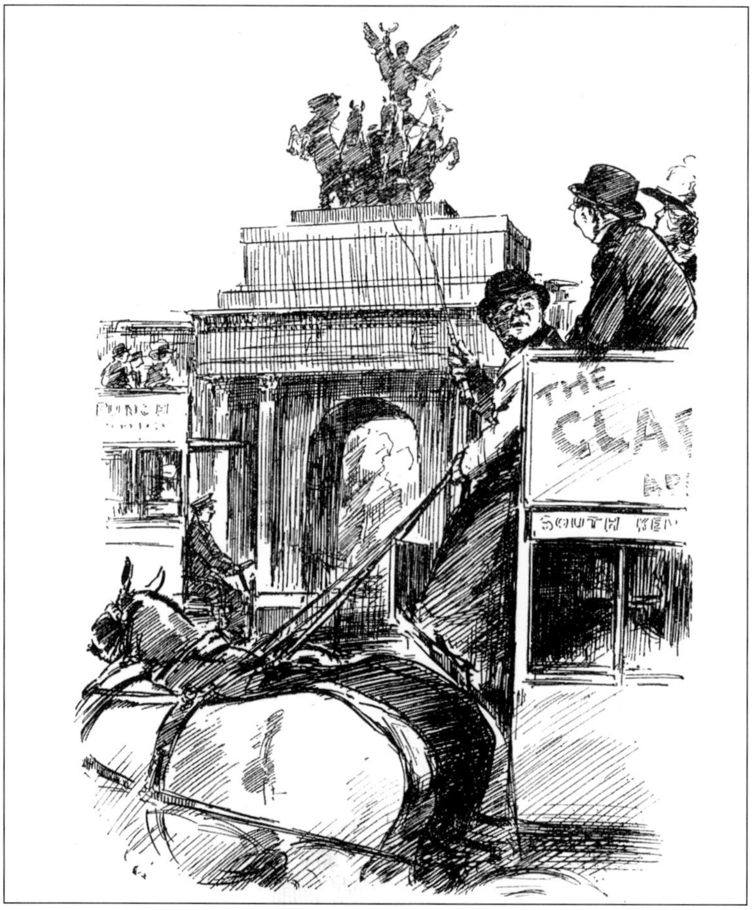

Punch cartoon, August 21, 1912. The caption read:
Driver (approaching Hyde Park Corner and pointing out the sights to country visitors): 'On the left is the statute erected to the great Dook o' Wellington, and that 'ere on the right's a statute erected to the memory of the pore ole 'oss 'buses wot's bin run orf the street by them stinkin' motors.'

Chapter Fourteen: 'The Dream in the Artist's Brain'
1912: The Peace Quadriga

Books which purport to be a history of a century are perforce written at some distance after most of the events described. Where that century is the 20th and the specific subject is art, sometimes narrowed to 'modern art', Adrian Jones may be passed over without mention. This happens because paintings receive more attention than sculptures, and because this artist was not part of the movement to free sculpture from resemblance. A reader is more likely to learn that the first decade of the 20th century saw the early development of abstract sculpture than that those years saw the completion of Adrian's Peace Quadriga, Europe's largest bronze statue, both a miracle of the hand and an achievement of the brain and the imagination. Like another great emblematic work, the Statue of Liberty, it gives a sense of delivering a better world: viewers raise their eyes to the heavens to see Peace achieving victory over War.

Adrian's contemporaries from the opening three or four decades of the 20th century would have been very surprised if they could have known that for the following four decades he would be largely forgotten. They had gone in their thousands or tens of thousands to see his statues ceremoniously unveiled, and for five years they had followed the progress to completion of the Quadriga itself, as recorded in the words and illustrations of a wide range of national newspapers, both popular and upmarket, the provincial press, and magazines. Even the *Great Central Railway Journal*, not the first name that springs to mind in the field of art appreciation, quoted to its readers the words of the art journalist Lewis Hind, written shortly before the Quadriga's inauguration:

> Captain Adrian Jones should feel happy this Spring. He sees his Quadriga on the Constitution Hill Arch gradually unfolding itself before a pleased populace; he sees the work of years out of his hands and in its appointed place, towering from as fine a site as a group of monumental sculpture could desire; he hears, if he travels up and down Piccadilly, the comments of Londoners – favourable and often enthusiastic. That is gratifying. Londoners do not often admire London's monuments. I ask myself, why does the man in the street look with appreciation on this Quadriga. Why does he feel elation at the vast figure? ... How imposing she is, how dominating and impressive! ... The reason we like it is because in designing his group the sculptor has remembered that if the design is half the battle the environment is the other half. In proportion, in angle, in scale, the Quadriga is harmonious with its spacious surroundings. Look at it from whatever point you like, the group asserts itself, and is in keeping with its environment.

Not only 'the man on the street' looked with approbation and gave Adrian cause to be happy. Two leading Royal Academy sculptors, George Frampton and Goscombe John, were among those who wrote letters of warm congratulations, and on the proposal of Goscombe John, Adrian was elected a member of the Royal

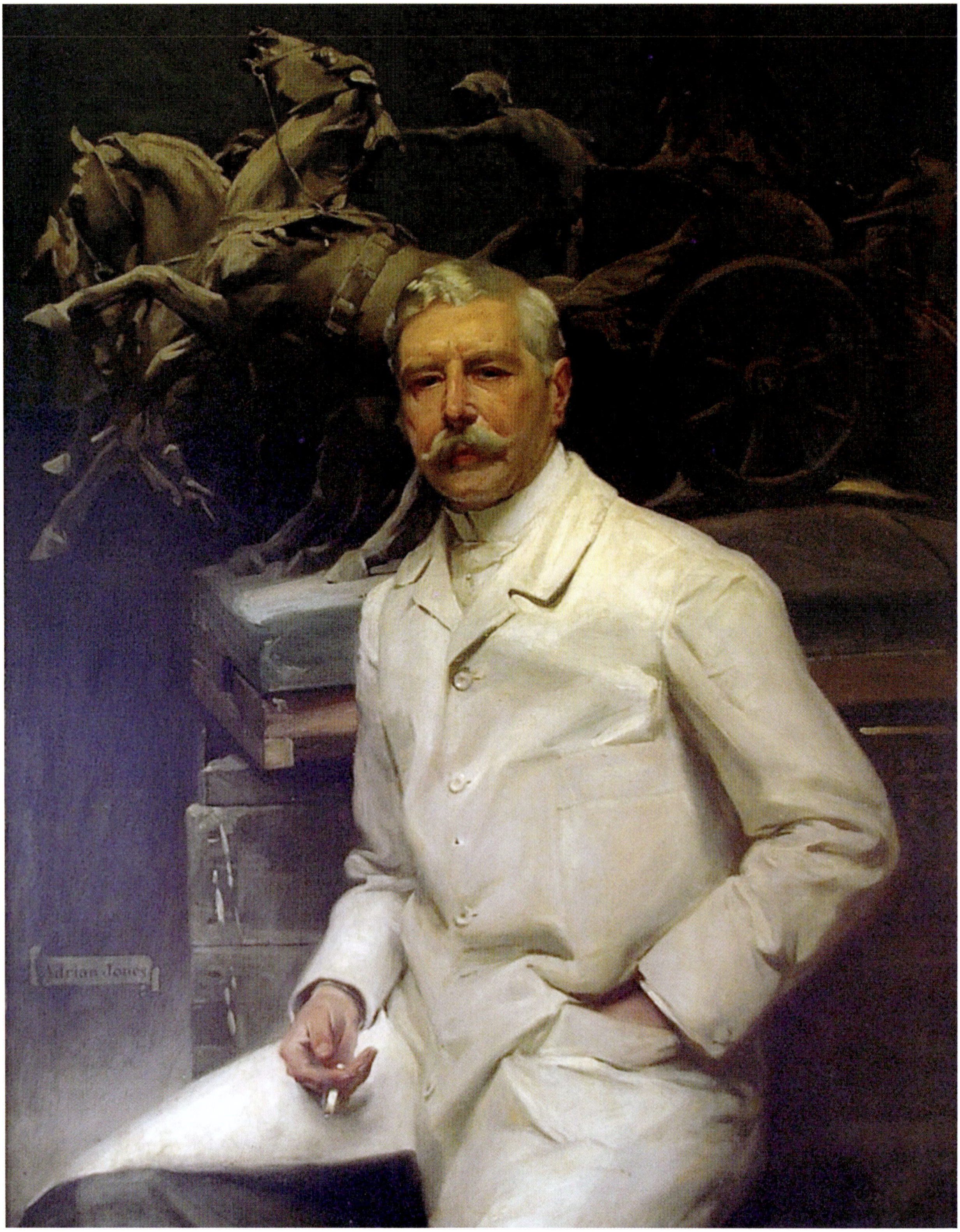

Captain Adrian Jones, by Alfred Priest, 1909.
Priest painted the portrait as a wedding present for Adrian's son. In the studio background is 'Triumph'.

Society of British Sculptors. But Lewis Hind was mistaken in thinking that the spring of 1912 would bring Adrian every happiness. It brought also one major disappointment.

The genesis of the Quadriga had been in 1891, when the Prince of Wales had been so taken with Adrian's Assyrian chariot exhibit 'Triumph' in the RA Summer Exhibition that he summoned Adrian and strongly encouraged him to sculpt a Quadriga to fill the empty site on top of the Wellington Arch (alternatively called the Decimus Burton Arch). Decimus, so christened because he was the tenth child in his family, had designed both the Stanhope Gate entrance to Hyde Park, later to be the impressive backdrop for Adrian's Cavalry of the Empire memorial, and the Wellington Arch. The Arch had been intended as a royal entrance to elaborate gardens planned by King George IV, but those plans had not come to fruition, so it was built in 1828 to serve the humbler role of an entrance to Green Park. Burton's design for the arch, like King George's gardens, was not fully completed. His intentions to add sculptural decorations and a Quadriga on the top were thwarted by a committee decision to make the Arch a national memorial to the Duke of Wellington. In 1836 the sculptor Wyatt's equestrian statue of George IV was erected in Cockspur Street and the interest it attracted led to Wyatt's being commissioned to sculpt an equestrian statue of Wellington for the arch. Burton protested in vain. The committee, led by the Duke of Rutland, was intent on paying full honour to the Iron Duke by putting up the largest statue imaginable. The 40-ton monster took three years to model, until in 1846 twenty-nine horses dragged it from studio to site, where Burton oversaw its lifting into position. Burton received no payment for that labour, but he nursed his wrath and in his will of 1881 left £2,000 for the statue's removal. The Commissioners of Woods and Forests consulted the Royal Academicians, whose firm opinion was that the gargantuan horse and rider should go. Ironically, the signatories to this opinion included Sir Frederick Leighton. While remaining confident that he had made the right aesthetic judgement, he may later have been irked that he had unwittingly helped to make possible the Prince's proposal that that non-Academician Adrian Jones should create a replacement. In 1883 the statue of Wellington was sent to Aldershot, and the top of the Wellington Arch stood deserted. Queen Victoria was glad. It had not seemed to her quite proper that when she passed through the central gateway of the Arch on ceremonial occasions (it was closed at other times), she should have to drive beneath the statue of one of her subjects.

After putting his idea for a Quadriga to Adrian, Prince Edward requested him to make a drawing of the Arch with 'Triumph' on top. Adrian did the drawing, affixed a photograph of the model, and sent the composition to the Office of Works. Time passed. Annually the Office informed Adrian that the project remained unforgotten but also unfunded. He kept his hand in by working on other life-size or larger statues, successfully submitting to the RA Summer Exhibition 'Duncan's Horses' in 1892, 'Maternal Care' in 1893, and 'Rape of the Sabines' in 1894. In 1895 he spent time at Sandringham, executing paintings of horses and dogs commissioned by Prince Edward and Princess Alexandra. He was planning to go to the USA that year with Emma, visiting New York, Philadelphia and Boston, and Alexandra helped to fund the journey by sending the cheque for her painting even before it had been completed. In Boston, where the local press reported the visit of Adrian and Emma under the headline 'Eminent English Sculptor' and spoke of Adrian's 'position in the front rank among English sculptors', he indulged himself by suggesting to Bostonians some heroic statuary of the kind he was currently being thwarted from producing in London. Boston's Copley Square, he thought, could be made a magnificent art centre by dignified treatment including 'a grandly symbolical or historical subject' group.

More time passed. Occasionally the press revived the matter of the Arch. In 1898 the *Globe* newspaper complained that it was shameful that Burton's Arch was still left uncompleted and insisted that the Quadriga Burton had intended should now be placed there without delay. A journal called the *Artist*, inspired by the *Globe*, entertained its readers with a ghost story. Two hours before dawn, a rider on a colossal horse reins up in front of the arch. 'Poor old thing, *still* without a top', he muses, and remembers how cold o' nights he had found it up there for seven-and-thirty years. He is the ghost of Wyatt's statue of the Duke of Wellington. His reflections are interrupted by the rumbling arrival of an antiquated coach. Out steps the ghost of a waxwork Napoleon, who asks the Duke what cause has brought him up from Aldershot. The Duke tells him of what he has read in *The Globe* and Napoleon comments, 'You English are certainly extraordinarily slovenly and careless about the beauty of your city.' Wellington explains: 'The idea of the authorities in this country has been ... that if a sculptor can model a man, he must, therefore, be able to model a horse. Look at my case. There are three of me now, and three of poor Copenhagen.' [The first had been Chantrey's equestrian statue of him, erected outside the Royal Exchange in 1844, but that plays no part in the story.] 'This sorry image I now bestride is number two.' Wellington next directs Napoleon's attention to Sir Edgar Boehm's statue of him. 'Look at that last effort over there in front of my old house. Who would ever imagine from that, that my dear Copenhagen was a thoroughbred? ... Copenhagen could gallop. Look at that horse there – heavy in front, and short and heavy in the neck – would you, sir, have trusted him over rough ground in a campaign? Of course you wouldn't. No, the only thing at all like him, as far as I have seen, is in a group by Adrian Jones, a tip-top modeller of animals.' Napoleon reminds Wellington that he has much personal experience of triumphal arches and gives his opinion that it would seem wise to commission a statue from Adrian, but wonders what is the general opinion. In response Wellington beckons across the Inniskilling Dragoon who is one of the four Waterloo soldiers standing guard round the pedestal of Boehm's statue, and orders him to inform Napoleon and himself of any comments on the Arch made by members of the public during his ten years of standing nearby. The dragoon replies that hardly a day passes without passers by expressing astonishment at the lack of attention and pride of the authorities, who seemed content year after year to leave the Arch lacking a Quadriga. This view was held by educated persons of every description, and indeed he had heard more than one Royal feeling very strongly on the subject. As for choice of artist, 'We don't want Germans or French to do our work. They say that there is but one Englishman living who can model a horse as it should be modelled, and that he has a magnificent Quadriga scheme at this very moment in his studio; and that this cast in bronze would be the very thing.'

'His name?' asks Wellington.

'Adrian Jones, General', replies the Inniskilling.

In that year of 1898, when the anonymous writer 'Vox' in *The Artist* was story-telling in his support, Adrian was back at Sandringham working on his fifth royal commission, a bronze statuette of Persimmon. The Derby winner was by then at stud and more filled out than in his racing days, but still obviously a horse of breeding and quality. Adrian spent hours in his stable. He found him an outstandingly good-tempered stallion, and as great thoroughbreds are not always easy of approach he decided to seize the opportunity to take full measurements. The immediate purpose of these was to ensure that the statuette was anatomically correct, but in addition he stored them against the day when Persimmon might be reincarnated in quadruple.

'Vox' had evidently not been the voice of those who controlled the purse strings. More years passed. Persimmon died. In 1905 Edward, by then King Edward, presented the skeleton to South Kensington Museum for display there. Adrian's foresight in preserving details of the horse was rewarded, though not yet with the commission for which he most hoped: the Jockey Club asked him for a one third larger than life statue of Persimmon which they intended as a gift for the King. Even those Royal Academicians who still felt annoyance at this self-taught sculptor's successes, and retained the power to block him from election to their ranks, could have no ground for complaint on this occasion. As the sculptor of the statuette which had admirably captured the chief points of the Derby and St Leger winner, and the possessor of numerous measurements, pencil sketches, oils 'notes' and wax models, he was the obvious choice. Though the gift was theoretically a surprise, Edward was aware of it. While Adrian had been working on the Persimmon statuette, when Edward was in residence at Sandringham, he would join Adrian in the horse's box to admire and comment on progress. Now he came frequently to the Chelsea studio to watch Adrian at work, making suggestions and complimentary remarks, and presumably taking an opportunity to express his regret that the Quadriga project remained stalled. The King accepted his present immediately before his 1905 Derby Day Dinner for Jockey Club members, and afterwards the diners went on from Buckingham Palace to join the ladies at a glittering ball given by Lady Devonshire at Devonshire House. The press reported on the princes and princesses, dukes and duchesses, earls and countesses, and lords and ladies present, and did not hesitate to add such details as that the King had worn the insignia of the Garter, the Duchess of Portland's 'jewels were gorgeous', the Countess of Dudley was 'beautifully dressed and wearing a tiara of pearls and diamonds' and Lady Mabel Crichton was 'one of the prettiest girls present'.

Adrian could have been forgiven for thinking that something comparable would be a welcome celebration after some future unveiling; but he had his own occasion a week later when he opened his studio to show the plaster cast of Persimmon before it went to the foundry. A splendid representation of the famous horse', reported the *Morning Post*, '... in all its magnificence as a stallion full of form, yet graceful and distinguished ... especially excellent is the modelling of the chest and legs, and the supple sweep of the curved lines of the back and the hindquarters'. Edward chose for its permanent site the stud yard at Sandringham, consulted Adrian on details of the pedestal, then in April 1906 had the bronze Persimmon placed on its base of Devon

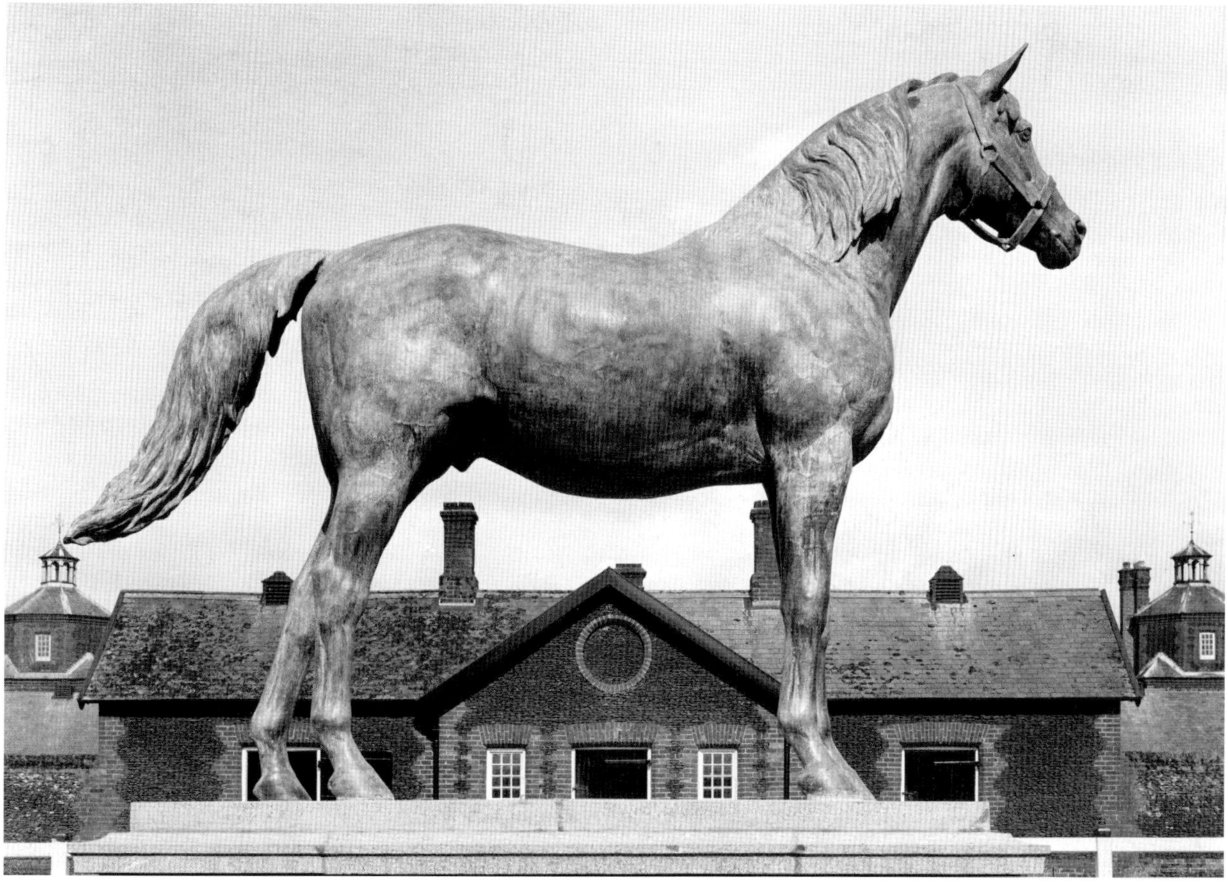

Persimmon, 1905, larger than life in the stud yard at Sandringham

granite, where it still stands. 'A magnificent piece of work… the whole suggests a perfect specimen of the thoroughbred', said the *Field*.

The visits of Lord Farquhar, Comptroller of the Royal Household, had been frustratingly negative but had led to a tacit understanding that when funding of the Quadriga did become available Adrian could expect to be the sculptor. Now finally, as Adrian relates in *Memoirs*: 'One day Lord Farquhar called and asked me to give him details of the proposed statue and particularly to consider the question of cost. I may have been a little irritable that morning, for I remember telling him plainly that I was tired of making estimates and plans, because I had made so many and there had been no result. Lord Farquhar ... assured me he was now prepared to talk business, and that he wanted particularly to know if I was prepared to start work, if he promised to see the job through. Naturally, I agreed at once, for I knew that if I could succeed with the Quadriga it would be the biggest work of my life.'

So in October 1907, sixteen years after Edward's initial proposal of the idea, Adrian was able to start work in earnest. By mid-December he had his sketch model positioned on a raised platform high enough to let him place an accurate drawing of the Arch to the same scale in front of it, and a photograph of this was safely lodged in the Office of Works. He had also decided on the size and attitude of the main components. The horses would be twice life size, and to show that their galloping had been suddenly arrested by the alighting of Peace on the chariot, they would be reared up, which in addition to giving him the artistic effect he wanted had the engineering advantage of placing each horse's centre of gravity well over the hind legs which, suitably strengthened, could therefore carry the considerable weight. Peace herself, because she would be furthest from viewers' eyes but had nevertheless to dominate the ensemble, would be bigger still, 14 feet tall, and 22 feet to her wing tips. In an article for *Pearsons Weekly* at the start of February 1908, Adrian wrote: 'I estimate my group for the Arch will take me three years to complete, working four or five hours a day.' That was to prove too optimistic.

The press seized on the story quickly. As early as 1 December 1907, *People* reported: 'It is authoritatively stated that Decimus Burton's Arch on Constitution Hill is, at last, to be completed by placing a four-horsed chariot on it.' It illustrated its report with a picture of 'The Quadriga as it will appear when completed'. In the same week the *Sphere* carried the same illustration of Adrian's model, described as 'the group for Decimus Burton's Arch'. In the accompanying account Adrian had to share the billing: 'a bronze Quadriga, the work of Captain Adrian Jones and the gift of Lord Michelham'. And in *People*, the headline had been 'Peer's Handsome Gift'. In his meeting with Adrian, Lord Farquhar had handled the question of costs deviously. Adrian commented: 'What he did not know about economising was not worth learning.' As soon as he had Adrian's undertaking to do the work, he spoke about expenditure without mentioning that the project now had the financial backing of a wealthy patron. Adrian presumed that the Quadriga's costs would fall upon the taxpayer, and he was confronted with the difficulty of estimating for a statue larger than any previously undertaken in Britain. 'But my heart was set on the job ... so that eventually I found myself agreeing to complete the work for a sum which was quite inadequate ... I had to dip pretty deeply into my own pocket to complete it to my own satisfaction.' It was only after terms had been agreed and the interview ended, that Adrian learned that the Quadriga was to be set up at no cost to the nation. Herbert Stern, the wealthy banker who two years previously had been ennobled as Lord Michelham, had undertaken to meet the cost. If Adrian had known this during the interview, he would certainly have sought a more realistic sum for his expenses and labour.

That labour was long, strenuous, difficult, at times even dangerous, and always demanding of accuracy. Fortunately, Adrian, now in his sixties, was still fit and was not scared of heights; otherwise the task would have been impossible. In 1906-07 he had been Chairman of Chelsea Arts Club, so there was no shortage of well-meaning advice from members about the huge undertaking that lay ahead. In his history of the Club Tom Cross narrates how Adrian was told in discussions of the project: 'So and so is good at animal figures, he can help you', and 'that chap over there has got time on his hands at the moment, he can give you a hand'. However, with memories of the 'Ghost' controversy still in his mind, Adrian had to be chary of such suggestions.

Having lived with the model for so long, Adrian had to waste little time on revising his thoughts. The idea of having a lion, emblematic of Great Britain, in the back of the chariot was abandoned early and replaced by cast down emblems of war which were more appropriate to the subject and more practical, giving Peace a perch to stand upon to add to her height. The other changes were for artistic effect: here a calculation on elongating to avoid a foreshortening effect when viewed from a long way below; there a shifting of masses to give the desired sense of central weight and airiness at the fringes. He had to precede all that with exhaustive processes of sketching, photographing, measuring and plumbing and then setting up the large, intricate iron armature, fixing to that a wooden skeleton shaped roughly like a horse, and then piling on masses of clay until the horse was sufficiently bulked up. Each horse in turn had to be fed with seven tons of clay, until it dwarfed everything else in the large studio, reducing the statuettes on wall shelves and the original 'Triumph' group in its corner to insignificance. Adrian and his helpers, endlessly shaping and moulding, became energetic pygmies. When the Camden Town Group painter James Manson visited the studio it made him understand how Gulliver must have felt in Brobdingnag. The work demanded hard labour, and behind the physical effort lay the mental anxiety of the studio being able to stable only one horse at a time, so that Adrian had to take care over his calculations for size and artistic effect to ensure that the constituent parts would later fit together as he wished. However, he had innate confidence in his ability, so the mental problems did not worry him unnecessarily; and for physical rest he and Emma often spent weekends in the cleaner air of Crystal Palace, there to stay in comfortable accommodation, to sit and walk in the beautiful grounds in the mornings, spend afternoons in the drawing room of the Crystal Palace Club, and appreciate seeing positioned in the Palace's North Nave his favourite imaginative statue, 'Duncan's Horses'. He relaxed also by switching occasionally to painting. But always the imperative remained to advance the Quadriga, to climb back up on to one of the wheeled stages to give his artist's finish to the clay which an assistant had roughly

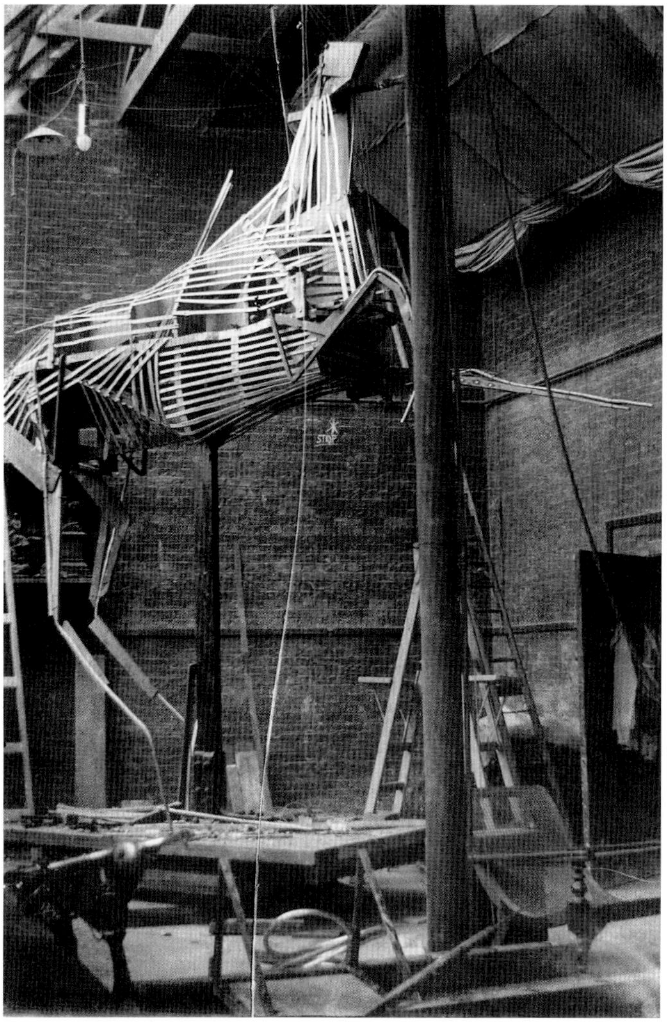

The **Quadriga**: the wooden skeleton of the first horse taking shape on the armature

piled on, to supervise the Italian workmen skilfully yet so messily throwing on the plaster mould layer, and finally to arrange for the plaster moulds to be carted to the trusted Burton's Foundry to receive their filling of molten bronze.

Press reports told the public how Captain Adrian Jones was 'proceeding apace' on 'his colossal task'. As early as August 1908 the *Illustrated London News* printed a full-page photograph on its front cover of Adrian shaping a horse's leg, and national and provincial papers published similar pictures. By 1909 journals such as the *Tatler* and the *Graphic* were showing eight or nine pictures of stages of the work in progress in a single issue. Lord Farquhar went with King Edward to Adrian's studio to see the work for himself. The general tone of the press remarks was highly optimistic. 'The Great Chariot For The Arch At Hyde Park Corner' would be ready for unveiling in the summer of 1910. But its progress did not prove so straightforward.

First Adrian tackled the challenge of the celestial female figure. She is the main character in the story the statue tells, and has to dominate the group. To do that, because she would be the furthest away from the viewer on the ground, she had to be enlarged even more than the twice life-size horses. Adrian used as his model Beatrice Stuart, in some ways a remarkable choice, for she had had one leg amputated above the knee and replaced by an artificial limb; but Dame Laura Knight remarked that 'by her grace and poise, as well as by her activity and apparent ease in climbing rocks on the Cornish shore, few people knew her terrible loss'. As a painter of numerous ballet and circus scenes, Dame Laura was a good judge of poise and activity, and these qualities, allied to classical features and statuesque beauty, made Beatrice an ideal choice as a model for Adrian. Now in her twenties, she was often depicted by Adrian's artist acquaintances, including John Singer Sargent and Augustus John, and his choice of her for the Quadriga further increased her fame. In 1912, the year of the Quadriga's inauguration, she sat for Dame Laura herself, Alfred Munnings and Sir Frank Dicksee. Dicksee's portrait of her head ('quite a success', wrote Munnings) shows her bold face in profile and her hair scraped back into a large bun. (Beatrice Stuart continued to model for leading artists up to and during the First World War, and in later life for a spell became secretary to Margot Asquith, the wife of the former Liberal prime minister.)

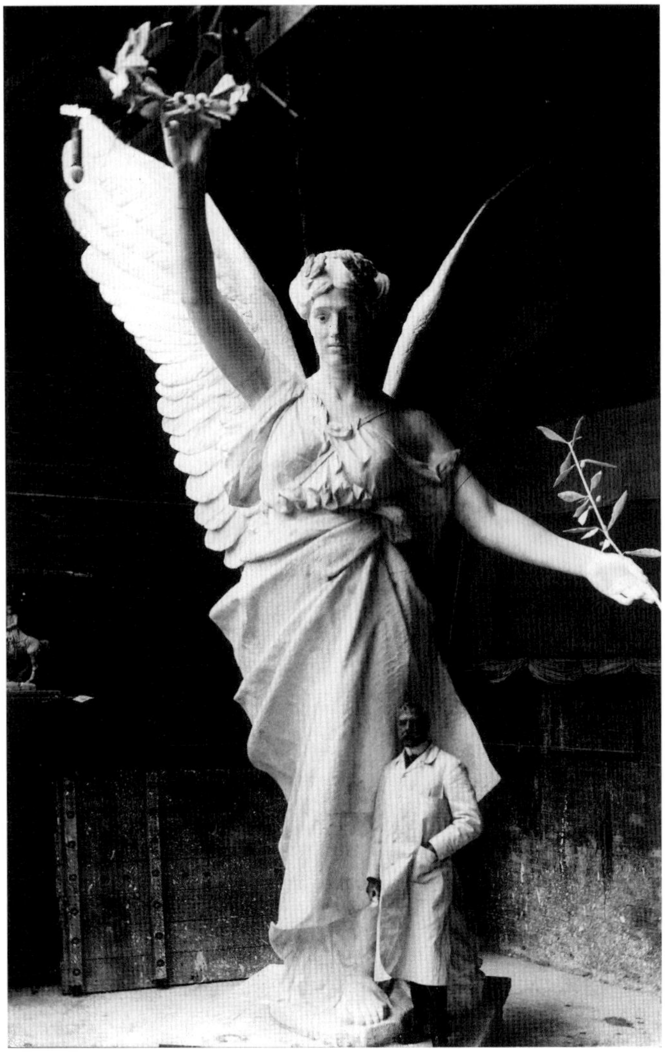

The **Quadriga**: Peace in the studio

Adrian established the dignified pose of Peace by a study of Beatrice from the nude, and next worked on her flowing robes. His idea of the composition he wanted was clear. He started the skirt folds at the left side of the waist, from where on the front they spray out almost like water from the lip of a waterfall, while to the left they swirl down and back to the billowing hem behind. Thus whether she is seen from the front, where the silhouette is of an outward sloping diagonal on her left and of fold ripples on her right, or from the side, there is no danger that the tall figure will look too thin. The angel's wings, by contrast, had to be thin in cross-section to look convincing, but because their great length demanded a considerable weight of clay, they also had to be strong. The armature for them therefore 'had to be constructed with particular nicety'. All passed off successfully, the wings remaining unbroken even when under pressure from the modelling tools used on them. In the figure's raised right hand Adrian placed a laurel wreath, whilst in her complementary diagonally lowered left hand she holds an olive branch. The greater prominence of the wreath has led some writers to refer to her as Victory. That is a mistake., but it seems legitimate to think of the statue, if one wishes, as the victory of Peace over War.

King Edward visited Adrian's studio to view in turn each figure in the composition as it neared completion. He would settle himself in a chair, Adrian would rotate the turntable to give him the view from all sides, and the King would usually make complimentary remarks. On seeing Peace, however, he asked: 'Could you not make the face prettier?' Adrian replied that he could, but explained that, at the distant height Peace would be from the viewer, only prominent facial features would register. Whatever the private regrets of the King, who considered that a lady who lacked beauty was deficient in a vital spark, whatever her other virtues, he told Adrian that he quite understood that it had to be so. This quick agreement typified Edward's supportive attitude. It was of course he who had encouraged Lord Michelham, one of his private 'set', to donate the money that now funded the project which he himself had proposed. He continued to take a close interest not just in the aesthetic aspects of the project but in the whole process. He was fond of going across to the clay bin, prodding it with his stick, and asking a stream of questions about the technical and engineering aspects of building the monument. In Adrian's words, 'He was in every way a very pleasant master to work under'.

Edward returned frequently to see progress, but by the time he went on holiday to Paris and Biarritz in March 1910 he sensed he was dying. It is said that he looked out from his hotel window at the Mediterranean and lamented that he would soon be leaving, 'perhaps for ever'. He returned from Biarritz in mid-April. In the remaining three weeks of his life, he went for a last time to the opera at Covent Garden, to his estate and racehorses at Sandringham, and to see the Quadriga being shaped in Church Street, Chelsea. He asked Adrian when the work would be completed and erected. Most was completed, but Adrian had to tell him that because of the difficulties which were having to be mastered in dealing with such a large group, casting at the foundry was lagging behind. 'Then', said the King, 'I am sorry, for I shall never see it'. Adrian was taken aback, for the poor state of the King's health was not known outside a tiny court circle, though when some days later the King failed to greet Queen Alexandra at Victoria Station on her return from holiday, a statement had to be issued that his condition was causing anxiety. On 8 May 1910 the Palace announced, 'The King is Dead'.

Despite this dreadful news, Adrian had to continue with his sculpture. When the first horse was half-complete, he sat down to tea with two assistants in the shell, and the photograph taken of the scene was to become the most popular image of his career. When the fourth horse was complete, he held his 1910 birthday party in his house and studio. His friends put on black tie and turned up in large numbers to celebrate, to admire and congratulate. Now with all four horses finished, there remained the task of modelling the chariot, its wheels eight feet in diameter, its body nine feet wide and eighteen feet long. On top of all the clay required for that, a further four or five tons would be needed for the gun and other symbols of war. Up on the stages, Adrian and his assistant advanced the work, its increasing weight supported by struts. In his autobiography, Adrian described what happened next:

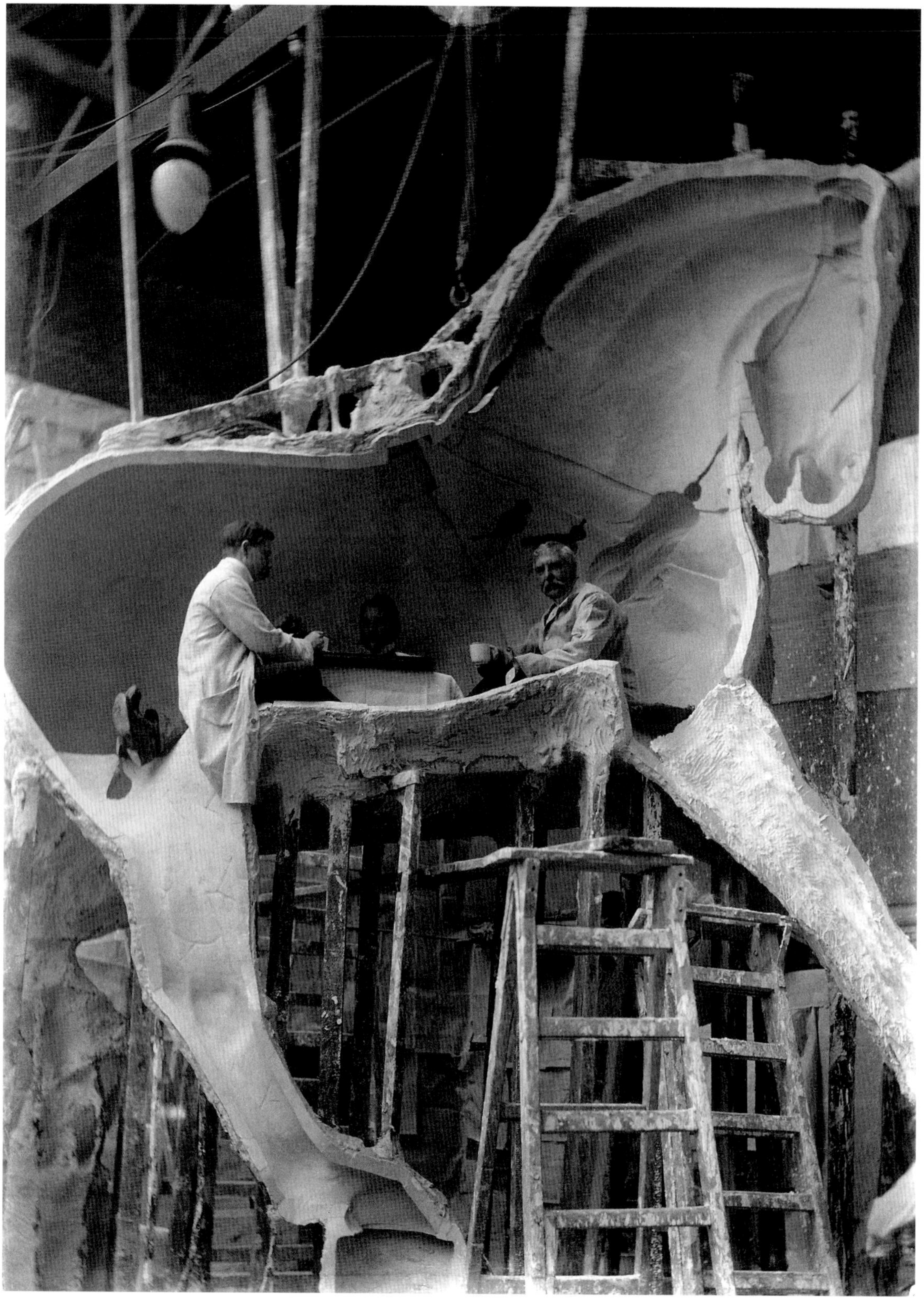

The **Quadriga**: Adrian, on the right, shares afternoon tea in the half shell of the first horse. This is the iconic photograph of Adrian's career as sculptor.

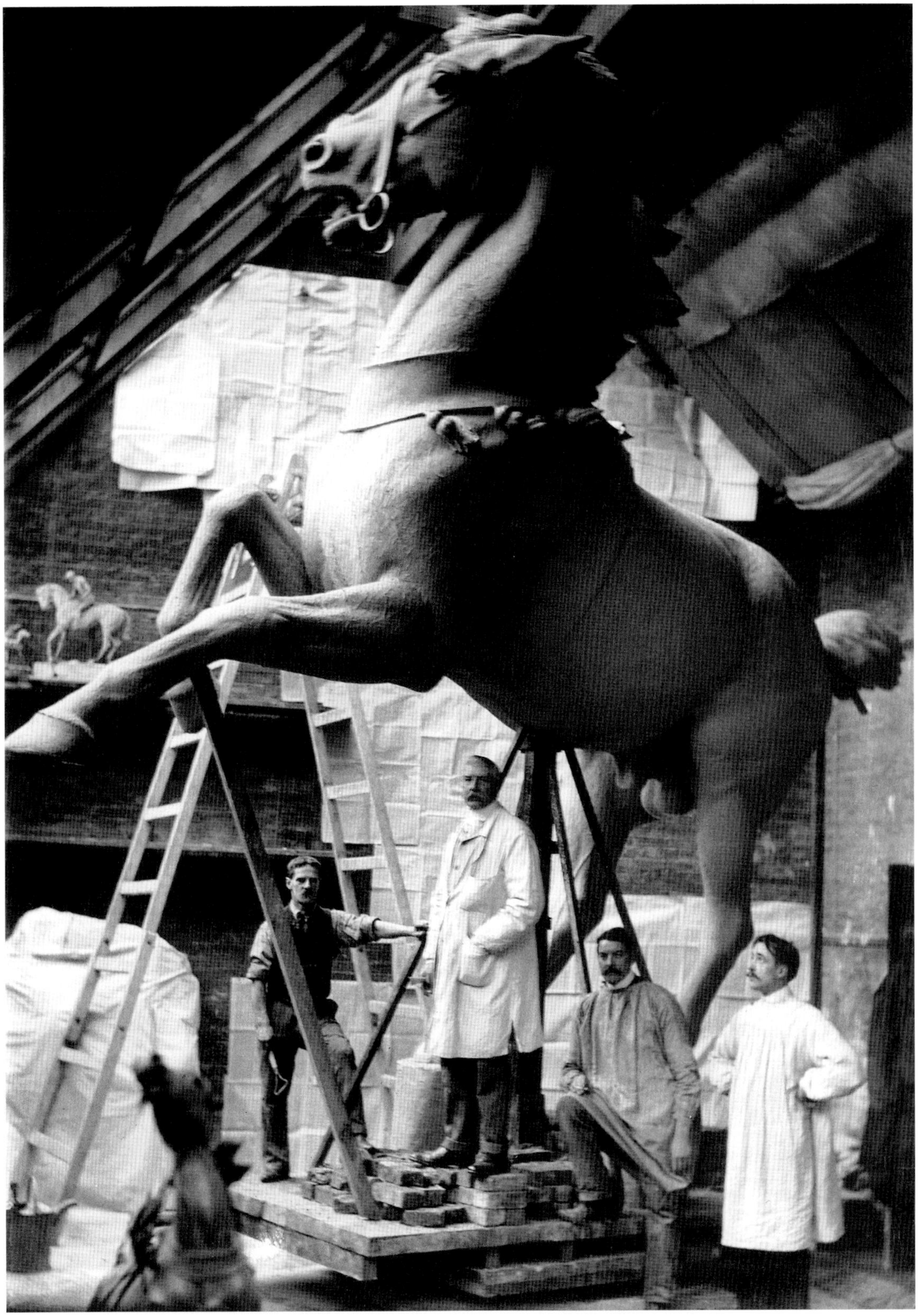

The **Quadriga**: a completed horse. 'Everything else in the place seemed to be suddenly dwarfed in stature. The groups, studies and statues which stood all around dwindled for the moment into insignificance.' J.B. Manson

It flashed across my mind that considering the weight now being borne by the struts, it would be a good idea to see if they were in a satisfactory condition. I came down and started to make a careful examination, my assistant remaining up above. I found certain evidence that the supports were not all that one might wish, and I immediately told my assistant to exercise the greatest caution, and be sure not to let any of his weight come on to the framework of the chariot. However, he ignored my warning; perhaps he was over-confident, or, in the enthusiasm of the moment, he sought to reach some part which was inaccessible without moving the stage ... He put his foot on some convenient part of the framework ... Down came the whole mass and crashed right through the studio doors into the garden, missing me by inches. Happily, my assistant was both young and athletic and, by a quick leap, he landed clear of the smash, but I have to thank a merciful Providence for a miraculous escape. I was more than a little shaken.

He went away for a few days to recover. Workmen repaired the studio doors and the chariot was resurrected from the confused mass of shattered clay, armature and props which littered the studio floor. Though the chariot's straightforward shape made it simpler than the horses to model, it felt wearisome doing it for a second time, and again Adrian had to pay close attention to strengthening. Peace had to appear gracefully ethereal, but the twenty-two-foot length to the tips of her topmost wing feathers added eight tons of loading; and whilst the bent-over young charioteer well captured the boyish slightness of Lord Michelham's son who had posed for it, if he could have been unfolded he would have stretched to ten feet tall, so he too added a giant's weight. The chariot had also to carry the cannon and other symbols of war that were essential to the artistic balance of the group and to perching Peace high enough not to be obscured in front view by the rearing horses. When he tired of the heavy handwork of wrestling with inanimate clay, Adrian returned to his recreation of painting a living object, usually equine, and at long last the sculpting in the studio was completed. Now the centre of activity moved to the furnace and fireclay moulding pit of Mr Burton's bronze foundry at Thames Ditton.

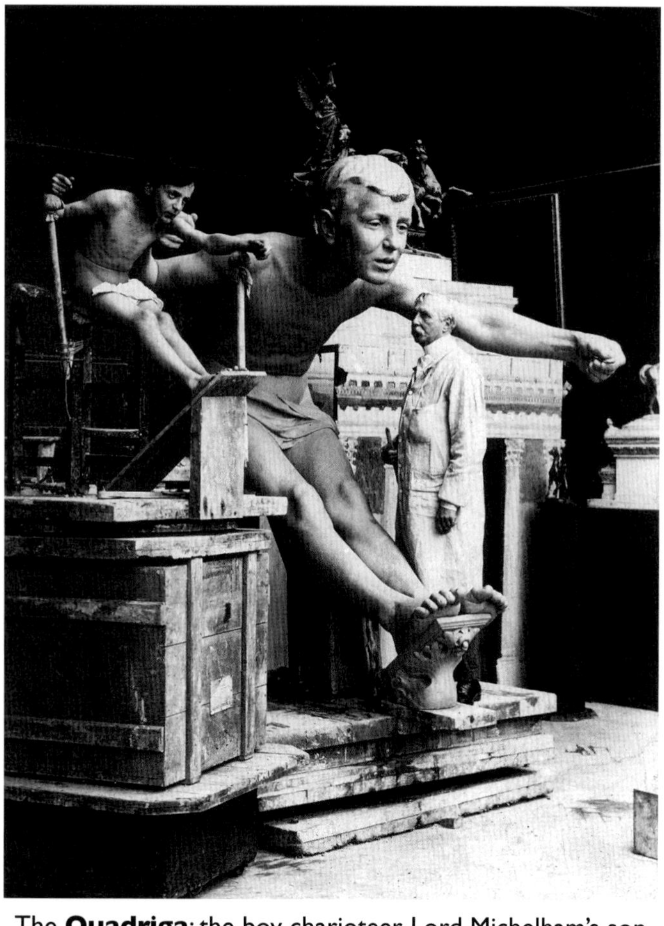

The **Quadriga**: the boy charioteer. Lord Michelham's son is stretched to ten feet.

There, in the first week of October, 1911, Adrian held a press viewing. The casting had been completed in August, and all the parts had been bolted together in one piece for the first time, initially with a wooden prop under one horse's chest to ensure that the group could not topple forward. Adrian placed great confidence in the skills of Burton, who had previously so successfully cast his Duke of Cambridge statue, but for help with problems demanding engineering expertise the two men called upon the services of Alexander Drew. After doing his calculations, Drew designed a steel platform to sit on the chariot's axle and wheel hubs and advised other internal load-bearing reinforcements. In an age which admired its engineers, the *Graphic* printed a drawing to show its readers how, inside the statue's hollow bronze, solid steel cores and rods were inserted under Peace's skirt, down the horses' hind legs, through two spokes of each chariot wheel, and into the flag of war that trailed from the chariot's tail. All these carried weight down to a platform of powerful rolled steel joists concealed in a forty-foot-long stone plinth which had been added to the roof of the arch. This work (none of which to most minds would constitute 'art'), and Alexander Drew's stress diagrams, were needed to satisfy the Board of Works that the colossal statue would not be a danger to the public. Adrian initially had difficulty in reassuring the Board that the rearing horses would not plunge forward over the front of the arch. But in addition to the extra metal in their hind legs, rods had been passed through their tails: these rods would be connected to the main chariot structure, anchoring the horses.

Adrian's and Alexander Drew's belt-and-braces policy satisfied the Board, and Adrian's viewing day enthused the press about 'this largest bronze in the country'. He pasted twenty-six reviews, all favourable, in his book of newspaper cuttings, and doubtless there were more. It is easily possible to compile from them a list of complimentary snippets that would rival those selected phrases displayed outside theatre box offices: 'It will challenge comparison with the best works of its kind in the world' (*Pall Mall Gazette*); 'will compare favourably with anything that other world capitals have to show' (*Nottingham Guardian*); 'beautiful proportions' (*Daily Express*); 'a valuable addition to our outdoor art treasures' (*Eastern Daily Press*); 'the reproach that London does not possess any large groups of statuary worthy of the name may possibly be removed at last' (the *Field*); 'an ornament to London' (the *Lady*); 'wonderfully effective ... a dignified and dominating crown to Decimus Burton's rather dull and Early Victorian archway' (*Birmingham Post*); et cetera. There must be a suspicion that the press was rather led to see the Quadriga as a new large jewel in the crown of the capital of the Empire. Even so, the ardour of the tributes is remarkable. Still more notable is the absence of any adverse criticism. Newspapers and magazines alike saw the Quadriga as destined to be, in the words of the *Evening News*, 'a lasting delight to lovers of art, whether native, colonial or foreign'. But that paper also warned: 'Probably the office of works will not be ready for an unveiling ceremony until next spring'.

Certainly much remained to do. The group erected and displayed in the foundry had to be taken to pieces again and in November 1911 moved, by a circuitous route dictated by the clearance heights of overhead railway bridges, to a storage compound at Hyde Park Corner. Orders went to London's smallest police station, sited in the Arch, to move out temporarily. Gangs of men erected a ten ton crane on the Arch, used it to hoist each heavy statue part, and bolted them together in their final position. The *Sphere* devoted the front cover of a February 1912 issue to a drawing of the workmen up on the scaffolding and the statue's plinth, hammering, plastering, checking. On 1st March, Frederick and Emmeline Lawrence's suffragette weekly *Votes For Women*, delighting in Adrian showing the female figure of Peace on top, both literally and in the 'narrative' of the composition, placed a large head-on picture of the Quadriga on its front page. London was watching, and looking forward to the ceremonial unveiling.

Newspapers whetted the public appetite. On October 4th the *Court Journal* announced 'The King has consented to unveil the quadriga which has just been completed by Captain Adrian Jones and is to be erected on the Arch of the Hyde Park Corner and of Constitution Hill'. The dailies, reminding readers of the long and warm interest the late King Edward VII had shown in the work, found consolation in the fact that he had lived to see all its main features completed except for the figure of the boy charioteer, and expressed the hope 'that all will be ready for unveiling when the King [George V] returns from India'. That unveiling was apparently to be no ordinary one, for Adrian 'had devised a most original and ingenious scheme'. Specialist publications

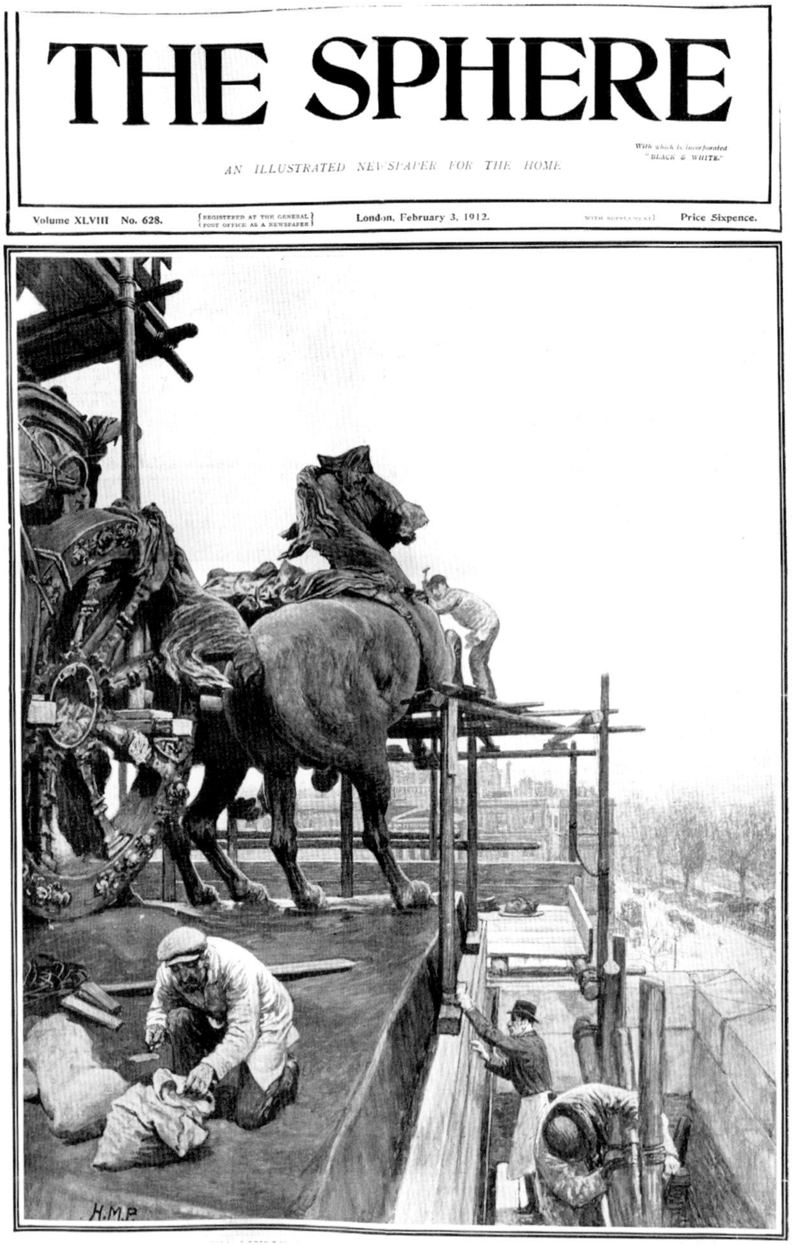

Cover picture: erecting the **Quadriga**

such as the *Building News* and the general press described how, instead of the sheeting normally used at such occasions, Peace and the horses would be shrouded in inflammable material which should be so chemically treated that it could be burnt away by a fuse connected to the royal dais below. This would be the first occasion on which a public monument was inaugurated with daylight fireworks. Trials of the new method would be made before the King Emperor's arrival home. The *Building News* reported confidently that 'there should be no difficulty about the matter'. Adrian entered into a contract for the carrying out of his idea.

And then the King returned to Britain – but the Quadriga's inauguration was far from being the grand ceremony so keenly awaited. Adrian himself said: 'When it appeared that there was to be no such ceremony, it cost me quite a lot of money to get out of the contract.' But the hurt was more than financial. The deepest wound came from the slighting of the great work which with royal encouragement he had dreamed of and laboured on so long. Instead of bands, a parade, speeches, crowds and fireworks, 'In quite an informal manner yesterday afternoon the King inaugurated Captain Adrian Jones's Peace group ... The arrangements had been kept private, and only a very few persons directly connected were present when the King, accompanied by the Queen and Prince Henry, drove up to the Arch. His Majesty shook hands with Captain Adrian Jones, the sculptor, and received others who were present' (the *Daily Graphic*, 3 April 1912). The others 'received' were the foundry expert, Mr Burton, and the donor, Lord Michelham. It was a low-key occasion with nothing cheeringly celebratory about it. On a cold early April day, the trees of Green Park not yet in leaf, King George and Queen Mary sat in their coach, and a handful of their subjects stood before them in dark heavy winter coats. The illustration in the *Graphic* showed in the background a single cyclist who had dismounted to watch.

Alexander Drew wrote Adrian an amazed letter:

> I am very astonished to notice the informal uncovering of the group, and cannot in the least understand why so important and ideal a sculpture should be treated with such scant courtesy; is it merely due to the thoughtlessness or pigheadedness on the part of those in authority, or to jealousy? Whatever the cause, the honour of producing such a masterpiece cannot be taken from you.

If Adrian thought he knew the answer to Drew's question, he did not reveal his thoughts in public. Perhaps he had too readily assumed that there would be a ceremonial unveiling of the Quadriga; but the press had stated unequivocally that the King would unveil it. Perhaps the King considered that Adrian had been presumptuous in planning details of an innovative ceremony in his absence. Perhaps some high court official felt his role had been usurped. Perhaps behind the scenes some influential Royal Academicians had manipulated the court to cause their rival discomfiture. Certainly Adrian was disappointed that the King, with whom he had chatted at race meetings, lowered the occasion from an unveiling to a featureless 'inauguration'. The disappointment was the deeper because he knew that if Edward had still been on the throne there would have been great fanfare. But as one who had served his Queen and Country, he was too loyal a subject even to hint at any criticism of the monarch. Among friends in the Chelsea Arts Club, however, he did voice his suspicion that Royal Academy displeasure might have been one reason for the lack of public celebration. In his history of the Club Tom Cross tells how some members, aware of how let down Adrian felt, later obtained the ear of the King, who consequently wrote Adrian a letter of congratulation that pleased him greatly.

Adrian's sense of injustice was surely justified. Even his planned subsidiary celebration, a dinner party to be held in the Arch's top large room prior to the inauguration, was stymied.He must have compared the Quadriga's insignificant inauguration with the pomp at the unveiling a year before of the Queen Victoria monument in front of Buckingham Palace at the other end of Green Park. That too had an angel figure (Victory) on top, and the emblematic groups lower down included Peace; but that statue's sculptor, Thomas Brock, *was* an RA After he had been presented to George V, the King called for a sword and forthwith knighted him KCB (Knight Commander of the Bath). Kaiser Wilhelm attended as the invited Guest of Honour. As a passing fancy, one could wish that instead of inviting the Kaiser to the 1911 ceremonial unveiling of the Victoria Monument, George V had organised a brilliantly impressive unveiling

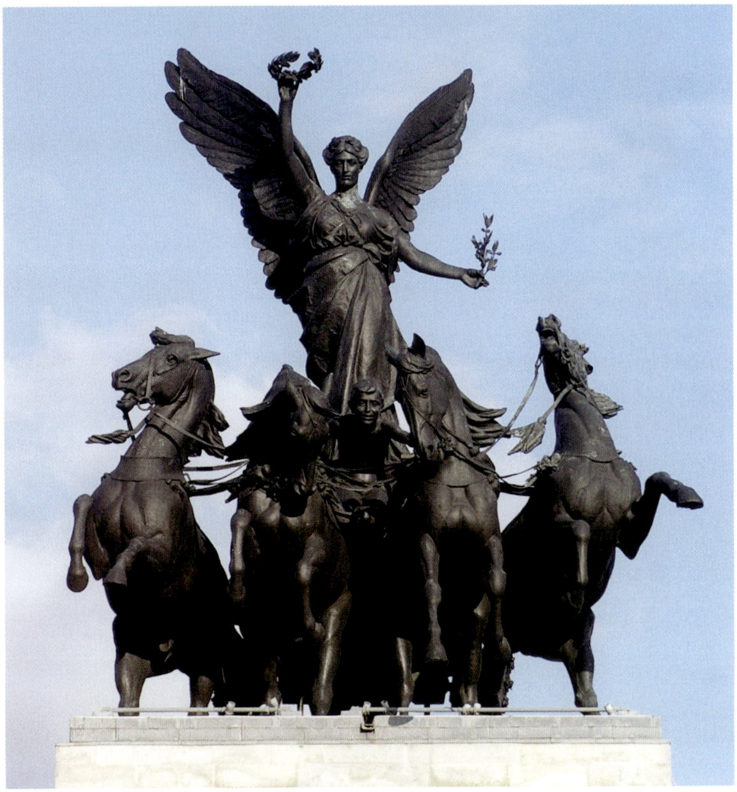

The **Peace Quadriga,** front

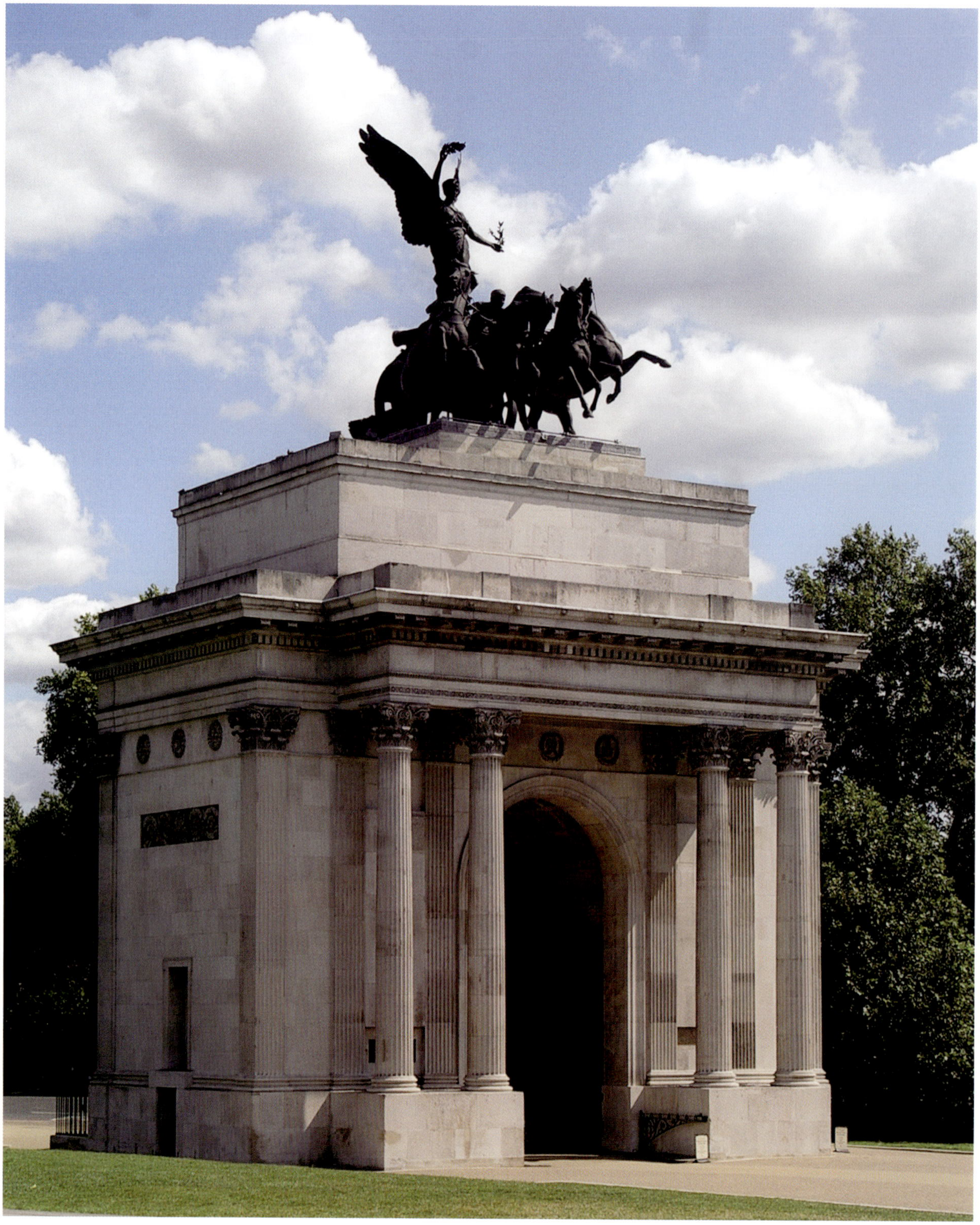

The **Peace Quadriga** on The Wellington (Decimus Burton) Arch. The great emblematic statue expresses hope for a better world. Viewers lift up their eyes and see Peace victorious over the forces of war.

in 1912 of the Quadriga, invited the Kaiser as guest, and thus impressed upon him the message of Adrian's Peace statue that war should be no more. Europe would have been spared the slaughter of 1914-18; and Adrian would never have had cause to carve a Kaiser Willy moustache on the dragon of evil war.

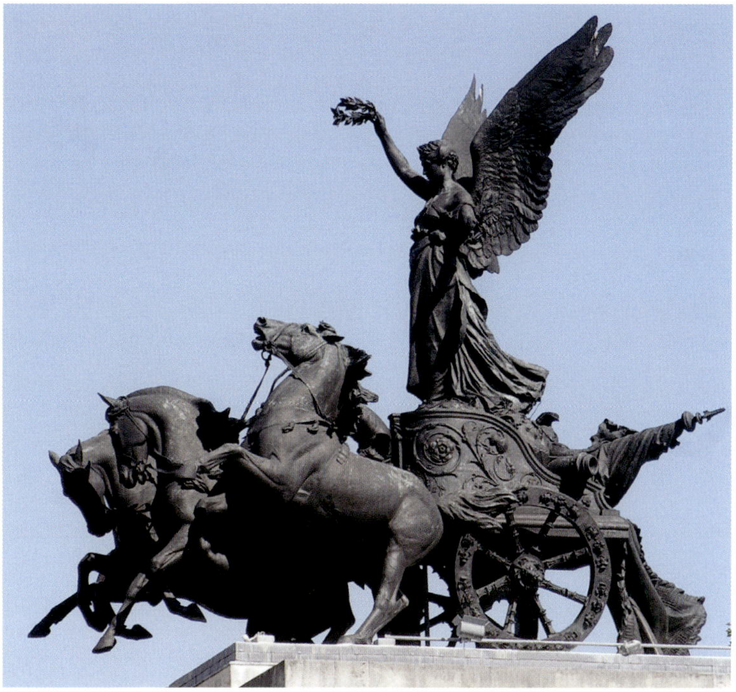

The **Peace Quadriga,** left side

Insult was added to injury a year after the Quadriga inauguration. In 1913 workmen affixed a commemorative plaque to the Arch. It read: 'The Quadriga surmounting this Arch was presented to the Nation as a mark of deepest loyalty and respect to the late revered Majesty Edward VII by Herbert, First Baron Michelham of Hellingley, KVO MCMXII'. No mention of Captain Adrian Jones, MVO. Years later his name was added, 'but even then only very indistinctly and in such a manner that it was almost impossible to read'. In compensation Adrian received appreciative letters and saw the statue quickly gain popular acceptance. *Punch* used it in cartoons. A replica was brilliantly modelled in cake and sugar at the 1912 Food and Cookery Exhibition: the caption to the press photograph proclaimed, 'In this case one may say without a suspicion of gush, 'Isn't it sweet!' Much more important than such trivia was the way the Quadriga became a focal point in the life of the nation at times of great joyous or sombre state occasions. Though after 1939-45 the increase in passing vehicles and then in the sixties remodelling as a traffic roundabout ruined the site, in the first third of the 20th century it was to the Quadriga that the *Daily Mirror* ('Certified Circulation Larger Than That Of Any Other Daily Picture Paper') and other papers sent their press photographers. There pictures for the front page were taken of the Victory Parade in July 1919, the gun carriage bearing the Unknown Warrior in November 1920, and the parades for royal weddings, homecomings from abroad and visiting foreign royalty. At the Victory Parade the crowd in the area of the Quadriga was estimated at 100,000. An official space was set aside for bereaved mothers, widows and orphans. The *Daily Telegraph* reported:

> To them belongs, as to no other section of our nation, both the past and the future. None may intrude in that sad and shadowy world of sweet and bitter memories of the bereaved ... None will dispute that Peace and its richest blessings belong to the children ... Was it not, too, of special significance that the dominating feature of this distinctive scene was the equestrian group by Captain Adrian Jones on the top of the Wellington Arch, with its central figure of Peace, holding in one hand the laurel crown, and in the other the olive branch? Chariot and charioteer seemed to stand out in gleaming bronze against the golden haze of the sky with new force and meaning... a spectacle worthy of the greatest city in the world ... Nowhere [else] on the route of the procession did the composition of pageant and people expand to such proportions in so fine an atmosphere.

Reading that account, Adrian must surely have felt that his art, King Edward's enthusiasm, Burton's foundry work, Drew's engineering and Lord Michelham's generosity had been recognised and rewarded. Even in 1912, whatever *his* disappointment over the lack of any opening ceremony, he could have a satisfying sense of a job well done. As his obituarist in the *Times* years later reminded readers when commending Adrian's extraordinary command of the mechanical and technical side of his art, 'Large-scale sculpture needs a great deal of knowledge and skill, not to speak of physical strength'. Adrian could reflect on a completed achievement, and compare it with Rodin's failure to complete his statue of 'Whistler's Muse', which had been commissioned in 1903, four months after the death of Adrian's friend 'Jimmy'. In the same week as the Quadriga's inauguration, the *Manchester Guardian* sent its reporters to Paris. They reported back to readers that Rodin could not yet fix a date for the delivery of the 50,000 francs commission because he could not work except when in creative mood. The commissioning committee had suggested to Rodin a subject more suited to Adrian, a winged Victory symbolising the triumph of Whistler's art over its enemies. Wisely Rodin, an experienced sculptor five years older than Adrian, rejected that and set about sculpting a powerful, more than life-size female figure. Its pose – one leg raised, head bowed, draped torso twisted – was difficult for his model Gwen John, sister of Adrian's Chelsea Arts Club acquaintance Augustus John, and progress remained intermittent. The statue's hand, which was intended to hold a medallion, never did so, for Rodin never got as far as sculpting the arms, and the chosen site on Chelsea Embankment, not far from Whistler's and Adrian's homes, stayed empty, never to be filled.

Meanwhile, the Quadriga stood in arrested motion on the Wellington Arch. Naturally, critical reactions differed. In the history of art, quadrigas had usually been fairly flat compositions, and there was some criticism of Peace's height and the group's triangular composition. Where the *Times* obituarist had seen it as 'rather ragged in silhouette', the fine art columnist of the *Bazaar* saw 'form and lines from every point of view clean, gracious and free from all entanglement'. Numerous reviewers described the emblematic details, although they cannot be readily seen from ground level: rose, thistle and shamrock on the chariot's sides and on its wheel rims, lion's heads on the wheel hubs, a ram's head (symbol of tranquillity!) on the end of the chariot pole. Perhaps surprisingly, no reviewer questions their appropriateness. Why should the chariot be a *British* vehicle of war? It is possible to come up with an answer, such as 'British military strength has been victorious in its imperial wars; now peace must rule in the Empire and, as Edward the Peacemaker desired, in Europe'. However, the answer is not altogether convincing, and though the emblematic scroll design on the chariot is attractive, it would have increased the universality of the statue had it not been given a national identity.

In reality, of course, viewers see the emblems barely if at all. Equally, they do not see the concealed problems of weight. They see a masterpiece which embraces the worlds of the divine (the Angel of Peace), the human (the charioteer) and the animal (the four horses, each head arrested in a different pose). They see Peace, rising high like a church spire, a heavenward symbol of evil overcome. One viewer may interpret this as eternal ethical virtue restraining mortal misdeed; another perhaps will simply see gentler female virtue checking the aggressive behaviour of men. Indeed, all who pause to look will carry away their own individual reactions, but these are all likely to reflect humankind's instinctive conviction that peace should triumph over war.

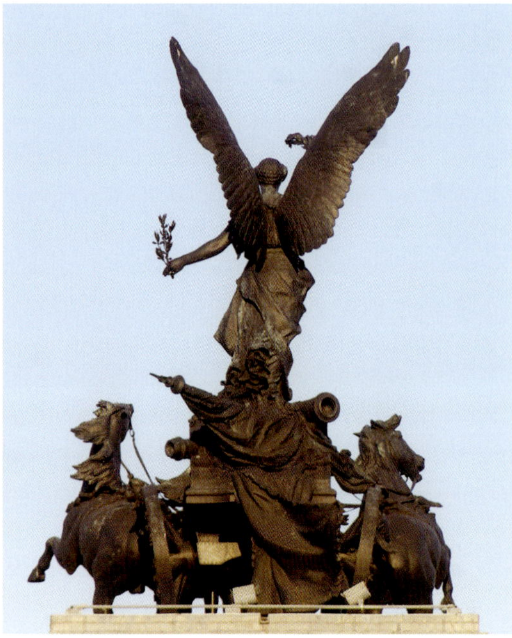

The **Peace Quadriga,** back

Chapter Fifteen: 'The World-Tragedy' 1914-1921: The Great War and afterwards

Life can deal out harsh ironies. The inauguration of Adrian's Peace Quadriga dedicated to the memory of Edward the Peacemaker was all too soon followed by the cataclysm of the 1914-18 Great War. Many of the hands that Adrian had shaken at his old school's 1912 prizegiving were soon clutching rifles. Two hundred and twenty-one boys and masters served in uniform; at least fifty-five of them died, were wounded or were invalided out, and exactly a quarter of the dead were members of the county regiment, the King's Shropshire Light Infantry. At the end of the fighting Adrian would both subscribe to the school's war memorial boards and sculpt the civic memorial for Bridgnorth.

Aged sixty-nine at the outbreak of the war, and feeling thoroughly fit, Adrian made a determined effort to join up. While realistic enough to recognise he could not expect a front line role, he felt sure that with his lengthy and comprehensive knowledge of horses he could serve usefully in the army's Remount Department. After all, three other Old Ludlovian former soldiers whom he knew through the Old Boys' Club or the Savage Club, had managed to get back into khaki despite now being above the normal age for military service. Adrian received an interview, but was turned down. Looking back in 1933, he still viewed that as 'a thousand pities, at least as I saw it, because when the world-tragedy came to its long-drawn-out end, I was still a vigorous man, and four years of hard work would have been very agreeable'.

One contribution he made to supporting the fighting troops came through his presidency of the Shropshire Society throughout the war years. For the duration, the Society's emphasis shifted to arranging for Shropshire men wounded and invalided home to London and suburban hospitals to be visited by members of the Society. Started in 1915, this work continued into 1916, and in 1917 it expanded to include sending funds from the Society to the County Fund for the comforts sent to Shropshire soldiers on active service. Another special grant was made for comforts for the troopers of the Shropshire Yeomanry.

Adrian's art works during the war years included 'patriotic' paintings depicting such scenes as 'Royal Artillery on the Dunes, Flanders' and 'Uhlan Debacle in Pripet Marshes', but his more major concern was a series of oils of great soldiers. These were expressive of his perceptions as a soldier, his skills as an artist, and his values as an honourable man of experience, and moreover, a spirit of generosity towards those who undertook the grave responsibilities of leadership. In that spirit, in 1914 he completed a sculpture that harked back to the Boer War, a posthumous bust of Sir George White of Ladysmith fame, who had attended the unveiling by Lord Roberts of the Carabiniers memorial in 1906. Referring to this marble bust in his *Memoirs*, Adrian chose not to add that this 'hero of Ladysmith', by his decision to stay in Ladysmith rather than man the more defensible line of the Tugela River, failed to save Natal.

Adrian had started his sequence of portraits of 'great soldiers' before the Great War began. He chose the medium of paint rather than sculpture, which gave him the opportunity to include more troops in the composition. He began the series of canvases with a portrait of Lord Roberts on active service in South Africa; it shows him on his horse on top of a kopje as his khaki-clad troops file past. The Royal Academy hung it (exhibit 445) in its Summer Exhibition of 1913, where it certainly caught the eye. The visiting art critic of the *New York Herald* termed it 'the feature of Gallery Six', and the *Observer* reported: 'This room is dominated by Mr Adrian Jones's equestrian portrait of Lord Roberts, heroic, not only in scale but in action of horse and rider.' Perhaps Adrian was too keen to ensure his painting was in the active, dramatic style of his Adelaide Boer War memorial and the Quadriga rather than more understated style of his Buller and Duke of Cambridge statues. The *Western Daily Mercury* commented bluntly on the figure of Roberts peering through binoculars for sight of the enemy: 'The body stiffened and thrown into a theatrical attitude is perhaps the least successful of the portraits of celebrities.'

Adrian returned to the RA Summer Exhibition the following year, 1914, with his bust of Sir George White (exhibit 2041) selected for the sculpture display, and another equestrian portrait of Lord Roberts, this one calmer and more colourful (exhibit 317). He had found a successful formula which he would use again two years later when he tackled painting Kitchener. Adrian had encountered Roberts during the Abyssinian War of 1867-8 at the expeditionary force's base camp at Zula, where both were involved in animal transport arrangements, but thereafter their paths diverged. Whereas Adrian served in India only at the start of his army career, Roberts could give his autobiography the title *Forty One Years in India*, which included no fewer than eight years as commander-in-chief – and after that, which already equalled Buller's total service, he went on to be Commander-in-Chief in Ireland, to supersede Buller in command in the Boer War, and finally to succeed Wolseley as Commander-in-Chief of the British Army before retiring in 1904. As that was the year in which Adrian started work on his bust and statue of Buller, he probably heard from his sitter an occasional uncomplimentary remark about Roberts and his 'Indian ring' of officers, but popular opinion held that Roberts was probably Britain's greatest field marshal since Wellington. At this time, Rudyard Kipling's *Barrack Room Ballads* was averaging 9,000 sales every year, and through his poetic alter ego, a cockney Tommy Atkins, the poet gave a fond portrait of 'Little Bobs, Bobs, Bobs, Pocket-Wellin'ton'. The poem, which required a title no longer than the widely known nickname 'Bobs', begins:

> There's a little red-faced man
> Which is Bobs,
> Rides the tallest horse 'e can –
> Our Bobs.

In his role as Commander-in-Chief of the army, Roberts had attended the unveiling of the Marines Memorial in 1903, and Adrian had stood beside him when the by then retired field marshal unveiled the Carabiniers' Boer War Memorial in 1906, so he well knew that his subject was pocket-sized in comparison to his own more typical military physique. He knew well also that it was a frequent fate of 11 feet by 9 feet paintings to be hung above eye level. So he painted horse and rider as seen from below, which enabled him to use perspective marginally to elongate Roberts's torso, and to raise Roberts above all the background detail. The spacious painting in no way dwarfs 'little Bobs'.

The press praised the 1914 picture enthusiastically. Irish newspapers, interested because Roberts hailed from Waterford and he and Adrian had both served in Ireland, were as enthusiastic as the English. The *Irish Times* commented on both the painting and its position in Gallery III: 'Over the portrait of the King is a large canvas by Mr Adrian Jones, giving a portrait of Lord Roberts mounted on his favourite white horse. Lord Roberts is in full uniform as Field Marshal, and the picture is a brilliant success.' The *Court Journal* also praised the painting, but perhaps in its choice of the epithet 'commanding' there is a hint of an eyebrow raised in mild astonishment: 'An equestrian portrait by Adrian Jones, "Field Marshal Earl Roberts, VC, KG", is a fine example of portrait and animal painting. The Earl is mounted on his charger, and the picture holds a commanding position over the King's portrait.' The Hampshire papers loyally referred to the painting's local relevance. Thus the *Hampshire Observer*: 'Very arresting is the equestrian portrait in Gallery III of Field Marshal Earl Roberts, Winchester's oldest Freeman ... It is an excellent likeness of the gallant officer on a white charger, with a landscape and troops in the background.' The wittiest comment came in the *Queen* magazine, which, alluding to the height of pictures hung level with Adrian's, observed: 'They are literally above criticism'. If Adrian too was privately amused at his painting 'commanding' King George V, who two years previously had snubbed his bold plan for the official opening of the Quadriga, as a loyal monarchist he did not say so.

Unquestionably commanding the painting, 'Bobs' sits on his Arab steed Volney, which Queen Victoria had honoured with medals for war service. He is wearing a scarlet full dress tunic, gold corded and gold laced, the blue sash of the Garter, the stars of his Orders and his medals on his chest, and in his right hand rests the baton of a field marshal. Adrian has filled the potentially uninteresting space behind the horse with British and Indian regimental cavalry officers and a union jack. The red, white and blue of the flag echo the red, white and blue worn by the horse and rider, and a breeze swirls the flag, the horse's tail and the cocked hat's plume of white and red feathers in a harmonious composition. On the right a column of cavalry stretches away into the distance until only the tiny triangles of the lancers' pennons can be distinguished.

The background conveys historical information. Roberts's career was mainly spent in India, so this is an 'important' painting, and has a function that goes beyond giving aesthetic pleasure. Here is a history, as seen through Adrian's mind, which in 1914 had an outlook moulded by his life in Victorian and Edwardian times, the heyday of Empire, and by his connection to the military in his career and in his art. In painting Empire history, Adrian is affirming a part of the British national identity as then seen. Roberts, as his title Earl of Kandahar, Waterford and Pretoria reflected, was a Briton who commanded men of other nations in those nations. A century later, were the painting in a public gallery, most viewers would bring to it a different mind set and a smaller body of knowledge about the Empire, so it would be understandable if the painting's narrative evoked less enthusiasm than it initially received. However, it actually hangs in the Royal United Services Institute, where those who pass it on the landing of the main staircase will understand Adrian's tribute to soldierly bearing and leadership. The picture, though brilliant and attractive, does not glamorise fighting. As is clear from his corpus of work, Adrian well knew that war involved men and animals in casualties as well as victories.

The *Daily Telegraph* reported after a few days: 'The colossal picture of Earl Roberts on his charger now being exhibited in the Royal Academy by Adrian Jones ... has aroused a lively interest among the admirers of the aged field marshal and the British Army ... The drawing of the charger shows the fine modelling of which the painter is a master, and the whole group is of remarkable historical interest.' The paper suggested that 'a fitting receptacle for the vast canvas' would be the fine theatre of the RUSI, the price being met by public subscription or a wealthy patron. Three months later the Great War broke out, and money had to flow in other directions. For Earl Roberts, the portrait became a valediction. That autumn he visited Indian troops in the field in France, and there he died of pneumonia. After the War, Adrian painted a reduced size replica of his Roberts portrait for the RUSI, and it was placed in one of the panels of the lecture theatre. The large canvas remained a prominent feature in Adrian's studio. After his death, Emma retained it, and at her own death she bequeathed it to the RUSI, so that finally after three decades it found the home the *Daily Telegraph* recommended for it in 1914.

After the outbreak of the war, Adrian's determined efforts to join the army having failed, he kept very busy in the studio. His portrait of Roberts having been so well received, he used the same formula for

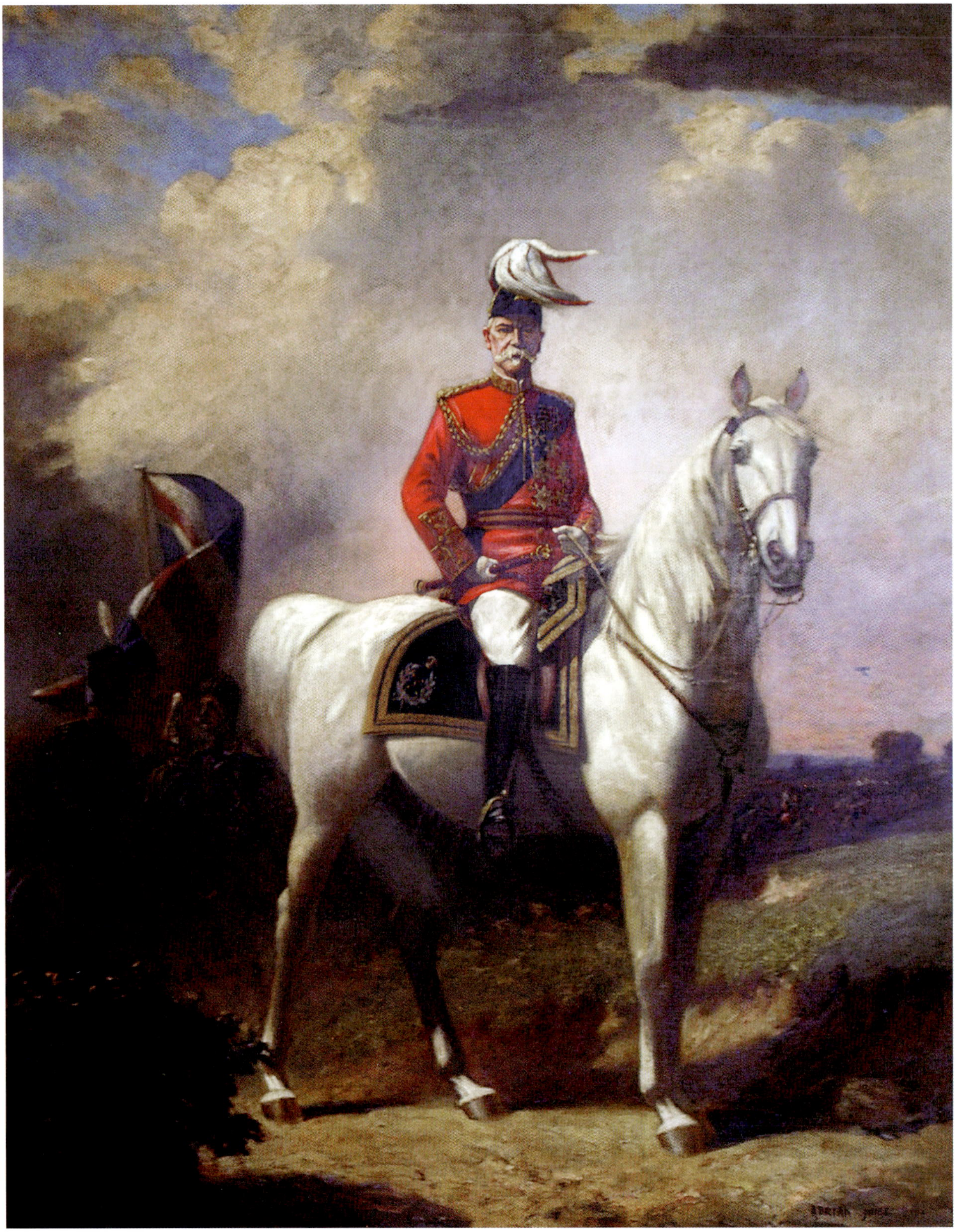

Field Marshal Lord Roberts, VC, KG, 11 by 9 feet oil on canvas, R.A. exhibit 1914; now Royal United Services Institute composing his next life-size oil. Again a great soldier sits on his stationary Arab steed; again in the distance columns of troops march across the landscape. This time Adrian's subject is Lord Kitchener, and the setting is Egypt, instantly recognisable from the Sphinx and the pair of Gizeh pyramids in the background. There is no attempt to be contemporary. Since August 1914 Kitchener had been in the civilian role of Secretary of State for War, a role which inevitably attracted criticism later when the arms supplies for the Western Front were considered inadequate and the Dardanelles campaign ended unsuccessfully. He had been in Egypt from 1911 to 1914, but that was as consul-general, not a job which involved commanding troops in the field. In this wartime painting Adrian is reminiscing about 1898 and Kitchener's defeat of the

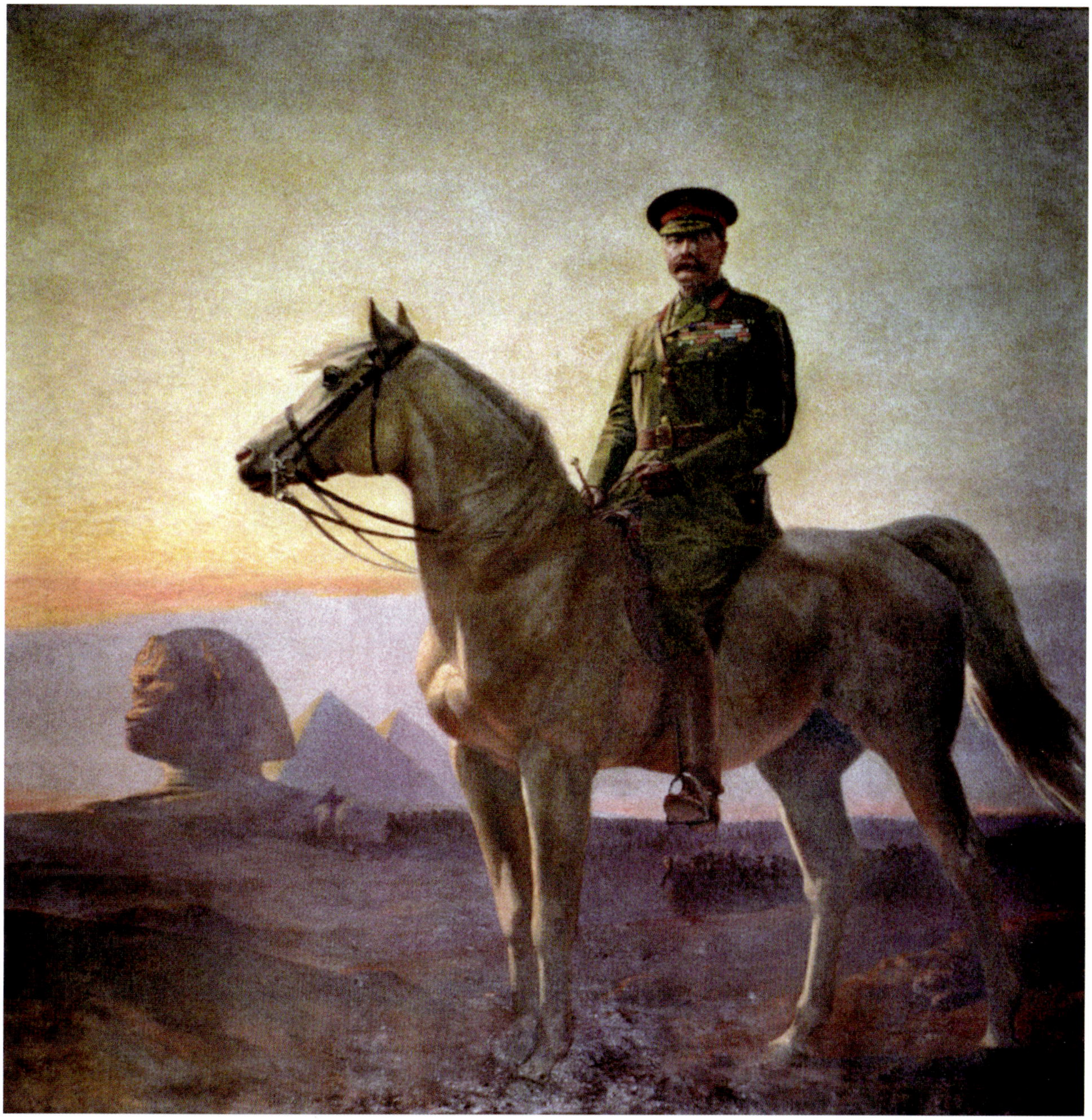

Field Marshal Lord Kitchener, large oil on canvas, 1915, Ipswich Town Hall

Mahdi. Its implicit purpose is to boost morale by evoking pride in imperial Britain's military achievement. It is too calm to be labelled jingoistic, but an accuser might wish to characterise its scenario, in which Kitchener so dominates the Egyptian Sphinx, as nationalistic. (The historian Sir Philip Magnus-Allcroft, who became a Governor of Ludlow Grammar School, titled one of his books *Kitchener: Portrait of An Imperialist.*)

The background scene is essential to the picture's narrative, but whereas in the portrait of Roberts the supporting cast of officers behind Volney is large enough to attract attention, everything in this composition except Kitchener and his horse is minor. Even the sky is undramatic. The only verticals are the horse's forelegs and breast, and the leg and upper body of Kitchener. Roberts is upright too, but the breeze which swirls the clouds and the flag also swirls his helmet plumes and the horse's tail. That and the proximity of his officers conjoin 'little Bobs' to his army and to India. Also, India's horizon lies halfway up Volney, and India's sky above Roberts's head occupies almost a quarter of the canvas. The sense of Kitchener in Adrian's depiction of him is very different. He was a big man, over six feet tall, who seemed to make everyone and everything around him tiny by comparison. The featureless sky's role is just to illuminate him; the mighty Sphinx and pyramids rise only to his knee; the other mounted officer is no more than a speck in shadow; the land of Egypt is beneath his boot. His steady gaze fixes on the viewer rather in the manner of the famous poster, 'Your Country Needs You'. Adrian captures the personality of a general who when in command in Egypt was admired and popular, but whose popularity, unlike that of the more 'human' Buller, came not from having a warm personality but from being trusted to win battles. This is achieved without any hint of caricature; the full cheeks and large moustache are true to life. To quote the war correspondent G.W. Steevens, whom he would have read, Adrian shows a face which 'neither appeals for affection nor stirs dislike'. For his tribute picture, Adrian had turned to that part of the past which best expressed Kitchener's determined will to win. But even that will could not save Kitchener from the fate he was about to meet. Sent to Russia on a fact-finding mission by the Cabinet, in June 1916 he was en route to Archangel on the cruiser *HMS Hampshire* when the vessel struck a mine off Orkney, and went down with the loss of most of the crew and of Kitchener himself. This enemy action made him the war's highest-ranking casualty. Adrian's painting of the lost Field Marshal sold quickly. Mr John Cobbold, of the brewing family, purchased it and presented it to Ipswich Town Hall, where it still hangs behind the Mayor's chair.

Like the Boer War, the Great War required a contribution from South Australia, as from the other parts of the Empire, but during the conflict its citizens still found time and energy to raise funds for a statue to honour one of their heroes from an earlier time. The statue was to commemorate Captain Charles Sturt, a great explorer whose discoveries may be said to have created the state of South Australia. Sturt had come to Australia as a soldier, but resigned his commission in order to pursue the thrills of exploration. In 1827, with a fellow explorer, two soldiers and eight convicts for company, he led an expedition inland from Sydney. They took with them a small boat on wheels, for there were rumours of a sea far in the interior, but where the sea was reported to be they found only a wilderness of reeds. However, they did discover the Darling River. The following year Sturt set out again, and swirled along the Murrumbidgee River by boat and raft until swept out onto what proved to be Australia's greatest river, the Murray. The expedition sped downstream for a month, surviving heat, famine and potentially hostile natives, and ended near the sea where Adelaide now stands. Not being equipped for seafaring, they had no option but to turn back and row against the stream. It took them two months to reach their base camping ground. Luckily there was a happy ending: as the small party shared out its last ounces of food supplies, a group of rescuers bringing stores found them, and they returned to Sydney in triumph. Sturt's epic journey of more than 2,000 miles had been Australia's greatest feat of exploration to date.

Five years later, in 1832, the state of South Australia was founded, and in 1838 Sturt became its surveyor-general. His undying sprit of adventure led him to head another expedition in 1844, its aim being to explore the depths of South Australia and discover what lay in the new territory's remote regions. Due north from the Murray and Darling rivers the expedition reached the desert and pressed uncomfortably on until they reached a spot where water welled up from rock. There they stayed for six months, their condition edging up from discomfort to agony, imprisoned as they were by a temperature of 130°F in the shade. They found only sterile areas around them, slow starvation brought on scurvy, and they had to turn for home. When they reached Adelaide they were far spent, Sturt himself suffering eye damage from the relentless glare of the sun.

Adrian's Boer War statue had been well received in Adelaide, so it was not surprising that the city commissioned him to create the Sturt memorial in 1916. Early in the War he had been busy in his studio with paintings. Now in 1916 he took up major sculpture again. The Adelaide commission appealed to him both because he admired Sturt's spirit of adventure and because of his personal experience of endurance in the field and of working with Australians. It was also, Adrian reported in his *Memoirs*, of 'very special interest ... because, among the English explorers in Australia was my own brother to whose tragic end a curious story attached'. Adrian goes on to devote an Appendix to the story of his elder brother Henry's death in a valley which was later named after him. He gives as his source the *Queenslander* of about 1855, and the story is said to concern a tragic misfortune from a quarter of a century earlier. The chronology is impossible, for in 1830 Henry had not yet been born. But though the date is mistaken, the yarn itself, involving the blood of a pioneer of a new country, is the kind of thing the Victorians saw as symbolic of the founding of the Empire. Here it is, briefly.

Henry Jones had founded Oak Park cattle farm in Queensland, doubtless naming the farm after Oakly Park, Lord Plymouth's estate near Ludlow. After some time he decided to seek more grazing country so that he could increase his cattle numbers. The only other man on the place was an uneducated aboriginal called Knowles. Taking five horses, some weeks' rations, his rifle, and Knowles, Jones set off. He was a thorough bushman who travelled with great care, by the compass always, and made notes of distances. After a week bearing through poor or rough country, they found the well-watered pasture paradise now called Jones's Valley. Henry was leading his horses when the hammer of his primitive, muzzle-loading rifle caught on a twig. The rifle discharged, and the bullet entered his spine. He knew that he was going to die, but that before he did, he must teach Knowles how to find his way back to Oak Park. Knowles knew nothing of compass work and could not read Henry's notes. So for the next two days and nights, even as he weakened, Henry lay on his side and rehearsed Knowles in memorising the notes in the pocket-book and gaining an understanding of compass points. At the end of the second day of teaching he lapsed into incoherence and died. Next morning Knowles made a grave and covered it as best he could, before making his way back, with much wandering and hardship, to Oak Park, to tell of how Henry had saved him from dying lost in the outback.

For this personal reason as well as his professional pleasure in a repeat commission, Adrian was very pleased to begin work on his statue of Sir Charles Sturt. He had pictures of Sturt from which to model, among them portrait postcards which had been sold to raise funds for the statue. In them Sturt's face – high forehead, prominent pointed nose, firm chin – was distinctive enough, but Adrian always preferred to work from life. Luckily the explorer's daughter was in England. She had inherited her father's looks, and she came to sit for Adrian. He considered that the final outcome owed much to her assistance; indeed she apparently helped him not just with capturing the face but also over initial difficulty he had with modelling the figure. As she was Sturt's daughter, not his son, that seems extraordinary. Presumably she gave helpful information about her father, rather than literally providing a likeness of his form. In his approach Adrian concentrated entirely

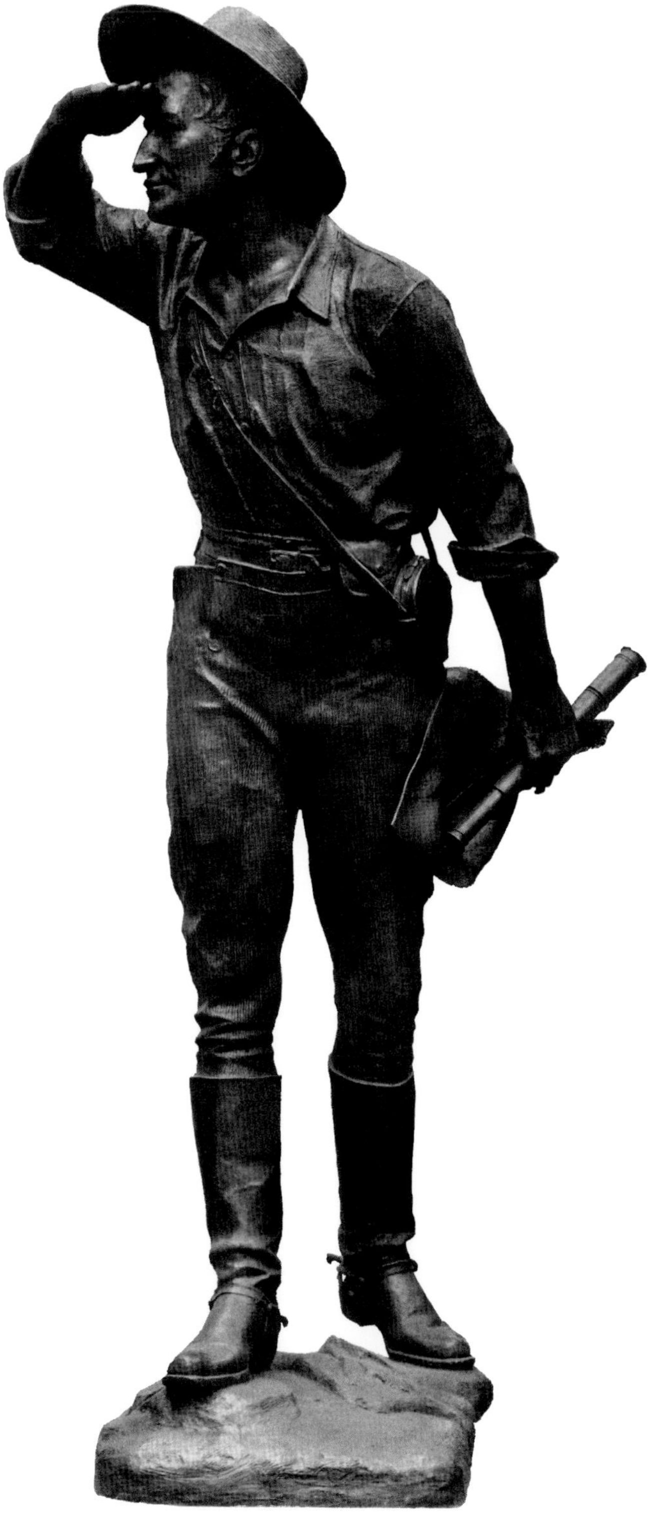

Captain Sturt, studio plaster statue, 1916

on Sturt as an explorer in a hot climate: a lean man in a shading hat, open-necked shirt with rolled up sleeves, breeches and high boots. He had seen an illustration of Sturt dressed thus accompanying an article in *My Magazine* entitled 'The Men Who Made Australia Known'. In that, Sturt holds a rifle, prepared if necessary to confront approaching spear-wielding aborigines. (In real life the gun had not been fired, as an aborigine of commanding presence interposed himself between rifle and spears and prevented any bloodshed.) Adrian eliminated the firearm as insufficiently expressive of surveying and exploration, and replaced it with a telescope held in Sturt's left hand, whilst the right shades his eyes to help him peer forward. It is a conventional, mildly theatrical pose. However, to emphasise the action of trying to see into the distance, Adrian showed Sturt bending slightly forward. A cable arrived from Adelaide requesting him to alter the shading hand and, more importantly, the stoop, which was considered undignified in a national hero. Adrian, preferring his original concept, jibbed. Opposition rumbled on, but diminishingly. By December 1916 the Sturt Statue was in South Australia, awaiting unveiling by the State Governor, Sir Henry Galway.

Because it was wartime, the ceremony on 21st December was particularly patriotic. The Police Band, having entertained the gathering crowd in central Adelaide, precisely at noon played 'God Save the King'; after the Governor's speech and the unveiling it played 'The Song of Australia'; and after the speeches of the State Premier and the Mayor of Adelaide, it led the singing of the National Anthem again. Adrian recorded in his *Memoirs* that 'everyone was satisfied'. The statue still stands there on its tall pedestal, Sturt being South Australia's equivalent of Keats's

... stout Cortes, when with eagle eyes
He stared at the Pacific –
... Silent, upon a peak in Darien.

Adrian believed that his statues should satisfy from every viewpoint. The most evocative view of this one is from the back. The front view of the gaze ahead can seem a hackneyed pose, and at some angles of the sun the hat brim and hand shade the face too much. Look rather from behind when a fierce sun beats down on the stooped back, empathise with Sturt's endurance of heat and fatigue, and share his view of the beyond – though that view today embraces not wilderness but high rise buildings.

After the armistice, Adrian worked on a sequence of war memorials commissioned both by military regiments and civic organisations – work which would use all his artistic skills and military experience, and would include what he himself regarded as some of his finest sculpture. At the same time – by way of contrast from these monumental works – he added to the sequence of portraits of great soldiers he had begun before the war.

In 1920, and with especial pleasure, he painted Lord Allenby. He recorded: 'I greatly enjoyed my association with this famous soldier.' Not everyone during the Great War enjoyed visits from Allenby. In the Middle East he would make unscheduled visits to units in the field, and if everything was not as he would expect it to be his reaction could be volcanic. Units would try to warn each other by sending the signal 'BBL', an agreed abbreviation for 'Bloody Bull's Loose'. James McBey, official war artist to Allenby's force, titles his small (35 by 25 inches) portrait oil painting of Allenby 'The Bull'. The choice of descriptive nickname as title, and the fierce look given to the subject of the painting (now in the Imperial War

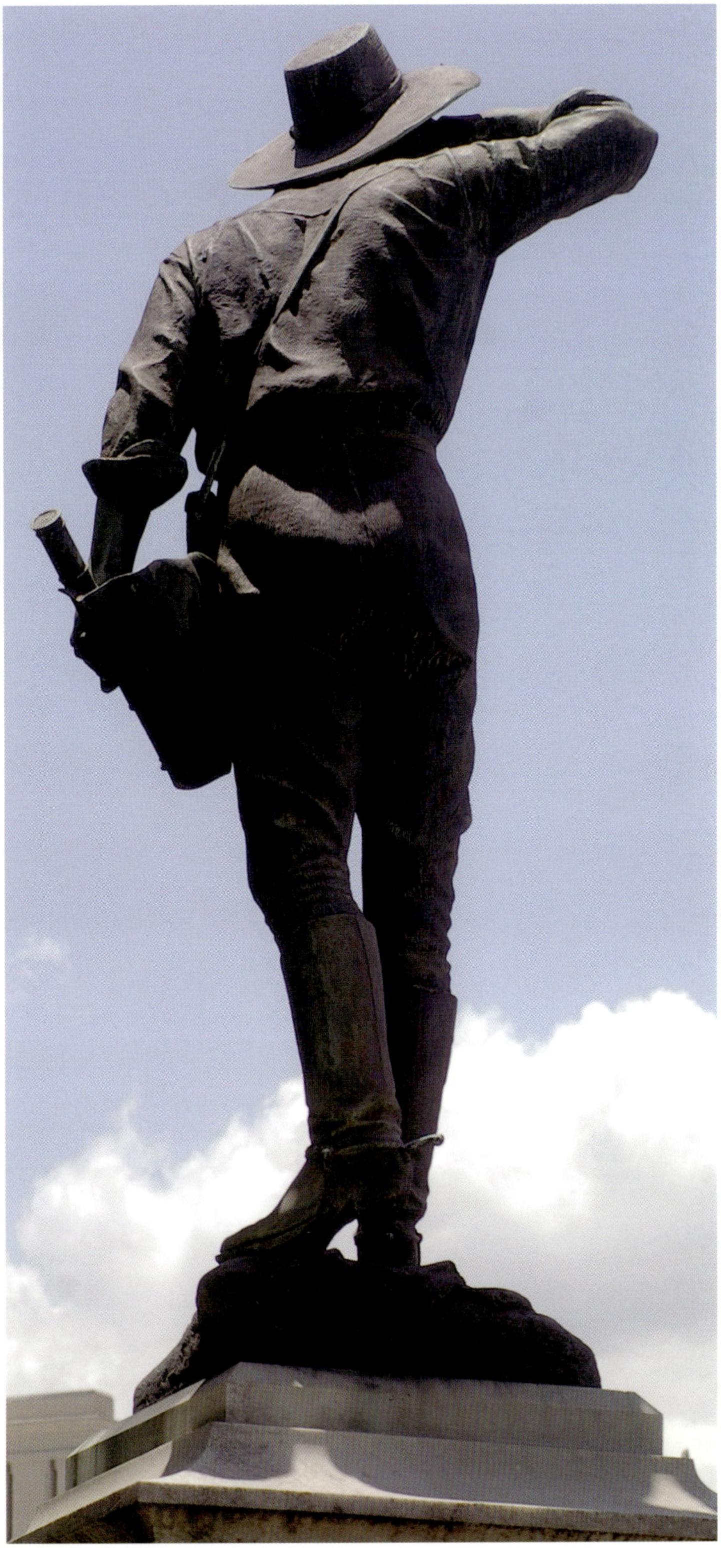

Captain Sturt, bronze statue, Adelaide. Adrian slightly realigned the telescope to give a more compact left side to the statue.

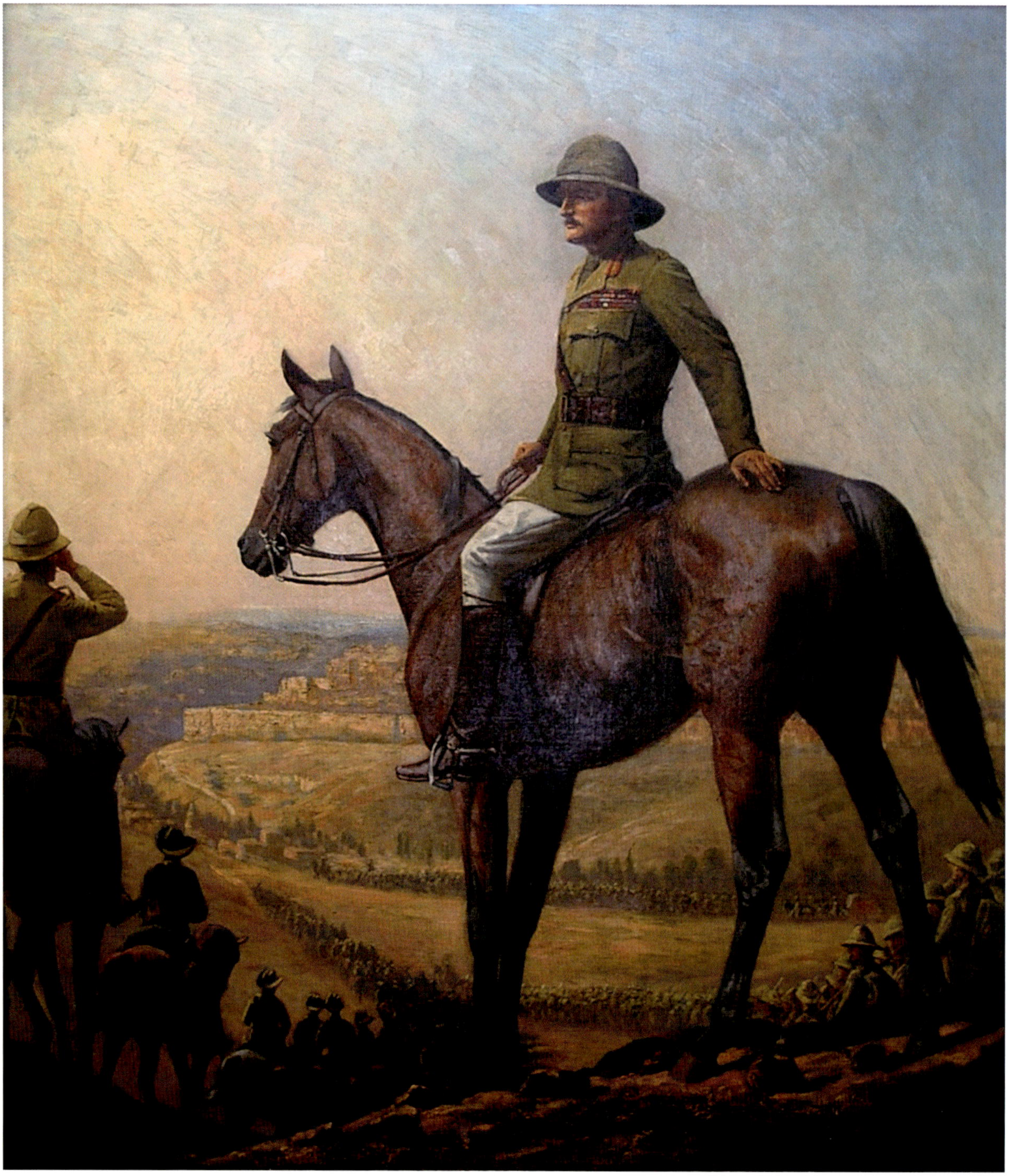

Field Marshal Lord Allenby, 5½ by 4 feet oil on canvas, 1920, Victory Services Club

Museum) hint at that occasional temper. McBey did an even smaller (18 by 23 inches) pen and watercolour painting of the same subject as Adrian's: Allenby at Jerusalem. He shows Allenby flanked by a French and an Italian colonel, walking quietly forward from the Jaffa Gate, so that he may meet Jerusalem's leading officials. Though the capture of Jerusalem was a momentous occasion, there is nothing heroic or triumphal in the little painting. One can imagine a picture in similar mood showing General Percival walking forward to surrender at Singapore in 1942. But this modest pedestrian picture, painted at the time of the event, is historically accurate: Allenby deliberately entered Jerusalem humbly.

Adrian's large equestrian painting is very different in style and purpose. It is not a contemporary recording of reality. This is 63 by 48 inches of commemorative art, something fit to be presented to a regiment or a military club. Allenby, like the Duke of Cambridge in Adrian's portrayal of him, is a big man on a big horse. Together they fill most of the picture. Unlike Roberts and Kitchener, Allenby looks not out at the viewer but across at his troops. His slouch-hatted cavalry column and his helmeted infantry column are converging without opposition on their objective, the walled town of Jerusalem in the middle distance. The picture is a celebratory composition. It offers neither realism – Allenby is painted as a credit to his batman, not in the disarray of hard campaigning – nor revelatory characteristics. It is Adrian's salute to a field marshal who by use of elaborate deception, surprise and speedy concentration forced the Turkish army into retreat and captured iconic Jerusalem. In making the portrait equestrian, Adrian was following in a long but now dead tradition. Then, great military leaders were invariably depicted on horseback, whereas in sculptures created since the Second World War the bronzes of celebrated generals simply *stand* and stare. So Adrian's portrait of Allenby is of its age. Some might call it dated; but the date of the picture as communicated by what is happening behind Allenby is one of its strengths. The backgrounds to Roberts and Kitchener represented an era in their lives. Allenby is shown at one particular moment in his life, an important moment which tells why across the generations we should still be interested in him. The picture is superbly painted, without ambiguity. Adrian has put Allenby literally on a horse and metaphorically on a pedestal. Paused before the painting, one is drawn into endorsing Adrian's admiration for a remarkable soldier. It was bought by Lord Rosebery, who presented it in 1937 to the Allenby Services Club (now the Victory Services Club). Adrian donated the purchase price to the trustees of the Allenby Memorial Fund.

In late 1922 Adrian completed the fourth of his large equestrian paintings of British field marshals. The painting's title did not include any name. It is called 'The Dawn', and is set at that time of day when the military habit was to 'stand to' in defence or to advance in attack, and it is a scene of action. Nevertheless, it is essentially a portrait, the subject this time being Earl Haig. He is a soldier around whom controversy has raged. Shaped in his military thinking and leadership by the pre-1918 world, he was judged – adversely – by the very different world after 1918. Adrian, however, as usual judged his fellow man generously. Like others, Haig had done his flawed best; the British Army had found no better general to replace him, and in 1918 he had brought the nation victory. Writing his *Memoirs* in the 1930s, Adrian still referred to Haig simply as 'the man who did so much for us all' and lamented that the selection of the sculptor for the taxpayer-funded statue of Earl Haig eventually erected in Whitehall in 1937 was not decided by open competition. At his age, he was not invited to submit a design.

By the 1920s there was little demand for conventional pictures of Tommies, against a backdrop wilderness of shattered trees, advancing with rifles at the carry and bayonets fixed. Such images had been featured countless times in photographs. Nor was there now much appetite for pictures of the-general-as-hero. As the years passed and unemployment made the land increasingly unfit for heroes, people thought more of the cost of victory and forgot the euphoria of achieving it. The painting of Haig remained unsold. As late as 1934 it was still in Adrian's studio when a reporter from the *Star* visited 'the finest of all British equestrian sculptors'.

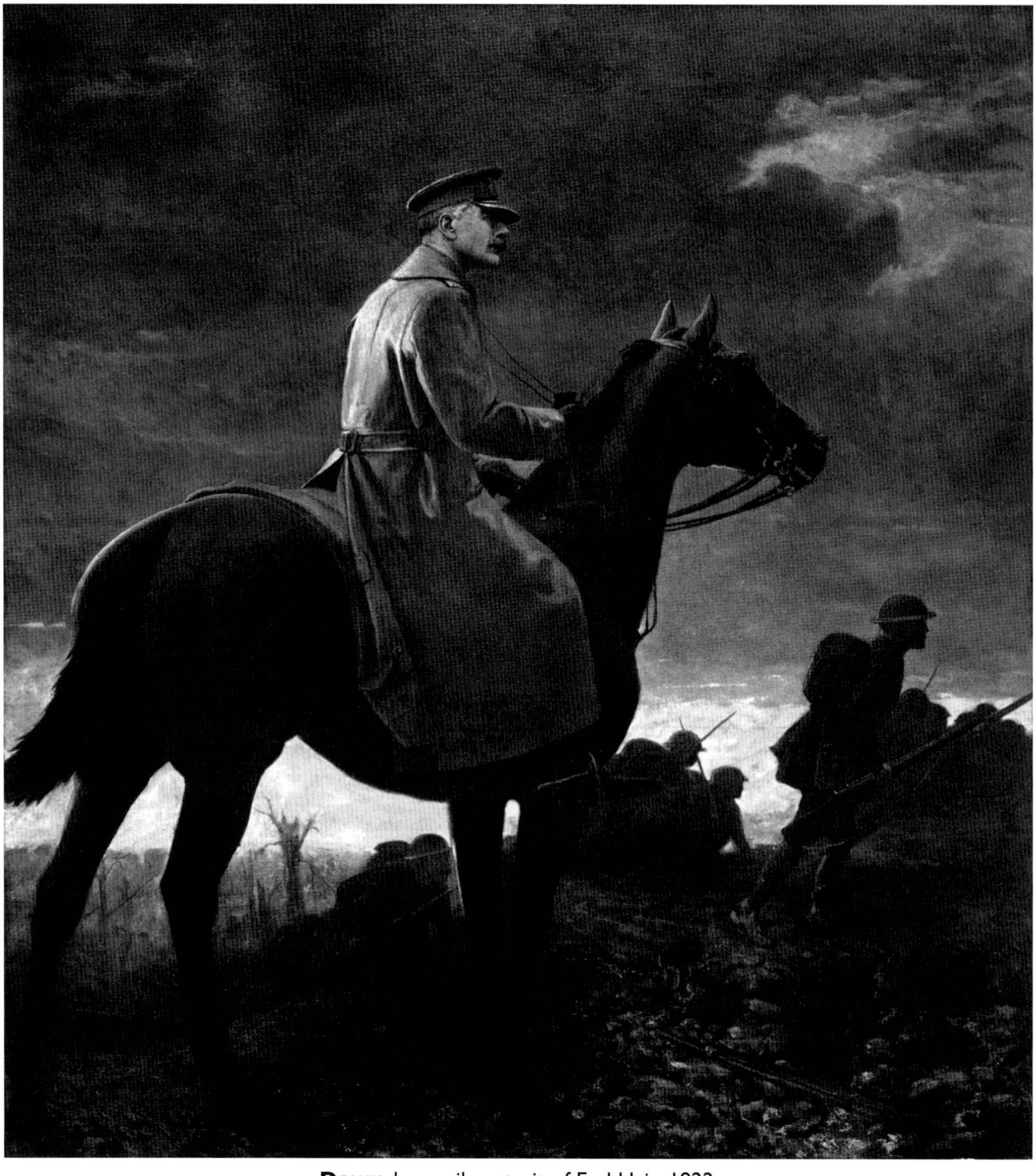

Dawn, large oil portrait of Earl Haig, 1922

When the journalist expressed interest in the large canvas of 'The Dawn', Adrian told him that it showed Haig just before the last 'big push'. In *Memoirs* Adrian says: 'It shows the great Field Marshal on his charger watching the commencement of an action.' Adrian's own sense of the painting, then, was of a prelude to final victory, as symbolised by the golden dawn which is set to banish the darkness of battle. As this is not a photograph but a painting, Adrian adds fiction to fact. It is fact that men went forward; it is fictional that Haig sat exposed so close to them. (Any literal-minded viewer must hope that the low sun is in the enemy's eyes rather than silhouetting the Field Marshal as an easy target.)

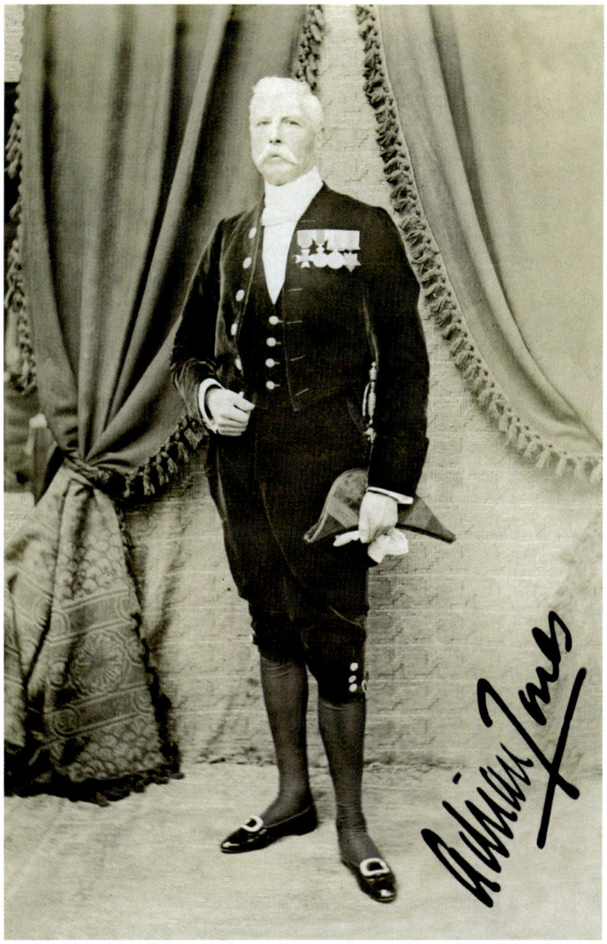

Adrian Jones in court dress, wearing his Member of the Victorian Order (MVO) and campaign medals

On occasion the painting would be moved from the studio to an exhibition. Appropriately, its appearance in the Army Officers' Art Society exhibition of 1928 attracted attention. The Society had been formed two years previously. Anyone holding or having held a regular commission in the Army or Marines could apply to join, and all profits from entrance charges and catalogue sales went to Haig's British Legion Poppy Day Appeal. Adrian was one of the three professional artists who supported it from the outset, in 1926 exhibiting paintings and his bronze statue 'Action Front'. The *Times* found the 1928 exhibition interesting, for overall it revealed some general characteristics of the soldier: 'conservatism, the habit of discipline, orderliness, an interest in detail, and neatness of execution; but these are acquired rather than temperamental characteristics'. The correspondent was perceptive, but he was commenting mainly on watercolours and drawings which were much smaller and less ambitious than 'The Dawn'. Of the exhibition's 369 works, only 56 were oils. The correspondent continues:

> Very properly, in view of the object of the exhibition – Earl Haig's Fund for Ex-Servicemen – the oil paintings are dominated by Captain Adrian Jones. It is a good military portrait, not without a certain grandeur of design, and since Lord Haig is quite recklessly exposed the incident represented may be supposed to be the taking over at dawn or sunset of a position from which the enemy has retired.

The writer was again perceptive. It was possible to conjecture that the painting showed a sunset because in recognition of the exhibition's charitable purpose Adrian had replaced the title 'The Dawn' with 'Field Marshal Earl Haig'; but the narrative imagined by the correspondent is more plausible than Adrian's own. 'Grandeur' is a striking word about what is certainly a striking picture. The ruined landscape in the background and the rifle abandoned, no longer needed by its Tommy, in the foreground are reminders of war's destruction and death, but the overall atmosphere of the picture, painted after the war had been won, is calmly hopeful. After years of stalemate and attrition, a bright end is in sight. The nearest soldier, though watchfully alert, holds his rifle casually in one hand rather than in the two-handed high carry position he would use if he was expecting imminently to shoot or jab. Haig sits unmoving and silent. Adrian catches the serene self-assurance that came from Haig's God-given sense of certain ultimate victory. The black and white illustration is from Adrian's family's archives. Where the picture is now, or if it still exists, the National Gallery does not know.

In the year in which Adrian's portrait of him was exhibited, Haig died. Lord Rosebery bought the portrait of Allenby as a memorial. The 'great soldiers' who had served Victoria, Edward and George V were passing away. But Adrian's long day's work was not yet done.

Civic memorials of the Great War

The post-war building throughout Britain of memorials, virtually all funded by the public, must constitute one of the greatest outbursts of artistic activity in the nation's history. Adrian's first commission for a civic Great War memorial came from the Shropshire town of **Bridgnorth**. It brought him two opportunities that appealed strongly. For the first time an open-air public statue of his design would appear in his native county; and while it would recognise the townspeople's service in all three branches of the armed forces, he could pay particular tribute to the King's Shropshire Light Infantry. He remarked in *Memoirs* that: 'it will not be forgotten by any men of the county that the Shropshire Regiment received from the French Government the Croix de Guerre for distinguished services in the field'. It would be forgotten least of all by Adrian; he had been involved during the War with charitable work for Shropshire's soldiers, and he knew that the attack which had won the KSLI the Croix de Guerre avec Palme had been led by a former pupil of Ludlow Grammar School whose portrait now hung with his own in the School's assembly hall. Geoffrey Bright, from the family of a well-known Ludlow firm of auctioneers, had been the senior subaltern in the 4th Battalion KSLI on 6 June 1918, when because the more senior officers were casualties he had commanded the battalion in a desperate counter attack to retake the Montagne de Bligny. This hill overlooked the Champagne country a few miles south-west of Rheims, and the permanent loss of such a key position would have forced a considerable general withdrawal. Bright ordered an uphill assault in three waves. It looked a forlorn hope. Had this been a military exercise, the umpires would have declared the Shropshires all dead. Extraordinarily, in the event their first wave rushed the fairly rudimentary German slit trench defences within five minutes, where work with bomb and bayonet drove the enemy to death, flight or surrender.

Later, such is the confusion of war, Bright received by runner an order from Brigade HQ to realign with the other remnants of the brigade at the foot of the hill. Not best pleased at the potential prospect of having to capture Bligny Hill a second time, and reinforced in his reaction by the string of colourful obscenities with which his second-in-command greeted the order, Bright diplomatically sent back word that the order was impossible to obey. Nothing more was heard of it, and Bright was heartened to receive another message, this time from the Divisional General: 'Stick it, Shropshires! I'm doing my best to send replacements.' At this time the 19th Division was under the command of the French 5th Army. Its Commandant, General Berthelot, issued a citation praising the 'magnificent dash' and 'superb valour' of the KSLI, awarded Bright (amongst others) a personal Croix de Guerre, and later announced the regiment would receive the supreme honour of that award 'avec Palme'. This was again in the news in 1922. As Adrian worked on the statue, the regiment was preparing the organisation of a parade in Shrewsbury when the fourth anniversary of the battle of Bligny would be marked by the presentation of the honour to the KSLI by General Berthelot in person. It was readily agreed that one face of the Bridgnorth statue's pedestal should carry, in addition to the badges of the Air Force, Army and Navy, the KSLI badge and the Croix de Guerre avec Palme. Some other decisions, however, were not arrived at so easily.

Bridgnorth's first sight of the memorial came in the form of a photograph of the model from which the bronze would be cast. It was placed in the window of the Mayor's High Street shop in August 1920, and the *Bridgnorth Journal* reported 'admiration of the design has been very generally expressed', The Executive Committee charged with implementing the decision to have a town memorial had appointed a sub-committee to visit London, look at the exhibition of war memorials on display there and choose a sculptor. It had reported back in April, recommending that Captain Adrian Jones, 'a sculptor of great distinction and a Shropshire man', should be appointed to execute the memorial at a cost not exceeding £700, and be requested to submit his design and visit Bridgnorth to select a site as soon as possible. As £750 had already been subscribed by the public, the executive committee moved forward swiftly and confidently. It met again just a week later, with Adrian present. He had already toured the town, and now proposed that the memorial be sited at the High Street crossroads. The committee voted forthwith to approve that choice, then further resolved that Adrian be entrusted to produce a statue along the lines of the sketch he had shown, at life size and a quarter. The last decision, to opt for a figure seven and half feet tall rather than simply life size, was the boldest of the evening, for Adrian had earlier given the Committee his informal estimate that such a figure would cost £1,000. He was asked to obtain exact tenders.

The early 1920s were a time of rising costs in labour and materials. For the next three months Adrian pursued estimates for the ten foot pedestal, the bronze panels, and the casting of the figure in bronze. On 21 August 1920, Adrian wrote to the committee chairman, regretfully informing him that because of increased costs the total bill would now be £1,400. The chairman replied urgently and told Adrian to do no further work before the committee met the following week. Within that week Adrian, realising the chairman's nervousness about the doubled cost, wrote back saying that under the circumstances he would waive the sum he had allowed for himself and thereby reduce the cost to £1,200. The committee duly met, with the photograph of the plaster cast on the table before them, and with Adrian present to comment and explain as required. The ensuing discussion was full, but at the end of it the executive committee voted, with no one opposing, to accept the Mayor's proposition 'That subject to the money being forthcoming, the sketch and site be approved and submitted to the General Council for adoption'. The meeting of the general committee, the umbrella body for the appeal and project, followed immediately. It was even more determined. To its motion of full approval for the scheme it added the clause, 'and the meeting pledges itself to do its utmost to successfully carry it out'. To learn the town's reaction, it convened an afternoon meeting in the town hall of its own members, subscribers and any others interested.

The small attendance of around thirty, even allowing for the inconvenient afternoon timing in days when a Shropshire town had fewer retired people than it has in the twenty-first century, suggests that, though opinions on both site and design were divided, passions were not violent. Certainly the subject of the meeting seemed to bring out the best in people. One speaker referred to criticism of the scheme which had been uninformed and casual, but none of that surfaced in the debate. The town's new mayor, Councillor A.G. Lloyd, presided, and established the tone in his opening address. He declared the meeting necessary because so much more money, involving more support from subscribers and townspeople, was required. It would be a great pity if their War Memorial, instead of being a united testimony, emblematic of the united action, vigour, and sacrifice of the men of their town, leading to victory, should be a bone of contention in their midst. Personally he was willing to sink any feeling he might have in order to obtain this united effort. He thought the statue in hand would be one of the best little statues in the country, and would so be accounted by those who would follow them. But the memorial would not be satisfactory if unity was not achieved on choice of site also.

The meeting agreed to consider site and statue as separate issues, though the Mayor reminded everyone that the latter debate would have to include consideration of costs. The discussion of the site initially followed predictable lines, the value of having the memorial in the heart of the town set against the disturbance of increasing vehicle traffic and the difficulty of manoeuvring large loads such as timber wagons past the proposed statue. But then Mr W.H. Foster, whose father had given the grounds of Bridgnorth Castle to the town and corporation for ever, made a decisive speech. He argued that a site at a busy crossroads would have 'no sanctity about it, and no feeling of reverence for all those names they would see inscribed upon it'. He advocated a quiet place, specifically the site originally proposed in the castle grounds, where everybody could see it and go up to it to read the names. He sat down to applause. (The verdict of history must be that when the meeting later voted unanimously for the castle grounds setting it was more far-sighted than Adrian. In recent times, the statue of General Buller in Exeter has been moved from a traffic island to the side of the road, and in London the Quadriga, the Cavalry Memorial and the Uxbridge War Memorial have been given greener surroundings. The Duke of Cambridge in Whitehall, like the Cenotaph, somehow manages to coexist with the traffic, but is certainly not easily approached. The most unfortunate is the Carabiniers Memorial; it has to compete with traffic, road signs and traffic lights.)

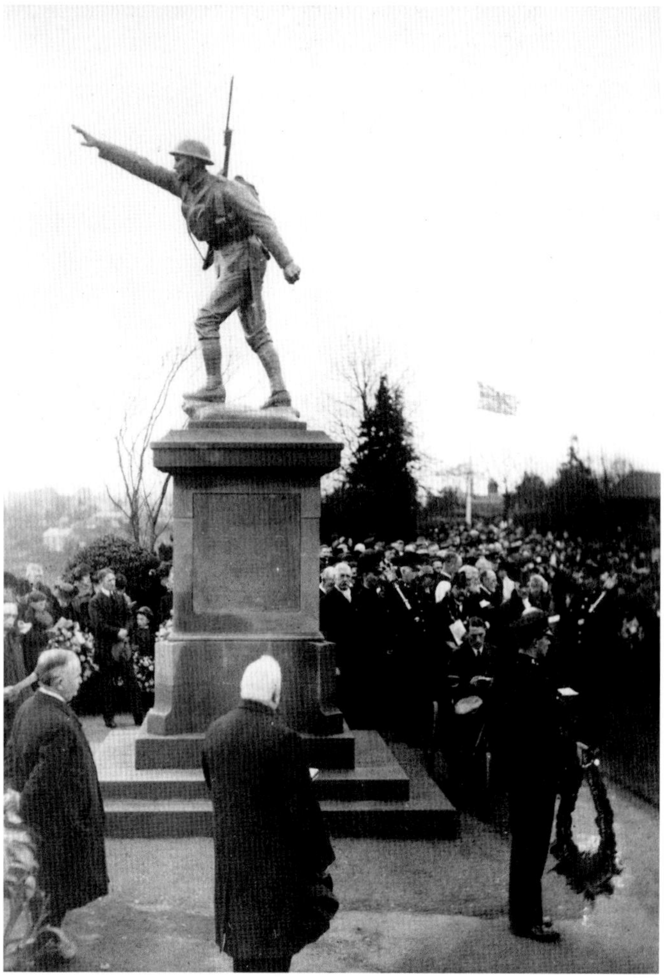

Bridgnorth War Memorial, 1922:
The day of the unveiling in the Castle Gardens. Adrian is standing immediately to the right of the plinth.

As for funding, despite some misgivings because £450 'was rather a tall order', confidence in generosity prevailed: 'In Bridgnorth, where so many had been touched by severe losses – sons had been killed and many maimed for life – everyone should wish to contribute his bit or her bit to the cost of commemorating their gallantry in the field.' It was even suggested that Adrian should not waive his fee as 'it would be rather derogatory for a town like this to get their work done for nothing'. It was the statue's design, however, which provoked the most heartfelt discussion. When the photograph of the plaster model had appeared in the High Street, the *Bridgnorth Journal*.had given as its opinion that: 'A more fitting symbol than that chosen – a realistic county soldier hurling a bomb with all his energy and strength and thus 'doing his bit' – could scarcely be found.' Adrian had been asked to design a statue which commemorated those who defended the country and returned, as well as those who had lost their lives. That ruled out anything along the lines of Lutyens' Cenotaph to 'our glorious dead'. Equally the request to show a defender meant that he could not use an angel of peace motif. He told the press his principle had been to show 'moral and military effort put forth'. One speaker at the meeting said she did not like the design at all: she would have liked to see a Tommy standing at attention. Another said a memorial should be one of peace and therefore he was rather disappointed: he had looked at it and said, 'Still at war, I see', though he recognised that there was no getting away from the fact that the Executive Committee had approved the design unanimously when Adrian had shown it to them. In the end, the meeting voted for the Castle Gardens site and the proposed design with no votes against. The mayor's call for a united effort had prevailed, and in due course united effort raised the necessary funds.

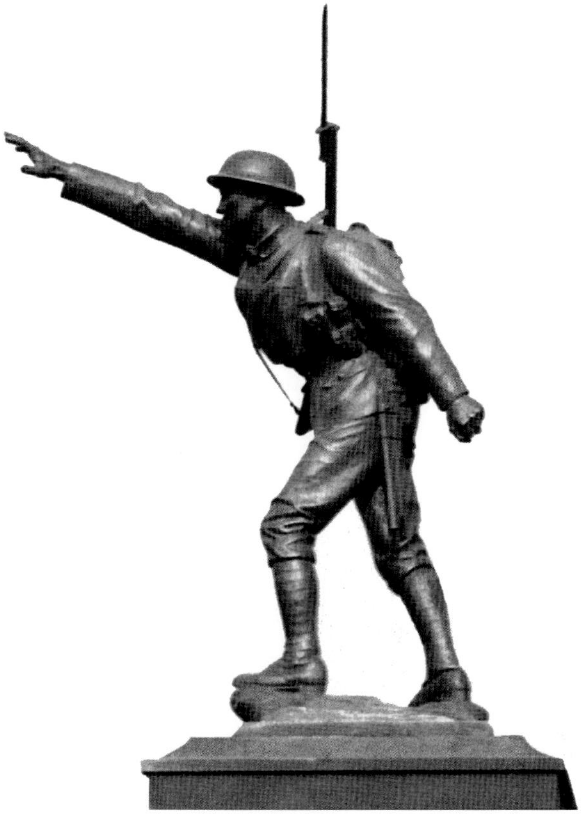

Bridgnorth War Memorial: the life-size plus a quarter bronze statue of a King's Shropshire Light Infantry 'Tommy'

Adrian had not been present at the meeting to defend or explain his design. Unquestionably the statue is 'still at war', and after its unveiling and dedication on 9 March 1922, a press illustration of it was accompanied by the statement that the bronze figure is 'throwing a bomb'. The use of the present tense is unjustifiable. There is no bomb of any description in the soldier's hand, nor anywhere among his kit. Even an assertion that this is a soldier who has just thrown a bomb would be unconvincing. A bomb was a short range weapon, and a soldier who had just hurled one would have had his rifle at the carry in his other hand rather than harmlessly still slung over the shoulder and across his back. The only possible credence for the bomb story is the soldier's open palm, for nothing else in his pose suggests throwing. The front leg is not braced for effort; rather it appears simply to be taking a slightly uphill step forward. Plainly if a sculptor intends to depict a bomber, he must include a hand grenade or similar device. It is more probable that Adrian was using the same idea as he used on the first bas relief panel of the Royal Gloucestershire Hussars memorial, unveiled one month after that at Bridgnorth: a soldier is urging advance on the enemy hilltop position ahead. He is expecting soon to be in close quarter action, for he has fixed his bayonet on his rifle, but first he has to move forward. With the engagement in which the KSLI won the Croix de Guerre avec Palme alluded to on the pedestal, Adrian may have imagined the Tommy's upward gaze and outflung arm indicating Bligny Hill.

The story of the KSLI's successful assault, common knowledge amongst Salopians in 1922, is now mainly known just among veterans who attend the annual Light Infantry and Rifles Reunion, held each year as near as possible to the battle's anniversary. The statue in its own high ground position remains a key feature of the Castle Hill gardens. The dedication, in the presence of Adrian, was carried out by the Bishop of Hereford, who had himself earned the Distinguished Service Order (DSO) during the war. And the unveiling was done by one of 'those who defended the country and returned'. He was not a general. Taking precedence on 9 March 1922, over the Mayor, the mace bearer and the mayoral procession, the unveiler was Private Eli

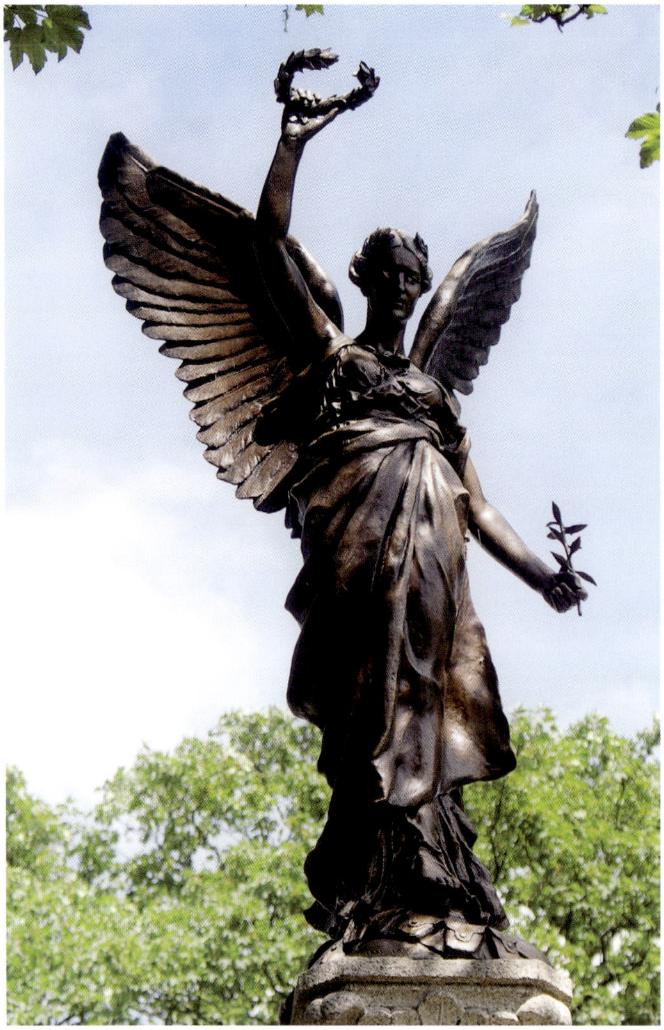

Uxbridge War Memorial: the victorious figure of Peace. The sky relates her to the world of angels, and the overarching leaves have the effect of making her a part of our world also.

Jones, KSLI, who had lost both his legs during the war.

Uxbridge had first considered a war memorial in 1921, but the proposed site had been spoilt by a road widening scheme. So in April 1924 a town meeting elected a new War Memorial Committee and delegated the duty of drawing up 'some scheme of a war or peace memorial' which would then be submitted to another town meeting. By that time, five and a half years after the Armistice of 1918, some saw it as a reproach to Uxbridge that nearly all the surrounding villages had erected war memorials but Uxbridge itself had not, and they felt that that must now urgently be remedied. Others argued that as several Uxbridge churches and the cricket club already had memorials, the plan now should be for something more useful than a statue. Undeterred, the committee approached Adrian and asked for a sketch design. Given the choice between 'a war or peace memorial', he opted for peace. This was not because of his experience at Bridgnorth, but because of his longstanding belief that Peace was a supreme value. He wrote in *Memoirs*: 'We had quite enough memorials that seemed to revive the war spirit rather than to consider peace, which is, after all, the aim and end of every great struggle.' He decided on a design strongly reminiscent of the figure of Peace he had placed on the Quadriga war chariot. The committee made it their final choice, and the local newspaper told its readers:

> We can well understand that the committee deem themselves fortunate in securing the cooperation of so distinguished a sculptor, one who undoubtedly occupies a front rank amongst British artists. Mr Adrian Jones carried out the Cavalry Memorial recently unveiled in Hyde Park, which is a really magnificent specimen of British sculpture, but he is more widely remembered by the Quadriga, that very vivid and stirring group of statuary over the Wellington archway.

For a second time a tall (six and a half feet), elegant and graceful symbolic angel of Peace took shape in Adrian's studio. From her shoulders sprang an attractive pair of feathery wings; as on the Quadriga, her raised right hand held a laurel victory wreath and her lowered left an olive branch; at her feet lay the now unused detritus of war, an abandoned tin helmet and ammunition pouches. The intention was that she would stand on a column of Cornish granite hewed from the quarry in one piece. This would replace a drinking fountain at a road junction beside the RAF station, and the ensemble would rise to a total height of seventeen and a half feet. However, when Adrian inspected the site he observed that a lamp standard beside the fountain rose to about twenty feet and thus would detract from Peace's impressiveness against the skyline. He returned to the committee and recommended a larger column and a revised total height of twenty-three feet, which would mean an increase in cost from £550 to £850. As in Bridgnorth, the committee decided on bold support. It resolved that it would be the larger scheme which would be put to the forthcoming town meeting.

The meeting, held in competition with a glorious July evening when most people wished to be out of doors, flowed with fundraising ideas. A Sunday collection, a flag day, a procession by the Fire Brigade, a tattoo by the RAF, an appeal to businesses, a house to house collection throughout the urban district: it was the duty and obligation of everybody to raise the necessary funding. Uxbridge may have been a late starter with its memorial, but it now moved swiftly. In August, on site, the Urban Council Surveyor met Adrian, who came accompanied by a full size model of the statue and its new sixteen-foot column. The Surveyor undertook to obtain authorisation for the removal of the water trough and the offending electric light standard, and as the granite and bronze statue would weigh over 20 tons he undertook to arrange for

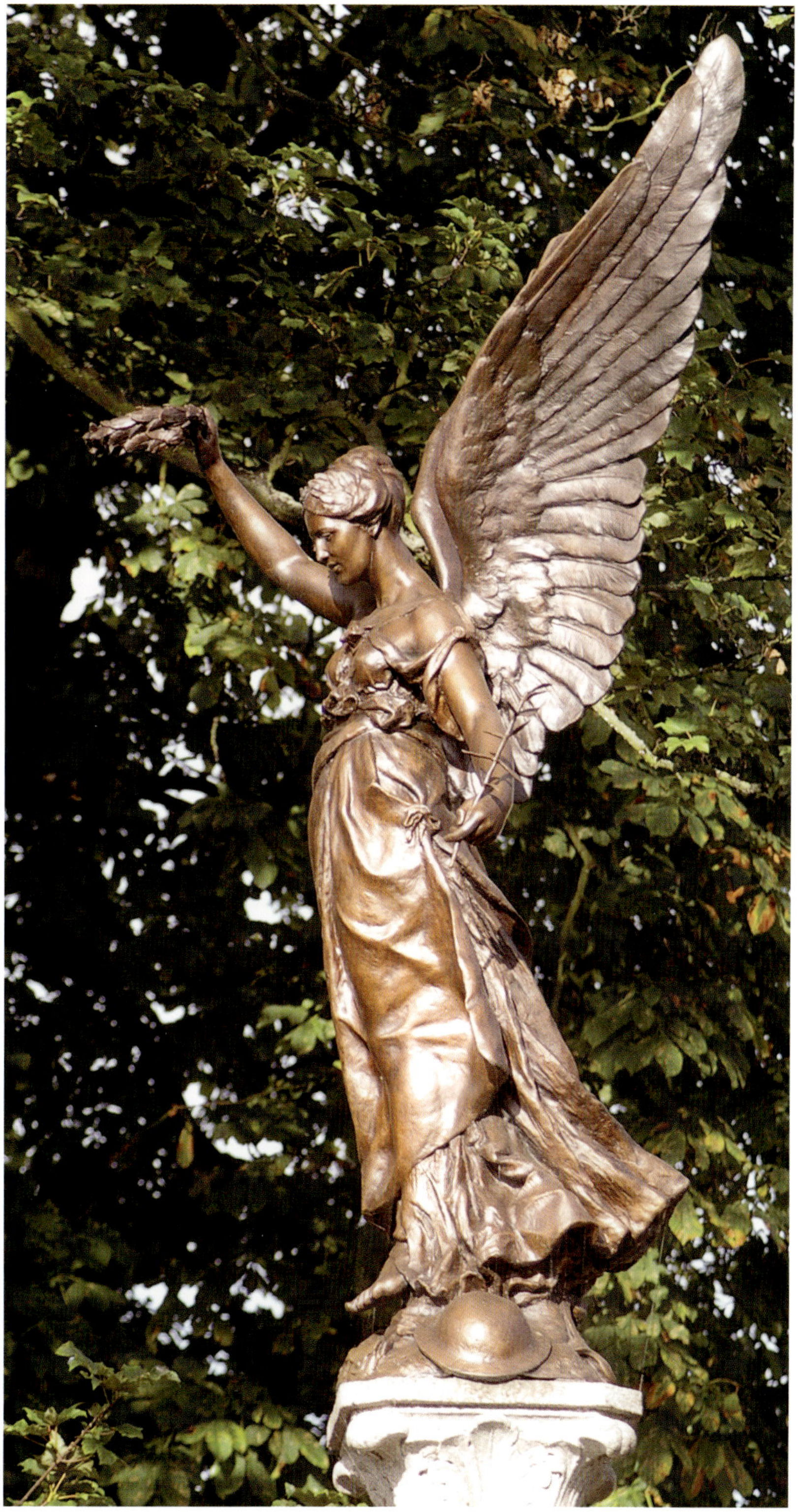

Uxbridge War Memorial: side view of Peace. Brilliantly modelled wings and draperies, all in 'a most attractive light golden colour'

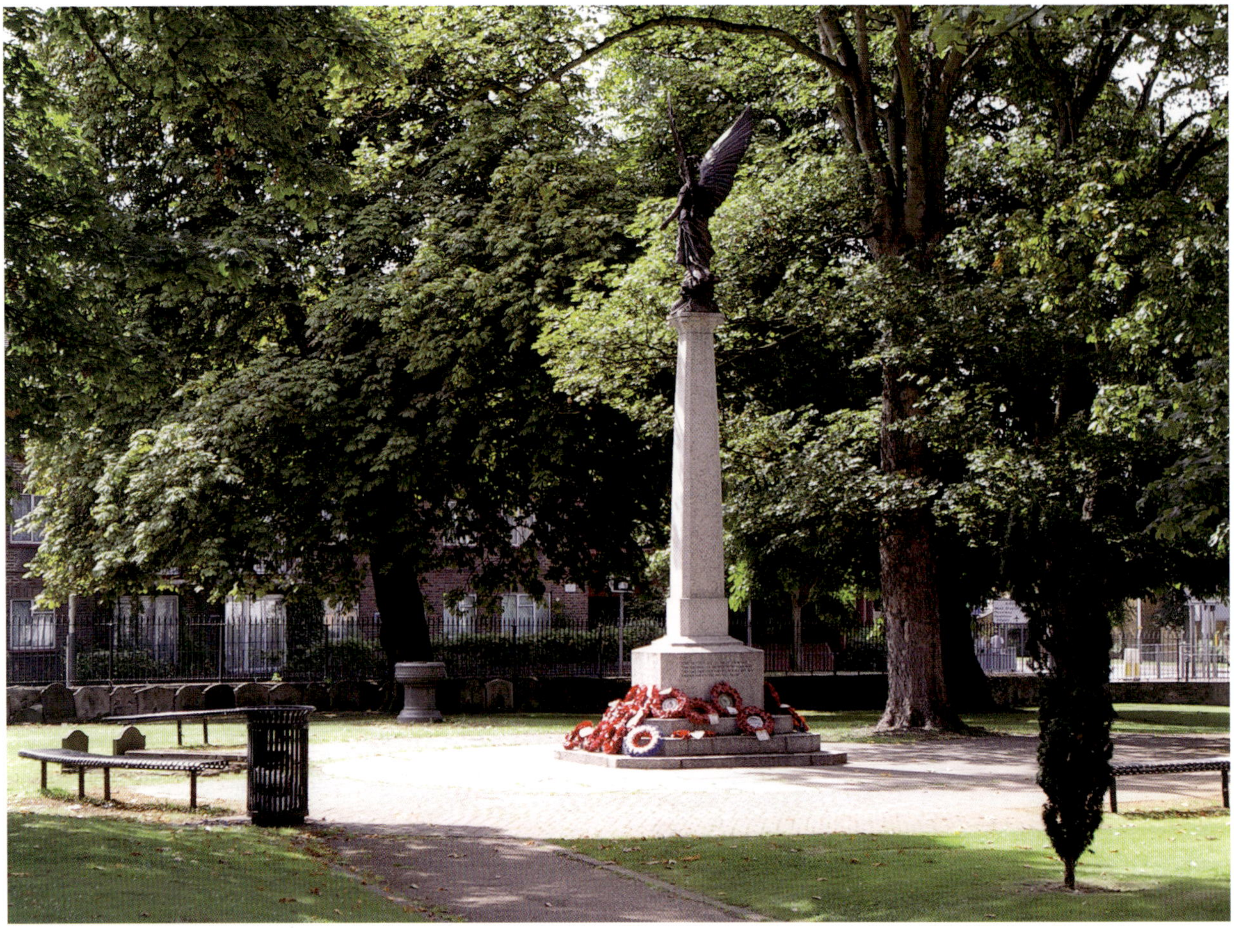

Uxbridge War Memorial, 1924. The memorial was originally sited outside the RAF Base.

Council workmen to lay a concrete foundation bed under the road surface. Their determination was to have everything done in time to permit an unveiling by Armistice Day, and they succeeded.

As usual, Adrian had entrusted the casting to the Thames Ditton foundry. He considered it 'singularly successful ... of a most attractive light golden colour'. Because the lapse of time since the Great War made it improbable that any list of the killed would be wholly accurate, the monument bears no inscribed names. It had been said at the town meeting that the names of the dead men were already cut deep in the hearts of those who had lost them, and the proposition that there be just a suitable general inscription had been passed unanimously. The Dowager Lady Hillingdon performed the unveiling in front of the RAF base, and, in a new experience for Adrian, the servicemen and band on parade were airmen.

The Uxbridge memorial, perhaps because it largely replicates Peace on the Quadriga, may be the least visited of Adrian's monuments, yet this personification of Peace is beautiful in her own right, a fine example of Adrian's superb modelling skills. She and her gleaming Cornish granite column survived the tramcars and other traffic of the twentieth century remarkably untarnished. They have now been moved to an appropriately peaceful site. Viewed from the quiet circle of benches, she is nearer than her Quadriga namesake. Her head on its long gracious neck is tilted forward as she looks down benignly. Adrian did not have to give her the severe face of the larger, more distanced Quadriga figure. (King Edward VII would have been pleased.) And perhaps an occasional visitor, noticing her somehow very human bare foot pressing down on the hardware of war, may reflect hopefully with Milton that 'Peace hath her victories / No less renowned than war'.

Chapter Sixteen: 'Something Very Satisfactory' Regimental Memorials of the Great War

Action Front (1921)

Reviewing the Sladmore Gallery's 1984 Retrospective Exhibition of Adrian's work, the *Financial Times* art critic David Piper identified as 'the sculptor's real, and remarkable, gift ... the capture of figures in motion ... his ability to model them turning on themselves in irresistible rhythm'. He went on to single out for particular praise the bronze statuette 'Action Front':

> Astonishing in its complexity is a group showing a field gun going into action, still limbered to its ammunition carriage and four horses, with five gunners. It is all caught, straining in a slope of battered mud, and mud clings to the wheels. The detail here, of uniforms, harness, gun equipment, is translated into bronze with loving completeness but in this case the swirl of the composition, drawing the onlooker compulsively round it, absorbs all its movement ... it is admirably realised, a virtuoso performance.

'Action Front' was one of Adrian's own favourite pieces. He put much time and trouble into the plaster model, and had it accepted for the 1921 Royal Academy Exhibition (exhibit 1248). Afterwards he worked it to exact scale, cast it in bronze and resubmitted it to the Royal Academy. The jury selected it again (exhibit 1418) for the 1925 Exhibition. 'Not a brilliant show', reported the *Yorkshire Observer*. 'No sensational picture of the year, despite two or three attempts to achieve notoriety ... No, the season's successes lie in the sculpture division; among them a statuette in bronze, entitled 'Action Front', by Captain Adrian Jones ... With the time fast approaching when mechanical traction will be substituted for horse, this little gem would be invaluable as a record of the horse tradition.' The *Observer* went on to tell its readers that Adrian was known as 'Quadriga' Jones to art circles, and that this exhibit combined correct detail with 'artistic composition'. That composition had been highly challenging to the artist. As he explained in *Memoirs*:

> It is an accurate representation of what would happen in given circumstances, but in order to bring it within the limits of sculpture, it is confined to a group consisting of guns and horses. A group of this nature is very long, and the great difficulty in making a sculptured representation lies in so arranging that the group presents a compact appearance and, while true in line and composition, remains equally true in detail.

The truth of the detail had always been a feature of his works, but in the 1920s he saw it as particularly important. As horses were replaced by mechanised transport, he wished to combine artistry with accurate historical record: 'This statue may well become a souvenir of the old system, and will, I hope, find some abiding place in one of our national museums, for I think it is one of the best pieces of work I have ever done.'

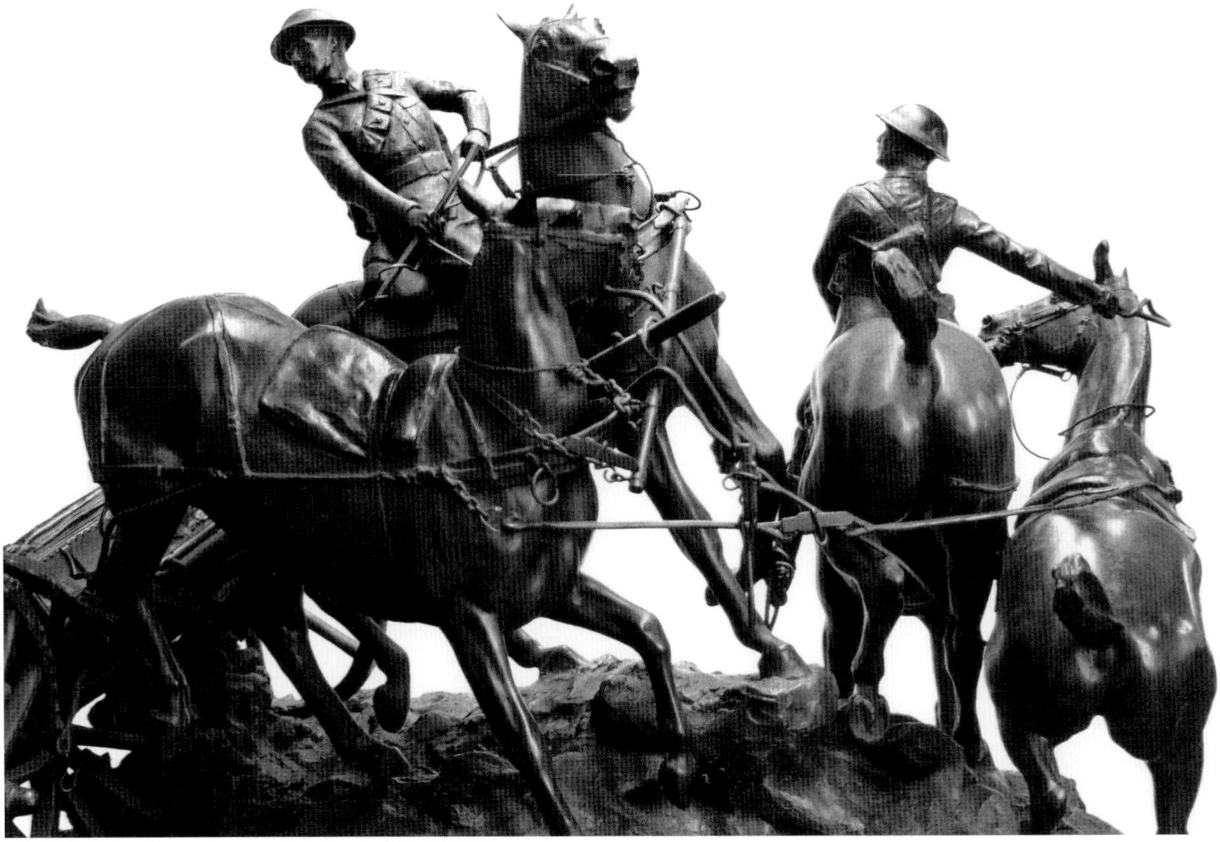

Detail: **Action Front**, anxious horses and anxious men

The statuette's current 'abiding place' is the St John's Wood Barracks Museum. As this is a private Royal Artillery museum (viewing by invitation), it does not qualify as 'one of our national museums'. Nevertheless, it is an abiding place which would surely have pleased Adrian because of his two spells of service there with the Royal Horse Artillery. The complex sculpture, so praised by David Piper and the press, proclaimed by Adrian 'one of the best pieces of work I have ever done', and described in *Regimental Heritage* (the Royal Artillery's record of its paintings and art objects) as a 'fine miniature bronze', sits compactly on its wooden base in the middle of the museum. The notice plate on the base, in uncomprising block capitals, reads:

AN UNSUCCESSFUL DESIGN FOR THE RA WAR MEMORIAL
HYDE PARK CORNER LONDON

That is doubtless not the inscription which Adrian would have chosen or wished. It would have been kinder simply to have displayed the bronze over its title: 'Action Front'. But the wording is justified as historical record, and though 'Action Front' is unquestionably, to use the Royal Artillery's own description, 'fine', the decision was right.

Artillery was the most important weapon of the Great War. In popular belief the machine gun had been the more murderous, but in fact over half the casualties on the Western Front were caused by field guns, heavy guns and howitzers. Their role was so crucial that in the course of the War the Royal Artillery trebled in size to nearly 1,800 batteries, and almost one soldier in five was a gunner. These gunners mastered

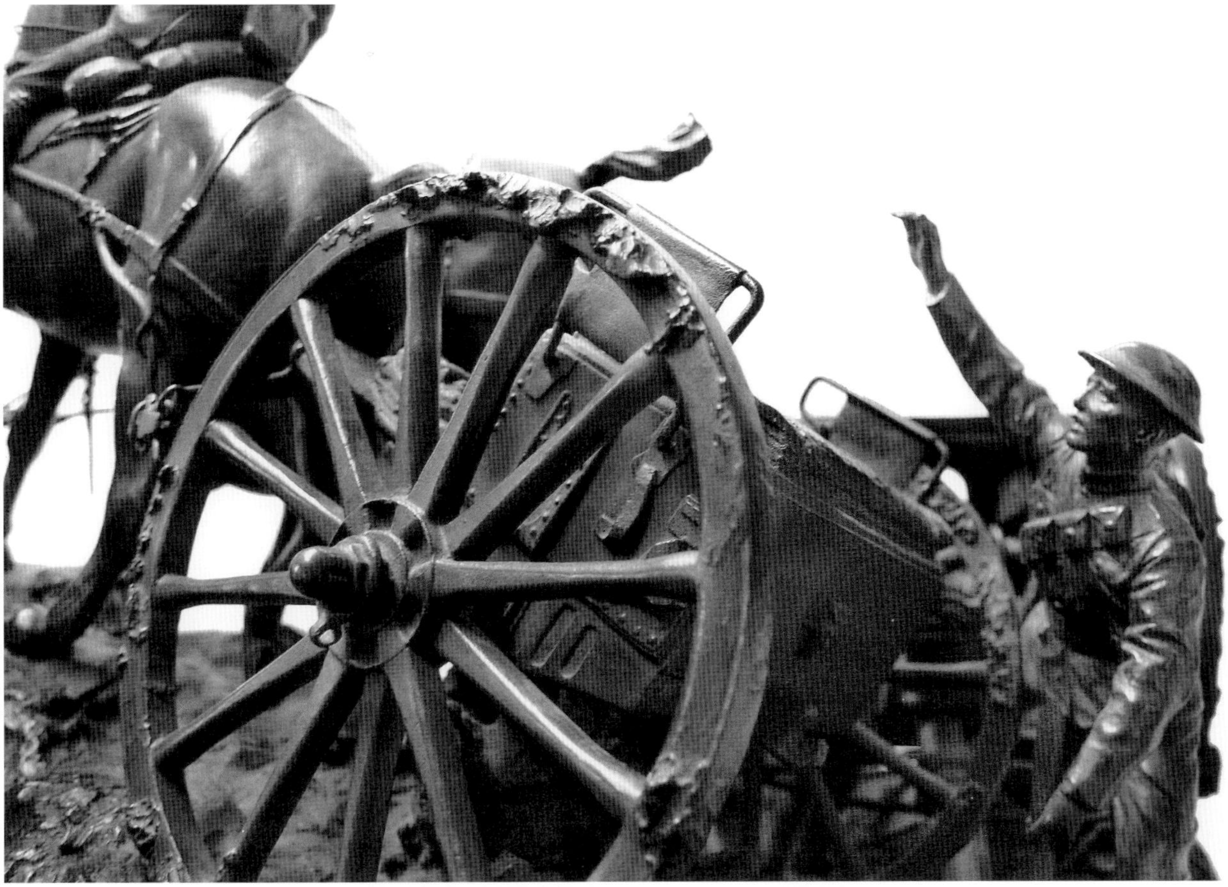

Detail: **Action Front**, the mud of Flanders on the wheels

new techniques such as the creeping barrage; and they worked hard, for whereas infantry were regularly rotated out of the line, gunners had to stay in position as long as any units in their division remained on the front.

The major memorial for this important royal regiment, erected in 1925, stands at Hyde Park Corner, close to Derwent Wood's Machine Gun Corps Memorial and Adrian's Peace Quadriga, and just across the road from his Cavalry of the Empire Memorial, which then stood at Stanhope Gate and had been unveiled the year before. While Adrian would have been pleased to have a hat trick of statues at Hyde Park Corner, if the commission was not to be his he would be content that it went to an artist forty years younger than himself who shared much of his approach to art. Like Adrian, Charles Jagger did not follow the modernist trends which were then increasingly characterising European sculpture: he continued in the tradition of classical figurative sculpture. Some of the principles Jagger expressed in his later book, *Modelling and Sculpture in the Making*, wherein he reviewed his practice, could almost have been written by Adrian: 'Exaggeration and modification of the forms of nature are the undisputed prerogative of the creative artist, and it is only the abuse of their legitimate licence which results in revolting deformity and malformation.' That replicates Adrian's distinction between craftsman and true artist. Or: 'Any emotional subject, teeming with drama and human tragedy, can only adequately be expressed by grim realism controlled and directed by the artist.' That could describe Adrian's approach to the realisation of the Marines Memorial.

Jagger's memorial, topped by a large howitzer pointing skywards, is an attention-compelling presence. Its dark, still statue of a standing gunner-driver, hung with equipment, tin-helmeted against shrapnel, caped against wet, leg-guarded against being crushed between horses, arms outstretched like a man crucified, demands reverent regard, though neither it nor the other three bronze figures have conventionally heroic postures or expressions (as later featured in Stalinist art). The *Architect's Journal* in 1925 complained that as Hyde Park Corner was the forecourt to the West End: 'However excellent the sculpture a war memorial that can only commemorate the brutality of war has no place here.' But whilst the inscription on the Machine Gun Corps Memorial is brutal – 'Saul hath slain his thousands but David his tens of thousands' – that on the Artillery memorial – 'Here was a royal fellowship of death' – has a different, more moving, impact. The key merit, however, is not the inscription but the way the bronze gunner figures address themselves full on to any person or parade that stands before them. The failure of Adrian's brilliant 'Action Front' *as a memorial* is that is essentially an artistic recreation of a moment of military action. That can be fully successful in a painting or bas relief. A viewer of Adrian's painting of the charge of the Lancers at Omdurman, for instance, is likely to be content to judge it as a depiction of action. The combatants are totally involved in their own world of the battle. Similarly, the gunners in 'Action Front' are completely absorbed in unlimbering and setting up the field gun ready to fire. Any onlooker is irrelevant to them.

If in one's imagination 'Action Front' is worked up from the 'to scale' miniature into a life-size monument for a public space, potential drawbacks become apparent. At the level of practicality, it would require a tall

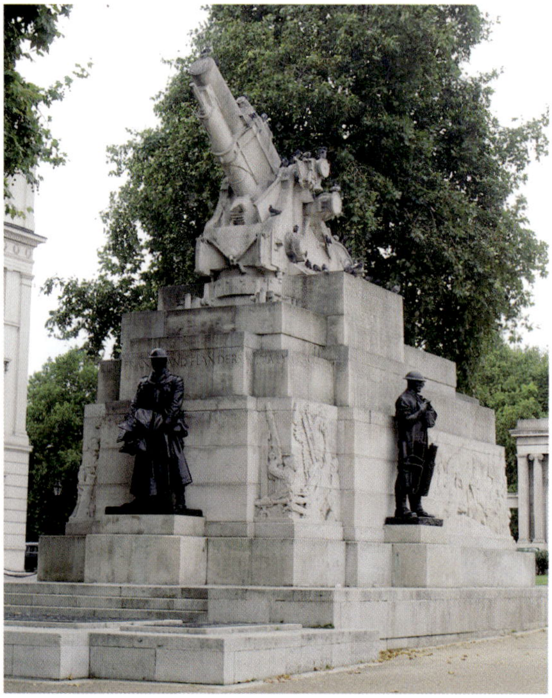

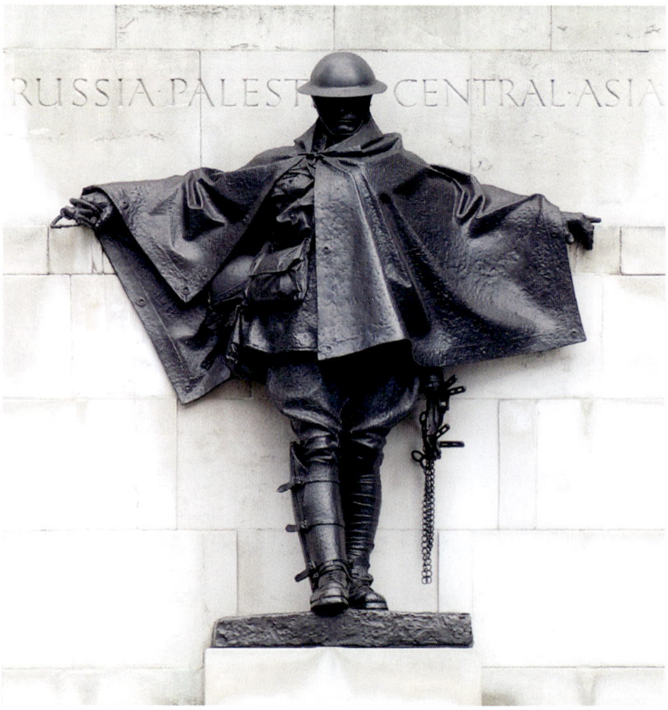

Left: **Royal Artillery Memorial,** Hyde Park Corner, by Charles Jagger, 1925. Unlike the highly animated Action Front, Jagger's memorial is a work of massive stillness, with any activity confined to the bas reliefs. The giant 9.2 inches howitzer gun mouth is capped. The artillery officer (near end) and the shell carrier (side) stand unmoving (and, not seen here, on the far end lies a gunner in the ultimate stillness of death).
Right: Detail: **Royal Artillery Memorial**: The Driver statue on the far side, facing the road. He also is still. In 1921 Jagger had destroyed his fussier designs for the artillerymen statues, and replaced them with these striking figures.

pedestal to make it inaccessible to those small boys who would love to climb all over it; yet it is a complex composition which can only be taken in at eye level or below. Also, though neither Jagger nor Adrian modelled the main British gun of the 1914-18 War, the 18-pounder field gun, Jagger's mammoth howitzer spoke of modern weaponry awesome in range and destructive power, whereas Adrian's horse-drawn, lighter 13-pounder harked back to the past and would soon be thought of as 'a souvenir of the old system'. The Artillery themselves judged that in comparison to Jagger's design, Adrian's would be less dignified. That could partly be a reaction against such realism as the mud on the wheels. More importantly, it was a recognition that the piece's frenzy of hurried action lacked solemnity, and the permanence and 'stillness' that need to characterise a memorial.

Adrian's doubly right-angled composition, which cleverly achieves a compact grouping in the statuette, would become a liability if magnified. Which side would be the face? It ought to be one of the rectangle's longer sides, and logically should surely be that which shows the gun pointing towards the front line's imagined enemy. Then, however, the viewer would not see the two men crouched behind the gun shield. The opposite side would give a view of these two soldiers preparing the field gun to fire, but now the gun barrel is hidden beyond the shield. Thus neither view would give full recognition to both the artillery men and the artillery. Jagger by contrast placed stationary men on separate foreground bases at the sides of a large plinth, placed the menacing aimed but inactive howitzer on top of the plinth, and portrayed activity only in the background bas reliefs. Each component is distinct.

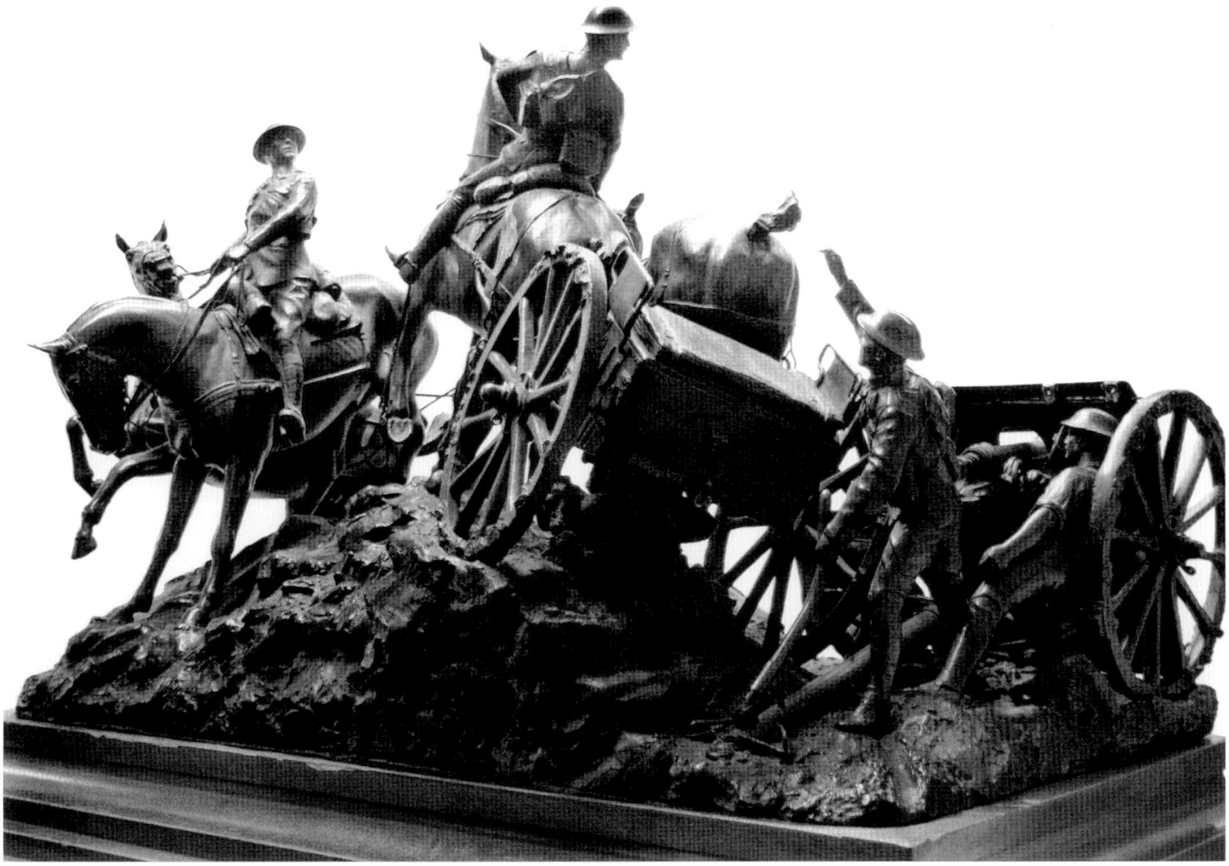

Action Front, statuette of Royal Horse Artillery field gun team; Royal Academy exhibit, 1921 (model) and 1925 (bronze)

In considering 'Action Front' it is better to forget the statue that never was and just look at the statuette that exists. Rightly it is in the museum of the King's Troop, who still fire thirteen-pounders ceremonially. It is exhibited below eye level in a position where it may be readily seen from all four sides. In both design and execution, it is a superb work. The accuracy of details of the portrayal of machinery, men and horses is beyond question; the whole conveys a complete picture of how a field gun was brought into action. The human element is even more striking than the hardware. Here is physical exertion and trained teamwork, each gunner fulfilling his ordered part though all are under the stress of urgency, best expressed in the strained expression of the man signalling to the riders, who look back anxiously while coping with the task of controlling two nervous horses sliding on the muddy terrain. The expertise and humanity of the sculpture well justify Adrian's assessment that it was one of the best pieces he ever did.

The Royal Gloucestershire Hussars Memorial (1922)

For a host of reasons, Adrian must have been pleased when a committee presided over by the Duke of Beaufort, Honorary Colonel of the Royal Gloucestershire Hussars, invited him to sculpt bas reliefs for their Great War regimental memorial. In the latter part of the 19th and into the 20th century the Duke of Beaufort had bred prize-winning foxhounds of the kind Adrian admired and sculpted. The yeomanry regiment had troops stationed in towns he knew – Monmouth and Newport through his first wife's family, and Cheltenham because of its horse-racing. He knew too from his own military experience the kind of Middle Eastern hot deserts over which those troops had fought. There the RGH had been brigaded with the 'sturdy Australian' mounted infantry, whom Adrian admired and had commemorated in Adelaide, and they had got on well with them. Also, many of Adrian's acquaintances had had contacts with the regiment: in the pre-War years, French, Roberts, Evelyn Wood and Allenby had all inspected it, and it had provided an escort for Baden-Powell when he received the freedom of Cardiff. But more material than any of that was that Field Marshal Allenby, while on leave from Palestine, gave Adrian sittings for the portrait of him watching his troops advancing on Jerusalem, and during those sessions would have spoken to Adrian, as one ex-Inniskilling Dragoons cavalryman to another, about the successful performance of the cavalry in his Egyptian Expeditionary Force's Palestine campaign. Adrian 'greatly enjoyed' his times with Allenby. The RGH commission was an opportunity both to play to his artistic strength of portraying horses and to pay tribute to part of the cavalry arm of Allenby's army. The memorial would be most unusual amongst 1914-18 memorials in that the commemoration would not be of deaths on the Western Front but of those of 'the forgotten soldiers' of the Great War. True, the men of the Egyptian Expeditionary Force had a higher survival rate then those of the British Expeditionary Force, (though even a slight wound could prove fatal if the man lay in the blazing sun without water), because the battles were smaller and briefer and the enemy's artillery firepower less overwhelming, but the discomforts of the campaign were just as great, and there was little or no chance of a Blighty leave. The memorial had been very well earned.

The RGH soldiers who fell in the Boer War had been commemorated by a stained glass window in Gloucester Cathedral Chapter House. The memorial for the World War was to be designed by the London architects Cash and Wright, and erected on the Cathedral's College Green. It is a tall cross which, with its pedestal, rises 35 feet high. The cross rests on an octagonal superbase that displays the regiment's badges and lists vertically in chronological order the countries and territory – Egypt, Gallipoli, Sinai, Palestine and Syria – in which it fought. The lower, again octagonal, pedestal holds a portrait format bronze panel of signed bas relief by Adrian on each of its four broader sides. Between them narrower side panels bear, in raised lettering in alphabetical, not rank, order, more than 200 names of those who lost their lives. The whole stands on a base approached over a wide three-stepped platform. It is a bold, simple symmetrical design, in harmony with its Christian setting, and comfortably fitting into daily life on the Green. In good weather cats from the houses of the Cathedral Close sunbathe on the platform until their place is taken by office workers and visitors eating their sandwiches. So on many days the public perch within a few inches of Adrian's remarkably narrative and interesting commemorative art. It never suffers graffiti attacks.

The funding for the memorial came from relatives of the fallen and members or ex-members of the regiment. The unveiling on 29 April 1922 was preceded by a memorial service. The large and representative congregation included hussars from the armoured car company which had replaced the cavalry in post-War reorganisation. Movingly, the anthem used had been composed by one of the regiment's subalterns, Lt. Graham Anderson, killed in action in December 1917. Afterwards everyone processed to the Union Jack-shrouded memorial, which was attended by a regimental guard of honour. General Sir Philip Chetwode, who had commanded Allenby's Desert Column, which at times included the RGH, carried out the unveiling. His address gave an account of the RGH's service and sacrifice, including the fighting in Gallipoli, where its active strength had been reduced from 390 to 69. He closed with a prescient warning that the future might again involve war: 'It may not be in our day, but in the day of our children, the cry will again be for men.' A carving of one of the regiment's tanks operating in the Western Desert, placed on the memorial's bottom tier after 1939-45, shows that his foreboding was fulfilled.

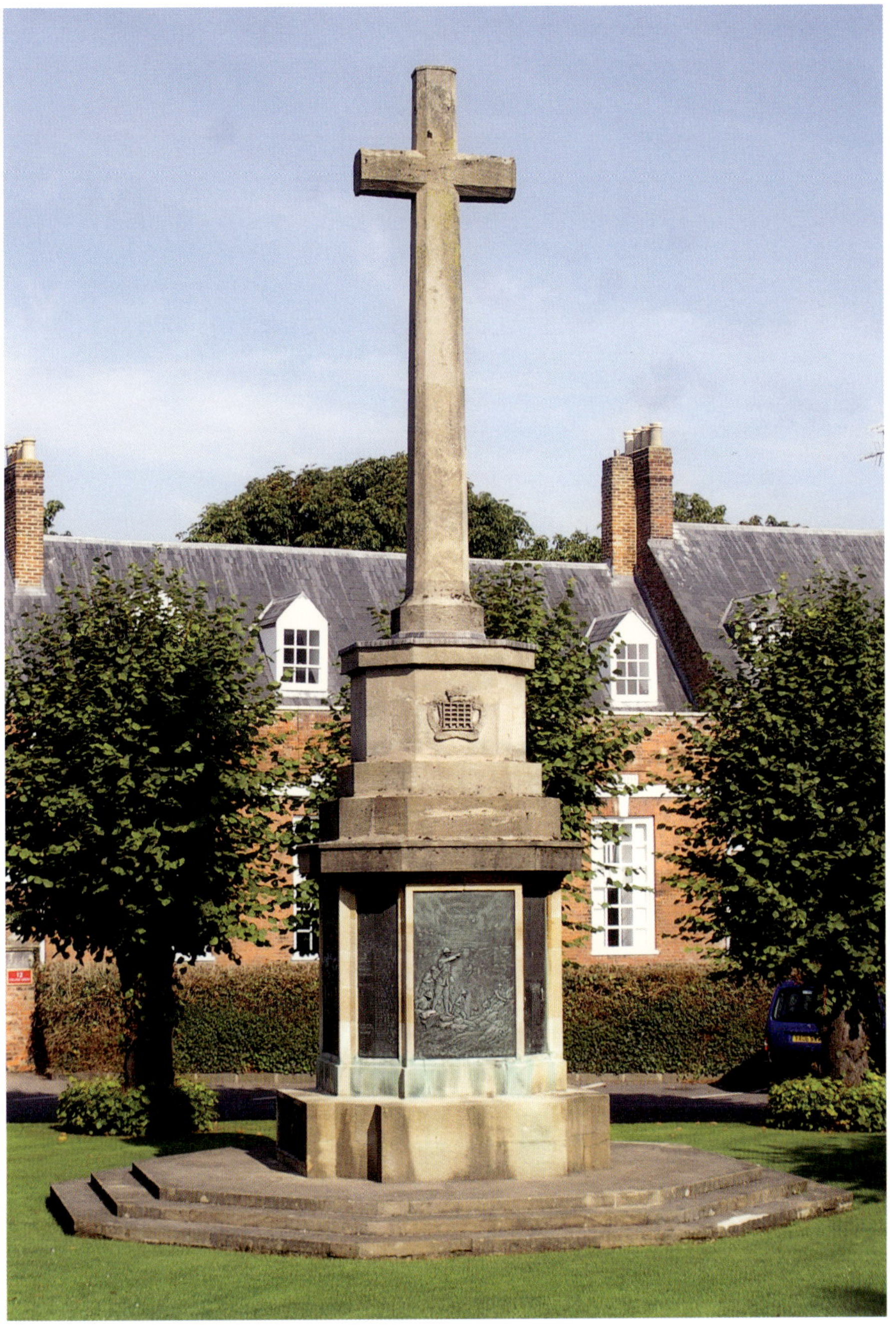

Royal Gloucestershire Hussars Memorial, 1922,
Gloucester Cathedral College Green

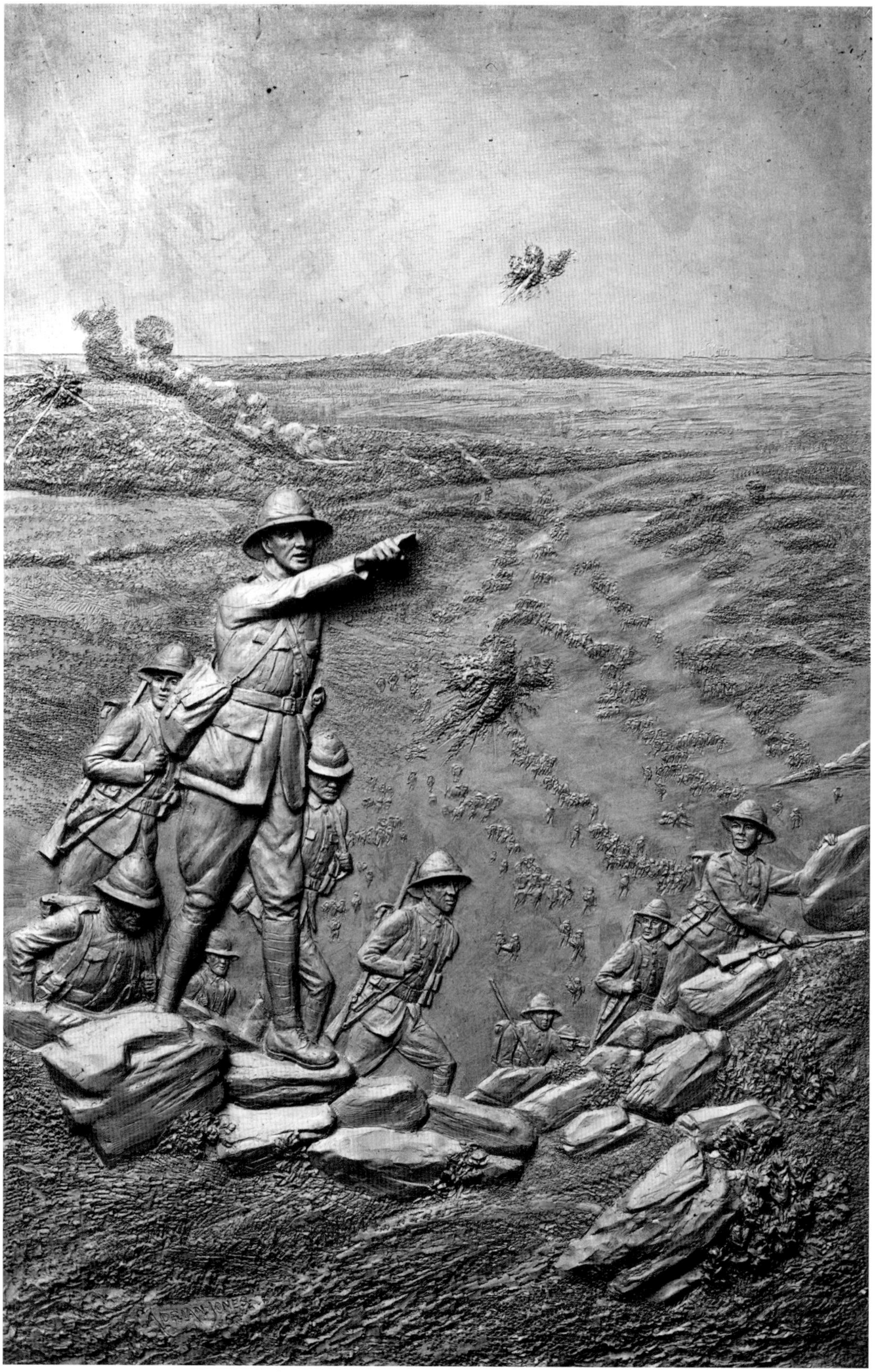
ADRIAN JONES

The Royal Gloucestershire Hussars Memorial: bas relief, Gallipoli 1915, Scaling Chocolate Hill Like many yeomanry and territorial units, the RGH spent most of the War's first year guarding Britain's east coast against the Germans who never invaded. They were then sent not to France but to the doomed campaign in Gallipoli. They disembarked first in Alexandria in April 1915, to be met by one of the trials that frequently lay ahead: a severe sandstorm. On the voyage out they had not lost a single horse or mule, a reflection of their good horsemastership and of how steamers had improved and shortened voyage times since Adrian's unfortunate troopship experiences. In August came the order to proceed to Gallipoli – dismounted. That last word can cause great chagrin in a cavalry regiment. The horses had to be left in Egypt; the men had to learn to use infantry equipment. However, the RGH were less dismayed by the transformation to infantry than others might have been. At pre-War inspection exercises 'Bobs' Roberts had forewarned them that although in a war they would continue to carry out the cavalry roles of reconnaissance and screening for the main force, they would undoubtedly also have to fight on foot. Now that rifles could kill at 2,000 yards it would be folly for cavalrymen to expose themselves as inviting sword-waving targets. The RGH took pride in their own shooting: they had a fine record of success in yeomanry competitions at pre-War Bisley rifle meetings and were keen on the prospect of taking on the enemy Turks and Germans. One hopes that Adrian heard how as the paddle steamer used in normal times by Isle of Man holidaymakers pulled away from the transport ship which had brought the RGH from Alexandria, an officer sounded 'Gone Away' on his hunting horn. The Hussars came ashore on 'A' Beach, Suvla Bay.

The Gallipoli campaign had been in progress, murderously, since April, though 'progress' is hardly the apt word, for the enemy had confined the beachhead to just 600 yards inland. On the panel facing the Cathedral, subscribed 'Gallipoli 1915', Adrian depicts the scene on 21 August 1915 when the 2nd Mounted Division (more accurately Dismounted Division), which included the RGH, took part in an attack on the Turkish lines at Suvla Bay. They are crossing the dry Salt Lake in the background and then scaling Chocolate Hill, another misnomer, as it was anything but a sweet place. An officer, fresh and confident in this, his first experience of real warfare, one arm thrown forward in a pose reminiscent of the Shropshire Tommy on Adrian's contemporary Bridgnorth Memorial, points the line of advance. Behind him troops burdened by infantry backpacks labour upwards. By 1922 Adrian considered that the nation had 'had quite enough of memorials that seemed to revive the war spirit'. Major-General Sir Ian Hamilton, then commander of the British force on Gallipoli, wrote of the 21st August operation:

> The advance of these English yeomen was a sight calculated to send a thrill of pride through anyone with a drop of English blood running in their veins. Such superb martial spectacles are rare in modern war. Here, for a mile and a half there was nothing to conceal a mouse ... not a man was there who hung back or hurried.

That is not the tone of Adrian's bas relief, which at first sight appears a remarkably low key evocation of a tragic day which claimed the lives of a dozen yeomen. He shows the complete lack of cover on Salt Lake, across which lines of men stretch into the distance until they are almost indistinguishable from the landscape. He shows too the problem of clambering up Chocolate Hill: its crest prevents the men engaging the enemy – hence the rifles slung unused over their shoulders. Meanwhile the Turks are able to drop death on the British from overhead shrapnel bursts. Adrian of course could not show a death in foreground close-up even if he had wanted to: with only twelve RGH men killed, distressed relatives would have been left wondering which of the twelve it was. Closer inspection reveals, to the left of the helmet of the extreme right hand yeoman, a distant small detail in very low relief of one or perhaps two prone casualties. Nowhere else on the four panels is death or injury portrayed.

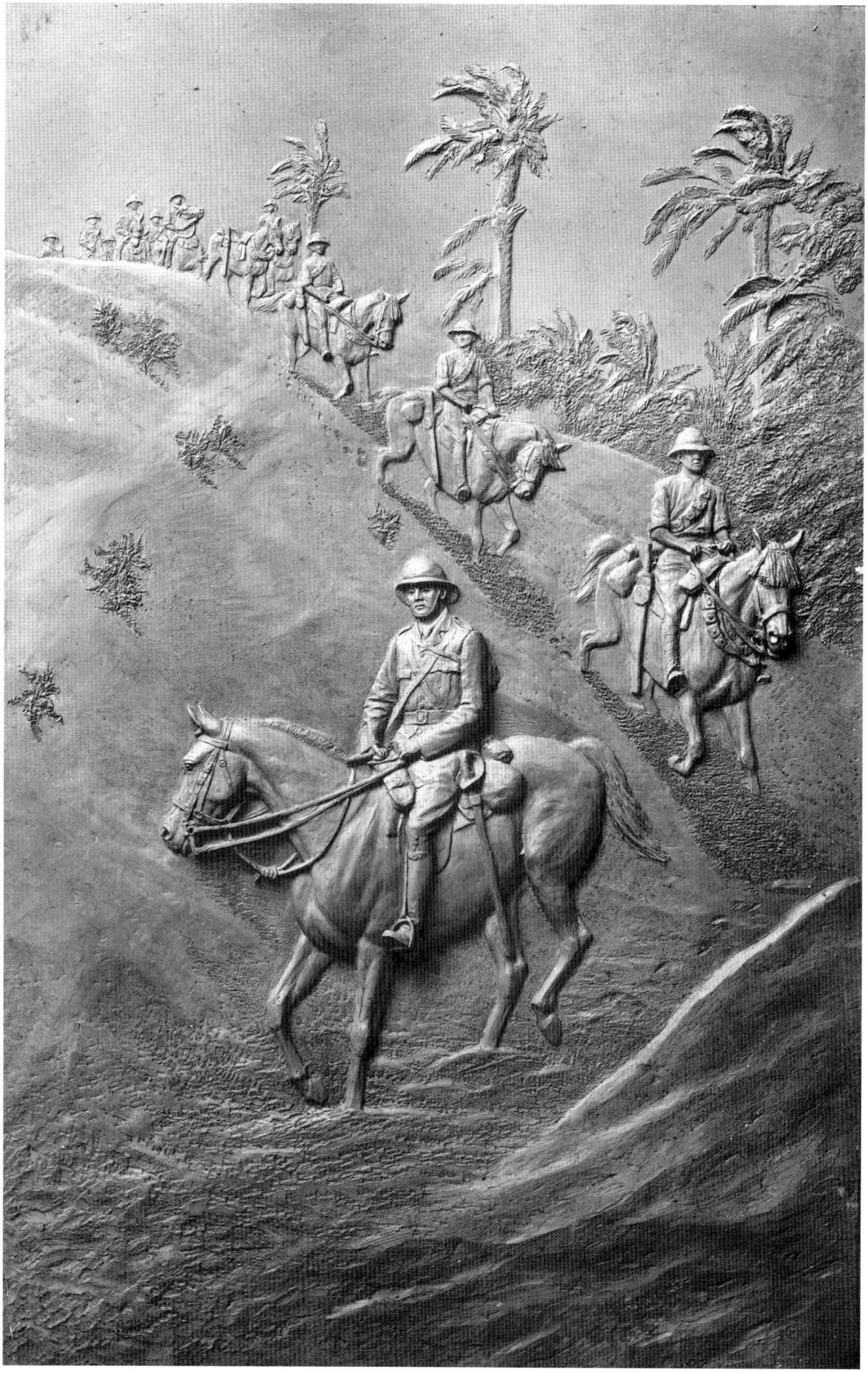

The Royal Gloucestershire Hussars Memorial: bas relief: Sinai 1916, The Sand of the Desert. On the side of the memorial facing away from the Cathedral, is the panel 'Sinai 1916'. 'The Sand of the Desert' is a scene based on a pocket camera snap taken at the time. An RGH patrol returning from a reconnaissance descends a sandhill past scrubby bushes. The eager, fresh faces of the officer and young soldiers of the first panel are gone. The leading officer's eyes are heavy-lidded, and his tired face is drained of all animation. There may have been a skirmish; the empty saddle of the led horse cresting the sandhill suggests at least one casualty suffered. But here there is no immediate danger. The officer's sword is sheathed, and each man's firearm is in its bucket. The enemy now is the desert itself. The hooves of the officer's horse are buried fetlock deep, and the troopers' horses, burdened with the extra weight of bandolier on man and beast, sink equally deep as they file down the soft sand slope. Such arduous cavalry patrolling had to be undertaken despite debilitating thirst. An RGH officer noted in his diary: 'Horses are constantly without water for thirty six hours.' Nothing heroic is happening. As Adrian knew from personal veterinary experience with desert columns, soldiering in the Middle East is a test of endurance.

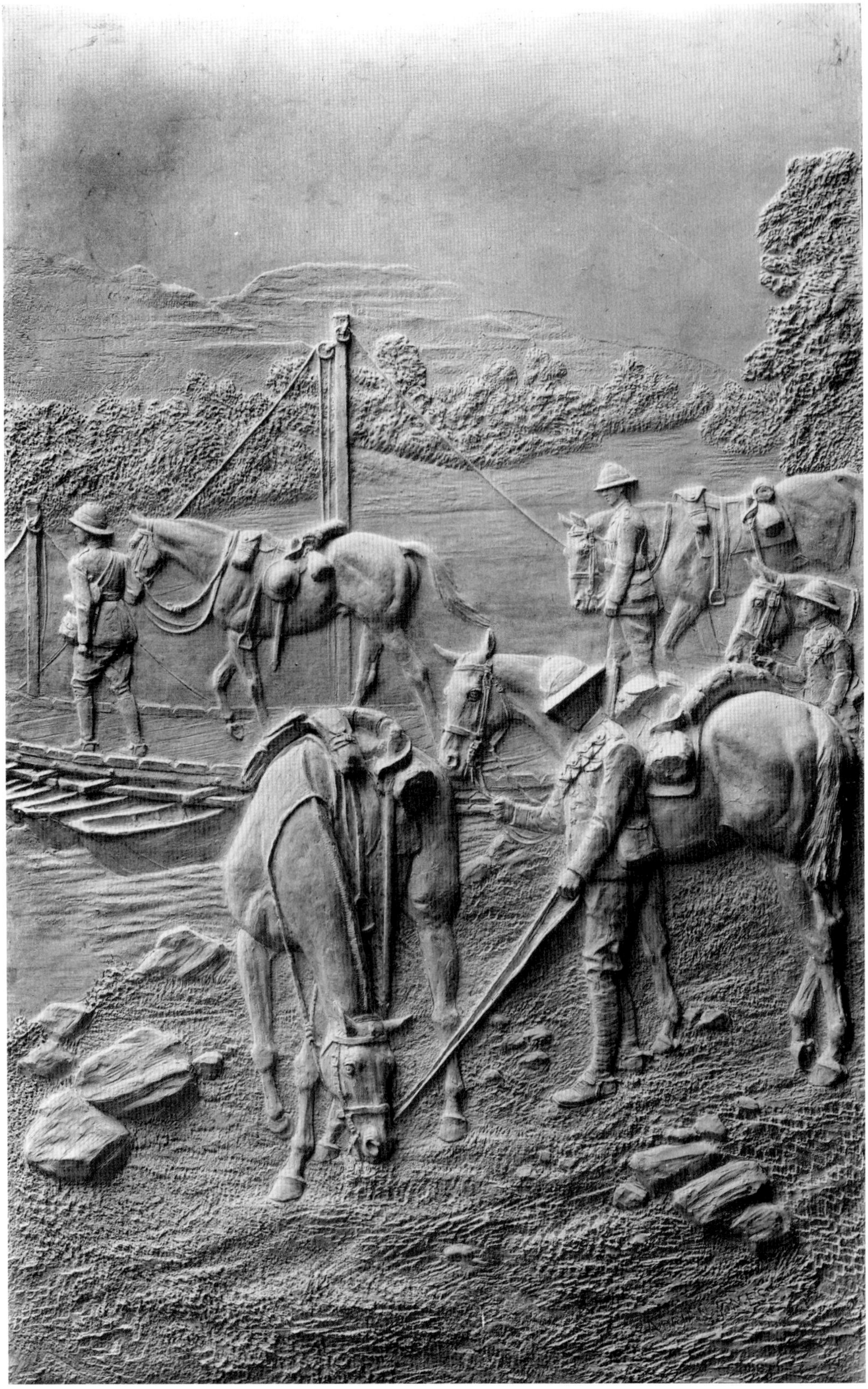

The Royal Gloucestershire Hussars Memorial: bas relief: Palestine 1917, Crossing the Jordan. The bas relief on the north face is 'Palestine 1917': 'Crossing the Jordan', (though the breakthrough crossing came in 1918 during Allenby's advance on Damascus). An officer leads his horse over a pontoon bridge of boats. Behind, troop horses are positioned showing left flanks. Adrian, ever a stickler for accurate and significant detail, thereby creates the chance to show that by this later stage in the campaign the regiment is fully re-equipped as cavalry: the hussars have their swords back. Though the middleground shows the symbolic moment of crossing the Jordan, the foreground interest is two horses being led not to the bridge but to the river bank to drink. It was a rare blessed moment when a surface stream could be used to water the horses and fill the men's water bottles.

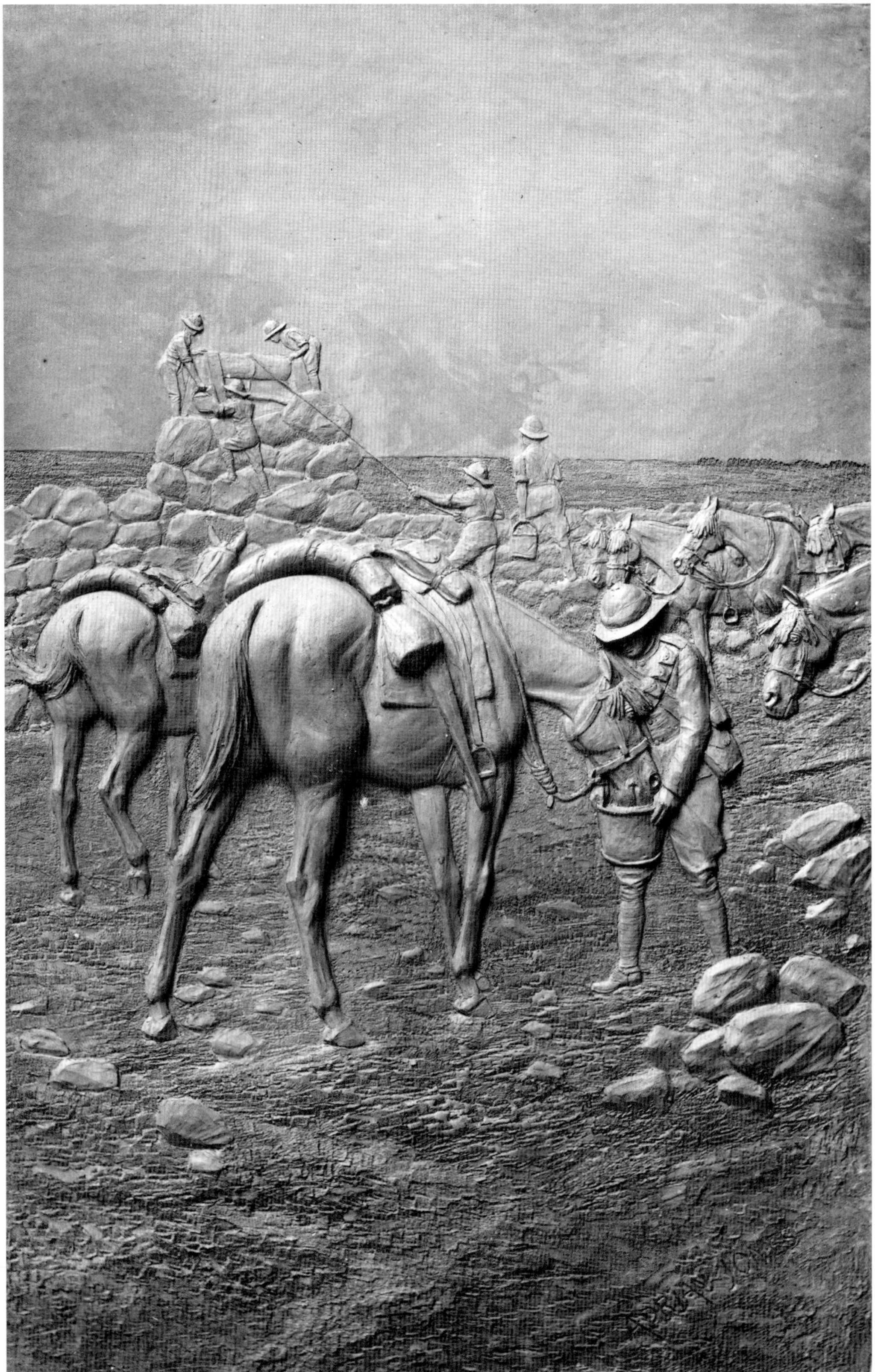

The Royal Gloucestershire Hussars Memorial: bas relief: Syria 1918, Watering Horses. Adrian returned to the vital matter of water for his last panel. This, on the south face, is 'Syria 1918': 'Watering Horses'. The regiment had spent summer in the inferno of the Jordan valley, well below sea level. Temperatures above 130°F, humidity, malaria-bearing mosquitoes, sand flies which caused septic sores, scorpions and lice, all contributed to produce dispirited horses and sick men. But the final stage of the campaign was one of pursuit of a fleeing enemy, as fast as possible. Wherever they could during their retreat the Turks destroyed the water-lifting apparatus of the wells, which were generally deep. An officer recorded that 'the watering of the horses was thus a task ranging from the tedious and difficult to the impossible'. Against a backdrop of cloudless, pitiless sky and barren desert, Adrian depicts men in shirtsleeve order toiling to raise and fetch water. He includes such telling details as the fly fringes above the horses' eyes, designed to give some protection from the persistent pests. The scene is an evocation of discomfort, heat, thirst and demanding labour, and at the same time emphasises the logistical imperative that in order to operate, cavalry must gain access to water.

The Royal Gloucestershire Hussars memorial is markedly more informative than most others. Adrian could have chosen more dramatic subjects from the regiment's wartime experiences. He could have shown A Squadron's outnumbered and outgunned defence of the oasis of Qatia in the Sinai province of Egypt in 1916, a sacrifice still remembered at the Memorial on the anniversary of the defeat; or, for something more heartening, the regiment's capture in 1918 of Nazareth, at the gallop with swords drawn in the highest cavalry tradition; or something horrific from the spell in static trench warfare at Gaza in 1917. However, his own wishes, and the dimensions of the panels, led him to eschew large scenes apart from the crossing of Salt Lake. It would be just possible to walk round the monument and think that the RGH never fired a shot in anger or took casualties – until the eye falls upon the narrower panels of names and the inscription 'Who Gave Their Lives'. The names remember the Hussars' dead; it is enough that the panels illustrate and commemorate their powers of soldiering on in tough campaigning in which the RGH first acquitted themselves resiliently as infantry and then as part of the most successful cavalry campaign in modern history. The restrained bas reliefs tell of lives which helped achieve complete and sweeping victory.

Artistically too the monument is a success. The command of composition and perspective, enhanced by the way the foreground components are in higher relief than those of the background, give a coherent pictorial presentation of what Adrian was commissioned to commemorate. Any weakness is in the background. Where the rains of most of a century have streaked the bronze with green, it can be difficult to recognise a very low relief shell burst or piece of scrub.

The local press was impressed enough by the memorial at its unveiling to report 'these panels being by Adrian Jones, RA'. He must have enjoyed reading that imagined elevation to Royal Academician – and he kept the newspaper cutting

Queen's Bays and Inniskilling Dragoons Regimental Memorials (1927 and 1929)

In his eighties, 'for love of my old regiment', Adrian designed and executed 1914-18 memorials for two of the cavalry regiments with whom he had served as a subaltern in his twenties and thirties. Whilst these were expressions of fond loyalty, and he charged only expenses, they also offered a different challenge. For his previous military memorials, in addition to intrinsic artistic considerations, he had to pay heed to the surroundings; now the extra consideration was portability. The regiments wished to transport the memorials with them in their postings around the world. That was hardly surprising. The Bays had been serving abroad almost continuously since 1914, and both they and the Inniskillings were in India when they conceived the idea of having a memorial to their regiment's dead. For easier implementation of the project, both entrusted planning and contact with Adrian to an English committee chaired by the Colonel of the Regiment.

The earlier approach to Adrian came from the Bays. His design in response to their request for a memorial was sent by the English Committee to India, and approved. The Bays had much to commemorate. They had gone out to France with the first contingent of the British Expeditionary Force and then soldiered on to play a part in many of the War's major engagements. Their experience was the opposite to that of the Royal Gloucestershire Hussars. Whereas the RGH, having first fought dismounted in Gallipoli, ended the War as fast moving cavalry under General Allenby's command in Palestine and Syria, the Bays on the Western Front began under Allenby in his Cavalry Division, and during the retreat from Mons in late August and the start of September 1914 did real traditional cavalry work in a war of movement; but as early as the first battle of Ypres in October and November they had increasingly to act as infantry. Unlike the yeomanry, the Bays and Inniskillings were to remain horsed units throughout the War, though when the troops went forward into the front lines, the horses remained behind, cared for by as few men as possible. After the exhausting hours in the saddle during the retreat from Mons, when the cavalry's protective screen saved the British

Expeditionary Force from being overwhelmed, and after the action at Nery when the Bays as part of the 1st Cavalry Brigade had severely damaged a whole German cavalry division, as the War became stuck in a pattern around the Ypres salient, life for men and horses became a routine of suffering.

Mud, barbed wire and cratered ground are the antitheses of what cavalry soldiers would want for their horses. In *The Last Hurrah* Richard Holmes quotes the words of Private Clarke of the Bays about the horses: 'How those poor creatures suffered ... they broke your heart, especially when you passed the injured ones, left to die, in agony and screaming with pain and terror'. At the first battle for Ypres, Private Clarke was but one man in a sustained clash of arms involving more men than any earlier battle in British military history. The Kaiser had arrived nearby to be ready for a triumphal entry when his determined army had taken the town; the British and French were determined it would not fall; neither force found it possible to advance against the other, so they dug in. It was the start of trench warfare and of an appalling rise in the numbers of wounded men and corpses. Above any other confrontation, the linchpin battle of First Ypres was the one most particularly remembered at the Bays' Service of Dedication for Adrian's portable memorial.

The later years of the war saw the Bays and Inniskillings doing spells in the trenches. By the end, the new battle honours that would be inscribed on Adrian's memorials could have been those of an infantry regiment. Thus the Inniskillings pedestal features familiar names such as Somme, Cambrai, Amiens, Hindenburg line, St Quentin Canal and Flanders. It had been tough for the cavalrymen to act as infantry. They had not undergone annual training in how to dig; they were less equipped than an infantry battalion with the equipment such as entrenching tools, camp cookers and periscopes which made trench life a little safer and more bearable; and because some men had to be kept back to feed, water and exercise the regiment's horses, they faced putting fewer men, more thinly spread, into their allocated section of the front line. Meanwhile they watched aeroplanes taking over reconnaissance, and tanks threatening to become technically efficient enough to replace them as the shock weapon. They also had the frustration of waiting to exploit the breakthrough that never quite came. To saddle up and then stand to, only to find nothing worthwhile happening afterwards, was dispiriting, though the British gift for humorous realism ensured that morale did not crack.

The Service of the Dedication of Adrian's Queen's Bays regimental war memorial at the Cavalry Barracks in Colchester on 17 July 1927 was both a parade and an Anglican service. It was a Sunday. The regiment's band led the parade and the crowd in the hymn 'Fight the Good Fight'; there followed prayers, readings of Psalm 123 and from Chapter Three of *The Book of Wisdom* ('Their going from us to be utter destruction ... As gold in the furnace hath he tried them, and received them as a burnt offering', which some of those listening must have thought searingly apt and accurate); two more hymns; prayers for the departed; benediction; Last Post and Reveille from the regiment's trumpeters, and 'God Save The King'.

With the extraordinary exception of the inauguration of his Peace Quadriga by King George V and Queen Mary, the unveilings of Adrian's works were big occasions. The Colchester ceremonial was for a 'private' memorial which would travel with the Bays, yet 5,000 spectators lined the sides of the barrack square. Women put on their cloche hats and brought their children, including babies still in their prams. Nevertheless, press accounts recorded that 'a silence deep in its solemnity reigned' when the Union Jack was pulled off the memorial, and the crowd's singing was 'moving and inspiring'. Monday's *Daily Mirror* published five photographs: four general views and a close-up of Adrian, present wearing his top hat. He was almost the most senior Bays veteran there, second only to another in his eighties who had joined in 1865. An impressive array of current and former military top brass had come also: at least seven generals, including Lieutenant General Sir Charles Briggs, who commanded the 1st Cavalry Division in the War, and the present Inspector-General of the Cavalry; all the colonels of the Colchester Garrison; and of course a host of Bays Old Comrades, officers and men in their civilian suits but wearing medals. For the Service, the Assistant Chaplain General to the Forces officiated, aided by three other chaplains. (When the Bays rededicated their war memorial, to which the names of the dead of 1939-45 had been added, at Chester in 1949, a time when Adrian's reputation was largely in eclipse, they still did their former officer proud. On that occasion the Chaplain General to the Forces took the service, and the unveiler was King George VI's racegoing consort Queen Elizabeth, who was familiar with and liked Adrian's equine statuettes and paintings in the Royal Collection.)

In 1927 Sir Hew Fanshawe, having unveiled the memorial, addressed the parade and crowd. After a deserved reference to the Bays' performance during the retreat from Mons and 'that brilliant action at Nery', he spoke of the crisis of First Ypres, 'where Allied faltering would have enabled the Germans to sweep round to Calais and occupy the Channel ports closest to England: in the words of Sir John French, there was not only the safety, but actually the very existence of the British Empire at stake. The whole Regiment, I feel sure, would have gladly given their lives for such a stake. They gained in battle the honours of which they are so proud. The memorial, I hope, will be a lasting example and encouragement to the present members of the Queen's Bays, who, I trust, will add further laurels to the Regiment's record'. In expressing hope and trust that the men on parade would emulate the brave deeds of those being commemorated, General Fanshawe was uttering sentiments appropriate for honouring the dead. Personal comment confided to reminiscences or diaries could be bitter. Private Clarke wrote of 'victims of man-made madness' and an officer in another of Adrian's former regiments, Sir Morgan Crofton of the 2nd Life Guards, called the struggle in the Ypres salient 'murder pure and simple'. General Fanshawe concluded by expressing his gratitude to Adrian, 'the designer and sculptor of the beautiful monument'. Then wreaths were laid, and the regiment marched by, followed by the Old Comrades, bowlers and trilby hats doffed in respect as they passed.

The memorial has a central oak panel, with side panels which can be swung to open or closed positions. Above, a pedimented board carries the inscription 'In memory of

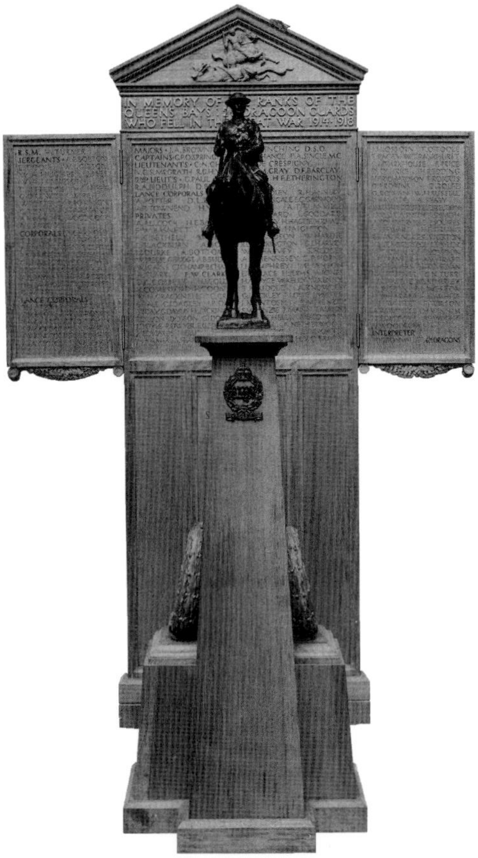

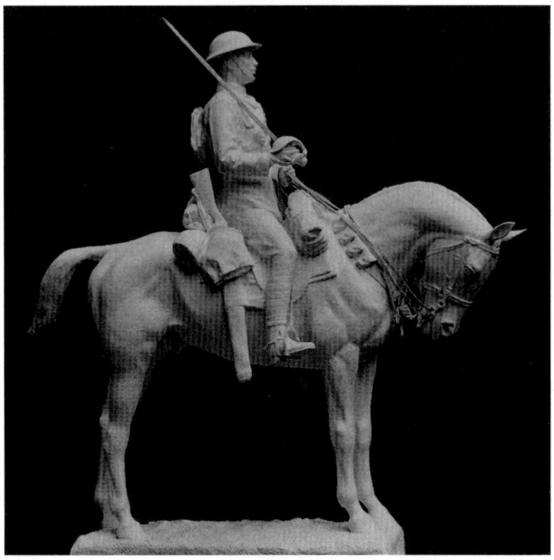

Above: **The Queen's Bays (transportable) Memorial**, 1927.
Below: Detail: **The Queen's Bays Memorial**, bronze mounted trooper statuette

all ranks of the Queen's Bays', and on the panels themselves are listed the 15 officers, 18 non-commissioned officers and 173 other ranks who fell in 1914-18. Before the panels a tapering pedestal, ornamented with the regiment's badge and recording on its sides the Bays' battle honours, reaches up to Adrian's statuette of a mounted trooper in war kit. The memorial is large enough to be a presence in the centre of a barrack square, especially when mounted on a ceremonial platform as it was for its unveiling, yet it can be packed into two cases and readily transported.

At a march past, the statuette is seen head on. Trooper and horse are stationary, the pose that of a mounted sentry. Adrian chose to portray a soldier of the Bays as he would have been in the early months of the War, the time when because the battlefield situation was still fluid the cavalry had opportunities to act in the traditional way. This Bay rests a 1908 pattern cavalry sword, at the slope, on his shoulder. In 1915 the British cavalry on the Western Front had these swords withdrawn as they were considered unsatisfactory for trench warfare. So Adrian's memorial of 1927 is nostalgic as well as dignified; it commemorates the men who died and the way they fought, a way, 'lest we forget', now passed into history.

The Inniskillings memorial for 1914-18

This was unveiled by Field Marshal Allenby at York Cavalry Barracks on 10 May 1929. Not just a way of fighting, but the 6th Inniskilling Dragoons themselves had then passed into history. In the post-War reduction in cavalry numbers, they had been amalgamated with the 5th Dragoon Guards. As the Inniskillings were the junior of the two regiments, they lost their number and their historic badge of Inniskilling Castle with St George's flag floating triumphantly above. Though, in a gesture of compensation, the badge was added to the new regiment's standard, the Inniskillings felt they had been absorbed rather than amalgamated. They determined that all ranks who had fought and died as 6th Inniskilling Dragoons should be remembered. In response to their Committee's approach, Adrian offered a design, which was approved, called 'The Empty Saddle'. This was an effective but not a new concept. The artist J.P. Beadle had painted a picture with that title which proved a popular success when exhibited in 1911 at the Royal Academy, where Adrian would have seen it. The depicted scene showed two mounted lancers in the Boer War returning across the veldt from a patrol. The second soldier is leading a third horse, which has the empty saddle, and as an indication that a comrade has been lost he is carrying both his own lance and the retrieved lance of the missing man. As related earlier in this chapter, on the Sinai bas relief panel of his RGH memorial Adrian had used a patrolling scene incorporating a led riderless horse, though with no dramatic emphasis on that component. Then in 1925 at the RA Summer Exhibition he had exhibited a statuette with the title 'The Empty Saddle', and now he used it again.

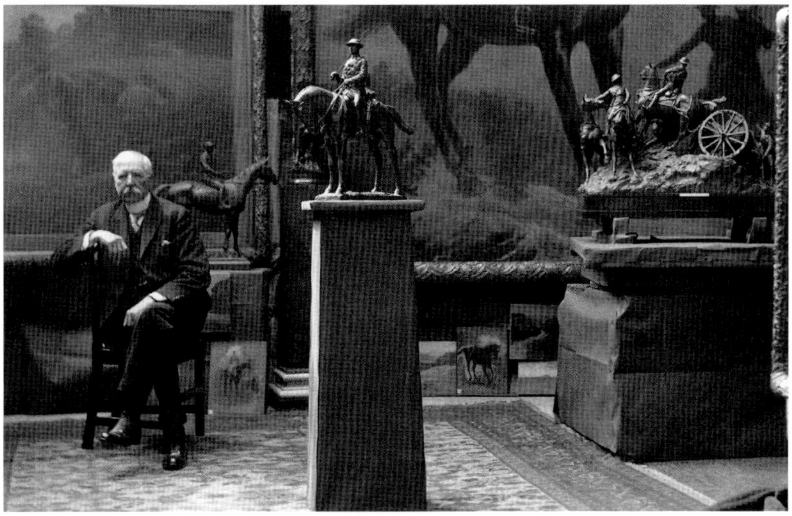

Adrian Jones amidst paintings and casts of statuettes in his studio's display area, c.1930

The memorial's overall design is similar to that of the Bays. The statuette stands upon a pedestal; the front bears the regiment's badge, and the sides list battle honours from the regiment's history and from 1914-

18. A three piece screen behind displays a cross of St George, the patron saint of cavalry, and carries the inscription and the names of 185 men who fell. It could quickly be dismantled and reassembled so that it could travel with the new regiment, and thus in post 1939-45 years it often became a British war memorial stationed in Germany. At its inauguration in York both ex-Inniskillings and ex-5th Dragoon Guardsmen paraded to pay it due honour.

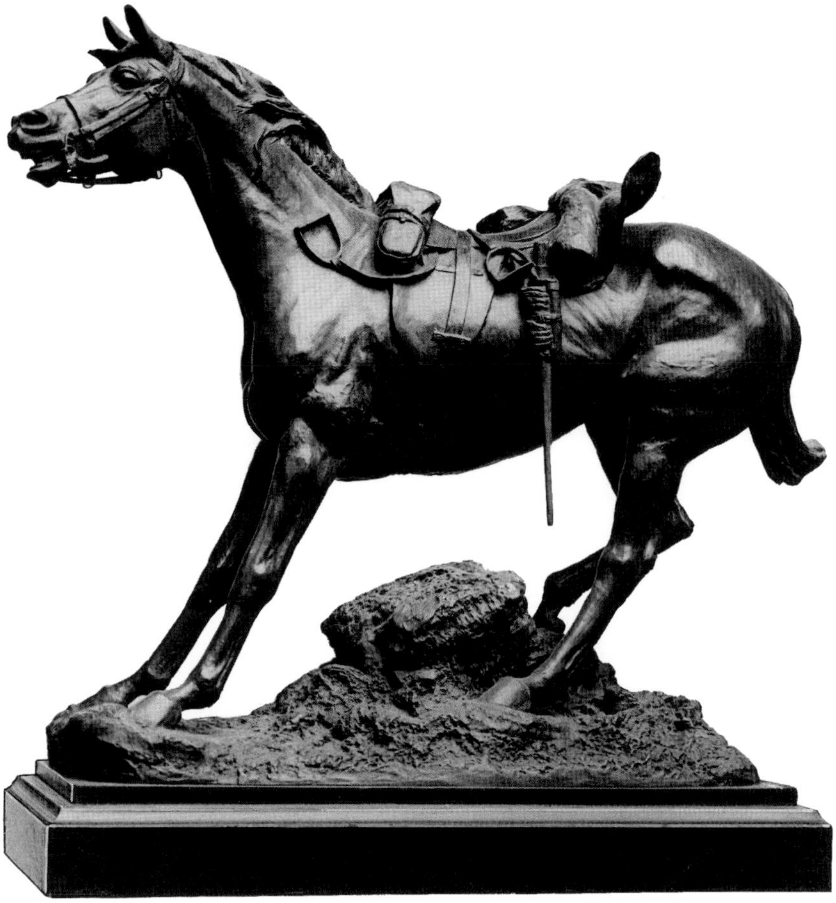

Detail: The **Inniskilling Dragoons Memorial**, 1929: **The Empty Saddle**, bronze statuette (part of transportable memorial)

As a war memorial it is unusual and striking: unusual in that it has no human figure, and striking in its portrayal of fright. The horse is terrified. Adrian's artistic task was to make it clear, even to an uninitiated or unknowledgeable viewer, that the saddle is not empty because of some everyday riding accident. Adrian wrote in *Memoirs:* 'A charger merely standing still with saddle and accoutrements would suggest to anyone conversant with cavalry that the owner had merely "taken a toss".' This memorial horse is certainly not 'merely standing still'. Its attitude is startled and tense, and the wild disorder of the stirrups – one has been thrown right over the horse's back – reflects the wild galloping and rearing of its flight. Key parts of the harness such as the reins are missing, and the saddle is damaged. In Adrian's words, the piece is 'suggesting that the rider has been carried away by a shell'. Like all too many human combatants, the horse has suffered shell shock. In Adrian's last memorial, the final word has gone to the War's most destructive arm, the artillery. The man has become one of war's victims off stage. In this arresting and original composition by an ex-veterinary surgeon artist, the dead Inniskillings are remembered, in the mind's eye, but through the image of a frightened horse. It is an image to be looked at with what the Victorian poet Coventry Patmore termed 'the synthetic eye': understanding what Adrian is showing deepens one's understanding of the sufferings of cavalrymen in the Great War of 1914-18. In his last memorial he had revisited his approach to his first large statue, 'Duncan's Horses': through images of maddened horses reflecting evils in the human world.

Chapter Seventeen: 'Old comrades of the Great War'
1924: The Cavalry of the Empire Memorial

Although the Cavalry of the Empire Memorial was not the last monument Adrian created to commemorate the dead of the Great War, it seems an appropriate one with which to end the account of his work as a sculptor of war memorials,. When in the last fifteen years of his life he reflected on his career in the army and in art, he took particular pleasure in knowing that people gathered annually at his war memorials to remember and honour the dead, and because of his own service with several cavalry regiments, he felt that most strongly about his Cavalry of the Empire memorial at Stanhope Gate in Hyde Park: 'I am glad to think that old comrades of the Great War gather round this memorial every year, distinguished soldiers attend to deliver addresses, and so we keep in touch with the past which may not be forgotten, even when the youngest of those who played a part in it is gathered to his Fathers.' In many ways too this particular statue is a fitting climax to the military career of one who had been so involved both with horses and the Empire.

The commission to sculpt the Cavalry War Memorial delighted Adrian. It came to him from a committee chaired by Brigadier-General the Honourable Osbert Lumley, who had also been in charge of the fundraising. Obviously Adrian, as an artist who had spent more than twenty years attached to horse artillery, dragoon guard, hussar and household cavalry regiments, was an appropriate choice. More relevantly still, he had a record of success in producing both life-size (or larger) military equestrian statues and bas relief cavalry scenes, and the commissioning committee had as their second and final idea a scheme requiring these two.

In the years immediately following the Second Boer War of 1899-1902 Adrian himself had considered the possible nature of a national monument to those men from different parts of the British Empire who had become brothers in death in South Africa. It would not place any emphasis on the defeat of the Boers. Rather it would seek to pay tribute to the spirit of loyalty, brotherhood and sacrifice which had brought volunteers across the seas to do their bit for Queen, then King, and Empire. While it would include infantrymen and gunners, it would have an equestrian group at its summit. That group would give the design a more heroic feel, but its main purpose would be to mark the major role played in the Boer War by mounted men. Adrian translated these ideas into a statuette model. The result was certainly ambitious. Four heraldic couchant lions guard a massive base with curved sides, and on a narrow platform at the front stands the winged allegorical figure of Fame, while at the back on a round mound suggesting the world stands winged Britannia. The two figures' wings rise above the top of the base towards a rocky outcrop on which are busily active British and colonial foot-soldiers, including a kilted soldier from a Highland regiment. Crowning the top is a group of three horsemen, their pith helmets and slouch hats again indicating varied nationalities. Like someone on a medieval battlefield, a trooper waves aloft a curling banner. To produce such an elaborate monument full scale in stone and bronze would have been extremely expensive, and the project proved stillborn, though not before the *Artist* had suggested that 'any committee which may hereafter be formed' could entrust sculpting the human figures to others 'but let the horses and the men they carry be done by the one man we have among us who alone is qualified to do justice to the theme'. It recommended the presumed committee 'to visit the studio of Adrian Jones'.

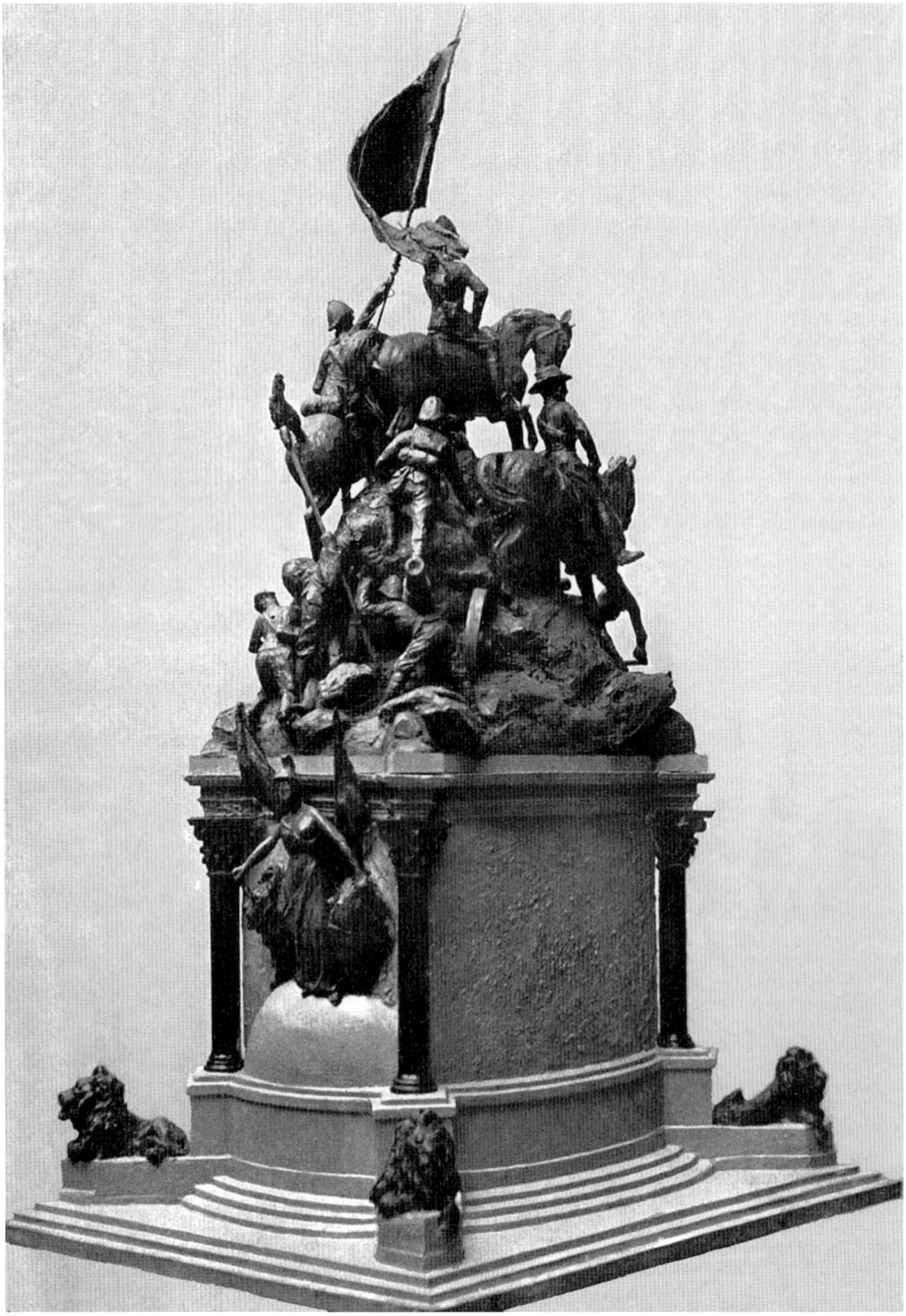

National Memorial to the Fallen in South Africa (Boer War), 1903, studio model, back view. The statue aimed to celebrate comradeship between soldiers from different nations in the British Empire. Adrian was eventually able to execute this idea twenty years later in his Cavalry of the Empire memorial.

Though Adrian's ideas failed to be realised in a National War Memorial for South Africa, he utilised some elements in other post-Boer War works. The mounted cavalryman scouting from the crest of rocks appeared in the South Australia Boer War Memorial of 1904. Soldiers on foot clambering up to the top of a hill to gain a scouting outlook appeared in bas relief in the Carabiniers' Boer War Memorial of 1905. Some ideas were even to appear twenty years later in the Cavalry Memorial. But before that, different proposals for Hyde Park Corner had to be rejected. In 1920 Adrian was amongst those who responded to an anguished cry of 'Why?' from the *Evening Standard* when there was a proposal to erect an Egyptian needle-style 'pylon' there. He gave the newspaper an interview in which he admitted that as the sculptor of the Quadriga he had a personal interest to declare, but nevertheless went on to vent scornful opposition:

> Will Londoners really allow this wonderful [Decimus Burton] arch to be removed or overshadowed by an Egyptian monument which might delight a Pharaoh but is not, therefore, suitable for a city where Pharaohs are at least few and far between? The Pylon would be a permanent slur on British art, a constant declaration to our Continental visitors that British art is so bankrupt in ideas that we have to burrow for artistic corn in Egypt ... A Pylon reminds us of mummies. Are these of any inspiration to an Empire struggling back to life after years spent in the Shadow of Death? ... I hope people will go on asking 'Why?' until the proposal is dropped.

It was.

However, the first proposal of the Cavalry Memorial Committee also involved a column. It had decided that the memorial should feature a symbolic St George, the patron saint of cavalry. This would take the form of a bronze column some fifty feet high inside Hyde Park, near Marble Arch. The column would be an enlarged replica of a field-marshal's baton, surmounted by the figure of St George and the dragon. This design was aimed at commemorating the fallen and simultaneously recording that four cavalry officers of the Great War gained such batons. Wishful thinking added the hope that the sight would give army recruits an incentive to opt for a cavalry regiment. Such incentive was the more necessary because in post-war retrenchment sixteen regiments were being amalgamated into eight, with a consequent effect on *esprit de corps* in an age when individual traditions still evoked strong loyalties. Moreover, a former source of recruits, the horse yeomanry regiments, had been largely wiped out when all but the ten most senior regiments had been told to abandon their horses and accept a mechanised role or disband. However, His Majesty's Office of Works refused to approve the baton scheme, so it lapsed.

Writing his autobiography in the 1930s, Adrian affirmed: 'The Cavalry had every reason to be proud of the part they played in the Great War.' By then that was far from a universally shared view. Opinions were being voiced that to have used a quarter of all shipping from Britain to France during the war to transport horse fodder represented gross misallocation of space that should have been used for munitions, that cavalrymen had led comparatively cosseted lives behind the front line doing nothing much while waiting to exploit breakthroughs that never came, and that Haig and other cavalry generals were moustached donkeys whose battle plans, drawn up in luxurious chateaux, butchered their own men. Such extreme criticisms have since rightfully been corrected (for a start, the vast bulk of the fodder was not for the cavalry's horses but for the 350,000 other horses used by the British army on the Western Front!), and certainly in the early 1920s the predominant mood, despite personal griefs, was gratitude for the great victories of 1918 which had won the war. So Adrian was delighted to receive the commission for the Cavalry Memorial and to carry it out.

'General Lumley asked me to prepare a sketch model design with St George ... for the main motive.' Adrian's first attempt was grandiose, towering up through five tiers. A dead dragon droops over the topmost tier; St George's horse, its stomach perilously close to the pointed scales on the dragon's back, straddles the dragon; and up in the saddle St George holds aloft a long lance. Around the tall middle tier of the pedestal, three cavalrymen of the 1914-18 War, mounted on horses standing on one of Adrian's trademark rocky outcrops, wave lance, sword and rifle towards St George. They are greeting him as a victor, but the sense is more 'Three cheers for St George' than disciplined military salute. St George meanwhile is not acknowledging their waves. Instead he gazes levelly into the distance on his right. Perhaps there he sees the civilians he has saved from the evil dragon standing on the battlemented walls or the hills to which they have fled for safety. The 'toy soldier', placed next to the model base for the studio photograph to give a sense of the planned size of the memorial, suggests that the scaled-up version would have been around forty feet high.

It is temptingly easy to be disparaging about the first design for the Cavalry of the Empire memorial because it is demonstrably inferior to the final one, and the temptation has not been resisted in the paragraph above. However, the subsequent changes were not dictated solely by artistic taste. Adrian had been too ambitious. As Britain slipped towards the severe slump of the 1920s, times were straitened. With no government funding, to raise money sufficient for casting in bronze four horses and their riders, a dragon and a rocky ground, was too demanding. The Committee appreciated the fact that Adrian had met its request that St George should be the dominant feature, and approved the inclusion of Great War soldiers, but asked Adrian for a smaller, more economical design. Their demand for something simpler, reinforced by his awareness that his entry for the Royal Artillery's 1914-18 War memorial was considered insufficiently dignified, was a good discipline for Adrian. He gave the matter 'careful consideration', revised the design and thereafter stuck firmly to his second decisions:

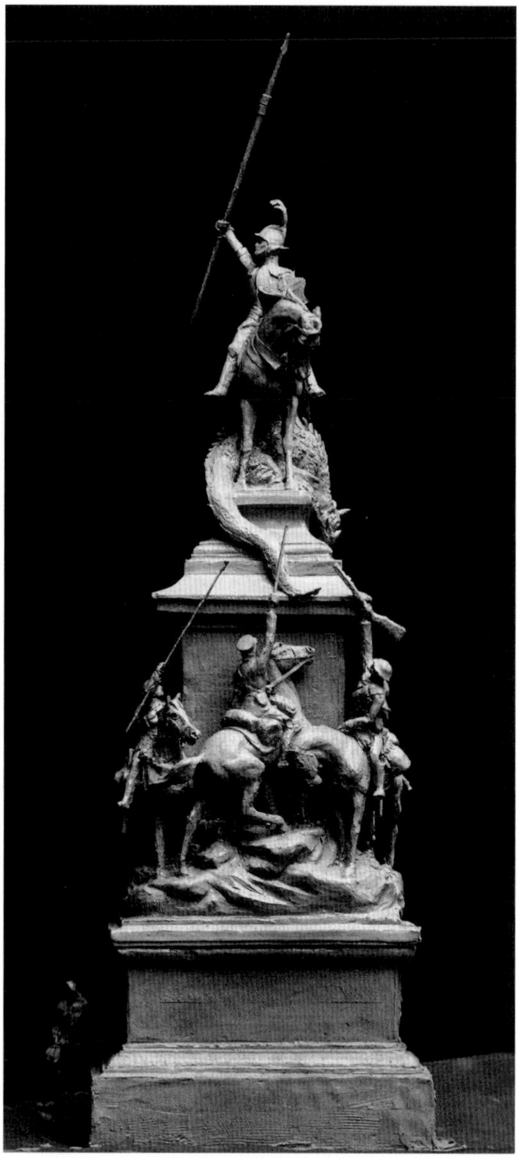

Cavalry of the Empire Memorial: studio model of the initial design, later abandoned

> When a sculptor has to erect a statue in a Royal Park, the situation bristles with difficulties and formalities. All manner of Departments seem not only to have requirements but the right to enforce their wishes, and the work must be submitted to many commissions, most of which will have suggestions, which I am sure they regard as being of value. There is only one thing for a man to do if he wants to survive all these unwelcome but unavoidable attentions; he must make up his mind about his design and allow nothing and nobody to alter it ... Present a firm front to the critics, and then ... face the consequences. If you do this you may succeed in pleasing, though success can never be certain.

He went on to produce a statue which was to lead Field Marshal Lord Allenby to write that 'My wife and I had a good look at the Memorial and think it is out and away the best war memorial in London. In imagination and in dignified execution you have achieved a monument worthy of the Cavalry Arm.'

Adrian adopted some details from the paintings of the Renaissance master Albrecht Dürer. Obviously he would pay some attention to Dürer's 'St George and the Dragon', but he may have paid attention equally to his 'Soldier on Horseback with a Lance' and his 'Knight, Death and Devil'. All three show a knightly figure sitting very upright in the saddle, legs thrust deeply down into low stirrups and feet angled out, helmet worn with visor up, reins held in the right hand. The pose of Adrian's horse, standing still with forelegs squarely planted, partly echoes that in Dürer's picture of St George, but there is no question of exact imitation. To an extent, to achieve the dignity he sought, Adrian had to idealise Dürer's heavier horse. More important than any resemblance of detail was the similarity in technique: both artists pile accurate detail upon accurate detail in pursuit of authenticity, and their supreme technical accomplishment is in the service of, not at the expense of, imagination and feeling. Adrian set himself to do what had never before been attempted in a London statue. He would portray St George in a complete, head to foot, suit of armour.

He was knowledgeable about contemporary military dress, but though he had sculpted a crusader in helmet and chain mail for his 'For the Faith' statuette exhibited (exhibit 1856) in the Royal Academy Summer Exhibition of 1903, he could not claim expertise in medieval armour. Very helpfully, the commissioning Committee obtained the services of a Fellow of the Society of Antiquaries. Major Victor Farquharson was an armour expert who in addition to advising Adrian lent him sketches and rare pieces of real armour. Further important help came from Garter King-at-Arms Sir Henry Burke, who provided pieces from which Adrian could model the arm, breast and back plates of armour, and the sword, spurs and gauntlets. Adrian copied other pieces from sketches of an effigy of the Earl of Warwick that dated from 1454, but replaced the effigy's inappropriate tilting helmet with a graceful light helmet extending over the back of St George's neck. This last piece, of English make and taken from Major Farquharson's private collection, completed the faithful presentation of St George in the character of knight as well as saint. The careful selection of the armour parts produced a late Gothic horseman who was both handsome and unique amongst London's statues. He sits on a powerful horse, sculpted with Adrian's customary anatomical accuracy, the strongly muscled neck reflecting that this is no gelding but a stallion. During the modelling of the statue, various Committee members visited Adrian's studio to view progress. Happily he found the visits of their Chairman, Brigadier Lumley, very welcome, because 'I never worked with a more charming man', and he appreciated the great encouragement he received on the several visits of Lord and Lady Allenby. But when a Viscount on the Committee proposed to him that he should alter the way St George was sitting in the saddle to make it conform to the riding style of the twentieth century cavalrymen whom the statue was commemorating, Adrian refused to change it. Chiefly he argued that then 'it would have been quite contrary to the style of the figure in armour', but also he was going to portray contemporary cavalry in the bas reliefs.

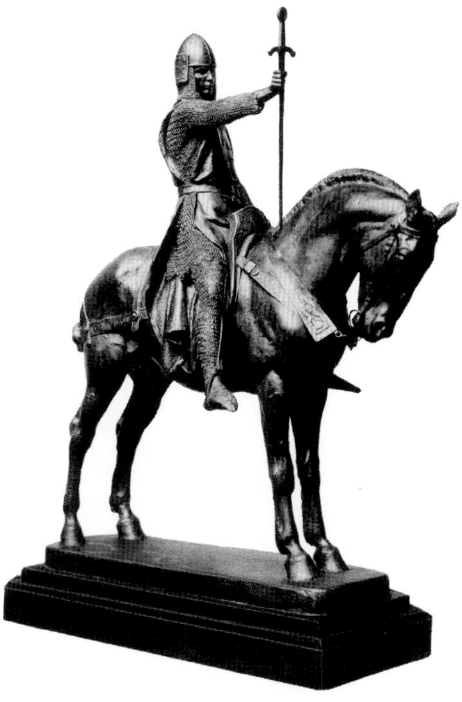

For the Faith, bronze statuette, RA exhibit, 1903

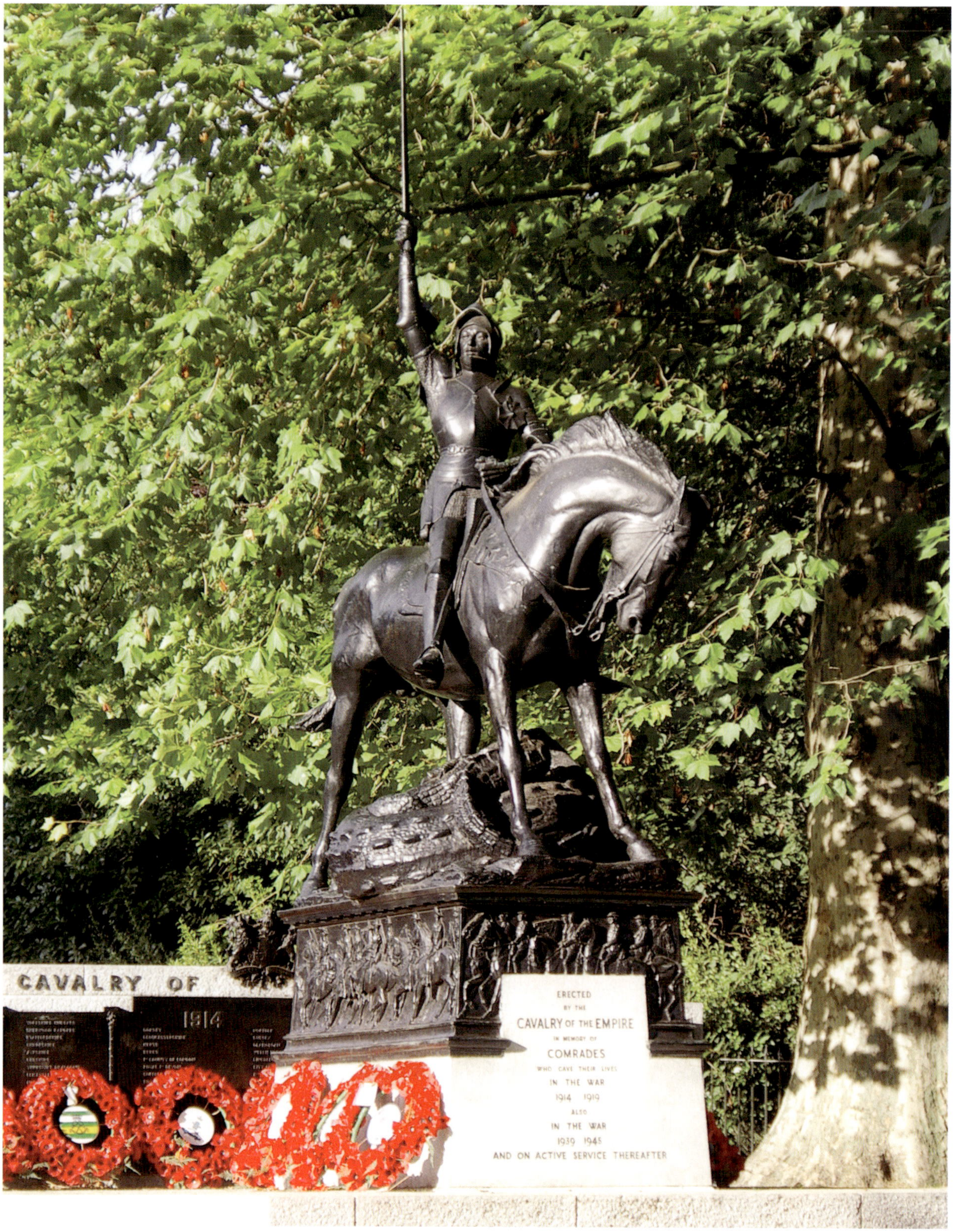

Cavalry of the Empire Memorial, 1924,
now repositioned beside the Serpentine Way, Hyde Park

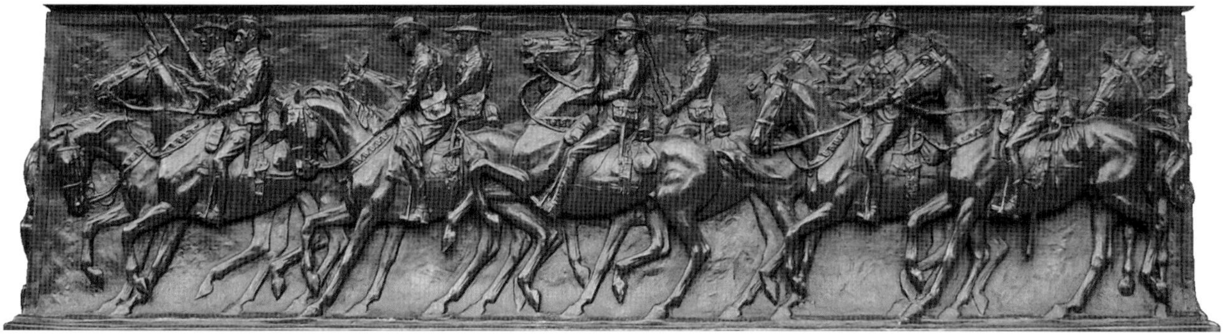

Cavalry of the Empire Memorial bas relief, right side panel. Round the bronze panels at the top of the statue's plinth trot the Cavalry of the Empire, Anzac, Canadian, South African, British and Indian, slouch-hatted, pith-or-tin helmeted, turbaned. Even when standing square to a side of the monument, the onlooker is aware that the line of comrades is indivisible. Standing on St. George's right, one sees all the horses moving left except for the horse at the extreme right of the panel, which is seen coming head-on as if emerging from the line on the panel on the front of the plinth.

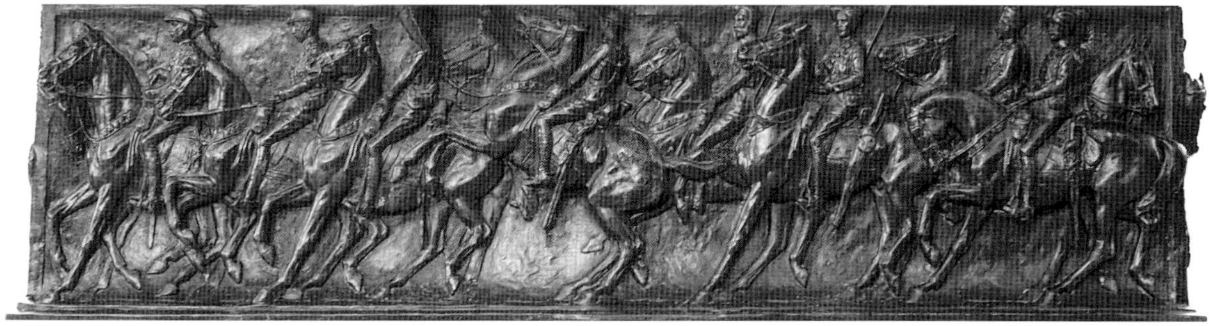

Cavalry of the Empire Memorial bas relief, left side panel. Walk round to the left side and one again sees the right hand horse head-on and beside it the silhouetted nose of its companion horse, for the cavalrymen are riding in informal column of two, with those in the outer column sculpted in higher relief.

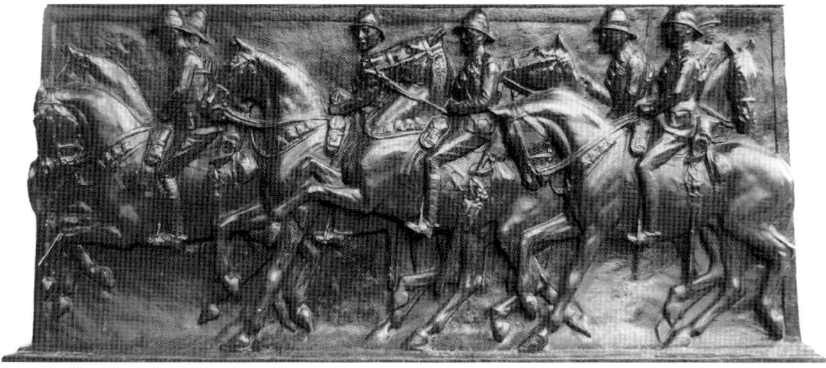

Cavalry of the Empire Memorial bas-relief, rear. Walk further round to stand at the back of the horse, and one sees Adrian using the same technique of presentation at the right of that panel. So the line is continuous, with no break in the comradeship of the nationalities. These are not men in full dress or any exact parade ground drill formation: the frieze depicts them in field dress for campaigning. But neither are the men actually fighting. Rifles are casually at the carry or slung over the shoulder as the cavalry move forward together. As in Adrian's other late memorials, the evocation is not of blood and guts.

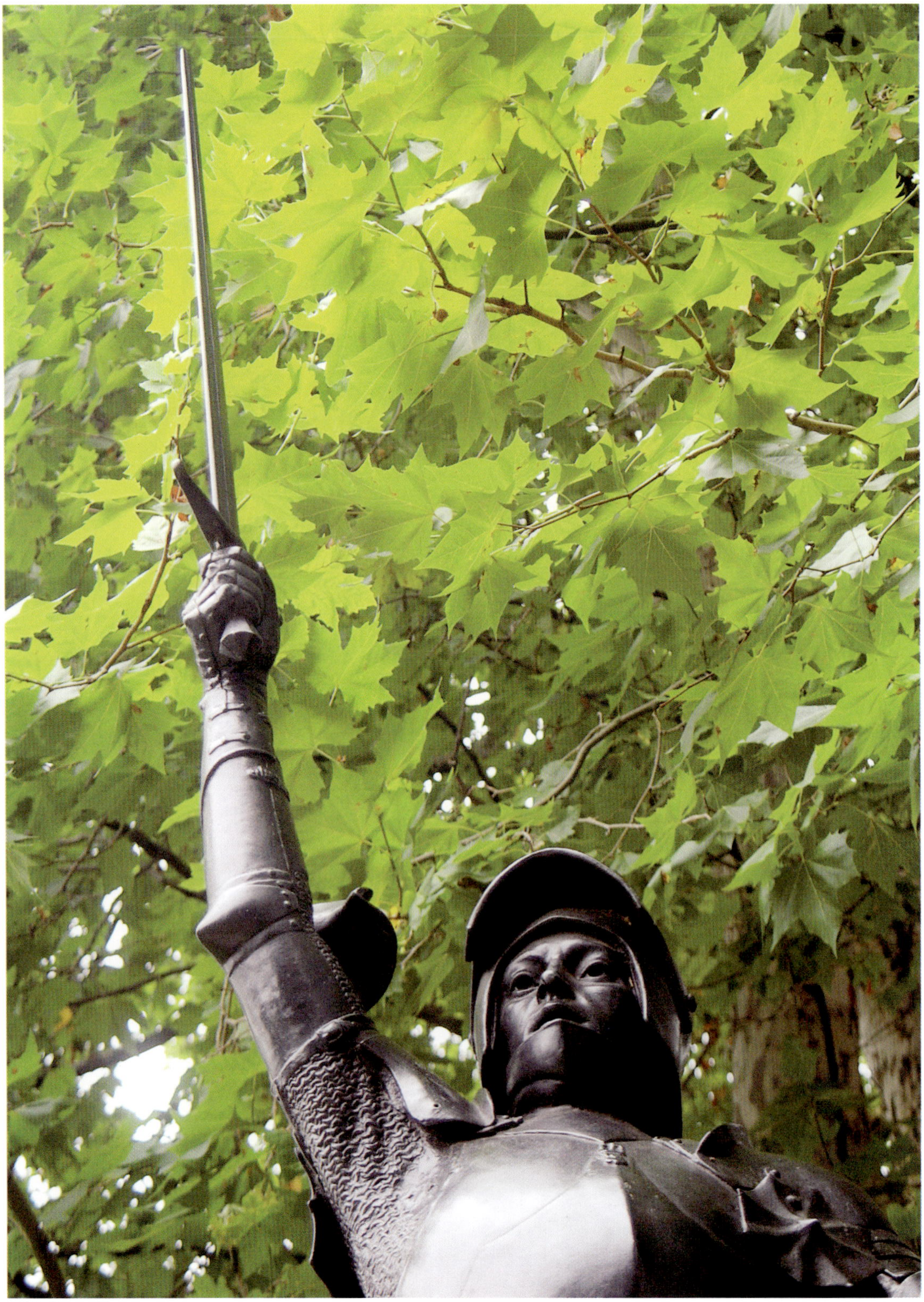

Detail: **Cavalry Memorial,** head of St. George.
Adrian had drawn pieces of armour in his sketching notebook before attempting their likeness in sculpture.

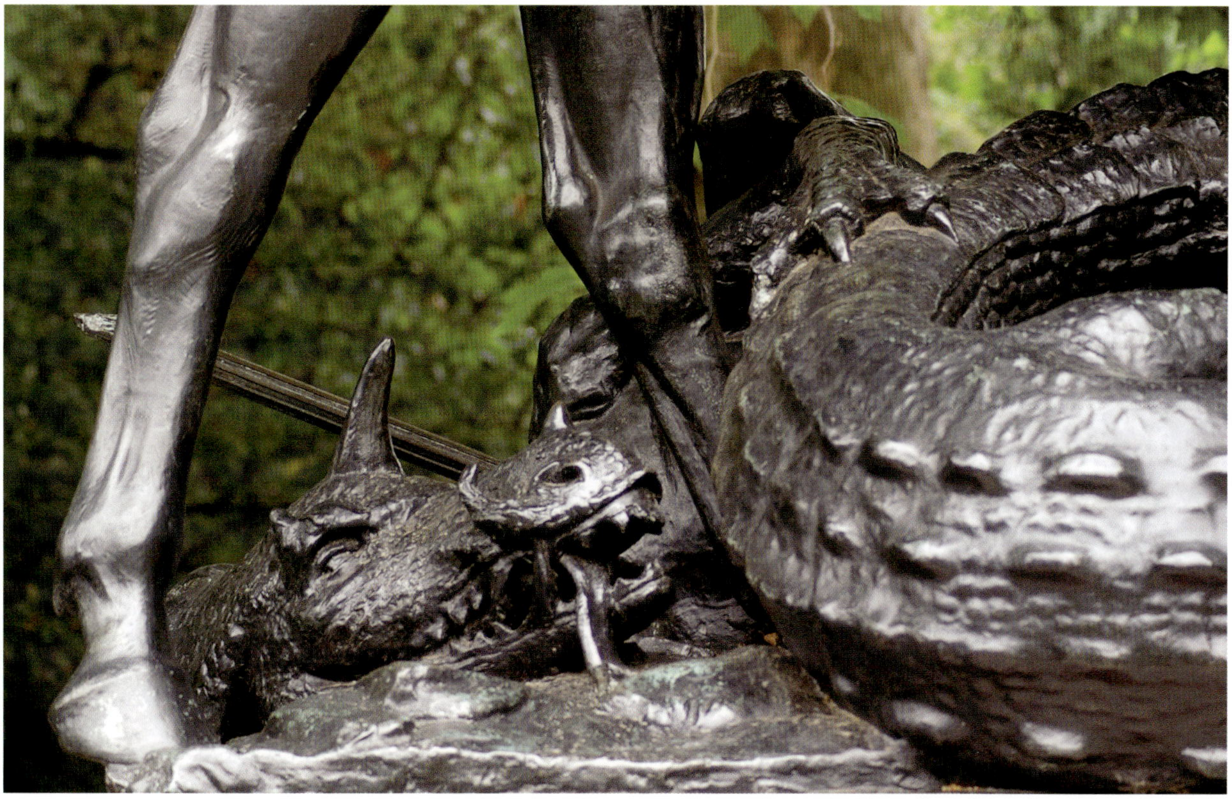

Detail: **Cavalry Memorial,** head of the dragon, featuring a stiff-pointed Kaiser Willy moustache

So too with the coiled dragon of evil beneath St George's steed. It is not writhing in death throes. It might be asleep, save that St George's broken lance protrudes from its vitals, so it is lying defeated in merited death. The thick body coil and the sharp pointed wing tips, which are emphasised by their protruding over the edge of the plinth, show how destructively powerful this enemy has been on land and in the air, though now it lies inoffensive. The *Shrewsbury Chronicle* wrote of the St George figure, 'He is the soldier from whom the passion of war is eliminated'. All fighting finished, he sits visor up and horse reined in. The first version's lance has been replaced by a sword: the handguard of the hilt forms the Christian symbol of the cross. St George still holds up his head as he salutes, but it is now turned only half-right, and his eyes appear to include anyone who stands in the obvious best viewing position to the right front of the horse, as well as any imagined distant people in the statue's 'story'. Recalling the invitation card to his studio private viewing on which a moustache resembling his own had been added to the face of the soldier carrying off the Sabine woman, and knowing that Edward VII had disliked his nephew Kaiser Wilhelm II, Adrian adorned the face of the dragon with a Kaiser Willy moustache. Adding a hint of ridicule to a solemn memorial must be risky, but here, being unobtrusive, it does not detract from the overall dignified effect. In this Cavalry of the Empire statue the guns of war have fallen silent, metaphorically and literally. Metaphorically, for the lance and sword of saint and knight St George have ended the dragon's fire. Literally, because the statue is made from guns captured by cavalry units during the Great War and melted down. It is perfectly right that our deep sense of gratitude may be accompanied by a touch of laughter.

Behind the statue runs a stone wall which carries bronze plaques, not executed by Adrian, though supervised by him and the architect, Sir John Burnet, ARA. (He was responsible for the layout and setting of the memorial in its first position at Stanhope Gate, where he reduced the entrance and exit gates from four to two and created between them an island for the statue. A painting of it there hangs on the first landing of the Cavalry and Guards Club. A further revision of traffic flows in the 1960s resulted in the statue's move to its present quieter location beside Hyde Park's Serpentine Road.) Vertical lists on the bronze plaques name every one of the Empire's cavalry units, and in a vestige of the original proposal for a column of field marshals' batons, four such batons stand between the lists to commemorate that four cavalry generals were promoted to field marshal: Edward Allenby, 1st Viscount of Megiddo; Douglas Haig, 1st Earl of Bemersyde; John French, 1st Earl of Ypres; and 'Wullie' Robertson, Baronet.

Sadly, just as King Edward did not live to see the inauguration of the Quadriga, Brigadier Lumley, whose energetic fundraising had made the Cavalry Memorial possible, died before its unveiling. Allenby was also absent. Though a keen supporter and admirer when home on leave, he was still the High Commissioner in Egypt. The act of unveiling was thus performed by French. When he moved forward to make his speech, Haig and Robertson moved with him. When he turned to address the parade and the crowd, Haig and Robertson turned beside him, the three field marshals united in homage. For though the field marshals had at times disagreed abusively during the War, knowledge of their acrimony had not yet filtered to the general populace and ex-servicemen. And though some historians have since passed harsh verdicts on the marshals, especially French and Haig, in 1924 they were still largely popular despite the critical books that were beginning to appear. French was to die just a year and a day after the unveiling. His ashes were placed in an oak coffin to lie in state in the Guards Chapel. Within two hours of the lying-in-state being opened to the public, over seven thousand people, most of them soldiers who had served with him, filed past. The pall bearers close to the gun carriage which carried the coffin in his funeral procession included Haig, Robertson and the Duke of Connaught, all of whom had attended the Cavalry Memorial unveiling. When Haig died three years later, the crowd who watched his funeral procession in London was estimated at more than a million, and when he lay in state in the High Kirk of St Giles in Edinburgh the queue to walk past his coffin stretched away for a mile in driving sleet.

So too it was a large throng who associated themselves by their attendance with the tribute being paid to the cavalry by the Great War's military leaders and by royalty at the unveiling of Adrian's commemorative statue. The occasion was unique. Never before or since has a member or representative of every cavalry regiment of the British Empire stood together in one parade. They included those regular and yeomanry regiments who since 1918 had been mechanised or adapted to a different role The order for the parade was 'service dress', but it was remarked that the cavalrymen had managed to give that order a large number of individual variations, each accentuating the distinctiveness of their regiment's history and customs. Yet in some ways it was a comparatively low key affair. In the days before the unveiling on May 21st the press carped over a War Office order that 'medals and decorations will be worn only by the troops on parade and not by spectators'. The *Star* said the order 'seems singularly uncalled for. What action is it proposed to take against any spectator who, having served his country in the war and having received a medal, presumes to attend the ceremony wearing it?' It is not easy to know what could have motivated such an unenforceable order. Someone must have wished the occasion not to be too 'big' and important. Whilst French had great admirers as a leader of cavalry, he also had his detractors, their virulence increased by the publication in 1919 of his book *1914*, which some saw as inaccurate and too favourable to himself in its judgements. King George had expressed displeasure; Herbert Asquith, in 1924 the leader of the Liberal Party, no longer thought highly of him; and in the military, other generals such as Smith-Dorrien, whom French had sacked as commander of the Second Army in France, had grievances. But as the supportive attendance of Haig and Robertson reflected, the unveiling was not seen as an occasion for parading animosity, and the following year Smith-Dorrien joined the field marshals as another pall-bearer at French's elaborately staged funeral procession. More probably there may have been anxiety in the War Office that the unveiling would be used for propaganda in favour of the cavalry arm, which military 'reformers' were seeking to cut back. If so, their anxiety was justified; French intended to deliver a fluent eulogy, so well rehearsed that he needed neither script nor notes.

And it proved to be a 'big' parade, though it lacked the pomp and colour that often characterises army ceremonial. In addition to the three field marshals, seventeen generals, including the Chief of the Imperial General Staff, the Earl of Cavan, attended. The line of them wore khaki service dress with medal ribbons. The Prince of Wales wore the beribboned khaki service dress of a cavalry regiment, the 12th Royal Lancers, for he was Colonel of that Regiment. The four hundred men of the Guard of Honour were in khaki too, but they had dressed wearing medals. The Royal Horse Guards Band wore khaki. Everyone on parade, from the Chief of the Imperial General Staff to the most junior boy trumpeter, was booted and spurred. Yet the only horses in sight were a few police horses; the Prince and other royalty and the generals had arrived by motor car. Then Park Lane and the interior roads of Hyde Park were closed to traffic.

The Chaplain-General opened the ceremony by announcing the singing of two verses of the hymn 'O God, our Help in Ages Past'. The threesome of Lord Ypres, Lord Haig and Sir William Robertson went forward, about turned and faced the assembly, and Lord Ypres delivered the Address. He declared the gathering one of the most impressive and solemn occasions in the history of the cavalry service. Never before

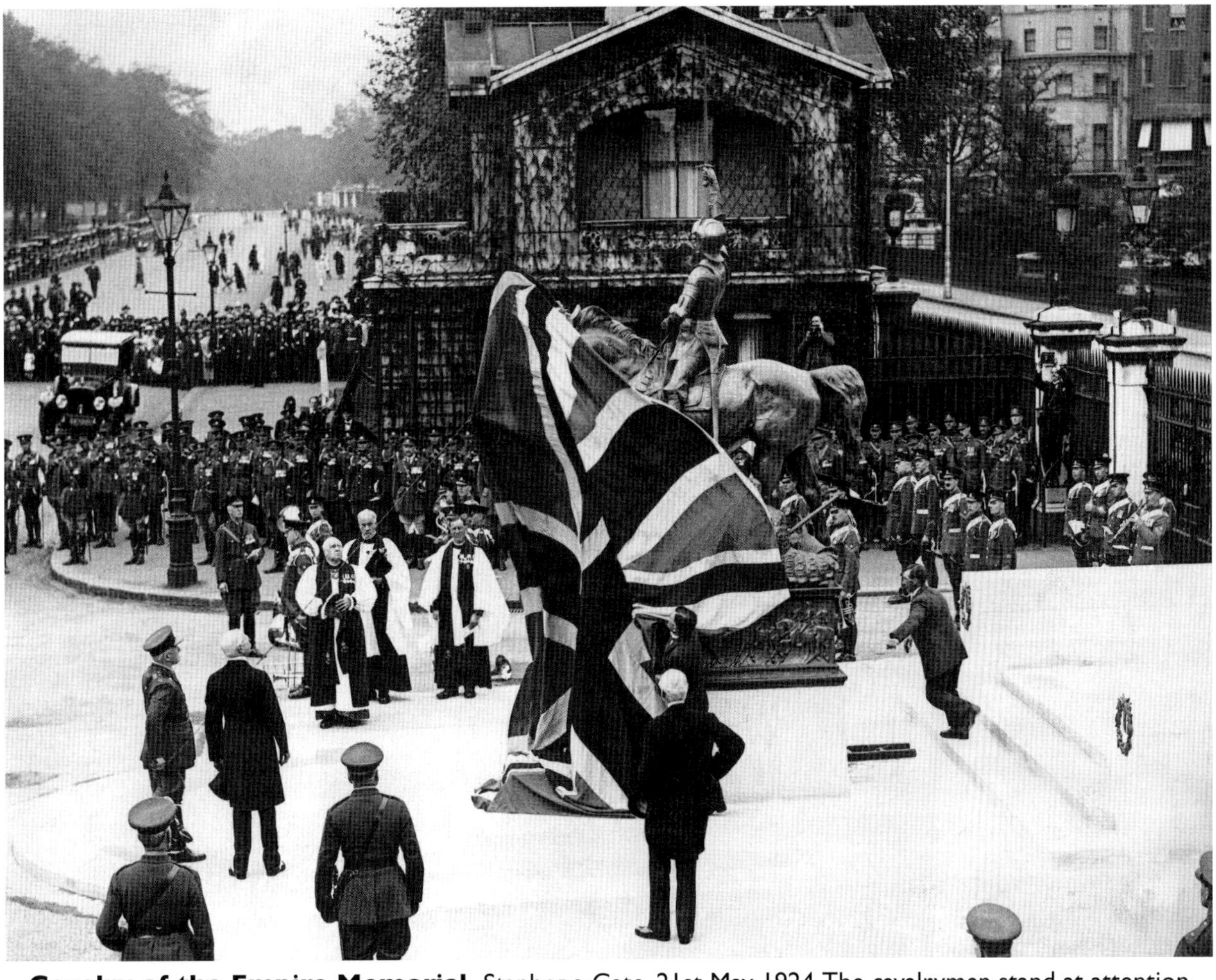

Cavalry of the Empire Memorial, Stanhope Gate, 21st May 1924. The cavalrymen stand at attention as Field Marshal Lord French, with Adrian beside him, pulls away the veiling Union Flag.

had the cavalry forces of the Empire been so united in a great war. Never before had they fought side by side on European battlefields. Never before had their joint services been recorded and the memory of their dead perpetuated by the erection of a monument in the heart of the Empire. Those glorious comrades whom the monument honoured had lost their lives in the greatest war the world had ever seen, a war in which the cavalry played a part which had never been surpassed in its history. Lord Ypres then recounted the 'splendid work' of the cavalry at Mons and in the retreat, on the Marne and the Aisne, the securing of Ypres and the Channel ports, the holding of the Wytschaete-Messines ridge and then, towards the close of the war, the victorious onslaught which rolled up the Turco-German armies on the eastern flank, which without doubt marked the beginning of the end. Doubtless also in the midst of many successes there were some few failures to attain this object sought for, but all showed the great cavalry spirit. Even in the new mechanical age there were many indispensable tasks in war which only the cavalry could perform. No General would undertake a command in the field without the assistance of mounted troops. He suggested therefore that they should be determined to keep the cavalry spirit ever alert, active and unimpaired, and be ready to emulate it when they were again called upon to take the field. 'Mounted troops', he said, 'are not done with yet'.

But they were. Adrian lived long enough to see every regular cavalry regiment except the ceremonial Household Cavalry and the Horse Artillery King's Troop lose their horses. His monument became a memorial not just to those who had given their lives but to the cavalry arm itself.

'In conclusion', French added, 'let me in the name of the Cavalry Service express our deep gratitude to Captain Adrian Jones, himself an old cavalry officer, the sculptor, and Sir John Burnet, the architect, for the beautiful monument they have designed and completed'. With that he released the covering Union Jack to reveal the figure of St George, and then unveiled the commemoration plates on the walled background. The Chaplain-General led final prayers. No saddening Last Post was played. The cavalry trumpets sounded

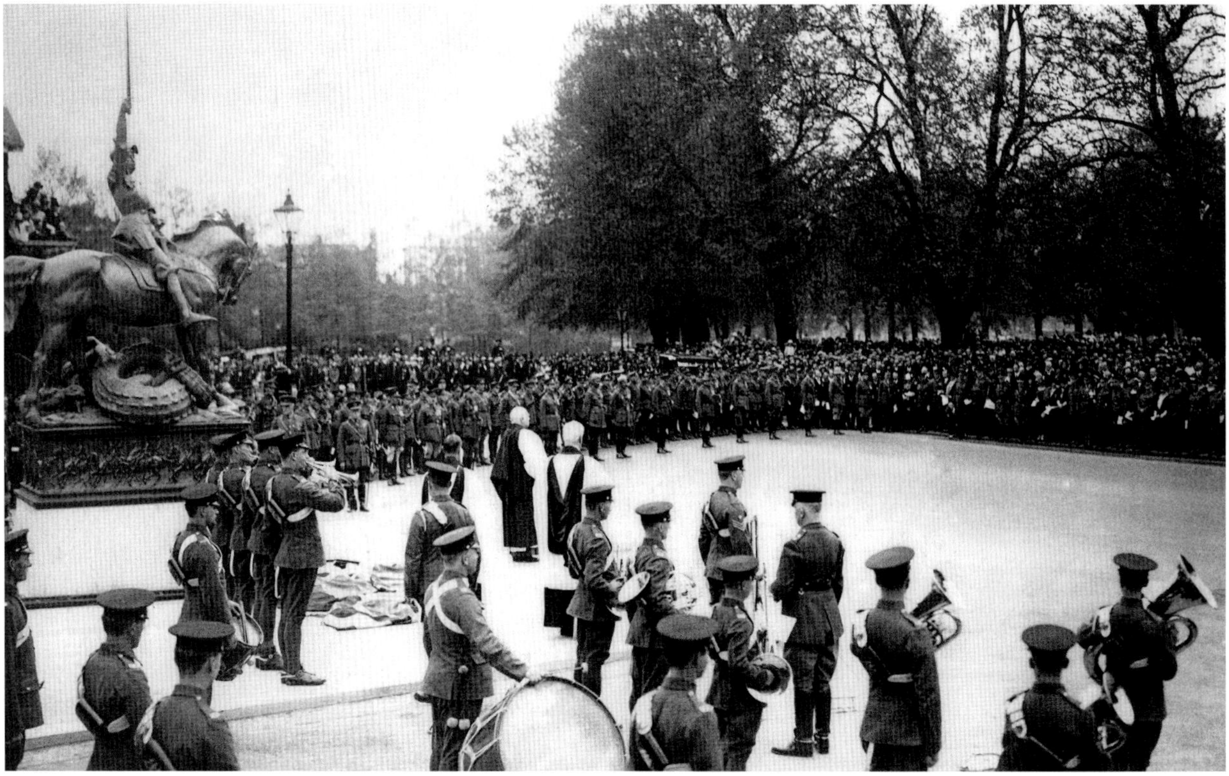

Cavalry Memorial: after the unveiling, the Horse Guards trumpeters sound the Reveille.

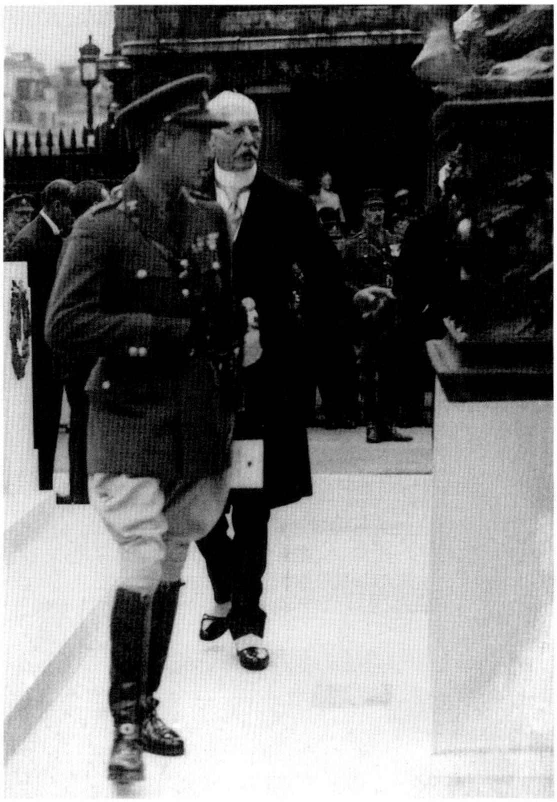

Cavalry Memorial: Adrian points out details of the bas relief to the Prince of Wales.

only the Reveille, and everyone sang 'For all the saints who from their labours rest'. The smallest boy trumpeter carried forward the main wreath to be laid, a huge harp-shaped laurel garland from all the Empire's cavalry regiments. The reporter from the *Sussex Daily News*, though primarily concerned to name the soldiers from the Sussex Yeomanry who had been in the parade, noted also that the trumpeter's 'self-assurance and military precision' would have done credit to any of the field marshals.

The ceremony over, the Prince of Wales could now leave his place at the front of the enclosure and make his own close inspection of the statue. The bronze panels showing horsed cavalrymen in campaigning dress appeared to arouse his special interest. Adrian was presented to him, and heartily congratulated on the success of his labours. The youthful Edward was the third Prince of Wales Adrian had known, and the third who had had occasion to congratulate him on his art.

A huge crowd had massed to watch, serried ranks on all sides, and the houses in Park Lane alive with ladies on the lower balconies, butlers and housekeepers a storey higher, and on the roof parapets maids in blue prints and white aprons. The Prince departed in his car and the parade dismissed. Suddenly the scene was informal. The troops and the crowd – a democratic mix of service dress hats, top hats, bowlers, cloth caps and ladies' bonnets – surged to surround the statue for their own close-up view. The *Daily Chronicle* felt moved at the sight of young soldiers fingering the inscriptions on the background panels, seeking to touch the name of their own regiment. The *Birmingham Post* was struck by how even red-tabbed senior staff officers went to pat the glossy neck of the Police Commissioner's beautiful horse, itself a war veteran with a band of medal ribbons across its forehead.

The *Times* reported: 'In the light of a spring afternoon the statue gave the impression of being cast in gold.' Reviews in the press were complimentary. Commentators liked the way Adrian had expressed valour in the knight and calm dignity in the saint. Two things particularly struck them. First, the beauty of the statue and its frieze of riders. Second, the statue's size, which made it one of London's smallest monuments. The *East Anglian Daily Times* termed it 'certainly one of the most delicately fashioned pieces of sculpture in the Metropolis'. The general verdict was that the statue succeeded both as 'art' and commemoration.

The only clumsy feature in the design is the way the inscription, 'Erected by the Cavalry of the Empire', cuts across the front frieze. The Quadriga remains Adrian's greatest achievement, and for many, 'Duncan's Horses' constitutes his most adventurous and striking art work. But probably for equally many, 'Cavalry of the Empire' is his most readily appreciated monument. One can walk right up to it in its quiet wooded glade, admire the supreme craftsmanship (much of it at eye level), reflect on Lord and Lady Allenby's opinion 'out and away the best war memorial in London', and – even without knowing the details of history – be moved by the sight of the wreaths still annually laid there by what are now nations of the Commonwealth. All this, and a funny moustache.

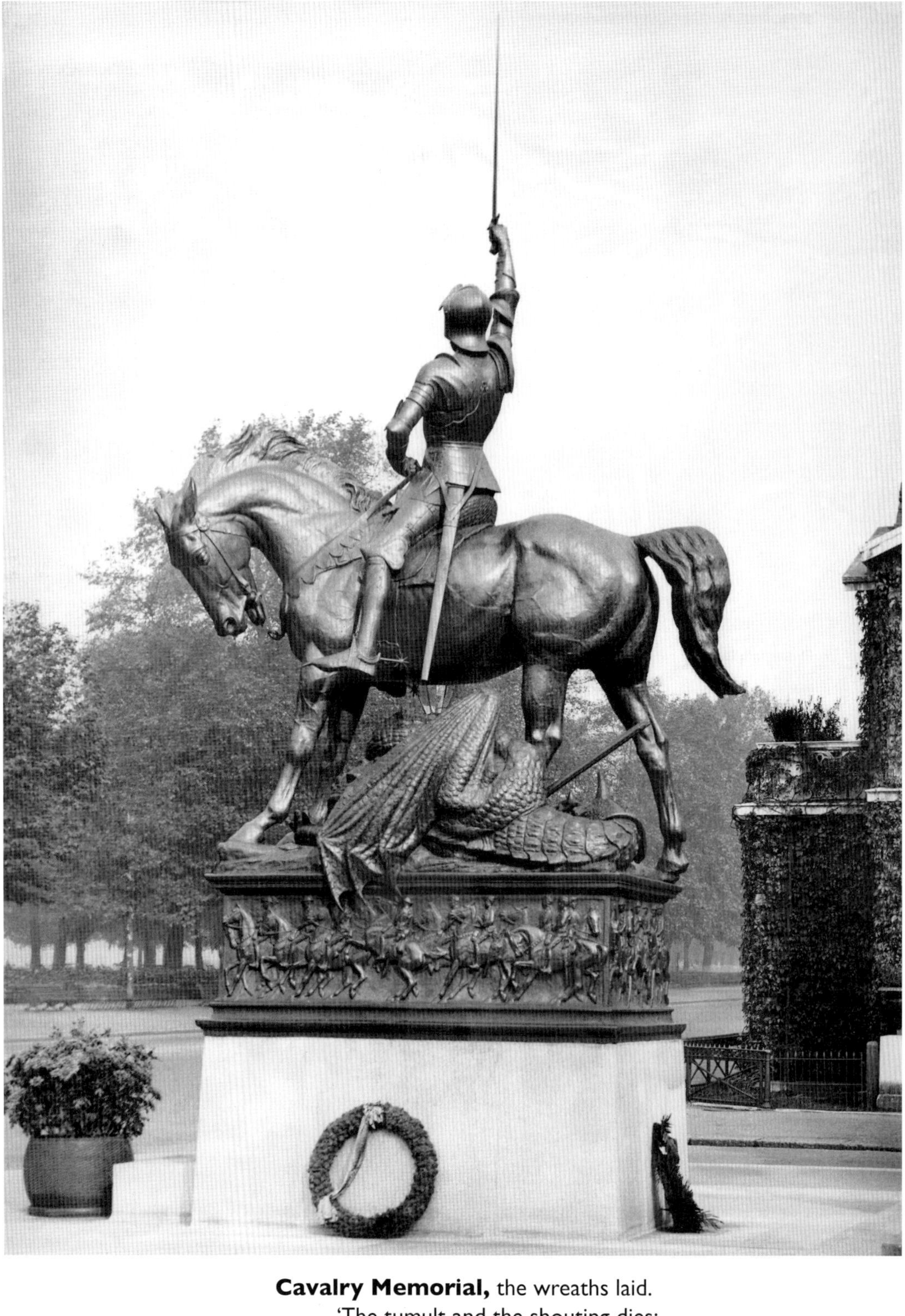

Cavalry Memorial, the wreaths laid.
'The tumult and the shouting dies;
The Captains and the Kings depart:
... Lord God of Hosts, be with us yet,
Lest we forget, lest we forget.'

Chapter Eighteen: 'Another Lease of Life'
1924-1938: Last Sculptures, Paintings and Memoirs

After the unveiling of the Cavalry of the Empire Memorial, the Honorary Secretary of the Savage Club wrote to Adrian:

> We have all of us naturally read with the greatest interest that the Cavalry Memorial dedicated by the Earl Ypres was executed by you. On behalf of us all, the Committee have asked me to convey to you their hearty congratulations on the success of your great work and to assure you that we feel it an honour that such a Memorial should have been designed and executed by a Brother Savage.

Because the good talk and the good fellowship of the Savage Club had been such an important source of relaxed happiness in his life, Adrian particularly valued this note of appreciation. Now seventy-nine, he could have been excused if he had decided that the unveiling in a royal park of a memorial to the cavalry, at a parade unique in the annals of the British Empire, would be a suitably climactic moment at which to retire with plaudits still ringing in his ears. Such a decision, however, would not have been in character, and he carried on working. Between 1920 and 1935, a bas relief and fourteen of his bronzes, both equine and human portrait statuettes, were accepted for Royal Academy Summer Exhibitions, his paintings were shown in numerous galleries, and he responded to requests to produce memorials.

Yet as a new generation of sculptors experimented with abstraction and the liberation of their art from conventional naturalistic forms and proportions, critics relegated Adrian to comparative obscurity. People in general could not look at a statue and say unerringly, 'That is an Adrian Jones' in the way they might say of a reclining figure with a hole in it, 'That is a Henry Moore'. Nevertheless, Adrian remained the sculptor who had created the largest number of prominent public statues in the nation's capital, and at the Jubilee of King George V in 1935, the *Children's Newspaper,* whose editorial board was as sound in judgement as those of adult papers, included him in its huge illustration of 'King George and His Hundred Men – Most Famous People of the Jubilee Reign'. (Number 1 was Neville Chamberlain and number 105, because a handful of women stood amongst the hundred men and thereby increased the total, was Sir Edwin Lutyens. Adrian, number 30, stands with the novelist John Galsworthy on his left and Sir John Reith, Director General of the BBC, on his right.) The *Sketch* marked the Jubilee by commissioning Rowland Hilder to make a drawing of the Royal Procession for the central spread of its Jubilee issue. Hilder chose for his subject the tumultuous reception King George and Queen Mary received when their coach emerged through the Quadriga archway, a passage which in 1935 was still reserved solely for royalty. The picture was titled 'In the Shadow of the Quadriga', which the accompanying paragraph recorded 'was designed by Captain Adrian Jones, MVO'. One may wonder if for a brief moment the King in his mind contrasted the crowds and cheering of his Jubilee appearance at the Arch with their absence at his inauguration of the Arch near the start of his reign, and speculate too if Adrian perhaps allowed himself a wry smile at the idea of the Quadriga overshadowing the monarch. In the picture itself the flag-adorned Arch and its Quadriga dwarf the royal progress below. Forgivably, Adrian put the picture into his book of news cuttings.

Adrian kept active in other fields also, and though these were fields in which he had worked before they could still bring new experiences. His continuing pleasure in horse statuettes and his previous acquaintance with the McCalmont military family took him back in the early 1920s to their home near Waterford in Ireland to make a sketch of their stallion Tetrarch, preparatory to making a statuette (see illustration on page 276). Hugo McCalmont, now Sir Hugh, and his lady were in residence, but the racehorse's owner was their son Dermot. He had designed for Tetrarch accommodation which was really too grand to be called a stable. Adrian referred to it as Tetrarch's 'mansion'. It was large and, uniquely, circular, more like a riding school than a stall, so its occupant could move around freely without any danger of injury from a corner or projection. It doubly pleased Adrian. First, it reflected the affection of Major Dermot McCalmont for a horse who had often carried his jockey first past the winning post. Second, Tetrarch was an outstanding horse 'full of quality and worthy of his home'. Adrian had previously seen Tetrarch gallop in training, 'and when he passed me, his power and force were really more suggestive of an express train than of a horse'.

This comparison to an express is a high compliment. He particularly admired the A1 class of 4-6-0 locomotives designed by H.N. Gresley, the chief engineer of the London and North Eastern Railway, to haul the LNER expresses. He was gratified when in 1924 no. 2549 was named 'Persimmon'. In the same year Gresley's 'Flying Scotsman' was exhibited in the Palace of Engineering at Wembley. Adrian went to see it and afterwards told a *Daily Mail* reporter that he did not see how that express engine could be improved from an artistic point of view: 'Were an artist to draw a picture of an imaginary locomotive which was intended to express the idea of speed and power, it is quite likely that it would not do so as effectively as this engine'. He added that in his view the appearance of mechanical products was improving generally with motor cars becoming more graceful and aeroplanes having far better lines than formerly. It would be a mistake to deduce from Adrian's love of beautiful horses that he was antipathetic towards modern machinery. Adrian would also have enjoyed painting Tetrarch, a distinctive horse with splotches of white on his grey coat, but there he had been anticipated by the equine artist A.C. Haigh, who had painted Tetrarch at the end of his racing career in 1914. However, Adrian took great pleasure in sketching and in making a study of the head, and then transforming those into a bronze, for although Tetrarch in retirement was no longer what many had judged to be perhaps the fastest horse that ever ran: 'I never modelled any horse quite so muscular and thick-bodied.' The resulting statuette won acceptance for the 1927 Royal Academy Summer Exhibition (exhibit 1642).

Another commission received in the early 1920s was also of a familiar kind. The Cottesmore Hunt wanted a bronze statuette of their retiring Master, the Earl of Lonsdale, on his horse Patsy, with a pair of hounds below; and the Hunt's farmer members wanted a statuette of one of the Earl's hunters – a real vote of appreciation, for back in 1911 Adrian had sculpted for the Cottesmore farmers the Earl's then favourite hunter, Mullagh. The statuette of him now, on the new favourite Patsy, won a place in the 1922 Royal Academy (exhibit 1412).

During the last fifteen years of active sculpting which remained to him thereafter, Adrian paid as much attention to humans as to horses. Between 1923 and 1935, several of his Royal Academy exhibits had the title of a man's name. Two of these were equestrian, but that familiar form portrayed distinctive subjects. The Cuban General Masceo was one, and the other and last, in 1935, was a Boer, General Botha. Adrian's first experience of war came in Abyssinia in 1868. Then his commander, Lord Napier, had picked out as a supreme benefit of the campaign a reforging of the bond of trust between the Indian and British troops who had marched and fought side by side. After that, in his statues and bas reliefs, and in ambitious studio models fated never to be cast in expensive bronze, Adrian had frequently emphasised the motif of military comradeship between the various nationalities of the British Empire. He had been gratified to execute some works for Hunts in post-war rural Britain: the continued existence of more than two hundred of them, each with hounds, hunters and hunt staff to maintain, benefited country districts with the circulation of millions of pounds. Yet it was surely fitting that the last of the thirty-three exhibits he successfully submitted to the Royal Academy should reflect not his love of the hunting field or the racecourse but instead his admiration for bravely given mutual support when needed in the cause of the Empire. General Botha had fought against the British in the Boer War but become a comrade in arms in the Great War. The ninety-year-old sculptor, sculpting tool in hand, posed beside the statuette for a press photo agency, and the photograph duly appeared under such headlines as 'Veteran Sculptor at Work'.

His reputation as a great sculptor and major contributor to the London street scene in key contexts such as Whitehall and Hyde Park Corner was now secure. King George V did not wait to send him a hundredth birthday telegram, as was the royal custom, but sent him a congratulatory telegram on his ninetieth. The Royal Society of British Sculptors, which had elected him to membership in 1912 and then made him a Fellow in 1923, in recognition of his great body of work declared him an Honorary Fellow in 1932. Finally, on 9 April 1935, at an evening presentation in Hyde Park Hotel, with its President Sir William Dick in the Chair, the Royal Society presented Captain Adrian Jones, MVO, MRCVS, FRBS, with the highest honour which can be bestowed upon a British sculptor, its Gold Medal. The event took place two years after the publication of Adrian's *Memoirs,* so there exists no public firsthand account of his feelings, but any sense he had of just reward for his half century of work in sculpture must surely have been given an extra edge by the knowledge that the distinguished audience present to see him receive this ultimate accolade included the current President of the Royal Academy, Sir William Llewellyn. To add to his pleasure in this occasion in his honour there was the attendance of his architect acquaintance Sir Edwin Lutyens, whose classical-style Cenotaph had since 1919 joined the Wellington Arch as a second major monumental landmark on London's processional route for great state occasions.

Most pleasant of all was the presence of Sir William Goscombe John, RA. He first appears in Adrian's *Memoirs* in a brief enigmatic anecdote. Adrian is chatting to the genre and historical painter Seymour Lucas RA at the Academy when Goscombe John joins them. Lucas says to John: 'You praise this man's work a great deal; why don't you help him?' To that Adrian adds a single sentence of comment to bring the chapter to an emphatic end: 'This helped me to realise that it was the sculptors, not the painters, who were up against me.' One might assume that the 'you' in Lucas's challenge was a rebuke to John personally, and that Adrian was including John in his accusation against sculptors. However, Adrian probably only recounted the incident to illustrate that he had been slow to comprehend the intensity of the professional jealousy most RA-trained sculptors felt towards him. Goscombe John was not one of them. The next time he appears in *Memoirs* he is writing in 1912 from his home in St John's Wood to congratulate Adrian warmly on the Quadriga: 'I like it very much indeed.' He goes on to praise its interest and charm and the appropriateness of its scale to the Arch. In that year John was himself particularly committed to commissions for the new Cardiff City Hall, but though busy there he was also a member of the RSBS Council and showed that his congratulations to Adrian on the Quadriga were not empty words by successfully proposing Adrian for membership. Adrian attended meetings of the Society in 1914, but then Goscombe John resigned membership after a dispute over the workings of the selection committee, and thereafter Adrian did not play an active part in the Society's affairs, preferring to give his time to the Savage and Chelsea Arts Clubs. John rejoined the RSBS in 1929, and in 1942 followed Adrian in receiving its Gold Medal.

The two men had some similarities: their links to Wales, their affable personalities, their artistic outlook and, though John was by fifteen years the younger, the timing of their working lives. John had spent some time in the Royal Academy Schools, but also the year 1886-87 training with Adrian's mentor Charles Birch. After a spell abroad he returned to London and settled in St John's Wood in 1892, the year of the 'Ghost' scandal. John was not then even an Associate of the RA (that came in 1899) and so not involved in any allegations against Adrian. For both, the 1890s saw the start of their fame and major successes, and both went on to unusually lengthy careers: Adrian exhibited at the Royal Academy from 1884 to 1935, and John, who started younger, for a remarkable sixty-two years (1886 to 1948). Across these decades neither changed to a modern style (John referred disparagingly to 'Easter Island'-style modern sculpture) and so despite collecting the top honour of a RSBS Gold Medal they shared the fate of being overlooked by opinion formers and art historians. But the public continue to notice their great outdoor statues. John's statues in the Liverpool area, for instance – the King's Liverpool Regiment Memorial near St. George's Hall, the Engine Room Heroes Memorial at the Pier Head, and the Port Sunlight War Memorial in the gardens beyond the Lever Art Gallery – are arguably the best known and most frequently admired by Liverpudlians. In all their activity, these two men of mutual regard were probably only once in direct competition. Adrian would have liked to have undertaken the statue of Viscount Tredegar, the leader of a troop in the Charge of the Light Brigade in the Crimean War, for Cathays Park in Cardiff, but the commission was won by Goscombe John, a son of Cardiff.

Adrian's relationship with John is evidence that although the conventional account of Adrian's being at odds with the sculptors of the RA establishment is broadly accurate, he was by no means ostracised by everyone. His range of friends and of friendly acquaintances in the art world was wide. By the time he published his autobiography, whatever reservations the avant-garde had towards the traditional nature of his art, there was near universal recognition of the greatness of his realised talent and the scale of his achievements as a sculptor.

His reputation as a painter does not match that. Indeed, when the Sladmore Gallery's 1984 retrospective exhibition of Adrian's work was being planned and Adrian's great nephew wrote to the Lord Chamberlain's Office in St. James's Palace to ask if any of Adrian's paintings which had been bought by royalty could be made available on loan, he received the reply: 'Dear Mr Cunningham, There are several paintings by Adrian Jones in the royal collection, but they are not, I am afraid, very good and many of them are not in particularly good order.' Mr Cunningham wrote back to ask if he might see them, and heard in response:

> It might be possible to show you the paintings by Adrian Jones later in the autumn' (of 1983) 'but the point I must reiterate is that they could *not* be lent to an exhibition because they need conservation treatment before they could be placed on show before the public. He is, I am afraid, an indifferent painter and his works have not, so far, received attention because there are so many more important paintings in the royal collection. My impression is, however, that his works in bronze are much more accomplished.

While there are some comforting words in the last sentence (and the Queen gave gracious permission for bronze statuettes of the Derby winner Diamond Jubilee and the Grand National winner Ambush II to be loaned to the Exhibition), and though it is incontestable (except perhaps by the Spirit of Edward VII?) that there are more important paintings than Adrian's in the royal collection, the tale of neglect and lack of appreciation a quarter of a century ago made depressing reading for the letter's recipient who, as a trained veterinary surgeon himself, admired the unequalled anatomical mastery in Adrian's painting and sculpture

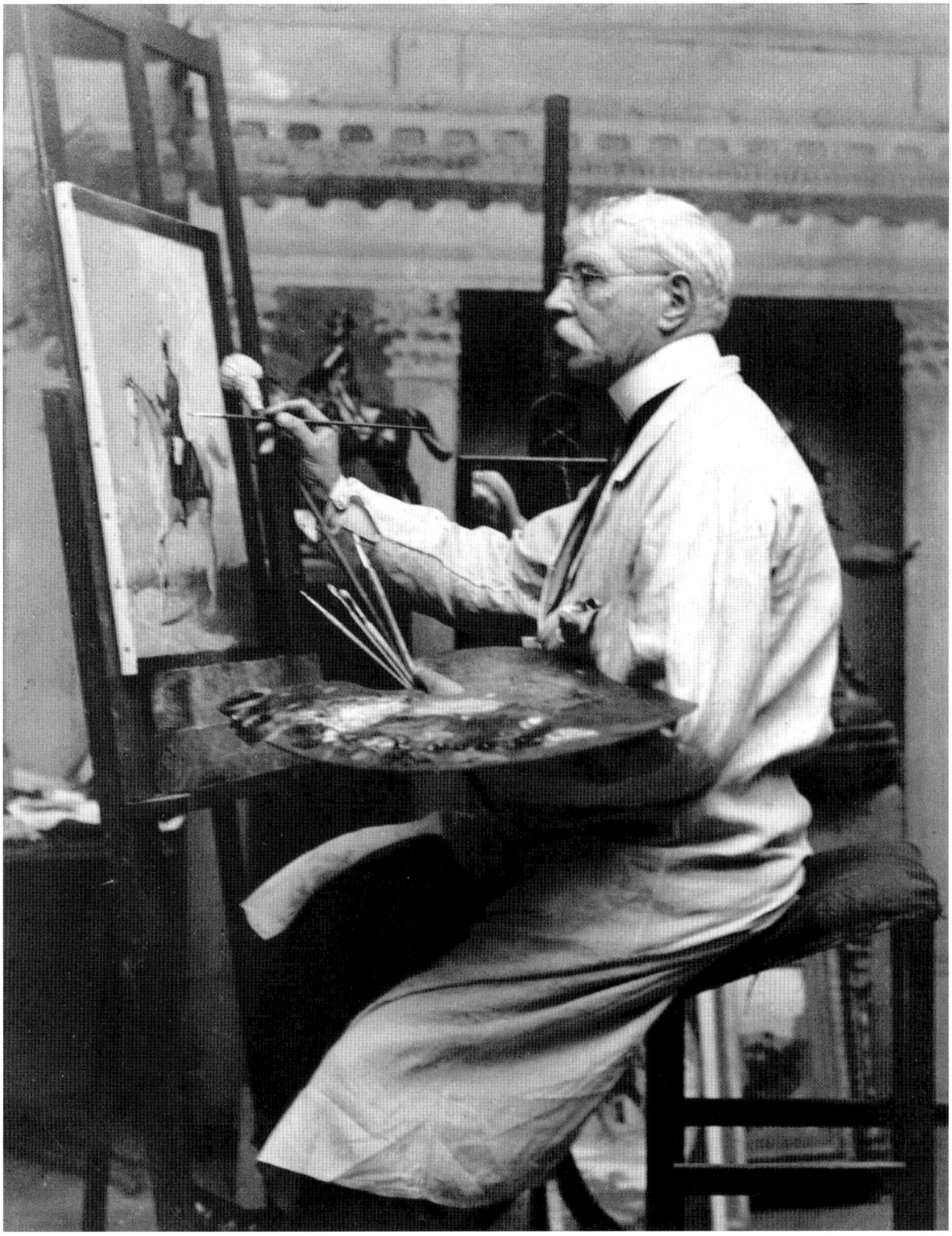

Adrian Jones, equestrian artist

that so enthused the Victorians and Edwardians. Two comments may be ventured. First, it is correct that Adrian's reputation as a great artist should finally rest upon his sculpture. Second, it is private collectors rather than museum curators who cherish Adrian's paintings. They like the straightforward representational accuracy, the focus on the beautiful animal, the highly sympathetic and appreciative approach to the subject, the overall harmony of subject and setting. The work of the even more popular Sir Alfred Munnings, by contrast, has a museum at Dedham dedicated to it, so there the equestrian artist's paintings *are* considered 'important'. Happily for a curator, because there is more of ancillary interest in a Munnings painting, there is more to talk about. It is impossible to envisage a painting by Adrian with the title 'My wife, my horse and myself'. Munnings painted such a picture, and most competent curators would back themselves to 'interpret' it and find a subtext. That is legitimate, and can be valuable; but Adrian's paintings offer less scope for it. Admire and enjoy.

This biography of Adrian Jones has been largely concerned with the mainstream of his work: military, equine and equestrian art. But he could be versatile when he chose. 'The Reapers' and 'Mrs Temple and Snow' were relaxed, uncommissioned works painted with affection, not placed on the market but kept in the family and passed on to relatives. The large canvas he chose to use for 'The Reapers' gave him the opportunity he took in several agricultural scenes to express his admiration for heavy working horses. The high horizon line five-sixths of the way up the picture embeds the men and horses firmly in their landscape of toil, and the tones of the men's clothing further identify them with the harvest. But the horses, men and machinery so fill the foreground of the painting with their size that they are the reverse of insignificant. The painting is a very British equivalent to Millet's very French 'The Gleaners'. Millet makes an overt appeal to the viewer's sympathies with his bent women scratching for the poor remains of harvest in a featureless flat landscape whilst in the background a swarm of workers also labour hard, but one man, presumably the owner of the land, sits idle on his horse overseeing the toil of others. Yet Adrian is just as imaginatively engaged as Millet with his subject. Much reaping remains to be done before the sun goes down, and even as the horses rest for a moment at the head of the field the farmer and labourer together wrestle with an adjustment to the reaping machinery. The dignity of animal, man and labour is recognised. As well as realism, there is celebration of the bountiful golden harvest and the beauty of the countryside.

'Mrs Temple and Snow' is an unusual work of Adrian's in that it is a domestic interior genre painting. His treatment of the life of his family as private included not selling paintings of it. Mrs Temple was a sister of Adrian's second wife, and her daughter was Adrian's goddaughter. She was therefore very much 'family'. So it seems right here to do little more than follow the exhortation above to 'admire and enjoy' the warm colours and cosy atmosphere of the fireside scene depicted, commenting only on the superb brushwork of Snow's coat, such a contrast to the smooth treatment of the quietly absorbed reader's face, and apologising for the fact that Snow's front paws in the illustration have been nipped off, possibly because of too close framing.

'Scene on the River Thames' instantly evokes the standard idyllic image of Edwardian summers and messing about in boats before the image was shattered by the slaughter of 1914. No one feature dominates. The difference between the technique used on the lightly painted sky and the thickly laid on paint of the riverside trees is remarkable, but Adrian has put his biggest artistic effort into the play of light on the river water in the foreground and contrasted it with the dark bend beyond. That darkness in this painting is not symbolic. The details in the scene are intended to evoke a mood, but it is certainly not a dark mood prefiguring a black end to the Edwardian idyll. Adrian is simply painting what he sees. But just as it is mistaken to seek to read a troubled 'message' into Adrian's sunny paintings, it would be equally mistaken to presume that he lived unaware of the Edwardian age's widespread troubles. In the heatwave summer of 1911 that contributed most to the image of constantly sunlit Edwardian Britain, as Adrian was literally sweating

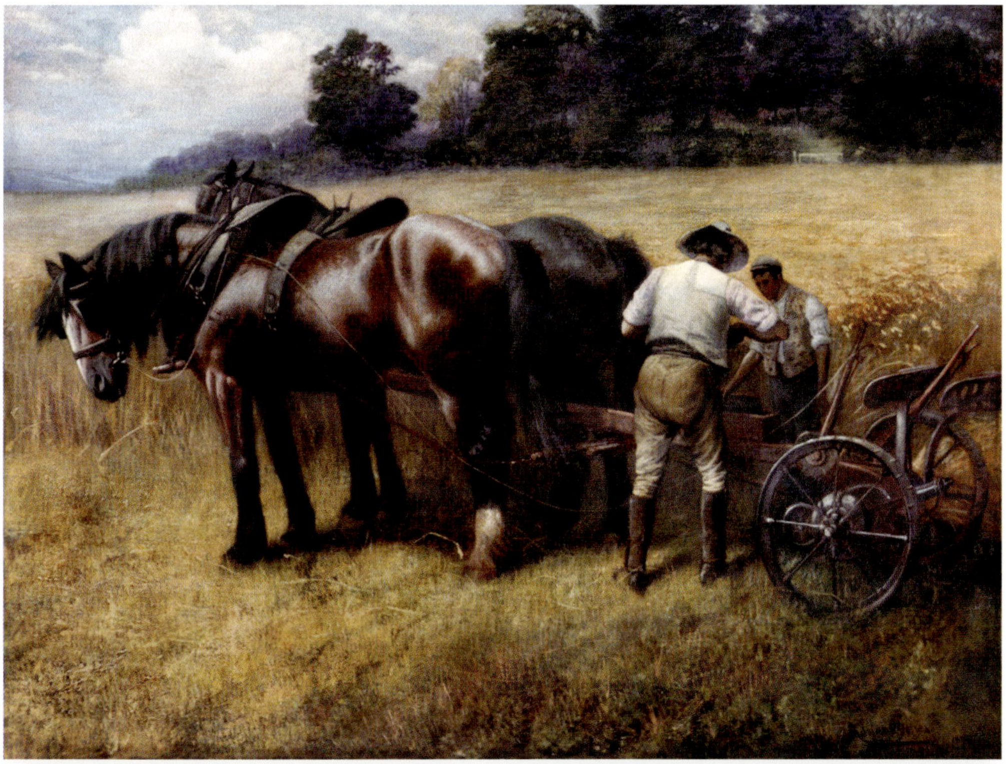

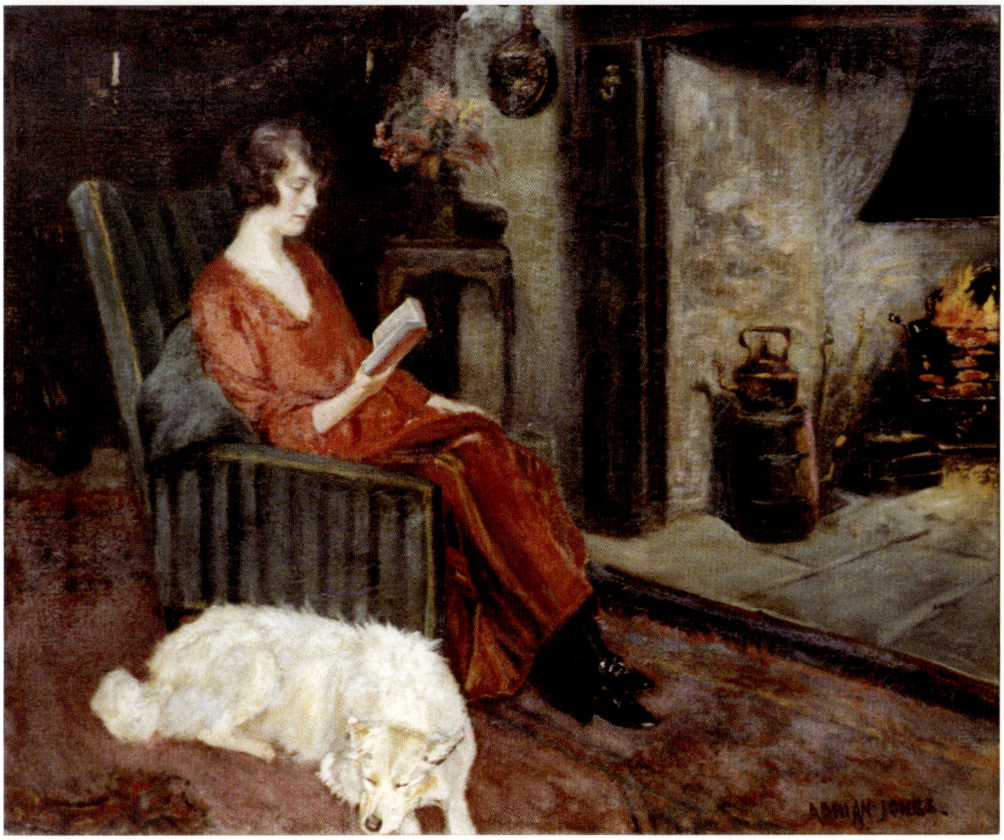

Above: **The Reapers**; Below: **Mrs Temple and Snow**

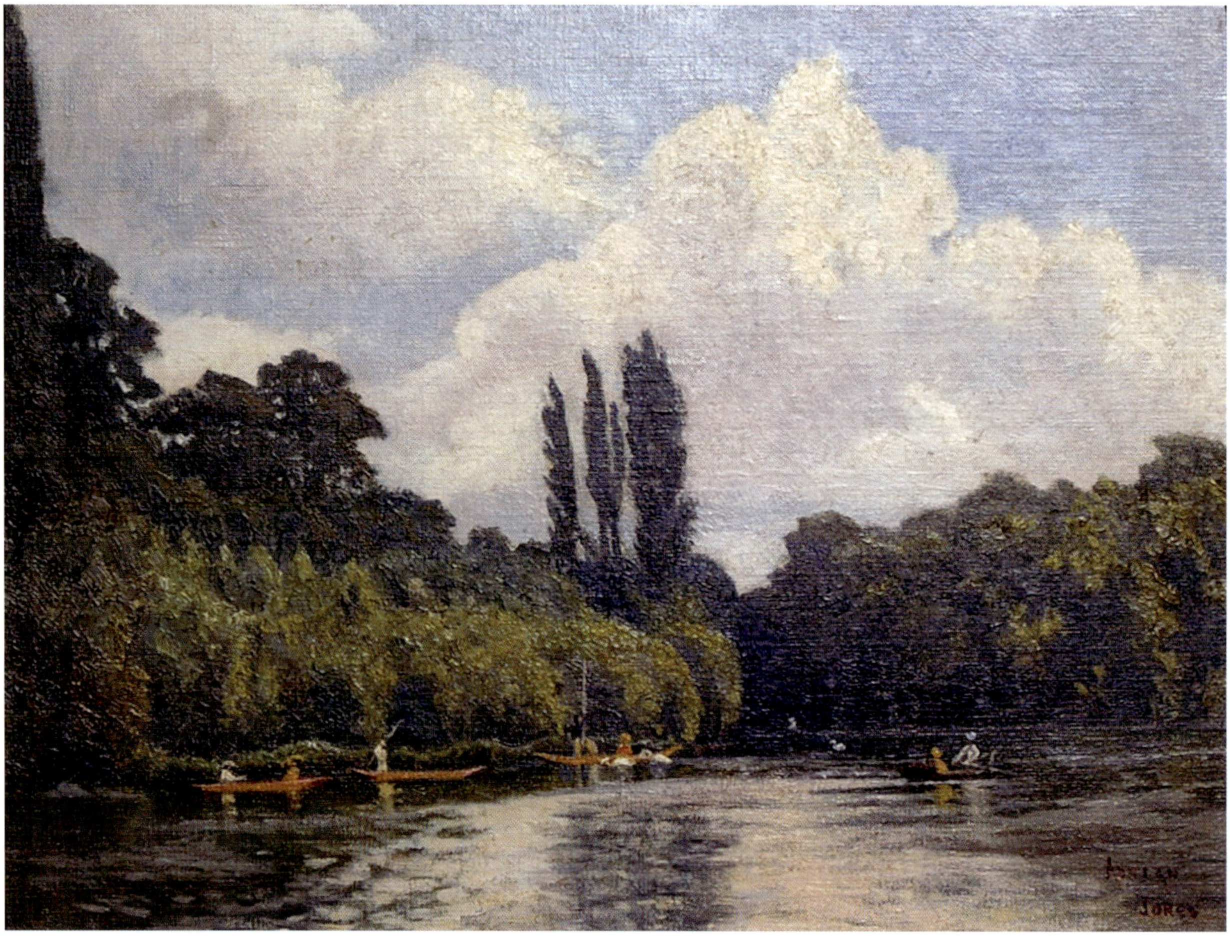

Scene on the River Thames

over the final stages of heavy work on the Quadriga for Hyde Park Corner, in Hyde Park itself and in nearby Kensington Gardens and St. James's Park areas of grass were crowded with tents for troops, present lest the strikes paralysing the London docks erupted into a revolutionary rising. It was a strange context in which to be working on Peace.

The context of Adrian's military sculptures was always clear, revealed in statue and bas relief. 'Meditation' is a 23-inch-high bronze nude without any apparent context, different from any other work Adrian produced before or after. His view, expressed in the epilogue to his *Memoirs,* was that sculpting the human form was less demanding than sculpting horses:

> The sculptor cannot pose his horse or his horses and then merely copy them ... he must understand their anatomy intimately ... he must be a close observer, able to commit action to memory so that he can reproduce the animal in any position that is necessary to the execution of his idea.

He also makes the points that critics ought not 'to think that a sculptor can be good in any field of work', and that a female figure, however well crafted, will be no more than a still life if it is without 'some big idea ... and a certain measure of originality'. In the light of such beliefs it is unsurprising that he did

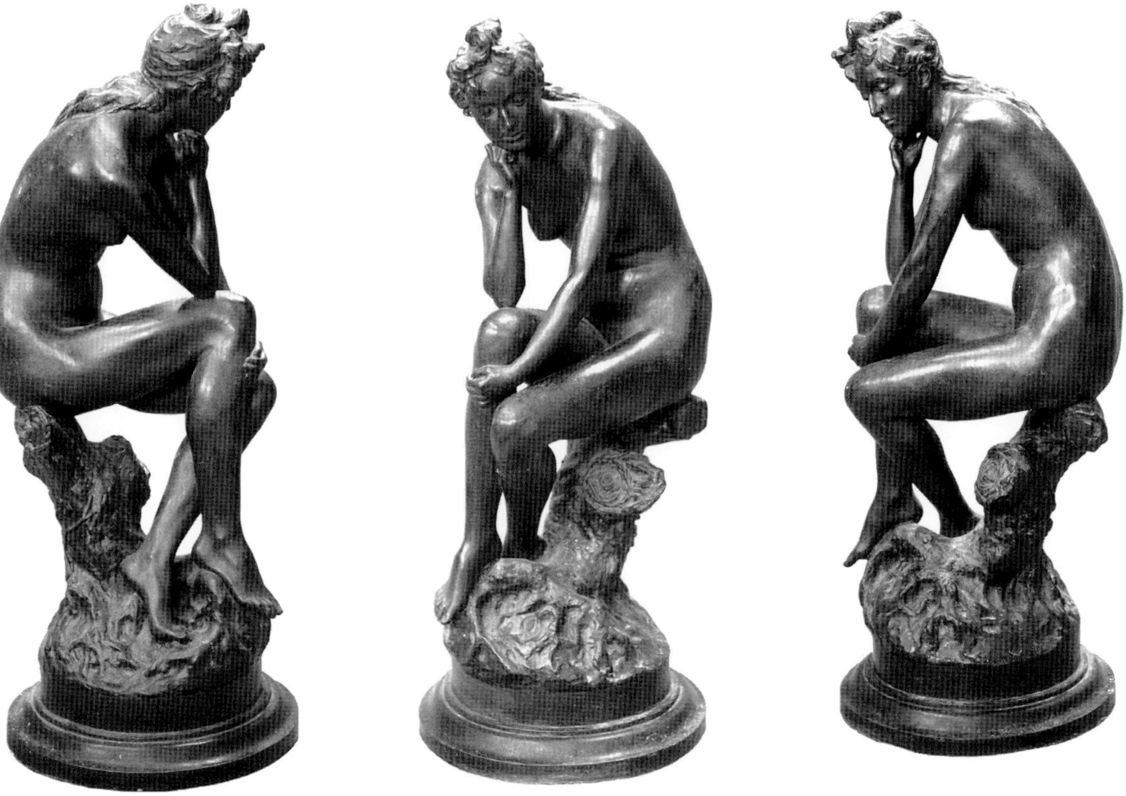

Meditation, bronze statuette

not make a practice of sculpting – or painting – nudes, and it remains slightly surprising that in 1902 he produced 'Meditation'. Speculation about his motivation might lead in several directions. The development of independent art galleries in the last part of the 19th century had increased opportunities for the exhibition in public and for the sale of nude figures, but Adrian was fully busy without commercial expansion into that field. In 1898 his ally Goscombe John in 1898 had used a nude, 'The Elf' (now in the National Museum of Wales), as his diploma piece for the Royal Academy; perhaps Adrian imagined that adding a nude to his body of work might help towards his eventual elevation to ARA. In the year his prize-winning 'Gone Away' had appeared in the sculpture section of the Royal Academy Exhibition, Edward Onslow Ford had exhibited in the same section his allegorical girl nude 'Peace', who poses with one arm raised and one lowered, much like Adrian's figures of Peace, and holds in her hands a dove of peace and the palm branch of victory. Perhaps memory of that encouraged Adrian to attempt his own allegorical nude. As a more general influence, the New Sculptors often used nudity because of their concern with surface effect; though Adrian was not formally of their school, he was fully cognisant of their practice. More probably, however, in 'Meditation' he was just showing that he was skilled enough to turn his hand to most things.

Perhaps he also had an idea, albeit not 'some big idea', for a quiet joke. Rodin had been working on 'The Thinker' off and on for the past twenty-two years. Adrian would quickly undertake and complete his own brooding figure and suggest a reference in its title: 'Meditation'. She sits in the attitude of Rodin's thinker, forward-leaning torso, head leaning on fist, elbow leaning on knee, other hand more loosely clasped on a leg, the feet – one to the side half-rear of the other – extended down the slope of the seating support. But the style is not that of Rodin. He mixes an idealised figure of graceful turn and beauty of form typical of

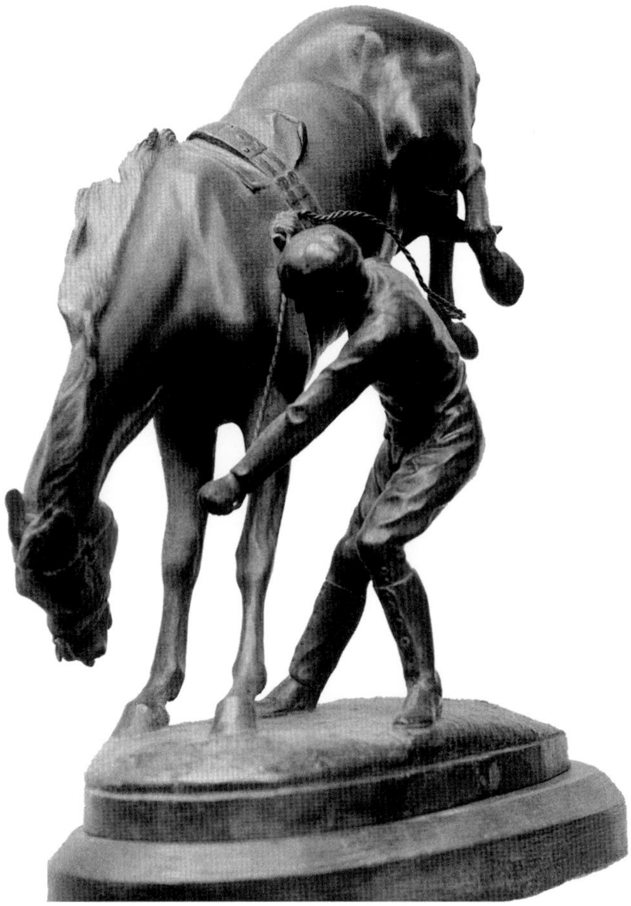

Breaking In a Two-year-old Horse, exhibited 1898 in one-man show at the Graves Gallery, Pall Mall

the aestheticists, with a show of different surface effects in hair, skin and base typical of the New Sculptors. It was a light-hearted effort, elegant but not, in the opinion of one owner who keeps the self-absorbed statuette in his bathroom, erotic. Jimmy Whistler might have called it 'Art for art's sake'.

The last illustration in this review of Adrian's versatility is 'Breaking In A Two Year Old'. He must have enjoyed this opportunity, impossible in his celebratory equestrian statues and commissioned equine statuettes, to sculpt a horse with hindquarters in the air. He chose it as one of the statuettes to be exhibited in his one man exhibition at the Graves Gallery in May 1898. The *Glasgow Herald*, perhaps alerted by the *Artist* magazine having devoted an article to Adrian's sculpture the previous month, and aware that 'in Scotland he is little known' although eight of his works were shown in the Glasgow Institute of Fine Art, sent along its art reviewer. Having first commented on the variety of the paintings of animals 'wherein is evident the artist's knowledge of the anatomy, movement, and temper of his subjects', he moved on to the small sculptures, 'remarkable for spirited and clean modelling'. He thought two bronzes 'particularly fine' – 'The Last Arrow', the statuette of a buffalo hunted by an Indian, and 'Breaking In'. The horse in the latter is described as 'kicking and plunging against the restraining bridle, with head down and forefeet firmly fixed and hind legs gathered in the air'. The strenuous vigour of the struggle between horse and horse-tamer for mastery is clear in the photograph from the Jones archives, but the 'restraining' end of the bridle is missing. It must have led to the horse from the lower side of the man's fist. The history of Adrian's artworks in general shows that sculptures, like paintings, require loving care and conservation.

When in November 1933 the firm of Stanley Paul published *Memoirs of a Soldier Artist* by Capt. Adrian Jones MVO, with his bold legible signature at the bottom right of the front cover just as if he were signing a canvas, it received extensive commendatory review. About fifty publications – national and regional newspapers, and journals ranging from the *Times Literary Supplement* to *Everybody's Weekly* – gave publicity to its contents and entertained their readers by retelling some of its amusing anecdotes. At the end of the Introduction to his *Memoirs*, Adrian declared that the story of his life would be 'my final task'. It was not to prove so, as he was to live on for a further five years. Nor did the newspapers and journals that printed a report or a review treat the book as solemn 'last words'. The *Parthenon* expressed the view that the 'memoirs have the merit of an unusual distinction inasmuch as they comprise a volume by one who is still a vital force' and 'run the gamut of the years in a correctly personal fashion ... the tale he tells is a veritable cavalcade ... midst a galaxy of genius'. As one might expect, publications which had a connection with Adrian were fulsome. The *British Legion Journal* reviewed under the headline 'A Soldier Artist's Genius'; the *Veterinary Record* used the heading 'A Great Veterinarian Sculptor' and reminded readers that an artist [i.e. painter] and sculptor of equestrian subjects 'must understand anatomy intimately ... this, surely, is the secret of Captain Adrian Jones' success'. The *Shrewsbury Chronicle* wrote of his 'immortal works ... proof against the barbs of professional jealousy'. Only the Irish press was partly grudging. As related in Chapter Three, the *Irish Independent* considered that Adrian had little to say of interest concerning Ireland; and the *Irish News* reviewer, writing from the standpoint of a trained artist, thought the self-taught Adrian immodest:

> It is amusing to see him set down discoveries of his own as if they were real discoveries in art but which the reviewer learned in his first year of clay-modelling ... this book accounts for the fact that he has never modelled a symbolic figure entitled 'Humility'.

In an article headed 'Contrasts in Best-Sellers', the *Times* reported: 'It has been a season of singular contrasts among the best sellers.' At one extreme, Sarah Bowes-Lyon, the twelve-year-old second cousin of the Duchess of York (afterwards Queen Elizabeth) had scored enviable success with her illustrated book *Horsemanship as it is Today*, and at the other, octogenarian soldier veterans such as Adrian Jones had written popular autobiographies. At twelve shillings and sixpence Adrian's book cost just five shillings more than that of the child author. The press must have felt that the November publication date implied suitability for the Christmas market. Many reviewers described rather than evaluated. *John O'London's Weekly* and the *Humorist* devoted the most space to the book, concentrating on Adrian as a raconteur and entertaining their readers by recounting many of his diverting anecdotes. In its review the *Times* opened by declaring 'This is a very pleasant book, preserving throughout the peculiar serenity of old age', and closed with 'Throughout the book there are interesting sidelights on famous people – all, or most of them, subdued by time to a friendly gleam.'

Adrian's own last years were also lit by 'a friendly gleam'. Thought to be the oldest sculptor in the world, he was still fit enough to work on statuettes and to paint; people commented on his straight back and the bold clarity of his handwriting. Artistic tastes had moved on, while he had not changed his style, so although there was universal recognition of his supreme craftsmanship, the avant-garde could dismiss him as a realist whose horses were no more or less than horses. It must have struck him as ironic that a quarter of a century earlier he had been briefly referred to as a surrealist on the ground that his Quadriga was no more than a fanciful creation.

The Royal Veterinary College invited him back in 1925 as an illustrious guest at the opening of their new research institute in animal pathology; and at their 1934 AGM they presented to him the diploma of Honorary Associate. Reporting on this occasion the next day, the press recorded in rather awed tones that he was 'still at work, although ninety years old'. Though he received this honour essentially as an equine sculptor, in his speech to the vet audience he told not of his art but of his experiences with animals as a vet officer in the campaigns of nearly seventy years previously.

But he always maintained that he was first and foremost an artist. He set out his principles for a final time in *A Testament of Beauty*, the article he wrote for the *Times* to mark his receipt of the RSBS Gold Medal in 1935:

> The principles first of all say that nothing human or animal of God's creation should be in any way distorted ... I don't want people to think that I suggest a facsimile ... All live things look bigger than dead ones ... A facsimile work of the model will never fill the eye or the sense of proportion. It has to be increased in different places without disturbing the anatomy to produce the effect of reality.

Three years later the *Times* obituarist, in referring to Adrian's article, commented that 'between "distorting" and "increasing" there is room for many differences of opinion, and the plain truth is that between them lies the art, as distinct from the craft, of sculpture'. Or, to quote the old adage, the truth may be plain but it is not simple. In the words of the Latin tag, *Quot homines, tot sententiae*: 'There are as many opinions as there are men'. Readers may wish to form their own opinion, but it is not essential to join the debate.

Importantly, Adrian believed that he had produced 'art'. Partly because of its subject matter, and partly because of his style, he had made a connection between art and the British people, with thousands or tens of thousands watching unveilings, buying postcards of all the major statues and of popular statuettes such as 'Waterloo', attending Remembrance ceremonies and gathering at the Quadriga in six figure numbers on national occasions. Whether it was an Industrial Exhibition at Earls Court or an Empire Exhibition at Wembley or a place of public resort such as the Crystal Palace, his 'finely sculptured groups' were selected for display. He was especially proud of those of his works that were sited permanently in London. He felt that to have helped to decorate any city was an honour, but to have helped to decorate the Mother City of an Empire was more. To an extent he was a 'grand old man' from the past: dressed in the flowing black cloak lined with scarlet which he had worn during the Abyssinian Campaign seventy years previously, he sat many evenings in the Savage or Chelsea Arts Club, recalling long dead celebrities such as Thomas Carlyle and James Whistler whom he had known in Chelsea, but also listening deferentially to the views of far younger, more radical artists. Even when he did not like what an artist did, he saw little point in saying so. But he did not have to think of himself as a 'has been'. Some of his best work had been done since the Great War; at times he was called back into public attention, as when Mussolini invaded Abyssinia and he was interviewed about fighting a war there, or when Sir David Campbell was appointed Governor of Malta and the press featured Adrian's painting of him as the Grand National winning jockey on 'The Soarer'; or when the Royal Veterinary College or Royal Society of British Sculptors gave him a further honour; and he celebrated his ninety-second birthday in quintessentially twentieth-century style with a cocktail party.

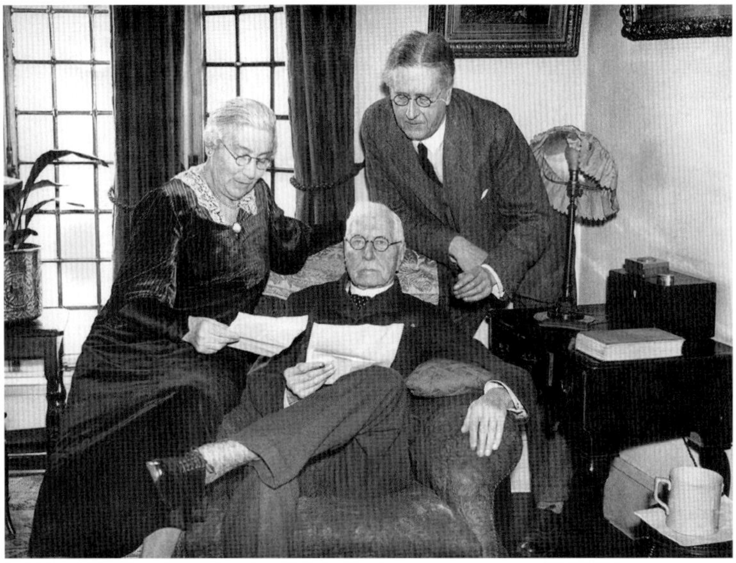

'Many happy returns': Adrian with Emma and his son. George V telegrammed: 'I send my hearty congratulations on your 90th birthday', and the celebrities of the art world gathered for his birthday party at Chelsea Arts Club, where Sir John Lavery spoke to the toast of 'Captain Jones'.

After a spell of influenza and bronchitis, Adrian died on 24 January 1938, within a fortnight of his ninety-third birthday. The *Times* obituarist wrote that 'Jones was universally popular, not to say beloved, in art circles in Chelsea, where he lived'. At his funeral service in Chelsea Old Church the following Friday morning, the seventeen family members present, led by Emma, Adrian and Nell, were joined by mourners from most strands of his life. There were fellow artists such as Wilson Steer and Sir Goscombe John; representatives of the Royal Society of British Sculptors, the Royal Army Veterinary Corps, the Veterinary Association, the Allenby Club, the Shropshire Society in London, the Royal Commission on Historical Monuments, and the Queen's Bays; and other army officers. The Trumpet Major of the Queen's Bays attended to sound any required trumpet calls, though Adrian had directed that his funeral should be as simple as possible. He had also directed that absolute proof of death should be furnished before his body was placed in the coffin, that he should be cremated, and that no unnecessary money should be spent on his grave. Cremation followed at Golders Green, and his ashes, marked by a plain tablet on the church's north outside wall, were laid to rest in the churchyard of St. Laurence's, Ludlow, close beside those of the poet A.E. Housman, who had died two years previously. The spot was just a little over a hundred yards from where he had been born, the same distance from where his South Australian yeomanry scout statue watched over events in the town hall, and a quarter of a mile from his schoolroom.

Memorials to Adrian Jones are also to be seen in the form of many of his works. In the 1930s his sculpture 'Duncan's Horses' found a home at the Crystal Palace, where, in what Adrian termed 'a miracle' it was the only major statue to survive the great fire that consumed the Palace in 1936. The next year Adrian made a gift of the cast to the Royal Veterinary College. Sadly, its misfortunes were not yet over. The college could not afford to cast the statue in bronze. A letter in the issue of the *Veterinary Record* dated 19 June 1937 announced the launch of 'the Adrian Jones Statue Appeal Fund'. £1,800 was required to meet the costs of moving the statue to the Vet College, repairing the minor injuries suffered at Crystal Palace, constructing a granite pedestal and foundations, and casting in bronze. The fund received a splendid send-off with an anonymous donation of £500 and other promises, but then the Second World War intervened. Industry had to manufacture munitions, and no resources could be spared to cast statues in bronze.

Until 1967 'Duncan's Horses' languished unseen in a furniture depository in Camden Town, but not forgotten by the Royal Veterinary College. In 1960 the College resolved to restore the horses so that they might one day become the centrepiece of the forecourt at their new field station in Hertfordshire. In 1967 the fund was used to transport the plaster cast there, place it on a plinth and coat it in polyester resin intended to weatherproof it. Expert advice gave assurances that the statue should now endure indefinitely. The experts were wrong. As wind and rain beat upon it and penetrated its weatherproofing defences, the wooden frame inside and the plaster outside expanded at different rates, and cracks opened up. The College Bursar, Derek Gordon-Brown, his fund largely exhausted just keeping the horses in one piece, was on the verge of losing hope of salvation for the statue when by chance he met Keith Grant, the Head of Art at Roehampton Institute of Higher Education. For Grant, Adrian Jones – soldier, veterinary surgeon, artist and devoted horseman – rated as a Renaissance figure whom he saw as very close to Stubbs as an anatomist of the horse. With Gordon-Brown he made a joint inspection of 'Duncan's Horses' and unhesitatingly declared that the sculpture must be saved. Thus fortified in resolution, Gordon-Brown approached the Market Harborough sculptor Geoffrey Tiney, who specialised in sporting and wildlife subjects, to take on the difficult task of restoring the horses. Because he was (to use his phrase) a dedicated admirer of Adrian Jones, and considered 'Duncan's Horses' to be his masterpiece, Tiney agreed. At last the statue, now with a bird's nest in it, was to be saved. A second 'Duncan's Horses' Appeal was launched immediately after 1984's annual memorial service at Jones's Cavalry of the Empire Memorial in Hyde Park. The Duke of Edinburgh acted as patron, Adrian's great nephew Jim Cunningham gave advice as necessary, and Edward Horswell, director of the Sladmore Gallery, arranged a retrospective exhibition of Adrian Jones's work and gave all profits to the Appeal. With the help of a generous benefaction from Paul Mellon the money flowed in swiftly, and within three years the target was reached. Geoffrey Tiney, helped by his skilled moulder Alex Ryman, and driven by his admiration for Jones, immersed himself in the fascinating and lengthy task of conservation.

So finally, on 26 June 1985, the oldest and largest veterinary college in Britain was able to celebrate the unveiling of the statue. The Principal invited HRH the Duke of Edinburgh to unveil what the Duke himself termed 'an appropriate and much prized work of art', assuring the large throng present that 'Duncan's Horses' would be 'the central feature in the campus life of the College for many, many years to come'. Now, 'many years' later, unharmed by wind or rain, and sited where Adrian by his gift intended it to be, it still draws the eye of the passer by, or of the student gazing through the glass wall of the College library and learning centre.

Because of its position in the middle of the Royal Veterinary College forecourt, visitors, before walking round it as Adrian would wish, have to walk towards it. The usual approach is from the direction of the college's main entrance. At middle distance the statuary group is already impressive, its more than life-size scale emphasised by its raised position atop a rockery mound and by its almost pyramidical line of composition. But it does not yet fully reveal itself or evoke a strong emotional response. Indeed, it may be rather baffling. Clearly enough there are a couple of horses, but what is the mass between their respective hind legs that diminishes the clarity of the outline by in-filling just where spatial separation would have been expected? Shadows cast by the planes and curves of the horses may further confuse the eye. And though an observer may come knowing the statue's title in advance and may perhaps have general knowledge of the play *Macbeth*, there will be no memory of any major plot advancement involving the king's horses. Going to view Millais's 'Ophelia', one imagines that one is going to see a beautiful maiden drowning, and that is indeed what one sees. But what is the story of Duncan's horses?

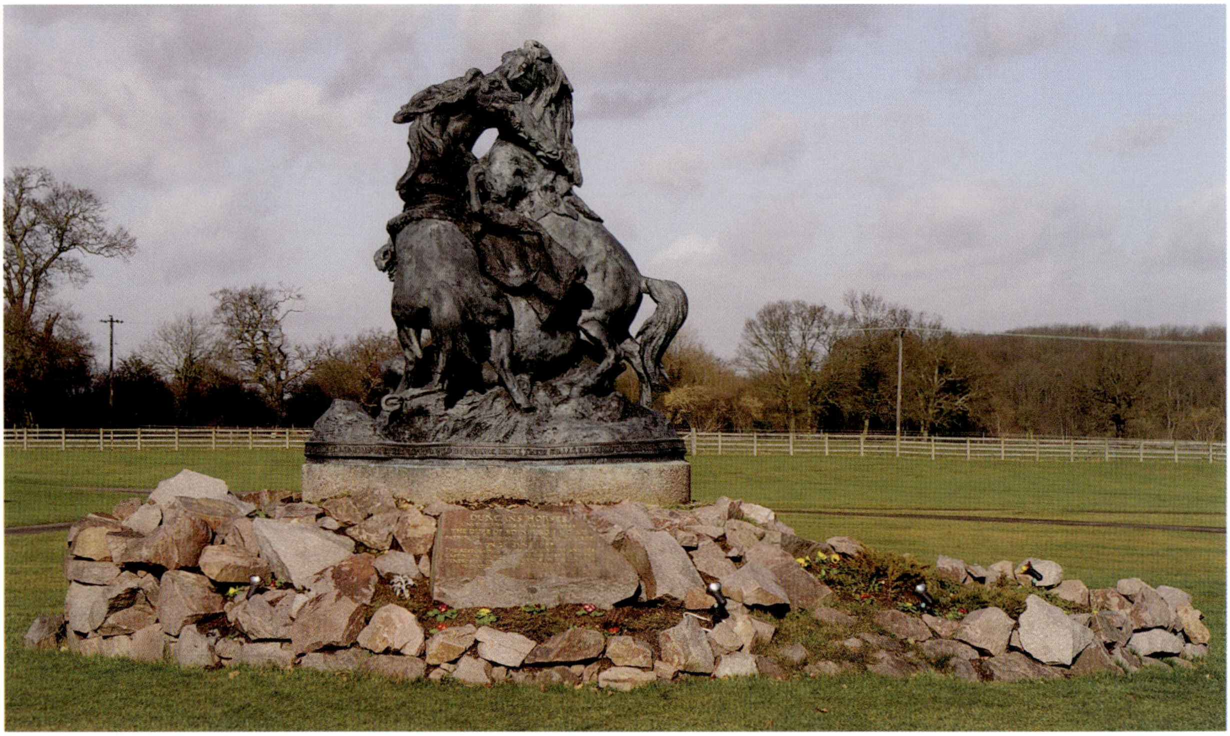

The bronze statue **Duncan's Horses** in the centre of the Royal Veterinary College forecourt. This is the viewer's first sight of the statue on approach from the College entrance.

Closer, the action in the statue is clearer. The infill is the haunches of a collapsed horse. Walk round, and the vigour of the action and the skill of the artist's execution are still more dramatic. Three, not the originally perceived two, horses are attacking each other, twisting and turning to gain supremacy. Running round the base is the quotation which inspired Adrian:

> Duncan's horses – a thing most strange and certain –
> Beauteous and swift, the minions of their race,
> Turn'd wild in nature, broke their stalls, flung out,
> Contending 'gainst obedience, as they would make
> War with mankind.

A glance at the sculpted horses shows that in the perspiration that followed inspiration he paid fullest attention not to the noble Ross's lines quoted, but to the Old Man's reply:

> Tis said they [i.e. the horses] eat each other.

The resulting statue is horrific, disturbing. The highest-reared horse crunches its teeth down onto the neck of the second, which writhes its head round, grasping and biting back. The third, pinioned between and below the others, struggles strenuously but futilely, seeking to contort its head into position to grapple in fight. These are horses out of their minds, literally maddened.

The focus is entirely on the horses. No murdered Duncan, no Macbeth nor his Lady, no horrified Ross watching in amazement; no added context of any kind. The sculpture is naturalistic, but the sculpted horse behaviour is unnatural. These are horses from fiction, behaving as only fictional horses could. But the group is far from being just another example of sometimes despised 'Victorian narrative art'. Many equine sculptures, Adrian's commissioned statuettes included, are records: loving, admiring portrayals of loved and admired horses. The emotions aroused by them are gentle and pleasurable. But in 'Duncan's Horses' Adrian advances equine sculpture to new possibilities, although because the sculpture is not the product of any '-ism' of modern experimental art it has been too often overlooked by art historians. The horses, though shown 'turn'd wild in nature', are not wild horses. They wear disordered pieces of primitive royal harness trappings. They have broken out into vicious behaviour only because they have been ill served by evil human action. Not spelt out, for this is not allegorical statuary, but tacitly, 'Duncan's Horses' is deeply significant in meaning.

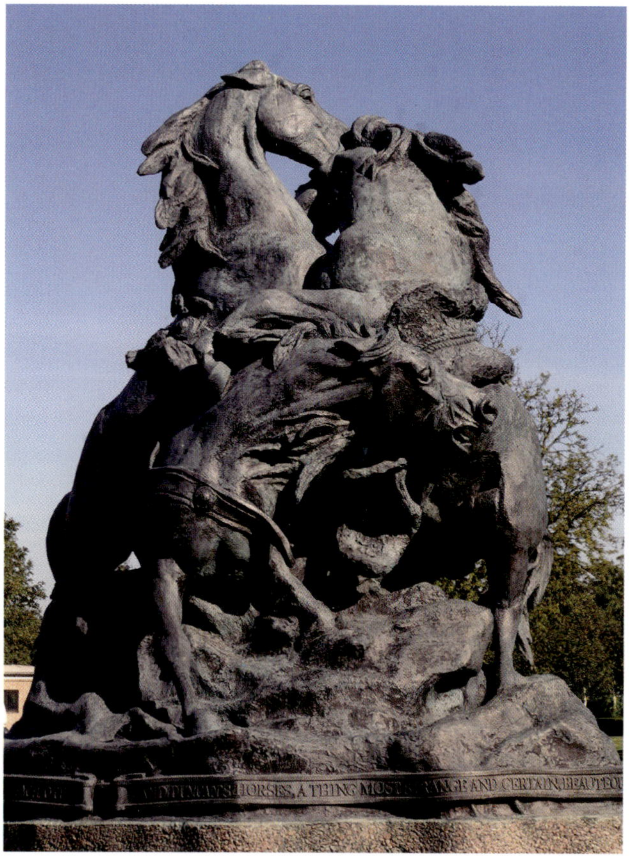

"Tis said they eat each other'

Another of Adrian's statues has recently been rescued – or at least a fragment of it has. The plaster cast of the South Australia Boer Memorial unveiled in Ludlow Town Hall in 1905 stayed there for many years. The Scout scanned countless Hall dances, social and charitable events for the next eighty-one years, and survived such exuberances as American servicemen relaxing from preparations for D-Day by clambering up to join him on the horse's back. In 1986, however, the Town Hall, by then the responsibility of the South Shropshire District Council, was declared unsafe and hastily – too hastily, admirers of the building thought – demolished. Horse and rider were lifted out by crane and injured in the process. The damage included exposure of the armature, and after years of storage in various locations chemical reactions inside the plaster ended in the disarticulated statue lying abandoned in a commercial warehouse. There had been a moment of hope when a delegation from Australia looked at the statue, while it was stored by the National Army Museum, to consider it as a national memorial to Australian soldiers to be sited near Adrian's Peace Quadriga at Hyde Park Corner; but assessment showed that the damage was irreversible. In 2005, the centenary of its arrival in Ludlow, the National Army Museum accepted that the horse was fit only for the knacker's yard, and it was decided that the broken plaster should be destroyed. Fortunately the Chairman of the Old Ludlovians' Association, Dr Jen Davies, was able to rescue the severed horse's head, and with the help of her husband transport it to Ludlow, where they repaired it, rewaxed it, and treated it with bronze gilding cream. Appropriately, they carried out this conservation in the Ludlow College classroom which had originally been a coach house. The restored head was unveiled at a former students' Annual Reunion, and is now on display on the College's Palmers Hall site, where it may be viewed close-up in the lobby of the staircase which leads to Upper Quadrangle, the Adrian Jones Gallery, and the schoolroom where Adrian received his education.

The plaster horse's head is not the only work of Adrian's to be seen in the town of his birth. A year after his death in 1938, his widow Emma presented to Ludlow Grammar School his equestrian bronze statuette of the Indian cavalry soldier Colonel Dowla. It was received by the Chairman of Governors, Mr E.H. Rickards, who had known Adrian Jones personally, and the headmaster announced that it would be cherished as a 'memorial to the art of the late Captain A. Jones'. It was placed in the medieval assembly hall. Since 2007 it has been gazed upon across the hall by a bronze bust of Adrian himself, attired in his sculptor's working clothes with artist's tools protruding from his breast pocket. Appropriately, the bust is the work of another Shropshire figurative artist, Jemma Pearson.

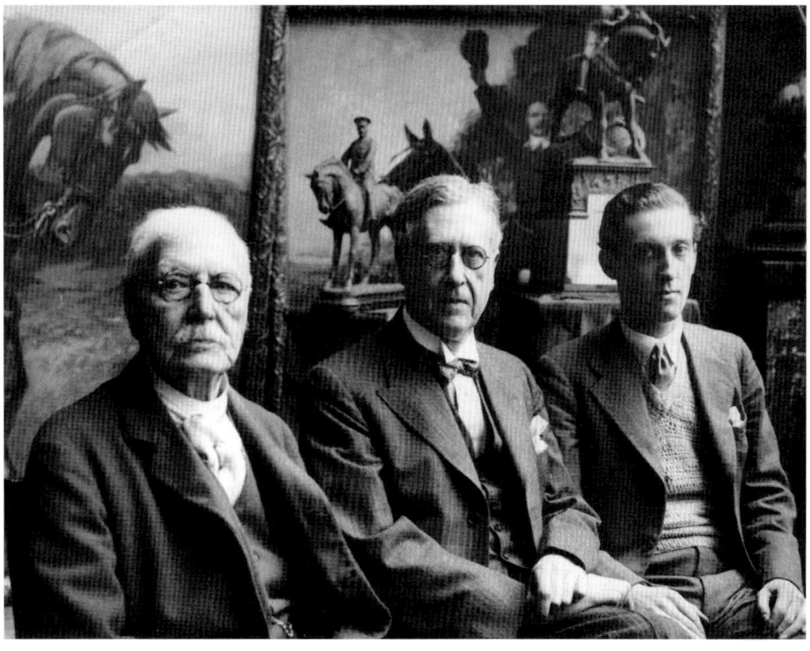

Three generations. Father Adrian, son Adrian and grandson Adrian

Another work of Adrian's to have received attention in recent years is the Quadriga. In 1997 English Heritage placed the Wellington Arch on its first Buildings at Risk register, whereupon the Government gave English Heritage responsibility for it. They undertook a £1.5 million restoration which included stripping the Quadriga of its blackened wax and returning it to the original bronze finish, and opening the interior and the balcony of the Arch to the public. It is now a cherished feature of the Princess Diana Memorial Way. Deprived of his planned pyrotechnic opening, Adrian would have loved to see it floodlit, and to observe the effects of such other lighting displays as the large poppies which float down the face at Remembrance time. James Manson, the first Secretary of the Camden Town Group of painters, writing an article on Adrian in 1912, concluded: 'The Quadriga was at first called "Triumph", and at last that is what indeed it is.' English Heritage's magnificent restoration deserves the same accolade.

One place with strong associations with Adrian Jones has no official memorial. In London, though his Chelsea home has been renamed Adrian House, it does not bear a blue plaque. In 2001 Mr Selwyn H. Pressinger, whose family had been fellow parishioners with Adrian and Monica at the Oratory and who had written about Adrian in the *Army Quarterly And Defence Journal* and elsewhere, proposed the affixing of a plaque. The Blue Plaques Secretary replied that their panel had decided not to pursue the suggestion. 'It was felt that much of his [i.e. Adrian's] reputation today rested on the Quadriga of Peace at Wellington Arch, and that this work itself stood as the best testimony of Jones' achievements.' Few if any would deny that a good example of work indeed constitutes 'best testimony', but if that criterion were to be universally applied to proposals for plaques, no creative artist who had ever produced a great painting or sculpture which could be seen by the public, no composer who had written a great work which could be heard in a concert hall, and no architect whose great

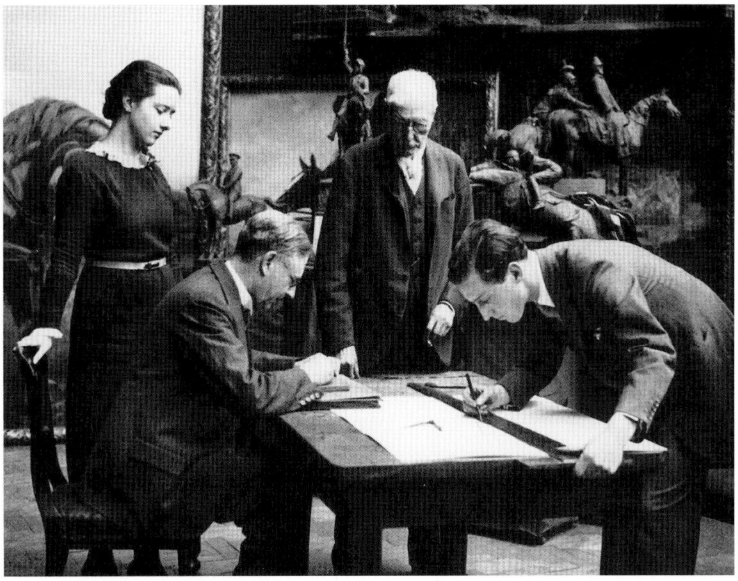

Adrian's granddaughter Monica joins the three Adrians.

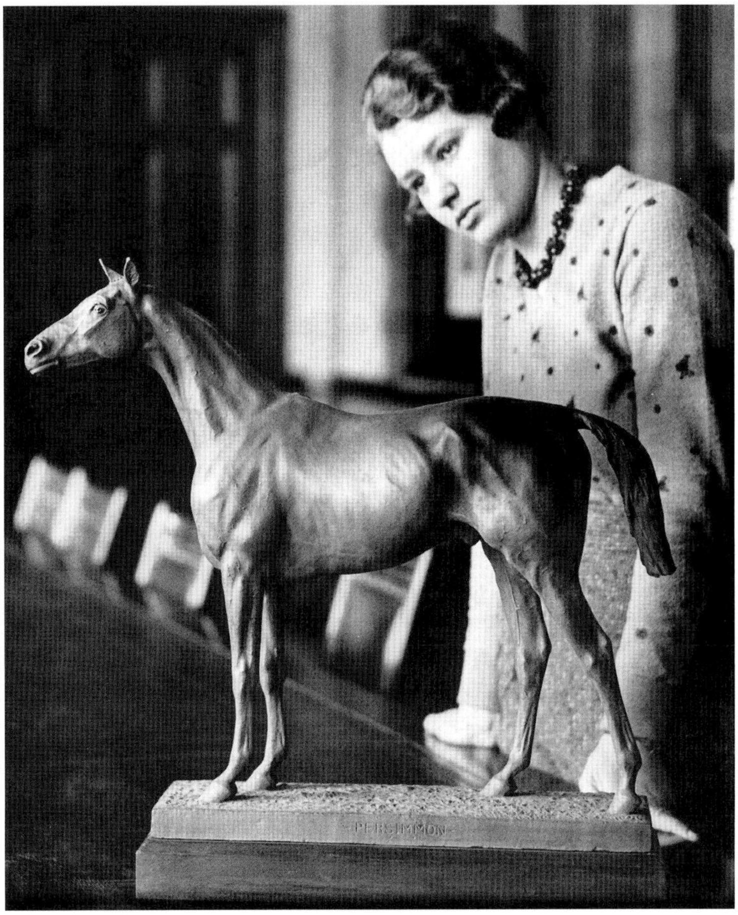

Persimmon as racehorse, bronze statuette, admired by Monica

building enhanced a London street would qualify for a blue plaque on his former dwelling place. In reality, many a house where a distinguished person lived comparatively fleetingly has its blue commemoration. 147 Church Street, where Adrian lived and worked for forty-seven years in the era when Chelsea was London's art quarter, remains unmarked.

A pleasure of Adrian's last years was that his son and his grown up grandchildren now lived in London, and all three had inherited artistic ability. As father, son and grandson were all named Adrian, the *Evening Advertiser* predicted that 'Adrian' Jones l, Il and lll will provide another headache for the historian'. Son Adrian had married a Catholic girl, Ellen Cunningham, originally from Limerick, five years younger than himself. Ellen, always known in the family as Nell, had spent some of her childhood in Cyprus, and was to spend many years of her married life abroad also, as Adrian was an engineer who built bridges around the world. Sadly she lost one child and was gravely ill herself with puerperal fever in Buenos Aires at the end of 1910, but happily, even if she did not fulfil the good wishes of the friend who wrote to assure her, 'You are still young [she was twenty-six] and I hope to see you the mother of half a dozen boys and girls yet', Adrian lll was safely born at Brighton in August 1912 and his sister Monica in Argentina in October 1913. Adrian and his family spent the war years there, sending parcels to troops on the Western Front, and Nell receiving the letters of her officer brother Arthur from Salonika in Greece, a minor theatre of the war. He was struck by the make-the-best-of-it humorous outlook of the troops, whether manning a trench or dressing as a 'simply ravishing girl' in an other ranks' pantomime. He told his sister, 'The British Tommy is certainly a twentieth century miracle.'

After further years in Argentina, once back in London Adrian Il became known as a watercolourist and as an etcher with a decisive and careful style. He joined the Society of Graphic Artists, and when he first exhibited at the Society's show in the Royal Institute Galleries in Piccadilly, the press praised the clearness and hardness of his etching 'Siesta', and reported that 'he came to the private view with his vigorous and upright father'. Adrian lll had the reputation of being a child prodigy, though it is hard to know what level of achievement lay behind a press report that he 'began painting at the age of three'. Certainly in 1934, at the unusually early age of twenty-one, he shared a two-man show in the Storran Gallery with the even younger Derek Hill, the designer of the scenery and costumes of that year's production of *Castor and Pollux* by Oxford University Opera Club. This Adrian became an architect, joined the Architectural Association, and showed his work at the AA's annual exhibitions in their Bedford Square premises. In the same year as his two man show, his watercolours, including one of Constantinople, were picked out as having 'real charm'. He continued his art during his 1939-45 service in the Royal Navy Volunteer Reserve. In 1945, by which time he had risen from Ordinary Seaman to Lieutenant, he was licensed by Naval Intelligence to sketch in Malta Dockyard, but his field of choice was limited, because the exclusions from the licence ranged from 'any fortifications' to 'any riotous or disorderly assembly'. After the war he designed a much admired architectural scheme of painted decoration for the Little Oratory chapel of London's Brompton Oratory, and with Monica contributed exhibits to grandfather Adrian's retrospective exhibition. He died in December 1985. Neither he nor Monica married, so the direct line of Adrian's descendants ended.

Adrian had waived his fee for several of the last memorials he designed, and he was not destined to be a rich man. His estate was valued at £3,142. After his death, Emma moved to a flat elsewhere in Chelsea. She suffered the vicissitudes of upheaval, wartime blitz, the death of one of her sisters and a spell of ill health which involved two months in a nursing home. In July 1941 she returned to Watchet. She told Adrian lll in a letter that it was 'a small house, and so far comfortable. My furniture and effects were sent here from the flat, Chelsea. Everything dreadfully damaged from the raid which partially destroyed the building'. She was replying to a letter from Adrian, who, by one of life's coincidences, was aboard *HMS Cottesmore,* named after the Hunt for which his grandfather had sculpted statuettes. He was very happy in his life at sea, which in the previous month had included his ship shooting down a German Heinkel 111 bomber which attacked it while it was on convoy duty. Emma commented that his life now was 'so absolutely different to what you had been accustomed'. From a seaport family, with a father and nephews who had been seamen, she 'was very pleased to hear that you are so happy in your new work'. Adrian had asked for information on his great grandmother, but Emma could tell him no more than he already knew, that she had been Jane Marshall and had lived somewhere near Badminton. As she explained sadly, 'I have not found any papers that would help ... When I left Church Street I had to destroy quantities of letters as the accumulation of forty seven years. It was tiring work.' She thought it was brave of his mother, Nell, to continue to live in Sydney Street in Chelsea. Later in the blitz that family home too was hit, so Adrian had to deal with the War Damage Commission over claims for immediate and then further repairs.

Events continued to bear out the truth of Adrian's obituary in the *Liverpool Daily Post* that his Peace Quadriga 'has become part of the London picture and it is only regrettable that since it was erected just before 1914 there has been barely any peace worth mentioning'. Britain continues to need soldier-artists. Eminent among them stands Captain Adrian Jones, rural, metropolitan and imperial man; keen horseman, soldier and artist; compared to Cellini as a craftsman, and with some qualities of genius; and withal a likeable and admirable personality.

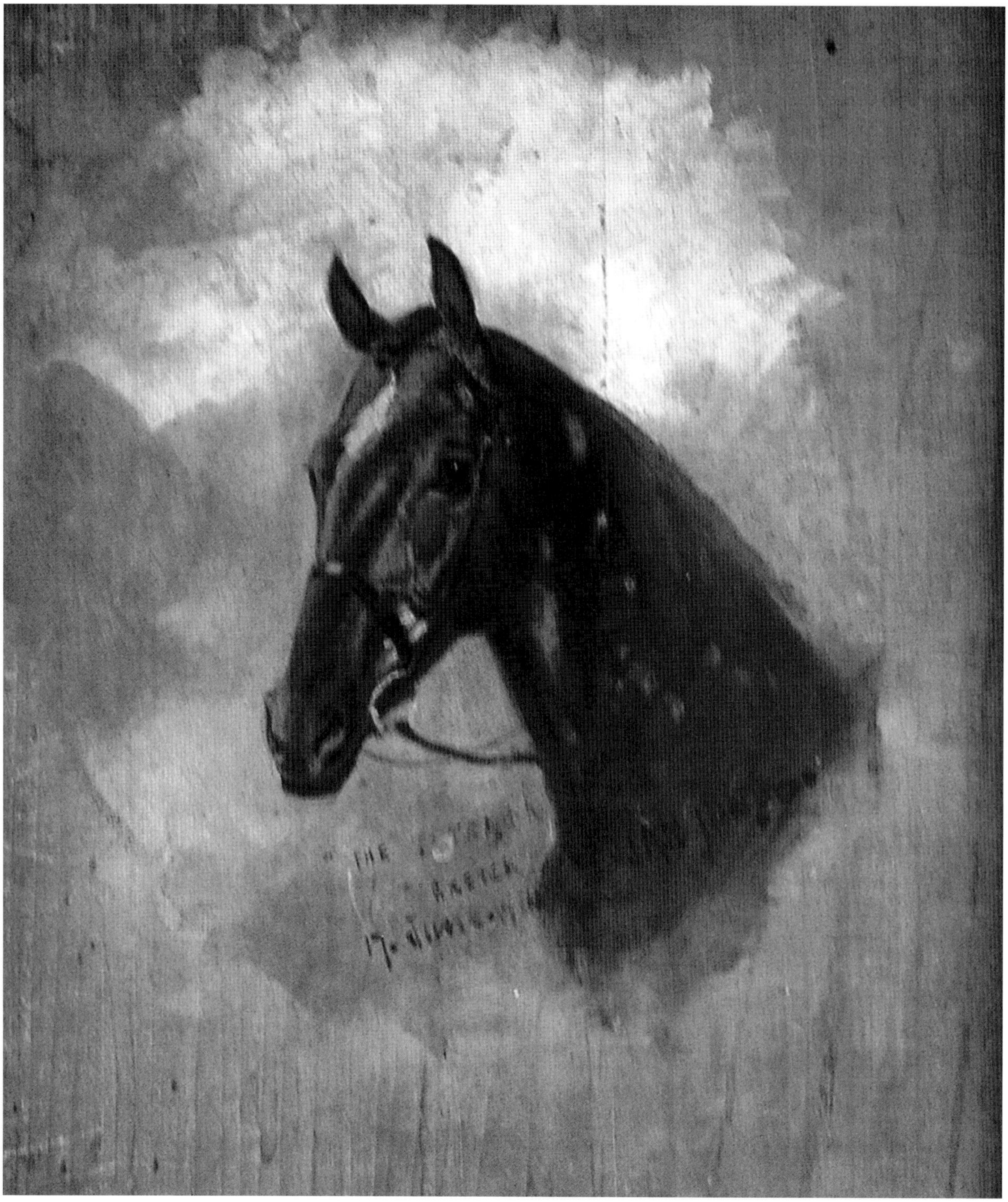

Tetrarch, sketch made in the early 1920s

Where to see the works of Adrian Jones

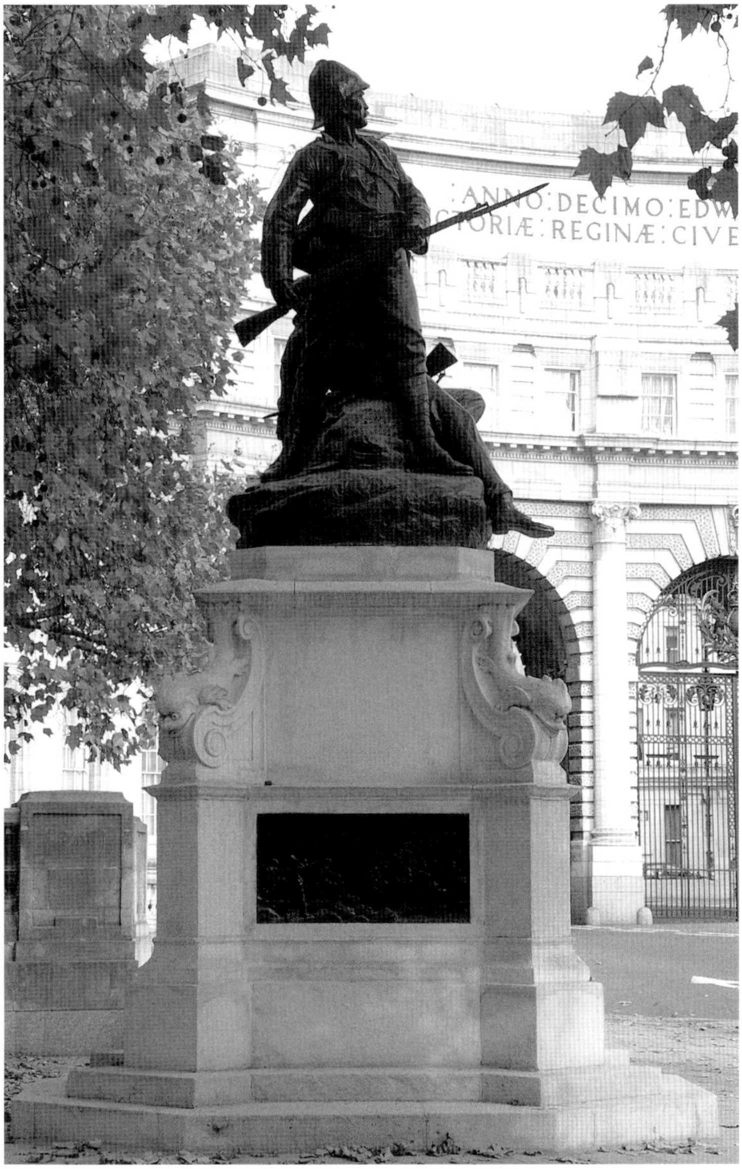

Royal Marines Memorial, repositioned after the Second World War on the north side of the Mall; Admiralty Arch in the background

Walking the Adrian Jones Trail

To see the quality of Adrian Jones's magnificent public sculptures, the best place is the nation's capital, London. The Adrian Jones Trail, described below, passes along handsome streets and through pleasant parks. Three quarters of an hour of unhurried walking is enough to complete it, but allow longer if you wish to look at the sculptures and bas reliefs in detail and if you intend to ascend the interior of the Wellington Arch, opened to the public by English Heritage, to view the three floors of exhibits and emerge on the balcony just beneath Europe's largest bronze sculpture, the Quadriga. The Trail can be walked in either direction, but the greater sense of climax comes from starting in Whitehall, as does the route outlined here.

Begin in Whitehall, near the Horse Guards sentries and museum, at the equestrian statue of the **Duke of Cambridge** (see Chapter Twelve). Next walk up Whitehall, in the direction of Trafalgar Square, but turn left through Admiralty Arch into the Mall. Near the top of the Mall, on the north (right hand) side, is the **Royal Marines Memorial** (Chapter Ten). Afterwards continue down the Mall, and then proceed through Green Park on a line alongside Constitution Hill Road to the right of Buckingham Palace. At the far end of Constitution Hill is Hyde Park Corner. Here is the Wellington Arch, home to English Heritage's exhibition on Adrian Jones. On top is the **Peace Quadriga** (Chapter Fourteen). If you plan to go inside the Arch, check opening times in advance). To finish, cross to Hyde Park, enter through the Stanhope Gate and bear left for a little distance along the Park's Serpentine Row. On the right hand side, a little set back, is the **Cavalry of the Empire Memorial** (Chapter Seventeen). To extend the walk by half an hour – or perhaps on another day! – walk south to the Albert Gate, cross Knightsbridge and go straight down Sloane Street, Lower Sloane Street and Chelsea Bridge Road to the Embankment. On the corner on the right, facing across to Chelsea Bridge, is the **Carabiniers Boer War Memorial** (Chapter Ten).

Visiting Museums

The biography has emphasised that Adrian Jones's statuettes and paintings are largely in royal and private collections, not in museums. The relevant army museums will show the military world in which Adrian Jones made his veterinary career, but one is likely to see more of his works of art at Sandringham than in any museum. However, a visit to any of the following museums will give fuller knowledge of the worlds of artists and racegoers which Adrian Jones also inhabited.

The **National Horseracing Museum,** High Street, Newmarket, has films of classic races, some from Victorian and Edwardian times, and equine statuettes by Jones, Munnings and others.

The **Ashmolean Museum**, Beaumont Street, Oxford, displays, in the nineteenth and early twentieth century galleries, bronze statuettes of Leighton's 'Athlete Struggling with a Python', Hamo Thorneycroft's 'General Gordon' and 'The Mower', Rodin's 'The Thinker' and 'Age of Bronze', and paintings by Leighton, Alma Tadema, Sickert and the Camden Town Group, Wilson Steer's 'Evening, Ludlow', etc. The museum also owns three paintings by James Manson who is quoted on the title page and elsewhere in *Triumph*, but they are not always on display.

The **Lady Lever Art Gallery**, Port Sunlight, holds numerous sculptures by Goscombe John, etc; Leighton's huge canvas 'The Daphnephoria', and his 'Garden of the Hesperides', painted in the year of the 'Ghost' controversy; other paintings by Alma Tadema, Frith, Sargent, Millais, Munnings, and enamels by Stubbs. Outside in the nearby gardens, Goscombe John's striking Port Sunlight War Memorial.

Add a visit to Liverpool to see John's King's Liverpool Regiment Memorial, his equestrian Edward VII, and 'Engine Room Heroes'; a portrait of Adrian Jones's patron Colonel Walker is in the entrance hall of the **Walker Art Gallery**, and two Adrian Jones paintings (Chapter Nine) are in **Croxteth Hall**.

Further Reading

Particular interests in aspects of Adrian Jones's life and art may be pursued in books listed here.

Schooling and Ludlow

D. Lloyd: *Country Grammar School: A History of Ludlow G.S.* (Studio Press, limited edition, 1977)
D. Lloyd and P. Klein: *Ludlow, A Historic Town in Words and Pictures* (Phillimore, 1984)
Ludlow Historical Research Group: *Victorian Ludlow* (Scenesetters, 2004)
H. Weyman: *Royal Visits to Ludlow* (Ludlow Chronicle reprint, 1911)

Veterinary Education and Service

E. Cotchin: *The Royal Veterinary College, London* (Barracuda Books, 1990)
Sir F. Smith: *A History of the R.A.V.C., 1796-1919* (Balliere, Tindall and Cox, 1927)

The Turf

S. Peters: *The Grand National* (Tempus Publishing, 2005)

Clubland

T. Cross: *Artists and Bohemians: 100 Years with the Chelsea Arts Club* (Quiller Press, 1992)

Campaigns and Commanders

P.J. Haythornthwaite: *The Colonial Wars Source Book* (Arms and Armour Press, 1995)
I. Hernon: *Britain's Forgotten Wars: Colonial Campaigns of the 19th Century* (Sutton Publishing, 2003)
G.A. Henty: *The March to Magdala* (Tinsley Brothers, 1868)
Earl Roberts: *Forty One Years in India: From Subaltern to Commander-in-Chief* (Macmillan, 1914)
P. Duckers: *The British-Indian Army, 1860-1914* (Shire Publications, 2003)
T.P.Dooley: *Irishmen or English Soldiers? Southern Catholic Irish in the British Army, 1876-1916* (Liverpool University Press, 1995)
H. Keown-Boyd: *A Good Dusting: The Sudan Campaigns, 1883-1899* (Martin Secker and Warburg, 1986)
R. Neillands: *The Dervish Wars: Gordon and Kitchener in the Sudan 1880-1898* (John Murray, 1996)
Veterinary Reports: Nile Expeditionary Force (HMSO, 1885)
M. Prior: *Campaigns of a War Correspondent* (Edward Arnold, 1912)
G.W. Steevens: *With Kitchener to Khartoum* (Nelson, 1900)
R.S.H. Moody: *Some Reminiscences* (serialised in *The Dragon* regimental journal of The Buffs (East Kent Regiment), 1924-25)
J. Symons: *Buller's Campaign* (Cresset Press, 1963)
G. Powell: *Buller: A Scapegoat?* (Leo Cooper, 1994)
P. Trew: *The Boer War Generals* (Sutton Publishing, 1999)

R. Holmes: *The Little Field Marshal: A Life of Sir John French* (Weidenfeld and Nicholson, 2004)
G. Corrigan: *Mud, Blood and Poppycock* (Cassell, 2003)
D. Winter: *Haig's Command: A Reassessment* (Viking, 1991)
D. Winter: *Death's Men: Soldiers of the Great War* (Allen Lane, 1978; Penguin Books, 1979)

Arms and Uniforms
P. Duckers: *British Military Rifles 1800-2000* (Shire Publications, 2005)
Dress Regulations For The Officers Of The Army, 1900 (HMSO, 1900)

Regimental Histories
Earl Dundonald: *My Army Life (2nd Life Guards)* (Edward Arnold, 1926)
F. Fox: *The Royal Gloucestershire Hussars Yeomanry, 1898-1922: The Great Cavalry Campaign in Palestine* (Philip Allan, 1923)
The Hon. E.G. French: *Goodbye to Boot and Saddle: The Tragic Passing of British Cavalry* (Hutchinson, 1951)
B. Harwood: *Chivalry and Command: 500 Years of Horse Guards* (Osprey, 2006)
E.S. Jackson: *The Inniskilling Dragoons* (Arthur Humphreys, 1909)
H. McCalmont: *Memoirs of Major-General Sir Hugh McCalmont, K.C.B., C.V.O (7TH Hussars)* (Hutchinson, 1924)
F. Manning: *Her Privates We (a novel, based on the King's Shropshire Light Infantry on the Somme, 1916)* (Serpentine Tail, 1999)
J.R.B. Mousdale: *The King's Shropshire Light Infantry* (Leo Cooper, 1972)
The Cocoanut Tree – and After: War Memories, 4th King's Shropshire Light Infantry, 1914-1918 (Shropshire Regimental Museum, 2004)
R. Pomeroy: *The Story of the 5th Royal Inniskilling Dragoon Guards, Volume II* (Blackwood and Sons, 1924)
J. Wanklyn: *Guns at the Wood: A Record of St. John's Wood Barracks* (limited private edition of 500 copies)
B. White-Spunner: *Horse Guards* (Macmillan, 2006)
F. Whyte and A. H. Atteridge: *History of the Queen's Bays, 2nd Dragoon Guards, 1685-1929* (Jonathan Cape, 1930)

Art
W. Baron: *Perfect Moderns, A History of The Camden Town Group* (Ashgate Publishing, 2000)
J. Baskett: *The Horse in Art* (Yale University Press, 2006)
S. Brindle and D. Robinson: *The Wellington Arch and the Marble Arch* (English Heritage, 2001)
M.R.D. Foot: *Art and War: Twentieth Century Warfare As Depicted By War Artists* (Headline Books, 1990)
J. Goodman: *What A Go! The Life of Alfred Munnings* (Collins, 1988)
P. Harrington: *British Artists and War: The Face of Battle in Paintings and Prints, 1700-1914* (Greenhill Books, 1993)
O. Humphrey and J. Mayer: *A Memoir of George Stubbs* (Pallas Athene, 2005)
R. Ironside: *Wilson Steer* (Phaidon Press, 1943)
N. Oliver: *Not Forgotten* (Hodder and Stoughton, 2005)
S.P.H. Pressinger: *Military and Equine Works of Captain Adrian Jones* (Sandilands Press, 2005)
B. Read: *Victorian Sculpture* (Yale University Press, 1982)
J. Ridley: *Edwin Lutyens, His Life, His Wife, His Work* (Pimlico, 2003)
Royal Veterinary College: *Adrian Jones, His Life and Works*: *Exhibition Catalogue*; also, *Save Duncan's Horses Appeal: Commemorative Brochure* (Sladmore Gallery, 1984)

List of Illustrations

Ceremonies

Other Artists' Works

Militaria

Shropshire Society

Buildings

General Index and Index of Works of Art

The titles of works of art are in italics beneath the artist's name. An italicised page number indicates illustration(s). Passages containing information about and critical review of major artworks are included also, unitalicised, among the general entries. All such passages are illustrated.

Jones, Captain Adrian

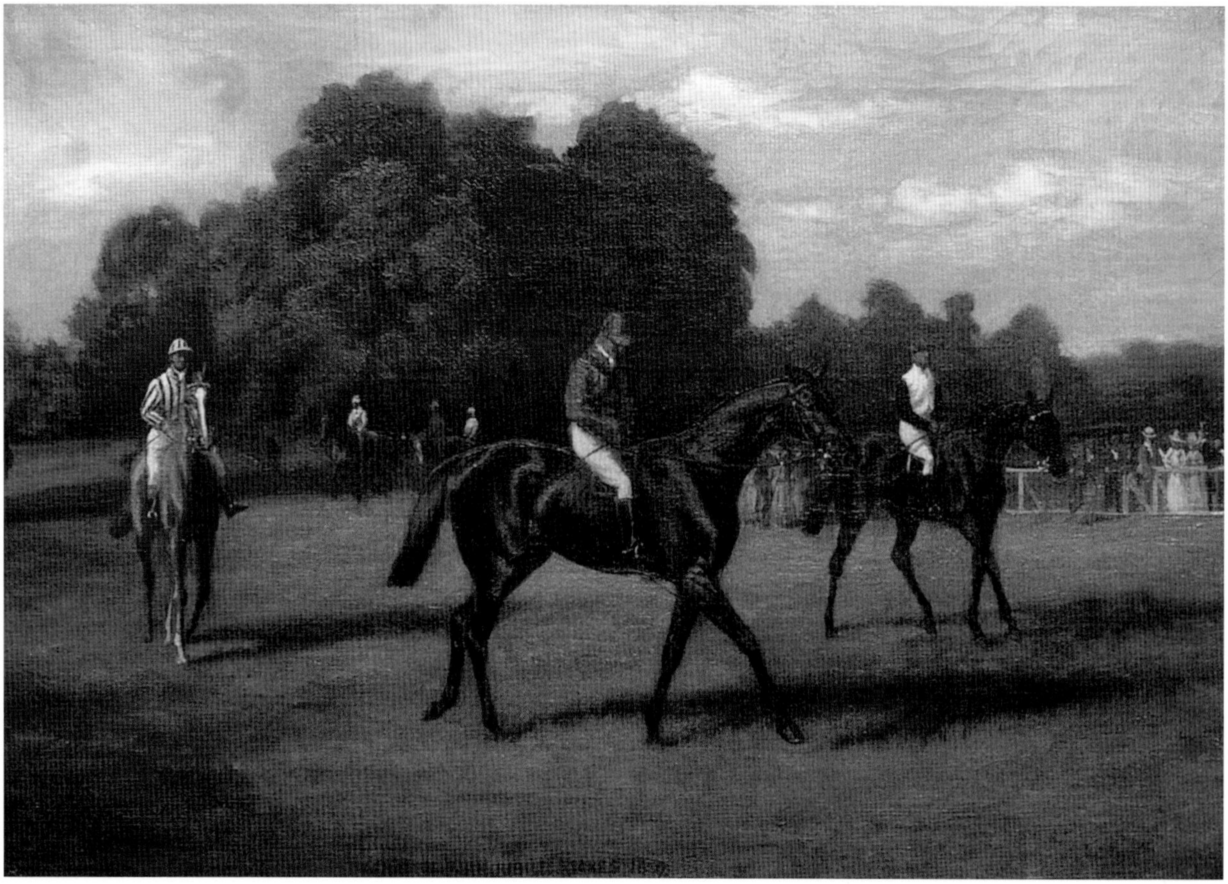

Kempton Park Jubilee Stakes, 1897. The racehorses are circling quietly, waiting for the starter's call. This is the kind of English scene that private collectors enjoy having on their walls.

Comp
medicine

Pocket
Neurology

Romée Snijders & Veerle Smit
Melissa van Kuik, Carlijn Veldman, Gwendolyn Vuurberg

Together for Healthcare

Want to know more about
Compendium Medicine?
Take a look at our website!

www.compendiummedicine.com

First edition, 2024

ISBN 9789083190990
BISAC MED056000
Thema MKJ

FSC www.fsc.org
MIX
Paper | Supporting responsible forestry
FSC® C118234

Preface

Welcome to the *Compendium Community!*

'Together for Healthcare' – these three simple words encapsulate the spirit of our collective mission and underscore the essence of our work. In an era where the complexity of healthcare is becoming increasingly interconnected, collaboration is not merely an option but an imperative. Our books symbolise the effectiveness of collaboration, knowledge sharing, and a joint commitment to improve and interconnect healthcare.

We proudly present the first edition of our pocket *Neurology*, with all the information you want to have at your fingertips. This comprehensive guide covers a wide range of clinical topics that will prove invaluable during your internship, traineeship, and night shifts. You can, for instance, explore chapters like neurological examination, conditions, and clinical reasoning, presenting examples of diagnoses to consider for specific symptoms.

The innovative *Compendium Method*©, designed for medical students and doctors, employs comprehensible illustrations for every medical condition, straightforward tables, icons, and useful mnemonics. It is visually appealing, to the point, and concise. We only focus on the essentials and make sure all the content is comprehensively presented.

Our strength lies in the diverse expertise of our close-knit medical team, consisting of students, doctors, and specialists from 15 hospitals and different specialties. This collaborative approach ensures that our content is comprehensive and accurate.

We are committed to inclusivity and aim to make our texts and images a reflection of the diversity of patients our readers provide care to. We aspire for every future doctor and patient to find themselves reflected in our books. Our team works continuously to improve and expand the selection of books. We welcome readers to share their feedback and suggestions, contributing to the continual improvement of our pocket series.

We sincerely wish to express immense gratitude to our team of medical students and healthcare professionals. The outstanding result of their contributions is this extraordinary pocket – a pocket for everybody in healthcare.

Enjoy reading and enjoy working, and we hope to hear from you soon!

Amsterdam, June 2024

Veerle Smit, MD & Romée Snijders, MD
Doctors and founders *Compendium Medicine*

Editorial staff

Want to know more about us?
Scan this QR code.

Editorial board

Romée J.A.L.M. Snijders, MD & Veerle L. Smit, MD

Chief editor

Gwendolyn Vuurberg, MD, PhD

Pocket editor

Current edition

Melissa A. van Kuik, MD, OLVG, Amsterdam

Previous edition

Carlijn Veldman, BSc, University of Groningen
Gwendolyn Vuurberg, BSc, University of Amsterdam

Authors

Current edition

Sabhat K. Akhtar, MD, Amsterdam University Medical Center
Demi van Bijlevelt, MD, St Jansdal Hospital, Harderwijk
Liza M.Y. Gelissen, MD, Amsterdam University Medical Center

Previous edition

Yvette de Haan, BSc, VU Amsterdam
Tim Halderman, BSc, VU Amsterdam
Paul Hendriks, BSc, University of Antwerp
An Hudepohl, BSc, University of Groningen
Joppe Lefebvre, BSc, Catholic University Leuven
Cas van der Made, BSc, Radboud University Nijmegen
Iris Verhagen, BSc, Utrecht University

Acknowledgements

Illustrators

Yente S. Beentjes, MD, Utrecht University
Hebe T.A. Boerhout, Utrecht University
Cas van Cruchten, Maastricht University
Susan Deelstra, University of Groningen
Floris Duetz, AVAG, Amsterdam
Lotte Dupuis, Radboud University Nijmegen
Gulizar Durak, Hogeschool Rotterdam
Astrid A.H. Feikema, Radboud University Nijmegen
Iza Hogenelst, Hogeschool Inholland Amsterdam
Dite L.C. de Jong, Maastricht University
Didi D.J. Juin, Hogeschool Utrecht
Jasmin Kaur, BSc, Hogeschool Rotterdam
Koen L.C. Ketelaars, MD, Radboud University Nijmegen
Robin Klabbers, Maastricht University
Rosalie C. Krijl, MD, VU Amsterdam
Sibylle Lange, Radboud University Nijmegen
Juliëtte M.E. Linskens, MD, Maastricht University
Sophie Reese, University of Groningen
Belle van Rosmalen, University of Amsterdam
Laura Sanchez, MSc, Catholic University Leuven
Esther Simons, Radboud University Nijmegen
Carlijn Sturm, Leiden University
Linda Xie, MD, Leiden University

Editorial coordinators

Laura M. Barrantes Rodríguez, MD, international relations manager
Pauline Blom, final editor
Vera den Boef, project manager
Jasmijn M.A. van Es, MD, illustration editor
Melanie Goedegebure, project manager
Charlotte Schoenaers, BSc, illustration manager
Charlotte Vinkenvleugel, BSc, manager diversity and inclusivity

Sounding board

Eva L. Brunner, MD, Public Health Service Hollands Midden
Estelle van Eijk, MD, Reinier de Graaf Hospital, Delft
Nathasja van Leeuwen, MD, St. Joseph Hospital, Kagondo
Merit E. Maas, MD, MSc, Centre for Youth and Family Rijnmond, Rotterdam
Chase Neff, MD, Radboud University Medical Center, Nijmegen
Naïlah Sint Jago, MD, Utrecht

Language support

Translation Agency Perfect
Mark Hannay, translator
Ruth Rose, editor

Graphic designers

Maria van Doorn, BASc
Ivana Kinkel

Content quality assurance

The editorial board extends its sincere appreciation to the many contributions of doctors, specialists, and professors from around the world who played a pivotal role in crafting this pocket. We wish to express our thanks to the entire international team for their dedicated efforts and invaluable expertise. Special appreciation is also extended to the team of specialists who actively participated in shaping the previous edition.

Current edition

Ernesto A.C. Beenakker, MD, PhD, MBA, Medical Center Leeuwarden
Tamara B. Kaplan, MD, Brigham and Women's Hospital, Boston
Prof. Peter Portegies, MD, PhD, Amsterdam University Medical Center
Kiki S.J. Post, MD, Ommelander Hospital Group, Groningen
Prof. Walter Royal, MD, Morehouse School of Medicine, Atlanta
Jolanda Schieving, MD, PhD, Radboud University Medical Center, Nijmegen
Bas J.J.W. Schouwenberg, MD, PhD, Radboud University Medical Center, Nijmegen

Previous edition

Ernesto A.C. Beenakker, MD, PhD, MBA, Medical Center Leeuwarden
Matthias M. Cabri, MD, Amsterdam University Medical Center
Stefan Graus, MD, Deventer Hospital
Yvette de Haan, MD, Amsterdam University Medical Center
Prof. Mario Maas, MD, PhD, Amsterdam University Medical Center
Bob W. van Oosten, MD, PhD, Amsterdam University Medical Center
Kiki S.J. Post, MD, Ommelander Hospital Group, Groningen
Jantine G. Röttgering, MD, Amsterdam University Medical Center
Jolanda Schieving, MD, PhD, Radboud University Medical Center, Nijmegen
Bas J.J.W. Schouwenberg, MD, PhD, Radboud University Medical Center, Nijmegen
Fianne H.M. Spaander, MD, PhD, Zaans Medical Center and OLVG, Amsterdam
Iris E. Verhagen, MD, Leiden University Medical Center
Philip Voets, MD, Gelre Hospital, Apeldoorn

The Compendium Method©
Manual

In *Compendium Medicine* we use the same concise, visual and schematic description of the various medical specialties. Everything is geared towards overview and structure, facilitating study and practice. We call this the *Compendium Method©*.

Fixed layout

All our medical specialties are presented in the same, recognisable way and each has its own colour and icon. The pockets have a fixed chapter structure. The table of contents of each pocket tells you exactly which topics are covered. The symbols in the corner of the page show what kind of information is being discussed.

- ATLS
- Anatomy
- Physiology
- Patient history
- Physical examination
- Diagnostics
- Treatment
- Differential diagnosis
- Conditions
- Clinical reasoning
- Appendices
- References
- Abbreviations
- Index

Illustrations

The figures provide at-a-glance insight into topics like anatomy or the typical patient. They are also intended for study and practice, such as checking whether you can identify the letters in a picture without looking at the caption.

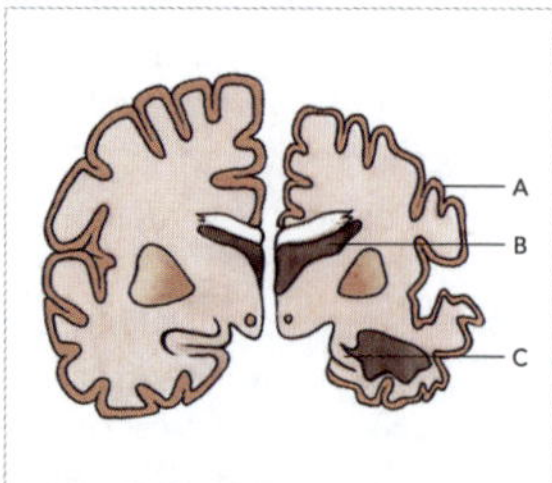

Figure 92 // Alzheimer's disease
A: Cortical atrophy **B:** Ventriculomegaly
C: Hippocampal atrophy

Conditions

Each condition in this pocket starts with a full-sentence definition followed by a telegram-style explanation. For each condition, the following icons (as applicable) are discussed. These visual cues that convey specific attributes or features of the condition are also useful when studying. You can cover the text and quiz yourself.

- D Definition
- E Epidemiology
- Ae Aetiology
- R Risk factors
- Hx Patient history
- PE Physical examination
- Dx Diagnostics
- Tx Treatment
  - General
  - Paramedical care
  - Pharmacological treatment
  - Invasive, non-pharmacological treatment
- P Prognosis
- ! Watch out/don´t forget

Tables

We use tables to arrange the information in a clear and structured manner, with columns representing different conditions and rows indicating features or characteristics. Centered formatting for matching features makes it easy to identify similarities and differences.

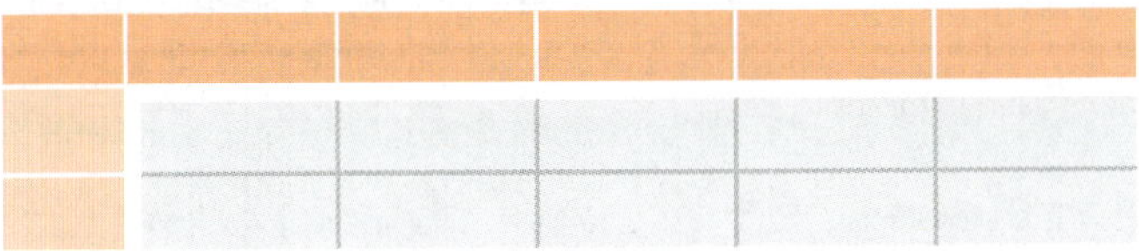

Diagrams

→ = positive/yes/+ → = negative/no/-

Diagrams help you reason clinically, starting from a particular symptom, using the green and red arrows as signposts. Always remember that the full differential diagnosis may consist of additional diagnoses.

Icons & frames

Fun fact: our founders are Dutch, and in the Netherlands, we refer to a mnemonic as a "donkey bridge". That's why the symbol for mnemonics in our books is a donkey.

Throughout this pocket you will find highlighted frames.

QR code	Note	Reference to another chapter
Alarm!	Description of the typical patient	Mnemonic
Formula		

Punctuation marks

The punctuation in our books also focuses on overview and ensures that the subject matters are covered concisely and effectively.

(--) Rare	(++) Most common	↓ Decrease/detoriation
(-) Uncommon	→ Consequence	♀ Female sex
(+) Very common	↑ Increase/improvement	♂ Male sex

Abbreviations

We make extensive use of abbreviations, medical terms and symbols for scientific units and quantities. Below are some examples of the abbreviations used in this pocket.

sec	second/seconds	d	day/days	min.	minimum
min	minute/minutes	wk	week/weeks	max.	maximum
h	hour/hours	mo	month/months	e.g.	for example
		y	year/years	L	litre/litres

Index

The pockets include a comprehensive and easy-to-use index. It contains all the topics covered in the books so you can quickly navigate and find the information you are looking for.

Appendices

In the pockets, you will find space for your notes, additional information, reminders, or insights. In addition, handy appendices have been added; these contain specific information that you would like to have at hand and are therefore located at the back of the pockets.

They/theirs

We realise that sex and gender identity are not binary and that there is more variation than just 'woman' or 'man'. For readability's sake (as well as for grammatical reasons) we have therefore chosen to use the pronouns 'they/theirs', regardless of sex or gender identity.

Warning

When studying this pocket, be mindful of the protocols within your own facility and adhere to the established guidelines. It is also essential to understand the circumstances under which you may or may not provide assistance in a given country, as this can potentially have legal consequences.

Want to know more about the Compendium Method©? Scan the QR code.

Table of contents
Neurology

Table of contents
Neurology

Table of contents
Neurology

ATLS

ABCDE approach

Advanced Trauma Life Support (ATLS) consists of performing a primary survey using the ABCDE approach (see Diagram 1). The ABCDE approach is a systematic, step-by-step approach to assess and treat trauma patients. Do not continue to the next step until the current step has been found to be stable, or treatment has been started whose effect cannot be evaluated immediately. If the patient deteriorates, restart from the top. If the patient is stable according to the primary survey, the secondary survey is performed (see Diagram 2).

Several function scales can be used to quickly map a patient's neurological condition, such as the Glasgow Coma Scale (GCS, see Table 1) and the AVPU score (see Table 2). The amount of blood loss can be estimated based on vital parameters (see Table 3).

Keep evaluating the patient throughout the ATLS trauma care. After starting treatment during the primary survey, reassess the patient starting with the first step.

EYE OPENING	MOTOR RESPONSE	VERBAL RESPONSE
1 No response	**1** No response	**1** No response
2 To pain	**2** Extension response to pain	**2** Sounds
3 To speech	**3** Abnormal flexion response to pain	**3** Words
4 Spontaneously open	**4** Normal flexion response to pain	**4** Confused
	5 Moves to localised pain	**5** Orientated
	6 Obeys commands	

Table 1 // Glasgow Coma Scale

A patient with a GCS ≤E1M5V2 is considered to be in a coma.

Primary survey: care and support based on the ABCDE approach
Secondary survey: complete examination if appropriate response during the primary survey
Tertiary survey: repeat the ABCDE approach and secondary survey one day after admission, incl. evaluation of any interventions

AVPU SCORE	
A	Patient is awake and alert
V	Patient responds only to verbal stimulus
P	Patient responds only to pain stimulus
U	Patient is unresponsive

Table 2 // AVPU score (Alert, Verbal, Pain, Unresponsive)

CLASSIFICATION OF HAEMORRHAGIC SHOCK

	I	II	III	IV
Blood loss (ml)	<750	750-1500	1500-2000	>2000
Blood loss (% blood volume)	<15	15-30	30-40	>40
Pulse (per minute)	<100	>100	>120	>140
Blood pressure (mmHg)	=	=	↓	↓
Pulse pressure	=/↑	↓	↓	↓
Respiratory rate (per minute)	14-20	20-30	30-40	>35
Urine production (ml/hour)	>30	20-30	5-15	Negligible
Central nervous system/mental status	Slightly anxious	Mildly anxious	Anxious, confused	Confused, lethargic

Table 3 // Classification of haemorrhagic shock

ABC**DE(FG): D**on't **E**ver **F**orget **G**lucose.

ABCDE approach

A Airway (+ C-spine)

Possible causes of instability:
- Aspiration of blood/vomit
- Atonia of the tongue due to unconsciousness
- C-spine injury
- Maxillofacial fractures

PE
- In case of no breathing → start CPR
- Airway clear
  - Does the patient talk?
  - Is the breathing audible (stridor, snoring)?
- Inspect mouth (foreign body/blood/vomit)

Dx Maxillofacial CT, C-spine CT, C-spine X-ray (in children)

Tx
- Head tilt/chin lift (consider cervical injury → jaw thrust, no head tilt)
- 15L/100% oxygen mask → oropharyngeal airway → orotracheal intubation → cricothyrotomy
- Monitor CO_2 after intubation

! Suspected cervical injury after trauma → immobilise the neck (manual immobilisation or head blocks). If diagnostic imaging is indicated, this is performed in the 5th step (E) when the patient is found stable.

B Breathing and ventilation

Possible causes of instability:
- Flail chest with lung contusion
- Haemothorax
- Open pneumothorax
- Tension pneumothorax
- Pulmonary oedema
- Bronchospasm

PE
- Respiratory rate
- Cyanosis
- Use of auxiliary breathing muscles
- Jugular vein distention
- Trachea deviation
- Symmetrical chest excursions
- Auscultation of lungs (presence/absence of respiratory sounds, crepitations, rhonchi, wheezing)
- Chest palpation (rib fractures, subcutaneous emphysema)
- Chest percussion

Dx
- Oxygen saturation
- Chest X-ray
- Blood gas
- Administration of oxygen therapy/ventilation: 15L/100% non-rebreathing mask, intubation as needed
- Tension pneumothorax → needle decompression at 5th intercostal space, midaxillary line (children: 2nd intercostal space, midclavicular line) and thoracic drain at 5th intercostal space, midaxillary line
- Open pneumothorax → close with valve → final closure in OR
- Massive haemothorax → intravenous (IV) and chest drain at 5th intercostal space, midaxillary line
- Pneumothorax → chest drain at 5th intercostal space, midaxillary line

C Circulation

> Possible causes of instability:
> - All forms of shock

PE
- Skin (colour, haematomas, clammy)
- Blood pressure, CVP
- Pulse
- Urine production
- Capillary refill
- Auscultation of the heart (heart sounds, murmurs)
- Abdominal palpation (abdominal rigidity with large haematoma)
- Long bone stability
- Rectal examination if indicated

Dx
- ECG
- (e)FAST ultrasound (free fluid in peritoneal, pericardial and pleural space, ventral pneumothorax)
- Lab, crossmatch testing
- Pelvic X-ray to diagnose/rule out pelvic fracture as cause of haemorrhagic shock

Tx
- IV access (low-threshold 2nd access route)
- Administer blood/fluids as needed
- Fixate fractures
- External bleeding: compression or tourniquet
- Internal haemorrhage: surgery or angioembolisation as needed, stabilise unstable pelvis with pelvic belt (over greater trochanter)
- Tranexamic acid (1 g in 10 min within 3h of accident, followed by 1 g in 8h at hospital)

! In the event of massive blood loss, atypical symptoms may occur in elderly people, children, athletes, and the chronically ill

D Disability

> Possible causes of instability:
> - Cerebral trauma
> - Intoxication
> - Hypoxaemia, Hypercapnia, Hypovolaemia (back to B and C)
> - Hypoglycaemia
> - Meningitis
> - Status epilepticus

PE
- Consciousness: GCS (see Table 1) and AVPU (see Table 2)
- Lateralisation
- Pupil reflexes
- Neck stiffness

Dx
- Blood glucose level
- Brain CT

Tx
- Loss of consciousness → return to A; intubate as needed and keep looking for treatable causes (intracerebral haemorrhage, epilepsy, hypoglycaemia, etc.)
- Bedside glucose → treat hypoglycaemia: administer glucose 10 g IV at a slow bolus rate (10 g = 100 ml gluc 10% = 20 ml gluc 50%, expected rise 2 mmol/L per 10 g) and check glucose <10 min, repeat as needed
- Cerebral oedema → hypertonic salt IV (NaCl 10%)

E Exposure

> Possible causes of instability:
> - Hypothermia

PE
- Body temperature
- Check fully undressed patient for wounds and lesions, but try to prevent iatrogenic hypothermia from undressing patient, so cover the patient again as soon as possible
- Assess back and complete spine (log roll)
- Rectal examination (if indicated)

Tx
- Hypothermia → warm up patient

In trauma, always consider major bleeding: external, legs, abdomen, chest, and pelvis.

During the ATLS trauma care, the area to be assessed should be undressed, e.g. to assess symmetrical chest excursions.

Intact circulation can be measured by e.g. capillary refill (<3 sec) and urine output (catheter urine: >0.5 ml/kg/hour).

GCS ≤8 (in a trauma situation) is an indication for intubation.

Nowadays, single-/multitrauma patients often undergo what is known as a total body CT. This CT is done as quickly as possible after the primary survey, but not before the patient is stabilised.

In traumatic resuscitation, consider **HOTT** (**h**ypovolaemia, **o**xygenation, **t**ension pneumothorax and **t**amponade).

During trauma care the CT is also known as the **Donut of Death**. The indication for a CT scan may be seen during trauma care according to the ABCDE approach, but a patient is not scanned untill they are stabilised. An unstable patient may die during a CT scan.

Secondary survey

1. AMPLE

The AMPLE method can be used to gain a better understanding of the patient's condition.

AMPLE
A: Allergies
M: Medications currently used
P: Past illness/pregnancy
L: Last meal
E: Events/environment related to injury

2. Head-to-toe examination

- Reassess vital parameters
- Comprehensive head/neck/back examination with log roll
- Comprehensive abdominal examination
- Comprehensive neurological examination with reassessment of GCS
- Comprehensive limb examination

3. Additional tests

- X-rays: chest X-ray (possibly primary), pelvis X-ray (possibly primary), spine X-ray, extremity X-ray
- CTs: chest CT, abdominal CT, pelvis CT, spine CT. Additional CT scan if necessary
- (Repeated) (e)FAST
- Lab
- Urinalysis

4. Treatment

- Wounds → clean as needed, suture, and/or administer tetanus shot as needed
- Treat fractures and other injuries

Diagram 2 // Secondary survey

Anatomy

Cerebrum

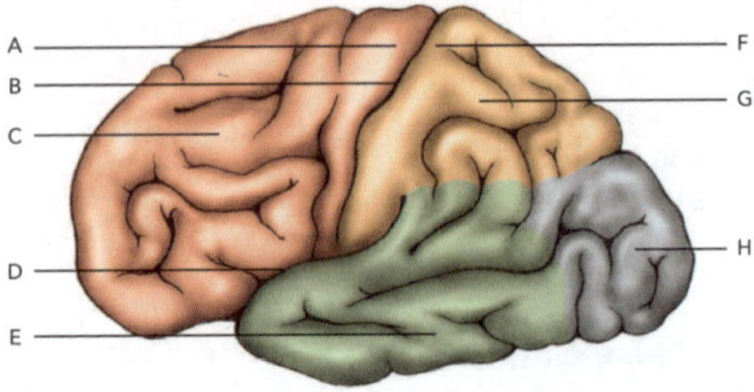

Figure 1 // Brain lobes

A: Precentral gyrus **B:** Central sulcus **C:** Frontal lobe **D:** Lateral sulcus **E:** Temporal lobe **F:** Postcentral gyrus **G:** Parietal lobe **H:** Occipital lobe

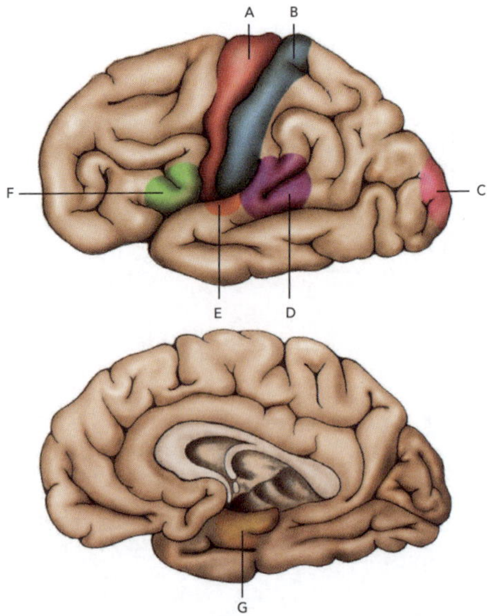

Figure 2 // Major regions of the brain

A: Primary motor cortex **B:** Primary sensory cortex **C:** Primary visual cortex **D:** Wernicke's receptive speech area **E:** Auditory cortex **F:** Broca's expressive speech area **G:** Primary olfactory cortex

Basal ganglia

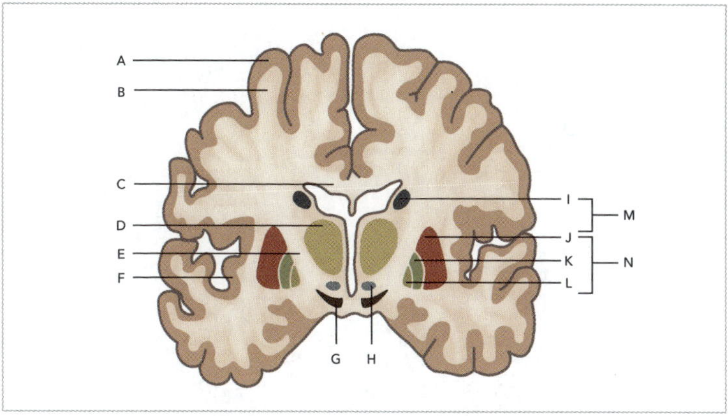

Figure 3 // Basal ganglia

A: Grey matter **B:** White matter **C:** Corpus callosum **D:** Thalamus **E:** Internal capsule **F:** Insula **G:** Substantia nigra **H:** Subthalamic nucleus **I:** Caudate nucleus **J:** Putamen **K:** External globus pallidus **L:** Internal globus pallidus **M:** Striatum **N:** Lentiform nucleus

Thalamus

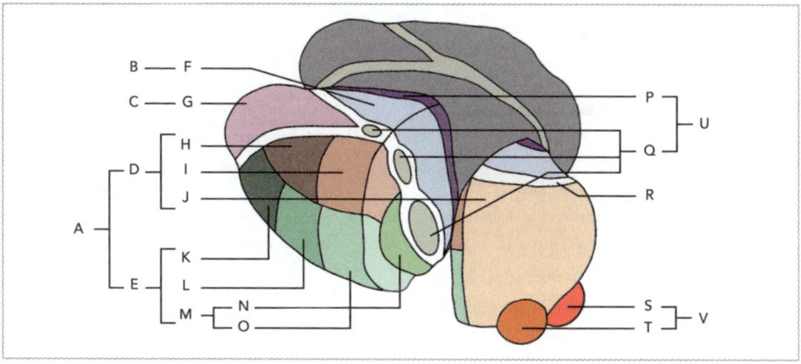

Figure 4 // Thalamus

A: Lateral nuclear group **B:** Medial nuclear group **C:** Anterior nuclear group **D:** Posterolateral nuclear group **E:** Ventrolateral nuclear group **F:** Medial dorsal nucleus **G:** Anterior nucleus **H:** Lateral dorsal nucleus **I:** Lateral posterior nucleus **J:** Pulvinar of the thalamus **K:** Anterior ventral nucleus **L:** Ventral lateral nucleus (ventral intermediate nucleus) **M:** Ventral posterior nucleus **N:** Ventral posterior medial nucleus (VPM) **O:** Ventral posterior lateral nucleus (VPL) **P:** Midline nuclear group **Q:** Intralaminar nuclei **R:** Internal medullary lamina **S:** Medial geniculate body **T:** Lateral geniculate body **U:** Non-specific nuclei **V:** Metathalamus

Hypothalamus

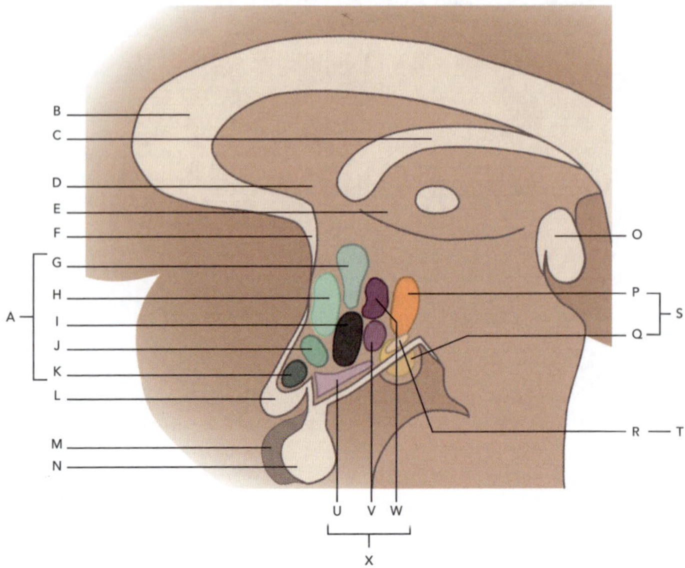

Figure 5 // Hypothalamus

A: Anterior nuclear group **B:** Corpus callosum **C:** Fornix **D:** Foramen of Monro **E:** Hypothalamic sulcus **F:** Terminal lamina **G:** Paraventricular nucleus **H:** Preoptic nucleus **I:** Anterior nucleus **J:** Supraoptic nucleus **K:** Suprachiasmatic nucleus **L:** Optic chiasm **M:** Adenohypophysis **N:** Neurohypophysis (circumventricular organs (CVO) inside the hypothalamus) **O:** Epiphysis (CVO outside the hypothalamus) **P:** Posterior nucleus **Q:** Mamillary body **R:** Lateral tuberal nucleus, medial tuberal nucleus, tuberomamillary nucleus **S:** Posterior (or mamillary) nuclear group **T:** Lateral nuclear group **U:** Infundibular nucleus (arcuate nucleus) **V:** Ventromedial nucleus **W:** Dorsomedial nucleus **X:** Medial (or tuberal) nuclear group

Adenohypophysis is the **a**nterior lobe of the pituitary gland.

Ventricular system

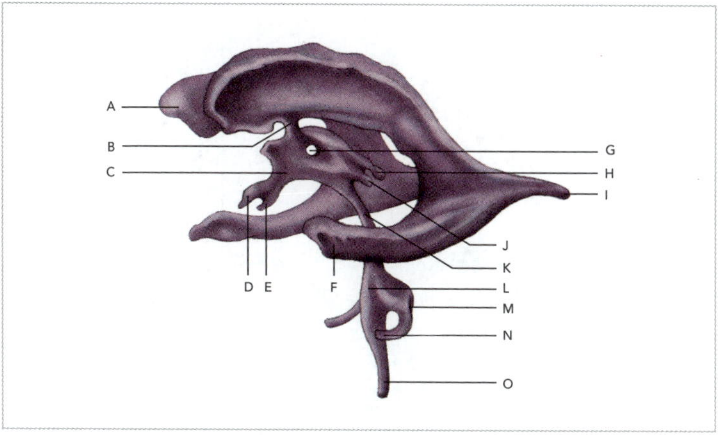

Figure 6 // Ventricular system

A: Lateral ventricle **B:** Foramen of Monro **C:** Third ventricle **D:** Supraoptic recess **E:** Infundible recess **F:** Temporal horn of the lateral ventricle **G:** Interthalamic adhesion **H:** Suprapineal recess **I:** Occipital horn of the lateral ventricle **J:** Pineal recess **K:** Cerebral aqueduct **L:** Fourth ventricle **M:** Median aperture (foramen of Magendie) **N:** Lateral aperture (foramen of Luschka) **O:** Central canal

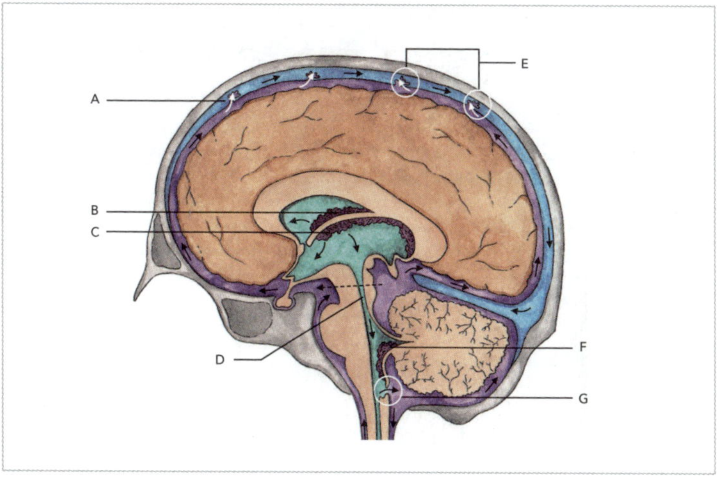

Figure 7 // Circulation of cerebrospinal fluid (CSF)

A: Superior sagittal sinus **B:** Choroid plexus of the lateral ventricle **C:** Choroid plexus of the third ventricle **D:** Cerebral aqueduct **E:** Arachnoid granulations **F:** Choroid plexus of the fourth ventricle **G:** Median aperture

Venous circulation

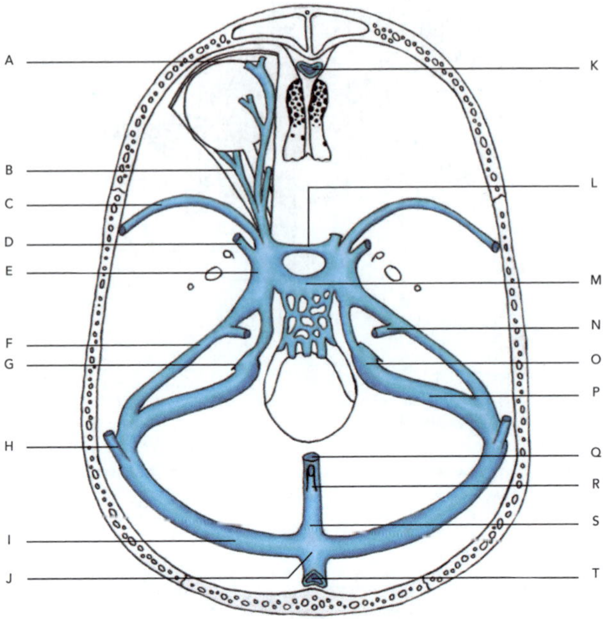

Figure 8 // Venous sinuses: caudal view

A: Superior ophthalmic vein **B:** Inferior ophthalmic vein **C:** Sphenoparietal sinus **D:** Superficial middle cerebral vein **E:** Cavernous sinus **F:** Superior petrosal sinus **G:** Jugular foramen **H:** Vein of Labbé **I:** Transverse sinus **J:** Confluence of sinuses **K:** Superior sagittal sinus **L:** Anterior intercavernous sinus **M:** Posterior intercavernous sinus **N:** Petrosal vein **O:** Superior bulb of the jugular vein **P:** Sigmoid sinus **Q:** Great cerebral vein (vein of Galen) **R:** Inferior sagittal sinus **S:** Straight sinus **T:** Superior sagittal sinus

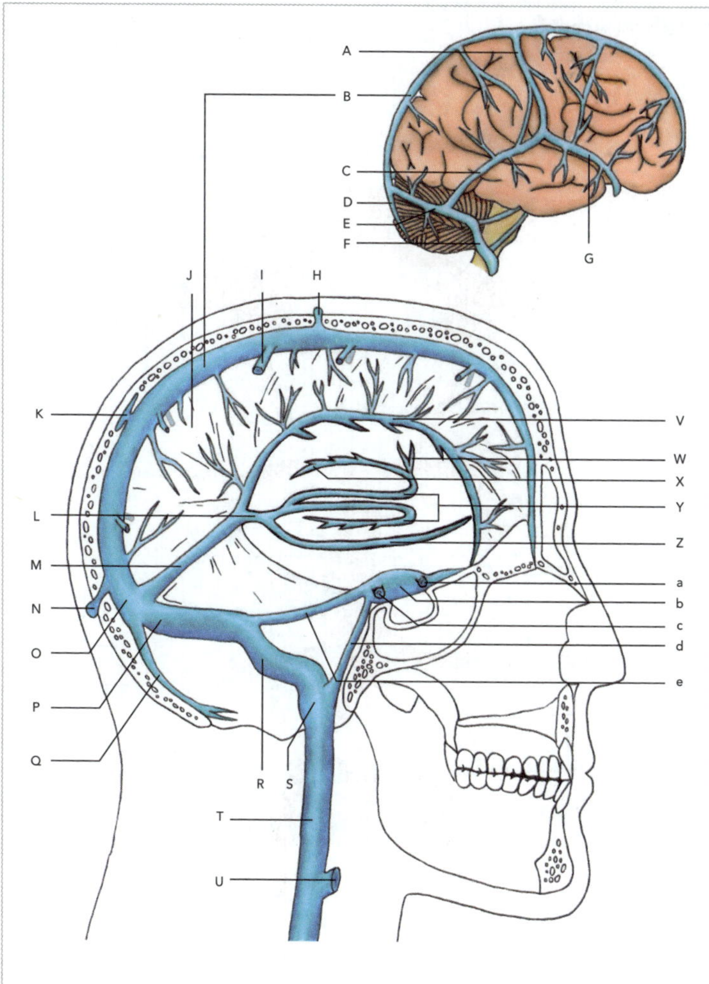

Figure 9 // Venous sinuses: lateral view

A: Vein of Trolard **B:** Superior sagittal sinus **C:** Vein of Labbé **D:** Occipital sinus **E:** Transverse sinus **F:** Sigmoid sinus **G:** Superficial middle cerebral vein **H:** Parietal emissary vein **I:** Vein of Trolard **J:** Falx cerebri **K:** Diploic vein **L:** Great cerebral vein (vein of Galen) **M:** Straight sinus **N:** Occipital emissary vein **O:** Confluence of sinuses **P:** Transverse sinus **Q:** Occipital sinus **R:** Sigmoid sinus **S:** Jugular bulb **T:** Internal jugular vein **U:** Facial vein **V:** Inferior sagittal sinus **W:** Thalamostriate vein **X:** Septal vein **Y:** Internal cerebral vein **Z:** Basilar vein **a:** Anterior intercavernous sinus **b:** Cavernous sinus **c:** Posterior intercavernous sinus **d:** Inferior petrosal sinus **e:** Superior petrosal sinus

Cerebral arteries

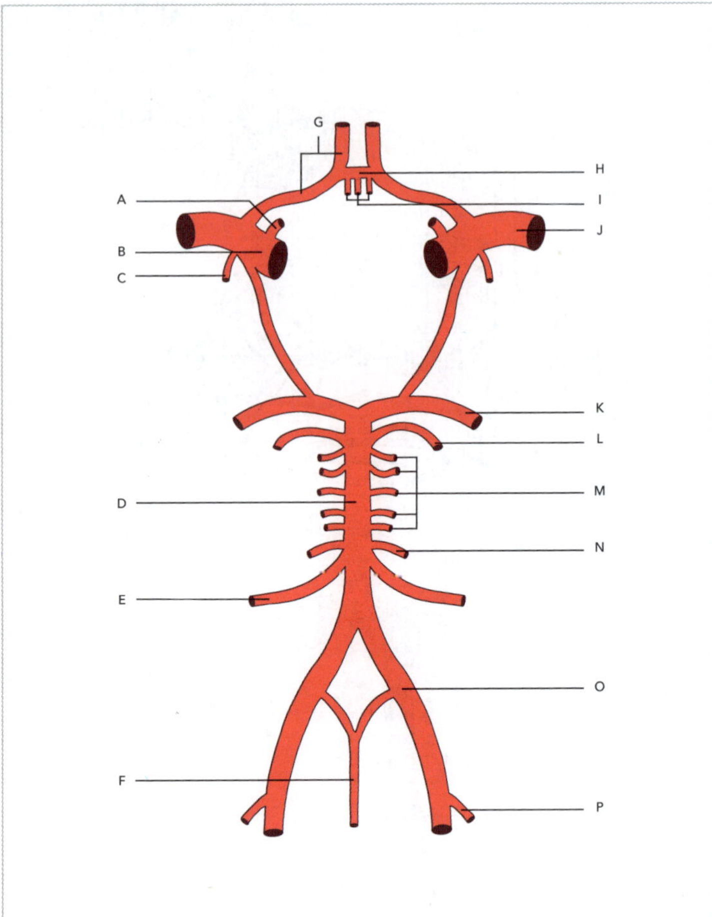

Figure 10 // Circle of Willis

A: Ophthalmic artery **B:** Internal carotid artery **C:** Anterior choroid artery **D:** Basilar artery **E:** Anterior inferior cerebellar artery (AICA) **F:** Anterior spinal artery **G:** Anterior cerebral artery (ACA) **H:** Anterior communicating artery **I:** Anteromedial central arteries **J:** Middle cerebral artery (MCA) **K:** Posterior cerebral artery (PCA) **L:** Superior cerebral artery (SCA) **M:** Mesencephalic arteries and pontine arteries **N:** Labyrinthine artery **O:** Vertebral artery **P:** Posterior inferior cerebellar artery (PICA)

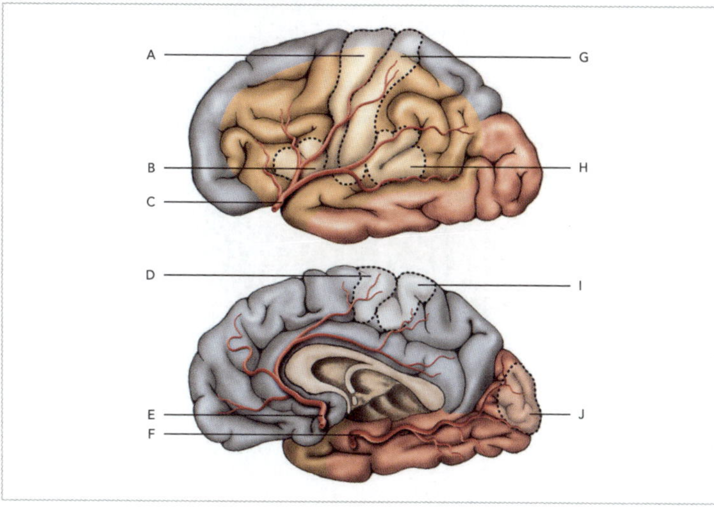

Figure 11 // Blood supply: cerebral arteries (yellow: middle cerebral artery, blue: anterior cerebral artery, red: posterior cerebral artery)

A: Motor cortex **B:** Broca's expressive speech area **C:** Middle cerebral artery **D:** Motor innervation leg and foot **E:** Anterior cerebral artery **F:** Posterior cerebral artery **G:** Sensory cortex **H:** Wernicke's receptive speech area **I:** Sensory innervation leg and foot **J:** Visual cortex

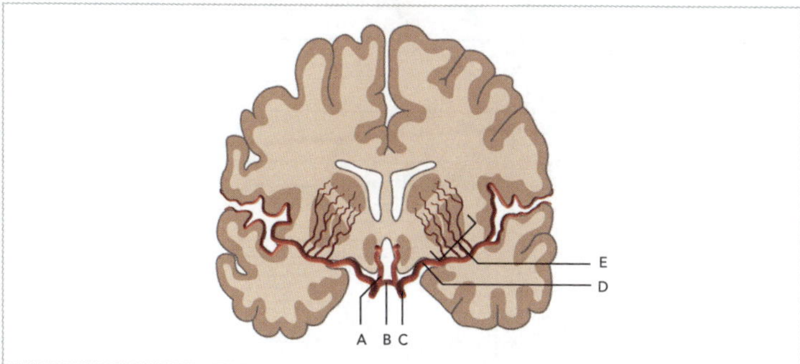

Figure 12 // Blood supply: middle cerebral artery (coronal view)

A: Anterior cerebral artery **B:** Anterior communicating artery **C:** Internal carotid artery **D:** Middle cerebral artery **E:** Anterolateral central arteries (perforating arteries)

Cerebellum

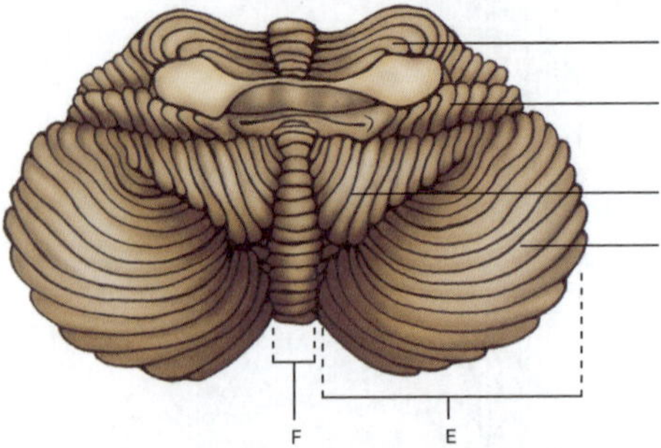

Figure 13 // Cerebellum

A: Anterior lobe of the cerebellum **B:** Flocculonodular lobe **C:** Cerebellar tonsil **D:** Posterior lobe of the cerebellum **E:** Cerebellar hemisphere **F:** Vermis

Cranial nerves

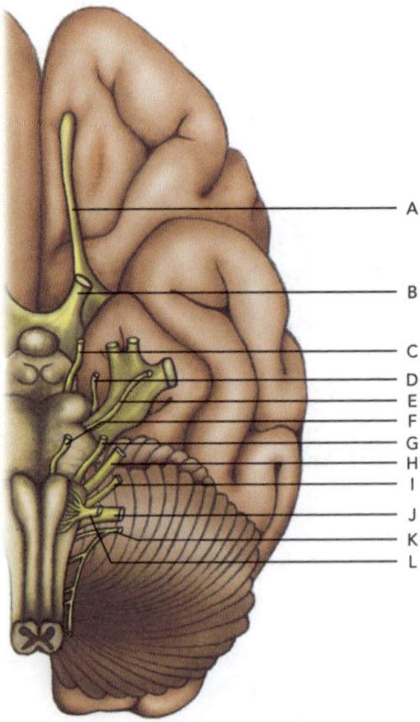

Figure 14 // Cranial nerves

A: Olfactory nerve (I) **B:** Optic nerve (II) **C:** Oculomotor nerve (III) **D:** Trochlear nerve (IV) **E:** Trigeminal nerve (V) **F:** Abducens nerve (VI) **G:** Facial nerve (VII) **H:** Vestibulocochlear nerve (VIII) **I:** Glossopharyngeal nerve (IX) **J:** Vagus nerve (X) **K:** Accessory nerve (XI) **L:** Hypoglossal nerve (XII)

The following sentence is a mnemonic for the cranial nerves:
On **o**ld **O**lympus' **t**owering **t**ops, **a** **F**inn **a**nd **G**erman **v**iewed **s**ome **h**ops.

You have one nose and two eyes:
- Cranial nerve I: smell
- Cranial nerve II: sight

Autonomic nervous system

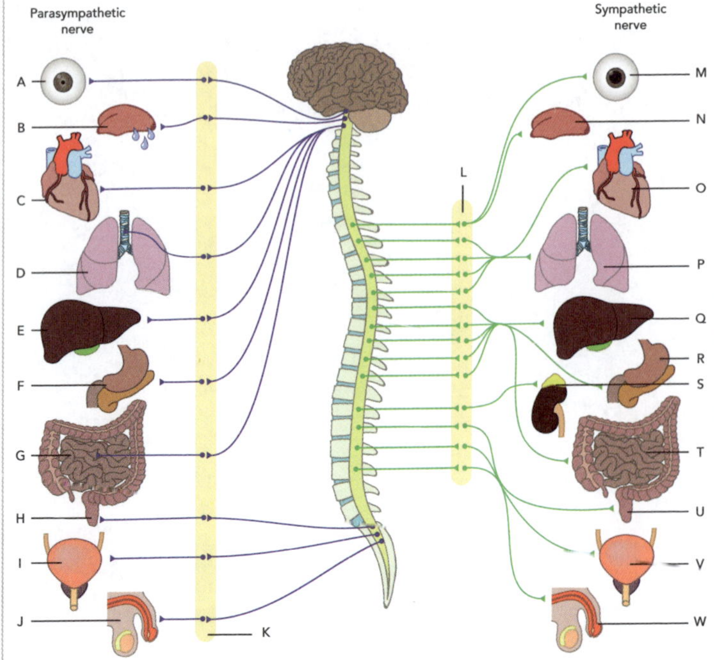

Figure 15 // Autonomic nervous system

A: Miosis **B:** Stimulates saliva production **C:** Lowers heart rate **D:** Bronchoconstriction **E:** Inhibits glucose release and stimulates gallbladder **F:** Stimulates gastric wall and pancreatic secretion **G:** Stimulates intestinal wall secretion **H:** Relaxes rectum **I:** Contracts bladder **J:** Stimulates sexual organs **K:** Parasympathetic ganglia (near target organs) **L:** Sympathetic trunk **M:** Mydriasis **N:** Inhibits salivary production **O:** Increases heart rate **P:** Bronchodilation **Q:** Stimulates glucose release and inhibits bile release **R:** Inhibits gastric wall and pancreatic secretion **S:** Stimulates adrenaline secretion **T:** Inhibits intestinal wall secretion **U:** Contracts rectum **V:** Stimulates and relaxes bladder **W:** Inhibits sexual organs

Motor and sensory pathways

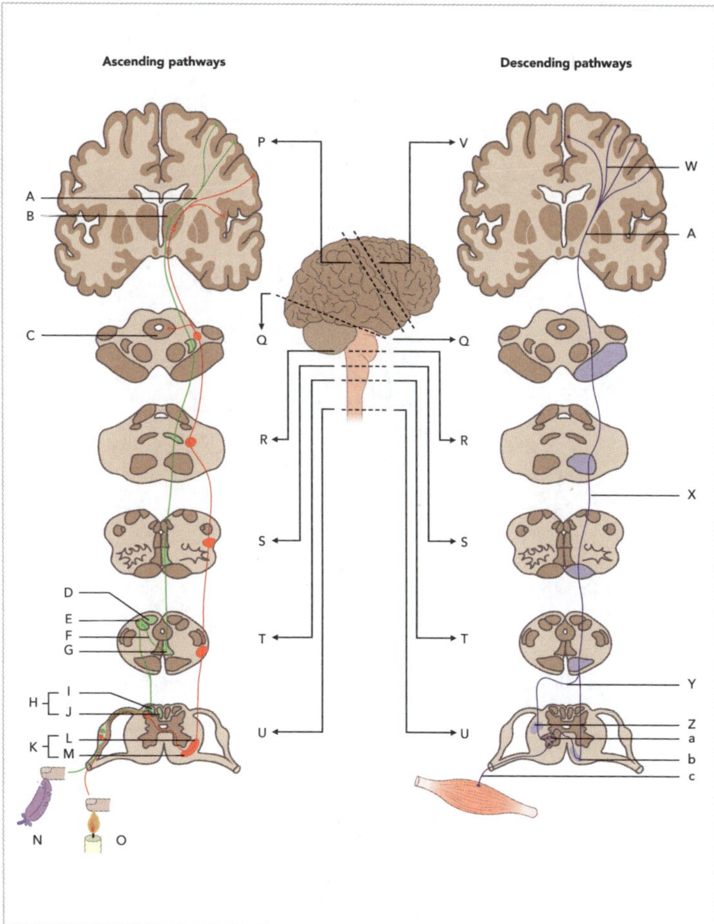

Figure 16 // Ascending and descending pathways

A: Internal capsule **B:** Thalamus (VPL nucleus) **C:** Periaqueductal grey (PAG) **D:** Gracile nucleus **E:** Cuneate nucleus **F:** Decussation of the lemnisci **G:** Medial lemniscus **H:** Lemniscal system **I:** Cuneate fasciculus **J:** Gracile fasciculus **K:** Anterolateral system **L:** Lateral spinothalamic tract **M:** Anterior spinothalamic tract **N:** Deep sensation **O:** Superficial sensation **P:** Sensory cortex **Q:** Mesencephalon **R:** Pons **S:** Medulla (high) **T:** Medulla (low) **U:** Spinal cord **V:** Motor cortex **W:** Corona radiata **X:** Corticospinal tract (upper motor neuron) **Y:** Pyramidal decussation **Z:** Lateral corticospinal tract **a:** Interneuron **b:** Anterior medial corticospinal tract **c:** Lower motor neuron

Spinal cord

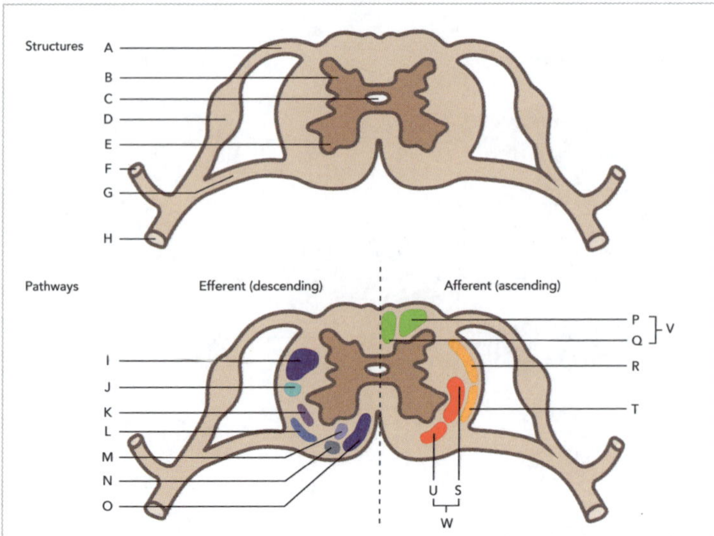

Figure 17 // Cross-section of the spinal cord

A: Dorsal root **B:** Dorsal horn **C:** Central canal **D:** Spinal ganglion **E:** Central horn **F:** Dorsal branch **G:** Ventral root **H:** Ventral branch **I:** Lateral corticospinal tract **J:** Rubrospinal tract **K:** Reticulospinal tract **L:** Vestibulospinal tract **M:** Pontoreticulospinal tract **N:** Tectospinal tract **O:** Medial corticospinal tract **P:** Cuneate fasciculus **Q:** Gracile fasciculus **R:** Posterior spinocerebellar tract **S:** Lateral spinothalamic tract **T:** Anterior spinocerebellar tract **U:** Anterior spinothalamic tract **V:** Dorsal system (deep sensation) **W:** Anterolateral system (superficial sensation)

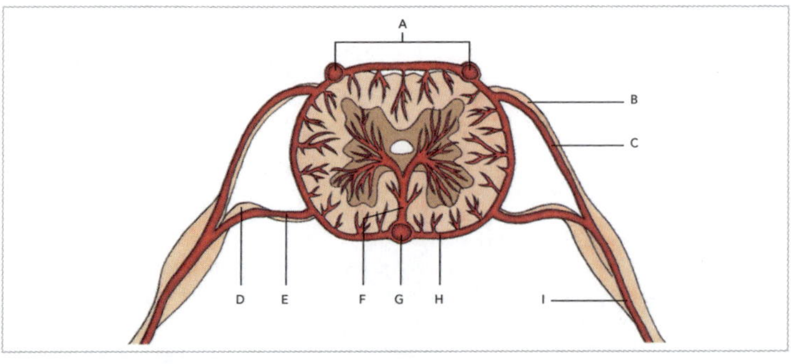

Figure 18 // Blood supply cross-section of the spinal cord

A: Posterior spinal arteries **B:** Posterior root **C:** Posterior radicular artery **D:** Anterior root **E:** Anterior radicular artery **F:** Sulco-commissural artery **G:** Anterior spinal artery **H:** Vasocorona **I:** Segmental spinal artery

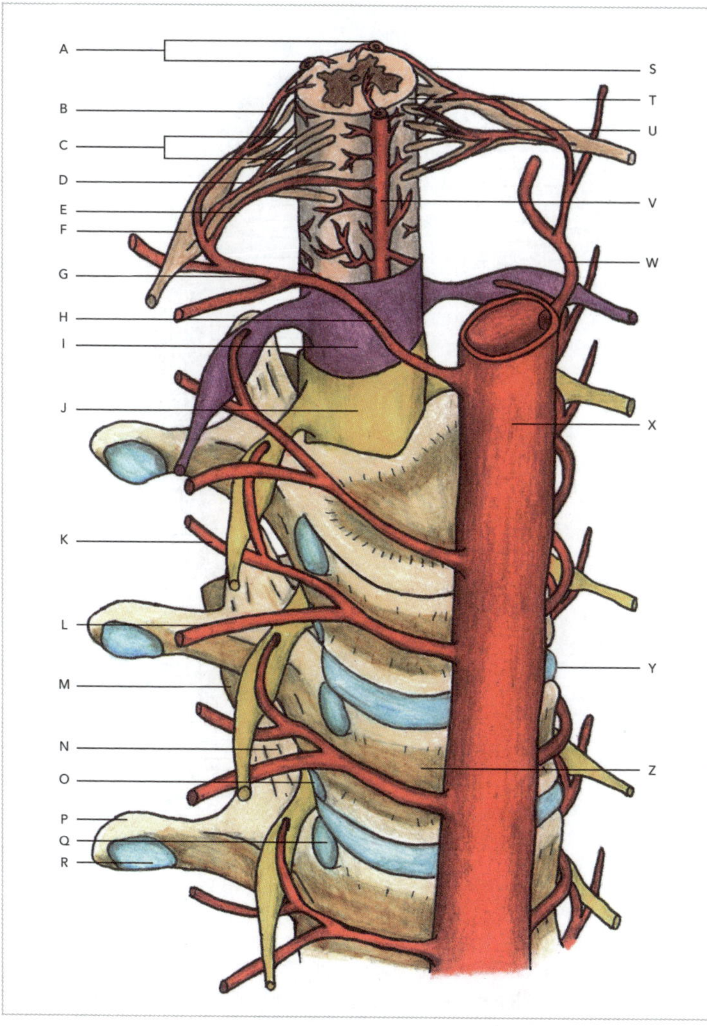

Figure 19 // Blood supply to the spinal cord, close-up view

A: Posterior spinal arteries **B:** Posterior radicular branch **C:** Anterior and posterior rootlets **D:** Anterior radicular branch **E:** Segmental medullary arteries **F:** Dorsal root ganglion **G:** Segmental spinal artery **H:** Right posterior intercostal artery **I:** Spinal arachnoid mater **J:** Spinal dura mater **K:** Medial cutaneous branch **L:** Lateral cutaneous branch **M:** Spinous process **N:** Superior articular process **O:** Inferior costal facet **P:** Transverse process **Q:** Superior costal facet **R:** Transverse costal facet **S:** Posterior radicular branch **T:** Spinal pia mater **U:** Anterior radicular branch **V:** Anterior spinal artery **W:** Left posterior intercostal artery **X:** Aorta **Y:** Intervertebral disc **Z:** Vertebral body

Vertebral column

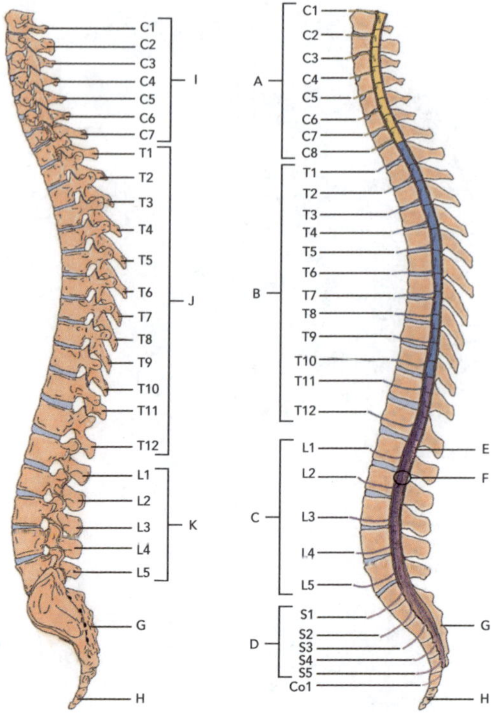

Figure 20 // Vertebral column

A: Cervical nerve roots **B:** Thoracic nerve roots **C:** Lumbar nerve roots **D:** Sacral nerve roots **E:** Conus medullaris **F:** Cauda equina **G:** Sacrum **H:** Coccygeal vertebrae **I:** Cervical vertebrae **J:** Thoracic vertebrae **K:** Lumbar vertebrae

A normal adult spine has cervical lordosis, thoracic kyphosis, lumbar lordosis and sacral kyphosis.

SAME (spinal cord):

- **S**ensory: **a**fferent
- **M**otor: **e**fferent

Dermatomes

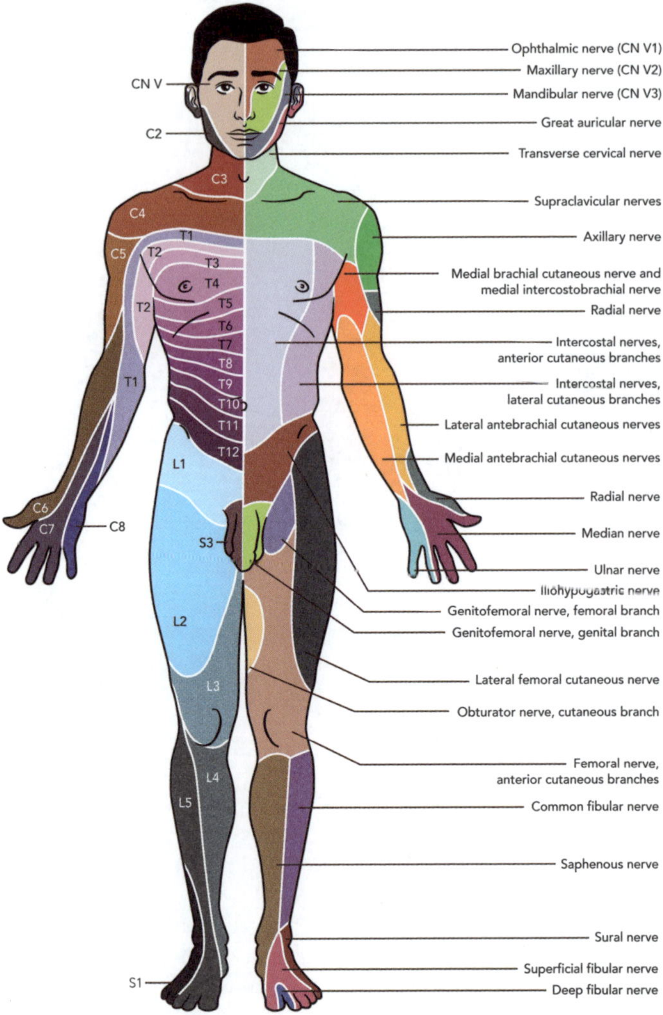

Figure 21 // Dermatomes and peripheral nerves
C, cervical; CN, cranial nerve; T, thoracic; L, lumbar; S, sacral

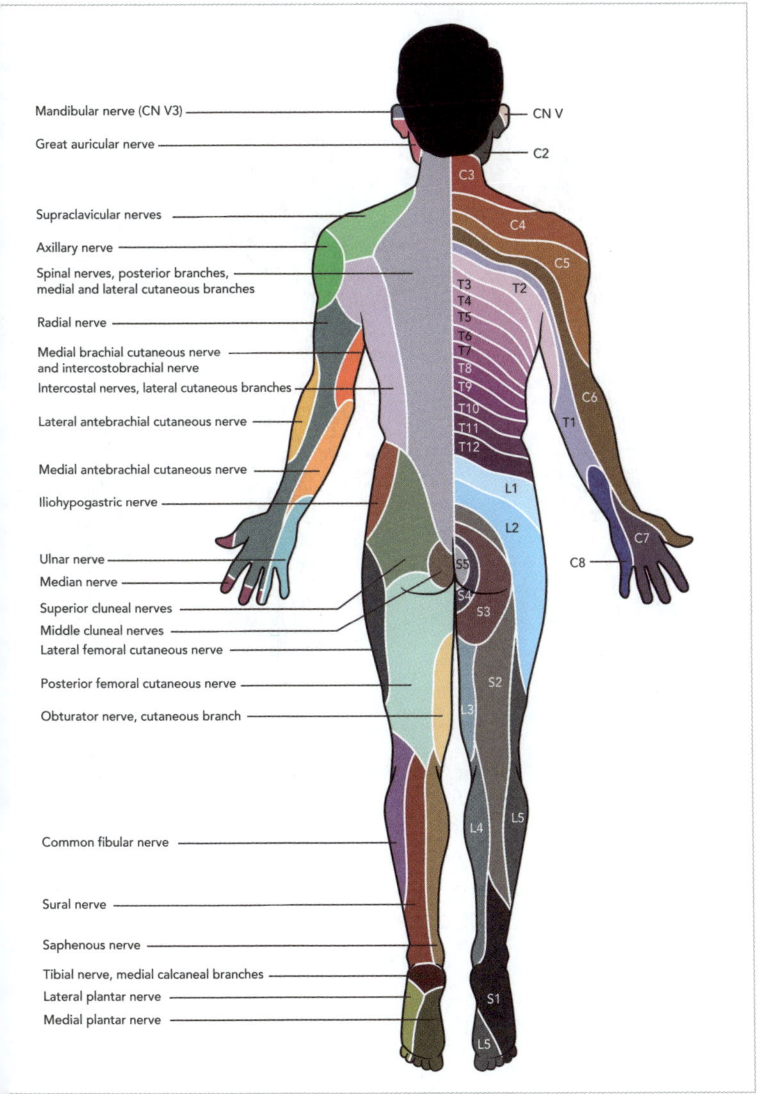
Mandibular nerve (CN V3)
Great auricular nerve
Supraclavicular nerves
Axillary nerve
Spinal nerves, posterior branches, medial and lateral cutaneous branches
Radial nerve
Medial brachial cutaneous nerve and intercostobrachial nerve
Intercostal nerves, lateral cutaneous branches
Lateral antebrachial cutaneous nerve
Medial antebrachial cutaneous nerve
Iliohypogastric nerve
Ulnar nerve
Median nerve
Superior cluneal nerves
Middle cluneal nerves
Lateral femoral cutaneous nerve
Posterior femoral cutaneous nerve
Obturator nerve, cutaneous branch
Common fibular nerve
Sural nerve
Saphenous nerve
Tibial nerve, medial calcaneal branches
Lateral plantar nerve
Medial plantar nerve
CN V
C2
C3
C4
C5
T2
T3
T4
T5
T6
T7
T8
T9
T10
T11
T12
C6
T1
L1
L2
C7
C8
S5
S4
S3
S2
L3
L4
L5
S1
L5

Innervation of the extremities

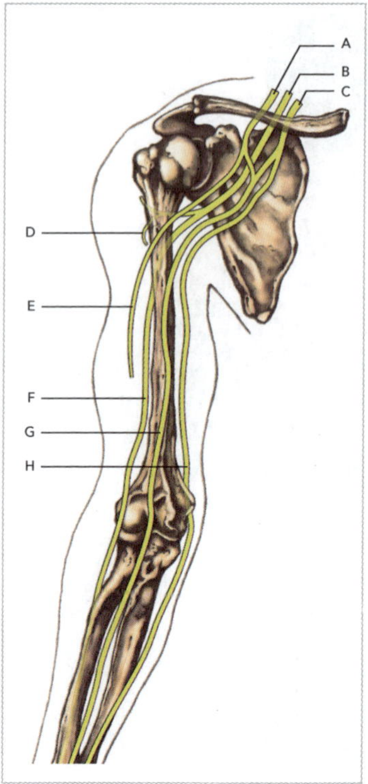

Figure 22 // Innervation of the upper extremities
A: Lateral fasciculus **B:** Posterior fasciculus **C:** Medial fasciculus **D:** Axillary nerve **E:** Musculocutaneous nerve **F:** Radial nerve **G:** Median nerve **H:** Ulnar nerve

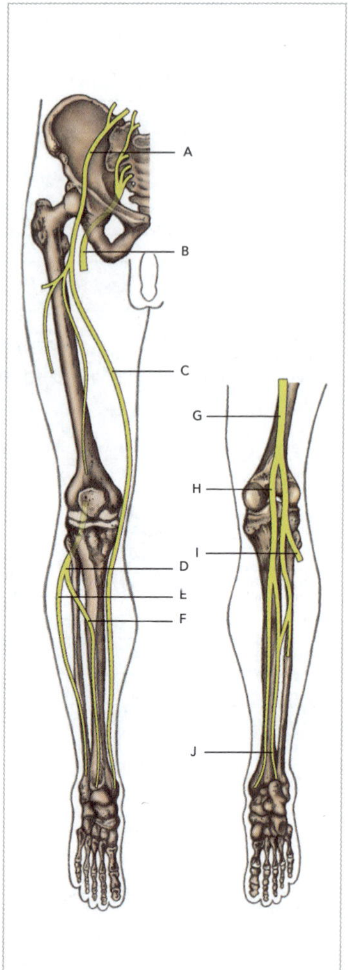

Figure 23 // Innervation of the lower extremities
A: Femoral nerve **B:** Sciatic nerve **C:** Saphenous nerve **D:** Common fibular (peroneal) nerve **E:** Superficial fibular (peroneal) nerve **F:** Deep fibular (peroneal) nerve **G:** Sciatic nerve **H:** Tibial nerve **I:** Common fibular (peroneal) nerve **J:** Sural nerve

Physiology

Somatotopic organisation of the cortex

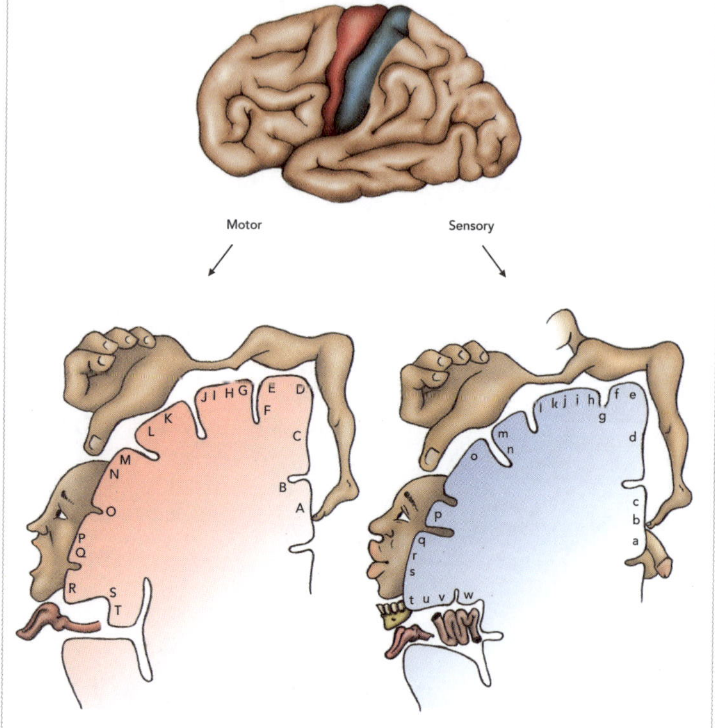

Figure 24 // Homunculus

A: Toes **B:** Ankle **C:** Knee **D:** Hip **E:** Torso **F:** Shoulder **G:** Upper arm **H:** Elbow **I:** Forearm **J:** Wrist **K:** Hand **L:** Fingers **M:** Thumb **N:** Neck **O:** Eye **P:** Face **Q:** Lips and jaw **R:** Tongue **S:** Pharynx **T:** Larynx **a:** Genitalia **b:** Toes **c:** Foot **d:** Leg **e:** Hip **f:** Torso **g:** Neck **h:** Shoulder **i:** Upper arm **j:** Elbow **k:** Forearm **l:** Wrist **m:** Hand **n:** Fingers **o:** Thumb **p:** Eye **q:** Nose **r:** Face **s:** Lips, teeth, gums **t:** Jaw **u:** Tongue **v:** Pharynx **w:** Abdomen

Synaps

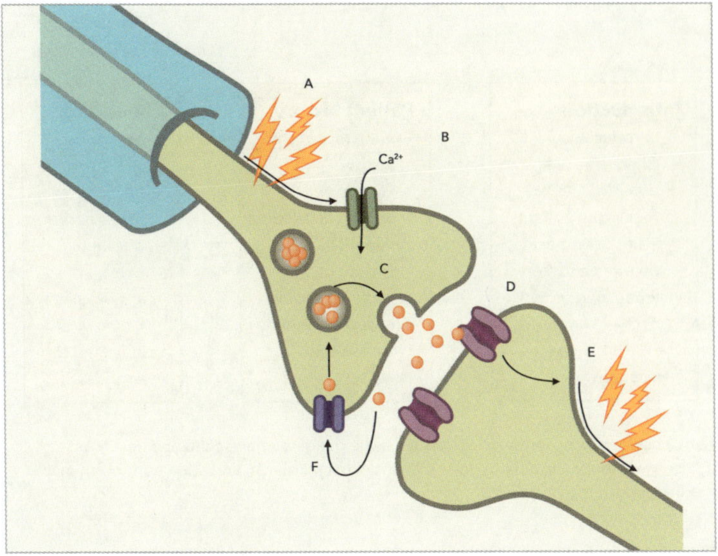

Figure 25 // Synapse between nerve cells

A: Action potential arrives at synapse **B:** Influx of calcium ions **C:** Neurotransmitter is released **D:** Neurotransmitter activates postsynaptic receptors **E:** New action potential **F:** Re-uptake of neurotransmitter molecules

Motor unit

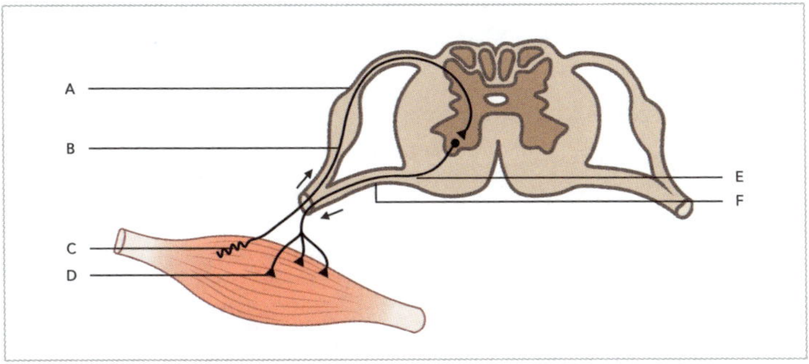

Figure 26 // Course of the nerve roots

A: Dorsal root ganglion and dorsal root **B:** Sensory nerve fibre (afferent) **C:** Muscle spindle **D:** Neuromuscular junction **E:** Motor nerve fibre (efferent) **F:** Ventral root

Patient history

Introduction
- Introduce yourself
- Check personal details
- Assess the patient: acute or non-acute, determine reason for encounter and/or chief complaint, nonverbal communication

→

Patient history
- General patient history
- History of presenting complaint/current illness
- History of relevant system (full review of systems if necessary)

→

Concluding
- Summarise your findings
- Patient's remarks and/or questions
- Explain physical examination and/or indicated diagnostics

Consider psychosocial variables such as language barriers, cultural differences between patients and physicians, financial backgrounds, and addiction, which may impact disease progression.

Diagram 3 // Patient history

General patient history

Medical history, medication use (exact dosage, frequency, last dose, administration form), history of substance use (smoking, alcohol, drugs), allergies (latex, plasters, medication, contrast agents), family history, psychosocial history, travel history, social history (home situation, work, study, social support), vaccinations, ill individuals in immediate vicinity.

If the patient is unable to provide a medical history due to reduced consciousness, additional help must be sought from someone who is familiar with the patient.

- When patients present with head trauma or acute onset neurological deficits, it is crucial to inquire about the use of anticoagulants (low-molecular-weight heparin (LMWH), vitamin K antagonist (VKA), or direct-acting oral anticoagulants (DOACs)), antiplatelet therapy (excl. acetylsalicylic acid monotherapy), or known coagulopathy (e.g. haemophilia).
- There are six critical cardiovascular risk factors that should be determined when a stroke/transient ischaemic attack (TIA) is suspected: hypertension, hypercholesterolaemia, previous cardiovascular diseases, family history (heart attack/stroke/TIA age <60), smoking, diabetes mellitus (DM).
- In case of a seizure, ask extensively about recent infections, drug and alcohol use, stress, sleep deprivation, and flashing lights, as these factors could provoke seizures.
- For several neurological diseases, a thorough family history is crucial (e.g. stroke, multiple sclerosis (MS), migraine, epilepsy, Huntington's disease).
- If the patient is unable to provide a medical history due to reduced consciousness, additional help must be sought from someone who is familiar with the patient.

Review of systems

General system

General well-being, itching, fever, chills, night sweats, appetite, weight change (deliberate/unintended), fatigue, exercise tolerance.

Watch for red flags/B symptoms (e.g. disabling fatigue, weight loss, unexplained fever, night sweats, itching, icterus). These symptoms may be associated with a serious condition, such as malignancy.

Circulatory system

Dizziness/lightheadedness (orthostatic), chest pain (on exertion or at rest), palpitations (e.g. fluttering, pounding, racing), dyspnoea (e.g. dyspnoea on exertion or at rest, orthopnoea), nycturia, intermittent claudication, cold extremities, peripheral oedema.

Orthostatic hypotension can be a sign of autonomic dysfunction, which can be caused by neurological disorders such as Parkinson's disease, multiple system atrophy (MSA), or MS.

Respiratory system

Dyspnoea, coughing (dry, sputum, nocturnal), audible breathing (e.g. wheezing, rhonchi), chest pain (worsens when breathing deeply), sputum (e.g. consistency, colour, blood), haemoptysis. ENT: sore throat, earache, tinnitus, voice (hoarse), recurrent respiratory infections.

> Ask specifically for respiratory symptoms like dyspnoea when suspecting a neuromuscular disorder, Guillain-Barré syndrome (GBS), or amyotrophic lateral sclerosis (ALS) as the cause of a patient's neurological symptoms.

Digestive system

Vomiting (e.g. frequency, blood), nausea, reflux, regurgitations, swallowing problems, abdominal pain, stool pattern (e.g. frequency, consistency, colour, blood or mucus, tenesmus), flatus, jaundice, diet, appetite changes.

Urogenital system

Miction (e.g. dysuria, stranguria, haematuria, pollakisuria, polyuria), bladder function, incontinence, flank pain, changes in bowel habits, sexual history. ♀: vaginal discharge, menstrual cycle, hot flashes. ♂: weak stream, feeling of incomplete emptying, dribbling, discharge, erectile dysfunction, testicular pain or swelling.

> Several neurological disorders can lead to problems with micturition, like incontinence or retention (e.g. MS, Parkinson's disease, MSA, spinal cord injury, cauda equina syndrome). Cauda equina syndrome (urinary retention in combination with saddle anaesthesia and dysfunction of the anal sphincter in complaints of back and/or leg pain) is a medical emergency.

Locomotor system

Warmth, redness, swelling, cramps, restless legs, joint pain, joint instability, morning stiffness, loss of function, action radius, muscle atrophy.

> Muscle atrophy may indicate a neurological problem of the peripheral nervous system.

Central nervous system

Concentration difficulties, amnesia, dizziness (spinning rotation), loss of consciousness, seizures, headache, impaired senses (e.g. hearing, smell, taste, vision), language, speech, mastication, swallowing, diplopia, abnormal sensation (e.g. numbness, tingling), loss of strength, gait disorders, balance problems, tremors or involuntary movements, psychiatric symptoms.

Mental health system

Cognitive functioning, sleep problems, anxiety, depression, mood swings, delusions, hallucinations, suicidal thoughts or self-harm.

> Several neurological disorders may involve psychiatric symptoms, sometimes even as a first symptom, e.g. in Alzheimer's disease, frontotemporal dementia, and Parkinson's disease.

Neurological history

Five examples of common neurological complaints and corresponding history-taking questions are discussed below.

Acute motor deficits

Time of onset (or time last seen well), acute/gradual onset, symptoms trajectory, symptoms still present, location of motor deficit, additional symptoms (sensory disorders, visual field loss, speech problems, language disorders, double vision, coordination disorder, vertigo), headache, lower back pain, neck pain, nausea, vomiting, prior head trauma or seizure, cardiovascular risk factors (hypertension, hypercholesterolaemia, smoking, DM, family history of cardiovascular disease age <60), use of anticoagulants, last time of administration.

Syncope

Moment of occurrence, prior/prodromal symptoms (lightheadedness, nausea, altered sense of smell or perception of surroundings, palpitations), uncontrollable muscle movements (tremor, shaking limbs), paleness, chest pain, tongue bite, urinary incontinence, symptoms afterwards (confusion, neurological deficit, headache), history of transient loss of consciousness, DM, alcohol or drug use, medication use (diuretics, antihypertensives, antidepressants, neuroleptics, calcium channel blockers, vasodilators).

Dizziness

Lightheadedness, spinning sensation, onset (acute/gradual), course (continuous/attacks), duration, triggering factors (head position changes), additional symptoms (blurred vision, double vision, speech problems, gait disturbances, coordination problems, headache, deafness, tinnitus, palpitations, nausea/vomiting), medication use (antiseizure medication, sedatives, aminoglycosides).

Headache

Onset (thunderclap headache, acute/gradual), course (continuous/attacks, frequency/duration of attacks), site, intensity, prior symptoms (blotches in visual field, flashing lights, obscurations, altered sensation in corner of mouth or one hand), additional symptoms (neurological deficits, blurred vision, nausea, vomiting, fever, spinning rotation, red eye, watering eye, nasal congestion, sweaty forehead, drooping or swelling eyelid), trauma, family history of primary headache syndromes (e.g. migraine, cluster headache), use of anticoagulants, use of analgesics, use of oral contraceptive pills, smoking, medical history (malignancy, immunocompromised).

Lower back pain

Onset (acute/gradual), course (constantly or only when walking), radiation (to one or both legs), worsening at pressure-increasing moments (coughing, sneezing, squeezing), muscle weakness (unable to stand on toes, foot drop, difficulty climbing stairs), sensation disorder (numbness on back of foot, big toe, lateral edge of foot, tinglings), altered sensation during micturition, urinary incontinence or retention, fecal incontinence, decreased sensation in the saddle area, trauma, fever, medical history (e.g. known infections, malignancy).

The essential components of a pain history can be recalled using the mnemonic SOCRATES.

Pain (SOCRATES)
Site
Onset (sudden/gradual)
Character (dull, sharp, stinging)
Radiation
Associated symptoms
Time course/duration
Exacerbating, relieving factors (urge to move, pain during transport)
Severity

Physical examination

The most important aspects of the general physical examination in Neurology are presented. Emphasis is placed on the importance of clear communication and patient comfort throughout the examination.

Introduction
- Permission (explain examination and consent)
- Wash your hands, use PPE
- Privacy
- Expose target body part

→

Physical examination
- General inspection
- Vital signs
- Target physical examination
- Tract-specific examination

→

Concluding
- Thank patient
- Dispose of PPE and wash your hands
- Summarise your findings
- Explain indicated diagnostics and/or next steps

Diagram 4 // Physical examination
PPE, personal protective equipment

Always perform the physical examination according to the patient's specific complaints and clinical history. Consider indications or any red flags for additional diagnostics. This chapter provides a focused exploration of the most common general and system-specific aspects of physical examination in Neurology rather than attempting to cover all aspects comprehensively.

In Neurology, the neurological exam is key to localising the patient's symptoms (central vs. peripheral) (cerebral, cerebellum, brainstem, spinal cord, nerve roots, plexus, peripheral nerves, neuromuscular junction or muscles).

General inspection

Gender, age (biological vs. calendar), state of consciousness, general behaviour, mood, posture, skin colour (e.g. pale, cyanotic, flushing/blushing, icteric), mobility, grooming, nutritional status (e.g. cachexia, BMI), and any medical equipment attached to the patient or in the bedspace.

During the general inspection, pay extra attention to neurological-related findings like presence of asymmetry, atrophy, fasciculations, tremors, and chorea movements.

Anthropometric data

Abdominal circumference, weight, height, BMI.

Vital signs

REFERENCE RANGES					
RR	15-20/min	**Systolic BP**	100-140 mmHg	**T**	36-38°C/ 96.8-100.4°F
SpO_2	>95%	**Diastolic BP**	60-90 mmHg	**CRT**	<2-3 sec
HR/pulse rate	60-100/min	**CVP**	R 4-9 cm H_2O (3-8 mmHg)		

Table 4 // Normal vital signs (Vx)
BP, blood pressure; CRT, capillary refill time; CVP, central venous pressure; HR, heart rate; RR, respiratory rate; SpO_2, oxygen saturation; T, temperature

Pulse

- Heart rate: 60-100 bpm
- Heart rhythm: regular or irregular rhythm (e.g. atrial fibrillation, atrioventricular blocks)
- Pulse character/pulse force: full, normal, weak, absent/non-palpable
- In emergency situations or when access to the radial artery is challenging, the carotid or femoral pulse can be palpated for assessment

MEWS

The modified early warning score (MEWS) is an objective parameter for early recognition of patients who are at risk of rapid deterioration (see Table 5). Different hospitals have different trigger scores for notifying physicians: verify that your facility uses the same point assignments listed here.

MEASUREMENT	+3	+2	+1	0	+1	+2	+3
RR (per min)		<9		9-14	15-20	21-29	≥30
Saturation (%)	<92	92-93	94-95	>95			
Supplemental O_2		Yes		No			
Temperature		<35°C/ <95°F		35.0-38.4°C/ 95-101.1°F		≥38.5°C/ 101.3°F	
Systolic BP (mmHg)	≤70	71-80	81-100	101-199		≥200	
HR (per min)		≤40	41-50	51-100	101-110	111-129	≥130
Consciousness (AVPU score)				Alert	Responds to voice	Responds to pain	Unrespon-sive

Table 5 // Modified Early Warning Score
AVPU, alert verbal pain unresponsive; BP, blood pressure; HR, heart rate; RR, respiratory rate

General physical examination

During a neurological consultation, a general physical examination is performed on indication. For example:

- Examine the heart, lungs, abdomen, skin, and extremities in case of fever to collect clues for an infection focus.
- Auscultate the heart to detect murmurs and inspect the skin (Janeway lesions, Osler nodes, splinter haemorrhages) when endocarditis is suspected.
- Inspect the limbs' skin colour and palpate for arterial pulsations and limb temperature in case of paraesthesia, numbness and/or paresis/paralysis of one limb, as acute arterial occlusion can also present with these symptoms.

See the pocket Cardiology for an extensive explanation of the components of the general physical examination.

Neurological examination

General

During neurological examination, the mental status (level of consciousness and cortical functions), cranial nerves, motor function, sensory function, coordination, balance, reflexes and gait are tested. Cognition, meningeal irritation, provocative tests for radiculopathy, vertigo tests and postural reflexes can be tested on indication.

Mental status

The GCS can help quantify a decrease in consciousness through the EMV score (see Table 6).

EYE OPENING	MOTOR RESPONSE	VERBAL RESPONSE
1 No response	1 No response	1 No response
2 To pain	2 Extension response to pain	2 Sounds
3 To speech	3 Abnormal flexion response to pain	3 Words
4 Spontaneously open	4 Normal flexion response to pain	4 Confused
	5 Moves to localised pain	5 Orientated
	6 Obeys commands	

Table 6 // Glasgow Coma Scale

To score consciousness, add the best score in each category. When the responses from the left and right sides differ, use the higher of the two scores.

Brainstem functions can be tested by means of the pupillary reflex, corneal reflex and vestibulo-ocular reflex. The presence, absence, or asymmetry of these reflexes can be used to locate the lesion in the brainstem.

During the medical history abundant information can be obtained about the patient's neurological condition, including attention, abstraction (ability to keep track of things), behaviour, memory, rate of thinking, orientation (to time, place and people), prosopagnosia (inability to recognise faces), arithmetic, speech and language (dysarthria, aphasia), astereognosia (inability to recognise objects by touching them), apraxia (inability to perform complex or everyday actions such as combing hair or brushing teeth), perceptual disorders and anosognosia (lack of awareness of disability).

Virtually all cortical functions can be examined. When deciding which cortical functions to test, take the patient and the presenting complaint into account.

To test the speech, the patient is asked to repeat sentences. The examiner pays attention to articulation, prosody (rhythm, emphasis, intonation) and volume. In dysarthria (speech disorder), there is impaired motor function of the muscles involved in speech (often occurring together with swallowing disorders). Dysarthria can have many different causes, and is therefore of little localising value.

Aphasia is a disorder in the production or understanding of language. An expressive aphasia (i.e. motor aphasia) involves damage to the Broca's area and is characterised by difficulties in producing language. A receptive aphasia (i.e. sensory aphasia) involves damage to the Wernicke's area and is characterised by impaired understanding of language. In conduction aphasia, the connections between the areas of Broca and Wernicke are interrupted and a patient is not able to repeat a sentence. Aphasia causes disorders in speed of speech ("fluency"), comprehension of language, naming, recitation of sentences, reading and writing. Note that good hearing is essential for understanding language. Therefore, always rule out a hearing problem.

Cranial nerves

The functioning of the twelve cranial nerves can be evaluated by checking whether their sensory and/or motor functions are still intact (see Table 7).

Not all tests listed in Table 7 are performed during a standard neurological examination.

<table>
<tr><th></th><th>NAME</th><th>FUNCTION TEST</th></tr>
<tr><td>I</td><td>Olfactory nerve</td><td>Smell test: offer patient different smells, testing each nostril separately while pressing the other nostril shut</td></tr>
<tr><td>II</td><td>Optic nerve</td><td>• Vision test: test both eyes separately using a vision chart (with and without glasses/contacts), if vision <1: test with stenopeic slit
• Pupillary responses (afferent branch)
• Central field of view with Amsler grid map
• Donders' test (see Figure 27)</td></tr>
<tr><td rowspan="2">III</td><td rowspan="2">Oculomotor nerve</td><td>• Inspection: ptosis, pupil size, symmetry and shape
• Pupillary responses (efferent branch)</td></tr>
<tr><td rowspan="2">• Convergence reaction
• Eye tracking
• Eye alignment based on the Hirschberg test
• Rapid saccades</td></tr>
<tr><td>IV</td><td>Trochlear nerve</td></tr>
<tr><td>V</td><td>Trigeminal nerve</td><td>• Facial sensibility (eyes closed): does it feel the same everywhere when the researcher's hands touch the face?
• Deep sensation (cotton wool), superficial sensation (sharp object): counting number of stimuli or location of stimuli
• Corneal reflex (afferent)
• Masticatory muscle force: have patient bite down on wooden depressor or bite down with the examiner's hands on their cheeks (force symmetry)</td></tr>
<tr><td>VI</td><td>Abducens nerve</td><td>• Eye alignment based on the Hirschberg test
• Eye tracking
• Rapid saccades</td></tr>
<tr><td>VII</td><td>Facial nerve</td><td>• Inspection: facial symmetry
• Taste test (anterior $^2/_3$ of the tongue)
• Acoustic reflex
• Facial motor function: facial expression
  - Upper half of the face: squinting, raising eyebrows
  - Lower half of face: closing mouth and puffing up cheeks, baring teeth, smiling
• Corneal reflex (efferent)</td></tr>
<tr><td>VIII</td><td>Vestibulocochlear nerve</td><td>• Inspection: nystagmus, balance tests
• Whispering
• Weber test
• Rinne test
• Vestibulo-ocular reflex</td></tr>
</table>

Table 7A // Cranial nerve function tests

	NAME	FUNCTION TEST
IX	Glossopharyngeal nerve	• Inspection: throat (pharyngeal arches), voice (hoarse, nasal speech) • Say 'eh' and 'ah': pharyngeal arch symmetry • Pharyngeal reflex/gag reflex (if indicated) • Swallowing • Taste test (posterior $^1/_3$ of the tongue)
X	Vagus nerve	
XI	Accessory nerve	• Inspection: asymmetry and/or atrophy of the sternocleidomastoid and trapezius muscles, drooping shoulder • Trapezius muscle: give resistance and have patient shrug shoulders • Sternocleidomastoid muscle: give resistance and have patient turn their head
XII	Hypoglossal nerve	• Inspection: tongue (protrusion in midline, atrophy, fasciculations) • Tongue motor function: sticking out tongue and alternately pressing tongue against cheeks

Table 7B // Cranial nerve function tests

Pupillary responses

Pupillary responses are checked by shining a directed light briefly into the patient's eyes. Physiologically, the input of light is detected by the optic nerve (afferent branch). Via the parasympathetic fibres originating from the Edinger-Westphal nuclei along the oculomotor branch (efferent branch), the sphincter pupillae muscle then contracts and causes myosis in the ipsilateral eye (direct response) and the contralateral eye (indirect reaction).

Donders' test

Donders' test is used to test the four quadrants of the peripheral visual field of both eyes. Have the patient cover one eye. The examiner sits about one metre across from the patient and covers the eye on the same side as the patient. The patient looks straight at the examiner with the eye to be tested. Patient and examiner should now have matching visual fields. While moving their fingers, the examiner moves their hand to the outer edge of their temporal visual field, equidistant from the examiner and the patient (see Figure 27). The patient reports when they can see the fingers move. If the patient cannot see the fingers move, the examiner incrementally moves the hand closer to the midline. To test the nasal visual fields, the examiner switches hands (covering their eye with the examining hand and performing the test with the other hand). The test is then repeated for the other eye.

The **menace reflex** is used as an alternative for patients with impaired attention or aphasia, who cannot undergo the Donders' test. For this test, the examiner performs a rapidly approaching movement from the patient's lateral visual field, causing the patient to blink.

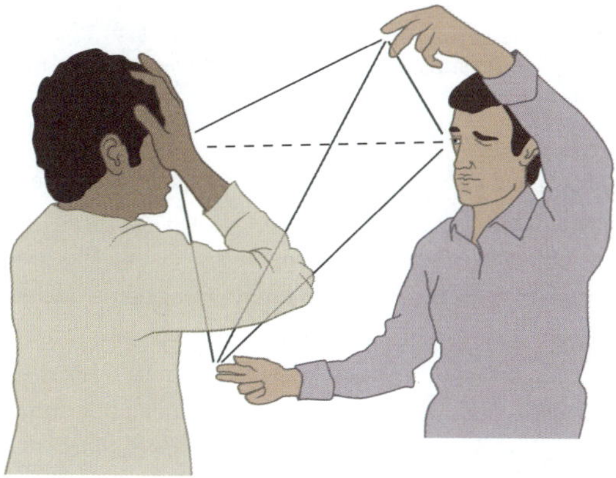

Figure 27 // Donders' test

Eye tracking

To test smooth eye tracking, the examiner slowly moves their finger, following the lines of the British flag, within a 45° angle of the sagittal plane in front of the patient's nose. The examiner looks for eye muscle paresis and asks the patient to report double vision. The examiner also looks for pathological nystagmus by keeping their finger still within a 45° angle. Nystagmus is a rhythmic, oscillatory eye movement with at least one slow phase. The most common type is jerk nystagmus, consisting of a slow phase followed by a fast phase. The less common pendular nystagmus consists of only slow phases. The jerk nystagmus can be described as downbeat, upbeat, horizontal, torsional or mixed nystagmus, according to the direction of the fast phase. In the lightest form, a first-degree nystagmus, the nystagmus is only present when gazing toward the fast phase direction. A second-degree nystagmus is also present when gazing forward, and a nystagmus is third-degree when the fast phase is opposite to the direction of gaze. Figure 28 shows the muscles and associated cranial nerves involved in eye tracking.

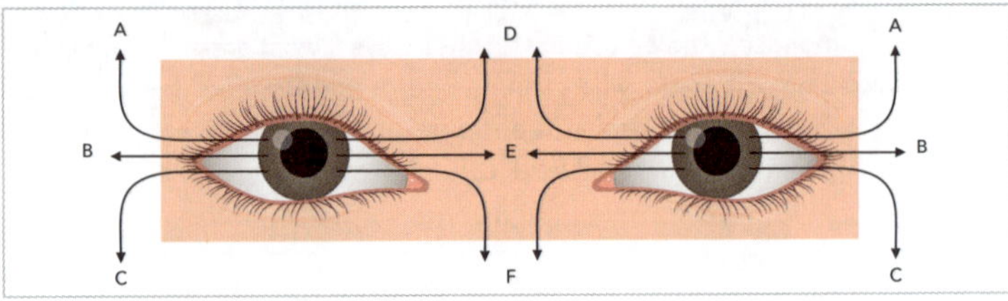

Figure 28 // Eye muscles and associated cranial nerves
A: Superior rectus muscle (CN III) **B:** Lateral rectus muscle (CN VI) **C:** Inferior rectus muscle (CN III) **D:** Inferior oblique muscle **E:** Medial rectus muscle (CN III) **F:** Superior oblique muscle (CN IV)

Saccades

Saccades are rapid conjugate eye movements that shift from one fixation point in the visual field to another (gaze movement). While testing saccades, the examiner holds an object (e.g. a pen) in one hand and raises a finger with the other. The patient is asked to fix their gaze on the pen first before shifting to the finger (or vice versa). A hypermetric saccade is a saccadic eye movement moving beyond the fixating target (overshoot), while a hypometric saccade is a saccadic eye movement which does not reach the fixating target (undershoot). The hypometric saccade can be seen in for example Parkinson's disease.

Convergence response

In the convergence test, the patient is asked to focus on the examiner's finger. The examiner moves their finger towards the patient's head from a distance of 30 cm, forcing their eyes to converge. During the test, the examiner looks for eye tracking and pupillary responses (myosis is physiological).

Hirschberg test

The Hirschberg test is used to assess ocular alignment. The patient is asked to focus on a target straight ahead. The examiner shines a light between both eyes (at a distance of 30 cm). If the light is not reflected in the centre of the cornea, the patient's eyes are misaligned.

Corneal reflex

To test the corneal reflex, briefly touch the cornea with a sterile gauze or cotton ball, moving from the peripheral to the central part. In normal situations, the patient would reflexively shut the eye (contraction of the orbicularis oculi muscle). Absence of the reflex indicates CN V impairment. If the eye turns upwards, CN V is intact but CN VII is impaired.

Oculocephalic reflex (doll's eyes)

To test the oculocephalic reflex, the eyes of the comatose patient are held open while the head is abruptly rotated from side to side in a horizontal plane. A positive reflex is observed when the eyes do not turn with the head, but move in the opposite direction, as if the patient is fixating on a single point in space. A negative reflex is observed when the eyes remain in the midline or move in the same direction as the head. This indicates dysfunction of the brainstem.

Motor exam

Passive motion tests

Passive motion tests serve to assess muscle tone. Increased muscle tone (hypertonia) can be classified into rigidity (extrapyramidal disorder) and spasticity (central motor neuron (CMN) lesion, late stage). Rigidity can be observed when an increased resistance is felt during passive movement of a patient's joint (e.g. wrist, elbow, ankle, knee). A continuous stiffness felt by the examiner during the movement of the patient's joint is called lead-pipe rigidity. A jerky movement is called cogwheel rigidity. Decreased muscle tone (hypotonia) indicates a peripheral motor neuron (PMN) lesion or myopathy. Hypotonia is also present in early-stage CMN lesions, e.g. secondary to a cerebral infarction. Inspection may reveal postural abnormalities (asymmetry), involuntary movements (fasciculations), or muscle atrophy or hypertrophy.

Active motion tests

Active motion tests serve to assess muscle strength. With loss of strength, the aim of the neurological examination is to locate the disorder in a CMN, in a PMN, in the neuromuscular transition or in the muscle(s). Muscle strength can be assessed by applying resistance against the specific movement caused by the muscle. Loss of strength of a muscle or muscle group says nothing about the nature and location of the disorder. Only the combination of various findings from the complete neurological examination gives a clue to the cause. In case of CMN disorders, neurological examination will reveal ipsilateral or contralateral loss of strength (paresis) with hyperreflexia, pathological reflexes and hypertonia of a particular body part (especially the arm and/or leg). In case of PMN disorders, neurological examination will reveal loss of strength with diminished/absent reflexes, hypotonia, atrophy or fasciculations. The disorder should then be localised in the nerve root, brachial or lumbosacral plexus, peripheral nerve or muscle.

Strength tests

To determine muscle strength, individual muscle groups are tested in optimal, isometric contraction. The patient contracts the muscle or muscle group in question, after which the examiner applies resistance. The Medical Research Council (MRC) scale is used to assess the muscle strength of all muscles and muscle groups (see Table 8). There is great physiological variance in muscle strength, but generally speaking, at peak strength most muscles will overcome the examiner's arm and/or hand resistance. If this is not the case, the patient usually has loss of strength. Table 9 lists several specific motor function tests. See Table 10 for a list of strength tests.

GRADE	MEANING
0	No contraction
1	Minimal contraction, no movement
2	Active movement with gravity eliminated
3	Active movement against gravity
4	Active movement against gravity and additional resistance
5	Normal strength

Table 8 // MRC scale for muscle strength

FUNCTION TEST	PROCEDURE
Pronator drift (Barré sign)	• Shut eyes, extend arms and supinate hands • In a paresis (corticospinal tract injury, cortical problem), the impaired arm will drift downwards and the forearm will pronate • See Figure 29
Mingazzini sign	• Lying supine, eyes shut, legs and hips at 90° • A drop of one or both legs indicates monoparesis or paraparesis • Trembling legs can be a sign of a proprioceptive disorder • This test might be too difficult for patients with weak abdominal muscles • See Figure 30
Trendelenburg sign	• Standing on one leg • Weakness in the hip abductor muscles can cause the buttock on the same side as the raised leg to drop • See Figure 31

Table 9 // Specific motor function tests

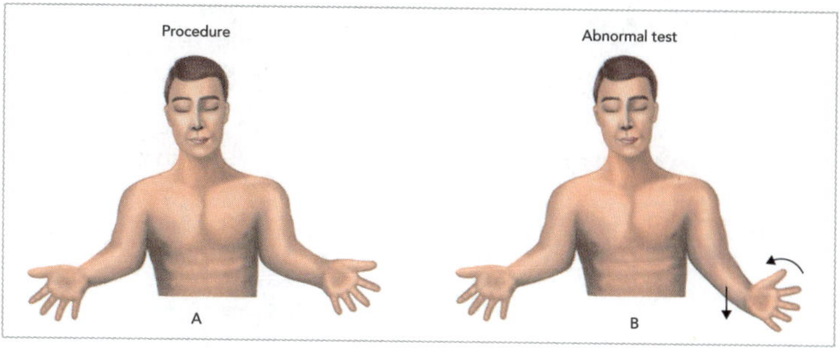

Figure 29 // Pronator drift (Barré sign)

A: Negative test **B:** Positive test: downward drift arm and pronation forearm

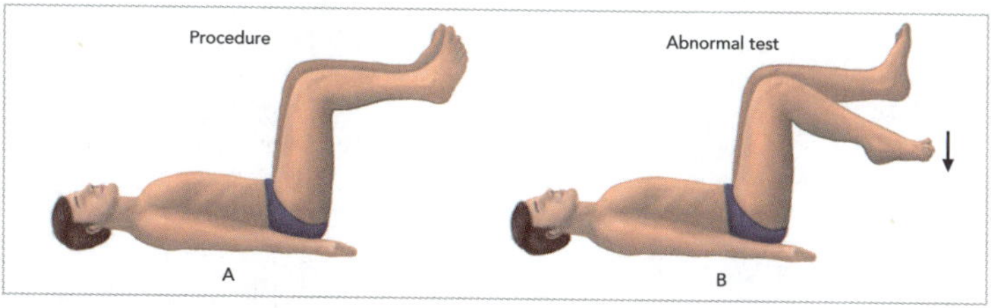

Figure 30 // Mingazzini sign

A: Negative test **B:** Positive test: one or both legs drop

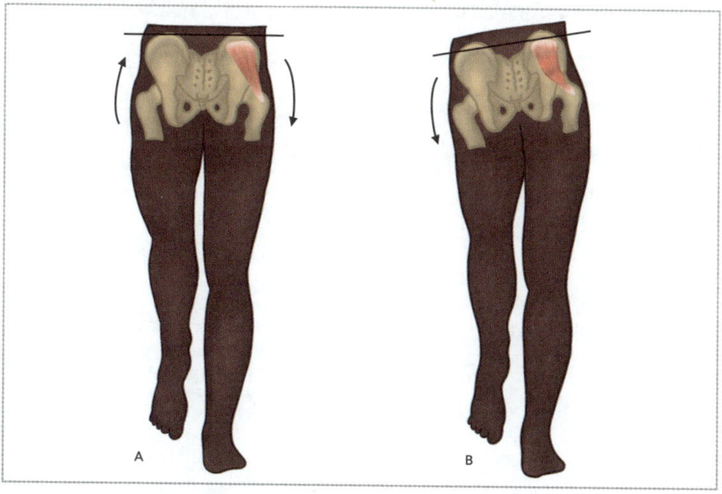

Figure 31 // Trendelenburg sign

A: Negative test **B:** Positive test: the contralateral buttock to the supporting leg drops

Because of the large physiological variation in muscle strength and tone, all function tests should be performed and compared bilaterally.

SEGMENT	MUSCLE(S)	INNERVATION	FUNCTION TEST
C2-C3-C4	Trapezius muscle	Accessory muscle	Shrugging shoulders
C3-C4-C5	Diaphragm	Phrenic nerve	Abdominal breathing, coughing (Valsalva manoeuvre)
C5-C6	Deltoid muscle	Axillary nerve	Abduction of upper arm beyond 15°
	Biceps brachii muscle	Musculocutaneous nerve	Supinated forearm flexion
	Supraspinatus muscle	Suprascapular nerve	Abduction of upper arm from 0° to 15°
	Infraspinatus muscle		Upper arm external rotation (in the shoulder)
C5-C6-C7	Serratus anterior muscle	Long thoracic nerve	Pushing motions and arm extension
C6-C7	Extensor carpi radialis longus muscle	Radial nerve	Extension and abduction of the hand relative to the wrist
C6-C7-C8	Triceps brachii muscle	Radial nerve	Forearm extension
C7-C8	Extensor digitorum communis muscle		Extension of the fingers at the MCP joint
	Extensor carpi ulnaris muscle		Extension and adduction of the hand relative to the wrist
	Abductor pollicis longus muscle		Abduction of thumb in plane of palm
C6-C7	Flexor carpi radialis muscle	Median nerve	Flexion and abduction of the hand relative to the wrist
C8-T1	Abductor pollicis brevis muscle		Abduction of thumb perpendicular to plane of palm
	Opponens pollicis muscle		Thumb to the tip of the little finger
C7-C8-T1	Flexor carpi ulnaris muscle	Ulnar nerve	Flexion and adduction of the hand relative to the wrist

Table 10A // Strength tests

SEGMENT	MUSCLE(S)	INNERVATION	FUNCTION TEST
C8-T1	Abductor digiti minimi muscle	Ulnar nerve	Abduction of the little finger
	Opponens digiti minimi muscle		Little finger to the tip of the thumb
	Palmar and dorsal interossei muscles		Adduction and abduction of the fingers
	Adductor pollicis muscle		Thumb adduction
T1 to T12	Intercostal muscles	Intercostal nerves	Deep inspiration
T6 to T12	Abdominals	Abdominal muscle nerves	Getting up from supine position, forceful expiration
L1-L2-L3	Iliopsoas	Femoral nerve	Thigh flexion at the hip, tucking knees
L2-L3-L4	Quadriceps femoris muscle		Lower leg extension at the knee
	Adductores femoris muscles	Obturator nerve	Pressing knees together
L5-S1-S2	Hamstrings	Sciatic nerve	Knee flexion
L4-L5	Gluteus medius muscle	Superior gluteal nerve	Internal rotation of the thigh with knee and hip flexion
	Gluteus minimus muscle		
L5-S1	Gluteus maximus muscle	Inferior gluteal nerve	Thigh extension at the hip
L4-L5	Posterior tibial muscle	Tibial nerve	Inversion of the foot
S1-S2	Gastrocnemius muscle		Plantar flexion of the foot, tiptoe walking
L4-L5	Anterior tibial muscle	Deep peroneal nerve	Dorsiflexion of the foot, heel walking
L5	Extensor hallucis longus muscle		Dorsiflexion of the great toe
L5-S1	Peroneus longus and peroneus brevis muscles	Superficial peroneal nerve	Eversion of the foot
	Flexor digitorum longus muscle	Tibial nerve	Flexion of the toes

Table 10B // Strength tests

Bradykinesia tests

Bradykinesia can be defined as slowness of movement and can be tested by letting the patient perform rapid alternating movements. The physician performs the movement and the patient imitates the movement with at least ten repetitions per movement. Tests which can be performed are finger tapping, fist open and close, pronation/supination of the hand, toe tapping and heel tapping. The movements must be performed as fast as possible and with the biggest possible amplitude. All tests are positive for bradykinesia if the speed and/or amplitude reduce over time.

Sensory exam

Sensory deficits can be localised by differentiating between the quality of the deficit (superficial and/or deep) and the associated failure area:

- Radiculopathy: nerve root disorder with failure following a dermatomal distribution;
- Mononeuropathy: peripheral nerve disorder with failure limited to the area innervated by the affected peripheral nerve;
- Polyneuropathy: distal bilateral failure symptoms, typically with a 'stocking-glove' distribution.

Dissociated sensory loss can occur in conjunction with a complete or incomplete spinal cord injury. This involves unilateral superficial sensory loss (see Table 11) and contralateral deep sensory loss (see Table 12).

The major peripheral nerves and dermatomes can be tested by checking for sensory loss in the areas they innervate and testing of the reflex arcs. An overview of the dermatomes and peripheral nerves can be found in the Anatomy section (see Figure 21).

When testing sensation, the object should always be tested on an unaffected dermatome first.

FUNCTION TEST	PROCEDURE
Sharp/dull discrimination	A sharp or blunt object is placed on the skin (dermatome or area innervated by peripheral nerve) in varying sequences and at various intervals. The patient identifies the stimulus as sharp or dull. If failure of a specific dermatome or peripheral nerve is suspected, test multiple stimuli at the border of the affected area.
Temperature sense	A collection tube is filled with hot or cold water and used to touch different areas of skin. The patient identifies the tube as hot or cold.

Table 11 // Superficial sensibility function tests

FUNCTION TEST	PROCEDURE
Sense of movement	With eyes shut, the patient indicates when they feel their big toe being moved. The examiner tries to find the smallest possible movement that the patient can still feel.
Joint position sense	With eyes shut, the patient identifies the position of the thumb/big toe: upward/neutral/downward. The examiner explains each position first.
Vibration sense	• A vibrating tuning fork (128 Hz) is used to touch: - Lower extremity: MTP, lateral malleolus, tibial tuberosity - Upper extremity: MCP, radial styloid, olecranon • When testing sense of vibration, it is important to place the tuning fork on bone, not on soft tissue. The patient reports when they perceive the vibration. Sense of vibration is tested from distal to proximal direction. If the sense of vibration is intact distally, the test need not be performed proximally.
Light touch	A cotton ball is used to touch different skin areas (dermatome or peripheral nerve area). The patient reports when they perceive the cotton ball touching them.
Tactile extinction	The patient will be touched by the examiner on two different body parts and will be asked to identify the body parts that are touched
Two-point discrimination	A sharp object (tweezers, paperclip) is used to touch the patient in two places that are very close together (distance depends on body part). The patient reports whether they can tell the two points apart.

Table 12 // Deep sensibility function tests
MCP, metacarpophalangeal joint; MTP, metatarsophalangeal joint

Coordination exam

For proper coordination and balance, the cortical (sensory) input and (motor) output structures, the basal ganglia, the cerebellum and the peripheral nerves all need to function adequately. Impaired coordination or balance may indicate a disorder in one of these structures. Functional coordination and balance tests include the tandem gait, Romberg, finger-to-nose, finger-to-finger, diadochokinetic, finger dexterity and heel-to-shin tests (see Table 13).

FUNCTION TEST	PROCEDURE
Tandem gait test / heel-to-toe test	• Ask the patient to walk in a straight line, one foot in front of the other (heel-to-toe) • An abnormal tandem gait (overstriding, wide gait) that improves after optical correction indicates a proprioceptive disorder (sensory ataxia) • An abnormal tandem gait (overstriding, wide gait) that does not improve after optical correction indicates a cerebellar disorder (cerebellar ataxia)

Table 13A // Functional coordination tests

FUNCTION TEST	PROCEDURE
Romberg test	• Have the patient stand upright with their feet together for 30 sec. If succesful, have the patient shut their eyes. • If proprioception is impaired, the patient will be unable to maintain balance with their eyes shut (positive Romberg test) • The inability to keep the feet together, with eyes open or eyes shut, may indicate a cerebellar disorder
Finger-to-nose test	• With arms in 90° abduction, have the patient alternately bring their left and right index finger to their nose, first with eyes open, then with eyes shut • Fluent movements that consistently land right next to the nose may indicate simulation or a functional neurological disorder • Delayed performance may indicate an extrapyramidal disorder When the movement is performed jerkily or clumsily with closed eyes and improves when the eyes are being opened, this may indicate sensory ataxia. If the abnormal movement does not improve with open eyes, this indicates cerebellar ataxia. An intention tremor may occur at the end of the movement if the movement is performed slowly.
Finger-to-finger test	• Have the patient move their finger to the examiner's finger as quickly as possible, after which the examiner immediately moves their finger again • Overshoot is a sign of dysmetria, indicating a cerebellar disorder
Diadochokinesis	• Have the patient quickly rotate their wrist in alternating directions, first with each hand separately, then with both hands simultaneously • Slow, clumsy or irregular movements indicate a cerebellar or extrapyramidal disorder
Dexterity	• Have the patient tap their fingers with their thumb in order as quickly as possible, first with each hand separately, then with both hands simultaneously • Slow, clumsy or irregular movements indicate a cerebellar or extrapyramidal disorder
Heel-to-shin test	• Have the patient place their heel on the knee and slide it down the tibia to their foot and big toe • Jerky or clumsy movement when performed with closed eyes, and improvement with open eyes, may indicate sensory ataxia. No improvement of the abnormal movement with open eyes may indicate cerebellar ataxia. An intention tremor may occur at the end of the movement if the movement is performed slowly.

Table 13B // Functional coordination tests

Reflexes

General

A reflex is an involuntary response to a standardised stimulus. In principle, patients do not have to actively cooperate with reflex tests, which means these can also be performed in patients with a decreased level of consciousness (as opposed to motor function and sensibility). There are three groups of reflexes:

- Proprioceptive reflex (muscle stretch reflex, deep tendon reflex): elicited by quickly and briefly stretching a tendon (by tapping the tendon with reflex hammer). Proprioceptive reflexes have a short reaction time and are tireless (they cannot be exhausted). Muscle stretch reflexes on the left side of the body are always compared with the right side of the body (e.g. biceps reflex, brachioradialis reflex, triceps reflex, knee reflex, Achilles reflex; see Figures 32, 33, 34, 35 and 36, respectively). Proprioceptive reflexes can be elicited while the patient is lying or sitting down.
- Exteroceptive reflex: skin reflexes in which touching a particular area of skin causes the superficial muscles in that area to contract (e.g. abdominal skin reflex and plantar response; see Figures 37 and 38, respectively).
- Pathological reflex: a certain muscle contraction elicited by administering a standardised stimulus that occurs only with a lesion in the reflex arc (e.g. the frontal release signs, also primitive reflexes, or Hoffmann's sign and Babinski's sign, indicating a problem in the corticospinal tract).

Muscle stretch reflexes are graded on a scale of 0 to 5+ (see Table 14). Absent reflexes, clonus or reproducible response differences between the left and right side or between the arm and leg are pathological responses (see Table 15). Overly brisk reflexes (hyperreflexia) can also be indicative of pathology.

SCALE	REFLEX
0	Absent
1+	Delayed, trace or brought out only with reinforcement
2+	Normal
3+	Brisk
4+	Subclonus (non-sustained clonus)
5+	Clonus (sustained clonus)

Table 14 // National Institute of Neurological Disorders and Stroke (NINDS) scale: grading of deep tendon reflexes

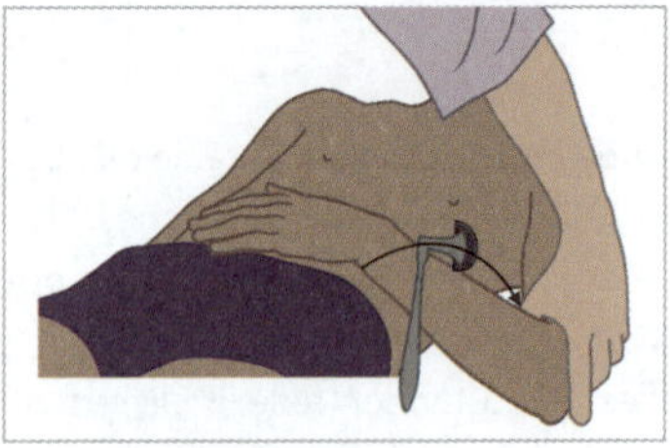

Figure 32 // Biceps reflex

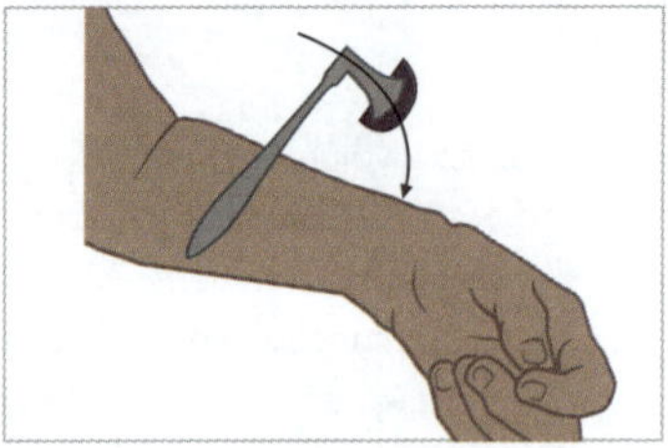

Figure 33 // Brachioradialis reflex

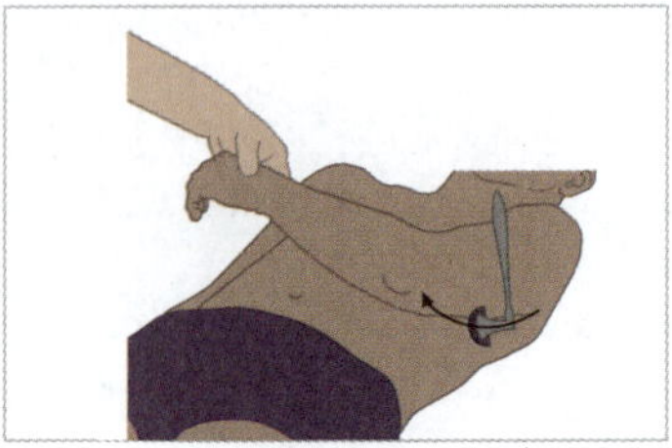

Figure 34 // Triceps reflex

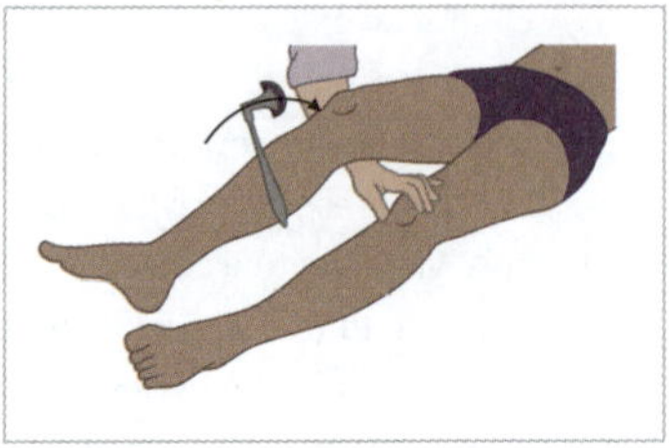

Figure 35 // Knee reflex

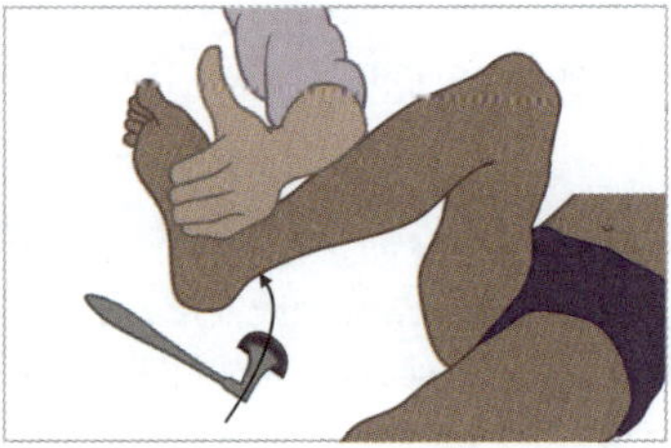

Figure 36 // Achilles reflex

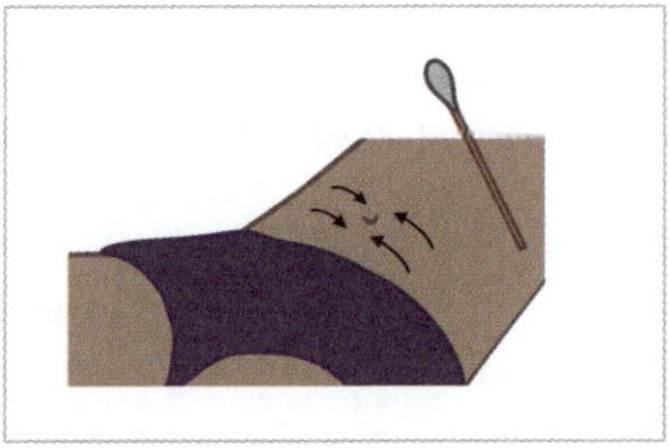

Figure 37 // Abdominal skin reflex

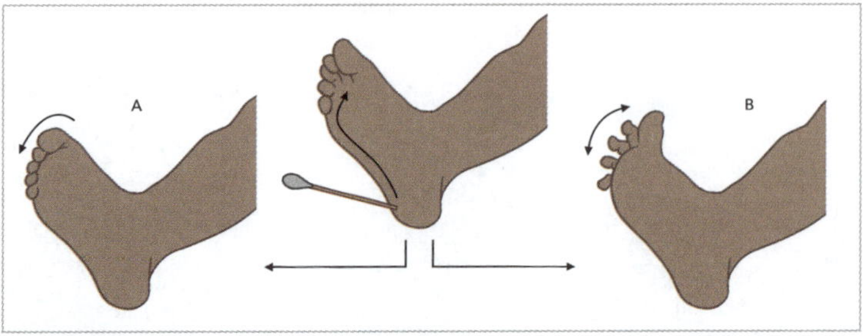

Figure 38 // Plantar response

A: Normal plantar response **B:** Abnormal Babinski's sign

RESPONSE	INTERPRETATION
Normal response	Ranges from low to brisk
Areflexia	• The absence of a reflex response after repeated stimuli • Can indicate a lesion of a peripheral nerve, a lesion of the central part of the reflex arc, an acute stage of a spinal cord injury or a deep coma
Clonus	• Series of short rhythmic contractions. Repetitive reflex in which the response to the previous muscle contraction provides a stimulus for the next muscle contraction. • May indicate a lesion of the CMN • In newborns (whose corticospinal tract is not yet fully myelinated) and patients with brisk reflexes, clonus can be physiological (if number of beats ≤4). A clonus >4 beats indicates pathology.
Differences in proprioceptive reflex responses	• Reproducible response differences between left and right • Hyporeflexia may indicate an ipsilateral lesion in the PMN • Hyperreflexia may indicate a contralateral lesion in the CMN
Hyperreflexia	• Enhanced reflex on one side or both sides of the body • May indicate a disorder in the tractus corticospinalis or late-stage haemiplegia. Symmetrical hyperreflexia may be indicative of myelopathy, but may also be physiological.

Table 15 // Interpretation of reflexes

Anal reflex

The anal reflex is a urogenital test that is performed to assess e.g. suspected spinal cord injury, cauda equina syndrome or lumbosacral radicular syndrome (see Table 16).

FUNCTION TEST	PROCEDURE
Anal reflex	• Contraction of the external sphincter (S4-S5) in response to stroking the skin around the anus (pudendal nerve) • An absent reflex response may indicate e.g. spinal cord injury or cauda equina syndrome

Table 16 // Urogenital function test

Gait exam

Gait is tested by asking the patient to walk back and forth, preferably barefoot. The examiner watches for how the patient starts and stops walking, gait speed, symmetry, suppleness, arm movements, stride width, stride length, rollover, turning, tiptoe walking and heel walking, and additional movements of e.g. the head and arms.

Tests on indication only

Cognition

Cognition can be tested in various ways. Well-known and widely used examples are the Mini Mental-State Examination (MMSE) (see Appendix 1), the Montreal Cognitive Assessment (MoCA) (see Appendix 2), and the Frontal Assessment Battery (FAB) for the cognitive functions of the frontal lobe (see Appendix 3). The MMSE, MoCA, and FAB are not reliable in the acute phase of neurological conditions.

Meningeal irritation

Meningeal irritation (neck stiffness) occurs in e.g. meningitis, subarachnoid haemorrhage (SAH), or tumours in the posterior cranial fossa that press on the meninges. Figure 39 shows signs of meningeal irritation.

The specificity of neck stiffness (also nuchal rigidity) (68%), the presence of Kernig's sign (95%), and Brudzinski's sign (95%) are high, but sensitivity is low at 30%, 5% and 5%, respectively.

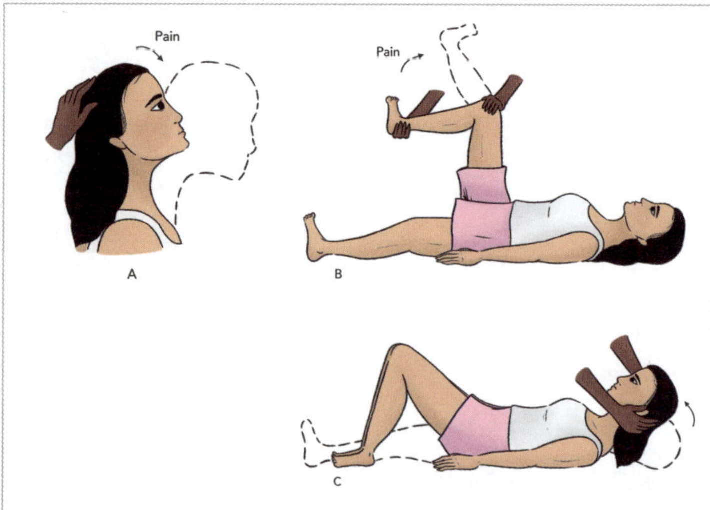

Figure 39 // Signs of meningeal irritation

A: Neck stiffness: pain and resistance with passive neck flexion **B:** Kernig's sign: pain and resistance when passively extending the leg flexed at the hip and knee **C:** Brudzinski's sign: reflexively leg flexion with passive neck flexion

Provocative tests for radiculopathy

In the provocative tests for radiculopathy, stress is deliberately applied to the exiting nerve roots (see Tables 17 and 18). The goal is to assess whether this stress elicits pain in the patient. The location and radiation of the pain provides additional information.

FUNCTION TEST	PROCEDURE
Lasègue test (cervical)	• Dorsally move arm into abducted position and head to contralateral side (see Figure 40) • Radicular syndrome gives radiating pain to the arm beyond the elbow and tingling at the end of a dermatome
Spurling test	• Move the neck back (extension) and sideways (lateroflexion) to the affected side. Axial pressure to the head can be applied. • Radicular syndrome gives radiating pain to the arm beyond the elbow and tingling at the end of a dermatome

Table 17 // Provocative tests for cervical radiculopathy

FUNCTION TEST	PROCEDURE
Lasègue test	• Lying supine, lift extended leg on affected side (see Figure 41) • Radicular syndrome at L5 or S1 gives radiating pain in the ipsilateral leg beyond the knee following a dermatome • If the Lasègue test is positive, take a note of the angle at which the pain is elicited • Radiating pain can also result from e.g. meningeal irritation or a peripheral lesion of the sciatic nerve
Crossed-over Lasègue test	• Lying supine, lift the unaffected, extended leg • Severe radicular syndrome gives pain in the contralateral leg beyond the knee along the sciatic pathway
Reversed Lasègue test	• In prone or lateral position, lift leg (see Figure 41) • Radicular syndrome at L3 or L4 gives radiating pain to the leg beyond the knee on the anterior side of the leg (as opposed to Lasègue and Bragard test, which elicit pain radiating through the sciatic tract)
Bragard test	• Lift extended leg to slightly below pain threshold, dorsiflex foot • Radicular syndrome gives radiating pain to the leg beyond the knee following a dermatome • The Bragard test is performed to confirm the Lasègue test

Table 18A // Provocative tests for lumbosacral radiculopathy

FUNCTION TEST	PROCEDURE
Kemp test	• In standing position, have the patient lean backwards and to the side of the suspected radicular syndrome (lateroflexion). Axial pressure to both shoulders can be applied. • Radicular syndrome gives radiating pain to the leg beyond the knee following a dermatome
Flip test	• The patient sits on the edge of the examination table with legs hanging down, the examiner stretches each leg • Radicular syndrome gives back extension (the patient lies down on the table)

Table 18B // Provocative tests for lumbosacral radiculopathy

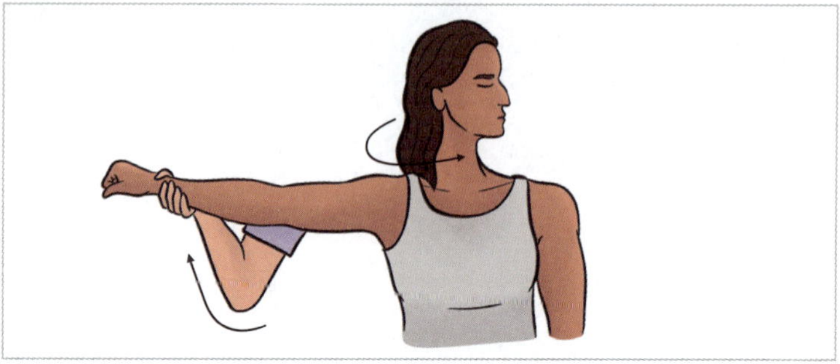

Figure 40 // Lasègue test (cervical). Move arm in 90° abduction dorsally with head rotated towards the non-painful side. Positive (abnormal) test: radicular syndrome gives radiating pain in the arm.

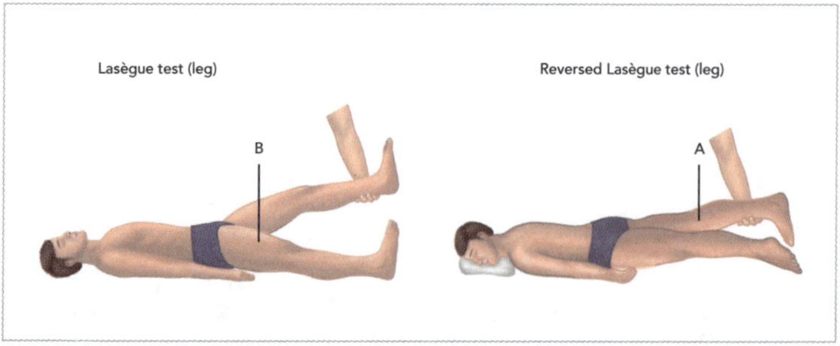

Figure 41 // Lasègue test and reversed Lasègue test

A: Patient lies prone on examination table. The leg is stretched and extended at the hip. The test is positive (abnormal) if it gives pain in the raised leg. **B:** Patient lies supine on the examination table. The leg is stretched and flexed at the hip. The test is positive (abnormal) if it gives pain in the raised leg.

Vertigo tests

Dix-Hallpike manoeuvre

The Dix-Hallpike manoeuvre should be performed in all patients complaining of positional vertigo to diagnose benign paroxysmal positional vertigo (BPPV). The patient sits on the examination table with their head in slight extension and 45° rotation to the affected side. Holding the patient's head with both hands, the examiner brings the patient to a supine position, with the head lower than the thorax, as quickly as possible. The patient should keep their eyes open during the test, so that the examiner can check for nystagmus (see Figure 42). Nystagmus in conjunction with vertigo occurring a few seconds after the manoeuvre and disappearing within a minute is an indicator of BPPV on the side of the downward-facing ear. The nystagmus pattern can be used to locate the semicircular canal from which the BPPV pathology originated.

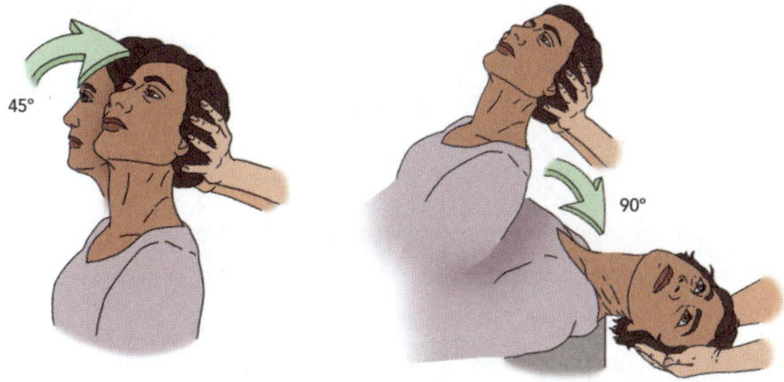

Figure 42 // Dix-Hallpike manoeuvre

Head Impulse Test (HIT)

The HIT can be performed in patients with acute vertigo which is present at the time of examination. The aim of the test is to distinguish between a peripheral and a central cause of the vertigo. The test comprises a rapid passive lateral rotation of the head, elicited by the examiner turning the patient's head while the patient fixates on the examiner's nose (see Figure 43). The test is positive when the eyes first move along in the direction of the lateral movement and then compensatory refixate to the nose of the examiner. When the patient can continue to fixate on the nose, the test is negative. A positive test indicates a disruption to the vestibulo-ocular reflex and increases the likelihood of a peripheral cause of the vertigo.

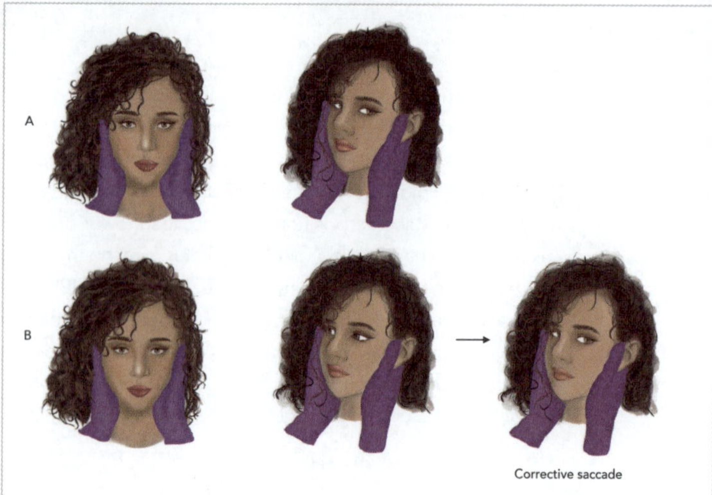

Figure 43 // Head Impulse Test
A: Negative test: patient keeps fixated on the nose **B:** Positive test: patient shows an corrective saccade

Test of Skew

The test of Skew can be performed in patients with acute vertigo which is present at the time of examination. It is performed by alternately covering the patient's eyes while the patient fixates on the examiner's nose (see Figure 44). During the movement of the examiner's hand from the one eye to the other, the uncovered eye is observed for any vertical and/or diagonal corrective movement. If abnormal movement occurs, often associated with vertical diplopia, a central cause of the vertigo becomes more likely.

> The HIT, nystagmus and test of Skew are often performed together and are called Head Impulse-Nystagmus-Test of Skew (HINTS).

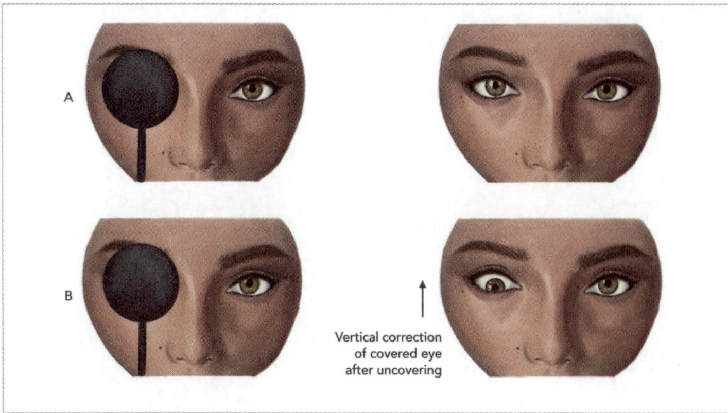

Figure 44 // Test of Skew
A: Normal test **B:** Abnormal test: vertical corrective movement

Postural reflexes

When testing postural reflexes, the patient is asked to stand with both feet together. The examiner stands behind the patient and gives them a sudden push forwards (propulsion), backwards (retropulsion) or sideways (lateropulsion), assessing the patient's stability.

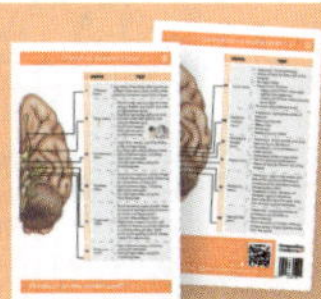

Diagnostics

Lab values

Reference values may vary between laboratories. Test results should preferably be compared to previous values. Request them from the patient's GP or another hospital if necessary.

While the following section provides examples of conditions associated with altered lab values, it is essential to acknowledge that the scope of medical diagnoses is vast and varied.

When interpreting laboratory results, it is crucial to consider them in the context of all findings. For example, an isolated thrombocytopaenia has a completely different differential diagnosis than thrombocytopaenia with anaemia and leukopenia (pancytopenia).

General blood count

LAB VALUE	EXPLANATION	INTERPRETATION
Haemoglobin (Hb)	Protein in erythrocytes that can bind and carry oxygen	↑ Polycythaemia: • Primary polycythaemia: - Congenital - Acquired: malignant bone marrow disease • Secondary polycythaemia: - Secondary to hypoxia: e.g. COPD or smoking, sleep apnoea, high altitudes, right-to-left shunts, congestive heart failure - Secondary to kidney disease - Secondary to EPO-producing tumour - Secondary to alcohol use disorder ↓ Anaemia, see Table 20
Haematocrit (Ht)	Measure of red blood cell volume in relation to total blood volume	↑ • Dehydration • Primary or secondary polycythaemia ↓ Anaemia

Table 19A // General blood count

CMV, cytomegalovirus; COPD, chronic obstructive pulmonary disease; DIC, disseminated intravascular coagulation; EBV, Epstein-Barr virus; EDTA, ethylenediamineetraacetic acid; EPO, erythropoietin; HIV, human immunodeficiency virus; ITP, immune thrombocytopenia; HELLP, hemolysis, elevated liver enzyme levels and low platelet levels

LAB VALUE	EXPLANATION	INTERPRETATION
Mean corpuscular volume (MCV)	Measure of the average volume of erythrocytes, see Table 20	↑ Macrocytic = Normocytic ↓ Microcytic
Platelet count (PLT)	• Platelets/thrombocytes • Are primary haemostasis by aggregation	↑ Thrombocytosis: • During/after infection/inflammation • Splenectomy/hyposplenism • Iron deficiency • Myeloproliferative disease • Paraneoplastic ↓ Thrombocytopenia: • Synthesis ↓: bone marrow insufficiency, e.g. tumour invasion/medication-induced, deficiencies (vitamin B12, folic acid), liver disease (e.g. liver cirrhosis), hyperthyroidism/hypothyroidism • Utilisation/degradation ↑: DIC, ITP, medication-induced immune thrombocytopenia, post-transfusion, preeclampsia/HELLP, viral infection (e.g. CMV, EBV, hepatitis B/C, HIV), parasitic infection (malaria), idiopathic, heparin-induced thrombocytopenia • Loss ↑: blood loss, splenomegaly (e.g. in portal hypertension) • Other causes: gestational trombocytopenia, hereditary thrombocytopenia (e.g. Bernard-Soulier syndrome) • Watch out for pseudothrombocytopenia: false lower result due to agglutination in EDTA tube
Red blood cell (RBC) count	• Erythrocytes: red blood cells • Transport O_2 and CO_2 between lungs and tissue	↑ Erythrocytosis: • Primary: polycythaemia vera, see Hb • Secondary to oxygen deprivation, see Hb ↓ Erythropenia: • Reduced synthesis: - Nutritional deficiency - Disrupted production in bone marrow • Increased degradation, e.g. autoimmune haemolysis, haemoglobinopathy, DIC, valve haemolysis
Mean corpuscular haemoglobin (MCH)	Average amount of oxygen-carrying haemoglobin per erythrocyte (Hb/erythrocytes)	↑ Hyperchromic anaemia: • Vitamin B12 deficiency • Folic acid deficiency

Table 19B // General blood count

LAB VALUE	EXPLANATION	INTERPRETATION
Mean corpuscular haemoglobin concentration (MCHC)	Average haemoglobin concentration per erythrocyte (Hb/Ht)	= Normochromic anaemia ↓ Hypochromic anaemia: • Iron deficiency • Haemoglobinopathy
Red blood cell distribution width (RDW)	A measure of MCV variance	↑ In case of high MCV variance, e.g. after a blood transfusion or in combined microcytic and macrocytic anaemia (MCV may be normal)
Reticulocyte count (RTIC)	• Reticulocytes: immature erythrocytes that still have RNA • Adequacy of a reticulocyte response depends on haematocrit levels. A deep anaemia should give a marked increase in reticulocyte count.	↑ Reticulocytosis: • Increased erythrocyte synthesis, e.g. haemolytic anaemia, bleeding ↓ Reticulopenia: • Reduced erythrocyte synthesis, e.g. medication-induced myelosuppression, aplastic anaemia, aneamia of chronic disease

Table 19C // General blood count

Anaemia - interpretation

HB	MCV	DIFFERENTIAL DIAGNOSIS
↓	↓	• Iron-deficiency anaemia (chronic blood loss) • Sideroblastic anaemia • Haemoglobinopathy • Other causes: lead poisoning ⊖, sideroblastic anaemia ⊖, hookworm infection ⊖
	↓/=	Anaemia of chronic disease (e.g. infections, malignancy, autoimmune diseases)
	=	• Acute blood loss • Long-term chronic kidney disease (EPO deficiency) • Malnutrition • Mixed-aetiology anaemias • Multiple myeloma
	=/↑	• Haemolysis • Medication-induced • Thyroid dysfunction (specifically hypothyroidism) • Haematological malignancy • Bone marrow disease: - Aplastic anaemia - Bone marrow filtration - Myelodysplastic syndrome

Table 20A // Anaemia - interpretation

HB	MCV	DIFFERENTIAL DIAGNOSIS
↓	↑	• Vitamin B12 deficiency (e.g. malabsorption, HIV) • Folic acid deficiency • Pregnancy • Toxic: alcohol use disorder, medication-induced (e.g. cytostatics)

Table 20B // Anaemia - interpretation

Electrolytes

LAB VALUE	EXPLANATION	INTERPRETATION
Sodium (Na^+)	• Main extracellular cation • Very important in water management	↑ Hypernatraemia: • Increased water loss: - Osmotic diarrhoea or diuresis (e.g. hyperglycaemia, mannitol) - Arginine vasopressin deficiency (e.g. cranial trauma, infections, autoimmune) - Arginine vasopressin resistance (e.g. drugs, amyloidosis, hereditary) • Increased sodium retention (iatrogenic with unchecked IV drip) • Insufficient fluid intake (with or without intact thirst stimulus) ↓ Hyponatraemia: often multiple causes • Water retention: - SIADH - Renal insufficiency stage 5 - Congestive heart failure - Liver cirrhosis - Blood loss (resulting in ADH ↑ to preserve volume) - Nephrotic syndrome • Increased sodium loss: - Gastrointestinal, e.g. diarrhoea, small bowel obstruction - Renal, e.g. diuretics, renal failure, osmotic diuresis (severe hyperglycaemia), Addison's disease - Transdermal, e.g. burns, excessive sweating • Other: - Tea & toast (malnutrition) - Polydipsia

Table 21A // Electrolytes

ACE, Angiotensin-converting enzyme; ADH, antidiuretic hormone; AST, Aspartate aminotransferase; IV, intravenous; LDH, Lactate dehydrogenase; NSAID, non-steroidal anti-inflammatory drugs; PPI, proton pump inhibitor; PTH, parathyroid hormone; SIADH, Syndrome of inappropriate antidiuretic hormone ADH release; TPN, total parenteral nutrition

LAB VALUE	EXPLANATION	INTERPRETATION
Potassium (K^+)	• Main intracellular cation • Regulates e.g. nerve impulse transmission, glycogen and protein synthesis	↑ Hyperkalaemia: • Extracellular redistribution (shift): - Metabolic or respiratory acidosis - Hyperosmolality - Insulin deficiency - Medication-induced, e.g. beta blockers, digoxin • Tissue breakdown (often in combination with LDH, AST, bilirubin): - Haemolysis - Tumorlysis - Rhabdomyolysis - Distal arterial occlusion • Impaired renal excretion: - Mineralocorticoid deficiency - Renal insufficiency - Medication-induced, e.g. ACE inhibitors, NSAIDs, potassium-sparing diuretics - Type IV renal tubular acidosis • Pseudohyperkalaemia (e.g. following blood collection) ↓ Hypokalaemia: • Intracellular redistribution: - Metabolic or respiratory alkalosis - Insulin use • Renal loss: - Renal conditions, e.g. type I and II renal tubular acidosis - Hyperaldosteronism - Medication-induced, e.g. diuretics, glucocorticoids - Hypomagnesaemia - Chronic metabolic acidosis • Extrarenal loss, e.g. gastrointestinal (diarrhoea) • Insufficient intake, e.g. chronic alcohol use disorder

Table 21B // Electrolytes

Ca^{2+} is partially bound to albumin. Low albumin levels may lead to a decrease in total Ca^{2+} and may be accompanied by normal ionised Ca^{2+}. Total Ca^{2+} can be corrected for the patient's albumin level using lab-specific formulas. Scan the QR code for the formula.

LAB VALUE	EXPLANATION	INTERPRETATION
Magnesium (Mg^{2+})	• 70% in bone, remainder is intracellular • Cofactor in enzymatic processes • Stabilises nucleic acids and ribosomes	↑ Hypermagnesaemia: • Renal insufficiency • Medication-induced, e.g. laxatives, lithium, antacids containing magnesium • Other: - Rhabdomyolysis - Hypothyroidism ↓ Hypomagnesaemia: • Gastrointestinal loss, e.g. diarrhoea, inadequate intake, malnutrition/malabsorption • Medication-induced, e.g. PPIs, diuretics, cisplatina, insulin, tacrolimus, cyclosporine • Renal loss, e.g. hyperaldosteronism, hyperthyroidism, diuretics • Other: - Chronic alcohol use - Hypercalcaemia - Hungry bone syndrome
Chloride (Cl^-)	• Main extracellular anion • Regulation closely linked to sodium metabolism	↑ Hyperchloraemia: • Chloride administration: secondary to administration of chloride-rich intravenous fluids • True water loss relative to chloride: - Renal: osmotic diuresis, postobstructive diuresis, arginine vasopressine resistance (formerly diabetes insipidus) - Extrarenal: fever, diarrhoea, burns, dehydration • Increase in tubular reabsorption: e.g. renal tubular acidosis, acetazolamide, neobladder ↓ Hypochloraemia: • Increased loss: - Gastrointestinal, e.g. vomiting - Renal - Ascites - True water gain relative to chloride: congestive heart failure, SIADH - High output stoma • Metabolic alkalosis

Table 21C // Electrolytes

LAB VALUE	EXPLANATION	INTERPRETATION
Calcium (Ca^{2+})	• 99% is stored in bone as a mineral, 50% of plasma calcium is free and biologically active (ionised), 40% is bound to albumin, 10% bound to organic molecules • Regulates e.g. nerve impulse conduction, muscle contractility, enzyme functioning, and clotting	↑ Hypercalcaemia: • Primary/tertiary hyperparathyroidism • Tumour-induced, e.g. bone metastases, multiple myeloma, PTH-like peptide • Endocrine: hyperthyroidism, adrenal cortex insufficiency, pheochromocytoma • Vitamin D excessive production or intoxication (e.g. sarcoidosis, lymphoma) • Pseudohypercalcaemia ↓ Hypocalcaemia: • Primary hypoparathyroidism • PTH resistance/pseudohypoparathyroidism • Vitamin D deficiency • Chronic renal insufficiency • Hypomagnesaemia • Medication-induced, e.g. corticosteroids, diuretics, anti-seizure medication • Malabsorption • Acute pancreatitis • Blood transfusions, including massive blood transfusions
Phosphate (PO_4^{3-})	• 75% in bone, remainder in muscle tissue and intracellularly • Main intracellular anion • Particularly important for cell energy metabolism	↑ Hyperphosphataemia: • Endogenous: rhabdomyolysis, haemolysis, intestinal infarction • Exogenous: supplementation, e.g. phosphate enemas • Reduced renal excretion: acute or chronic renal insufficiency, hypoparathyroidism, medication-induced (e.g. vitamin D supplementation) • Shift from intracellular: lactate acidosis, ketoacidosis • Pseudohyperphosphataemia: hyperbilirubinaemia, extreme hypertriglyceridaemia, heparin ↓ Hypophosphataemia: • Redistribution: refeeding syndrome, respiratory alkalosis, diabetic ketoacidosis, hungry bone syndrome, medication-induced (e.g. insulin) • Renal loss: hyperparathyroidism, vitamin D deficiency, medication-induced (e.g. diuretics, glucocorticoids) • Reduced absorption: TPN, malabsorption, anorexia nervosa, alcohol use disorder, chronic/non-chronic diarrhoea, vitamin D deficiency, medication-induced (e.g. overuse of antacids)

Table 21D // Electrolytes

Liver tests and pancreatic tests

LAB VALUE	EXPLANATION	INTERPRETATION
Alanine transaminase (ALT)	Enzyme found primarily in hepatocytes	↑ • Liver conditions: - Hepatitis, e.g. viral, toxic, alcoholic (ALT<AST), autoimmune, ischaemic - Non-alcoholic steatohepatitis - Liver cirrhosis - Hepatocellular carcinoma/liver metastases - Medication-induced liver injury - Liver abscess - Acute liver failure - Haemochromatosis - Wilson's disease - Primary biliary cholangitis/primary sclerosing cholangitis • Bile duct obstruction, see ALP • Chronic/acute pancreatitis • Budd-Chiari syndrome • Preeclampsia-eclampsia/HELLP • Hypotension, i.e. septic shock
Aspartate aminotransferase (AST)	Enzyme found mainly in liver and striated (i.e. cardiac, skeletal) muscle tissue	↑ • In all diagnoses mentioned in ALT • May also be elevated in: - Myocardial infarction/heart failure - Muscle conditions, e.g. rhabdomyolysis, dermatomyositis
Alkaline phosphatase (ALP)	Enzyme found primarily in liver parenchyma, bile epithelium, and osteoblasts	↑ • Bile duct obstruction: - Cholelithiasis - Cholangitis - Hepatocellular carcinoma, cholangiocarcinoma, liver metastases - Pancreatic malignancy - Medication-induced - Pregnancy • Liver conditions: - Hepatitis, e.g. alcoholic - Primary biliary cholangitis - Primary sclerosing cholangitis • Bone disease (isolated elevation of ALP): - Hyperparathyroidism - Bone metastases - Paget's disease - Osteomyelitis or fractures

Table 22A // Liver tests and pancreatic tests

LAB VALUE	EXPLANATION	INTERPRETATION
Gamma-glutamyltransferase (GGT)	• Enzyme present in virtually all cells • Serum GGT generally comes from the hepatobiliary system	↑ • Bile duct obstruction, see ALP • Liver conditions: - Primary biliary cholangitis - Primary sclerosing cholangitis - Hepatitis, e.g. alcoholic • Alcohol use • Obesity
Lactate dehydrogenase (LDH)	Enzyme involved in glycolysis in various tissues	↑ • Increased cellular death in: - Liver conditions - Myocardial infarction - Muscle conditions - Haemolysis • Malignancies (specifically lymphoma, haematological malignancy)

Table 22B // Liver tests and pancreatic tests

A combination of elevated AST and ALT (liver enzymes) indicates hepatocellular damage. The AST/ALT ratio can provide information about the underlying condition. ALT>AST could indicate viral or autoimmune hepatitis and AST>ALT could indicate alcoholic hepatitis. A combination of bilirubin ↑, ALP ↑, and GGT ↑ indicates cholestasis.

A decrease in the synthetic function of the liver indicates severe liver disease. The common assessing liver synthetic function are albumin, prothrombin test (PT)/international normalised ratio (INR), and glucose.

Proteins

LAB VALUE	EXPLANATION	INTERPRETATION
Albumin	• Half of all blood proteins • Produced by the liver • Main protein for osmotic pressure, also a transport protein • Negative acute-phase protein • Non-specific marker of liver synthetic function • Necessary for interpretation of calcium level	↑ Hyperalbuminaemia: • Dehydration ↓ Hypoalbuminaemia: • Reduced synthesis: - Liver disease (e.g. liver cirrhosis, hepatitis, malignancy) - Inflammatory processes - Malnutrition/malabsorption - Hypothyroidism • Increased degradation: - Cushing's syndrome - Malignancies - Hyperthyroidism • Increased loss: - Renal, e.g. nephrotic syndrome - Gastrointestinal, e.g. IBD - Ascites (exudate) - Burns • Haemodilution

Table 23 // Proteins
IBD, inflammatory bowel disease

Inflammatory markers

LAB VALUE	EXPLANATION	INTERPRETATION
Erythrocyte sedimentation rate (ESR)	• Erythrocyte sedimentation rate (mm/h) • Elevated with increased concentration of acute-phase proteins and/or immunoglobulin-mediated surface charge alteration, causing erythrocytes to repel each other less and sink faster	↑ • Increased blood protein levels: - Infections - Autoimmune diseases - Rheumatic conditions - Malignancies - Monoclonal and polyclonal gammopathies - Infarction - Hypothyroidism • Anaemia • Pregnancy, obesity, older age, smoking ↓ • Abnormalities of erythrocytes, e.g. polycythaemia, sickle cell disease • Congestive heart failure • Hypogammaglobulinaemia
C-reactive protein (CRP)	• Positive acute-phase protein • Produced in the liver	↑ • Infections • Inflammation • Rheumatic conditions • Malignancies • Trauma • Thrombosis
White blood cell (WBC) count	• Leukocytes: white blood cells • Part of the immune system	↑ Leukocytosis: • Infections • Inflammatory processes • Autoimmune diseases • Myeloproliferative disease, e.g. leukaemia • Medication-induced, e.g. steroids • Smoking ↓ Leukopenia: • Infections (due to utilisation) • Medication-induced/iatrogenic, e.g. chemotherapy, immunosupressants, antibiotics • Bone marrow deficiency • Splenomegaly (e.g. in portal hypertension) • Benign leukopenia, seen in individuals of African, Middle Eastern, and West Indian descent • Other causes: B12 and folate deficiency

Table 24A // Inflammatory markers

LAB VALUE	EXPLANATION	INTERPRETATION
Leukocyte differential	Breakdown of total leukocytes by subtype	↑ Neutrophilia: • Bacterial infection, sepsis, myeloproliferative diseases ↓ Neutropenia: • Decreased production: severe infections, medication-induced/iatrogenic • Increased utilisation/destruction: medication-induced antibody formation ↑ Lymphocytosis: • Infection, smoking, hyposplenism, lymphoproliferative disease ↓ Lymphopenia: • Infection, HIV, renal failure ↑ Monocytosis: • Bacterial/parasitic infection, myeloproliferative diseases, Hodgkin's disease, neutropenia, steroids ↓ Monopenia: • In neutropenia, hairy cell leukaemia, cytotoxic agents (e.g. chemotherapy) ↑ Eosinophilia: • Parasitic infection, allergic reactions, skin diseases, myeloproliferative diseases, hypereosinophilic syndrome ↑ Basophilia: • Allergic reactions, iron deficiency, chronic myeloid leukaemia, systemic mastocytosis, allergic reaction

Table 24B // Inflammatory markers

In various inflammations, e.g. in acute pancreatitis an elevated WBC precedes an increase in CRP (approx. 24 hours).

Renal function tests

LAB VALUE	EXPLANATION	INTERPRETATION
Creatinine	Degradation product of creatinine phosphate from muscle tissue, mainly excreted by glomerular filtration	↑ • Acute kidney injury, chronic kidney disease • Medication-induced, e.g. trimethoprim, supplements • Dehydration • Muscle breakdown (e.g. rhabdomyolysis, myocardial infarction) • Excessive meat consumption ↓ • Significant fluid overload • Low protein intake, e.g. malnutrition • Reduced muscle mass, e.g. increasing age, females • Hyperthyroidism
Creatinine-clearance	Plasma (in ml) cleared of creatinine per minute by glomerular filtration and secretion. Both serum creatinine and urine creatinine (24h collection) levels are needed.	• Prerenal kidney disease (decreased renal perfusion): e.g. hypovolaemia, hypotension, decreased circulating volume (e.g. congestive heart failure, hepatorenal syndrome), renal artery stenosis, medication-induced • Renal kidney disease (reduced clearance due to impaired glomeruli and/or tubules): e.g. acute tubular necrosis (e.g. ischaemia, nephrotoxic drugs), acute interstitial nephritis, diabetes mellitus, medication-induced • Postrenal kidney disease (urinary tract obstruction): e.g. urolithiasis, prostate carcinoma, benign prostatic hyperplasia, urinary retention
Estimated glomerular filtration rate (eGFR, CKD-EPI)	• Estimation of GFR based on serum creatinine, sex, age, and weight as a marker for muscle mass • Relevant in chronic kidney disease (stages 1-5) • Only reliable in more or less stable kidney function	
Urea	• Waste product of hepatic protein metabolism • Reabsorbed in the kidneys	↑ • Prerenal, renal, or postrenal kidney disease (if urea/creatinine ratio ↑: prerenal) • Dehydration • Increased protein degradation, e.g. tissue damage, upper gastrointestinal bleeding • High-protein diet ↓ • Haemodilution • Pregnancy • Malabsorption/malnutrition • Severe liver damage

Table 25 // Renal function tests

CKD-EPI, Chronic Kidney Disease Epidemiology Collaboration

Clotting markers

LAB VALUE	EXPLANATION	INTERPRETATION
International normalised ratio (INR)	• Calculation based on PT • Measure of the extrinsic and common pathway of the coagulation cascade • Monitoring vitamin K anticoagulant therapy • Patient plasma PT / normalised plasma PT	↑ • If prolonged PT + normal aPTT: - Use of coumarines (vitamin K antagonists) or warfarin - Isolated factor VII deficiency - Coagulation disorders, e.g. coagulopathy or mild vitamin K deficiency - In acute or chronic liver failure. If chronic → progression of advanced liver cirrhosis. - Acute DIC • If prolonged PT + prolonged aPTT: - Factor I, II, V, X, or fibrinogen deficiency, combined factor deficiencies - Liver failure - Acute DIC - Severe vitamin K deficiency - Anticoagulants (e.g. warfarin, direct thrombin inhibitors, others) ↓ Activation of clotting in early disseminated intravascular coagulation
Prothrombin test/ time (PT)	Test for the extrinsic and common pathway of the coagulation cascade	
Activated partial thromboplastin test/time (aPTT)	• Test for the intrinsic and common pathway of the coagulation cascade • Monitoring unfractionated heparin therapy	↑ If prolonged aPTT + normal PT: • Factor VIII (hemophilia A), factor IX (hemophilia B), factor XI (hemophilia C) deficiency • Factor XII deficiency • Von Willebrand's disease • Anticoagulants (unfractionated heparin therapy) • Lupus anticoagulant ↓ • Strong elevation one or more clotting factors (e.g. factor VIII due to stress) • Activation of coagulation in early DIC • Pregnancy (factor VIII ↑ and fibrinogen ↑)

Table 26A // Clotting markers
t-PA, tissue plasminogen activator

Laboratories use different techniques to measure PT, which makes PT values very difficult to compare. The INR is therefore used to correct for differences between labs.

LAB VALUE	EXPLANATION	INTERPRETATION
D-dimer	Degradation product of fibrinolysis	↑ • Venous thrombosis (high sensitivity but low specificity) • Pulmonary embolism (high sensitivity but low specificity) • Disseminated intravascular coagulation • Other causes (low specificity): - Pregnancy - Infection - Renal insufficiency - Trauma - Malignancies - Aortic dissection
Fibrinogen	• Coagulation factor produced in the liver • Converted into fibrin by thrombin • Positive acute-phase protein	↑ • Inflammatory processes • Trauma • Pregnancy ↓ • Decreased synthesis, e.g. liver disease • Increased degradation: - DIC - Fibrinolysis • Increased loss, e.g. after bleeding • Medication-induced, e.g. t-PA, streptokinase

Table 26B // Clotting markers

Coumarin derivative therapy can be monitored by tracking INR, heparin therapy by tracking aPTT, and LMWH therapy by tracking anti-Xa activity. Monitoring of therapy with DOACs is employed in specific cases, e.g. when using DOACs in patients with a gastric bypass. Therapy with platelet aggregation inhibitors is not monitored in practice.

Miscellaneous

LAB VALUE	EXPLANATION	INTERPRETATION
Ammonia	Degradation product of proteolysis	↑ Hyperammonaemia: • Congenital urea cycle enzyme defects • Acquired: - Liver cirrhosis (90%) - Infections - Multiple myeloma - Acute leukaemia - Medication-induced
Glucose	• Blood sugar • Main energy source for all cellular processes	↑ Hyperglycaemia: • Impaired glucose tolerance, DM, diabetes gravidarum • Acute stress: trauma, sepsis, myocardial infarction, cerebrovascular accident • Medication: corticosteroids • Endocrinopathy: Cushing's syndrome, acromegaly ↓ Hypoglycaemia: • Medication-induced, e.g. sulphonylurea derivatives, insulin • Insulinoma • Fasting/malnutrition, alcohol • Liver failure • Endocrinopathy: hypocortisolism, panhypopituitarism
Glycated haemoglobin (HbA1c)	• Glycosylated haemoglobin, measure of average blood glucose concentration over the past 6-8 wk • Monitoring adherence and treatment effectiveness	↑ • DM or poorly controlled DM • Erythrocyte lifespan ↓ (falsely lower result), e.g. haemoglobinopathy • Target range in diabetics ≤53 (7%) to ≤64 mmol/mol (8%) depending on age, treatment, and duration of DM
Creatine kinase (CK)	• Enzyme needed for e.g. muscle contraction • Predominantly found in skeletal muscle, brain, and heart • Has various isoenzymes	↑ Increased cellular death in: • Muscle conditions: myositis, rhabdomyolysis, overtraining, IM injection, hereditary muscle diseases, malignant hypertension • Myocardial infarction (often used to estimate infarction size) • Epilepsy • Hypothyroidism • Trauma/postoperative

Table 27 // Miscellaneous
IM, intramuscular

Nutritional panel

LAB VALUE	EXPLANATION	INTERPRETATION
Vitamin B1 (thiamine)	• Water-soluble vitamin • Involved in carbohydrate, fat and protein metabolism; cellular respiration and oxidation of fatty acids; mitochondrial energy production, protein synthesis, neurotransmitter synthesis	↓ • Poor intake: inadequate diet, chronic alcohol use disorder, bariatric surgery • Poor absorption: malabsorption syndrome, bariatric surgery, short bowel syndrome, vomiting, malnourishment • Increased utilisation: refeeding syndrome, pregnancy, breastfeeding, hyperthyroidism • Increased loss: dialysis, infection, diarrhoea, vomiting, systemic disease, medication-induced (e.g. diuretics)
Vitamin B9/B11 (folic acid or folate)	• Water-soluble vitamin • Necessary for protein and nucleic acid synthesis	↓ • Poor intake: inadequate diet, chronic alcohol use disorder • Poor absorption: diseases involving the jejunum (e.g. celiac disease, short bowel syndrome, amyloidosis), bariatric surgery, elevated pH • Increased loss: dialysis • Medication-induced (e.g. methotrexate, phenytoin, trimethoprim) • Pregnancy • Can cause megaloblastic anaemia
Vitamin B12 (cobalamin)	• Water-soluble vitamin • Cofactor in DNA, fatty and amino acid metabolisation, maturation of red blood cells and myelin synthesis	↑ Hypercobalaminaemia: • Excessive supplementation • Liver disease • Kidney disease • Diabetes mellitus • Haematological malignancy • Solid tumour ↓ • Pernicious (megaloblastic) anaemia • Poor intake: diet lacking of animal products • Poor absorption: bariatric surgery, terminal ileum disease (e.g. Crohn's disease, celiac disease, parasites, intestinal bacterial overgrowth) • Recreational use of nitrous oxide

Table 28 // Nutritional panel

DNA, deoxyribonucleic acid; pH, potential of hydrogen

When a vitamin B12 deficiency is suspected but vitamin B12 serum levels are in the low/low-normal ranges, determine its metabolites, homocysteine, and methylmalonic acid (MMA) to diagnose a functional deficiency:

- MMA: MMA needs vitamin B12 as a cofactor to be converted. If the amount of available vitamin B12 is too low, this conversion cannot take place and MMA serum levels will be higher. A combination of a low/low-normal vitamin B12 and increased MMA level indicate a functional vitamin B12 deficiency.
- Homocysteine: homocysteine breaks down into methionine and cysteine when interacting with vitamin B12. When B12 levels are in the low/low-normal range, a high level of homocysteine can be found. This indicates a functional B12 deficiency.

Lipid profile

LAB VALUE	EXPLANATION	INTERPRETATION
Total cholesterol	• Total amount of cholesterol in the blood • Cholesterol is required for the biosynthesis of bile acids, steroid hormones, and vitamin D • Important modifiable cardiovascular risk factor	↑ • Dyslipidaemia • Hypothyroidism • Renal disease: e.g. nephrotic syndrome, chronic kidney disease • Cholestatic liver disease • Use of anabolic steroids ↓ • Medication (e.g. lipid-lowering agents) • Hyperthyroidism • Advanced liver cirrhosis • Malnutrition/malabsorption
Low-density lipoprotein (LDL)	• 60-70% of serum cholesterol • Transports cholesterol from the liver to tissues • Important modifiable risk factor for the development of atherosclerotic plaque	
High-density lipoprotein (HDL)	• Transports cholesterol from tissues to the liver • Inversely correlated with cardiovascular risk	↑ • Regular exercise and BMI ↓ • Smoking cessation • Medication: statins ↓ • Dyslipidaemia
Lipoprotein A (Lp(a))	• Type of LDL • Promotes atherosclerosis and thrombosis by affecting fibrinolysis, inflammation, endothelial function, and oxidative stress • Independent risk factor for athero-sclerotic cardiovascular disease • Lp(a) levels are mainly genetically determined	↑ • Genetic • Sub-Saharan African and South Asian descent

Table 29 // Lipid profile

Neurological diagnostics

Electroencephalogram (EEG)

An EEG records the electrical activity of the brain through small scalp electrodes attached to the head in a fixed pattern (e.g. international 10-20 system, see Figure 45). The electrodes measure potential differences which are displayed for each EEG channel. The electrical activity can be described in terms of location, amplitude, frequency, morphology, symmetry and continuity. Based on the frequency different common waveforms can be distinguished: alpha, beta, delta, and theta activity. Abnormalities in the activity include decelerations or epileptiform changes (see Figure 46). Furthermore, the state of the patient determines which waves are normal and abnormal (see Table 30). Brain activity can be influenced (e.g. amplitude, pattern) by opening and closing of the eyes. Hyperventilation or flashing lights may provoke abnormal activity.

An EEG can be used to e.g. determining the focus, type or risk of relapse of epilepsy, encephalitis, sleeping disorders, low consciousness without focus, intraoperative monitoring, prognosis after cardiac arrest, determining brain death, and dementia.

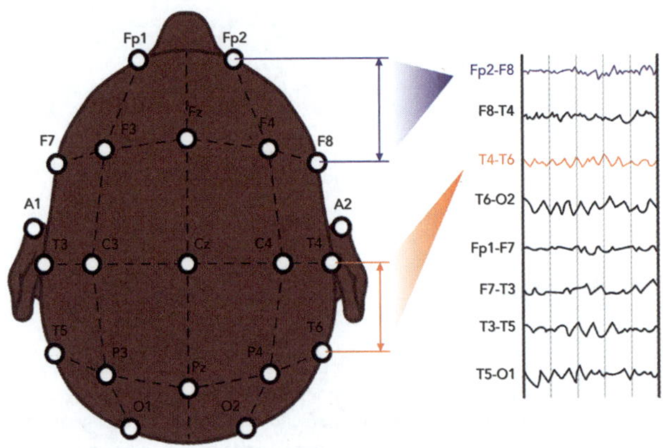

Figure 45 // The 10-20 system (l) with the potentials perceived by the EEG (r)

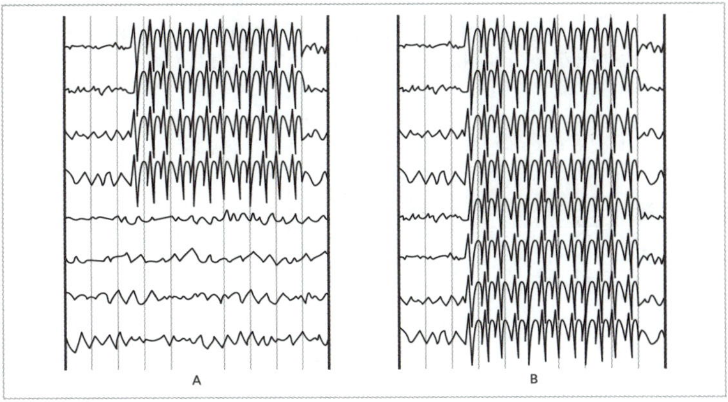

Figure 46 // EEG

A: Partial seizure: the lower four leads show a normal EEG, without epileptiform activity. Epileptiform activity appears as an increase in vertical deflections. **B:** Generalised seizure

TYPE	FREQUENCY	PHYSIOLOGICALLY	PATHOLOGICALLY
Alpha	8-12 Hz	In an awake state, localised in the occipital regions	In comatose state, diffuse alpha activity (alpha coma), e.g. • Encephalitis • Hypoxic-ischaemic encephalopathy • Traumatic brain injury • Metabolic disorders • Drug overdose
Beta	13-30 Hz	In an awake state, localised in the frontal and central head regions	• Asymmetrical amplitudes • Hemisphere with lower waves: infarction or subdural collections • Local decreased or increased activity: brain abscess, vascular malformation, tumours or cortical dysplasia
Delta	0.5-4 Hz	During deep sleep, localised in the fronto-central regions	In an awake state, e.g. • Encephalopathy • Sedative medication • Cerebral infections • Focal cerebral dysfunction (e.g. traumatic brain injury, tumour, ischaemic stroke, intracerebral haemorrhage)
Theta	4-7 Hz	During drowsiness and early sleep stages, localised in the fronto-central regions	In an awake state, e.g. in one location or predominantly in one hemisphere: increased chance of underlying disease such as meningioma, low-grade glioma and ischaemic stroke

Table 30 // EEG waveforms

Hyperventilation, sleep deprivation and photostimulation can sometimes provoke epileptiform abnormalities on EEG.

EEG can be used to determine the focus, type, and recurrence risk of epilepsy, but the clinical picture forms the basis for diagnosis, as EEG abnormalities may not be clinically relevant.

Evoked potentials

Evoked potentials reflect the electrophysiological response of the cerebral cortex to external stimuli. Repeated external stimuli are administered and the cortical responses are measured via electrodes on the scalp (EEG). Single stimuli are followed by small cortical responses that cannot be measured because the response of the stimulated part of the cortex is indistinguishable from the internal EEG noise. By frequently repeating the external stimulus over a short period of time, it becomes easier to distinguish the response to the external stimulus from normal cortical activity. Conversely, the cortex can also be stimulated to measure the response of the peripheral nervous system (see Table 31).

TYPE OF POTENTIAL	TEST	INDICATIONS
Brainstem evoked auditory potentials (BEAP)	Record response of auditory temporal cortex to auditory stimuli (see Figure 47)	Suspected deafness (especially in newborns)
Motor evoked potentials (MEP)	Record response of contralateral adductor digiti minimi (ulnar nerve) and anterior tibial (peroneal nerve) muscles to magnetic stimulation of the motor cortex	Suspected lesion in myelum that cannot be diagnosed in any other way
Somatosensory evoked potentials (SSEP)	Record response of the sensory parietal cortex of the contralateral hemisphere to distal sensory stimulation of median nerve, peroneal nerve or posterior tibial nerve	Prognosis in postanoxic encephalopathy
Visual evoked potentials (VEP)	Record response of occipital cortex to visual stimulation	Optic nerve conduction (e.g. in MS)

Table 31 // Indications of evoked potentials

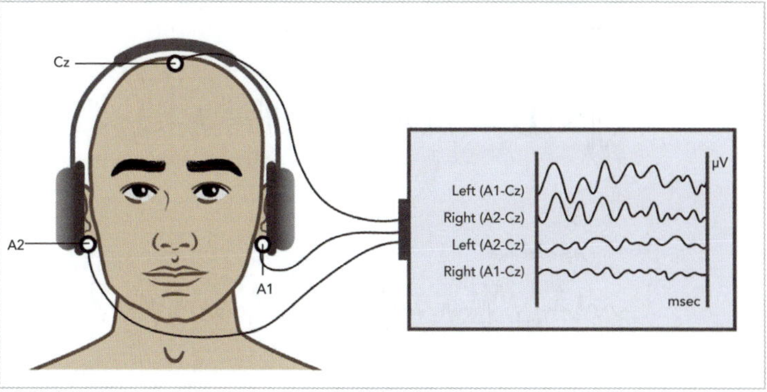

Figure 47 // Brainstem evoked auditory potentials (BEAP)

Electromyogram (EMG)

EMG is a diagnostic procedure used to study the muscle tissue and the corresponding motor neurons. Electrical signals from motor neurons cause muscle contraction which is measured with needle electrodes directly inserted into a muscle. The measurements are visualised on an oscilloscope, where a specific wave pattern is drawn. Any nerve lesion from the spinal motor neuron to the peripheral nerve branches can result in a rising fibrillation on the oscilloscope. Additionally, a nerve conduction study can be performed, where electrode stickers are applied to the skin to determine the speed and strength of signals traveling between two measuring points.

EMGs could be used in cases of pain, sensory symptoms and/or muscle weakness to determine muscle or peripheral nerve dysfunction. The results can be used to diagnose multiple conditions including muscular dystrophy, polymyositis, myasthenia gravis, ALS, or peripheral nerve dysfunction (e.g. carpal tunnel syndrome, peripheral neuropathies).

In myogenic disease, a concentric needle can be used to measure the electrophysiological activity of muscle fibres. In myopathic disease, muscle action potentials are often short-lasting and have a lower amplitude than normal (see Figure 48, part B).

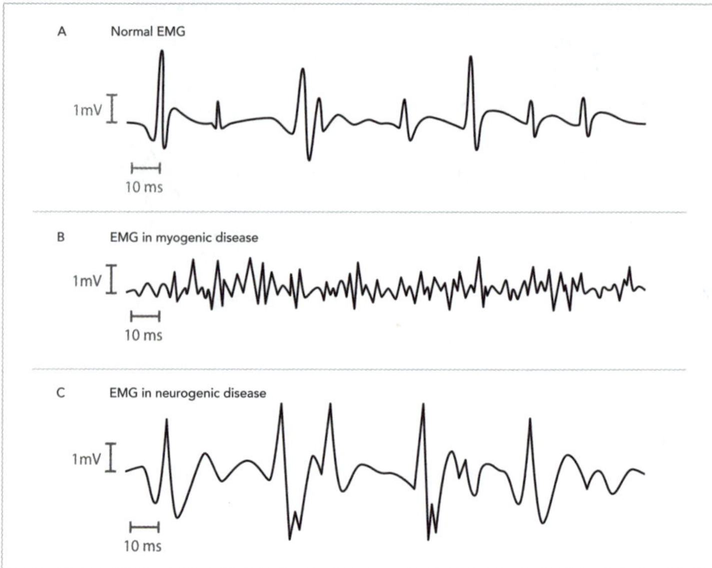

Figure 48 // EMG

A: Normal situation with mild muscle tone. **B:** The nerve of the motor unit being examined is intact, but several muscle fibres are inactive due to myopathic disease. This is reflected by the small-amplitude potentials. **C:** The nerves of several motor units are affected, because there are only a small number of motor unit potentials. The potentials do have a large amplitude because the intact nerves have taken over the muscle fibres of the affected nerves, resulting in larger motor units.

In neurogenic disease, the nerve conduction velocity can be determined by stimulating the nerve and measuring the response time of the associated muscle using surface electrodes. Severely reduced conduction velocity is suggestive of a demyelinating disease (see Figure 48, part C). Decreased action potential amplitude is suggestive of axonal disease. Spontaneous activity is found in the muscles at rest (fibrillations, positive sharp waves).

Needle EMGs are also performed for neurogenic diseases (e.g. polyneuropathy). Spontaneous muscle fibre activity at rest is consistent with neurogenic disease.

A single-fibre EMG measures the action potentials of an individual muscle fibre. It is used to help detect disorders of neuromuscular transition (e.g. myasthenia gravis).

Nerve ultrasound

Nerve ultrasound is an exam that uses sound waves to visualise a nerve. It can be used to measure the cross-sectional area of a nerve. Increased cross-sectional nerve area may indicate compression, causing the nerve to swell, as in carpal tunnel syndrome. Other indications include ulnar neuropathy, fibular neuropathy, and demyelinating polyneuropathies. Nerve ultrasound is more patient-friendly and easier to perform than an EMG (dynamic, quick), but EMG is better for identifying the severity of the condition.

Lumbar puncture (LP)

General

In an LP, a needle is used to puncture the CSF space (L3-L4 or L4-L5) between the spinous processes to obtain CSF (see Figure 49). This is done below the point where the spinal cord ends (L1/L2). See Figure 50 for the correct positioning. Prior to CSF collection, CSF pressure can be measured with the patient lying down by attaching a pressure gauge to the needle and holding it vertically. In the lateral position, the CSF pressure at the puncture site is equal to the intracranial pressure, provided CSF communication between both spaces is unimpeded.

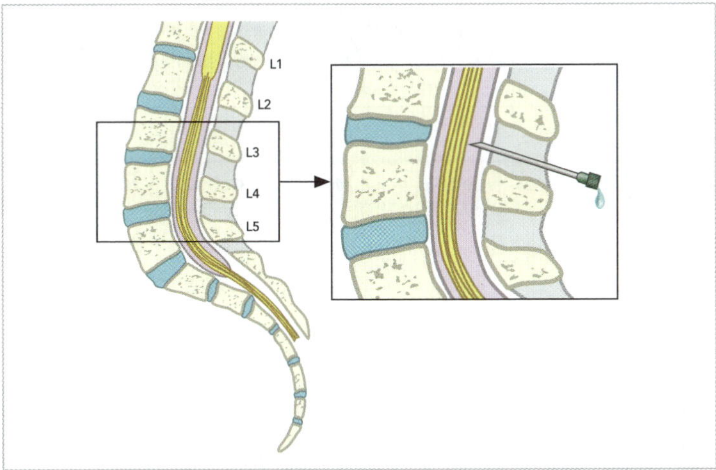

Figure 49 // LP between the spinous processes (L3-L4 or L4-L5)

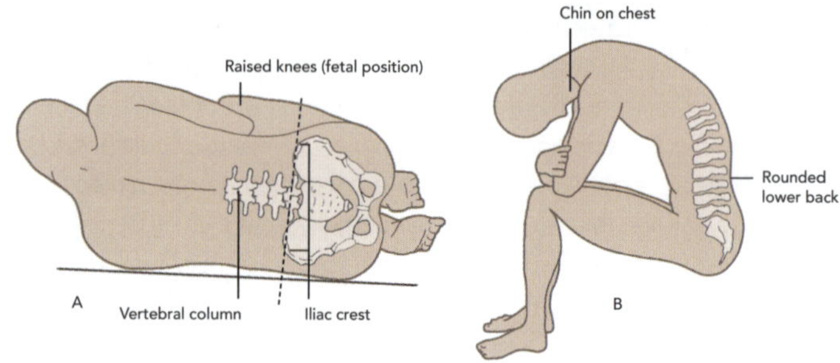

Figure 50 // LP positioning
A: Left lateral lying position **B:** Sitting position

Indications

CSF analysis is indicated in case of suspected bacterial meningitis, viral meningitis/encephalitis (CSF pleocytosis, culture, PCR), cerebral venous thrombosis (CVT) or idiopathic intracranial hypertension (increased CSF opening pressure), SAH (CSF spectrophotometry for bilirubin), leptomeningeal metastasis (cytology for neoplastic cells), MS (IgG index, oligoclonal bands), central nervous system (CNS) localisation lymphoma (cytology, immunophenotyping, MYD88), dementia (tau, amyloid beta (Aβ42)) and Creutzfeldt-Jakob disease (14-3-3, RT-QuIC). See Table 32 for a few of these indications and corresponding findings.

CONDITION	CSF PRESSURE ($cm\ H_2O$)	LEUKOCYTES ($/mm^3$)	GLUCOSE (mmol/L)	TOTAL PROTEIN (g/L)
Normal	5-20	≤5	50-65% of blood glucose	0.2-0.6 (age-dependent)
Bacterial meningitis	↑	↑↑	↓	↑
Viral meningitis	=/↑	↑	=	=/↑
Viral encephalitis	=	↑	=	↑
Guillain-Barré syndrome	=	=/↑	=	↑

Table 32 // CSF abnormalities

Contraindications

Contraindications for an LP are an increased intracranial pressure due to space-occupying lesions (SOL) with increased risk of herniation, locally infected skin, use of anticoagulants, coagulopathy, and thrombocytopenia. If there are signs of increased intracranial pressure, a brain computed tomography (CT) prior to the LP is indicated to avoid potential cerebellar tonsillar herniation through the foramen magnum due to a reduction of intraspinal pressure.

Complications

Post-puncture headache due to intracranial hypotension is a common complication of LP. This type of headache occurs mainly in a vertical position. CSF produced in the choroid plexus replenishes the CSF and the headache slowly disappears. On the rare occasions this fails to happen, a 'blood patch' can be performed, taking venous blood from the patient and re-injecting it epidurally. The clot will close the hole in the dura almost immediately. Rare complications of LP include subdural haematoma and CVT.

Cells

An increase in leukocyte count can indicate an infection. Bacterial meningitis is characterised by polynuclear cell predominance, viral meningitis by mononuclear cell predominance. See Table 32 for other differences between bacterial and viral meningitis. Following a traumatic puncture, erythrocytes enter the CSF. In the centrifuged specimen the supernatant will be colourless and clear. If the erythrocytes were already present before the puncture, e.g. in SAH, the supernatant will be yellow. Cytological exams can also be performed to confirm or rule out suspected leptomeningeal metastases or lymphoma.

Protein

Elevated protein levels are an unspecific finding, as they occur in many CNS disorders, e.g. bacterial infections, viral infections, and GBS.

Glucose

In the physiological state, the CSF glucose level is $^2/_3$ of the blood glucose level. CSF glucose measurements should therefore always be accompanied by venepuncture. Glucose consumption by bacteria in a bacterial infection may be one reason for a lower CSF glucose level.

Microorganisms

A gram stain and bacterial culture test can be done to diagnose a bacterial infection. A polymerase chain reaction (PCR) can be done to diagnose a bacterial or viral infection.

Immunoglobulins

Immunoglobulins can leak through the blood-brain barrier or be produced in the CNS. Patients with MS may, for example, have a higher CSF immunoglobulin G (IgG) level than serum IgG level. In addition, in case of autoimmune encephalitis, specific autoantibodies and/or a paraneoplastic panel can be tested in the CSF.

IgG index

Intrathecal IgG production (autoimmune) can be determined with the IgG index (see Formula 1). Indications include infectious diseases (e.g. neuroborreliosis) and autoimmune disorders (e.g. MS).

$$\text{IgG index} = \frac{\text{CSF IgG}}{\text{serum IgG}} : \frac{\text{CSF albumin}}{\text{serum albumin}}$$

Formula 1 // IgG index

Xanthochromia describes CSF yellowing due to the presence of blood breakdown products (bilirubin). The puncture itself can also cause blood admixture (traumatic puncture), manifesting as fresh blood in the CSF.

Imaging

Carotid duplex ultrasound

In Doppler ultrasounds, blood flow is shown in colour. With a colour Doppler, blood flowing towards the probe is shown in red (positive Doppler shift), blood flowing away from the probe is shown in blue (negative Doppler shift), and turbulent flow is shown in green. Depending on the velocity and direction of the blood, a frequency difference is measured between the transmitted frequency and the received frequency of the sound wave (Doppler shift). The Doppler shift (vertical axis) is plotted against time (horizontal axis) (see Figure 51). Doppler ultrasounds are used to calculate and visualise flow direction, flow velocity, flow resistance (also called resistive index), peak systolic pressure, end-systolic pressure and more.

Duplex ultrasounds are also known as duplex Doppler ultrasonography and combine Doppler with sonography. An indication for duplex ultrasound is arterial stenosis. Arterial stenoses are measured by dividing peak systolic velocity in the stenosis by peak systolic velocity pre- or post-stenosis. The more severe the narrowing, the higher the peak systolic velocity in the stenosis (Bernoulli's principle).

In neurology, a duplex ultrasound is indicated in patients with a recent ischaemic stroke or TIA to diagnose large vessel disease (i.e. significant carotid stenosis) as the underlying aetiology.

For more information on neuroimaging, see the pocket *Radiology*.

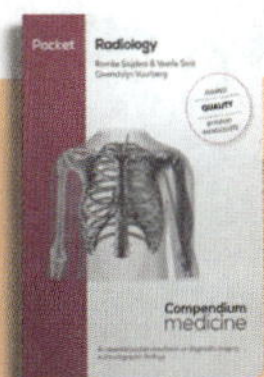

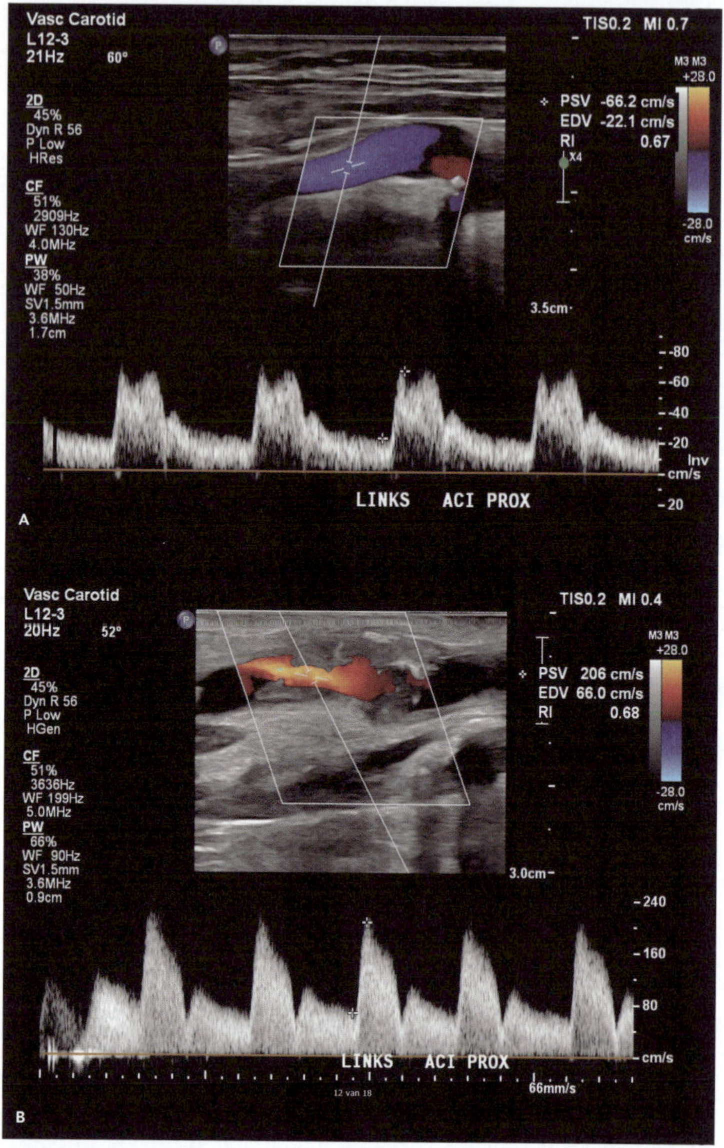

Figure 51 // Carotid duplex ultrasound. Proximal part of the left internal carotid artery.
A: Without atherosclerosis; **B:** With atherosclerosis leading to a stenosis of 50-69%.

Computed tomography (CT)

CT uses X-rays, just like a conventional X-ray. CT is a type of imaging in which an X-ray tube rotates around the patient to capture three-dimensional cross-sections of the body. The detectors measure how much radiation passes through the patient. This lets the computer calculate the degree of attenuation and convert it into greyscale values (see Table 33). Depending on the level of attenuation, structures appear white (hyperdense) or grey/black (hypodense). CT images are made in the axial plane, looking up at the patient from below (the left side of the image is the right side of the patient). These images can be used to make reconstructions in other planes (e.g. sagittal and coronal). CT images can be made with IV contrast and without contrast (non-contrast CT). Administering contrast can reveal an abscess, malignancy, or blood vessels.

Indications for a non-contrast brain CT include trauma, subarachnoid and intracranial haemorrhage, ischaemia and hypoxia. Brain CT is the modality of choice for identifying traumatic brain injury (TBI). A brain CT after TBI is indicated if at least one of the criteria is met (see Table 35). Be aware that local guidelines may incorporate additional criteria from internationally validated tools (e.g. Canadian CT Head Rule, New Orleans criteria or CT in Head Injury Patients (CHIP) prediction rule). For a roadmap to read a brain CT, see Appendix 5.

STRUCTURE	APPEARANCE	COLOUR
Osseous	Hyperdense	
Grey matter	Mildly hyperdense	
White matter	Mildly hyperdense	
Cerebrospinal fluid	Isodense	
Fat	Hypodense	
Air	Hypodense	

Table 33 // Appearance of structures on CT

SITUATION	APPEARANCE	TIME
Hyperacute	Isodense	<1h
Acute	Hyperdense	Hours to several days
Subacute	Isodense	10-14d
Chronic	Hypodense	>3 wk

Table 34 // Appearance of haemorrhage on CT

A CT can be performed quickly for identifying a suspected ischaemic or haemorrhagic condition. A brain haemorrhage can be seen on CT immediately, while an ischaemic event may reveal itself hours after onset (see Table 34). In acute situations, a CT may be performed to rule out haemorrhage in case of clinical suspicion of an ischaemic event. If haemorrhage has been ruled out, a CT angiography can be performed to detect a possible occlusion. Haemorrhage must be ruled out before starting IV thrombolysis (IVT). See Figures 52 to 55 for possible findings on a brain CT.

TIMING FOR CT SCAN	CRITERIA BRAIN CT
<1h	• GCS ≤12 on initial assessment • GCS <15 2h after injury • Focal neurological deficits • >1 episode of vomiting • Post-traumatic seizure • Suspected open or depressed skull fracture • Sign of basal skull fracture (e.g. battle sign, CSF leakage from ear/nose, bilateral periorbital haematoma, haemotympanum)
<8h*	Loss of consciousness or amnesia and one of the following: • Age ≥65 years • Coagulopathy/anticoagulant**/antiplatelet therapy (excluding acetylsalicylic acid monotherapy) • Dangerous mechanism of injury • >30 min retrograde amnesia

Table 35 // Indications brain CT after TBI in patients ≥16 years
Please note: brain CT is recommended if any one of the criteria is met
* Or <1h in case of delayed presentation (>8h after injury)
** Anticoagulant treatment includes VKAs, DOACs or (low-molecular-weight) heparins

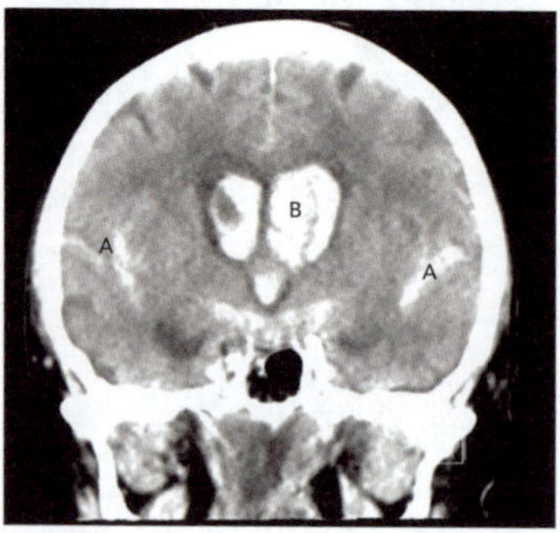

Figure 52 // Coronal section of a CT showing SAH. Subarachnoid blood spread across both hemispheres, at the site of the Sylvian fissure (A), prepontine and in the basal cisterns. Substantial amount of intraventricular blood in both lateral ventricles (B), third ventricle and fourth ventricle.

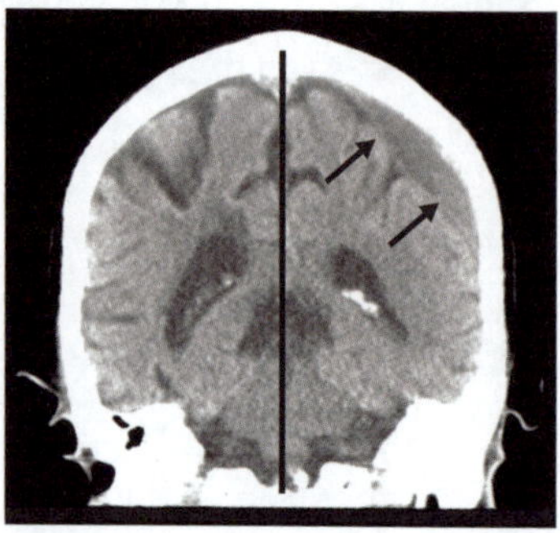

Figure 53 // Coronal section of a CT showing a subdural hypodense area (black arrows) over the left convexity. It is not as hypodense as CSF and is therefore suggestive of the presence of blood. There is no midline shift (black line).

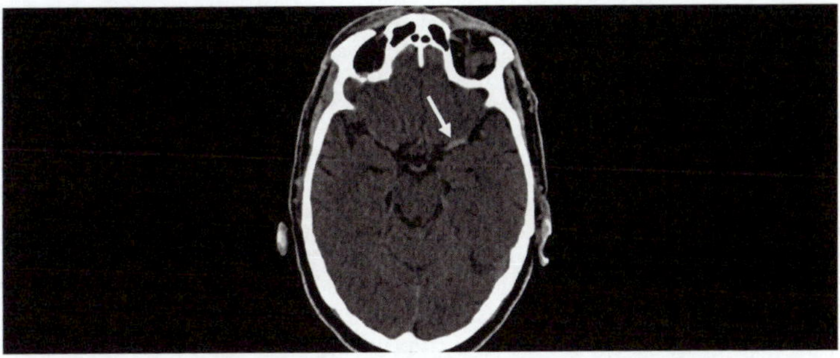

Figure 54 // Non-contrast CT (axial plane) showing a dense artery sign in the left middle cerebral artery (MCA, white arrow). Visible hyperdensity is caused by a thromboembolism in the vascular lumen. This is an initial sign of infarction that can be seen within 90 min of the infarction onset.

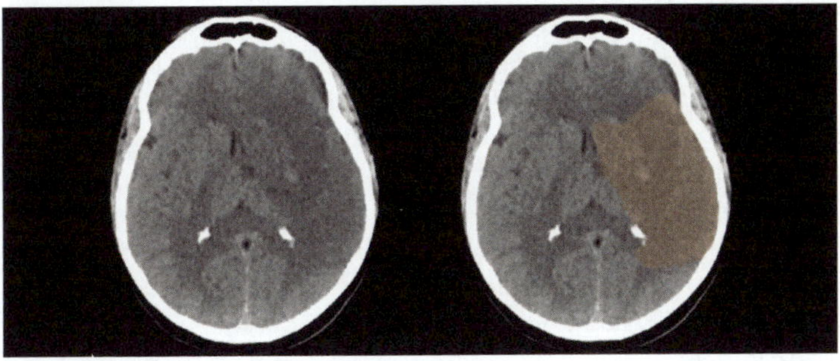

Figure 55 // Non-contrast CT (axial plane) showing a hypodense area on the left, indicative of ischaemic stroke (supplied by the MCA). The CT was acquired four hours after onset of symptoms.

CT angiography (CTA)

A CTA is a CT of the intracranial and extracranial blood vessels (carotids, vertebrobasilar system), in which contrast is injected into the blood vessels. The contrast blocks the X-rays, outlining the blood vessels on the scan. Depending on when the scan is performed, the choice can be made between CTA or CT venography (CTV).

Indications for a CTA include suspected acute cerebral infarction, SAH, carotid dissection, vascular malformations. A CTV is indicated in case a CVT is suspected. MR angiography (MRA, see Figure 56) is as sensitive as CTA, but is more difficult to perform in a restless patient. Additionally, not every hospital or clinic has access to MRI in acute settings.

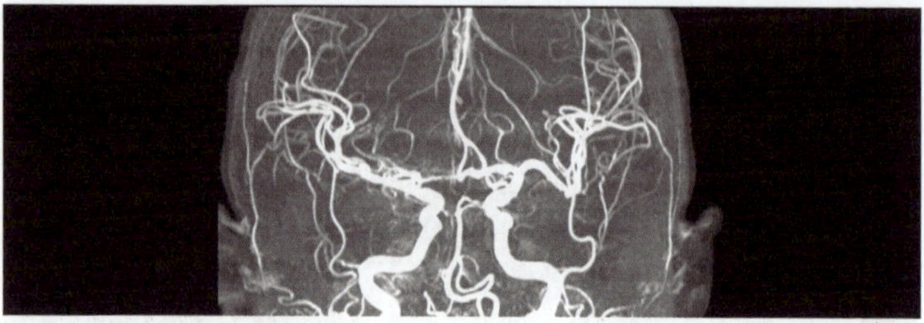

Figure 56 // MRI angiography. Complete recanalisation after transient ischaemia of almost the entire right temporal pole, the putamen and the head of the caudate nucleus.

CT perfusion (CTP)

A CTP is a CT scan of the brain that uses iodine contrast to calculate the perfusion of brain tissue based on different flow parameters. After intravenous administration of iodine contrast cerebral blood flow (CBF), cerebral blood volume (CBV) and mean transit time (MTT) are calculated and displayed in different colours. Depending on the software, red areas represent high perfusion and blue areas represent low perfusion. Based on these series the infarct core (unsalvageable tissue) and penumbra (salvageable tissue) of an ischaemic stroke are calculated. Mostly, the core is displayed in red and the penumbra in green (see Figure 57). A CTP is used in most centres in addition to a non-contrast brain CT and CTA to increase the diagnostic accuracy for the indication of acute interventions in ischaemic strokes.

- If the penumbra is larger than the core (mismatch), IVT can be administered up to 12h after stroke onset and mechanical thrombectomy can be executed up to 24h after onset.
- Note that the exact time window for 'late' IVT and thrombectomy differs worldwide, therefore always consult the local guidelines in acute treatment of an ischaemic stroke.

Inaccurate perfusion maps may be due to cardiovascular disease (e.g. a poor cardiac output, atrial fibrillation (AF), severe arterial stenosis) or inadequate placement of regions of interest (e.g. arterial and venous density regions).

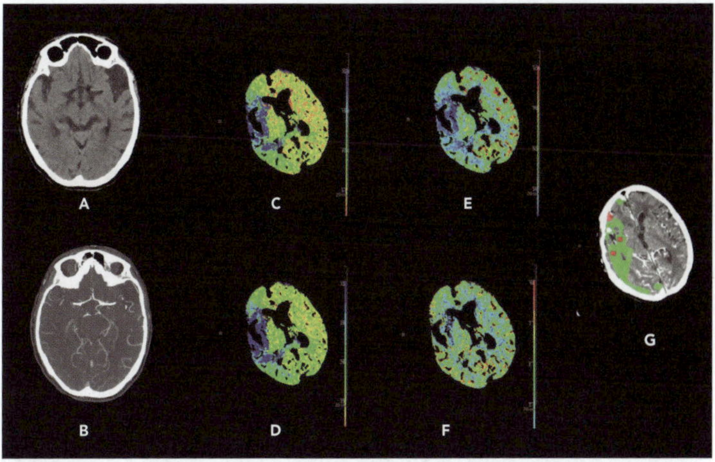

Figure 57 // CT perfusion with a defect in the right MCA supply area

A: Brain CT without contrast. **B:** CTA showing an occlusion of the right middle cerebral artery with **C:** increased MTT, **D:** increased time to peak (TTP), **E:** decreased CBF, and **F:** decreased CBV of the affected area. **G:** Calculated perfusion with large penumbra in right hemisphere (green) and no evident infarct core (red).

Magnetic resonance imaging (MRI)

An MRI is made using a magnetic field. Magnetic field gradients and radiofrequency pulses can be combined to create different images (sequences). Combining various different sequences makes it possible to compare different brain structures. The most commonly used sequences are:

- **T1**-weighted images: fluid → hypointense/fat; spinal cord → hyperintense
- **T2**-weighted images: fluid → hyperintense/fat; spinal cord → hypointense

See Figure 58 for a T1-weighted and T2-weighted MRI image. Indications for an MRI include ischaemia, CVT, vascular malformation, infection, tumours, dementia, congenital abnormalities, epilepsy, metabolic disorders, pituitary pathology, internal auditory pathology, disc herniation, MS, myelopathy, and radiculopathy. See Table 36 for the differences between CT and MRI.

Acute cerebral infarction can be demonstrated with a DWI-ADC sequence (DWI: diffusion-weighted imaging; ADC: apparent diffusion coefficient). These images show the calculated coefficient without T2 effects (ADC) based on the motion of water molecules (DWI: isotropic weighted T2 image). As a result, two images can be displayed from one scan based on water molecule diffusion, which depends on e.g. cell membrane integrity. In the acute phase, increased DWI signal and decreased ADC signal are observed in ischaemic tissue. As time passes, the signal changes. The inverse is true for old infarctions: increased ADC signal and decreased DWI signal.

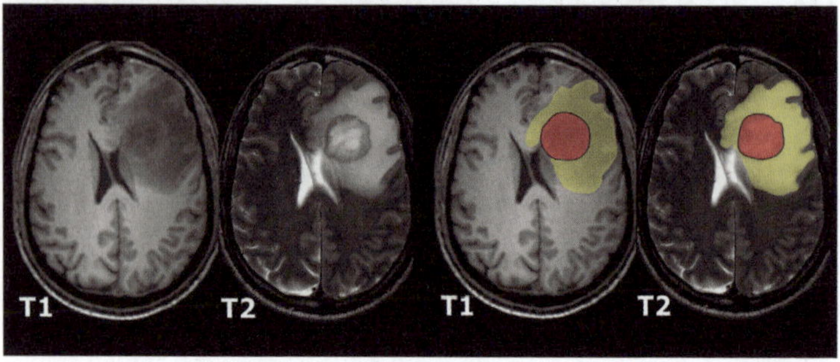

Figure 58 // A T1- and T2-weighted transverse MRI image showing a brain tumour in the left hemisphere with frontoparietal surrounding reactive oedema. Both the tumour (red area) and the oedema (yellow area) have high signal intensity on the T2-weighted image.

FEATURE	CT	MRI
Exam duration	Minutes	Minutes to an hour
Indications	E.g. osseous or pulmonary abnormalities	E.g. soft tissue abnormalities
Radiation	Radiation exposure	No radiation exposure
Osseous structures	1st choice for suspected fracture	E.g. bone oedema, angiosarcoma

Table 36 // CT vs. MRI

Contraindications for MRI:
- Metal in the body (metal splinters in the eye);
- Implanted devices/prostheses (e.g. implantable cardioverter defibrillator (ICD), pacemaker, implanted insulin pump or cochlear implant);
- Unstable patients (given the long scan duration);
- Claustrophobia;
- Patients who are unable to remain still (e.g. small children).

Note: Nowadays, many prostheses/implants are suitable for MRI. For more information, visit *MRIsafety.com*.

MRI is preferred in children because of the radiation exposure involved in CT.

The FLAIR sequence (fluid attenuation inversion recovery) is another type of MRI. This is a T2-weighted image on which CSF would normally be hyperintense. In a FLAIR sequence the CSF appears hypointense, bringing out abnormalities in the nearby brain parenchyma. The FLAIR sequence is particularly useful in conditions where there are many abnormalities adjacent to CSF spaces, such as MS, in which periventricular lesions are common.

Functional MRI scan (fMRI)

fMRI provides functional information about cortical activity based on differences in blood flow created by cortical activity (e.g. following stimuli). During an fMRI scan the patient has to lie still and perform tasks. The brain regions activated by these tasks receive more oxygenated blood, producing a different colour on the 3D MRI. Currently, fMRI is only indicated for scientific research or in preparation for neurosurgical procedures at some facilities.

Nuclear imaging

Functional imaging can be used to visualise the anatomical structure and brain function in a 3D image. This is done with single photon emission computed tomography (SPECT) or positrion emission tomography (PET). Both modalities use radioactively labelled substances (isotopes) to visually demonstrate the functioning of certain neurotransmitters based on the amount of radiation. This is combined with a CT to verify the anatomical location.

Possible indications for dopamine transporter SPECT (DAT-SPECT) include Parkinson's disease and atypical parkinsonism. Indications for an fluorodopa (F-DOPA) PET scan include Parkinson's disease and atypical parkinsonism. An fluorodeoxyglucose (FDG) PET scan can be used in Parkinson's disease, atypical parkinsonism, and Alzheimer's disease. Specifically in Alzheimer's disease also an amyloid PET scan can be helpfull. Depending on the condition other tracers may be usefull.

Treatment

General

Lifestyle management

Lifestyle interventions play a major role in cardiovascular risk management (CVRM) and improving overall health. Reducing the cardiovascular risk is essential in primary, secondary, and tertiary prevention. The most important modifiable cardiovascular risk factors are hypertension, smoking, DM, overweight, physical inactivity, and dyslipidaemia.

Smoking

Smoking cessation is essential to lowering cardiovascular risk and should be advised to all patients. Individual follow-up support, stop-smoking support programmes, nicotine replacement therapy, varenicline, and bupropion can be offered.

Physical activity

Physical activity reduces cardiovascular risk regardless of body weight. It is recommended to perform at least 150-300 min a week of moderate-intensity physical activity (e.g. walking at a brisk pace, slow cycling), or 75-150 min of vigorous-intensity physical activity (e.g. jogging, cycling, heavy gardening). Cardiac rehabilitation programmes are recommended in tertiary prevention settings.

Nutrition and lipid management

Cholesterol and lipid management are cornerstones of CVRM, demanding precise dietary decisions. A diet rich in fruits, vegetables, and whole grains should be adopted. Saturated fats, salt intake, and alcohol consumption (maximum 100g per week, i.e. six glasses of wine or seven beers) should be restricted. Additional pharmacological treatment of dyslipidaemia is often necessary.

BMI

Weight reduction improves dyslipidaemia, blood pressure, and glucose intolerance. A BMI of 18-25 kg/m^2 should be pursued by a maintainable wholesome diet in combination with physical activity.

Mental disorders are associated with an increased risk of cardiovascular disease. Patients with both cardiovascular risk factors and mental disorders require intensified attention and support in changing their lifestyle. These patients should be offered evidence-based mental healthcare and interdisciplinary guidance.

Pharmacological treatment

Analgesics

	MEDICATION	MECHANISM OF ACTION	ADVERSE EFFECTS
	Paracetamol	Analgesic and antipyretic properties via unknown mechanism	Mild adverse effect profile: risk of liver damage at high doses (>150 mg/kg) and in cases of alcohol use disorder and pre-existing liver damage
NSAIDS	**Diclofenac**	Classic non-selective inhibitors of the COX enzyme with analgesic, antipyretic and anti-inflammatory properties	• GI: risk of peptic ulcer • Renal: peripheral oedema, acute/chronic renal insufficiency especially in patients on RAS inhibitors, diuretics, pre-existing renal insufficiency, heart failure, dehydration, sepsis • Cardiovascular: potential ↑ risk especially with COX-2 inhibitors and diclofenac, including risk of heart failure
	Ibuprofen		
	Naproxen		
	Celecoxib	Selective COX-2 inhibitor with fewer renal and GI adverse effects	

Table 37 // Analgesics
ASA, acetylsalicylic acid; COX, cyclooxygenase; GI, gastrointestinal; PMHx, past medical history; OAC, oral anticoagulants; RAS, renin-angiotensin system; SSRI, selective serotonin reuptake inhibitor

Opioids

	MEDICATION	MECHANISM OF ACTION
OPIOIDS	**Codeine**	• Opiate receptor agonist: - μ receptor: analgesia (main effect) - κ and δ receptor: spinal and peripheral analgesia • Fentanyl is more potent than morphine and can be administered transdermally ($t_{1/2}$ 17h), via IV ($t_{1/2el}$ 6-8h) and nasally ($t_{1/2}$ 3-4h) • Codeine is a prodrug of morphine that has unpredictable variability in conversion to morphine (10x less potent) • Tramadol and buprenorphine are partial agonists. Tramadol also has an SNRI mechanism of action
	Tramadol	
	Morphine	
	Oxycodone	
	Fentanyl	

Table 38 // Opioids
SNRI, serotonin-norepinephrine reuptake inhibitors; TCA, tricyclic antidepressant

To prevent constipation, always prescribe **opioids** in combination with a **laxative**: e.g. docusate sodium/calcium, bisacodyl, macrogol, lactulose, magnesium sulfate/ citrate, methylnatrexone, naloxegol, or an enema.

Legend

- 💡 = Additional information
- ● = Indication for prescribing medication
- ⇔ = Interaction with drugs or high-risk groups
- ⊗ = Indication for stopping with medication
- ▲ = Intoxication management
- 🇺🇸 = United States of America (USA)

NOTES
⇔ Administer lower dose in cases of alcohol use disorder, chronic malnutrition, hepatic failure or dehydration ▲ Antidote: N-acetylcysteine (cysteine derivative)
● Prescribe PPI in patients aged >70, peptic ulcer in PMHx, or age >60 with DM, heart failure or use of corticosteroids, SSRIs, OAC or ASA ● In combination with low doses of ASA: PPI in patients aged >80, >60 with ulcer in PMHx, or >70 using corticosteroids, OAC, SSRIs or clopidogrel

ADVERSE EFFECTS	NOTES
• CNS: respiratory depression (especially high-risk in COPD), miosis, delirium, sedation, dependence • Pulmonary: bronchoconstriction • GI: motility ↓ (constipation, nausea and vomiting)	⇔ Risk of constipation ↑ due to immobility, poor water and fibre intake, and use of anticholinergics, antidepressants and diuretics ↑ ● So do not forget to prescribe a laxative when starting an opioid ⇔ Risk of respiratory depression and sedation ↑ with alcohol and CNS depressants (anaesthetics, anxiolytics, TCA, hypnotics and sedatives) ⇔ Tramadol combined with SSRIs produces ↑ risk of serotonin syndrome ▲ Naloxone (competitive antagonist) as an antidote for opioid-induced adverse effects 💡 Consider opioid rotation in case of adverse effects or poor effect

STEP 1	Start with paracetamol and add an NSAID if pain relief is insufficient. Diclofenac is 1st choice for colic pain. Consider selective COX-2 inhibitors with CIs for classic NSAIDs.
STEP 2	Add a weak-acting opioid (tramadol) or substitute the non-opioid. Codeine is still used primarily as an antitussive and not for additive pain relief.
STEP 3	Combine a strong oral or transdermal opioid (morphine, fentanyl, oxycodone) with a non-opioid. Fentanyl patches provide relief for nausea, vomiting and small bowel obstruction.
STEP 4	Opt for subcutaneous or IV route.

Table 39 // Treatment of nociceptive pain (World Health Organization (WHO) analgesic ladder)

Neuropathic pain treatment

	MEDICATION	MECHANISM OF ACTION	INDICATIONS
NEUROPATHIC PAIN TREATMENT	**Tricyclic antidepressants (TCA)** (amitriptyline, nortriptyline)	• Synaptic reuptake of noradrenalin and serotonin (5-HT) ↓ • Voltage-gated sodium channel blockade • Central and spinal cord level NMDA receptor blockade	• Neuropathic pain • Tension headache, migraine • Depression
	Gabapentinoids (pregabalin, gabapentin)	• Exact mechanism unknown • Number of available CNS presynaptic voltage-dependent calcium channels ↓ → release glutamate, norepinephrine, substance P ↓	• Neuropathic pain • Epilepsy • Anxiety disorders
	Carbamazepine	• Exact mechanism of action unknown • Anticonvulsant, psychotropic, and mildly anticholinergic action • Voltage-dependent sodium channel antagonist → repetitive neural discharges ↓, synaptic propagation of excitatory impulses ↓ and catecholamine conversion ↓ and glutamate release ↓	• Trigeminus neuralgia • Focal epilepsy, primary generalised tonic-clonic seizures • Acute mania, bipolar disorder
	Serotonin-norepinephrine reuptake inhibitors (SNRIs) (duloxetine, venlafaxine)	• Reuptake of 5-HT and noradrenalin ↓ • Dopamine reuptake ↓ (weak effect) • Potentiation of descending inhibitory CNS pain pathways	• Neuropathic pain, trigeminus neuralgia • Anxiety disorders

Table 40 // Neuropathic pain treatment
5-HT, serotonin; CI, contraindication; CYP, cytochrome P; MI, myocardial infarction; NMDA, N-methyl-D-aspartate; SJS, Stevens-Johnson syndrome

Anticoagulants

	MEDICATION	MECHANISM OF ACTION	INDICATIONS
PLATELET AGGREGATION INHIBITORS	**Acetylsalicylic acid (ASA)** (aspirin)	Platelet aggregation inhibition: • ASA irreversibly inhibits the COX enzyme (→ production of platelet aggregation-stimulating thromboxane A2 ↓) • P2Y12-inhibitors irreversibly inhibit activation via the ADP receptor on the platelet	Treatment of ACS, AP and PAD, secondary prevention after MI, CABG, TIA and ischaemic stroke
	P2Y12-inhibitors (clopidogrel, ticagrelor, prasugrel)		Secondary prevention after MI, ACS, TIA or ischaemic stroke. Combine with ASA in ACS without ST elevation or after PCI.

Table 41A // Anticoagulants
ACS, acute coronary syndrome; ADP, adenosine diphosphate; AP, angina pectoris; CABG, coronary artery bypass graft; DVT, deep vein thrombosis; PAD, peripheral arterial disease; PCI, percutaneous coronary intervention; Pgp, P-glycoprotein; VTE, venous tromboembolism

ADVERSE EFFECTS	NOTES
• Anticholinergic → dry mouth, dizziness, obstipation, voiding disorders, erectile dysfunction and confusion (elderly) • Antinoradrenergic → orthostatic hypotension • Antihistaminergic → sedation, weight gain	⇔ CI: after recent MI and long QT syndrome ⇔ Orthostasis, falling risk ↑ during dehydration (fever, vomiting, diarrhoea), diuretics, antihypertensive medication
Somnolence, sedation, dizziness, headache	Decrease dose in case of renal insufficiency
• Neutropenia and thrombocytopenia, GGT ↑, hyponatraemia, effect on oestrogen metabolism (oral contraceptives clearance ↑) • Dizziness, drowsiness, fatigue, nausea, vomiting, ataxia, diplopia, allergy, urticaria, risk of neural tube defect in fetus ↑ • Idiosyncratic: rash, agranulocytosis, SJS, aplastic anaemia, hepatotoxicity	⇔ Strong inducer of CYP3A4, CYP2C9 and CYP1A2, it is metabolised by CYP3A4. It expedites the metabolism of other agents (e.g. statins, VKAs, DOACs, opioids and macrolides) when used concomitantly
Nausea, dry mouth, somnolence, headache	⇔ CI: liver dysfunction, chronic kidney disease (<30 ml/min), uncontrolled hypertension

ADVERSE EFFECTS	NOTES
• Hypersensitivity (urticaria, exanthema, angioedema) • Bleeding risk ↑ (haematoma, epistaxis, GI bleeding) • GI (stomach problems)	⇔ Bleeding risk in the elderly and patients using corticosteroids, other NSAIDs and SSRIs ↑ Prior to procedures with a high risk of bleeding complications, such as neurosurgery: stop ASA/P2Y12-inhibitors 5-7 days in advance. Due to irreversible binding, the duration of action of both drugs is 7-10 days. Perioperative platelet transfusion in case of acute haemorrhage secondary to ASA or P2Y12-inhibitors use
• Bleeding risk ↑ (haematoma, epistaxis, GI bleeding) • Abdominal pain, diarrhoea, dyspepsia	

Double the dosage of clopidogrel or choose another P2Y12 inhibitor or ASA/dipyridamole in CYP2C19 intermediate metabolisers. Choose another P2Y12 inhibitor or ASA/dipyridamole in CYP2C19 poor metabolisers.

	MEDICATION	MECHANISM OF ACTION	INDICATIONS
VITAMIN K ANTAGONISTS (VKAS)	**Acenocoumarol**	Inhibition of vitamin K and with it the synthesis of coagulation factors II/VII/IX/X	Indicated for: • AF (CHA_2DS_2-VASc >1) • Mechanical valve prosthesis • VTE (DVT, pulmonary embolism); duration: 3 months (1st VTE episode provoked by transient risk factor), 6 months (first idiopathic VTE), >1 year (recurring VTE)
	Phenprocoumon		
	Warfarin		
HEPARIN GROUP	**Factor Xa inhibitor** (fondaparinux)	Binding to antithrombin III → factor Xa inhibition	Used to treat venous and arterial thromboembolic disorders before starting OAC, also used as prophylaxis for surgical patients and for bridging. Therapeutic (6 months) in VTE secondary to malignancy.
	Heparin	Heparin (SC/IV) activates antithrombin (factor III) and thus indirectly inactivates factors Xa and IIa (thrombin)	
	LMWH (nadroparin, enoxaparin)	LMWHs SC contain fragments of heparin with higher anti-Xa activity and lower anti-IIa activity. LMWHs are renally cleared.	
DIRECT ORAL ANTI-COAGULANTS (DOACS)	**Direct IIa inhibitors** (dagibatran)	Competitive and reversible inhibition of activated factor II	• Prevention of ischaemic stroke and systemic embolism in nonvalvular AF • Treatment of DVT and pulmonary embolism and prevention of recurrent VTE
	Factor Xa inhibitors (rivaroxaban, apixaban, edoxaban)	Selective inhibition of activated factor X	

Table 41B // Anticoagulants

ACS, acute coronary syndrome; ADP, adenosine diphosphate; AP, angina pectoris; CABG, coronary artery bypass graft; DVT, deep vein thrombosis; PAD, peripheral arterial disease; PCI, percutaneous coronary intervention; Pgp, P-glycoprotein; VTE, venous tromboembolism

All antiplatelet drugs require an initial loading dose, often higher, followed by a lower maintenance dose for continued treatment.

LMWHs have a longer $t_{1/2}$ and more stable serum levels, and no anti-Xa activity monitoring is needed. In case of reduced LMWH renal clearance, the dose should be adjusted based on anti-Xa levels.

ADVERSE EFFECTS	NOTES
Bleeding risk ↑	⇔ Bleeding risk ↑ due to: • Corticosteroids and NSAIDs (ulcerogenic) • SSRIs combined with platelet aggregation inhibitor (thrombocytopathy) • Nonadherence • Alcohol consumption • Low vitamin K intake • Febrile illness • Enhanced action of VKA due to cotrimoxazole or after sudden discontinuation of carbamazepine or rifampicin For haemorrhage management: see following pages
• Bleeding risk ↑ • Heparin-induced thrombocytopenia type I/II • Anaphylaxis • Transaminases ↑	Bridging: before any invasive procedure with bleeding risk, a short-acting medication (LMWH/ heparin) is administered to bridge the discontinuation of the OAC ● Following acute haemorrhaging, discontinue heparin/LMWH and administer protamine (partially inhibits anti-Xa activity, less so with LMWH) IV as an antidote For more information on therapeutic blood monitoring, see the following pages
• Bleeding risk ↑ • Anaemia • GI: dyspepsia, diarrhoea, nausea, vomiting • Kidney function ↓	⇔ Bleeding risk ↑: • Corticosteroids and NSAIDs • Platelet aggregation inhibitors combined with SSRIs • Thrombolytics • Nonadherence • Alcohol consumption • Febrile illness • Pgp inhibitors such as ciclosporin, itraconazole, ketoconazole, amiodarone and verapamil ▲ In case of active haemorrhaging on dabigatran, idaruzicimab can be administered as an antidote

The efficacy of **VKAs** (coumarin derivatives) depends on the INR. In case of haemorrhage or elevated INR, vitamin K can be given orally (effect after 8 hours) or intravenously (after 6 hours). Vitamin K treatment lasts 24 hours and must be repeated, certainly with phenprocoumon (long $t_{1/2}$). In life-threatening situations like intracranial haemorrhages a four-factor prothrombin complex concentrate (II, VII, IX, X) should also be administered.

> **DOACs** are taken orally and do not require routine INR monitoring, reducing patient burden. DOAC treatment is as effective as VKA treatment, with less severe (intracerebral) bleeding complications, but a higher risk of GI haemorrhage. Excercise caution when prescribing DOACs to frail elderly patients.

> **DOACs** are not indicated in patients with mechanic heart valves. These patients should be treated with VKAs.

INR

The INR is the rate at which blood clots. The physiological INR is 1. An INR of 2 means that blood clots twice as slowly. The target value of INR is between 2.0-3.5, depending on the thrombotic risk.

Bridging

Bridging involves temporarily administering a short-acting agent (LMWH or occasionally unfractionated heparin) to bridge a period without VKA. Coumarin derivatives must be discontinued prior to any invasive procedure with a high bleeding risk. Due to their respective elimination half-lives, acenocoumarol should be discontinued 3-4 days and phenprocoumon 5-7 days prior to surgery. Bridging is indicated in patients with an increased risk of thrombosis. This risk can be estimated with the CHA_2DS_2-VASc score, which uses validated risk factors to evaluate ischaemic stroke risk in patients with AF. Preoperative discontinuation of DOACs is not an indication for bridging because of the short $t_{1/2}$.

Bridging with LMWH is indicated for:

- Very high arterial thromboembolism risk: AF with CHA_2DS_2-VASc score 8-9, mechanical or bioprosthetic heart valve, or a ischaemic stroke/TIA <6 months ago.
- Very high VTE risk: <3 months after first or recurrent idiopathic DVT/pulmonary embolism.

The CHA_2DS_2-VASc score:

Congestive heart failure	1 point
Hypertension	1 point
Age >75	2 points
Diabetes mellitus	1 point
Stroke/TIA/thromboembolism	2 points
Vascular disease	1 point
Age 65-74	1 point
Sex **c**ategory (female = 1, male = 0)	1 point

For the latest information about doses, adverse effects, and more:

- United Kingdom: *www.medicines.org.uk/emc*
- Canada: *go.drugbank.com*
- Netherlands: *www.farmacotherapeutischkompas.nl*

Intravenous thrombolysis (IVT)

IVT is designed to restore cerebral blood flow in patients experiencing acute ischaemic stroke, aiming to minimise any additional damage to the affected brain tissue. A specialised stroke team is available at the emergency department to conduct rapid evaluation when there is suspicion of an acute ischaemic stroke. This includes prompt neurological assessment (e.g. National Institutes of Health Stroke Scale (NIHSS) score, see Appendix 4), vital parameters, INR, and glucose levels. A brain CT without contrast is acquired to rule out intracranial haemorrhage and to look for early signs of ischaemia, followed by CTA and CTP. If there are no contraindications for IVT, the patient is administered recombinant tissue plasminogen activator (rtPA, alteplase) through a peripheral venous catheter.

Alteplase is a thrombolytic agent that functions by converting plasminogen to plasmin. The enzyme plasmin cleaves fibrin. This process results in the dissolution of the thrombus and restores the perfusion of the previously blocked cerebral artery. The prescribed dosage is in total 0.9 mg/kg (up to a maximum of 90 mg). It is administered as a 10% bolus, followed by the remaining dose as a continuous infusion over a 60-minute period.

Indications

- IVT can be administered <12h after onset of symptoms, but yields the best results when performed within 4.5h of onset time

- Clinical diagnosis of acute ischaemic stroke with disabling deficits
- Favourable characteristics on CTP (core-penumbra mismatch) or brain MRI (DWI-FLAIR mismatch) if onset time is 4.5-12h ago at time of presentation. The decision to administer IVT in the early phase (onset <4.5h) does not depend on the CTP characteristics.

Contraindications

CONTRAINDICATIONS FOR IV THROMBOLYSIS

- Coagulopathy (platelet count <100,000/mm³, INR >1.7, aPTT >40 sec, or PT >15 sec, use of VKA, DOAC, therapeutic LMWH or heparin)
- Acute intracranial haemorrhage
- History of intracranial haemorrhage
- Acute head trauma
- Severe head trauma <3 mo
- Prior ischaemic stroke <3 mo
- Intracranial neoplasm
- GI malignancy or recent GI bleeding event <21d
- Intracranial/intraspinal surgery <3 mo
- Glucose <2.7 mmol/L
- (Suspected) infectious endocarditis
- Aortic dissection
- Blood pressure systolic ≥185 mmHg or diastolic ≥110 mmHg

Table 42 // Contraindications IV thrombolysis

The conditions under which IVT can be administered to patients with use of anticoagulants vary widely. Please refer to your local guidelines for these conditions.

Contraindications may differ per country, check your local guidelines.

Complications

- Intracranial haemorrhage (e.g. haemorrhagic transformation of infarction)
- Major systemic haemorrhage
- Angioedema

Antiseizure medication

	MEDICATION	MECHANISM OF ACTION	INDICATIONS
ANTISEIZURE MEDICATION	**Barbiturates** (phenobarbital, primidone)	• GABA agonist • Primidone is converted to phenobarbital in the body	• Generalised and focal epilepsy • Status epilepticus • Off-label 1st choice for neonatal convulsions
	Benzodiazepines (clonazepam, diazepam, clobazam, lorazepam, midazolam)	• GABA action on benzodiazepine receptor in the GABA-A receptor-chloride-ionophore complex ↑ • GABA → nervous system ↓ via hyperpolarisation → anticonvulsant, anxiolytic, hypnotic, muscle relaxant action	• Clonazepam (oral, IV): current or imminent status epilepticus; maintenance therapy focal and generalised epilepsy • Diazepam (rectal, IV): current or imminent status epilepticus, anxiety disorders • Clobazam (oral): maintenance therapy for therapy-resistent epilepsy • Lorazepam (IV): current or imminent status epilepticus • Midazolam (nasal, IV): current or imminent status epilepticus, febrile convulsions, insomnia
	Carbamazepine	• Exact mechanism of action unknown • Anticonvulsant, psychotropic and mildly anticholinergic action • Recurrent high-frequency neural discharges ↓ • Synaptic propagation ↓ • Catecholamine conversion and glutamate release ↓	• Maintenance therapy for focal epilepsy and primary generalised tonic-clonic seizures • Trigeminal neuralgia
	Valproic acid	• Exact mechanism of action unknown • GABA concentration ↑ (likely) and sodium and potassium channel sensitivity ↓	• Maintenance therapy generalised and focal epilepsy • Status epilepticus (high-dose IV)

Table 43A // Antiseizure medication

AV, atrioventricular; ECG, electrocardiogram; GABA, gamma-aminobutyric acid; PCOS, polycystic ovary syndrome; SVA2, synaptic vesicle protein 2; UGT, uridinedifosfaat-glucuronosyl-transferase

Elderly patients generally metabolise antiseizure medication at a slower rate and are therefore more susceptible to dose-related adverse effects.

ADVERSE EFFECTS	NOTES
• Fatigue, lethargy, headache, dizziness, vomiting, nausea, ataxia, nystagmus, diplopia, acute psychotic reactions • Cardiorespiratory depression • Idiosyncratic: rash	⇔ CYP3A induction ⇔ Concentration ↑ due to valproic acid
• Sleepiness, fatigue, psychomotor activity ↓, dizziness • Muscle relaxation • Habituation/dependence	⇔ Other antiseizure medication Exercise caution in cases of severe liver disease, chronic pulmonary insufficiency, spinal or cerebral ataxia, acute alcohol or drug intoxication, porphyria, elderly and debilitated patients ▲ Caution, overdose may cause respiratory depression ⊖ ▲ Antidote: flumazenil
• Neutropenia and thrombocytopenia, GGT ↑, hyponatraemia, effect on oestrogen metabolism (oral contraceptives clearance ↑) • Dizziness, drowsiness, fatigue, nausea, vomiting, ataxia, diplopia, allergy, urticaria, risk of neural tube defect in foetus ↑ • Idiosyncratic: rash, agranulocytosis, SJS, aplastic anaemia, hepatotoxicity	⇔ CI: generalised tonic-clonic seizures with myoclonuses or absences: risk of counterproductive effect ⇔ Strong inducer of CYP3A4, CYP2C9 and CYP1A2, Pgp and UGT substrate of CYP3A4, watch out for interaction with CYP3A4 inhibitors ⇔ Teratogenic
• Tremor, nausea, sedation, parkinsonism, hair loss, amenorrhoea, risk of neural tube defect in foetus ↑, risk of PCOS ↑ • Idiosyncratic: hepatotoxicity, pancreatitis	⇔ CYP2C9 ↓, Pgp ↑ ⇔ Plasma phenytoin level ↓, enhanced action of barbiturates ⇔ Teratogenic

Testing serum concentrations of antiseizure medication is useful in case of treatment with phenytoin, use of multiple antiseizure medication, dose-related adverse effects, suspicion of noncompliance, possible interactions, dialysis and during pregnancy.

	MEDICATION	MECHANISM OF ACTION	INDICATIONS
ANTISEIZURE MEDICATION	**Phenytoin**	• Exact mechanism of action in epilepsy unknown • Improves AV conduction by suppressing spontaneous depolarisation of atrial and ventricular tissue	• Maintenance therapy focal epilepsy or tonic-clonic seizures in generalised epilepsy • Status epilepticus (high-dose IV)
	Ethosuximide	Blockage of voltage-gated calcium channels	1st choice for children with absences
	Lacosamide	• Exact mechanism unknown • Selective slow inhibition of voltage-dependent potassium channels → stabilisation hyperexcitable neuronal membranes	• Maintenance therapy for focal epilepsy, monotherapy or adjuvant (age >2 y) • Adjuvant maintenance therapy for primary generalised tonic-clonic seizures in idiopathic generalised epilepsy (age >4 y)
	Lamotrigine	Inhibition of voltage-gated sodium channels → glutamate release ↓	Adjuvant or monotherapy for focal and generalised epilepsy
	Levetiracetam	• Exact mechanism of action unknown • Influence on intraneuronal calcium level, GABA and glycine channel sensitivity, interaction with SVA2	• Monotherapy for focal epilepsy, with or without secondary generalisation (age >16) • Monotherapy for generalised epilepsy • Adjuvant therapy for focal epilepsy (age >1 mo), myoclonic seizures in juvenile myoclonic epilepsy (age >12 y) and primary generalised tonic-clonic seizures in idiopathic generalised epilepsy (age >12 y) • Status epilepticus (high-dose IV)

Table 43B // Antiseizure medication

AV, atrioventricular; ECG, electrocardiogram; GABA, gamma-aminobutyric acid; PCOS, polycystic ovary syndrome; SVA2, synaptic vesicle protein 2; UGT, uridinedifosfaat-glucuronosyl-transferase

ADVERSE EFFECTS	NOTES
• Nausea, constipation, dizziness, ataxia, nystagmus, tremor/dyskinesia, confusion, speech disorder, apathy, neuropathy, visual disturbances, arrhythmia, effect on oestrogen metabolism (oral contraceptives clearance ↑) • Idiosyncratic: gum hyperplasia, rash	⇔ CI: generalised tonic-clonic seizures with myoclonuses or absences: risk of counter-productive effect ⇔ Strong CYP3A4 inducer ⇔ Blood level in conjunction with carbamazepine ↓, with e.g. alcohol consumption ↑ ⇔ Teratogenic ⊗ CYP2C9 polymorphism: manifested as noticeably more or more severe adverse effects 💡 IV administration only with continuous ECG and respiratory monitoring because of risk of hypotensia, arrhythmias, and CNS depression 💡 Measure free fraction in case of hypoalbuminuria and watch for displacement of albumin by valproic acid
• Nausea, vomiting • Drowsiness, headache, dizziness	⇔ CI: concurrent use of alcohol or sedatives
• Nausea, headache, dizziness, diplopia, ataxia • In children: (naso)pharyngitis, fever	⇔ CI: second- or third-degree AV block 💡 Be careful when prescribing to patients with cardiac problems or elderly. Check ECG for PR interval ↑ before prescription. 💡 Myoclonic seizures can occur or worsen during titration period
• Headache, agitation, nausea • Idiosyncratic: rash, SJS	⇔ Skin rash is more likely to occur with concomitant use with valproic acid 💡 Myoclonic epilepsy may worsen 💡 Abrupt cessation → withdrawal seizures
• Nasopharyngitis, headache, drowsiness, ataxia, sedation • Idiosyncratic: rash	💡 Dosage should be adjusted to renal function

Medication tapering is preferred for women who are actively looking to conceive and patients who have been in remission for >2 years.

Lamotrigine and levetiracetam are the first-choice maintenance therapies for women of childbearing age, preferably as monotherapy at the lowest effective dose.
Carbamazepine, phenytoin, and valproate are known to be teratogenic. Valproate has been shown to carry the highest risk of major congenital malformations. Therefore, these agents should not be prescribed to women of childbearing age.

Antipsychotics

	MEDICATION	MECHANISM OF ACTION	INDICATIONS
ANTIPSYCHOTICS	**Clozapine** (atypical)	• Dibenzodiazepine derivative with antipsychotic and sedative action • Antagonist of D4 and 5-HT2 receptor, weaker antagonist of adrenergic, cholinergic, histaminergic and other dopaminergic and serotonergic receptors	• Schizophrenia (therapy-resistant) • Psychotic disorders in Parkinson's disease and Lewy body dementia
	Haloperidol (classic)	• Butyrophenone derivative with antipsychotic and minor sedative effect • D2 and α1 receptor antagonist	Delirium, tic disorders, chorea in Huntington's disease, aggression/psychotic symptoms in Alzheimer's disease/vascular dementia
	Risperidone (atypical)	5-HT2, D2, and α1 receptor antagonist	• Continuing aggression in moderate/serious Alzheimer's disease, mental retardation or behavioural disorders • Off-label: delirium

Table 44 // Antipsychotics

Because many antiseizure medication induce the CYP mechanism, close attention must be paid to how different antiseizure medication can lower or raise each other's levels when prescribed together.

Many antiseizure medication have a major effect on driving ability.

In case of **brain tumour-related epilepsy (BTRE)**, the use of levetiracetam, lacosamide, or valproic acid have been proven effective. If levetiracetam is ineffective, lacosamide and valproic acid can also be used as add-on medication.

ADVERSE EFFECTS	NOTES
• Granulocytopenia/agranulocytosis • Myocarditis/cardiomyopathy in persistent tachycardia or symptoms of heart failure, drowsiness, dizziness, constipation, hypersalivation	Check leukocyte and neutrophil counts before and during treatment Monitor blood pressure (standing and lying down) in patients with Parkinson's disease during the first weeks of use ⇔ Do not combine with alcohol ⇔ Smoking cessation → CYP1A2 ↓ → blood level ↑
Agitation, headache, drowsiness, extrapyramidal symptoms, hyperkinesia, tardive dyskinesia, orthostatic hypotension, dry mouth, constipation, depression, QT interval ↑, malignant neuroleptic syndrome (if suspected, discontinue treatment immediately!)	⊗ CYP2D6 polymorphism: noticeably more or more severe adverse effects ⇔ CI: QT-extending agents Exercise caution with agents that cause CYP3A4 ↓ ⇔ CI: Parkinson's disease or a recent MI
• Extrapiramidal → parkinsonism, acathisia, dyskinesia, dystonia • Antihistaminergic → drowsiness, sedation, headache, insomnia • Dopaminergic → hyperprolactinaemia: galactorrhea, loss of libido, gynaecomastia • Leukopenia/neutropenia, QT interval ↑, malignant neuroleptic syndrome	⊗ CYP2D6 polymorphism: noticeably more or more severe adverse effects Increased risk of cardiovascular/cerebrovascular adverse effects ⊗ Malignant neuroleptic syndrome: muscle rigidity, hyperthermia, autonomic dysregulation, consciousness ↓ secondary to dopamine receptor blockade

Cholinesterase inhibitors

	MEDICATION	MECHANISM OF ACTION	INDICATIONS
CHOLINESTERASE INHIBITORS	**Galantamine**	• Forms a complex with acetylcholinesterase → enzyme temporarily inactivated → time spent by acetylcholine in synaptic cleft ↑ • Provides cognitive improvement in small number of patients	• Light/moderately severe Alzheimer's disease • Light/moderately severe dementia in Parkinson's disease • Rivastigmine: Lewy body dementia
	Rivastigmine, donepezil		

Table 45 // Cholinesterase inhibitors

Parkinson's medication

	MEDICATION	MECHANISM OF ACTION	INDICATIONS
PARKINSON'S MEDICATION	**Levodopa**	• Dopamine precursor which is capable of crossing the blood-brain barrier and after conversion to dopamine acts as agonist of the D2 receptor • $T_{1/2}$ 1.5 hours (in elderly 25% ↑)	• 1st choice for Parkinson's disease • Parkinsonism
	Dopamine agonists Non-ergot dopamine agonists (pramipexole, ropinirole rotigotine, apomorphine)	Selective activation of D2 receptors especially and to a lesser extent of D1 receptors	• Parkinson's disease • Parkinsonism
	MAO-B inhibitor (rasagiline, safinamide, selegiline)	Selectively inhibits the MAO-B enzyme → dopamine degradation ↓	Parkinson's disease
	COMT inhibitor (entacapone, tolcapone)	Selectively inhibits the COMT enzyme → peripheral conversion of levodopa ↓ and fluctuation of plasma level ↓	Parkinson's disease (especially in the later stage, with levodopa response fluctuations)

Table 46A // Parkinson's medication

ACh, acetylcholine; COMT, catechol-O-methyltransferase; MAO-B, monoamine oxidase-B

ADVERSE EFFECTS	NOTES
Nausea, vomiting	💡 No effect on disease course ⇔ CI: severe heart failure, AV block and syncope due to risk of syncope and rhythm or conduction disorders
• Nausea, vomiting, diarrhoea, anorexia, dizziness, insomnia, anxiety, cholinergic (bradycardia, hyperhidrosis) • Especially in Parkinson's disease: fall frequency ↑ • Sometimes: syncope and rhythm or conduction disorders	

ADVERSE EFFECTS	NOTES
Hyperkinesias/dyskinesias, paraesthesias, rigidity, anorexia, headache, hallucination, confusion, somnolence/insomnia, dizziness, angina pectoris, palpitations, fatigue, orthostatic hypotension (especially in initial stage), nausea, vomiting	💡 Levodopa may be prescribed in combination with a decarboxylase inhibitor (benserazide, carbidopa) → peripheral conversion of levodopa ↓ 💡 Levodopa is least effective against speech problems, balance problems and delayed movement initiation (especially in later-stage Parkinson's disease) 💡 Effect ↓ as monotherapy in progressing Parkinson's disease
Nausea, vomiting, dizziness, confusion, hallucinations, drowsiness, impulse control disorders	💡 Effect ↓ as monotherapy in progressing Parkinson's disease 💡 Lesser effect on hypokinesia and rigidity than levodopa, but longer $t_{1/2}$ (clinical effect lasts longer) ⇔ Dopamine agonists potentiate levodopa action → dosage ↓
Insomnia, delusions, blood pressure ↓	💡 Effect over time ↓ ⇔ Tyramine degradation ↓, indication for a low-tyramine diet. Symptom of tyramine ↑: severe, throbbing headache.
Nausea, vomiting, delusions, hallucinations	💡 The effect of adding MAO-B inhibitors alongside levodopa appears similar to that of entacapone

	MEDICATION	MECHANISM OF ACTION	INDICATIONS
PARKINSON'S MEDICATION	**Amantadine**	• Presynaptic dopamine re-uptake ↓, dopamine release from nerve endings ↑ • Suppresses hyperkinesias and dyskinesias (adverse effect of levodopa) • Antiviral: Influenza A ↓	Parkinson's disease, uncomplicated phase with mild functional impairment
	Anticholinergics (biperiden, trihexyphenidyl)	ACh receptor antagonist → improved dopamine-acetylcholine balance	• Parkinson's disease • Medication induced extrapyramidal symptoms

Table 46B // Parkinson's medication

ACh, acetylcholine; COMT, catechol-O-methyltransferase; MAO-B, monoamine oxidase-B

Riluzole

MEDICATION	MECHANISM OF ACTION	INDICATIONS
Riluzole	• Exact mechanism of action unknown • Blocks glutaminergic neurotransmission in the CNS	ALS

Table 47 // Riluzole

ULN, upper limit of normal range

Triptans

	MEDICATION	MECHANISM OF ACTION	INDICATIONS
TRIPTANS	**Sumatriptan**	• Exact mechanism of action unknown • 5-HT1 receptor antagonist (especially 5-HT1B and 5-HT1D)	Cluster headache, migraine (acute treatment)
	Other triptans (almotriptan, eletriptan, frovatriptan, naratriptan, rizatriptan, zolmitriptan)		• Acute migraine treatment • Frovatriptan, zolmitriptan: prophylaxis in menstrual migraine

Table 48 // Triptans

ADVERSE EFFECTS	NOTES
Ankle oedema, livedo reticularis (especially in women), delusions, hallucinations	Effect over time ↓ CI: cognitive impairment due to ↑ risk of hallucinations
Memory disorders, blurred vision, urinary problems, potency disorders, dry mouth, palpitations, intraocular pressure ↑	Mainly inhibits trembling, saliva production, and perspiration Used almost exclusively for therapy-resistant tremor due to adverse effect profile (beta blocker preferred in elderly patients)

During levodopa treatment, adjuvant treatment with dopamine agonists, MAO-B inhibitors and COMT inhibitors are effective in the later complicated phases with response fluctuations, e.g. 'on-off' and 'wearing-off'.

ADVERSE EFFECTS	NOTES
Fatigue, nausea, liver dysfunction (often <3 mo after starting)	Monthly check of ALT for 1st 3 mo (thereafter every 3 mo) ⊗ ALT ≥5 ULN

ADVERSE EFFECTS	NOTES
Bad taste (nasal spray), local reaction to injection (e.g. pain, swelling, bruising), dizziness, drowsiness, paraesthesia, hot flushes, retrosternal pain, dyspnoea	Sumatriptan should not be used as a prophylactic due to the risk of chronic headache and exacerbation ↑ ⇔ CI: PMHx: MI, ischaemic heart disease, coronary artery spasm, stroke, TIA, peripheral vascular disease, liver disease
Nausea, abdominal pain, vomiting, dry mouth, dysphagia, sensory disturbances, dizziness, headache, muscle weakness/pain	⇔ CI: Concomitant use of other 5-HT1B/1D agonists ⇔ PMHx: MI, ischaemic heart disease, coronary artery spasm, stroke, TIA, peripheral vascular disease

Anti-inflammatory drugs

	MEDICATION	MECHANISM OF ACTION	INDICATIONS
ANTI-INFLAMMATORY DRUGS	**Methylprednisolone**	Anti-inflammatory and immunosuppressive agent: • Blocking promotor sites proinflammatory genes, promoting expression anti-inflammatory gene products, inhibiting synthesis inflammatory cytokines • Synthesis of COX-2 • Reversing capillary permeability, suppressing fibroblast and leukocyte migration, controlling protein synthesis, stabilising cellular lysosomes • Inhibiting cell-mediated immunologic functions dependent on lymphocytes	Treatment of inflammatory responses (e.g. MS relapse, ADEM, neuromyelitis optica, cerebral oedema secondary to cerebral neoplasm, autoimmune encephalitis, giant cell arteritis with visual loss)
	Intravenous immunoglobulin (IVIG)	Extensive immunomodulatory actions including binding and neutralising of autoantibodies to factor VIII, modulating of the complement system, inhibiting Fc mediated effects and modulating cellular immunity and activity of endothelial cell proliferation	GBS, autoimmune encephalitis, myasthenia gravis, CIDP, dermatomyositis

Table 49 // Anti-inflammatory drugs
ADEM, acute disseminated encephalomyelitis; CIDP, chronic inflammatory demyelinating polyneuripathy; IgA, immunoglobulin A

ADVERSE EFFECTS	NOTES
Headache, peptic ulcer, weight gain, cushingoid features, hypertension, muscle weakness and wasting, fluid retention, insomnia, mood disorders	⇔ CI: ventricular or duodenal ulcers 💡 Increases susceptibility of infections and causes increased severity of infections with masking of clinical signs and symptoms 💡 May cause increased insuline demands in DM patients 💡 Effects of cholinesterase inhibitors can be decreased in myasthenia gravis
Headache (e.g. migraine, tension headache), flu-like symptoms (nausea, vomiting, fever, flushing, fatigue), urticaria, eczema, hypotension, arrhythmia, diarrhoea, muscle or joint pain	⇔ CI: hypersensitivity to human immunoglobin, (selective IgA deficiency with anti-IgA antibodies) 💡 Expected to be correlated with thromboembolic diseases due to a relative increase of viscosity of the blood caused by the inflow of immunoglobin. Be cautious in obese patients or when risk factors for thrombotic events are present. Administer at the lowest possible infusion rate.

Multiple sclerosis disease-modifying therapies (DMTs)

	MEDICATION	MECHANISM OF ACTION	INDICATIONS
FIRST LINE THERAPY	**Interferon-beta 1a**	Binds to type I interferon receptors → increased expression of anti-inflammatory agents and downregulation of proinflammatory cytokines expression	CIS, RRMS
FIRST LINE THERAPY	**Interferon-beta 1b**	Binds to type I interferon receptors → increased expression of anti-inflammatory agents and downregulation of proinflammatory cytokines expression	RRMS, active SPMS
FIRST LINE THERAPY	**Glatiramer acetate**	Shifts the immune response from a proinflammatory state comprised of Th1 T-cells to regulatory, non-inflammatory Th2 T-cells	RRMS, active SPMS
FIRST LINE THERAPY	**Teriflunomide**	Selective and reversible inhibitor of dihydroorotate dehydrogenase → reduced proliferation of active B- and T-lymphocytes	CIS, RRMS, active SPMS
FIRST LINE THERAPY	**Fumarates** (dimethyl fumarate, diroximel fumarate, monomethyl fumarate)	Activates transcription of Nrf2 and up-regulates Nrf2-dependent antioxidant genes → anti-inflammatory a nd immunomodulatory effects	CIS, RRMS, active SPMS
FIRST LINE THERAPY	**Ponesimod**	Selective S1P-1 receptor modulator	CIS, RRMS, active SPMS
FIRST LINE THERAPY	**Ozanimod**	Selective S1P-1 and S1P-5 receptor modulator	CIS, RRMS, active SPMS
SECOND LINE THERAPY	**Fingolimod**	Unselective S1P receptor modulator	CIS, RRMS, active SPMS

Table 50A // Multiple sclerosis DMTs

CIS, clinically isolated syndrome; IgM, immunoglobulin M; JC virus, John Cunningham virus; Nrf2, nuclear factor erythoid 2-related factor 2; PPMS, primary progressive multiple sclerosis; RRMS, relapsing remitting multiple sclerosis; S1P, sphingosine 1-phosphate; SPMS, secondary progressive multiple sclerosis; SC, subcutaneous

ADVERSE EFFECTS	NOTES
Flu-like symptoms, fever, muscle pain, injection site reactions, lymphopenia, headache, nausea, liver enzymes ↑	⇔ CI: severe depression or suicidality 💡 IM injections
	⇔ CI: severe depression or suicidality, liver dysfunction 💡 SC injections
Injection site reactions, fever, chills, aches, flushing, shortness of breath, palpitations, tachycardia	⇔ CI: kidney dysfunction, cardiovascular diseases 💡 SC injections
Headache, diarrhoea, nausea, ALT ↑, hair density ↓	⇔ CI: immunocompromised, liver dysfunction, bone marrow function ↓, anaemia, leukopenia, neutropenia, thrombocytopenia, active infections, hypoproteinaemia, kidney dysfunction 💡 Tablets
Nausea, diarrhoea, abdominal pain, flushing, liver enzymes ↑, lymphopenia	⇔ CI: immunocompromised, active infections, liver dysfunction, lymphopenia, active malignancy, kidney dysfunction 💡 Tablets
Infections (upper respiratory tract, urinary tract, nasopharyngitis), headache, liver enzymes ↑, hypertension, peripheral oedema, insomnia, vertigo	⇔ CI: immunocompromised, active infections, liver dysfunction, unstable angina pectoris, heart failure, active malignancy, second-/third-degree AV block, recent MI, sick-sinus syndrome without pacemaker 💡 Tablets
Infections (upper respiratory tract, urinary tract, herpes zoster, nasopharyngitis), liver enzymes ↑, lymphopenia, bradycardia, hypertension	⇔ CI: immunocompromised, active infections, liver dysfunction, unstable angina pectoris, heart failure, active malignancy, second-/third-degree AV block, recent MI, sick-sinus syndrome without pacemaker 💡 Tablets
Back pain, diarrhoea, fatigue, GI disturbance, headache and upper respiratory tract infections, bradycardia (only after administration), macular oedema	⇔ CI: immunocompromised, active infections, liver dysfunction, unstable angina pectoris, heart failure, active malignancy, cardiac arrhythmias treated with class Ia or class III antiarrhythmic agents, second-/third-degree AV block, recent MI, sick-sinus syndrome without pacemaker, QTc interval ≥500 msec 💡 Tablets

	MEDICATION	MECHANISM OF ACTION	INDICATIONS
SECOND LINE THERAPY	**Cladribine**	Deoxyadenosine analogue prodrug, resulting in lymphocyte apoptosis	RRMS, active SPMS
	Siponimod	Selective S1P-1 and S1P-5 receptor modulator	CIS, SPMS
	Ofatumumab	Monoclonal anti-CD-20 antibody	CIS, RRMS, active SPMS
	Alemtuzumab	Monoclonal anti-CD-52 antibody	RRMS, active SPMS
	Natalizumab	Monoclonal antibody, reduces lymphocyte migration over the blood-brain barrier	CIS, RRMS, active SPMS
	Ocrelizumab	Monoclonal anti-CD-20 antibody	CIS, RRMS, active SPMS, PPMS
	Rituximab	Monoclonal anti-CD-20 antibody	RRMS

Table 50B // Multiple sclerosis DMTs

CIS, clinically isolated syndrome; IgM, immunoglobulin M; JC virus, John Cunningham virus; Nrf2, nuclear factor erythoid 2-related factor 2; PPMS, primary progressive multiple sclerosis; RRMS, relapsing remitting multiple sclerosis; S1P, sphingosine 1-phosphate; SPMS, secondary progressive multiple sclerosis; SC, subcutaneous

ADVERSE EFFECTS	NOTES
Lymphopenia, fatigue, herpes virus-associated infections, alopecia, nausea, headache, skin rash, somnolence	⇔ CI: immunocompromised, liver dysfunction, kidney dysfunction, active malignancy, tuberculosis Indicated when response to other DMT is inadequate Tablets
Headache, hypertension, liver enzymes ↑, lymphopenia, AV block, bradycardia, infections (herpes zoster)	⇔ CI: immunocompromised, active infections, liver dysfunction, unstable AP, heart failure, active malignancy, second-/third-degree AV block, recent MI, sick-sinus syndrome without pacemaker, bradycardia, homozygous CYP2C9*3 (poor metaboliser) Tablets
Infections (upper respiratory tract, urinary tract, herpes zoster, nasopharyngitis), injection-related reactions (skin and/or systemic), headache	⇔ CI: immunocompromised, active infection, active malignancy SC injections
Infusion-related reactions (headache, rash, nausea, fever), infections (upper respiratory tract, herpes zoster, varicella zoster), cardiovascular events, neutropenia, secondary autoimmunity	⇔ CI: immunocompromised, active infection, hypertension, history of cardiovascular diseases Indicated when response to ≥2 other DMTs is inadequate IV infusion
Urinary tract infections, nasopharyngitis, vertigo, headache, nausea, progressive multifocal leukoencephalopathy	⇔ CI: immunocompromised, active infections, liver dysfunction, JC virus positivity, malignancy IV infusion or SC injections
Infusion-related reactions, headache, nasopharyngitis, flu-like symptoms, bacterial infections, viral infections, bronchitis, leukopenia, (febrile) neutropenia, thrombocytopenia, urinary tract infections, IgG ↓ and IgM levels ↓/↑	⇔ CI: immunocompromised, active infections (hepatitis, herpes zoster), cardiac failure, active malignancy IV infusion
Infusion-related reactions, bacterial infections, viral infections, bronchitis, leukopenia, (febrile) neutropenia, thrombocytopenia, upper respiratory tract infections, urinary tract infections, IgG ↓ and IgM ↓/↑	⇔ CI: hypersensitivity to murine proteins, immunocompromised, active infections (hepatitis, herpes zoster), cardiac failure, active malignancy IV infusion Rituximax is used off-label for the treatment of MS

Invasive, non-pharmacological treatment

Mechanical thrombectomy

Mechanical thrombectomy, also known as intra-arterial thrombectomy (IAT), is an angiography-guided procedure in which clots are removed from the brain following an ischaemic stroke. The common femoral artery, or in some cases the radial artery, is punctured using the Seldinger technique. A guidewire is used to lead the diagnostic catheter to the cerebral arteries and localise the clot using fluoroscopy and iodinated contrast. After localisation of the clot, the diagnostic catheter is removed, and a therapeutic catheter is guided over the wire. The clot can be subsequently removed using an aspiration catheter or with a stent retriever (see Figure 59). The stent retriever folds around the clot, after which it can be removed. A combination of these two techniques can also be used.

Indications

- Mechanical thrombectomy can take place <24h after onset of symptoms, but yields the best results when performed within 6h of onset time
- Proven ischaemic stroke with severe neurological deficits (NIHSS ≥6, see Appendix 4). Mechanical thrombectomy may be considered in patients with a NIHSS score of 0-5 in case of disabling deficits, clinical worsening after IVT, or a contraindication for IVT.
- Approachable thrombus location. This may be as distal as the M3/M4 segment of the MCA, or the ACA or PCA (see Figure 60).
- Favourable characteristics on CTP (core-penumbra mismatch) or brain MRI (DWI-FLAIR mismatch) if onset time is 6-24h prior to time of presentation at the emergency room. For the decision to perform early mechanical thrombectomy (onset <6h) finding a large vessel obstruction on brain CTA is sufficient. A CTP or MRI is not required.

Contraindications

- Intracranial haemorrhage (e.g. haemorrhagic transformation of infarction)
- Very high pre-existing patient morbidity

Complications

- Occlusion of another (mostly distal) vessel caused by a clot breaking off
- Damage to the vessel wall resulting in intracranial haemorrhage
- Reperfusion oedema causing neurological deterioration after treatment due to cerebral herniation

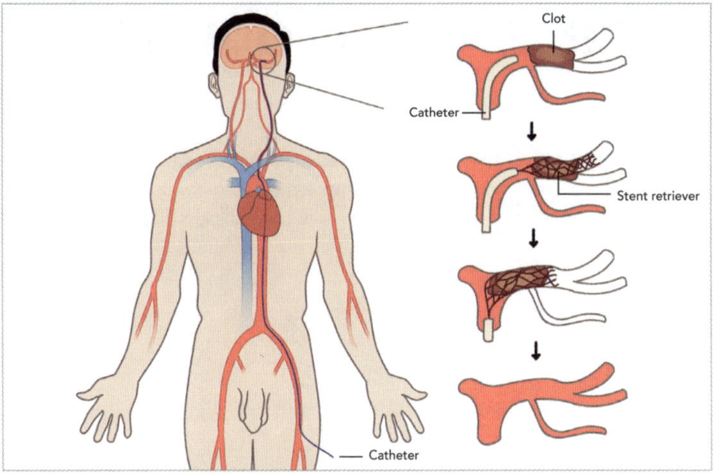

Figure 59 // Removal of an intracranial clot using a stent retriever

Mechanical thrombectomy is also an option in occlusion of the basilar artery, although its effectiveness is not yet demonstrated.

Mechanical thrombectomy is not performed in all hospitals, so patient transfer may be needed.

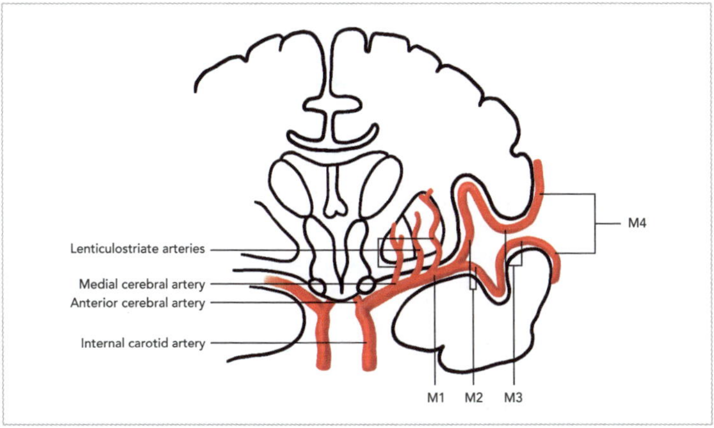

Figure 60 // Segments of the medial cerebral artery

Differential diagnosis

This section lists several examples of diagnoses to consider for specific presenting complaints. Important! The diagnoses listed in this section are not exhaustive and serve only as examples. You can take notes in the margins.

Loss of consciousness

Transient loss of consciousness

- Trauma:
  - Mild TBI (EMV $\geq$13)
- Cerebral:
  - Haemorrhagic cerebrovascular disease (SAH)
  - Ischaemic cerebrovascular disease (brainstem TIA)
  - Epileptic seizure
- Cardiovascular:
  - Orthostatic hypotension
  - Reflex syncope (e.g. vasovagal, situational, sinus carotid syndrome)
  - Cardiac syncope (arrhythmia, structural heart disease, lung condition, or large vessel disease)
- Psychogenic:
  - Hyperventilation
  - Psychogenic non-epileptic seizures
  - Psychogenic pseudosyncope

SAH and a TIA in the brainstem can be accompanied by transient loss of consciousness, but this is rare.

Long-term

- Neurological:
  - Head trauma
  - Brainstem ischaemia
  - Diffuse anoxia
  - Intracranial haemorrhage
  - Hydrocephalus

- Diffuse cerebral oedema
- Meningitis
- Encephalitis
- Brain abscess
- Intracranial neoplasm
- End-stage neurodegenerative disease
- Status epilepticus (or postictal state)

◆ Metabolic:
- Intoxication: alcohol, medication (e.g. benzodiazepine, opioids, antipsychotics, antidepressants), gamma-hydroxybutyric acid (GHB), carbon monoxide (CO)
- Hypo- or hyperthermia
- Hypo- or hyperglycaemia
- Hypothyroidism
- Hypoadrenalism
- Thiamine deficiency
- Hepatic failure
- Renal failure
- Electrolyte abnormality (elevated Na^+, Ca^{2+}, Mg^{2+})

◆ Cardiopulmonary:
- Cardiopulmonary arrest
- Hypoxia
- Shock

◆ Psychiatric:
- Silent delirium
- Psychogenic coma

> The most common cause of transient loss of consciousness at all ages is vasovagal syncope. Characteristic symptoms are:
> - Short-term unconsciousness (a few seconds)
> - Prodromal symptoms (pallor and sweating)
> - Temporary vision loss
> - Sometimes incontinence
> - Jerking movements
> - Slow to very slow pulse (vagus nerve stimulation)

An epileptic seizure is more often accompanied by a lateral tongue bite. Vasovagal syncope is more likely to be accompanied by a distal tongue bite.

Diplopia

- Ocular:
  - Refractive errors
  - Diabetic retinopathy
  - Retinal infarction
  - Glaucoma
  - Chorioretinitis
  - Cataract
  - Lens dislocation
  - Decompensated latent strabismus
- Cranial nerve dysfunction:
  - Trauma
  - Ischaemic neuropathy (e.g. DM, hypertension, temporal arteritis)
  - Aneurysm or vascular malformations
  - SOL (e.g. primary tumor, abscess, or metastases)
  - Idiopathic intracranial hypertension (IIH)
  - CVT
  - Infectious (e.g. meningitis, neurosyphilis, neuroborreliosis)
  - MS
  - Wernicke encephalopathy
  - Miller Fisher syndrome
- Neuromuscular junction:
  - Myasthenia gravis
- Cerebral:
  - Migraine
  - TIA
  - Ischaemic stroke
  - Intracranial haemorrhage
  - SOL (e.g. tumour, abscess, or metastases)
- Functional:
  - Convergence spasm

Dizziness

- Vertigo:
  - Peripheral:
    - BPPV
    - Vestibular neuritis
    - Ménière's disease
    - Herpes zoster oticus (Ramsay Hunt syndrome)
    - Labyrinthine concussion
    - Vestibular schwannoma
    - Perilymphatic fistula
    - Superior semicircular canal dehiscence syndrome (SSCDS)
  - Central:
    - Vestibular migraine
    - Brainstem ischaemia
    - Cerebellar ischaemic or haemorrhagic stroke
    - Chiari malformation
    - MS
- Lightheadedness:
  - Cardiovascular:
    - Orthostatic hypotension
    - Cardiac arrhythmia
    - Ischaemic heart disease
    - Heart failure
  - Hyperventilation
  - Intoxication (CO intoxication, alcohol, drugs, medication)
  - Adverse affect of medication

> Acute vertigo accompanied by other neurological symptoms (e.g. dysarthria, ataxia, paresis, diplopia) may indicate an urgent medical condition (e.g. ischaemic or haemorrhagic stroke).

> Dizziness is an adverse effect of many different drugs, e.g. benzodiazepines, antidepressants (SSRI, TCA), antihypertensives, antiseizure medication, beta blockers.

Dysarthria

- Upper motor neuron (bulbar):
  - Cerebrovascular disease
  - Demyelinating disorders (MS)
  - ALS (pseudo-bulbar)
  - Huntington's disease
- Lower motor neuron (bulbar):
  - Cerebrovascular disease
  - Poliomyelitis
  - Demyelinating disorders (MS)
  - ALS (bulbar)
  - Syringobulbia
- Extrapyramidal:
  - Parkinson's disease
  - Atypical parkinsonism
- Cerebellum:
  - Demyelinating disorders (MS)
  - Cerebrovascular disease
  - SOL
  - Hereditary ataxia (e.g. Friedreich's ataxia)
- Myasthenia gravis
- Intoxication (medication, alcohol, drugs)
- Hypothermia

In case of speech disorders, always consider loose dentures as a cause of dysarthria. Good hearing is very important for language comprehension (hearing problem, suboptimal hearing aid settings).

Memory loss

- Cerebral:
  - Mild cognitive impairment
  - Alzheimer's disease
  - Vascular dementia
  - Frontotemporal dementia
  - Lewy body dementia
  - Wernicke encephalopathy
  - Korsakoff syndrome

- Creutzfeld-Jakob disease
- Transient global amnesia
- Cerebrovascular disease
- Hydrocephalus
- Head trauma (retrograde and post-traumatic amnesia)

◆ Metabolic disorders:
- Dehydration
- Hypoglycaemia/hyperglycaemia
- Hyponatraemia/hypernatraemia
- Hypothyroidism/hyperthyroidism

◆ Psychiatric:
- Delirium
- Post-traumatic stress disorder
- Depression
- Psychotic disorder
- Dissociative disorder

> **Transient global amnesia** is acute onset isolated anterograde and retrograde amnesia which is temporary with a maximum duration of 24 hours (typically up to 8 hours). Known triggers are exercise, emotional stress, sexual intercourse, acute illness, and extreme temperatures.

Loss of sensation

◆ Cerebral:
- Cerebrovascular disease

◆ Brainstem:
- Cranial nerve palsy (e.g. trigeminal nerve)
- Cerebrovascular (Wallenberg syndrome)

◆ Spinal cord:
- Trauma
- Spinal degeneration
- Spinal disc herniation
- Transverse myelitis (e.g. MS)
- Viral myelitis
- Epidural abscess
- Ischaemia
- Spinal haemorrhage (e.g. epidural, subarachnoid, intramedullary)

- Vascular malformation
- Epidural metastases
- Intramedullary tumour
- Subacute combined degeneration (e.g. nitrous oxide)
- Radiation myelopathy
- Syringomyelia

- Peripheral nervous system:
  - Plexopathy (DM, trauma, SOL, inflammatory, infectious, post-radiation therapy, idiopathic)
  - Radiculopathy (spinal disc herniation, degenerative, trauma, SOL)
  - Radiculitis (varicella zoster virus (VZV), Lyme)
  - Mononeuropathy (compression, trauma)
  - Polyneuropathy:
    - DM
    - Alcohol use disorder
    - Vitamin B12 deficiency
    - Uraemia
    - Infectious (syphilis, HIV, Lyme, lepra)
    - Drug-induced (chemotherapy)
    - GBS

In many cases of polyneuropathy, no aetiology is found. This is known as chronic idiopathic axonal polyneuropathy (CIAP).

The malfunction of multiple peripheral nerves in an extremity may indicate brachial plexus or lumbosacral plexus disease.

Visual field defects

- Ocular:
  - Cataract
  - Retinitis pigmentosa
  - Retinal detachment
  - Macular degeneration
  - Optic neuritis (MS)
- Optic chiasm:
  - Pituitary tumour

    - Aneurysm of the internal carotid artery, anterior communicating artery, or ACA
    - Meningioma
    - Craniopharyngeoma
- Optic radiation or cortex:
    - Cerebrovascular disease (occipital/parietal)
    - SOL
- Functional neurological disorder

Headache

Acute

- Primary thunderclap headache
- Primary cough, exertional or sexual activity headache
- Haemorrhagic stroke (SAH, intracerebral)
- Reversible cerebral vasoconstriction syndrome
- CVT
- Head trauma
- Dissection of the carotid artery or vertebral artery
- Acute hypertensive crisis
- Posterior reversible encephalopathy syndrome (PRES)
- Pituitary apoplexy
- Acute glaucoma

Paroxysmal headache

- Primary:
    - Migraine
    - Cluster headache
    - Tension-type headache
    - Paroxysmal hemicrania
- Inflammatory:
    - Temporal arteritis
- Neurogenic:
    - Trigeminal neuralgia
- Endocrine:
    - Pheochromocytoma

Continuous headache

- Primary:
  - Tension-type headache
- Cerebral:
  - Increased intracranial pressure (IIH, SOL, hydrocephalus)
- Infectious:
  - Sinusitis
  - Meningitis/encephalitis (bacterial, viral)
  - Cerebral abscess
- Inflammatory:
  - Temporal arteritis
- Medication overuse headache
- Referred pain:
  - Cervical spine / muscle pain
  - Dental problems
- Chiari malformation
- Metabolic disorders:
  - Dehydration
- Intoxication (CO intoxication, alcohol, drugs)
- Withdrawal symptom
- Ocular:
  - Refractive errors
- Jaw joint inflammation

Horner syndrome

- First-order (central):
  - Demyelination (e.g. MS)
  - Cerebrovascular disease of the hypothalamus or brainstem (e.g. Wallenberg syndrome/lateral medullary syndrome)
  - Arnold-Chiari malformation
  - Encephalitis
  - Meningitis
  - Tumour (intracranial or spinal cord)
  - Syringomyelia
- Second-order (preganglionic):
  - Apical lung tumour (Pancoast tumour)
  - Cervical rib

- Mediastinal tumour
  - Thoracic aneurysm
  - Thyroid malignancies
  - Iatrogenic (e.g. thoracic surgery, chest tube placement)
- Third-order (postganglionic):
  - Internal carotid artery aneurysm/dissection/thrombosis
  - Cluster headache or migraine
  - Cavernous sinus thrombosis
  - Nasopharyngeal carcinoma/lymphoma
  - Temporal arteritis
  - Herpes zoster infection

Epileptic seizure

- Cerebral:
  - Epilepsy
  - SOL
  - Post-traumatic
  - Post-stroke
  - Cavernous or arteriovenous malformation
  - Eclampsia
  - Infectious (abscess, meningitis, encephalitis, tuberculosis (TB), neurocysticercosis (pork tapeworm taenia solium), malaria)
- Metabolic disorders:
  - Dehydration
  - Hypoglycaemia
  - Electrolyte disorders (hyponatraemia/hypernatraemia, hypomagnesaemia, hypocalcaemia)
  - Uraemia
  - Thyrotoxicosis
- Intoxication
- Withdrawal symptom

Loss of strength

- Cerebral:
  - Cerebrovascular disease
  - SOL
  - Demyelinating disorders (MS)

- Postictal paresis
- Spinal cord:
  - Trauma
  - Spinal degeneration
  - Spinal disc herniation
  - Transverse myelitis (e.g. MS)
  - Viral myelitis
  - Epidural abscess
  - Ischaemia
  - Spinal haemorrhage (e.g. epidural, subarachnoid, intramedullary)
  - Vascular malformation
  - Epidural metastases
  - Intramedullary tumour
  - Subacute combined degeneration (e.g. nitrous oxide)
  - Radiation myelopathy
  - Syringomyelia
- Anterior horn cell disorders:
  - ALS
  - Progressive spinal muscular atrophy (PSMA)
  - Primary lateral sclerosis (PLS)
- Neuropathies:
  - Radiculopathy (trauma, spinal disc herniation, degenerative, SOL, infectious)
  - Plexopathy (DM, trauma, SOL, inflammatory, infectious, idiopathic, radiation therapy)
  - Mononeuropathy (trauma, compression, DM, inflammatory, infectious, iatrogenic)
  - Polyneuropathy (GBS, DM, alcohol use disorder, vitamin deficiencies, infectious, inflammatory)
- Neuromuscular junction:
  - Myasthenia gravis
  - Lambert-Eaton myasthenic syndrome (LEMS)
- Myogenic:
  - Sarcopenia
  - Cachexia
  - Substance abuse
  - Inflammatory myopathy (dermatomyositis, polymyositis)
  - Metabolic myopathy

- Muscular dystrophy
- Metabolic disorders:
  - Hypoglycaemia
  - Hyponatraemia
  - Hypokalaemia/hyperkalaemia

A SOL can involve various aetiologies, such as a tumour, abscess, haematoma, etc.

Low back pain

- Idiopathic/aspecific
- Myogenic
- Scoliosis
- Spinal disc herniation
- Spondylarthrosis/facet arthrosis
- Spondylolisthesis
- Malignancy (multiple myeloma, vertebral metastases, leptomeningeal metastases)
- Vertebral compression fracture
- Infectious (Lyme, VZV, spondylodiscitis, epidural abscess, spinal TB (Pott's disease))
- Ankylosing spondylitis (Bechterew's disease)
- Sacroiliitis

When diagnosing a radicular syndrome, remember that the cervical and lumbar nerve roots are numbered differently. Cervical nerve roots originate above the corresponding vertebra, lumbar nerve roots originate below the corresponding vertebra.

Peripheral paraesthesia (tingling)

- Polyneuropathy:
  - Acute:
    - GBS
  - Chronic:
    - DM
    - Alcohol use disorder
    - Vitamin deficiencies

  - Infectious
  - Inflammatory
- Radiculopathy:
  - Spinal disc herniation
  - Spinal degeneration
  - Infectious (e.g. Lyme, VZV)
  - Neoplasm (e.g. leptomeningeal or vertebral metastases)
- Mononeuropathy:
  - DM
  - Compression
  - Infectious
  - Inflammatory
  - Iatrogenic

Tremor

Resting tremor:

- Parkinson's disease
- Holmes tremor
- Drug-induced tremor (e.g. antiseizure medication, lithium, chemotherapeutic agents)
- Functional tremor
- Essential tremor
- Peripheral neuropathy

Action tremor:

- Postural tremor:
  - Essential tremor
  - Exaggerated physiological tremor
  - Holmes tremor
  - Neuromuscular disorders
  - Functional tremor
  - Cerebellar tremor
  - Peripheral neuropathy
- Kinetic tremor:
  - Intention tremor (ataxic tremor):
    - Cerebellar tremor
    - Drug-induced tremor (e.g. antiseizure medication, lithium, chemotherapeutic agents)

- Essential tremor
    - Holmes tremor
  - Simple kinetic tremor:
    - Essential tremor
    - Functional tremor
    - Peripheral neuropathy
    - Cerebellar tremor
  - Task-specific tremor:
    - Functional tremor
    - Exaggerated physiological tremor
    - Essential tremor
- Isometric tremor:
  - Exaggerated physiological tremor
  - Orthostatic tremor

Altered gait

- Central:
  - Intoxication
  - Parkinson's disease
  - Huntington's disease
  - Cerebral ischaemia
  - MS
  - Friedreich's ataxia
  - Wernicke encephalopathy
  - Neurosyphilis
  - Hydrocephalus
  - MSA
- Peripheral:
  - Musculoskeletal
  - Mononeuropathy lower extremities
  - Chronic polyneuropathy
  - Radiculopathy
  - GBS

> Gait disorders can be classified into motor, sensory, sensorimotor, atactic, extrapyramidal and functional gait disorders.

Confusion (acute)

- Substance abuse:
  - Intoxication
  - Withdrawal symptoms
- Cerebral:
  - Delirium
  - Dementia
  - Cerebrovascular disease
  - Hypoxia
  - Postictal
  - Meningitis/encephalitis
  - Cerebral abscess
  - Wernicke encephalopathy
- Metabolic disorders:
  - Hypoglycaemia/hyperglycaemia
  - Sepsis
  - Thyrotoxicosis
  - Uraemia
- Drug-induced
- Functional

Transient neurological deficit

- Cerebral:
  - TIA
  - Transient focal neurological episodes (cerebral amyloid angiopathy (CAA))
  - Migraine
  - Transient tumor attacks
- Metabolic disorders:
  - Hypoglycaemia
  - Hyponatraemia, hypokalaemia/hyperkalaemia
- Functional neurological disorder

Central nervous system disorders

Traumatic disorders

Mild traumatic brain injury (TBI)

D Mild TBI is defined as an initial GCS score ≥13, post-traumatic anterograde amnesia <24h and post-traumatic loss of consciousness <30 min.

E 90% of all neurotraumas are mild TBIs

Ae
- Falls ⊕⊕, traffic accidents ⊕, violence ⊖, sports ⊖, work ⊖
- Depending on the type of trauma, diffuse or focal brain damage can occur: blow to the head (→ focal brain damage, see Table 51) and torsional motion (→ diffuse axonal injury (DAI) with minor cerebral capillary haemorrhage)

Hx Low-energy trauma, short-term consciousness ↓ (max. 30 min), post-traumatic amnesia (max. 24h), headache, nausea, vomiting, blurred vision, aversion to light (photophobia), aversion to sounds (phonophobia), tinnitus, hearing loss

PE GCS ≥13, disorientation, retrograde/anterograde amnesia, imprinting disorder, pupillary reflexes, focal neurological deficit, evidence of skull base fracture (spectacle haematoma, liquorrhoea, battle sign)

Dx Brain CT without contrast: cerebral contusion, SAH, subdural or epidural haematoma (see Table 35 for the indications for a brain CT)

Tx In-hospital observation if GCS <15, CT abnormalities, seizures, abnormal coagulation parameters, or neurological deficits

Conservative management (e.g. oral analgesics, antiemetics)

P Often full recovery within 7-10 days (post concussion syndrome)

! Note that current diagnostic decision has a high sensitivity, but low specificity in order to also diagnose asymptomatic patients → 90-95% no intracranial injury

	COUP INJURY	CONTRECOUP INJURY
D	Mild traumatic brain injury at impact site.	Mild traumatic brain injury opposite impact site.
Ae	Direct impact from an object while stationary	Acceleration-deceleration mechanism (e.g. moving head colliding with a stationary object)
Hx	Consciousness ↓, headache, dizziness, amnesia, nausea, vomiting, loss of strength, visual disturbances, sensory disturbances, girdling across abdomen or chest, clear fluid from ear or nose	
PE	Focal neurological deficits, localised directly below contact surface (see Figure 61)	Focal neurological deficits, diagonally across from contact surface, often localised at base of the skull (see Figure 61)
Dx	Brain CT: assess cerebral contusion and intracranial haemorrhage	
Tx	Apply ATLS, regularly monitor pupillary responses and GCS score for first 12h, symptomatic: treat pain and nausea	
P	• Most patients recover <6 mo • Generally no residual symptoms • 50% of patients have persistent post concussion symptoms after 3 months • Mortality <1%	
!	Post concussion symptoms: headache, fatigue, dizziness, insomnia, concentration and memory impairment	

Table 51 // Traumatic brain injury: coup-contrecoup injuries

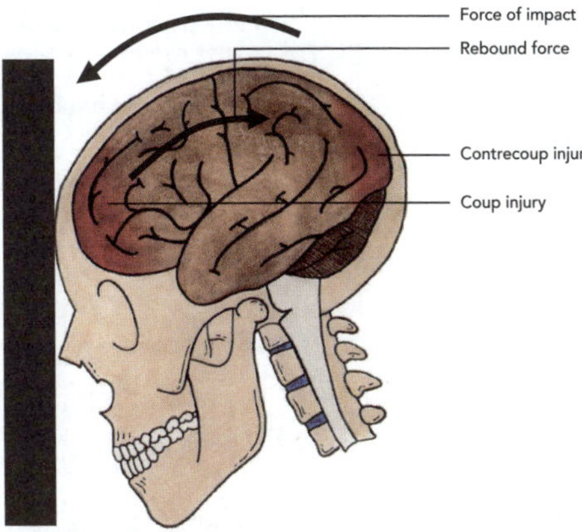

Figure 61 // Coup-contrecoup injuries

Moderate-severe TBI

D Moderate TBI is defined as a GCS score 9-12. Severe TBI is defined as GCS ≤8.

E 10% of all head injuries are moderate-severe TBIs

Ae Depending on the type of trauma, diffuse or focal brain damage can occur: blow to the head (→ focal brain damage) and torsional motion (→ DAI with minor cerebral capillary haemorrhage)

Hx High-energy trauma (HET), consciousness ↓, post-traumatic amnesia, seizures, headache, nausea, vomiting, blurred vision, photophobia, phonophobia, tinnitus, hearing loss

PE Hypertension, bradycardia, respiratory irregularities

GCS <13, disorientation, retrograde/anterograde amnesia, imprinting disorder, pupillary reflexes, focal neurological deficit, evidence of skull base fracture (spectacle haematoma, liquorrhoea, battle sign)

Dx
- Consider diagnostics as indicated per ATLS protocol (e.g. X-ray, e-FAST, lab)
- Brain CT: intraparenchymal and subarachnoid haemorrhage, haemorrhagic cerebral contusion, subdural/epidural haemorrhage, pinpoint haemorrhage (see Table 35 for the indications for a brain CT)
- Brain MRI: to rule out DAI (pinpoint haemorrhages)

Tx Apply ATLS, monitor vital signs, prevent secondary injury

Monitor and treat increased intracranial hypertension: osmotic agents IV (mannitol, hypertonic saline)

Consider neurosurgical intervention: hemicraniectomy

P Most patients recover <6 mo, 10% severely disabled (cognitive/motor), 3-5% vegetative state, mortality 33%

!
- Secondary cranial brain injury (subdural/epidural haematoma, focal oedema, herniation)
- Autonomic dysregulation (tachycardia, hypertension, tachypnoea, sweating, stretching cramps) in first days to weeks
- 3-5% post-traumatic epileptic seizures

Epidural haematoma

D An epidural haematoma is caused by bleeding from a meningeal artery between the skull and dura mater (see Figure 62).

E 8.2% of TBI

Ae HET, non-traumatic cause ⊝ (e.g. coagulopathy, vascular malformation, abscess, or surgical complication)

Hx Trauma mechanism, consciousness ↓ (with lucid interval), amnesia, headache, nausea, vomiting

PE Ipsilateral pupil dilation, pupils unreactive to light, seizures, contralateral hemiparesis

Dx Brain CT: convex (lens shaped) hyperdensity

Tx Surgical evacuation (emergent decompressive craniectomy or burr holes)

P Depending on severity, localisation, and time to intervention

!
- Frequently associated with skull fracture → infection risk
- Watch out for herniation!

The period of time that the victim is lucid before lapsing into unconsciousness is also called the **lucid interval**.

Subdural haematoma (SDH)

	ACUTE	CHRONIC
D	Acute haemorrhage between the dura mater and arachnoid mater, mostly combined arterial/venous.	Chronic haemorrhage between the dura mater and arachnoid mater from bridging vein (see Figure 62).
E	In 10-20% of severe TBI	Incidence 1.7-20.6:100,000
Ae	Trauma	Minor trauma (especially in the elderly and patients on oral anticoagulants)
R	Age 31-47, ♂, diffuse cerebral atrophy	Increased fall risk due to alcohol use disorder or old age, use of anticoagulants, old age (brain atrophy → vulnerable bridging veins that are more exposed → more likely to rupture after a minor blow, e.g. hitting head on kitchen cupboard)
Hx	Trauma, acute onset, consciousness ↓, headache, nausea, vomiting	No obvious trauma, insidious onset, initiative ↓, cognition ↓, drowsiness, confusion, behavioural changes, gradual neurological deficits, headache, incontinence
PE	Contralateral hemiparesis, consciousness ↓, increased intracranial pressure (anisocoria, cranial nerve palsy, ataxia, meningeal irritation, coma)	Insidious declining consciousness, focal neurological deficit
Dx	Brain CT: concave hyperdensity (see Figure 63)	
Tx	Wait-and-see for minor haemorrhage Reversal of anticoagulation, analgesics, antiemetics • Surgical decompression (e.g. burr hole drainage, decompressive craniectomy, or craniotomy) • Middle meningeal artery embolisation	
		Middle meningeal artery embolisation
P	Mortality 50% (esp. in elderly >65y)	Mortality rate 0-32%
!	Watch out for herniation!	

Table 52 // Acute vs. chronic SDH

Subarachnoid haemorrhage (SAH)

	TRAUMATIC	NON-TRAUMATIC
D	Haemorrhage between the arachnoid mater and the pia mater (see Figures 62 and 64).	
E	More common than non-traumatic type	Incidence 6-7:100,000 per year
Ae	Trauma	Aneurysm rupture (85%), perimesencephalic haemorrhage (10%), other causes (5%)
R	N/A	Age 35-65, ♀, positive family history (FHx), smoking, alcohol consumption, hypertension
Hx	• Asymptomatic (++) • Symptoms of mild traumatic head/brain injury: consciousness ↓, headache, nausea, vomiting	Thunderclap headache, 'popping' sensation, nausea, vomiting, prior physical exertion (25%)
PE	• Slight T ↑ Consciousness ↓, focal neurological deficits	
	Asymptomatic (++)	• BP ↑, hypoxaemia • Meningeal irritation several hours after onset • Fundoscopy: intraocular haemorrhage (Terson syndrome)
Dx	Brain CT: hyperdensity at the subarachnoid space, usually near a skull fracture or cerebral contusion (see Figure 64)	• Brain CT: hyperdensity at the subarachnoid space (often aneurysm near the circle of Willis) • LP: xanthochromia after 12h (if no CT <6h) • CTA: location of aneurysm
Tx	Apply ATLS Reversal of anticoagulation, analgesics, antiemetics Surgical treatment of additional intracranial damage upon indication	Bed rest Nimodipine to prevent ischaemia, analgesics Coil or clip aneurysm
P	Often benign, additional damage can impact the prognosis	Mortality 50%, 75% residual symptoms, high risk of recurrence without treatment
!	N/A	Watch out for secondary cerebral ischaemia, hydrocephalus, intracerebral haemorrhage, recurrent SAH

Table 53 // Traumatic vs. non-traumatic SAH

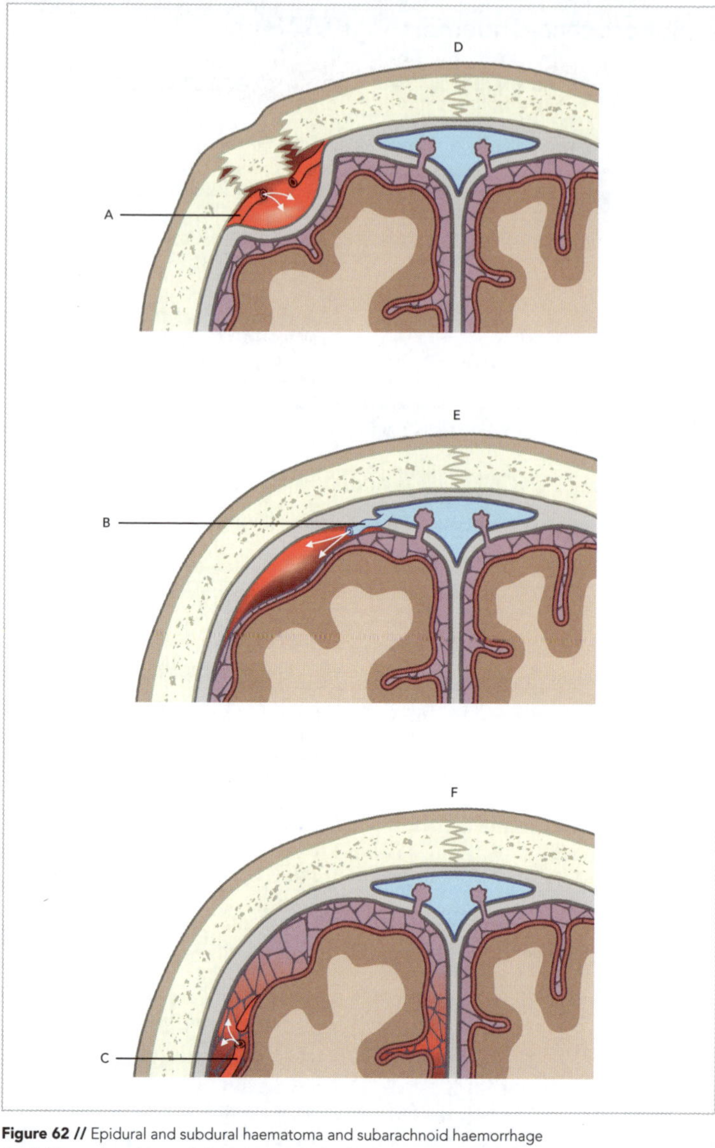

Figure 62 // Epidural and subdural haematoma and subarachnoid haemorrhage

A: Middle meningeal artery **B:** Bridging vein **C:** Cerebral artery **D:** Epidural haematoma **E:** Subdural haematoma **F:** Subarachnoid haemorrhage

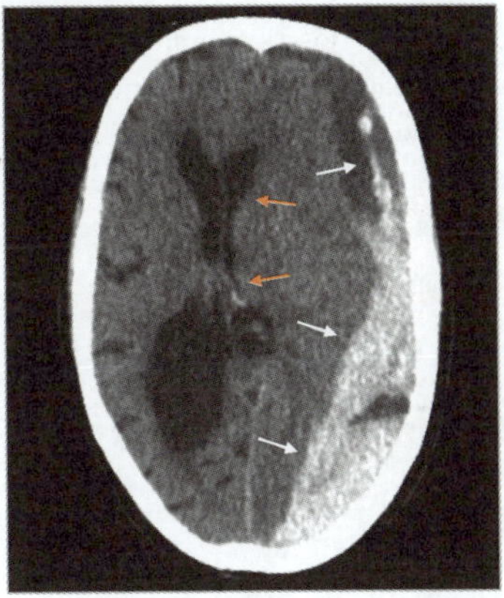

Figure 63 // Axial soft-tissue window setting: SDH along the left convexity (white arrows) with mass effect on the ventricular system (orange arrows). The acute component is hyperdense (white), the chronic component is hypodense (dark grey).

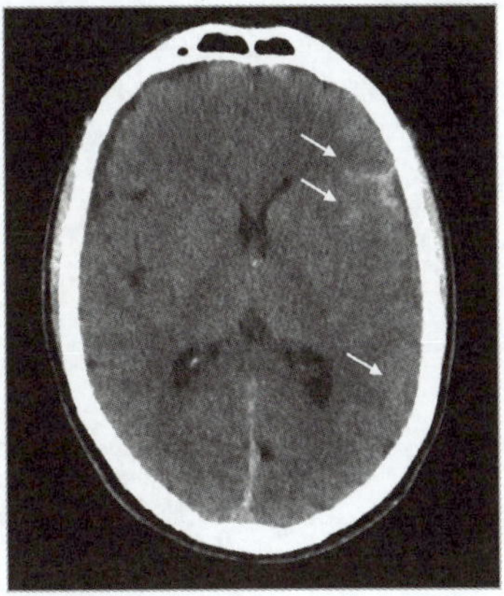

Figure 64 // Axial soft-tissue window setting: SAH with blood in the sulci (white arrows).

Skull base fracture

D In a skull base fracture, depending on the site of the fracture a distinction is made between anterior, middle and posterior skull base fractures (see Figure 65).

E Unknown

Ae Falls, HET

Hx Trauma mechanism, headache, nausea, vomiting, consciousness ↓

PE
- General: cranial nerve palsy
- Frontal skull base: nasal CSF leak, spectacle haematoma (see Figure 66)
- Middle skull base: auricular CSF leak, haematotympanum, facial nerve palsy, battle sign (see Figure 66)

Dx
- Brain CT, facial CT: visible fracture line, concomitant intracranial haemorrhage
- Nasal fluid leakage: test for β2-transferrin (positive if CSF)

Tx Apply ATLS, monitor vital signs, prevent secondary injury
Consider IV antibiotics (ABx)
Consider neurosurgical intervention in risk of herniation: hemicraniectomy

P Determined mainly by concomitant TBI, most patients recover <6 mo, 10% severely disabled (cognitive/motor), 3-5% vegetative state

Watch out for meningitis, cerebral abscess, hearing loss, loss of smell (olfactory nerve damage), vision loss (optic nerve damage), concomitant intracranial injury (subdural/epidural haematoma, focal oedema, herniation)

Battle sign: haematoma behind the ear caused by haemorrhage in the mastoid.

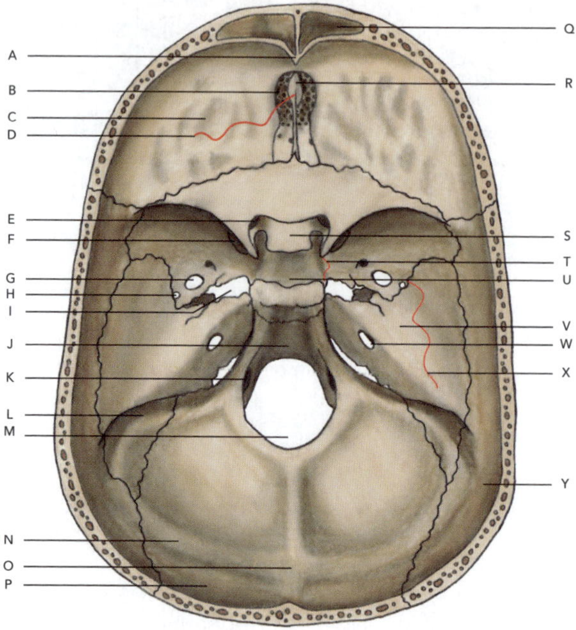

Figure 65 // Skull base fracture: types

A: Frontal crest **B:** Lamina cribrosa **C:** Frontal bone **D:** Fracture of the anterior cranial fossa **E:** Optic foramen **F:** Superior orbital fissure **G:** Foramen ovale **H:** Foramen spinosum **I:** Foramen lacerum **J:** Clivus **K:** Hypoglossal canal **L:** Groove for sigmoid sinus **M:** Foramen magnum **N:** Groove for transverse sinus **O:** Internal occipital protuberance **P:** Occipital bone **Q:** Frontal sinus **R:** Crista galli **S:** Tuberculum sellae **T:** Fracture of the sphenoid bone **U:** Sella turcica **V:** Temporal bone **W:** Internal auditory canal **X:** Fracture of the petrous part of the temporal bone **Y:** Parietal bone

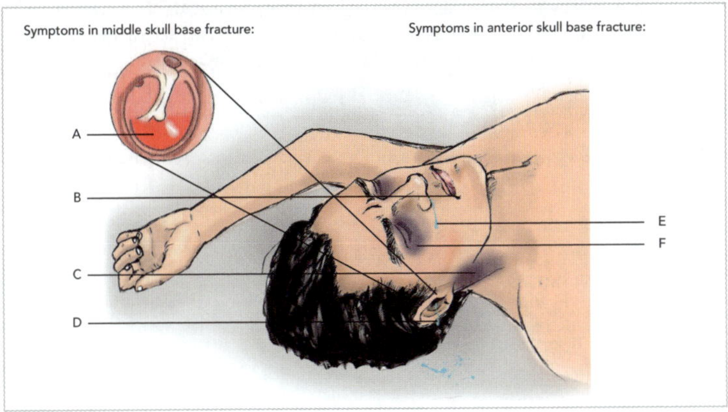

Figure 66 // Skull base fracture

A: Haematotympanum **B:** Facial nerve palsy **C:** Battle sign **D:** Auricular CSF leak **E:** Nasal CSF leak **F:** Spectacle haematoma (racoon eyes)

Herniation

D Herniation is the displacement of brain tissue to another compartment due to increased intracranial pressure. There are several different types (see Table 54 and Figure 67).

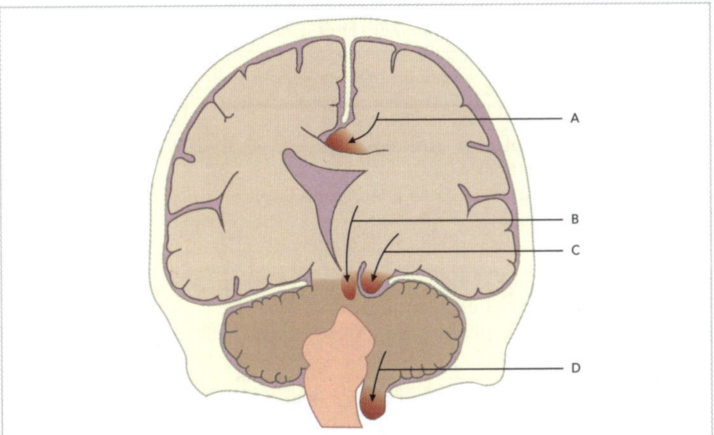

Figure 67 // Types of herniation

A: Subfalcine herniation **B:** Central transtentorial herniation **C:** Lateral transtentorial herniation **D:** Tonsillar herniation

	SUBFALCINE HERNIATION	CENTRAL TRANSTENTORIAL HERNIATION	LATERAL (UNCAL) TRANSTENTORIAL HERNIATION	TONSILLAR HERNIATION
D	Bifrontal ischaemia caused by brain tissue herniation below the falx.	Brain tissue moves from centrally above to below the tentorium, causing herniation.	Unioccipital or bioccipital ischaemia due to the herniation of temporal brain tissue under the tentorium.	Herniation of the cerebellar tonsils in the foramen magnum.
Ae	Unilateral, lateral SOL → brain tissue is pushed under falx cerebri	Diffuse cerebral oedema or acute hydrocephalus → brain tissue is pushed down by hiatus of the tentorium cerebelli		SOL/major infarction in cerebellar hemisphere → cerebellar tonsils are pushed through foramen magnum
Hx	Consciousness ↓, mental changes, urinary incontinence	Consciousness ↓		
PE	Paraparesis	Onset: consciousness ↓, miosis, Cheyne-Stokes respiration, normal or abnormal flexion in response to pain stimuli	Onset: ipsilateral oculomotor nerve palsy (widened pupil), contralateral hemiparesis	• Onset: neck pain, consciousness ↓ • Later: tetraparesis with respiratory depression
		Later: motor function ↓, no pupillary responses, no oculocephalic and oculovestibular responses, abnormal extension in response to pain, loss of autonomic functions		
Dx	Brain CT: to detect displaced and herniated brain tissue			
Tx	Temporary interventions: mild hyperventilation, osmotic agents IV (e.g. mannitol, hypertonic saline), dexamethasone (e.g. for oedema due to SOL) Surgical decompression by means of a hemicraniectomy			
!	Cushing's triad: hypertension, bradycardia and irregular breathing			

Table 54 // Types of herniation

Brain death

D Brain death is a complete, irreversible loss of brain and brainstem function. Cardiac activity and circulation can be maintained for some time with mechanical ventilation and medication.

E Unknown

Ae Severe TBI or herniation

PE EMV 3: no response to pain stimuli, abscence of brainstem reflexes, positive apnoea test, spinal reflexes remain intact in early stages

Dx
- Diagnostics to rule out hypothermia, hypotension, intoxication/medication, neuromuscular junction blockade, metabolic/endocrine disorders
- Isoelectric EEG, intracranial circulatory arrest (CTA), cerebral circulatory arrest (transcranial Doppler)

Tx No benefit of further medical or neurosurgical intervention

P Irreversible, circulatory arrest due to vascular tonus loss after days to weeks

! Determining brain death is relevant for organ donation

> **Clinical criteria of brain death:** EMV 3, apnoea, and absent brainstem reflexes (lack of spontaneous respiration, unresponsive pupils, absent corneal reflex, loss of eye movements, absent cough reflex, absent oculocephalic and oculovestibular reflex).

Cerebrovascular disease

Haemorrhagic stroke

D A haemorrhagic stroke includes bleeding from one of the intracranial blood vessels. Haemorrhagic strokes are less common than ischaemic strokes (ratio 1:4).

E Incidence 25:100,000 per year

Ae
- Vessel malformation, CAA, aneurysm, trauma, tumour → lobar haemorrhage → brain tissue compression → symptoms (see Figure 68 and 69)
- Chronic hypertension → weaker small vessels → basal ganglia haemorrhage (see Figure 69)

R Advanced age, hypertension, use of anticoagulants, coagulation disorders, CVT, presence of tumour/metastases, cocaine/amphetamine use (→ BP ↑), dark skin, Asian descent

Hx Signs of motor, sensory and other neurological deficits, headache, nausea, vomiting, neck stiffness, consciousness ↓

PE
- BP ↑
- Focal neurological deficit depending on localisation

Dx
- Brain CT: hyperdense lesion, hypodense oedema
- CTA intracranial arteries: detect aneurysm or vascular malformation

- Brain MRI: CAA (cerebral microbleeds, superficial siderosis), tumour
- Labs: coagulation disorder
- Consider LP in SAH: presence of xanthochromia (see Table 53)

Tx Admit to Stroke Unit, monitor vital signs, prevent complications

Treat underlying cause (lower BP, reversal of anticoagulation)

- Brainstem herniation/compression: emergency surgical evacuation of haematoma
- Arteriovenous malformation (AVM): surgical removal, embolisation, stereotactic radiotherapy
- Aneurysm: clip or coil

P
- Depends on aetiology, size and localisation
- Mortality high in first few days

> The typical patient with haemorrhagic stroke presents with acute onset focal neurological deficits suggestive of the site of the haemorrhage. In severe cases, the patient presents with symptoms of increased intracranial pressure and decreased consciousness.

Ischaemic stroke

D An ischaemic stroke is localised ischaemia of part of the brain, caused by vascular occlusion leading to neurological deficit. Ischaemic strokes are more common than cerebral haemorrhagic strokes (ratio 4:1). In a TIA, the deficit disappears within 24 hours. A TIA usually lasts several minutes to hours.

E Incidence 98.6:100,000 per year

Ae Atherosclerosis with thrombus formation (intracranial or extracranial), carotid stenosis, cardiac source of embolism (AF, prosthetic valve, endocarditis), arterial dissection, coagulation disorder, vasculitis, malignancy (see Figure 69)

R Hypertension, smoking, cardiovascular diseases (esp. AF and MI), DM, hyperlipidaemia, obesity, advanced age, ♂, bedridden, positive FHx, previous ischaemic stroke

Hx Sudden onset neurological deficits (e.g. motor, sensory, aphasia, vertigo) depending on the stroke territory (see Table 55), headache, usually not progressive

PE
- BP ↑, RR ↓/=
- Neurological deficits depending on supply region (see Table 55 and Figure 68)
- Score according to NIH Stroke Scale (NIHSS, see Appendix 4)

Dx
- Labs (exploratory): whole blood count, INR, aPTT, PT, kidney function, electrolytes, blood lipids (total cholesterol, LDL, HDL, triglycerides), glucose
- Brain CT without contrast: exclude haemorrhage, ischaemic area (hypodense area (see Figure 70) with loss of gray-white matter differentiation (visible after several hours), dense vessel sign ⊖)
- CTA and CTP (onset <24h): intra-arterial occlusion, infarct core and/or ischaemic penumbra, significant carotid stenosis
- Brain MRI: ischaemia (restriction of diffusion on DWI/ADC)
- Carotid duplex ultrasound: significant carotid stenosis
- Cardiac embolism evaluation: ECG and 24h cardiac monitoring (detect e.g. AF), echocardiography, ambulatory Holter monitoring

Tx
- Admit to Stroke Unit, monitor vital signs, prevent complications, treat underlying cause
- Secondary prevention: lifestyle interventions

Physiotherapy, speech therapy, occupational therapy

- IVT (rtPA, e.g. alteplase)
  - Onset <4.5h and no contraindications (see Table 42)
  - Onset between 4.5h and 12h, no contraindications and favourable characteristics on CTP (core-perfusion mismatch) or brain MRI (DWI-FLAIR mismatch)
  - Secondary prevention: platelet aggregation inhibitor, statin, antihypertensives and (in case of immobility) LMWH
- Intra-arterial/mechanical thrombectomy:
  - Onset <6h and confirmed and approachable thrombus location what may be as distal as the M3/M4 segment of the MCA, or the ACA or PCA
  - Onset between 6h and 24h, confirmed and treatable intra-arterial large vessel occlusion and favourable characteristics on CTP (core-perfusion mismatch) or MRI-brain (DWI-FLAIR mismatch)
- In case of intracranial herniation (malignant MCA infarction): hemicraniectomy
- Significant carotid artery stenosis (>50%): carotid endarterectomy <2 wk

P
- Mortality <1 mo: 13.5%, due to herniation, infections (especially pneumonia), cardiac sources
- Most recovery occurs <3 mo

! Complications: post IVT haemorrhage, aspiration pneumonia, malignant MCA infarction

The exact time window for extended IVT and mechanical thrombectomy may vary between countries.

Similar to a CTA and CTP, an MRI may be used to diagnose recent ischaemia. An MRI shows a DWI-FLAIR mismatch: a visible lesion on DWI, without a visible lesion on the FLAIR sequence.

The typical patient with ischaemic stroke is known to have cardiovascular risk factors and presents with acute onset hemiparesis, visual field defect and/or aphasia suggestive of the site of the occlusion.

Wallenberg's syndrome arises from a ischaemic stroke in the lateral part of the medulla oblongata. The syndrome often starts with sudden vertigo, vomiting, dysphagia, nystagmus, dysphonia and hiccups. Further symptoms are highly dependent on the affected structures.

OCCURENCE	ANTERIOR CEREBRAL ARTERY	MIDDLE CEREBRAL ARTERY	POSTERIOR CEREBRAL ARTERY	BASILAR ARTERY
(++)	Contralateral hemiparesis, leg > arm	Contralateral hemiparesis, contralateral central facial paresis, sensibility deficits deep > superficial	Homonymous hemianopsia	Tetraparesis, pseudobulbar paresis, horizontal gaze palsy, vertigo, nausea, nystagmus
(+)	Cognitive problems, frontal symptoms	Spasticity, ipsilateral head and gaze deviation, aphasia if located in language area, neglect if located in parietal lobe (right > left)	Behavioural disorders, memory disorders	Ataxia, consciousness ↓, irregular breathing if reticular formation is affected
(−)	Disorientation or apathy	N/A	Bilateral infarction → visual agnosia	Locked-in syndrome, Wallenberg's syndrome

Table 55 // Neurological deficits by supply region

Locked-in syndrome is a severe paralytic condition in which patients can only voluntarily perform vertical eye movements. However, they are not in a coma and are aware of their surroundings.

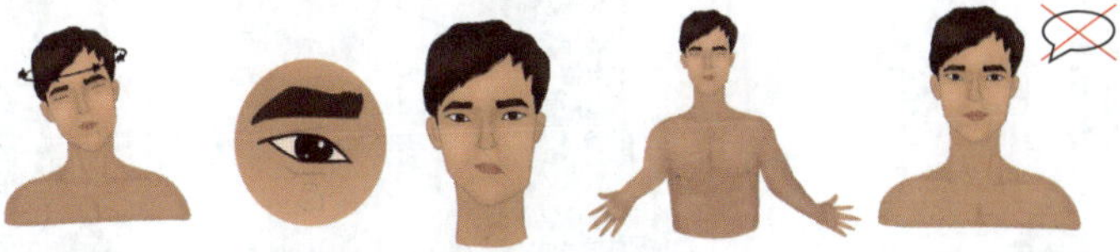

B: Balance: Sudden loss of balance?
E: Eyes: Sudden loss of vision?
F: Face: Facial asymmetry? Drooping mouth?
A: Arms: Can the patient raise both arms?
S: Speech: Incoherent or incomprehensible speech?
T: Time: Note what time the symptoms started and call the emergency line!

Figure 68 // BE-FAST rule

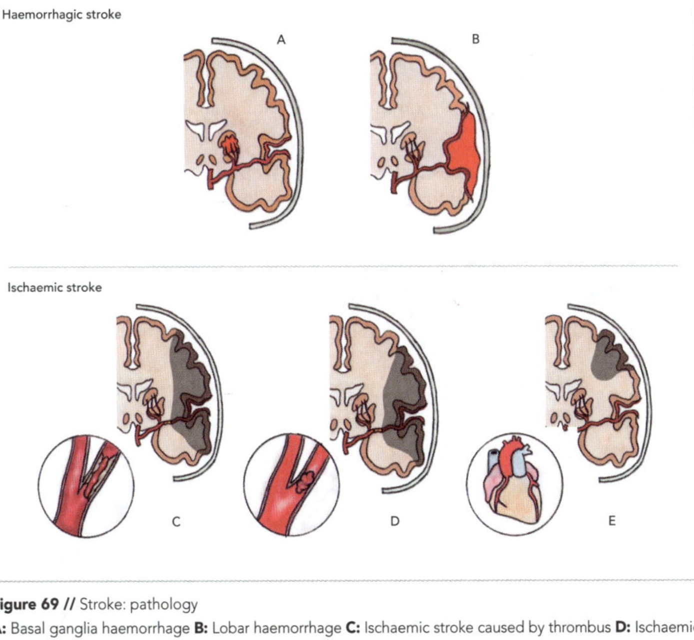

Figure 69 // Stroke: pathology

A: Basal ganglia haemorrhage **B:** Lobar haemorrhage **C:** Ischaemic stroke caused by thrombus **D:** Ischaemic stroke caused by embolus **E:** Ischaemic stroke caused by watershed infarctions

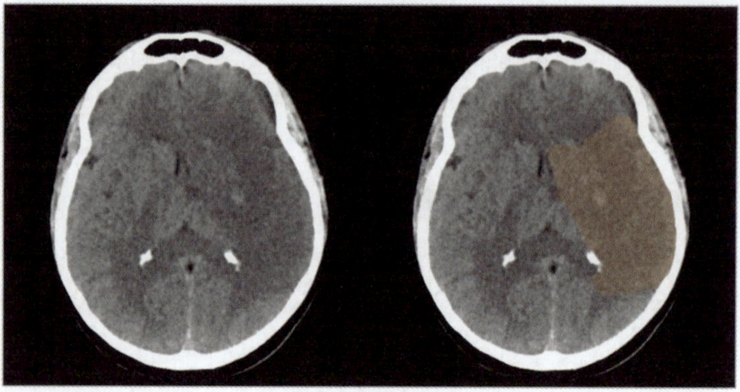

Figure 70 // CT showing hypodense area in left hemisphere consistent with ischaemic stroke

Cerebral venous thrombosis (CVT)

D CVT is a condition in which the blockage of a cerebral venous sinus by a thrombus can cause headache, increased intracranial pressure, seizures and focal deficit symptoms.

E Incidence 1-3:100,000

Ae Coagulation disorders, trauma, infections, inflammation, LP, neurosurgical intervention

R ♂:♀ = 1:4, coagulation disorder, oral contraception, pregnancy, postpartum period, infection, malignancy, traumatic brain injury

Hx Gradual or acute headache, vomiting ⊖, seizures, diplopia

PE
- Visual field defects, consciousness ↓ ⊖, focal neurological deficits
- Fundoscopy: papilloedema

Dx
- Brain CT without contrast: venous haemorrhage (cortically or peripherally localised, cashew nut sign (juxtacortical intracerebral haemorrhage resembling a cashew nut)), ischaemic area (venous origin), vasogenic oedema, dense sinus/vein sign
- CTV or MR venography (MRV): sinus filling defects, empty delta sign (triangular filling defect superior sagittal sinus)
- Labs: detect genetic or non-genetic coagulation disorders, infection, or inflammation
- LP: CSF pressure ↑

Tx
- LMWH SC or heparin IV in acute phase, switch to OAC if clinically stable (VKA or DOAC)

- Antiseizure medication in case of seizures

Endovascular thrombectomy

P Mortality 2-5%, risk of recurrence 2-4%

! Haemorrhagic transformation eventually occurs in 30-40% of venous infarctions

Infectious disease

	BACTERIAL MENINGITIS	VIRAL MENINGITIS
D	Rapidly progressing bacterial infection of the meninges with a high mortality rate.	Viral infection of the meninges usually characterised by a benign course and spontaneous recovery.
E	• Incidence Western countries: 0.7-3:100,000 • Incidence Sub-Saharan Africa: 0-40:100,000	Incidence 3-15:100,000 per year
Ae	• Haematogenous spread, direct contiguous spread from adjacent anatomic structures (e.g. otitis media, sinusitis), foreign objects, or after surgical procedure • Newborns: Escherichia coli, group B streptococci, Listeria monocytogenes • Children aged <5: Neisseria meningitidis, Streptococcus pneumoniae, Haemophilus influenzae • Children aged >5 and adults: Streptococcus pneumoniae, Listeria monocytogenes, Neisseria meningitidis, Haemophilus influenzae, Staphylococcus aureus, TB • Immunocompromised patients: Streptococcus pneumoniae, Neisseria meningitidis, Haemophilus influenzae, Listeria monocytogenes, Cryptococcus, TB, Nocardia	• Herpes simplex virus (HSV) type 1 and 2, VZV, enteroviruses, parechovirus, measles, mumps, flaviviruses • Immunocompromised patients: HIV, HSV type 2, CMV, VZV, EBV, enterovirus, arbovirus, JC virus
R	Age <5, DM, alcohol use disorder, immunodeficiency or use of immunosuppressants, recent cranial trauma, CSF leak, otitis, sinusitis or pneumonia, IV drug use	Seasonal variation (summer and fall: enterovirus, arbovirus, parechovirus), childhood
Hx	Rapid clinical deterioration, fever, headache, nausea (++), vomiting (++), photophobia (++), consciousness ↓	Nausea, vomiting, headache, generalised muscle pain, fever
PE	T ↑↑ (++), positive glass test: rash does not fade under pressure (see Figure 71) • Meningeal irritation: neck stiffness, Kernig's and/or Brudzinski's sign (see Figure 39) • Confusion, consciousness ↓, coma, neurological deficits, epileptic seizures, papilledema • Meningococcal sepsis: petechiae (see Figure 71), purpura	T ↑, exanthema • Meningeal irritation: neck stiffness (−) • No loss of consciousness or neurological deficit

Table 56A // Bacterial and viral meningitis

	BACTERIAL MENINGITIS	VIRAL MENINGITIS
Dx	• Labs: complete blood count, CRP ↑, glucose, electrolytes, kidney function, liver function • LP: CSF culture and PCR, CSF analysis (see Table 57) • Brain CT: before performing LP if there is potential intracranial pressure ↑ → risk of cerebellar/tonsillar herniation	
	• Labs: coagulation (if signs of petechiae or purpura) • Blood culture	• Labs: serology
Tx	• Dexamethasone IV before administering ABx (mortality and morbidity of pneumococcal meningitis ↓) • ABx IV, select ABx based on age and presence of risk factors • Targeted ABx based on culture results • Meningococcal meningitis: reportable, isolation, start close contacts on prophylactic treatment (rifampicin or ciprofloxacin)	Symptomatic For suspected herpes virus: aciclovir IV
P	• Depends mainly on time until start of treatment • Subacute (++), rapidly progressive • Mortality of meningococcal meningitis 4-7%, mortality of pneumococcal meningitis 20-30% • Residual symptoms: hearing loss, cognitive decline, sluggishness	• Spontaneous recovery within 1-2 wk • Long-term symptoms: anxiety, depression, neurocognitive dysfunction
!	• Watch out for sepsis and respiratory failure • Anticipate acute hydrocephalus and cerebral oedema	Mumps meningitis: parotitis, orchitis

Table 56B // Bacterial and viral meningitis

CSF PARAMETER	BACTERIAL MENINGITIS	VIRAL MENINGITIS
Pressure	↑	=/↑
Cells	↑↑	↑
Protein	↑	=/↑
Glucose	↓ (<60% of blood glucose)	=
Colour	Cloudy, purulent	Bright, opalescent

Table 57 // CSF-based differentiation between bacterial and viral meningitis

The typical patient with bacterial meningitis is ill and presents with a high fever, headache, photophobia and vomiting that arose within a day. Patients usually present with decreased consciousness and meningeal irritation.

The classical triad fever, neck stiffness, and altered mental state only occurs in 41-51% of the patients with bacterial meningitis. Absence of these characteristics do not rule out bacterial meningitis.

In case of suspected bacterial meningitis, start dexamethasone and ABx immediately after taking blood cultures. Before performing an LP perform a CT if necessary.

- In patients with history of CNS disease, new onset seizure, focal neurological deficits, immunocompromised state, moderate to severe impaired consciousness or papilloedema, perform brain CT to rule out displacement of intracranial structures before performing LP.
- LP may lead to herniation if internal structures have been displaced.
- CN III and CN VI palsy is suggestive of increased intracranial pressure.

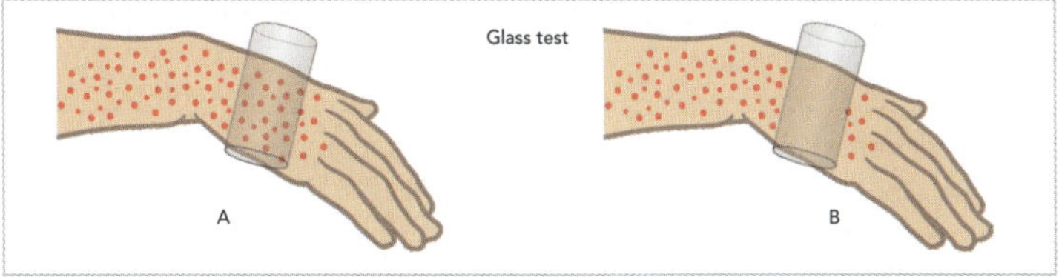

Figure 71 // Glass test: if the rash does not fade under pressure, the patient has petechiae. This may indicate meningococcal meningitis or sepsis.
A: Rash does not fade under pressure: petechiae **B:** Rash fades under pressure: not petechiae

Viral encephalitis

D Viral encephalitis is a subacute viral inflammation of the brain.

E Incidence: 19.3:100,000 person-yr, Western countries < South Asia and Sub-Saharan Africa

Ae
- HSV type I, VZV, arboviruses, rabies virus, EBV, measles, mumps
- Immunocompromised patients: HSV, VZV, arboviruses, CMV, human herpesvirus 6 (HHV-6)

R Immunocompromised, unvaccinated

Hx
- Malaise, fever, headache, nausea, vomiting, photophobia, seizures, focal neurological deficits
- Specific finding in herpes simplex encephalitis: personality changes, hallucinations, cognitive impairment and word-retrieval difficulty, fever, epilepsy, paresis

PE • T ↑

- Consciousness ↓ (−), focal neurological deficits (−), seizures (−)
- LP: CSF pleocytosis, PCR, CSF culture
- Brain MRI: T2 hyperintensity of affected cortex and white matter

Tx Symptomatic

For suspected herpes virus: aciclovir IV

P Course varies from mildly to rapidly progressive with mortality or residual symptoms

! Herpes simplex encephalitis mortality 60-70% (untreated)

Cerebral abscess

D A cerebral abscess is a localised collection of pus in the brain that gives site-specific focal neurological deficits.

E Europe incidence 0.4-1.3:100,000, developing countries 8% of intracranial masses

Ae
- Parameningeal focus of infection (otitis media, sinusitis), haematogenous (jaw abscess, bacterial endocarditis), penetrating brain trauma/neurosurgical surgery, sepsis
- Pathogens: streptococci, staphylococci, Escherichia coli, Proteus mirabilis
- In immunocompromised patients: Aspergillus fumigatus, Candida albicans, Cryptococcus neoformans, Listeria, Nocardia, TB, Toxoplasmosis
- After dental treatment

Hx Depending on site and size: headache, fever, consciousness ↓, nausea, vomiting, cognitive impairment

PE Fever (++)

- Focal neurological deficit (++), seizure (+), neck stiffness (−)
- Fundoscopy: papilloedema (−−)

Dx
- Labs: leukocytes ↑, ESR ↑, CRP ↑
- Blood culture: detect and identify bacterial pathogen
- Brain CT with IV contrast: hypodense lesion with peripheral enhancement
- Brain MRI with IV contrast: T2 hyperintense lesion with peripheral enhancement, and diffusion restriction within the abscess

Tx Treat underlying cause

ABx IV, dexamethasone

Aspiration (stereotactic guided) or exision in case of a large abscess → consult neurosurgeon

P 1-year mortality 20%

!
- 25% of patients have residual symptoms (especially focal epilepsy)
- LP may cause brain tissue displacement and herniation
- Cerebral abscesses are underdiagnosed on noncontrast CT

Autoimmune encephalitis

D Autoimmune encephalitis is an immune-mediated inflammatory response of the CNS, usually with a (sub)acute presentation of fluctuating or progressive neuropsychiatric symptoms.

E Prevalence 13.7:100,000 in the USA, unknown for other countries

Ae Autoantibodies targeted against extracellular proteins (e.g. NMDAR, LGI1, CASPR2, GABABR, AMPAR, DPPX, GlycineR, GABAAR, IgLON5, mGluR1, mGluR5), or intracellular proteins (e.g. Hu, Yo, CV2, Ri, Ma1, Ma2, amphiphysin, Tr/DNER, KLHL-11, GFAP). An underlying malignancy is often the cause of the development of the antibodies (paraneoplastic syndrome).

R Ovarian teratoma, thymoma, mammary carcinoma, small cell lung cancer, lymphoma, testicular carcinoma

Hx Behavioural changes, short-term memory loss, speech disorder, seizures, lethargy, autonomic symptoms, pain, double or blurred vision, weakness, sensory disorder, movement disorder

PE Cognitive problems, psychiatric symptoms (++), autonomic symptoms

Consciousness ↓, nystagmus, opsoclonus, ataxia, dysarthria, movement disorders (e.g. catatonia, chorea, dyskinesia, dystonia, stereotypic movements, orofacial dyskinesias)

Dx
- Labs: presence of autoantibodies (less sensitive compared to CSF)
- LP: presence of autoantibodies, lymphocytes =/↑ and protein =/↑, IgG index ↑, and the presence of oligoclonal bands in 50% of the patients
- Brain MRI: often normal in early disease course, abnormalities in >50% (cortical thickening, T2/FLAIR signal ↑ in the medial temporal lobe, abscence of diffusion restriction and haemorrhage)
- EEG: epileptic or slow activity
- Screening for the presence of an underlying malignancy

Tx Treatment of underlying cause (e.g. in case of malignancy multidisciplinary treatment of the tumour)

Methylprednisolone IV, optionally with IVIG

	ANTI-NMDA RECEPTOR ENCEPHALITIS	ANTI-LGI1 ENCEPHALITIS
D	Autoantibodies against the GluN1 subunit of the NMDA receptor, causing internalisation of the receptor.	Antibodies against leucine-rich glioma-inactivated 1 (LGI1) region of the voltage-gated potassium channel (VGKC) complex.
E	Incidence 1.5:1,000,000 per year	Incidence 0.83:1,000,000 per year

Table 58A // Two most common subtypes of autoimmune encephalitis

	ANTI-NMDA RECEPTOR ENCEPHALITIS	ANTI-LGI1 ENCEPHALITIS
Ae	Tumour (ovarian teratoma ⊕), herpes simplex encephalitis	Tumour (thymoma) in 5%
R	♀:♂ 4:1, young adults	♂ 60%, 60-70 years
Hx	• Prodromal headache and/or fever • Psychiatric symptoms ⊕ incl. anxiety, agitation, bizarre behaviour, hallucinations, delusions, disorganised thinking, psychosis • Sleep disorder, memory deficits, seizures	Memory deficits, cognitive problems, sleep disorder
PE	Autonomic instability (e.g. hyperthermia, fluctuations of blood pressure, tachycardia, bradycardia, hypoventilation) Consciousness ↓, language dysfunction (e.g. mutism), catatonic features, dyskinesia	Cognitive dysfunction, faciobrachial dystonic seizures
Dx	• Labs: antibodies against GluN1 • LP: CSF antibodies against GluN1, lymphocytic pleocytosis, oligoclonal bands • EEG: slow disorganised activity ⊕, epileptic activity, extreme delta brush • Brain MRI: normal or non-specific findings (e.g. abnormal FLAIR or T2 hyperintensity in the medial temporal lobe, cerebral/cerebellar cortex, basal ganglia, and brainstem) • Abdominal CT: screening for an underlying malignancy	• Labs: hyponatraemia ⊕, antibodies against LGI1 • LP: antibodies against LDI1 in CSF (testing in both CSF and serum is recommended), pleocytosis • Brain MRI: medial temporal lobe hyperintensity, unilateral hippocampal lesions
Tx	Methylprednisolone IV, optionally with IVIG Tumour resection in case of underlying neoplasm	
P	Mortality 10%, relapse occurs in 15-24%	Mortality 2.8%, relapse occurs in 1/3 of the patients
!	Usually causes diffuse encephalitis	Usually causes limbic encephalitis

Table 58B // Two most common subtypes of autoimmune encephalitis

Headache and facial pain

Headache

D Headache is a common complaint at all ages. In most cases, the condition is harmless (see Table 59 and Figure 72).

	MEDICATION OVERUSE HEADACHE	MIGRAINE	TENSION-TYPE HEADACHE
D	Headache induced by chronic medication use.	Recurring attacks of throbbing unilateral headache.	Oppressive headache that feels like a band around the head.
E	Prevalence 1-1.5%	Prevalence 14-15% of all headache diagnoses, ♀>♂	Prevalence 26%
Ae	• Genetic predisposition to a different type of headache, behavioural factors and central sensitisation • Other type of primary headache	• Neurovascular, exact aetiology unknown • Spreading depolarisation across brain → trigeminal nerve activation → meningeal inflammation → headache • Neuronal depolarisation in the brain → vasoconstriction → compensatory vasodilatation → throbbing headache due to sudden increase in blood flow	Idiopathic, no link to stress or muscle tone
R	• ♀, psychiatric comorbidity (anxiety, depression), especially with migraine • Most common for opioids, aspirin, caffeine, paracetamol, triptans or NSAIDs	• Positive FHx, seizures in periods of rest, ♀:♂ = 3:1 • Highly individualised triggers: alcohol, sleep deprivation, stress, disappearance of stress, menstruation	♀
Hx	• Daily headaches • Headache when waking up • Accompanied by weakness, nausea, difficulty concentrating, memory problems, irritability	• Average frequency 2x/mo • Episodes: unilateral, frontotemporal, throbbing/pulsating, moderate-serious pain • Duration 4-72h • Worsens with exertion • Nausea, vomiting, photophobia, phonophobia • Preceded by aura (usually visual) or prodromal symptoms (changes in taste and smell, yawning)	• Bilateral, tight/clenching, band-like mild-moderate pain, mild nausea • Duration: 30 min-7d

Table 59A // Types of headaches and facial pain

	MEDICATION OVERUSE HEADACHE	MIGRAINE	TENSION-TYPE HEADACHE
PE	Criteria: • Excessive drug use: simple analgesics (paracetamol and NSAIDs) >15 days/mo for >3 mo, triptans/opiates >10 days/mo for >3 mo • Headache ≥15 days/mo in a patient with pre-existing headache syndrome • No other explanation	Criteria migraine: • Headache 4-72h (untreated) • ≥2 of: moderate or severe, unilateral, throbbing pain, worsening with exertion • ≥1 of: photophobia and phonophobia, or nausea and/or vomiting Criteria aura: • ≥2 attacks with: - ≥1 fully reversible symptoms (e.g. sensory, motor, speech/language, visual, brainstem, retinal) - ≥3 of the following: ≥1 aura symptoms spread gradually over ≥5 min, ≥1 unilateral, individual aura symptoms last 5-60 min, ≥2 occur in succession, ≥1 aura symptoms are positive (e.g. scintillations, pins and needles), aura accompanied or followed by headache (within 60 min) • Not better accounted for by another headache diagnosis	Criteria: • >10 episodes, <180 days/yr or headaches <15 days/mo • Headache 30 min-7d • 2 of: oppressive pain, bilateral pain, mild/moderate pain, not worsening with exertion • No nausea • Not photophobia plus phonophobia (only one) • No other explanation
Tx	Education, psychological support, abrupt cessation of excessive drug use (gradual tapering in case of opioid use) • Symptom relief: long-acting NSAIDs (if this was not the excessively used medication) • Treat withdrawal symptoms if applicable	• Acute treatment: paracetamol, NSAIDs, triptans, anti-emetic (metoclopramide) • Prophylactic (>2 episodes/month): propranolol, metoprolol, candesartan, botulinum toxin, calcitonin gene-related peptide (CGRP) inhibitors, valproic acid, topiramate, amitriptyline	Education • Paracetamol, NSAIDs • Prophylactic: amitriptyline or nortriptyline, physiotherapy with biofeedback

Table 59B // Types of headaches and facial pain

	MEDICATION OVERUSE HEADACHE	MIGRAINE	TENSION-TYPE HEADACHE
P	72% have no symptoms after 1-6 mo or a >50% decrease in symptoms after quitting	• Episodes can occur frequently for an extended period of time before a prolonged absence • Can progress into a chronic form	Chronic intermittent course
!	Withdrawal symptoms for 2-10 days	• Migrainous infarction in the occipital lobe • Status migrainosus • Migraine aura status	• Chronic use of analgesics may perpetuate headaches • Concomitant depressive symptoms

Table 59C // Types of headaches and facial pain

	TEMPORAL ARTERITIS	CLUSTER HEADACHE	TRIGEMINAL NEURALGIA/NEUROPATHY
D	A type of vasculitis that mainly affects the carotid artery and its branches, including the temporal artery (formerly known as giant cell arteritis).	Severe episodic pain around the eye with autonomic symptoms.	Unilateral repetitive short episodes of pain occurring in the area of a trigeminal nerve branch.
E	Incidence age >50 10-50:100,000 per year	Prevalence 0.1% of the population	Incidence 4-8:100,000 per year
Ae	Idiopathic inflammatory disease, possibly accompanied by occlusion of the carotid nerve and its branches (e.g. temporal artery)	Suspected hypothalamus activation → activation of the trigeminal-autonomic reflex	• Trigeminal nerve compression • Primary: neurovascular conflict • Secondary to MS, inflammation, tumour (e.g. schwannoma, meningeoma)
R	Age >50, ♀:♂ = 3:1	♀:♂ = 1:3-4, smoking, head trauma, positive FHx	Age >50

Table 59D // Types of headaches and facial pain

	TEMPORAL ARTERITIS	CLUSTER HEADACHE	TRIGEMINAL NEURALGIA/NEURO-PATHY
Hx	• Unilateral temporal or occipital headache • Jaw claudication, scalp tenderness, visual disturbances, general malaise • Frequently associated with polymyalgia rheumatica	• Occurs in bouts lasting weeks to months • Episodes characterised by very severe, piercing unilateral pain behind the eye (see Figure 72), lasting 15-180 min, 1 attack per 2 days up to 8/day • Ipsilateral autonomic symptoms (watering, red eye, rhinorrhoea or nasal congestion, Horner's syndrome) • Restlessness or agitation • Triggers: alcohol, histamine, nitrates, low blood oxygen, tension, sleep deprivation	• Neuralgia: attacks lasting several sec to min with severe shock-like pain, trigeminal neuralgia (tic douloureux) in the nerve's supply region (ophthalmic nerve, maxillary nerve, mandibular nerve), unilateral, several times a day • Neuropathy: esp. sensory disorders • Triggers: touching specific triggerpoints, cold air, jaw movements
PE	• Unilateral and temporal, red, swollen, tender temporal artery and skin • Absent pulsations of the temporal artery • Fundoscopy: cotton wool spots, optic nerve ischaemia	Non-contributing	Hyperaesthesia of affected nerve branch
Dx	• Labs: ESR ↑↑, Hb ↓, CRP ↑, leukocytes ↑, platelets ↑ • Temporal artery biopsy: vasculitis with mononuclear cell infiltrate, possibly granuloma formation and giant cells • Duplex temporal artery: halo sign	Non-contributing	Brain MRI to rule out secondary causes of trigeminal neuralgia

Table 59E // Types of headaches and facial pain

Temporal arteritis often occurs alongside polymyalgia rheumatica: symmetrical pain/stiffness in shoulders, hips and neck, worsening with physical exertion.

Horner's syndrome is caused by sympathetic fibre function loss. The clinical features are a combination of ptosis, miosis and anhidrosis on the ipsilateral side of the lesion.

	TEMPORAL ARTERITIS	CLUSTER HEADACHE	TRIGEMINAL NEURALGIA/NEURO-PATHY
Tx	Prednisone (oral), administer higher dose via IV for ophthalmic symptoms	• Acute treatment: inhale 100% O_2 (≥12L/min, 15 min), sumatriptan SC or nasal spray • Prophylactic: verapamil, pitozifen, lithium	Carbamazepine, gabapentin, pregabalin, amitriptyline for neuropathy Jannetta surgery (trigeminal nerve decompression), coagulation of Gasser's ganglion (Sweet procedure), Gamma knife stereotactic surgery
P	• Depends on presence of visual disturbances, thoracic aneurysm/aortic dissection and ischaemia • Start treatment → rapid symptom ↓ • Irreversible vision loss (optic nerve ischaemia, 10%)	80% still have complaints after 15 years	Intermittent course, condition usually prompts an intervention
!	Amaurosis fugax, thoracic aneurysm, frequent exacerbations	Chronic paroxysmal hemicrania: ♀>♂, more frequent attacks, shorter duration, responds well to indomethacin	Watch out for MS in younger patients, especially with bilateral symptoms

Table 59F // Types of headaches and facial pain

Alarm symptoms in acute headache:

- Acute onset of severe headache
- Consciousness ↓
- Vomiting and nausea (except migraine)
- Combination of headache with BP ↑ and HR ↓
- Combination of headache with neurological deficit
- Diplopia
- Pain worsens during pressure-increasing moments
- Fever
- Focal neurological deficits
- Neck stiffness
- Vomiting in the morning
- Age >50

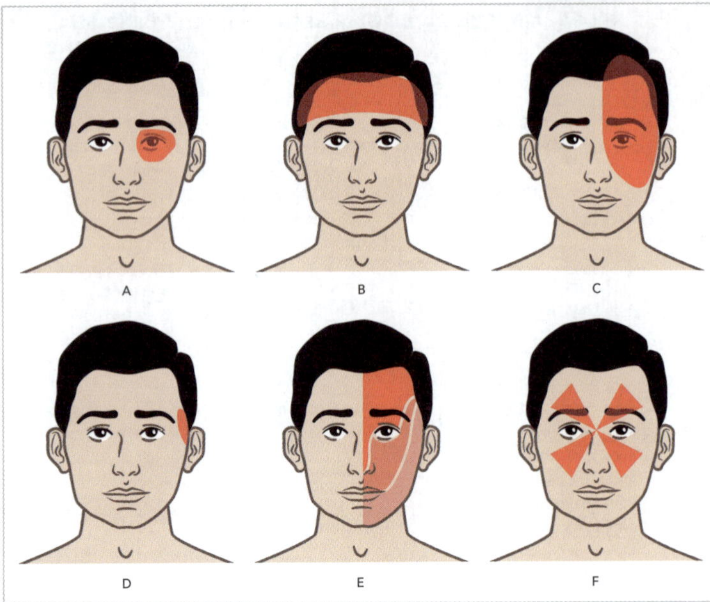

Figure 72 // Localisation of pain in different headache types
A: Cluster headache **B:** Tension headache **C:** Migraine **D:** Temporal arteritis **E:** Trigeminal neuralgia **F:** Sinusitis

Peripheral vestibular disorders

Benign paroxysmal positional vertigo (BPPV)

D BPPV is the most common peripheral vestibular disorder that causes intermittent, brief episodes of dizziness provoked by head motion. Three types can be distinguished: posterior ⊕⊕, horizontal ⊕ or anterior ⊖ semicircular canal BPPV.

E Prevalence 10-140:100,000, often >60 years, ♀:♂ 2.4:1

Ae
- Idiopathic ⊕⊕, secondary cause ⊕ (e.g. surgery, trauma, migraine, infection, or prolonged recumbent position)
- Pathophysiology: accumulation of otoliths in the semicircular canals/cupula → activates vestibular system

R ♀, age >60, head trauma, vestibular neuritis

Hx Intermittent vertigo (<1 min) induced by head motion, nausea, vomiting, imbalance ⊖, absence of focal neurological deficits

PE • HINTS test (signs for peripheral vertigo): HIT shows corrective saccade, unidirectional/rotational nystagmus, no vertical skew deviation
- Posterior BPPV: Dix-Hallpike manoeuvre → vertigo, rotational and up-beating nystagmus
- Anterior BPPV: Dix-Hallpike manoeuvre → vertigo, rotational and down-beating nystagmus
- Horizontal BPPV: supine head roll test → vertigo and horizontal nystagmus

Dx Not indicated

Tx • Posterior/anterior BPPV: (modified) Epley manoeuvre (see Figure 73) or Semont manoeuvre, Brandt-Daroff exercises
- Horizontal BPPV: Gufoni manoeuvre or Barbecue roll manoeuvre

P Recurrence <1 year (+)

! A vertebrobasilar stroke can mimic symptoms of BPPV → look for brainstem findings to differentiate between these two diseases

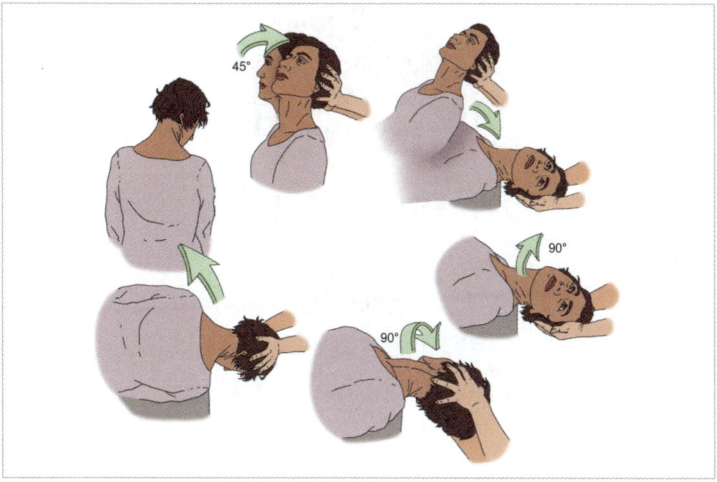

Figure 73 // Epley manoeuvre

Ménière's disease

D Ménière's disease is an auditory-vestibular disease with episodic vertigo, hearing loss and tinnitus.

E Incidence 17-200:100,000

Ae Idiopathic

R Genetic predisposition, recent viral infection, autoimmune disease

Hx Vertigo episodes (20 min - 12h), fluctuating hearing loss, low-frequency tinnitus, sensation of fullness in affected ear, nausea, vomiting (see Figure 74)

PE
- Rotatory or horizontal nystagmus
- Tuning fork test: lateralisation to unaffected ear (Weber), bilateral positive (Rinne)

Dx Audiometry (perceptive/sensorineural hearing loss), vestibular function testing

Tx
- Symptomatic: benzodiazepine, antiemetics
- Chronic: consider betahistine/diuretics (low evidence)

P Fluctuating trajectory of vertigo for years, long-term hearing loss (++), imbalance in the elderly (+)

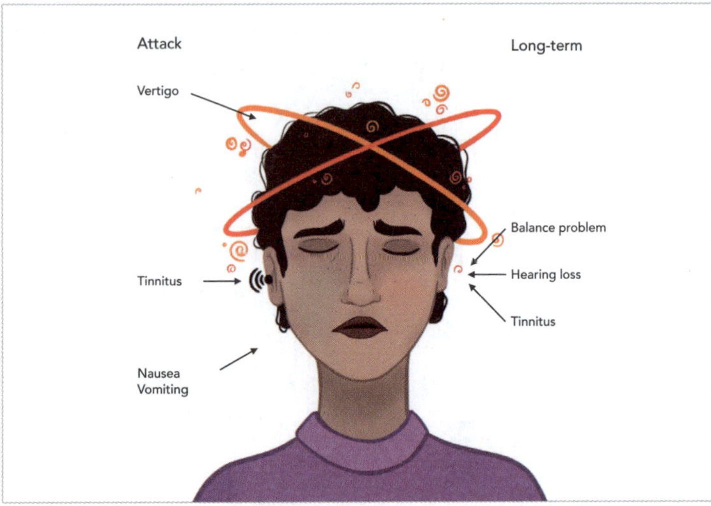

Figure 74 // Ménière's disease: clinical features

Vestibular neuritis

D Vestibular neuritis is the inflammation of the vestibular nerve and is associated with acute onset of vertigo with nausea and vomiting for several days.

E Incidence: 3.5-15.5:100,000

Ae Exact aetiology unknown, hypothetically triggered by viral infection or ischaemia of the anterior vestibular artery

R Age 30-60, prior viral infection

Hx Abrupt continuous vertigo >24h, nausea, vomiting, imbalance, no neurological or cochlear symptoms

PE HINTS test: HIT shows corrective saccade, unidirectional/rotational nystagmus, no vertical skew deviation. Absence of focal neurological deficits.

Dx Not indicated

Tx Vestibular rehabilitation therapy

Symptomatic: antiemetics

P Self limiting

Epileptic disorders

Generalised onset seizures

D In generalised onset seizures, seizure activity starts simultaneously over both sides of the brain. Types of primary generalised seizures are absences, myoclonic, atonic, tonic, and tonic–clonic seizures (see Table 60).

E Prevalence 65 million patients worldwide with epilepsy, lifetime prevalence generalised onset seizures 7.6 per 1,000 persons

Ae
- Genetic predisposition, intoxications or alcohol withdrawal
- Na^+ and Ca^{2+} ion channel dysfunction → overexcitable neurons → electrical discharge in the brain

R Positive FHx, prematurity

	TONIC-CLONIC SEIZURES	ABSENCE SEIZURES
D	Epileptic seizure beginning with tonic muscle contractions followed by rhythmic twitches (see Figure 75).	Brief, frequent attacks of impaired consciousness that the patient cannot remember afterwards (see Figure 76).
E	25% of all epilepsy patients	Prevalence 6.3-8:100,000
Ae	Genetic predisposition	Genetic predisposition
	Intoxications or alcohol withdrawal	
R	• Age of onset 3-25 • Alcohol use disorder • Seizure triggers: e.g. missed medication, alcohol, drugs, fever, sleep deprivation, flashing lights, stress	Age of onset 3-10, ♀

Table 60A // Two most common types of generalised onset epileptic seizures

	TONIC-CLONIC SEIZURES	ABSENCE SEIZURES
Hx	• Emotional distress in hours or days preceding seizure • Epigastric rising sensation, sensory perceptions (sound, flashes of light, smell of burnt rubber), anxiety or derealisation may precede aura • More commonly: acute onset without warning signs and occasional scream (chest muscle and diaphragm contraction) • Tonic phase with bilateral muscle contractions (stiffening) and loss of consciousness (typically 10-30 sec) • Clonic phase with bilateral twitches or jerking and open eyes (typically 30-60 sec) • Postictal somnolence, confusion, agitation • Average seizure duration 2-3 min	• Seizures lasting 5-10 sec with acute impaired consciousness, blinking, absent gaze, lack of reactions, no memory of seizure, may be provoked by hyperventilation • Atypical seizures: longer seizures with gradual onset and end, with possible muscle tone change in the extremities
PE	Postictal confusion, lateral tongue bite, Todd paresis, urinary incontinence	Normal neurological exam
Dx	• EEG: generalised spikes and spike waves during seizure, normal or sporadic spikes and spike waves between seizures • Brain MRI: to rule out underlying pathology	• EEG: generalised 3 Hz spike waves during seizure, elicited by hyper-ventilation, flashing lights, fatigue • Brain MRI: to rule out underlying pathology
Tx	Treat or avoid seizure triggers Valproic acid, lamotrigine or levetiracetam	Ethosuximide, valproic acid or lamotrigine
P	±70% of adults are seizure-free within 20y	• 75% spontaneous remission <20y after disease onset • <10% develop tonic-clonic seizures
!	• Injuries, status epilepticus • If age of onset >25 → suspected focal to bilateral tonic clonic seizure with underlying cause • Sudden unexpected death in epilepsy (SUDEP)	• Later age of onset → greater risk of tonic-clonic seizures • Impact on school performance

Table 60B // Two most common types of generalised onset epileptic seizures

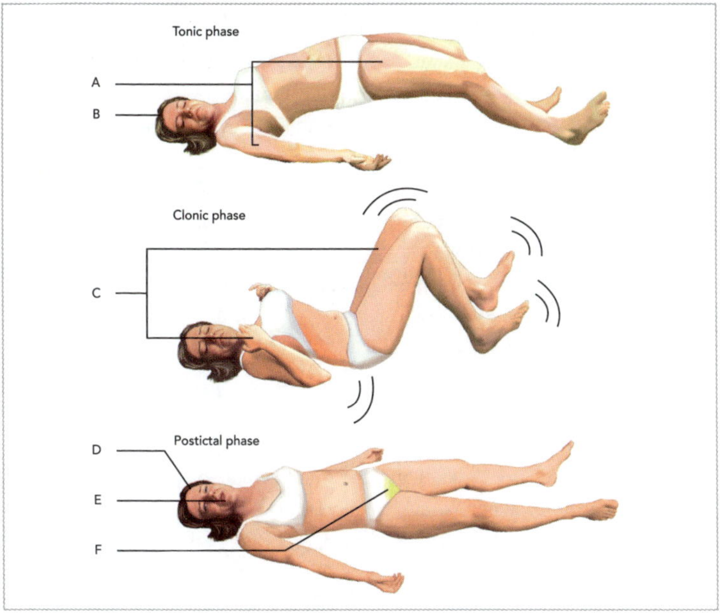

Figure 75 // Generalised onset epileptic seizure: tonic-clonic
A: Bilateral and symmetrical muscle contractions **B:** Loss of consciousness **C:** Bilateral and symmetrical clonic muscle contractions **D:** Confusion **E:** Lateral tongue bite **F:** Urinary incontinence

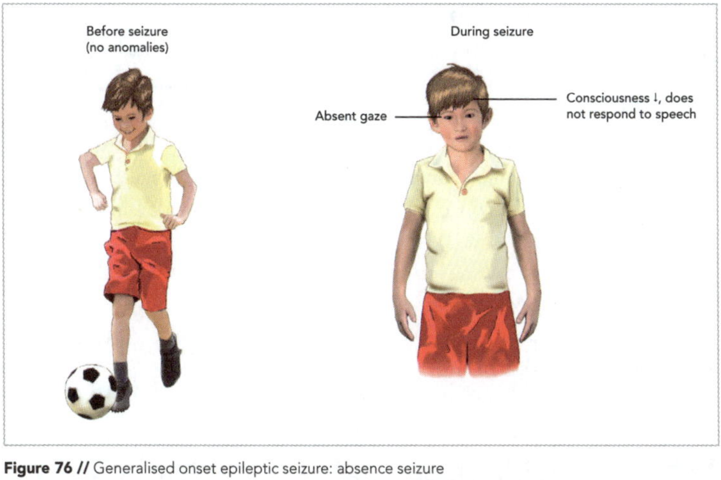

Figure 76 // Generalised onset epileptic seizure: absence seizure

Status epilepticus

D A generalised convulsive status epilepticus is a generalised onset epileptic seizure lasting >5 min or multiple seizures without recovery of consciousness, and total duration >5 min. A focal status epilepticus lasts >30 min.

E Incidence 1.3-81:100,000 per year

Ae Any cause leading to an epileptic seizure

R Tonic-clonic seizures, structural brain abnormality, alcohol, stress, infection, drugs, sleep deprivation

Hx
- Like epileptic seizures, but continuous or recurrent
- Loss of consciousness >5 min

PE Depends on type of epilepsy

Dx Ictal EEG: generalised spikes and spike waves

Tx
1. Seizure >5 min: midazolam or lorazepam
2. Not effective >5 min: repeat midazolam or lorazepam
3. Not effective >5 min: high dose antiseizure medication IV (e.g. phenytoin, levetiracetam, or valproic acid)
4. Not effective <20 min: midazolam, propofol, or thiopental IV (often in ICU)

P Mortality 3-50%

! Watch out for aspiration pneumonia, cardiac complications, cerebral oedema due to anoxia

Focal seizures with preserved awareness

D Focal seizures with preserved awareness are caused by acute and synchronous firing of cerebral neurons in one part of one hemisphere. No loss of consciousness occurs.

E Prevalence 65 million patients worldwide with epilepsy

Ae Metabolic disturbances (metabolic seizures) or structural brain abnormalities: trauma, tumour, infection, congenital, vascular malformation, stroke

R
- Adults > children
- Seizure triggers: e.g. missed medication, alcohol, drugs, fever, sleep deprivation, flashing lights, stress

Hx Depends on localisation (see Table 61)

PE Preserved consciousness, Todd paresis

Dx
- MRI to rule out structural cerebral abnormalities
- Ictal EEG: focal epileptic discharges

Tx Treat underlying cause, treat or avoid seizure triggers

- Antiseizure medication (e.g. carbamazepine, lacosamide, lamotrigine, levetiracetam, oxcarbazepine, valproic acid)
- Consider surgical removal of seizure focus

P Depends on underlying aetiology. High recurrence risk if unknown aetiology.

! Focal to bilateral tonic-clonic seizures, focal status epilepticus

Todd paresis: temporary paresis (<1 day) after an epileptic seizure.

	PRECENTRAL CORTEX	SUPPLEMENTARY MOTOR CORTEX	FRONTAL CORTEX
D	Also known as Jacksonian seizures.	Also known as adversive seizures.	N/A
E	Unknown		
Hx	• Start in finger or mouth • Spread to hand, arm, ipsilateral trunk and occasionally to the leg in 20-30 sec	• Jerky turning of the head, eyes and trunk • Speech arrest	• Automatisms, especially of the lower extremities (cycling or walking movements) • Often while sleeping

Table 61A // Localisation of focal epilepsy

	PARIETAL CORTEX	OCCIPITAL CORTEX	TEMPORAL CORTEX
D	N/A		
E	Rare		Most common
Hx	Sensory seizures (paraesthesias) that may spread to adjacent parts of the body or progress to motor symptoms	Visual symptoms (distortions and colours) in visual field contralateral to the focus	• Auditory, olfactory or gustatory hallucinations • Autonomic symptoms • Cognitive symptoms (déjà vu or jamais vu: anxiety attacks)

Table 61B // Localisation of focal epilepsy

Focal seizures with impaired awareness

D Focal seizures with impaired awareness occur when the initial focal epileptic discharge spreads across multiple lobes of the brain, resulting in decreased awareness.

E 36% of all epilepsy patients

Ae Structural brain abnormality (temporal ⊕⊕, frontal ⊕, parietal ⊖, occipital ⊖): trauma, tumour, infection, congenital, vascular malformation, stroke, metabolic disturbances

R
- Adolescence, hippocampal sclerosis, CNS infection, AVM, tumour
- Seizure triggers: e.g. missed medication, alcohol, drugs, fever, sleep deprivation, flashing lights, stress

Hx
- Aura (epigastric rising sensation, visual symptoms, olfactory symptoms, derealisation/déjà vu)
- Followed by consciousness ↓ with routine actions such as chewing, lip smacking, dressing
- Absent impression
- Presence of a seizure trigger (e.g. sleep deprivation)
- Frequent generalised seizures during sleep

PE Short-term postictal confusion, Todd paresis

Dx
- MRI to rule out structural cerebral abnormalities
- Ictal EEG: unilateral or bilateral paroxysms

Tx Treat underlying cause, treat or avoid seizure triggers

Antiseizure medication (e.g. carbamazepine, lacosamide, lamotrigine, levetiracetam, oxcarbazepine, valproic acid)

Consider surgical removal of seizure focus

P
- Depends on underlying aetiology. High recurrence risk if unknown aetiology.
- If hippocampal sclerosis → progressive epilepsy that becomes therapy-resistant

!
- Injuries and aspiration during a seizure
- SUDEP
- Focal to bilateral tonic-clonic seizures, focal status epilepticus

> The typical patient with an epileptic seizure presents with shaking and jerking symptoms, a lateral tongue bite, urinary incontinence and postictal confusion.

Febrile convulsions

D Febrile convulsions, also known as febrile fits, are generalised epileptic seizures that occur in children during a fast-rising fever (see Figure 77).

E Prevalence in Western countries 2-5% of all children, incidences vary worldwide up to 14%

Ae Upper respiratory tract infection (++), gastrointestinal infection (+), childhood maculopapular disease (–), pneumonia (–), meningitis (–)

R Age 6 months-5 years, positive FHx, previous febrile convulsion

Hx Generalised tonic or tonic-clonic seizure lasting <15 min, one convulsion during fever episode, postictal confusion followed by full recovery

PE
- T ↑, HR ↑, cold, lymphadenopathy, drowsiness (postictal)
- Identify febrile focus: pulmonary, abdominal, urogenital, neurological

Neurological examination to rule out meningitis

Dx Consider tests to confirm focus of infection or in case of severe illness: urinalysis (to rule out urinary tract infection), PCR (to rule out viral upper respiratory tract infection), chest X-ray (to rule out pneumonia), LP (to rule out meningitis), blood culture (to detect pathogen)

Tx Wait-and-see

Benzodiazepines if a febrile convulsion >3 min

P Recurrence rate 30%, risk to develop epilepsy 1-1.5% for typical febrile convulsions and 4-15% for atypical febrile convulsions

!
- EEG is not indicated for typical febrile convulsions nor does it predict recurrence
- Consider meningitis in children with a fever lasting >24h prior to seizure

- **Typical (simple) febrile convulsion:** generalised, one convulsion per fever episode, lasting <15 min in children aged 6 mo to 5y.
- **Atypical (complex) febrile convulsion:** focal characteristics, multiple convulsions per fever episode lasting >15 min.

Antipyretics, e.g. paracetamol, reduce fever but do not prevent febrile convulsions. Many parents believe they do, so it is important to explain.

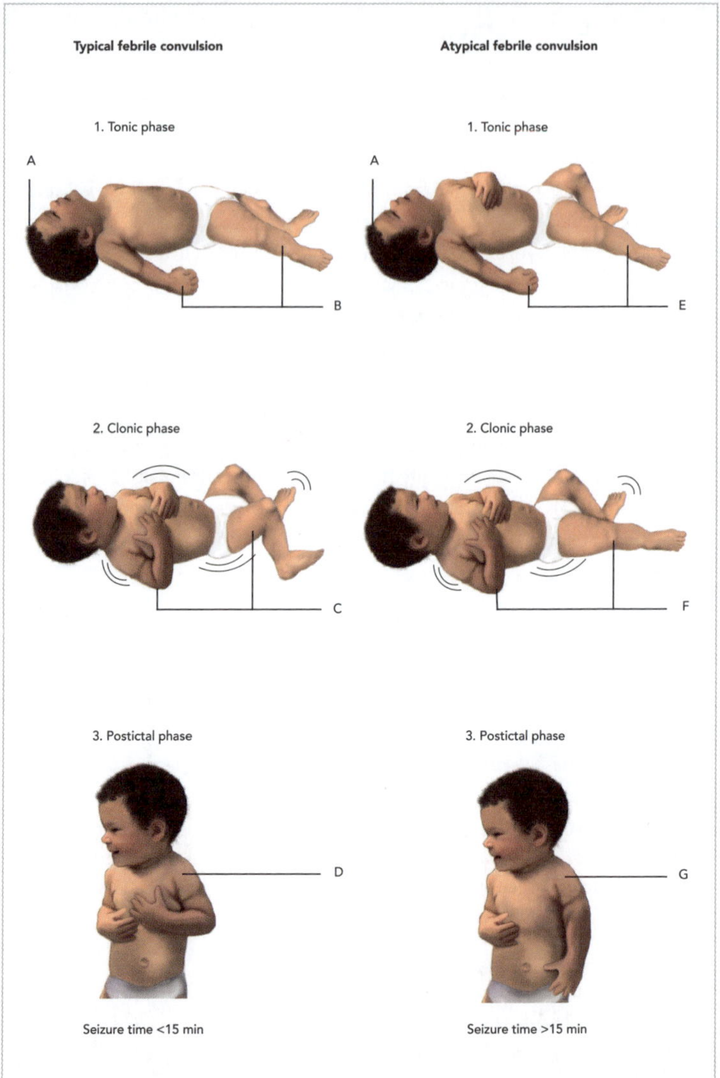

Figure 77 // Febrile convulsions: typical and atypical

A: Fever (>38°C) **B:** Bilateral and symmetrical muscle contractions **C:** Bilateral and symmetrical muscle contractions **D:** Full recovery without residual symptoms **E:** Asymmetric muscle contractions **F:** Asymmetric muscle twitching **G:** Deficit symptoms (e.g. difficulty moving, talking)

Hydrocephalus

D Hydrocephalus is a neurological disorder characterised by dilation of the ventricular system caused by an abnormal buildup of CSF in the ventricles of the brain. There are two main types of hydrocephalus: obstructive hydrocephalus with blockage of the CSF flow within the ventricular system, and communicating hydrocephalus with blockage of the CSF after it exits the ventricles (see Figure 78).

E Live birth prevalence ±85:100,000

Ae
- Obstructive hydrocephalus: ventricular haemorrhage, tumour, stenosis, vascular malformation, Chiari malformation
- Communicating hydrocephalus: occlusion of arachnoid granulations due to meningitis or SAH
- Blocked CSF circulation or resorption → CSF pressure ↑ → dilated ventricular system
- Normal pressure hydrocephalus (NPH): CSF absorption probably ↓

R ♂, positive FHx, neural tube defects, CNS malformations, CNS infections, CNS tumours

Hx Headache, vomiting, cognitive impairment, urinary incontinence, gait disorders, blurred vision

PE Consciousness ↓, slow pupillary responses, upgaze vertical gaze paresis, papilloedema, gait disorders (unsteady gait, swaying)

Dx
- Brain CT/MRI: dilated ventricular system, increased callosal angle, transependymal oedema, and a potential cause of obstruction of CSF flow (e.g. intraventricular haemorrhage, tumour, Chiari malformation, aqueduct stenosis)
- For NPH a high volume LP with 10-min walking test before and after LP: positive if >20% decrease in number of steps or seconds

Tx Treat underlying cause

CSF drainage: external ventriculocardial or ventriculoperitoneal drain, surgical: ventriculostomy if obstructive

P Depends on underlying cause

Hakim's triad is a set of three characteristic clinical symptoms of NPH: reversible memory impairment, urinary incontinence and gait disturbances.

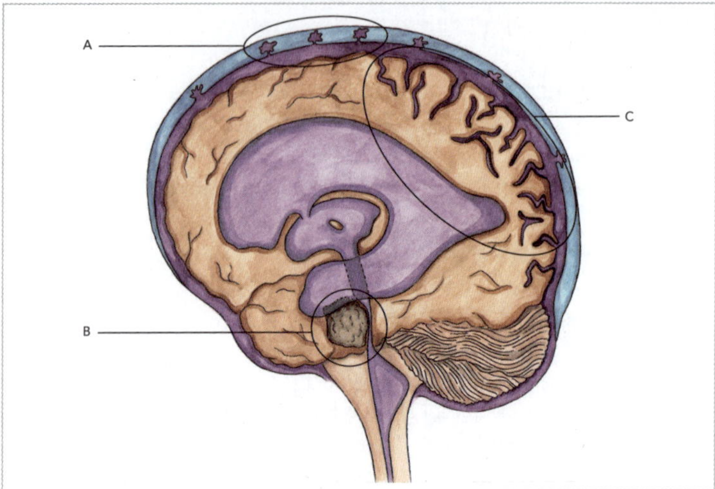

Figure 78 // Hydrocephalus

A: Communicating hydrocephalus secondary to narrowed/occluded arachnoid granulations **B:** Obstructive hydrocephalus secondary to tumour **C:** Cerebral atrophy leading to CSF space enlargement (hydrocephalus ex vacuo)

Oncology

Glioma

D A glioma is the most common primary malignant tumour of the CNS and arises from glial tissue (astrocytic, oligodendroglial and ependymal), see Figure 81. The WHO classifies gliomas (grades I-IV) based on depth of invasion and degree of malignancy (see Table 62). Gliomas rarely metastasise, but do invade surrounding tissue.

E Incidence 6:100,000 per year

Ae
- Astrocytoma: isocitrate dehydrogenase (IDH) mutation, intact 1p/19q
- Oligodendrogliomas: IDH-mutation, 1p/19q-codeletion
- Glioblastoma: IDH-wild type
- Ependymoma: neurofibromatosis type 2, zinc finger translocation associated (ZFTA) fusion-positive, yes-associated protein 1 (YAP1) fusion-positive

R PMHx: radiotherapy head/neck area

Hx Headache, vomiting (due to increased intracranial pressure) (++), epilepsy (+), behavioural changes, mood disorders, focal neurological deficits

PE
- Neurological deficits linked to tumour site

- Fundoscopy: papilloedema secondary to increased intracranial pressure

Dx
- Brain CT: iso-hypodensity, occasionally with mass effect and vasogenic oedema
- Contrast brain MRI: glioblastomas are often characterised by thick, irregular enhancement with central necrosis, frequently with surrounding oedema. Low-grade gliomas often appear as hyperintensities on T2 sequences and may be fully or partially enhanced.
- Histology of stereotactic biopsy
- Molecular biomarkers: e.g. IDH, 1p/19q, O6-methylguanine-DNA methyltransferase (MGMT), p53

Tx
- See Table 62
- Multidisciplinairy treatment approach (neurologist, neurosurgeon, oncologist, radiotherapist)
- Gliomas (except for grade 1 astrocytomas) have a diffuse growth pattern → radical resection or curative treatment not possible. Adjuvant chemoradiation is necessary.
- Wait-and-see approach is warranted in patients aged <40 with a small, non-enhancing tumour and a single epileptic seizure as sole clinical symptom
- Deep or strategic localised gliomas (thalamus, mesencephalon, brainstem) are unresectable. Only a biopsy is possible to obtain a tissue diagnosis.

Symptomatic: dexamethasone, antiseizure medication

P See Table 62

! In patients who have undergone radiotherapy, it may be challenging to differentiate tumour progression from radionecrosis based on imaging

> Intracranial tumours may be surrounded by oedema on radiological imaging. The exact cause of the oedema is unknown.

	GRADE I: low-grade	GRADE II: diffuse low-grade astrocytoma or oligodendroglioma	GRADE III: anaplastic glioma	GRADE IV: glioblastoma
T	• Dexamethasone for cerebral oedema • Antiseizure medication for epilepsy			
	Wait-and-scan approach Surgical resection: grade I gliomas are surgically curable. Grade II gliomas require surgical resection with radiological follow-up.		Surgical resection, adjuvant radiotherapy and chemotherapy (temozolomide), radiological follow-up	
P	10y survival rate: 50%		Median survival: • Astrocytoma 3-4y • Oligodendroma >7y	Median survival 6-12 mo, MGMT methylation improves survival

Table 62 // WHO classification of gliomas

Intracranial meningioma

D An intracranial meningioma is a tumour arising from the meninges (see Figure 81). Based on parameters including mitotic count, infiltration and biological behaviour, meningiomas are classified into three WHO grades: I (benign, 78-81%), II (atypical, 15-21%), III (malignant or anaplastic, 1-4%). Grade II and III meningiomas can recur.

E Incidence 6:100,000 per year

Ae
- Genetic predisposition: chromosome 22 deletion (locus of neurofibromatosis type 2 (NF2) gene)
- Often arises sporadically from arachnoid cells

R Head/neck radiotherapy, genetic predisposition: NF2, tumour growth during pregnancy/exposure to exogenous sex hormones, ♀, peak age 40-70, ionising radiation

Hx
- Asymptomatic (++)
- Headache, vomiting (due to elevated intracranial pressure) (+)
- Epilepsy (+), behavioural changes, cognitive impairment, symptoms consistent with obstruction of CSF circulation (see Hydrocephalus)
- Focal neurological deficits

PE Focal neurological deficits based on tumour location

Dx
- Brain MRI
  - T1: isointense or hypointense lesion relative to grey matter (often with dural tail sign) and contrast enhancement (see Figure 79)
  - T2: isointense or hyperintense lesion relative to grey matter and hyper-

intense surrounding oedema (see Figure 80)

- Histological biopsy: confirm meningioma

Tx Asymptomatic or slow-growing (<10% growth in 1y): annual/semi-annual check-up (wait-and-scan)

- Resection if symptomatic/growing (>10%), consider adjuvant radiotherapy and/or chemotherapy (for grade III meningioma or incompletely resected grade I and II meningioma)
- Inaccessible or smaller lesions: stereotactic radiotherapy

P
- 5y survival rate of atypical meningiomas: 73%
- 5y survival rate of anaplastic meningiomas: 42%

! Most meningiomas are asymptomatic and discovered by chance

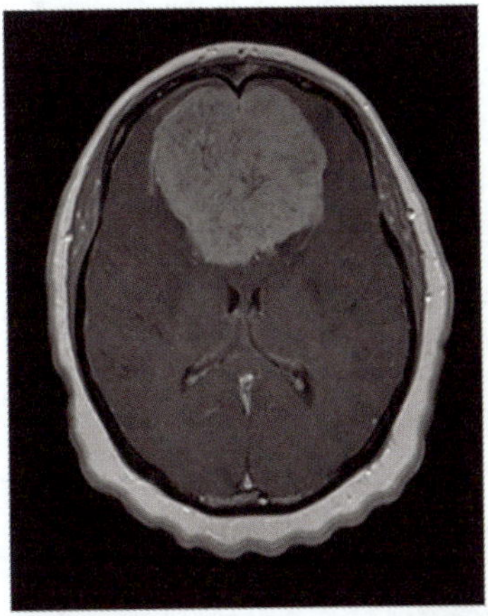

Figure 79 // Transverse section of a T1-weighted MRI showing frontal intracranial meningioma with contrast (meningioma is enhanced)

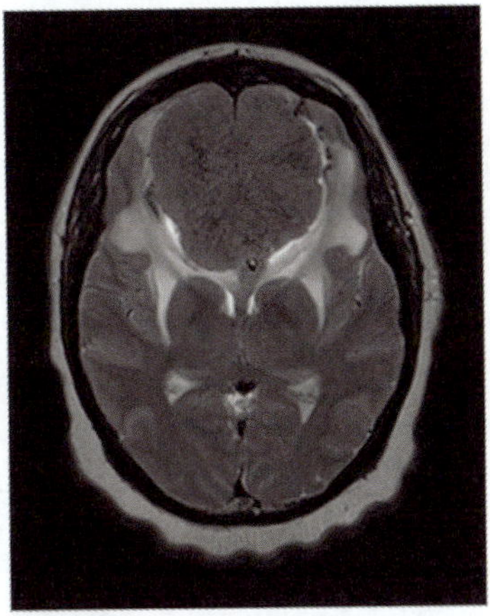

Figure 80 // Transverse section of a T2-weighted MRI showing frontal intracranial meningioma (oedema is enhanced)

Spinal tumours

D Spinal tumours are classified by location (see Figure 81). Epidural tumours are usually metastases and are not discussed here. Intradural tumours are often primary tumours and are located extramedullary (e.g. meningeoma, neuroma). Intramedullary tumours are a distinct group of spinal cord tumours, often of glial type (e.g. astrocytoma, ependymoma).

E Incidence 1-2.5:100,000 per year

Ae Idiopathic

Hx • Local back pain, sometimes radiating pain, lying down → pain ↑ (++)
• Urinary/faecal incontinence, impotence
• Motor/sensory deficit symptoms

PE Progressive spinal cord injury, motor and/or sensory deficits, hyper-reflexia

Dx • Spinal MRI: detect tumour (radiographic features vary per tumour type)
• Consider histopathology: confirm tumour cells and type through biopsy

Tx Surgical resection with spinal stabilisation
In case of incomplete resection: adjuvant chemotherapy

P • Survival rate depends on tumour type
• Benign, extramedullary tumour: neurological deficits often recovers fully
• Intramedullary tumour: recovery depends on deficits before surgery and type of tumour, full recovery from spinal cord injuries is rare

! Preferred location of intramedullary tumours: thoracic (adults), cervical (children and adolescents)

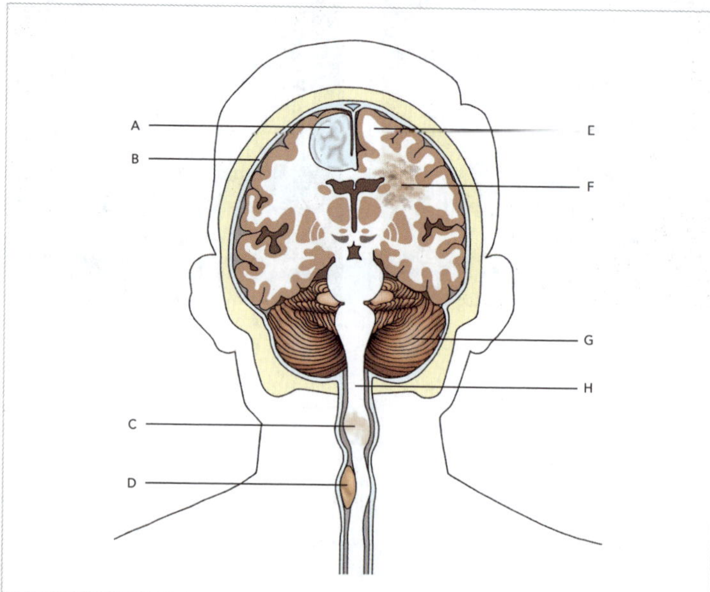

Figure 81 // Glioma, meningioma, spinal cord tumours
A: Intracranial meningioma **B:** Meninges **C:** Intradural intramedullary spinal cord tumour **D:** Intradural extramedullary spinal cord tumour **E:** White matter **F:** Glioma **G:** Cerebellum **H:** Start of spinal cord

Vertebral metastases

D Vertebral metastases are bone metastases located in the vertebral column caused by haematogenous dissemination of cancer cells. Epidural extension can lead to nerve root entrapment or spinal cord compression (see Figure 82).

E Incidence 15-30% in patients with underlying malignancies

Ae Primary tumour: breast (21%), lung (19%), and prostate cancer (7.5%)

R Unknown

Hx Asymptomatic ⊕, local/radiating neck or back pain, pain increasing during the night, numbness, tingling, gait disturbance, muscle weakness, incontinence, ataxia

PE Radiating pain in a specific dermatome

Paresis, dysesthesia, hypo- or areflexia (nerve root entrapment), hyperreflexia, and Babinski's sign (spinal cord compression)

Dx
- Biopsy when primary tumour is unknown, a chest/abdominal CT may be indicated to identify more suitable biopsy sites
- Spinal X-ray: pathological compression fracture
- Spinal CT/MRI: extensiveness of metastases and spinal instability, expansion into the spinal canal with spinal cord compression and/or nerve root entrapment

Tx
- Analgesics
- Steroids (oedema reduction) and chemotherapy (tumour treatment)

- Radiotherapy (pain)
- Consult spinal surgeon for decompression and/or stabilisation

P 2y survival 10-20%

! Metastatic compression of the spinal cord is an oncological emergency in vertebral metastasis and occurs in ±5-10% of patients with cancer, it can progress quickly (few days)

Intramedullary metastases are rare (±5% of patients with intramedullary lesions).

- In 50% lung cancer is the primary malignancy
- The metastases are most often localised in the cervical spine and are diagnosed with MRI
- Prognosis is poor, up to 67% of patients die within 6 mo of diagnosis

Leptomeningeal metastases, also known as carcinomatous meningitis or meningeal carcinomatosis, are metastases in the leptomeninges.

- They occur in 5-8% of patients with solid tumours and 5-15% of hematogenous cancers
- Diagnosis can be made using MRI with contrast and LP
- The median overall survival is 2.4 mo
- Treatment with intrathecal chemotherapy and radiotherapy may extend survival to 6-10 mo

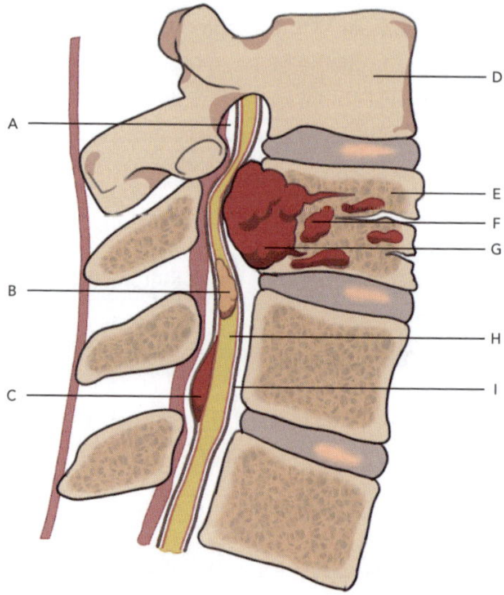

Figure 82 // Vertebral metastasis, leptomeningeal metastasis, intramedullary metastasis
A: Epidural space **B:** Intramedullary metastasis **C:** Leptomeningeal metastasis **D:** Normal vertebrae **E:** Partially collapsed vertebrae **F:** Vertebral metastasis **G:** Epidural extension **H:** Spinal cord **I:** Dura

Brain metastases

D Brain metastases are malignant growths that have spread to the brain. They are the most common neurological complication of solid tumours in adults.

E
- Most common intracranial tumours in adults (>50% of brain tumours)
- Occur in 15-40% of adults with cancer. Solitary lesion in 50% of patients.

Ae Primary carcinomas, e.g. lung, breast, melanoma, kidney and colorectal

R Age >30-40

Hx
- Symptoms depend on the location of the metastases
- Headache, vomiting (due to increased intracranial pressure) ⊕
- Epilepsy ⊕, behavioural changes, cognitive impairment, symptoms consistent with obstruction of CSF circulation (see Hydrocephalus)

PE Neurological deficit symptoms, depending on location of metastases

Dx
- Brain CT: hypointense, isointense, or hyperdense lesions, vasogenic oedema
- Brain MRI: T1 isointense or hypointense lesion, T2 hyperintense lesion with hyperintense vasogenic oedema, contrast enhancement
- Chest/abdominal/neck CT: diagnosis of primary tumour and staging

Tx
- Symptomatic: antiemetics, antiseizure medication, analgesics, dexamethasone
- Depending on primary tumour: systemic therapy (e.g. immunotherapy or chemotherapy)

Surgical resection, stereotactic radiosurgery, radiotherapy

P
- Survival rate depends on primary tumour
- Median life expectancy without treatment: 1-2 mo
- Median life expectancy after radiotherapy: 4-6 mo

Cranial nerve disorders

Cranial nerve disorders

D Cranial nerve disorders often involve single or multiple cranial nerve palsy. The cause and symptoms depend on the nerve involved (see Table 63).

> The parasympathetic fibres of CN III peripherally enclose the central motor fibres of CN III like a tube. As a result, CN III entrapment at the superior border of the petrous part of the temporal bone will first result in parasympathetic deficits (pupil dilation) followed by motor deficit at a later stage.

	NERVE	FUNCTION	SYMPTOMS OF CRANIAL NERVE PALSY
I	Olfactory nerve	Smell	Anosmia, parosmia, kakosmia, hyposmia
II	Optic nerve	Vision, pupillary responses	Visual disturbances, colour vision ↓, visual field defects, pupil does not respond to light (afferent pupil defect), papilloedema
III	Oculomotor nerve	• Motor innervation of the eye (superior, medial and inferior rectus muscles and inferior oblique muscle), eyelid (levator palpebrae superioris muscle) • Pupillary responses	Hypotropia and exotropia, crossed horizontal diplopia, ptosis, dilated pupil unresponsive to light (efferent pupillary defect), torticollis (see Figure 83)
IV	Trochlear nerve	Motor innervation of the eye (superior oblique muscle)	Esotropia and hypertropia, downgaze diplopia (climbing stairs, reading) → diagonal diplopia, compensatory torticollis (see Figure 83)
V	Trigeminal nerve	Sensory innervation of the face, motor innervation of masticatory muscles and tensor tympani muscle, corneal reflex (sensory)	Trigeminal neuralgia, neuropathy, facial sensation disorders, pain, masticatory muscle deficit ⊖
VI	Abducens nerve	Motor innervation of the eye (lateral rectus muscle)	Esotropy, gazing into the distance → uncrossed horizontal diplopia (see Figure 83)
VII	Facial nerve	Facial muscles, innervation of the platysma and stapedius muscle, sense of taste in the anterior $2/3$ of the tongue, tear secretion, corneal reflex (motor)	• Peripheral facial nerve palsy: ipsilateral paresis of one side of the face, sense of taste ↓, tear secretion ↓ (see Figure 84) • Central facial nerve palsy: contralateral paresis of the lower half of the face (see Figure 84)
VIII	Vestibulocochlear nerve	Balance, vestibulo-ocular reflexes, optokinetic nystagmus, hearing	Balance disorders, vertigo, nystagmus, tinnitus, sensorineural deafness

Table 63A // Cranial nerves with their function and the causes and symptoms of cranial nerve palsy
AION, anterior ischaemic optic neuropathy; PION, posterior ischaemic optic neuropathy

CAUSES OF CRANIAL NERVE PALSY

- Inflammatory: allergic/viral upper respiratory tract infection or sinusitis, meningitis
- Miscellaneous: cranial trauma, smoking, olfactory meningioma, Parkinson's disease, Alzheimer's disease, sarcoidosis, congenital, idiopathic

---

- Vascular: non-arteritic anterior or posterior ischaemic optic neuropathy (AION/PION), arteritic AION (temporal artritis), vasculitis
- Inflammatory: optic neuritis (e.g. in MS), papillitis, meningitis
- Optic chiasm compression due to pituitary masses, aneurysms, or cysts
- Miscellaneous: vitamin B1/B12 deficiency, toxic neuropathy, Leber hereditary optic neuropathy, trauma

---

- Vascular: microvascular (e.g. DM, hypertension), vasculitis, mesencephalic infarction or haemorrhage, aneurysm
- Inflammatory: herpes zoster infection, meningitis
- Compression: tumour, intracranial pressure ↑, entrapment trauma
- Miscellaneous: connective tissue disorders, orbital or cavernous sinus pathology

---

Congenital, microvascular (e.g. DM, hypertension), trauma, orbital or cavernous sinus pathology, iatrogenic, infectious, brainstem syndrome

---

Compression by tumour or blood vessel, trauma, herpes zoster infection, connective tissue disease, neurinoma, MS, vasculitis

---

Microvascular (e.g. DM, hypertension), aneurysm, vasculitis, trauma, increased intracranial pressure, tumour, infectious, inflammatory, orbital or cavernous sinus pathology

---

- Vascular: DM, hypertension
- Infectious: VZV, Borrelia, otitis media
- Inflammatory: MS, GBS
- Miscellaneous: Bell paresis (idiopathic), trauma, tumour compression, brainstem disorders, toxic, amyloidosis, nuclear aplasia

---

Fracture of the petrous temporal bone, vestibular schwannoma, bacterial meningitis, vestibular neuritis, medication

NERVE		FUNCTION	SYMPTOMS OF CRANIAL NERVE PALSY
IX	Glosso-pharyngeal nerve	Innervation of the salivary glands, sensory innervation of pharyngeal and laryngeal muscle tissue, sense of taste of the posterior 1/3 of the tongue, carotid sinus	Swallowing disorders, speech problems (hoarseness), deviated uvula pointing to contralateral (healthy) side (see Figure 85)
X	Vagus nerve	Innervation of the salivary glands, motor innervation of pharyngeal and laryngeal muscle tissue, digestive tract, vocal cords	Swallowing disorders, speech problems (hoarseness), deviated uvula pointing to contralateral (healthy) side (see Figure 85)
XI	Accessory nerve	Innervation of the sternocleidomastoid muscle and trapezius muscle	Sternocleidomastoid muscle and trapezius muscle strength ↓
XII	Hypoglossal nerve	Innervation of tongue muscles	Swallowing disorders, speech problems, tongue atrophy, tongue deviates to affected side when extended (see Figure 85)

Table 63B // Cranial nerves with their function and the causes and symptoms of nerve malfunction
AION, anterior ischaemic optic neuropathy; PION, posterior ischaemic optic neuropathy

The following sentence is a mnemonic for remembering whether a cranial nerve provides **s**ensory innervation, **m**otor innervation or **b**oth: "**S**ome **S**ay **M**oney **M**atters, **B**ut **M**y **B**rother **S**ays **B**ig **B**rains **M**atter **M**ost!"

CAUSES OF CRANIAL NERVE PALSY
Pathology of the jugular foramen, vertebral artery aneurysm, iatrogenic
Pathology of the jugular foramen, vertebral artery aneurysm, intrathoracic pathology, tumour compression, iatrogenic
Iatrogenic, trauma, tumour compression

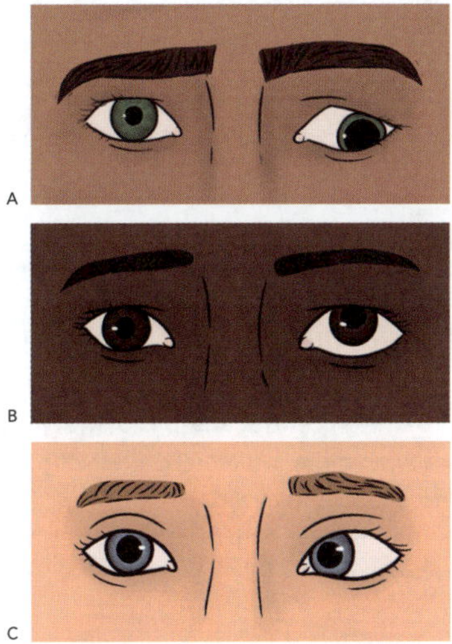

Figure 83 // Clinical presentation of oculomotor, trochlear and abducens nerve palsies when patient looks forward

A: Oculomotor nerve palsy (ptosis, mydriasis, down and out position eye) **B:** Trochlear nerve palsy (upward position affected eye) **C:** Abducens nerve palsy (inward turn of affected eye (esotropia))

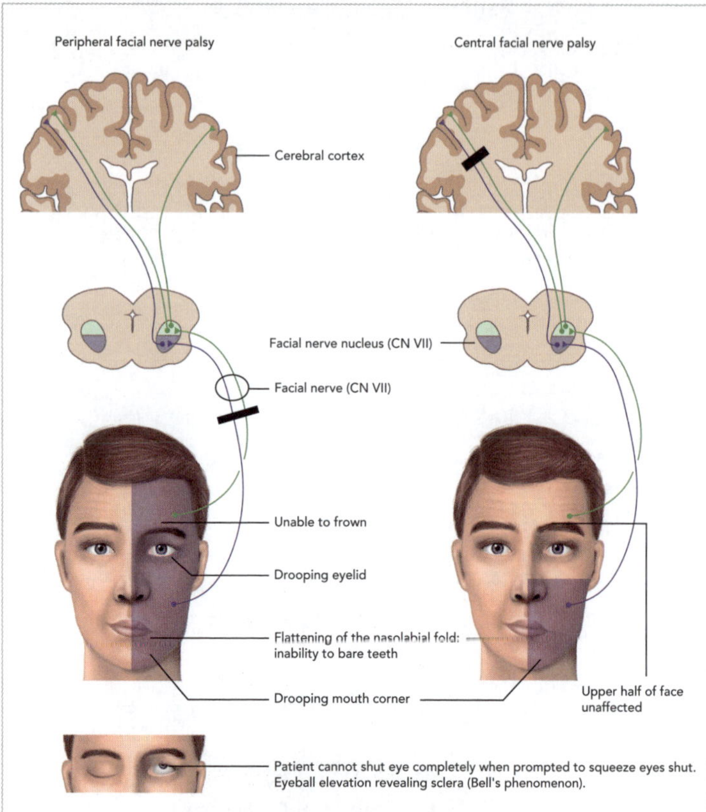

Figure 84 // Peripheral and central facial nerve palsy

Distinction between **central and peripheral facial nerve palsy:**

- Peripheral: complete ipsilateral paresis of one side of the face (including forehead and eyelid)
- Central: contralateral paresis of the lower half of the face (excluding forehead and eyelid)

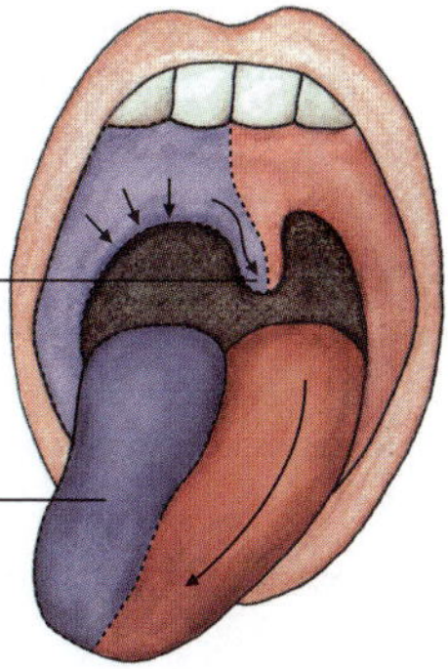

Figure 85 // Glossopharyngeal nerve, vagus nerve and hypoglossal nerve palsy
A: Right-hand-side glossopharyngeal nerve and vagus nerve paresis: uvula deviates to the left **B:** Right-hand-side hypoglossal nerve paresis: tongue deviates to the right.

Multiple sclerosis

Multiple sclerosis (MS)

D MS is a demyelinating autoimmune disorder of the CNS that in most cases is initially characterised by alternating, transient neurological deficits at different sites. At a later stage, the course is more progressive (see Figure 86).

E Prevalence varies worldwide: Europe 143:100,000; America 117:100,000; Africa 8.8:100,000; South East Asia 8.6:100,000; Western Pacific 4.8:100,000

Ae
- Inflammation, demyelination, axonal degeneration
- Most likely cause is an autoimmune disorder with activated lymphocytes

R Age 20-40, ♂:♀ = 1:2-3, positive FHx, smoking, autoimmune disorders, geographical factors (closer to equator → risk ↓)

Hx
- Depends on site of demyelination, subacute onset, sometimes gradual onset, fatigue (++), walking difficulties, sensation of walking on cotton wool, tingling, diplopia, painful eye movements, vision loss, loss of strength, micturition disorders, erectile dysfunction, depression, cognitive symptoms
- Triggers for exacerbation: heat (fever, physical exertion, sauna), stress/emotions

PE
- Sensation: loss of deep sensation > loss of superficial sensation, Lhermitte's sign (see Figure 87)
- Motor innervation: paresis, spasticity

- Reflexes: abdominal reflexes absent, hyperreflexia, Babinski sign
- Coordination: ataxia, dysarthria, balance disorders, tremor
- Visual disturbances: optic neuritis

Dx
- McDonald criteria: dissemination of symptoms in space and time (see Table 64)
- Brain MRI: detect white matter lesions consistent with neurololgical deficits. Hyperintense lesions on T2-weighted images. Black holes on T1-weighted image. Lesion areas specific for MS: periventricular, infratentorial, juxtacortical, spinal.
- LP: CSF cell count =/↑, lymphocytes ↑, IgG index ↑, oligoclonal bands present in CSF, absent in blood
- Expanded disability status scale: quantify and monitor limitations in MS

Tx
Symptomatic
- To influence exacerbation frequency and neurodegeneration: DMT (see Table 50)
- Treat exacerbations (relapses): methylprednisolone IV or oral

P
- 80% relapsing-remitting, of which 2/3 ultimately develop a secondary progressive course (see Figure 86)
- 15-20% primary progressive course, 10% no progression (benign MS)
- 1/3 mildly impaired, 1/3 moderately impaired, 1/3 severely impaired
- Life expectancy shortened by ±7y

The typical patient with MS is a young woman presenting with subacute transient neurological deficit symptoms, with new or recurrent deficit symptoms occurring months to years later, with white matter abnormalities on MRI.

Lhermitte's sign: an electric shock-like sensation along the back and extremities that occurs with flexion of the neck.

Progressive multifocal leukoencephalopathy (PML) is a rare and possibly fatal CNS disease, caused by JC virus, which gives asymptomatic and latent infection in immune competent patients. Reactivation can occur in patients with reduced cellular immunity (e.g. patients with HIV or MS patients treated with natalizumab), leading to PML.

In addition to DMTs, **haematopoietic stem cell transplantation** (HSCT) is available as treatment for MS. It is most effective in patients with highly active RRMS despite taking DMTs.

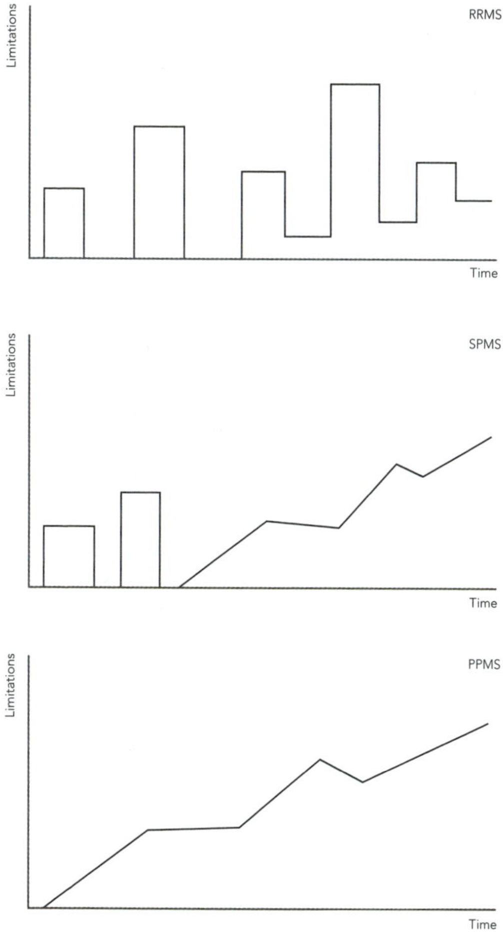

Figure 86 // Multiple sclerosis: disease courses

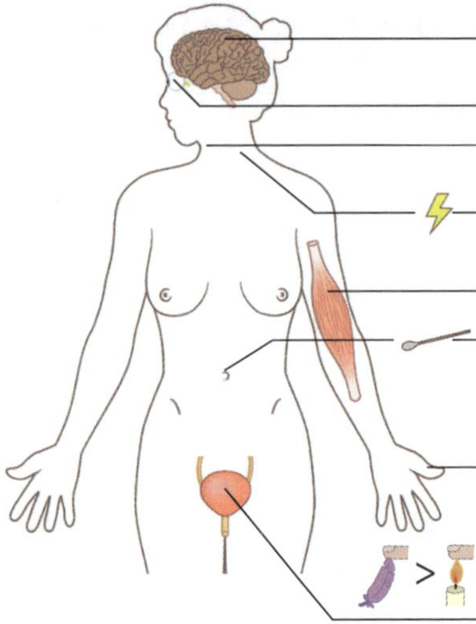

Figure 87 // Multiple sclerosis: clinical features

MCDONALD CRITERIA
Diagnose relapsing-remitting MS when one of the following criteria is met:
• ≥2 clinical attacks and ≥2 lesions with objective clinical evidence • ≥2 clinical attacks and ≥1 lesion with objective clinical evidence, plus good historical evidence • ≥2 clinical attacks and ≥1 lesion with objective clinical evidence, plus dissemination in space by a further clinical episode at another site or by MRI • 1 clinical attack and ≥2 lesions with objective clinical evidence, plus dissemination in time by a further clinical episode, by MRI or the presence of CSF oligoclonal bands • 1 clinical attack and 1 lesion with objective clinical evidence, plus dissemination in space by a further clinical episode at another site or by MRI and dissemination in time by a further clinical episode, by MRI or the presence of CSF oligoclonal bands
Diagnose primary progressive MS when the follow criteria are met:
1 year of disability progression (retrospectively or prospectively determined) independent of clinical relapse, plus two of the following criteria: • ≥1 T2-hyperintense lesions characteristic for MS in one or more of the following regions: periventricular, cortical, juxtacortical, or infratentorial • ≥2 T2-hyperintense lesions in the spinal cord • Presence of CSF-specific oligoclonal bands

Table 64 // McDonald criteria

Movement disorders

Dystonias

D Dystonias are abnormal, often repetitive movements or postures caused by involuntary (unintended) muscle contractions. Dystonias can be focal (e.g. torticollis and blepharospasm), unilateral or generalised (e.g. dystonia musculorum deformans). They can also be classified as primary torsion dystonia (often genetically based), secondary dystonia (e.g. cerebrovascular diseases), heredodegenerative dystonia (e.g. parkinsonism, Huntington's disease and metabolic disorders such as Wilson's disease and Fahr's disease), or drug-induced dystonia (e.g. SSRIs or levodopa).

	BLEPHAROSPASM	SPASMODIC TORTICOLLIS (CERVICAL DYSTONIA)	TORSION DYSTONIA (DYSTONIA MUSCULORUM DEFORMANS)
D	Contraction of the orbicularis oculi muscle, also known as closing the eyelids.	Neck and shoulder muscle contractions.	DYT-TOR1A dystonia. Contractions of almost all muscles, also called generalised dystonia.
E	Prevalence 2-13:100,000	Prevalence 2-40:100,000	Prevalence 1-4:1,000,000
Ae	Possible brainstem disorder	Possible impairment of muscle control due to defective sensory processing in the basal ganglia	Autosomal dominant inheritance, DYT1 gene defect on chromosome 9q34
R	Typical age 50-70 ♀:♂ = 3:1	Adult age	Age of onset <25
Hx	• Blinking frequency ↑ • Meige's syndrome: also dystonia of the lower half of the face	• Neck pain, fatigue • Trigger: emotion • No complaints while sleeping	• Focal onset in foot or hand causing children to tiptoe • Followed by generalisation to the rest of the body, especially torsion dystonia (see Figure 88)
PE	Eye irritation with photophobia	Intermittent rotation of the head that can briefly be corrected (see Figure 89)	Inversion and plantar flexion of the foot
Dx	Non-contributing		

Table 65A // Types of dystonias

	BLEPHAROSPASM	SPASMODIC TORTICOLLIS (CERVICAL DYSTONIA)	TORSION DYSTONIA (DYSTONIA MUSCULORUM DEFORMANS)
Tx	Touch can temporarily relieve dystonia Botulinum toxin injections	Touch can temporarily relieve dystonia Botulinum toxin injections, anticholinergics	Incurable Occupational therapy, physiotherapy, speech therapy Botulinum toxin injections, anticholinergics DBS
P	Spontaneous remission rare		Less generalisation in patients with advanced age of onset
!	Watch out for functional blindness!	Can often be corrected by 'sensory tricks', e.g. touching the chin	Watch out for contractures!

Table 65B // Types of dystonias
DBS, deep brain stimulation

Patients with dystonia may experience typical writer's cramp, in which increasing hand cramp occurs while writing, both in the writing hand and to a lesser extent in the contralateral hand.

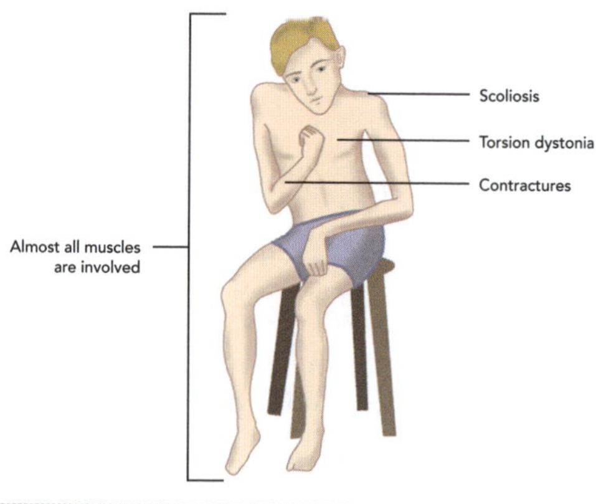

Figure 88 // Torsion dystonia

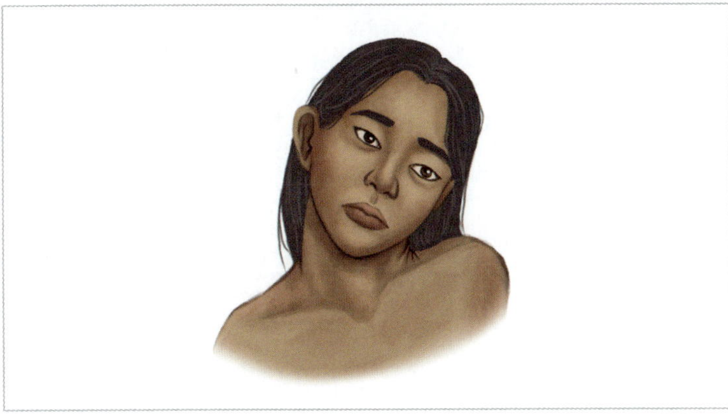

Figure 89 // Torticollis

Gilles de la Tourette syndrome

D Gilles de la Tourette syndrome is a neuropsychiatric disorder characterised by various types of tics and compulsions presenting from childhood.

E Prevalence 50-500:100,000

Ae
- Strong genetic component, autosomal dominant inheritance
- Possible disorder in the striato-thalamo-cortical system

R Age of onset <11, ♂>♀ 4:1, behavioural disorders (obsessive-compulsive disorder (OCD), attention deficit hyperactivity disorder (ADHD), aggression)

Hx
- Initial stage: simple motor tics (blinking, pursing lips) (see Figure 90)
- Later: emergence of sensory tics (pressure, itching, stinging sensation, pain), vocal tics (coughing, echolalia, coprolalia) and motions (jumping, kicking)
- Symptoms vary in severity and scope and can be temporarily suppressed, slightly less than half also have sleep disorders, emotional distress → symptoms ↑

PE Observe tics

Tx
Behavioural therapy, psychoeducation
Antidopaminergic agents such as atypical antipsychotics (e.g. risperidone) and neuroleptics (e.g. haloperidol)
DBS

P
- Some patients experience spontaneous reduction or total remission of symptoms in adulthood
- Many comorbidities, e.g. ADHD and OCD

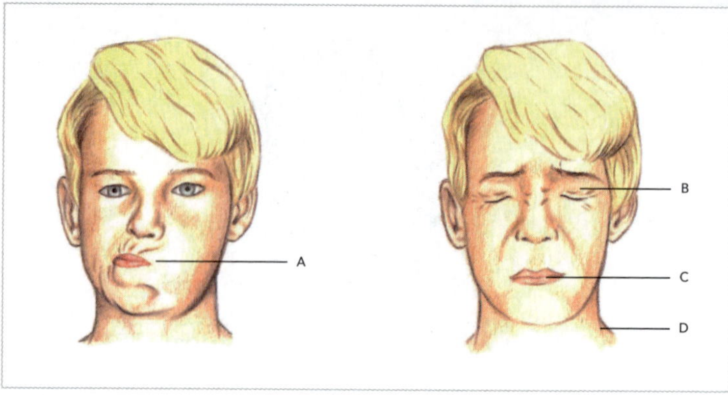

Figure 90 // Gilles de la Tourette syndrome
A: Motor tic of the mouth **B:** Motor tic of the eye **C:** Vocal tics **D:** Neck muscles affected

Tremors

D A tremor is a rhythmic, trembling and involuntary movement. Depending on the circumstances in which a tremor occurs, the following subdivisions can be made:

- Resting tremor: when the body part is completely relaxed (e.g. in Parkinson's disease, Holmes, drug-induced, functional tremor)
- Action tremor:
  - Postural tremor: when a body part is held against gravity (e.g. essential tremor, exaggerated physiological tremor, Holmes, neuromuscular disorders, functional tremor)
  - Kinetic tremor
    - Intention tremor (ataxic tremor): when a directed movement is made (cerebellar tremor, drug-induced)
    - Simple kinetic tremor
    - Task-specific tremor
  - Isometric tremor: when contracting muscles, while keeping the body part still (e.g. when making a fist)

Note that resting tremor, postural tremor and intention tremor are clinically the most relevant types of tremor (see Table 66).

	CEREBELLAR TREMOR	ESSENTIAL TREMOR	FUNCTIONAL TREMOR
D	Low-frequency, coarse tremor that occurs at the end of a movement.	A postural or action tremor which commonly involves the hands or arms, without any other neurological conditions.	A tremor which is often a combination of rest, postural and kinetic tremors, usually involving hands and arms.
E	Unknown	• Most common movement disorder • Prevalence 1-2% of the population	Unknown
Ae	Cerebellar disorder (difficulty coordinating movement), alcohol use disorder	Autosomal dominant inheritance	Organic cause unlikely
R	MS, stroke, Wilson's disease, alcohol use disorder	Age of onset around 20, positive FHx	Stressful experience, prior physical trauma, surgery, or infection
Hx	Target overshoot or undershoot, tremor worsens with precise movements	• Emotional distress, fatigue → symptoms ↑ • Alcohol → symptoms ↓	Acute onset, symptoms vary with severity of tremor
PE	• Intentional tremor of arms and legs, shaking of head (++) • Low-frequency, coarse tremor Coordination: ataxia, dysmetria	• Bilateral, symmetrical, postural (++) or intention tremor (+), upper extremities, head and voice • High-frequency, fine tremor Coordination: abnormal finger-to-nose test	Tremor disappears with passive movement or distraction, no rhythmic movements
Dx	Brain CT/MRI: to assess extent of MS lesions, ischaemic or haemorrhagic stroke, tumour, atrophy (e.g. spinocerebellar ataxia), or cerebellitis (infectious or autoimmune)	Thyroid test in case of suspected thyroid problem	Non-contributing
Tx	Thalamotomy or thalamic stimulation in severe cases	Non-selective beta blockers, antiseizure medication, benzodiazepines • Consider DBS of the thalamus • High-intensity focused ultrasound therapy	Cognitive behavioural therapy, responds well to placebo
P	88% of cases improve after surgical intervention	Chronic progression	Best chance of recovery if treatment is started <6 mo after tremor onset

Table 66 // Different types of tremors

Neurodegenerative disorders

Huntington's disease

D Huntington's disease is a neurodegenerative movement disorder involving chorea, personality changes and dementia (see Figure 91).

E Prevalence 4-5:100,000, North-America and Europe > Africa and East-Asia

Ae
- Genetic (autosomal dominant): elongated cytosine-adenine-guanine (CAG) sequence on chromosome 4p16.3 (Huntington gene (HTT))
- Neurodegeneration → severe brain atrophy of the caudate nucleus and putamen in particular

R Age of onset 30-50, positive FHx

Hx
- Onset: behavioural problems, personality changes (agitation, paranoia)
- Later: motor disorders with chorea, cognitive decline, psychiatric complaints (mood disorders, anxiety symptoms, obsessive-compulsive thoughts, delusions, hallucinations), poor impulse control, addiction, dysphagia (→ severe emaciation), urinary and faecal incontinence

PE
- Gait pattern: unsteady gait, broad-based gait
- Chorea, hyperreflexia, dystonia, slower eye tracking

Dx DNA testing: demonstrate causal mutation

Tx
- Dopamine antagonists (haloperidol, tiapride or pimozide) or dopamine reuptake inhibitors (tetrabenazine) → suppress chorea
- Antidepressants or anxiolytics

P Average disease duration 20y. Death due to respiratory failure or suicide. Age of onset <20 → faster transition to progressive course. Higher number of CAG repeats → more severe disease course.

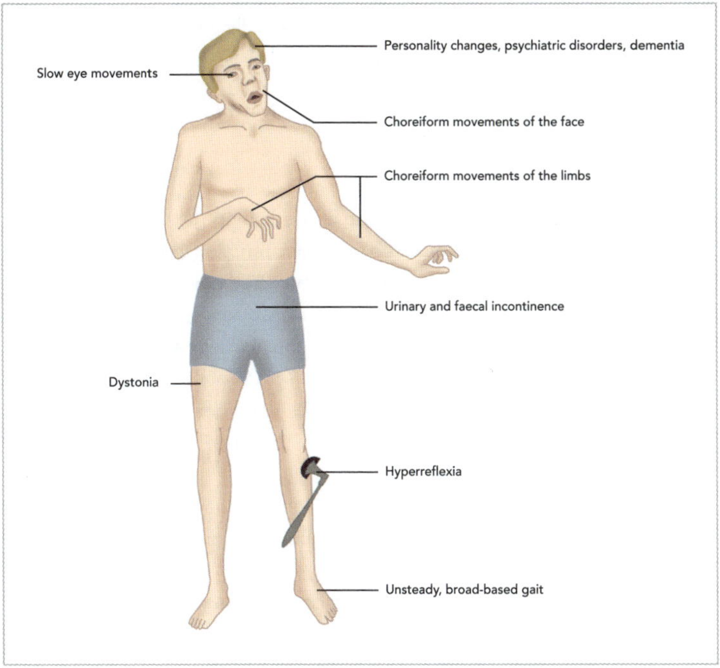

Figure 91 // Huntington's disease

Parkinson's disease

D Parkinson's disease is a neurodegenerative movement disorder that is clinically characterised by a hypokinetic-rigid syndrome.

E Prevalence 60-400:100,000

Ae
- Neurodegenerative: neuronal atrophy and depigmentation in substantia nigra → degeneration of dopaminergic nigrostriatal pathways → striatal dopamine deficiency (especially in the putamen) (see Figure 92)
- Later: all neurotransmitter systems are affected

R Age 50-70, positive FHx, traumatic brain injury, toxins: pesticides

Hx
- Core symptoms: bradykinesia, rigidity, tremor, hypokinesia, balance disorder (see Figure 93)
- Early symptoms: unilateral arm swing ↓, micrographia, clumsiness, olfactory disturbances, rigidity, muscle pain (+), fatigue (++), akinesia, hypokinesia, bradykinesia (++), rest tremor

- Late symptoms: cognitive impairment, sleep disorders, depression, constipation and autonomic function disorders, visual hallucinations, bradyphrenia

PE
- Dysarthria, low-volume speech
- Motor symptoms: asymmetric rest tremor ⊕, cogwheel phenomenon, hypertonia
- Gait: shuffling, short-stepped gait (festinating gait), involuntary rapid walking, freezing, diminished arm swing, en bloc turning
- Posture: impaired postural reflexes, hunched posture, facial masking

Dx
- Brain MRI: to rule out other causes of parkinsonism
- Consider DAT-SPECT scan: presynaptic dopamine receptor defect in striatum (if in doubt about diagnosis)

Tx
- Choice of drug treatment depends on symptoms, age and comorbidity: levodopa is most effective (always combined with peripheral decarboxylase inhibitor)
- After several years of levodopa → duration of action and effect ↓, motor complications ↑, on/off fluctuations ↑ → consider adding 2nd drug with longer $t_{1/2}$
- Increase in dopaminergic activity: dopamine agonist, COMT inhibitor, MAO-B inhibitor
- Delayed dopamine reuptake: amantadine
- Inhibition of cholinergic activity: anticholinergic
- Treat additional symptoms with e.g. antidepressants

DBS

P Slowly progressive (even with treatment), culminating in severe disability, median life expectancy varies: 4-22y, 40% risk of depression, 70% of patients have dementia after 10y

! Risk of psychiatric disorders due to medication in combination with cholinergic deficiency syndrome

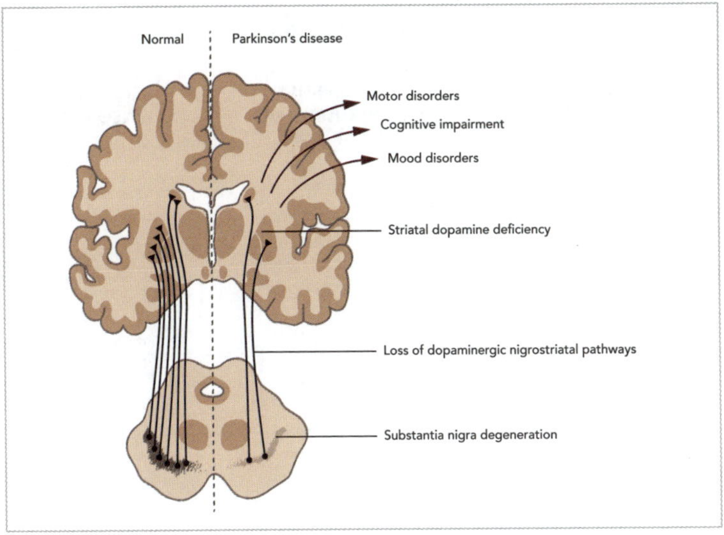

Figure 92 // Pathophysiology of Parkinson's disease

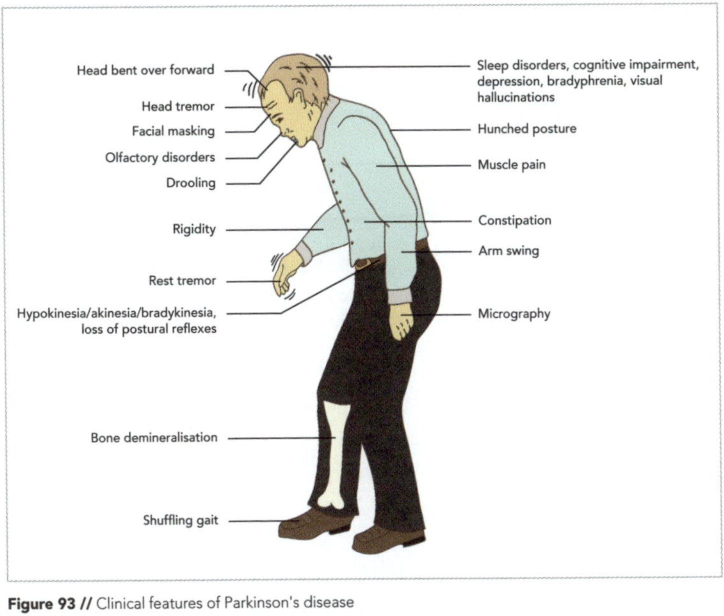

Figure 93 // Clinical features of Parkinson's disease

Atypical parkinsonian syndromes

	MULTIPLE SYSTEM ATROPHY (MSA)	PROGRESSIVE SUPRANUCLEAR PALSY (PSP)	VASCULAR PARKINSONISM (lower body parkinsonism)
D	Heterogeneous group of progressive disorders characterised by autonomic dysfunction and parkinsonism (see Figure 94).	Progressive brain disorder characterised by parkinsonism with axial rigidity and increased fall risk, vertical eye movement disorders and dementia (see Figure 95).	A condition in which ischaemic cerebral damage in strategic areas leads to parkinsonism.
E	Prevalence 3-5:100,000		Unknown
Ae	Presynaptic dopamine deficiency with postsynaptic receptor dysfunction	• Brainstem, cerebellar and diencephalic atrophy • Tau-protein aggregation	• Infarction in the basal ganglia and frontal lobes • Periventricular and subcortical white matter lesions
R	Age 50-70	Age >50	Hypertension, PMHx: ischaemic stroke
Hx	• Autonomic functional disorders (++): orthostatic hypotension, incontinence, erectile dysfunction, constipation • Several types: with parkinsonism (MSA-P) or with cerebellar ataxia (MSA-C), see Figure 94	Trunk and neck rigidity (++), autonomic function disorders, frequent falls	Mainly affects lower extremities
PE	Antecollis, tremor, dysarthria, dyskinesias	Primitive reflexes, vertical gaze paresis (++), severe postural instability (++), pyramidal signs, hypokinesia, upright posture, blinking frequency ↓	• Muscle tone: parkinsonism of the lower extremities in particular • Gait: wide strides and shuffling gait • Pseudobulbar symptoms, pyramidal/cerebellar disorders
Dx	• Brain MRI: putaminal abnormalities • DAT-SPECT scan: postsynaptic dopamine receptor defect in striatum	Brain MRI/CT: to rule out NPH, multiple ischaemic strokes	Brain MRI/CT: vascular lesions

Table 67A // Atypical parkinsonian syndromes
MSA-P, multisystem atrophy with parkinsonism; MSA-C, multisystem atrophy with cerebellar ataxia

	MULTIPLE SYSTEM ATROPHY (MSA)	PROGRESSIVE SUPRANUCLEAR PALSY (PSP)	VASCULAR PARKINSONISM (lower body parkinsonism)
Tx	• Poor response to dopaminergic therapy • Antihypotensive drugs for orthostatic hypotension	• No response to dopaminergic therapy • Antidepressants have limited effect	Poor response to dopaminergic therapy
P	Progressive, median survival 4-10y	Progressive, median survival 6y	Variable progression
!	N/A	• Risk of subcortical dementia ↑ • Watch out for progressive swallowing disorders, aspiration pneumonia	Early cognitive impairment

Table 67B // Atypical parkinsonian syndromes
MSA-P, multisystem atrophy with parkinsonism; MSA-C, multisystem atrophy with cerebellar ataxia

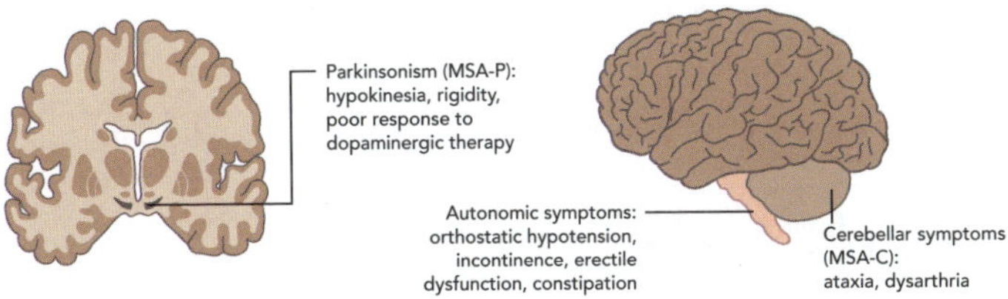

Figure 94 // Multiple system atrophy

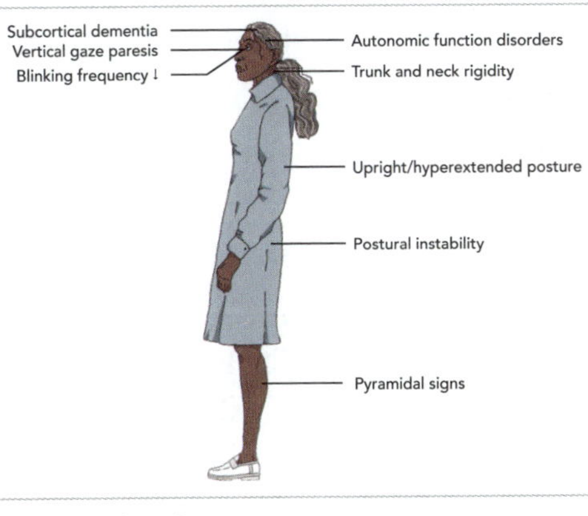

Figure 95 // Progressive supranuclear palsy

The **DAT-SPECT scan** gives information on the dopaminergic function of presynaptic terminals. It can be used to confirm or exclude a diagnosis of dopamine deficient parkinsonism. However, it is not able to distinguish between Parkinson's disease and atypical parkinsonian syndromes.

Spinocerebellar ataxia

D Spinocerebellar ataxia is a rare group of neurodegenerative disorders affecting the cerebellum and often the long tracts of the spinal cord and causing coordination disorders (see Table 68).

	AUTOSOMAL DOMINANT SPINOCEREBELLAR ATAXIA	FRIEDREICH'S ATAXIA
D	Heterogeneous group of hereditary disorders characterised by progressive cerebellar ataxia.	Hereditary disorder that often arises in adolescence and is characterised by ataxia and later by cardiomyopathy.
E	Prevalence 4:100,000	Prevalence 2-3:100,000
Ae	Cerebellar degeneration, possibly involving other systems and tracts	
Ae	Autosomal dominant, expanded CAG repeat → toxic effect of mutated protein	Autosomal recessive, expanded GAA repeat in the FRDA gene → intracellular frataxin level ↓
R	Positive FHx	
R	Age of onset 20-60	Age of onset 10-15
Hx	Depends on type, mainly coordination difficulties, progressive clumsiness	Difficulty walking, numbness of extremities, dysphagia, progressive clumsiness
PE	Different phenotypes (Harding's classification): • Type I: extremity ataxia, dysarthria, dementia, eye movement disorders, optic nerve atrophy, extrapyramidal and pyramidal disorders • Type II: ataxia (see Figure 96), retinal degeneration • Type III: limited to ataxia	• Progressive extremity ataxia, eye movement disorders, areflexia, Babinski reflex, spasticity, dysarthria, pyramidal weakness, deep sensory deficit • Hollow feet and swan neck deformity • Later: cardiomyopathy

Table 68A // Types of spinocerebellar ataxia
GAA, acid α-glucosidase; FRDA, Friedreich's ataxia

	AUTOSOMAL DOMINANT SPINOCEREBELLAR ATAXIA	FRIEDREICH'S ATAXIA
Dx	DNA testing: demonstrate causal mutation	
	Brain MRI: assess cerebellar atrophy and rule out other causes (SOL, stroke)	• ECG abnormalities (arrhythmia) • Brain MRI: medullar and spinal atrophy, no cerebellar atrophy, rule out other causes: SOL, stroke
Tx	No causal therapy, adaptations and aids to stay independent for as long as possible Symptomatic: support by multidisciplinary teams (physiotherapy, speech therapy, occupational therapy)	
P	• Progressive: patients are wheelchair-bound after 10-15y from onset of symptoms • Average life expectancy 56y	• Slowly progressive: 50% of patients are wheelchair-bound around age 25 • Average life expectancy 37y

Table 68B // Types of spinocerebellar ataxia
GAA, acid α-glucosidase; FRDA, Friedreich's ataxia

> The typical patient with spinocerebellar ataxia presents with ataxia and dysarthria.

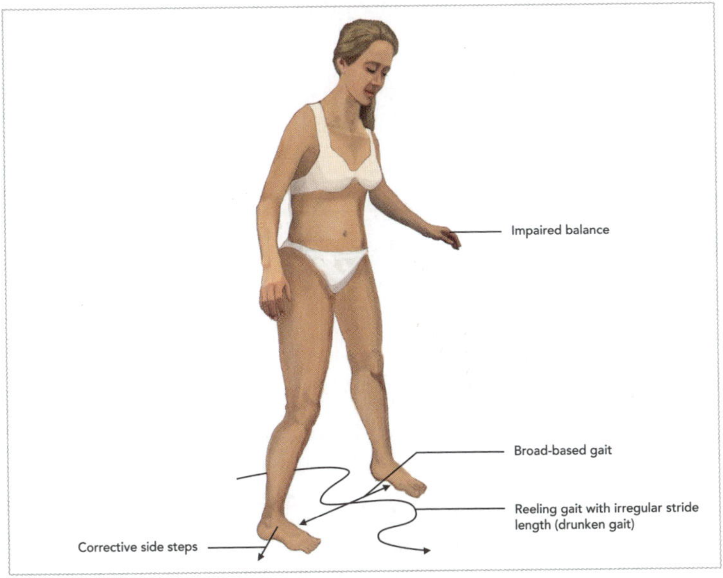

Figure 96 // Ataxic gait

Wernicke encephalopathy and Korsakoff syndrome

	WERNICKE ENCEPHALOPATHY	KORSAKOFF SYNDROME
D	Acute neuropsychiatric disorder that often precedes Korsakoff syndrome. The condition can be mild, sometimes going unnoticed.	Chronic neuropsychiatric disorder and often a long-term consequence of Wernicke encephalopathy, in which memory impairment is particularly prominent.
E	0-2% of Western population	
Ae	Vitamin B1 deficiency → caused by alcohol use disorder (±80%), malabsorption, poor nutritional intake, increased metabolism, loss of water-soluble thiamine (e.g. in renal dialysis)	
		TBI, SAH, secondary ischaemia after SAH, meningitis, multiple small infarctions
R	More common in men, but women are more susceptible to developing Korsakoff, age >50	
Hx	Memory impairment (esp. short-term memory), disorientation (esp. in time), confabulations, euphoria, difficulty planning activities	
PE	Classic triad (10-33%): ocular dysfunction (e.g. horizontal gaze-evoked nystagmus, bilateral abducens palsy), altered mental status, ataxia	Abnormalities found in Wernicke encephalopathy may disappear or persist after administering thiamine
Dx	• Clinical diagnosis • Labs: vitamin B1 deficiency • Brain MRI: reversible cytotoxic oedema, symmetrical lesions on T2-weighted/FLAIR images in the thalamus, periaqueductal gray, mammillary bodies, and tectal plate	
Tx	Lifestyle advice on diet and alcohol Restore nutritional status High dose thiamine IV (or IM), vitamin B-complex, vitamin C	Oral thiamine
P	IV thiamine corrects ophthalmoplegia within a week	
	• Untreated: consciousness ↓ → coma • Up to 80% of surviving patients progress to Korsakoff syndrome (alcoholic > non-alcoholic)	Memory recovery in <20%

Table 69 // Wernicke encephalopathy and Korsakoff syndrome

Confabulation: memory gaps are filled with fantasies.

Always administer thiamine before administering glucose. Because of the involvement of thiamine in carbohydrate metabolism, administering glucose may lead to an acute situation or worsening of the thiamine deficiency.

Spinal disorders

Chiari malformation

D A Chiari malformation is a displacement of the brainstem and cerebellar tonsils in the foramen magnum. Concomitant high-seated odontoid process can lead to compression of the medulla oblongata. See Table 70 and Figure 97.

E Live birth prevalence type I 1:1,000, type II 0.44:1,000

Ae Disorder of the skull base, cerebellum and brainstem combined with increased pressure

R Spina bifida, neurofibromatosis type I, Noonan syndrome

Hx Neck pain, headache in pressure-inducing situations (cerebellar tonsils descend further), ataxia, deafness, hoarseness, difficulty swallowing, difficulty breathing during sleep

PE Cranial nerve palsy, deep sensory and motor deficits

Dx Brain/brainstem MRI: detect Chiari malformation

Tx Asymptomatic: conservative management

Symptomatic or CSF obstruction: surgical decompression

	TYPE I CHIARI MALFORMATION	TYPE II CHIARI MALFORMATION "ARNOLD-CHIARI MALFORMATION"	TYPE III CHIARI MALFORMATION
D	Cerebellar tonsils displaced caudal into spinal canal.	• Caudal herniation of cerebellum and medulla into spinal canal • 95% myelomeningocele • Obstructive hydrocephalus due to malformation	Caudal displacement of medulla with low occipital or high cervical encephalocele.
E	Prevalence 1% of population	Prevalence 0.44:1,000 births	⊖
P	Benign and asymptomatic (++)	Decreased incidence with folate therapy	• Severe mental and motor retardation • Mortality 14%

Table 70 // Types of Chiari malformation

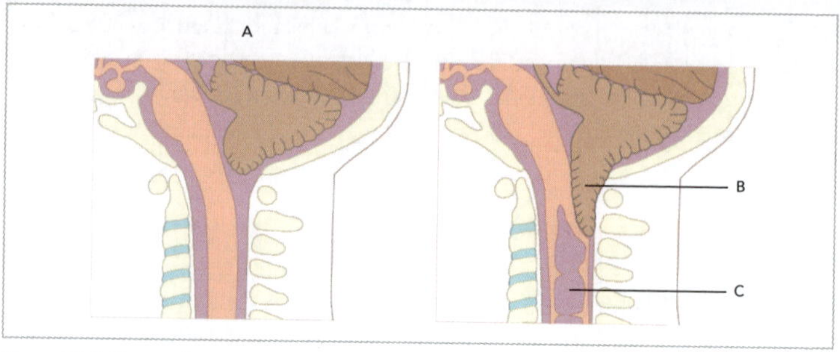

Figure 97 // Chiari malformation
A: Normal **B:** Descended cerebellar tonsil **C:** Syrinx

Syringomyelia

D Syringomyelia is a slowly progressive condition in which a central cavity develops in the spinal cord. The condition is most common in the cervical spinal cord. The medulla oblongata is rarely affected (syringobulbia).

E Prevalence in children 2-8:100,000

Ae Idiopathic ⊕⊕, sometimes secondary to spinal cord tumour or traumatic spinal cord injury → abnormal CSF circulation → central cavity in the spinal cord ↑ → neurological deficits ↑

R ♂:♀ = 2:1, basilar impression, Chiari malformation, intramedullary tumour, traumatic spinal cord injury, vascular spinal cord injury

Hx Early stage: hand injuries and burns ↑

PE
- Early stage: areflexia of the arms, superficial sensation ↓
- Advanced stage: sympathetic failure → bilateral Horner's syndrome ⊕, oedematous skin ⊕, ulcers ⊕, Charcot joint ⊖
- Early stage: atrophy and motor deficits in the hands and arms
- Final stage: motor deficits and loss of deep sensation in the legs

Dx Spinal MRI: detect central cavity in spinal cord

Tx
- For neuropathic pain: amitriptyline or carbamazepine
- For spasticity: diazepam or baclofen

Consider inserting shunt between syrinx and spinal CSF space or syringopleural shunting

P Gradually progressive with prolonged stable periods, spontaneous remission is rare

! Chiari malformation type 1 may present with syringomyelia

Spina bifida

D Spina bifida is a complex malformation characterised by spinal deformity and dysfunction, usually in the lumbosacral region (see Figure 98). A distinction is made between spina bifida occulta (lesion covered by skin) and spina bifida aperta (neural tissue visible).

E
- Global incidence 1-10:1,000 births
- Spina bifida aperta 5-6:100,000 births
- Spina bifida occulta 12% of population

Ae Neural plate fails to fuse or does not fuse completely in the first 28 days after conception

R Hereditary factors, folic acid deficiency, maternal DM, use of antiseizure medication during pregnancy

Hx Depending on type: paralysis and sensory deficit of the lower extremities, urinary and faecal incontinence, constipation, minor swelling and/or tuft of hair on the back

PE Depending on type: minor swelling and/or local tuft of hair on the back; red, fleshy plaque, mostly in lumbosacral region, covered with fragile transparent membrane and an elongated segment of embryonic neural plate tissue in the midline

Dx
- Prenatal (16-20 wk): ultrasound, labs and amniocentesis: alpha-foetoprotein ↑
- Postnatal (if clinically suspicious): spinal ultrasound, detect spina bifida with brain and spinal MRI

Tx
- Prevention: folic acid prior to conception or as early as possible in the pregnancy (up to 3 mo)
- Lifelong follow-up of neurological function

Prophylactic ABx immediately after birth

- Surgical closure preferably as early as possible after birth in case of spina bifida aperta or tethered cord in spina bifida occulta
- Fetal surgery can be performed in specialised centers
- Shunt in case of hydrocephalus

P 75% reach young adult age, long-term prognosis depends on level of lesion

! Watch out for hydrocephalus due to CSF circulation disorder in Chiari-II malformation, or syringomyelia

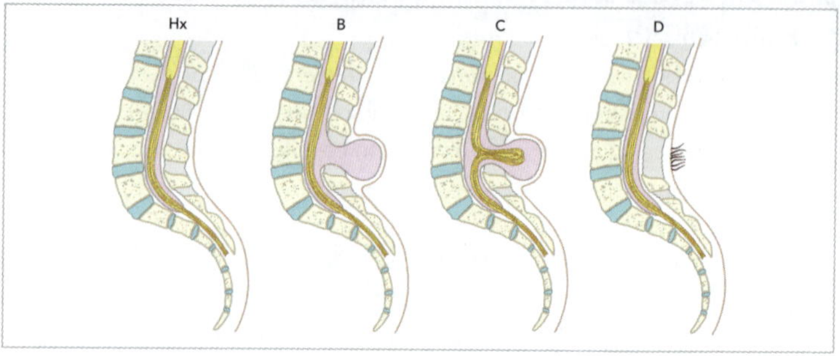

Figure 98 // Spina bifida
A: Normal **B:** Meningocele **C:** Myelomeningocele **D:** Spina bifida occulta

Central cord syndrome

D Central cord syndrome is a motor function and superficial sensation disorder caused by a lesion of the central part of the spinal cord (see Figure 99).

E 10% of all spinal cord syndromes

Ae
- Hyperextension of the neck (e.g. fall on chin) → selective central spinal cord contusion
- Syringomyelia, tumour

R Elderly patients with a narrow spinal canal (degenerative disorders)

Hx Latent interval, neck pain near lesion, bladder dysfunction

PE
- With limited lesions: loss of superficial sensation (thermoanalgesia) and areflexia in the affected areas
- With extensive lesions: disrupted corticospinal tract → central pareses of the arms with relative sparing of the legs and loss of sensibility with sacral sparing

Dx Spinal MRI: localisation of spinal cord lesion or syringomyelia

Tx Neck immobilisation with rigid cervical collar

Physical therapy, occupational therapy

Glucocorticoids no longer recommended

P Recovery depends on nature and severity of the injury

Traumatic spinal cord injury

D Traumatic spinal cord injury is characterised by severe traumatic compression or disruption of the spinal cord, leading to neurological deficits caudal to the lesion (see Figure 99).

E Incidence 10.5:100,000 per year

Ae Traffic and sports accidents, violence → force perpendicular to the axis of the spine, overextension or overflexion → spinal cord injury

R ♂, age 15-30, osteoporosis, osteoarthritis or rheumatoid arthritis (→ narrow spinal canal → compresses more easily)

Hx Trauma mechanism

PE
- First weeks: spinal shock (hypotonic paralysis, anaesthesia, areflexia, orthostatic hypotension, paralytic ileus, absent bladder control)
- Later: hyperreflexia with loss of deep and superficial sensation, atrophy, paralysis, impaired sweat secretion, impaired blood pressure regulation, impaired bladder function and sexual functions in region caudal to lesion
- Incomplete lesion: some functions are preserved

Dx Spinal MRI: diagnose extent and localisation of spinal cord injury

Tx Surgical decompression and stabilisation

P
- Functional outcome is described by the American Spinal Injury Association (ASIA) impairment scale (A-E)
- Lesion between C3-C5 → respiratory failure → high mortality
- Spinal cord oedema exacerbates symptoms

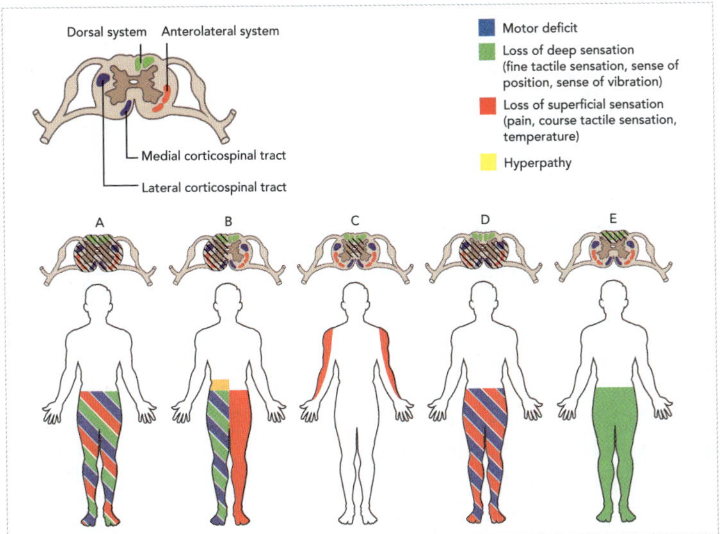

Figure 99 // Types of spinal cord syndromes

A: Complete spinal cord injury **B:** Brown-Séquard syndrome **C:** Central cord syndrome **D:** Anterior cord syndrome **E:** Posterior cord syndrome

Brown-Séquard syndrome

D Brown-Séquard syndrome is caused by penetrating injury, resulting in a spinal cord hemisection and a specific deficit pattern (see Figure 99).

E 2-4% of all traumatic spinal cord injuries

Ae Stab and gunshot injuries (trauma), unilateral tumour (metastasis or meningioma), vascular spinal cord injury, MS

Hx Spinal hemisection → motor and sensory symptoms: loss of strength, and loss of fine tactile sensation on the affected side. Loss of gross touch several levels below the injury on the contralateral side.

- At lesion level: paresis, atrophy, analgesia, ipsilateral hyperpathy
- Caudal of lesion: central paresis and ipsilateral loss of discriminative sensation, contralateral loss of superficial sensation

PE
- At lesion level: paresis, atrophy, analgesia, ipsilateral hyperpathy
- Caudal of lesion: central paresis and ipsilateral loss of deep sensation, contralateral loss of affective sensation

Dx Spinal MRI: detect spinal cord hemisection

Tx Surgical decompression depending on underlying cause

P Unknown

> In Brown-Séquard syndrome there is a loss of vibration sensation ipsilaterally, and loss of pain and temperature contralaterally, starting several levels below the hemisection.

Neurocognitive disorders

Alzheimer's disease

D Alzheimer's disease is a neurodegenerative disorder and the most common cause of dementia (70%). It presents with memory, language and/or executive function disorders that arise gradually.

E Annual incidence 2.8%

Ae
- Mostly unknown
- Altered amyloid precursor protein (APP) → APP accumulation → beta-amyloid is released and forms aggregates → neurotoxic → cerebral cortex atrophy, hippocampal atrophy and ventriculomegaly (see Figure 100)
- Beta-amyloid plaque formation and tau-protein tangle formation → loss of neurons

R Advanced age, positive FHx, Down syndrome, stroke, hypertension, head trauma, smoking

Hx
- Initial stage: memory disorders (anterograde episodic and executive memory affected first, retrograde episodic and semantic memory affected later), word-finding difficulties, inability to perform everyday actions properly (apraxia), inability to recognise persons, objects, sounds, etc. (agnosia), behavioural changes (disinterest, indecisiveness, aggression), olfactory disorder, difficulty sleeping, mood disorders, delusions, visual hallucinations
- Later stage: severe language disorders with echolalia and perseveration
- Final stage: speechlessness (mutism), lack of emotion, enthusiasm or motivation (apathy), incontinence, periods of screaming

PE Initial stage: neurological examination reveals no abnormalities; later stage: tremor, myoclonia, hypertonia, primitive reflexes

Dx
- Labs: to rule out other causes
- LP: beta-amyloid 1-42 ↓, tau and p-tau protein ↑
- Brain CT/MRI: hippocampal and tempoparietal cortical atrophy, atrophy precuneus, medial temporal lobe atrophy (MTA) score ↑, posterior atrophy score ↑
- PET: biparietal reduced glucose metabolism
- Neuropsychological examination: MMSE ↓, MoCA ↓, Cambridge cognition examination (CAMCOG) ↓

Tx Symptomatic, incurable, treat comorbidities (sleep disorders, mood disorders, delirium, psychosis)

Cholinesterase inhibitor (rivastigmine or galantamine), NMDA antagonist (memantine), lecanemab

P Slowly progressive, average duration of disease 8y, longer if onset at younger age, death due to cachexia, uraemia, cardiovascular disease, (aspiration) pneumonia

! 10-20% develop epilepsy at later stage

Episodic memory is the collection of past personal experiences and events. **Semantic memory** is the collection of context-independent general concepts, facts and meanings.

The typical patient with Alzheimer's disease is >65y old, has a positive FHx and presents with memory disorders. Diagnostics reveal no signs of vascular cerebral damage.

Alzheimer's disease diagnostic criteria (1 major criteria with ≥1 minor criteria)

Major criteria:

- Gradual progressive decline >6 mo
- Measurable episodic memory impairment
- Isolated memory deficit or combined with other cognitive impairments

Minor criteria:

- Atrophy medial temporal lobe (MRI)
- Abnormal CSF biomarker
- Positive FHx for genetic mutation
- Low glucose uptake in bilateral temporoparietal areas (PET/SPECT)

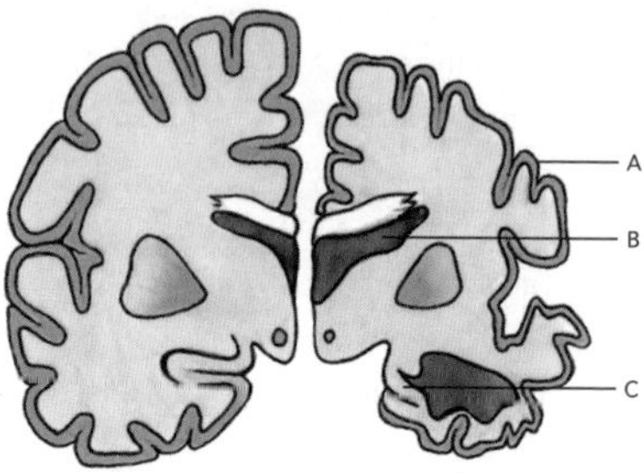

Figure 100 // Alzheimer's disease
A: Cortical atrophy **B:** Ventriculomegaly **C:** Hippocampal atrophy

Other conditions with dementia

	FRONTOTEMPORAL DEMENTIA	LEWY BODY DEMENTIA	VASCULAR DEMENTIA
D	Heterogeneous group of three behavioural syndromes caused by frontotemporal degeneration (see Figure 101).	A progressive disease involving cognitive decline and parkinsonism (see Figure 101).	A dementia syndrome characterised by sluggishness, difficulty organising thoughts and lack of initiative. It is thought to be caused by cerebrovascular damage (see Figure 101).

Table 71A // Other types of dementia
REM, rapid eye movement; TDP-43, transactive response DNA binding protein of 43 kDa

	FRONTOTEMPORAL DEMENTIA	LEWY BODY DEMENTIA	VASCULAR DEMENTIA
E	5% of patients with dementia, prevalence 2-31:100,000	5% of patients with dementia	10-20% of patients with dementia
Ae	10-25% autosomal dominant inheritance, frontotemporal degeneration secondary to tau pathology, TDP-43 pathology with and without ubiquitin	• Hypopigmentation of the substantia nigra and locus caeruleus • Lewy bodies in brainstem, limbic cortex and neocortex	• Large infarctions or multiple small infarctions → loss of neurons • Temporal correlation between detection of cerebrovascular abnormalities and symptoms
R	Positive FHx of for dementia or psychiatric disorders	Parkinsonism, REM sleep, behavioural disorders	Hypertension, ischaemic stroke, haemorrhagic stroke, MI, smoking, DM, AF, peripheral vascular disease
Hx	• Behaviour: loss of initiative, disinterest (apathy syndrome), disinhibited behaviour (sexual disinhibition, gluttony), compulsive acts and loss of empathy • Language: word-retrieval difficulty, syntax errors, grammatical errors (primary progressive aphasia) • Motor function: tremor, ataxia, gait disorders and frequent falls	• Initial stage: fluctuating cognition (executive functions) with fluctuating alertness, recurrent visual hallucinations, parkinsonism with poor response to levodopa • Later stage: memory disorders, language disorders, apraxia • REM sleep disturbances, delusions, frequent falls	• Initial stage: sluggishness, difficulty organising thoughts, lack of initiative, memory disorders, personality changes, lack of facial expressions, low-volume speech • Later stage: pseudobulbar syndrome, incontinence
PE	Tremor, gait disorders, ataxia	Symptoms of parkinsonism	Focal neurological deficit, gait disorders, ataxia, paresis, hyperreflexia
Dx	• Brain MRI: frontotemporal atrophy • Neuropsychological examination to identify type of cognitive impairment, FAB	• DAT-SPECT scan: dopamine uptake in basal ganglia ↓ • Neuropsychological examination to identify type of cognitive impairment	• Brain CT/MRI: lacunar and cortical infarcts or leukoaraiosis • Neuropsychological examination to identify type of cognitive impairment
Tx	Symptomatic	Cholinesterase inhibitors (rivastigmine)	Prevention: combat risk factors

Table 71B // Other types of dementia

REM, rapid eye movement; TDP-43, transactive response DNA binding protein of 43 kDa

	FRONTOTEMPORAL DEMENTIA	LEWY BODY DEMENTIA	VASCULAR DEMENTIA
P	Rapidly progressive, average disease duration <5y	Highly fluctuating course, average disease duration 7y	Slowly progressive, fluctuating course
!		First generation antipsychotics (haloperidol) are contraindicated	

Table 71C // Other types of dementia
REM, rapid eye movement; TDP-43, transactive response DNA binding protein of 43 kDa

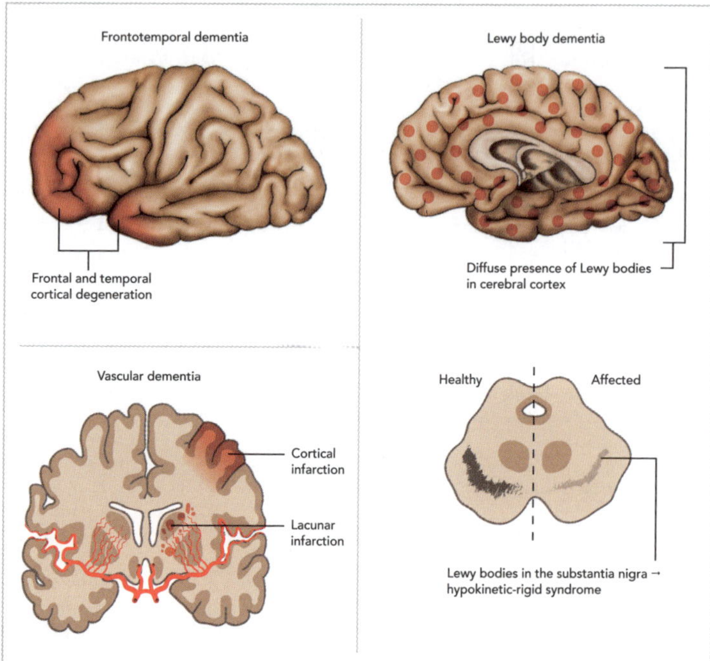

Figure 101 // Types of dementia

The one-year rule is used to distinguish between Lewy body dementia and Parkinson's disease. In Lewy body dementia, cognitive symptoms appear >1y earlier than the motor symptoms. The opposite occurs in Parkinson's dementia.

Narcolepsy

D Narcolepsy is a sleep disorder characterised by daytime sleepiness, sleep paralysis, hypnagogic hallucinations and interrupted sleep. Narcolepsy type 1 is the most common form and is accompanied by cataplexy. Type 2 is narcolepsy without cataplexy.

E Prevalence 25-50:100,000

Ae Lack of neurons producing hypocretin in the hypothalamus. Hypocretin activates various brain structures responsible for wakefulness, inhibits REM sleep and is involved in the regulation of sleep-wake rhythms. There is some debate on whether narcolepsy has an autoimmune or genetic aetiology.

R Positive FHx

Hx Daytime sleepiness, vivid dreams (hypnagogic hallucinations), paralysis during emotions such as laughing or crying (cataplexy), paralysis just after waking up

PE Non-contributing

Dx
- Polysomnography: shortened time to REM sleep, sleep efficiency ↓ and frequent spontaneous awakening
- Multi Sleep Latency Test (MSLT): reduced sleep latency with REM sleep
- LP: CSF hypocretin levels reduced or absent

Tx Schedule daytime naps, psychological support, evaluate ability to drive

Sodium oxybate, wakefulness promoting agents (e.g. modafinil, amphetamines), antidepressants, or benzodiazepines

P Chronic condition, people can live normal lives with lifestyle changes

!
- Often associated with obstructive sleep apnea syndrome (OSAS)
- Sleep deprivation → cataplexy ↑

Peripheral nervous system disorders

Radiculopathies

Radicular syndrome

D A radicular syndrome is caused by irritated nerve roots, usually due to a bulging intervertebral disc (spinal disc herniation), spinal stenosis, and bone spurs. This can lead to radiating pain, paraesthesias, motor and/or sensory deficits, and impaired reflexes. In most cases, spontaneous recovery follows within a few months. Disc herniation is caused by a bulging intervertebral disc that impinges the inferior or superior nerve root. Disc herniation can occur lumbosacrally (90%), cervically and, exceptionally, thoracically (see Table 72).

E Prevalence of lumbosacral radiculopathy 3,000-5,000:100,000, cervical radiculopathy 1-6:100,000

Ae
- Degeneration of intervertebral disc → fissures in annulus fibrosus → protrusion of nucleus pulposus → nerve root compression (see Figure 103)
- Other: trauma, infections (Borrelia, VZV), malignancy (leptomeningeal and vertebral metastasis), ischaemic (DM)

R Disc herniation: age 25-50, ♂:♀ = 2:1, previous episodes of back pain

Hx
- Radiating pain and paraesthesias in a dermatome
- Sharp, stabbing pain
- Disc herniation: pain ↑ in pressure-inducing situations (coughing, sneezing, straining) and when nerve root is stretched

PE
- Reflexes ↓ and muscle weakness, depending on localisation (see Table 72)
- Dysaesthesias or paraesthesias in a dermatome
- Cervical: Lasègue test and Spurling test (see Table 17 and Figure 40)
- Lumbosacral: Lasègue test, crossed-over Lasègue test, reversed Lasègue test, Bragard test, and Kemp test (see Table 18 and Figure 41)

Dx Spinal MRI: disc herniation with nerve root compression

Tx
- Analgesia following WHO analgesic ladder
- Nerve root block: corticosteroid injection

In cauda equina syndrome, rapid increase in motor deficit symptoms, conservative treatment ineffective, untreatable pain: discectomy

P 80% recover spontaneously within wk/mo

Watch out for cauda equina syndrome (medical emergency)

The typical patient with spinal disc herniation presents with progressive tingling, radiating pain and/or numbness in an arm or leg with a dermatomal distribution.

Cauda equina syndrome (see Figure 102): compression across width of entire cauda equina → bilateral loss of sensation in saddle area (radiculopathy), urinary retention (atonic bladder), bladder and rectal sphincter tone ↓, sexual dysfunction, pain in back and/or legs, positive Lasègue test, and weakness or paresis.

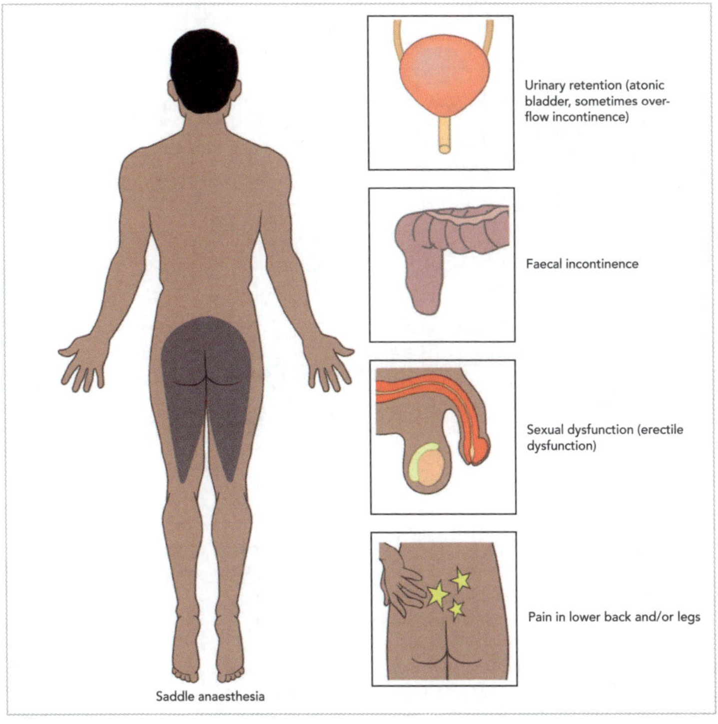

Figure 102 // Cauda equina syndrome

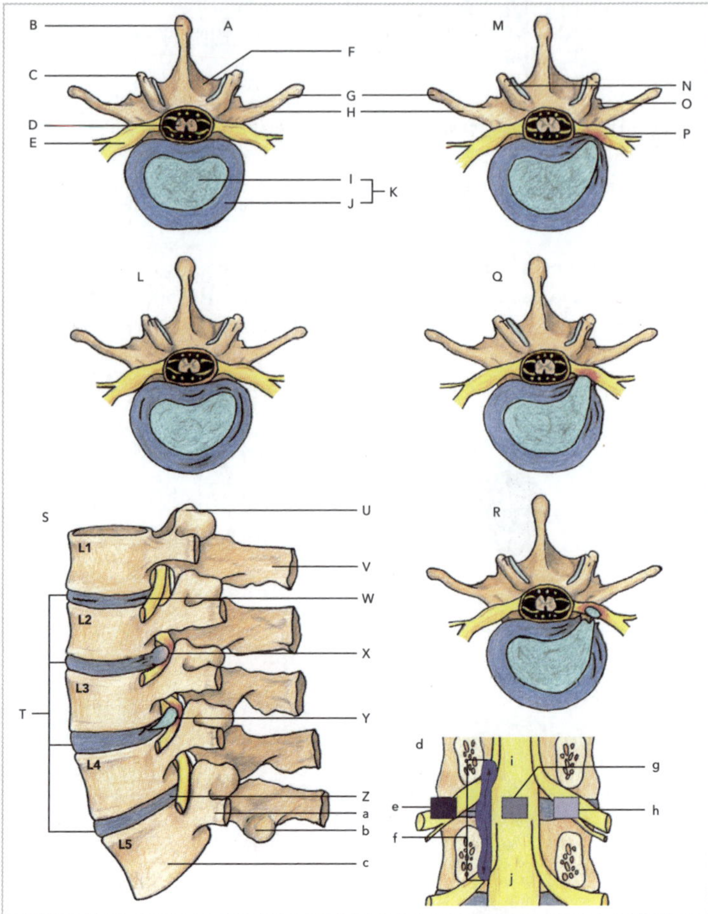

Figure 103 // Spinal disc herniation

A: Normal disc at lumbar vertebra **B:** Spinous process **C:** Mammillary process **D:** Medullary cone **E:** Nerve root **F:** Lamina of the vertebral arch **G:** Costal/transverse process **H:** Pedicule of the vertebral arch **I:** Nucleus pulposus **J:** Annulus fibrosus **K:** Intervertebral disc **L:** Degenerative disc in lumbar vertebra **M:** Prolapsed disc at lumbar vertebra with nerve root compression **N:** Superior articular process **O:** Accessory process **P:** Compression **Q:** Herniated disc at lumbar vertebra with nerve root compression **R:** Sequestrated disc at lumbar vertebra with nerve root compression **S:** Lateral view of L1-L5 **T:** Intervertebral disc **U:** Mamillary process **V:** Spinous process **W:** Degenerative disc **X:** Prolapse with root compression **Y:** Herniation with root compression **Z:** Normal disc **a:** Costal/transverse process **b:** Inferior articular process **c:** Vertebral body **d:** Posterior view of spinal canal and vertebrae **e:** Lateral herniation **f:** Paracentral herniation **g:** Central herniation **h:** Foraminal herniation **i:** Superior migration **j:** Inferior migration

DISC HERNIATION (frequency)	ROOT	PARAESTHESIAS	PAIN	PARESIS		REFLEXES
C5-C6 (25%)	C6	Lateral forearm, thumb	Neck, shoulders, scapula	Biceps brachii muscle, wrist extensors	Elbow flexion, wrist extension	Biceps reflex ↓
C6-C7 (60%)	C7	Anterior forearm, index finger, middle finger	Neck, shoulder, medial arm, and medial hand	Triceps brachii muscle, finger extensors	Elbow extension, wrist flexion, finger extension	Triceps reflex ↓
C7-T1 (8%)	C8	Medial forearm, ring finger, little finger	Neck, shoulder, medial forearm, and medial hand	Triceps brachii muscle ⊖, finger flexors	Elbow extension ⊖, flexion fingers	Triceps reflex ↓ ⊖
L3-L4 (10-20%)	L4	Knee, medial lower leg	Lower back, and front of the thigh	Vastus medialis muscle (part of quadriceps femoris)	Knee extension	Knee reflex ↓
L4-L5 (40-45%)	L5	Lateral side of the thigh, knee and lower leg, medial side of the foot, thumb	Lower back, dorsal side upper leg radiating to the lateral side of the lower leg	Tibialis anterior muscle, extensor hallucis muscle	Dorsal flexion of the foot, inversion/eversion of the foot	N/A
L5-S1 (40-45%)	S1	Dorsal side of the thigh, lateral side of the lower leg, lateral side of the foot, little finger	Lower back, unilateral radiating to the lower leg	Foot and toe flexors	Plantar flexion of the foot	Achilles reflex ↓

Table 72 // Different types of spinal disc herniation

Neuropathies

Plexopathy and mononeuropathy

D Plexopathy is a disorder of the brachial or lumbosacral plexus. A mononeuropathy is a dysfunction of a single nerve (see Table 73).

Ae Depending on location, compression ⊕, trauma ⊕, ischaemia ⊕, infection ⊖, tumour ⊖

Dx EMG: conduction velocity ↓↓ or amplitude ↓↓

Tx Wait-and-see

In neurotmesis: surgical nerve repair

P
- Neuropraxia: axon and nerve sheath intact → spontaneous recovery within hours to weeks
- Axonotmesis: axon damaged, nerve sheath intact → spontaneous recovery within months to years (1 mm/day)
- Neurotmesis: axon and nerve sheath damaged → little to no recovery

NERVES	FUNCTION	CAUSES OF DYSFUNCTION	SYMPTOMS OF DYSFUNCTION
Upper brachial plexus (C5-C7)	Motor and sensory innervation of the arm	• Birth trauma, avulsion trauma • Inflammation: neuralgic shoulder amyotrophy	Erb-Duchenne paralysis/Erb palsy: weakness with external rotation of the shoulder, scapula alata, sensibility of upper arm and radial part of the forearm ↓, dropped shoulder
Lower brachial plexus (C8-T1)		• Birth trauma, trauma, lung tumour • Inflammation: neuralgic shoulder amyotrophy	Klumpke's palsy: paralysis of small muscles of the hand, hand and finger flexors, sensory innervation of ulnar part of the forearm and hand ↓, claw hand
Ulnar nerve	Adduction of thumb, extension of ulnar 2 digits, closing and spreading fingers, sensory innervation of ulnar 1.5 digits	Compression, especially in the cubital tunnel (iatrogenic during surgery, fracture of the medial epicondyle)	Claw hand, loss of fine hand motor skills, tingling, sensory innervation of ulnar 2 digits ↓ (see Figure 104)
Median nerve	Opposition of the thumb, flexion of fingers, sensory innervation of inside of the radial 3 digits	Trauma due to venipuncture, glass injury to the wrist, humeral fracture or upper arm compression (honeymoon palsy), pressure on carpal root, carpal tunnel syndrome	Preacher's hand, hand and finger flexor deficit, tingling or numbness in palm of the hand (see Figure 104)
Radial nerve	• Extension of fingers, wrist and forearm, supination of hand, sensory innervation of lateral side of the arm • Innervation of triceps brachii and brachioradialis muscles	Humeral fracture, compression on upper arm or axilla (Saturday night palsy or crutch palsy)	Dropping hand/dropping fingers, arm extensor deficit, absent triceps reflex, sensory innervation of radial side of the arm, radial 3 digits ↓ (see Figure 104)

Table 73A // Overview of peripheral nerves

NERVES	FUNCTION	CAUSES OF DYSFUNCTION	SYMPTOMS OF DYSFUNCTION
Axillary nerve	Upper arm abduction from 15°, innervation of deltoid muscle	Dislocation or reposition of humerus	Dropped shoulder, deltoid muscle atrophy
Musculocutaneous nerve	• Flexion and external rotation of elbow, sensation of front and lateral side of the arm • Innervation of biceps brachii muscle	Trauma	Sensation of lateral part of the forearm ↓, atrophy: biceps brachii muscle
Suprascapular nerve	• External rotation of shoulder, abduction of upper arm to 15° • Innervation of supraspinatus and infraspinatus muscles	Trauma, compression	Atrophy: infraspinatus muscle, supraspinatus muscle
Long thoracic nerve	• Pulls shoulder blade around chest • Innervation of serratus anterior muscle	Trauma, sports injury, mastectomy with axillary lymph node resection, neuralgic shoulder amyotrophy	Scapula alata
Lumbar plexus (L2-L4)	Motor and sensory innervation of the leg	Trauma, haematoma in iliopsoas muscle, pregnancy/birth, tumour, diabetic amyotrophy	Acute failure of knee extensors and hip flexors, drop foot, absent patellar reflex, medial lower leg and anterior thigh pain
Femoral nerve	Flexion of hip, extension of knee, sensation of front of the thigh, inside of front of the lower leg, innervation of quadriceps femoris muscle	Pelvic surgery, compression by a pelvic mass or peritoneal haematoma, stretch injury of the inguinal structures	Weak knee extensors and hip flexors, sensory innervation of front thigh and inside of front of the lower leg ↓
Obturator nerve	Adduction of thigh, sensory innervation of medial side of the thigh	Compression during complicated delivery (in women), pelvic trauma, pelvic surgery	Weakness of the leg adductor muscles causing gait instability, atrophy, and numbness of the medial thigh
Sciatic nerve	Knee flexion, innervation of hamstrings	Posterior hip dislocation, acetabular fracture, hip surgery, prolonged compression of the buttocks, Borrelia infection, overextension of hip, injection in buttock region	Atrophy: hamstrings

Table 73B // Overview of peripheral nerves

NERVES	FUNCTION	CAUSES OF DYSFUNCTION	SYMPTOMS OF DYSFUNCTION
Tibial nerve	Plantar flexion of foot, flexion of toes, sensory innervation of back of the lower leg and sole of the foot	Ankle fracture or distortion, compression after trauma, tarsal tunnel syndrome	Paraesthesia or hypaesthesia of sole of the foot and back of the lower leg, absent Achilles reflex, calf atrophy
Fibular nerve	• Dorsal flexion of foot, sensory innervation of dorsum of the foot and anterolateral part of the lower leg • Innervation of tibialis anterior muscle and peroneus muscles	Compression (cast, tight socks, crossed legs), stretch injury (foot inversion), trauma	Foot drop, hypaesthesia of dorsum of the foot and lateral part of the lower leg, steppage gait ⊕, atrophy peroneus muscles and tibialis anterior muscle
Superior gluteal nerve	External rotation, internal rotation, flexion and abduction of the thigh	Trauma, total hip replacement	Gluteal muscle atrophy, Trendelenburg's sign
Inferior gluteal nerve	Extension and external rotation of the thigh	Unknown	Gluteal muscle atrophy
Lateral femoral cutaneous nerve	Sensory innervation of the lateral thigh	Nerve compression or stretching in fascia lata, usually near superior anterior iliac spine due to tight-fitting clothing	Painful paraesthesia and sensory innervation of lateral side of the thigh ↓, known as meralgia paraesthetica
Posterior femoral cutaneous nerve	Sensory innervation of back of the thigh and buttock	Unknown	Sensory innervation of back of the thigh and buttock ↓

Table 73C // Overview of peripheral nerves

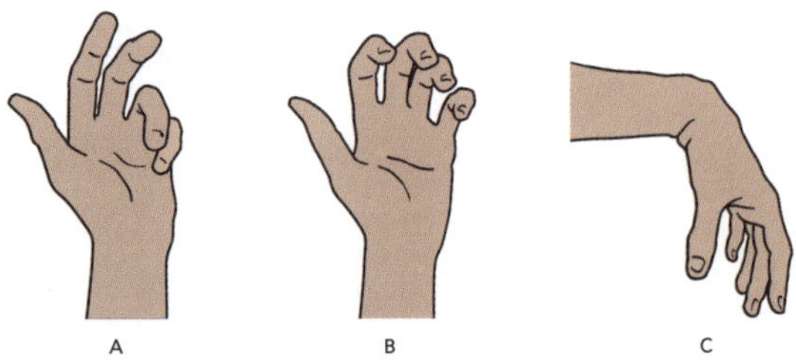

Figure 104 // Clinical features of median, ulnar and radial nerve dysfunction
A: Preacher's hand (median nerve lesion) **B:** Claw hand (ulnar nerve lesion) **C:** Dropping hand (radial nerve lesion)

Carpal tunnel syndrome (CTS)

D CTS is a neuropathy caused by distal compression of the median nerve in the carpal tunnel.

E Prevalence 1-5%

Ae
- Median nerve compression in the carpal tunnel (see Figure 105)
- Carpal tunnel narrowing due to inflammation, anatomical changes or tendon compression

R ♀, pregnancy, obesity, osteoarthritis, rheumatoid arthritis, DM, hypothyroidism, acromegaly, tendovaginitis, polyneuropathy, trauma

Hx
- Tingling in the hand, palmar side from radial 3.5 digits (see Figure 105)
- Nighttime complaints with interrupted sleep
- Shaking hands → symptoms ↓
- Asymmetrically bilateral ⊕

PE
- Thenar atrophy, palmar numbness, sensation ↓
- Impaired pincer grasp and fine motor function
- Hyperflexion of the wrist and throbbing near ligament → complaints ↑ (Tinel's test)

Dx
- Nerve ultrasound: nerve thickening
- EMG: prolonged conduction time of median nerve over wrist

Tx Wrist slightly extended using splint

Corticosteroid injection

Decompression of the median nerve

P Sometimes spontaneous remission, often recurrent

The typical patient with carpal tunnel syndrome complains of numbness in the palm accompanied by tingling in the radial 3.5 digits. This sensation often occurs at night and can be relieved by shaking one's hand.

The letters of the word **MEDIAN TRAP** correspond to the causes of carpal tunnel syndrome: **m**yxoedema, o**e**dematous (pre-menstrual), **D**M, **i**diopathic, **a**cromegaly, **n**eoplasm, **t**rauma, **r**heumatoid arthritis, **a**myloidosis and **p**regnancy.

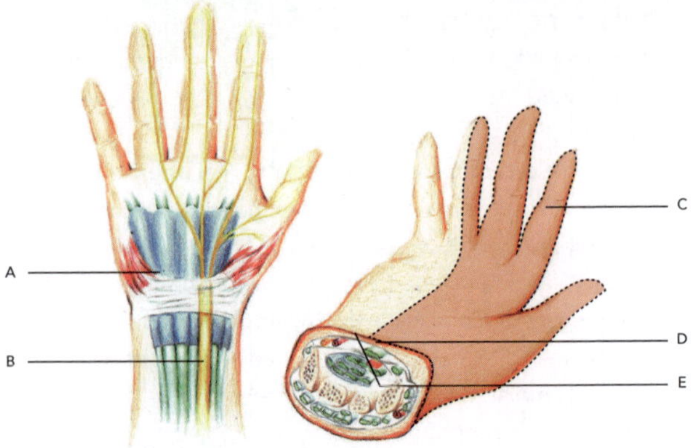

Figure 105 // Carpal tunnel syndrome
A: Flexor retinaculum of the hand **B:** Median nerve **C:** Soreness and numbness **D:** Median nerve entrapment **E:** Carpal tunnel

Ulnar neuropathy

D Ulnar neuropathy is a compression of the ulnar nerve (funny bone) in the cubital tunnel at the elbow (cubital tunnel syndrome, see Figure 106) or in Guyon's tunnel in the wrist (ulnar tunnel syndrome, see Figure 107).

E Prevalence cubital tunnel syndrome 5.9%, prevalence Guyon canal syndrome unkown

Ae Hamate fractures, ganglia, synovitis, aneurysm/thrombosis of ulnar artery, pisotriquetral osteoarthritis

R Compression of the nerve due to overexertion/posture

Hx Pain and paraesthesias in ulnar 2 digits and hypothenar region, muscle weakness ⊖

PE Pain and paraesthesias in ulnar 2 digits, hand muscle atrophy with typical clawing of ulnar 2 digits, difficulty spreading fingers, positive Tinel test

Dx
- EMG: conduction delay or abnormal amplitude decay
- Ultrasound in case of clinical suspicion and normal EMG: thickened ulnar nerve

Tx Rest, possibly ergonomic advice

Consider a splint. Night splinting is the 1st choice for treating cubital tunnel syndrome.

Decompression of the ulnar nerve in Guyon's tunnel or the cubital tunnel. In cubital tunnel surgery, a distinction can be made between simple decompression of the ulnar nerve (1st choice), medial epicondylectomy and anterior transposition of the ulnar nerve (freeing the ulnar nerve and moving it to the flexor side).

P Good

! • After surgery, it may take some time (months to 1y) for symptoms to disappear entirely
• Surgical decompression at the elbow is associated with myriad complications (paraesthesias)

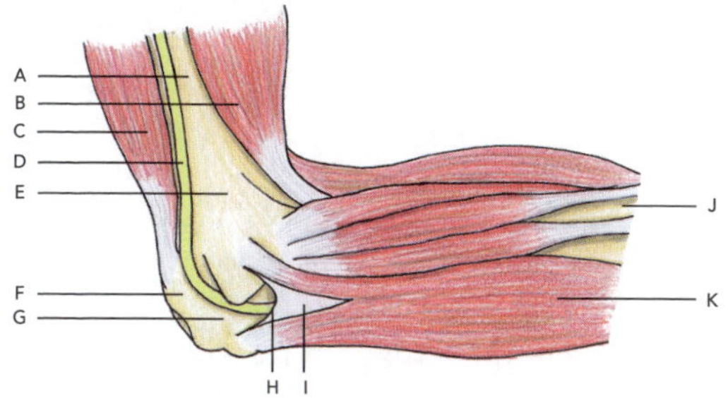

Figure 106 // Cubital tunnel syndrome

A: Humerus **B:** Biceps brachii muscle **C:** Triceps brachii muscle **D:** Ulnar nerve **E:** Medial epicondyle **F:** Olecranon **G:** Ulna **H:** Cubital tunnel **I:** Aponeurosis **J:** Radius **K:** Flexor carpi ulnaris muscle

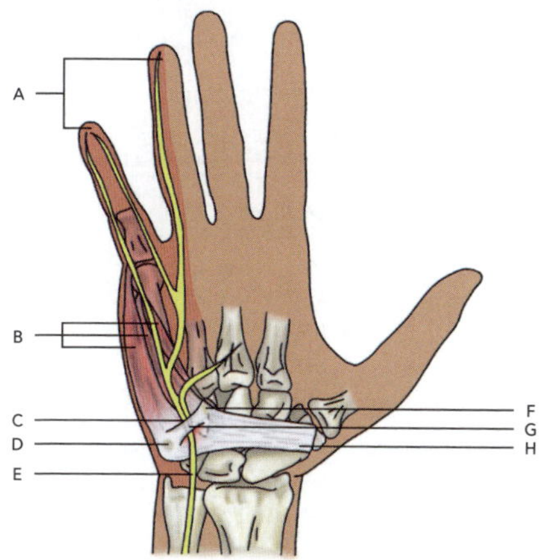

Figure 107 // Ulnar tunnel syndrome

A: Pain/paraesthesia in the ulnar 2 digits **B:** Hypothenar atrophy **C:** Guyon's canal **D:** Pisiform bone **E:** Ulnar nerve **F:** Hook of the hamate bone **G:** Pisohamate ligament **H:** Flexor retinaculum (= roof of the carpal tunnel)

Polyneuropathy

D Polyneuropathy is a symmetrical and generalised dysfunction of especially peripheral nerves (see Table 74 and Figure 108).

	AXONAL NEUROPATHY	DEMYELINATING NEUROPATHY	SMALL FIBRE NEUROPATHY
D	Axonal transport is affected, causing dysfunction.	Schwann's cells are affected, causing dysfunction.	The small unmyelinated (superficial) nerves are affected.
E	Most common	Unknown	Unknown, diagnosis is often missed and explained as somatic symptom disorder
Ae	DM, deficiencies (vitamin B1, B6, B12 or folic acid), alsohol use disorder, toxicity (vitamin B6), HIV or leprosy infections, medication, renal failure, CIP, connective tissue disorders, paraneoplastic	GBS, CIDP (+), hypothyroidism, neuroborreliosis, viral infections with cytomegalovirus, diphtheria or herpes/varicella zoster, paraproteinaemia, Charcot-Marie-Tooth disease (HSMN)	DM, thyroid dysfunction, neurotoxic drugs, vitamin B12 deficiency, HIV
R	Smoking, cardiovascular diseases, disregulated diabetes, alcohol use disorder, long-term bedridden/ICU admission	Recent infection, tick bite, positive FHx for HMSN	DM, thyroid dysfunction, neurotoxic drugs, vitamin B12 deficiency, HIV, autoimmune disease
Hx	• Initial stage: numbness (++), pain (+) or tingling (++) in the toes • Then spreads to feet and lower legs, followed by toe and foot weakness (extensors > flexors) • Culminates in symptoms spreading to fingers and hands or trunk (see Figure 108)	• Painful paraesthesias • Deep sensation: starts distal before spreading in proximal direction • Autonomic symptoms (cardiac arrhythmia, orthostatic hypotension, constipation, diarrhea, impotence, sweating abnormalities, trophic changes)	• Superficial sensory disorders are most noticeable, burning, tingling pain, electric shock-like pain lasting several seconds • Autonomic symptoms (+)

Table 74A // Types of polyneuropathy

CIP, critical illness polyneuropathy; HSMN, hereditary motor sensory neuropathy

	AXONAL NEUROPATHY	DEMYELINATING NEUROPATHY	SMALL FIBRE NEUROPATHY
PE	• Symmetrical sensory deficits (stocking-glove pattern) • Distal weakness • Distal hyporeflexia or areflexia	• Early symptom: absent/ low reflexes • Deep sensation disorders are more common • Proximal and distal loss of strength • Foot abnormalities (e.g. pes cavus, hammer and claw toe deformity)	Symptoms occur mainly in feet, sense of pain and temperature ↓, normal reflexes
Dx	• Labs to identify possible causes: ESR, complete blood count, glucose, HbA1c, liver function, creatinine, thyroid stimulating hormone (TSH), paraprotein, vitamin B1, vitamin B12. Extend laboratory test on indication. • EMG (to distinguish between axonal/demyelinating), consider nerve biopsy, skin biopsy: axon count ↓		
Tx	Treat underlying cause, lifestyle changes In severe cases: physiotherapy Pain relief with amitriptyline, pregabalin, nortriptyline		
!	Polyneuropathy may be an initial sign of a paraneoplastic syndrome		

Table 74B // Types of polyneuropathy
CIP, critical illness polyneuropathy; HSMN, hereditary motor sensory neuropathy

In many cases of polyneuropathy (±25%), the cause is unknown. This is known as CIAP.

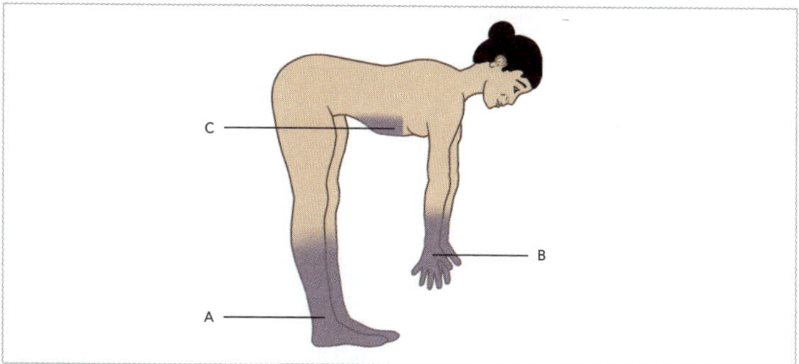

Figure 108 // Polyneuropathy
A: Symmetrical sensory disturbances in the feet, weakness of the toes and feet, delayed/absent Achilles reflex/knee reflex, progresses in distal to proximal direction **B:** Symmetrical sensory disturbances in the hands, progresses in distal to proximal direction **C:** Autonomic function disorders

Guillain-Barré syndrome

Guillain-Barré syndrome (GBS)

D GBS is an acute demyelinating polyneuropathy caused by a dysregulated immune response following bacterial or viral infection.

E Prevalence 0.8-6.4:100,000

Ae
- Dysregulated immune response → myelin sheath inflammation → segmental nerve demyelination → conduction velocity ↓
- 2/3 after bacterial or viral infection (e.g. upper respiratory tract infection, gastroenteritis)
- Cross-reaction between microorganism and peripheral nervous system ('molecular mimicry')

R ♂:♀ = 1.5:1

Hx
- Starts with general malaise, muscle pain, typically located in the back and extremities
- Progressive ascending muscle weakness
- Superficial and deep sensation disorders (e.g. paraesthesias, numbness, dysaesthesias)

PE Autonomic dysfunction (hypertension/hypotension, tachycardia/bradycardia, fever, urinary retention, ileus), decrease of vital capacity, decrease of single breath count

- Progressive symmetric muscle weakness of the legs, spreading to the arms and face (e.g. peripheral facial nerve palsy, see Figure 109)
- Muscle stretch reflexes: ↓/ absent

Dx
- LP: cell count =, protein ↑
- EMG: conduction blocks and severe conduction delay of both motor and sensory nerves

Tx
- Treatment of symptoms
- Hospital admission for monitoring. Indications for intensive care unit (ICU) admission: rapid disease progression, severe autonomic or swallowing dysfunction, respiratory distress, Erasmus GBS Respiratory Insufficiency Score (EGRIS) >4.

IVIG, or plasma exchange if inability to walk >10 m independently, rapid progression, severe autonomic, bulbar or respiratory dysfunction

P
- Mortality despite treatment 3-10%
- After 4 wk of disease activity: plateau phase lasting weeks to months, followed by gradual spontaneous recovery
- 25% develop respiratory failure
- 25% residual symptoms or chronic fatigue
- Recurrences are rare

The severity of disability in GBS can be quantified using the GBS Disability Scale and the EGRIS.

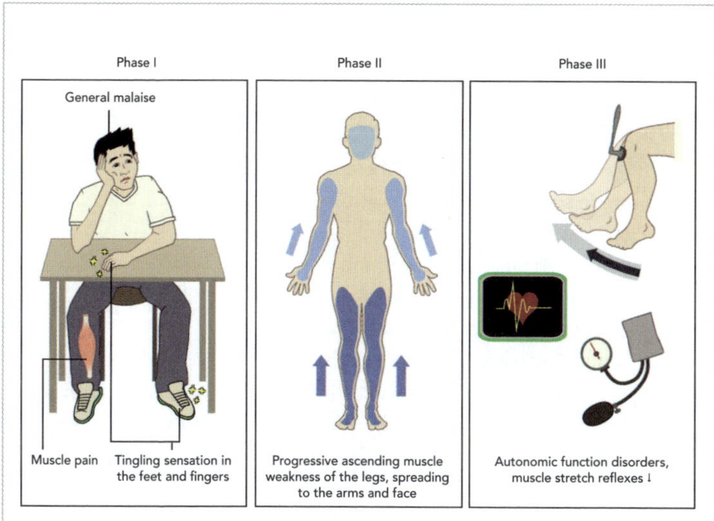

Figure 109 // Guillain-Barré syndrome: different stages

Neuromuscular disorders

Duchenne's muscular dystrophy

D Duchenne's muscular dystrophy is an X-linked recessive hereditary disorder characterised by progressive muscle weakness (see Figure 110).

E Live birth incidence ♂ 1:3,600, prevalence 30:100,000,000

Ae
- Mutation in the dystrophin gene (locus Xp21) → dystrophin level low or absent
- X-linked recessive inheritance
- $^1/_3$ spontaneous mutation
- Muscle tissue is replaced with connective tissue and fat

R Age of onset 2-3, positive FHx, mostly ♂ affected, ♀ are carriers (may experience mild symptoms)

Hx
- Proximal muscle weakness → learning to walk at 18 mo: frequent falls, Gowers' sign (see Figure 111)

- Growth restriction, 1/3 also mental retardation
- Carriers: mild muscle weakness, cardiomyopathy

PE Waddling gait, hyperlordosis, pseudohypertrophic calves, scoliosis

Dx
- Labs: CK ↑↑
- Echocardiography: dilated cardiomyopathy
- Muscle biopsy: dystrophic abnormalities
- Absence of dystrophin protein in muscle tissue (muscle biopsy)
- DNA test: Xp21 gene mutation

Tx Physiotherapy, occupational therapy
- Prednisone → improves muscle strength and progression of cardiomyopathy ↓
- Studies on pharmacological and gene therapy are ongoing, but these novel treatments are not yet standard practice

- Correct scoliosis and stabilise spine
- Ventilation in late stage

P Slowly progressive until all skeletal muscles of the trunk and limbs are affected, patients are wheelchair-bound around age 11, max. life expectancy 40y, eye, mouth, swallowing muscles and diaphragm are spared for a long time

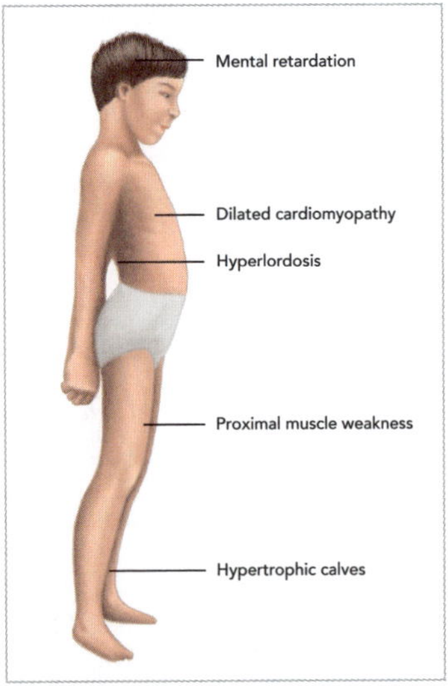

Figure 110 // Duchenne's muscular dystrophy

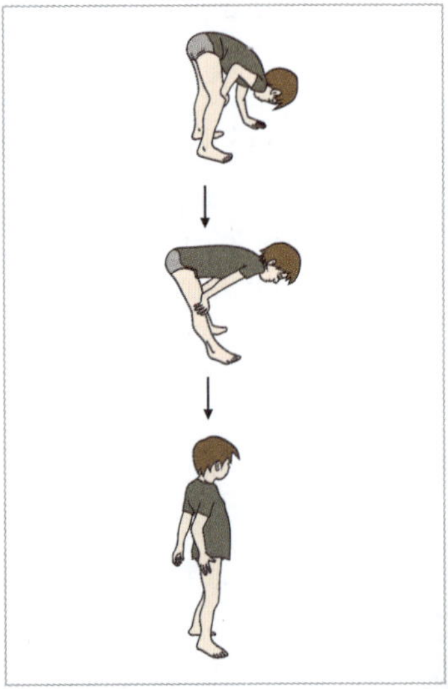

Figure 111 // Duchenne's muscular dystrophy: Gowers' sign

The typical patient with Duchenne's disease presents with delayed motor development and progressive proximal muscle weakness, leading to severe disability.

Becker's muscular dystrophy

D Becker's muscular dystrophy is an X-linked recessive hereditary disorder characterised by progressive muscle weakness. Becker's muscular dystrophy is seen as a relatively mild variant of Duchenne's disease.

E Live birth incidence ♂ 3:100,000, prevalence 10:100,000,000

Ae
- X-linked recessive inheritance
- Mutation in dystrophin gene → abnormal dystrophin level

R Age of onset <10, positive FHx, only ♂ affected, ♀ carriers, genetic: mutation in dystrophin gene

Hx Often detected in connection with cardiac complaints, muscle cramps, mental retardation ⊖

PE Muscle weakness (less pronounced than in Duchenne's disease)

Dx
- Labs: CK ↑
- Echocardiography: dilated cardiomyopathy
- Muscle biopsy: dystrophin level ↓
- DNA testing: demonstrate causal mutation

Tx Exercise therapy

Surgical deformity correction, heart transplant if indicated

P More rapidly progressive, wheelchair-bound around age 30, life expectancy 20-80y

Myotonic dystrophy

D Myotonic dystrophy is a multisystem disease characterised neurologically by myotonia and muscle weakness.

E Prevalence 13:100,0000

Ae CTG repeat expansion on the long arm of chromosome 19, autosomal dominant inheritance

R ♂:♀ = 1:1, age of onset 15-30

Hx Cataract is often the first symptom, myotonia especially of the hands (relaxation disorder)

PE
- Type I: muscle weakness starting in distal muscles, atrophy, mental retardation, cardiac arrhythmia, gastrointestinal disorders (see Figure 112)

- Type II: proximal muscle weakness, fewer cardiac symptoms (see Figure 113)

Percussion myotonia

Dx
- EMG: myotonia
- DNA analysis: trinucleotide repeat on chromosome 19

Tx Physiotherapy, occupational therapy

Sometimes medication for muscle cramps

P Slowly progressive, ultimately disabling in late life

! Anticipation (earlier age of onset in every subsequent generation), many complications in pregnancy, complications with anaesthesia

Myotonia: delayed relaxation after muscle contraction.

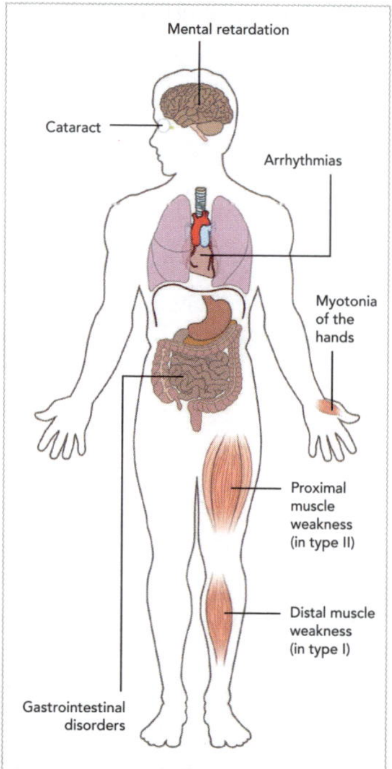

Figure 112 // Myotonic dystrophy: general symptoms

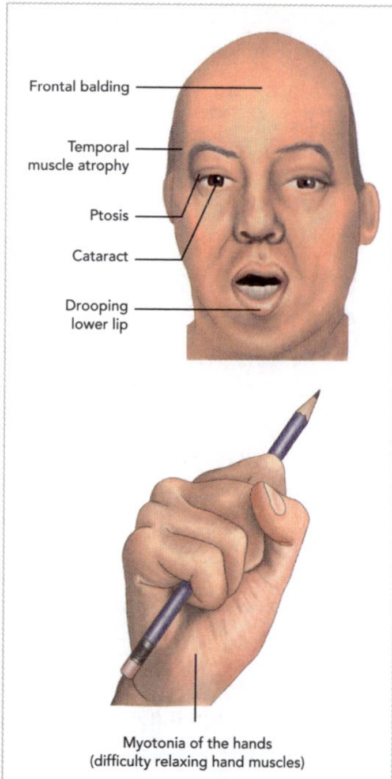

Figure 113 // Myotonic dystrophy: myotonia and facial features

Neuromuscular junction disorders

D Neuromuscular junction disorders are associated with myasthenia. Myasthenia is an abnormal muscle weakness affected by fatigue. See Table 75 for neuromuscular junction disorders.

	MYASTHENIA GRAVIS	LAMBERT-EATON MYASTHENIC SYNDROME (LEMS)
D	Autoimmune disorder in which antibodies to the AChR or MuSK cause variable muscle weakness (see Figure 114).	Autoimmune disorder, often arising as a paraneoplastic symptom, usually secondary to a lung carcinoma.
E	Prevalence 10-20:100,000	Prevalence 2.5:1,000,000
Ae	IgG autoantibodies to the postsynaptic AChR or MuSK → neuromuscular junction blockade (see Figure 115)	• IgG autoantibodies to presynaptic VGCC → release of acetylcholine ↓ (see Figure 116) • 55% small-cell lung carcinoma (paraneoplastic phenomenon)
R	Common onset age ♀: 20-39y, peaks at both early and late onset, ♂: 50 and 70y, only peaks at late onset	• Non tumour LEMS ♂:♀ = 1:1 • Paraneoplastic LEMS ♂:♀ = 3:1
Hx	• Varying muscle weakness: worse at the end of the day, under stress or after exertion, and improves after rest • >50% presents with ocular symptoms (ptosis, diplopia) • Generalised weakness (proximal limbs, axial muscles), bulbar weakness (dysarthria, dysphagia) • Dropped head syndrome at the end of the day • Anti-MuSK type: mainly weakness of cranial and bulbar muscles with neck and respiratory involvement	• Initial stage: mainly muscle weakness in upper legs (difficulty getting up and walking) • Autonomic dysfunction (dry mouth, impotence, constipation, orthostatic hypotension) • Later: bulbar symptoms, ocular symptoms, spreading muscle weakness (proximally to distallly, and caudally to cranially) • Symptoms do not vary during the day
PE	Paresis of affected muscles (can be elicited with provocation tests), muscle atrophy, ptosis, diplopia	Reflexes ↓ (brisk after prior contraction, ptosis, diplopia, muscle weakness, muscle strength increases after repeated contractions or stimulation, no atrophy

Table 75A // Types of neuromuscular junction disorders
AChR, acetylcholine receptor; MuSK, muscle-specific tyrosine kinase; VGCC, voltage-gated calcium channels

	MYASTHENIA GRAVIS	LAMBERT-EATON MYASTHENIC SYNDROME (LEMS)
Dx	• Labs: anti-AChR antibodies, anti-MuSK antibodies • EMG: repetitive stimulation → subsequent muscle action potentials are 10% smaller than preceding potentials (decremental pattern) • Mediastinum CT: thymoma	• Labs: anti-VGCC antibodies • EMG: repetitive stimulation → initially low muscle action potentials, increase after contraction (incremental pattern) • Chest CT/bronchoscopy: lung carcinoma
Tx	Acetylcholinesterase inhibitors (e.g. pyridostigmine), immunosuppressants (e.g. prednison, azathioprine), IVIG, plasmapheresis • Thymectomy • For respiratory muscle paralysis: mechanical ventilation	Treat underlying lung carcinoma • 3,4-diaminopyridine • Immunosuppressants if symptoms persist
P	• Slowly progressive, spontaneous remission and exacerbations possible, 10% spontaneous remission after 10-15y • 15% also thymoma → more severe disease	Progresses within weeks to months, course depends on aetiology (tumour often determines prognosis)
!	• Myasthenic crisis: acute deterioration with paralysis of swallowing, or breathing muscles • Some medication is contraindicated → they can cause exacerbation of myasthenia gravis symptoms • Neonatal myasthenia gravis: antibodies pass through placenta, duration 18 days	Survival of non tumour LEMS comparable to general population

Table 75B // Types of neuromuscular junction disorders

AChR, acetylcholine receptor; MuSK, muscle-specific tyrosine kinase; VGCC, voltage-gated calcium channels

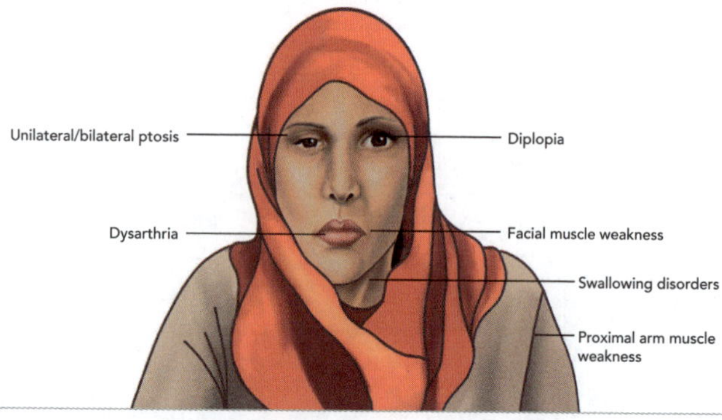

Figure 114 // Myasthenia gravis: typical facial features

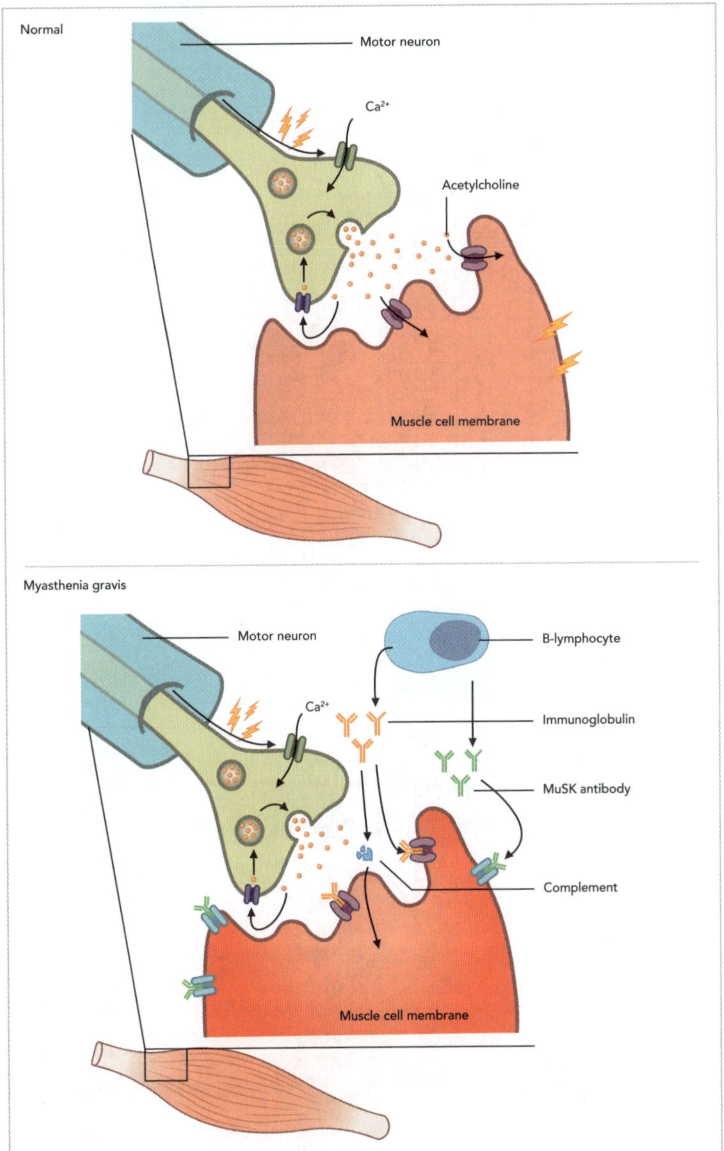

Figure 115 // Myasthenia gravis

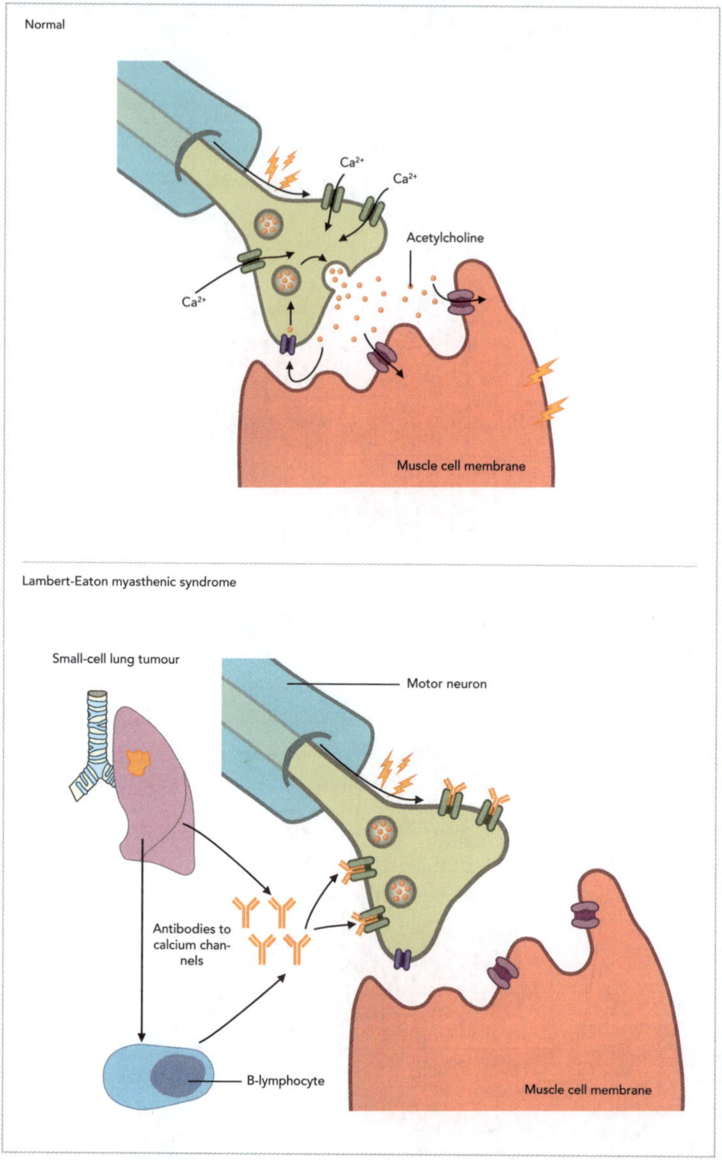

Figure 116 // Lambert-Eaton myasthenic syndrome

Anterior horn disorders

Amyotrophic lateral sclerosis (ALS)

D ALS is a neurodegenerative disorder affecting both central motor neurons and peripheral motor neurons. It therefore has features of both central and peripheral motor disorders.

E Incidence 2-3:100,000 per year

Ae
- Anterior horn motor cell degeneration → axonal loss and gliosis (scarring)
- 5-10% familial (autosomal dominant inheritance)
- Possible correlation with glutamate metabolism, intoxication, oxidative stress and intracellular calcium homeostasis abnormalities

R Age 50-60, ♂:♀ = 3:2, positive FHx

Hx
- Initial stage: muscle cramps and progressive asymmetric loss of strength hands (fine finger movements ↓) and/or feet (difficulty walking) (see Figure 117)
- Fasciculations, spasticity, weight ↓
- Later: bulbar muscles → swallowing disorder (dysphagia), dysarthria
- Pseudobulbar reflexes: compulsive laughing and crying
- Higher cerebral functions, control of eye movements and sensory innervation remain intact

PE
- Initial stage: paresis of the feet (drop foot), hands, bulbar muscles ⊖, hypertonia, hyperreflexia, atrophy
- Later: generalised paresis, fasciculations, muscle stretch reflexes ↑, pathological reflexes

Dx
- EMG: acute and chronic denervation symptoms
- Brain or spinal MRI: rule out other causes

Tx Physiotherapy, occupational therapy
- Glutamate antagonist (riluzole) → slightly delays course
- Anticholinergics, botulinum injections

Percutaneous endoscopic gastrostomy (PEG) tube, ventilation

P Progressive, median survival 3-5y, death from respiratory failure, 10-20% live longer than 10y

! 60-70% spreads in fixed order: e.g. affected leg → contralateral leg → ipsilateral arm → contralateral arm

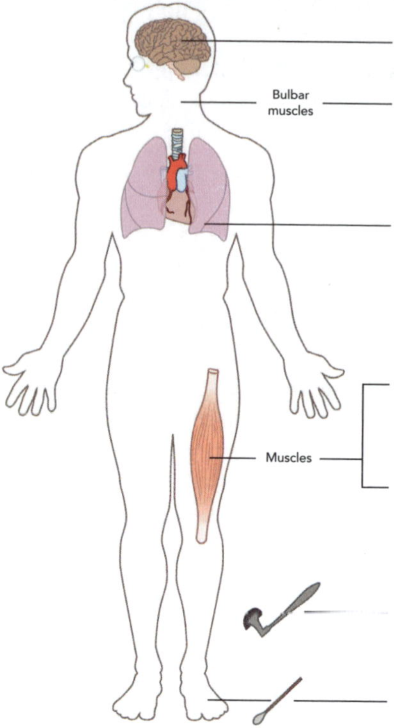

Figure 117 // Amyotrophic lateral sclerosis

Spinal muscular atrophy (SMA)

D SMA is a hereditary disorder resulting from degeneration of anterior horn motor cells that is characterised by muscle weakness, atrophy, fasciculations and reduced muscle stretch reflexes. See Table 76 for three different types.

E Live birth incidence 8-10:100,000 per year

> **Fasciculations** are typical of PMN disorders, especially those involving anterior horn motor cells.

	TYPE I	TYPE II	TYPE III
D	Werdnig-Hoffmann disease, infantile	Intermediate; Dubowitz syndrome	Wohlfart-Kugelberg-Welander disease
E	Most common type, 50% of SMA patients	34% of SMA patients	16% of SMA patients
Ae	Autosomal recessive inheritance, defects on chromosome 5, SMN1 gene defect → no functional SMN protein production		
R	Age of onset <6 mo	Age of onset 6-18 mo	Age of onset 18 mo to 20y
Hx	• Limited fetal movements during pregnancy • Difficulty crying, swallowing, sucking • Child unable to sit independently • Little spontaneous motor activity • Preserved facial expressions	Stalled motor development (child learns to sit but not to walk) after 3 mo, loss of previously acquired skills	• Learns to walk, later loss of motor skills • Starts in thigh and pelvic muscles, followed by shoulder, trunk and neck weakness
PE	• Initial stage: hypotonia (floppy infant, see Figure 118), contractures, tongue fasciculations • Later stage: paralysis of trunk, neck and extremity muscles	• Initial stage: proximal muscle weakness (legs > arms), atrophy, finger tremor, scoliosis • Later: tetraplegia, contracture formation and severe kyphoscoliosis	• Finger tremors, proximal leg paresis, atrophy • Tongue and distal muscles not affected until late stage
Dx	• EMG: reduced conduction velocity and/or reduced amplitude • Muscle biopsy: dystrophic abnormalities • DNA testing: demonstrate causal mutation		
Tx	Symptomatic: nutrition, ventilation, orthopaedic aids In severe cases: physiotherapy Nusinersen (Spinraza): improves SMN2 function → increases SMN protein production		
P	Life expectancy max. 2y	Adulthood reached, but shortened life expectancy (10-40y)	Often wheelchair-bound, life expectancy not shortened
!	N/A	Watch out for respiratory failure	N/A

Table 76 // Types of hereditary proximal spinal muscular atrophy
SMN, survival motor neuron

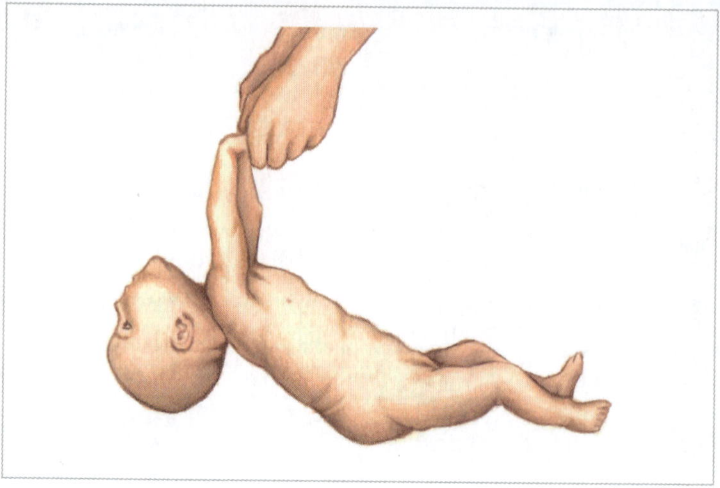

Figure 118 // Hereditary proximal spinal muscular atrophy (floppy infant)

Clinical reasoning

This section lists several examples of diagnoses to consider for specific symptoms.

Headache

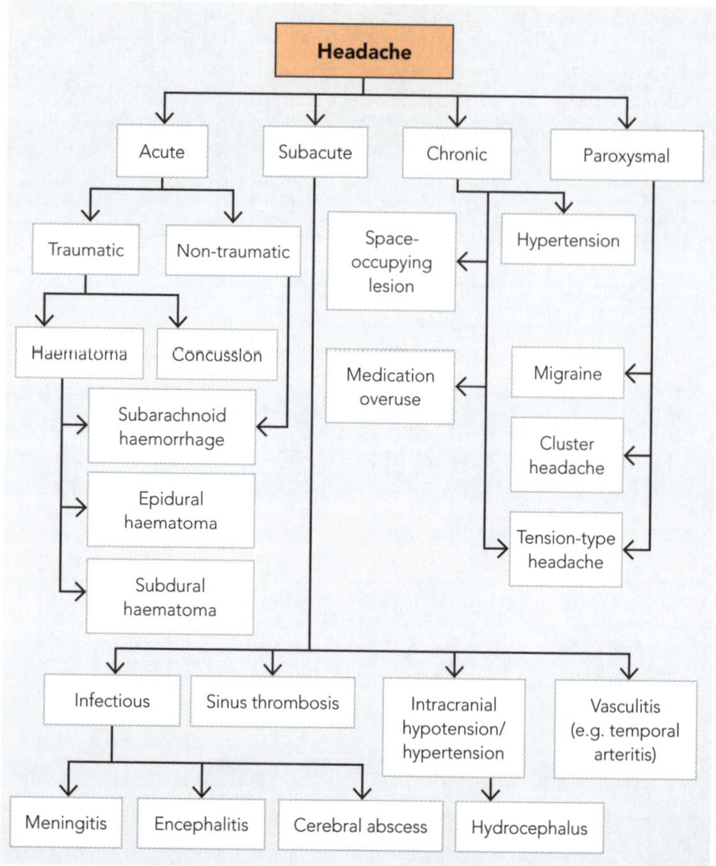

Diagram 5 // DDx Headache

Transient loss of consciousness

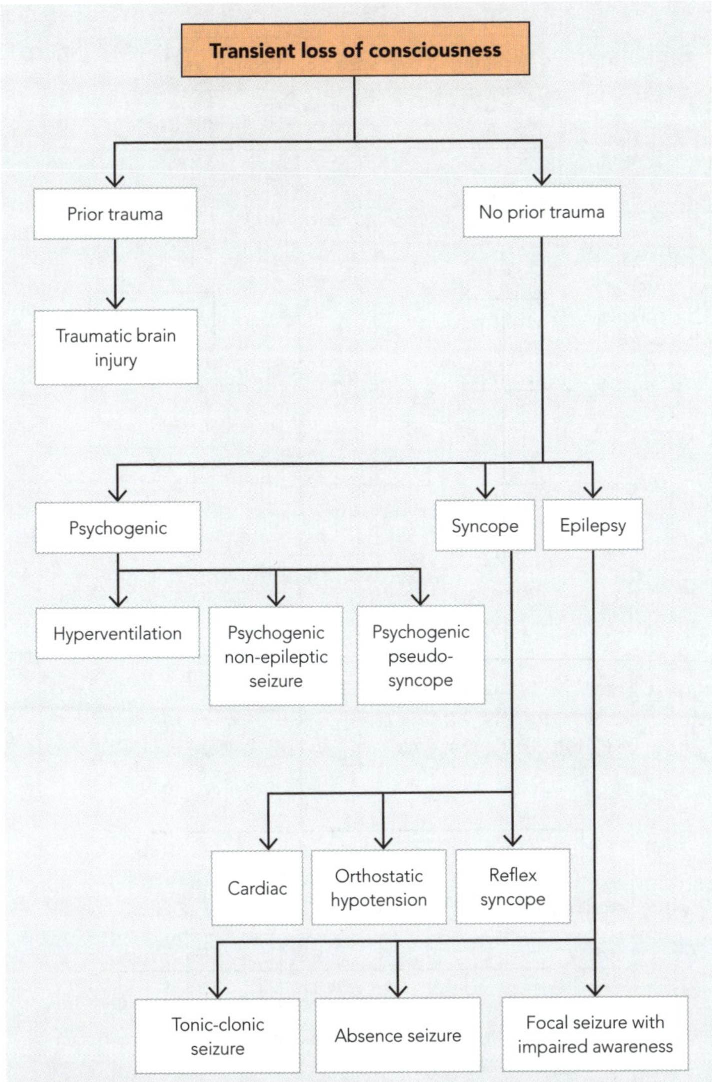

Diagram 6 // DDx Transient loss of consciousness

Prolonged decreased consciousness

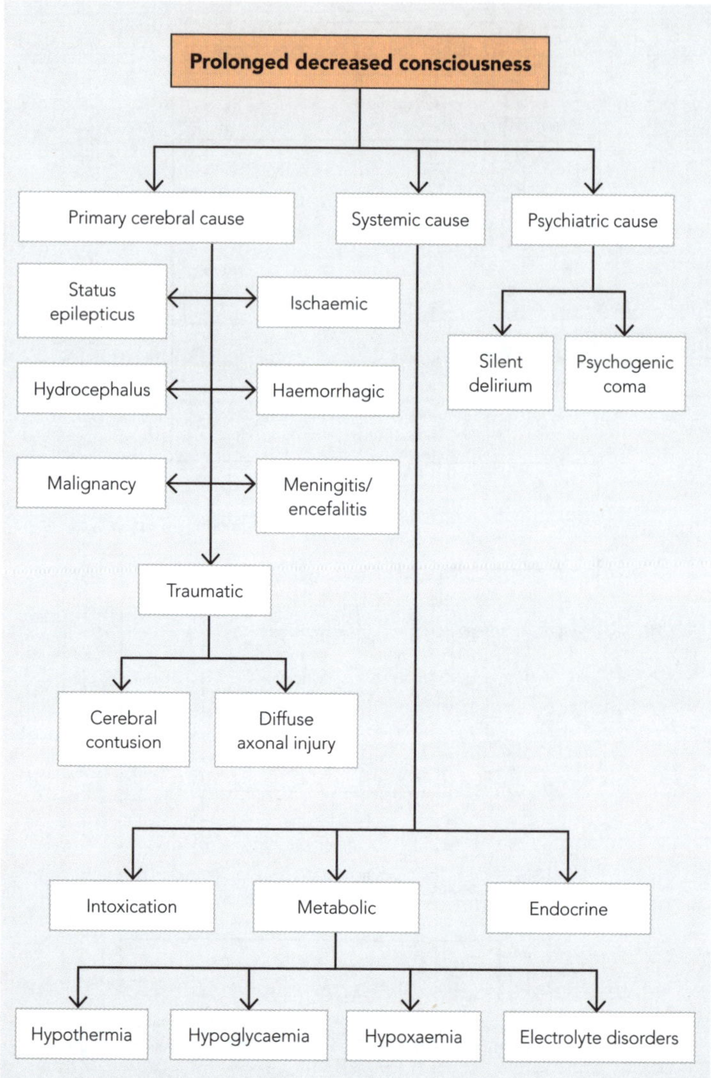

Diagram 7 // DDx Prolonged decreased consciousness

Dizziness

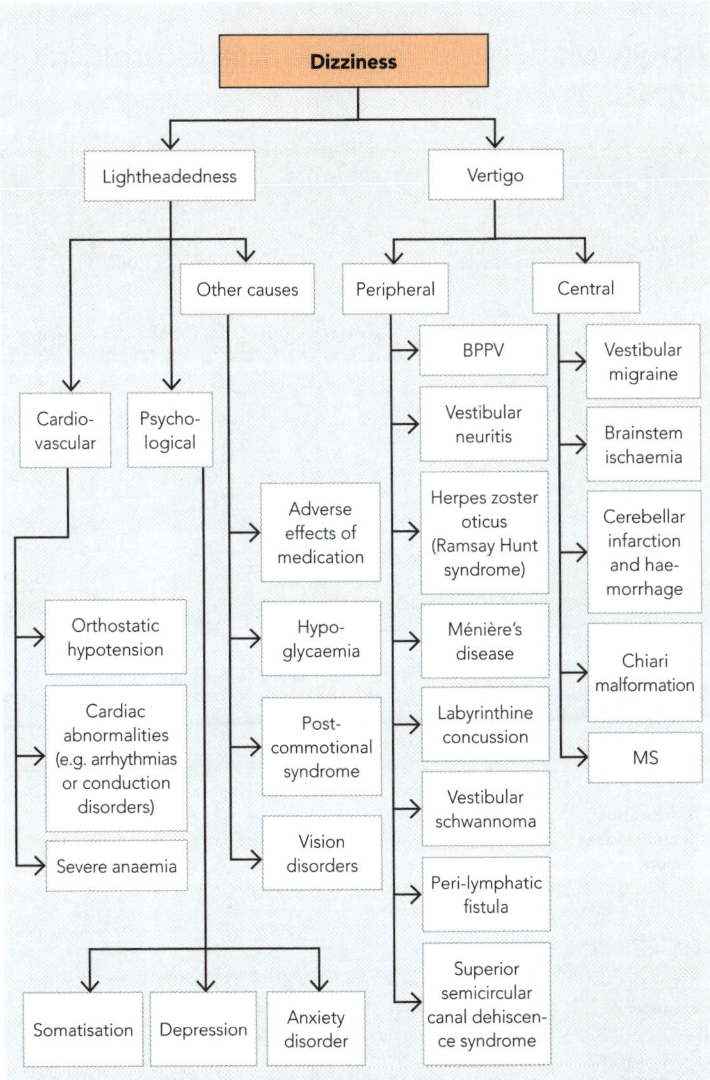

Diagram 8 // DDx Dizziness

Appendices

Appendix 1: Mini Mental-State Examination (MMSE)

Give a brief introduction to the MMSE.

'I will now ask you a few questions and give you a few problems to solve. Try to answer the questions to the best of your ability.'

ASSIGNMENT	INSTRUCTIONS	SCORE
1. Orientation in time	a. What year is it? b. What season is it? c. What month of the year is it? d. What day is it? e. What day of the week is it?	Total: 0-5
2. Orientation in space	a. Which province are you in now? b. Which place are you in now? c. Which building are you in now? d. What is the name of the ward you are in now? e. What floor are you on now?	Total: 0-5
3. Registration	I will now list three items. Please repeat all three after me. 'Apple, key, cupboard' • 1 point for each correct answer, repeat up to five times until the patient knows all the answers.	Total: 0-3
4. Attention and calculation	a. Subtract 7 from 100 and subtract 7 from the result until I say stop. • When the patient stops, repeat the same instructions three times, giving it up to 1 minute. b. Can you spell the word 'world' backwards?	Total: 0-5
5. Recall	Can you repeat the same items as before? (Assignment 3)	Total: 0-3
6. Language (naming)	What is this? And what is that? • Point at a pen and a watch. 1 point for each correct answer.	Total: 0-2
7. Language (repeat)	Please repeat the following sentence: 'No ifs, ands, or buts' • 1 point for a complete, correct sentence.	Total: 0-1

Table 77A // Mini Mental-State Examination (MMSE)

ASSIGNMENT	INSTRUCTIONS	SCORE
8. Language (comprehension)	Please read the words and follow the instructions. • Show the patient a sheet of paper that reads the following in a sufficiently large font: 'Close your eyes.'	Total: 0-1
9. Language (comprehension)	Take this piece of paper with your right hand, fold it in two and put it on your lap. • 1 point for each action performed correctly.	Total: 0-3
10. Language (writing)	Can you write a full sentence for me on this sheet of paper? • 3 points if the sentence has a subject (1 point), predicate (1 point) and meaning (1 point).	Total: 0-3
11. Copying	Can you copy this image? • 1 point if the patient draws the image correctly. 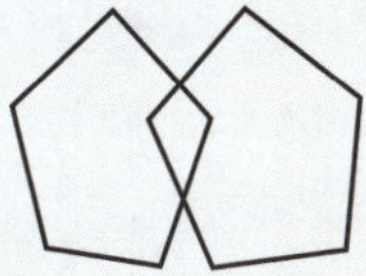	Total: 0-1
		Score ≥24: normal

Table 77B // Mini Mental-State Examination (MMSE)

Appendix 2: Montreal Cognitive Assessment (MoCA)

COGNITIVE DOMAIN	INSTRUCTION	SCORE
1. Visuospatial / executive	Draw the line, start from a number to a letter in ascending order, from 1 – A – 2 …. (1 point) 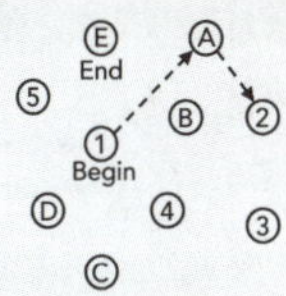 Copy the cube (1 point) 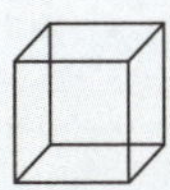 Draw a clock and set the time to 10 past 11 (contour 1 point, numbers 1 point, hands 1 point)	

Table 78A // Montreal Cognitive Assessment (MoCA)

COGNITIVE DOMAIN	INSTRUCTION	SCORE
2. Naming	Name the following animals (1 point for each correct answer) 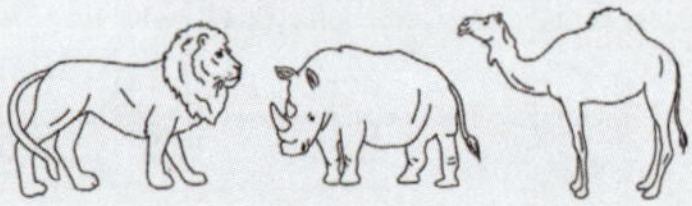	
3. Memory	Read the following list of the words: Face – Velvet – Church – Daisy - Red The patient must repeat them. Do 2 trials. Do a delayed recall after 5 min.	No points
4. Attention	Repeat in forward order: 2 - 1 - 8 - 5 - 4 (1 point) Repeat in backward order: 7 - 4 - 2 (1 point) Read the list of letters (1 letter/second). The patient must tap with his hand at each letter A. (Correct = 1 point. No points if ≥2 errors) F B A C M N A A J K L B A F A K D E A A A J A M O F A A B Serial 7 substraction starting from 100 (93 - 86 - 79 - 72 - 65) 0 correct = 0 point 1 correct = 1 point 2-3 correct = 2 points 4-5 correct = 3 points	
5. Language	Repeat: • I only know that John is the one to help today (1 point) • The cat always hid under the couch when dogs were in the room (1 point) Name maximum number of words in one minute that begin with the letter F (1 point if ≥11 words)	
6. Abstraction	Similarity between e.g. banana and orange = fruit • Train - bicycle (1 point) • Watch - ruler (1 point)	

Table 78B // Montreal Cognitive Assessment (MoCA)

COGNITIVE DOMAIN	INSTRUCTION	SCORE
7. Delayed recall	Recall the words from 'memory' (1 point for each uncued word) • Face • Velvet • Church • Daisy • Red	
8. Orientation	Ask the following questions (1 point for each correct answer) Tell me the: • Date • Month • Year • Day (of the week) • Place • City	
		Total*

Table 78C // Montreal Cognitive Assessment (MoCA)
*Normal total score ≥26 points

Appendix 3: Frontal Assessment Battery (FAB)

The FAB is a tool for evaluating frontal cognitive functions.

ITEM	INSTRUCTIONS	SCORE	
1. Conceptua-lisation	In what way are a banana and an orange alike? A table and a chair? A tulip, a rose and a daisy?	For every correct response	1
2. Fluency	The examiner asks the patient to say as many words as they can beginning with the letter 's' for 1 minute (excluding people and place names).	• 3 words • 3-5 words • 6-9 words • 9 words	0 1 2 3

Table 79A // Frontal Assessment Battery (FAB)

ITEM	INSTRUCTIONS	SCORE	
3. Motor sequences	The examiner demonstrates the Luria sequence. The patient is asked to follow along first, after which the patient is asked to repeat the motions independently. Perform the following motions: 1. fist, 2. edge of the hand on the table (little finger at the bottom), 3. palm flat on the table. The examiner performs three sequences together with the patient, after which the patient continues independently.	• Patient cannot perform the sequence with the examiner • Patient cannot perform the hand motions independently, but can follow along • Patient can independently perform three successive sequences • Patient can independently perform six successive sequences	0 1 2 3
4. Conflicting instructions	Instructions: 'Tap twice when I tap once.' (The examiner performs a sequence of three single taps: 1-1-1) 'And tap once when I tap twice.' (The examiner performs a sequence of three double taps: 2-2-2 The examiner then taps the following sequence: 1-1-2-1-2-2-2-1-1-2)	• Patient copies sequence four times • 2 mistakes • 1-2 mistakes • 0 mistakes	0 1 2 3
5. Go/No-go	Instructions: 'Tap twice when I tap once.' (The examiner performs a sequence of three single taps: 1-1-1) 'And do not tap when I tap twice.' (The examiner performs a sequence of three double taps: 2-2-2. The examiner then taps the following sequence: 1-1-2-1-2-2-2-1-1-2)	• Patient copies sequence four times • 2 mistakes • 1-2 mistakes • 0 mistakes	0 1 2 3
6. Prehension	The examiner asks the patient to place their hands on the table with their palms up. Next, they tell the patient: 'Do not take my hands', before bringing their hands close to the patient's hands or touching them. If the patient takes the hands, the examiner repeats the same instruction: 'Do not take my hands', before bringing their hands closer to the patient a second time.	• Patient takes examiner's hands every time • Patient takes examiner's hands without hesitation • Patient hesitates and asks what they have to do • Patient does not take the examiner's hands	0 1 2 3

Table 79B // Frontal Assessment Battery (FAB)

Appendix 4: NIH Stroke Scale (NIHSS)

CATEGORY	EXTRA INSTRUCTIONS	SCALE	SCORE
1a. Level of consciousness		0 = Alert 1 = Not alert, but arousable 2 = Not alert, requires repeated stimulation to arouse or moves to pain stimulation 3 = Unresponsive or response with reflex	
1b. Question: month and age	Ask the month and age	0 = Both correct 1 = One correct/unable to speak (intubation/orotracheal trauma/severe dysarthria, language barrier) 2 = Neither correct (or aphasia/stuporous)	
1c. Command	Close eyes, squeeze hand (pantomime if communication barrier)	0 = Performs both tasks correctly 1 = Performs one task 2 = Neither task performed	
2. Horizontal gaze movement		0 = Normal 1 = Partial gaze palsy 2 = Forced deviation	
3. Visual fields		0 = No visual loss 1 = Partial hemianopia 2 = Complete hemianopia 3 = Bilateral hemianopia	
4. Facial palsy	Raise eyebrows, close eyes, show teeth	0 = Normal 1 = Minor paralysis (flattened nasolabial fold, asymmetry on smiling) 2 = Partial paralysis ((near)total paralysis of lower face) 3 = Complete paralysis (one or both sides)	
5a. Motor left arm	Extend arm for 10 sec • Sitting position: 90° • Supine position: 45°	0 = No drift 1 = Drift 2 = Some effort against gravity 3 = No effort against gravity 4 = No movement UN* = amputation or joint fusion	

Table 80A // NIH Stroke Scale (NIHSS)
*UN = Untestable

CATEGORY	EXTRA INSTRUCTIONS	SCALE	SCORE
5b. Motor right arm	Extend arm for 10 sec • Sitting position: 90° • Supine position: 45°	0 = No drift 1 = Drift 2 = Some effort against gravity 3 = No effort against gravity 4 = No movement UN* = amputation or joint fusion	
6a. Motor left leg	Hold the leg at 30° for 5 sec	0 = No drift 1 = Drift 2 = Some effort against gravity 3 = No effort against gravity 4 = No movement UN* = amputation or joint fusion	
6b. Motor right leg	Hold the leg at 30° for 5 sec	0 = No drift 1 = Drift 2 = Some effort against gravity 3 = No effort against gravity 4 = No movement UN* = amputation or joint fusion	
7. Limb ataxia		0 = Absent 1 = Present in 1 limb 2 = Present in 2 limbs UN* = amputation of joint fusion	
8. Sensation		0 = Normal 1 = Mild-to-moderate sensory loss 2 = Severe-to-total sensory loss	
9. Aphasia		0 = No aphasia 1 = Mild-to-moderate aphasia 2 = Severe aphasia 3 = Mute, global aphasia	
10. Dysarthria		0 = Normal 1 = Mild-to-moderate dysarthria 2 = Severe dysarthria UN* = Intubated or other physical barriers	
11. Extinction and inattention		0 = No abnormality 1 = Visual tactile, auditory, spatial or personal inattention 2= Profound extinction or hemi-inattention ≥1 modality	

Table 80B // NIH Stroke Scale (NIHSS)

*UN = Untestable

Appendix 5: Brain CT assessment

1. Patient information

- Name patient, date of birth, hospital-specific patient identification number
- Acquisition date and time CT scan

2. Brain

- Asymmetry or flattening of the gyri and sulci
- Abnormal grey and white matter differentiation
- Hypodense/hyperdense abnormalities (location, size, good/bad delineation)
- Oedema
- Mass effect or signs of herniation. Sufficient liquor (space) surrounding the brainstem? Midline shift?

3. Haemorrhage

- Type, cause and location (frontal, parietal, temporal, occipital)
- Subarachnoid cisterns: Sylvian fissure (between the temporal and frontal lobes), quadrigeminal cistern (W-shape on transverse images), suprasellar cisterns (pentagon on transverse images), prepontine cisterns (crescent on transverse images), great cistern (caudal of cerebellum and dorsal of medulla oblongata)

4. Ventricular system

- Hydrocephalus
- Intraventricular blood (hyperdensity), blood-fluid level

5. Skull

- Extracranial soft tissue swelling
- Fracture and secondary signs of fracture e.g. pneumocephalus (air in cranial space)
- Air retention of the sinuses and mastoid, air-fluid (blood) levels in the sinus

6. Compare with previous scans

New/changed findings compared with previous scans

Appendix 6: Neurological status

Tables 81 and 82 show clinical notes for a neurological examination in an unaffected patient.

ITEM	NOTE
General	Patient is alert, GCS/EMV 4-6-5, oriented to person, space and time, no lateralisation, no dysphasia or dysarthria, no meningeal irritation.
Cranial nerves	Isocoric pupils, both reactive to light. Normal oculomotor activity, no diplopia or nystagmus. Fields of vision intact. No ptosis, symmetrical eyes in normal position/ no strabismus. Sensation and motor skills face symmetrically intact. Pharyngeal arches symmetrical, tongue in midline. Bilateral trapezius muscle and sternocleidomastoid muscle strength MRC 5/5.
Sensory innervation	Sense of touch, vibration, position, movement, and temperature intact. Good sharp-dull discrimination.
Motor innervation	No atrophy, no pareses, no tremor, no fasciculations. Negative Barré test and negative Mingazzini test. Symmetrical upper and lower extremity strength, tested separately (MRC 5/5). Normal muscle tone.
Reflexes	Biceps reflex 2/2, triceps reflex 2/2, knee reflex 2/2, achilles reflex 2/2, plantar reflex bilateral. Abdominal skin reflex symmetrical.
Coordination	Diadochokinesis normal, finger-to-nose test and shin-to-heel test symmetrical and unimpaired, tandem gait normal. Negative Romberg test.
Gait	Normal gait, normal stride length, normal arm swing. Heel walking/tiptoe walking normal.

Table 81 // Specific motor function tests

When describing a patient's sense of vibration, note where their sense of vibration is impaired, e.g. 'sense of vibration impaired distal to medial malleolus'.

When testing motor function, use the MRC scale to describe the strength of individual muscles: MRC left/MRC right (see section on Neurological examination).

UPPER EXTREMITY (RIGHT/LEFT)	LOWER EXTREMITY (RIGHT/LEFT)
• Serratus anterior muscle 5/5 • Deltoid muscle 5/5 • Biceps brachii muscle 5/5 • Triceps brachii muscle 5/5 • Wrist extensors 5/5 • Wrist flexors 5/5 • Finger extensors 5/5 • Finger flexors 5/5 • Opponens pollicis muscle 5/5 • Interossei muscles 5/5	• Gluteus medius and minimus muscles (lying and standing) 5/5 • Iliopsoas muscle 5/5 • Quadriceps muscle 5/5 • Hip adductors 5/5 • Hamstrings 5/5 • Tibialis anterior muscle 5/5 • Gastrocnemius muscle 5/5 • Peroneus muscle 5/5 • Extensor hallucis longus muscle 5/5 • Flexor hallucis longus muscle 5/5

Table 82 // List of muscles to include in neurological exam notes with MRC scale

With isocoric and bilaterally light-reactive pupils, **PEARL** is often used as acronym for **P**upils **E**qual **A**nd **R**eactive to **L**ight.

A nystagmus is named for its fast phase. Nystagmus can occur horizontally or vertically, or be accompanied by a rotational nystagmus.

- 1st degree: nystagmus occurs when gazing towards the fast phase
- 2nd degree: nystagmus also when gazing ahead
- 3rd degree: nystagmus occurs when gazing towards the slow phase

You use the **gas**trocnemius muscle to step on the gas.

Quick reference cards for this specialty are available online. Go to our website *www.compendiummedicine.com* or scan the QR code.

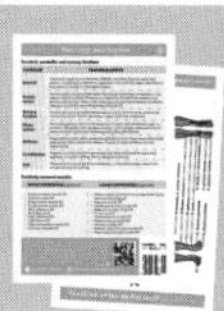

References

1. Adams RD, Fisher CM, Hakim S, Ojemann RG, Sweet WH. Symptomatic occult hydrocephalus with 'normal' cerebrospinal-fluid pressure. A treatable syndrome. N Engl J Med. 1965 Jul 15;273:117-26. doi: 10.1056/NEJM196507152730301. PMID: 14303656.
2. Aggarwal R, Charles-Schoeman C, Schessl J, Bata-Csörgő Z, Dimachkie MM, Griger Z, Moiseev S, Oddis C, Schiopu E, Vencovský J, Beckmann I, Clodi E, Bugrova O, Dankó K, Ernste F, Goyal NA, Heuer M, Hudson M, Hussain YM, Karam C, Magnolo N, Nelson R, Pozur N, Prystupa L, Sárdy M, Valenzuela G, van der Kooi AJ, Vu T, Worm M, Levine T; ProDERM Trial Group. Trial of Intravenous Immune Globulin in Dermatomyositis. N Engl J Med. 2022 Oct 1;387(14):1264-1278. doi: 10.1056/NEJMoa2117912. PMID: 36198179.
3. Aguiar de Sousa D, von Martial R, Abilleira S, Gattringer T, Kobayashi A, Gallofré M, Fazekas F, Szikora I, Feigin V, Caso V, Fischer U. Access to and delivery of acute ischaemic stroke treatments: A survey of national scientific societies and stroke experts in 44 European countries. Eur Stroke J. 2019 Mar;4(1):13-28. doi: 10.1177/2396987318786023. Epub 2018 Jul 20. PMID: 31165091; PMCID: PMC6533860.
4. Albuja AC, Khan GQ. Absence Seizure. In: StatPearls [Internet]. Treasure Island (FL, United States): StatPearls Publishing; 2022 Oct 10 [cited 2023 Oct 7]. Available from: https://www.ncbi.nlm.nih.gov/books/NBK499867/.
5. Alport AR, Sander HW. Clinical approach to peripheral neuropathy: anatomic localization and diagnostic testing. Continuum (Minneap Minn). 2012 Feb;18(1):13-38. doi: 10.1212/01.CON.0000411546.13207.b1. PMID: 22810068.
6. Ameer MA, Peterfy RJ, Khazaeni B. Temporal Arteritis. In StatPearls [Internet]. Treasure Island (FL, United States): StatPearls Publishing; 2023 Aug 8 [cited 7 Oct 2023]. Available from: https://www.ncbi.nlm.nih.gov/books/NBK459376/.
7. Anderson D, Woods B, Abubakar T, Koontz C, Li N, Hasoon J, Viswanath O, Kaye AD, Urits I. A Comprehensive Review of Cubital Tunnel Syndrome. Orthop Rev (Pavia). 2022 Sep 15;14(3):38239. doi: 10.52965/001c.38239. PMID: 36128335; PMCID: PMC9476617.
8. Armstrong JR, Mosher BD. Aspiration pneumonia after stroke: intervention and prevention. Neurohospitalist. 2011 Apr;1(2):85-93. doi: 10.1177/1941875210395775. PMID: 23983842; PMCID: PMC3726080.
9. Armstrong MJ, Weintraub D. The Case for Antipsychotics in Dementia with Lewy Bodies. Mov Disord Clin Pract. 2016 Jun 24;4(1):32-35. doi: 10.1002/mdc3.12383. PMID: 30713945; PMCID: PMC6353494.
10. Arts NJ, Walvoort SJ, Kessels RP. Korsakoff's syndrome: a critical review. Neuropsychiatr Dis Treat. 2017 Nov 27;13:2875-2890. doi: 10.2147/NDT.S130078. PMID: 29225466; PMCID: PMC5708199.
11. Arumugham VB, Rayi A. Intravenous Immunoglobulin (IVIG). In: StatPearls [Internet]. Treasure Island (FL): StatPearls Publishing; 2023 Jul 3 [cited 2023 Nov 18]. Available from: https://www.ncbi.nlm.nih.gov/books/NBK554446/.
12. Ascoli M, Ferlazzo E, Gasparini S, Mastroianni G, Citraro R, Roberti R, Russo E. Epidemiology and Outcomes of Status Epilepticus. Int J Gen Med. 2021 Jun 28;14:2965-2973. doi: 10.2147/IJGM.S295855. PMID: 34234526; PMCID: PMC8254099.
13. Atroshi I, Gummesson C, Johnsson R, Ornstein E, Ranstam J, Rosén I. Prevalence of carpal tunnel syndrome in a general population. JAMA. 1999 Jul 14;282(2):153-8. doi: 10.1001/jama.282.2.153. PMID: 10411196.
14. Attal N, Cruccu G, Baron R, Haanpää M, Hansson P, Jensen TS, Nurmikko T. EFNS guidelines on the pharmacological treatment of neuropathic pain: 2010 revision. Eur J Neurol. 2010 Sep;17(9):1113-e88. doi: 10.1111/j.1468-1331.2010.02999.x. Epub 2010 Apr 9. PMID: 20402746.
15. Au KS, Ashley-Koch A, Northrup H. Epidemiologic and genetic aspects of spina bifida and other neural tube defects. Dev Disabil Res Rev. 2010;16(1):6-15. doi: 10.1002/ddrr.93. PMID: 20419766; PMCID: PMC3053142.
16. Bae CH, Na HG, Choi YS. Current diagnosis and treatment of vestibular neuritis: a narrative review. J Yeungnam Med Sci. 2022 Apr;39(2):81-88. doi: 10.12701/yujm.2021.01228. Epub 2021 Aug 9. PMID: 34411472; PMCID: PMC8913909.
17. Bai QK, Zhao ZG, Lu LJ, Shen J, Zhang JY, Sui HJ, Xie XH, Chen J, Yang J, Chen CR. Treating ischaemic stroke with intravenous tPA beyond 4.5 hours under the guidance of a MRI DWI/T2WI mismatch was safe and effective. Stroke Vasc Neurol. 2019 Feb 11;4(1):8-13. doi: 10.1136/svn-2018-000186. PMID: 31105973; PMCID: PMC6475081.
18. Barichello T, Rocha Catalão CH, Rohlwink UK, van der Kuip M, Zaharie D, Solomons RS, van Toorn R, Tutu van Furth M, Hasbun R, Iovino F, Namale VS. Bacterial meningitis in Africa. Front Neurol. 2023 Feb 14;14:822575. doi: 10.3389/fneur.2023.822575. PMID: 36864913; PMCID: PMC9972001.
19. Barkhof F, Hazewinkel M, Binnewijzend M, Smithuis R. Dementia- Role of MRI [Internet]. Radiology Assistant. 2021 Jan 09 [updated 2022 Mar 03; cited 2023 Oct 07]. Available from: https://radiologyassistant.nl/neuroradiology/dementia/role-of-mri.
20. Bar-Or A, Pachner A, Menguy-Vacheron F, Kaplan J, Wiendl H. Teriflunomide and its mechanism of action in multiple sclerosis. Drugs. 2014 Apr;74(6):659-74. doi: 10.1007/s40265-014-0212-x. PMID: 24740824; PMCID: PMC4003395.
21. Barton, JJS. Benign paroxysmal positional vertigo [Internet]. UpToDate. 2022 Jun 23 [cited 2023 Oct 11]. Availa-

ble from: https://www.uptodate.com/contents/benign-paroxysmal-positional-vertigo.
22. Bassetti CLA, Kallweit U, Vignatelli L, Plazzi G, Lecendreux M, Baldin E, Dolenc-Groselj L, Jennum P, Khatami R, Manconi M, Mayer G, Partinen M, Pollmächer T, Reading P, Santamaria J, Sonka K, Dauvilliers Y, Lammers GJ. European guideline and expert statements on the management of narcolepsy in adults and children. J Sleep Res. 2021 Dec;30(6):e13387. doi: 10.1111/jsr.13387. Epub 2021 Jun 25. PMID: 34173288.
23. Basura GJ, Adams ME, Monfared A, Schwartz SR, Antonelli PJ, Burkard R, Bush ML, Bykowski J, Colandrea M, Derebery J, Kelly EA, Kerber KA, Koopman CF, Kuch AA, Marcolini E, McKinnon BJ, Ruckenstein MJ, Valenzuela CV, Vosooney A, Walsh SA, Nnacheta LC, Dhepyasuwan N, Buchanan EM. Clinical Practice Guideline: Ménière's Disease. Otolaryngol Head Neck Surg. 2020 Apr 1;162(2_suppl):S1-S55. doi: 10.1177/0194599820909438
24. Batool A, Kasi A. Leptomeningeal Carcinomatosis. In: StatPearls [Internet]. Treasure Island (FL, United States): StatPearls Publishing; 2023 Mar 27 [cited 7 Oct 2023]. Available from: https://www.ncbi.nlm.nih.gov/books/NBK499862/.
25. Bear MF, Connors BW, Paradiso MA. *Neuroscience: Exploring the Brain*, 4th ed. Philadelphia: Wolters Kluwer; 2016.
26. Beghi E. The Epidemiology of Epilepsy. Neuroepidemiology. 2020;54(2):185-191. doi: 10.1159/000503831. Epub 2019 Dec 18. PMID: 31852003.
27. Van den Berg B, Walgaard C, Drenthen J, Fokke C, Jacobs BC, van Doorn PA. Guillain-Barré syndrome: pathogenesis, diagnosis, treatment and prognosis. Nat Rev Neurol. 2014 Aug;10(8):469-82. doi: 10.1038/nrneurol.2014.121. Epub 2014 Jul 15. PMID: 25023340.
28. Beynon GJ, Jani P, Baguley DM. A clinical evaluation of head impulse testing. Clin Otolaryngol Allied Sci. 1998 Apr;23(2):117-22. doi: 10.1046/j.1365-2273.1998.00112.x. PMID: 9597280.
29. Bhattacharyya N, Gubbels SP, Schwartz SR, Edlow JA, El-Kashlan H, Fife T, Holmberg JM, Mahoney K, Hollingsworth DB, Roberts R, Seidman MD, Steiner RW, Do BT, Voelker CC, Waguespack RW, Corrigan MD. Clinical Practice Guideline: Benign Paroxysmal Positional Vertigo (Update). Otolaryngol Head Neck Surg. 2017 Mar;156(3_suppl):S1-S47. doi: 10.1177/0194599816689667. PMID: 28248609.
30. Bhattarai J, Sumerall S. Current and Future Treatment Options for Narcolepsy: A Review. Sleep Sci. 2017 Jan-Mar;10(1):19-27. doi: 10.5935/1984-0063.20170004. PMID: 28966734; PMCID: PMC5611768.
31. Bigley GK. Chapter 67: Sensation. In: Walker HK, Hall WD, Hurst JW, editors. Clinical Methods: The History, Physical, and Laboratory Examinations, 3rd edition [Internet]. Boston: Butterworths; 1990 [cited 2023 Sept 20]. Available from: https://www.ncbi.nlm.nih.gov/books/NBK390/.
32. Bleyl S, Brauer PR, Schoenwolf GC, Francis-West PH. *Larsen's human embryology*, 5th ed. Philadelphia: Elsevier; 2014.
33. Blumenfeld, H. *Neuroanatomy through Clinical Cases*, 3rd ed. New York: Oxford University Press; 2022.
34. Bodilsen J, D'Alessandris QG, Humphreys H, Iro MA, Klein M, Last K, Montesinos IL, Pagliano P, Sipahi OR, San-Juan R, Tattevin P, Thurnher M, de J Treviño-Rangel R, Brouwer MC; ESCMID Study Group for Infections of the Brain (ESGIB). European society of Clinical Microbiology and Infectious Diseases guidelines on diagnosis and treatment of brain abscess in children and adults. Clin Microbiol Infect. 2024 Jan;30(1):66-89. doi: 10.1016/j.cmi.2023.08.016.
35. Borhani Haghighi A, Edgell RC, Cruz-Flores S, Feen E, Piriyawat P, Vora N, Callison RC, Alshekhlee A. Mortality of cerebral venous-sinus thrombosis in a large national sample. Stroke. 2012 Jan;43(1):262-4. doi: 10.1161/STROKEAHA.111.635664. Epub 2011 Oct 13. PMID: 21998058.
36. Born G, Patrono C. Antiplatelet drugs. Br J Pharmacol. 2006 Jan;147 Suppl 1(Suppl 1):S241-51. doi: 10.1038/sj.bjp.0706401. PMID: 16402110; PMCID: PMC1760725.
37. Bozzi F, Alabau-Rodriguez S, Barrera-Ochoa S, Ateschrang A, Schreiner AJ, Monllau JC, Perelli S. Suprascapular Neuropathy around the Shoulder: A Current Concept Review. J Clin Med. 2020 Jul 22;9(8):2331. doi: 10.3390/jcm9082331. PMID: 32707860; PMCID: PMC7465639.
38. Bragazzi NL, Kolahi AA, Nejadghaderi SA, Lochner P, Brigo F, Naldi A, Lanteri P, Garbarino S, Sullman MJM, Dai H, Wu J, Kong JD, Jahrami H, Sohrabi MR, Safiri S. Global, regional, and national burden of Guillain-Barré syndrome and its underlying causes from 1990 to 2019. J Neuroinflammation. 2021 Nov 11;18(1):264. doi: 10.1186/s12974-021-02319-4. PMID: 34763713; PMCID: PMC8581128.
39. Van den Brande R, Cornips EM, Peeters M, Ost P, Billiet C, Van de Kelft E. Epidemiology of spinal metastases, metastatic epidural spinal cord compression and pathologic vertebral compression fractures in patients with solid tumors: A systematic review. J Bone Oncol. 2022 Jul 9;35:100446. doi: 10.1016/j.jbo.2022.100446. PMID: 35860387; PMCID: PMC9289863.
40. Brandstadter R, Katz Sand I. The use of natalizumab for multiple sclerosis. Neuropsychiatr Dis Treat. 2017 Jun 28;13:1691-1702. doi: 10.2147/NDT.S114636. PMID: 28721050; PMCID: PMC5499927.
41. Bressman SB, Sabatti C, Raymond D, de Leon D, Klein C, Kramer PL, Brin MF, Fahn S, Breakefield X, Ozelius LJ, Risch NJ. The DYT1 phenotype and guidelines for diagnostic testing. Neurology. 2000 May 9;54(9):1746-52. doi: 10.1212/wnl.54.9.1746. PMID: 10802779.
42. Brex P, Williams V. Updated criteria for diagnosing Multiple Sclerosis [Internet]. Denmark Hill, UK: ACNR; 2019 Jan 18 [cited 2023 Oct 5]. Available from: https://acnr.co.uk/articles/updated-criteria-for-diagnosing-multiple-sclerosis/.
43. Brignole M, Moya A, de Lange FJ, Deharo JC, Elliott PM, Fanciulli A, Fedorowski A, Furlan R, Kenny RA, Martín A, Probst V, Reed MJ, Rice CP, Sutton R, Ungar A, van Dijk JG; ESC Scientific Document Group. 2018 ESC Guidelines for the diagnosis and management of syncope. Eur Heart J. 2018 Jun 1;39(21):1883-1948. doi: 10.1093/eurheartj/ehy037. PMID: 29562304.

44. Britton JW, Frey LC, Hopp JL, Korb P, Koubeissi MZ, Lievens WE, Pestana-Knight EM, St. Louis EK. Electroencephalography (EEG): An Introductory Text and Atlas of Normal and Abnormal Findings in Adults, Children, and Infants [Internet]. Chicago: American Epilepsy Society; 2016 [cited 2023 Sept 30]. Available from: https://www.ncbi.nlm.nih.gov/books/NBK390354/.
45. Bromfield EB, Cavazos JE, Sirven JI, editors. Chapter 3: Neuropharmacology of Antiepileptic Drugs. In: An Introduction to Epilepsy [Internet]. West Hartford (CT): American Epilepsy Society; 2006 [cited 2023 Oct 7]. Available from: https://www.ncbi.nlm.nih.gov/books/NBK2513/.
46. Brott T, Adams HP Jr, Olinger CP, Marler JR, Barsan WG, Biller J, Spilker J, Holleran R, Eberle R, Hertzberg V, et al. Measurements of acute cerebral infarction: a clinical examination scale. Stroke. 1989 Jul;20(7):864-70. doi: 10.1161/01.str.20.7.864. PMID: 2749846.
47. Bubuioc AM, Kudebayeva A, Turuspekova S, Lisnic V, Leone MA. The epidemiology of myasthenia gravis. J Med Life. 2021 Jan-Mar;14(1):7-16. doi: 10.25122/jml-2020-0145. PMID: 33767779; PMCID: PMC7982252.
48. Caplan LR. Overview of the evaluation of stroke [Internet]. UpToDate. 2023 Mar 23 [cited 2023 Oct 07]. Available from: https://www.uptodate.com/contents/overview-of-the-evaluation-of-stroke.
49. Carpenter CR, Hussain AM, Ward MJ, Zipfel GJ, Fowler S, Pines JM, Sivilotti ML. Spontaneous Subarachnoid Hemorrhage: A Systematic Review and Meta-analysis Describing the Diagnostic Accuracy of History, Physical Examination, Imaging, and Lumbar Puncture With an Exploration of Test Thresholds. Acad Emerg Med. 2016 Sep;23(9):963-1003. doi: 10.1111/acem.12984. Epub 2016 Sep 6. PMID: 27306497; PMCID: PMC5018921.
50. Chadwick DR. Viral meningitis. Br Med Bull. 2006 Feb 10;75-76:1-14. doi: 10.1093/bmb/ldh057. PMID: 16474042.
51. Chaudhuri KR, Ondo WG. *Movement Disorders in Clinical Practice*, 1st ed. London: Springer London; 2010.
52. Cheung V, Hoshide R, Bansal V, Kasper E, Chen CC. Methylprednisolone in the management of spinal cord injuries: Lessons from randomized, controlled trials. Surg Neurol Int. 2015 Aug 24;6:142. doi: 10.4103/2152-7806.163452. PMID: 26392918; PMCID: PMC4553662.
53. Chisari CG, Sgarlata E, Arena S, Toscano S, Luca M, Patti F. Rituximab for the treatment of multiple sclerosis: a review. J Neurol. 2022 Jan;269(1):159-183. doi: 10.1007/s00415-020-10362-z. Epub 2021 Jan 8. PMID: 33416999; PMCID: PMC7790722.
54. Chiu RG, Mehta AI. Spinal Metastases. JAMA. 2020 Jun 16;323(23):2438. doi:10.1001/jama.2020.0716. PMID: 32543685.
55. Chokhawala K, Stevens L. Antipsychotic Medications. In: StatPearls [Internet]. Treasure Island (FL, United States): StatPearls Publishing; 2023 Feb 26 [cited 2023 Oct 7]. Available from: https://www.ncbi.nlm.nih.gov/books/NBK519503/.
56. Chun J, Hartung HP. Mechanism of action of oral fingolimod (FTY720) in multiple sclerosis. Clin Neuropharmacol. 2010 Mar-Apr;33(2):91-101. doi: 10.1097/WNF.0b013e3181cbf825. PMID: 20061941; PMCID: PMC2859693.
57. Clinical Guidelines for Stroke Management [Internet]. Stroke Foundation. 2017 July 25 [cited 2023 Oct 30]. Available at https://informme.org.au/en/Guidelines/Clinical-Guidelines-for-Stroke-Management.
58. Cloud LJ, Jinnah HA. Treatment strategies for dystonia. Expert Opin Pharmacother. 2010 Jan;11(1):5-15. doi: 10.1517/14656560903426171. PMID: 20001425; PMCID: PMC3495548.
59. Cohen JA, Comi G, Arnold DL, Bar-Or A, Selmaj KW, Steinman L, Havrdová EK, Cree BA, Montalbán X, Hartung HP, Huang V, Frohna P, Skolnick BE, Kappos L; RADIANCE Trial Investigators. Efficacy and safety of ozanimod in multiple sclerosis: Dose-blinded extension of a randomized phase II study. Mult Scler. 2019 Aug;25(9):1255-1262. doi: 10.1177/1352458518789884. Epub 2018 Jul 25. PMID: 30043658; PMCID: PMC6681431.
60. Cohan SL, Hendin BA, Reder AT, Smoot K, Avila R, Mendoza JP, Weinstock-Guttman B. Interferons and Multiple Sclerosis: Lessons from 25 Years of Clinical and Real-World Experience with Intramuscular Interferon Beta-1a (Avonex). CNS Drugs. 2021 Jul;35(7):743-767. doi: 10.1007/s40263-021-00822-z. Epub 2021 Jul 6. PMID: 34228301; PMCID: PMC8258741.
61. Colás R, Muñoz P, Temprano R, Gómez C, Pascual J. Chronic daily headache with analgesic overuse: epidemiology and impact on quality of life. Neurology. 2004 Apr 27;62(8):1338-42. doi: 10.1212/01.wnl.0000120545.45443.93. PMID: 15111671.
62. Colović MB, Krstić DZ, Lazarević-Pašti TD, Bondžić AM, Vasić VM. Acetylcholinesterase inhibitors: pharmacology and toxicology. Curr Neuropharmacol. 2013 May;11(3):315-35. doi: 10.2174/1570159X11311030006. PMID: 24179466; PMCID: PMC3648782.
63. Connolly BS, Lang AE. Pharmacological treatment of Parkinson disease: a review. JAMA. 2014 Apr 23-30;311(16):1670-83. doi: 10.1001/jama.2014.3654. PMID: 24756517.
64. Cooksley T, Rose S, Holland M. A systematic approach to the unconscious patient. Clin Med (Lond). 2018 Feb;18(1):88-92. doi: 10.7861/clinmedicine.18-1-88. PMID: 29436445; PMCID: PMC6330912.
65. Cortese I, Reich DS, Nath A. Progressive multifocal leukoencephalopathy and the spectrum of JC virus-related disease. Nat Rev Neurol. 2021 Jan;17(1):37-51. doi: 10.1038/s41582-020-00427-y. Epub 2020 Nov 20. PMID: 33219338; PMCID: PMC7678594
66. Covell T, Siddiqui W. Korsakoff Syndrome. In: StatPearls [Internet]. Treasure Island (FL, United, States): StatPearls Publishing; 2023 Jan 30 [cited 2023 Oct 7]. Available from: https://www.ncbi.nlm.nih.gov/books/NBK539854/.
67. Crossman AR, Neary D. *Neuroanatomy: An illustrated Colour Text*, 4th ed. Edinburgh: Elsevier Churchill Livingstone; 2010.
68. Darras BT. Spinal muscular atrophies. Pediatr Clin North Am. 2015 Jun;62(3):743-66. doi: 10.1016/j.pcl.2015.03.010. Epub 2015 Apr 11. PMID: 26022173.
69. Electronic medicines compendium [Internet]. Datapharm; [cited 2023 Nov 18]. Available from: https://www.medicines.org.uk/emc.

70. Dean L, Kane M. Clopidogrel Therapy and CYP2C19 Genotype. In: Pratt VM, Scott SA, Pirmohamed M, et al., editors. Medical Genetics Summaries [Internet]. Bethesda: National Center for Biotechnology Information (US); 2012 [cited 28 Oct 2023]. Available from: https://www.ncbi.nlm.nih.gov/books/NBK84114/.
71. Deeks ED. Cladribine Tablets: A Review in Relapsing MS. CNS Drugs. 2018 Aug;32(8):785-796. doi: 10.1007/s40263-018-0562-0. Erratum in: CNS Drugs. 2019 Feb;33(2):193. PMID: 30105527; PMCID: PMC6353806.
72. Defazio G, Hallett M, Jinnah HA, Conte A, Berardelli A. Blepharospasm 40 years later. Mov Disord. 2017 Apr;32(4):498-509. doi: 10.1002/mds.26934. Epub 2017 Feb 10. PMID: 28186662; PMCID: PMC5941939.
73. Delank KS, Wendtner C, Eich HT, Eysel P. The treatment of spinal metastases. Dtsch Arztebl Int. 2011 Feb;108(5):71-9; quiz 80. doi: 10.3238/arztebl.2011.0071. Epub 2011 Feb 4. PMID: 21311714; PMCID: PMC3036978.
74. Delatycki MB, Corben LA. Clinical features of Friedreich ataxia. J Child Neurol. 2012 Sep;27(9):1133-7. doi: 10.1177/0883073812448230. Epub 2012 Jun 29. PMID: 22752493; PMCID: PMC3674491.
75. Dementia facts & figures [Internet]. Alzheimer's Disease International; [cited 2023 Oct 07]. Available from: https://www.alzint.org/about/dementia-facts-figures/.
76. Derex L, Nighoghossian N. Intracerebral haemorrhage after thrombolysis for acute ischaemic stroke: an update. J Neurol Neurosurg Psychiatry. 2008 Oct;79(10):1093-9. doi: 10.1136/jnnp.2007.133371. Epub 2008 Jan 25. PMID: 18223014.
77. Devasagayam S, Wyatt B, Leyden J, Kleinig T. Cerebral Venous Sinus Thrombosis Incidence Is Higher Than Previously Thought: A Retrospective Population-Based Study. Stroke. 2016 Sep;47(9):2180-2. doi: 10.1161/STROKEAHA.116.013617. Epub 2016 Jul 19. PMID: 27435401.
78. Diener HC, Limmroth V. Medication-overuse headache: a worldwide problem. Lancet Neurol. 2004 Aug;3(8):475-83. doi: 10.1016/S1474-4422(04)00824-5. PMID: 15261608.
79. Dishion E, Tadi P. Doll's Eyes. In: StatPearls [Internet]. Treasure Island (FL, United States): StatPearls Publishing; 2023 May 1 [cited 2023 Oct 5]. Available from: https://www.ncbi.nlm.nih.gov/books/NBK551716/.
80. Dobesh PP, Stacy ZA. Chapter 2 - Pharmacology of oral anticoagulants. In: Flaker G. Stroke Prevention in Atrial Fibrillation [Internet]. St. Louis: Elsevier; 2019 [cited 2023 Oct 12]. p. 11–34. Available from: https://doi.org/10.1016/b978-0-323-55429-9.00002-9.
81. Doble A. The pharmacology and mechanism of action of riluzole. Neurology. 1996 Dec;47(6 Suppl 4):S233-41. doi: 10.1212/wnl.47.6_suppl_4.233s. PMID: 8959995.
82. Dresser L, Wlodarski R, Rezania K, Soliven B. Myasthenia Gravis: Epidemiology, Pathophysiology and Clinical Manifestations. J Clin Med. 2021 May 21;10(11):2235. doi: 10.3390/jcm10112235. PMID: 34064035; PMCID: PMC8196750.
83. Drew LB, Drew WE. The contrecoup-coup phenomenon: a new understanding of the mechanism of closed head injury. Neurocrit Care. 2004;1(3):385-90. doi: 10.1385/NCC:1:3:385. PMID: 16174940.
84. D'Souza D, Sriselvakumar S, El-Feky M, et al. Dural venous sinus thrombosis [Internet]. Radiopaedia.org. 2023 Aug 01 [cited 2023 Oct 05]. Available from: https://radiopaedia.org/articles/dural-venous-sinus-thrombosis.
85. Dubois B, Feldman HH, Jacova C, Dekosky ST, Barberger-Gateau P, Cummings J, Delacourte A, Galasko D, Gauthier S, Jicha G, Meguro K, O'brien J, Pasquier F, Robert P, Rossor M, Salloway S, Stern Y, Visser PJ, Scheltens P. Research criteria for the diagnosis of Alzheimer's disease: revising the NINCDS-ADRDA criteria. Lancet Neurol. 2007 Aug;6(8):734-46. doi: 10.1016/S1474-4422(07)70178-3. PMID: 17616482.
86. Eddy CM, Rickards HE, Cavanna AE. Treatment strategies for tics in Tourette syndrome. Ther Adv Neurol Disord. 2011 Jan;4(1):25-45. doi: 10.1177/1756285610390261. PMID: 21339906; PMCID: PMC3036957.
87. Edlow JA, Newman-Toker D. Using the Physical Examination to Diagnose Patients with Acute Dizziness and Vertigo. J Emerg Med. 2016 Apr;50(4):617-28. doi: 10.1016/j.jemermed.2015.10.040. Epub 2016 Feb 16. PMID: 26896289.
88. EFNS Task Force on Diagnosis and Management of Amyotrophic Lateral Sclerosis:; Andersen PM, Abrahams S, Borasio GD, de Carvalho M, Chio A, Van Damme P, Hardiman O, Kollewe K, Morrison KE, Petri S, Pradat PF, Silani V, Tomik B, Wasner M, Weber M. EFNS guidelines on the clinical management of amyotrophic lateral sclerosis (MALS)--revised report of an EFNS task force. Eur J Neurol. 2012 Mar;19(3):360-75. doi: 10.1111/j.1468-1331.2011.03501.x. Epub 2011 Sep 14. PMID: 21914052.
89. Eggers SDZ, Bisdorff A, von Brevern M, Zee DS, Kim JS, Perez-Fernandez N, Welgampola MS, Della Santina CC, Newman-Toker DE. Classification of vestibular signs and examination techniques: Nystagmus and nystagmus-like movements. J Vestib Res. 2019;29(2-3):57-87. doi: 10.3233/VES-190658. PMID: 31256095; PMCID: PMC9249296.
90. Eisen A, Aminhoff MJ, Wilterdink JL. Disorders affecting the spinal cord [Internet]. UpToDate. 2021 Feb 4 [cited 2023 Oct 7]. Available from: https://www.uptodate.com/contents/disorders-affecting-the-spinal-cord.
91. Elbaroody M, Mostafa HE, Alsawy MFM, Elhawary ME, Atallah A, Gabr M. Outcomes of Chiari Malformation III: A Review of Literature. J Pediatr Neurosci. 2020 Oct-Dec;15(4):358-364. doi: 10.4103/jpn.JPN_135_19. Epub 2021 Jan 19. PMID: 33936298; PMCID: PMC8078634.
92. Emmady PD, Anilkumar AC. EEG Abnormal Waveforms. In: StatPearls [Internet]. Treasure Island (FL): StatPearls Publishing; 2023 May 1 [cited 2023 Oct 7]. Available from: https://www.ncbi.nlm.nih.gov/books/NBK557655/.
93. Engelborghs S, Niemantsverdriet E, Struyfs H, Blennow K, Brouns R, Comabella M, Dujmovic I, van der Flier W, Frölich L, Galimberti D, Gnanapavan S, Hemmer B, Hoff E, Hort J, Iacobaeus E, Ingelsson M, Jan de Jong F, Jonsson M, Khalil M, Kuhle J, Lleó A, de Mendonça A, Molinuevo JL, Nagels G, Paquet C, Parnetti L, Roks G, Rosa-Neto P, Scheltens P, Skårsgard C, Stomrud E, Tumani H, Visser PJ, Wallin A, Winblad B, Zetterberg H, Duits F, Teunissen CE. Consensus guidelines for lumbar puncture in patients with neurological diseases.

Alzheimers Dement (Amst). 2017 May 18;8:111-126. doi: 10.1016/j.dadm.2017.04.007. PMID: 28603768; PMCID: PMC5454085.

94. Evans RQ, Whitlow CT. Acute mild traumatic brain injury (concussion) in adults [Internet]. UpToDate. 2022 Feb 22 [cited 2023 Oct 05]. Available from: https://www.uptodate.com/contents/acute-mild-traumatic-brain-injury-concussion-in-adults.

95. Fanous AA, Siddiqui AH. Mechanical thrombectomy: Stent retrievers vs. aspiration catheters. Cor et Vasa. 2016 Apr;58(2):193-203. doi: 10.1016/j.crvasa.2016.01.004.

96. Fearon C, Doherty L, Lynch T. How Do I Examine Rigidity and Spasticity? Mov Disord Clin Pract. 2015 Mar 28;2(2):204. doi: 10.1002/mdc3.12147. PMID: 30363919; PMCID: PMC6183506.

97. Nederlandse Vereniging voor Neurologie (NVN) [Dutch Neurology Association]. Richtlijn Licht traumatisch hoofd/hersenletsel (LTH) [Guideline Mild traumatic head/brain injury] [Internet]. FMS Richtlijnendatabase. 2010 Jan 6 [cited 2018 Jun 15]. Avaliable from: https://richtlijnendatabase.nl/richtlijn/licht_traumatisch_hoofd_hersenletsel_lth/licht_traumatisch_hoofd_hersenletsel_-_startpagina.html.

98. Feghali J, Yang W, Huang J. Updates in Chronic Subdural Hematoma: Epidemiology, Etiology, Pathogenesis, Treatment, and Outcome. World Neurosurg. 2020 Sep; 141:339-345. doi: 10.1016/j.wneu.2020.06.140. Epub 2020 Jun 25. PMID: 32593768.

99. Feigin VL, Brainin M, Norrving B, Martins S, Sacco RL, Hacke W, Fisher M, Pandian J, Lindsay P. World Stroke Organization (WSO): Global Stroke Fact Sheet 2022. Int J Stroke. 2022 Jan;17(1):18-29. doi: 10.1177/17474930211065917. Erratum in: Int J Stroke. 2022 Apr;17(4):478. PMID: 34986727.

100. Ferro JM, Canhao P. Cerebral venous thrombosis: Etiology, clinical features, and diagnosis [Internet]. UpToDate. 2023 Sep 25 [cited 2023 Oct 07]. Available from: https://www.uptodate.com/contents/cerebral-venous-thrombosis-etiology-clinical-features-and-diagnosis.

101. Ferro JM, Canhao P. Cerebral venous thrombosis: Treatment and prognosis [Internet]. UpToDate. 2022 Dec 05 [cited 2023 Oct 05]. Available from: https://www.uptodate.com/contents/cerebral-venous-thrombosis-treatment-and-prognosis.

102. Fink KR, Fink JR. Imaging of brain metastases. Surg Neurol Int. 2013 May 2;4(Suppl 4):S209-19. doi: 10.4103/2152-7806.111298. PMID: 23717792; PMCID: PMC3656556.

103. Finnerup NB, Attal N, Haroutounian S, McNicol E, Baron R, Dworkin RH, Gilron I, Haanpää M, Hansson P, Jensen TS, Kamerman PR, Lund K, Moore A, Raja SN, Rice AS, Rowbotham M, Sena E, Siddall P, Smith BH, Wallace M. Pharmacotherapy for neuropathic pain in adults: a systematic review and meta-analysis. Lancet Neurol. 2015 Feb;14(2):162-73. doi: 10.1016/S1474-4422(14)70251-0. Epub 2015 Jan 7. PMID: 25575710; PMCID: PMC4493167.

104. Fischer MA, Jan A. Medication-Overuse Headache. In: StatPearls [Internet]. Treasure Island (FL, United States): StatPearls Publishing; 2023 Jun 26 [cited 7 Oct 2023]. Available from: https://www.ncbi.nlm.nih.gov/books/NBK538150/.

105. Flynn JP, Gerriets V. Ocrelizumab. In: StatPearls [Internet]. Treasure Island (FL, United, States): StatPearls Publishing; 2023 Jun 26 [cited 2023 Oct 12]. Available from: https://www.ncbi.nlm.nih.gov/books/NBK547750/.

106. Folmer H, Deckers C, Knoester PD, De Haan GJ. Epilepsie: Farmacotherapeutische richtlijn [Epilepsy: Pharmacotherapeutic guideline] [Internet]. Nederlandse Huisartsen Genootschap [Dutch General Practitioner Association]. 2003 [cited 2016 Feb 2]. Available from: http://goedehuisarts.nl/FTP_NHG/standaarden/FTR/Epilepsie_text.html.

107. Fons K, Jnah AJ. Arnold-Chiari Malformation: Core Concepts. Neonatal Netw. 2021 Aug 1;40(5):313-320. doi: 10.1891/11-T-704. PMID: 34518383.

108. Fornasari D. Pharmacotherapy for Neuropathic Pain: A Review. Pain Ther. 2017 Dec;6(Suppl 1):25-33. doi: 10.1007/s40122-017-0091-4. Epub 2017 Nov 24. PMID: 29178034; PMCID: PMC5701897.

109. Foroughipour M, Gazeran S. Effectiveness and side effects of dimethyl fumarate in multiple sclerosis after 12 months of follow up: An Iranian clinical trial. Iran J Neurol. 2019 Oct 7;18(4):154-158. PMID: 32117551; PMCID: PMC7036051.

110. Frey J, Malaty IA. Tourette Syndrome Treatment Updates: a Review and Discussion of the Current and Upcoming Literature. Curr Neurol Neurosci Rep. 2022;22(2):123–142. doi: 10.1007/s11910-022-01177-8. Epub 2022 Feb 2. PMID: 35107785; PMCID: PMC8809236.

111. Furman JM, Barton JJS. Evaluation of the patient with vertigo [Internet]. UpToDate. 2022 May 27 [cited 2023 Oct 5]. Available from: https://www.uptodate.com/contents/evaluation-of-the-patient-with-vertigo.

112. Furman JM. Causes of vertigo [Internet]. UpToDate. 2021 Mar 23 [cited 2023 Oct 6]. Available from: https://www.uptodate.com/contents/causes-of-vertigo.

113. Furman JM. Vestibular neuritis and labyrinthitis [Internet]. UpToDate. 2022 Jun 28 [cited 2023 Oct 11]. Available from: https://www.uptodate.com/contents/vestibular-neuritis-and-labyrinthitis.

114. Gaillard F, Baba Y, Ranchod A, et al. Cerebral venous thrombosis [Internet]. Radiopaedia.org. 2008 Aug 26 [updated 2023 Jul 9, cited 2023 Oct 5]. Available from: https://radiopaedia.org/articles/cerebral-venous-thrombosis.

115. Gaillard F, Ranchod A, Smith D, et al. Wernicke Encephalopathy [Internet]. Radiopaedia.org. 2009 Feb 28 [updated 2023 Feb 26; cited 2023 Oct 13]. Available from: https://radiopaedia.org/articles/wernicke-encephalopathy.

116. Gaillard F, Sharma R, El-Feky M, et al. Leptomeningeal metastases [Internet]. Radiopaedia.org. 2 May 2008 [updated 7 Aug 2023; cited 7 Oct 2023] Available from: https://radiopaedia.org/articles/leptomeningeal-metastases.

117. Galvin R, Bråthen G, Ivashynka A, Hillbom M, Tanasescu R, Leone MA; EFNS. EFNS guidelines for diagnosis,

therapy and prevention of Wernicke encephalopathy. Eur J Neurol. 2010 Dec;17(12):1408-18. doi: 10.1111/j.1468-1331.2010.03153.x. PMID: 20642790.
118. Gardner-Thorpe J, Love N, Wrightson J, Walsh S, Keeling N. The value of Modified Early Warning Score (MEWS) in surgical in-patients: a prospective observational study. Ann R Coll Surg Engl. 2006 Oct;88(6):571-5. doi: 10.1308/003588406X130615. PMID: 17059720; PMCID: PMC1963767.
119. Garre-Olmo J. Epidemiologia de la enfermedad de Alzheimer y otras demencias [Epidemiology of Alzheimer's disease and other dementias]. Rev Neurol. 2018 Jun 1;66(11):377-386.
120. Gladstone DJ, Oh J, Fang J, Lindsay P, Tu JV, Silver FL, Kapral MK. Urgency of carotid endarterectomy for secondary stroke prevention: results from the Registry of the Canadian Stroke Network. Stroke. 2009 Aug;40(8):2776-82. doi: 10.1161/STROKEAHA.109.547497. Epub 2009 Jun 18. PMID: 19542057.
121. Glauser T, Shinnar S, Gloss D, Alldredge B, Arya R, Bainbridge J, Bare M, Bleck T, Dodson WE, Garrity L, Jagoda A, Lowenstein D, Pellock J, Riviello J, Sloan E, Treiman DM. Evidence-Based Guideline: Treatment of Convulsive Status Epilepticus in Children and Adults: Report of the Guideline Committee of the American Epilepsy Society. Epilepsy Curr. 2016 Jan-Feb;16(1):48-61. doi: 10.5698/1535-7597-16.1.48. PMID: 26900382; PMCID: PMC4749120.
122. Goodin DS. The epidemiology of multiple sclerosis: insights to disease pathogenesis. Handb Clin Neurol. 2014;122:231-66. doi: 10.1016/B978-0-444-52001-2.00010-8. PMID: 24507521.
123. Goodman AD, Anadani N, Gerwitz L. Siponimod in the treatment of multiple sclerosis. Expert Opin Investig Drugs. 2019 Dec;28(12):1051-1057. doi: 10.1080/13543784.2019.1676725. Epub 2019 Nov 3. PMID: 31603362.
124. Gorelick PB. Risk factors for vascular dementia and Alzheimer disease. Stroke. 2004 Nov;35(11 Suppl 1):2620-2. doi: 10.1161/01.STR.0000143318.70292.47. Epub 2004 Sep 16. PMID: 15375299.
125. Gregorian T, Lewis J, Tsu L. Opioid-Induced Constipation: Clinical Guidance and Approved Therapies. US Pharm. 2017;42(12):15-19.
126. Guarnera C, Bramanti P, Mazzon E. Alemtuzumab: a review of efficacy and risks in the treatment of relapsing remitting multiple sclerosis. Ther Clin Risk Manag. 2017 Jul 14;13:871-879. doi: 10.2147/TCRM.S134398. PMID: 28761351; PMCID: PMC5522829.
127. Guo Y, Tian X, Wang X, Xiao Z. Adverse Effects of Immunoglobulin Therapy. Front Immunol. 2018 Jun 8;9:1299. doi: 10.3389/fimmu.2018.01299. PMID: 29951056; PMCID: PMC6008653.
128. Hahn CD, Emerson RG. Electroencephalography and Evoked Potentials. In: Daroff RB, Jankovic J, Mazziotta JC, Pomeroy SL. Bradley's Neurology in Clinical Practice, 7th ed. Amsterdam: Elsevier;2015. P348-365.
129. Hallett M. NINDS myotatic reflex scale. Neurology. 1993 Dec;43(12):2723. doi: 10.1212/wnl.43.12.2723. PMID: 7802740.
130. Hanewinckel R, van Oijen M, Ikram MA, van Doorn PA. The epidemiology and risk factors of chronic polyneuropathy. Eur J Epidemiol. 2016 Jan;31(1):5-20. doi: 10.1007/s10654-015-0094-6. Epub 2015 Dec 23. PMID: 26700499; PMCID: PMC4756033.
131. Harris JA, Murphy JA. Lacosamide and epilepsy. CNS Neurosci Ther. 2011 Dec;17(6):678-82. doi: 10.1111/j.1755-5949.2010.00198.x. Epub 2010 Oct 15. PMID: 20950330; PMCID: PMC6493858.
132. Hasbun R. Aseptic meningitis in adults [Internet]. UpToDate. 2023 Jun 20 [cited 2023 Oct 07]. Available from: https://www.uptodate.com/contents/aseptic-meningitis-in-adults.
133. Hasbun R. Clinical features and diagnosis of acute bacterial meningitis in adults [Internet]. UpToDate. 2022 Oct 11 [cited 2023 Oct 07]. Available from: https://www.uptodate.com/contents/clinical-features-and-diagnosis-of-acute-bacterial-meningitis-in-adults.
134. Hauser SL, Bar-Or A, Cohen JA, Comi G, Correale J, Coyle PK, Cross AH, de Seze J, Leppert D, Montalban X, Selmaj K, Wiendl H, Kerloeguen C, Willi R, Li B, Kakarieka A, Tomic D, Goodyear A, Pingili R, Häring DA, Ramanathan K, Merschhemke M, Kappos L; ASCLEPIOS I and ASCLEPIOS II Trial Groups. Ofatumumab versus Teriflunomide in Multiple Sclerosis. N Engl J Med. 2020 Aug 6;383(6):546-557. doi: 10.1056/NEJMoa1917246. PMID: 32757523.
135. Headache Classification Committee of the International Headache Society (IHS). The International Classification of Headache Disorders, 3rd edition. Cephalalgia. 2018 Jan;38(1):1-211. doi: 10.1177/0333102417738202. PMID: 29368949.
136. Hijdra A, Koudstaal PJ, Roos RAC. *Neurologie [Neurology]*, 7th ed. Amsterdam: Bohn Stafleu van Loghum; 2016.
137. Hidalgo JA, Tork CA, Varacallo M. Arnold-Chiari Malformation. In: StatPearls [Internet]. Treasure Island (FL): StatPearls Publishing; 2023 Aug 4 [cited 2023 Oct 6]. Available from: https://www.ncbi.nlm.nih.gov/books/NBK431076/.
138. Hodgens A, Sharman T. Corticosteroids. In: StatPearls [Internet]. Treasure Island (FL, United States): StatPearls Publishing; 2023 May 1 [cited 7 Oct 2023]. Available from: https://www.ncbi.nlm.nih.gov/books/NBK554612/.
139. Holroyd KA, O'Donnell FJ, Stensland M, Lipchik GL, Cordingley GE, Carlson BW. Management of chronic tension-type headache with tricyclic antidepressant medication, stress management therapy, and their combination: a randomized controlled trial. JAMA. 2001 May 2;285(17):2208-15. doi: 10.1001/jama.285.17.2208. PMID: 11325322; PMCID: PMC2128735.
140. Isen DR, Kline LB. Neuro-ophthalmic Manifestations of Wernicke Encephalopathy. Eye Brain. 2020 Jun 30;12:49-60. doi: 10.2147/EB.S234078. PMID: 32636690; PMCID: PMC7335288.
141. Iyer S, Kim HJ. Cervical radiculopathy. Curr Rev Musculoskelet Med. 2016 Sep;9(3):272-80. doi: 10.1007/s12178-016-9349-4. PMID: 27250042; PMCID: PMC4958381.
142. Jain S, Iverson LM. Glasgow Coma Scale. In: StatPearls [Internet]. Treasure Island (FL, United States): StatPearls

Publishing; 2023 Jun 12 [cited 2023 Oct 14]. Available from: https://www.ncbi.nlm.nih.gov/books/NBK513298/.

143. Jayarangaiah A, Theetha Kariyanna P. Lambert-Eaton Myasthenic Syndrome. In: StatPearls [Internet]. Treasure Island (FL, United States): StatPearls Publishing; 2022 Jul 12 [cited 2023 Oct 7]. Available from: https://www.ncbi.nlm.nih.gov/books/NBK507891/

144. Johnson KS, Sexton DJ. Lumbar puncture: Technique, indications, contraindications, and complications in adults [Internet]. UpToDate. 2023 [cited 2023 Oct 7] Available from: https://www.uptodate.com/contents/lumbar-puncture-technique-indications-contraindications-and-complications-in-adults.

145. Jones J, Baba Y, Sharma R, et al. Intracerebral hemorrhage [Internet]. Radiopaedia.org. 2023 Aug 29 [cited 2023 Oct 05]. Available from: https://radiopaedia.org/articles/6132.

146. Józefowicz RF. The five-minute neurological examination [Internet]. Rochester: URMC [cited 2023 Oct 5]. Available from: https://www.urmc.rochester.edu/MediaLibraries/URMCMedia/neurosurgery/images/5-minute-neuro-exam-handout.pdf.

147. Kammerman S, Wasserman L. Seizure disorders: Part 1. Classification and diagnosis. West J Med. 2001 Aug;175(2):99-103. doi: 10.1136/ewjm.175.2.99. PMID: 11483551; PMCID: PMC1071497.

148. Kang C, Blair HA. Ofatumumab: A Review in Relapsing Forms of Multiple Sclerosis. Drugs. 2022 Jan;82(1):55-62. doi: 10.1007/s40265-021-01650-7. Erratum in: Drugs. 2021 Dec 29;: PMID: 34897575; PMCID: PMC8748350.

149. Kandel SA, Mandiga P. Cluster Headache. In: StatPearls [Internet]. Treasure Island (FL, United States): StatPearls Publishing; 2023 Jul 4 [cited 2023 Oct 7]. Available from: https://www.ncbi.nlm.nih.gov/books/NBK544241/.

150. Karibe H, Hayashi T, Hirano T, Kameyama M, Nakagawa A, Tominaga T. Surgical management of traumatic acute subdural hematoma in adults: a review. Neurol Med Chir (Tokyo). 2014;54(11):887-94. doi: 10.2176/nmc.cr.2014-0204. Epub 2014 Oct 31. PMID: 25367584; PMCID: PMC4533344.

151. Keene CD, Montine TJ. Epidemiology, pathology, and pathogenesis of Alzheimer disease [Internet]. UpToDate. 2022 Aug 23 [cited 2023 Oct 07]. Available from: https://www.uptodate.com/contents/epidemiology-pathology-and-pathogenesis-of-alzheimer-disease.

152. Kessler SK, McGinnis E. A Practical Guide to Treatment of Childhood Absence Epilepsy. Paediatr Drugs. 2019 Feb;21(1):15-24. doi: 10.1007/s40272-019-00325-x. PMID: 30734897; PMCID: PMC6394437.

153. Khan Z, Bollu PC. Horner Syndrome. In StatPearls [Internet]. Treasure Island (FL, United States): StatPearls Publishing. 2023 Apr 10 [cited 2023 Oct 7]. Available from: https://www.ncbi.nlm.nih.gov/books/NBK500000/.

154. Khatami R, Luca G, Baumann CR, Bassetti CL, Bruni O, Canellas F, Dauvilliers Y, Del Rio-Villegas R, Feketeova E, Ferri R, Geisler P, Högl B, Jennum P, Kornum BR, Lecendreux M, Martins-da-Silva A, Mathis J, Mayer G, Paiva T, Partinen M, Peraita-Adrados R, Plazzi G, Santamaria J, Sonka K, Riha R, Tafti M, Wierzbicka A, Young P, Lammers GJ, Overeem S; European Narcolepsy Network. The European Narcolepsy Network (EU-NN) database. J Sleep Res. 2016 Jun;25(3):356-64. doi: 10.1111/jsr.12374.

155. Khoury C. Chiari malformations [Internet]. UpToDate. 2023 Aug 10 [cited 2023 Oct 07]. Available from: https://www.uptodate.com/contents/chiari-malformations.

156. Kieseier BC. The mechanism of action of interferon-β in relapsing multiple sclerosis. CNS Drugs. 2011 Jun 1;25(6):491-502. doi: 10.2165/11591110-000000000-00000. PMID: 21649449.

157. Kim J, Lee SJ. Traumatic Subarachnoid Hemorrhage Resulting from Posterior Communicating Artery Rupture. Int Med Case Rep J. 2020 Jun 26;13:237-241. doi: 10.2147/IMCRJ.S254160. PMID: 32617022; PMCID: PMC7326191.

158. Kleindorfer DO, Towfighi A, Chaturvedi S, Cockroft KM, Gutierrez J, Lombardi-Hill D, Kamel H, Kernan WN, Kittner SJ, Leira EC, Lennon O, Meschia JF, Nguyen TN, Pollak PM, Santangeli P, Sharrief AZ, Smith SC Jr, Turan TN, Williams LS. 2021 Guideline for the Prevention of Stroke in Patients With Stroke and Transient Ischemic Attack: A Guideline From the American Heart Association/American Stroke Association. Stroke. 2021 Jul;52(7):e364-e467. doi: 10.1161/STR.0000000000000375. Epub 2021 May 24. Erratum in: Stroke. 2021 Jul;52(7):e483-e484. PMID: 34024117.

159. Koelman DLH, van Kassel MN, Bijlsma MW, Brouwer MC, van de Beek D, van der Ende A. Changing Epidemiology of Bacterial Meningitis Since Introduction of Conjugate Vaccines: 3 Decades of National Meningitis Surveilptodlance in The Netherlands.u Clin Infect Dis. 2021 Sep 7;73(5):e1099-e1107. doi: 10.1093/cid/ciaa1774. PMID: 33247582; PMCID: PMC8423501.

160. Kohil A, Jemmieh S, Smatti MK, Yassine HM. Viral meningitis: an overview. Arch Virol. 2021 Feb;166(2):335-345. doi: 10.1007/s00705-020-04891-1. Epub 2021 Jan 3. PMID: 33392820; PMCID: PMC7779091.

161. Koleva M, De Jesus O. Hydrocephalus. In: StatPearls [Internet]. Treasure Island (FL, United States): StatPearls Publishing; 2023 Jul 24 [cited 7 Oct 2023]. Available from: https://www.ncbi.nlm.nih.gov/books/NBK560875/.

162. Kristoffersen ES, Harper CE, Vetvik KG, Zarnovicky S, Hansen JM, Faiz KW. Incidence and Mortality of Cerebral Venous Thrombosis in a Norwegian Population. Stroke. 2020 Oct;51(10):3023-3029. doi: 10.1161/STROKEAHA.120.030800. Epub 2020 Sep 4. PMID: 32883194.

163. De Krom MC, Kester AD, Knipschild PG, Spaans F. Risk factors for carpal tunnel syndrome. Am J Epidemiol. 1990 Dec;132(6):1102-10. doi: 10.1093/oxfordjournals.aje.a115753. PMID: 2260542. doi: 10.1093/oxfordjournals.aje.a115753. PMID: 2260542.

164. Kuks JBM, Snoek JW. *Klinische neurologie [Clinical neurology]*, 16th ed. Houten, Bohn Stafleu van Loghum; 2007.

165. Kumar R, Lim J, Mekary RA, Rattani A, Dewan MC, Sharif SY, Osorio-Fonseca E, Park KB. Traumatic Spinal Injury: Global Epidemiology and Worldwide Volume. World Neurosurg. 2018 May;113:e345-e363. doi: 10.1016/j.wneu.2018.02.033. Epub 2018 Feb 14. PMID: 29454115.

166. Larson, EB. Evaluation of cognitive impairment and dementia [Internet]. UpToDate. 2022 Nov 02 [cited 2023 Oct

07]. Available from: https://www.uptodate.com/contents/evaluation-of-cognitive-impairment-and-dementia.

167. Lassiter G, Melancon C, Rooney T, Murat AM, Kaye JS, Kaye AM, Kaye RJ, Cornett EM, Kaye AD, Shah RJ, Viswanath O, Urits I. Ozanimod to Treat Relapsing Forms of Multiple Sclerosis: A Comprehensive Review of Disease, Drug Efficacy and Side Effects. Neurol Int. 2020 Dec 3;12(3):89-108. doi: 10.3390/neurolint12030016. PMID: 33287177; PMCID: PMC7768354.
168. Lee AG. Third cranial nerve (oculomotor nerve) palsy in adults [Internet]. UpToDate. 2017 Jun 19 [cited 2023 Oct 5]. Available from: https://www.uptodate.com/contents/third-cranial-nerve-oculomotor-nerve-palsy-in-adults.
169. Lee AG, Ponce CMP, Vickers A. Sixth cranial nerve (abducens nerve) palsy in adults [Internet]. UpToDate. 2023 May 22 [cited 2023 Oct 5]. Available from: https://www.uptodate.com/contents/sixth-cranial-nerve-abducens-nerve-palsy.
170. Lee JH, Lee JK, Park JS, Kim DH, Baek JH, Yoon BN, Kim S, Ha C, Cho WM, Han SH. Characteristics of surgically treated Guyon canal syndrome: A multicenter retrospective study. J Plast Reconstr Aesthet Surg. 2022 Sep;75(9):3269-3278. doi: 10.1016/j.bjps.2022.04.049. Epub 2022 Apr 27. PMID: 35654688.
171. Lee KS. How to Treat Chronic Subdural Hematoma? Past and Now. J Korean Neurosurg Soc. 2019 Mar;62(2):144-152. doi: 10.3340/jkns.2018.0156. Epub 2018 Nov 30. PMID: 30486622; PMCID: PMC6411568.
172. Lee SE. Frontotemporal dementia: Clinical features and diagnosis [Internet]. UpToDate. 2021 July 27 [cited 2023 Oct 07]. Available from: https://www.uptodate.com/contents/frontotemporal-dementia-clinical-features-and-diagnosis.
173. Lee SH, Kim JS. Benign paroxysmal positional vertigo. J Clin Neurol. 2010 Jun;6(2):51-63. doi: 10.3988/jcn.2010.6.2.51. Epub 2010 Jun 30. PMID: 20607044; PMCID: PMC2895225.
174. Lenka A, Jankovic J. Tremor Syndromes: An Updated Review. Front Neurol. 2021 Jul 26;12:684835. doi: 10.3389/fneur.2021.684835. PMID: 34381412; PMCID: PMC8350038.
175. Lenka A, Louis ED. Revisiting the Clinical Phenomenology of "Cerebellar Tremor": Beyond the Intention Tremor. Cerebellum. 2019 Jun;18(3):565-574. doi: 10.1007/s12311-018-0994-6. PMID: 30565088.
176. Leonhard SE, Mandarakas MR, Gondim FAA, Bateman K, Ferreira MLB, Cornblath DR, van Doorn PA, Dourado ME, Hughes RAC, Islam B, Kusunoki S, Pardo CA, Reisin R, Sejvar JJ, Shahrizaila N, Soares C, Umapathi T, Wang Y, Yiu EM, Willison HJ, Jacobs BC. Diagnosis and management of Guillain-Barré syndrome in ten steps. Nat Rev Neurol. 2019 Nov;15(11):671-683. doi: 10.1038/s41582-019-0250-9. Epub 2019 Sep 20. PMID: 31541214; PMCID: PMC6821638.
177. Lew C, Punnapuzha S. Migraine Medications. In: StatPearls [Internet]. Treasure Island (FL, United States): StatPearls Publishing; 2023 May 1 [cited 7 Oct 2023]. Available from: https://www.ncbi.nlm.nih.gov/books/NBK553159/.
178. Li Z, Richards S, Surks HK, Jacobs A, Panzara MA. Clinical pharmacology of alemtuzumab, an anti-CD52 immunomodulator, in multiple sclerosis. Clin Exp Immunol. 2018 Dec;194(3):295-314. doi: 10.1111/cei.13208. Epub 2018 Oct 1. PMID: 30144037; PMCID: PMC6231011.
179. Liao Q, Zhang Y, He J, Huang K. Global Prevalence of Myotonic Dystrophy: An Updated Systematic Review and Meta-Analysis. Neuroepidemiology. 2022;56(3):163-173. doi: 10.1159/000524734. Epub 2022 Apr 28. PMID: 35483324.
180. Links KA, Merims D, Binns MA, Freedman M, Chow TW. Prevalence of primitive reflexes and Parkinsonian signs in dementia. Can J Neurol Sci. 2010 Sep;37(5):601-7. doi: 10.1017/s0317167100010763. PMID: 21059505.
181. Lipka AF, Boldingh MI, van Zwet EW, Schreurs MW, Kuks JB, Tallaksen CM, et al. Long-term follow-up, quality of life, and survival of patients with Lambert-Eaton myasthenic syndrome. Neurology. 2020;94(5):e511-e520. [cited 2024 Mar 3].
182. Longstreth WT Jr, Koepsell TD, Ton TG, Hendrickson AF, van Belle G. The epidemiology of narcolepsy. Sleep. 2007 Jan;30(1):13-26. doi: 10.1093/sleep/30.1.13. PMID: 17310860.
183. Löscher W, Klein P. The Pharmacology and Clinical Efficacy of Antiseizure Medications: From Bromide Salts to Cenobamate and Beyond. CNS Drugs. 2021 Sep;35(9):935-963. doi: 10.1007/s40263-021-00827-8. Epub 2021 Jun 18. Erratum in: CNS Drugs. 2021 Aug 17;: PMID: 34145528; PMCID: PMC8408078.
184. Lunde HMB, Assmus J, Myhr KM, Bø L, Grytten N. Survival and cause of death in multiple sclerosis: a 60-year longitudinal population study. J Neurol Neurosurg Psychiatry. 2017 Aug;88(8):621-625. doi: 10.1136/jnnp-2016-315238. Epub 2017 Apr 1. PMID: 28365589; PMCID: PMC5537547.
185. Ma H, Campbell BCV, Parsons MW, Churilov L, Levi CR, Hsu C, Kleinig TJ, Wijeratne T, Curtze S, Dewey HM, Miteff F, Tsai CH, Lee JT, Phan TG, Mahant N, Sun MC, Krause M, Sturm J, Grimley R, Chen CH, Hu CJ, Wong AA, Field D, Sun Y, Barber PA, Sabet A, Jannes J, Jeng JS, Clissold B, Markus R, Lin CH, Lien LM, Bladin CF, Christensen S, Yassi N, Sharma G, Bivard A, Desmond PM, Yan B, Mitchell PJ, Thijs V, Carey L, Meretoja A, Davis SM, Donnan GA; EXTEND Investigators. Thrombolysis Guided by Perfusion Imaging up to 9 Hours after Onset of Stroke. N Engl J Med. 2019 May 9;380(19):1795-1803. doi: 10.1056/NEJMoa1813046. Erratum in: N Engl J Med. 2021 Apr 1;384(13):1278. PMID: 31067369.
186. Maas AIR, Menon DK, Manley GT, Abrams M, Åkerlund C, Andelic N, Aries M, Bashford T, Bell MJ, Bodien YG, Brett BL, Büki A, Chesnut RM, Citerio G, Clark D, Clasby B, Cooper DJ, Czeiter E, Czosnyka M, Dams-O'Connor K, De Keyser V, Diaz-Arrastia R, Ercole A, van Essen TA, Falvey É, Ferguson AR, Figaji A, Fitzgerald M, Foreman B, Gantner D, Gao G, Giacino J, Gravesteijn B, Guiza F, Gupta D, Gurnell M, Haagsma JA, Hammond FM, Hawryluk G, Hutchinson P, van der Jagt M, Jain S, Jain S, Jiang JY, Kent H, Kolias A, Kompanje EJO, Lecky F, Lingsma HF, Maegele M, Majdan M, Markowitz A, McCrea M, Meyfroidt G, Mikolić A, Mondello S, Mukherjee P, Nelson D, Nelson LD, Newcombe V, Okonkwo D, Orešič M, Peul W, Pisică D, Polinder S, Ponsford J, Puybasset L, Raj R, Robba C, Røe C, Rosand J, Schueler P, Sharp DJ, Smielewski P, Stein MB, von Steinbüchel N, Stewart W, Stey-

erberg EW, Stocchetti N, Temkin N, Tenovuo O, Theadom A, Thomas I, Espin AT, Turgeon AF, Unterberg A, Van Praag D, van Veen E, Verheyden J, Vyvere TV, Wang KKW, Wiegers EJA, Williams WH, Wilson L, Wisniewski SR, Younsi A, Yue JK, Yuh EL, Zeiler FA, Zeldovich M, Zemek R; InTBIR Participants and Investigators. Traumatic brain injury: progress and challenges in prevention, clinical care, and research. Lancet Neurol. 2022 Nov;21(11):1004-1060. doi: 10.1016/S1474-4422(22)00309-X. Epub 2022 Sep 29. Erratum in: Lancet Neurol. 2022 Oct 7; PMID: 36183712; PMCID: PMC10427240.

187. Manivannan S, Spencer R, Marei O, Mayo I, Elalfy O, Martin J, Zaben M. Acute subdural haematoma in the elderly: to operate or not to operate? A systematic review and meta-analysis of outcomes following surgery. BMJ Open. 2021 Dec 3;11(12):e050786. doi: 10.1136/bmjopen-2021-050786. PMID: 34862284; PMCID: PMC8647543.
188. Mansfield M, Smith T, Spahr N, Thacker M. Cervical spine radiculopathy epidemiology: A systematic review. Musculoskeletal Care. 2020 Dec;18(4):555-567. doi: 10.1002/msc.1498. Epub 2020 Jul 25. PMID: 32710604.
189. Martin TJ. Horner Syndrome: A Clinical Review. ACS Chem Neurosci. 2018 Feb 21;9(2):177-186. doi: 10.1021/acschemneuro.7b00405. Epub 2017 Dec 20. PMID: 29260849.
190. McBride, W. Intracranial epidural hematoma in adults [Internet]. UpToDate. 2022 May 03 [cited 2023 Oct 05]. Available from: https://www.uptodate.com/contents/intracranial-epidural-hematoma-in-adults.
191. McCormack PL. Natalizumab: a review of its use in the management of relapsing-remitting multiple sclerosis. Drugs. 2013 Sep;73(13):1463-81. doi: 10.1007/s40265-013-0102-7. PMID: 23912625.
192. McGill F, Griffiths MJ, Bonnett LJ, Geretti AM, Michael BD, Beeching NJ, McKee D, Scarlett P, Hart IJ, Mutton KJ, Jung A, Adan G, Gummery A, Sulaiman WAW, Ennis K, Martin AP, Haycox A, Miller A, Solomon T; UK Meningitis Study Investigators. Incidence, aetiology, and sequelae of viral meningitis in UK adults: a multicentre prospective observational cohort study. Lancet Infect Dis. 2018 Sep;18(9):992-1003.
193. McKay LI, Cidlowski JA. Physiologic and Pharmacologic Effects of Corticosteroids. In: Kufe DW, Pollock RE, Weichselbaum RR, et al., editors. Holland-Frei Cancer Medicine, 6th edition [Internet]. Hamilton (ON): BC Decker; 2003 [cited 2023 Oct 12]. Available from: https://www.ncbi.nlm.nih.gov/books/NBK13780/.
194. McKinley W, Santos K, Meade M, Brooke K. Incidence and outcomes of spinal cord injury clinical syndromes. J Spinal Cord Med. 2007;30(3):215-24. doi: 10.1080/10790268.2007.11753929. PMID: 17684887; PMCID: PMC2031952.
195. Medina A, Mahjoub Y, Shaver L, Pringsheim T. Prevalence and Incidence of Huntington's Disease: An Updated Systematic Review and Meta-Analysis. Mov Disord. 2022 Dec;37(12):2327-2335. doi: 10.1002/mds.29228. Epub 2022 Sep 26. PMID: 36161673; PMCID: PMC10086981.
196. Mescher AL, Junqueira LC. *Junqueira's basic histology: Text & atlas*, 12th ed. New York; McGraw-Hill Education; 2010.
197. NICE Clinical Guidelines, No. 75. Metastatic Spinal Cord Compression: Diagnosis and Management of Patients at Risk of or with Metastatic Spinal Cord Compression. Cardiff (UK): National Collaborating Centre for Cancer (UK); 2008 Nov [cited 2023 Oct 14]. Available from: https://www.ncbi.nlm.nih.gov/books/NBK55011/.
198. Miller AE, Chitnis T, Cohen BA, Costello K, Sicotte NL, Stacom R; National Medical Advisory Committee of the National Multiple Sclerosis Society. Autologous Hematopoietic Stem Cell Transplant in Multiple Sclerosis: Recommendations of the National Multiple Sclerosis Society. JAMA Neurol. 2021 Feb 1;78(2):241-246. doi: 10.1001/jamaneurol.2020.4025. PMID: 33104165.
199. Miller DJ, Simpson JR, Silver B. Safety of thrombolysis in acute ischemic stroke: a review of complications, risk factors, and newer technologies. Neurohospitalist. 2011 Jul;1(3):138-47. doi: 10.1177/1941875211408731. PMID: 23983849; PMCID: PMC3726129.
200. Miller RG, Jackson CE, Kasarskis EJ, England JD, Forshew D, Johnston W, Kalra S, Katz JS, Mitsumoto H, Rosenfeld J, Shoesmith C, Strong MJ, Woolley SC; Quality Standards Subcommittee of the American Academy of Neurology. Practice parameter update: the care of the patient with amyotrophic lateral sclerosis: drug, nutritional, and respiratory therapies (an evidence-based review): report of the Quality Standards Subcommittee of the American Academy of Neurology. Neurology. 2009 Oct 13;73(15):1218-26. doi: 10.1212/WNL.0b013e3181bc0141. Erratum in: Neurology. 2009 Dec 15;73(24):2134. Erratum in: Neurology. 2010 Mar 2;74(9):781. PMID: 19822872; PMCID: PMC2764727.
201. Mills KR. The basics of electromyography. J Neurol Neurosurg Psychiatry. 2005 Jun;76 Suppl 2(Suppl 2):ii32-5. doi: 10.1136/jnnp.2005.069211. PMID: 15961866; PMCID: PMC1765694.
202. Moeller J, Haider HA and Hirsch LJ. Electroencephalography (EEG) in the diagnosis of seizures and epilepsy [Internet]. UpToDate. 2023 Jan 31 [cited 2023 Oct 7]. Available from: https://www.uptodate.com/contents/electroencephalography-eeg-in-the-diagnosis-of-seizures-and-epilepsy.
203. Mokin M, Ansari SA, McTaggart RA Society of NeuroInterventional Surgery, et al. Indications for thrombectomy in acute ischemic stroke from emergent large vessel occlusion (ELVO): report of the SNIS Standards and Guidelines Committee. Journal of NeuroInterventional Surgery 2019;11:215-220. doi: 10.1136/neurintsurg-2018-014640. Epub 2019 Jan 4. PMID: 30610069.
204. Moore WS, Barnett HJ, Beebe HG, Bernstein EF, Brener BJ, Brott T, Caplan LR, Day A, Goldstone J, Hobson RW 2nd, et al. Guidelines for carotid endarterectomy. A multidisciplinary consensus statement from the ad hoc Committee, American Heart Association. Stroke. 1995 Jan;26(1):188-201. doi: 10.1161/01.str.26.1.188. PMID: 7839390.
205. Moskowitz HS, Dinces EA. Meniere disease: Evaluation, diagnosis and management [Internet]. UpToDate. 2022 Nov 02 [cited 2023 Oct 11]. Available from: https://www.uptodate.com/contents/meniere-disease-evaluation-diagnosis-and-management.
206. Moulin DE, Hagen N, Feasby TE, Amireh R, Hahn A. Pain in Guillain-Barré syndrome. Neurology. 1997

Feb;48(2):328-31. doi: 10.1212/wnl.48.2.328. PMID: 9040715.
207. Mulero P, Midaglia L, Montalban X. Ocrelizumab: a new milestone in multiple sclerosis therapy. Ther Adv Neurol Disord. 2018 May 10;11:1756286418773025. doi: 10.1177/1756286418773025. PMID: 29774057; PMCID: PMC5952271.
208. Muzumdar D, Jhawar S, Goel A. Brain abscess: an overview. Int J Surg. 2011;9(2):136-44. doi: 10.1016/j.ijsu.2010.11.005. Epub 2010 Nov 16.
209. Nadarajan V, Perry RJ, Johnson J, Werring DJ. Transient ischaemic attacks: mimics and chameleons. Pract Neurol. 2014 Feb;14(1):23-31. doi: 10.1136/practneurol-2013-000782. PMID: 24453269; PMCID: PMC3913122.
210. Nakashima T, Pyykkö I, Arroll MA, Casselbrant ML, Foster CA, Manzoor NF, Megerian CA, Naganawa S, Young YH. Meniere's disease. Nat Rev Dis Primers. 2016 May 12;2:16028. doi: 10.1038/nrdp.2016.28. PMID: 27170253.
211. Nasr DM, Brinjikji W, Cloft HJ, Saposnik G, Rabinstein AA. Mortality in cerebral venous thrombosis: results from the national inpatient sample database. Cerebrovasc Dis. 2013;35(1):40-4. doi: 10.1159/000343653. Epub 2013 Feb 14. PMID: 23428995.
212. Nasreddine ZS, Phillips NA, Bédirian V, Charbonneau S, Whitehead V, Collin I, Cummings JL, Chertkow H. The Montreal Cognitive Assessment, MoCA: a brief screening tool for mild cognitive impairment. J Am Geriatr Soc. 2005 Apr;53(4):695-9. doi: 10.1111/j.1532-5415.2005.53221.x. Erratum in: J Am Geriatr Soc. 2019 Sep;67(9):1991. PMID: 15817019.
213. National clinical guideline for stroke for the UK and Ireland, 6th edition [Internet]. Intercollegiate Stroke Working Party, Royal College of Physicians. 2023 May 4 [cited 2023 Oct 05]. Available from: https://www.strokeguideline.org/.
214. Nayak CS, Anilkumar AC. EEG Normal Waveforms. In: StatPearls [Internet]. Treasure Island (FL): StatPearls Publishing; 2023 Jul 24 [cited 7 Oct 2023]. Available from: https://www.ncbi.nlm.nih.gov/books/NBK539805/.
215. Nayak L, Lee EQ, Wen PY. Epidemiology of brain metastases. Curr Oncol Rep. 2012 Feb;14(1):48-54. doi: 10.1007/s11912-011-0203-y. PMID: 22012633.
216. Naylor R, Rantner B, Ancetti S, de Borst GJ, De Carlo M, Halliday A, Kakkos SK, Markus HS, McCabe DJH, Sillesen H, van den Berg JC, Vega de Ceniga M, Venermo MA, Vermassen FEG, Esvs Guidelines Committee, Antoniou GA, Bastos Goncalves F, Bjorck M, Chakfe N, Coscas R, Dias NV, Dick F, Hinchliffe RJ, Kolh P, Koncar IB, Lindholt JS, Mees BME, Resch TA, Trimarchi S, Tulamo R, Twine CP, Wanhainen A, Document Reviewers, Bellmunt-Montoya S, Bulbulia R, Darling RC 3rd, Eckstein HH, Giannoukas A, Koelemay MJW, Lindström D, Schermerhorn M, Stone DH. Editor's Choice - European Society for Vascular Surgery (ESVS) 2023 Clinical Practice Guidelines on the Management of Atherosclerotic Carotid and Vertebral Artery Disease. Eur J Vasc Endovasc Surg. 2023 Jan;65(1):7-111. doi: 10.1016/j.ejvs.2022.04.011. Epub 2022 May 20. PMID: 35598721.
217. Neuropathic pain in adults: Pharmacological management in non-specialist settings [Internet]. London: National Institute for Health and Care Excellence (NICE); 2013 Nov 20 [updated 2020 Sep 22, cited 2023 Oct 12]. Available from: https://www.nice.org.uk/guidance/cg173.
218. Nicolas S, Nicolas D. Triptans. In: StatPearls [Internet]. Treasure Island (FL, United States): StatPearls Publishing; 2023 Mar 7 [cited 2023 Oct 7]. Available from: https://www.ncbi.nlm.nih.gov/books/NBK554507/.
219. Norkett W, McLone DG, Bowman R. Current Management Strategies of Hydrocephalus in the Child With Open Spina Bifida. Top Spinal Cord Inj Rehabil. 2016 Fall;22(4):241-246. doi: 10.1310/sci2204-241. PMID: 29339864; PMCID: PMC5108507.
220. Obata H. Analgesic Mechanisms of Antidepressants for Neuropathic Pain. Int J Mol Sci. 2017 Nov 21;18(11):2483. doi: 10.3390/ijms18112483. PMID: 29160850; PMCID: PMC5713449.
221. Ocejo A, Correa R. Methylprednisolone. In: StatPearls [Internet]. Treasure Island (FL): StatPearls Publishing; 2022 Dec 11 [cited 2023 Nov 18]. Available from: https://www.ncbi.nlm.nih.gov/books/NBK544340/.
222. O'Connor E, Simpson BS, Houlden H, Vandrovcova J, Matharu M. Prevalence of familial cluster headache: a systematic review and meta-analysis. J Headache Pain. 2020 Apr 25;21(1):37. doi: 10.1186/s10194-020-01101-w. PMID: 32334514; PMCID: PMC7183702.
223. Olek MJ, Howard J. Clinical presentation, course, and prognosis of multiple sclerosis in adults [Internet]. UpToDate. 2023 Aug 30 [cited 2023 Oct 5]. Available from: https://www.uptodate.com/contents/clinical-presentation-course-and-prognosis-of-multiple-sclerosis-in-adults.
224. Olsson T, Boster A, Fernández Ó, Freedman MS, Pozzilli C, Bach D, Berkani O, Mueller MS, Sidorenko T, Radue EW, Melanson M. Oral ponesimod in relapsing-remitting multiple sclerosis: a randomised phase II trial. J Neurol Neurosurg Psychiatry. 2014 Nov;85(11):1198-208. doi: 10.1136/jnnp-2013-307282. Epub 2014 Mar 21. PMID: 24659797; PMCID: PMC4215282.
225. Oncel MY, Ozdemir R, Kahilogulları G, Yurttutan S, Erdeve O, Dilmen U. The effect of surgery time on prognosis in newborns with meningomyelocele. J Korean Neurosurg Soc. 2012 Jun;51(6):359-62. doi: 10.3340/jkns.2012.51.6.359. Epub 2012 Jun 30. PMID: 22949965; PMCID: PMC3424176.
226. Onyike CU, Diehl-Schmid J. The epidemiology of frontotemporal dementia. Int Rev Psychiatry. 2013 Apr;25(2):130-7. doi: 10.3109/09540261.2013.776523. PMID: 23611343; PMCID: PMC3932112.
227. Ortiz R, Scheperjans F, Mertsalmi T, Pekkonen E. The prevalence of adult-onset isolated dystonia in Finland 2007-2016. PLoS One. 2018 Nov 20;13(11):e0207729. doi: 10.1371/journal.pone.0207729. PMID: 30458031; PMCID: PMC6245745.
228. Ortiz Gómez, J.A. The incidence of vertebral body metastases. Int Orthop. 1995;19(5):309-11. doi: 10.1007/BF00181116. PMID: 8567140.
229. Palm A, Vataja R, Talaslahti T, Ginters M, Kautiainen H, Elonheimo H, Suvisaari J, Lindberg N, Koponen H. Incidence and mortality of alcohol-related dementia and Wernicke-Korsakoff syndrome: A nationwide register

study. Int J Geriatr Psychiatry. 2022 Aug;37(8):10.1002/gps.5775. doi: 10.1002/gps.5775. PMID: 35789035; PMCID: PMC9546078.

230. Paulsen F, Waschke J, Hombach-Klonisch S, Klonisch T. *Sobotta atlas of human anatomy: Head, neck and neuroanatomy*, 15th ed. München: Urban & Fisher; 2011.

231. Payer S, Mende KC, Westphal M, Eicker SO. Intramedullary spinal cord metastases: an increasingly common diagnosis. Neurosurg Focus. 2015 Aug;39(2):E15. doi: 10.3171/2015.5.FOCUS15149. PMID: 26235013.

232. Payne AB, Adamski A, Abe K, Reyes NL, Richardson LC, Hooper WC, Schieve LA. Epidemiology of cerebral venous sinus thrombosis and cerebral venous sinus thrombosis with thrombocytopenia in the United States, 2018 and 2019. Res Pract Thromb Haemost. 2022 Mar 7;6(2):e12682. doi: 10.1002/rth2.12682. PMID: 35284775; PMCID: PMC8901465.

233. Perez EE, Shehata N. Intravenous immune globulin: Adverse effects [Internet]. UpToDate. 2022 Nov 14 [cited 2023 Nov 18]. Available from: https://www.uptodate.com/contents/intravenous-immune-globulin-adverse-effects.

234. Pfeuffer S, Rolfes L, Hackert J, Kleinschnitz K, Ruck T, Wiendl H, Klotz L, Kleinschnitz C, Meuth SG, Pul R. Effectiveness and safety of cladribine in MS: Real-world experience from two tertiary centres. Mult Scler. 2022 Feb;28(2):257-268. doi: 10.1177/13524585211012227. Epub 2021 May 12. PMID: 33975489; PMCID: PMC8795224.

235. Pohl D, Rostasy K, Reiber H, Hanefeld F. CSF characteristics in early-onset multiple sclerosis. Neurology. 2004 Nov 23;63(10):1966-7. doi: 10.1212/01.wnl.0000144352.67102.bc. PMID: 15557527.

236. Poon MT, Bell SM, Al-Shahi Salman R. Epidemiology of Intracerebral Haemorrhage. Front Neurol Neurosci. 2015;37:1-12. doi: 10.1159/000437109. Epub 2015 Nov 12. PMID: 26588164.

237. Pourmemari MH, Heliövaara M, Viikari-Juntura E, Shiri R. Carpal tunnel release: Lifetime prevalence, annual incidence, and risk factors. Muscle Nerve. 2018 Oct;58(4):497-502. doi: 10.1002/mus.26145. Epub 2018 May 18. PMID: 29665085.

238. Powers WJ, Rabinstein AA, Ackerson T, Adeoye OM, Bambakidis NC, Becker K, Biller J, Brown M, Demaerschalk BM, Hoh B, Jauch EC, Kidwell CS, Leslie-Mazwi TM, Ovbiagele B, Scott PA, Sheth KN, Southerland AM, Summers DV, Tirschwell DL. Guidelines for the Early Management of Patients With Acute Ischemic Stroke: 2019 Update to the 2018 Guidelines for the Early Management of Acute Ischemic Stroke: A Guideline for Healthcare Professionals From the American Heart Association/American Stroke Association. Stroke. 2019 Dec;50(12):e344-e418. doi: 10.1161/STR.0000000000000211. Epub 2019 Oct 30. Erratum in: Stroke. 2019 Dec;50(12):e440-e441. PMID: 31662037.

239. Puppala VK, Dickinson O, Benditt DG. Syncope: classification and risk stratification. J Cardiol. 2014 Mar;63(3):171-7. doi: 10.1016/j.jjcc.2013.03.019. Epub 2014 Jan 7. PMID: 24405895.

240. Queremel Milani DA, Davis DD. Pain Management Medications. In: StatPearls [Internet]. Treasure Island (FL): StatPearls Publishing; 2023 Jul 3 [cited 2023 Oct 7]. Available from: https://www.ncbi.nlm.nih.gov/books/NBK560692/.

241. Rahimi A, Corley JA, Ammar A, Shlobin NA, Rolle M, Mekary RA, Park KB. The unmet global burden of cranial epidural hematomas: A systematic review and meta-analysis. Clin Neurol Neurosurg. 2022 Aug;219. doi: 10.1016/j.clineuro.2022.107313. Epub 2022 Jun 6. PMID: 35688003.

242. Rajan KB, Weuve J, Barnes LL, Wilson RS, Evans DA. Prevalence and incidence of clinically diagnosed Alzheimer's disease dementia from 1994 to 2012 in a population study. Alzheimers Dement. 2019 Jan;15(1):1-7. doi: 10.1016/j.jalz.2018.07.216. Epub 2018 Sep 7. PMID: 30195482; PMCID: PMC6531287.

243. Rajesh S, Wonderling D, Bernstein I, Balson C, Lecky F; Guideline Committee. Head injury: assessment and early management-summary of updated NICE guidance. BMJ. 2023 May 30;381:1130. doi: 10.1136/bmj.p1130. PMID: 37253484.

244. Reed MJ. Approach to syncope in the emergency department. Emerg Med J. 2019 Feb;36(2):108-116. doi: 10.1136/emermed-2018-207767. Epub 2018 Nov 23. PMID: 30470687.

245. Robinson LR. Traumatic injury to peripheral nerves. Muscle Nerve. 2022 Dec;66(6):661-670. doi: 10.1002/mus.27706. Epub 2022 Sep 7. PMID: 36070242.

246. De Robles P, Fiest KM, Frolkis AD, Pringsheim T, Atta C, St Germaine-Smith C, Day L, Lam D, Jette N. The worldwide incidence and prevalence of primary brain tumors: a systematic review and meta-analysis. Neuro Oncol. 2015 Jun;17(6):776-83. doi: 10.1093/neuonc/nou283. Epub 2014 Oct 13. PMID: 25313193; PMCID: PMC4483114.

247. Rodolico C, Bonanno C, Toscano A, Vita G. MuSK-Associated Myasthenia Gravis: Clinical Features and Management. Front Neurol. 2020 Jul 23;11:660. doi: 10.3389/fneur.2020.00660. PMID: 32793097; PMCID: PMC7390870.

248. Roth EJ, Park T, Pang T, Yarkony GM, Lee MY. Traumatic cervical Brown-Sequard and Brown-Sequard-plus syndromes: the spectrum of presentations and outcomes. Paraplegia. 1991 Nov;29(9):582-9. doi: 10.1038/sc.1991.86. PMID: 1787982.

249. Sadler B, Kuensting T, Strahle J, Park TS, Smyth M, Limbrick DD, Dobbs MB, Haller G, Gurnett CA. Prevalence and Impact of Underlying Diagnosis and Comorbidities on Chiari 1 Malformation. Pediatr Neurol. 2020 May;106:32-37. doi: 10.1016/j.pediatrneurol.2019.12.005. Epub 2020 Jan 21. PMID: 32113729; PMCID: PMC7156318.

250. Sánchez S, Rincon F. Status Epilepticus: Epidemiology and Public Health Needs. J Clin Med. 2016 Aug 16;5(8):71. doi: 10.3390/jcm5080071. PMID: 27537921; PMCID: PMC4999791.

251. Sawires R, Buttery J, Fahey M. A Review of Febrile Seizures: Recent Advances in Understanding of Febrile Seizure Pathophysiology and Commonly Implicated Viral Triggers. Front Pediatr. 2022 Jan 13;9:801321. doi: 10.3389/fped.2021.801321. PMID: 35096712; PMCID: PMC8793886.

252. Scammell, TE. Clinical features and diagnosis of narcolepsy in adults [Internet]. UpToDate. 2022 Jul 12 [cited 2023 Oct 07]. Available from: https://www.uptodate.com/contents/clinical-features-and-diagnosis-of-narcolepsy-in-adults.
253. Scharf JM, Miller LL, Gauvin CA, Alabiso J, Mathews CA, Ben-Shlomo Y. Population prevalence of Tourette syndrome: a systematic review and meta-analysis. Mov Disord. 2015 Feb;30(2):221-8. doi: 10.1002/mds.26089. Epub 2014 Dec 8. PMID: 25487709.
254. Schieving JH. Kinderneurologie [Paediatric Neurology] [Internet]. Kinderneurologie.eu. 2009 Oct 25 [cited 2019 May 15]. Available from: https://www.kinderneurologie.eu.
255. Schwingenschuh P, Deuschl G. Functional tremor. Handb Clin Neurol. 2016;139:229-233. doi: 10.1016/B978-0-12-801772-2.00019-9. PMID: 27719841.
256. Shankar Kikkeri N, Nagalli S. Trigeminal Neuralgia. In: StatPearls [Internet]. Treasure Island (FL): StatPearls Publishing; 2022 Jul 9 [cited 2023 Oct 7]. Available from: https://www.ncbi.nlm.nih.gov/books/NBK554486/.
257. Siddiq F. Nonaneurysmal subarachnoid hemorrhage [Internet]. UpToDate. 2023 Feb 13 [cited 2023 Oct 07]. Available from: https://www.uptodate.com/contents/nonaneurysmal-subarachnoid-hemorrhage.
258. Silvis SM, Aguiar de Sousa D, Ferro JM, Coutinho JM. Cerebral venous thrombosis. Nat Rev Neurol. 2017 Sep;13(9):555–565. doi: 10.1038/nrneurol.2017.104. Epub 2017 Aug 18. PMID: 28820187.
259. Singh G, Sander JW. The global burden of epilepsy report: Implications for low- and middle-income countries. Epilepsy Behav. 2020 Apr;105:106949. doi: 10.1016/j.yebeh.2020.106949. Epub 2020 Feb 20. PMID: 32088583.
260. Sizar O, Genova R, Gupta M. Opioid-Induced Constipation. In: StatPearls [Internet]. Treasure Island (FL, United States): StatPearls Publishing. 2023 Aug 7 [cited 28 Oct 2023]. Available from: https://www.ncbi.nlm.nih.gov/books/NBK493184/.
261. Smith EE, Wright CB. Etiology, clinical manifestations, and diagnosis of vascular dementia [Internet]. UpToDate. 2023 Apr 24 [cited 2023 Oct 07]. Available from: https://www.uptodate.com/contents/etiology-clinical-manifestations-and-diagnosis-of-vascular-dementia.
262. Smits M, Dippel DW, Steyerberg EW, de Haan GG, Dekker HM, Vos PE, Kool DR, Nederkoorn PJ, Hofman PA, Twijnstra A, Tanghe HL, Hunink MG. Predicting intracranial traumatic findings on computed tomography in patients with minor head injury: the CHIP prediction rule. Ann Intern Med. 2007 Mar 20;146(6):397-405. doi: 10.7326/0003-4819-146-6-200703200-00004. PMID: 17371884.
263. So YT. Wernicke encephalopathy [Internet]. UpToDate. 2020 Feb 11 [cited 2023 Oct 7]. Available from: https://www.uptodate.com/contents/wernicke-encephalopathy.
264. Southwick FS. Pathogenesis, clinical manifestations, and diagnosis of brain abscess [Internet]. UpToDate. 2021 Dec 03 [cited 2023 Oct 07]. Available from: https://www.uptodate.com/contents/pathogenesis-clinical-manifestations-and-diagnosis-of-brain-abscess.
265. Steiner TJ, Stovner LJ. Global epidemiology of migraine and its implications for public health and health policy. Nat Rev Neurol. 2023 Feb;19(2):109-117. doi: 10.1038/s41582-022-00763-1. Epub 2023 Jan 24. PMID: 36693999.
266. Stiell IG, Wells GA, Vandemheen K, Clement C, Lesiuk H, Laupacis A, McKnight RD, Verbeek R, Brison R, Cass D, Eisenhauer ME, Greenberg G, Worthington J. The Canadian CT Head Rule for patients with minor head injury. Lancet. 2001 May 5;357(9266):1391-6. doi: 10.1016/s0140-6736(00)04561-x. PMID: 11356436.
267. Stovner LJ, Hagen K, Linde M, Steiner TJ. The global prevalence of headache: an update, with analysis of the influences of methodological factors on prevalence estimates. J Headache Pain. 2022 Apr 12;23(1):34. doi: 10.1186/s10194-022-01402-2. PMID: 35410119; PMCID: PMC9004186.
268. Stroke and transient ischaemic attack in over 16s: diagnosis and initial management [Internet]. London: National Institute for Health and Care Excellence (NICE); 2019 May 1 [updated 2022 Apr 13, cited 2023 Oct 05]. Available from: https://www.nice.org.uk/guidance/ng128.
269. Strupp M, Brandt T. Vestibular neuritis. Semin Neurol. 2009 Nov;29(5):509-19. doi: 10.1055/s-0029-1241040. Epub 2009 Oct 15. PMID: 19834862.
270. Subbarao BS, Silverman A, Eapen BC. Seizure Medications. In: StatPearls [Internet]. Treasure Island (FL, United States): StatPearls Publishing; 2023 Jul 10 [cited 7 Oct 2023]. Available from: https://www.ncbi.nlm.nih.gov/books/NBK482269/.
271. Subbe CP, Kruger M, Rutherford P, Gemmel L. Validation of a modified Early Warning Score in medical admissions. QJM. 2001 Oct;94(10):521-6. doi: 10.1093/qjmed/94.10.521. PMID: 11588210.
272. Sullivan R, Yau WY, O'Connor E, Houlden H. Spinocerebellar ataxia: an update. J Neurol. 2019 Feb;266(2):533-544. doi: 10.1007/s00415-018-9076-4. Epub 2018 Oct 3. PMID: 30284037; PMCID: PMC6373366.
273. Tam SKP, Chia J, Brodbelt A, Foroughi M. Assessment of patients with a Chiari malformation type I. Brain Spine. 2021 Dec 3;2:100850. doi: 10.1016/j.bas.2021.100850.
274. Termsarasab P, Thammongkolchai T, Rucker JC, Frucht SJ. The diagnostic value of saccades in movement disorder patients: a practical guide and review. J Clin Mov Disord. 2015 Oct 15;2:14. doi: 10.1186/s40734-015-0025-4. PMID: 26788350; PMCID: PMC4710978.
275. Thada PK, Bhandari J, Umapathi KK. Becker Muscular Dystrophy. In: StatPearls [Internet]. Treasure Island (FL, United States): StatPearls Publishing; 2023 Jul 19 [cited 2023 Oct 7]. Available from: https://www.ncbi.nlm.nih.gov/books/NBK556092/.
276. Atlantic Clinical Indications and Criteria for Intravenous and Subcutaneous Immunoglobulin (IVIG/SCIG) Version 2.0 [Internet]. Halifax, NS: The Atlantic IVIG Utilization Working Group (2021); 2022 Apr [cited 2023 Oct 14]. Available from: https://www.gov.nl.ca/hcs/bloodservices/resources/ivig/.
277. The ISPN Guide to Pediatric Neurosurgery. Epidemiology of Spina Bifida Occulta and Tethered Cord Syndrome in Children [Internet]. New York, USA: The International Society for Pediatric Neurosurgery; 2017 May 9 [cited

2023 Oct 07]. Available from: https://ispn.guide/congenital-disorders-of-the-nervous-system-in-children/spina-bifida-occulta-and-tethered-cord-syndrome-in-children-homepage/epidemiology-of-spina-bifida-occulta-and-tethered-cord-syndrome-in-children.
278. Theys T, Janssen P. Neurofysiologie [Neurophysiology], 3rd ed. Leuven: Acco; 2018.
279. Thomalla G, Simonsen CZ, Boutitie F, Andersen G, Berthezene Y, Cheng B, Cheripelli B, Cho TH, Fazekas F, Fiehler J, Ford I, Galinovic I, Gellissen S, Golsari A, Gregori J, Günther M, Guibernau J, Häusler KG, Hennerici M, Kemmling A, Marstrand J, Modrau B, Neeb L, Perez de la Ossa N, Puig J, Ringleb P, Roy P, Scheel E, Schonewille W, Serena J, Sunaert S, Villringer K, Wouters A, Thijs V, Ebinger M, Endres M, Fiebach JB, Lemmens R, Muir KW, Nighoghossian N, Pedraza S, Gerloff C; WAKE-UP Investigators. MRI-Guided Thrombolysis for Stroke with Unknown Time of Onset. N Engl J Med. 2018 Aug 16;379(7):611-622. doi: 10.1056/NEJMoa1804355. Epub 2018 May 16. PMID: 29766770.
280. Titulaer MJ, Lang B, Verschuuren JJ. Lambert-Eaton myasthenic syndrome: from clinical characteristics to therapeutic strategies. Lancet Neurol. 2011 Dec;10(12):1098-107. doi: 10.1016/S1474-4422(11)70245-9. PMID: 22094130.
281. Treadwell SD, Thanvi B. Malignant middle cerebral artery (MCA) infarction: pathophysiology, diagnosis and management. Postgrad Med J. 2010 Apr;86(1014):235-42. doi: 10.1136/pgmj.2009.094292. PMID: 20354047.
282. Tunkel AR, Hartman BJ, Kaplan SL, Kaufman BA, Roos KL, Scheld WM, Whitley RJ, Practice Guidelines for the Management of Bacterial Meningitis. Clin Infect Dis, 2004 Nov 1;39(9):1267-84. doi: 10.1086/425368. Epub 2004 Oct 6. PMID: 15494903.
283. Turc G, Isabel C, Calvet D. Intravenous thrombolysis for acute ischemic stroke. Diagn Interv Imaging. 2014 Dec;95(12):1129-33. doi: 10.1016/j.diii.2014.10.002. Epub 2014 Nov 15. PMID: 25465121.
284. Ulivi L, Squitieri M, Cohen H, Cowley P, Werring DJ. Cerebral venous thrombosis: a practical guide. Pract Neurol. 2020 Oct;20(5):356-367. doi: 10.1136/practneurol-2019-002415. PMID: 32958591.
285. Vaamonde-Gamo J, Flores-Barragán JM, Ibáñez R, Gudín M, Hernández A. DaT-SCAN SPECT en el diagnóstico diferencial entre demencia con cuerpos de Lewy y enfermedad de Alzheimer [DaT-SCAN SPECT in the differential diagnosis of dementia with Lewy bodies and Alzheimer's disease]. Rev Neurol. 2005 Sep 1-15;41(5):276-9.
286. Van Calenbergh F. *Neuroanatomie: de schedel en de hersenvliezen, de functionele systemen en de craniale zenuwen [Neuroanatomy: the skull and the meninges, the functional systems and the cranial nerves]*, 2nd ed. Leuven: Acco; 2018.
287. Van de Beek D, Brouwer M, Hasbun R, Koedel U, Whitney CG, Wijdicks E. Community-acquired bacterial meningitis. Nat Rev Dis Primers. 2016 Nov 3;2:16074. doi: 10.1038/nrdp.2016.74. PMID: 27808261.
288. Van de Beek D, Cabellos C, Dzupova O, Esposito S, Klein M, Kloek AT, Leib SL, Mourvillier B, Ostergaard C, Pagliano P, Pfister HW, Read RC, Sipahi OR, Brouwer MC; ESCMID Study Group for Infections of the Brain (ESGIB). ESCMID guideline: diagnosis and treatment of acute bacterial meningitis. Clin Microbiol Infect. 2016 May;22 Suppl 3:S37-62. doi: 10.1016/j.cmi.2016.01.007. Epub 2016 Apr 7. PMID: 27062097.
289. Van der Plas A. Startpunt Radiologie [Internet]. 2017 Dec 20 [cited 2019 May 15]. Available from: http://www.startpuntradiologie.nl/.
290. Vecht C, Royer-Perron L, Houillier C, Huberfeld G. Seizures and Anticonvulsants in Brain Tumours: Frequency, Mechanisms and Anti-Epileptic Management. Curr Pharm Des. 2017;23(42):6464-6487. doi: 10.2174/138161282 3666171027130003. PMID: 29076421.
291. Ventafridda V, Saita L, Ripamonti C, De Conno F. WHO guidelines for the use of analgesics in cancer pain. Int J Tissue React. 1985;7(1):93-6. PMID: 2409039.
292. Venugopal V, Pavlakis S. Duchenne Muscular Dystrophy. In: StatPearls [Internet]. Treasure Island (FL, United States): StatPearls Publishing; 2023 Jul 10 [cited 2023 Oct 7]. Available from: https://www.ncbi.nlm.nih.gov/books/NBK482346/.
293. Vilensky JA, Robertson WM, Suárez-Quian CA. The Clinical Anatomy of the Cranial Nerves: The Nerves of 'On Olympus towering Top' [Internet]. Chichester UK: Wiley-Blackwell; 2015 [cited 2023 Oct 7]. Available from: https://enarm.com.mx/catalogo/32.pdf.
294. Visseren FLJ, Mach F, Smulders YM, Carballo D, Koskinas KC, Bäck M, Benetos A, Biffi A, Boavida JM, Capodanno D, Cosyns B, Crawford C, Davos CH, Desormais I, Di Angelantonio E, Franco OH, Halvorsen S, Hobbs FDR, Hollander M, Jankowska EA, Michal M, Sacco S, Sattar N, Tokgozoglu L, Tonstad S, Tsioufis KP, van Dis I, van Gelder IC, Wanner C, Williams B; ESC National Cardiac Societies; ESC Scientific Document Group. 2021 ESC Guidelines on cardiovascular disease prevention in clinical practice. Eur Heart J. 2021 Sep 7;42(34):3227-3337. doi: 10.1093/eurheartj/ehab484. Erratum in: Eur Heart J. 2022 Nov 7;43(42):4468. PMID: 34458905.
295. Walton C, King R, Rechtman L, Kaye W, Leray E, Marrie RA, Robertson N, La Rocca N, Uitdehaag B, van der Mei I, Wallin M, Helme A, Angood Napier C, Rijke N, Baneke P. Rising prevalence of multiple sclerosis worldwide: Insights from the Atlas of MS, third edition. Mult Scler. 2020 Dec;26(14):1816-1821. doi: 10.1177/1352458520970841. Epub 2020 Nov 11. PMID: 33174475; PMCID: PMC7720355.
296. Wang H, Zhao S, Wang S, Zheng Y, Wang S, Chen H, Pang J, Ma J, Yang X, Chen Y. Global magnitude of encephalitis burden and its evolving pattern over the past 30 years. J Infect. 2022 Jun;84(6):777-787. doi: 10.1016/j.jinf.2022.04.026. Epub 2022 Apr 19.
297. Ward MD, Jones DE, Goldman MD. Overview and safety of fingolimod hydrochloride use in patients with multiple sclerosis. Expert Opin Drug Saf. 2014 Jul;13(7):989-98. doi: 10.1517/14740338.2014.920820. PMID: 24935480.
298. Ward TN, Levin M, Phillips JM. Evaluation and management of headache in the emergency department. Med Clin North Am. 2001 Jul;85(4):971-85. doi: 10.1016/s0025-7125(05)70354-0. PMID: 11480268.
299. Warner JJ, Harrington RA, Sacco RL, Elkind MSV. Guidelines for the Early Management of Patients With Acu-

te Ischemic Stroke: 2019 Update to the 2018 Guidelines for the Early Management of Acute Ischemic Stroke. Stroke. 2019 Dec;50(12):3331-3332. doi: 10.1161/STROKEAHA.119.027708. Epub 2019 Oct 30. PMID: 31662117.

300. Waruiru C, Appleton R. Febrile seizures: an update. Arch Dis Child. 2004 Aug;89(8):751-6. doi: 10.1136/adc.2003.028449. PMID: 15269077; PMCID: PMC1720014.
301. Weigel R, Schmiedek P, Krauss JK. Outcome of contemporary surgery for chronic subdural haematoma: evidence based review. J Neurol Neurosurg Psychiatry. 2003 Jul;74(7):937-43. doi: 10.1136/jnnp.74.7.937. PMID: 12810784; PMCID: PMC1738576.
302. Wein S, Baba Y, Feger J, et al. Intramedullary spinal metastasis [Internet]. Radiopaedia.org. 22 Aug 2012 [updated 20 Aug 2022; cited 7 Oct 2023] Available from: https://radiopaedia.org/articles/intramedullary-spinal-metastasis-1.
303. Williams CT, De Jesus O. Friedreich Ataxia. In: StatPearls [Internet]. Treasure Island (FL, United, States): StatPearls Publishing. 2023 Jun 27 [cited 2023 Oct 7]. Available from: https://www.ncbi.nlm.nih.gov/books/NBK563199.
304. Williamson C, Venkatakrishna R. Traumatic brain injury: Epidemiology, classification, and pathophysiology [Internet]. UpToDate. 2023 May 2023 [cited 2023 Oct 7]. Available from: https://www.uptodate.com/contents/traumatic-brain-injury-epidemiology-classification-and-pathophysiology.
305. Wiseman D. Cauda Equina Syndrome [Internet]. Washington: American Association of Neurological Surgeons [cited 2023 Oct 6]. Available from: https://www.aans.org/en/Patients/Neurosurgical-Conditions-and-Treatments/Cauda-Equina-Syndrome.
306. Wolk DA, Dickerson BC. Clinical features and diagnosis of Alzheimer disease [Internet]. UpToDate. 2021 Oct 08 [cited 2023 Oct 07]. Available from: https://www.uptodate.com/contents/clinical-features-and-diagnosis-of-alzheimer-disease.
307. Wolters EC, Groenewegen HJ. *Neurologie: structuur, functie en dysfunctie van het zenuwstelsel,* 3rd ed. Houten: Bohn Stafleu van Loghum; 2010.
308. Wu J, Ji S, Niu P, Zhang B, Shao D, Li Y, Xie S, Jiang Z. Knowledge mapping of syringomyelia from 2003 to 2022: A bibliometric analysis. J Clin Neurosci. 2023 Apr;110:63-70. doi: 10.1016/j.jocn.2023.01.004. Epub 2023 Feb 21. PMID: 36822071.
309. Wu V, Sykes EA, Beyea MM, Simpson MTW, Beyea JA. Approach to Ménière disease management. Can Fam Physician. 2019 Jul;65(7):463-467. PMID: 31300426; PMCID: PMC6738466.
310. Yamada M, Komatsu J, Nakamura K, Sakai K, Samuraki-Yokohama M, Nakajima K, Yoshita M. Diagnostic Criteria for Dementia with Lewy Bodies: Updates and Future Directions. J Mov Disord. 2020 Jan;13(1):1-10. doi: 10.14802/jmd.19052. Epub 2019 Nov 8. PMID: 31694357; PMCID: PMC6987529.
311. Yang W, Huang J. Chronic Subdural Hematoma: Epidemiology and Natural History. Neurosurg Clin N Am. 2017 Apr;28(2):205-210. doi: 10.1016/j.nec.2016.11.002. Epub 2017 Feb 1. PMID: 28325454.
312. Zahoor I, Shafi A, Haq E. Chapter 7: Pharmacological Treatment of Parkinson's Disease. In: Stoker TB, Greenland JC, editors. Parkinson's Disease: Pathogenesis and Clinical Aspects [Internet]. Brisbane (AU): Codon Publications; 2018 Dec 21 [cited 2023 Oct 7]. Available from: https://www.ncbi.nlm.nih.gov/books/NBK536726/.
313. Zhang R, Wang Y, Fang J, Yu M, Wang Y, Liu G. Worldwide 1-month case fatality of ischaemic stroke and the temporal trend. Stroke Vasc Neurol. 2020 Dec;5(4):353-360. doi: 10.1136/svn-2020-000371. Epub 2020 Jul 13. PMID: 32665364; PMCID: PMC7804064.
314. Zhang Q, Zhou X, Li Y, Yang X, Abbasi QH. Clinical Recognition of Sensory Ataxia and Cerebellar Ataxia. Front Hum Neurosci. 2021 Apr 1;15:639871. doi: 10.3389/fnhum.2021.639871. PMID: 33867960; PMCID: PMC8046926.
315. Zhao L, Zhao W, Hou Y, Wen C, Wang J, Wu P, Guo Z. An Overview of Managements in Meningiomas. Front Oncol. 2020 Aug 21;10:1523. doi: 10.3389/fonc.2020.01523. Erratum in: Front Oncol. 2020 Sep 24;10:599431. PMID: 32974188; PMCID: PMC7473392.
316. Zhou F, Yu B, Luo J, Ma Y, Li J, Zhang T, Yu G. Global trends in the research on benign paroxysmal positional vertigo: A 20-year bibliometric and visualization analysis. Front Neurol. 2022 Oct 17;13:1046257. doi: 10.3389/fneur.2022.1046257. PMID: 36324379; PMCID: PMC9618818.
317. Zimmerman B, Hubbard JB. Deep Tendon Reflexes. In: StatPearls [Internet]. Treasure Island (FL, United States): StatPearls Publishing. 2023 Jul 24 [cited 2023 Oct 5]. Available from: https://www.ncbi.nlm.nih.gov/books/NBK531502/.
318. Ziu E, Viswanathan VK, Mesfin FB. Spinal Metastasis. In: StatPearls [Internet]. Treasure Island (FL): StatPearls Publishing; 2023 Aug 14 [cited 2023 Oct 14]. Available from: https://www.ncbi.nlm.nih.gov/books/NBK441950/.
319. Zorginstituut Nederland [Healthcare Institute]. Farmacotherapeutisch Kompas [Pharamcotherapeutical Compass] [Internet]. [Cited 2019 May 15]. Available from: https://www.farmacotherapeutischkompas.nl/.
320. Zou W, Li Q, Peng F, Huang D. Worldwide Meniere's disease research: A bibliometric analysis of the published literature between 2002 and 2021. Front Neurol. 2022 Oct 12;13:1030006. doi: 10.3389/fneur.2022.1030006. PMID: 36313500; PMCID: PMC9597620.

Are you missing a resource or topic? Or is there a new guideline that isn't yet listed here? Let us know! Together we can keep Compendium Medicine up to date.

Illustrations & figures

Illustrators

Yente S. Beentjes: *figure 109 (modification), figure table 78A, 78B*
Hebe T.A. Boerhout: *figures 31 (modification), 39 (modification), 40 (modification), 45 (modification), 68 (modification), 74, 83*
Cas van Cruchten: *figures 8, 9, 18, 19, 65, 103, 106, 107*
Susan Deelstra: *figures 10, 16, 67, 72, 97*
Floris Duetz: *figures 88, 89, 90, 91, 118*
Lotte Dupuis: *figure 85*
Gulizar Durak: *figure 28*
Astrid A.H. Feikema: *figures 61, 95, 108*
Iza Hogenelst: *figures 7, 78*
Dite de Jong: *figures 71, 114, 115, 116*
Didi D.J. Juin: *figures 42, 73, 89 (modification)*
Jasmin Kaur: *figures 43, 44, 105*
Koen L.C. Ketelaars: *figures 6, 11, 12, 13, 14, 17, 19, 21, 22, 23, 24, 25, 26, 27, 32, 33, 34, 35, 36, 37, 38, 45, 46, 47, 48, 49, 62, 81, 92, 94, 98, 99, 104, 112, figure table 77B*
Robin Klabbers: *figures 4, 5, 109*
Rosalie C. Krijl: *figures 1, 2, 3, 15, 47 (modification), 69, 100, 101, 108 (modification), 114 (modification)*
Sibylle Lange: *figures 87, 102, 117*
Juliette M.E. Linskens: *figure 50*
Sophie Reese: *figure 39*
Belle van Rosmalen: *figures 66, 75, 76, 77, 96*
Laura Sanchez: *figures 20, 95 (modification)*
Esther Simons: *figures 93, 111*
Carlijn Sturm: *figures 29, 30, 31, 40, 41, 67, 68, 84, 110, 113*
Linda Xie: *figures 59, 60, 71 (modification), 82, 102 (modification)*

Sources

01. Figure 51: K.M. Kasius, MD, PhD, neurologist, clinical neurophysiologist and somnologist OLVG Amsterdam
02. Figures 52, 53, 54, 55, 56, 79, and 80: Prof. Mario Maas, MD, PhD, radiologist, Amsterdam University Medical Center
03. Figures 57, 63, 64, and 70: Gwendolyn Vuurberg
04. Figure 58: A. van der Plas, MD, radiologist, Maastricht UMC+, www.startpuntradiologie.nl
05. Figure cover and beginning pages: Traité complet de l'anatomie de l'homme: comprenant la médicine opératoire 1831-1844 / Bourgery, Jean Baptiste Marc; Jacob, Nicolas Henri/ Public domain

Epilogue

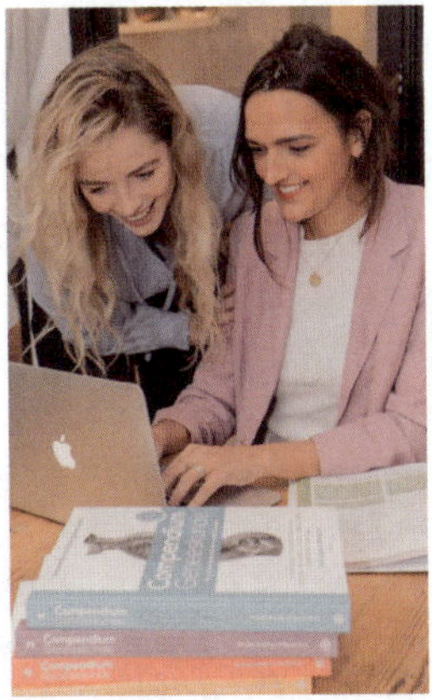

Veerle Smit (L) & Romée Snijders (R)

Through the collaborative effort of an incredible team consisting of students, illustrators, graphic designers, and medical specialists, with this pocket we have successfully translated our vision into reality. Our goal was to ensure that you, as students and doctors, have access to essential information – literally at your fingertips, regardless of your location.

A heartfelt thank you, Melissa, for spearheading the publication of our third English pocket! We extend our gratitude to Gwen for her comprehensive involvement in the Neurology project. To Sabhat, Demi, and Liza – what an incredible journey we have embarked upon together! Your contributions and enthusiasm have been instrumental every step of the way. This has been an intense yet uniquely rewarding process, for which we also want to thank the authors of the previous edition: Yvette, Tim, Paul, An, Joppe, Cas, and Iris.

We are enormously grateful to all the medical professionals who provided valuable feedback and content support, elevating the quality of the text. Your contributions were integral to achieving this result.

This pocket could not have turned out so visually successful without all the illustrators – also often medical students – who collaborated on this pocket. Thanks to our team for their exceptional ability to comprehensibly cover the specialty in their graphic work.

We gratefully acknowledge our graphic heroes, Maria and Ivana, whose efforts gave this pocket its recognisable *Compendium Medicine* look. Special thanks also go to Melanie, Vera, Pauline, Charlotte, and Jasmijn for ensuring the smooth functioning of the entire process.

Last, a sincere thank you to all our colleagues who have *Compendium Medicine* on their bookshelves. Your support has been indispensable in realising our dreams.

We are incredibly proud of this team and hope to see you again soon, in or outside the hospital!

Amsterdam, June 2024

Veerle Smit, MD & Romée Snijders, MD
Doctors and founders of *Compendium Medicine*

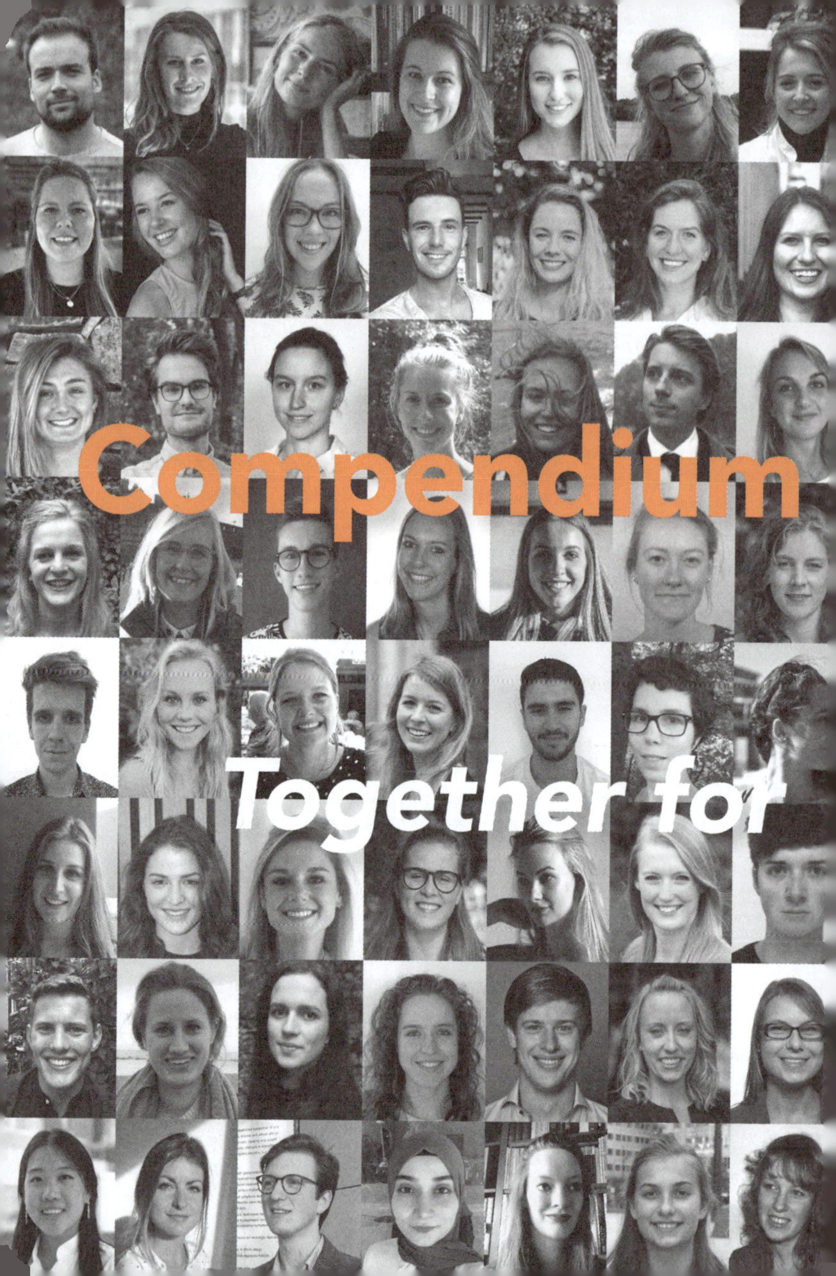
Compendium
Together for